ENCYCLOPAEDIA OF NORTH-EAST INDIA

ENCYCLOPAEDIA
OF
NORTH-EAST INDIA

(In 3 Volumes)

(Sikkim, Nagaland, Tripura)

(Vol. 3)

T. RAATAN

KALPAZ PUBLICATIONS

DELHI-110 052

Encyclopaedia of North-East India

Rs. 2200 (In 3 Volumes Set)

ISBN: 81-7835-068-8 (Set)
ISBN: 81-7835-275-3 (Vol. 3)

Published in 2004 in India by
Kalpaz Publications
C-30, Satyawati Nagar
Delhi-110 052
E-mail: kalpaz@hotmail.com

Lasertypesetting by: Varsha Graphics, Delhi
Printed at: Mehra Offset Press, Delhi

Contents

Preface

Third and last volume of the series—*Encyclopaedia of North-East India* also comprises of three sections which represent three states. These are Sikkim, Nagaland and Tripura respectively. Like other states of North-East, all these three States also hold special significance in the region and highly important to be documented.

Sikkim comprised in Section I of the book is surrounded by Bhutan in the east, Tibet in north, Nepal in the west and West Bengal in the south corner. State lies in the heart of high eastern Himalayan range. Blessed with a land which people of all communities live in harmony, it has world's third highest mountain regarded as the guardian deity of Sikkim. Most of Sikkim consists of mountain terrain interspersed with ravines and green valleys. Two main rivers of the state are Teesta and Rangit.

Nagaland is State of Section II of the Volume. Having remained an area centrally administered by the Governor of Assam, it was known as the Naga Hills Tuensang Area on December 1, 1963, formally made the State of Indian Union, it is situated in the extreme north-east of the country and is surrounded by Arunachal Pradesh in north, Assam in west, Manipur in south and Myanmar in east.

Last section of the book is on *Tripura* which attained complete statehood in 1972. Tripura is strategically located between the river valleys of Myanmar and Bangladesh. Encircled almost on three directions by Bangladesh, it is connected with the States of Assam and Mizoram in the north-east.

Following the trend from the first two volumes, here also, first chapter of each state is committed to basics about the land and also of people living in it. Chapter 2 of Sikkim is about political and administrative developments in the state and Chapter 3 about state of education in Sikkim. Fourth and last chapter is on class structures in Sikkim which deals with both old and new setup that has emerged with the spread of education.

Regarding Nagaland, second chapter gives description of pre- and post-organisation of state period. Chapter 3 is about culture, customs, and traditions of Nagas and 4th one on role of women in Naga tribal society. Naga festivals and songs have been discussed in 5th chapter and last chapter is about development planning in 2001.

Finally, contents of Tripura have been divided into five chapters. Chapter 2 talks about measures for land reformation and their implementation. Chapter 3 is devoted to gods/goddesses and their images in Tripura. Chapter 4 gives a brief account of rich land resources and other natural and man-made resources. Last chapter, like most of the states of the series deals with the economic aspect., i.e., planned economic development in the state.

The volume will make an interesting reading for readers and provide valuable information to researchers and academicians.

T. Raatan

Introduction

Last volume of the series is about Sikkim, Nagaland and Tripura. Since these three States also share so much in common that it is not even reproducable in one volume, so they have been brought here together. But this nowhere means that they do not have their uniqueness. Each State has its distinct features which find place in the various chapters of the book.

Sikkim with 1096 sq. km. area and capital Gangtok is a blessed land where people from all communities and religions live in complete harmony. It is recorded that the early history of Sikkim begins from the 13th century when the signing of blood brotherhood treaty between the Lepcha Chief Thekong Tek and Tibetan Prince Khye Bumsa at Kabi Lungstok in northern part of the state took place. After this what is said to have happened is the visit of three great saints to kingdom in 1641 in western region of Sikkim where they met Phutsog Namgyal, a sixth generation descendent of Khye-Bumsa. He was formally appointed the first Chogyal of Sikkim at Yuksam in 1642 and this marked the beginning of the Namgyal dynasty in the region. Alongwith the march of events, Sikkim finally became an integral part of modern union in 1975. Population, population between the age of 0-6, is shown below.

Table 1
Population, Decadal Growth Rate, Sex Ratio and Density of Sikkim: Census 2001

State/District	*Population*			*Decadal Growth Rate*		*Sex Ratio*		*Density*	
	Person	*Male*	*Female*	*1981-91*	*1991-01*	*1991*	*2001*	*1991*	*2001*
	(1)	(2)	(3)	(4)	(5)	(6)	(7)	(8)	(9)
Sikkim	**540,493**	**288,217**	**252,276**	**28.47**	**32.98**	**878**	**875**	**57**	**76**
North	41,023	23,410	17,613	18.09	31.32	828	752	7	10
West	123,174	63,835	59,339	30.55	25.48	915	930	84	106
South	131,506	68,227	63,279	29.78	33.37	892	927	131	175
East	244,790	132,745	112,045	28.60	37.17	859	844	187	257

Obviously, the economy of the State is basically agriculture-based. Maize, rice, wheat, potato, large cardamom, ginger and orange have been the main crops. Sikkim is known for largest area and maximum production of cardamom in entire country. Ginger, potato, orange and off-season vegetables are other cash crops in the State. Of total land being utilised in the state, merely 12 per cent is used for cultivation. Since the possibilities of enhancing producing through area expansion are almost nil, so, the emphasis is laid on maximising production and net income per unit area. Efforts for development of commercial land and horticulture crops and floriculture are also in the process.

Table 2
Population, Population in the Age Group 0-6 of Sikkim: Census 2001

State/ District	*Total Rural Urban*	*Population* Person	Male	Female	*0-6 Population* Person	Male	Female
Sikkim	**Total**	**540,493**	**288,217**	**252,276**	**77,170**	**38,856**	**38,314**
	Rural	**480,488**	**255,386**	**225,102**	**71,340**	**35,827**	**35,513**
	Urban	**60,005**	**32,831**	**27,174**	**5,830**	**3,029**	**2,801**
North	Total	41,023	23,410	17,613	6,250	3,139	3,111
	Rural	39,775	22,642	17,133	6,080	3,048	3,032
	Urban	1,248	768	480	170	91	79
West	Total	123,174	63,835	59,339	19,780	10,056	9,724
	Rural	121,350	62,809	58,541	19,550	9,948	9,602
	Urban	1,824	1,026	798	230	108	122
South	Total	131,506	68,227	63,279	20,819	10,224	10,595
	Rural	127,560	66,083	61,477	20,438	10,021	10,417
	Urban	3,946	2,144	1,802	381	203	178
East	Total	244,790	132,745	112,045	30,321	15,437	14,884
	Rural	191,803	103,852	87,951	25,272	12,810	12,462
	Urban	52,987	28,893	24,094	5,049	2,627	2,422

This state too has been declared as an industrially backward one. Thus, the Department of Industries in the state lay special emphasis on evolution and promotion of various small-scale industries. Training for skill upgradation as well as learning in art and craft given to the youth by the Directorate of Handloom and Handicrafts at Gangtok. There are also three public sector undertakings in the state. Sikkim Industrial Corporation, setup in 1977, perform function of both State Financial Corporation as well as Small Industrial Development Corporation.

Total population of the state is of three principal ethnic communities—Bhutias, the Lepchas and the Nepalese. As per records, Maghey Sankranti, Durga Puja, Laxmi Puja and Chaite Dasai are the principal festivals celebrated by the Nepalese community. Pang-Lhabsol, Losoong and Losor are celebrated by the Bhutia community. Festivals of Lepcha community are Namsoong and Tendong HCO Run Faat.

Significant tourist places are Gangtok, Bakim, Yumthang, Dzongri, Varsey, Tashiding, Rumtek monastry, Pemayantse monastry, Tsomgo and Phodong monastry.

About **Nagaland,** it is said that just like other inhabitants of the north-east region, the Nagas too have their share of legend and folklore about their origin and evolution through the ages. Nagas are predominantly tribal people and each tribe has its own effective system of self-governance since time immemorial. During the 12th and 13th century, gradual contact with the Ahoms of the present-day Assam was established but it did not make any significant impact on traditional Naga style of living. After the British penetration, the area was brought completely under their control. After independence, Nagaland was declared formally a State of Indian Union in 1963. Population, population between the age of 0-6, ratio and density of Nagaland (districtwise). Decadal growth rate, sex are shown below :

Table 3
Population, Decadal Growth Rate, Sex Ratio and Density of Nagaland : Census 2001

State/District	*Population*			*Decadal growth rate*		*Sex Ratio*		*Density*	
	Person	*Male*	*Female*	*1981-91*	*1991-01*	*1991*	*2001*	*1991*	*2001*
	(1)	(2)	(3)	(4)	(5)	(6)	(7)	(8)	(9)
Nagaland	**1,988,636**	**1,041,686**	**946,950**	**56.08**	**64.41**	**886**	**909**	**73**	**120**
Mon	259,604	138,005	121,599	58.98	73.42	872	881	84	145
Tuensang	414,801	216,888	197,913	69.87	78.10	889	913	55	98
Mokokchung	227,230	118,428	108,802	52.39	43.48	912	919	98	141
Zunheboto	154,909	79,627	75,282	32.68	61.00	964	945	77	123
Wokha	161,098	83,620	77,478	42.80	95.01	917	927	51	99
Dimapur	308,382	166,335	142,047	55.16	73.30	830	854	192	333
Kohima	314,366	161,701	152,665	68.98	49.96	879	944	67	101
Phek	148,246	77,082	71,164	44.66	45.12	880	923	50	73

The State of Nagaland is predominantly agrarian. Main crops grown are rice, wheat, maize and pulses.

Regarding industrialisation, the process of industrialisation is not upto the mark but the necessity to establish more and more industries have now been recognised. Nagaland Sugar Mill at Dimapur, pulp and paper mill at Tuli and a plywood factory at Tizit are worth mentioning with cooperative industries are managing handloom and handicraft cottage industries. The Nagaland Industrial Development Corporation is the premier promotional organisation in offering guidance and capital aid to entrepreneurs.

Transport services are not very good. Dimapur is only state where rail and air services have been provided.

Finally, important festivals of the State are Sekreyni, Moatsu, Tuluni and Tokhu Emong. Entire tribal clans celebrate their disinct seasonal festivals with colourful spirit and musical feasts.

Table 4
Population, Population in the Age Group 0-6 of Nagaland : Census 2001

State/District	*Total Rural Urban*	*Population* *Person*	*Male*	*Female*	*0-6 Population* *Person*	*Male*	*Female*
Nagaland	**Total**	**1,988,636**	**1,041,686**	**946,950**	**280,172**	**141,852**	**138,320**
	Rural	**1,635,815**	**846,651**	**789,164**	**233,511**	**117,741**	**115,770**
	Urban	**352,821**	**195,035**	**157,786**	**46,661**	**24,111**	**22,550**
Mon	Total	259,604	138,005	121,599	37,464	18,968	18,496
	Rural	243,485	129,235	114,250	34,778	17,518	17,260
	Urban	16,119	8,770	7,349	2,686	1,450	1,236
Tuensang	Total	414,801	216,888	197,913	57,044	28,836	28,208
	Rural	385,147	200,263	184,884	53,065	26,816	26,249
	Urban	29,654	16,625	13,029	3,979	2,020	1,959
Mokokchung	Total	227,230	118,428	108,802	22,866	11,412	11,454
	Rural	196,026	101,288	94,738	19,589	9,702	9,887
	Urban	31,204	17,140	14,064	3,277	1,710	1,567
Zunheboto	Total	154,909	79,627	75,282	24,593	12,619	11,974
	Rural	132,100	67,117	64,983	21,508	10,986	10,522
	Urban	22,809	12,510	10,299	3,085	1,633	1,452
Wokha	Total	161,098	83,620	77,478	21,204	10,608	10,596
	Rural	123,402	63,219	60,183	16,626	8,296	8,330
	Urban	37,696	20,401	17,295	4,578	2,312	2,266
Dimapur	Total	308,382	166,335	142,047	45,780	23,109	22,671
	Rural	184,490	96,088	88,402	29,565	14,752	14,813
	Urban	123,892	70,247	53,645	16,215	8,357	7,858
Kohima	Total	314,366	161,701	152,665	44,915	22,700	22,215
	Rural	235,782	119,668	116,114	34,404	17,285	17,119
	Urban	78,584	42,033	36,551	10,511	5,415	5,096
Phek	Total	148,246	77,082	71,164	26,306	13,600	12,706
	Rural	135,383	69,773	65,610	23,976	12,386	11,590
	Urban	12,863	7,309	5,554	2,330	1,214	1,116

Tripura is the last State of the Volume of the series. Tripura has a long historic past, its distinct culture and a fascinating folklore. Historical background of Tripura can be better understood from *Rajmala* Chronicles of King Tripura that find detailed treatment in first Chapter Land and the People of Nagaland are finds reference of Tripura. Even in epic like 'Mahabharata' and 'Puranas'. Referring to Rajamala series rulers were known by the surname 'Fa' meaning Father. It is also recorded that the rulers of Bengal helped Tripura Monarchs in the 14th century. Kings of Tripura countered Muslim invasions and defeated them but they could not resist British interference. Initially, a part 'C' State, Tripura became State in full fledged form in 1972.

Tripura too is pre-dominantly an agriculture based State. Total irrigation area in the State is 64,665 hectares and additionally 1.17 lakh hectares is expected to be brought under the same with a thermal power plant to be taken up under NEEPCO, the State is likely to become power-surplus State.

Decadal Growth rate, sex ratio and density of Tripura

Population, population between the age of 0-6 are shown below :

Table 5
Population, Decadal Growth Rate, Sex Ratio and Density of Tripura : Census 2001

State/District	*Population 2001*			*Decadal growth rate*		*Sex Ratio*		*Density*	
	Person	*Male*	*Female*	*1981-91*	*1991-01*	*1991*	*2001*	*1991*	*2001*
	(1)	(2)	(3)	(4)	(5)	(6)	(7)	(8)	(9)
Tripura	**3,191,168**	**1,636,138**	**1,555,030**	**34.30**	**15.74**	**945**	**950**	**263**	**304**
West Tripura	1,530,531	783,825	746,706	32.53	18.29	944	953	427	505
South Tripura	762,565	391,179	371,386	40.30	6.10	951	949	229	243
Dhalai	307,417	158,480	148,937	33.69	10.79	931	940	125	139
North Tripura	590,655	302,654	288,001	30.86	26.44	943	952	222	281

Important festivals of the State Maker Sankranti, Holi, Ashokashtmi, Brahmakund festival at Mohanpur, Rash festival, Bengali New Year, Garia, Biju and Hozagiri festivals etc. Some more festivals to be celebrated are: Boat race, Mansa Mangal, Ker, Kharchi, Sarad, Diwali, Christmas and Buddha Purnima.

Table 6
Population, Population in the Age Group 0-6 of Tripura : Census 2001

District	*Total Rural Urban*	*Population* *Person*	*Male*	*Female*	*0-6 Population* *Person*	*Male*	*Female*
Tripura	**Total**	**3,191,168**	**1,636,138**	**1,555,030**	**427,012**	**216,244**	**210,768**
	Rural	**2,648,074**	**1,359,288**	**1,288,786**	**376,018**	**190,067**	**185,951**
	Urban	**543,094**	**276,850**	**266,244**	**50,994**	**26.177**	**24,817**
West Tripura	Total	1,530,531	783,825	746,706	188,847	95,212	93,635
	Rural	1,123,030	577,030	546,000	150,974	75,760	75,214
	Urban	407,501	206,795	200,706	37,873	19,452	18,421
South Tripura	Total	762,565	391,179	371,386	108,052	55,068	52,984
	Rural	708,498	363,023	345,475	103,161	52,519	50,642
	Urban	54,067	28,156	25,911	4,891	2,549	2,342
Dhalai	Total	307,417	158,480	148,937	46,912	23,811	23,101
	Rural	288,546	148,507	140,039	44,825	22,757	22,068
	Urban	18,871	9,973	8,898	2,087	1,054	1,033
North Tripura	Total	590,655	302,654	288,001	83,201	42,153	41,048
	Rural	528,000	270,728	257,272	77,058	39,031	38,027
	Urban	62,655	31,926	30,729	6,143	3,122	3,021

Finally, tourist centres worth seeing are: Ujjayanta Palace, Jaggan Nath Temple, Laxmi Narayan Temple, Uma Maheshwari Temple, Benu Bari Vihar, State Museums, Rabindra Kanan at Agartala, 14 Goddesss temple at Agartala, Brahmakunda, Kamla Sagar, Sepahijala and Trishna Wildlife Sanctuaries, Dumboor lake, Sundari and Bhubaneshwari Temples and Jampuri Hills. A list of tourist places of the State indicates that inhabitants of the region are predominantly religion minded and god-fearing people.

In nutshell, Mughal invasions and British monopolisation has distorted the state and its economy to a large extent. Even people have received cultural setbacks with advent of Christianity and English ways of living. Now, after independence of media and conferring the title of complete statehood to Tripura, things have started changing for the better. Central as well as State Governments are contributing their share to the development of the religion with introduction of sophisticated technology, establishment of more industrial units and spread of education through more institutes. What is needed the most is sincere commitment and good coordination between the centre and the State. Cooperation from the inhabitants of the region will be of utmost significance with all this, there is no doubt that the state and region will be united in the strong economies of the country.

Section-I
Sikkim

1

Land and the People

As is evident to all, the description of any State starts with the geographical details of that State. So, here are basics about Sikkim. Sikkim, the 22nd State of the Indian National Union is essentially a Himalayan enclosed basin. It is mountainous State hemmed in on the west by Nepal, on the north by Tibet, on the south by West Bengal and on the east with Bhutan. Surrounded thus, Sikkim enjoys, and still retains unusual distinctiveness. It is somewhat rectangular in shape, 113 kilometres long and 64 kilometres wide. The total spread area of Sikkim is 7,096 square kilometres. For the sake of administrative convenience, the State is divided into four districts, viz. North, South, East and West. Every district comes under the direct administrative control of a District Collector. For the North district, the headquarters is situated in Mangan region. Namchi is the headquarters of South district. The West district has its headquarters at Gualshing. While the East district headquarters is situated in Gangtok, which also happens to be the State capital of Sikkim.

Various Ethnic Groups

The present population of the State is primarily composed of Lepchas, Bhutias, Nepalese and the plains people who represent different ethnic groups settled in the State at different times. The plains people are largely the business communities (Marwaris of Rajasthan and Baniyas of Bihar and Uttar Pradesh), Brahmins, Kshatriyas, and others who come from the Indo-Gangetic plains that covers Bihar, Uttar Pradesh, Haryana, Punjab, Kerala, West Bengal, Tamil Nadu and Andhra Pradesh.

The Marwaris and Baniyas play a significant role in the State trade and commerce while others have job in the academic and administrative spheres. The oldest residents of Sikkim are the *Rongs* or *Lepchas.* Though it is only a notion and no historical records exist as to show how they came to inhabit this country, the Lepchas are said to have migrated via Assam to this mountain State. They are fair in complexion, of medium height and possess pronounced Mongoloid features. Religiously, they are from Lamaist Buddhism. Besides, there are considerable number of Lepchas who are mainly the Christian converts. Lepchas maintain their own ethnic group identity in Sikkim. They have their own language. It is contended that the language they speak is of the Tibeto-Burmese family. The Lepchas have no caste distinction but they are said to belong to either of the five patrilineal clans which originated from supernatural and mythological ancestors.

The Lepchas have a custom of polyandry. In marriage, they have a tradition of paying bride-price. Among the Lepchas, the property is divided equally among sons. The exclusive Lepcha settlement can be noted only in the Dzongu area of present day Sikkim. The Bhutias are descendants of immigrants from the Tibetan province of Kham and Bhutan during 17th century, who played an important role in establishing the kingdom of Sikkim. 'Bhutia' is the ancient name for Tibet, and all those whose ancestors had Tibetan origin identify themselves usually as Bhutias. Bhutias are big built, tall, strong, sturdy and fair in complexion with pronounced Mongolian features and vary from the Lepchas. The Bhutia social structure is patriarchal and they have an old tradition of polyandry. In marriage, they also have a tradition of paying bride-price.

Normally, the Bhutias reside in a joint family. There is no caste distinction among the Bhutias. Marriage is usually arranged and settled by the parents. Religiously, the Bhutias are most of the time Buddhists with a few exceptions of Christians. Nepali mass immigration in Sikkim started after the Bhutia settlement (especially during the British reign in India). Nepalese are people either whose forefathers had come from Nepal or those who had origin in Nepal. Their forefathers were the settlers who hailed Nepal, coming in from the beginning of the nineteenth century. Indeed, Nepalese come from a society which may be regarded as an 'organic whole'[1] in the sense that though its constituent parts represent religious and cultural diversity, yet Nepali language, Nepali dress and way of life have unified them into a one strong community. Besides, the majority of them are migrants to Sikkim and a large number of their brethren are in Nepal than in Sikkim.

Being immigrants gets them with a sense of unity.[2] They have retained their own cultural identity, distinct from Lepchas and Bhutias. The Nepalese ethnic group in Sikkim is inclusive of the following sub-cultural sections.

Among the castes of Nepalese origin who settled down in Sikkim the Bahuns, Thakuris and Chetris are important. The *Bhuns* have the highest position among the Nepalese caste people. They are quite orthodox patriarchal Hindus and would not normally have any matrimonial relations with other lower castes. The Bahuns are basically monogamous but some of them were previously known to be polygynous. Traditionally, the ideal age for a girl's marriage is six.[3] They would not even eat together with other non-Bahuns. Then in social rank are the *Thakuris.* They are Hindus. *Chetris* are also Hindus and their social rank is higher next only to the Thakuris. Chetris also wear sacred threads. In fact, they have little difference with the Bahuns and Thakuris in terms of ritual practices and social ceremonies. Though, inter-marriage is common they usually prefer marriage only within their own clans. Marriage is usually arranged among all higher castes Nepalese.

Among the low caste groups, there are *Kamis, Sarkis* and *Damais* etc., who are also regarded as Scheduled Castes in Sikkim. They are the artisans and are engaged in trades which are prohibited for the high castes Nepalese. The *Kamis,* who are blacksmiths by profession, have social standing superior to *Damais,* the tailors and *Sarkis,* the cobblers. All these three caste varieties are untouchables and in no way related to caste Hindus. Their family system is patriarchal and by religion they are Hindus. Marriage is arranged mostly by parents.

Apart from castes, there are several tribes normally enumerated as *Kiratis.* Among the Kiratis, the Limbus, Sherpas, Tamangs, Rais, Mangars, Gurungs are important. The *Limbus* are mostly Hindus, though some Limbus are still found as animists in the interior part of Sikkim. Limbus too believe that they are indigenous people of Sikkim. In reality, they are supposed to have been immigrants, but are identified with a region covering eastern Nepal and Western Sikkim and traditionally called Limbuan.[4] The Limbus speak their Limbu language which is recognised as one of the State languages in Sikkim. Though, Limbus are regarded equal by other middle caste Nepalese, yet they are not fully assimilated into the Nepali caste hierarchy.

At present, the Limbus want to retain their own identity in contrast to the Nepali identity. *Sherpas* were generally grouped with Kirati tribes in earlier periods. Though, the Sherpas are not assimilated into Nepali caste hierarchy, yet they are represented as *nepalese* in wider context. They have their own dialect and religiously they belong to Lamaist Buddhism. Simultaneously, they maintain their Sherpa identity alongwith Nepali identity. But under the Constitution of India, Sherpas are subsumed under the term 'Bhutia'.[5]

Tamangs also were enumerated with Kiratis. Tamangs in a similar way retain their distinct Tamang identity and are represented as *nepalese* in a broader context. Tamangs are not normally included in the Nepali caste hierarchy, but they are considered equal to the other Nepalese middle castes in Sikkim.

Religiously, they also belong to Buddhism. In fact, Sherpas and Tamangs maintain marginal culture in this area, because they celebrate both Hindu as well as Buddhist festivals/ceremonies. Like Sherpas the Tamangs also have their own Tamang dialect. *Rais* had enumerated previously with Kirati tribes. Among the Nepalese, the Rais are now treated as middle caste people. They are mainly the Hindus and also have their own Rai dialect. Right now, they are completely assimilated into the Nepalese culture. *Manager* also were regarded previously as Kiratis, but at present they are treated as middle caste among the Nepalese.

They are more Hindus and probably embraced the Hindu faith soon after the Chetris and so have been absorbed in the mainstream of Hinduism more than the other Kirati tribes. *Gurungs* also were enumerated in the past with Kiratis. At present, they are treated as middle caste among the Nepalese and profess Hinduism. Gurungs also have their own old Gurung dialect. They are also completely assimilated into the Nepalese culture. *Newars* in Sikkim are regarded as equal by other Nepalese middle castes. Though they are mostly Hindus but worship both Hindu and Buddhist deities together and combine rituals of both faiths in their religious and domestic levels. They have their own Newari dialect largely for domestic use and use Nepali language for outside communications. Newars are predominantly traders, but in Sikkim they are also seen as agriculturists.

Monastery and the Religion of Lamaism

In the state of Sikkim, lamaist religion is a real force that moulds the socio-cultural pattern of the people belonging to this faith. The powers and influence of the monasteries which are the strongholds of this religion i.e., lamaism are insurmountable. The monasteries are the centres of all social activities since the monasteries and the lamas are involved in all occasions in the life of a Buddhist family right from birth to death. It is a common practice that the second son of most Bhutia families in Sikkim is dedicated to the Monastery.[6] Education has always been one of the traditional functions of the Buddhist monastery. Lamas are usually recruited both from Lepchas and Bhutias. People are eager for their sons to become lamas. They commonly think that if a son is intelligent and healthy, he should be sent for monastic training.[7] The census data showing all Scheduled Tribes with their religions is given below.

Table 1
Religion for Scheduled Tribes

Scheduled Tribe	*Rural*			*Urban*		
	Total	*Males*	*Females*	*Total*	*Males*	*Females*
1	2	3	4	5	6	7
ALL SCHEDULED TRIBES						
All Religions	**83,486**	**43,477**	**40,009**	**7,415**	**4,027**	**3,388**
1. Buddhists	78,678	40,993	37,685	6,654	3,648	3,006
2. Christians	2,759	1,401	1,358	523	266	257
3. Hindus	1,869	981	888	220	102	118
4. Jains	7	6	1	0	0	0
5. Muslims	24	15	9	4	4	0
6. Sikhs	2	1	1	0	0	0
7. Other Religions and Persuations	147	80	67	14	7	7

Source: Census 1991.

The monastery is the place where Buddhists receive their ideal education, and join their ideal profession with the lamas from the intellectual elite of society with an exceedingly high prestige. The monastic training starts between the age of five and ten. At the start of the training, the parent or guardian of the boy prepares a feast for the lamas of the gonpa. The real training begins with thue rank of Tongpa. The initial successive ranks of Tongpa and Kunyel are in the nature of novitiate. The real priesthood begins from the stages of Chinyel, Nyepo, Chenjipa and Chutempa. Once the pupil passes the rank of Chinyel, he is regarded as professional lama, who may be asked by the village people to perform ceremonies.

In fact, these series of ranks represent the various roles of priests in the monastic organisation and play an essential part in the prayer services and festivities in the gonpa. The status of Dorjee-Lopen (the head of the gonpa) is regarded top among the Lamas. The payment increases as the qualifications (the rank acquired in the process of training) of lamas go higher. Fee is usually received in cash together with drinks and mid-day meals and high tea at the house.[8] In comparison to the Nepalese, the lamaist have a largest consumption rate. It is mainly because the lamaist have to feed the monks regularly to earn merit; they have to denote in cash and kinds to the monasteries; and give free labour service for repairing the heavy structured gonpas (monasteries). The lamaists themselves feed their priests and their rituals require use of country liquor, which is made of rice or millet. This is heavy economic drain on their limited resources.[9]

Agricultural and Industrial Developments

This is the mainstay of the people of Sikkim and its economy is primarily based on agriculture. The total cultivated area in Sikkim is about two lakh acres (196,547.89 acres). In spite of different measures to increase per acre production, the State continues to be dependent upon foodgrain import. In the high mountains till the limit of human habitation, agriculture is undertaken side by side with cattle rearing and cottage industries. The census data about various types of workers are as follows:

Table 2
Agricultural and Farming Functions including Labourers and Other Workers (Statistics): Census 2001

Total/ Rural/ Urban	*Persons/ Males/ Females*	*Cultivators Labourers*	*Agricultural Industry Workers*	*Household Workers*	*Other*
Total	Persons	131,422	16,939	3,250	111,709
	Males	70,154	8,614	2,287	84,902
	Females	61,268	8,325	963	26,807
Rural	Persons	131,400	16,914	3,057	87,654
	Males	70,137	8,592	2,141	66,612
	Females	61,263	8,322	916	21,042
Urban	Persons	22	25	193	24,055
	Males	17	22	146	18,290
	Females	5	3	47	5,765

In the mountains where rice cannot be grown successfully there barley, maize, millet and potatoes are important crops. The principal crops grown are maize, paddy, millet, wheat, barley, cardamom, apple, potato, oranges, buck wheat, pine-apple, banana, etc. Again, terrace system is the most prevailing type of rice

Table 3
Agricultural and Farming Functions including Labourers and Other Workers (Districtwise): Census 2001

District	Cultivators			Agricultural labourers			Household industries			Other workers		
	P	M	F	P	M	F	P	M	F	P	M	F
North	9,174	4,815	4,359	2,097	1,067	1,030	285	176	109	12,078	9,115	2,963
West	35,757	20,612	15,145	4,087	2,355	1,732	913	788	125	12,374	9,495	2,879
South	48,527	24,982	23,545	2,675	1,212	1,463	530	344	186	18,021	13,712	4,309
East	37,964	19,745	18,219	8,080	3,980	4,100	1,522	979	543	69,236	52,580	16,65

cultivation. In few cases 'Jhum' cultivation has continued to the present times as another type of agriculture practice. Rice is grown upto about 1600 metres wherever water is available. Wet paddy is interspersed with maize in dry fields and the latter is grown even till heights of 3000 metres. Oranges and cardamom constitute the two principal cash crops. In the wet middle altitude valleys cardamom is grown and fruit like oranges have been planted extensively upto about 1500 metres.

The other important cash crops of Sikkim, excluding cardamom and oranges, are ginger and potato. In fact, Sikkim has achieved a lot on the agriculture front since its association with the Indian union in 1975. Since almost 85 per cent[10] people inhabit in rural area and the agricultural products constitute the mainstay of the state's agricultural people, its development becomes important for improving the rural economy of the State. Efforts have been made to orient agriculture development in such a manner as to raise productivity by adopting right programmes and policies of making best utilisation of limited land resources. Sikkim has a limited potential for expanding arable land. The government has, therefore, laid great emphasis on the development of animal husbandry as a subsidiary occupation in rural areas. The main commercial establishments are controlled mainly by the Marwaris, Baniyas and other traders from the plains. They are mainly moneylenders, general merchants, clothiers, wholesale dealers, hoteliers and wine vendors. A number of Nepalese, Bhutias, etc., can be seen engaged in trade in Sikkim. A network of commercial and a variety of small scale and medium scale industrial establishments have been developed in Sikkim. Through the development plans sponsored by the Central Government, a huge capital has been invested in efforts to raise the standard of living of the people and boost welfare programmes. A census data about total, main, marginal and non-workers are given below :

Table 4
The Survey of Main Workers, Marginal Workers and Non-Workers (Statewise): Census 2001

Total Rural Urban	*Persons Males Females*	*Total workers*	*Main workers*	*Marginal workers*	*Non-workers*	*Total Workers (main + marginal)*
Total	Persons	263,320	212,478	50,842	277,173	263,320
	Males	165,957	146,666	19,291	122,260	165,957
	Females	97,363	65,812	31,551	154,913	97,363
Rural	Persons	239,025	190,152	48,873	241,463	239,025
	Males	147,482	129,620	17,862	107,904	147,482
	Females	91,543	60,532	31,011	133,559	91,543
Urban	Persons	24,295	22,326	1,969	35,710	24,295
	Males	18,475	17,046	1,429	14,356	18,475
	Females	5,820	5,280	540	21,354	5,820

Table 5
The Survey of Main Workers, Marginal Workers and Non-Workers (Districtwise) : Census 2001

District	*Total workers*			*Main workers*			*Marginal workers*			*Non workers*		
	P	M	F	P	M	F	P	M	F	P	M	F
North	23,634	15,173	8,461	17,572	13,050	4,522	6,062	2,123	3,939	17,389	8,237	9,152
West	53,131	33,250	19,881	45,169	30,298	14,871	7,962	2,952	5,010	70,043	30,585	39,45
South	69,753	40,250	29,503	57,272	36,015	21,257	12,481	4,235	8,246	61,753	27,977	33,776
East	116,802	77,284	39,518	92,465	67,303	25,162	24,337	9,981	14,356	127,988	55,461	72,527

This has resulted in the development of education, public health, communication and consequently, the setting up of industries though at a mini level. The leading industries are Sikkim Distilleries at Rongpo; Government Fruit Preservation Factory at Singtam; Jewel Factory; Government Cottage Industries; Sikkim Time Corporation; also Cigarette Factories at Mazitar, Rongpo and Jorethang; Sikkim Mining Corporation. The minor industries are like this, carpet weaving units 65; handicrafts 5; printing press 6; wooden products 6; motor repairing 13; bakery 10; paddy 8; match factory 1; candle factory 2; leather products 4; and miscellaneous are 50.[11] State Report Agricultural Census (1976-77) reveals that agriculture is the main occupation of the rural population in which cultivators number 90,380 and agriculture labourers are 4,207 while others are busy in mining 59; manufacturing, processing, servicing, repair etc., 406; construction 3,793; transport, storage and communication 1,778; persons involve in factory, fishing, hunting, plantation 619; industry 1,033; trade and commerce 2,338; and others 6,944.

The members of non-workers are 98,236.[12] While 1981 census reveals that total number of main workers as 147,436 of which 60.10 per cent are cultivators, 3.32 per cent are agricultural labourers and 1.08 per cent are associated with household industry and 35.51 per cent are other workers. Out of the total population main workers are 46.60 per cent and the marginal workers are 1.70 per cent, while on the other hand, the total non-workers are 51.70 per cent.[13] With the growing encouragement given by the government in these spheres in recent times, the number of persons engaged in those particular occupations has increased to a considerable extent. Thus, the State of Sikkim represents a variety of people, cultures and occupation.

References

1. Thanka B. Subba, *Dynamics of a Hill Society,* p. 29.
2. A.C. Sinha, "Resource Distribution and Multiple Ethnic Identity in Sikkim", in Haimendorf, C. Von. Fiirer (ed.), *Asian High Land Societies,* p. 193.
3. T.B. Subba, *op. cit.,* p. 29.
4. S.K. Chaube, *"Ethnicity and Politics in Sikkim",* in Raha, M.K. (ed.) *The Himalayan Heritage,* p. 65.
5. *Census of India,* Sikkim Series, p. 112.
6. Tulku Ringu, *"Monastic Education in Sikkim", Educational Change in Sikkim,* Annual Number, 1977, p. 10.
7. Chie Nakane, "A Plural Society in Sikkim: A Study of the Interrelations of Lepchas, Bhutias and Nepalis," in Haimendorf, C. Von. Fiirer (ed.), *Caste and Kin in Nepal, India and Ceylon* (New Delhi), p. 227.
8. *Ibid.,* pp. 227-29.
9. A.C. Sinha, *op. cit.* p. 198.

10. *Census of India,* Sikkim Series, 1981.
11. State Report Agricultural Census, 1976-77, Government of Sikkim, quoted in Jha, S.K., and Mishra, *Sikkim: Government and Politics*, p. 9.
12. *Ibid.*
13. *Census of India,* Sikkim Series, 1981.

2

Socio-cultural and Linguistic Set-up of Sikkim

Lingustic Aspects

It is a nice development that with the rising rates of literacy and the gradual spread of education some gifted young poets have started composing their *verses* in the Sikkimese-Bhutia language.

The Lepcha or *Kye* language had no script. Under such conditions no literature could have been produced in the *Kye* language. In fact, Chador Namgyal, the third Chogyal invented a script for this language. However, no attempt could be made to develop a type for Lepcha script. It was not possible to print books in this language. Some enthusiastic Lepcha zealots started bringing out a hand written magazine in this language. But because of several difficulties., particularly the want of finances and patronage, the attempt had to be abandoned.

It is a fact that about two-third of the people living in Sikkim are Nepalese; they speak different Nepalese dialects. The sub-sects of the Nepalese, i.e., Rais, Gurangs, Limbus, and Tamangs use their different dialects. The Nepalese language and literature have now come to flourish in Sikkim, particularly when there are no restrictions on the free expression by people in any language of one's choice.

A "Nepali Study Circle" has been constituted by some Nepalese interested in the development and furtherance of their language, literature, culture and tradition. The circle has been successfully bringing out a quarterly magazine in the Nepali language. This organ has been providing opportunities to promising Nepalese poets, story writers, essayists and journalists. The circle also brings out a monthly in English language, but a majority, of the articles included in this magazine are by the Nepali contributors. This monthly magazine has been given the name of *Premula.* Tulsi Aptan, Ramdatt Lal Thakur, Raghunath Suvedi, Santosh Barweda and Shanti Pradhan are those Nepali poets of Sikkim who have made a mark.

In fact Bhutia language was the language of the State. Nonetheless, English had been widely used and continues to be used in government offices and educational institutions. However three language formula has been adopted in schools. Besides English and a native language the school students are to learn

Hindi from class IV to class VIII. Such a policy is a right step towarsd national integration and the meaningful development of the regional languages. The census data relating to language spoken by all Scheduled Tribes is indicated below :

Table 1
Mother Tongue for Scheduled Tribes

Scheduled Tribe / *Mother Tongue*	*Number of Speakers*					
	Rural			*Urban*		
	Total	*Males*	*Females*	*Total*	*Males*	*Females*
1	2	3	4	5	6	7
All Scheduled Tribes						
Adi	6	3	3	0	0	0
Anal	2	2	0	0	0	0
Angami	1	1	0	0	0	0
Ao	2	1	1	0	0	0
Arabic/Arbi	6	5	1	0	0	0
Bengali	2	1	1	2	1	1
Bhili/Bhilodi	1	1	0	0	0	0
Bhotia	30,190	15,544	14,646	2,762	1,644	1,118
Bhumij	4	1	3	0	0	0
Coorgi/Kodagu	55	31	24	1	1	0
Deori	11	8	3	0	0	0
Dimasa	10	9	1	1	1	0
Dogri	1	0	1	1	0	1
English	28	15	13	12	6	6
Gangte	1	0	1	0	0	0
Gujarati	3	2	1	1	1	0
Hindi	55	41	14	15	11	4
Juang	2	1	1	0	0	0
Kashmire	1	1	0	0	0	0
Khandeshi	5	5	0	0	0	0
Korku	2	1	1	0	0	1
Lalung	1	0	1	0	0	0
Lepcha	27,982	14,602	13,380	755	415	340
Limbu	287	149	138	3	1	2
Lotha	4	2	2	0	0	0
Lushai/Mizo	2	1	1	0	0	0
Malayalam	2	1	1	2	1	1
Malto	3	0	3	0	0	0
Manipuri	14	7	7	2	1	1
Marathi	4	1	3	1	0	1
Miri/Mishing	2	2	0	0	0	0
Mishmi	4	1	3	3	1	2
Mogh	4	0	4	1	0	1
Nepali	7,539	3,868	3,671	1,763	895	868
Paite	1	0	1	0	0	0
Punjabi	8	4	4	1	1	0

(Contd.)

(Contd.)

1	2	3	4	5	6	7
Sanskrit	3	3	0	1	0	1
Sherpa	12,980	6,750	6,230	348	186	162
Tamil	2	1	1	0	0	0
Telugu	6	6	0	0	0	0
Tibetan	1,765	1,031	734	731	394	337
Tulu	1	1	0	0	0	0
Urdu	0	0	0	2	2	0
Wancho	2	1	1	0	0	0
Others	2,482	1,373	1,109	1,007	465	542

Source: Census 1991.

Way of Living

The people of Sikkim mostly live in small houses in villages. The houses by and large are similar to primitive dwellings. However, the Bhutia and Lepcha houses are different than the Nepalese houses. The Lepcha and Bhutia dwellings are constructed on taller stone foundations and they are often supported by poles made up of tree-trunks.

The economically well-developed communities dress up in different fashions. The Nepalese women folk tie a cloth, around their waiste for a skirt and cover the upper torso with a blouse. The head-gear is called *majetro* which is a two metre long *dupatta.* The Lepcha and the Bhutia women dress up themselves in *Bakkhu,* a long double breasted gown. This gown is fitted to the body with the help of a long cloth piece tied along the waiste. Inside the gown a loose blouse with long sleeves is put on. The married women carry a long appron like cloth hanging from the waiste. This cloth is often brocaded on both the corners. The old women put on embroidered caps. On festive occasions *Oonjiyoo,* i.e., a silken coat is put on by those who can afford it. The Bhutia man too wear *Bakkhu* with long sleeves. They put on trousers also. The Lepchas use the dress similar to the Naga dress. In all probability, since they came to Sikkim after having settled in Nagaland for generations they stuck to their old dress. A cap carrying multi-coloured feathers of different birds is their head dress. However, with the passage of time it has become difficult to identify people from their dresses since many Nepalese flaunt Bhutia dresses and *vice versa.*

Moreover, with increasing contact with the people from other parts of India, *shalwar kameez* shirt, pantaloon, coat, neck-tie have made enroads. Educated people now prefer to dress themselves in the western fashion. The Educated female now often support bobbed cut hair. Shukla is right when he says, "Thus Sikkim these days is a big cultured laboratory, where different blends are being mixed up and a synthetic culture part Bhutia, part Nepali and part Indian—is coming up."

The women love jewellery. The Bhutia women have a preference for Tibetan type of ornaments. The Nepali woman like golden necklaces studded with costly stone heads. In remoter areas large ear rings looking like bracelets are still used.

The woman on the whole are soft spoken, labourious and attractive. In Sikkim there is no seclusion for women and they work shoulder to shoulder with man in performing their functions. A census data relating to age, sex and marital status for all Scheduled Tribes is given below :

Table 2

Age, Sex and Marital Status for Scheduled Tribes

Age group	*Total*	*Never Married*	*Married*	*Widowed*	*Divor-ced*	*Unsp-ecified*
ALL SCHEDULED TRIBES						
Rural						
All ages	**83,486**	**50,813**	**30,310**	**2,063**	**287**	**13**
0 - 9	22,395	22,395	0	0	0	0
10-14	11,475	11,315	152	2	6	0
15-19	8,917	8,121	783	3	10	0
20-24	7,498	4,197	3,257	13	30	1
25-29	6,758	1,871	4,804	43	40	0
30-34	5,070	715	4,253	75	26	1
35-39	4,609	385	4,061	118	45	0
40-44	3,543	220	3,153	145	25	0
15-44	36,395	15,509	20,311	397	176	2
45-49	3,001	170	2,653	150	28	0
50-54	2,655	128	2,271	231	25	0
55-59	1,901	84	1,605	199	13	0
60-64	1,983	106	1,517	343	17	0
65-69	1,074	46	773	247	7	1
70-74	737	34	471	225	7	0
75-79	351	13	219	118	1	0
80+	401	46	204	144	6	1
Age not stated	1,118	967	134	7	1	9
URBAN						
All ages	**7,415**	**4,533**	**2,755**	**108**	**17**	**2**
0 - 9	1,291	1,291	0	0	0	0
10-14	943	930	9	1	2	1
15-19	977	934	43	0	0	0
20-24	890	638	250	2	0	0
25-29	831	330	491	8	1	1
30-34	598	126	464	4	4	0
35-39	477	50	420	6	1	0
40-44	323	26	285	9	3	0
15-44	4,096	2,104	1,953	29	9	1
45-49	256	14	232	9	1	0
50-54	212	26	175	10	1	0
55-59	151	17	119	14	1	0
60-64	156	16	123	16	1	0
65-69	73	7	54	11	1	0
70-74	47	7	34	6	0	0
75-79	26	2	23	1	0	0
80+	37	5	21	10	1	0
Age not stated	127	114	12	1	0	0

Source : Census 1991.

Marriage ceremony was spread over eighteen days but now it has been limited to three days only. The maternal uncle of the bride holds a very prestigeous position in the matrimonial affairs. At the time of bethrothal (engagement) unless his consent is obtained no deal can be stuck. Obviously he is the first to receive gifts including money and liquor. Only after the he has accepted the gifts the engagement stands binding, irrevocable and final. After engagement, the would be bridegroom is required to work with his prospective in-laws. On the day of wedding the would be couple and their parents gather togather on a watir spring sprouting from beneath a massive monolith. At this spot the bride and bridegroom are blessed. The price usually consists of a milch cattle, a calf, bronze and brass utensils, ornaments, a poney or a horse. The bride is taken to her in-laws a year after the wedding ceremony. On all these occasions the relatives of both the sides are feasted on delicacies and liquor. Till recently divorce had no sanction in this region.

In Sikkim there is a common school system. About 98 per cent of the educational institutions are managed and funded by the government which provides free universal education including cost free text books and free mid-day meals to primary schools children. The State follows the national cirricular framework prepared by the National Council of Educational Research and Training. The three language formula has also been implemented. The national language Hindi is being taught from class four to class eight.

The provision of proper facilities in the State for the education of disabled children and youths is a recently implemented programme. With cent per cent State support education is about 30 mentally retarded children is being provided in Paljor Namgyal Girl's School. To rehabilitate blind and physically handicapped youths vocational training-*cum*-production centre is bieng run at Jore-thang in South Sikkim. On November 14, 1987, the foundation stone of the Jawaharlal Nehru Memorial Institute for the Handicapped was laid at Bomtar in Namchi district. In order to make education an effective tool for the cultivation of social, and moral values, moral education component has already been incorporate in the curriculum of the primary stage. An another census data indicating ever/currently married women with their no. of surviving children is given on next page.

Table3
Ever Married and Currently Married Women Belonging to Scheduled Tribes by Present Age, Number of Surviving Children and Total Number of Surviving Children by Sex

Present Age	*Total ever/ currently married women*	*Ever/currently married women with number of serviving children*						*Total surviving children*		
		0	1	2	3	4	5+	*Total*	*Males*	*Females*
1	2	3	4	5	6	7	8	9	10	11
ALL SCHEDULED TRIBES										
RURAL										
Ever Married										
All ages	16,328	3,173	2,069	2,452	2,281	1,872	4,007	47,031	24,485	22,546
Less than 15	80	73	4	3	0	0	0	10	4	6
15-19	622	405	136	28	4	5	0	224	117	107
20-24	2,219	689	655	519	178	58	18	2,557	1,337	1,220
25-29	2,782	464	450	709	628	300	160	5,839	2,948	2,891
30-34	2,139	316	189	353	435	376	426	6,115	3,108	3,007
35-39	1,930	210	113	219	318	346	689	7,034	3,596	3,438
40-44	1,538	204	64	136	180	191	733	6,478	3,337	3,141
45-49	1,286	159	84	108	139	184	582	5,391	2,862	2,529
50-54	1,060	134	81	91	120	123	489	4,367	2,351	2,016
55-59	728	101	62	68	86	73	323	2,955	1,590	1,365
60-64	778	147	88	90	79	88	262	2,670	1,403	1,267
65-69	463	91	48	43	51	53	151	1,485	829	656
70-74	305	68	38	44	30	30	82	896	470	426
75-79	160	33	32	14	13	15	45	459	239	220
80 +	176	49	21	18	17	24	38	446	238	208

(Contd.)

1	2	3	4	5	6	7	8	9	10	11
Currently Married										
All ages	**15,010**	**2,884**	**1,891**	**2,292**	**2,137**	**1,724**	**3,654**	**43,240**	**22,425**	**20,815**
Less than 15	76	70	4	2	0	0	0	8	3	5
15-19	615	399	135	28	4	5	0	223	116	107
20-24	2,196	677	648	517	177	58	18	2,543	1,328	1,215
25-29	2,732	447	439	697	623	300	157	5,769	2,917	2,852
30-34	2,082	306	180	339	424	371	420	5,995	3,041	2,954
35-39	1,854	196	99	210	311	331	676	6,846	3,500	3,346
40-44	1,438	191	54	121	166	180	699	6,140	3,161	2,979
45-49	1,192	145	68	101	123	170	559	5,113	2,703	2,410
50-54	933	109	66	79	108	105	445	3,956	2,124	1,832
55-59	624	86	50	60	73	59	282	2,565	1,365	1,200
60-64	572	102	63	61	58	67	204	2,046	1,059	987
65-69	308	58	30	25	33	37	105	1,016	573	443
70-74	169	33	20	27	19	17	43	494	254	240
75-79	86	21	21	7	6	7	21	218	123	95
80 +	79	20	10	9	9	11	18	216	111	105
URBAN										
Ever Married										
All ages	**1,508**	**346**	**228**	**358**	**223**	**132**	**208**	**3,454**	**1,780**	**1,674**
Less than 15	9	9	0	0	0	0	0	0	0	0
15-19	32	21	5	3	0	1	0	15	6	9
20-24	190	80	61	35	8	3	2	180	84	96
25-29	307	69	70	110	32	13	8	509	266	243
30-34	233	44	29	72	47	26	15	526	249	277
35-39	202	18	14	61	51	27	31	570	306	264
40-44	116	24	9	20	25	13	24	315	167	148
45-49	109	12	9	19	17	18	33	371	213	158
50-54	79	12	5	9	8	8	36	313	156	157
55-59	67	14	5	9	10	9	20	210	114	96
60-64	72	10	8	10	11	8	24	235	111	124

(Contd.)

1	2	3	4	5	6	7	8	9	10	11
65-69	31	9	3	4	4	4	6	93	47	46
70-74	22	11	4	2	2	0	3	33	19	14
75-79	16	6	2	4	3	0	1	25	6	19
80 +	17	6	2	0	2	2	5	48	32	16
Currently Married										
All ages	**1,408**	**323**	**219**	**338**	**213**	**113**	**189**	**3,177**	**1,640**	**1,537**
Less than 15	6	6	0	0	0	0	0	0	0	0
15-19	32	21	5	3	0	1	0	15	6	9
20-24	189	80	61	35	8	2	2	176	82	94
25-29	299	68	67	107	32	12	8	496	260	236
30-34	227	41	29	69	47	26	15	520	247	273
35-39	198	18	13	60	50	26	31	560	301	259
40-44	107	24	8	18	24	9	23	284	150	134
45-49	100	11	9	14	16	17	32	349	203	146
50-54	71	11	5	7	7	6	34	284	142	142
55-59	54	10	5	8	9	5	17	174	96	78
60-64	59	9	7	10	8	6	18	184	81	103
65-69	20	7	1	2	3	2	4	51	29	22
70-74	18	8	4	2	2	0	2	25	15	10
75-79	15	6	2	3	3	0	1	23	6	17
80 +	8	2	2	0	1	1	2	26	18	8

Sources: Census 1991.

Notes: 1. 'All ages includes 'age not stated'.

2. Number of ever/currently married women in column 4 includes women not reporting number of surviving children.

3. The age groups having nil return are not shown.

3

Political and Administrative Developments

Not only Sikkim represents homogeneous arrangements of heterogeneous population, but as a state, Sikkim, the erstwhile Himalayan Kingdom, too offers a singular example of modernisation of a backward area in the Himalayas within a short span of time. In all spheres of life—political processes, social structure, state economy, culture and style of life this state has witnessed unusual changes since the turn of century. The processes of change, though slow during the initial stage, were greatly accelerated since its merger with the Indian Union in 1975. In this chapter an attempt has been made to briefly recount these changes, specifically the changes that had taken place in the administrative structure of the state in the pre-merger and post-merger periods. In this regard, modernisation of state bureaucracy means the introduction of certain administrative forms and values prevalent in India.

Pre-merger Times

Before its incorporation into India, Sikkim had remained, administratively, for many years, in relative isolation. The socio-political structure centred around an hierarchy of lamas and monasteries and the temporal ruler called Chogyal. The kingdom with its system of feudal, aristocratic bureaucracy was formed by the immigrant Bhutias in co-operation with the local Lepcha chiefs. Prior to the Bhutia immigration there was no central political power in Sikkim but only local Lepcha Chiefs[1] were there in order to administer their respective villages. The installation of first King Phuntso Namgyal in 1642 was recognised by the Dalai Lama in Tibet. Hence, the Bhutia leadership headed by King Phuntso Namgyal under the Tibetan influence made the beginning of the Lepcha subservience to the Bhutia theocratic feudalism. Then, Phuntso Namgyal with the help of Tibetan lamas and aristocracy made the first attempt to provide a viable administrative structure and the new chieftancy in Sikkim. To fulfil this purpose, Phuntso Namgyal appointed 12 Kalons (Ministers) from the Bhutia immigrants.[2] But the Lepchas at that time were not just the 'sons of the soil', but were also better cultivators and the entire land was in their hands. Therefore, gaining favour of Lepchas was very important for better administration. Due to this, the "Bhutia ruler adopted a magnificent device for courting the Lepcha loyalty by recognising the 12 important Lepcha

Chiefs heads as the Dzongpens (the governors or administrators of the forts) and by dividing the country into 12 Dzongs (districts)."[3]

"It is said that the traditional political system under the Namgyal dynasty in Sikkim had involved an intricate devolution of administrative powers and functions that have sometimes been characterised . . . as 'feudal'. The Chogyal (king) of Sikkim was vested with absolute authority, and the government was operated as if the country were a private estate. At the central level (the palace or Durbar, as it was commonly called) the Chogyal was assisted by one or more officials bearing the designation Chandzoh—the equivalent of a 'confidential secretary' in contemporary Sikkimese terminology—and a personal attendant called the Dronyer (literally 'introducer of guests or visitors'). There was no departmental system as such with a vertical distribution of administrative functions. Whatever administrative requirements arose were handled by either the Chandzohs or Dronyer, as was deemed appropriate by the Chogyal. Regional and local administration was vested in the Dzongpens (district officers) appointed by the Chogyal or, for their private estates, in the Kazis (land owning mobility of Bhutia/ Lepcha descent)".[4]

The colonial feudalism in the state had emerged in 1888 when the British Government of India appointed John Claud White as the first political officer of Sikkim to clear the untidy administrative mess and also to checkmate the Tibetan influence in the state.[5] He appointed a State Council in place of traditional council, the Lhadi Medi, which had remained a larger and more representative body than its successors. The Chogyal was temporarily deprived of his political powers and functions owing to this appointment of a 'political officer' alongwith the concurrent policy implemented by the British Government of India.

This at the same time resulted in a basic reorganisation of the administrative structure in Sikkim. A number of departments were established for the first time headed by officers to be held directly responsible to the political officer. In fact, the State Council had no direct administrative duties at the central level, as it was a consultative body whose advice the political officer would get at his own discretion. In spite of that, the political officer had to depend largely upon the members of the State Council. As some of the members were most powerful and influential persons among the Sikkimese, their concurrence was usually sought on important policy decisions. Besides, like Kazis and Thikadaris, the Council members too were a crucial link in the regional and local administrative structure, virtually functioning in the capacity of district officers.[6] With the appointment of J.C. White as political officer by the British Government of India, a systematic land revenue realisation was introduced. He administered the state affair with the support of a State Council consisted of the Lamas and the Kazis. He stipulated the granting of *illakas* (areas) on contract to the lessees who were held accountable for the revenue, public works, justice, law and order, in their respective *illakas*.

This situation continued till 1950, when the system was abolished. The central administration was under the strict supervision of a secretariat which consisted of three members who were answerable to the Council and Chogyal. Excepting a few, in major cases, higher servants were appointed mainly from the aristocracy. Moreover, it was the abolition of each Kazi house to send an intelligent and enlightened member for the Ruler's service. Apart from this, for filling even the higher posts in the government, no competitive tests were administered. Even, at times, Buddhist clergymen were assigned to look after the administrative jobs.[7] Indeed, prior to 1949, the British had set up a rudimentary form of government in which the Ruler was the repository of all authority. Certain departments had been established in the secretariat in Gangtok, all of which were answerable to the Chogyal (King). Apart from a police force and minimal departments for forests and public works, there was hardly something resembling a local administration.[8]

In 1949, the appointment of the Dewan (the principal Administrative Officer) initiated the pace of bureaucratisation of Sikkim in a non-lamaist pattern. In the landlord abolition programme, the crucial step, of course, was the establishment of two tahsils (districts), Eastern Sikkim and Western Sikkim, in August 1949. The tahsildars (district officers) were endowed to perform most of the functions previously allocated to the lessee landlords: revenue collector, judicial magistrate and registrar of land transaction activities.[9] In 1953, the Executive Council was formed as a first substantial step in the direction of an effective rationalisation of the administrative process.

A dyarchical system of administration was discovered, under which the administrative departments of Sikkim were divided into reserved and transferred subjects. The reserved subjects were administered by the order of President (then called Dewan or Principal Administrative Officer) while the transferred subjects were administered by executive councillors. The transferred subjects were these; education, health, agriculture, animal husbandry, press and publicity, transport, public works, excise, and bazaars departments. Reserved subjects too included finance, land revenue, state enterprise, home, external affairs. Establishments were entrusted to the charge of elected members of the Executive Council, each of whom was personally responsible to the State Council for the administration of the department.[10] A host of bureaucratic appointments were made to fill the void created by the eradication of the lessee system. Besides, the introduction of the First Seven Year Plan (1954-61) made it imperative for the administration to be sufficiently geared up in order to successfully fulfil the requirements of the development plans. As a result, Sikkim was divided into four districts with district officials: North, West, South and East.

The administration was handled by the secretariat headed by the Chief Secretary under whom the developmental secretaries of finance, revenue, trade and industry, panchayats and many other directors functioned. The district officer in each district was assisted by a number of other officials appointed by the Sikkim Durbar, which included a deputy development officer, an extension officer, a revenue inspector, and officers deputed to the district level by the various departments of the secretariat. The district officer had a huge variety of functions and powers encompassing virtually all aspects of administration in his area. He was the leading judicial authority acting as the magistrate of the district court and as the head of the district police unit. He also functioned as the development officer, and all development programmes came within his jurisdiction. Land revenue collection was one of the district officer's primary responsibilities and he also approved the registration of any changes in land ownership.

At last, he was granted broad powers of supervision and control over local Panchayats. At the village level Panchayats, have been established from 1966, which are responsible for village administration and coordination of the development programmes. Anyway, the April 1973 upheaval and tripartite agreement of May 8, 1973 had left Chogyal as a constitutional head of the state. In the agreement, certain changes in both the electoral and administrative set-ups were introduced. At the central level, virtually all of existing political administrative institutions were affected either directly or implicitly. Under these conditions, for instance, it was specifically provided that the prime minister now termed the Chief Executive—shall be appointed by the Chogyal on the nomination of the Central Government.

The dyarchical administrative system was also abolished. The power and status of the Chogyal were seriously diminished by the agreement. While he is still the head of the state, his capacity to control and manipulate the administrative and political systems was substantially reduced. His scope for initiative in virtually almost all fields of government was now superseded by the Chief Executive who emerged as the real head of the government. The Chief Executive was called Chief Executive Officer and his power and position were elaborately defined in the 8th May 1973 agreement. He was to have a special responsibility to ensure the right implementation of the constitutional and administrative changes in Sikkim, the smooth and efficient running of its administration, the continued enjoyment of certain basic rights and fundamental freedoms by all sections of the population of Sikkim and the optimum utilisation for the benefit of the people of Sikkim, of the funds sanctioned for economic and social development of Sikkim. The elected assembly was granted the authority to propose and pass laws concerning all of the departments of the state government.

Earlier power structure in the society comprised the former feudal structure together with Buddhism and a caste system which largely determined the occupational and status hierarchy within society and also the (Hindus/Buddhists) cultural ethos. The basic productive unit was the family. Direct inheritance of occupational position and loyalty to the king was quite common. A civil servant was expected to have allegiance not to the system but to the Ruler. This was very much evident from the pattern of the recruitment and the pattern of functioning of the forums for the bureaucrats.

The recruitments to the higher civil service were made on personal considerations through certain networks of influence at the highest level. The most effective network consisted of the patricians and the political entrepreneurs. The Government of India provided training facilities for the candidates entering the higher bureaucracy. The selection of even these mentioned trainees was not based on any competitive test. The major sources of the recruitment to the Sikkimese bureaucracy had been the feudal elements—like the Kazi houses and the Newars; and at the ethnic level, the Bhutias.[11] In fact, there was as yet no civil service nor was there any regular system of recruitment to the administration and most government positions were recommended by the Durbar. A large population of the apex posts in the Sikkimese administrative and technical services was held by the Indians. Initially, most of these officers were brought into the Sikkimese service since there were few Sikkimese with the required education or experience to fill these posts.

Later, however, the top assistants in some of these departments were Sikkimese. Various bureaucrats in science and technology was low and few Sikkimese came forward to man the available posts.[12] Thus, before the merging of Sikkim in the Indian Union the bureaucracy in Sikkim, though it had got its size swollen and expanded in comparison with the past, basically remained traditional in nature. As the treaty of 1861 between Sikkim and the British in India, the state inherited a colonial administration built up by a succession of British Political Officers to fulfil the purpose of establishing law and order in the State. But, due to recognition of the existing rulers as Maharajas the British Government and afterwards the Indian Government left the local administration in the state untouched, mostly loose and arbitrary in a feudal background. That is how Sikkim came to have a feudal administrative arrangements at the time of its integration with the Indian Union.

Development in the Post-merger Period

During this period, the 1973 agreement between the two governments was superseded by the terms under which Sikkim acceeded to the Indian Union. The monarchy was abolished and Sikkim turned one of the democratic states of the Indian Union operating under all the constitutional and administrative rules and procedures applicable elsewhere in India. The state has already started to suit the democratic set up and as a part and parcel of India its people have become the citizens of the democratic Indian Union. Right now, the administrative machinery of Sikkim is not different from that of the other States of the Indian Union.

During the reign of the Rulers in past the state was basically feudal but after its merging with India the state has become democratic and its bureaucracy and political order streamlined so as to conform to the all India pattern. So, it can be said without doubt that the history of modern Sikkim began in May 1975.

Further, the administration has expanded remarkably since the merger of the state with India in 1975. There is now a governor who is the constitutional head of the State. There is one elected chief minister and other ministers in the cabinet. Each minister is in charge of the administration of the departments allotted to his care. A Minister may be in charge of more than one department and for this, the allotment of department to a minister is usually determined by political factors. The minister is advised by the secretary and also joint secretary of the respective departments. After the merger of Sikkim in the Indian Union in 1975, the seretariat was reorganised into various departments and branches. Each department was placed under a secretary. Besides, several new departments have been set up and the old departments expanded remarkably. With its integration the state has come under the National Planning Commission. The departmental activities have been multiplied and expanded significantly. Since 1975, the secretariat has a chief secretary, secretaries, assisted by joint secretaries, deputy secretaries and under secretaries.

Indeed, the administration of the state is run by the secretariat headed by the Chief Secretary, the seniormost officer in the state under whom departmental secretaries and respective directors are responsible for individual departments. The Public Works Department has its own secretariat with its chief engineer as secretary. Apart from this, recently a secretariat has been established for the Power Department in Gangtok with its own secretary. Moreover, the Education Department also keeps its own secretariat and apart from its secretary, has directors. There is a development commissioner for the state to draw up development programmes and evaluate the progress of planning and execution. The Police Department has been expanded and placed under an inspector-general of police.

There is now also a chief conservator and conservators of forest and a supporting array of subordinates and field officers. Like other states, the judiciary is independent of the executive. There is a high court for the state which comprises of a chief justice and other judges. Moreover, there are also judicial officers at Gangtok and magistrates at each of the district headquarters. Indeed, the growth and expansion of various departments after merger of Sikkim has been phenomenal.

Further, in the State of Sikkim the first ever Public Service Commission came into being in 1981.[13] There is now State Civil/Police/Forest Service, each having junior officers in junior scale, senior officers in senior level and seniormost officers in the selection grade.

At present, recruitment to the different levels of state administration even at the lower levels has become more methodical, universalised and also democratic as in the other states of India. In this way, the past traditional and feudal agrarian-cum-administrative system has given way to the new modernised bureaucracy. Over the past decade it has grown in Sikkim and has taken a firm root in response to the organic necessities of a backward, isolated state, with the augmentation in the state activities for implementing various plans and programmes, and for expending the administration in remote parts, the number of employees in the state government services has steadily increased.

Since most of the employees belonging to Class II and Class III categories are recruited locally, expansion in their numbers is directly related to the expansion of the educational system. In Sikkim, the State government being almost the only employer, the demand for the expansion of the bureaucracy consequently places a call for the increase in the educational facilities. This is precisely the reason for including the above discussions in this chapter on the background and development of state bureaucracy in Sikkim. This background information is also necessary to understand the formation of a new class consisting of educated, naval class bureaucrats. In the following chapters this relationship between education and bureaucracy on the other hand and class formation on the other will become more visible.

References

1. Chie Nakane, "A Plural Society in Sikkim: A Study of the Interrelations of Lepchas, Bhotias and Nepalis", in Haimendorf, C.Von Fiirer (ed.), *Caste and Kin in Nepal, India and Ceylon* (New Delhi), p. 216.
2. Quoted in A.C. Sinha, *Politics of Sikkim*, p. 55.
3. *Ibid.*, pp. 13-14.
4. Leo E. Rose, "*Modernizing a Traditional Administrative System: Sikkim 1890-73*", in Fisher, James, F. (ed.), *Himalayan Anthropology: The Indo-Tibetan Interface*, pp. 205-06.
5. A.C. Sinha, *op. cit.*, p. 19.
6. Leo E. Rose, *op. cit.*, pp. 206-07.
7. A.C. Sinha, *op. cit.*, p. 56.
8. J.S. Lall, (ed.), *The Himalaya: Aspects of Change*, p. 229.
9. *Sikkim Secretariat File*, 1949, quoted in Leo E. Rose, *op. cit.*, pp. 217-218.
10. S.K. Jha and S.N. Mishra, *Sikkim: Government and Politics*, pp. 39-40.
11. A.C. Sinha, *op. cit.*, pp. 56-57.
12. V.H. Coelho, *Sikkim and Bhutan*, pp. 45-46.
13. S.K. Jha and S.N. Mishra, *op. cit.*, p. 49.

Since most of the [illegible] Class II and Class III category [illegible] the state government being almost the only employer [illegible]

[illegible]

[illegible] the first [illegible] in the southern [illegible]. In 1954, the Tashi Namgyal Academy was [illegible] the first modern public

4

Background and Post-Merger Achievements in Education

Plato, the first political philosopher has said that the "ultimate function of state is padagogic". This has become true in the state of Sikkim which has professed beyond expectation in the field of education. Especially after merging with the Indian Union, miraculous developments have taken place in this regard. Here, we are presenting a brief history and the education profile of the State of Sikkim.

Background

Prior to the immigration of Tibetans no historical evidence or written documents are available to show the existence of any type of educational system in Sikkim. With the immigration of the Tibetans from Tibet during the early 17th century,[1] the religious based monastery education was started. The immigrant Tibetans instituted monarchy in Sikkim and changed the indigenous people into Lamaism and imparted monastery based education in which religious texts were taught to the students. But this form of education was confined to the lamas, young and old, and not meant for the laity.

Thus in course of time a literati centering around the monasteries was built up. The monks knew very well the art of paper making, printing and a number of arts and crafts. Some of them were experts in medicine, treatment of diseases using both mundane and spiritual means. But this kind of education being esoteric in nature did not benefit the common man. The history of modern formal education in the state of Sikkim begins with the establishment of a missionary school in 1883 in Gangtok by Reverend McFarlene, a Scottish missionary. Thereafter, two schools were set up in 1906, one for the Bhutia boys named as Bhutia Boarding School and another named as Nepali Boarding School for Nepalese boys. But, very soon in 1924 both the Bhutia and Nepali Boarding Schools were amalgamated into one high school which was named after the then Maharaja Tashi Namgyal of Sikkim. Around that time the very first girls' school was also established but at a primary level by the Christian missionaries.

Since 1944, the education and educational agencies were brought under the direct control of the then king Maharaja Tashi Namgyal. In 1954, the first Education Directorate was set up. After 1954, initiative was made to impart formal education in the state in a planned and systematic manner.[2] In 1964 the Tashi Namgyal Academy was established with pure elitist prejudice as the first modern public school in Sikkim at government expenses. The older institution—Tashi Namgyal High School continued to function as a general school for the children of the people other than the ruling elite class. Prior to the establishment of Tashi Namgyal Academy, the children of ruling elitist section of Sikkimese society were usually sent abroad or to better public schools in India either through government scholarships or through individuals' own expenses. Undoubtedly, such advantages were confined only to the Sikkimese elitist section. This Tashi Namgyal Academy undoubtedly was set up in order to fulfil the demand for modern education among the children of Sikkimese elite within Sikkim itself because there were many problems in sending their children to distant places. Moreover, there was a growing demand of modern education for the Sikkimese elites to perpetuate and control their power within the state.[3] The opportunities for modern education during the pre-merger period under discussion were concentrated particularly to the ruling classes of Sikkimese social set up in whose hands mostly the political powers were vested. There was a distinct influence of interests of the ruling classes in spreading and facilitating the progress of modern education in Sikkim in order to perpetuate their elitist position in Sikkimese society. This can be substantiated by citing the following remark made by D.P. Dahal (1978)—who has been an ex-Education Minister of Sikkim Government. "In forties even the education in Sikkim was meant for the aristocracy".[4] Such indifference primarily generated a grievance among the commoners, particularly the Nepalese who by then had become the majority. The demand of more and more schools were made, fresh schools (private) were opened, and pressures were created on government to take them over. Obviously, the Durbar reacted not favourably to such activities and made the following announcement which appeared to be a forewarning to parents and guardians.

"Responsible quarters of the Durbar have grave misgivings about the 'mushroom growth' of the schools in Sikkim. This fault may be partly mitigated by the unusual urge for education exhibited by the public in recent years. All the same, parents, guardians and those interested in education should note that this vital service of the community must be treated less casually if it is to serve its ultimate purpose. The limited resources of our small country must be fully utilised. A new school should be set up only when it is absolutely necessary. Instead of asking for more centres of teaching would it not be better to improve the existing schools in staffing and equipments thereby raising general standard of education, while at the same time safeguarding the moral and physical well-being of the children. You can rest assured that the Durbar would always consider such objective requests most sympathetically".[5]

This type of demand was raised mainly by the Nepalese because of the other commoners like Bhutias and Lepchas who were Buddhists, ideal education had been in the traditional way: in maximum cases it was natural for them to be inclined to take monastic education (training) rather than formal education.[6] And it was more important and necessary for them to become lamas, Since importance of lama in the traditional Sikkimese society had been overwhelming. During the times of Maharaja Kumar Thendup Namgyal, the trend of Tibetan influence in educational development was evident.

For instance, the establishment of Enchey School which imparted education in Buddhist scripture to young lamas and others, the establishment of Sheda Nyngma College in 1963 as a unique type of institution of higher education in Sikkim under government patronage. The primary objective of this institution was to impart higher education to the prospective lamas who would join monasteries. Still, one important feature of this institution was that the Government had officially recognised the courses offered by it as equivalent to those of Bachelor Degree of some other universities. Although the main thrust of curriculum in this institution had been on Mahayana Buddhistic texts and Tibetan language, few secular subjects had also been started to modernise the course. The study of English too had been in the curriculum in order to make it more relevant from the angle of modern usage. At present this institution has been purely as a residential institution with an yearly in-take of 40 students. It is presently affiliated to the Sampurnanda Sanskrit University of Benaras.[7]

Right now, the Enchey School has been continued as one of the government secondary schools in Sikkim. The curriculum is also the same as that of the other government secondary schools in the state.

Not only this, during his reign the Namgyal Institute of Tibetology for higher learning in the study of Mahayana Buddhism was also established in 1958. At present, this institution is situated at Deorali in Gangtok and has become a full-fledged research institution in this direction. However, during the later half of Chogyal regime and just before the merger of Sikkim with India the then Maharaja Tashi Namgyal and later Maharaja Kumar Thendup Namgyal himself took the lead in the issue of educational expansion and a number of schools were established during his time with the co-operation and assistance given by the Government of India. With large-scale Indian assistance and import of teachers from other states, the various endeavours had a positive effect to enhance the literacy in Sikkim among the common people so much so that by 1917 the literacy rate had increased to 17.14 per cent from 2.98 per cent in 1931.

The state had a very well-organised and fairly result-oriented educational system at the time of its integration with the Indian Union in 1975. But even then, by and large the educational facilities available to the common masses fell short of the actual requirement. Indeed, major changes in, and impetus to, education, educational planning and development in Sikkim have been possible only after its integration with the Indian Union. In fact, the year 1975 may be considered as a watershed in the history of educational development in Sikkim. Since then a systematic attempt has been made to plan and improve education in the state in accordance with the National Educational Policy. Now the people of Sikkim have the equality of opportunity for entry into any educational institution.

The government too paid special attention to impart formal education to the people of rural and remote areas of Sikkim. In fact, to cope with the tempo of modernisation, expanding system of bureaucratisation and professionalisation, the state government has laid great emphasis on the expansion of various educational programmes and plans.

Education is regarded as the main instrument for the removal of backwardness from the state. It is felt that education prepares the minds of the people for acceptance of developmental programmes and also encourages their participation in the developmental process. The educated people are expected to spearhead the socio-economic changes in the state and support the people to rise up from the poverty-level.

Whether this noble objective has been achieved or not needs to be examined very closely. In the following pages of the chapter, an attempt has been made to quantify in concrete terms the nature of educational development that has taken place in post-merger Sikkim.

On the whole, as expected the urban literacy level is higher in all the districts, as compared to the literacy rate in the rural areas of the districts. There is also a marked difference in male and female literacy in urban and rural areas. The overall male literacy rate is quite high in urban (61.44 per cent) and in rural areas (40.25 per cent) compared to that of the female literacy levels in urban and rural areas (45.42 per cent backward, 18.24 per cent respectively). It seems that women are more backward educationally in the rural areas of the different districts than in the urban parts. It is low in almost all the rural areas of all the districts, ranging from 12.60 per cent literacy rate in the West District to 22.85 per cent in the East District. While compared to this situation the male literacy rates in the rural areas of the four districts range from 32.57 per cent in the West District to 45.20 per cent in the East District region.

Facilities Regarding Education

Education is practically free in Sikkim. In addition, needy and meritorious students are being further assisted in the form of scholarships and free boarding. Text books are supplied free of cost to children going in classes I to XII in the government schools. A good number of boys and girls are also receiving higher education and vocational training in other states of India and in foreign nations. A number of students are being sent to different parts of India to join higher level professional colleges in the fields like agriculture, medical science, engineering and veterinary science.

Apart from this, a Teachers' Training Institute, a Degree College and a Law College are all situated in the East District. Thus, the East District has now a larger part of the educational institutions than any of the other districts. To keep abreast with the growing need for school education at all levels, the government has started a larger number of schools during the last few years. A number of schools were also upgraded.

It appears that during this period a major emphasis has been given to develop the primary education. A large number of pre-primary schools have been upgraded as lower primary schools and also number of lower primary schools (145) have been upgraded as upper primary schools. A number of upper primary schools (113) have been upgraded as junior high schools. Same kind of noteworthy expansion has also taken place in the number of high/secondary schools.

Educational Set up

As per the pre-primary education scheme, 328 pre-primary centres function in the state at present. These centres can be counted not so much as an educational institution, as a mother and child care centre. Since 1976, the pre-primary centres have been functioning and before that they did not exist in Sikkim. These centres are managed by trained 'school mothers'. Now, these centres have become very popular because working mothers are able to leave their children at the centre during their working hours and also, the children in the age group of 3-5 get initiated into a school atmosphere. These pre-primary centres are mainly one teacher schools and the teacher of the pre-primary centre is generally named as school mother.

Schooling at Primary Level

In state, there are 232 lower primary schools and 250 upper primary schools in Sikkim. Lower primary schools impart education upto the Class III stage while upper primary schools run upto class V stage. In the primary level, Nepali, Bhutia, Lepcha and Limbu languages are taught. There is a primary school within the radius of two kilometres of a village and enrols almost each child in the 6-11 years age group. Schooling at the primary stage and the curricula help to equip the young students for possible entry into immediate higher educational institutions, namely, Junior High Schools.

Schooling at Secondary Level

Now there are 122 junior high schools which are graded upto Class VIII. The examination at the end of the junior high school is conducted by the Sikkim Junior High School Examination Board. Sikkim has now 54 government high/ secondary schools graded upto Class X, and one high/secondary school run by the Catholic Missionaries. There is no state board to hold the final examination[8] at the end of this stage, which is conducted by the Central Board of Secondary Education, Delhi. This three-tier system of school education, primary, junior high school and high/secondary school, leads to the next stage of the higher/senior secondary school. The state now has 13 higher/senior secondary schools that prepare students for the higher/senior secondary examination[9] of the Central Board of Secondary Education, Delhi. Besides this, there is Tashi Namgyal Academy which function as a public school. It prepares students for the Indian students for the Indian School Certificate Examination conducted by the Board for such schools at Delhi. The higher/senior secondary examination ensures possibility the entry for young students into higher educational institutions, namely, college and university.

Teaching Staff

During the pre-merger days, most of the teachers in Sikkim were recruited from different parts of India. Very few teachers could be found locally. But the situation has quite changed in recent years—the number of local recruits is gradually increasing.[10]

In accordance with the Census of 2001, indeed a comprehensive survey of literates and literacy rates have come on the surface as helpful guide for us. It has vividly covered the regions of North, West, South and East of Sikkim State. In fact a comparative study has been made in connection with the local population of male and female. The female as shown below is the clear indication.

Table 1
Literates and Literacy Rates by Sex—Sikkim : Census 2001

Union Territory/ Districts		*Literates*			*Literacy Rate of 2001*	
	Persons	*Males*	*Females*	*Persons*	*Males*	*Females*
Sikkim	**322,828**	**191,326**	**131,502**	**69.68**	**76.73**	**61.46**
North	24,033	15,673	8,360	69.11	77.32	57.65
West	61,326	36,147	25,179	59.31	67.21	50.75
South	75,400	43,251	32,149	68.12	74.57	61.02
East	162,069	96,255	65,814	75.57	82.05	67.74

NFE and Adult Education

Alongwith this, it will be relevant to point out that the government is concentrating upon not merely on formal education, but is also giving due importance to adult and non-formal education to supplement school based formal education. The department of education has adopted and introduced the National Adult Education Programme and Non-Formal Education in all the nooks and corners of the state for those who cannot attend regular schools. In order to implement such programmes, the government has set up quite a good number of Adult Education Centres and Non-Formal Education centres.

Current Position

Undoubtedly the state government is concerned about improving the standard of education in the state. The notional objective of the state in education is to develop a system of national education. It means among other aspects, universal free elementary education, removal of adult illiteracy, adoption of state languages as well as Indian languages as medium of instructions at all levels, diversification of secondary education and so on. There are other goals that relate to the creation of a population which would be aware of the modern world outside Sikkim state and the development of educated citizens loyal to the nation and its people. To cope with the evergrowing demand for education from every corner of Sikkim, it has not only opened new schools but has also upgraded some of the existing schools keeping in view the needs of the people.

Thus, in conclusion, it may be said that the most notable feature of the state educational system after its merger with the Indian Union has been the phenomenal expansion. The growth and expansion of education and demand for education and educational facilities within the state have been highly momentous. The number of educational institutions has increased rapidly as a result of the initiative taken by the government as well as by the increased demand for education. This educational spread has undoubtedly benefited almost all sections of the people of Sikkim although the shares of the benefits differ according to the location (rural and urban), gender, district, communities and socio-economic status of the people. There has been substantial progress during this post-merger period in the proportion of young students who are in some sense ready for higher education.

References

1. P.N. Chopra, Sikkim, p. 43.
2. D.G. Bhattacharya, *A Study of Educational Development in Sikkim,* pp. 104-10.
3. *Ibid.,* pp. 111-12.
4. quoted in *Ibid.,* p. 112.
5. Sikkim Herald, 1959, quoted in *Ibid.,* p. 113.
6. Chie Nakane, "A Plural Society in Sikkim: A Study of the interrelations of Lepchas, Bhotias and Nepalis", in Haimendorf, C. Von. Fiirer (ed.), *Caste and Kin in Nepal, India and Ceylon* (New Delhi), p. 261.
7. D.S. Bhattacharya, *op. cit.,* p. 112.
8. *Ibid.,* p. 29.
9. *Ibid.,* p. 30.
10. *Ibid.,* p. 30.

3. *Ibid.*, p. 111-112.

9. [illegible]
10. *Ibid.*, p. 30.

5

Emergence of a New Class

I

In the previous chapter, we have seen what developments have taken place in the field of education with state and central Government's efforts as well as individual endeavours. An obvious outcome of education is emergence of a new class structure with dominant educated class. In this chapter, we shall discuss the certain aspects of old and new class structure in Sikkim.

Theories of Class

Among the sociologists and social anthropologists, there is still a confusion about the theory of social class and more broadly, of social satisfaction. 'Stratification'[1] refers to any hierarchical ordering of social groups or strata in a society. Its main forms are caste, class, estate and status groups, and each of these types of social stratification is undoubtedly complex. There are many unsettled questions about the basis and features of classes and status groups, just as about castes and estates. Furthermore, in the context of classes, the membership of modern social classes generally is less stable than that of other types of hierarchical groups. The individual is born into a particular social class, just as he is born into a caste or estate; but he is almost less likely to remain at the social level in which he was born and he or his family may rise or fall in the social hierarchy. If he desires, he needs no patent of mobility, no kind of official recognition, to confirm his new status and positions. It will be enough for him to be wealthy, to have a specific economic and occupational role, and perhaps to acquire some of the secondary cultural characteristics of the social stratum into which he has moved.[2] In this regard, it may be said that the class position in the society is to some extent transitional in this modern phase of the world.

Indeed, the class-based inequalities are a universal phenomenon and its amount and extent may differ from society to society. In a very general sense, classes are groups of people into which society is classified. All sociologists and social anthropologists admit that society is not homogeneous and it consists of a large number of strata and social groups. But views are not the same when one comes to the question of what lies at the basis of this stratification.[3] Broadly, in this study the term 'class' is viewed in the Weberian framework, as it is realised that it provides a realistic explanation of emerging 'class' situation in post-merger

Sikkim. Apart from this, the concept of 'class' is used here as a instrument for social analysis of recent trends of changes in the contemporary Sikkimese society as a whole.

1. Marx. Most recent sociological work about the theory of class is based on a distinction between Weberian and Marxist approaches. Marx defines class as conceived of groups in terms of relations of production. He says that the relations of production in terms of ownership of means of production determine class structure, that is positions of superordination and subordination.

Thus, he has given a two class model: the bourgeoisie and the proletariat. The bourgeoisie does own and control the means cf production, directs labour power and also appropriates the surplus product. While the proletariat does not own or control means of production and they are in a position to sell their labour power. Hence, Marx affirmed 'the economic basis of classes'[4] which in turn meant the increasing separation and polarisation of the bourgeoisie and the proletariat. But Karl Marx's two-class model cannot adequately account for the complex divisions of contemporary societies. G.D.H. Cole felt that Marx's interpretation of class due to being dependent on relation to means of production, does not satisfactorily explain the existence of other classes in society besides the two main classes—those having the means of production and those not owning the means of production.[5]

Dahrendorf[6] notes that all forms of distinction cannot be traced back to man's share in effective personal property as Marx tried to show. So, the ownership and non-ownership of means of production cannot be said as the only determinant factors of the classes in the modern society which is highly complex in nature.

2. Max Weber. On the other hand, Max Weber, in presenting 'a comprehensive alternative'[7] to the Marxist theory, said that stratification on the basis of occupation, prestige, consumption and style of life is particularly important in capitalist societies. He observes that stratification generate a hierarchy of continuously graded positions based on a variety of factors, not just the ownership of productive property. In this opinion it is impossible to conceive of the class system of contemporary societies as consisting of two opposed classes. According to Weber, the term 'class' refers to any group of people that is seen in the same 'class situation'. He writes that we may speak of class when a number of people have common life chances and these chances represent financial interests in terms of the possession of goods and opportunities for income and under the conditions of commodity or labour markets. These three points, as per Weber, refer to 'class situation'.[8] Weber also argued that " 'property' and 'lack of property' are, therefore, the basic categories of all class situations. Within these categories, however, classes, the process by which classes are formed and an outline of the class situations are further differentiated: on the one hand, according to the kind of property that is usable for returns; on the other hand, according to the kind of services that can be offered in the market".[9]

The way this suggests, property ownership is the basic criterion for class membership, and among unpropertied workers, classes are differentiated along occupational lines. This, he too has meant that "those who have no property but who offer services are differentiated just as much according to their kinds of services as according to the way in which they make use of these services in a continuous or discontinuous relations to a recipient. But, always that is the generic connotation of the concept of class: that the kind of chance in the market is the decisive moment which presents a common condition for the individual's fate. 'Class situation' is, in this sense, ultimately 'market situation".[10]

Hence, Weber's definition of social class illustrates the centrality of occupations and occupational mobility in his concept of class structure.[11] In this connection, it is important to write here that according to Weberian model, "if class is defined in terms of market opportunities, then interpretation of class conflict must centre on the struggles between groups over access to the market. This will, however, neglect the more fundamental mechanisms which control such access."[12]

3. Sorokin. Famous thinker Sorokin[13], is Weberian in his conception of class and he argued that class system moves around the stratification of occupational roles. Gradients of inequality among occupations leads to three principal strata. Mobility is predictably confined between these broad strata, at the top, entrepreneurs are "Economically independent . . . their own 'bosses' . . . and [then] activity consists either exclusively, or at least partially, in an organisation and control of their 'business' and their employees. Enterpreneurs own property and/or capital. Below this group are higher employees, who do not own property but engage in professional, technical and non-managerial pursuits. The work of this group is limited to non-manual activities. Wage earners are the third group. Compared with 'Higher employees', they are also unpropertied but 'receive lower remuneration [and] are subordinate in function, being mainly manual workers."

Here, strata is internally differentiated with finer gradations corresponding to increasingly detailed specifications of occupational roles.

4. Mills. Mills[14] another Weberian, also says that it is occupation rather than property which is the basis of class stratification in contemporary societies. He is thus unequivocally and explicitly Weberian in his stress on the occupational order as the basis of class. Mills gives more specific reasons for the growth of New Middle Class occupations. One, technological changes have resulted in greater labour productivity. As a consequence, for fewer productive workers are needed. Next. large-scale enterprise has required large scale marketing and distribution. Hence, there has been an increase in the numbers of people indulged in selling, transportation, communication and in those financial sectors to do with merchandising, credit-financing and banking. Thirdly, the growth in the size of the business and the quite greater scope of government activities has meant an increased demand for people to coordinate, administer and manage. Mills suggests his view that these are changes in the occupational structure.

5. Giddens. In this context, Giddens is also Weberian in his emphasis on market capacity as the crucial determinant of class position and the chief factor affecting market capacity is the possession and non-possession of recognised skills. He advances the idea that class structure are, in a very large measure, consolidated by societal mobility regimes. Being a reason, he specifies that by a process called mediate structuration by him, market conditions are linked with class relationships, resulting in the rudimentary growth of class structure. The role of mediate structuration in the labour market is most clearly reflected by the mobility regime of a society. Giddens says that 'the greater the degree of 'closure' of mobility chances . . . the more this facilitates the formation of identifiable classes . . . is facilitated by the degree to which mobility closure exists in relation to any specified form of market capacity."[15]

Class structure is shaped by the pressures imposed by mobility regimes. Mobility closure defines class boundaries and the extent of closure determines their permeability. Mediate structuration functions by limiting opportunities for mobility on the basis of differential market advantages among competing groups and individuals. Three factors are mainly responsible for the closure of mobility chances. They are the ownership of property and/or capital; the possession of educational and/or technical qualifications; and the membership of manual-labour power. He also distinguishes mediate structuration from proximate structuration. The combination of mediate and proximate structuration create a class structure based on market capacity. Corresponding to these market capacities, three major categories constitute the class structure of quite advanced capitalism: an upper class of property and/or capital owners; a middle class possessing technical and/or educational qualifications; and a working class which depends on its labour.[16]

6. Parkin. Parkin proposes the idea of closure as unifying the analysis of all forms of inequality. He unlike Giddens or Sorokin does not present a set of division corresponding to class structures. Still, his discussion of social class provides insight into the conditions responsible for class formation and reproduction. He adopts the Weberian premise that classes exist by virtue of being "social closure." Social closure is "the process by which social collectivities seek to maximise rewards by restricting access to resources and opportunities to a confined circle of eligibles."[17] Structured inequality results from one group systematically excluding another from valued social resources. As a condition for class formation, he argues that "Strategies of exclusion are the predominant mode of closure in all stratified systems".[18]

Exclusionary practices are an important means of closure in the exchange of personnel between occupations. He emphasises the formative role of credentials and credential-enforcing organisation in the evolution of class structure, Parkin says elsewhere, "the backbone of the class structure and indeed of the entire reward system of modern Western society, is the occupational order."[19]

7. Lockwood. One more Weberian, Lockwood defines class in terms of three factors: Market situation 'consisting of source and size of income, degree of job-security, and avenue for upward occupational mobility', work situation, or 'the set of social relationships in which the individual is involved at work by virtue of his status in the division of labour'; and status situation, or the position in the hierarchy of prestige.[20]

8. Ossowski. Through reviewing a number of definitions of class, Ossowski considers class as a particular and specially important aspect of social structure. He gives some common points to the conceptions of a " 'class' society; the class constitutes a system of the most comprehensive groups in the social structure; the class division concerns social status connected with a system of privileges and discriminations not determined by biological criteria. The membership of individuals in a social class is relatively permanent."[21]

Ossowski also suggets a 'scheme of gradation' to understand social structure. Gradation denotes both subjectively evaluated and objectively measured rank. He classifies gradation into simple and synthetic categories. By simple gradation in the set up of social classes he understands a conception of social structure in which the relation of higher and lower classes is based on the grading of some objectively measurable criteria like the gradation of wealth, the amount of property, or the size of a person's share in the national income. Therefore, he talks of a simple gradation in conceptions of social structure by referring only to a scheme of economic gradation. He states, when two or more incommensurable criteria are involved in settling the levels in the social structure, it would involve synthetic gradation. He also stresses that "one might for instance set up a gradation of classes with educational levels as the basis of the gradation . . . The level of education is at times an important dimension in a synthetic gradation . . .[22]

Hence, we have seen that the meaning of class has been changing since the introduction of Marxian theory of class. The fundamental viewpoint so far discussed above offer useful starting points in which the ideas about class proposed by the various scholars like Marx, Weber and other neo-Weberians have been discussed. Special attention is devoted to the non-Marxist concepts of social class advocated by Weber, Sorokin, Mills, Lockwood, Giddens, Parkin and Ossowski.

All the theoretical discussions as proposed by the various scholars establish that the occupational position and education together are important attributes to determine one's class hierarchy in the society. And, it is in this theoretical context that the present study has been undertaken to deal with the fundamental theme which is to ensure the fact that education acts as one of the most important contributing factors to the emergence of a new class in Sikkim. Thus, education may be regarded as one of the most important operative factors in the formation of a new class and the emergence of this new class brings about changes in the existing social relations and thus, contributing to social change. It is not necessary that the aspects contributing to the development of classes should be similar in all societies, they may differ from one society to another. Society is not a static phenomenon and it changes in the due course of time. Therefore, there may arise new situations and new factors which might have considerable influence over the formation of classes and social change. Here has been observed that "in the less developed countries or developing countries the validity and general applicability of the class theory remains to be tested. This is all the more important since education has been assigned in the plans of these countries the decisive instrumental role of bringing about a modern, developed, industrial and just society."[23]

II

Emergence of New Class

The word 'new class' is very recent and has begun to appear with ever increasing frequency in discussions of the contemporary new American scene. Its usage delineates the fact that a new important class, or say, new dominant class or a new privileged class is emerging. The new class attempts to relate those trends to one-another to release the changing economy to a changing occupational structure in which education has very important and significant role and which, in turn, is related to a changing society.

About new class D.P. Moynihan emphasises that "The social legislation of the middle third of the century created 'social place' for a new class whose privilege (or obligation) it is to dispense services to populations that in various ways/wards of the state". [24] While Norman Podhoretz uses the term new class politically, he stresses, "The nature of the New Politics movement is easy enough to describe in sociological terms. The movement is made up largely of educated, prosperous people, members of the professional and technical intelligentsia and their wives and children, academics and their students: the group . . . presently identified as a New Class long before it came to consciousness of itself as a class and as a potential political force".[25]

In this regard, Irving Kristol emphasizes that ". . . these people constitute what one may simply call, for lack of better name 'the new class'. The new class is not easily defined but may be vaguely described. It consists of a goodly portion of those college educated people whose skills and vocations proliferate in a 'post-industrial society' . . . It is, by now, a quite numerous class; it is an indispensable class for our kind of society; it is a disproportionately powerful class; it is also an ambitious and frustrated class."[26]

But, David T. Bezelon thought to be the new class as ". . . non-property holding individuals whose life conditions are determined by their position within or relation to, the corporate order . . . people gaining status through organisational position. They achieve their positions—or at least are permitted to enter the race—mostly by virtue of educational status. People who mostly organise and administer, and criticise and comment on the activities of others . . . the technologists and administrative intellectuals.[27]

Milovan Djilas produced a book *The New Class* in which he delineated the emergence of new class in the communist world, particulary the USSR. Djilas deliberately stressed that "Everything happened differently in the USSR and other communist countries from what the leaders—even such prominent ones as Lenin, Stalin, Trotsky and Bukharin—anticipated. They expected that the state would rapidly wither away, that democracy would be strengthened. The reverse happened. They expected a rapid improvement in the standard of living—there has been scarcely any change in this respect and, in the subjugated East European countries, the standard of living has been declined. In every instance, the standard of living has failed to rise in proportion to the rate of industrialisation, which was much more rapid. It was believed that the differences between cities and villages, between intellectual and physical labour would slowly disappear; instead these differences have increased. Communist anticipation in other areas—including their expectations for developments in the non-Communist world—have also failed to materialise. . . In 1936, when the new Constitution was promulgated, Stalin announced that the "exploiting class" has ceased to exist. The capitalist and other classes of ancient origin had in fact been destroyed, but a new class, previously unknown to history had been formed . . . This new class, the bureaucracy, or more accurately the political bureaucracy, has all the characteristics of earlier ones as well as some new characteristics of its own."[28]

"The new class may be said to be made up of those who have special privileges and economic preferences because of the administrative monopoly they hold.[29] Djilas further says that the new class, however, is not the proletariat as a whole but instead a class of officials who rule in socialist states. "Government of persons" continues, state Djilas, with "special privileges and economic preferences" for a "special stratum" of administrators. Djilas is prepared to call them a class since they have "control of the national income and national goods."[30]

About the idea of the new class, B. Bruce Briggs observes that interesting hints of the idea of the new class can be found as well in the diffuse writings of Marx and Engels. Their texts were detailed when it became apparent toward the end of the nineteenth century, that something other than the Marxist projection of increasing bourgeois-proletarian polarisation was taking place. Intermediate groups were appearing; salaried workers, owning no productive property but relatively well paid and enjoying considerable status. In Germany, all these came to be labelled "the new middle class" and in America "White Collar" workers. Marxist theoreticians wrestled mightily with these unforeseen groups, and the alternative was to identify them as "a stratum" and not "a class" and to label them as "the intelligentsia", a Russian word that first appeared in the 1880s to identify the small group with a (Western) formal education, most of whom were employed in precapitalist Russia as teachers or bureaucrats.[31] In this regard, Max Nomad similarised the Soviet System with the class rule of the intellectuals. He stresses: that system has evolved in enormous hierarchy of intellectuals who are bureaucrats at the same time; administrative office-holders, technical managers and engineers, judges, servants, journalists, writers, professors, higher transport and postal employees, Marx-theologians, army officers, actors, singers, scientific spies, bank accountants, trade unionists and sports organisers—all of them government employees who owe their bourgeois comfort to the labour of the uneducated workers and peasants . . . The badge of admission to this new privileged class is a certain amount of education or training exceeding the average level of the manual workers . . . This class which, being identified with the government, has become the collective owner of the country's socialised economy—its industries and its land."[32]

About this subject, John Kenneth Galbraith wrote regarding the emergence of the new class in his book *Afluent Society.* In that book he emphatically mentioned that "We have barely noted that the leisure class has been replaced by another and much larger class to which work has none of the older connotation of pain, fatigue, or other mental or physical discomfort. We have failed to appreciate the emergence of this New Class, as it may be simply called, largely as the result of one of the oldest and most effective obfuscations in the field of social science."[33] And to him what these new class people get as "pay is not unimportant. Among other things it is a prime index of prestige. Prestige—the respect, regard and esteem of other—is in turn one of the most important sources of satisfaction associated with this kind of work. But, in general who do this kind of work expect to contribute their best regardless of compensation."[34]

Here, it is important that though Galbraith did not delineate the new class, he included within its college professors, school teachers, surgeons, maximum of those who pay income surtax rates and politicians. But, "overwhelmingly the qualification is education. Any individual whose adolescent situation is such that sufficient time and money is invested in his preparation and who has at least the talents to carry him through the formal academic routine can be a member. There is a hierarchy within the class. The further and rapid expansion of this class should be a major social goal of the society. Since education is the operative factor in expanding the class, investment in education, qualitatively as well as qunatitatively, becomes very close to being the basic index of social progress. It enables people to realise dominant aspirations . . . Were the expansion of the New Class a deliberate objective of the society this, with its emphasis on education and its ultimate effect on intellectual, literacy, cultural and artistic demands would greatly broaden the opportunities for membership."[35]

Hence, it may be considered that if property and inheritance form the basis and mode of access in the capitalist system, then technical skill and education are the base and mode of access to status, position, and power/authority/influence are reward in a post-industrial system. The ideology of the new class is the idea of the career open to talent, the idea of meritocracy. Its defence is in the democratic ideal and in the idea of the equality of opportunity.

At the moment, when the economic and educational systems have become more open due to the need for professional skills and breakdown of social class barriers, the idea of meritocracy has come under attack on the very ground that it would generate a new privileged class system and thus exclude those who are unable to meet the educational or skill requirements.[36] In order for the new class to be a class in existence, Daniel Bell suggests that "an ideology is necessary, and correctly nominates 'meritocracy'. That idea might be extended further—define book learning as 'merit', school grades as 'talent', formal education as 'skill', terms and numbers as 'theoretical knowledge'.[37] Schelsky has summed up these new class interests in a convincing formula: "Belehrung, Betreuung, Beplanung",—indoctrination, caring, and planning, all justified as promoting the better services and welfare of the general population.[38]

Concept of the new class can also be found in the idea of service class employed by Dahrendorf. He stresses that the members of the service class are bureaucrats whose main function is the administration of laws, thereby acting as a bridge within rulers and the ruled. Dahrendorf admits that bureaucrats differ a good deal from one another, especially in that there may be a large gap between those at the apex of the ladder and those at the bottom. However despite these differences Dahrendorf still insists that bureaucrats should be considered together as the service class, because they are all on a bureaucratic ladder together whatever their relative positions.[39]

III

Old Class Structure

Broadly speaking, the traditional society in Sikkim was characterised by three strata: the Clergy; the Nobles and Aristocrats; and Commoners.[40]

Among the clergy, the monks were taken from the high born Bhutias and Lepchas. These monks were variously trained as painters, embroiders, carvers, and skilled craftsmen, and during their training they enjoyed free maintenance at their monasteries. In Sikkim, they usually did not teach the laity nor did they preach to the commoners.

Besides, the monks could work in the secular fields as well. Also, these monks were used as emissaries, mediators, and settlers of various state affairs. Even also the monks occupied important positions in internal administration. Along with this, they were also appointed to the State Council. They played an important role in the management of monastery estates, administered justice and even helped the laity in fighting against the enemies. They were very much influential both in the court and in the public life, even if they were economically dependent.

In fact, in collaboration with the Kazis these clergymen managed the affairs of the state. Among the monks, the lamas had to bear a rigorous training[41] for years in learning the doctrines, scriptures and practices before they attained higher ranks. The monks used to get partial sustenance from their relatives during their training period. Among the monks, the head lamas of the important Gonpas were recruited. These were mostly of Tibetan and Kazi origin. Further, these lamas also held a good number of civil posts.[42]

They were made up of mainly Kazis with few Newars (the immigrant Nepalese) who had risen to a socio-economic prominence and were drawn into policy making and administrative channels in the Chogyals' time in pre-merger Sikkim. Among the aristocrats, the Kazis constituted a fluid "social class".[43] In reality, the Lepchas as well as the Bhutias have an old tradition of polyandry and Lepcha conversion to Lamaism paved the way for a social intercourse at the uppermost level with the Bhutia aristocracy around the monasteries. The new Bhutia rulers inveigled them into a ritual bond of blood brotherhood. That was how a new social class of the Kazis came in Sikkim.[44] The Kazis were the regional lords and had authority to command the regional territories. Aside from using some authority and adjudicating minor disputes, the Kazi also assessed the revenue payable by all the people settled on the land within his jurisdiction; paid over to the ruler a sum of fixed contribution and kept the greater portion for himself. The Kazis had no proprietory right in the land although they did have a kind of hereditary title to their position.[45] The Kazis were the kinsmen of Rulers and had some tradition of religious education. They were widely respected and their favour was always solicited.

Again, they usually manned the council alongwith various official positions in the state. Besides, they also commanded the contingent against the foes. In this way, they wielded sufficient authority in the realm. By following the Tibetan tradition these Kazis were named after the localities they ruled. The Kazis also overtook ministerial positions and were commanded to maintain two residential provisions; one at their provincial estates (the size of which also varied) where they ruled, and another in the capital near the palace of the king where they were traditional functionaries of the Durbar. With the withdrawal of the British from the Indian subcontinent, democratic movements were used to be organised in Sikkim. The Sikkimese ruler was obliged to abolish landlordism, but the Kazis found berths in the bureaucracy. The Kazis through their long association with the Durbar and the management of the state affairs, were the most obvious choice for recruitment to government posts. That was the reason there was a disproportionate preponderance of the members of the Kazi houses in the Sikkimese bureaucracy.[46] In this way, these patricians, with their wealth, social status and bureaucratic position, use to be able to fill high posts in the new administrative set up until the state merged into the Indian Union.

Commoners. Finally, the people who were regarded as commoners constituted the common class in the society of traditional Sikkim. These people belonging to the common class were mostly the wage-earning working people either as tenants or *bustiwallas* (villagers) and other skilled, semi-skilled and unskilled workers in old set up of Sikkim.

IV

Modern Class

Today society in Sikkim is characterised broadly by four distinct strata: Agrarian class; Business class; Wage-earning working class; and the New Class.

1. Agrarian Class. Structure of this class may be defined in terms of a hierarchically organised landowning groups depending on their size of land-holding. It comprises four main class groups. These are—the landlords-cum-big landowners, medium-sized landowning farmers, small-sized landowning farmers and landless farmers (Kutias/Adhyars). The landless agricultural labourers may be better categorised as belonging to wage-earning working class because they usually use their labour power for earning daily wages by working in the agricultural fields.

2. Business Class. The Business class is economically independent and its activity consists, either exclusively or at least partially, of the organisation and control of their business. They keep property and/or capital. They are mainly big and petty businessmen and also few small scale industrialists.

3. Wage Earning Class. The wage-earning working class people are mainly the skilled, semi-skilled and unskilled manual workers. They usually do not own any productive resources but they keep their own labour power.

4. New Class. New class which has emerged in present day Sikkim, the central theme of this research study, which comprises members with an educational background.

The central point of discussion for highlighting the emergence of the new class in Sikkim has mainly been the period since its merger with India in 1975, that is the post-merger duration of Sikkim. During the last fifty years or so Sikkim has seen a number of major changes in the functioning of the state power. With its merger in the Indian Union since 1975, all the inorganic and organic resources in the state have been designated as 'public goods' under the direct control and utilisation by the state. The change has been the rise of social services and large state expenditures for public welfare, utilisation of public goods in the state for its development, administration and execution of law and order and the like. Allocation and distribution of the state's resources and rewards are carried out in an equally democratic manner.

The development of state machinery is intended to increase the state's revenue and earnings for promoting the development of its people. There is a concentration on the evolution of state bureaucracy in all areas of life like agriculture, health and family welfare, education, administration, communication, law and crime, forestry, irrigation and power, land and revenue, and many other economic as well as development spheres, all of which are public services. The greater scope of government activities has meant a growing demand for people to coordinate, manage and administer in the present day Sikkim. The acceptance of the principle of welfare arises from the need of inclusion of its people into citizenship in the society. Another factor arising from the endeavours to incept the technological revolution in terms of communication and transportation and technical machinery for public welfare, is the increasing degree of interdependence in the society, so that the spill over effects are no longer local but upon the society as a whole in the state of Sikkim. Besides the growth of state power as an independent force subjected to the Indian Constitution, the whole machinery of state administration and public services is set up to direct, control and guide people to the state's way.[47] In this way there have emerged new opportunities, for instance, the avenues of employment in various administrative, technical, professional, white-collar occupations in the state. The demand for these occupational positions has been increasing everyday together with the augmentation of state activities.

A new class of educated minor officials, teachers and bureaucrats has come up in Sikkim to cope with the expandnig bureaucratisation and professionalisation of public services in the state. As the most important political and social shift of the twentieth century, the new class has risen to prominence in Sikkim and it now acts as an instrument to bring about changes in the Sikkimese society and community. In fact, the transition from a feudal, peasant, agrarian society to a modern, democratic society cannot be accomplished without solid social changes. One of these changes, the alteration of the class-structure deserves special attention because it involves entire incentive system of the society.[48]

After Sikkim mingled with the Indian Union, the state authorities paid special attention in this direction and in assistance with the Central Government of India, the state government has been making necessary measures to make it one of the modern and developed states in India. It is therefore not out of context to place a premium on education as the main instrument to modernisation of a backward society like Sikkim. As Neelsen notes "credo of bourgeois society has been the open society"[49]—right from a backward, theocratic, closed society to an open, more universalised society. However, this does not mean levelling out of the variations in property, income, prestige and power, etc., in the society; but rather their distribution according to individual achievement. The task set for society is, thus, to enable each individual to compete on an equal footing, while the rewards are to be distributed inequally according to position within the hierarchical and differential occupational structure. As these positions are allocated primarily on the basis of formal educational qualifications, these facts preclude the establishment of a better egalitarian society. Thus, education reproduces the new type of inequality by bringing about the new class structure within the society in Sikkim. Therefore, the schooling order in Sikkim may be considered as the process of societal transformation which implies the dissolution of the traditional and simultaneous existence of a new structure of inequality. It is now generally accepted that an educational system particularlyin the developing countries reflects much more closely the forming shape of social and economic development. Nowadays, the state government has taken the initiative towards 'man-power planning' and to diffuse it throughout the state targetting to cope with the expanding bureaucratisation and government activities. The urgency of planned growth and also the tendency towards mass education especially because of the spread of democracy, have resulted in the growth of popularity of educational planning in Sikkim for properly introducing changes in the various aspects of the societies. In the present day Sikkim, the educational aspirations are part and parcel of both popular hopes for the future national plans and for economic progress of the state.

Therefore, the educational planning plays a prominent part in the modern government of Sikkim. Its aim is to forecast the number of individuals with various occupational qualifications (formal education) needed by the society. Thus, as a result, the present day Sikkim needs to order the educational division of labour. The state government has conferred more importance and special attention upon encouraging the educational sub-system leading to various occupational positions within the society. Due to this reason, the state government has been encouraging its members to educate themselves by extending various educational facilities available for secondary, higher secondary and higher education.[50] As an outcome, the people of Sikkim have a remarkable tendency to go through formal education for achieving 'requisite' qualifications as an entry to hierarchical division of labour in terms of occupational positions within the state government services. Besides, education in present day Sikkim is imparted in schools and emphasis is put on learning how to do something new so as to be able to join the government and work for the society and its people. There is now a complete and significant relation between formal education and the state government services in Sikkim. The state government of Sikkim is itself now the leading agency for job creation and has been a chief source of employment for educated local people and thus functions as an internal labour market.[51]

Economically, Sikkim is an agricultural society like the rest of the states within the Indian Union. Its economy is primarily based on agriculture and a majority of the population depends on agriculture. Severe lack of transport facilities and non-availability to sufficient raw materials are major obstacles to the development of Sikkimese economy in terms of industry, wide scale trade and commerce. Therefore, even at present, it can be said that the state is neither developed nor industrialised and can be classified as backward due to the scarcity in resources. So far, the collection of revenues is derived mainly from income and sales tax, excise, bazaars forest, state nationalised transport, etc.

There are many taxes including land revenue which considerably add to the state income. The earnings from the total collected revenues are insufficient to fulfill all the needs of the state for implementing various plans and programmes of the state government. As a result, it is largely dependent upon the financial support from the Central Government for implementing various developmental plans for the progress of the state and its people.

Currently, the state is endeavouring to augment its earning and to increase the collection of state revenues, but the success is very little due to scarce resources available in the state. Even today the extent of trade and commerce is not significant; it is privately held in the state. On the other hand, the employment situation in the state government services is fast expanding with day to day increase in the state government activities in planning, formulation, management and administration. The state government functionaries have been performing a major role in running the state government administration and thus they provide a guarantee to the maintenance of the progressive profile of Sikkim. They are, indeed, a part of the decision-making process of the state comprising increasingly powerful elite in present day Sikkim, and can be counted as quite a significant and distinct group in the society. It is undoubtedly the fact that under normal conditions the power positions of the fully developed state bureaucracy is even overwhelming[52] in the state.

Along with the expansion and growth in the state activities the government needs a large work-force to maintain its various functions in all the fields of development: institutional financing of plans and programmes, supervising the various developmental activities, bureaucratic expansion, expansion of education, implementation of various health and social welfare programmes, to name a few. All of them demand the supply of educated manpower at different educational levels. Hence, in Sikkim the function of education presently is to ensure that there is an educated[53] labour force in accordance with the needs of situation. The new class in Sikkim may be conceived as the collectivities[54] of persons in which class position individuals are defined in terms of their occupational position in the internal labour market. The access in the internal labour market is ensured by the essential formal educational qualifications. Therefore, the occupational position which is the essential determinant of the new class is defined primarily in terms of essential formal educational qualifications.

Thus, the new class comprises a large part of educated government employees and it may be defined in terms of occupational position, formal education, and income as salaries largely form the government. In this manner the new class structure is constituted hierarchically by the rank and file of school teachers, salaried professionals of all type, government employed administrators, managers, white-collar workers and those who hold their position inside the occupational hierarchy of the government by virtue of possession of professional and literary skills usually obtained through formal education. Hence, the new class structure may be delineated as into the following sub-class categories

(a) Professional. State employed and salaried professionals of all kinds like physicians, veterinary doctors, members of judiciary, university and college teachers, etc., and even including a number of workers, e.g., scientists, engineers, computer programmers; technical and kindred but less obvious professional like school teachers, librarians, etc.

(b) Official. Government employed managers, administrators and kindred persons.

(c) White-Collar. Government employed clerical and kindred like accountant, cashier, auditor, office supervisor, stenographer, typist-cum-personal secretaries-cum-office assistants, inspectors in various departments; technicians and kindred.

In this manner, this chapter aims at providing coverages upon education, occupational position and its corresponding influence on the distribution of income and privileges, as main attributes for determining the new class in Sikkim. Occupational position is important because in modern as well as modernising society like Sikkim the special occupational position is used in common social interaction as a major means of locating the individual within the social system. Besides, in the absence of hereditary feudalism like the state class differences come to rest primarily on occupational position.[55] The occupation, education, income and privileges of the new class may be accounted for changes in their life style, ideas and opinion which in turn bring about changes in the society.

This said new class may be conceived as internally stratified and differentiated according to position in the occupational hierarchy, range of skills, function, income as salaries as per pay scales, education, authority-cum-power and responsibility related to particular position, status and privileges. Indeed, the occupational positions of the new class in the government are of course, overlapping in many cases which make it difficult to formulate a unique hierarchical ordering of the new class. However, this calls for more research in the area of sub-divisions in emerging class structure. Nevertheless, on the basis of these attributes the new class may be classified into two broad hierarchical set ups: higher and lower. The new class may also be classified as into three hierarchical sub-orders which are as below.

New Class Hierarchy

New Class	*Hierarchical Position*	*Status*
(a) Professional	Class I	Higher
	Class II	Higher
	Class III	Lower
(b) Official	Class I	Higher
	Class II	Higher
(c) White-collar	Class II	Lower

(a) Class I. It consists of higher professionals and officials who occupy senior gazetted ranks in the occupational hierarchy. They have special privileges in terms of monetary and educational preferences because of the administrative monopoly they hold this way or that way within the government. It includes salaried senior doctors, engineers, senior members of the judiciary, university professors, higher technicals, scientists, certain senior managers and administrators, departmental heads at state and district level and kindred who occupy senior gazetted levels in the government. It is the highest position in the occupational hierarchy and the members of this group possess a higher social status in the society.

(b) Class II. The members of this class also possesses gazetted ranks but relatively junior than those of Class I. It is practically distinguished from the other groups of the new class, e.g., Class III employees by generally superior qualifications, income according to pay-scale, by the kind of work done in usual combination with supervisory functions over a larger number of members of Class III employees. It also comprises professionals like doctors, engineers, junior scientists, computer programmers, members of the judiciary, college teachers, chair persons of the institutions like schools including post graduate teachers of higher secondary schools, administrators and managers also including other management staff like assistant managers and kindred. The members of this group also enjoy a comparatively higher social status in the society.

(c) Class III. This group encompasses a large number of general members of the new class who are in the more routinal clerical and administrative posts, occupying lower and middle level non-gazetted positions in the occupational hierarchy of the government. In terms of education, income privileges and certain responsibility related to occupational position they have a fairly crystallised social status though below Class I and Class II employees in the society. It includes all types of white-collar workers including lower and obviously less professionals like junior engineers, school teachers and kindred.

While the new class is internally satisfied, yet all its members should be considered together as the new class whatever their relative positions since they are all government functionaries.

1. All do Mental Work. All these new class members perform essentially non-manual and mental work. The new class is conceived as class because it comprises comprehensive and separable collectivities of individuals, those can be distinguished as a broad and distinct strata of the society in Sikkim. The membership of the new class is relatively permanent and assigned by the achieved position. Permanence may be interpreted as a high degree of probability that an individual will remain in his class position throughout his life.

The status in the new class is attained in terms of education, occupational position and income which are used as the most reliable measures of socio-economic status. Among the members of the new class, a difference of income depending on the specific pay-scale and position in the government produces a hierarchy of prestige and power as per variations in its size and responsibility. Prestige of the new class thus depends on the level of skill the job entails, the degree of education or training required, the amount of control-cum-authority and responsibility involved in the performances of work, the income which is typically received as salary according to salary scale including the variation in privileges—to mention the most readily apparent factors in determining the social status of the new class. Thus, social status of the new class is not dependent on crude economic power but rather on the combination of these attributes. Therefore, for instance, an ordinary member of new class, e.g., white-collar may be economically worse off than a small enterpriser of skilled manual worker, but is superior to them in terms of staff rank of the occupational status in the government, education, degree of responsibility and control, style of life which help surely to distinguish them separately from others in the societal order.

2. Common Sense of Income. It is a class because the members of this new class have the same source of income and the source here is the state government. Thus, they have differential share in the national income. Further, the members of the new class are all non-self employed and perform duties as assigned to the posts they hold. The members of the new class enjoy certain other privileges like job security, promotion opportunity, i.e., opportunity for upward occupational mobility and other privileges available to the government employees. Class interest of the new class is to perform services for the general public in accordance with their particular occupational positions in the bureaucracy. All this involves caring, improving, planning, financing, maintenance of all public works and programmes. The interest of the new class is indeed subservient to the interest of the state.

The new class being a class, an ideology is necessary and that may be conceived as the idea of career and higher aspirations that involves the personal advancement by acquiring higher skills and work experience. The new class members are much concerned about the career of their children that involves the personal emancipation of their children also through acquiring good education, one that will allow them to obtain higher qualifications and well paid jobs in the government. Therefore, it may be said that the new class has relatively a permanent ideology.[56] The class consciousness of the new class results from sharing a common class interest for the fulfilment of their needs in the society.

Their class consciousness may also be conceived as the consequence of their work situation which makes them more conscious about their status and class position in the society. Since the new class members have relatively a permanent ideology, specific class interest and class consciousness of their position being a functional group—for the most part, they have relatively same social attitudes, work habits and occupational outlook and style of life—have distinguished them as a separate strata alienated from the other classes in the society.[57]

3. Class Boundaries. The class boundaries of the new class are felt as barriers to the mobility of common men. In fact, this kind of occupational position (essential determinant of the new class) is more closed owing to the fact that such position is conditional upon the possession of the specific skills acquired through formal education and thus restricting access to the positions to those who have required educational qualifications and excluding those who do not have such education.[58]

Further, in the context of the new class, the class boundary may also be evident in occupational position clustering. There are two complex dimensions about class boundary of the new class: firstly, there is difference in skills, occupational position and status. Secondly, the other privileges like promotion, job security, pension and the like; and the autonomy. Autonomy refers to the fact that the new class members are more organised workers and enjoy more autonomy in the workplace by virtue of the power checked by certain rules and regulations acquired through organised action. Hence, the distance of the new class from other classes in the society is much more prominent and highly significant.

Involvement of New Class in Politics

In the olden days, the leadership of the society in Sikkim rested with the ruling aristocrats, kinship based upon inheritance and the incarnated lamas. But now things have changed. Nowadays, it is definitely education more than the brawn which is valued. Naturally, with the growth of modern formal education, the leadership of the state has gone from the king, ruling aristocrats, lamas to modern educated people. There has been now a large and continuous increase of the educated people in the ruling political elite. The table that follows will be all the more relevant to understand the impact of the educated class on the composition of ruling political elite in Sikkim. It presents a significant trend of increase in the number of formally educated members in the Sikkim State Legislative Assembly from 1974 to 1985. The most notable fact that may be said is that in the year 1985, none of the members have been either illiterate or have any religious education. It reflects that in the year 1985, there has been a substantial growth in the number of members (53.13 per cent) who are highly educated. Finally, it articulates the fact that there has emerged an educated class who constituted the current ruling political elite in Sikkim.

Presently, the growing educated class in Sikkim has facilitated the rise of the new class. In the absence of industrialisation in Sikkim, an educated person can find practically one opportunity of career, namely government service. Since the merger of Sikkim with the Indian Union, the existence of continually growing education and large job opportunities in the government has ensured the rise of the new class in Sikkim. And, the power position of the new class in Sikkim has increased substantially due to ever growing use of government power in all aspects of the people's life in the present day society.

In democratic politics, mass support is necessary to achieve political power.

To attain such support in favour of political party, the new class has achieved greater importance because they possess the skills of analysing, criticising, moralising, persuading and other means like the mass media and the educational institutions. Under conditions of political freedom, it can shape debate, determine agendas, define standards and objective, and evaluate policies. Therefore, the new class has the ability as well as the opportunity to mobilise people in favour of particular parties since they have now a larger audience in the society. In this way, the political influence of the new class has increased sufficiently.

Emergence of the new class has also a significant impact on the composition of ruling political elite and the standards and processes through which its members are recruited. In times of rapid social change, this has resulted in the increasing number and influence of new class representatives and the declining role of businessmen, agriculturists and priests in the polity. The presence of the new class in the ruling political elite has been signalled by the changing educational and occupational characteristics of its members.

An analysis about the occupational background of the legislators of State Assembly has been shown in the following table. It appears from the table that during 1974-85 the number of members of farmers, politician-cum-agriculturists, lamaist and even self-employed businessmen has declined significantly. While, in 1985 and afterwards, the number of members who were in government service before joining politics has increased substantially. This shows not only the general occupational trends within the society in Sikkim but also substantiates the fact of rising number of new class representatives in ruling political elite of the today's Sikkim. Of the total 16 members of the new class in Legislative Assembly, 7 were professional, 6 were white-collar and 3 were officials.

State Ministry	*New Class Background*	*Number*
Chief Minister	Professional	1
Cabinet Minister	Professional	3
	Official	1
	White Collar	2
Total		2
State Assembly		
Speaker	Professional	1
Member	Professional	2
	Official	2
	White Collar	4
Total		9
Grand Total		16

Source: *Who's who,* published by Sikkim Legislative Assembly Secretariat, Gangtok, Sikkim, Febrruary, 1987, pp. 13-57.

Amongst the state ministry, out of total 11 ministers majority of the ministerial position, 7 are held by the members of the new class. The chief minister himself has the background of new class. Besides, the position of the Speaker in the Legislative Assembly also is conducted by a member of the new class. The number of ministers-cum-members and other members of the Legislative Assembly having new class background has been given in preceding paragraph. Apart from the ministerial positions, a number of legislators with the new class background have held chairmanship in the different departments under the state government. In the opposition party a number of leading party positions have been held by the members of the new class. In this context, incomplete data, which are available, have been shown below to substantiate this point.

Political Party	*Party Position*	*New Class background*	*Number*
Sikkim Pradesh	Vice Presidents	Official	2
Congress Committee (I)	General Secretary	Official	1
	Convener	Professional	1
Naya Sikkim Party	President	Professional	1
Krantikari Morcha	President	Professional	1

Source: Member of Sikkim Pradesh Congress Committee (I), Gangtok, Sikkim.

All these figures substantiate the fact of rising number of new class members in the ruling political elite and their ever increasing influence and importance in politics of present day Sikkim. It may also be concluded here that the political power in Sikkim has passed in the hand of modern educated class who come with the new class background. In addition to all this, it will be relevant to point out that with the emergence of the new class a type of association has emerged in the society.

For instance, there are two associations in Sikkim, namely, Sikkim Government Employees' Association and Sikkim Government Employees' Federation. Both associations practically seek to protect and promote the interests of the employees, improve the service conditions of the members, bring them at par with the employees in other parts of the country and work for the unity and fellow-feeling within the employees. Apart from these objectives these associations also play a greater role and exert influence in determining the voting behaviour, evolution of political ideas and views of the employees because these associations are related to a political party this or that way. Therefore, these associations also play an indirect role but important in influencing common people in determining their political ideas and views.

Very recently, in 2001, there had been sizeable progress in the field of education, agriculture and also economic structure. The state government is indeed well-aware of their difficulties and with new innovative measures and financial assistance of the Central Government, there have been launched new projects which have come up as prominent steps of welfare schemes for a common man living in the far-flung areas of the state. Road-building, starting a primary school in a village, a small dispensary to take care of the public, raising of local security force, to carve out several areas for community projects, to develop and protect forests, to contain the water in ponds in order to streamline irrigation schemes, to produce the crop of rice, fishery, sheep and goats after improving their quality, to take care of religious institutions, to inculcate the feeling of secularism, to generate the spirit of patriotism among the people, to devise scheme for the health and welfare of children, women and old people, to promote handicraft work and export of the local production of Indian sub-continent—all these schemes have been launched by the Government during the period 2000-2001. And the planning of several projects have been made which have deep and strong bearing on the future development of the state. Indeed, the idea is to remove its economic backwardness so that masses of the state should have the healthy trend in resolving complex and difficult issues.

References

1. M.N. Shrinivas, "Caste", *Current Sociology,* Volume VIII, No. 3, 1959, quoted in Bottomore, T.B., *Classes in Modern Society,* p. 15.
2. T.B. Bottomore, *Classes in Modern Society,* p. 17.
3. Sharit Bhowmick, *Class Formation in the Plantation System,* p. 16.
4. T.B. Bottomore, *op. cit.* p. 17.
5. G.D.H. Cole, *Studies in the Working Class Structure,* p. 181.
6. R. Dahrendorf, *Class and Class Conflict in Industrial Society,* p. 137.
7. N. Apercrombie, and J. Urry, *Capital, Labour and the Middle Classes,* p. 7.
8. Max Weber, "Class, Status, Party", in Gerth, H.H. and Mills, C. Wright, (edited and translated), *From Max Weber: Essays in Sociology,* p. 51.
9. *Ibid.,* p. 182.
10. Max Weber, "Class, Status and Party", in Bendix, R. and Lipset, S. Martin (eds.) *Class Status and Power,* p. 22.
11. C. Mathew Snipp, "Occupational Mobility and Social Class: Insights from Men's Career Mobility", *American Sociological Journal,* Vol. 50, No. 4, August 1985, p. 476.
12. N. Abercrombie, and J. Urry, *op. cit.,* p. 9.
13. P. A. Sorokin, *Social Mobility,* pp. 107-08.
14. C.W. Mills, *White Collar.*
15. A. Giddens, *The Class Structure of the Advanced Societies,* p. 107.
16. Quoted in C.M. *shipp, op. cit.,* pp. 476-77.
17. F. Parkin, *Marxism and Class Theory: A Bourgeois Critique,* p. 44.
18. *Ibid.,* p. 45.
19. F. Parkin, *Class Inequality and Political Order,* p. 18.
20. D. Lockwood, *The Black Coated Worker,* p. 12.
21. S. Ossowski, *Class Structure in the Social Consciousness,* p. 11.
22. *Ibid.,* p. 42.
23. J.P. Neelsen, "Education and Social Mobility", *Comparative Education Review,* Vol. XIX, No. 1, 1975, pp. 129-143.
24. D.P. Moynihan, "Equalizing Education: In Whose Benefit?", *Public Interest,* Fall, 1972, quoted in Briggs, B. Bruce, *The New Class?* (ed.), Transaction Books, 1979, p. 2.
25. N. Podhoretz, "Between Nixon and the New Politics", *Commentary,* September 1972, quoted in Priggs, B. Bruce, *Ibid.,* p. 2.
26. I. Kristol, "Business and the New Class", *Wall Street Journal,* 19th May 1975, quoted in Briggs, B. Bruce, *op. cit.,* p. 4.
27. T. David Bazelon, *Power in America: The Politics of the New Class,* quoted in

Brigs, B. Bruce, *op. cit.*, p. 7.

28. Milovan Djilas, *The New Class*, pp. 37-38.
29. *Ibid.*, p. 39.
30. Quoted in Andrew, Hacker "Two New Classes' or None?" in Briggs, B. Bruce, *op. cit.*, p. 157.
31. B. Bruce Briggs, (ed.), *The New Class?* pp. 11-12.
32. Max Nomad, "Masters Old and New", in Calverton, V.L. (ed.), *The Making of Society*, pp. 882-93, quoted in Briggs, B. Bruce, *Ibid.*, p. 13.
33. John Kenneth Galbraith, *Afluent Society*, p. 340.
34. *Ibid.*, p. 342.
35. *Ibid.*, pp. 343-345.
36. Danial Bell, *"The New Class: A Muddled Concept,"* in Briggs, B. Bruce, *op. cit.*, p. 182.
37. Quoted in B. *Bruce Briggs, op. cit.*, p. 209.
38. Quoted in P.L. Berger, "The Worldview of the New Class," in Briggs, B. Bruce, *op. cit.*, p. 53.
39. R. Dahrendorf, "The Service Class," in Burns, T. (ed.), *Industrial Man*, pp. 140-50.
40. A.C. Sinha, *The Politics of Sikkim*, p. 18.
41. The ideal training is expected to continue through all stages and ranks of the priesthood, ending with the rank of Dorze-Lopen (the head of the Gonpa). Each rank requires certain qualifications acquired in the process of training, according to which all lamas are ranked from the top to the bottom. Nankane, Chie, A Plural Society in Sikkim: A Study of the Interrelations of Lepchas, Bhotias and Nepalis, in Haimendorf, Christopher Von Fiirer, (ed.), *Caste and Kin in Nepal, India and Ceylon*, pp. 227-228.
42. A.C. Sinha, *op. cit.*, pp. 39-40.
43. *Ibid.*, p. 19.
44. *Ibid.*, p. 5.
45. N. Hope, "The Sikkimese Theory of Land-holding and the Darjeeling Grant", *Bulletin of Tibetology*, Vol. III, No. 2, 1966, p. 48.
46. A.G. Sinha, *op. cit.*, p. 47.
47. All these must be taken into account that given occupational positions involve specific powers over other people not only in the actual courses of work but also outside the job areas by virtue of their relations and interdependencies in the society.
48. Kingsley Davis, "The Role of Class Mobility in Economic Development", in Goode, William, J. (ed.), *The Dynamics of Modern Society*, p. 385.
49. J. P. Neelsen, "Class Structure, Education and Social Change in India: Results of an Empirical Case Study in Dhanbad/Bihar", in Neelsen, J.P., (ed.), *Social Inequality and Political Structures*, p. 67.
50. Due to inadequate facilities of college and higher education available in Sikkim, the meritorious students are usually given scholarships and sent by the state government to different parts of India to join higher level of professional colleges and universities in the field of science, arts and commerce. Besides, the government employees also being sent on deputation by the state to join in the higher level professional and other diploma courses

and training to different parts of India. In addition, those student who are intended to have higher education in the field of science/arts/commerce and can afford they often go outside state to take admission in the colleges and universities located in the adjacent hills and plains of West Bengal and other states of India.

51. The job opportunities in the government has expanded rapidly more than production of goods and materials because of the ecological handicaps on agricultural expansion and development and lag in advanced technological application as well as lack of industrialisation, and because of the persistence of individual and small scale entrepreneurial units which are mainly in the hands of plains people and rich 'locales, while the internal labour market has been enlarged remarkably for educated labour force in the society.
52. Max Weber, "Bureaucracy", in Gerth, H.H. and Mills, C. Wright, *op. cit.*, p. 232.
53. Since the job opportunities for educated local people in tremendous the unemployment situation for the educated is yet to emerge in Sikkim. That is why this study did not have the opportunity to deal with them. Despite that it may be said that in such a situation the class membership of an unemployed educated individual is to be determined on the basis of his family (parents) class origin, until he achieves any occupational position in the society.
54. It is a social collectivities because it comprises of a group of individuals living in the society who are relatively similar in terms of educational, occupational, income privileges, power and status background; common class interest, ideology and class consciousness; similar social attitudes, work habits and occupational outlook, and similar styles of life—the similar life chances.
55. Today, the occupational position rather than property is the main source of income for most of those who receive any direct income as salary. The possibilities of selling their services in the internal labour market now determine the life-chances of new class. Education in this regard is one of the most vital attributes in the present day society.
56. It plays effective role to perpetuate new class in the society. Because, children of its members are carefully indoctrinated in the importance of finding better occupational position through education. Thus, new class also hs continuity. Besides, this ideology provides a unique symbol of recognition which may effect on the behaviour pattern of the individual creating personality-cum-individuality of that member.
57. All these common grounds may diminish ethnic differences among the new class members who are form diverse ethnic groups, but it requires indepth study on ethnic consciousness of new class in real situation.
58. In this regard, it is relevant to point out that though education in Sikkim is free and everybody has equal right for education, nevertheless, there are number of various major educational constrains which have been in continuous operation in excluding as well as deterring major part of the people to achieve educational qualifications necessary for such positions in the society (This has been elaborately discussed in the Chapter VIII with concluding remarks in the conclusion Chapter IX).

Section-II
Nagaland

6

Land and the People

Though a separate state Nagaland has been formed for convenience of administration and consolation of revolutionaries who wanted the same but Nagas are spread almost all over the North-East. And also observe more or less common culture and ways of living. Boundaries may not be able to break all that which these simple tribesmen share in common.

(a) Formation of State

With slim surging streams, verdant luxuriant hills, everchanging clouds, serpentine paths and numerous colourful tribes, Nagaland is one of the smallest states of India (now Sikkim is the smallest). It was carved out in the Indian map as sixteenth state of the Union on 1st December 1963 and inaugurated by the then President of India, Dr. S. Radhakrishnan. The State of Nagaland has been formed with the erstwhile Naga Hills Districts of Assam (established in 1881) and the Tuensang Division of NEFA.

The administrative unit, previously known as Naga Hills and Tuensang Area (NHTA) came into being on 1st December 1957, following the acceptance by the Government of India of a resolution passed in the first Naga People's Convention held at Kohima on 22nd August 1957. In another convention at Mokokchung in October 1959 it was advised to rename the areas as 'Nagaland'. The Governmennt of India accepted the recommendation and renamed the area on 18th February 1961. It was a mere preliminary step to the Constitution of Nagaland as a full-fledged State. On the same day an Executive Council consisting of five members with a Chairman called the Chief Executive Councillor and an interim body of 42 members were constituted.

The Executive Council acted as a 'de facto' Council of Ministers for Nagaland and the interim body 'de facto' Legislature of the state. Dr. Imkongliba Ao, the first Chairman of the Interim Body was killed on 21st September 1961 and Mr. T.N. Angami was elected in his place. Mr. Chubatoshi Jamir, who was nominated as the only M.P. from Nagaland occupied his seat in the Lok Sabha in November 1961. The Nagaland five-men Executive Council was sworn in on 16th March 1961 at Raj Bhawan capital, Shillong. It included Mr. P. Shilu Ao (Chairman), Mr. D. Jasokie, Mr. Chiten Jamir, Mr. Hokishe Sema and lastly Mr. Akum Imlong.

In the most important endeavour, the then PM Jawaharlal Nehru introduced a Bill on 21st August 1962 to legalise the formation of the state of Nagaland. He also introduced in the house the Constitution (13th Amendment) Bill incorporating certain special features. These included a provision that the single person would be appointed as the Governor of Assam and Governor of Nagaland, and the existing jurisdiction of Assam High Court would continue. Again, the Governor would have special responsibility for law and order during the transitional period or so long as disturbances carry on. Another important aspect of it needs to be mentioned that "No Act or Law passed by the Union Parliament affecting the following subjects shall have legal force in Nagaland till specially applied to it by a majority vote of the Nagaland Legislative Assembly:

(a) Religion or Social Practices
(b) Customary Naga Laws and Procedures
(c) Civil and Criminal Justice insofar all these concern decisions according to Naga Customary Law. The existing laws relating to administration of Civil and Criminal Justice as provided through the Rules for the Administration of Justice and Police in the Naga Hills District shall continue to be in force.
(d) The ownership and transfer of land and its resources.

Just forty days after the inauguration of the State, General Elections were held in Nagaland. The initial strength of the Legislative Assembly was 46. It was increased to 60 after ten years. Due to its enchanting scenic beauty and pleasant climate the state is called "Switzerland of the East.

As we know, the Nagas belong to Indo-Mongoloid family. According to Dr. Suniti Kumar Chatterjee, they are in fact the Kirats known in Sanskrit literature.

(b) Background and Geographical Set Up

The word 'Naga' has been derived from the Sanskrit word "Nagna' which means naked. In the remote past, the Nagas used to wear scanty clothes or no clothes at all. This may be true even today in case of the far away places in dense forest areas. But in the light of a *Mahabharat* story, the word 'Naga' is derived from 'Nag' (Pannag), 'Nag' means snake. The story runs as follows:

"After having lost the Kingdom to the Kauravas, Arjun, the third Pandava had been wandering in different parts of India. Once he met Ulupi in a remote dark land. Infatuated, she took Arjun to her private chamber. Astonished, Arjun asked to know the identity of the charming youthful beauty. She replied:

"Oirabat Kule Jatah Kauravya Nam Pannagah.
Tasyasmiduhita Rajannulupi Nam Pannagi."

"Born in Oirabat race, the snake-King Kauravya is my father. I am her daughter, princess Ulupi." Enchanted Arjun married Ulupi, then went to the neighbouring state of Manipur. Chitrangada, Princess of that land also offered herself to the third Pandava in wedlock. Rabindranath has beautifully narrated that love-story in his verse-drama 'Chitrangada'."

It is evident to all of us, both Nagaland and Manipur are the neighbouring states and here, it is to be noted that while the princess of one land had introduced herself as the 'daughter of a snake-King' the other was an emancipated man well-trained in horse-riding, war-fare, etc. In many folk-tales of the Nagas it is imagined that human being originated from different animals. It, however, certainly gives some explanation of the self-introduction of Ulupi. Maybe the land of Ulupi is Nagaland now. Whatever may be, what is the harm if we imagine it as a romantic place of Mahabharata?

It is said that there is another place in Nagaland which is related to some anecdote of *Mahabharata* which does not need mention here.

Total population of this state is about eight lakh. There are fourteen main tribes, namely—Ao, Angami, Sema, Lotha, Rengma, Chakhesang, Sangtam, Yimchunger, Konyak, Phom, etc., and Chang, Zeliang, Kuki, Khiemnugan (Khienmuanghan) and some minor tribes—Pochury, Kochari, etc. Bengalis and Assamese are the majority communities among the people those who have been working in different State and Central Government offices.

Besides, Punjabis are mostly the contractors, Marwari and Biharis business community. A remarkable populations are Nepalis who have been living in the state since long. Nepalis girls, with their yellowish complexion, reddish cheek, stubbed nose, chubby figure have similarity with the local tribal groups and have compatibility in their hair do and dress as well.

As per law, no outsider (people from the plains) is allowed to purchase any land in the state and live permanently over here. There are only a few exceptions who had settled long back and in case of Nepalis who came from other hilly regions. The area of Nagaland spread 6,366 sq. mile (16,579 sq. km). The state lies between 25.06' and 27.04' North and 93.20' and 95.15' East. On the south it is surrounded by Manipur, with Burma to the east, Arunachal Pradesh to the north and all along the western foot-hills lies the valley of the Assam plains region. The state consists of a long narrow strip of hilly country running more or less parallel to the left bank of the Brahmaputra river. Most of the villages stand at three to four thousand feet high. The Nagas prefer to build their houses on the apex point of hills at higher elevation.

The longest peak in the state, Saramati in Tuensang district, is about 12,600 feet (3,840 metre) high above the sea level.

Next comes Japvo in the Kohima district is 9890 ft. (3,014 m), Kapu 9320 ft. (2841 m), Paona 9156 ft. and Kapamezu 7970 ft. Doyang, Dikhu, Dhansiri, Tizu and also Melak (Jhanji) are the main rivers of the state which flow through the Assam plains to join the mighty Brahmaputra.

Popular Doyang, the biggest river of the Nagaland is navigable for a few kilometres before it enters the valley of Assam.

Originated from the southern part of the state it goes through Wokha and Zunheboto districts in the north and then turns towards west to meet Brahmaputra in Assam.

Dikhu, a tributary of powerful Brahmaputra which is also navigable for a short distance, flows through Mokokchung and Tuensang districts. Dhansiri rises from the south-west corner of the Naga Hills and flows a north-westerly course for about 23 km. She then turns at right angles to the north-east parts and as far as Dimapur forms the northern boundary of the district.

As it flows along a few miles from the outer range of hills it receives a large number of tributaries with the only exception of Diphupani which is barely 47 km in length, all others are small and unimportant. The next river that deserves mention is Rengmapani which falls into Doyang.

In Nagaland there is no lake and waterfall. It is mostly cold round the year, but the low regions like Dimapur is quite hot during the summer when the mercury runs between 60º–110º F.

In Nagaland, monsoon starts in May-June and continues till August-September Heavy rains are recorded in June-July. The average rainfall is between 70"–100". The hills of Nagaland are covered with lush green thick forests where wild flowers, plants, luxuriant orchids, cactus, creepers, peepal, Rhododendron, ferns are seen. Tree ferns and wild ginger are clung to the rocky cliffs. Rice, maize, wheat, millet, gram, mustard, potato, tapioca, cotton are cultivated. Also grown here are pineapple, apple, sugarcane, apricot, plaintain,. chillies and an inferior quality of tea in some low sloping lands. Inside the forest are found wild elephants (in the downhills), tiger, bison, buffalo, barking deer, sambar, leopard, monkey, jackal, wild pig, bear, dog, cat, rat, snake, lizard, toad eagle, vulture, skylark, owl, crow, hornbill, bulbul, maina, fowl and many more vanishing due to indiscriminate hunting.

The Nagas think all animals and birds eatable. Among the domestic animals they rear mithun (cross breed of buffalo and cow), buffalo, cow, goat, lamb and the like.

Maximum of the Nagas, almost 73 per cent, are agriculturists. They generally practise *Jhum* or shifting cultivation. After winter a part of hill side or jungle is marked off for *Jhum*. It is generally cleared by lopping off the undergrowth and branches of trees, which are allowed to dry in the sun for some time. Shortly before the arrival of rains the dry leaves and bushes are set on fire. They take care that the fire does not spread into the forest. The fire kills the weeds and insects and the ashes also fertilize the ground. Then the farmer comes, clear the field and sow seeds. As the rains come, the seeds begin to sprout. They collect the harvest as crop ripens. After a year or a few years, depending on the suitability, they select another virgin or near virgin hilly forest and then repeat the same process. As the jhum cultivation has not been proved much productive, the government is trying to bring more and more land within permanent terrace cultivation.

Now, Nagaland has been striving for industrial development as well. There is a Sugar Mill at Dimapur, a Pulp and Paper Mill and Tuli and Forest Product at Tijit. The State Government extends all encouragement for the progress of small scale industries and enrichment of handloom technology.

(c) Various Districts of the State

State of Nagaland consists of seven districts—Kohima, Phek, Wokha, Zunheboto, Mokokchung, Tuensang and Mon.

1. Kohima

The area of Kohima district is about 4041 sq. km. and has a population of more than two lakh and a half. The density of population is 62 per sq. km. in which Angami, Kuki and Zeliang tribes are found in the majority. The rate of literacy is almost 50 per cent. In the district there are four sub-divisions, i.e., Dimapur, Peren, Tseminyu, Pughoboto, seventeen town circles and 346 villages.

Both oil and gas are available here. Also there are sugar mill, bee keeping and sericulture farms, etc.

2. Phek

This district, carved out of Kohima in December 1973 is the home of Chakhesang and Pochury tribes. Phek is situated at about 1,444 metres above the sea level consisting of an area of 2,026 sq. km. and a population of 70,618 of which 40 per cent is literate. Meluri and Pfutsero are the two sub-divisions, with eight town circles and some 96 villages. Limestone, base metal, citronella farm, etc., are available in the district.

3. Wokha

Like Phek, this was carved out of Mokokchung district (also Zunheboto) in December 1973 where Lotha tribe is in majority. It is situated at around 1,500 metres above sea level. Area of Wokha district is 1628 sq. km. and population about 58 thousand. The rate of literacy is almost 46 per cent in the district. It has only one sub-division, Bhandari, and Wokha and Baghty are the two block headquarters with eight town-circles and some 95 villages. The forest is very rich in the district and it is dense near the rivers Doyang and Baghty where trees like timber, orchid, medicinal plants, bonsum, titachapa, hollock, bamboo, cane, etc., are found. Wild mithuns roam about in the green woods close to the foothills. In the Chunky valley there is a deposit of coal and oil has been found close to Changang in Bhandari circle. *Jhum* cultivation is largely in vogue in the district. The principal crops are paddy, maize, barley, pulses, vegetables, rapeseed, mustard, groundnut and the like. Apple, peach, banana, pineapple, orange, musambi, papaya, etc., are also grown. Sericulture farms, pineapple fibre unit, citronella farm, etc., are situated in this district.

4. Zunheboto Town (1874 m)

This is the headquarters of the district with an area of 1,255 sq. km. and a population of about 62 thousand where Sema Nagas are the majority. Literacy rate is 46 per cent. It has one sub-division, Aghunato, two block headquarters, Zunheboto and Tokiye, ten administrative town circles and around 155 villages.

There are Cottage-Industry Training Centre, Citronella Farm, Distillation Units, etc., in the district.

5. Mokokchung (1325 m)

This is called the Paris of Nagaland where Ao Nagas are in majority, is the most advanced district in Nagaland. With its pastoral beauty, it has an area of 1615 sq. km. and also a population of more than one lakh and five thousand. The density of population is 65 per sq. km. and literacy about 62 per cent. Alongwith Mokokchung, it has another sub-division, Tuli and nine administrative towns and villages. In the district the plain parts are in Chunky valley where land is very fertile and terrace cultivation extracts its full benefit. The main rivers flowing through the district are Melak, Dikhu and Desoi. Timber, Bamboo, grass, palm leaves are in plenty in the forest. Rice is the leading crop. Also cultivated are maize, tapioca, ginger, potato, sugarcane, betel leaf, mustard, etc. The land underneath is quite rich in coal, limestone, cobalt, magnestic, cromite, nickel, etc. There is also a pulp and paper mill at Tuli which is the main industry of the district.

6. Tuensang

On the eastern part near the border of nation Burma lies Tuesang district (1372 m) which has an area of 4228 sq. km. with a population of more than one lakh and fifty-three thousand. The density of population is 36 per sq. km. and literacy rate is about 40 per cent. The district has six sub-divisions namely—Kiphire, Longleng, LongKhim, Noklak, Shamatorp and Tobu and 17 towns and total 236 villages. It is mostly inhabited by Chang and Konyak tribes followed by Sangtam, Yimchunger, Khiemnugan and Phom. Here in Kiphire sub-division live mostly the Sangtam and Yimchunger Nagas. The districts is covered with steep hills and gorges with Saramati, the highest peak of Nagaland. The main rivers flow from here are Dikhu, Zungki and Tizu. The soil of the district is quite acidic. The minerals available are cromite, nickel, copper, bauxite, manganese and iron ore. Pine, timber, bonsum, bamboo, cane, cherry, walnut, orchids, and last but not the least banana are found in the forest. The industries are forest-based. There are Cottage Industry Training Centre, Sericulture Farm, one handicrafts-cum-production centre, Bee keeping Farm, Citronella Farm, Distillation Unit, District Industrial Centre and many more. People are mostly agriculturist who practise both the *Jhum* and terrace cultivation and produce maize, millets, etc., apart from many other products.

7. Mon

Mon (898 m) district covers an area of 1786 sq. km. with a population of 79 thousand. The density of population is 44 per sq. km. and literacy 20 per cent. Konyak and Phom are the leading inhabitants of the district besides a small number of Chakhensang and Angami tribes. Konyaks usually maintain the old tradition. They usually get their tatoo marked and put on head-gears decorated with feathers of birds. Mon has three sub-divisions—Naginimara, Tizit and Champang with seven town circles and 82 villages. The district has good reserves of coal, oil and gas. There are Cottage Industry Training Centre, Sericulture Farm; Plywood Factory, Citronella Farm and also a Distillation Unit. Covered with forest, from this predominantly hilly district flows the river Dikhu. Maize, millet, tapioca, etc., largely are grown in the district.

Education

In Nagaland, a far-flung State in the Himalayas, the early initiative for the development of education was taken up by the Christian missionaries, particularly by E.W. Clark of the American Biptist Mission. As early as in 1908-1909, there were 21 Government schools, the total number of pupils being 561 boys and 550 girls. The increase was phenomenal. So in 1931, there was a total of 42 schools at the Kohima Sadar sub-division alone.

After independence, several schools were started. So far so, in 1967, there were three colleges, 16 high, 66 middle and 268 primary schools. Many schools have libraries. Hindi has been included in the school curriculum.

In the leading institutions, local dances, sports, various games, arts, carpentry, and social services are taught to the young boys and girls. A few so institutions have started their magazines to boost the academic faculties of the students. The sconting and National Cadet Corps training have been started in several institutions. Besides Teachers' Training Centres have been opened.

Table 1
Literates and Literacy Rates by Sex—Sikkim : Census 2001

Union Territory/ Districts	*Literates*			*Literacy Rate of 2001*		
	Persons	*Males*	*Females*	*Persons*	*Males*	*Females*
Nagaland	**1,146,523**	**645,807**	**500,716**	**67.11**	**71.77**	**61.92**
Mon	93,859	55,586	38,273	42.25	46.70	37.12
Tuensang	183,513	105,249	78,264	51.30	55.97	46.12
Mokokchung	172,208	92,188	80,020	84.27	86.14	82.20
Zunheboto	90,864	49,205	41,659	69.73	73.43	65.80
Wokha	113,704	62,565	51,139	81.28	85.69	76.46
Dimapur	205,230	117,677	87,553	78.15	82.16	73.34
Kohima	200,137	113,205	86,932	74.28	81.44	66.64
Phek	87,008	50,132	36,876	71.35	78.97	63.08

Besides standard Public Schools, a few colleges have been started at Kohima and Dimapur where English, Arts, Commerce, History, Economics, Logic, Geology, Botany and other subjects are taught.

Language

Grierson has included the Nagaland dialects in the Tibeto-Burman family of languages. He has further sub-divided these dialects into Western, Eastern and Central sub-groups. The Angami, Rengma, Sema and Chakesang dialects come under the Western sub-group. Besides the Central sub-group includes the dialects spoken by Aos, Lothas and Phoms, while the eastern sub-group is made up of the dialects principally spoken by the Changs and Konyaks.

In fact the tribal languages have been put down to the Roman alphabet, but it is Angami Rengma and Ao languages which have had a small corpus of a written literature in the form of school text books and some publications under the auspices of the Christians. The census data related to Scheduled Tribes for their language spoken by them is given as follows :

Table 2
Mother Tongue for Scheduled Tribes

Scheduled Tribe Mother Tongue	Number of Speakers					
	Rural			Urban		
	Total	Males	Females	Total	Males	Females
1	2	3	4	5	6	7
All Scheduled Tribes						
Adi	90	51	39	21	15	6
Anal	13	9	4	1	1	0
Angami	34,325	17,317	17,008	13,482	6,698	6,784
Ao	1,29,178	65,545	63,633	36,505	18,572	17,933
Arabic/Arbi	10	7	3	4	3	1
Assamese	2,311	1,233	1,078	355	174	181
Bengali	2,099	1,095	1,004	176	116	60
Bhili/Bhilodi	9	5	4	1	0	1
Bhotia	2	1	1	1	0	1
Bishnupuriya	5	3	2	0	0	0
Bodo/Boro	4,665	2,426	2,239	356	199	157
Chakhesang	12,494	6,634	5,860	4,752	2,571	2,181
Chakru/Chokri	42,181	21,739	20,442	1,841	1,008	833
Chang	24,646	12,756	11,890	5,933	3,117	2,816
Dimasa	1,923	964	959	16	13	3
Dogri	7	5	2	0	0	0
English	602	336	266	133	53	80
Gadaba	19	9	10	2	2	0
Gangte	33	17	16	0	0	0
Garo	1,548	840	708	215	122	93
Gondi	17	7	10	3	1	2
Gujarati	43	24	19	0	0	0
Halabi	61	28	33	7	3	4
Halam	1	0	1	1	0	1
Hindi	1,259	736	523	224	140	84
Hmar	5	1	4	5	3	2
Ho	12	12	0	3	2	1
Jatapu	13	2	11	2	2	0
Juang	1	0	1	0	0	0
Kabui	2,388	1,201	1,187	36	19	17

(Contd.)

(Contd.)

1	2	3	4	5	6	7
Kannada	1	1	0	1	0	1
Karbi/Mikir	94	46	48	32	18	14
Kashmire	3	1	2	2	2	0
Khandeshi	6	3	3	5	0	5
Kharia	10	9	1	14	5	9
Khasi	20	10	10	29	16	13
Khezha	22,647	11,624	11,023	655	360	295
Khiemnungan	20,265	10,497	9,768	1,566	876	690
Khond/Kondh	4	2	2	1	0	1
Kinnauri	1	0	1	0	0	0
Kisan	88	55	33	1	0	1
Koch	4	2	2	0	0	0
Koda/Kora	5	4	1	0	0	0
Kolami	7	3	4	0	0	0
Kom	0	0	0	3	2	1
Konda	8	4	4	1	0	1
Konyak	1,28,448	66,448	62,000	7,490	4,079	3,411
Korku	7	4	3	0	0	0
Korwa	21	8	13	4	3	1
Koya	0	0	0	4	2	2
Kui	1	1	0	0	0	0
Kuki	14,024	7,144	6,880	1,101	598	503
Kurukh/Oraon	145	82	63	3	2	1
Lahnda	4	4	0	0	0	0
Lalung	5	1	4	3	3	0
Lepcha	0	0	0	1	1	0
Liangmei	4,176	2,121	2,055	26	10	16
Limbu	0	0	0	2	1	1
Lotha	64,608	32,838	31,770	17,310	9,139	8,171
Lushai/Mizo	149	84	65	30	16	14
Malayalam	175	114	61	54	30	24
Malto	0	0	0	2	2	0
Manipuri	24	19	5	6	1	5
Mao	3,812	1,918	1,894	814	446	368
Maram	4	2	2	1	0	1
Marathi	21	11	10	5	3	2
Miri/Mishing	22	16	6	6	3	3
Mishmi	27	12	15	0	0	0
Mogh	15	8	7	3	0	3
Monpa	5	3	2	0	0	0
Munda	26	16	10	8	4	4
Mundari	119	79	40	5	2	3
Nepali	1,822	1,030	792	231	131	100
Nicobarese	2	2	0	1	1	0
Nissi/Dafla	7	6	1	0	0	0
Nocte	371	189	182	4	1	3
Oriya	42	32	10	5	3	2
Pabha	21	14	7	5	3	2
Paite	30	15	15	5	5	0

(Contd.)

(Contd.)

1	2	3	4	5	6	7
Pawi	9	6	3	9	5	4
Phom	54,682	29,548	25,134	727	419	308
Pochury	10,413	5,375	5,038	66	38	28
Punjabi	9	7	2	17	12	5
Rengma	26,822	13,354	13,468	2,711	1,441	1,270
Sangtam	46,611	23,682	22,929	3,383	1,864	1,519
Santali	13	9	4	5	3	2
Sema	1,41,597	71,785	69,812	17,945	9,266	8,679
Sindhi	5	4	1	14	5	9
Tamil	30	22	8	4	2	2
Tangkhul	362	207	155	305	160	145
Tangsa	12	6	6	2	1	1
Telugu	43	23	20	2	1	1
Thado	613	308	305	39	21	18
Tibetan	53	26	27	5	1	4
Tripuri	21	11	10	6	2	4
Tulu	22	14	8	2	1	1
Urdu	14	8	6	7	7	0
Vaiphei	5	2	3	1	1	0
Wancho	4	4	0	0	0	0
Yimchungre	41,542	21,144	20,398	3,137	1,756	1,381
Zeliang	27,195	14,103	13,092	1,283	682	601
Zemi	9,019	4,625	4,394	17	9	8
Zou	3	2	1	0	0	0
Others	52,790	26,819	25,971	4,476	2,278	2,198

Source: Census 1991

Angami is the language recognised upto matriculation standard at the secondary level. The other tribes while using Angami and Ao as a medium for primary and middle standards, have made efforts to develop their respective alphabets. The Ao language is found in various villages. In fact Chongli is the dominant and shows signs of gradually becoming the language of the Ao tribes. Indeed the spread of the Chongli dialects has received great impetus from the work of the Mission. The translation works have been done in this language.

Agricultural and Industrial Developments

It is an agrarian State and about 80 per cent of its population depend upon agriculture. Nagaland is essentially an agrarian state of the country. About 80 per cent of its total population is directly dependent on agriculture. In some of the tribes of Nagas, working in jobs others than farming, hunting, forestry and gathering is considered as a taboo. Although sedentry agriculture is practised but it is insignficant and confined to terraces around Kohima and in the aarrow rive. terraces adn alluvial fans. Shifting cultivation is the dominant agricultural system. It is therefore imperative to discuss the salient features of the shifting cultivation known as Jhuming in North East India.

The crops grown, the agricultural operations done in an agricultural year differ from latitude to latitude and meso to micro agro-climatic regions.

Nevertheless, the major agricultural activities and *Jhuming* operations may be broadly classified under the following headings.

1. Search for *Jhum* land.
2. Felling of trees and clearing of Jungles.
3. Burning of trees and dried vegetation.
4. Allotement of land.
5. Sowing and plantation of crops.
6. Digging and hoeing of fields.
7. Plantation of vegetables, dibbling and sowing of seeds.
8. Weeding and harvesting of vegetables.
9. Harvest of main crops.
10. Fallowing.
11. Collection of ratoon crops.

I some Naga tribes, clearing of the jungle is considered the primary responsibility of the entire village. Generally the sowing season for terraced rice-fields is April-May. The grain ripens towards October. The *Jhum* paddy seed is sown during the spring time; in many cases the plant sprouts in May, followed in July by weeding, the grain ripens in July but sometimes the ripening season may go as late as September.

After Independence there have been significant development in the field of industry.

Spinning and Weaving. Spinning and weaving is a household industry in Nagaland. Weaving is one of the most important duties of females. Weaving of cloths is forbidden for a man to share, with the exception that the spots of dark blue with which white *'Lengta'* bands are often decorated are invariably embroidered by man and never by a women.

Dyeing. Nagas have several techniques of dyeing. Dyes are prepared from the leaves of indigo *Strobilanthes flaccidifolius* which is cultivated for this purpose both in plots in heavy, shady jungles and in the sun, leaves grown in shade and in sun being needed at different stages of the process.

Pot Making. Pots are made generally by women as it is a taboo for males to make pots. The non-Christians, still observe the old restriction and obtain their cooking pots generally from the Phom District.

Wood and Cane Work. Nagas are pretty skilful in wood cane work. Cane being profuse is largely utilised for works in craft. Picturesque cane crafts comprising bowls mugs and containers with multi-coloured engravings on them are made by all tribes. Other varieties such as fillets as part of ornamentation have elaborately worked out design. Cane helmets and hot frames are many. Among the Nagas a cane-rain proof hot is also made. Mats woven of cane strings with fine texture have decorative value.

Manufacturing of Salt. From the brine springs, salt is locally excavated and manufactured, by boiling water on the fire over the iron cauldrons or *Chungas,* especially designed, the lid having been tightly compressed until the water becomes evaporated and turned out into solid salt. Such enterprises are carried in Jalukie, Peletkie and Mbaupungwa or Mbangpanlwa (Zeliangroun area), and Akhegwo, Yis, Purr, Molen and Ozeho villages (Chakhesang area). The census data relating to agricultural workers, household workers and industrial workers are as follows :

Table 3

Agricultural and Farming Functions Including Labourers and Other Works (Statewise): Census 2001

Total/ Rural/ Urban	*Persons/ Males/ Females*	*Cultivators Labourers*	*Agricultural Industry Workers*	*Household Workers*	*Other*
Total	Persons	544,433	33,852	18,072	253,625
	Males	271,608	18,141	6,529	191,489
	Females	272,825	15,711	11,543	62,136
Rural	Persons	537,861	32,842	14,702	151,981
	Males	268,540	17,673	4,923	107,504
	Females	269,321	15,169	9,779	44,477
Urban	Persons	6,572	1,010	3,370	101,644
	Males	3,068	468	1,606	83,985
	Females	3,504	542	1,764	17,659

Table 4

The Survey of Main Workers, Marginal Workers and Non-workers (Statewise): Census 2001

Total Rural Urban	*Persons Males Females*	*Total workers*	*Main workers*	*Marginal workers*	*Non-workers*	*Total Workers (main + marginal)*
Total	Persons	849,982	708,455	141,527	1,138,654	849,982
	Males	487,767	424,236	63,531	553,919	487,767
	Females	362,215	284,219	77,996	584,735	362,215
Rural	Persons	737,386	606,601	130,785	898,429	737,386
	Males	398,640	341,298	57,342	448,011	398,640
	Females	338,746	265,303	73,443	450,418	338,746
Urban	Persons	112,596	101,854	10,742	240,225	112,596
	Males	89,127	82,938	6,189	105,908	89,127
	Females	23,469	18,916	4,553	134,317	23,469

Besides there are industries of stone work, smithery, fire making, sugar mill, seri-culture, paper making, carpentry and other small scale industry.

Religion

In fact the Christian population dominate in the State. Others are the tribal religions.

Naga tribal religion being a mixture of theism, animism, supernaturalism and superstition is connected with the practice of sorcery, exorcism and magic.

Table 5
Agricultural and Farming Functions including Labourers and Other Workers (Districtwise) : Census 2001

District	*Cultivators*			*Agricultural labourers*			*Household industries*			*Other workers*		
	P	M	F	P	M	F	P	M	F	P	M	F
Mon	108,212	57,113	51,099	5,907	3,458	2,449	1,521	734	787	13,275	10,733	2,542
Tuensang	152,324	76,327	75,997	6,333	3,299	3,034	1,562	630	932	24,990	19,824	5,166
Mokokchung	65,366	32,547	32,819	6,892	3,109	3,783	4,056	1,785	2,271	32,465	23,171	9,294
Zunheboto	27,659	14,980	12,679	1,724	612	1,112	776	261	515	31,898	16,745	15,153
Wokha	36,627	16,493	20,134	668	318	350	1,435	487	948	17,723	14,126	3,597
Dimapur	28,994	17,689	11,305	4,680	2,923	1,757	2,776	913	1,863	65,810	55,790	10,020
Kohima	73,157	33,379	39,778	6,287	3,682	2,605	4,504	1,241	3,263	50,741	38,016	12,725
Phek	52,094	23,080	29,014	1,361	740	621	1,442	478	964	16,723	13,084	3,639

Table 6
The Survey of Main Workers, Marginal Workers and Non-Workers (Districtwise) : Census 2001

District	*Total workers*			*Main workers*			*Marginal workers*			*Non workers*		
	P	M	F	P	M	F	P	M	F	P	M	F
Mon	128,915	72,038	56,877	108,367	63,263	45,104	20,548	8,775	11,773	130,689	65,967	64,722
Tuensang	185,209	100,080	85,129	157,760	86,811	70,949	27,449	13,269	14,180	229,592	116,808	112,784
Mokokchung	108,779	60,612	48,167	82,291	48,427	33,864	26,488	12,185	14,303	118,451	57,816	60,635
Zunheboto	62,057	32,598	29,459	50,375	27,453	22,922	11,682	5,145	6,537	92,852	47,029	45,823
Wokha	56,453	31,424	25,029	50,614	28,992	21,622	5,839	2,432	3,407	104,645	52,196	52,449
Dimapur	102,260	77,315	24,945	86,785	70,483	16,302	15,475	6,832	8,643	206,122	89,020	117,102
Kohima	134,689	76,318	58,371	114,669	67,780	46,889	20,020	8,538	11,482	179,677	85,383	94,294
Phek	71,620	37,382	34,238	57,594	31,027	26,567	14,026	6,355	7,671	76,626	39,700	36,926

Naga priests receive special training for wording off evil spirits and for the conduct of ceremonies. Several practices are held to avert epidemics, believed to be a representation of an evil spirit's shadow, which in cases of failures of being appeased, has come to ravage the village. A sacrificial offering in such situations consists of eggs laid in the path wrapped in a leaf, while the village paths are strewn with pieces of ornamental decorations and clothings. Invocations to such a spirit are made to ward him off. But the system of invocation and appeasement of spirits varies from tribe to tribe, from village to village and from one houshold to another. Sacrifices are also offered with a cooked liver, entrails and slices of meat in addition to eggs. The census data for religion adopted by Scheduled Tribes is as follows :

Table 7
Religion for Scheduled Tribes

Scheduled Tribe	*Rural*			*Urban*		
	Total	*Males*	*Females*	*Total*	*Males*	*Females*
1	2	3	4	5	6	7
ALL SCHEDULED TRIBES						
All Religions	**9,33,145**	**4,78,579**	**4,54,566**	**1,27,677**	**66,577**	**61,100**
1. Buddhists	109	50	59	72	39	33
2. Christians	9,17,662	4,70,396	4,47,266	1,26,475	65,947	60,528
3. Hindus	10,914	5,753	5,161	821	423	398
4. Jains	30	21	9	3	2	1
5. Muslims	552	262	290	90	44	46
6. Sikhs	33	16	17	5	2	3
7. Other Religions and Persuations	3,832	2,075	1,757	210	119	91
8. Religion not stated	13	6	7	1	1	0

Source: 1999

Religious Officials

The Nagas know nothing of any priestly caste, or priesthood upon which special powers have been conferred by consecration. For the simple ceremonies of the home and field a man acts as his own priest. For ceremonies such as the Mithan sacrifice, where the clan as a whole is concerned. One of the clan priest is called in. There are old men who have been councillors and their qualifications are age, experience and free from any serious deformity. Each clan in a village may have from one to four priests, the number varying from village to village. Public opinion dictates who among the old men are fitted to be priests. Attached to each priest is another old man who acts as his assistant takes his place, and a new assistant is chosen. A simple ceremony is performed by a new priest to celebrable his entry into office. He kills a cock in front of his house and announces that he is following the customs of his ancestors. For most village ceremonies the priests take it in turn to act, but at the bigger festivals they are all expected to be present.

7

Pre- and Post-Reorganisation Era

Nations and states at international as well as national level mark delimitation to create borders and boundaries. But at the same time, famous Council of Europe used the phrase "Borders are scars of history".[1] This indicates a problem which is especially difficult for the ethnic groups, national minorities and divided nations. The scars of Naga history are the boundaries that divided the Nagas into Nagaland, Manipur, Assam and Arunachal Pradesh, and eastern Nagaland now in Burma. The Nagas today feel deeply that they had been wrongly separated by the frontiers made by the British and Indians. As a speaker at Naga Students' Federation stated, "Blood is thicker than an imaginery line. It is natural that a people divided by foreigners suffer immensely but sooner or later they are always reunited. Take the case of Germany. A few years ago the Germans themselves said Germany would never be united in a thousand years but it happened so soon and so fast. The unification of the Nagas will be a historical necessity.[2]

Of course, it is true that the Naga areas were first divided by the British in the 19th century. But the creation of Nagaland state in 1963 put the "divide and rule" policy into real practice. In recent history, the Nagas have gone through a time of rapid change. In the 19th century when the Nagas first came in contact with the Europeans, Mr. S.E. Peal had predicted that the Naga tribes would soon turn "reformed and hopelessly sophisticated."[3] J.H. Hutton noted the remarkable rapidity with which Nagas were changing and commented that in the first 50 years of their relation with Europeans, the Nagas had gone through "a period of rapid change such as huminity has probably never before experienced."[4]

A brief study of the present situation shows that the organisation of Nagaland state was by and large responsible for further accelerating the pace and nature of this change.

British Penetration into Nagaland

Both the British military expedition in this region and the American missionary activities commenced almost simultaneously. In 1832 the first military expedition to the Naga Hills was undertaken and the very first batch of missionaries made their appearance in the area in 1836.[5] Generally our sources illustrate that the transition from the traditional to contemporary society was accompanied by many forces of confrontation and conflict.

The Naga Tribal Society was tempted by the manifestations of colonial culture on one hand, but was curious to preserve their autonomy, tribal organisation and indigenous culture on the other, as has been with many tribal societies in the world. But one finds that the transition from the pre-modern onto modern was always historically inevitable. This historical inevitability was further strengthened by the occupation of the Naga Hills by the British in the 19th century.

The Nagas until that time had not been exposed to the temptations of material culture which their neighbours both in Burma and in India had experienced for centuries under different changing dynastic rulers and maharajahs. Among the various operative forces which penetrated into Nagaland with the British entrance, ecclesiology performed a very important role in the entire process of social change among the Nagas. To quote Terhuja in this regard, "If one responsible dynamic factor were to be singled out for an overall change in the life of the Nagas it would undoubtedly be the introduction of Christianity among them."[6]

With the course of time, missionaries with their firm determination operated carefully taking note of various problems facing the Nagas. They opened up schools and stressed medical care. These developmental activities and favours of the missionaries associated with the religious cause left a deep impression on the tribal mind. We find that in the last days of the British rule and just a decade after they left, the number of Naga Christians rose tremendously.[7]

The general education of the people at the hands of the missionaries opened up the eyes of the Nagas to a different world. The education of the tribes which form one of the major themes in the process of conversion laid down the basis for future development and this way helped to create a new educated elite. After acquiring a good education a number of Nagas entered the Civil Services under the British India Government. Mr. A. Kevichusa became the first Naga graduate in the year 1924 and went on to become a Deputy Commissioner.[8] Entering these various professions not only provided an impetus to shift to a new life-style but gave employment opportunities to widen their outlook, and they inbibed fresh ideas for improving their agriculture, various arts and crafts, and exploitation of the forest resources. Obviously, the economic development within the Naga community expanded the social division of labour and served to modify the tribal organisation of settled agricultural villages.

Side by side, effort to enhance the opportunities of carrying out trades with distant parts and the importing of various articles of daily use also improved. This increased the mobility within the Naga society together with the help of the British administration which ensured the construction of roads that linked up the various areas in Nagaland. All these measures monetised the economy and gradually undermined the barter system. It was during the British times that some events of historical significance took place. The formation of the Naga Club and its memorandum which was submitted to the famous Simon Commission in 1929.

This short and succinct document illustrates the far-sightedness and political vision that the Naga leaders had for their people in those days. In reality, it impressed the British so much that it became an issue for debate in the British Parliament.

The emergence of the Naga National Council that started in 1946 was another important event, as it was the foundation of guiding light for all subsequent Naga nationalistic aspirations and movements. Just a year after its inception the leaders met Gandhi and the dialogue which took place between them in July 1947 is known to all the Nagas. It is important to put in record the correct words of what Gandhi said to the Naga leaders on that day. "We do not want the British and they are going. If you say that you are not Indians and your country does not belong to India then the matter must end there. Nobody will force you to join the Indian Union."

After Independence Developments

Very shortly, this exchange followed by the Independence of India and Gandhi's assassination. The Indian Army shifted into Nagaland and a few years later the war for Naga Independence commenced in the 1950s. During this time, one of the major blunders was committed by the Naga People's Convention (NPC) and their 16 Point Agreement. Some petty Government officials along with some opportunists started a dialogue with the Indian Government.

A careful study of the 16 Point Agreement shows that it was not an agreement at all but a clever enumeration of luring offers. The NPC leaders made a list of their demands and the external affairs legal adviser answered the questions regarding the Naga demands so cleverly and graciously that the NPC leaders felt they had an agreement. The legal adviser said that the demands had been recorded but the decision would depend on various steps including constitutional amendments. At this point, the NPC leaders had the upper hand and could have insisted on their demands because at that time the Naga movement was so strong that Nehru could have banned down. If the NPC leaders had insisted on the re-transference of the Reserve Forest from Assam to Nagaland, it could have been implemented and at present there would have been no border issue with Assam. But they were in such a hurry to return to Nagaland to become ministers of the new state that they did not follow through this and other clauses.

There were also many superfluous as well as contradictory points. There was a clause which demanded the creation of a Naga Regiment. The whole idea of a Naga Regiment would help only to strengthen the Indian Army to fight against the Nagas. Only Mr. A. Kevichusa refused to sign the agreement and withdrew from the NPC saying that if there were to be an agreement in case, it should be directly between the NCC and the Indian Government—the role of a third party, i.e., NPC intervention, being necessarily limited to that of mediator or go-between. But unfortunately the wisdom of this old man was rejected by the Government of India and other NPC leaders.

Creation of Nagaland as a State

Notwithstanding the protests, the 16 Point Agreement resulted in the creation of Nagaland as a State. This marked the bifurcatiion of Naga political aspiration into 2 directions. On one hand, those who ascribed to the idea of statehood within the Indian Union followed the political funda of the rest of India and came to view politics not in its sense of shaping the destiny of people, but saw no further than the elections, power and money. On the other hand, a huge section of Nagas kept alive their quest for a sovereign nation state. The creation of Nagaland State also further divided the Nagas emotionally as well as politically. More than half of Nagaland was left out of the new state. Thus, Nagas was divided into five administrative units; Nagaland, Assam, Manipur, and Arunachal Pradesh and lastly Eastern Nagaland in Burma. Some Nagas who were not included in the new state voiced a protest that the Nagas in the newly formed Nagaland were enjoying the fruit of the blood-shed by all the Nagas both within and outside the fresh state as the state was direct result of the armed conflict with India. Others, however, held the view that the state is just a temporary phase in Naga history in the same manner that Naga Hills was a district of Assam under the British, and believed that the "Promised Land" was yet to be reached. To quote Horam here, "Nagaland, a greater and sovereign country, is the goal of the nationalist Nagas who have been fighting for this for the last 30 years".

Thus, India felt the need for a concerted effort to persuade the Nagas to abandon their goals and ideals. She used military might to confront the Nagas and also material inducement in terms of crores of rupees in order to divert their attention. India's generosity cannot be dismissed. But the sad thing is that the state politicians now depend entirely on Delhi to solve their smallest troubles. Nagaland has roads, buildings, water supply systems—all of which do not work. For some decades Nagas have stopped exercising their self-determination. An apathy is gradually but surely gripping the people. The spirit that sustained them in their villages for centuries and preserved the Nagas as an admirable people who maintained an orderly society has been shaken and disused.

Development of the State

Of course, the creation of Nagaland state was also accompanied by a new phase of development. Huge amounts of money were pumped into the new state for the objective of development. The politicians and officials who were responsible for handling this money became corrupted as they succumbed to the temptation of quick wealth. The person, who before had been a simple villager with virtually no possession to speak of, could not handle this sudden and overwhelming exposure to money and all its associated benefits. Thus corruption became, in a sense, a way of life as there was no accountability for these funds.

Many new industrial establishments were formed and the extension of bureaucracy following statehood created new employment facilities. The plans for education, social welfare and medical facilities got improved. Side by side, the Marwaris and other Indian business communities made their influx reaping the advantages of this fresh frontier of economic enterprise. All these changes facilitated the formation of a nouveau rich class and an uneven social structure. The nature of political activities were mainly responsible for the emergence of the bourgeoisie and this in turn provided them the initial capital to multiply further their resources through business, transport or construction works. All this led to the social stratification based on material prosperity. The exploitation of the Nagas by the fellow tribesmen commenced speedily, for the first time Naga millionaires came into existence. The ex-ministers and bureaucrats became quite wealthy landlords in Dimapur area investing crores of rupees on multi-storey buildings and farms employing illegal Bangladeshi refugees.

Administration of the State

One more drastic change that has taken place in the state is in terms of administrative organisation. Prior to this, the Naga Social Organisation was governed by the village council and chief who would settle down conflicts and other problems in the clan or village. The newly imposed government led to the erosion of the traditional authority of the village council. There has been a great loss of autonomy even at this lowest level of functioning.

Also at the cultural level, an overflow of money and the introduction, through education, to western modes of dress, behaviour and thought has led to a superficial understanding and assimilation of some aspects of Western culture. This superficial westernisation in matters of dress, food habits, music and other activities became popular. These developments have strongly challenged the traditional way of life. For instance, take the matter of a wedding in a Naga society. In earlier times wedding was a simple affair, the whole ceremony was performed with minimum fuss, especially regarding material arrangements. But the scene is now much changed. There is a great pre-occupation with physical arrangements that tends towards extravagance, sometimes involving thousands of rupees and the slaughter of a large number of animals for feasting purposes.

Because, the traditional society and values have been eroded due to modernisation without any new positive direction to take its place, the Naga society is, now, in limbo. Although modernisation has ushered in the benefits of better social welfare and medical facilities and a more mobile infrastructure in terms of say, transport, communications and physical development, a decidedly disturbing attendant result is seen in the way of modernisation is viewed by the new generation which is product of the net process. Most are confused with what the term implies for the Nagas and the direction it should take. Many are swept into the concept that modernisation equals those of fast cars, videos, pop music, a slavish following of the latest western fashions and race to increase one's social and material status and the adoption of other superficial aspects of western life culture. Although modernisation in the true sense of the term is a historical necessity, it is this misconception of the term that has created confusion in the minds of the Naga people.

In this process, the rhythm of tribal production has been seriously disturbed. The migration from the village is leading to the gradual disappearance of tribal arts and handicrafts such as weaving, basketry, masonry and the like. This sudden upheaval of a mass of people going away from their roots has led to a very grave social and economic crisis. Since ages past the indigenous mode of production has been footed on the land, and its products have been preserved for time immomorial. But due to the shift in economy, timber has become a lucrative industry. There is a mere temptation for every young man to make quick money in this line which has led to the destruction of irreplaceable tracts of forest land, which is even causing a major ecological imbalance. The shift from the village to town life has also resulted in a process of alienation. The ties of clan and family which held together the fabric of Naga social way of living and governed modes of conduct and interaction are to a large extent, gradually loosening if not actually severed. Accompanying this process also is a loss of one's roots and one's identity. The Nagas have been essentially sons of the soil, working and living in rhythm with the seasons and nature. Their history has been handed down from generation to generation by word of mouth and with the help of songs, festivals and legend. The migration to towns has stripped off much of this sense of identity, of knowing who and what one is the past.

In the political arena, the Nagas seem to be living in a modern world which the Yogoslav writer, Milovan Djalas, has said as "Living today in tomorrow's world with yesterday's ideas". Today, the Nagas are confused and disappointed by the changes that have come about as a result of this fast development. As a Naga thinker so succinctly puts it, "The Nagas, by large, are perplexed and dissatisfied with the political offspring that the struggle has produced. The disappointment is understandable because we too regard ourselves as a people and we have failed to achieve our declared goal. Our loyalty to our aspirations on one hand and our inability to cope with what has happened on the other, has resulted in the present ironic situation: electoral politics which ponder to our baser tendencies prevails overground, while the politics that reflects the true feelings of our people has gone underground.

In various fields the fast pace of modernisation has carried in its wake many attendant evils, and this traumatic period has left a deep emotional stress on the minds of the Nagas. As T. Sakhrie puts it, "The Nagas made a leap, as it were, from a distant past into the glare of the present century . . . found the world greatly changed. They looked about with uncertainty and pinched themselves to be assured that all that was really true . . . people became suddenly restive with the existing state of affairs. There was social unrest, economic unrest, political unrest. Everywhere there were crisis for better, bigger, nobler things. The era brought a new impetus to all fields of human endeavour."

Despite, we must remember that Naga society has never been stagnant. As Julian Jacobs rightly puts, "It would be altogether wrong to see Nagas as passive victims of a process of deculturation. There has been never prisitine or unchanging Naga society. Rather, we may discern the ways in which Naga ethnicity is being actively and consciously remoulded in the era. What emerges here is a vigorous sense of history and identity at the level of individual, tribe and nation." It is probably too early to predict what Nagaland will become because the state is still too young. But some of the damage already done will definitely effect the course of the history of the Nagas.

References

1. Caux Brochere 1991 "Democracy starts with me".
2. Naga Students Federation Seminar, March 1991 "Nagas Towards AD 2000".
3. J.H. Hutton, *The Angami Nagas,* London 1921, p. VIII.
4. *Ibid.*
5. F.S. Downs, *Christianity in North East India* Delhi 1983.
6. K. Terhuja, "The Christian Church among the Angami Nagas" in *Tribal Situation in India,* Vol. 13. edited by K.S. Singh.
7. Joseph Puthenpurakal, *Bapist Mission in Nagaland Shillong* 1984.
8. Interview with Mr. A. Kevichusa.

8

Society and Customs

I. Culture

Each community and a tribe has its distinct identity. This is true in the case of Nagaland also. Every Naga tribe has its own characteristics in respect of language, dress, festival, culture, etc. With the advent of modern civilisation some common features are going to be mingled in them. But those who have been living in the remote areas in the opaque jungle are still maintaining their own identity, culture and tradition. There is no caste system among the Nagas. Each tribe is divided into different clans. Marriage among the same clan is banned.

According to the Census Reports the largest tribe is Konyak followed by Ao, Sema and Angami whereas the smallest tribes are Phom, Rengma and Zeliang. Among the tribes who possess the intervening place are Chakhesang, Lotha, Sangtam, Yimchunger. More or less the same population pattern, it can be said, has been maintained over the years.

1. Aos. Aos are among the most advanced tribes who are mainly the inhabitants of Mokokchung region. The Ao villages are situated at the highest points of the long straight ranges. The main road running along the top of the range going through the villages and in many places there are avenues flanked by Oak trees presenting a pleasant shade. Ao houses are more spaciously and more airy than the dwellings of their southern neighbours, Lothas and Rengmas. Village Aos, like Semas and Lothas, cut their hair in such a way that it looks like a cap.

There we find Morungs in certain villages. Morung is the more ornamental and remarkable than other houses in the Naga village. It is a dormitory for the unmarried young men of the village who usually sleep here in the night. Strangers and guests are entertained and public affairs transacted here.

The function of the Morung may vary from clan to clan, but it generally serves as a recreation club, centre of education, art and discipline and ceremonial purposes. Earlier it was the guard-house to save from any possible attack from the enemies. Still dwellers of the Morung come out to face any eventuality and in time of emergency. The institution of Morung has made immense impact on the Naga-life through the ages. The life of the Naga youth moulds here as they set to learn the basic principles of community living, mutual understanding and necessity of helping one another. It serves as a cultural-centre as the young ones revel in folk dance, song and fool-lores over here which pass on from one generation to another through their memory in spoken language. They learn the art of weaving, wood-carving, cane and bamboo work, etc., also in the Morung which is on the wane due to the negative influence of the modernity.

We see that there is free mixing among the boys and girls of both the Morungs. Morungs are however not found in Angami areas. In many of the villages in Ao, Lotha, Khiemmgan and Phom areas Morungs still exist. Near the Morungs are placed drums made of wood.

About diet, rice is the staple food of Aos. They believe in deities and spirits like other tribes. Aos are a bit darker than the other tribes. Men are not tatooed, but girls are usually tatooed on their chin, breast, arms, legs.

Aos wear a piece of black cloth round their waist which touches the knee. A white cloth made of cotton and decorated with designs and cowries is also hung in frontside. Sometimes they cover their upper part with a jacket-type garment. From their right shoulder they put on a coloured scarf. They wear ornaments, necklaces made of glass beeds, wild bear task, cowri shells, etc. They wear a head-gear, made of bear's hair on which feathers of hornbill are fixed. They put on ivory armlet, wristlet, etc., and tie a cotton string round their waist and fasten a dao (cutter) by it in a wooden sheath.

About females Ao women put on a red coloured decorated cloth from their waist to knee and white blouse with sleeves to cover the upper part. They use a lot of ornaments, e.g., necklaces of red and blue coloured cornelian beads, crystal ear trinket, brass rings, brass made bracelets, hornbill feathers, etc. Ao girls are conspicuous for their lovely hair style and charm.

Despite the fact that Aos are endogamous people, of late inter-tribe marriage is also taking place. They have no bride price as is prevalent among some other tribes. The marriage custom is quite simple. Divorce is common among them. The Aos are among the first Naga tribe to accept Christianity. In 1894 the American Missionaries founded an American Baptist Mission at Impur village. There was a school to which some Chiefs and rich villagers began to send their children. The missionaries were not only pioneers in education but also in health education and services.

These Aos observe Moatsu festival after the sowing is done and mother earth begins to show the sign of fertility in May. The other festival, Tsungrem Mong is celebrated on the occasion of harvest in August.

2. The Angamis. One of the most prominent tribes, i.e., Angamis inhabit in the south-eastern part of Kohima district. Angamis and Chakhesangs are commonly known as southern Angamis who are economically well-off. Their houses are built haphazardly and closely near the road.

In appearance, Angamis are generally tall with brownish complexion and slanted eyes. They wear a short cloth round their waist which comes down to the knee. Two scarves with quite attractive designs are hung cross-wise from their shoulder to chest. They put on ear-rings of wing feathers, balls of puffed cotton, thick ivory armlet made, necklaces made of stone-beads and their legs are decorated with cane-rings. Their women wear a piece of black coloured stripped cloth round their waist upto knee. A sort of sleevless blouse with designs cover their upper part of the body. Ornaments like necklace, bracelet, armlets, etc., are also used by them. But these type of dresses and ornaments are used by them occasionally and for celebrations and in remote villages. Modern men just put on shirt and pant and women mekhala type of lower garment, blouse and a chadar, and not much ornament. As far as their language is concerned Angami, has some similarity with Burmese, Chinese and even Japanese. The Angamis do not keep any bride-price, but some presents are offered to the parents of the girl customarily. They are not allowed to marry in the same Khel, i.e., clan. They are mainly monogamous and only sons inherit the property of the father. Unmarried Angami girls crop their hair and let it grow only after having got married.

These Christian Angamis however do not observe this custom. They bury dead relatives near their house inside a wooden box with a dao (cutter), two sticks, some amount of paddy, etc. Monolithic monuments are prepared for the dead. Their most important festival Sekrenyi is celebrated in February. Terhunyi, another festival is performed in December after the harvest is complete. They drink rice bear, 'Zu' in a mug made of horn, specially during the festival time.

3. The Sema Nagas. They are shorter physique with strong Mongolian features, are the inhabitants of Zunheboto and Wokha districts. The traditional dress of all the Naga tribal people are basically more or less the same with variation in colour and design. The same can be said about their head-gears and some ornaments. It may however be mentioned that members of the southern tribes like Zeliang, Angami and Chakhesang wear a black Kilt embroidered in cowrie shells. Men of the central and eastern tribes like Konyak, Phom, Sema, Chang, Khemnugan, Yimchunger, etc. wear a belt with an apron. Some tribes embroider the length with cowrie shells.

One more important aspect regarding the dress must be mentioned that only the warriors who had hunted many enemy heads or persons who gave a number of feasts are competent to put on the finest and most decorative Naga dress. Their dress is indicative of their valour and social position. They make good use of cowries, feathers, goat's hair dyed red, shells, bone, coloured cane, ivory, etc., in their dress.

Like we have said earlier while the educated modern Nagas of all the tribes have accepted western type of dress, common men and women in general put on Naga chadar, scarf and shawl. Here, it may, however, be mentioned that the Sema women are the best weavers. The traditional Semas are migratory in nature. High bride-price is prevalent among them. They are monogamous, but their chief can take three or four wives. The eldest son of the first wife has to be the next chief. The property of the deceased father of course is divided among all the sons. Divorce is not common among them. Widow remarriage is also prevalent. They bury the dead bodies near the house. Their main festival, Tuluni, is celebrated in the second week of July. More festivals are Saghu, Awona Kuchu, etc.

4. Lothas. They are the inhabitants of Wokha district who have some similarities in custom and dress with the Angamis and the Aos. They are even today maintaining Morungs. The Lothas, strong and muscular, are smaller and darker than the Angamis. They also pay bride-price. Widow remarriage is allowed. Divorce is almost nil. Lothas are great experts in the cultivation of cotton. After paddy cotton is their main product. Tokhu Emong, their important festival, is celebrated in the first week of November.

5. Zeliangs. The Zeliang Nagas mainly live in Kohima district. They are Indo-Mongoloid in appearance with sharp slanted eyes, thick black hair, brownish complexion and strong-built. Their language comes under the Sino-Tibetan group. They are quiet, gentle and friendly. They rear domestic animals like cow, goat, pig, fowl, etc. Zeliang females are expert in handloom while the men-folk do handicrafts with bamboo and cane. They are well-known for their attractive, symbolical dances and exquisite hand-woven embroidered textiles.

They pay bride price and their bride price consists of mithun, land, ornament and money. Sons inherit their father's property and the youngest son gets the maximum share. The daughters get only the ornaments from their mother. If a man has no son his property goes to the closest male relative. A younger brother of the deceased can marry the widow of the elder brother, but never the widows of the younger brother. A man is allowed to marry his wife's younger sister, but never her elder sister. They are generally monogamous. Divorce is allowed. When a wife wants to be separated from her spouse, she has to return the bride-price paid earlier by her husband. Nga-Ngai, their main festival is celebrated in the last week of the month of December.

6. The Chakhesangs. These Indo-Mongoloid people live in the southern part of Phek district, who are medium in structure, strong and sturdy. Their complexion is brown but fair. Erunyi, their main festival is celebrated in December after the harvest is brought home. They observe Tsukhenyie in the month of March/April.

7. The Rengmas. This, one of the smallest Naga tribes, also lives in Phek district who are darker and shorter in structure than the other Nagas. These Rengmas have no priest. The elders perform the rituals and make sacrifices in their festivals who believe in many deities and spirits. Morung occupies a pious place among the Rengmas which is regarded as a sanctuary also. Even if a notorious criminal once takes shelter in it, no one can hurt him till his case is settled in the village council. Ngada, their harvest festival, is celebrated in the last week of November.

8. Sangtams. In the southern area of Tuensang district live the Sangtam Nagas who belong to Indo-Mongoloid family. They were head-hunters till 1946. Mongmong, worship of the God of the house has been their important festival, observed in the first week of September.

9. The Yimchungers. They also live in Tuensang, since the Yimchunger men remained pre-occupied in warfare with neighbouring tribes their women could not evolve the art of decorative weaving. Even today they wear a simple black dress. There had been traditional enmity between the Yimchungers and the Khemnugan and they would hunt each others heads to take revenge. The situation of late has been changed after a peace conference arranged by the Government functionaries in 1965 (26th July). Metemneo is their main festival observed in the second week of August after the harvest of millet.

10. Khemnugans. Yet one tribe live in this district. They are the Khemnugan Nagas who were head-hunters till 1963. They are polygamous people and take even five or six wives. A Khemnugan can kidnap a girl whom he likes and marry her. This medieval custom of marriage by capture is still prevalent among them. There is, however, no bride-price like some other tribes. Divorce is quite easy and simple among them. Their main festivals are Miu and Tsokum. Miu is the festival prior to the sowing of the seeds in the first week of April while Tsokum is associated with harvesting, celebrated in the second week of October. Both the Yimchunger and the Khemnugan have almost the same number of population, around seventeen thousand each.

11. The Chang Tribes. They are dominant in Tuensang. They are also polygamous and take four to six wives. Chang women are expert in weaving. The Changs are one among the very few Naga tribes that use poisoned arrows not only for hunting wild animals but even for killing their enemies when they find it extremely necessary. Naknyulum is their main festival celebrated in the first week of July.

12. The Konyaks. Among the largest tribes (60,000) who live in Mon district, i.e., Konyaks were head-hunters till 1961. They are somewhat backward and do not have much knowledge in weaving which is reflected in their scant dress. They also tatoo their bodies with various designs. During the pre-Independence era when the British invaded the Naga Hills and grew poppy in the valley of Mon district so that they could control this fierce tribe easily, as a result the Konyaks did got addicted to opium and became less enterprising. The status of the chief is important among the Konyaks. It is hereditary past and the chief can marry more than once. A Chief's son will marry only another Chief's daughter and vice versa.

As the Konyaks live very near to Burma border they have kinship and matrimonial relations with the people of the villages of Burma. Some sort of trial marriage is exercised among the tribe and enjoy more freedom in pre-marital sex life.

In appearance, Konyaks are of medium stature, yellow-brownish in complexion with mesocephalic head, platyrrhine nose and straight hair. Aolingmonyu is their main festival celebrated at the end of March when sowing is complete in Konyak villages.

13. Phoms. There had been traditional opposition with the Phoms, the inhabitants of Mon districts who were formerly grouped under the Konyak. It is one of the smallest tribes of eastern region. They speak their own dialect. Since they live in a small place in between the Konyaks and the Chang area, their culture has greatly been impacted by the Konyaks on the northern side and the Changs on the south. They excel in the art of wood carving like the Konyaks. Monyu is their great festival observed in the first week of April soon after the sowing season.

14. The Pochury Nagas. They live in the south-eastern part of Phek district. This Indo-Mongoloid tribe, earlier a part of Chakesang, are comparatively simple. They also keep relations with the villages of Burma border because of living nearby.

Lastly, the Kukis are not exactly one of the Naga tribes who live in the southern part of Kohima district. They were of course head-hunters like Nagas previously.

We find that there are some features common among all the Naga tribes. The village headman and priest play a vital role in their social and spiritual life. Most of the Nagas have their village councils in which their disputes regarding land, marriage, inheritance, theft, etc., are settled.

For the councils, the headmanship is hereditary. The village Nagas are traditionally animist. The bury the dead relations inside or close to their house or at the outskirt of the village. They keep a space in front of their house for burying the bodies. The place is fenced around with wooden posts and bamboo and marked by stone pieces. They also keep food stuff and materials used by the person who is no more in the graveyard for some time.

Close to the Morung a huge log drum is placed at many villages which occupies an important and sacred place in their life. Log drum is made out of a hollowed trunk of a tree through carving of a Mithun head at one end and the tail at the other. The drum, struck with the pestles on the slit by men lined up on either side, can be listened from miles away.

Earlier, it served the purpose of a war drum, but nowadays it is beaten to announce a festival or ceremony or in emergency like fire break, etc. Marriage is performed in the presence of village elders, headman and near relatives in a simple ceremony. In most cases bride price is given to the parents of the girl some money, domestic animal, food stuff, etc., and the girl a few ornaments. Most of the Nagas practise *jhum* cultivation, but slowly they are taking to terrace cultivation. Their festivals are mainly related to harvesting and crop-collection. Nagas believe in deities and spirits and they have numerous superstitions.

Thus all Naga tribes have their own identity and their own style of living which is somewhat different from the others. In many aspects, they are common to one another but this has not put a question mark on their existence since they are very conscious of their culture and rituals.

II. Customs about Marriages

"Young Nitiko Angami, attendant to our household, got married to Crimino. Nikito is an animist and non-Christian. His marriage ceremony was very simple." This is a quak by an eye witness English educated Nagas are all Christians. Their marriage ceremonies are held according to Christian rites. Most of the Christian Nagas people have their separate churches, like Angami Baptist Church, Sema Church, Lotha Catholic Church, etc. Marriage of different Nagas usually take place in those churches. Marriage customs of all the Christians, whether they belong to Naga tribe or any other community, are the same, just the outward pomp and show may vary according to one's financial and social position.

Here is a dialogue between a researcher and a tribal.

"When you decide to marry how do you proceed?"

"Some village elder is sent to the house of the chosen girl. He makes the preliminary talks. The opinions of the would-be-married get priority."

"How does the bride respond to the groom's proposal?"

"Even if the girl considers the boy fit for the match she does not give her consent immediately. She contemplates over the proposal for some time. If she feels good at heart, gets some indication of good omen, then only arrangements for marriage are put forward."

Nikito, the tribal, gave some more information.

At times, at the bride's house a test is taken by strangling a fowl and watching the way in which it crosses its legs when dying. If the legs are placed in an inauspicious posture, the match is forthwith broken off, but if it ends in a favourable way, further negotiations take place. Even at this stage the girl can use her 'veto' if she does not feel for it, dreams a bad dream or finds something unfavourable. But if all go favourably, the marriage day is fixed. There is a feast on the day at the bride's house. At times some fowls are presented by the groom to his parents-in-law. In the presence of both parents and guardians of both the parties and gaon-burrahs, the marriage is solemnised.

We have mentioned earlier that 'bride price' is prevalent among some tribes. The girl's parents become happy when their daughter marries a man of their own village or a closeby village. Then the girl will live quite close and be able to help them in need like illness, etc.

Some part of 'bride-price' can be paid off by the groom with his labour. This is possible if he stays nearby and can look after his own field and also his father-in-law's as well. This too has been discussed that the Naga tribes are exogamous and they do not marry in the same clan. Sexual relation among the persons of same clan is also not allowed.

1. Konyak chiefs take more than one wife and his principal wife must be from his own clan which is not in practice in other tribes. Any common Konyak will of course take only one wife. The chiefship among the Konyaks has been very sacrosanct and they try to keep their heredity safe by marrying in their own clan.

2. We have read that the Angamis are monogamous, but the Semas are polygamous and keep as many wives as they can maintain. Even Christianity has not been able to deter them from this practice. It should be mentioned that even the effusive rebellion Naga leader Kaito Sema had two wives. Also the 'Ato Kilonser'

(Prime Minister) of the so called 'Naga Federal Government', Kughato Sema has two wives.

From the Lothas only a rich Naga can take a second wife. The Khemnugans may have any number of wives as they like. Marriage by capture is also present among them. If a Khemnugan boy wants to marry a particular girl he expresses it to his guardians and they abduct the girl at an opportune time when the girl goes to fetch water from the spring or river, or to the field to do farming. Thereafter the boy and the girl live as husband and wife.

But different from this, in the towns and educated parts, people get married with mutual understanding and consent.

Pre-marital relations are not frowned upon in the Naga society. Angami girls can have their lovers. The Semas are of course not that liberal since their daughter bring 'bride price'. If the girl gets involved in any adultery, the 'bride price' will get reduced considerably, or if she marries according to her choice, there will be no scope for getting 'bride price'.

In this case, the Ao society is more acquiescent. Ao girls enjoy the independence of free mixing. Pre-marital intimate relation is common among the Konyaks. Though free mixing is permitted in the Naga society, yet it is definitely neither liked nor encouraged if someone sleeps with a girl today and with another tomorrow. Divorce is not at all problematic among the Nagas. Probably the incidents of divorces are more among the Aos, on the other hand Semas are not generally inclined to get divorced. It pulls them into financial obligation. Among the Khemnugans it is rather easy. In case a husband proves his wife's guilt of adultery, he can abandon her even by keeping the ornaments brought by her at the time of marriage and claim fine from her paramour. But if a husband ill-treats his wife she can also walk out on him and demand the return of her jewellery and valuables from him.

Naga people are very practical and pragmatic as far as their sex-life is concerned. No body will accuse an Ao if he behaves friendly to a women when her husband is away, or if a Lotha permits his brother to live close to his wife when he goes away for a long. But everything is done within the limits of accepted social norms and conventions.

This might sound baffling that the oldest profession of the world has also set its net in Nagaland. Earlier it was confined only to the Chakhesang area, particularly in Kazabama (Chizami). But as more and more outsiders have been coming to the state, the demand for women of easy virtue is increasing and flesh trade thriving. There are prostitutes in Kohima and Dimapur.

Thus, women are vulnerable in one way or the other, be it modern civilised society or an age-old original tribal set up. Need of gender sensitisation is equally there at both places.

Tradition of Head Hunting

It can generally be stated that head-hunting is no longer practised in Nagaland.

The practice had the basis in the cultural and religious life of the Naga people in the olden days. Taking a head during a raid was the greatest honour for a man which specially conferred on him the right to put on certain dresses and jewellery. In many Naga shawls there are designs of mithun symbolising wealth of the owner, elephant and tiger valour of the man and human head indicating his success during head-hunting.

It is said that Chang Moh Nei or Cowrie shawl could not be worn unless a man had taken six or more heads in war.

Also, the art of wood carving among the different Naga tribes had been under the practice of head hunting and Morung institution. Carvings on the beams and pillars of a warrior men's house and Morung primarily include human heads. Head-hunting was the inspiration of Naga painting also.

Background

Originally this was unknown to the Nagas. As per a folk-tale current among them once a bird dropped a berry from a tree. A lizard and a red ant fought for it. Some Nagas got to see the ant cut off the lizard's head and thus they learnt to take heads, they say. There had been a faith among the Nagas that the human head contained a lot of power and energy. The super-natural power of a soul is also stored in the head. When a head is taken from another village, power and energy also come with it. This is useful for human and animal fertility. It inspired the crops to grow better, more especially when the head is of a woman with long hair. A young Naga who had taken a head held a great position over his comrades in attracting the most graceful girl of the village for marriage. If a youth was unable to take a head, in olden days, he found considerable difficulty to getting a wife. Head-hunting inspired wonderful dances as well. In fact, the practice of head-hunting had been an inevitable part of the Naga life and culture.

Even today they decorate morung, their houses and themselves with human and animal hair. They dye hair sometimes to add beauty. It may also be mentioned that women and children were not spared in head-hunting. Rather they used to become the easy prey to head-hunting. By killing women folk, the enemy population could be restricted and reduced. Even in March 1963 in Chilso, a tiny village in the Noklak region of Tuensang district, when three girls of Khemnugan Naga went down to the stream in the valley below to fish, lost their heads.

Besides Khemnugan, one other tribe live in the area is Yimchunger and these two tribes had been at loggerheads all the time. Naturally Khemnugan asserted, attacked the Yimchunger inhabitants and set their houses on fire to avenge the death of the three girls of their tribe. Thirty-two Yimchunger heads were cut by the Khemnugan warriors. In the same year on 21st October they hunted another head of a noted Yimchunger dobhashi (interpreter), called Kichingham. Some other incidents of head-hunting can be mentioned.

It should be disclosed here that Yengpang, a village near the Burmese border, had an old animosity with another village called Kojok. The people of Yengpang were not very strong. In 1936 they contacted a strong village, Pangsha to attack Kojok on their part and promised them number of mithuns, a prized animal. It was a common practice in those days. The Pangsha people did as they were asked to do. As a punitive measure the then administrative authority burnt the Pangsha village after the fact of the head-hunting was investigated and confirmed, but the real culprit, village Yengpang was not punished. It enraged Pangsha very much. To add fire to their fury they were not paid mithuns also as promised. Naga memories are not short. In October 1954 the son of one of the most important Pangsha headman was ambushed and then beheaded. First the Pangsha village could not understand who were responsible for it. But when the Yengpang people performed a special ceremony to celebrate victory in the head-hunting raid, they realised who were the culprits. Before the administration could do anything, the Pangsha warriors attacked the much smaller and weaker village, Yengpang, and took a toll of fifty-seven heads including the local school teacher, his wife and even a small child. This was a perfectly normal act of revenge of the Nagas.

Pangsha of course in the past were punished more than once for their head-hunting activities. Pangsha is in the Tuensang district. The people of this area were known for their indomitable fearless spirit. Earlier in 1909 a team consisting of the British administrators had come to this part of Nagaland to punish the head-hunters. On reaching there they first asked for the people who were guilty for taking heads. To this the Tuensang people replied—"Does a hunter give away his hounds?"

Following demand was for a fine in money. The reply from the uninhibited tribals was—"We have no coins. We hear the Government make coins. If they are short, let them make some more."Last and the third demand was for mithuns, the customary fine for head-hunting in British days. This time no reply came, but the animals were found tied up outside the village entrance. We have also heard of another interesting anecdote in this regard. Mr. Shilu Ao was the first Chief Minister of Nagaland. He had visited Delhi in October 1963, then appointed as Chairman of the Executive Council, in connection with negotiations about the future of the Naga Hills and to hold discussion about law and order problem in the state. Mr. Ao was quite a witty person and indulged in easy pranks whenever an occasion came his way. While he was in Delhi a hefty shopkeeper asked him confidentially if it was true that Nagas were cannibals.

"Yes" replied Shilu Ao with all gravity, "why do not you turn up at my hotel. We are six there and you'll make a good meal for six of us." The shopkeeper did return at the hotel and what happened afterwards—readers can imagine. There was no respect of head-hunting by the Lotha and Rengma Nagas after 1880, Ao and Angami left this habit in 1905, Sema Nagas in 1909. Sangtam Nagas did the head-hunting till 1947 and Konyaks till 1962. Chang Nagas abdicated it in 1959 excepting the happening when in March 1969 a few China trained Angami underground Nagas were butchered by them as mentioned earlier. The Yimchungers stopped this practice in 1963.

Though it is true that the Nagas have given up the habit of head-hunting which had been a powerful part of their cultural life a few decades back. But of late in the Naxalite movement in Bengal, Bihar and Andhra Pradesh was it not practised more vehemently? At places were not the heads of petty land-owners hung around the wooden poles? And what are the civilised countries doing now with their modern arms and ammunitions. In fact, it takes ages to leave negative practices. Strict laws and strong will power is required for this.

9

Women in Naga Tribal Society

Introduction

It is said that status of women in any society is the index of growth and civilisation and Naga women enjoy many social rights as their men-counterparts. One may be astonished to learn that on the question of social status and individual liberty, they are in quite better position than their sisters in other states of India who claim to be more advanced. They stand equal to men in every walk of life and need not entirely depend on the earnings of the male members. Often they complement family earnings by their own which sometimes surpass the husband's earning.

They being very painstaking and industrious never feel helpless even if the husband dies or divorces the wife. She steers clear the helm with the help of her competent hand.

I. Social Status

The ability of the Naga women to put in physical labour in the farms and the fields ensure economic independence for them even if they fail to secure job in Government or private concerns due to inadequate or little academic education. That is why even when a girl without much beauty fails to win a groom does not become a burden to the family. On the contrary, her ability to earn money often lures young men to approach his parents asking for her hand.

These Naga women are well-built, though a little short in stature, are hard working and fairly good-looking. They never stay idle, instead all the time doing something or other like bringing water and wood, cooking food, weaving cloth, brewing country liquor besides working in the field. There is no check in free mixing among boys and girls in Naga society. But it has its limitation. Everybody obeys norms and custom. Parents permit their daughters to go on a picnic or an excursion with their mates of the opposite sex without any objection. Naga girls can espouse their life partner according to their choice.

Unfaithful wives are of course punished as per social norms. The life of grand parents of the bygone years was naturally very simple, but in modern time their life has become complicated. Marital knots are usually tied in their own tribe, but inter-tribe marriage is not rare, and sometimes inter-state marriages also take place. Punjabi, Assamese, Nepali and Bengali inhabitants at times get married to Naga girls. The number of such marriages is not however high. The people of other states also do not remain behind in this regard.

Also, there are separate morungs—dormitary for girls in some villages. Unmarried girls sleep there in the night. It is a place for their recreation, dance and music, weaving and the like. "Do the boys visit the girls morung during the night?" The answer was in affirmative. "They gossip, play, sing and dance together."

"How long do they stay with their girl friends?"

"It is often until the cock's crow"—as someone puts it.

Some years back a foreign lady interested in Naga culture while travelling in the Naga country went to a Chang village in the Tuensang district. One night she went to a morung for the girls. She asked the girls about their boy friends. The girls in the morung answered all her queries without any inhibition. They accepted that their mates used to visit a little late in the night and leave towards morning. They also invited the women to stay for the night with them. The lady made a plea that their boy friends might object. An articulate girl readily said—"Don't worry, we can easily arrange one more friend for you!"

There is no doubt that the modern women are gradually becoming ease-loving, and luxurious. The spread of Christianity also made a whale of change in their thinking. The number of girls has increased considerably not only in schools and colleges, but in offices as well. Naga women occupy high positions in the Nagaland Public Service Commission, the education department and in many other fields. Rani Gaidiliu has become a legend in her life-time because of her fearless fight against the British. Rano Saiza, a niece of the self-exiled rebel Naga leader, A.Z. Phizo fought an Assembly seat with the then Chief Minister. It indicates their advancement in the political field.

There is a case, suddenly Lily Sema, draped in a silken sari appeared at the door-step. She looked beautiful in a sari as well. It suited her as she wore it smartly. The green printed sari with designs of plants and flowers, embraced her well-formed body. When Lily came to learn about the contents of my writing she gave me some more information. The percentage of literate women was more than any other Indian State except for West Bengal and Assam.

Some Naga girls got higher education even from the various universities of America. Lily at last had purchased a Fiat car. She invited me to have a run with her. While driving she attracted my attention to a building constructed on the roadside. Masons and labourers were working there. And also a respectable fair-looking lady with a coloured scarf tied on the top of head was working with the labourers, in fact she was breaking stones to be used obviously for the building under construction.

"Do you know her?"—Lily asked me, then she added, "Her husband is an important political leader, a former MP and once a minister in the State Cabinet. They are building their own house."

It could give shock to anyone.

If not more, at least in the north-eastern border of our country there prevails the dignity of labour in this small state of Nagaland. If occasion demands, wives of ministers, MPs or MLAs do not hesitate to resort to physical labour. Nobody gets ashamed of it. They join in farming as well. Even the school, college and office going Naga boys and girls work in the field during sowing, reaping or harvesting whenever it becomes necessary. Early in the morning one finds in Kohima batches of teenagers, young and old women are moving towards the field with Khang's (a basket made of cane and bamboo) on their back, and again returning in the evening. Even an old woman, with numerous wrinkles on her face, carry so much of load in her basket on the back that will make a strong young man of the plains blush.

Naga women take active part during all festivals and functions. They are expert in weaving, embroidery, bamboo work, wood carving, knitting, pot making and the like. Every Naga wife presents at least one shawl woven by herself to her husband. If someone fails to do it she feels miserable and will be laughed at in the community.

Here, it is heartening to state that in the early 1980s Air India brought out a calender on 'Indian Brides', including one from the Zeliang Naga. Evale Meru was surrounded by three other beauties of the state, Evale Meru appeared on the cover of *Namaskar,* the international magazine of India. Many outsiders, as said earlier, have accepted girls as their wives. Once one marries a Naga girl he is accepted in the Naga society and afterwards can inhabit in Nagaland permanently. In case, some outsider wants to mix up with Naga girls with bad intentions just to have 'good time' during their short stay, he will be rewarded with suitable punishment.

An incident can be narrated here which took place before my eyes. A Bengali young man had just joined his first posting in a Central Government Office at Capital city Kohima. Without any guardian and restriction around he started flying very soon. The Naga girls are simple and free from any inhibition. The Bengali young man grew intimacy with an Angami girl. One day we heard that he had tied the marital knot with her. Some well-wishers gave this good news to his parents in Calcutta and immediately they appeared in the scene. But by that time a lot of water had flowed down both the Doyang and Dhansiri rivers, the Naga wife was expecting a baby.

Fierce and delicate dispute started since the guardians wanted their 'good boy' to return home leaving the Naga wife behind. At last they reached at a mutually agreed decision—the 'Naga wife' would withhold her right as a wife, would not accompany the Bengali man but get life-long maintenance amount for herself and the child instead. The condition was not only verbal, an agreement was signed by both the parties and experienced by many Government and non-Government responsible men.

Many years later, the researcher, happened to meet that man. Still he was sending the alimony amount to his former Naga wife and progeny.

But some other Bengalis did not involve themselves in this type of fix. They married Naga girls and then settled in this state, are living in the homes of their Naga wives. Their children obviously speak in their mother tongue.

There is another story to be narrated by an eye witness, "In the three-storied wooden building where there is a bright example of a national integration. This building has been requisitioned by our Central Government Office where we all work. There are many rooms in this building. To my left is an Assamese family, a Nepalese to the right, down below in different rooms are staying people from Kashmir, Haryana and MP Above us on the top are persons from Tamil Nadu, Kerala and Bihar.

To the Kashmiri family the other day came an attractive girl of about seventeen-eightcen. In the Khang on her back she carried about 20 kg. of rice. Though she put on Naga chadar and shawl, her sharp features, large eyes and golden complexion distinctly made her different from the Naga girls.

I came to know afterwards that she was the daughter of one Kashmiri Pandit who had settled here long back. (I saw him leading the procession of Sekrenyi festival of the Angami Nagas throughout the town. He also attracted everybody's attention due to his sharp feathers, fair complexion and brilliant disposition). He married an Angami girl in course of time and Somani, the 'sweet seventeen' is the daughter of the Kashmiri-Angami couple.

His Kashmiri wife is still alive in Srinagar and he also maintains a connection with her. But now he is an important person in Kohima village and one of the 'Gaoburahs' as well.

However, Somani started coming to our building that rather frequently. I noticed her, she came to me also as she had been very social and friendly. (As there has been 'someone' always present unseen to guard over me and as she is very jealous I could not venture to develop friendship with Somani.) But after some time no more Somani was seen in our building.

One afternoon 'Haryanvi Bhabiji' told me the reason. A way-ward young brother of the U.P. wala came a few days back over here to spend his holidays. Somehow he developed friendship with Somani. He used to go to Barabasti, upwards Kohima town to Somani's house, also to the field where Somani would go to do farming. And one day both of them found locked to each other in a secluded hilly corner. Her father gave him a good dressing down and kept Somani under his strict surveillence. The Somani-affair has ended there.

What about the evil effects of modern age on Naga women?

Is there any atrocity committed on Naga women which has become so common nowadays?

Is it possible to escape from this bane?

Let us look at some of the happenings.

In August 1985 a fifteen year old girl was found raped and murdered at Goriphema, in the remote Northern Angami area about 60 km from Kohima.

On hearing the incident a police party rushed to the spot walking about 40 km through difficult terrain and arrested one person having criminal records. A case under Section 302 IPC was registered against him."

Particularly, this incident was described as the first sex crime in Nagaland. But certainly the claim is disputable since many crimes are generally not reported at all and nobody knows what is happening in the remote inaccessible areas of the countryside.

On this, the Voluntary Action Bureau of Nagaland Social Welfare Board, a State Government body, expressed its deep grief in October, the same year, at the alarming increase in cases of atrocities against women and children in the state. A meeting of the Bureau took place under the chairmanship of Mrs. Lushi Haralu, who was the chairperson of the welfare board, said that a strong protest against act of such heinous crimes should not be viewed as criticism of the government. A statement released by Mrs. Haralu after the meeting listed as many as seven cases of rape murder and assault on women or children.

This is more significant in the state where women have traditionally been treated far better as compared to those in most of the country. Here is a case of DSP attempted to rape a woman, in another a political leader tried to violate four girls inside his own house, Mrs. Haralu also mentioned the reported killing of a baby sister of the DFO (Forest), Mon and the murder of a girl at Zunheboto. Even a girl was shot at by a minister, at Dimapur in September of the year 1980. Mrs. Haralu regretted that all these cases were either hushed up, withdrawn by the government or settled outside the court by the sides concerned. She observed that the Bureau was "pained to note the degeneration in public moral by readily accepting cash or other kinds of offers in cases where heinous and disgusting crimes are involved."

Above are some of the instances to present a consolidated picture of Naga society vis-a-vis Naga women today. The picture will not be complete if we do not depict the other side of the story also.

Once, two Naga girls were arrested for committing dacoity—A news item was published in *The Warrior,* April 1982, a news magazine published by the Department of Information and Publicity, Government of Nagaland. The news item said that for alleged dacoity and theft in Kohima, two females had been arrested by the Kohima Police. Miss Mesile Rengma of Tesofenugyu village and Miss Tesile Rengma of Suniyu village were arrested by a police party dictated by Inspector Vijetuyo. Besides, stolen property worth more than 30 thousand, 32 pistols and five live cartridges were also found from the houses of these girls. Mesile and Tesile were alleged to have been connected in eight dacoities committed in Kohima town itself. After questioning session, the police came to know about other people who were involved in these crimes. They were not connected with the rebel Nagas. It does not solicit any comment. In fact, nobody will have an iota of doubt that modern civilisation has invaded with all its ingredients of good and evil!

II. Women Leadership

While talking of warriors of Nagaland, the names of the underground rebel Naga leaders like Kaito Sema, Kughato Sema, T. Muiva Angami and A.Z. Phizo are mentioned very frequently. But the Naga woman who had fought the British valiantly during the pre-Independence era, who was called 'The Joan of Arc of the Naga hills' is hardly mentioned nowadays. She was the only person from Nagaland to be honoured as a 'Freedom Fighter' by the Union Government alongwith the freedom fighters of other states.

1. Rani Gaidiliu. The name of this dauntless lady is Rani Gaidiliu. The first premier of India, Pandit Jawaharlal Nehru endowed her with this appellation, 'Rani', in 1937 when he had come to know about her while travelling in Assam.

The epithet adorns her till date, she is still regarded as a 'Rani'—a queen—a leader by her people. She was born in a distant secluded village, Longkayo in a Rongmei tribe on 27th January in 1915. Her cousin, Jadunang of Tamenglong part in Manipur state started a religious movement called the 'Haraka' cult. It was a kind of old animistic religion of three concerned tribes, i.e. Zemi, Liangmei and Rongmei. Jadunang propagated to his people that if they worshipped and made human and mithun sacrifices before the God creator Tingwang, he would give them plenty of food and drinks, there would be no illness and they would enjoy unrestrained freedom.

Slowly, the new faith attracted the simple Nagas of the Zemi, Liangmei and Rongmei tribes of the Zeliang area and conjoining Tamenglong area of Manipur and North Cachar in Assam.

The followers and admirers of the new faith came to be known as Khampais. Khampai rites had some resemblance with the Hindu Tantric cult. Jadunang was very highly against the spread of Christianity in Nagaland and harangued about the liberation movement. As he used to ask his Khampai followers to make human sacrifices before the God, they were abducting people and slaying them.

Once they caught and killed four Manipuri traders who were on their way to Assam and offered their blood to the deity in a temple near Nungkao. Alarmed at the dangers of the Haraka worship the British Government decided to put an end to it. Jadunang was caught, charged for homicide, tried and hanged on 29th August 1931 at Imphal now capital city of Manipur.

What else even after Jadunang's execution the temper of movement was not smothered. Gaidiliu was only seventeen at that time. She took over the leadership and went on with the liberation movement in the Zeliangrong area. In fact from the age of thirteen she was associated with her cousin, Jadunang in all his activities to resuscitate their old tribal religion, throw the British out from Nagaland and attain complete independence.

Gaidiliu started sending around the message of revolt against the British in the Naga hills. With a heavy hand the British Government tried to suppress it and troops were sent to capture her. Consequently, Gaidiliu got underground, restricted her activities and manoeuvred the fight from her hideout in the deep forest. A reward of Rs. 500 was announced for providing information about her whereabouts or leading to her arrest. Also it was announced that if any village helped the Government in capturing her that whole village would be exempted from paying renenue for ten years.

If any of her acolytes was arrested severe punishment was given to him to extract information. Gaidiliu formed a band of dauntless, well-organised guerillas. Voluntarily people would help them offering food and cash. Under the protection of her followers she swiftly moved from one place to another and after some months she had to flee to Haflong in Assam. Meanwhile her people refused to pay taxes to the Government and extend unpaid labour to the Government officials.

Jungle Stay and Arrest

Gaidiliu shifted to further east. In the thick jungle of Pulomi village she made a wooden fortess. There were arrangement for accommodation for 4,000 fighters inside it. She told her followers that it was a fight in which either they would be victorious or perish. In fact, it was her challenge against the strong well-equipped Assam Rifles in the north-east region. Also, British started a massive attack against her. Troops were sent from all directions, outposts were kept at strategic points and continuous patrolling went on. At last she was arrested by the Assam Rifles near Henima village in early 1933.

In chain she was brought to present capital, i.e. Kohima via Khonoma village. This young fiery freedom fighter was treated no better than a wild animal by the British. A rope had also been tied round her waist.

The very next day Gaidiliu along with her young brother was mercilessly beaten in Kohima jail. Their muscles were torn, clothes were also removed from their bodies. The winter cold badly shivered them to the bones. Those were the most difficult, painful and trying period of her life. She passed through the ordeal, but she did not break down. She spent quite a many tortured days in the Imphal Jail. At last she was tried and sentenced to life imprisonment for practising a dangerous cult and carrying out insurgency against the British Government. Meanwhile many of her followers were also captured, imprisoned and they expired in the British jail. But the struggle for freedom did not stop, it went on.

At the time of touring eastern India in 1937 during his political activities Jawaharlal Nehru came to know about Gaidiliu. He was deeply moved when he listened about indomitable spirit, bravery and heroism of the young Naga girl. In his book *Unity of India* he expressed his feelings, sympathy and bitterness towards her imprisonment—"This heroic girl was captured and sentenced for transportation for life. And now she lies in some prison in Assam, wasting her bright young womanhood in dark cells and solitude. Six years she has been there. What torment and suppression of spirit they have brought to her, who in the pride of her youth dared to challenge an empire! And India does not even know of this brave child of the hills. But her own people remember their Gaidiliu, the Rani and think of her with love and pride. And a day will come when India also will remember her and cherish her, and bring her out of her prison cell."

During the same year Indian National Congress tried to get her released, Jawaharlal, sought help from the then British MP, Lady Astor. But according to the British Government she was still "very potential source of danger" and freedom struggle was in full swing. The release of Gaidiliu would provide more strength and inspiration to the struggle for independence. So Gaidiliu was made to spend her days and nights behind the bars year after year. She was transported from one jail to another jail and every time she thought that it was her last journey as the British Raj shifted a convict to a new place before the execution.

Release from the Jail

In the year 1946 when an Interim Government was set up, she was eventually released from the prison and Nehru gave her the title 'Rani' and she came to be known as such. INC considered her movement as a part of national movement for liberation against the foreign rule and she was sanctioned a monthly pension as a political sufferer.

Gaidiliu had spent a period of more than thirteen years in various jails. Now she returned to the hills to her people and stayed with her brother to take rest for some days. But how long? The second chapter of her struggle started again. Rani Gaidiliu again went underground in 1960. This time, she reactivated the Khampais as a counter-force against the underground rebel Nagas. The secessionist leader A.Z. Phizo and his followers asked for a separate Independent sovereign Naga State and formed the so-called 'Naga Federal Government'. Rani also established a civil and military administration named the 'Zeliangrong Government of Rani Party'. This parallel menace was an irritant to the rebel Nagas and they tried their best to oust the Rani and her acolytes. But they failed to make any headway in the Khampai stronghold.

On the other hand on 29 January 1965 these Khampais kidnapped nine underground Nagas from the village Ngulong in Kohima district when they had gone there to collect taxes forcefully as the underground rebel Nagas used to do. These nine underground Nagas were killed by them. It naturally created a great uproar within the rebel Nagas.

In the meanwhile the State Government succeeded in bringing Gaidiliu overground (The effort of a Bengali Dy. Commissioner of Kohima in this regard is highly commendable). She went to Kohima on 20 January 1966. Later she met the Prime Minister Jawaharlal in Delhi on 21st February the same year. Rani extended her loyalty to the Government of India. She, however, demanded the creation of a separate Zeliangrong Unit covering the contiguous Zeliangrong parts of Manipur, Nagaland and Assam. On 24th September, the same year, her three hundred and twenty Khampai followers surrendered at Henima and some half of them were absorbed in the Nagaland Armed Police.

Social Reforms of Gandhiji

Apparently, living through the patronage of the State Government Rani Gaidiliu helped in the upliftment of the Naga society. She tried to remove poverty and spread education within the backward people. But her activities did not remain restricted in the field of social welfare for a long. Again she came out with her previous demand for a creation of a Zeliangrong state with a vengeance. As the president of the Zeliangrong People's Convention (ZPC) she led a delegation to national capital Delhi with a demand for a creation of Zeliangrong state comprising of Zeliangrong inhabited areas of Manipur, Nagaland and Assam and met with the Prime Minister and the Home Minister with the demand in mid-August 1987. The sixth conference of the ZPC convention took place at Haflong, Assam on 15 October 1988 with Rani Gaidiliu in the Chair.

Around some 1200 delegates from Assam, Nagaland and Manipur who participated in the convention reiterated their demand for a separate state. It was also decided in this conference that peaceful agitation in the form of bandh, demonstrations, picketings, economic blockade, non-payment of taxes, different types of hunger strikes, courting arrests and non-co-operation with the Government would be taken up.

Also the conference stressed the need for continuous struggle and sacrifices for the cause of the Zeliangrong unification into a separate homeland. They too condemned the atrocities committed by the Manipur Police on hundreds of innocent workers in Manipur and demanded unconditional release of all the ZPC workers in the jail. The legendary freedom fighter was expected to lead a high level delegation of the ZPC to New Delhi in the second week of November 1988 to give the ultimatum for creation of a Zeliangrong state within the Indian Union by 1st January 1989.

The state is now there but her bravery being a woman form a background area is undoubtedly beyond praise. The census data relating to married, unmarried, divorced/separated women and data relating to ever married/currently married women with their surviving children are given on next few pages.

Table 1
Age, Sex and Marital Status for Scheduled Tribes

Age group	*Total*	*Never Married*	*Married*	*Widowed*	*Divor-ced*	*Unsp-ecified*
ALL SCHEDULED TRIBES						
Rural						
All ages	**9,33,145**	**6,01,904**	**3,11,995**	**16,812**	**2,333**	**101**
0 - 9	2,27,560	2,27,560	0	0	0	0
10-14	1,24,578	1,23,019	1,406	46	105	2
15-19	1,13,248	1,08,758	4,307	40	115	28
20-24	86,303	69,452	16,397	202	249	3
25-29	70,066	35,188	34,194	376	299	9
30-34	52,898	13,425	38,552	623	295	3
35-39	51,435	5,783	44,572	878	196	6
40-44	43,903	3,001	39,455	1,268	176	3
15-44	4,17,853	2,35,607	1,77,477	3,387	1,330	52
45-49	40,431	1,672	37,124	1,461	173	1
50-54	31,497	1,114	28,297	1,927	158	1
55-59	21,239	654	19,025	1,445	113	2
60-64	20,507	556	17,669	2,156	126	0
65-69	12,506	268	10,636	1,518	84	0
70-74	9,794	251	7,882	1,578	82	1
75-79	5,736	133	4,558	999	46	0
80+	9,348	368	6,685	2,202	90	3
Age not stated	12,096	10,702	1,236	93	26	39
Urban						
All ages	**1,27,677**	**84,480**	**41,901**	**1,039**	**153**	**104**
0 - 9	35,631	35,631	0	0	0	0
10-14	17,508	17,225	266	11	6	0
15-19	15,579	14,754	808	8	8	1
20-24	12,252	8,416	3,778	25	19	14
25-29	11,254	3,795	7,310	62	27	60
30-34	8,914	1,153	7,620	112	18	11
35-39	7,858	456	7,255	121	15	11
40-44	5,762	199	5,417	125	21	0
15-44	61,619	28,773	32,188	453	108	97
45-49	4,019	100	3,816	97	6	0
50-54	2,698	89	2,479	114	16	0
55-59	1,196	35	1,102	57	2	0
60-64	967	65	796	104	2	0
65-69	417	13	348	48	8	0
70-74	342	37	258	46	1	0
75-79	141	5	105	31	0	0
80+	520	167	280	70	1	2
Age not stated	2,619	2,340	263	8	3	5

Source : Census 1991.

Table 2

Ever Married and Currently Married Women Belonging to Scheduled Tribes by Present Age, Number of Surviving Children and Total Number of Surviving Children by Sex

Present Age	Total ever/ currently married women	Ever/currently married women with number of serviving children						Total surviving children		
		0	1	2	3	4	5+	Total	Males	Females
1	2	3	4	5	6	7	8	9	10	11
ALL SCHEDULED TRIBES										
RURAL										
Ever Married										
All ages	**1,73,848**	**42,436**	**16,140**	**19,306**	**19,916**	**19,921**	**53,163**	**5,39,293**	**2,82,704**	**2,56,589**
Less than 15	772	719	9	34	0	0	0	77	43	34
15-19	3,527	2,307	782	205	37	44	0	1,479	789	690
20-24	12,797	4,900	3,420	2,337	1,076	381	242	14,242	7,371	6,871
25-29	22,993	5,735	3,527	4,747	3,925	2,692	1,915	46,463	24,116	22,347
30-34	22,438	4,733	1,796	3,018	3,662	3,549	5,379	64,641	33,666	30,975
35-39	24,245	4,569	1,140	2,152	3,041	3,622	9,446	87,683	45,543	42,140
40-44	20,506	3,919	919	1,487	1,911	2,632	9,397	81,584	42,517	39,067
45-49	18,682	3,490	791	1,248	1,630	2,215	9,105	78,370	41,027	37,343
50-54	14,009	2,976	860	1,066	1,408	1,501	6,023	53,796	28,434	25,362
55-59	9,106	1,887	546	693	866	1,002	3,979	35,584	18,718	16,866
60-64	8,636	2,130	740	804	813	883	3,096	29,242	15,522	13,720
65-69	5,309	1,376	462	497	562	509	1,805	17,702	9,488	8,214
70-74	4,062	1,213	443	366	407	347	1,182	11,820	6,410	5,410
75-79	2,340	766	226	239	216	194	634	6,445	3,440	3,005
80 +	3,682	1,291	437	346	314	305	847	8,954	4,965	3,989

(Contd.)

(Contd.)

1	2	3	4	5	6	7	8	9	10	11
Currently Married										
All ages	**1,60,414**	**38,125**	**14,251**	**17,784**	**18,514**	**18,706**	**50,520**	**5,08,534**	**2,66,178**	**2,42,356**
Less than 15	700	657	8	27	0	0	0	62	36	26
15-19	3,402	2,221	756	197	37	42	0	1,429	764	665
20-24	12,464	4,731	3,309	2,308	1,071	379	239	14,035	7,266	6,769
25-29	22,506	5,576	3,364	4,677	3,880	2,674	1,904	45,882	23,840	22,042
30-34	21,864	4,566	1,665	2,934	3,608	3,494	5,325	63,635	33,171	30,464
35-39	23,521	4,359	1,051	2,046	2,941	3,548	9,325	86,060	44,696	41,364
40-44	19,495	3,631	781	1,385	1,803	2,517	9,166	79,008	41,170	37,838
45-49	17,470	3,184	668	1,105	1,489	2,065	8,792	75,000	39,242	35,758
50-54	12,492	2,550	682	910	1,202	1,337	5,675	49,814	26,266	23,548
55-59	8,001	1,600	432	568	740	887	3,671	32,403	16,965	15,438
60-64	6,953	1,606	511	616	663	739	2,716	25,207	13,378	11,829
65-69	4,165	1,032	327	355	424	389	1,567	14,830	7,939	6,891
70-74	2,899	825	281	228	289	254	962	9,246	4,998	4,248
75-79	1,640	494	154	148	147	142	511	5,014	2,657	2,357
80 +	2,201	727	230	222	180	198	565	5,831	3,208	2,623
URBAN										
Ever Married										
All ages	**21,595**	**4,317**	**2,447**	**3,094**	**3,116**	**3,062**	**5,390**	**64,086**	**32,852**	**31,234**
Less than 15	169	146	10	13	0	0	0	36	17	19
15-19	724	450	180	54	13	10	0	367	193	174
20-24	2,970	895	772	723	361	126	52	4,097	2,119	1,978
25-29	4,906	977	699	1,055	1,016	677	441	11,136	5,650	5,486
30-34	3,923	517	293	511	735	864	978	12,681	6,543	6,138
35-39	3,397	443	157	329	454	642	1,360	13,167	6,671	6,496
40-44	2,028	266	100	136	212	300	1,003	8,561	4,401	4,160
45-49	1,354	183	65	80	123	208	691	6,011	3,139	2,872
50-54	818	121	47	73	73	121	378	3,423	1,780	1,643
55-59	358	65	18	31	38	42	162	1,493	728	765

(Contd.)

(Contd.)

1	2	3	4	5	6	7	8	9	10	11
60-64	333	65	39	26	27	26	145	1,282	668	614
65-69	144	30	10	20	15	20	49	543	261	282
70-74	127	36	19	5	17	3	46	444	226	218
75-79	52	16	5	5	6	0	20	153	78	75
80 +	155	49	23	16	11	10	41	389	219	170
Currently Married										
All ages	**20,695**	**4,106**	**2,278**	**2,972**	**3,015**	**2,958**	**5,200**	**61,738**	**31,628**	**30,110**
Less than 15	164	141	10	13	0	0	0	36	17	19
15-19	710	438	178	54	13	10	0	365	192	173
20-24	2,936	881	756	721	360	126	51	4,067	2,107	1,960
25-29	4,833	959	674	1,041	1,005	674	439	11,027	5,592	5,435
30-34	3,819	503	264	502	715	847	963	12,423	6,412	6,011
35-39	3,299	428	141	306	437	629	1,346	12,915	6,550	6,365
40-44	1,923	248	84	115	201	289	977	8,269	4,250	4,019
45-49	1,284	169	54	73	117	200	667	5,790	3,025	2,765
50-54	715	98	40	59	62	98	353	3,097	1,606	1,491
55-59	310	55	11	28	33	34	147	1,334	650	684
60-64	239	36	25	16	23	15	120	1,021	515	506
65-69	102	20	5	13	9	14	41	424	208	216
70-74	92	28	11	4	13	1	34	322	160	162
75-79	41	14	3	4	6	0	14	111	55	56
80 +	97	33	12	6	8	8	25	247	137	110

Source: Census 1991.

Notes: 1. 'All ages includes 'age not stated'.

2. Number of ever/currently married women in col.4 includes women not reporting number of surviving children.

3. The age groups having nil return are not shown.

10

Naga Festivals and Songs

Each society, tribal or non-tribal has its culture and folks. So is true of people of Nagaland and also who observe their festivals and sing folks with great enthusiasm.

I. Festivals

These people are fond of festivals, dance and music and of course, feasts. All the tribes have their separate festivals. Most of these festivals move round agriculture. Over 90 per cent of the population of Nagaland is mainly dependent on agriculture. They live in thousand and odd villages, many of them on high hills.

During their festivals they offer prayers for a bountiful harvest and prosperity to a Supreme Being having different names in various Naga dialects—Gawang to Konyaks, Tsungren to Aos, Alhou or Timilhou to Semas and so forth and so on. There are some very important festivals like the Angamis celebrating Sekrenyi, the Aos Moatsu, the Semas Tuluni, etc. These festivals present an intimate picture of the culture and social life style of the Nagas. Sekrenyi is a momentous festival of the Angamis. It is called as 'Phousanyi' also which implies 'protection of life' in general.

People take prominent part in this festival, performing the different rituals. It is believed that if they do not observe the function properly the deity will get annoy which will result in misfortune and sufferings for them. Sekrenyi starts on the 25th day of the second Naga month, 'Kezei' (or Kenuyo)—which mostly falls in the month of February and continues for ten days. 'Sekre' means 'pure' and 'nyi' 'festival'. 'Gaonbura'—the Naga priest performs this 'pure festival'.

1. First day. The Serenyi festival commences with a ritual, 'Kizie'. The lady of the house sprinkles a few drops of rice-soaked water, called 'Zumho', taken from the top of a jug, on the three wood made posts, covered with leaves, which are specially erected near the main gate of the house. The first day starts when all the men, young or old, go to the village-well to bathe. In the evening when the elder ones take rest young men go to the well to clean it. Some of them protect the well in the night so that no one is allowed to fetch water after having cleaned it. The women-folk are not allowed to touch the well-water that time, as such they store water before hand.

2. Second day. Maximum sacred is the day, 'Sekre' (pure). All the male members go to the well to have a bath and then put on war-dress. The young men also don two fresh shawls—white 'Mhoushu' and black 'Lohe' and spatter water on their chest, knees and right arms. They believe that all their ills and misfortunes have therefore been washed away by the purified well-water.

After their return home the oldest male member of the house offers food to the tutelary god. In the name of each male member and female member a cock and a hen respectively are always sacrificed separately. When the cock or hen is throttled the concerned member of the house says his or her prayer to the deity.

It is considered a good omen if the right leg of the fowl falls over the left leg when it collapses on the ground. Then the male members gather the fowls for cooking. No women will take part in it. The men-folk will cook the fowls in a new hearth using new utensils. There will be prayer before eating. After prayer they take country liquor, 'Mahopiva', specially prepared by them for the occasion. Till they finish their drinking no woman is permitted to take food.

3. Thekra Hie. The fourth day of the festival, is meant for the young to sing and dance. It continues for three days. All the young boys and girls wear their ceremonial costumes, drink jugs of rice bear, eat plates full of meat and then sing and dance their traditional songs. It may however be mentioned here that till the fifth day is over sexual relation is 'genna'—prohibited.

4. On the seventh day, the young men go for hunting.

5. Eighth day. The highly important is the eighth day when gate-pulling ceremony is performed. A perfect and suitable tree, selected beforehand, out of which a gate is made and kept at a fixed place. Different artistic designs are carved on the gate according to their beliefs and practices. The length of the gate is about 8 to 10 ft., breadth being a little less than this.

In the morning time, 'Gaonbura', the village headman goes to the gate with a little 'madu' (country liquor), a baked cake and a fowl. On a sheet of banana leaf a small 'madu' is spattered and then the fowl is let off. If the cock drinks 'madu' it is accepted as a good omen. The village headman along with his companions touches the gate through a rope made of creeper and says—

"We'll now take you to the—roper place. Villagers and good people with respect will pull you on. On your arrival, there will be plenty of crops and domestic animals in our village, we will have uninterrupted prosperity."

Two unmarried nude boys who never have had any sexual relations, help knot the gate with strong rope of creepers. The gate is tied by two sides. Many pieces of extra ropes are tied with each other to make it long. Other strong jute ropes are also fastened to it. Holding the two ropes bound by two sides, people with ceremonial war costume on both sides of the road start pulling the gate towards Kohima village. Christian Nagas also join in gate pulling.

In Kohima town, current Deputy Commissioner and other high officials also join the gate pulling procession. Hundreds of people gather to see the procession. No one is permitted to cross the procession. The Nagas make different sound imitating the animals while pulling the gate. When they reach the village all on-lookers and also women are asked to remain inside the village. Some more rituals and dances are performed after the gate is installed at the entrance of the village.

Previously, the gate was erected to obstruct the enemy to enter the village. Now it has become a symbol to drive away the evil forces. The gate pulling ritual is however not performed every year.

6. Ninth day. On the ninth day feasts celebrations take place. The rich Nagas offer feast and thereby earn a respectable place in the society. These are called 'Feasts of Honour'.

7. 'Thenyi Mi' and 'Thora' are on the eleventh and twelfth day respectively which indicate closing of the festival. Until the close of the festival is declared no one goes to the field. All work in the field and farm remain closed during the festival days.

About women, young unmarried girls with closely shaven heads sit down with the young boys and sing songs of bygone days, of about valour and bravery. There is an honourable place of 'Genna Bura' in the Sekrenyi festival. 'Genna' means the prevailing customs, rites and rituals. Also it shows 'forbidden'. 'Genna Bura' is the Naga priest who advises regarding rites, rituals and customs of all the festivals and functions. Sekrenyi is celebrated according to his instructions althrough the ceremony.

We hear that there are some common features in all the festivals of different tribes. Every tribe takes a meticulous care in observing the details related to a festival. The details are considered sacrosant. Before the commencement of the festival, villages are given a lift-up, approach roads are cleared and repaired, wells are cleaned, departed souls remembered, feasts given. Sexual indulgence becomes taboo during the period of festivals, at least for some days. No field work is done, women-folk are not allowed to do any household chores for a number of days as well.

In this the participation of younger ones is very significant. They learn the rituals and customs so that they can take over in future for celebration. They don their ceremonial dresses, dance and sing their traditional songs. Each and every family takes part in the festival. If some one or family has any problem the community as a whole takes care of it.

Significant festivals bring equality and unity among all the villagers. Feasts are hosted by the rich, work is done by all and joy shared by the whole community.

II. Folk Songs

No ritual celebrations complete without folk songs and especially music occupies a vital place in the life of Angamis. The stream of Naga songs has been flowing through their memory. Even when we go into the period of recorded history, nothing has been found in writing about them. There is a beautiful legend among the hill people about the absence of written traditional history of the Nagas.

"God gave men skins of deer on which he told them to write their traditions. The people of the plains obeyed his command and wrote down; but the hillmen, hungry and omnivorous, cooked and ate their writing materials, with the result that they were unable to keep any written record of their past to leave for the posterity."

Now, with the spread of education all-round development is taking place in Nagaland and efforts are being made to preserve their traditional literature like folk-lore, folk-songs, folk-tales, etc. in Ura Akademy.

In this context, the incident of individual gallantry, death of a noble soul or a dear one, feud between two hamlets and its results, fight between two heroes, special quality of a person, ill-treatment of a step-mother, tradition and custom, harvest, love for a friend and sacrifice, emotion of a lover, perpetual feelings of human being, romantic love, etc., are subjects of songs of different Naga tribes.

(a) Musical Formation of Songs. The hallmark of the Angami poems are that syllables are taken into consideration. There are nine syllables in a line and every line is almost a poem by itself. All other songs are restricted to famous nine notes excepting the dittys which are sung by the Shepherds in the forest and solo singers. If a line consists of nine syllables it can be rendered possibly into music and if the text is considered suitable they tilt it conveniently in different functions. They like to give more stress on the style of singing and the expression. There is, however, no hard and fast rule as far as rhythm and metres are concerned. It depends on the style of singing. These folk songs have five distinct intonation.

The same word can indicate five different meanings according to its modulation. As a result meaning gets changed if style of enunciation is altered.

(b) Singing at Functions. Of course, music is an indispensable part of each the Angami function. During the festivals young boys and girls spend hours after singing together. Singing continues through the feasts. Younger ones, thus, get their lessons in singing. They croon while they work in field in various seasons as well.

(c) Different Songs for Different Festivals. Their emotions get spontaneous expression through music. Singing provide them relief in their hard work. While singing the Angamis play a string instrument named 'Chotu'. 'Theku' is one more string instrument. Flute is also used whenever they find it necessary. Most of the Naga songs begin with syllables ' . . . oh, iho au ho', and at times they are repeated for four times or so without rendering any particular meaning.

Here is the free translations of a few Angami songs. I have put more stress on the internal meaning and taken freedom while interpreting these songs.

"Every night Mehouviu walks about
Morusa's house in Kidema basti in his sleep.
There they take together
Madu and ju:
May be it's just a comely dream
'Cause Mehouviu was not wedded
to Morusa in reality-
They exist only in the tales of village folk"

(Madu—Country liquor; u—Jaga food)

Since everything has not been told in this folk song. One who does not know the back drop, it will not convey much meaning to him. It is a story of the great warrior named Morusa who was a good looking young man. He wanted to marry, but could not find a match in his own village. He came to know of Mehouviu, an alluring woman in the neighbouring village. He sent the marriage proposal to her through one of his followers. Mehouviu also heard about his gallantry and extended her consent.

The day of nuptial was fixed. Morusa wanted to show the specimen of his bravery on the day of wedlock. He went up to the adjacent hamlet for head-hunting and brought a head on the day of matrimony. All his friends gathered on that day and were busy with drinking, singing and merry-making. According to the custom they had been waiting for the bride to come for marriage since evening, but even till mid-night Mehouviu did not turn up. Morusa thought that she had deceived him. But at last he came to know that no, Mehouviu did not delude him.

The tragedy of fate was that the head which he had hunted from the adjoining Kraal was none other than his would-be-wife Mehouviu's.

Song below is an exposition of the gallant Naga life which was surrounded by numerous dangers, and also of undying human love :

"You were born like a luminous star,
You had all the glaze of youth,
After we started our life together
You went to trap birds in the forest
That year early morning one day.
Alas, villagers brought the message-
You were slaughtered by the enemies,
I ran to you with the caressing shawl
Which had never wrapped your body earlier.
We could not understand each other that much.
You never went away leaving me behind,
Now, when we started comprehending each other
You left me for ever, O dear, O darling!"

The title of the following poem is 'AVU NEI HU'—'No more Now'. The poem is very simple, but when it is presented in duet, it becomes interesting. It is very famous among the students of schools and colleges.

"I wanted to make my playmate life partner,
My parents declared—'we don't approve this match';
An unknown damsel became my wife,
My playmate, I envy your would be husband."

"I went to my parent's house one day

Tieing the child on my back with cloth.
My old lover was present there-
Oh, how I spent an hour with uneasiness!"

The boy drew the girl by a thread-loop
And sighed glaring at her face,
He untied the knot of the loop tenderly
And took her in his arms easily.
"What will be your child's name?"—he asks
And adds "How pretty—soft like butter";
His emotions got swelled up-
"Please give his name Zerothrienuyo".

He took out his costly necklace affectionately
And put it around the child's neck saying-
"If his father asks—'who has given this necklace?'
Mention my name not, tell it's gifted by your Mom."

While working in the field the Angami boys and girls sing the following song:

"Ruditsou, scatter seeds by your hands
They'll grow like you-fresh and effusive.
When I recollect sweet memories of the past
O dear, love overflows my heart.
When you were young, I loved you ten times
That love has not diminished even today.
If I ever hurt you unknowingly
Bury all those today beneath the ground.
The girls seldom keep their promise.
So, swear you would'nt dupe me ever.
Even if you said playfully—you loved me-
Honour it, 'cause lying is a sin.
Number of girls I meet here and there
None is as charming as you are.
I want to shout—'only you are my lady-love.'
But lest my friends tease me, I keep my mouth shut.
If I go to you in the night to express my love
Neighbours will ask next morning
'Who visited you last night?'
Lock your lips, bring some other topic gravely."

Finally, it's a marriage song. When the bride comes back to her parent's house after marriage her friends tell her—

"O devoted bride! you are lost
In thinking of your new family
Recollecting your new environment, new companions.
As if you've forgotten us altogether
Your playmates, friends of the past;
But how can we forget you so early?
When we play, dance and sing,
or go to the field, do farming-
Your memory haunts us always,
We all remember you every now and then.
How can we blame you even if you forget
It's but natural for a maiden
Leaving behind parent's house, Kith and Kin,
Departs to keep house with her husband and in-laws
This is the life of a wench, this our custom."

Is the story portrayed in the above song of a newly married damsel of the North-East any different from her sisters of the other parts of India?

III. Folk Stories

This is heard that in Angami folk-tales Gakripu or Mache is very amusing and witty character. He had been a deceitful person and flourishing at the cost of others.

(1) There is a story:

"Once he was going on a trading mission with only one hundred rupees in his pocket. On the way while passing through a forest he was attacked by a bear. He confronted the animal valiantly, but in the process his money was scattered on the ground. Meanwhile, riding on a horse, another man was also going through that place. Gakripu told him that the bear had defecated the money and if he fought the bear it would relieve more money for him also. The man believed it, got down from his horse and started to wrestle with the bear. At this opportunity Gakripu collected his money, mounted the horse and galloped away. The stranger went on fighting with the bear without of course the expected result.

Riding merrily Gakripu came to a stream. There he met an old woman and her daughter. They wanted to go across the rill, but water was too deep for them. Gakripu came forward to help them. He put the daughter on the horse and told the old woman that he would return after dropping her daughter on the other side.

And what did Gakripu do?
He did what was natural for him.
He just ran away with the wench."

People narrate another interesting legendary character, Zosheto. Before that here are two more folk-tales of the Angami Nagas.

It is a story of olden days. "Selupvra Angami fathered a daughter out of wedlock. As he was very much ashamed of it he used to keep his daughter away from other's glare.

Gradually Crimino, his daughter, reached the marriageable age. One day he called her and ordered—"Go out and bring any one home whoever you may find outside."

She went out and looked here and there, but could not find any one.

Crimino was afraid of her father. Since childhood she got nothing but strict instructions from her father. Her father had commanded to take someone home, so when she failed to get any one else she just took a dog home who appeared before Crimino and presented it to her father.

The dog was large, there were white patches in his eyes. Selupvra was amazed to see the choice of his daughter!

"Hi lass! If the dog is your choice then marry this animal." He said, dejected. Crimino did not dare to protest. She married that dog. Selupvra got a boat after their marriage, placed some amount of food and water in it and asked them to start for a far off place.

After a long and arduous journey this odd couple reached a secluded bank of Jhanji river. They got down from the boat and decided to settle there. They built a small hut and started their life. Soon they had many children within a few years.

Years passed by. Suddenly one day Selupvra remembered that he did not get any information from his daughter and 'son-in-law'. At once he set out to make enquiry about them. As nobody knew where they had settled, he had to return without making any headway. Even then he did not lose hope altogether. He used to ask other villagers if any one of them had any information of his daughter and 'son-in-law'. Thus, one day he came to know that someone had heard human voices inside the dense forest on the bank of Jhanji river.

Hearing this then and there he started towards Jhanji river. With great difficulty he found out their abode. The moment his canine 'son-in-law' saw, welcome him barking.

When Selupvra entered their hut Crimino offered him various fruits and wild bear meat. While eating he wanted to see his grand children. Crimino called them and they came running from their play ground. Selupvra saw that the complexion of all his grand children was white. Such whiteness he never saw earlier in his life. Enjoying their hospitality for a few days he returned to his village. Before departure he invited his grand children to come to him when they would come of age."

After that incident many-many years rolled on. Nobody knows as to how a peculiar belief ingrained among the Angami Nagas that the white people are the descendants of that unnatural odd pair. This notion has still been current among the traditional Nagas. This tale must appear to be very weird and grotesque. But this 'queerness' is the kind of idiosyncrasy of the Naga folk-tales and many other folk stories as well.

(2) We are presenting here another folk tale. It is a story of an Angami girl and a Kinnari man.

"Long ago an Angami girl became very famous for her beauty far and wide. Her beauty attracted all the Naga youths and they desired to marry her. But Crisivilo decided to give her hand to a young man who was both very rich and handsome. So she turned down all the proposals from the poor or moderately well-to-do Nagamen.

Gradually the frangrance of her beauty reached even the Kinnarlok of high hills. One night she was walking about the morung (dormitary for unmarried girls). The silver rays of the moonlight bathed her body. Suddenly a good looking Kinnar young man appeared before her from nowhere. In the bright moonlit night Crisivilo seemed to be moving in a dreamland. In this enchanting atmosphere it seemed to her quite natural when the unknown Kinnar proposed to marry her. She assured him that if he was very rich he could go to her parents with the proposal and Crisivilo would give her consent.

Next day the Kinnar went to her parents and said that he came of a high family, the roof of his house was made of glasses of the sunbeams, from there one could observe the heavenly beauty. He was so rich that the same utensils were not used for the second time.

Crisivilo's parents were so moved by the handsome looks and charming behaviour of the Kinnar young that they agreed to marry their daughter with him. They did not feel any necessity to verify his whereabouts or his family background.

Without any pomp and show Crisivilo was wedded to the Kinnar man according to simple Naga custom. After marriage the Kinnar took his wife home. There Crisivilo found to her utter dismay that what he had told about his financial and social position was all false. He had no house of his own, but lived in a cave. The sunlight of course, played over the head as there was no shed over them and many heavenly scenes were visible there. It was also true that he did not use the same plate for the second time since those were tree-leaves thrown after use. Her husband was the poorest in the Kinnar society.

Crisivilo could do nothing at the turn of event but to curse her own fate and lack of wisdom. She just tried to adjust herself with the reality. But it was indeed a very difficult job.

Since they had no house of their own they had to shift from one place to another according to the varying moods of nature. Meanwhile two daughters were born to them. Crisivilo could not take to the surroundings. When she thought of her parents who did not have plenty of money but had a comfortable living, she felt her life unbearable. She pined for coming out of her miserable married life every moment.

The Kinnar also did not have enough interest in Crisivilo as earlier. He began feeling enamoured of the women of his own community, spent time in their company.

Not even a handful of foodgrain was in their house one day. Both the daughters were crying for food. The Kinnar did not care. Rather he went out well-dressed and spent the night in a dancing Kinnari's house alongwith his friends. When he returned home after midnight he was dead drunk and slept like a deadman. He was least bothered about Crisivilo and the two little daughters whether or not they had any food.

So long Crisivilo put up with all sufferings, which had them stretched to the limit. She left the terrible place that night leaving behind the two daughters.

She went alone through the uneven terrain, valley, deep forest, stream and reached her parents in the Naga village after an arduous journey of ten days. Her parents were mortified to hear her sufferings of all those years. They advised her to start life afresh and forget the past.

And Crisivilo did not err the second time. At last she married an Angami from her own community. He was a widower and not good looking but had enough property, foodgrain and domestic animals.

In Zosheto, a legendary character, one may find some qualities of modern Casanova. His accomplishments are quite mirthful—with a tinge of sexuality. J.P. Mills narrated Zosheto's sexual adventures in his book, *Rengma Nagas*.

Once Zosheto took all the women of his Khel (clan) down to the stream for fishing. He told them that he would go upstream and mix poison with river water. Then they should take off their shawls (lower garments) and stand naked in the water down stream holding their shawls so as to make a blockade to stop the fish going down.

The women carried out his instructions. But Zosheto, instead of mixing fish poison used a wild root called Ayirha with an intoxicating juice of plants. The mixture of the wild root and exhilarating fluid was cascaded down the rill water and entering the women's sexual organs. It made them mad with desire. They begged Zosheto to satisfy them. He readily agreed and satiated all of them but one girl.

The girl was very obedient and when approached told that she must ask for her father's permission before having any physical relation with Zosheto. As she was also very much inebriated she started running to her house to obtain assent from her father. Zosheto, as enterprising as he had been, reached her house earlier by another way. Since the girl's father was not home at that time he hid himself inside the house and when the girl came in the outer room and said "Zosheto has had sex with all other women of our Khel. May I have physical connection with him?". Zosheto pretending her father from the inner room said in an artificial voice "When Zosheto has had connection with all other women of our Khel you can also have it with him".—The girl returned to the river side where Zosheto had reached earlier again by a short cut.

Then both of them enjoyed to their satisfaction."

So, these are the folk story which have remained part and parcel of Naga life and belief and of course, another indication of their culture.

11

New Planning in 2001

We have read in previous chapters that a number of developments both good as well as bad have taken place in Nagaland after its emergence as a state. If on one front, insurgency has disturbed the economy, free flow of aid by central government has flourished its social and economic life. Changing socio-political and economic scenario have led to new planning also which has primarily been in agricultural sector since agriculture is the main means of livelihood of Nagas. But it has definitely touched other aspects also which are as below:

A. On the agrarian scene, the control over land utilisation today falls under five main heads:

1. The State Government of Nagaland
2. The village and/or community
3. The clan
4. Lineage
5. The Individual.

B. While the traditional land system used to be:

1. Collective land ownership
2. Individual land ownership

Under the collective ownership, these were:

(a) Lineage
(b) Clan
(c) Village

C. Individual land ownership was Traditional Patta.
Table 10.1 presents a better picture of the above:

In the new planning, measures have also been adopted by state with alterations State measures are like this:

1. The Village Council
2. The Range Council
3. The Tribal Council

Above said socio-economic bodies which deal with disputes and cases involving breaches of customary laws and also usages.

The fact is that all Naga tribes depend directly on land and forest for their livelihood. They subsist for this on editable leaves and roots, honey, wild games and fish. They build their homes with timber and bamboo and practise certain cottage crafts with the help of local raw materials. They make use of herb and medicinal plants with a purpose to cure their diseases, and even their religion and folklore are woven around the spirits and concerns of forests.

In Naga society the community land under *Jhum* is in the process of privatization as per a particular specific plot being cultivated by 'X' within class 'Y' and 'X' cultivating it again in the recurrent Jhum cycles the way it is among the Konyaks and Angamis. In some cases, the payment of a nominal amount to the village authority or clan in question by its members has been another factor that too is very important.

The Zubza farmers are now classified as given below:

1. Big land-owners
2. Small land-owners
3. Landless labourers

From the above, it is obvious that a very serious problem would arise if proper attention is not given to agricultural development and in this regard, if appropriate education is not imparted to the masses in relation to agricultural activity/activities.

Undoubtedly it is a well-known fact that technological advancement, modern education, mobility and this changing occupation structure etc. have greatly contributed to Naga social change. In this so-called Naga egalitarian society, the fact that social differentiation was always present cannot be denied. But anyhow, caught between tides of modernisation on the one side, and an embedded social structure on the other, the transformation of Naga agrarian situation in Nagaland requires further investigation as to help us in knowing numerous details so far not investigated by various researchers.

Section-III
Tripura

12

Land and the People

Each social group, each state has a history and a culture of its own which is an account of political and social developments, irrespective of the fact that whether these developments are positive or negative. So, Tripura state too has a historical background.

I. Ancient Period

In ancient period, prior to the establishment of the Muslim rule in Bengal, Tripura had no distinct political status. It had virtually no significance at that time. The archaeological evidences found in the region prove the fact that a huge portion of this region, particularly south-western part of the present state of Tripura, was politically attached to the Kingdoms of Eastern Bengal known as Samatata Vanga and Harikela.[1]

(a) Gupta Dynasty. From the year 507 B.C. to 8th century Maharaja Vainyagupta, a member of the dynasty of Imperial Guptas, ruled over Samatata and granted lands in Tripura region. The seat of his kingdom was situated in or close to Tripura region. At first he was a local governor under an imperial Gupta monarch, but subsequently he became an independent ruler. After Vainyagupta, Gopachandra, Dharmaditya and Samachardeva ruled over Samatata between circa A.D. 525–A.D. 575.

It appears that these three kings ruled from a place, wherefrom Vainyagupta also had ruled before them. This locality was somewhere either in the eastern Dacca or in northern Tippera district which formed the central part of the kingdom of these monarchs.[2]

Huien Tsang who visited India in the first half of the 7th century referred to the Kingdom of Samatata which included the major part of Vanga proper. According to his account, it had included within its political boundaries a part of the Central Bengal in addition to the region of the district Tippera.[3] Huien Tsang also tells that a line of Brahmin Kings ruled there in the first half of 7th century, Silabhadra of Nalanda Monastery belonged to that dynasty.

(b) Nath Dynasty. The Tippera Copper Plate grant of Samanta Lokanatha brings into lime light a line of feudatory chiefs that ruled East Bengal in the region round Tippera in the middle of the 7th century. According to this inscription Lokanatha, Jivadharana and Jayaturgavarsha were feudatories of a common sovereign whose title was Paramesvara. On behalf of his suzerain Paramesvara,

Lokanatha, defeated Jayatungavarsha and Jivadharana. This inscription also contains a short history of four or five generations of the Natha family. They were the followers of Saivism. The first King's name ending in natha is missing in the copper plate because of corrosion but he is described as having sprung from the good family of the sage Bharadvaja and also that he was a renowned King, having the right to the use of the paramount title of *Adhimaharaja.* The second feudatory of this dynasty whose name was Srinatha, acquired much fame as a matchless warrior. The name of his accomplished and virtuous son was Bhavanatha and Lokanatha came after him.

(c) The Rata Dynasty. Virtually, nothing is known about Paramesvara or Jayatunga-varsha. However, some details about Jivadharana are contained in another copper plate found at Kailan, a village south-west of Comilla. The charter was issued by Shridharana the Rata ruler of Samatata and son of Jivadharana who is also called the Lord of Samatata. Reference is made to Devaparvata, the capital of this Rata family. This Devaparvata was encircled by the river Kshirode which is identified with modern Khira, a dried up river course still traceable as branching off from the Gumti exactly west of the Comilla town. The river surrounds the southern end of the Mainamati hills, where the ancient hill-fort of Devaparvata seems to have been situated.[4] These two Rata rulers, who nominally acknowledged the suzerainty of some overlord, were practically independent. After the Ratas, came the Devas who also had their capital at Devaparvata and the Kings Viradeva, Anantadeva, Bhavadeva and Kantideva belonged to this dynasty. They were the Buddhists whereas the Ratas were the Vaishnavites.

(d) Khadga Dynasty. Famous Asrafpur plates of the Khadga dynasty proved the fact that a large portion of Tripura was under the control of the Khadga dynasty. The name of four Kings of the Khadga dynasty known to all are Khadgodyama, Jatakhadga, Devakhadga and Rajarajabhatta, each being the son of the predecessor. From the Chinese evidences, it appears that the Khadga dynasty ruled in the second half of the 7th century A.D. and their kingdom comprised nearly the whole of the Eastern and Southern Bengal including Tripura. Two copper plate grants of Devakhadga, were issued from the royal camp of Karmanta Vasaka that was their capital. This city has been identified with modern Barkamta, a police station situated twelve miles west of Comilla. The Khadgas were also the Buddhist followers.

(e) Chandra Dynasty. Next dynasty with personal names suffixed by the word 'Chandra' ruled in Eastern Bengal from about 875 to 1035 A.D. It is stated that the original home of this dynasty was in Rohitagiri which is identified wth Lalmai Hills close to Comilla by N.K. Bhattasali.

> The fact that quite a large number of inscriptions of this family have been found in the region of Lalmai Hills near Comilla strongly supports the identification proposed by Bhattasali.[5]

Here, it is interesting to note in this connection that one Chandra dynasty was also ruling in the Arakan Kingdom. We are not sure whether the Chandras of Arakan had any relation with the Chandras of the East Bengal. From the coins and inscriptions found in Arakan it is proved beyond doubt that about twenty kings of the Chandra dynasty ruled in Arakan. Whether these Chandras extended their political influence in Tripura or its adjoining regions before the setting up of the Chandra dynasty of East Bengal is not certain.

They were seven Kings of the Chandra dynasty of Eastern Bengal, Purna Chandra, Suvarna Chandra, Trailakya Chandra, Shri Chandra, Kalyan Chandra, then Ladaha Chandra and finally Govinda Chandra. Although Purna Chandra and Suarna Chandra were the followers of Brahmanical religion, the successors of Suvarna Chandra became Buddhists. The Baghaura image inscription and one more inscription engraved on an image of Ganesa discovered in the village of Narayanpur in the Tippera district shows that some portions of Tripura were included in Samatata, which itself was below the suzerainty of Mahipala I. Probably, he wrested it from Ladaha Chandra. But that Ladaha Chandra recovered it is proved by the Bharella image inscription King Govinda Chandra, the last heard Chandra King was defeated by the army of Rajendra Chola and finally the Chandra dynasty was defeated and ousted by Karna, the great Kalachari ruler.

(f) Varman Dynasty. With the fall of the Chandras, the Varmans became powerful in East Bengal. Jata Varman, Hari Varman, Samala Varman were all powerful rulers who ruled in Vikrampura. Bhoja Varman the last heard ruler of East Bengal was overthrown by Vijayasena of Sena dynasty.

(g) Small Kingdoms of Burma and Pattikara. The emergence of the small Kingdom of Pattikara in the district of Tippera may be traced back to the 11th century. The Burmese chronicles contain many references to this Kingdom. According to Hmannan, the kingdom of the Burmese king Anartha during 1044–1077 A.D. was bounded on the west by Pattikara. The same text narrates a romantic story of love between the prince of Pattikara and Sweinthi, the daughter of the ruler of Burma.

There was an intimate intercourse between the Burma and Pattikara during the 12th century. The origins of the Pattikara Kingdom can be traced back in the accounts of the Burmese chronicles. The Burmese chronicles state that the Shans invaded Arakan in the tenth century, and Northern Arakan was conquered by Anaratha. At this period, of political turmoil, the Chandras were ousted from Arakan and a branch of them settled at Pattikara. The existence of the kingdom of Pattikara in the thirteenth century is proved by an inscription engraved on a copper plate got from the neighbourhood of Comilla.

It records a grant of land in favour of a Buddhist monastery built at Pattikara, by Dhadi-eba, the Chief Minister of Sri Harikeladeva Ranavankamalla in 1220, that was the seventeenth year of his reign. Harikeladeva Ranavankamalla, who ascended the throne in 1203-04 and ruled till 1220, was undoubtedly an independent ruler. The name of the father of Dhadi-eba had been recorded as Mamhedi-eba and the name of the writer of the grant was Madeni-eba. The ending suffix "eba" in the names discloses their Burmese origin. Whether King Harikeladeva Ranavankamalla belonged to the old royal family of Pattikara or to Deva family, is not known and after him there is no mention of the name of the Kingdom of Pattikara. It was most possibly absorbed in the growing kingdom of the Deva family.

(h) Deva Family of Nadiya. Madhumathanadeva, the head of the Deva family, set up an independent kingdom in the eastern region of the river Meghna shortly after or before the Muslim raid on Nadiya. His grandson Damodardeva was a powerful king whose kingdom comprised the modern districts of Tippera, Noakhali and Chittagong.[6] Dasarathadeva, the son of Damodardeva, conquered Vikrampura and came into the control of the Sena kingdom in East Bengal in the second half of the 13th century. The title Ariraja Danuja Madhava borne by Dasrathadeva makes it very probable that he is identical with Danujarai, the King of Sonargaon who according to Ziauddin Barani, entered into an agreement with Ghiyasuddin Balban that he would guard against the escape of the rebellious Tughril Khan through the water ways. Dasarathadeva was a Vaishnava and his capital was at Sonargaon near Dacca. This Deva dynasty had lost its power and glory due to the Muslim advance in Eastern part of Bengal.

(i) Deva Family of Srihatta. Presence of another family in Srihatta is proved by two copper plates discovered at Bhatara, about 32 km from the Sylhet town. Govinda Kesavadeva of this family was a powerful ruler whose kingdom "extended also over the southern part of the district of Sylhet, south of the river Kusiyara, portions of Cachar district (including Karimganj subdivision) and possibly portions of northern Tripura also.[7] This prince was anyway, overthrown by Shahajallal who invaded Sylhet in A.D. 1257.

Above said all these historical facts definitely prove that the present state of Tripura was not founded in an ancient period. Most of the western and southern parts of Tripura was politically attached to Eastern Bengal under various dynasties and so had that time, no separate political entity.

There might be some tribes in ancient period living in the hilly north-eastern part of Tripura but they had no political importance at that time. Among all these tribes, the Tipras were numerous and well-organised. After the fall of the Deva dynasty, they were able to establish a kingdom in this region which afterwards came to be known as the Tripura kingdom. Modern scholars hold the opinion that the name Tripura is a sanskritised form of Tipra, a tribe to which the ruling family belonged.[8] Some writers think that the ancient Tripura kingdom was originally situated between north-eastern Tripura and North Cachar. *Rajmala,* a chronicle of the Tripura royal family, also narrates that the ancestors of this family changed their capital from Nowgong district to the district of Cachar on the bank of the river Barak and afterwards proceeded to south-westward and came to Dharmanagar and set up a capital on the bank of the river Juri. It was from Dharmanagar that they gradually moved further south-westward and came to the centre of the present Tripura state.

Medieval Period

(a) Tipra Tribe. While the Deva dynasty was declining in Eastern Bengal, the chief of the Tipra tribe rose in the hilly region of Tripura. They gradually extended their hold in the plain lands of Tripura region and a collision with the Islamic power, which was firmly established in Bengal in the meantime, was inevitable. The earliest chief of the Tipra tribe who successfully defended his country against the Muslim power of Bengal as written in *Rajmala* was Chhengthung Fa. According to *Rajmala,* a large army was sent against Chhengthung Fa from Gour as a retaliatory measure against the Tripura Chief for one incident: one Hiravant Khan was allegedly plundered of his wealth on his way to Gour to present a gift to the Sultan. Chhengthung Fa wished to sue for peace, but his wife protested against this type of cowardice, and herself led the Tripuri force against the enemy's troops and routed them. The kingdom which they established in this region came to be known as Tripura kingdom. They adopted the title Manikya, dropped the original Fa and their dynasty came to be known as the Manikya dynasty.

According to *Rajmala,* this family belonged to the lunar dynasty of the Kshatrya 'Jati'. Most modern scholars believe that the Tripuris like the Chacharis and other tribes of eastern India were Mongolian in origin. Suniti Kumar Chatterji classified them with the Indo-Mongoloids or Kiratas. They use the Bodos language. The Bodos who settled on the bank of the river Brahmaputra, gradually occupied the Garo Hills and Nowgong distict in state of Assam. From Nowgong district their area of occupation extended to Cachar (particularly in the North Cachar Hills) and into Sylhet, and from Cachar and Sylhet they went further to the south, to the Tripura State.[9] At present it appears somewhat difficult to ascertain the actual date of their migration to Tripura. Only we can presume that they entered Tripura long before the emergence of the Muslim rule in Bengal.

(b) Dharma's Father–Maha Manikya. Periodical *Rajmala* refers to an inscription dated A.D. 1458 of Dharma Manikya. In this inscription Maha Manikya was regarded as the father of Dharma Manikya and according to Tripura Vamsabali, Dharma Manikya ruled between A.D. 1431 to A.D. 1462. Therefore it can be presumed that Maha Manikya ruled before A.D. 1431 and he was the earliest known king of Tripura having the Manikya title. As per some modern scholars it was Maha Manikya who founded a kingdom during the early years of the reign of Raja Ganesa of Bengal and his newly founded kingdom was lying between Chittagong and Sylhet regions. They also presume that the original name of Maha Manikya was Chhengthung Fa.[10] It is not very unlikely that after successfully defending his newly formed kingdom against the Muslim power, Chhengthung Fa assumed the title Maha Manikya.

(c) Dharma Manikya. Dharma Manikya, the son of Maha Manikya, was a strong ruler and his reign constitutes an important landmark in the history of Tripura.

Although we find no coin of Dharma Manikya times the *Rajmala* talks of a copper plate of Dharma Manikya dated 1458. According to Tripur Vamsabali Dharma Manikya ruled from 1431 to 1462. He was a great patron of learning. It is said that he employed the priest Durlabhendra and two Brahmins, named, Sukreswar and Baneswar, to write a history of the dynasty. He donated lands to a large number of Brahmins in his realm and was himself a committed and devout Hindu. Dharma Manikya had paternal affection for his subjects. He excavated the famous Dharmasagar Tank at Comilla and built temples.

(d) Ratna Manikya—The Descendant of Dharma. Ratna Manikya who ascended the throne of Tripura at the death of Dharma Manikya, may be considered the earliest of the coin issuing rulers of Tripura. These coins belonged to the period between 1464 and 1467. These coins carry some common characteristics with the Muslim coins of Bengal. According to *Rajmala,* he was the youngest son of King Dangar Fa. From chronological angle, King Dangar Fa and Dharma Manikya were the same person. According to *Rajmala* and local traditions, King Dangar Fa divided his kingdom into seventeen divisions and placed them with his seventeen princes. Ratna Fa, the youngest son of Dangar Fa, was sent to Gour as hostage from Tripura. The Sultan of Gour was highly pleased with the charming manners and out of common intelligence of the prince. There the Sultan and the Prince came to an unholy alliance. The Prince got military help from the Sultan to capture entire Tripura for himself. With the help of mercenary powers, he defeated his elder brothers and declared himself the King of Tripura.

As a mark of gratitude Ratna Fa presented the Sultan with some elephants and a valuable ruby. In return, the Sultan recognised Ratna Fa as Ratna Manikya.[11] The Assamese envoys who went to Tripura in the early part of the eighteenth century stated that Ratna Manikya was conferred with the Manikya title by the Sultan of Gour.[12] It is generally believed that during his period, a large number of Brahmins, Vaidyas and Kayasthas came from various parts of Bengal and settled in Tripura. It is said that he introduced some administrative reforms which were based on the pattern prevalent in Bengal. His capital as mentioned in the coins was known as Ratnapur. Sultan Ruknuddin Barbak Shah, 1455 to 1476, of Bengal was the contemporary of Ratna Manikya and also it was probably from him that Ratna Manikya secured assistance to usurp the kingdom.

(e) Pratap Manikya's Time. Following the death of Ratna Manikya, his son Pratap Manikya became the ruler of Tripura. According to *Rajmala,* he was cruel and unpopular. The leaders of the army who became very much powerful after the death of Ratna Manikya, killed him.

(f) Mukut Manikya's Time. Ruler Pratap Manikya was succeeded by his younger brother Mukut Manikya. A coin of Mukut Manikya dated 1489 has been found. His reign lasted for a very short time and appears to have come to an end before 1490 because Dhanya Manikya already released a coin in that year. According to *Rajmala,* Dhanya Manikya succeeded his younger brother Pratap

Manikya II. But we find that Mukut Manikya issued a coin just prior to the accession of Dhanya Manikya. So Pratap Manikya II must be placed before Mukut Manikya. An inscription issued in the year 1488 mentioned the name of one Vijay Manikya who was a minor king at that time.

According to D.C. Sircar, it is possible that Vijay Manikya I, 1410-1488, was Mukut's elder brother who is known as Pratap Manikya II in the *Rajmala* and may have ruled for a very short reign.[13] D.C. Sircar is of the opinion that Dhanya Manikya whose coins are dated 1490 immediately after Mukut Manikya who issued coins in 1489, are dated have been the son but not the grandson of Mukut Manikya as stated by *Rajmala.*[14]

(g) Dhanya Manikya. Dhanya Manikya who took over the throne in the year 1490 may be regarded as the greatest ruler of Tripura in the medieval period. He crushed the rebellious feudal chiefs and army officers. Taking advantage of the disorder and chaotic state in Bengal prior to the accession of Husain Shah, Dhanya Manikya annexed to his kingdom some portions of Bengal such as Pattikara, Gangamandal, Meherkul and Khandal. He too reduced the Kukis to obedience. In the year 1506 he issued a coin and took the title 'Vijayindra' or conqueror. We find a coin of Dhanya Manikya issued in the year 1513 with the words inscribed 'Conqueror of Chittagong' which indicates that he conquered Chittagong in that year. It was during his reign that Sultan Husain Shah, 1493 to 1519, of Bengal made strenuous attempts to conquer Tripura.

(h) Muslim attacks. An inscription seen on the door of a mosque at Sonargaon dated 1513 recording the name of the builder as the Sher-e-Lasker of Tripura indicates that at least a portion of Tripura was conquered by Husain Shah prior to the year 1513. According to *Rajmala,* Husain Shah despatched his army on several occasions. But the people of Tripura fought heroically and successfully defended their country. *Rajmala* indicates Husain Shah not very much successful in his military expeditions against Tripura.

Dhanya Manikya was a great patron of art and literature. He took care to spread the Bengali language among the masses by having some Sanskrit works translated into Bengali. He built several temples, the greatest of these being the famous temple of Tripura Sundari at Udaipur in the year 1501. He also constructed a very big tank at Kasba (Kamala Sagar) to be named after his beloved and reputed queen Kamaladevi. According to Tripur Vamsabali, he died in the year 1515. The available coins of times of Dhanya Manikya prove that he ruled for about 25 years.

(i) Dhwaja Manikya's Rule. In fact, very little is known about the rule of Dhwaja Manikya who was probably the eldest son of Dhanya Manikya. According to Tripur Vamsabali he ruled for six years. Some writers maintain that he ruled just for one year. The old *Rajmala* does not mention his reign.

(j) Deva Manikya's Rule. The earliest available coin of Deva Manikya, who were the brother of Dhwaja Manikya, dated 1520 proves the fact that Deva Manikya became the ruler of Tripura in the year 1520. In that year he conquered

Bhulua or Noakhali. These coins of Deva Manikya dated 1528 and 1530 which described him as the conqueror of Sonargaon (Suvarnagram Vijayi) prove the fact that he successfully led expeditions in Sonargaon. As per *Rajmala,* Deva Manikya a devout Sakta, was murdered in a conspiracy and his son Indra Manikya became the ruler of Tripura. But he ruled only for one year and the army revolted and put Vijay Manikya on the throne.

(k) Vijay Manikya's Rule. Vijay Manikya, the son of Deva Manikya was a capable ruler and had a long reign. Some coins of Vijay Manikya which are available belonged to the period between 1532 to 1563. The existence of these coins shows that Vijay Manikya reigned for more than thirty years. He made some administrative reforms, reorganised army and recruited some Afghan cavalry in his army. Like Dhanya Manikya, Vijay Manikya was too, a great conqueror. He conquered Sylhet and recovered Chittagong from the Afghans.

Taking advantage of the Mughal-Afghan contest, Vijay Manikya invaded Sonargaon and plundered it. That his army moved up to the river Padma during the years 1557 to 1563 of his reign, is proved by some contemporary coins issued by Vijay Manikya. According to James Long, "At this time Vijay Raja of Tripura marched to Bengal with an army composed of 26,000 infantry, and five thousand horses besides artillery; he went by 5,000 boats along the streams Brahmaputra and Lakhi to Padma."[15] Vijay Manikya was a contemporary of King Akbar. The Ain-i-Akbari refers to his reign in the following words. "Adjoining Bhati is an extensive tract of territory inhabited by the Tipperah Tribes. The name of the ruler is Vijay Manik. Whoever obtains the Chieftainship bears the title Manik after his name and the nobles that of Narayan. He has a force of two hundred thousand footmen and a thousand elephants. Horses are scarce."[16]

(l) Gopi Prasad's Rule. Next, Ananta Manikya, the son of Vijay Manikya was not an efficient ruler. He was completely under the control of his father-in-law Gopi Prasad who from humble origins rose to the height of position and power. He usurped the throne of Tripura during the year 1567 and took the title Udai Manikya and issued coins in the same year. He changed the name of his capital from Rangamati to Udaipur, excavated a tank called Chandra Sagar and built a temple of Chandra Gopinath. According to *Rajmala* he ruled for five years.

(m) Amar Manikya Rule. Amar Manikya, son of Deva Manikya, restored the traditional dynasty to its proper place after ousting Joy Manikya, the son of Udai Manikya in 1577. He was an energetic ruler. He defeated the ruler of Tarap, Bhulua and Sylhet, and released a coin in 1581 to commemorate his victory over Sylhet. He constructed a big tank known as Amar Sagar and made his residence in a place which came to be known as Amarpur.

It is generally said that the second part of the *Rajmala* was compiled during his reign. Ralf Fitch, a European traveller on his way to Chittagong, visited Tripura during the reign of Amar Manikya and made these remarks. "From Satagan, I travelled by the country of the King of Tippera with whom the Mogen have almost continual wars. The Mogen which be of the Kingdom of Recon and Rame, be stronger than the king of Tippera; and so that Chittagong or Portogrando, is often times under the King of Recon."[17] As per *Rajmala,* Amar Manikya conquered Chittagong and invaded Arakan with the help of some Portuguese adventurers. But Sikandar Shah, the King of Arakan, defeated him and took over Chittagong. The Arakani force plundered Udaipur and massacred people. Amar Manikya left Udaipur and took shelter in the forest on the bank of the river Manu. There also he had been harassed by the Kukis. Being mentally depressed, Amar Manikya committed suicide by taking poison.

(n) Rajdhar Manikya's Rule. Rajdhar Manikya, the son of Amar Manikya, took over in 1586 and issued a coin that year. He shifted his capital back to Udaipur which was ransacked by the Mogs. He kept himself away from the battlefield and devoted life to religious pursuits. He was a great patron of the Vaishnava cult. According to *Rajmala,* Rajdhar Manikya ruled for twelve years. After his death one Iswar Manikya ascended the throne and released a coin in the year 1600; very little is known about him. In the same year Yasodhar Manikya ascended the throne of Tripura.

(o) Yasodhar Manikya's Period. Yasodhar Manikya, the son of Rajdhar Manikya, took over the throne in 1600 and had a coin issued that year. The image of Krishna with a flute inscribed on his coins indicates that he was a Vaishnava. In order to secure a fit base for a military operation against the King of Arakan, Ibrahim Khan Fatehjang, the governor of Bengal, under Jahangir's order launched an expedition vis-a-vis Tripura in 1618. Two land forces and one fleet was despatched against the King of Tripura. According to Baharistan-i-Ghayabi, the King of Tripura resisted the Mughals with the help of an army of "one thousand cavalry, sixty thousand infantry and two hundred elephants."[18] The king was defeated and Udaipur was occupied by the Mughals. The king was caught with his wives in the forest and they were sent to Jahangirnagar alias Dacca to Ibrahim Khan. Probably he was confined within the Mughal territory and died in 1623. Meanwhile the Mughal army continued to hold the country in military occupation of the most cruel king until after two and a half years, they were forced by an epidemic to leave the country. The occupied portion of Tripura entered into the Mughal rent roll as "Sarkar Udaipur."

(p) Kalyan Manikya's Times. The Mughals had left Udaipur just after two years and six months of occupation. The people selected Kalyan Manikya as their King. He was the son of Kachu Fa, a successor of Gagan Fa who was the son of Maha Manikya. A coin released by Kalyan Manikya in the year 1626 proves the fact that he became the ruler of Tripura at least in or before the year 1626. Kalyan Manikya restored peace and order, remodelled his army and also recovered most of the lost portions of his territory. Petter Heleys, a European visitor, mentioned in 1652 that the rulers of Tripura had frequent fights with the Mughals.[19] One more Muslim account *Naubahari Murshid Quli Khani* noted:

> Tipara is a country extremely strong by reason of abundance of its trees, the loftiness of its forts, and the difficulty of its roads. The Raja is proud of his strength and the practices of conch blowing and idol worship prevail there. Sultan Shuja during his governorship of Bengal, left his eldest son Zainuddin Muhammad as his deputy in Rajmahal, came to Dacca, and sent his chief minister Jan Bag Khan towards Tipara, but the Khan's men failed to take any of the forts of that country even after labouring for one year. At last he had to content himself with annexing the district of Mirzapur, and making it the frontier of the imperial dominions. Many of his soldiers died from the badness of the air.[20]

Like this, conquered portion of Tripura was enlisted as Sarkar Udaipur in the Revenue Records of Bengal Subha prepared in 1658. Nakshatra Roy, the second son of Kalyan Manikya, was sent to the court of Shuja like a hostage. Kalyan Manikya constructed a big tank known as Kalyan Sagar and build a Kali temple at Kasba. He devoted himself to religious pursuits and donated lands to the Brahmins.

(q) Govinda Manikya and Nakshatra Roy's Times. After the death of Kalyan Manikya, his first son Govinda Manikya ascended the throne in 1660. But Nakshatra Roy, the step-brother of Govinda Manikya, secured the help of the Mughals and took over Udaipur. Govinda Manikya was forced to leave Tripura. Nakshatra Roy took the title Chhatra Manikya and issued a coin in 1661. Chhatra Manikya ruled probably for six years.

With the support of the king of Arakan, Govinda Manikya recovered his throne in 1667. According to *Rajmala,* Govinda Manikya became the ruler of Tripura for the second time after the expiry of Chhatra Manikya. But the Assamese envoys who visited the court of Ratna Manikya II recorded a speech of King Mahendra Manikya which stated that Chhatra Manikya was killed by Govinda Manikya.[21] Govinda Manikya made peace with the Mughals by agreeing to give them five elephants as tribute annually. The name of Govinda Manikya became immortal through Tagore's well famous plays *Visharjan* and *Rajarshi.* It is generally believed that the third part of *Rajmala* was compiled during his reign. *Brihannarada Purana* was translated into Bengali below his patronage.

After the death of Govinda Manikya, his son Ramdeb Manikya became the ruler of Tripura in 1676. The temple of Tripura Sundari which had been struck and destroyed by lightning was repaired by Ramdeb Manikya in the year 1681. Tavernier, a French traveller who visited India during the reign of Shahjahan and also came to Bengal during the reign of Chhatra Manikya of Tripura, has left some interesting accounts about Tripura and its merchants. He wrote:

> I met with three, one at Dacca and two others at Patna. They were men of very few words; whether it were their own particular disposition, or the general habits of the country. They cast up their accounts with small stones like agats, as big as man's nail, upon every one of which was a cipher. They

had every one their weights, like a steller; though the beam were not of iron but of a certain wood as hard as Brazile; nor was the ring that holds that weight, and is put through the beam to mark the weight of iron, but a strong silk rope. Thus they weighed from a dram to ten of our pounds. If all the natives of the kingdom of Tipra were like the two merchants which I met at Patna, I dare affirm them to be notable topers; for they never refused whatever strong liquor I gave them, and never left till all was out; and when I told them by my interpreter that all my wine was gone, they clapped there hands upon their stomachs and sighed. These merchants travelled all three through the kingdom of Arakan, which lies to the south and west of Tipra, having some part of Pegu upon the winter west. They told me also, that it was about fifteen days journey to cross through their country; from whence there is no certain conjecture of the extent to be made by reason of the inequality of the stages. They ride upon oxen and horses, which were low but very hardy. As for the king and the nobility, the ride in the palleki or upon their elephants of war. They are no less subject to wens under their throats than those of Boutan; in so far much that the women have wens hanging down to their nipples; which proceeds from the badness of the waters. There is nothing in Tipra which is fit for strangers. There is a mine of gold, but the gold is very coarse and there is a sort of very coarse silk which is all the revenue the king has. He exacts no subsidies from his subjects, but only that they, who are not the prime nobility should work for six days in a year in his mine, or in his silk works. He sends his gold and silk into China for which they bring him back silver, which he coins into pieces to the value of ten sols. He also makes their pieces of gold like to the Aspers of Turkey; of which he has two sorts, four of the one sort making a crown, and twelve of the other.[22]

(r) Ratna Manikya II Period. King Ratna Manikya II, the son of Ramdeb Manikya, ascended the throne in 1685 at the age of five. His reign was full of conspiracy and quarrels among the members of the royal family. It was during his rule, Rudra Singha, the King of Assam, sent Ratna Kandali and Arjundas Vairagi as diplomatic envoys to Tripura. The object of Rudra Singha was to establish friendly relations with Tripura in furtherance of his purpose to organise a confederacy of the Hindu rulers against the Mughals. This was probably the first Assamese mission to Tripura. Ratna Kandali and Arjundas were humbly received by Ratna Manikya. Ratna Manikya sent Rameswar Bhattacharjee Nayalankar and Udainarayan Biswas to the Court of Assam in 1710. They reached Rangpur the new capital of Assam state where king Rudra Singha received the Tripura envoys amidst pomp and ceremony. Rudra Singha sent Ratna Kandali and Arjundas as envoys to Tripura for the second time. They had been formally received by the Tripura King Ratna Manikya on 15th April, 1712. They delivered a secret letter of Rudra Singha in which Tripura king was requested to inform Rudra Singha what support he could render against the Mughals.

During their stay at Udaipur the Assamese envoys and their camp followers were invited to the celebrations and festivities connected with the worship of Madan—the God of love and affection.

(s) Mahendra Manikya's Rule. Mahendra formally met the Assamese envoys on 24 July, 1712 and sent an envoy named Aribhim Narayan with them to the court of Ahom king. Mahendra Manikya expressed his intention to strengthen his friendship with the Ahom king monarch. He died in 1713 after a rule of fourteen months. Ratna Kandali and Arjundas Vairagi who visited the Tripura as envoys of King Rudra of Assam on three separate occasions between the years 1709 and 1715 recorded their impressions which throw sidelights on the social, economic and political conditions of medieval Tripura.[23] They observed that the people living in places adjoining the river Gumti were prosperous. Among agricultural products there were paddy, potato, cotton, sugarcane, oil-seeds, etc. The mango, coconut and jackfruit were found in the region in abundance. They witnessed market places at Udaipur on the bank of the river Gumti. One of these markets was called Rajhat where utensils made of copper, brass, etc., and articles like cotton, sugar, salt, milk and ghee were sold.

They mentioned some areas viz. Meharkul, Khandal, Mandal, Vakachai, Lohagarh, Tisna, Mirzapur, Lomagar, Bhusana, Kulasar and also Dharmanagar where paddy, pulses and corn of good quality were grown. The envoys also witnessed men of different professions who lived at Udaipur around a big tank called Amar Sagar. There were weavers, goldsmiths, carpenters, and washermen. There were also Brahmins, Kayasthas, Vaidyas and Gardeners who lived in between two tanks Amar Sagar and Vijay Sagar. The monarch lived in a house built with bricks. It housed also an armoury. The nobles also lived in houses built of bricks. Revenue of some parganas were allotted for the expenditure of the queens and members of the Royal family. There were many temples in the capital dedicated to Vishnu, Siva and other gods and goddesses. The *sati* system or the burning of the wife alongwith the dead body of her husband was prevalent in Tripura at that time. They recorded that all the wives of Ratna Manikya immolated themselves with their husband, permission being sanctioned for that act by their mother-in-law.

(t) Dharma Manikya II's Rule. Following the death of Mahendra Manikya, his brother Durjoy Singha took the title Dharma Manikya and ascended the throne in 1713 and issued a coin in the year 1714. The Ahom King Rudra Singh once again sent Ratna Khandali and Arjundas as envoys to Tripura for the third time.

They were received by Dharma Manikya on 13 May 1715 and were given final farewell from the court on 31 May 1715 with letters and presentation to the King Rudra Singha conveying general assurance of friendship. No envoy was sent this time from Tripura. The kingdom of Tripura fell down from its position of glory during the reign of Dharma Manikya II. Dharma Manikya failed to give regular tribute to the Nawab of Bengal, so the Nawab was displeased with him.

The old *Rajmala* wrote that the Nawab of Dacca sent an army against him.

Dharma Manikya defended his country with the help of his general Ranabhim Narayan for eight months. The Mughal army went back to their own country without achieving success. The old *Rajmala* also states that Jagatram a descendent of Chhatra Manikya, tried to seize the throne of Tripura but was defeated. Jagatram got the assistance of Aka Sadik, a zamindar of Patpasha Pargana. Aka Sadik, being intimately acquainted with an officer Mir Habib by name, recommended the cause of Jagatram to him, and looked for the favourable opportunity of subjugating Tripura. The Mughal army under the leadership of Mir Habib had crossed the Brahmaputra river and entered Tripura before the King came to know everything about it. They were accompanied by Jagatram whose cause they apparently espoused. Aided by such a guide, they had reached the capital before the King could make any preparation for his defence. "Absolutely unprepared for such an attack, the Raja fled to the neighbouring hills, whereupon the fort of Chandigarh, which had been his residence, was stormed by the invaders and the whole of his kingdom fell under the latter's control." Mir Habib incursion with Tripura had been corroborated by *Tariki-Bangla* and *Riaz-us-Salatin.*

(u) Jagat Manikya's Period. Jagatram was enthroned with the condition of paying a substantial portion of the revenue to the Nawab of Bengal. In order to guard Jagat Manikya alias Jagatram against Dharma Manikya, and at the same time to obtain loyalty, a Mughal troop was kept at Udaipur under the command of Aka Sadik, who was nominated as Foujdar. Nawab Sujauddin being pleased with this incident honoured Mir Habib and conferred him the title 'Khan' and called conquered provinces of Tripura as Roshnabad meaning the land of light.' Sujauddin became the Nawab of Bengal in 1727 and so this incident took place not prior to this year. Dharma Manikya, however, appealed to the Nawab and recovered his throne. The Nawab granted him the zamindari right of the district of Roshnabad on a yearly rent of rupees five thousand. From then, the king of Tripura had been in possession of Roshnabad simply at Zamindar.

(v) Mukunda Manikya's Rule. Dharma Manikya was succeeded by his younger brother Chandramoni who assumed the title Mukunda Manikya in the year 1729. He was taken possession by the Mughals on the ground that he failed to pay tributes of elephants as wanted by the Mughals. He committed suicide after ten years of reign.

(w) Joy Manikya's Times. Rudramoni, next descendent of Jagannath Thakur, brother of Govinda Manikya, organised a national militia against the Mughals and made a surprise attack on Udaipur and occupied it. The Mughals being unable to counter his attack came to terms and left the capital. As a reward for this act of bravery, people selected him as King in preference to the sons of Mukunda Manikya. Rudramoni adopted the title Joy Manikya and ascended the throne in 1739. In the mean time Indra Manikya, a son of Mukunda Manikya, secured military help from the Nawab of Bengal and occupied the throne and released a coin in the year 1744. Joy Manikya left the capital and carried on administration from the Motai hills and with the help of some zamindars he repeatedly tried to regain power.

(x) Shamser Gazi's Rule. Vijay Manikya passed away at Dacca and Krishnamoni, Indra Manikya's brother, tried to recover Udaipur, the capital of Tripura. Shamser Gazi, an upstart Muslim of Dakshin-sik at the junction of Chittagong, Noakhali and Sabroom gave defeat to Krishnamoni and occupied Udaipur. The dethroned Krishnamoni wandered in the hills and forest for about a decade. Shamser Gazi set up Lakshman Manikya, a grandson of Dharma Manikya, like a puppet king for three years and later on took the throne for himself. He excavated many tanks, and granted rent free lands.[24] He also committed dacoities in many places.[25] According to *Krishnamala*, he was made captive and was shot dead at the mouth of a cannon by the order of the Nawab of Bengal. Ghe *Ghazinama,* however, stated that Abu Bakar, the Governor of Chittagong, was not happy with him and shot him dead at the mouth of a cannon at Rangpur Ghoraghat. Taking advantage of this situation, Krishnamoni recovered the power and was recognised by the Nawab as the ruler of Tripura.

III. Modern Period

(a) Krishna Manikya's Rule. With the fall of Shamser Ghazi, Krishnamoni, the son of Mukunda Manikya, took the title of Krishna Manikya and ascended the throne in 1760. Old Agartala became his capital. Very soon Krishna Manikya was indulged in quarrels not only with Reza Khan, the Foujdar of Chittagong, but also with the British. Taking advantage of the confusion caused by the revolution of 1760 at Murshidabad, the king of Tripura stopped the payment of revenues. So Reza Khan first sent his *dewan* to Tripura and afterwards he personally came in 1760 but the king refused to surrender. The representation of the East India Company stationed at Calcutta were keen to acquire territory and got interested in this matter and interfered. On 20 January, 1761, Governor Vansittart instructed the President and Council of the Factory in Islamabad to take action against the ruler of Tripura.[26]

Accordingly, Verlest, the chief of Islamabad, despatched Lieutenant Mathews with two hundred sepoys and two guns to Tripura on 25 February, of the year 1761. Realising that he could not stand against the Foujdar and the British, the two great enemies at the same time, Krishna Manikya submitted. Thus the English flag was hoisted over the plain parts of Tripura.[27]

Collector Marriot was made from the Chittagong Council on 15 March to settle and receive the revenues of Tripura. The Collector found the province desolated by the Nawab's troops and was compelled to take payments in instaiments as the Raja was very low in cash. The king was made to sign two agreements: in one he agreed to pay the original revenue of Rs. 1,00,001 together with Rs. 45,463 to pay for the accuses of the troops, and in the other to pay a Salami or Nazarana of Rs. 1,11,191 annas 6 and pies 3 both the thirteen monthly instalments[28].

Ralph Leak was then appointed the first Resident of Tripura and this way, the hitherto independent, Tripura was subjugated by the British. It is stated in the

Krishnamala, a life history of Krishna Manikya, that one Balaram Manikya, the heir of Jagat Manikya was recognised as the ruler of Chakla Roshnabad by the Nawab of Bengal. But within a short time Krishna recovered it with the support of Verlest, the Governor of Chittagong Factory. Abdul Razzak who was appointed as ruler of Chakla Roshnabad by Shamser Gazi began to harass Krishna Manikya by sudden invasions. He was arrested and killed by the Nawab of Murshidabad.

The revolt of the Khuchung Chan of the Kuki tribe was also suppressed by the king. During the later years of his rule, a dispute arose with the British over the settlement of Roshnabad. However, this dispute was settled and in 1782, the British Resident, Leak under the instruction of the Government of Bengal, took over the Zamindari of Chakla Roshnabad into Khas or direct management for ten years and finally was returned to the ruler of Tripura. The temple of Satero-Ratna or Seventeen jewels situated at Jagannathpur the foundation of which was laid by Ratna Manikya II, was completed by Krishna Manikya. He performed many sacrifices and donated lands to the Brahmins. He passed away on 11th July, 1783.

After the death of Krishna Manikya, quarrels broke out over succession. There were mainly two claimants to the throne—Rajdhar Manikya, the nephew of Krishna Manikya and Shri Durgamoni, the son of Lakshman Manikya. To avoid civil war, queen Jahnavi Devi took the administration into her own hands and ruled for about two years. During her rule, the subjects suffered from the worst famine in 1784–85.

(b) Durga Manikya's Period. The conflict between Rajdhar Manikya and Durgamoni Thakur was finally settled by Warren Hastings in 1785, who declared Rajdhar Manikya the king and Durgamoni the Yuvaraj respectively. After the expiry of Rajdhar Manikya in 1804, the quarrels again broke out on the same issue. The succession of Ramaganga Manikya, the son of Rajdhar Manikya, was challenged by Durgamoni. The ministers and members of this royal family were divided into two camps. Ramaganga Manikya occupied the throne in 1804, Durgamoni sought the British judgement in the court. In 1808 the British Government titled Durgamoni king and ultimately in 1809, Durgamoni ascended the throne under the title Durga Manikya. Durga Manikya died in 1813.

(c) Ram Ganga Manikya's Rule. A new litigation started in the British court between Ramganga Manikya on the one hand and three other claimants, Ramchandra Thakur, Maharani Sumitradevi and Sambhu Chandra Thakur. The British Government pushed forward the claim of Ramganga Manikya who ascended the throne for the second time in 1813 and died in 1826. Sambhu Chandra Thakur revolted but Kashi Chandra Manikya, who was the brother of Ramganga Manikya, ascended the throne in 1826 and died in 1829, made a peaceful settlement with Sambhu Chandra Thakur by offering him a pension of rupees five hundred every month.[29]

(d) Krishna Kishore Manikya's Rule. Krishna Kishore Manikya, the son of Ramganga Manikya, took over the throne in 1829. He shifted his capital westward to Natun Haveli. During his reign, the Kukis disturbed the British frontier villages on several occasions and the instigators of these raids were the friends and relatives of the King. It was for this reason, that Krishna Kishore Manikya was involved in trouble with the British government of India. Krishna Kishore Manikya gave most of his time in hunting, sports and merry making. As a result the state and zamindari reached the stage of bankruptcy at the time of his death. He passed away with lightning shock in 1849.

(e) Ishan Chandra Manikya's Times. Next, Ishan Chandra Manikya, the son of Krishna Kishore Manikya, succeeded the throne of Tripura on 1st February, 1850. To solve the financial problem, he appointed Balaram Hazari, the *dewan* who tried to collect taxes from the subjects in a very cruel manner. The outcome was that some tribal people under their two leaders Kirti and Parikshit revolted against the king.

This revolt which is known as Tipra Revolt of 1850 was ultimately suppressed by the King. The British government's soldiers of the 34th Native Infantry stationed at Chittagong revolted in 1857. They entered the territory of the king of Tripura and sought protection. But the king was not in favour of those sepoys. He gave orders to arrest and to deliver them to the British authorities. The Kukis accompanied by some dissatisfied citizens of the king raided Tripura in 1860 and 1861. They even crossed Tripura and plundered some villages within the British territory. The British government was highly displeased with the king of Tripura because of the latter's inability to prevent the trespass of the Kukis into British territory.

(f) Bir Chandra Manikya's Rule. With the death of Ishan Chandra Manikya, his brother Bir Chandra Manikya became the ruler of Tripura in 1862. With the accession of Bir Chandra Manikya, a new age ushered in Tripura. By introducing certain reforms in the western pattern, he made Tripura a modern state. The justice was administered more rapidly and systematically than before; the revenue increased; a budget system was introduced, and there were numerous other signs of progress in the government of Tripura. He abolished slavery and *sati* system. In internal reforms his chief adviser was Babu Nilmoni Das whom he appointed his *dewan* in 1873.

(g) English Annexation. Taking benefit of the Lushai revolt, the British government took away a tract of 850 square miles from Longai river to Dhaleswari river in an unjust manner. In 1871 a political agent was appointed to inhabit at Agartala with the special object of protecting British interests on the frontier, which suffered from Lushai raids carried out through the state into British territory. This post was abandoned in 1878. Bir Chandra Manikya was a versatile genius, a linguist and a musician. He composed hundreds of lyrics. It was he who first found the genius in young Rabindranath after reading his collection of poems *Bhagna-Hriday* (the Broken Heart). His court was full of great musicians, poets and scholars. Bir Chandra is compared to Vikramaditya of old India.

(h) Radha Kishore Manikya's Rule. Radha Kishore Manikya who succeeded the throne in 1897 was also like his father, a great reformer. He introduced modern system of education, reformed the departments of public health, agriculture and police and remodelled them on European lines. A thorough land reform had been carried out in his times and the result was that during his reign land revenue increased. He was a benevolent ruler who did his best to promote the well-being of his subjects. He established the Victoria Memorial Hospital at Agartala. He also built a temple of Jagannath, a school and a museum. The old residential palace was badly destroyed by an earthquake in 1897 and a new palace called the *Ujjayanta* was constructed at his behest. Radha Kishore Manikya was a famous patron of literature and learning. The *Tripura State Gazette* an official newspaper was first published during his reign. While setting up the Santiniketan Brahmacharya Vidyalaya and Visva Bharti, Rabindranath Tagore got a substantial amount of financial assistance from him. The Bengal Technical Institute of Calcutta which formed the nucleus of the present Jadavpur University, got a handsome donation from him.

Radha Kishore gave financial assistance to the great scientist Jagadish Chandra Bose for his researches in science. He also gave financial help to the blind poet Hem Chandra Bandopadhayaya. This enlightened and benevolent ruler expired in a motor accident at Benaras, in 1909.

(i) Birendra Kishore Manikya's Time. Just like his father, Birendra Kishore Manikya was also an enlightened and benevolent ruler. He founded a school for agriculture and constructed a small but beautiful palace on a mound at Kunjaban. The most noteworthy achievement of Birendra Kishore was the introduction of tea industry in Tripura. This industry increased the revenue of the state and gave employment opportunities to the people. He himself was an artist and also a painter. He patronised drama, music and literature. He died in 1923 at the young age of forty.

(j) Bir Bikram's Rule. Maharaja Bir Bikram, the son of Maharaja Birendra Kishore Manikya, ascended the throne in 1923. He was a minor at that time so the administration was entrusted to a Council of administration. His investiture ceremony happened in the year 1927. He was an enlightened benevolent ruler who did his best for an all-round development of Tripura. Prior to the commencement of the Second World War, Maharaja made a world tour and visited several places of Far East, Europe and America. These long tours enabled him to gain firsthand knowledge regarding the thoughts and ideas of the modern world. He improved agriculture and encouraged the *jhum* cultivators to take to plough cultivation. He also spent a large amount for the development of internal communication. It was due to his initiative that an aerodrome was constructed at Singerbeel near Agartala. He planned to establish not only a college, but a rural unversity under a scheme popular as the "Vidyapathan Plan".[30]

For this purpose he acquired a big plot of land now known as College Tilla on the south eastern side of Agartala town. But the Maharaja expired before the fulfilment of his dream. His desire for reforms could not be implemented due to the Second World War and during the war, he extended his co-operation to the British authority. The very first Tripura Rifles and the Tripura Mahabir Legion earned undying fame in the Arakan and Burma warfields.[31] To put a check to the tribals' desires to embrace Christianity, the Maharaja provided impetus to Buddhism and founded a Buddha Mandir at Agartala in 1946 known as Benuban Bihar. Nir Mahal, a palace built by the Maharaja on an island in the centre of the lake Rudrasagar, is one among the finest beauty-spots in Tripura. He composed many songs and wrote a historical drama 'Jayabati'. On the eve of 80th birthday of Rabindranath the Maharaja held a special Darbar and conferred the hororfic title 'Bharat Bhaskar' or Sun of India on the poet. The Maharaja died on 17 May, 1947 at the age of thirtynine. Prior to his death he decided to accede Tripura to the Indian Union.

(k) Kirit Bikram's Rule. Following the death of Maharaja Bir Bikram, his son and successor Kirit Bikram became the Maharaja of Tripura. He was a minor, so a Council of Regency under the presidentship of Kirit Bikram's mother Kanchan Prava Devi, was formed in order to run the administration. Within a few months after the death of Maharaja Bir Bikram, Tripura faced a great crisis.

The Muslims of Tripura and Comilla headed by Abdul Barik Khan also known as Gedu Mia conspired with a few persons of the palace for the annexation of the state to Pakistan and preparations had been made to invade Tripura. The Government of India took immediate cognizance of the situation and Tripura was protected and saved.[32] On the advice of the Government of India, the Council of Regency was then dissolved and Maharani Kanchan Prava Devi became the sole Regent on 12 January, 1948.

The Tripura Merger Agreement was signed on 9 September 1949 in New Delhi. Maharani Kanchan Prava Devi made the agreement on behalf of her minor son as well as in her capacity as the Regent of the state. After this agreement an administrator had been appointed who took up the administration of Tripura as Chief Commssioner on the 15 October, 1949. It became a Part 'C' State of India. There was no record of the status of the impartible zamindary of Chakla Roshnabad in this agreement. It was included into erstwhile East Pakistan, now Bangladesh.

Under the provisions of the North Eastern Areas Law of 1971, Tripura became a full-fledged State in 1972. The revolutionary activities and ideas in India had their impact on Tripura and the outcome was the growth of political consciousness in Tripura in the first half of the 20th century. The political movement in Tripura had two aspects; it gave its full favour to the national struggle for freedom in India and at the same time it launched a movement against oppressive measures of the princely administration. The side of the terrorist movement reached and shook Tripura. Many underground activities of Anusilan and Jugantar parties of Bengal used to come to Tripura not merely for political activities but also for the truth that Tripura was a safer shelter for them as the British police had ordinarily no authority to enter Tripura. Regarding the activities of Anusilan Samity in Tripura, R.C. Majumdar said:

> "For the purpose of training members the Anusilan had two farms at Belonia and Udaipur in Hill Tipperah. These were outwardly, and in part really, agricultural farms but they served mainly as centres for training. During day time the members worked as labourers in the field but at night they were given training in the use of different kinds of arms, and practised shooting in the neighbouring hills. They had to work hard and lived under strict military discipline."[33]

Famous *Chhatra Sangha* established probably in 1927 was also a centre of revolutionary activities in Tripura. Its members were supporters of the Anusilan Samity of Bengal. Within a very short time after the martyrdom of Lala Lajpat Rai, some pupils formed an organisation known as *Bhratri Sangha* which was originally a physical and cultural society and later became an important centre for revolutionary movement in the region, i.e., Tripura. Most of the members of the *Chhatra Sangha* became the members of the *Bhratri Sangha.* Besides these two *Sanghas* there were also other small pockets in different areas known by different names, like *Milan Sangha, Matri Sangha,* etc.

Then political robbery was committed on the 23rd day of Chaitra of 1932 at 8 p.m. in a shop near Agartala Municipality office. Five members of the Anusilan Samity who belonged to the group of Satish Pakrasi of Dacca had committed this dacoity. Money and ornaments were looted from the said shop. Three members of this party were arrested and sentenced to rigorous imprisonment. On 26 January 1930, some members of the *Bhratri Sangha* called for a strike in schools and observed independence day. The government expelled some students from their schools and arrested certain youth leaders of this organisation.

The Tripura Government signed a pact with the British Government by which it was decided that the British Government could arrest any suspected man or woman from the territory of Tripura. Most of the members of the *Bhratri Sangha* were released by the Government before 1938. In a meeting held in December, 1938 at Agartala, the members of the *Bhratri Sangha* prepared a resolution by which it was decided that they would follow the line of Congress. Henceforth, a new organisation came into existence in place of *Bhratri Sangha* and this was named as *Tripura Rajya Gana Parisad.* Sachindra Lal Singha, Hariganga Basak, Sukhamoy Sengupta, Umesh Lal Singha, etc., were the pioneers of this organisation.

This organisation tried to make itself popular among the people of Tripura and tried to establish relations with other political organisations of India. Its ideas and objects were same as of the Indian National Congress. It gave expression to public resentment against feudal privileges and championed the cause of poor peasants by putting forward the demands for land reforms. This organisation released a bulletin from time to time. It sent its representatives, Sukhamoy Sengupta and Tarit Mohan Dasgupta to the All India States Peoples' Conference held at Gwalior in the year 1946.

The Janamangal Samity

It was formed by some young and energetic youths of Agartala in 1937-38. It raised the demand for 'responsible government under the aegis of the Maharaja'. Bansi Thakur, Biren Datta, Pravat Roy, Sukumar Bhowmik and also Kirti Singha were the leaders of this organisation. In 1945, *Tripura Rajya Jana Sikhya Samity* was formed. This organisation had an important role in spreading mass education in the region, i.e., Tripura. Many primary schools were opened at many places. Biren Datta, Dasarath Deb, Sudhanya Deb Barma, Aghore Deb Barma, Nilmani Deb Barma and many more were the members of this Samity.

Tripura Rajya Praja Mandal was formed in 1946. This organisation was composed of the ex-members of *Janamangal Samity, Janasikshya Samity* and of certain communist-minded people. It fought for the realisation of responsible government by elected people. Jogesh Chandra Deb Barma and Bir Chandra Deb Barma were the president and secretary respectively of the said organisation. This organisation sent Biren Datta, Sudhanya Deb Barma and Bir Chandra Deb Barma as representatives in the All India States Peoples' Conference which took place at Gwalior in the year 1946. *Tripura Rajya Gana Parishad* also sent their representatives to this conference.

Disputes arose between the two delegations as to who really represented Tripura. Any way, both were allowed to attend the conference as fraternal delegations, without recognition being accorded to any one of them. During 1938–39 a Harijan organisation was started below the leadership of Sukhamoy Sengupta. Tripura Motor Workers Association was organised in 1940–41 with the initiative of Monohar Bandopadhyay, Ajamin Das and lastly Girija Chakraborty of Akhaura, *Dharmanagar Hitasadhani Samity* which was formed in 1940 by Kala Chandra Nath Choudhury of Dharmanagar and Makbul Ali Bhuiyan was basically a socio-economic organisation of Hindu-Muslim unity. Abdul Barik Khan alias Gedu Mia formed *Anjuman Islamia* in 1945 at Agartala.

It set up its branches in all Moslem majority areas of Tripura. Its aim and objects were to improve the integrity of the Muslims of Tripura in every sphere of their lives. Around the same time another socio-religious organisation was formed under the name *Tripura Rajya Moslem Praja Majlish* by Arman Ali Munshi and Farid Mia of Udaipur. This organisation functioned as a rival institution of *Anjuman Islamia* among the Moslem agriculturists. Revolutionary activities enhanced in the early part of 1939. Many revolutionaries were expelled from Tripura. Some of them like Sachindra Lal Singha, Sukhamoy Sengupta, Umesh Lal Singha and Ashu Mukhopadhayaya started to deliver their speeches against the government of Tripura in its bordering places.

So they were arrested by the British Government and handed over to the Tripura State Police who kept them in Agartala Central Jail without any trial and they were then released in the early 1945.

All complete political meetings as well as agitations were declared illegal during the Second World War. On 6 September 1942, the Government of Tripura issued a notification by which (i) the Congress Working Committee, (ii) The All India Congress Committee (AICC) and (iii) All Provincial and District Congress Committees were declared unlawful associations. To meet the effects of public agitation, the Maharaja approved Tripura Constitution in the year 1941. But these reforms failed to pacify the people who demanded a democratic government responsible to the public. In 1942-43 the Reangs led Ratanmani began their movement against the oppressions of the feudal system of society. However, their movements were suppressed ruthlessly by the royal forces. The year 1946 witnessed the formal inauguration of the *Tripura State Congress*. The *Tripura Rajya Gana Parishad* was merged with *Tripura State Congress.* Sachindra Lal Singha, Sukhamoy Sengupta, Umesh Lal Singha and Tarit Mohan Dasgupta and also many others were in the leadership of the Congress. It was then functioning as a district unit under the Bengal Provincial Congress Committee. They pleaded evil of untouchability, for spinning with *Charkha* and demanded a responsible government in the State. Their movement along the line of Indian freedom movement went on.

Language

In Tripura, the official language is Bangla. It is also the medium of instruction in several schools of the State. But in public schools catering to the children of the elite class and institutions of higher learning England language is used. In government offices English language is used.

In fact Bangla being the *lingua franca* of the State, it is commonly used in schools, colleges, offices, several clubs, theatres, cities and towns. So far so, Bangla dominates the scenario in majority of the newspapers, and out of about fifty five daily, weekly, fortnightly and monthly newspapers, magazines and journals as many as forty-eight appear in Bangla language.

It is, however, interesting to note that in English and Tripuri languages only two each appear while in the Manipuri languages three such publications. The census data spoken by all Scheduled Tribes in Tripura is as follows :

Table 1
Mother Tongue for Scheduled Tribes

Mother Tongue	*Number of Speakers*					
	Rural			*Urban*		
	Total	*Males*	*Females*	*Total*	*Males*	*Females*
1	2	3	4	5	6	7
All Scheduled Tribes						
Adi	9	6	3	3	1	2
Angami	5	1	4	3	2	1

(Contd.)

(Contd.)

1	2	3	4	5	6	7
Assamese	17	14	3	4	4	0
Bengali	1,03,637	52,702	50,935	3,492	1,749	1,743
Bhili/Bhilodi	1,265	642	623	0	0	0
Bhotia	1	1	0	0	0	0
Bishnupuriya	8	5	3	0	0	0
Bodo/Boro	6	4	2	0	0	0
Coorgi/Kodagu	1	0	1	0	0	0
Dogri	1	1	0	0	0	0
English	124	60	64	29	17	12
Garo	8,627	4,354	4,273	139	76	63
Gondi	2	0	2	0	0	0
Gujarati	734	372	362	0	0	0
Halabi	3	2	1	1	1	0
Halam	24,900	12,582	12,318	53	32	21
Hindi	2,574	1,388	1,186	82	43	39
Kabui	2,399	1,225	1,174	0	0	0
Kannada	6	4	2	0	0	0
Khandeshi	4	1	3	0	0	0
Kharia	2	1	1	0	0	0
Khasi	201	108	93	4	2	2
Kinnauri	1	1	0	0	0	0
Koch	30	15	15	2	0	2
Koda/Kora	2	1	1	1	0	1
Konda	3	3	0	0	0	0
Konyak	1	0	1	0	0	0
Korku	1	1	0	0	0	0
Korwa	6	6	0	0	0	0
Kui	1	0	1	0	0	0
Kuki	1,621	833	788	10	5	5
Kurukh/Oraon	4,313	2,189	2,124	41	12	29
Lahnda	16	9	7	0	0	0
Lepcha	0	0	0	8	3	5
Limbu	4	3	1	0	0	0
Lushai/Mizo	4,585	2,362	2,223	90	51	39
Malayalam	26	24	2	0	0	0
Malto	34	15	19	0	0	0
Manipuri	2	1	1	0	0	0
Mao	1	0	1	1	0	1
Maram	7	5	2	0	0	0
Marathi	11	8	3	0	0	0
Mishmi	1	0	1	0	0	0
Mogh	28,064	14,352	13,712	49	34	15
Munda	6,987	3,596	3,391	27	14	13
Mundari	87	52	35	0	0	0
Nepali	142	68	74	34	16	18
Oriya	2,013	1,050	963	69	39	30

(Contd.)

(Contd.)

1	2	3	4	5	6	7	8
	Paite	6	4	2	7	5	2
	Pochury	1	0	1	0	0	0
	Punjabi	1	1	0	1	1	0
	Santali	2,488	1,297	1,191	76	53	23
	Sindhi	10	6	4	0	0	0
	Tamil	73	39	34	1	0	1
	Telugu	14	7	7	0	0	0
	Tibetan	20	14	6	1	1	0
	Tripuri	6,35,398	3,22,724	3,12,674	9,632	5,194	4,438
	Tulu	15	10	5	1	0	1
	Urdu	48	26	22	0	0	0
	Others	8,705	4,546	4,159	220	129	91

Source: Census 1991.

Education

In the far-flung State of Tripura, the system of education could not make headway since long. But offer the integration of Tripura in India, consistent efforts have been made to provide basic educatinal facilities to the young boys and girls at Primary and Middle School stage. The next step in this direction was towards the advancement of High School and College education. The Census data for the literates and literacy rate by sex is given below:

Table 2
Literates and Literacy Rates by Sex—Tripura : Census 2001

Union Territory/ Districts	*Persons*	*Literates Males*	*Females*	*Literacy Rate of 2001 Persons*	*Males*	*Females*
Tripura	**2,036,159**	**1,156,824**	**49.65**	**73.66**	**81.47**	**65.41**
West Tripura	1,044,135	585,440	55.15	77.82	85.02	70.24
South Tripura	460,710	267,269	41.37	70.39	79.52	60.75
Dhalai	160,368	95,480	54.29	61.56	70.90	51.57
North Tripura	370,946	208,635	44.42	73.10	80.09	65.73

Source: 1991 Census

The general college are located in Sadar sub-division. The Sanskrit College of the State is situated at Agartala. About eight thousand students attend these colleges where about four hundred teachers impart instructions. Besides there are fourteen professional and vocational institutes wherein about three thousand students receive training in different professions and vocations under the supervision of 250 instructors.

As a result of this new development in the field of education, well-lettered, awakened and enlightened and socio-economically advanced section of the population is receiving different useful training and skill for job opportunities in future.

Table 3
Age, Sex and Marital Status for Scheduled Tribes

Age group	*Total*	*Never Married*	*Married*	*Widowed*	*Divor-ced*	*Unsp-ecified*
ALL SCHEDULED TRIBES						
Rural						
All ages	**8,39,264**	**4,64,812**	**3,45,796**	**23,996**	**4,572**	**88**
0 - 9	2,45,264	2,45,264	,0	0	0	0
10-14	1,08,011	1,06,980	889	59	70	13
15-19	78,738	68,429	9,934	84	278	13
20-24	61,529	27,326	33,135	297	770	1
25-29	70,345	10,366	58,448	648	877	6
30-34	56,438	2,561	52,405	795	675	2
35-39	53,639	990	50,874	1,251	521	3
40-44	36,198	435	34,026	1,365	371	1
15-44	3,56,887	1,10,107	2,38,822	4,440	3,492	26
45-49	31,080	214	28,921	1,689	255	1
50-54	25,044	169	22,216	2,435	222	2
55-59	16,433	93	14,553	1,700	87	0
60-64	18,821	126	15,225	3,316	154	0
65-69	10,036	57	7,989	1,920	70	0
70-74	10,586	95	7,609	2,817	64	1
75-79	5,290	47	3,738	1,468	37	0
80+	10,119	204	5,633	4,135	115	32
Age not stated	1,693	1,456	201	17	6	13
Urban						
All ages	**14,081**	**7,646**	**5,953**	**440**	**35**	**7**
0 - 9	2,712	2,712	0	0	0	0
10-14	1,744	1,725	13	3	1	2
15-19	1,744	1,601	142	0	1	0
20-24	1,337	821	503	5	8	0
25-29	1,467	451	993	19	4	0
30-34	1,202	155	1,030	12	5	0
35-39	1,200	51	1,116	23	10	0
40-44	705	27	646	30	2	0
15-44	7,655	3,106	4,430	89	30	0
45-49	609	15	561	32	1	0
50-54	381	13	319	49	0	0
55-59	283	9	227	46	1	0
60-64	223	7	166	50	0	0
65-69	127	8	79	40	0	0
70-74	124	3	70	51	0	0
75-79	50	1	25	24	0	0
80+	113	6	49	56	1	1
Age not stated	60	41	14	0	1	4

Table 4

Ever Married and Currently Married Women Belonging to Scheduled Tribes by Present Age, Number of Surviving Children and Total Number of Surviving Children by Sex

Present Age	*Total ever/ currently married women*	*Ever/currently married women with number of serviving children*						*Total surviving children*		
		0	*1*	*2*	*3*	*4*	*5+*	*Total*	*Males*	*Females*
1	2	3	4	5	6	7	8	9	10	11
ALL SCHEDULED TRIBES										
RURAL										
Ever Married										
All ages	**1,95,365**	**21,672**	**30,891**	**32,752**	**32,514**	**27,629**	**46,639**	**5,90,920**	**3,08,624**	**2,82,296**
Less than 15	603	511	47	21	0	0	0	89	49	40
15-19	8,901	4,856	2,947	648	116	52	0	4,799	2,463	2,336
20-24	25,303	6,534	9,396	5,893	2,195	649	206	31,485	16,045	15,440
25-29	35,526	3,720	7,469	9,780	8,083	4,173	1,948	79,437	40,818	38,619
30-34	27,613	1,599	2,958	5,190	6,768	5,679	5,188	85,633	43,877	41,756
35-39	23,140	920	1,564	3,039	4,544	5,055	7,842	87,616	45,191	42,425
40-44	16,843	658	1,165	1,950	2,621	3,203	7,088	69,056	36,028	33,028
45-49	13,904	491	915	1,464	2,120	2,433	6,323	59,706	31,506	28,200
50-54	11,439	509	909	1,318	1,700	1,850	4,935	47,624	25,423	22,201
55-59	7,704	325	680	836	1,103	1,147	3,477	32,556	17,440	15,116
60-64	8,196	489	870	942	1,135	1,132	3,329	31,986	17,208	14,778
65-69	4,739	265	509	489	617	694	2,009	19,056	10,292	8,764
70-74	4,524	297	551	483	580	604	1,786	17,165	9,101	8,064
75-79	2,356	148	291	212	314	349	906	8,881	4,800	4,081
80 +	4,461	321	604	470	607	597	1,582	15,582	8,248	7,334

(Contd.)

(Contd.)

1	2	3	4	5	6	7	8	9	10	11
Currently Married										
All ages	**1,75,022**	**19,448**	**27,418**	**29,965**	**29,656**	**25,078**	**41,316**	**5,30,023**	**2,76,185**	**2,53,838**
Less than 15	539	457	41	19	0	0	0	79	44	35
15-19	8,594	4,687	2,858	636	111	44	0	4,639	2,382	2,257
20-24	24,502	6,249	9,027	5,817	2,177	640	201	30,849	15,726	15,123
25-29	34,486	3,462	7,062	9,572	8,004	4,146	1,930	78,098	40,107	37,991
30-34	26,627	1,420	2,658	4,967	6,643	5,607	5,141	83,933	43,016	40,917
35-39	21,932	777	1,335	2,781	4,326	4,890	7,680	84,595	43,659	40,936
40-44	15,648	547	974	1,732	2,401	3,041	6,828	65,540	34,183	31,357
45-49	12,532	392	761	1,237	1,879	2,213	5,945	55,235	29,110	26,125
50-54	9,502	372	687	1,029	1,372	1,555	4,368	41,143	21,958	19,185
55-59	6,468	253	537	679	909	950	3,057	28,091	15,002	13,089
60-64	5,622	295	542	606	751	797	2,497	23,290	12,485	10,805
65-69	3,267	173	292	348	432	486	1,474	13,808	7,462	6,346
70-74	2,437	157	271	262	290	312	1,061	9,830	5,216	4,614
75-79	1,284	76	153	111	162	198	542	5,197	2,815	2,382
80 +	1,488	111	206	154	189	187	574	5,469	2,902	2,567
URBAN										
Ever Married										
All ages	**3,184**	**399**	**691**	**811**	**496**	**302**	**392**	**7,510**	**3,925**	**3,585**
Less than 15	14	10	1	0	0	0	0	1	1	0
15-19	127	74	36	9	2	1	0	64	32	32
20-24	398	101	167	85	27	4	3	449	230	219
25-29	653	96	198	219	92	28	13	1,144	601	543
30-34	507	31	115	190	92	51	21	1,133	578	555
35-39	455	35	54	137	106	60	60	1,250	672	578
40-44	261	12	27	53	62	41	62	870	446	424
45-49	203	7	23	43	38	45	43	649	347	302
50-54	149	8	20	19	22	25	49	529	270	259
55-59	111	3	8	16	17	16	44	433	239	194

(Contd.)

(Contd.)

1	2	3	4	5	6	7	8	9	10	11
60-64	90	8	14	12	11	13	26	287	147	140
65-69	67	5	8	6	10	3	25	220	113	107
70-74	64	3	10	9	9	5	21	207	108	99
75-79	24	0	1	4	2	6	7	83	36	47
80 +	51	2	7	8	5	4	17	179	97	82
Currently Married										
All ages	**2,781**	**356**	**630**	**749**	**442**	**253**	**295**	**6,351**	**3,343**	**3,008**
Less than 15	9	6	1	0	0	0	0	1	1	0
15-19	126	74	35	9	2	1	0	63	32	31
20-24	390	99	164	83	26	4	3	439	225	214
25-29	633	87	195	212	92	28	13	1,127	593	534
30-34	494	31	109	186	92	49	21	1,111	566	545
35-39	424	26	50	131	99	57	58	1,184	635	549
40-44	235	12	26	49	57	35	54	782	403	379
45-49	175	5	20	35	36	41	34	558	299	259
50-54	108	5	15	16	16	15	38	388	210	178
55-59	70	3	2	8	9	10	32	288	164	124
60-64	47	5	3	7	4	7	19	170	85	85
65-69	32	1	4	5	5	1	14	128	65	63
70-74	20	2	3	3	3	3	5	63	36	27
75-79	5	0	0	2	0	1	2	19	9	10
80 +	7	0	1	2	0	1	1	18	12	6

Source: Census 1991.

Notes: 1. 'All ages includes 'age not stated'.

2. Number of ever/currently married women in columns includes women not reporting number of surviving children.

3. The age groups having nil return are not shown.

Women

The folk dances and classical dances are a passion with the Bengali women living in Tripura State. Besides fine arts, instrumental and vocal music seem attractive to their natural taste. When Rabindra Nath Tagore started a silent crusade for the development of dancing and singing as fine arts, the echoes of the crusade were heard and felt in Tripura also. Today, although the *Devadasi* tradition has not been revived in the shrines of Tripura, yet in many families the young girls receive training in classical dancing at the hands of some gurus.

There have been much development to impart education to young girls, including higher education, in the urban areas. In the rural areas, efforts are being made to impart 3 Rs to the younger generation. Indeed women are becoming conscious of their basic rights besides performing numerous domestic duties. In the urban areas, more and more females are becoming library minded. The census data relating to married, unmarried, divorced/separated women and data relating to ever married/currently married women with their surviving children are given on just previous pages.

References

1. R.G. Basak, *History of North-Eastern India,* 1967, p. 223.
2. *Ibid.,* p. 231.
3. R.C. Majumdar, *History of Ancient Bengal,* 1971, p. 8.
4. *Ibid.,* p. 81.
5. *Ibid.,* p. 214.
6. *Ibid.,* p. 275.
7. K. Gupta, *Copper Plate* 5 of *Sylhet,* 1967, p. 194.
8. R.C. Majumdar, *Bangla Desher Itihals, Vol. II,* 1973, p. 480.
9. S.K. Chatterjee, *Kirata-jama-Krti,* 1974, pp. 45-46.
10. R.C. Majumdar, p. 486.
11. Tripura Education Directorate, *Rajmala,* Agartala: The Directorate, 1967, pp. 18–19.
12. S.K. Bhuyan, ed., *Tripura Buranji,* 1962, pp. 34-35.

13-14. N.R. Roychoudhury, *Tripura through the Ages,* 1977, p. IV.

15. James Long, "Analysis of the Rajmala" *Journal Asiatic Society of Bengal,* (1850), p. 13.
16. Abul Fazal, *Ain-i-Akbari, Vol. II,* translated by Jarret and Sarkar, Calcutta 1942, p. 130.
17. Kailas Chandra Singha, *Rajmala,* 1896, p. 62.
18. *Baharistan-i-Ghaybi,* Vol. II, translated by M.I. Bora, p. 537.
19. *Bengal: Past and Present, October, 1907,* pp. 50-52.
20. "Naubahar-i-Murshid Quli Khani" *Bengal: Past and Present,* Vol. 69, No. 132.

21. Bhuyan, p. 85.
22. *Travernier's Travel in India,* translated by John Philip. Calcutta: Bangabasi Office, 1905, pp. 551-52.
23. Bhuyan, pp. ix-xi.
24. J.N. Sarkar, ed., *History of Bengal, Vol. II,* pp. 425-26.
25. Singha, pp. 125-26.
26. *Noakhali District Gazetteer,* p. 23.
27. *Chittagong District Records, Vol. I (1760-1773),* Calcutta, 1923, p. 143.
28. Abdul Majed Khan, *The Transition in Bengal, 1756-75.* Cambridge: Cambridge University Press, 1969, p. 39.
29. Sinha, p. 159.
30. S.N. Sen, "Rulers of Tripura", *Chunta Prakash,* 6 January, 1929.
31. Tripura State Gazette *Sankalan,* 1971, p. 311.
32. Sardar Patel's Correspondence, 1973, Vol. V, pp. 426-27.
33. R.C. Majumdar, *History of Freedom Movement in India,* Vol. II, 1975, pp. 268-69.

13

Measures for Land Reforms and Their Implementation

Tripura is basically an agriculture based economy like most of other states of North-East. So, disputes regarding land are obvious and so are reforms to hand these disputes. Thus, certain land reforms have been introduced. The objectives of these land reforms have been "to remove such motivational and other impediments to the increase in agricultural production as arise from the agrarian structure inherited from the past and also to eradicate all elements of exploitation and social injustice within the agrarian system"[1]. For achieving these objectives, the Tripura Land Revenue Reforms Act, 1960 (hereinafter referred to as Tripura Land Reforms Act) provides for as below:

(a) The elimination of intermediaries,
(b) The tenancy reform targeted to scale down rent and confer on *under-raiyats* including share-croppers the security of tenure till they are brought into direct relationship with the government of the state,
(c) The fixation of ceiling on land-holdings and thus distribution of surplus land,
(d) The prevention of fragmentation over agricultural holdings.

Both government and people of Tripura welcomed cultivating immigrants from other neighbouring states as there was plentiful supply of virgin land in the valleys. But the influx of refugees resulted in the two-and-a-half times increase in population during the time 1951 to 1971 (from 6.5 lakhs in 1951 to 15.56 lakhs in 1971). The rapid growth of the population caused heavy pressure of population on land in this industrially backward state. The stress of population on land, combined with the effects of transfer, partition and forced sale to money-lenders, has led to the systematic increase in sub-division of holdings. As a consequence, the general tendency has been for the number of uneconomic holdings to increase. The percentage of operational holdings below 1 hectare increased from 62 in 1961[2] to 70 in 1972.[3] In 1971 around 89 per cent of the operational holdings in the state were below 2 hectares.[4] The smallness of the holdings caused a bottleneck in the utilisation of certain indivisible resources such as manpower, bullock-power and resulted in all types of dis-economies and deterioration of economic condition of the owners of uneconomic holdings. Another serious defect of the agrarian structure in Tripura is the inequality with the distribution of land. The Agricultural Census (1970-71) revealed that while 70 per cent of the households operate only 28 per cent of the total area of operational holdings, 11 per cent of the households use 46 per cent of the total area of operational holdings.

Also in the plains of Tripura, like in other states, the land-holdings are not only small in size but also fragmented. The fragmentation of holdings stood as a serious obstacle to agricultural development and complete utilisation of the land. Along with this factor, a large number of rural households in Tripura are landless. The landless people mostly depend on employment in agriculture which is not only seasonal but also irregular too. Only some of them cultivate leased-in land under share-cropping system.

The extent of land hunger in the state can be understood from the fact that in 1973 about 2.59 lakh people in rural parts including Scheduled Castes and Scheduled Tribes were landless.

"With a view to protect the interests of the tribal population, the tribal reserve areas were created by the erstwhile rulers of the state, but the boundaries of the reserve area were not well-defined and a large number of tribals have been living outside these areas. Taking advantage of the ineffective enforcement of law and poor financial conditions of the tribals, the non-tribals have acquired land from the tribals both within and outside the tribal reserve areas. Then again, the refugees from the erstwhile East Pakistan acquired land from the tribals without observing legal formalities and restrictions. As a result, a large number of the economically backward tribals have become either landless or holders of tiny plots of land" quotes a researcher.

Therefore, the review shows that the agrarian structure of Tripura have developed many defects which are obstacles to the improvement of agricultural efficiency as well as economic lot of the agriculturists. The Tripura Land Reforms Act, 1960 was passed and subsequently amended substantially 'with a view to removing the impediments against increase in agricultural production and removal of social injustice in agrarian system of the state'. After this, an attempt will be made:

(i) to analyse the provisions of land reform law and to evaluate its implementation,
(ii) to study the impact of land reforms over the rural economy, and
(iii) to suggest the appropriate steps for improving land reform legislation and its enforcement.

Elimination of Intermediaries

There existed various types of intermediaries between the state and the *raiyat* under the land system prevailing in Tripura prior to its integration with the Indian Union in 1949. The present Tripura Land Reforms Law provides that the Government may, by notification, acquire all estates and all rights, title and interests of every intermediary in such estates free from all encumbrances. After acquisition, every tenant holding or any land under the intermediary shall hold the same directly under the government as a *raiyat*. The intermediaries are entitled to retain homestead lands, lands under their individual cultivation, lands held as mortgaged, lands comprised in orchards or used for the purpose of live-stock breeding, poultry farming or dairy farming, lands comprised in and required for tea garden, mill, factory or even workshop.

All lands possession of which is retained by the intermediary will be offered for settlement with him as a *raiyat* under the government and he will be liable to pay land revenue at full rate also applicable to similar lands in the locality. The intermediaries are entitled to compensation as a sliding scale varying inversely with the amount of income from 2 times to 15 times of the net income, relying on the income group to which the claimant may belong to. In Tripura all intermediary interests were abolished. The tenants of the erstwhile intermediaries have turned *raiyats* under the state and as a result now their rights are permanent, inheritable and transferable.

The intermediary rights of about 29,000 intermediaries were eliminated and as many as 70,000 tenants occupying nearly 35,000 hectares of land have acquired *raiyati* rights under the government. The abolition of intermediaries and the direct settlement of land have caused a stronger sense of ownership in the minds of the tenants and provided the much needed incentive to them for the improvement of land. The land records maintained by the officials of the previous rulers were incomplete and unreliable. Now, under the provisions of Tripura Land Reforms Act, the government has prepared a record of rights for the whole state. The record of rights is not just beneficial for the *raiyats* but also useful to the state for effectively implementing the land reform measures. Thus, the abolition of intermediaries has resulted in the formation of direct contact between the state and the tenants, an improvement in the tenurial status of the tenants, the achievement of a uniform system of land revenue administration in the state and growth in land revenue.

(B) Reform Related to Tenancy

In Tripura leasing of land in *barga* system (share-cropping) is a common feature and an extensive area is cultivated under this system. During the course of the 1961 Census, an intensive study of sample households engaged in cultivation was done and 17 per cent of the land cultivating households cultivated leased land held from private persons or institutions for payment in money, kind or share and even more than 16 per cent of the cultivating households cultivated land partly held from the government and partly from private persons for payment in money, kind or share.

Though the proportion of *bargadars* (share-croppers) is not shown differently, yet it is estimated that the percentage of *bargadars* to total number of persons cultivating leased land is considerably high. Till the enactment of the Tripura Land Reforms Law of 1960 the *under-raiyats* and *bargadars* had no legal protection against rack-renting and insecurity of tenure. Under the said Act the rent payable by a *bargadar* has been fixed at one-fourth of the produce where the *raiyat* (landlord) supplies plough, and cattle and one-fifth of the produce where the *raiyat* does not supply plough and cattle. Also, in the case of rent payable by an *under-raiyat* in the upper limit has been fixed at four times the land revenue. The interests of an *under-raiyat* including *bargadar* in any land possessed by him as such is heritable but not transferable. An *under-raiyat* cannot be evicted from land except under any of the following grounds:

(i) if the land has been reserved for individual cultivation of the *raiyat* and is within the 'permissible limit',
(ii) if the *under-raiyat* has intentionally and wilfully committed such acts which impair the cost or utility of the land for agricultural purposes,
(iii) if the *under-raiyat* could not pay rent within the prescribed time, and
(iv) if the *under-raiyat* has sub-let the land even without the consent of the *raiyat.*

But, at the same time, the *under-raiyat* holding land *under-raiyat* owning more than a 'basic holding' (0.80 standard hectare in area) is allowed to retain some land.

Further, the *raiyat,* who has taken possession of land after evicting an *under-raiyat* therefrom, on the ground of personal cultivation, fails to cultivate such land personally in any year during the time of four years next following, the *under-raiyat* is entitled to be restored to possession of land from which he has been evicted. In order to prevent the malafide surrender of land, the law provides that the *under-raiyat* shall surrender land held by him only to the government which shall lessee out the surrendered land to any other deserving person and the lease shall receive the rights of the *under-raiyat.* The Act further provides that the government may, by notification with effect from any specified date, declare all lands held by *under-raiyats* in any local part to be their non-resumable lands. The amount of compensation payable by an *under-raiyat* for the non-resumable land will be determined by the government of Tripura.

This law aims at the protection of *under-raiyats* and *bargadars* against rack-renting and eviction. But the legislation, in the absence of effective implementation, failed to lower the rates of rent and alter the traditional system of sharing the cost of cultivation and the produce of the land. The Act fixed rent between one-fourth and one-fifth of the produce but even after eighteen years of its execution, the half of the produce is the common rate of rent in all the districts.

Though the rights of resumption of land by the *raiyats,* owning more than the basic hoilding, have been confined yet the eviction of a *bargadar* is a very common feature. In the absence of a record of rights of the *bargadars* and the effective enforcement of the legislative measures, the landlords are in a state to realise exorbitant rents from the *bargadars,* who are competing for the use of land, and evict them taking advantage of their inferior financial and bargaining power. During a field study of the Sekerkot village,[6] it has been identified that the landlords realise from the *bargadars* half of the produce as rent and evict them as per their whims and fancies.

What is worst is that most of the *bargadars* are not even aware of the legal provisions regarding rent or their rights over land. It is important to note that in order to evade the law, most of the landlords conceal the fact of share-cropping and take sufficient precautions to avoid the possibility of their leased-out land being recorded. Taking advantage of the existing land hunger and weak bargaining capacity of the *bargadars,* the landlords are able to lease-out land under 'concealed share tenancy' or outside the record arrangement.'[7] The collected data revealed that in 1974, 28 per cent of the cultivators in Sekerkot village were *bargadars.*

In Tripura, there are around 2.5 lakh operational holdings and if 5 per cent of them are assumed to be under share-tenancy then the number of operational holdings under share-tenancy will be about 12,500. But as per the Agricultural Census (1970-71), in 1971 the number of operational holdings under share tenancy was only 454.90 in North Tripura District, 116 in South Tripura District and 248 in West Tripura District. This shows that there was either large scale eviction of *bargadars* or widespread concealment of share tenancy after enactment of Tripura Land Reforms Act, 1960.

After second amendment, the Act of 1974 provides for the recording of interests of the *bargadars* in the record of rights for effective implementation of the legislative measures but this belated attempt with the existing enforcement machinery failed to achieve much success.

In view of this the government has recently launched a programme *Operation Barga* for recording the rights of *bargadars.* The same programme is being implemented with the active co-operation of the officials of the Department of Settlement and Land Records, the Sub-Divisional Officers, the Block Development Officers (BDOs), and the Village Panchayats. The government has decided to pay to the *bargadars* legal expenses upto Rs. 350 to enable them to establish their *barga* rights. As said earlier, in the absence of record of rights of the *bargadars* and sincere and serious attempts on the part of the administrative machinery, the *bargadars* are exposed to rack-renting and eviction. Further, in the absence of security of tenure, the *bargadars* are not in a position to get loan on easy terms for purchasing agricultural inputs.

Thus, the legislative measures could neither protect the interest of the *bargadars,* nor could they create the necessary conditions for improving agricultural productivity. Now an attempt is being made by the government for recording the rights of the *bargadars* within the land records to ensure security of tenure to the *bargadars* till ownership right is conferred on them.

Truely, the legislative measures for protecting the interests of *bargadars* and *under-raiyats* are ambitious, but the effective enforcement of these measures will remain a complex and difficult task so long as the *intense* demand for land continues to exist. With the past experience, it may be said that even if the existing share-tenancy is abolished legally by shifting ownership right to the existing *bargadars,* it will reappear in a different form only to complicate and confuse landlord-tenant relations. A lasting solution is possible only if the pressure of population from agriculture to non-agricultural pursuits.

(C) Ceiling over Land-holdings

The un-economic size of the large majority of land-holdings, inequality in ownership and use of land, and landlessness of a considerable portion of the serious defects of the agrarian system in the state. So the ceiling legislation in Tripura, as in other states, seeks to impose limits on the amount of land that may be held by a family. The Tripura Land Reforms Act, 1960 decided the ceiling limit at 10 standard hectares for a family of five members. For each additional members above five, the ceiling could be raised by 2 standard hectares subject to a limit of maximum of 20 standard hectares. For the purpose of ceiling a standard hectare means one hectare of *loonga* or *nal* (low land) or three hectares of *tilla* (high land) land. Then, the Act was amended and the Tripura Land Reforms (Second Amendment) Act, 1974 lowered the ceiling limit to 7.20 standard hectares with retrospective effect from the 24 January, 1971. The law provides for the fixation of ceiling at different levels, varying between 2 and 7.20 hectares, for families of different sizes. The ceiling has been fixed at 2 standard hectares for an adult single unmarried person or a sole surviving member of a family and 4 standard hectares for a family consisting of 5 members. In case of a person having a family of more than 5 members, the ceiling limit can be increased by 0.60 hectare for each additional member subject to a maximum of 7.20 standard hectares.

It is important to note that while under the principal Act a family of a person included all children and grand-children as per the Tripura Land Reforms (Fourth Amendment) Act, 1976, the family does not include married and unmarried adult sons who hold any land. The following types of land have been exempted from the operation of the Act:

(i) The lands held for the purpose of cultivation of tea, coffee or rubber and purposes ancillary to the cultivation of these products.
(ii) The sugar-cane farm operated by a sugar factory,
(iii) Farm used for cattle breeding, dairy or wool raising functions.
(iv) An efficiently managed farm on which heavy investments have been made,
(v) The land in compact block used as an orchard, and
(vi) The land held by a co-operative society.

The limit of ceiling on land-holdings is expected to reduce the disparities in the ownership of land, to increase the size of un-economic holdings by redistribution of land, and to make available surplus land for the purpose of rehabilitation of landless cultivators. But the fixation of ceiling at a very high level, the relaxation of ceiling limit for orchards, the efficiently managed farms and the inordinate delay in the enforcement of legislative measures rendered ceiling legislation ineffective; in that it failed to achieve its objectives.

It is estimated that the net available surplus land will be only about 800 hectares in the state.[8] This way, the fixation of ceiling, which is the most radical land reform measure, proved to be of little importance. According to the 1961 Census figures, about 89 per cent of the holdings in Tripura are below 2 hectares and only about .05 per cent of the holdings are above 12 hectares.[9] The Agricultural Census conducted by the Department of Settlement and Land Records showed that 89 per cent of the operational holdings are below 2 hectares and only about .02 per cent of the operational holdings (excluding tea gardens) are above 10 hectares.[10]

Thus, there was no justification in fixing ceiling limit at 10 standard hectares for a family of five members with the provision of additional 2 standard hectares for every member in excess of five, subject to the maximum limit of 20 standard hectares. It is a common experience that the intensity of cultivation is higher in smaller farms than in the larger farms. A family holding which coincides with a 'plough unit' is likely to be most productive if intensive method of cultivation is practised. A family holding is equal to 2.5 standard hectares as per section 2(h) of the Tripura Land Revenue and Land Reforms Act, 1960.

In Tripura, a holding of 2 standard hectares may be taken as a family holding and on the basis of this ceiling limit may be decided at 6 standard hectares, i.e., three times the family holding.[11] To ensure a reasonable standard of living to the cultivating family, some relaxation is essential in case of *tilla* land which is of inferior quality. But too much relaxation not only stands in the way of making available sufficient land for redistribution but also takes away incentives in order to improve land. On the basis of the recommendations of the Chief Ministers' Conference held in New Delhi on 23 July, 1972, the State Government has amended the Land Reforms Law and fixed the ceiling limit for families of different sizes at different levels ranging between 2 standard hectares and 7.2 standard hectares. But lowering of the ceiling is not possible to make sufficient land available for redistribution because of the following factors:

(a) 'Standard hectare' was defined as one hectare of *loonga* or *nal* or three hectares of *tilla* land. The big land-holders in Tripura in most of the cases, own, both *loonga* and *tilla* land. Information regarding the number of holdings and total land about to come under the operation of ceiling is not available. The intensive study of the sample households engaged in cultivation conducted during the 1961 Census reveals that only 1.1 per cent of the holdings are of the size, 5 hectares and above, including both *loonga* and *tilla* lands. As per the Agricultural Census only about 1.6 per cent of the operational holdings including both *loonga* and *tilla* lands are of the size of 5 hectares and above. So the available information shows that much land will not be found surplus even after lowering of the ceiling limit.

(b) It is quite possible that many substantial land owners have transferred land in anticipation of fixation of ceiling limit at a lower level. By lowering the ceiling with effect from 24 January, 1971 the legislation failed to rule out the possibility of such anticipatory land transfer. Then again, the change in the definition of the term 'family' enabled many substantial owners to retain land in the names of their major sons, who may or may not be interested in farming. It is also possible that unscrupulous persons may take advantage of inactive enforcement of legislative measures and evade law by resorting to *benami,* i.e., transfer of land on to friends and relatives. After this, the problem is that sufficient surplus land will not be available even after lowering the ceiling limit.

Whereas the land is needed for the purpose of rehabilitation of the landless agricultural workers, for the enlargement of the size of un-economic holdings and also for the settlement of the *joomias.* So it is desirable that the government should obtain from the tea estates all land in excess of their bonafide requirements. The fixation of ceiling is not an appropriate measure in case of tea plantations, but there is no justification in allowing the tea planters to keep vast area unutilised under their possession and to dispose land at the market price after it ceases to be used for the cultivation of tea. Out of 19,827 hectares of land settled along with the tea estates, less than 5,600 hectares are under the cultivation of tea. So sufficient land will be found surplus in the tea estates even after meeting their requirements of land for the purpose of cultivation of tea and purposes ancillary thereto.

The redistribution of surplus and un-utilised land under the tea estates together with the available culturable waste land of about 98.8 thousand hectares[12] will be there for the rehabilitation of the landless people. This appraisal leads to the broad conclusion that the impact of the fixation of ceiling on land-holdings has come far short of the expectations. However, there is the possibility of further reducing the ceiling limit and acquiring sufficient land from the tea estates specifically.

(D) Prevention of Fragmentation of Land

The Tripura Land Reforms Act provides to prevent fragmentation of holdings by prohibiting partition and transfer of land by way of sale, exchange, gift, bequest or mortgage with possession which create fragments, meaning thereby, a holding of below 0.80 standard hectares. It is common knowledge that smallness of a holding results in high cost of cultivation and consequently low returns. So prevention of fragmentation is a highly important land reform measure. But available information shows that the provisions of the Act relating to prevention of fragmentation have not been strictly enforced. Undoubtedly, the regulation of partition is not free from administrative difficulties. The co-sharers, unwilling for joint cultivation, may avoid formal partition and sub-divide land informally and it might be administratively difficult to prevent this.

The regulation of transfer by sale or mortgage, which are generally to be registered, is easier if the Department of Settlement and Land Records is sincere about it. It is indeed surprising that neither the principal Act nor the subsequent Amendments provide for consolidation of holdings. It is well-known that fragmentation of holding is a great obstacle to the fuller utilisation of land and development of agriculture. A meaningful and enthusiastic implementation of the consolidation programme, after conferment of ownership right over the tenants of the erstwhile intermediaries and *under-raiyats* (in respect of non-resumable land), and distribution of surplus land in excess of ceiling limit, will contribute considerably to the hike in agricultural productivity and output.

In Tripura, the problem of fragmentation of holdings is not as serious as it is in many other states. In the hilly parts, where *jooming* is practised, the question of partition or transfer does not arise and in the plains people have been living permanently for few generations with right to transfer interest in land. But still in the plains adjoining Bangladesh, where both Hindu and Muslim immigrants started taking settlement of land since the enactment of *Rajaswa Sambandhiya Niyamabali* in 1880, maximum of the holdings are fragmented.

The unrestricted right of transfer, partition and insistence of each co-sharer on getting plots in each type of soil area resulted in fragmentation of holdings.

(E) Special Provisions for Scheduled Tribes Category

Taking advantage from poor financial condition of the tribals, the non-tribals acquired land both within and outside the tribal reserve areas. As a result, a large number of the economically backward tribals have become either landless or holders of dwarf holdings. With a view to put restriction on transfer of land from tribals to non-tribals, the Tripura Land Reforms Act, 1960 provided that no transfer of land by a person who is a member of the Scheduled Tribes shall be valid until: (i) the transfer is to another member of the Scheduled Tribe, or (ii) where the transfer is to a person who is not a member of any such tribe, it is made with the prior permission of the government, or the transfer is by way of mortgage to a co-operative society.

Thus, the Act prohibited transfer of land by tribals to non-tribals without previous permission of the government. But owing to ineffective implementation of this legislative measure, an indiscriminate transfer of land from tribal to non-tribal took place in contravention of the legal provisions. Subsequently, the said (Second Amendment) Act, 1974 provided for the restoration of all lands transferred on or after January 1, 1969, in contravention of the Act, to the transferor or even this successor-in-interest. By keeping the lands transferred before 1st January, 1969 outside the scope of the Land Reforms Act, legal recognition was given to the transfer of land made before that date. This has been done as it is very difficult to restore to the tribals control of lands transferred long ago. The problem of restoration of tribal land is also highly complicated in view of the fact that in many areas the boundaries of the tribal reserve areas are not well decided. Then again, in many cases the present land-holders purchased land from non-tribals who earlier acquired land illegally from members of Scheduled Tribes.

It is also a reality that tribal lands have not only been grabbed by unscrupulous persons and money-lenders, but in many cases poor refugees from Bangladesh acquired such lands without necessary grant from the government due to their ignorance and contributed greatly to the development of land. If they are evicted from land, they will be displaced for the second time. Socio-economic considerations need that the interests of the economically backward tribal population of the state should be adequately safeguarded and at the same time care should be taken for a proper settlement of the economically poor non-tribals. The state government is quite aware of the problems of both the tribals and non-tribals. The work of restoration of alienated lands to the transferors is progressing satisfactorily. New resettlement scheme for the rehabilitation of about 3,000 non-tribal families affected by restoration of alienated lands, has also been finalised. Thus, the state government is executing the legislative measure regarding the restoration of illegally transferred land to the members of the Scheduled Tribes without causing any serious hardship to the economically poor non-tribals. The Tripura Land Reforms (Second Amendment) Act, 1974 repealed the orders of the former rulers (Tribal Reserve Orders of 1931 and 1943) under which the 'tribal reserve' was constituted. The 'tribal reserve' was generated to safeguard the interests of only five classes of tribals. There are nineteen classes of tribals in Tripura and majority of the tribals are living outside the tribal reserve. So the making of the tribal reserve was discriminatory in nature. Then again, the tribal reserve was not serving any useful purpose as transfer of land took place on wider scale in the reserved area. Even the king dereserved a part of tribal reserve in 1948 for increasing land revenue and rehabilitation of the refugees hailing from the erstwhile East Pakistan.

As the Tripura Land Reforms Act prohibits the transfer of land throughout the state from tribals to non-tribals without previous permission of the government, there is no requirement for retaining the concept of the tribal reserve. In order to protect interests of the members of Scheduled Tribes in the areas predominantly inhabited by tribals, the Tripura Land Reforms (Third Amendment) Act 1975 says that if any person not belonging to Scheduled Tribes intends to sell land within 42 *tahsils* and 133 villages specified in the Act, then the members of the Scheduled Tribes shall have the preferential right to purchase such land."

The Act provides for financial accommodation on easy terms for purchase of land by economically handicapped persons belonging to Scheduled Tribes. The right of pre-emption will not, however, bring any instant tangible benefit to the tribals, though in the long run it will give them an opportunity to acquire land with financial aid from the government. The Tripura Tribal Areas Autonomous District Council Bill, 1979 has been invoked for the purpose of constituting an Autonomous District Council for the areas predominantly covered by the tribals. The Bill is yet to receive assent of the President of India. It is expected that the proposed Autonomous District Council will be able to protect the interests of the members of Scheduled Tribes in a better and more effective way.

(F) Land Records of Rights

The preparation and maintenance of latest record of rights are essential pre-requisites for effective implementation of land reforms. The land records prepared during the rule of the former Maharajas were neither fully done nor reliable. In view of this the Tripura Land Reforms Act provided for preparation of a complete record of rights for the whole state. But the land records prepared during the last two decades do not show correct and uptodate position. So it has been decided by the state government to make a complete revision of record of rights in a phased manner over a period of 5 years starting from 1978-79.

Apart from updating the land records, the revision operation will be oriented towards recording of interests of the *bargadars* and *under-raiyats*.

Quick conclusion that emerges from the foregoing analytical study of the land reform measures and their implementation is that the impact of land reforms has fallen short of the expectations. The legislative provisions for the elimination of intermediary tenures have been implemented fairly effectively, but tenancy reform failed to bring any tangible benefit to the *bargadars* and *under-raiyats*. The fixation of ceiling on land holdings, that is the most radical land reform measure, proved to be of little importance. In the absence of any legislative measure for the consolidation of holdings, the agricultural holdings left fragmented. For a considerable period after enactment of land reform legislation, the Scheduled Tribes failed to get the protection they had been granted by the enactment. It has been observed that the implementation and enforcement of the legislative measures in most of the cases, are slow and ineffective. Legislation was enacted without generating the proper atmosphere, studying the likely impact and strengthening adequately the implementing machinery. A large section of the villagers are still negligent about the reform measures and the benefits flowing from them, and as a result, there is the lack of the needed local support for the implementation of land reforms. The preparation of total and uptodate record of rights, (including the record of rights of the *under-raiyats* and *bargadars*), which is a pre-requisite for the implementation of land reform measures, did not receive the importance it deserved. Therefore, the defective legislation and its ineffective implementation led to the frustration and disappointment of the small land-holders, share-croppers, landless agriculturists and economically poor Scheduled Tribes on the one hand, and enabled the well-to-do section to evade law, on the other.

The Act has been amended with a view to plugging the loopholes and removing the shortcomings, and there is still further scope for improvement. But even an ideal legislation is likely to remain a lifeless letter if it is not effectively implemented and enforced. It is also to be realised that delay in the implementation gives scope for evasion, creates feeling of uncertainty and retards agricultural development.

Thus, a separate and well-organised Land Reforms Wing should be created in the Revenue Department for a speedy implementation of land reform measures, keeping watch over the working of the land reform law and tackling future problems relating to land reforms. Land Reform Committees of the beneficiaries should be constituted at the village and block levels for enlisting local support and also well-planned educative propaganda should be launched in order to make the villagers conscious about their rights and responsibilities. The record-of-righs of the *bargadars* should be prepared as fast as possible. In case of any dispute regarding share tenancy, the onus of proof should lie on the landlord. Surplus land over the revised ceiling limit should be taken over immediately without giving any scope for its evasion. The lands found surplus over ceiling limit, culturable waste lands and surplus lands in some tea-estates should be distributed in a planned way for the rehabilitation of those who are landless (including Scheduled Tribes) and enlargement of the size of dwarf agricultural holdings. The work of restoration of illegally transferred land to the members of Scheduled Tribes should be done as early as possible. This will have a salutory effect on the tribal population from psychological point of view. Due care should be taken for the re-settlement of the non-tribals hurt by restoration of land to the tribals. The Tripura Land Reforms Act should be amended to restrict transfer of land from a tribal to another tribal with a view to checking land transfer from poor tribals to affluence tribals. Suitable measures should be taken to prevent *benami* transfer of land in the name of a tribal for the benefit of a non-tribal. Law should be enacted for the purpose of consolidation of fragmented holdings and in the initial stage consolidation programme should be implemented in selected areas. As a supplementary measure, adequate financial provisions should be made to fulfil the credit requirements of the beneficiaries of land reforms. A sound agrarian economy can be ushered in through scientific farm management, extension of credit facilities and just price policy, only after necessary ground is prepared by implementing fully the programmes of land reforms.

References

1. W.W. Hunter, *A Statistical Account of Bengal*, pp. 503-06.
2. *Census of India 1961*, Vol XXVI, Part III, p. 36.
3. Government of Tripura, *State Report on World Agricultural Census (1970-71) in Tripura*, pp. 36-37.
4. *Ibid.*
5. Government of Tripura, *Fifth Five Year Plan Proposals*, Vol. 2.
6. Sekerkot is one of the villages selected for intensive socio-economic survey during 1961 Census. It is situated at a distance of 14 kilometres from Agartala. Agriculture is the principal means of livelihood of the villagers.
7. N.C. Dutta, *Land Reforms and Agrarian Relation in Tripura*, Agartala, Directorate of Census Operations, p. 9.
8. Government of Tripura, *Draft Five Year Plan 1978–83*, p. 64.
9. Census of India, 1961, *op. cit.*
10. Government of Tripura, *State Report on World Agricultural Census (1970-71) in Tripura*, pp. 36-37.
11. The Committee on Size of Holdings of the Panel on Land Reforms, set up by the Planning Commission in 1955, recommended three times th^ family holding as the limit for ceiling. *Source:* Planning Commission, Reports of the Committees of the Panel on Land Reforms, p. 101.
12. Government of Tripura, *Fifth Five Year Plan Proposals*, Vol. 2.
13. Government of Tripura, *Draft Five Year Plan 1978–83*, p. 61.

14

Mythology and Archaeology

Religion occupies the highest place in any culture or community. And it is expressed through various ways like worship. But in Tripura, it is expressed through art and archaeology. This state has flourished as a repository of ancient religion and sculpture for centuries. It has archaeological evidence to show the presence of Buddhism, Brahmanism and various indigenous tribal religions at one time or the other in its past. The fact that Buddhism flourished in different parts of Tripura from very early times has been attested by the discovery of varous archaeological materials. The immigration of the people of plains ushered in the rise of Brahmanism and its diverse sectarian beliefs and practices in Tripura. This has also been substantiated by the archaeological stuff. The religious history of ancient Tripura is in fact the religious history of Samatata, the kings who ruled the region upto the twelfth century. The religious history of Tripura before the twelfth century is inextricably mixed with the religious history of ancient Sylhet, Samatata, Noakhali and Chittagong.[1] Hinduism is the earliest religion of Tripura and its different sects in their full-fledged form flourished here for long.

(a) Vaisnavism

The truths of Hindu religious history like the rise of the *Bhagavata* cult,[2] the dedication and worship of Vasudeva and his identification with Krishna are all shrouded in obscurity. It is difficult to ascertain rightly the antiquity of Vaisnavism in Tripura. In the Pauranic period, the worship of Vishnu, Narayana and Vasudeva were intermingled and formed the laterVaisnavism. Bhagvat and *Pancharatra* sects, the two moves of religious thought have been mentioned in *Harshacharita*.[3] The image inscriptions[4] show that no distinction existed between Narayana and Vasudeva or Vishnu.

The God of Puranas was the famous deity of the *Vaisnava* form of Hinduism, and Pauranic Vaisnavism was the most widely prevalent and popular religion of Tripura region from the sixth century AD.[5] A copper plate inscription of about Gunaigarh in Comilla speaks of a temple of *Pradyumnesvara* in Tippera. The discovery of a copper-plate of *Lokanath*[6] from Tippera proves that the worship of *Ananta Narayan* was existent in Tripura region during the seventh century. Another copper-plate inscription of Kailan also indicates that *Sridharanarata* was a *Paramavaisnava* and a worshipper of Purpushottam, a ruler of Tippera during the seventh century A.D. Therefore Vishnu in his different forms represents the existence of Vaisnava sect in this region from the sixth and seventh centuries A.D.[7] From the eighth century onwards, the growth of Vaisnavism may be proved by a number of Vishnu images of the Pala and Sens periods, discovered in different parts of Tripura. For the want of sufficient materials, it has not yet been feasible to identify the exact nature of early Vaisnavism in Tripura. During its formative period, Vaisnavism was probably influenced by Vishnu of *Vedic Brahmanism*, Narayana of the *Pancharatras* and also Krishna-Vasudeva of the Satvants.[8] Vaisnavism was the predominant religion during the ancient and medieval times. The doctrines of Vaisnavism, in course of time, have undergone changes and one of the major changes in Vaisnavism came about by the addition of the concept Vasudeva-Krisna. The earliest image of Radha-Krishna in Tripura dates back just to seventeenth century only. A copper-plate inscription of Bhajavarma[9] of Samatata, belonging to the 11th century A.D. has been found at Balaba in Dacca, thereby, attesting that *Samatata* was accustomed to *Brajalila* since this period. The worship of *Avataras* of Vishnu, of course, is a remarkable feature of Vaishnavism. A few specimens of the Narasimha icon from Tripura indicate that the devotees of Vishnu in Tripura, had not forgotten the *Avatara Narasimha.*[10] In this state, the discovery of the icons of Kurmavatara of Vishnu testifies to the prevalence of the worship of this *Avatara* during 11th and 12th centuries. In iconography, Kurmavatara though, has not been represented in hybrid form but in the sculpture the actual tortoise is carved. An interesting image of monkey-god Hanuman[11] is found standing in the *Virasana* pose at Unakoti in Tripura. This particular image shows the prevalence of the cult of Rama in Tripura during the eleventh and twelfth centuries. A very important noteworthy fact is that a big slab of stone with two human foot prints is depicted at Unakoti and this has been traditionally revered as a symbol of the Visnupada.[12]

(b) Saivism in Tripura

Vedic religion did not extend Tripura during the ancient period. The indigenous religious life of ancient Tripura centred round the worship of the fourteen gods of the tribals[13] and the aboriginal *lingas* and afterwards Brahmanical religion entered into Hill Tripura.

The non-Aryan god Siva's worship might have been prevalent in Tripura before the entry of Brahmanical religion. Linga worship of the non-Aryans was not just popular in Tripura, but during the early historical period it had also radiated its influence on people of the neighbouring states. The Vratyas[14] have proceeded to Tripura from other areas and they grasped the religious thought of *linga*-worshipper in the name of Pasupata cult.[15] Saivism also attained a predominant position alongwith Vaisnavism in Tripura during the 6th century A.D.

The copper-plate inscription of Gunaighar in Comilla also shows that the cult of Siva had secured royal patronage, in Tippera region. Saivism, as identified in the above inscription, is a federation of cults, which had combined in it the different cults of Rudra, Siva and the *Lingas.*[16] So far as Tripura is concerned, a collection of Siva, antiquities, attributable to the period from A.D. 700-1200 has come to light from Unakoti, Pilak and some areas of Tripura. Throughout the historical period, the various areas of Saiva images and Siva *lingas* are excellently carved in sculpture.

(c) Worship of Sakti

Sakti has been highly popular since very early times among its devotees seeking her grace for granting them good fortune. Saktism is the blend of Aryan and non-Aryan streams of thought. It is a federation of cults,[17] where the leading principle is the *tantric* way to reach the goal. Sakti worship prevailed originally among the Indo-Mongoloid[18] race of Tripura as *Mataikatarma. Tantricism* was practised and this tantric worship slowly developed in iconography. Tantricism was the predominant religion of Tripura from the eighth to the fifteenth centuries. The gods and goddesses representing the Saiva form of Hinduism became the deities of the Sakta-Tantra. But, it is difficult to establish conclusively the beginnings of this Sakta tendency in Saivism. In the religious history of Tripura Sakti appears to be the active goddess who enjoyed wide popularity in the 7th century.[19] An excellently carved bronze image of Sarvani has been discovered in Tripura and it belongs to early times of the Christian era. A large number of sculptures found in Tripura bear evidence to the popularity of the Sakta cult.

(d) Small Sects

Ganesa is not a Vedic god but is a Pauranic deity.[20] People took to his worship sometimes in the eighth century and this deity became considerably popular by the 11th and 12th centuries. It is very interesting to learn that there is evidence to prove the existence of the Ganesa cult in Tripura. The sculptures of Tripura also indicate that Ganesa has been worshipped as the elder son of Siva-Durga. He also accompanies his parents. There is also ample evidence to the popularity of the Surya cult in Tripura. The cult of the Sun appears to have come from North India where the Sakadvipi Brahmans[21] initially introduced the solar cult.

The inscribed image of Surya discovered from Deulbadi[22] in Tripura belongs to the seventh century and it appears to have become important during the medieval times. The images of Sun-god discovered in Tripura indicate the wide worship of Sun-god from eighth to the fifteenth century A.D.

(e) Icon Worship

The system of icon-worship had its roots in the non-Aryan devotion or *Bhakti*. The people have been paying homage to the icons of countless deities all over India. It is very difficult to ascertain exactly the antiquity of icon-worship in the state but it, however, occupied an important place in the religious life of the people of ancient Tripura.

(f) Cult of Vishnu Images

The majority of Vishnu images carry four arms bearing *sankha, chakra, gada* and *padma.* According to the disposition of the four attributes in different arms, twenty-four various forms of Vishnu have been identified.[23] The *Sayana* form of extant Vishnu images have not yet been discovered in Tripura. The Samapada Sthanaka types of Vishnu images are found everywhere in Tripura. The earliest Vishnu image made of stone seen at Pilak is an interesting variety of Trivikrama. It is a four-armed figure, its back right and back left hands are placed on the heads of the Gadadevi and Chakrapurusa respectively; the right front appears to have been in the *abhaya* pose, the left one probably holding a conch shell. This image is assigned to the eighth century.

The commonest form of the Vishnu image in Tripura belongs to the variety called *Trivikrama* as laid down in the *Agni Purana, Padma Purana* and the *Rupamandana.*[24] An image of Vishnu of the eleventh and twelfth centuries discovered at Baddarghat near Agartala, is a considered specimen of black stone sculpture, and the arrangement of attributes in its four hands follows the order of *Trivikrama.* The *gada* and *chakra* are held by the right upper and left upper hands, and *padma* and *sankha* through the lower right and left hands. The stone image of Vishnu of the 11th and 12th centuries from Unakoti belongs to the Acyuta[25] variety. The god stands in the *Sthanaka* posture. The *padma* and *chakra* are held by the right upper and left upper hands and *gada* by the lower right hand, while the rest is missing.[26]

The contemporary image of ten-armed Vishnu[27] standing in *Sthanaka* posture, accompanied by Lakshmi and Sarasvati, is of great iconographic importance. This image was found at Noagaon. The god carries in his eight hands *chakra, hala, dhanuk, sankha, gada, khadga, sara* and lastly *padma.* Its back right back left hands are placed on the heads of Lakshmi and Sarasvati respectively. An independent carving of Narasimha[28] in a well preserved condition has been seen at Unakoti. The god has a visible face of a lion and six hands. The god stands in the *alidha* pose on a half-round plain pedestal; has an ornamental crown over head, and the usual ornaments, necklace with a hanging locket, *vanamala,* sacred thread, etc., are displayed. His upper pair of hands hold *chakra,* and *sankha.* With two hands he is ripping open the entrails of Hiranyakasipu. The middle left hand holds the head of the demon, while the right is in the *Abhoya mudra.* This image may be assigned to the eleventh and twelfth centuries. The tortoise-incarnation, the second *Avatara of Visnu,* was found at Unakoti. In iconography *Kurmavatara* has not been represented in hybrid form; but in the sculpture the actual tortoise is carved.

(g) Icons of Saiva

Among the Unakoti sculptures are to be seen two representations of *Chaturmukha Lingas*[29] and both the specimens are assigned to the eighth and ninth centuries.[30] A *Chaturmukha Linga* is now worshipped at an elevation of the Unakoti hills. Famous three faces of Siva are carved on the three sides of its *Rudra-bhaga* and the back-face is damaged. Another *Chaturmukha Linga* of Unakoti bears four well-carved figures shown till the waist on the four sides of its *Puja-*

Bhaga.

There is uniformity in the four figures of *Yogi Siva.* In *Ekamukhalinga*[31] of the eleventh and twelfth centuries is now kept on the upward slope of the Unakoti hills. The shape of this *Mukha-Linga* is spherical and the face of Siva is carved on it. Though *Nrtyamurtis* of Siva were got all over India, yet Southern India is really rich in the images of the dancing Siva. An unique image of a twelve-handed Nataraja[32] of the eleventh and twelfth centuries was found at Khowai. The image comprises of a conical stele, with *Kirtimukha* in the centre, Ganga—on the right and Gauri on the left are also present. Between them, the god is shown dancing on the back of his mount. Two exactly normal hands hold the *veena;* two other hands are clasped over the head and two more hands make a canopy over the head with the Nagasesa holding it by the head and tail. The rest three right hands have *damoru, aksamala* and *varada mudra;* of the three left hands the lower one holds *kamandulu* and the rest contain *trisula* and *kapala,* i.e. the head. Uma-Mahesvara *murtis* have been discovered from different parts of Tripura. This type of composite Siva icons had gained popularity in Tripura. A nicely executed image of Uma-Mahesvara made of black stone was found at Udaipur, in which Siva is shown in *Sukhasana* with his consort Uma. The god and goddess are represented as bugging each other. He has the *utpala* in his upper right hand, while the normal right hand is placed on the right breast of Uma. The left normal hand embraces the goddess's waist below her left breast. The other left hand catches the trident. The right hand of the goddess embraces the neck of the god and the left hand holds a mirror.

This image is of the twelfth century A.D. Vaivahika or Kalyanasundara[33] forms of composite *Siva* icons indicate the story of Siva's marriage with Uma. A broken Kalyana sundara *murti* of Siva made of sand-stone was found at Unakoti. The image is badly mutilated and the lower part of the god alongwith the figure of goddess is damaged. The god stands on *Padmapitha* in the middle of a stele. The goddess stands in front of Siva; their feet partly rely on the two feet of the god. Near the waist of the god and on its left side stand the figures of a male and a female, representing probably Himayat and Menaka pouring water from *Kusha;* this illustrates the *Abhisekakriya.* This said image is also attributed to the eleventh-twelfth centuries. Siva's images of both *Ugra* and *Soumya* types, are illustrated by icons. The god Aghora-Rudra, *Ugra* form of Siva, was represented in a medieval sculpture of Tripura.

A unique colossal head-image of Aghora-Rudra[34] is carved on the rock-wall of the Unakoti-hills and this gigantic head bears the terrific aspects of Rudra-Siva. It keeps a vertically set third eye marked on the forehead. It wears an ornamented conical crown and ear-rings. The right half of the moustache is prominent while the left half is missing. The upper lip and the lower lip are marked by the two horizontal lines only. The vertical teeth are shown in between these two horizontal lines. The face bears the double contour lines on the upper part of the eyes and the brows are absent. The nose is flat and also the nostrils are flaring.

This image also belongs to the eleventh and twelfth centuries. Siva as Bhairava represents himself in a terrible form as the healer of all evils.

The image of Bhairava alongwith his consort *Bhairavi* was found carved on the stone-wall of the Unakoti-hills facing the stream Unakoti Chhaua. The colossal panel of the god and the goddess image measures 12 m × 10 m × 70 cm × 25 cm. The three-eyed god presses the rosary against his breast with his left hand while the right hand is missing. He wears the decorated crown, ear-rings and a pactoral round his neck.

(h) Images of Sakti

Images of Sakti in both *Ugra* and *Soumya* forms are carved on bronze or stone as the consort of Siva by the devotees who have organised a distinct cult after the eighth century.[35] Besides the *Ugra* form of Sakti different varieties of *Soumya* aspect have also been brought to light. An exceedingly charming bronze image of Sarvani is discovered at Hrishya-Mukha.[36] The eight-handed goddess stands in *Sthanaka* posture on the central *Padmapitha*. The front surface of the pedestal below the lotus seat is fully covered by floral and vegetal devices and a figure of conchant lion with one of its paws raised in the right corner. On the left side, all arms are missing excepting the lower one which holds a *ghanta*. On right, four hands are partly extant, and the first, third and fourth hands hold a conch, a discus and a sword respectively, while the remaining is missing. This image is assignable to the seventh and eighth centuries. A fine specimen of two-armed Durga[37] (*Soumya*) found at Unakoti is shown standing at the back of a lion. She wears a short necklace and a *Sari* fastened with an ornamental belt at the waist. This image is attributed to eleventh and twelfth centuries. The most significant icon is the *Mahisa Mardini* type whose independent worship is still popular throughout Tripura. Many images of Durga in her *Ugra* form have been discovered in Tripura. The goddess is almost invariably represented with ten-arms, while in the early medieval sculptures found in Tripura, she is very often found having only eight arms.

A different image of eight-armed *Mahisa-Mardini*[38] in stone was found at Pilak and is now housed in the temple of the Rajesvari Ashram at Muhuripur. The goddess stands in *alidha* pose. The right leg of the image is strongly placed on the head of the buffalo-demon and the left one rests on a plain pedestal. In the four hands on the right, the goddess carries the *asi, chakra, sara,* and *trisula* thrust into the physique of the buffalo and the four hands on the left holds the *dhanu, tanka, sarpa* and tail of the buffalo-demon. This image is dated to circa eighth century A.D. old.

A very interesting sand-stone image of Mahisa-Mardini of the twelfth century is erroneously worshipped as Kali in a temple near Kamalasagar at Kasba.[39] The ten-armed goddess holds in her hands *nakusa, trisula, sakti, chakra* and *abhaya,* yet other attributes are not clear. She wears *jatamukuta,* and the *Jatas* are spread over both the sides of the head in an orderly manner. The *vahana,* the lion is shown in the middle part of the stele. The kneeling demon with folded hands rests on a plain pedestal.

A *sivalinga* is present in front of the demon and this is a rare evidence in the field of Hindu iconography. This image has been assigned to the 15th century A.D. An interesting sand-stone image of eight-armed Vaisnabi[40] of the fifteenth century A.D. from Amarpur is shown seated in the *lalitasana*-posture with Garuda below her seat. The goddess gracefully holds *sankha, chakra, gada, khadga, dhanu, sara.* The famous icon of the four-armed goddess, Kali, locally called Tripurasundari[41] is worshipped in the temple of the Tripurasundari at Udaipur. The goddess stands in *Sthanaka* pose on the body of Siva. She wears the *jatamukuta,* a *mundamala* comprising of thirteen human skulls. The upper and lower hands on the right hold the *vara* and *abhaya* and those in left, *Khadga* and *Munda.* This image is attributed to the fourteenth and fifteenth centuries back.

(i) Miscellaneous Images

Several images of the Sun-god have been discovered from different parts of Tripura. A very important image Surya[42] was found at Pilak and is now worshipped in Rajesvari Asram at Muhuripur. This image comprises of a semi-circular stele. The lower part of the Sun-god is hidden up to thigh by the body of the car. The Sun chariot is drawn by seven horses. The central horse kept in a rectangular shaped niche faces outwards and the remaining six, three on each side, are represented as prancing. Aruna is placed in front of the deity and the two side-figures have their knees and legs uncarved and indicated as inserted in the pedestal. In the present example the Pala style of the eighth century is well-marked. A sand-stone icon of Surya of the eleventh century found somewhere in Tripura presents some development in the treatment of the iconic type. This image is now preserved in the house of Maharaj Kumar Sahadev Bikram Kishore Debbarman of capital, i.e., Agartala.

Further, four images of Ganesa were found at Unakoti. Of them, the two *Sadra-Bhuja* and *Astabhuja* Ganesa deserve attention. They are rather unusual[43] and are of considerable iconographical interest. They stand in *Stanaka* posture. *Sadra-Bhuja* Ganesa has three tusks and *Asta Bhuja* Ganesa has four tusks. They hold *Narakapala, Akshamala, Gada, Khadga, Trisula* and *Pasa,* etc. The images are datable to the eleventh and twelfth centuries old.

Another seated Ganesa[44] is found on the same rock-wall of Unakoti. His four hands are very small. The god holds the *trisula, gada, sankha,* and *padma.* In the sculptures of Unakoti, another nicely executed image of four-armed Ganesa[45] made of sand-stone is shown seated and he holds *Parasu, Sankha, Aksamala* and *Vara-Mudra.* Both the images are assignable to the eleventh and twelfth centuries A.D. A stone image of four-armed Ganesa[46] of the eighth and ninth century from Pilak deserves special attention in this connection. It appears that the upper right and left hands carries *Kalpalatas* and the lower right hand *Modaka* and the lower left hand is not clear. The long trunk is lying across the chest and belly and is turned towards the right, perhaps touching *Modaka*. Below *Padmapitha,* also a rat vehicle is extant.

(j) Buddhism

State of Tripura and its adjoining regions became an important unit of Buddhism since the period of Asoka and continued to be so for several centuries thereafter. A copper-plate of Gunaighar proves that Buddhism flourished here around A.D. 507-508.[47] Prior to the sixth century, the *Mahayana* form of Buddhism, had found its way all over Tripura. The renowned Chinese pilgrim, Hiuen Tsang, came to India during the seventh century A.D.[48] In the course of his visit of Bengal, he found in Samatata thirty Sangharamas with about 2000 priests, all of the *Sthavira* school.[49]

Another Chinese pilgrim Sen-Chi stayed in Samatata, and he found that Mahayana Buddhism had been established in different parts of Samatata mainly through the patronage of the Khadga dynasty. In this regard, a copper-plate of Sridharana Rata[50] gives us the information that, at the request of Joyanatha, a royal gift was made in favour of the Ratanatraya, although Sridharana Rata was a Vaisnava. It is right from the eighth century onwards that Tantric Buddhism flourished and it became the most widely prevalent and popular religion of Tripura from the eighth to the twelfth centuries. Tantricism slowly found expression in iconography and the gods and goddesses of *Tantric* Buddhism became the common deities in the Tripura of the eighth century. The art and iconography of the same duration prove that this time the *Mahayana* sect began to be eclipsed by Vajrayana Buddhism.

(k) Viharas in Archaeology

These Viharas have been a symbol of religious sculpture and these may be said to be cloisters of Buddhist monks. The Buddhist Vihara became an important religious and cultural centre throughout Tripura from the sixth century till date. The monasteries were the centres of education and religion.

The monastery at Gunaighar was a great centre of Buddhism learning around A.D. 507-508.[51] Gunaighar is a place near Comilla where there was definitely an ancient Vihara. Salavana Vihara was another such centre situated inside the Lalmai-Mayanamati mountain range. The famous archaeological exacavations under the auspices of the Government of Pakistan have traced this Vihara. It was established by the Deba dynasty in the seventh or eighth century A.D.[52] A huge Buddhist establishment existed in the ancient Pattikera near Comilla[53] in the eleventh century. There is yet enough scope of study about the Pilak Vihara which was situated at Belonia in South Tripura. On the evidence of the mounds still found at Pilak we know that this holy place was a Mahayana Buddhist centre in the eighth and ninth centuries. This Vihara is infested with various mounds, icons of Buddhist and Hindu deities and ruins of temples. A number of old images, gold coins, terracotta temple-plaques and the sealing with the clear depiction of the *stupa* and the Buddhist creed have been found here.[54]

Stupas

A *stupa,* i.e., pillar generally constructed as part of the religious architecture particularly relating to the Mahayana sect. The inscribed terracotta seals found at Pilak depict the Buddhist *stupas* in miniature. These antiquities of Pilak, tell us that the *stupa* was as popular here as elsewhere. However, in Tripura *stupa*-worship was not probably given due importance. The icon, instead, became the major object of worship.

Iconography

Several standing and seated images of Buddha of the medieval period have been discovered at different places in south Tripura. These icons indicate the great popularity of image-worship. In stone, the most notable instance is the standing image of Buddha[55] at Pilak. The image consists of a conical stele of which right half is broken alongwith right arm. The left hand holds the hem of the garment. The head is shown with an *Usnisa* and the conventional close-curled hair is not clear. A miniature *stupa* is placed on the left side of the head of Lord Buddha. The image can be dated to circa the eighth century A.D. A sand-stone image of seated Buddha is also found at Pilak. The Buddha is shown seated in *Buddha-Padmasana* on a semi-circular *Padmapitha* with his hands in *Yoga-Mudra.* The image is depicted with an *Usnisa* and the conventional close-curled hair and ear-lobes hang downward. The image may be attributed to the ninth century A.D of course so old. Avolokitesvara, the god of love and compassion, was a favourite god of Tripura and in it the traces of the grace and attributes of both Visnu and Siva of Hinduism are discernible.[56] Avolokitesvara was popular in *Mahayana and Vajrayana* sects of Buddhism. A broken image of standing Avolokitesvara[57] endowed with two arm was seen at Pilak and is now preserved in the Tripura Government Museum.

This bronze image consists of a semi-circular background with a beaded and edged border. The border is ornamented with flames at intervals and a conical motif at the top is properly placed. The god stands in the *sthanaka* pose on a double petalled lotus resting on a plain pedestal. The left hand carries a lotus with a stalk and the right being in *Varada-Mudra.* This image also may be assigned to ninth century A.D. The terrific god Hevajra[58] is associated with *Akshobhya* and in him one finds resemblance with the terrific aspect of Siva.

A fine image of Hevajra,[59] Saktibirahita, seen at Dharmanagar in north-east Tripura is of great iconographic interest. The image has a thin coating of gold. The god is shown standing in *Ardha-parvanka-Nrtyasana* pose. On left side, the palms of the five hands are missing. He has eight heads, and sixteen hands, which carry skull-caps containing various animals and a deity. Miniature dancing figures of eight goddesses are kept in eight directions round the god. This image belongs to the eleventh century A.D.

God Marichi holds a place in the Mahayana and *Vajrayan* pantheon and she is *Vairocanakulodbhava.* An interesting stone image of Marichi[60] of the eighth and ninth centuries was found at Pilak and is now worshipped in a temple known Vasudev-badi at Muhuripur. The goddess stands in *Pratyalidha* pose on a plain pedestal. The image of this three-faced and six-armed goddess is badly mutilated and has suffered badly from peeling. The three right hands hold possibly the *sara, vajra* and *parasu* while *dhanu, parna-pichchhika* and *Tarjani Mudra* are in her three left hands. An image of the goddess Chunda[61] formed of sand-stone was found at Pilak and is now worshipped in the Rajeswari Ashram at Muhuripur.

The image is badly mutilated. The eighteen-armed goddess is placed in *Vajaparyankasana* on the central *Padmapitha.* The two normal hands hold *Dharmachakra Mudra. Vajrasattva, Ghanthapani* and five *Dhyani* Buddhas with their individual halos are carved over the upper part of the stele. This image is datable to circa eighth and ninth centuries. The census data about religions adopted by the people of Tripura is given below :

Table 1
Religion for Scheduled Tribes

Scheduled Tribe	*Rural*			*Urban*		
	Total	*Males*	*Females*	*Total*	*Males*	*Females*
1	2	3	4	5	6	7
ALL SCHEDULED TRIBES						
All Religions	**8,39,264**	**4,26,741**	**4,12,523**	**14,081**	**7,484**	**6,597**
1. Buddhists	1,26,006	64,179	61,827	777	440	337
2. Christians	41,547	21,429	20,118	939	562	377
3. Hindus	6,70,900	3,40,738	3,30,162	12,305	6,460	5,845
4. Jains	23	13	10	4	0	4
5. Muslims	445	200	245	28	11	17
6. Sikhs	4	3	1	0	0	0
7. Other Religions and Persuations	331	176	155	28	11	17
8. Religion not stated	8	3	5	0	0	0

Tripura, thus, to conclude, has been a haven for the coexistence of several religious sects and denominations such as Vaisnavism, Saivism, Sakhtism, Buddhism alongwith their respective cults of animatism, animism, magic and fertility and the like. The kings from time to time took active interest in the diffusion of religion. Archaeological evidence further proves that there was toleration among the various sects. A king of one religion is generally found donating land for the cause of another religion. Religious bigotry never did vitiate the atmosphere. In spite of the existence of several religious sects, the people led a peaceful life. The rise and fall of all these sects had never been at the cost of bloodshed. It stands in sharp contrast to the horrible state of affairs in medieval Europe caused by genocide in the name of the Inquisition unfortunately.

References

1. N.R. Roy, *Bangalir Itihasa: Adiparva,* Reprinted ed. Calcutta, 1959, p. 446.
2. H.C. Roy Choudhury, *Materials for the Study of the Early History of the Vaisnava Sect,* (Calcutta, 1936), p. 161.
3. Bana, *Harshacharita,* Uchchhvas VIII.
4. *Epigraphia Indica.* Vol. XXVII, p. 27; *Epigraphia Indica.* Vol. I, p. 124; *Epigraphia Indica.* Vol. II, p. 359.
5. *Indian Historical Quarterly* 6 (1930), p. 40.
6. *Epigraphia Indica.* Vol. XV, p. 301.
7. R.C. Majumder, *Bangla Desher Itihasa, Prachin-Yuga,* Calcutta, 1973, p. 35.
8. K.G.A. Goswami, *A Study of Vaisnavism,* p. 4.
9. *Epigraphia Indica.* Vol. XII, p. 37.
10. JAS. Vol. XVIII, Nos. 1-4, Calcutta, 1976; Ph. No. 12.
11. Tripura, Directorate of Education, *Unakoti* (Agartala, 1972) Plate XVI.
12. *Ibid.,* Plate XX.
13. *Tripura District Gazetteers;* (Agartala, 1975), p. 388.
14. R.C. Majumdar, ed., *History of Bengal,* Vol. I, Calcutta, *1971,* p. 404.
15. R.G. Bhanderkar, *Vaisnavism, Saivism and minor Systems,* (Poona, 1928), pp. 121-24.
16. R.C. Majumdar, (ed.), *History of Bengal,* Vol. I, (Calcutta, 1971), p. 404.
17. Swami Tattwananda, *The Vaisnava Sects, Saiva Sects, Mother Worship,* Calcutta, p. 13.
18. J.N. Sarkar, *India through the Ages* (Calcutta, 1951), p. 35.
19. N.K. Bhattasali, *Iconography of Buddhist and Brahmanical Sculptures in the Dacca Museum* (Delhi, 1972), pp. 203-05.
20. Vasudeva Upadhyay, *The Socio-religious Condition of North India* (Varanasi, 1964), p. 269.
21. H.D. Bhattacharya, "Minor Religious Sects" in R.C. Majumdar, ed., *The Age of Imperial Unity* (Bombay, 1953), p. 465.
22. R.C. Majumdar, *History of Bengal,* Vol. I, p. 549.
23. V.V. Vidyabinod, *Varieties of the Vishnu Image,* Calcutta, 1920.
24. V.V. Vidyabinod, *Vishnu Murti Parichay,* (Calcutta, 1917), p. 5.
25. Kalpana Desai, *Iconography of Visnu,* p. 157.
26. Tripura Unakoti, Directorate of Education (Agartala 1972), Plate VII.
27. *Tripura District Gazetteers* (Agartala, 1975), Plate V.
28. ASI, AR, 1921-22 (1924).
29. Tripura Directorate of Education, Unakoti (Agartala, 1972), Plates VIII, IX, X.
30. R.D. Banerji, *East Indian School of Medieval Sculpture* (Delhi, 1933) p. 111, Plates II (b) and (d).

31. Tripura, Directorate of Education, Unakoti (Agartala, 1972), Plate IV.
32. Bhattasali, pp. 110-16.
33. R.C. Majumdar, ed., *History of Bengal,* Vol. I, 1971, pp. 445-46.
34. N.R. Roy, p. 623, ASI, AR. 1921-22 (1924). Calcutta, pp. 86-87.
35. R.C. Majumdar, ed., *History of Bengal,* p. 407.
36. *Tripura District Gazetteers* (Agartala, 1975), Plate IV.
37. ASI, AR. 1921-22 (1924). Calcutta, pp. 86-87.
38. JAS. Vol. XVIII, Nos. 1-4; Calcutta, 1976, Photo No. 8.
39. Bhattasali, p. XIX.
40. K.P. Sengupta, ed., *The Rajmala;* Vol. III, Agartala, p. 163.
41. Tripura, Department of Education, Director General of Archaeology, Inspection Notes, 1952, p. 3.
42. JAS. Vol. XVIII, Nos. 1-4, Calcutta, 1976, Photo No. 9.

43-45. ASI, AR. 1921-22 (1924), Calcutta, pp. 86-87.

46. JAS. Vol. XVIII, Nos. 1-4; Calcutta, 1976, Photo No. 15.
47. *Indian Historical Quarterly,* Vol. 6 (1930), p. 55.
48. M.L. Roy Choudhury, *Bharatvarser Brhattar Parichay* (Calcutta, 1959), p. 171.
49. S.B. Dasgupta, *Obscure religious cults* (Calcutta, 1962), p. 10.
50. R.G. Basak, *History of North-Eastern Frontier,* (Calcutta, 1917) p. 249.
51. *Indian Historical Quarterly,* Vol. 6 (1930), p. 40.
52. *Desh,* No. 15, (1969), p. 195.
53. N.R. Roy, p. 633.
54. *Tripura District Gazetteers* (Agartala, 1975), p. 390.
55. JAS. Vol. XVIII; Nos. 1-4, Calcutta, 1976. Photo No. 5.
56. J.N. Banerjea, "Iconography", in R.C. Majumdar, ed., *The Age of Imperial Kanauj* (Bombay, 1955), p. 277.
57. *Tripura District Gazetteers* (Agartala, 1975), Photo VI; JAS. Vol. XVIII, Nos. 1-4, Calcutta, 1976, Photo No. 1.
58. Bhattacharya, *The Indian Buddhist Iconography* (Calcutta, 1958), pp. 157-58.
59. Bhattasali, p. XIX.
60. JAS. Vol. XVIII, No. 1-4; Calcutta, 1976; Photo No. 25.
61. *Ibid.,* Photo No. 10.

15

Rich Land and Other Resources

As we have already stated elsewhere that economy of a state depends largely on its stock of natural resources. Culturable land is the most basic wealth of a State since it is available for perennial use to yield products year after year. The quantum of reproducible resources does not depend simply on what is given in nature but also on the skill with which these are put to productive use conserving their total stock and improving upon their productive capacity. The land surface in Tripura can be largely divided into hilly terrain and low and flat valleys. The latter, being better culturable, can obviously support more persons per hectare than the former. Therefore, the population concentration in Tripura reflects the relative abundance of flat valley lands.

This proves for the fact that the density of population is not evenly distributed among the three districts of nearly equal size in area as shown by the table that comes next.

(a) Distribution of Area and Population in Districts

Every district in Tripura is so small in size that the district may conveniently be taken as the unit for the purpose of delineating the spatial distribution of resources. Land, rivers and forests are the major natural resources in the state. The Oil and Natural Gas Commission (ONGC) has undertaken drilling operations only recently in search of mineral oil and natural gas. Table 1 shows the broad pattern of the district-wise distribution of natural resources in Tripura. Physiographically, the lands in Tripura may be broadly divided into river valleys, mid-uplands with intermittant broad/narrow *loongas,* i.e., broken plateau and hill ranges/sub-ranges. The soil texture in the flat river basins ranges from sandy clay loam to clayey and is also suitable for cultivation of *aus, amom* and *boro* paddy, sugarcane, jute, potato, mustard, *rabi* and *kharif* vegetables, etc. These are the main agricultural crops produced in the state. It is, therefore, easy to draw that the district having the largest area of flat river basins will also be agriculturally most resourceful and prosperous. These are mainly rain-irrigated lands and there is scope for providing other types of irrigation arrangements. West Tripura with the largest area of river valleys is, therefore, most densely populated and intensively cultivated.

For the purpose of cultivation, next in importance are mid-uplands with intermittent *loongas,* i.e., broken plateaus with coarse sandy loam to loam in soil texture. On uplands of normal slope upto 15° land slope, the *aus* paddy, mesta, sugarcane and ground-nut, chillies and *kharif* vegetables can be raised. These lands are exclusively rain-irrigated and there is little scope for any other type of irrigation and also for growing more than one crop in a year.

Table 1
District-wise Distribution of Natural Resources in the State

Description of Resources	*West Tripura*	*North Tripura*	*South Tripura*
1. Hill Ranges	Parts of Baramura and Atharamura Ranges.	Longtarai, Shakhanunokoti and Jampai ranges	Debtamura Baramura (major parts), Kalajhari – Atharamura (Small part), Takka Tulsi Ranges.
2. River Valleys	Khowai, Howrah and part of Gumti major river valleys and Kalachara, Sonainala, Jahar Nala, Burima and Rangapania Nala, etc. minor river valleys.	Dhalai, Manu, Deo and Juri	Larger part of the Gumti (above 90 per cent Muhari and Manu Nala (Minor)
3. Hydro-electric Project and Water/River power potential.	Dam on Khowai river to control floods and improve irrigation.	Earth Dam on river Manu to control floods and improve irrigation.	Gumti Hydro-Electric Project: already installed with 10 MW power production capacity.
4. Average Annual Rainfall.	250 cm.	231 cm.	307 cm.
5. Forests Reserved and Protected forests	1,434.88 sq. km.	2,364.39 sq. km.	2,161.30 sq. km. 5,960.57 sq. km.
6. Mineral Deposits (as estimated by Geological Survey of India).	Glass sand 200,000 tonnes Plastic clay 914 tonnes, Natural gas and oil.	Limestone (not economically exploitable), Lignite (not economically exploitable), Clay deposits suitable for ordinary pottery and roofing tiles.	Lignite (not economically exploitable), small pockets of plastic clay and several gas seepages.
	Ground Water (artesian condition)	Ground water (artesian condition)	Ground water (artesian condition)

Source : Department of Agriculture, Govt. of Tripura.
Geological Survey of India.

Those uplands having more than 20° land slope are suitable only for horticultural and forest plantations. The soil in fat valley lands at the foot of hills and hillocks ranges from sandy clay loam to clayey loam. These lands are highly fertile where *aus* and *amon* paddy, sugarcane, jute, groundnut, sesamum, chillies, pulses, *rabi* and *kharif* vegetables are generally grown. Sandy loam to silty clay soil dominate the main hill ranges and sub-ranges. These are suitable for forest and horti-plantations.

The slope of the ranges are, of course, put to use for raising agricultural crops by the shifting cultivators. This is possible since top soils on the hill slopes become fertile as a result of accumulated leaf falls though this is mined out, so to say, in one agricultural operation by the *Joomias* (shifting cultivators). Thus, after one agricultural season the plot becomes barren.

(b) District-based Distribution of Land Resources in the State

In the West Tripura District come parts of Barramura and Atharamura ranges and the Khowai, Howrah and parts of Gumti Major river valleys besides five minor river valleys, named, Kala Chara, Sonainala, Johar nala, Burima nala and also Rangapania nala. This district contains the largest area of plains watered by river basins. No wonder, almost one-half of the total population of the State is concentrated in this district.

The second half of the population is nearly equally divided between the North and South Tripura Districts. The South Tripura District contains Deotamura—Baramura (major part), Kalajhari—Atharamura (small part) and Tulsi hills ranges. The river valleys falling in this district are the largest part of Gumti (above 90 per cent) and Muhari and the main river valley, Manu Nala. Most of the hilly terrain comprises the North Tripura District where lie the major hill ranges, named, Longtarai, Shakhan—Unakoti and Jampal.

Five rivers—the Dhalai, Manu, Deo and Juri flow from this district but their basins are of narrower dimensions. There are 1,212 villages in the district inhabited by 4,05,009 persons according to the 1971 census.

Here, the district-wise classification of agricultural area, irrigated area and production of agricultural crops are indicated and it can be seen that the West Tripura District produces the largest amount of rice that is the staple food in the State. Since the density of population is also the highest here, a large amount of food is imported into area from another two districts. The total irrigated area in the state is very meagre, being just about 10 per cent of the entire area under rice production. Because of the predominance of flat lands, both the West and the South Districts are better irrigated than the North District.

In both these districts, there is still vast scope for spread of irrigation facilities and to raise 3 crops in a year in larger areas in the districts. It is also possible here to further diversify the crop pattern, specifically, in growing *rabi* crops, such as, wheat, oilseeds, pulses and potato. Sugarcane has been successfully raised on the flat mounds (tillas) in the state so that with availability of finance, the production of this crop can be enhanced substantially in the North and South Districts. This will, of course, depend on the development of sugar and/or *gur* making industries. The one sugar mill recently began in the South District has raised demand for sugarcane in the area, but it is facing stiff competition with the *gur*-producing cottage industries in the matter of sugarcane procurement.

Jute and mesta production is focussed in the West and South Districts which will further go up with the growing demand for raw jute and mesta from the jute mill under construction close to Agartala in West Tripura District. The pattern of development that has been emerging clearly indicates that while West Tripura grows more rice, *rabi* and fibre crops, the North Tripura area will have to produce more rice and *rabi* crops besides sugarcane and the South Tripura should produce more rice, *rabi* crops, sugarcane and fibre crops.

The distribution of land resources again suggests that both the North and South Districts have considerable prospects for the development of various kinds of plantations on the hill slopes. Though land is one of the most significant and scarce resources of the State, yet it has been subjected to heavy erosion on account of the practice of shifting cultivation on the hill slopes. The adverse effects on soil are not confined to the hills alone. Even the plains are affected as these are subjected to frequent floods when the silted up rivers burst their banks following heavy rainfall. Thus, any plan for proper management and utilisation of lands must essentially be based on proper soil conservation measures including the solution of the difficulty of shifting cultivation.

(c) Livestock Population

Tripura has a great number of livestock population consisting of cattle, buffaloes, goats, ducks, pigs, fowls, pigeons, rams, etc. The district-wise distribution of livestocks as shown in the following table closely looks the proportionate distribution of human population. This is because, livestock rearing is still not undertaken on a commercial basis but as a part of subsistence economy by the rural households who often combine agriculture, animal husbandry and poultry to provide for the subsistence needs of the family. This is the reason why the breeds are all indigenous and of poor quality.

Therefore, under the plans many schemes have been undertaken to improve the breeds, as large areas on the uplands can be suitably developed as grazing fields, and fodder production can be augmented by using hill slopes that are otherwise unsuitable for agricultural operations.

(d) Fisheries Business

Due to hilly terrain, very few rivers in Tripura provide perennial water resource for fishing purpose. It is estimated that the state has a total impounded water area of 4480.55 hectares distributed among the districts as below:

Regarding the water area the South District leads, particularly following the construction of Gumti Water reservoir as a part of the Gumti Hydro-Electric Project. In the North District, at Kumarghat, the Regional Fish Breeding Farm, as per the North Eastern Council scheme has recently been started over an area of 20 hectares to produce 40 million fish seeds per annum for distribution within the North Eastern States.

(e) Forests

Big parts of the hill ranges having slopes above 20° are not suitable for permanent form of cultivation. These ranges were once covered by virgin forests. But as a consequence of reckless felling of trees, especially during the Second World War and afterwards, and the widespread practice of shifting cultivation, valuable forest resources have been very much depleted. Most of the hill ranges are now without any useful tree forests but are covered by unproductive low vegetal cover of shrubs and coarse grasses. Only some fire-hardy species of trees stand in isolated patches: 3,885 sq. km. of reserved forest area covers 36.4 per cent of the total geological area of the State but tree forests cover only 370 sq. km. area while the rest, 774 sq. km., is under unproductive low vegetal growth and bamboo forests.

Thus, there is vast scope for undertaking plantation of valuable forest species in the catchment areas of rivers. This is also necessary to erosion of hill slopes and silting up of river beds and recurrent floods in the plains. From the time of First Five Year Plan, the stress was laid on the afforestation programme. The District-wise distribution of reserved and guarded forests and new plantations raised are shown in following table.

Since most of the major hill ranges fall in North Tripura, the area under forests is the largest there 66.75 per cent and South Tripura comes next with 60 per cent. West Tripura, having the largest area of river valleys and plains, has the maximum area under agricultural crops and the smallest area under forests 42.6 per cent. According to the Forest Department's estimates, the growing stock of forests in the state is 8,54,271 cubic metre of plywood, 41,303 cubic metre of match-wood, 19,91,557 cubic metre of other hard wood, 80,67,165 tonnes of bamboo and 10,00,000 tonnes of thatch grass.

The estimated annual present yield of timber is 94,290 cubic metre and this is quite inadequate for the population of the state. With the progress of economic development and urbanisation, per capita consumption of timber will gradually rise from the present level of 0.05 cubic metre per capita per annum. The physiographical characteristic of the state clearly indicates that forestry, besides agricultural cash crops, will have to act as the main base for industrialisation programme in the state.

Already, wooden furniture industry has emerged as one of the most flourishing cottage industries. The state government too has planned to start one paper mill in the North District and a plywood factory in the South District. There are good prospects for the development of rubber-based industries which will thrive on the recent rubber plantations in the state. Over the last ten years, the state sponsored the raising of rubber plantations in about 625 hectares through an investment of Rs. 22 lakhs. These plantations yielded 20,600 tonnes of rubber in 1978 and it is expected to go up to 25,000 tonnes in 1979. It is being planned to raise high-yielding rubber plantations under an area of 5,000 hectares.

Most of the rubber plantations are now concentrated in the South District though in future it may be raised in the other two districts also. For meeting the growing needs of timber and fire-wood and industries, as also to serve as the main soil conservation and *joomia* rehabilitation measures, growth of forests almost holds the key to achieving a steady socio-economic development of the State. Tripura's undulating terrain has a heavy annual rainfall suitable for tea and certain other plantations. The best form of use of lands on the hill slopes and mounds would be through the raising of plantations. For this would make it possible to raise annual crops continuously without generating soil erosion. But for a variety of reasons, excepting some small-sized tea plantations, no other organised plantation industry was developed till recently.

Under the Five-Year Plans, certain schemes have recently been undertaken for raising rubber, cashew nut, citronella, coffee, and horticulture plantations. Except for rubber and horticulture, other plantations are still in the highly nascent stage. Whatever development has taken place in this regard, a distinct locational pattern has already emerged. While most of the tea plantations are focussing at the North and West Districts, most of the rubber plantations fall in the South District. Pineapple is the most important item in horticulture plantations, and the West District leads in its production, even if the North and South Districts also produce substantial quantities..

(f) Shifting Cultivation vis-a-vis Soil Conservation

The whole gamut of land-use planning in Tripura is vitally linked with the soil conservation measures particularly aimed at checking soil erosion caused by shifting cultivation. In fact, the scheme for settling the *joomias* by establishing colonies in plains was undertaken right from the First Five Year Plan, so that they could take to plough cultivation. The scheme continued up to 1968-69 settling 21,747 *joomia* families in some 59 *joomia* settlement colonies. By and large, they were allotted valley-lands suitable for paddy cultivation. Though a good number of families deserted the colonies yet it cannot be ruled out that many *joomia* families have since taken to wet rice cultivation. But the problem of *joomia* rehabilitation still remains. Since the beginning of the Fourth Five Year Plan, it has become the practice of settling the *joomias* on *tilla* lands through adoption of suitable soil conservation measures, such as, bench terracing and graded bunding of the plots.

Again, the Forest Department has also been rehabilitating the *joomias* in the forest lands under the *taungia* system of plantation.

(g) North Eastern Council (NEC) Scheme of Fifth Plan

In the Fifth Plan, NEC's *joom* control scheme has been started in a few river catchment areas in the state. It is an integrated approach to the problem of settling the *joomias* in permanent cultivation as a part of soil conservation steps. It covers all aspects of agriculture, horticulture, forestry and soil engineering. The forest department is engaged in executing the scheme in the upper reaches of the following river catchment parts in the North and the West Tripura Districts:

(a) North Tripura

1. Kewribari sub-catchment of Juri catchment (2 units)
2. Dasda-Anandabazar sub-catchment of Deo catchment (2 units)
3. Chailangta sub-catchment of Manu catchment (2 units)

(b) West Tripura

1. Ganganagar sub-catchment of Khowai catchment.

According to a report, "In each unit will be developed 62.5 hectares of orchards, 10 hectares of forest plantations, 2 hectares of water area for pisciculture, 5 hectares of rubber plantation, 40 hectares of homestead land, one school, one ringwell, 50 units of poultry, 50 units of piggery and approximately one km of approach road from the main road and 30 hectares of reclaimed land for permanent cultivation. The Agriculture Department on the other hand, has been executing the scheme in the West Tripura District on the 4 units Howrah River Catchment area at Patni, Belabari, Sib-thakurpara and Jarulbachai.

Here each family will be provided with 1.4 hectares of developed land fit for raising two crops a year. The *tilla* lands will be developed by bench terracing or graded bunding, depending on the degree of the slope. In addition, one hectare of land will be allotted for homestead, poultry farming, kitchen gardening and horticulture. For each unit, thirty hectares of horticultural crops and twenty hectares of other plantation crops will be developed. The water reservoirs will be constructed for providing irrigation and pisciculture.

The NEC scheme may be quite suitable for the river catchment areas but this alone cannot solve the problem of shifting cultivation and the solution to this problem has to be sought within the larger context of planning proper soil use. It is an accepted fact that any plan for Tripura's land use must tackle the problem of putting the hill slopes and uplands to continuous productive uses. All such lands are not equally suitable for all types of uses. Some are suited to agriculture, some to horticulture and other plantations and some to forestry. These lands, therefore, require to be classified into capability classes on the basis of slope, soil texture, soil structure, soil depth and the susceptibility to erosion. Pending the detailed survey, lands may roughly be classified according to the degree of slope alone. Agriculture may be undertaken on lands up to 20° slopes under appropriate soil conservation measures. Beyond this and up to 45° slopes orchards and pastures may be raised. For forest plantations all lands having above 45° slopes may be used."

(h) Power/Energy

Tripura's power resources are quite meagre. The Gumti river in the South Tripura District is only source of hydro-electricity in the State. The Gumti Hydro-Electric Project, completed in 1976, has a capacity of 10 MW. Due to non-availability of coal, the thermal power potential can also not be explored in the state. If, however, natural gas is found commercially exploitable, the thermal power may be generated in West Tripura District region from the natural gas. At present the power needs of North Tripura and parts of West Tripura Districts are met from power supplied by state of Assam.

The land-use pattern and general demographic characteristics do not yet indicate any sharp differences in the levels of development of the three districts. One of the cause for this is that, since Tripura's overall development is as yet extremely low, the regional disparities within the State have not yet been exposed. The development of the three following sectors, still, contain possibilities for the West District's development at a quicker pace than for the other two. Agartala, located in the West District is the capital city and is a sprawling urban agglomeration. The pace of development of urban amenities in this town in respects of communication, transport, education, treatment of disease and water-supply is the maximum. Institutions of higher education and hospital facilities are all concentrated heavily in West Tripura as is evident in the following table.

We have already said that Tripura is industrially backward. In the absence of any mineral deposits and an adequate transport network, whatever industries have so far been developed are all in the cottage and small industrial sector. In the Fifth Plan, of course, the establishment of three medium-scale industries was planned. And accordingly one *Khandeswari* mill has been set up at Bagafa in the South District; one Jute mill is under construction near Agartala in the West District while the said proposed paper mill to be set up at Kumarghat in North District is yet uncertain. The district-wise distribution of medium-scale and small-scale units and industrial estates as shown in Table 14.9 shows the disparities in development. Unless positive steps are taken to jack up the industrialisation programme in the two other districts, the regional disparities within the state will carry on and may be further accentuated.

When Tripura joined the Indian Union in 1949, this infrastructure was so precarious that even the state capital, Agartala, was not linked with the sub-divisional headquarters. Communication between the capital and mofussil regions, during the princely rule, was maintained through the neighbouring districts of Bengal which were located in East Pakistan (now Bangladesh). Therefore, in the

Five-Year Plans high priority has consistently been extended to the building of roads. With the construction of 200 km long Assam-Agartala road, Tripura's isolation from the rest of the country has ended. It also helped in making a link between Agartala and the sub-divisional headquarters in the northern part of the state, such as Khowai, Kamalpur, Kailasahar and Dharmanagar by constructing feeder roads. Next in list of importance was the completion of the building of all-weather Agartala-Sabroom road which links the state capital to the different sub-divisional headquarters in the South District region.

Also the construction of a network of roads has to large extent helped in exploitation of resources which are widely spread out. The railway lines are almost non-existent except for a short stretch of 12.35 km. from Patharkandi in Assam to Dharmanagar. The joining of the remote interiors with the centres of growth, markets, towns and the national highway is of vital importance. At the same time, the construction of roads in Tripura is quite difficult and costly on account of the hilly terrain, and the problems of availability of road building materials and workers. Yet, over the last 30 years road development in Tripura has been highly impressive. The total length of all kinds of roads now exceeds 4000 km as against just 300 km when Tripura joined the Indian Union. The district-based distribution of non-municipal PWD roads stands as follows:

1.	West Tripura	898.15 km.
2.	North Tripura	1274.77 km.
3.	South Tripura	1408.24 km.
	Total	3581.16 km.

This expansion of roads may look like a levelling up of inter-district disparities in economic development. South Tripura, otherwise lying behind West and North Tripura, is much ahead of them in respect of roads.

Thus, to conclude Tripura is though an agricultural state, it contains numerous natural resources. The only problem is that utilisation of these resources could not be made well. Now that the phase of development has commenced and things have began to change for the better, there is a lot of scope for improvement of this state of North-Eastern India.

16

New Planning

In the previous chapter, we have had a peep into natural resources of Tripura and this chapter presents a picture of planned economic development. Present chapter which is an edited version of a write up of Arun Kumar Gangopadhyay give accounts of development till 1970s in Tripura.

"Economic planning is essentially a process of adjustment between economic ambition and limitations. The adjustment may not only be a painful experience but quite often it is so. Tripura today presents a poignant scene of a grim compromise between economic ambitions and limitations. This situation serves as the back-drop of the development drama that goes on in Tripura.

The Tripura of yesteryear had a stagnant, semi-feudal and subsistence economy in the pre-independence period. But the princely state was free from economic stresses and strains at that time. The reasons are not far to seek. With a small population and economic aspirations, it did not experience the strangling hold of the severe limitations of resources. There was neither the pressure of population on land, nor the pressure of unemployment on the social structure and economic potential. Tripura was self-sufficient in food, and did not feel the need for industrial enterprise. Before 1949, it was all quite on the economic front in Tripura despite a very backward economy.

Since its merger in the Indian Union in 1949, Tripura has made a gradual and almost interrupted progress in all sectors of its economy. Though the process of developmental planning of the successive five-year plans has made itself felt, yet the state is in the grip of serious economic problems even till today. A rapid increase of population and an even more rapid rise of economic aspirations of the urban people have starkly exposed the scarcity of resources in Tripura. A steeply increasing population includes a section which aspires to enjoy greater and greater economic well-being. But the capacity to achieve larger additions to income and employment opportunities is becoming more and more restricted because of limitations of physical and financial resources. As a result, the rates of growth of income and employment tend to lag increasingly behind the needs and desires of the people. It is no wonder, therefore, that economic problems have multiplied while the economy has moved forward. What has made the situation all the more critical is that the rate of increase of money income has far exceeded the rate of increase in the supply of goods and services. This has resulted in a huge excess of demand for goods and services. The excess demand, in turn, pulls up prices and encourages unscrupulous trading practices.

(a) Agriculture

Tripura is primarily dependent on agriculture. But the growth of agricultural output has been inadequate to meet the increasing demand. Before 1949, Tripura felt itself secure from the scarcity of foodgrains. This was, however, due to low demand and not due to agricultural prosperity as such. The yield per acre was exceedingly low. The proportion of land utilised in agriculture was very small, and modern farming techniques were not known to the agriculturalists. But, unfortunately, Tripura has gradually lost self-sufficiency in food since 1949 and has instead become a food-deficit area. The present food deficit is not due to stagnation in agriculture. Agricultural output has increased but this increase does not compare favourably with the sharp rise of demand resulting from the growth of population and the desire of the urban people for a better life.

Since the inception of economic planning in our country in 1951, measures have been taken in Tripura to make cultivation more extensive as well as more intensive. During the First Five-Year Plan, the efforts were directed towards extensive cultivation. The reclamation of waste land, construction of minor irrigation projects, and activisation of horticulture were the measures taken for extending agricultural activity during this plan period. The emphasis in the second plan shifted to intensive cultivation through the use of improved farming techniques, better seeds, manures and insecticides. Because of these measures, the output of rice, pulses, sugarcane and potato increased appreciably. The Third Five Year Plan laid still greater emphasis on the expansion of agricultural output. The rising trend in the production of agricultural output and particularly in the production of foodgrains also continued in the Fourth Plan period. Efforts to conserve soil had been intensified and the use of improved varieties of seeds and manures had been stepped up in the Fourth Plan. There had been considerable fluctuations in the output of rice between 1973-74 and 1976-77. In order to increase the production of foodgrains substantially during the Fifth Plan, more areas have been brought under cultivation of high-yielding varieties of paddy and wheat. The use of fertilizers has been increased. Plant protection services have been extended. Mechanized cultivation and the adoption of improved farming techniques have been tended to become more and more acceptable to farmers.

While agricultural production expanded, the population shot up sharply from 6,45,707 to 15,56,342, an increase of about 141 per cent, between 1951 and 1971. The gains in agricultural productivity were neutralised by population growth and also an upward trend in demand. What is, therefore, needed now is accelerated growth of agricultural output in general and of foodgrains in particular. In spite of the deficiency in physical resources, some improvement in the rate of growth of agricultural output may be effected through the simultaneous implementation of a few measures. There is ample fallow land in Tripura. No efforts should be spared to cultivate the hitherto uncultivated land. Even to-day many cultivators in Tripura do not get improved varieties of seeds and manures nor any know-how to make use of these. It is essential to make more seeds and manures available to cultivators. Increased distribution of improved varieties of seeds and fertilizers will be economically meaningful only if farmers can effectively utilise them. This requires expansion of education and training in agriculture. Farming techniques must be modernized as far as possible. But changes in farming techniques should be closely in unison with the experience of the farmers. Endeavour should also be made to bring about a change in the outlook of tribal cultivators inculcating a liking for a switch over from shifting cultivation to settled cultivation. The flow of institutional credit into the agricultural sector must be expanded substantially and speedily. The census data relating to agricultural labourers and household workers is as follows:

Table 1
Agricultural and Farming Functions including Labourers and Other Workers (Statewise): Census 2001

Total/ Rural/ Urban	*Persons/ Males/ Females*	*Cultivators Labourers*	*Agricultural Industry Workers*	*Household Workers*	*Other*
Total	Persons	311,378	278,334	33,535	534,943
	Males	221,211	163,926	13,568	432,613
	Females	90,167	114,408	19,967	102,330
Rural	Persons	308,613	274,869	30,428	368,725
	Males	218,602	160,996	11,986	296,372
	Females	90,011	113,873	18,442	72,353
Urban	Persons	2,765	3,465	3,107	166,218
	Males	2,609	2,930	1,582	136,241
	Females	156	535	1,525	29,977

Some of these measures have already been taken. Firstly, several minor irrigation projects have been commissioned to bring as much area under irrigation as possible through the construction of seasonal bunds, distribution of pump-sets at subsidy, and the installation of artesian flow tubewells and shallow tubewells. Secondly, the implementation of rural electrification programme has already begun. Thirdly, an area of 1,04,300 hectares has been brought under high-yielding varieties of paddy by 1975-76 and this area has further increased to nearly 1,16,000 hectares by 1977-78. An intensive campaign was launched during 1975-76 for bringing more area under wheat cultivation by providing farmers with required inputs resulting into an increase in such area from 550 hectares to 2044 hectares. Fourthly, the liquidation of rural indebtedness was invoked because it is a pre-requisite for improving productive efficiency in the agricultural sector. The Tripura Agricultural Debtors Act 1975 has been enacted for the purpose of liquidating rural indebtedness and the Tripura Agricultural Debtor Relief Rules 1976 came into force from March, 1976. Moreover, the Tripura Agricultural Credit Operations Act 1976 has

Table 2

Agricultural and Farming Functions including Labourers and Other Workers (Districtwise): Census 2001

District	*Cultivators*			*Agricultural labourers*			*Household industries*			*Other workers*		
	P	*M*	*F*	*P*	*M*	*F*	*P*	*M*	*F*	*P*	*M*	*F*
West Tripura	112,359	81,535	30,824	113,760	69,318	44,442	17,012	7,773	9,239	289,528	238,200	51,328
South Tripura	103,983	69,969	34,014	92,250	51,544	40,706	5,128	2,473	2,655	101,670	81,833	19,837
Dhalai	41,597	27,838	13,759	40,232	22,079	18,153	2,883	971	1,912	42,675	32,291	10,384
North Tripura	53,439	41,869	11,570	32,092	20,985	11,107	8,512	2,351	6,161	101,070	80,289	20,781

been enforced in order to expand the flow of institutional credit to the rural sector. A State Level Co-ordination Committee has been set up to ensure adequate flow of agricultural credit. Fifthly, the implementation of agricultural land ceiling and speedy distribution of surplus land are an integral part of these scheme of agricultural development and rural reconstruction. The Tripura Land Revenue and Land Reforms (Fourth Amendment) Act 1976 has been enforced for the purpose of effective implementation of agricultural land ceiling and speedy distribution of surplus land. Moreover, 1644.18 hectares of land in tea estates of Tripura had been declared surplus. The government has ensured the distribution of 49,000 hectares of land among 48,750 landless families. The government has also issued temporary licenses to unauthorised occupants of government land in order to permit them to cultivate such land temporarily. These land reform measures are expected to remove some of the motivational and other impediments. Sixthly, the two Forest and Agriculture Departments of Tripura have been implementing a scheme of *joomia* settlement since 1974-75 for curbing shifting cultivation in Tripura.

(b) Industry

The key to economic growth is rapid industrial development. Tripura can never be expected to attain economic prosperity unless ways and means are found to promote industrial activity. The organised industrial units in Tripura are very few. Before 1951, there was hardly any industrial enterprise worth the name. This lack of industrial enterprise did not cause any concern at that time as there existed no pressure of demand for large increase in income and employment opportunities. But, with the rapid growth of population and the multiplication of needs of the people, the continued creation of additional income and employment opportunities has become imperative.

It is true that attempts were made in the course of the five plans to create a base for industrial activity in Tripura. The attempts made during the first four plans were too modest to make any noticeable impact on the economy of the state. During the first plan period, industrial institutes were setup to provide training facilities and financial assistance was given to small industrial units. Obviously, these modest measures did not give a thrust to industrial activity and nor were they expected to do so. In the second and third plans, the promotion of industrial training facilities and the development of village and small-scale industries became the hallmarks of industrial development. The only improvement in these periods was an increase in the intensity of the stress laid on village and cottage industries, special attention was paid to developmental activities in the handloom, sericulture, Khadi and Village industries, and handicrafts sectors. Training facilities were expanded. Financial assistance to small industrial units was also enlarged during the third plan period. Apart from these, a raw material depot was set up to ensure a regular supply of raw materials to industrial units, and arrangements were made to sell products of industrial units, through government sales emporia. Two industrial estates were set up to facilitate planned development of industries. The industrial programme in the fourth plan was more or less a somewhat magnified version of that in the Third Plan. These developmental efforts in the industrial sector were virtually insignificant relative to the ever increasing demand for more income and employment opportunities. Little attempt had been made in the first, second, third and fourth five-year plans to add new dimensions to the very small industrial sector of Tripura. The lack of a dynamic approach and obsession with stereotyped programmes were manifest in plans for industrial development. Census datas about all types of workers. Districtwise and statewise are as follows :

Table 3
The Survey of Main Workers, Marginal Workers and Non-Workers (Statewise) : Census 2001

Total Rural Urban	*Persons Males Females*	*Total workers*	*Main workers*	*Marginal workers*	*Non-workers*	*Total Workers (main + marginal)*
Total	Persons	1,158,190	906,487	251,703	2,032,978	1,158,190
	Males	831,318	740,153	91,165	804,820	831,318
	Females	326,872	166,334	160,538	1,228,158	326,872
Rural	Persons	982,635	743,447	239,188	1,665,439	982,635
	Males	687,956	604,711	83,245	671,332	687,956
	Females	294,679	138,736	155,943	994,107	294,679
Urban	Persons	175,555	163,040	12,515	367,539	175,555
	Males	143,362	135,442	7,920	133,488	143,362
	Females	32,193	27,598	4,595	234,051	32,193

The paucity of capital, deficiency in the supply of power, scarcity of raw materials, transport and communication bottlenecks, and the absence of entrepreneurs rule out the possibility of broad-based industrialisation in the near future. However, there is scope for modest expansion. Firstly, there is a good scope for industrial operations based on forest resources. Secondly, the possibilities of developing agro-based industries like dairy and poultry farming, fruit canning, sericulture, rice-milling, oil and flour-milling, etc., should be fully explored. Thirdly, the steps may be taken to encourage unemployed educated youth for self-employment in service industries. Fourthly, the plantation industry should be patronised and promoted. The planners should seriously consider whether it is feasible to take measures for expanding the rubber industry in Tripura. Fifthly, there is scope for the expansion of certain small-scale and cottage industries like handloom, saw-mills, brick kilns, tanneries, leather goods, grassworks, etc. The National Council of Applied Economic Research recommended investment for the development of such industries. The Government of Tripura has taken steps to set up a jute mill, a spinning mill, a sugar mill, a paper and pulp factory, and a plywood factory and steps to start large-scale and medium-sized industries were also initiated during the fifth plan period.

Table 4

The Survey of Main Workers, Marginal Workers and Non-Workers (Districtwise) : Census 2001

District	Total workers			Main workers			Marginal workers			Non workers		
	P	M	F	P	M	F	P	M	F	P	M	F
West Tripura	532,659	396,826	135,833	434,075	359,204	74,871	98,584	37,622	60,962	997,872	386,999	610,873
South Tripura	303,031	205,819	97,212	224,749	179,441	45,308	78,282	26,378	51,904	459,534	185,360	274,174
Dhalai	127,387	83,179	44,208	91,955	72,789	19,166	35,432	10,390	25,042	180,030	75,301	104,729
North Tripura	195,113	145,494	49,619	155,708	128,719	26,989	39,405	16,775	22,630	395,542	157,160	238,382

The strategy of the government to develop large-scale and medium-sized industries, is definitely a proper strategy from the point of view of long-run growth of income and employment. But the priorities in an economic plan should be fixed by reference to both the long run considerations and immediate requirements. Just as a big push to dynamize the economy is a necessity, so also is an immediate improvement of the employment situation. The blue-print for large-scale and medium-sized industries has been designed to dynamize the economy but not to effect a substantial increase immediately in the level of employment. There is always a time lag between the making of investment decisions and the implementation of these decisions in the case of large-scale and medium-sized industries. This time-lag must be quite long in a backward region like Tripura. Before investments are made in large-scale industries, and medium-sized industries, the infrastructure for the availability of raw materials, skilled labour, electric power and transport facilities has to be ensured. Tripura is beset with problems of deficiency in the supply of power, extreme shortage of skilled labour and inadequacy of transport facilities. These deficiencies are to be corrected before substantial investments are made in such enterprises. It will take considerable time to overcome the deficiencies in transport facilities and in supplies of skilled labour and electric power. The supply of power has improved, to some extent, because of the commissioning of one unit of 5 MWs of the Gumti Hydel Project and because of the implementation of an accelerated power programme. But the supply of power is still far from adequate for meeting the requirements of cheap electric power to large and medium industries. Thus, the steps to establish these industries will yield results only after a few years, provided, in the meanwhile the basic deficiencies are rectified. But the pressure of unemployment should be reduced immediately.

It is in the context of the need for immediate creation of additional employment that village and small-scale industries assume special importance. In a region like Tripura, which has a predominantly rural economy, the village and small-scale industries help to achieve maximum utilisation of local resources and ensure maximum local consumption in the short-run. The deficiencies in transport facilities and supply of power and shortage of skilled labour rule out large-scale industrialisation in the short-run. But village and small-scale industries can be developed despite these deficiencies. The best strategy for a rural economy is a strategy in which the emphasis in the short run is on the development of village and small scale industries and the rectification of basic deficiencies.

(c) Transport and Communications

The lack of adequate transport and communication facilities is a serious obstacle to economic development in Tripura. The extension of transport and communication facilities is vital for the future growth of the economy. It is, therefore, necessary to build up a network of transport and communications.

About a century ago, there was no road worthy of the name in Hill Tepperah. In the pre-independence days, the network of railways running through the eastern region of Bengal adjoining Tripura was the only means of external communication. As this region became part of East Pakistan (now Bangladesh), Tripura became isolated from the rest of India after the rigid partition. Moreover, Tripura's internal communications were extremely undeveloped at the time of its merger with India. Under Five Year Plans, the programmes of road construction have been implemented for developing Tripura's internal communications. In the first three plans, many roads were constructed in the densely populated areas of Tripura. In the Fourth and Fifth Plan periods some roads were constructed to join backward and hilly areas with the main centres of economic activity. The construction of bridges has also progressed simultaneously with the road construction. Tripura now wears a somewhat new look because of roads and bridges constructed since the inception of economic planning in 1951. But there are still many areas which are practically but off from the main places of economic activity. With the increase of population and the rise in demand, the trading activities have also expanded considerably. The development of internal transport facilities has not been commensurate with the growth of the internal trade. While internal transport and communication facilities leave much to be desired, the external transport and communication facilities are still extremely limited.

(d) Social Services

An index of economic development is the rate of growth of social services. Without substantial expansion of educational, medical and housing facilities, economic growth loses much of its significance. It is, therefore, necessary to take account of the extent to which these facilities have so far been expanded in Tripura. During the first three plans a remarkable improvement took place in the facilities for education at different levels. There was an impressive increase in the number of schools and teachers. The total enrolment of students multiplied several times. New colleges, including an Engineering College, were started. Moreover, facilities for physical education were enlarged. The expansion in educational facilities continued during the Fourth and Fifth Plans. A Postgraduate Studies Centre has been set up. It is expected that increased facilities for education will effect a qualitative change of manpower. Such a qualitative change is an essential ingredient in economic development. However, in spite of the large increase in educational facilities, the available facilities still remain far from sufficient. There are two reasons for this. Firstly, the educational facilities in Tripura were very limited before 1951. Secondly, the demand for educational facilities has increased at a very fast rate because of a growing desire for a better life. Since initially, the facilities were very limited and since the demand has subsequently increased steeply, even a striking expansion of educational facilities has not been enough for meeting the demand for such facilities.

The case with medical facilities is similar. The government of Tripura has taken various steps for promoting public health. Yet, the medical facilities that are now available here are far from adequate for providing proper medical care to the people. The reasons are again utter deficiency of such facilities before 1951 and the sharp rise in demand for these year after year.

(e) The Bane of Unemployment

The problem of unemployment has assumed critical proportions. One aspect of this problem is the high incidence of under-employment among the rural working force and the educated young persons. The number of job-seekers registered in the local employment exchange was 56,758 in 1977 and it stands at about 60,000 at present. The absorption of the unemployed educated youths in productive employment is impossible without industrial development. But we can hardly expect any substantial development of industries in Tripura in the near future. The service industries, and agro-based and forest-based industries, may, to some extent, provide additional employment immediately, if these industries are developed in a planned manner. Moreover, if unemployed young persons are absorbed only in government offices and educational institutions, money income increases without a corresponding increase in output. Our inability to broaden the sources of employment opportunities has forced us to reconcile ourselves to a precarious compromise between our aspirations and limitations. This poses a threat to social peace and security in Tripura.

Tripura's Five Year Plan

(a) The Perspective on the Plan

In the light of the foregoing analysis, the perspective on Tripura's Five Year Plan for the period 1978-79—1982-83 may be considered. The perspective of development in Tripura's Sixth Five Year Plan has been formulated in the light of the performance of the economy during the Fifth Plan. It will incorporate the outlook for the immediate future and the long run considerations of growth of income and employment.

Three imperatives stand out from an appraisal of the performance of the Fifth Plan. Firstly, there is the need for creating as much activities as possible within the state for reducing the economic dependence of Tripura upon other states. Exhorting the State Planning Board, the State Chief Minister Nripen Chakraborty commented that the "... money is being pumped in, but, at the same time, the same money is being pumped out through imports of essential commodities ..." With a view to reduce imports and the outflow of financial resources, efforts must be directed towards promoting as much economic activities as possible within the state. The principal reason for excessive dependence on imports is the negligible existence of industries in the state. Secondly, the removal of poverty is a pressing need. The percentage of population living below the poverty line has been on the increase. The efforts in this direction call for the rapid generation of additional income and employment and the reduction of inequality in the distribution of income and wealth. Thirdly, the problem of unemployment has assumed so serious proportions that the employment objective must, of necessity, be an explicit objective in the Sixth Plan. The steps must be taken to mitigate the incidence of both under-employment in rural areas and unemployment of the educated youth in urban and semi-urban areas.

In addition, some imperatives emerge from the outlook for the immediate future. Firstly, there is the need for rapidly expanding the state's capacity for both capital formation and adequate consumption. The emphasis should be on the satisfaction of local demands. Secondly, there should be maximum possible mobilisation of local resources for investment. Thirdly, the developmental activities should be labour-oriented and attention should be paid to the absorption of the local labour force in development projects. Fourthly, a high priority must be accorded to the promotion of economic welfare of the tribal population. In particular, the tribal *Joomias* must be provided with land, credit facilities, and inputs for agricultural and allied activities.

Besides, three imperatives follow from long-term considerations of growth of income and employment. Firstly, there is the need for annual monitoring and evaluation of developmental activities and the consequent readjustments of sectoral allocations and targets. Also, long-term considerations of growth of income and employment call for close links between successive five year plans. Secondly, the application of science and technology in the promotion of economic activities will assume importance in the context of long-term planning. Thirdly, decentralisation should be the characteristic feature of long-term economic planning in Tripura, as also in any other state of India.

(b) The Approach to Future Planning

Given the perspective of the Fifth Five Year Plan for Tripura for the years 1978-79—1982-83, we would formulate an approach to the Sixth Five Year Plan of the state. The Planning Commission has tentatively fixed an outlay of Rs. 125 crores for the Sixth Five Year Plan of this state. So, on an average, an annual outlay of Rs. 25 crore has been tentatively fixed for the State Plan. In addition to this, more money will be available to the state. Amounts that will be spent under the North-Eastern Council schemes, Central Government aided schemes, and centrally-sponsored schemes transferred to the state for economic development. The tentatively fixed size of the State Plan is obviously small in the context of the high incidence of poverty, the severe pressure of unemployment and under-employment, the glaring deficiencies in the infra-structure of the economy, the over-dependence on other states for supplies of essential goods, and the deplorable economic conditions of an overwhelming majority of the tribal population. Since thue proposed size of the State Plan is small, when judged in the context of massive problems faced by the state, it is imperative that the limited financial resources be fully utilised. When the size of a Plan is small, it is desirable and necessary that the level of implementation of the Plan should, in financial terms, reach cent per cent or nearly cent per cent of the approved outlay. In Tripura, where paucity of financial resources is a major constraint in planning exercises, the implementation of development programmes has so far been none too satisfactory even in financial terms. In 1977-78, the total expenditure under the annual State Plan was Rs. 1340.182 lakhs out of an approved outlay of Rs. 1638 lakhs; actual outlays under North-Eastern Council schemes and Central and Centrally-sponsored schemes were Rs. 102.317 lakh and Rs. 271.046 lakh respectively out of respective approved outlays of Rs. 179.830 lakh and Rs. 488.576 lakh. The levels of implementation of programmes relatively to approved outlays were 81.8 per cent for the State Plan, 56.90 per cent for North-Eastern Council schemes, and 55.50 per cent for Central and Centrally-sponsored schemes.

The levels of implementation has been particularly low in the case of North-Eastern Council schemes and Central and Centrally-sponsored schemes, while the level of implementation had been far from satisfactory in the case of State Plan. Taking the State Plan, North-Eastern Council schemes and Central and Centrally-sponsored schemes together, there was a shortfall of nearly Rs. 593 lakh in expenditure out of an approved outlay of about Rs. 2306 lakh; the shortfall amounted nearly 25.7 per cent of the approved outlay. Thus, ironically enough, a state, which suffers from a chronic paucity of financial resources, had failed to utilize even two-thirds of the small quantum of funds provided for the financing of development programmes in 1977-78. Such a poor performance should be abstained in future because poor implementation of a small plan robs the economic planning of much of its significance. Hence, the first point to be stressed in an approach to the Sixth Five Year Plan for Tripura is that, given the serious constraint of paucity of financial resources, there should be full or nearly full utilisation of funds provided for development programmes from all sources.

Apart from the financial constraint, there are several physical constraints also which are obstacles to planning exercises in Tripura. One formidable constraint is the deficiency in the availability of cement. In 1977-78, several projects could not either be completed or taken up because of the shortage of cement. It is high time that the planning authorities in Tripura should identify whether shortage of cement is a recurring bottleneck or a random disturbance. If it is just a random disturbance, then there may not be much cause for concern regarding the availability of cement during the Sixth Plan period. But, as it appears from past experience, the deficiency in the availability of cement for construction activities of the development projects appears to be of recurring nature. Hence, the availability of cement should be treated as a strategic variable in the Sixth Plan.

The second physical constraint is the extreme dearth of capital goods and accessories and spare parts. This rules out broad-based industrialisation in the organised sector and the application of sophisticated technology in agriculture and allied sectors even on a very limited scale during the Sixth Plan period. A third physical constraint is the scarcity of raw materials except for certain types of agro-based and forest-based industries which must constitute the core of the industrialisation in the Sixth Plan. The fourth physical constraint is the severe shortage of power. Both in respect of the consumption of electricity in industries and irrigation and in respect of rural electrification, Tripura is one of the most backward states in India. During 1975-76, the per capita consumption of electricity in Tripura was only 8.8 units as compared with the all-India average of 120 units. Even at present, the per capita consumption of electricity in Tripura is only 10 units or so. The shortage of power is a major hindrance to the development of agriculture, irrigation and industry.

Fifthly, there is the deficiency of transport and communication facilities both within the state and also with the other states. One of the pre-requisites of self-sustained economic development is that various modes of transport be available for carrying inputs into production units in different sectors of the economy and for carrying their outputs to different markets. But there is a glaring deficiency of transport facilities, particularly in rural areas of Tripura. In the remote villages, there are practically no roads. Therefore, the construction of new roads and expansion of road transport are a pressing necessity for the development of Tripura's rural economy. The expansion of railways in Tripura is also needed to give a push to the rural economy. If a new railway line is constructed in Tripura for connecting Dharmanagar to Kumarghat, there will be an impact on the villages in the neighbourhood of the railway line, and this will, in turn, bring in many effects in the economy. Furthermore, the hilly areas are more backward than plain areas and these areas should, therefore, receive special attention in the matter of development of transport and communications during the Sixth Plan period.

The sixth physical constraint is the low availability and the still lower utilisation of irrigation facilities. The partly accounts for the low productivity in agriculture and the wide prevalence of the system of single cropping in Tripura. About 90 per cent of the population of Tripura (to be precise, 89.57 per cent, according to 1971 Census) lives in villages. As stated in the state's Draft Five Year Plan 1978–83, 83.8 per cent of the population of Tripura was below the poverty line in 1973-74. The incidence of poverty is higher in rural areas than in urban areas. Therefore, the development of the rural economy must be the focal point of economic planning in Tripura. Since, according to 1971 Census, 74.37 per cent of the working force in Tripura is employed in agriculture, while another 2.23 per cent is employed in allied sectors, the highest priority in Tripura's Sixth Five Year Plan must be accorded to agriculture. Agricultural labourers, marginal farmers, small farmers, and tribal families practising shifting cultivation constitute target groups in the agricultural sector.

In order to relieve the pressure of under-employment in the agricultural sector, to increase output in the rural economy, to raise incomes of agricultural labourers, marginal farmers and small farmers, and also to promote economic conditions of the tribal population, a part of the manpower engaged in agriculture should be transferred to allied sectors like forestry, horticulture, dairy farming, poultry farming and animal husbandry. In development programmes relating to agriculture and allied sectors, the major emphasis must be laid on the promotion of infrastructural facilities, the provision of inputs for agriculture and allied sectors, and the inflow of credit into the rural economy.

The communication and transport facilities must be improved for connecting villages with main markets. The irrigation facilities must be expanded and fully utilised for better utilisation of land, seeds and fertilizers, reclamation of cultivable waste, and the extension of the system of double or multiple cropping. The rural electrification must be undertaken on an impressive scale, both for expanding irrigation facilities and for developing agro-based and forest-based rural industries. Manure, fertilisers, and high-yielding varieties of seeds must be supplied to cultivators at controlled prices. They should also be taught to make the best use of these inputs. Agricultural marketing facilities must be promoted and institutional credit must be provided to farmers, village artisans and other engaged in primary economic activities on liberal terms. The educational facilities in rural areas should be so oriented that education becomes related to the needs of the rural people, and educational programmes should be functional in nature and correlated to employment and production programmes in rural area. The co-operative societies must play an active role in promoting productive activities in villages. These societies must pay constant attention to the needs of farmers, artisans and others engaged in primary production. They should provide finance, seeds, fertilizers, non-agricultural inputs, marketing facilities, etc., to villagers. A pool of common funds of agricultural inputs under the control of co-operative societies should be developed, the people have very sad experience of the co-operative movement in Tripura where it is almost imposed from the above and the people participation is virtually non-existent. The loans extended by the co-operative societies are considered as non-refundable help from the government. A range of additional causes like the misappropriation, mismanagement, lack of earnestness and bureaucratic mentality of the managerial staff have operated behind the liquidation of so many local co-operative societies. Unless such cases are properly dealt with, the co-operatives will continue to be in the red.

Village-level workers should play a crucial role in the development of the rural economy. They should be readily available for rendering assistance to villagers. In order to dynamise the rural economy, the village and small-scale industries should be promoted as a key instrument of diversification of economic activities. There are prospects for industrial operations based on forest resources like teak, *sal, garjan, chamal, karai, jam,* bamboos and canes. Secondly, the opportunities for promoting agro-based industries like fruit canning, sericulture, production of *gur* and *khandsari,* rice-milling, oil-milling, etc. should be fully exploited. Thirdly, proper arrangements should be made for the expansion of the handicrafts sector.

There are trained artisans in various crafts. Fourthly, there is the scope for expansion of small-scale and cottage industries like handloom, blacksmithy, saw mills, brick kilns, potteries, tanneries, leather goods, soap factories, match factories, bakeries and ceramics. Small-scale industries should be promoted in urban areas also with a view to reduce the incidence of urban unemployment.

It will be necessary to ensure active participation of the people in the formulation and implementation of plan programmes. The planning from below is of fundamental importance for making economic planning meaningful and the participation of the rural people in planning exercises should be organised through village *panchayats.*

It may be noted, finally, that the deplorably under-developed state of the economy of Tripura is substantially due to the under-lying relations of production. The means of production are directly and indirectly owned mainly by a few rich families. Economic power is more or less concentrated in the hands of a few rich land-owners and businessmen. The vast majority of the rural poor has only marginal control over the means of production. Without social control over ownership of the means of production, it may not be possible to achieve optimum utilisation of the forces of production. The tenancy rights in lands must be protected. Share-croppers must be freed from exploitation by land-owners and the land should be provided to landless agricultural labourers. There should be speedy restoration of the possession of land alienated by tribals.

More important than the question of land-ownership is the question of ownership in the economy of Tripura. Both finance capital and real capital in the private sector are concentrated in the hands of a few rich land-owners and businessmen. There is neo-colonial exploitation of farmers and artisans in rural areas by urban traders who have massive control over the rural economy. Therefore, the social control over trade and the use of capital are necessary for achieving a desirable pattern and a satisfactory rate of economic growth in Tripura."

Now, after more than fifty years of Independence, things are starting to take positive turn just like Haryana of North-India. Tripura in North-East, has been politically neutral and non-controversial state, so has not been able to attract much attention of Central Government which have been the case in Nagaland. This too has slowed down the process of development in the state.

Index

Y

Z

ENCYCLOPAEDIA OF NORTH-EAST INDIA

ENCYCLOPAEDIA
OF
NORTH-EAST INDIA

(In 3 Volumes)

(Arunachal Pradesh, Manipur, Mizoram)

(Vol. 2)

T. RAATAN

KALPAZ PUBLICATIONS

DELHI-110 052

Encyclopaedia of North-East India

Rs. 2200 (In 3 Volumes Set)

ISBN: 81-7835-068-8 (Set)
ISBN: 81-7835-274-5 (Vol. 2)

Published in 2006 in India by
Kalpaz Publications
C-30, Satyawati Nagar
Delhi-110 052
E-mail: kalpaz@hotmail.com

Lasertypesetting by: Varsha Graphics, Delhi
Printed at: Vishal Kaushik Printers Delhi

Contents

Preface

Volume II of the series—*Encyclopaedia of North-East India* is combination of three States *viz.* Arunachal Pradesh, Manipur and finally Mizoram. These three states represent three sections of the book respectively. It is not wrong to say that all eight states of the present series are associated with one another in one respect or the other. They share a lot about their culture and economy in common. Their volumisation has been done for the convenience of presentation.

Section I, i.e., **Arunachal Pradesh,** the erstwhile North-East Frontier Agency has its international boundaries in common with Bhutan, China, Tibet and Burma in the West, north and north-east and east respectively. Internally, it touches the states of Assam and Nagaland. The terrain comprises submantane and mountainous ranges sloping down towards plains in Assam state, divided into valleys by the rivers—Kameng, Subansiri, Siang, Lohit and Tirap. Prior to 1962, the area was popularly called North-East Frontier Agency, constitutionally a part of Assam and due to its strategic importance, it was administered by the Ministry of External Affairs. Thus a study of basics of the state is of utmost importance.

Section II of the volume, i.e., **Manipur** is geographically divided into two tracts: the hills part comprising of five and plains of four districts the state is surrounded by Myanmar on the east Nagaland on the North, Assam and Mizoram on the West and Myanmar and Mizoram towards the South. With its strategic location and simplicity of culture, it attracts researchers and tourists towards itself.

Last section is about **Mizoram** that is basically a mountainous region which attained complete statehood in 1987. Sandwiched between Myanmar on the East and South and Bangladesh towards the west, Mizoram occupies an area of great strategic importance in the north-eastern corner of the country. Further it has great natural beauty and an endless variety of landscape. Also, the state is rich in fauna and flora. Needless to say that all this is more than sufficient to raise curiosity of any to know more and more about the state and its culture.

As usual, the Chapter 1 of all three sections is about the basic about the land and people living in it. Chapters 2, 3 and 4 on Arunachal Pradesh throw light on main occupation of the state, i.e, Agriculture, and other allied activities; Forest resources and mineral resources respectively. Chapter 5 is about economy of trade of the State and last chapter is on development in the field of education and handicrafts.

Now Section II that contains details about Manipur Chapter 2 is on background of administrative and political movement in Manipur. Chapter 3 and

4 respectively discuss principle deities and popular dances of Manipur. Last chapter is devoted to economic development in the State.

Final section of the volume which is Mizoram talks in 2nd Chapter about major political parties in the state. Consequences of terrorism and a picture of administrative set-up have been given in 3rd and 4th chapters. Last Chapter, titled New Planning gives an account of economic background and planning in pre and post-independence period.

T. Raatan

Introduction

Arunachal Pradesh, Manipur and Mizoram, now three different complete states, have been at some point of time linked with one another in one way or the other. Even today, they share a lot in common as well as their social set up, culture and traditions are concerned.

Arunachal Pradesh, whose no records are practically available that can narrate the history of the area except some verbal literature and a number of historical ruins found largely in the foot hills. Subsequent discoveries for exploration and excavation have identified these ruins as dating back almost from the early Christian era. However, historical proofs indicate that the area was not only popular but the people living on the land had close relations with rest of the country. Modern history of the state begins with advent of British rule in Assam following the Treaty of Yandaboo concluded in 1826. As already stated elsewhere, Arunachal Pradesh got the status of full fledged state in 1987 only.

Like most of other North-Eastern states, agriculture is the main occupation of the people of Arunachal and had largely depended on Jhum cultivation. Promotion is being given to the cultivation of cash crops like potatoes horticulture crops like apples, pine apples and oranges etc. Total Population, 0-6 years population, decadal growth rate, sex ratio and density of the districts are shown as follows :

Table 1

Population, Decadal Growth Rate, Sex Ratio and Density of Arunachal Pradesh: Census 2001

State/District	*Population*			*Decadal growth rate*		*Sex Ratio*		*Density*	
	Person	*Male*	*Female*	*1981-91*	*1991-01*	*1991*	*2001*	*1991*	*2001*
	(1)	(2)	(3)	(4)	(5)	(6)	(7)	(8)	(9)
Ar. Pradesh	**1,091,117**	**573,951**	**517,166**	**36.83**	**26.21**	**859**	**901**	**10**	**13**
Tawang	34,705	17,676	17,029	30.14	22.69	844	963	13	16
West Kameng	74,595	42,638	31,957	35.74	32.21	822	749	8	10
East Kameng	57,065	28,743	28,322	17.92	13.24	962	985	12	14
Papum Pare	121,750	64,122	57,628	83.24	67.21	831	899	21	35
Lower Subansiri	97,614	49,184	48,430	14.06	17.37	957	985	9	10

(Contd.)

(Contd.)

	(1)	(2)	(3)	(4)	(5)	(6)	(7)	(8)	(9)
Upper Subansiri	54,995	27,873	27,122	27.09	9.80	867	973	7	8
West Siang	103,575	54,139	49,436	31.64	15.17	873	913	11	13
East Siang	87,430	45,131	42,299	30.26	21.66	877	937	18	22
Upper Siang	33,146	17,844	15,302	31.50	19.32	822	858	4	5
Dibang Valley	57,543	31,280	26,263	39.03	33.61	788	840	3	4
Lohit	143,478	77,252	66,226	57.85	30.78	797	857	10	13
Changlang	124,994	65,608	59,386	53.56	30.84	863	905	20	27
Tirap	100,227	52,461	47,766	28.70	17.21	862	911	36	42

Table 2
Population, Population in the Age Group 0-6 of Aruncachal Pradesh : Census 2001

State/ District	*Total Rural Urban*	*Population Person*	*Male*	*Female*	*0-6 Population Person*	*Male*	*Female*
Arunachal Pradesh	**Total**	**1,091,117**	**573,951**	**517,166**	**200,055**	**102,010**	**98,045**
	Rural	**868,429**	**453,560**	**414,869**	**164,650**	**84,139**	**80,511**
	Urban	**222,688**	**120,391**	**102,297**	**35,405**	**17,871**	**17,534**
Tawang	Total	34,705	17,676	17,029	6,535	3,340	3,195
	Rural	30,249	15,259	14,990	5,776	2,959	2,817
	Urban	4,456	2,417	2,039	759	381	378
West Kameng	Total	74,595	42,638	31,957	12,181	6,221	5,960
	Rural	67,910	39,024	28,886	11,314	5,773	5,541
	Urban	6,685	3,614	3,071	867	448	419
East Kameng	Total	57,065	28,743	28,322	11,702	5,819	5,883
	Rural	42,100	20,855	21,245	8,492	4,243	4,249
	Urban	14,965	7,888	7,077	3,210	1,576	1,634
Papum Pare	Total	121,750	64,122	57,628	20,160	10,195	9,965
	Rural	59,868	31,140	28,728	10,866	5,539	5,327
	Urban	61,882	32,982	28,900	9,294	4,656	4,638
L. Subansiri	Total	97,614	49,184	48,430	17,582	8,809	8,773
	Rural	85,325	42,799	42,526	15,535	7,751	7,784
	Urban	12,289	6,385	5,904	2,047	1,058	989
U. Subansiri	Total	54,995	27,873	27,122	10,543	5,307	5,236
	Rural	39,527	19,797	19,730	7,602	3,821	3,781
	Urban	15,468	8,076	7,392	2,941	1,486	1,455
West Siang	Total	103,575	54,139	49,436	17,329	8,913	8,416
	Rural	82,907	42,500	40,407	14,215	7,335	6,880
	Urban	20,668	11,639	9,029	3,114	1,578	1,536
East Siang	Total	87,430	45,131	42,299	15,243	7,780	7,463
	Rural	65,458	33,484	31,974	11,908	6,115	5,793
	Urban	21,972	11,647	10,325	3,335	1,665	1,670

(Contd.)

(Contd.)

Upper Siang	Total	33,146	17,844	15,302	6,223	3,084	3,139
	Rural	33,146	17,844	15,302	6,223	3,084	3,139
	Urban	–	–	–	–	–	–
Dibang Valley	Total	57,543	31,280	26,263	10,221	5,251	4,970
	Rural	47,437	25,544	21,893	8,813	4,521	4,292
	Urban	10,106	5,736	4,370	1,408	730	678
Lohit	Total	143,478	77,252	66,226	27,686	14,338	13,348
	Rural	116,882	62,639	54,243	23,472	12,197	11,275
	Urban	26,596	14,613	11,983	4,214	2,141	2,073
Changlang	Total	124,994	65,608	59,386	24,733	12,691	12,042
	Rural	112,682	58,662	54,020	22,926	11,743	11,183
	Urban	12,312	6,946	5,366	1,807	948	859
Tirap	Total	100,227	52,461	47,766	19,917	10,262	9,655
	Rural	84,938	44,013	40,925	17,508	9,058	8,450
	Urban	15,289	8,448	6,841	2,409	1,204	1,205

Since the state has good reservoirs of Minerals, so far the purpose of conservation and exploration of these vast minerals, Arunachal Pradesh Mineral Development and Trading Corporation Limited (APMDTCL) was established in the year 1991. There are also two industrial training institutes at Roing and Doporifo in order to provide training to craftsman in different trades. Presently, there are 88 crafts and weaving units and 18 medium state industries alongwith a mini cement plant, a fruit processing plant and also one citronella oil distillery.

Regarding festivals, some important ones are Mopin and Solung of Adis, Losar of Monpas and the Sherdukpens, Boori-boot of the Hill Mirris etc. Dree, Si-Doynee, Reh and Nyokum are important festivals of different clans. Animal sacrifice is a common practice in most of the festivals.

Finally, the significant tourist places in Arunachal Pradesh are: Tawang, Dirang, Bondila, Tipi, Itanagar (Capital) Malinithin, Likabai, Pasighat, Along, Tezu, Miao, Roing, Doporijo, Namdapha, Bhismaknagar, Parashuram, Kund and Khonsa. There are some small worth seeing places also all over the state.

Manipur, next state of the volume, like most of the states of the region, suffer from non-availability of records as far as its origin and early background is concerned. As per the historians, Pakhaugba ascended the throne of one of the small leading principalities in 33 A.D. and founded the long dynasty that ruled over Manipur till close of nineteenth century, i.e., 1891. It is also said that though ancient hoes of ground stone have been found in the region, the earliest recorded history goes back only to A.D. 900. Start of Manipur in more recent history dates back to 1762 on when Raja Jai Singh concluded a treaty with the British for repel an invasion from Myanmar. The territory later got associated with India through the treaty of Yandaboo at the end of Indo-Burmese war. It was merged with Indian Union as part 'C' state in 1949. Manipur attained complete statehood in 1972. With this, a legislative assembly comprising 60 members was established.

Table 3
Population, Decadal Growth Rate, Sex Ratio and Density of Manipur : Census 2001

State/District	*Population*			*Decadal growth rate*		*Sex Ratio*		*Density*	
	Person	*Male*	*Female*	*1981-91*	*1991-01*	*1991*	*2001*	*1991*	*2001*
	(1)	(2)	(3)	(4)	(5)	(6)	(7)	(8)	(9)
Manipur	**2,388,634**	**1,207,338**	**1,181,296**	**29.29**	**30.02**	**958**	**978**	**82**	**107**
Senapati	379,214	196,646	182,568	36.13	81.96	942	928	64	116
Tamenglong	111,493	57,994	53,499	38.51	29.23	935	922	20	25
Churachandpur	228,707	114,740	113,967	31.00	29.81	931	993	39	50
Bishnupur	205,907	102,772	103,135	27.52	13.90	984	1,004	364	415
Thoubal	366,341	183,338	183,003	26.34	24.62	980	998	572	713
Imphal West	439,532	218,947	220,585	26.14	15.42	979	1,007	734	847
Imphal East	393,780	197,710	196,070	29.41	19.16	966	992	466	555
Ukhrul	140,946	73,413	67,533	31.74	28.98	884	920	24	31
Chandel	122,714	61,778	60,936	25.81	72.80	913	986	21	37

Table 4
Population, Population in the Age Group 0-6 of Manipur : Census 2001

State/District	*Total Rural Urban*	*Population*			*0-6 Population*		
		Person	*Male*	*Female*	*Person*	*Male*	*Female*
Manipur	**Total**	**2,388,634**	**1,207,338**	**1,181,296**	**312,691**	**159,448**	**153,243**
	Rural	**1,818,224**	**923,428**	**894,796**	**241,815**	**123,648**	**118,167**
	Urban	**570,410**	**283,910**	**286,500**	**70,876**	**35,800**	**35,076**
Senapati	Total	379,214	196,646	182,568	40,233	20,045	20,188
	Rural	379,214	196,646	182,568	40,233	20,045	20,188
	Urban	–	–	–	–	–	–
Tamenglong	Total	111,493	57,994	53,499	15,236	7,813	7,423
	Rural	111,493	57,994	53,499	15,236	7,813	7,423
	Urban	–	–	–	–	–	–
Churachandpur	Total	228,707	114,740	113,967	29,393	15,256	14,137
	Rural	228,707	114,740	113,967	29,393	15,256	14,137
	Urban	–	–	–	–	–	–
Bishnupur	Total	205,907	102,772	103,135	27,565	14,320	13,245
	Rural	132,639	65,842	66,797	17,844	9,375	8,469
	Urban	73,268	36,930	36,338	9,721	4,945	4,776
Thoubal	Total	366,341	183,338	183,003	59,305	30,073	29,232
	Rural	235,071	117,832	117,239	39,244	19,986	19,258
	Urban	131,270	65,506	65,764	20,061	10,087	9,974

(Contd.)

(Contd.)

Imphal West	Total	439,532	218,947	220,585	52,347	26,631	25,716
	Rural	196,860	98,719	98,141	26,129	13,500	12,629
	Urban	242,672	120,228	122,444	26,218	13,131	13,087
Imphal East	Total	393,780	197,710	196,070	52,634	26,928	25,706
	Rural	285,540	144,081	141,459	40,091	20,506	19,585
	Urban	108,240	53,629	54,611	12,543	6,422	6,121
Ukhrul	Total	140,946	73,413	67,533	20,182	10,251	9,931
	Rural	140,946	73,413	67,533	20,182	10,251	9,931
	Urban	–	–	–	–	–	–
Chandel	Total	122,714	61,778	60,936	15,796	8,131	7,665
	Rural	107,754	54,161	53,593	13,463	6,916	6,547
	Urban	14,960	7,617	7,343	2,333	1,215	1,118

About two-third of the people Methei who live in the Manipuri Valley are largely Hindus. Women in Methei conduct most of the trade in the valley and enjoy high social status. Hindus constitute almost 60 per cent of population some 34 per cent population comprises of the Scheduled Castes. Some of the Nagas have converted to Christianity. Manipuri is the dominant of English is the official language of the state.

Polo and Hockey are the most popular sports in the state. Manipur has given birth to an indigenous form of classical dance known as Manipuri. Dance and Dramas are said to be an integral part of Manipuri religious life. Themes are mostly derived from the life of Krishna, the pastoral god of Hinduism. Manipur was introduced to the rest of India by famous Bengali poet Ravindranath Tagore in 1917. Important festivals of the state are Lai Haraoba Rasaleela', Chieraoba, Ningol Chakkouba, Ratha Jatra, Id-ul-Fitre, Imoinu Irapta, Gaon Naga, Kut and Christmas etc.

In Manipur, agriculture is the single largest means of livelihood of majority of the rural people and is leading source of economy of the state. The state has rich forest resources also. A large area falls under reserved forests and protected forests also. Manipur is also the sole home of brown deer and has only floating national park of the world.

Lastly, with rich resources and committed people, it is making fast more towards industrialisation and has 8,991 registered industrial set-ups by the end of March 2001. Special thrust has been shifted towards revitalisation of various industrial corporations and development of infrastructure with this pace, the state can make progress in no time.

Mizoram, the last state of the present volume attained statehood in 1987 only. The origin of word 'Mizo' is not known till date. It is recorded that the Mizos came under the influence of the British Missionaries in 19th century and presently, most of them are part of Christianity. Mizo language too has no script of its own. The missionaries are said to have started the Roman script for Mizo language and formal education.

Agriculture is the main occupation as well as source of income of the state. Around 60 per cent of the population in state is engaged in agricultural pursuits. Pattern followed for agriculture is largely, 'Jhorm' or shifting cultivation. Horticulture is also performed in the state. Main crops are oranges, lemon, kagzi lime, passion fruits, hatkora, pineapple, jamir, papaya and the like. Cash crops of the state are sugarcane, tapioca and cotton. Now, there has been started extensive cultivation of ginger and cash crops.

Table 5
Population, Decadal Growth Rate, Sex Ratio and Density of Mizoram : Census 2001

State/District	*Population 2001*			*Decadal growth rate*		*Sex Ratio*		*Density*	
	Person	*Male*	*Female*	*1981-91*	*1991-01*	*1991*	*2001*	*1991*	*2001*
	(1)	(2)	(3)	(4)	(5)	(6)	(7)	(8)	(9)
Mizoram	**891,058**	**459,783**	**431,275**	**39.70**	**29.18**	**921**	**938**	**33**	**42**
Mamit	62,313	32,766	29,547	23.57	-3.50	891	902	21	21
Kolasib	60,977	31,874	29,103	26.82	36.01	924	913	32	44
Aizawl	339,812	173,930	165,882	57.23	39.24	917	954	68	95
Champhai	101,389	51,869	49,520	32.31	29.77	969	955	25	32
Serchhip	55,539	28,445	27,094	20.36	18.45	959	953	33	39
Lunglei	137,155	71,353	65,802	28.79	23.10	910	922	25	30
Lawngtlai	73,050	38,425	34,625	52.68	34.78	885	901	21	29
Saiha	60,823	31,121	29,702	47.72	33.16	939	954	33	43

Table 6
Population, Population in the Age Group 0-6 of Mizoram : Census 2001

District	*Total Rural Urban*	*Population*			*0-6 Population*		
		Person	*Male*	*Female*	*Person*	*Male*	*Female*
Mizoram	**Total**	**891,058**	**459,783**	**431,275**	**141,537**	**71,817**	**69,720**
	Rural	**450,018**	**233,718**	**216,300**	**79,440**	**40,153**	**39,287**
	Urban	**441,040**	**226,065**	**214,975**	**62,097**	**31,664**	**30,433**
Mamit	Total	62,313	32,766	29,547	10,919	5,592	5,327
	Rural	51,510	27,100	24,410	9,285	4,698	4,587
	Urban	10,803	5,666	5,137	1,634	894	740
Kolasib	Total	60,977	31,874	29,103	9,760	4,964	4,796
	Rural	24,806	13,133	11,673	4,385	2,203	2,182
	Urban	36,171	18,741	17,430	5,375	2,761	2,614

(Contd.)

(Contd.)

Aizawl	Total	339,812	173,930	165,882	47,473	23,999	23,474
	Rural	90,960	47,073	43,887	14,287	7,214	7,073
	Urban	248,852	126,857	121,995	33,186	16,785	16,401
Champhai	Total	101,389	51,869	49,520	17,074	8,656	8,418
	Rural	63,265	32,632	30,633	11,140	5,600	5,540
	Urban	38,124	19,237	18,887	5,934	3,056	2,878
Serchhip	Total	55,539	28,445	27,094	9,115	4,577	4,538
	Rural	26,333	13,340	12,993	4,667	2,328	2,339
	Urban	29,206	15,105	14,101	4,448	2,249	2,199
Lunglei	Total	137,155	71,353	65,802	22,526	11,467	11,059
	Rural	79,002	41,069	37,933	14,221	7,239	6,982
	Urban	58,153	30,284	27,869	8,305	4,228	4,077
Lawngtlai	Total	73,050	38,425	34,625	13,747	7,004	6,743
	Rural	73,050	38,425	34,625	13,747	7,004	6,743
	Urban	-	-	-	-	-	-
Saiha	Total	60,823	31,121	29,702	10,923	5,558	5,365
	Rural	41,092	20,946	20,146	7,708	3,867	3,841
	Urban	19,731	10,175	9,556	3,215	1,691	1,524

As far as industrial growth is concerned, entire Mizoram is a Notified Backward Area and is thus categorised as 'no industry district'. Despite this, sincere efforts were made in the past decade to speed up the growth of industries. Also, the government formed an industrial policy in 1989 and following this, some establishments/plants have been started in different parts of the state. Improvement of tea industry/garden and enhancing Tooklai approved varieties of tea seedlings has been taken up by the Government around state areas.

System of transportation is also on the improve. Rail link in Mizoram has been started at Bairabi. Aizawl is linked through air. PWD of the state is quite active now.

Now let us talk about Mizo festivals. As already said, people in the state are basically agriculturalists and therefore all their activities revolve around 'Jhum' cultivation and their festivals are focussed on such agricultural functions. 'Kut' the local term used for festivals. Three major festivals of Mizos are: Chapchar Kut, Miva Kut and Pawl Kut. Celebration of festivals is also expression of religious sentiments at times.

There are also famous tourist centres in the state. Aizwal which is situated some 4000 feet above sea level in 94 ethical and cultural centre of the state Champhai at Myanmar border is an attractive resort. Natural lake—Tamdil, Saitual resort, Vantawng falls are also attractive centres for tourists. Department of Tourism is progressing fast by expanding its activities in the area.

Thus, all three states have some unique features which separate them from one another and establish their own independent identity.

Section-I
Arunachal Pradesh

1

The Land and the People

Documentation of information of any geographical region starts with not land only but also people living in that land. Talk about them becomes even more important if the people are the tribals or a part of them are tribals. So is the case about Arunachal Pradesh. While, we find, on the one hand, silent ridges, peaks and rivers with shining sand deposits where the people fish in cheer and take rest in course of their tours, there are, on the other hand, noisy villages where they sing, dance and make merry argue freely and settle their disputes in absolute frankness. There are around 110[1] tribes and sub-tribes that constitute the base-population, inhabiting the narrow valleys as well as top of the hills and cut off from one another because of the hills and the ridges.

I. District Kameng

A detailed account of various important tribes may be preceded by the following table, giving an idea of their strength in the district.

Table 1
Numerical Strength of Different Tribes[2] in East Kameng

Name of Tribes	*Population*		
	Total	*Male*	*Female*
(1)	(2)	(3)	(4)
All Scheduled Tribes			
Total	43,116	21,240	21,876
Rural	43,116	21,240	21,876
1. Abor			
Total	9	6	3
Rural	9	6	3
2. Adi			
Total	123	68	55
Rural	123	68	55
3. Adi Gallong			
Total	31	17	14
Rural	31	17	14
4. Adi Minyong			
Total	6	2	4
Rural	6	2	4
5. Adi Padam			
Total	1	1	0
Rural	1	1	0
6. Adi Pasi			
Total	1	1	0
Rural	1	1	0
7. Aka			
Total	929	469	460
Rural	929	469	460
8. Apatani			
Total	92	63	29

(Contd.)

(1)	(2)	(3)	(4)
Rural	92	63	29
9. Bagi			
Total	250	132	118
Rural	250	132	118
10. Bangni			
Total	34,383	16,746	17,637
Rural	34,383	16,746	17,637
11. Bangro			
Total	75	31	44
Rural	75	31	44
12. Bogum			
Total	2	2	0
Rural	2	2	0
13. Bokar			
Total	1	1	0
Rural	1	1	0
14. Bolok Tangsa			
Total	1	0	1
Rural	1	0	1
15. Bomdo			
Total	2	2	0
Rural	2	2	0
16. Bori			
Total	2	1	1
Rural	2	1	1
17. Darok Tangsa			
Total	8	2	6
Rural	8	2	6
18. Deori			
Total	18	11	7
Rural	18	11	7
19. Degaru/Taraon Mishmi			
Total	3	2	1
Rural	3	2	1
20. Gallong			
Total	46	22	24
Rural	46	22	24
21. Hill Miri			
Total	8	4	4
Rural	8	4	4
22. Hotang Tangsa			
Total	3	2	1
Rural	3	2	1
23. Idu/Chulikata Mishmi			
Total	8	7	1
Rural	8	7	1
24. Katin Tangsa			
Total	1	0	1
Rural	1	0	1
25. Khamba			
Total	3	1	2
Rural	3	1	2
26. Khampti			
Total	6	6	0
Rural	6	6	0
27. Khrodeng Bangni			
Total	1	0	1
Rural	1	0	1
28. Komkar			
Total	12	6	6
Rural	12	6	6
29. Kongbo			
Total	1	1	0
Rural	1	1	0
30. Langkai Tangsa			
Total	1	1	0
Rural	1	1	0
31. Liju Nocte			
Total	1	1	0
Rural	1	1	0
32. Longchang Tangsa			
Total	5	4	1
Rural	5	4	1
33. Longphi Tangsa			
Total	8	4	4
Rural	8	4	4
34. Longri Tangsa			
Total	1	1	0
Rural	1	1	0
35. Lowang Tangsa			
Total	1	1	0
Rural	1	1	0
36. Meyor			
Total	6	4	2
Rural	6	4	2
37. Miji			
Total	1,027	527	500
Rural	1,027	527	500
38. Mikir			
Total	2	0	2

(Contd.)

(1)	(2)	(3)	(4)
Rural	2	0	2
39. Millang Abor			
Total	5	3	2
Rural	5	3	2
40. Mishing/Miri			
Total	29	15	14
Rural	29	15	14
41. Mishmi			
Total	9	6	3
Rural	9	6	3
42. Momba			
Total	1	1	0
Rural	1	1	0
43. Monpa			
Total	66	42	24
Rural	66	42	24
44. Morang Tangsa			
Total	8	3	5
Rural	8	3	5
45. Ngimong Tangsa			
Total	2	1	1
Rural	2	1	1
46. Nishang			
Total	1,663	830	833
Rural	1,663	830	833
47. Nissi			
Total	970	491	479
Rural	970	491	479
48. Nocte			
Total	11	8	3
Rural	11	8	3
49. Nonong			
Total	6	4	2
Rural	6	4	2
50. Padam			
Total	6	4	2
Rural	6	4	2
51. Panchen Monpa			
Total	4	2	2
Rural	4	2	2
52. Pongkong			
Total	5	2	3
Rural	5	2	3
53. Ponthai Nocte			
Total	7	4	3
Rural	7	4	3
54. Rangai Tangsa			
Total	1	0	1
Rural	1	0	1
55. Rongrang Tangsa			
Total	1	0	1
Rural	1	0	1
56. Sherdukpen			
Total	17	13	4
Rural	17	13	4
57. Simsa Tangsa			
Total	4	1	3
Rural	4	1	3
58. Singpho			
Total	3	0	3
Rural	3	0	3
59. Siram			
Total	17	12	5
Rural	17	12	5
60. Sulung			
Total	2,916	1,516	1,400
Rural	2,916	1,516	1,400
61. Sulung Bangni			
Total	7	3	4
Rural	7	3	4
62. Tagin			
Total	61	30	31
Rural	61	30	31
63. Tagin Bangni			
Total	6	3	3
Rural	6	3	3
64. Tanggam			
Total	3	1	2
Rural	3	1	2
65. Tangsa			
Total	16	7	9
Rural	16	7	9
66. Taram			
Total	3	0	3
Rural	3	0	3
67. Unclassified			
Total	191	89	102
Rural	191	89	102

Source : Census 1991.

Note: 1. All Scheduled Tribes includes figures for 'unclassified'.

2. Tribes having nil return are not shown.

Table 2
Numerical Strength of Different Tribes in West Kameng

Name of Tribes	Population		
	Total	Male	Female
(1)	(2)	(3)	(4)
All Scheduled Tribes			
Total	29,900	15,069	14,831
Rural	27,956	14,067	13,889
Urban	1,944	1,002	942
1. Abor			
Total	15	9	6
Rural	14	8	6
Urban	1	1	0
2. Adi			
Total	188	104	84
Rural	82	48	34
Urban	106	56	50
3. Adi Gallong			
Total	63	38	25
Rural	63	38	25
4. Adi Minyong			
Total	16	13	3
Rural	13	11	2
Urban	3	2	1
5. Adi Padam			
Total	7	5	2
Rural	7	5	2
6. Adi Pasi			
Total	17	12	5
Rural	16	11	5
Urban	1	1	0
7. Aka			
Total	2,807	1,351	1,456
Rural	2,757	1,330	1,427
Urban	50	21	29
8. Apatani			
Total	214	128	86
Rural	126	69	57
Urban	88	59	29
9. Ashing			
Total	5	2	3
Rural	4	1	3
Urban	1	1	0
10. Bangni			
Total	233	139	94
Rural	179	109	70
Urban	54	30	24
11. Bangro			
Total	1	1	0
Urban	1	1	0
12. Bogum			
Total	1,039	536	503
Rural	1,018	523	495
Urban	21	13	8
13. Bokar			
Total	5	2	3
Rural	2	1	1
Urban	3	1	2
14. Bolok Tangsa			
Total	1	1	0
Rural	1	1	0
15. Bomdo			
Total	1	0	1
Rural	1	0	1
16. Bori			
Total	10	6	4
Rural	9	5	4
Urban	1	1	0
17. But Monpa			
Total	658	330	328
Rural	657	329	328
Urban	1	1	0
18. Dafla			
Total	2	2	0
Rural	2	2	0
19. Darok Tangsa			
Total	1	0	1
Rural	1	0	1
20. Deori			
Total	35	18	17
Rural	30	15	15
Urban	5	3	2
21. Degaru/Taraon Mishmi			
Total	6	1	5
Rural	6	1	5

(Contd.)

(1)	(2)	(3)	(4)
22. Dirang Monpa			
Total	4,976	2,474	2,502
Rural	4,645	2,316	2,329
Urban	331	158	173
23. Gallong			
Total	29	15	14
Rural	12	6	6
Urban	17	9	8
24. Haisa Tangsa			
Total	43	21	22
Rural	43	21	22
25. Havi Tangsa			
Total	68	23	45
Rural	62	22	40
Urban	6	1	5
26. Hill Miri			
Total	22	11	11
Rural	18	9	9
Urban	4	2	2
27. Hotang Tangsa			
Total	13	6	7
Rural	12	6	6
Urban	1	0	1
28. Idu/Chulikata Mishmi			
Total	22	6	16
Rural	22	6	16
29. Karka			
Total	4	0	4
Rural	3	0	3
Urban	1	0	1
30. Khalim Tangsa			
Total	6	3	3
Rural	6	3	3
31. Khamba			
Total	4	3	1
Rural	1	1	0
Urban	3	2	1
32. Khamiyang			
Total	4	3	1
Rural	4	3	1
33. Khampti			
Total	30	18	12
Rural	12	7	5
Urban	18	11	7
34. Khowa			
Total	14	8	6
Rural	9	5	4
Urban	5	3	2
35. Khrodeng Bangni			
Total	1	0	1
Rural	1	0	1
36. Komkar			
Total	1	1	0
Rural	1	1	0
37. Kongbo			
Total	2	2	0
Rural	1	1	0
Urban	1	1	0
38. Lichi Tangsa			
Total	2	1	1
Rural	2	1	1
39. Lish Monpa			
Total	8	4	4
Rural	8	4	4
40. Longphi Tangsa			
Total	1	0	1
Rural	1	0	1
41. Lowang Tangsa			
Total	1	0	1
Rural	1	0	1
42. Meyor			
Total	2	1	1
Rural	2	1	1
43. Miji			
Total	3,406	1,735	1,671
Rural	3,343	1,696	1,647
Urban	63	39	24
44. Mikir			
Total	7	2	5
Rural	7	2	5
45. Millang			
Total	2	2	0
Rural	2	2	0
46. Miniyong			
Total	14	6	8
Rural	4	2	2
Urban	10	4	6
47. Mishing/Miri			
Total	28	19	9
Rural	23	15	8
Urban	5	4	1

(Contd.)

(1)	(2)	(3)	(4)
48. Mishmi			
Total	14	4	10
Rural	12	4	8
Urban	2	0	2
49. Moglum Tangsa			
Total	5	4	1
Rural	4	3	1
Urban	1	1	0
50. Momba			
Total	3	0	3
Rural	2	0	2
Urban	1	0	1
51. Monpa			
Total	11,737	5,913	5,824
Rural	11,247	5,654	5,593
Urban	490	259	231
52. Morang Tangsa			
Total	8	4	4
Rural	5	2	3
Urban	3	2	1
53. Mossang Tangsa			
Total	5	2	3
Rural	4	1	3
Urban	1	1	0
54. Muktum			
Total	2	1	1
Rural	2	1	1
55. Namsang Tangsa			
Total	2	0	2
Rural	2	0	2
56. Ngimong Tangsa			
Total	2	2	0
Rural	2	2	0
57. Nishang			
Total	80	48	32
Rural	70	43	27
Urban	10	5	5
58. Nissi			
Total	130	76	54
Rural	84	51	33
Urban	46	25	21
59. Nocte			
Total	25	18	7
Rural	20	15	5
Urban	5	3	2
60. Padam			
Total	3	0	3
Urban	3	0	3
61. Panchen Monpa			
Total	69	34	35
Rural	66	32	34
Urban	3	2	1
62. Pongkong			
Total	1	1	0
Rural	1	1	0
63. Ramo			
Total	3	3	0
Rural	3	3	0
64. Rongrang Tangsa			
Total	2	2	0
Rural	2	2	0
65. Sanke Tangsa			
Total	1	1	0
Rural	1	1	0
66. Sherdukpen			
Total	2,824	1,405	1,419
Rural	2,733	1,362	1,371
Urban	91	43	48
67. Simsa Tangsa			
Total	4	1	3
Rural	3	1	2
Urban	1	0	1
68. Singpho			
Total	1	1	0
Rural	1	1	0
69. Siram			
Total	2	2	0
Urban	2	2	0
70. Sulung			
Total	6	2	4
Rural	6	2	4
71. Tagin			
Total	40	28	12
Rural	23	19	4
Urban	17	9	8
72. Tangsa			
Total	11	8	3
Rural	5	4	1
Urban	6	4	2
73. Unclassified			
Total	886	447	439
Rural	425	226	199
Urban	461	221	240

Source: Census 1991.

Note: 1. All Scheduled Tribes includes figures for 'unclassified'.

2. Tribes having nil return are not shown.

(a) Bangni Tribe. Total number of Daflas/Bangnis/Nissis/Nissang claim to be descendant from one ancestor who begot three sons who, in turn, are believed to have been the forefathers of the three groups of clans, namely Dapum, Dodum and Dol.[3]

Further each of the above three groups is sub-divided into phratries and exogamous clans. Bangni tribe comprises Dafla, Tagin Bangni, Yano Bangni, Sulung Bangni and Khrodeng Bangni. This particular tribe inhabits the East Kameng. They are individualistic by nature comparatively and the whole tribe of Sulung has been their slaves.

They used to dispose and purchase the slaves till recently, at the price of 2 mithuns (a domesticated animal bearing high indigenous exchange value) and one piece of Endi cloth (Assam made) for every slave person of either sex.[4] Besides, a pig was sacrificed to ceremonise the deed. But now-a-days, the trade in slavery has almost been brought to standstill and stopped by the Administration. The Bangnis confined to shifting cultivation only and that also in light manner. Hence, they are by and large not self-sufficient in foodgrain production. Weaving is continued by the female folk. Other crafts called, blacksmith, pottery etc., are least known to them. At the same time they are skilled in cane carving.

They are very much conservative and usually suspect strangers coming across them. The Bangnis rear Mithun, Cow, Goat, Pig, Poultry bird, that is hen, mainly for meat purposes including occasional exchange and sacrifice, and no better economic benefit is derived. They practise polygamy socially.

(b) Monpa Tribe. Because of the second major tribes in Kameng District, the Monpas live in the north-west part of the region, that is, within the radius of five miles of Tawang, the valley of Dirang and the southern-west of Kalaktang region. The Dirang Monpas are Daling and Kolan. They are supposed to be the immigrants from Tibet through Bhutan. The garments of men folk are half-sleeved jackets called *Chuba,* over which full-sleeved maroon coloured coat, *aliphudum* is also put on. Waist is tied with a cloth called *Kichin.* Their female folk put on *Shinka, Totung, Tenga-khima* and *Kichin* also.

Their village bears a singularity in the sense that 'mane'-wall is there at the entrance of every village and inside the village there are *lakhpirs* and *chubirmanos.* Marriage by service is prevalent but divorce is prohibited traditionally. According to their tradition, dead bodies are cut into 108 pieces.

Financially, this tribe is one of the advanced tribes of Arunachal Pradesh. They are skilled weavers, keen traders and agriculturists. They rear animal for economic benefit and use wool, milk and milk-made products. They utilise the available agricultural land intensively and use animal driven plough. They have also *adopted* the hill slopes, terracing them for cultivation. They use manure of jungle leaves, cowdung, pig, chicken dung etc.

The waste of human being is also utilised by them as manure. The carpet weaving of the Monpas is famous and attractive. Indigenous paper as household industry is also existent among them. They are highly fond of dance, music and arts. Their art is well demonstrated by the door and window frames, *beautifying* their cosy stone built houses. The Monpas profess 'Mahayana Buddhism' and also are exceptionally more kind to their domesticated animals and children as compared to their other counterparts in the region.

The impact of compassionate Lord Buddha is very much perceptible amongst them. They are also very much influenced by the Tibetans, even in their way of life and food habits. For an example, the tea prepared by the Monpas with salt and butter is well liked by the strangers who happen to visit them. The background or base of the traditional organisation in Kameng among the Monpas is the village council chosen by all adult members of the village. Among the elected members, the *'Tsorgen'* (the Chief) is elected who administers the affairs of each group of village.

This way, the Monpas are having a well developed body of customary laws and the council administers the common property of the village and also decides the criminal disputes.

(c) The Miji Tribe. These people are confined to east-south of the district of United Kameng. The Mijis follow shifting cultivation mainly and resemble the neighbouring Akas. For the commercial goods, they rely on the Akas. Their dress and style of putting on the ornaments are also very much influenced by those of Akas. But the Mijis are more conservative as well as relatively poorer than certain other tribes like Akas.

(d) Sulung Tribe. Due to being the oldest, they are generally found in inaccessible high hills of the East Kameng District, that is, former Seppa Sub-division. The Sulungs have been slaves to the Bangnis, a major tribe of the region and work as forced labourers in the fields without any right to claim for wages. The services of the Sulungs to their masters during cultivation season in particular have been unavoidable: and they neither much will nor even find time to attend to their own cultivation and, consequently, have to depend on the jungles for food throughout the year. Most popular food is 'Rangbang', a jungle tree. They are blacksmiths and accurate archers. Weaving for their women is essential.

(e) The Akas Tribe. They profess the practice of painting their faces profusely and that is why the people in Assam gave this name to them. But they call themselves Hrusso. As the history of the area goes, Akas played a very significant role in the past.

The Akas have been brave and warriors as well demonstrated during their raid under the command of Tagi Raja which ultimately caused wiping out of a British outpost at Balipara in 1835.[5] Generally, every Aka village is supposed to be of a particular clan. However, the special feature of this community is its 'Rani' (Queen) system. For an instance, Jamiri village and Hushi-gaon (village) has a Rani (Queen) who is locally known as *Nigum.* The Rani is devotee of wealth, status and economic stability. She is also supposed to be the patron of her village and expected to help the needy persons.

Unlike the other tribal society, rank and property are the leading determinant of any one's status. The Akas marry their own cross cousin but marriage with own cousin (Uncle's son/daughter) is prohibited. The *'Posa'* system may be explained better as a tribute-money paid to two groups of the Akas mainly, the Hazarikhowas[6] and the *'Kapaschors'* (tealers who lurk amid the cotton plants) for maintaining peace.

However, observes A. Mackenzie that the former group was expected to give a share of its collections to the latter group. The Akas live in the upper as well as lower region of the Pradesh. Although primarily they are cultivators, their interest lies in trade and as a result they act as the middlemen between the Mijis and the other neighbouring tribe, the Bangnis. Due to being progressive in attitude, they have very close relation within the Mijis. The customs among these two tribes are also almost similar. Even inter-tribe marriage is also existing. Due to their contact with outside world, their women put on silver ornaments, bought from the markets of Assam. These contacts are also having good bearing on their garments but in their own tribal fashion only. So far their spiritual belief is concerned, those who inhabit the upper belt practise the traditional religion but those who inhabit the lower belt are *'Vaishnavites'*. The area of the Akas is bounded by the Mijis on the north, the Darrang district of Assam, on the south, the Bangnis, on the east and by the Sherdukpens, on the west who live around Rupa.

(f) The Sherdukpen Tribe. Their residence is the south-western part of West Kameng. The inhabitants of Rupa are locally known as *'Thongjis'*, and Shergaon as *'Senjis'*, and traditionally they claim that they came from Tibet. They also say their ancestors to be in *'Be Strongtsen Gompo'*, the Tibetan king who married an Assamese princess who begot two sons.

Of these two sons, the elder one became heir the Kingdom of Bhutan and the younger, Tabdung Ngowang Namje, took over the present territory of the Sherdukpens. The Sherdukpens, however, would pay tributes to the Akas, Miji and Monpa in the past.

The tributes were paid to each of the six Miji-kings in kind amounting one bullock, one head load each of salt and Jabrang spice, (indigenous spice looks like black pepper) two goats and a cowrie waist-belt. Besides, one goat, one small and one large piece of endicloth and 'dao' were paid on the every fifth year. These had been the tributes meant for only the Mijis chiefs.

However, there followers usually raided the houses of well-to-do persons. The Sherdukpens used to pay three bullocks, ten woven bags, one large and six small pieces of cloth, ten head loads of salt, twelve head loads of jabrang seeds, twenty-three fowls and two goats to each of the Aka kings also as tribute every year. The Sherdukpens were not free from the Monpas rulers of Tawang too, and therefore, used to pay 18 pieces of endicloth, 20 seers of rice and 40 seers of paddy once in every three years.

It is interesting here to note that Tawang Monpa officials also used to make return gift of coats, hats, shoes, blankets and necklace to the poor Sherdukpens. The forefathers of Sherdukpens, Japtang Bura, once met his maternal grandfather at Sibsagar (Assam), the then Ahom king who knew no bounds of happiness and ceded all the territory between Dhansiri and the Gabru (Balsiri) rivers alongwith its revenue to his grandson. At the time of departure of Japtang Bura (Old man); the Ahom king gave him a huge amount of porters and servants who, in turn, subsequently formed his reutinue.

Since then the heirs of the Sherdukpen king are known as Thongs, whereas the same of the porters and servants are known as Chhaos. Irrespective of their regular payment to tributes to others, the Sherdukpens would also collect taxes from the Kachari villages which they regarded to be their own territory. It is amazing to mention here that on the one hand the Sherdukpens used to offer tributes to the Tawang Monpa, they, on the other hand, collected taxes from Kalaktang Monpas in the Southwest of the district.[1] The Sherdukpens, being very small tribe in number, are confined to Rupa, Jigaon and Shergaon. The Khowas and Akas find their territory on the east, Thungri Jabrang fall on the south, the Monpas of Kalaktang areas on the west side and on the north falls a high hill rising as high as 10,000 feet and Rupa which itself is 5,500 feet above the sea-level.[8]

The Sherdukpens are divided into 'Thongs' and 'Chhaos' classes. They all are essentially traders rather than cultivators and as such migrate to Doimara in Assam plain, during winter. It is their annual but regular migration. They inhibit at Doimara in the temporary structure for about three months. They also profess Buddhism.

(g) The Khowa Tribals. This also known as Bugun, is another tribe with separate entity and confined to seven villages only in the west of the district. The Khowas are in the neighbourhood of the Sherdukpens, and they practice only to shifting cultivation. They are very backward economically. Their religious life is influenced by the major Buddhist tribe of the district, namely, Monpas. Weaving is known to their females but they mostly depend on the market of Bomdila. This tribe is divided into 'Exogamous' clans for the purpose of marriage.

(h) Bangro Tribe. This is a tribe inhabiting in the Eastern Kameng and akin to Bangnis. They also follow shifting cultivation and are poor. Being the smallest tribe in number in the district of Kameng, the sex-ratio of females to males comes out to be the highest amongst all, as borne out from tableabove.

II District of Subansiri

We find a large number of tribes living in this district. The numerical strength and sex-ratios of the major ones may be noted from the table is shown as follows:

Table 3
Main Tribes of Lower Subansiri District[9] (1991)

Name of Tribes	*Population*		
	Total	*Male*	*Female*
(1)	*(2)*	*(3)*	*(4)*
All Scheduled Tribes			
Total	1,10,609	55,083	55,526
Rural	96,020	47,556	48,464
Urban	14,589	7,527	7,062
1. Abor			
Total	52	17	35
Rural	40	11	29
Urban	12	6	6
2. Adi			
Total	1,954	1,067	887
Rural	493	289	204
Urban	1,461	778	683
3. Adi Gallong			
Total	603	319	284
Rural	125	65	60
Urban	478	254	224
4. Adi Minyong			
Total	134	78	56
Rural	45	33	12
Urban	89	45	44
5. Adi Padam			
Total	119	67	52
Rural	43	29	14
Urban	76	38	38
6. Adi Pasi			
Total	70	33	37
Rural	21	8	13
Urban	49	25	24
7. Aka			
Total	46	30	16
Rural	28	21	7
Urban	18	9	9
8. Apatani			
Total	18,970	9,382	9,588
Rural	11,722	5,770	5,952
Urban	7,248	3,612	3,636
9. Ashing			
Total	8	5	3
Rural	4	3	1
Urban	4	2	2
10. Bangni			
Total	139	77	62
Rural	86	50	36
Urban	53	27	26
11. Bangro			
Total	830	431	399
Rural	830	431	399
12. Bogum			
Total	1	0	1
Urban	1	0	1
13. Bokar			
Total	17	8	9
Rural	9	5	4
Urban	8	3	5
14. Bomdo			
Total	3	2	1
Rural	2	1	1
Urban	1	1	0
15. Bori			
Total	13	4	9
Rural	9	2	7
Urban	4	2	2
16. Dafla			
Total	549	253	296
Rural	549	253	296
17. Darok Tangsa			
Total	7	6	1
Rural	7	6	1
18. Deori			
Total	179	104	75
Rural	50	28	22
Urban	129	76	53
19. Degaru/Taraon Mishmi			
Total	6	6	0
Rural	6	6	0
20. Dirang Monpa			
Total	3	1	2
Rural	3	1	2
21. Gallong			
Total	231	114	117
Rural	57	28	29
Urban	174	86	88
22. Hill Miri			
Total	4,111	2,021	2,090
Rural	3,884	1,892	1,992
Urban	227	129	98

(Contd.)

(1)	(2)	(3)	(4)
23. Hotang Tangsa			
Total	83	39	44
Rural	72	37	35
Urban	11	2	9
24. Idu/Chulikata Mishmi			
Total	9	6	3
Rural	3	2	1
Urban	6	4	2
25. Kaman/Miju Mishmi			
Total	5	3	2
Rural	1	0	1
Urban	4	3	1
26. Khamba			
Total	2	1	1
Urban	2	1	1
27. Khamiyang			
Total	2	2	0
Rural	2	2	0
28. Khampti			
Total	107	65	42
Rural	32	23	9
Urban	75	42	33
29. Khowa			
Total	2	1	1
Rural	1	0	1
Urban	1	1	0
30. Komkar			
Total	7	5	2
Rural	4	3	1
Urban	3	2	1
31. Kongbo			
Total	6	2	4
Rural	4	0	4
Urban	2	2	0
32. Libo			
Total	1	1	0
Urban	1	1	0
33. Lichi Tangsa			
Total	2	1	1
Rural	2	1	1
34. Liju Nocte			
Total	2	1	1
Rural	2	1	1
35. Lowang Tangsa			
Total	2	1	1
Rural	1	1	0
Urban	1	0	1
36. Miji			
Total	66	31	35
Rural	40	20	20
Urban	26	11	15
37. Mikir			
Total	787	439	348
Rural	778	436	342
Urban	9	3	6
38. Millang Abor			
Total	1	0	1
Rural	1	0	1
39. Miniyong			
Total	86	43	43
Rural	15	10	5
Urban	71	33	38
40. Mishing/Miri			
Total	410	213	197
Rural	223	112	111
Urban	187	101	86
41. Mishmi			
Total	27	24	3
Rural	18	17	1
Urban	9	7	2
42. Momba			
Total	9	7	2
Rural	1	0	1
Urban	8	7	1
43. Monpa			
Total	372	221	151
Rural	119	85	34
Urban	253	136	117
44. Morang Tangsa			
Total	2	1	1
Rural	2	1	1
45. Mossang Tangsa			
Total	6	2	4
Rural	6	2	4
46. Muktum			
Total	8	4	4
Rural	1	1	0
Urban	7	3	4
47. Ngimong Tangsa			
Total	39	21	18
Rural	39	21	18
48. Nishang			
Total	16,793	8,501	8,292
Rural	16,051	8,077	7,974
Urban	742	424	318
49. Nissi			
Total	60,962	29,947	31,015
Rural	58,485	28,656	29,829

(Contd.)

(1)	(2)	(3)	(4)
Urban	2,477	1,291	1,186
50. Nocte			
Total	123	73	50
Rural	42	26	16
Urban	81	47	34
51. Nonong			
Total	62	30	32
Rural	57	27	30
Urban	5	3	2
52. Padam			
Total	181	107	74
Rural	126	73	53
Urban	55	34	21
53. Pailibo			
Total	1	1	0
Rural	1	1	0
54. Panchen Monpa			
Total	33	16	17
Rural	32	15	17
Urban	1	1	0
55. Pangi			
Total	40	22	18
Rural	24	13	11
Urban	16	9	7
56. Pasi			
Total	15	5	10
Rural	11	5	6
Urban	4	0	4
57. Phongle Tangsa			
Total	8	5	3
Rural	6	3	3
Urban	2	2	0
58. Pongkong			
Total	1	0	1
Rural	1	0	1
59. Ponthai Nocte			
Total	1	1	0
Rural	1	1	0
60. Ramo			
Total	2	2	0
Rural	1	1	0
Urban	1	1	0
61. Rangai Tangsa			
Total	2	2	0
Rural	2	2	0
62. Rongrang Tangsa			
Total	1	1	0
Rural	1	1	0
63. Sherdukpen			
Total	58	32	26
Rural	25	17	8
Urban	33	15	18
64. Simong			
Total	2	1	1
Rural	2	1	1
65. Simsa Tangsa			
Total	1	1	0
Rural	1	1	0
66. Singpho			
Total	13	11	2
Rural	9	9	0
Urban	4	2	2
67. Siram			
Total	6	4	2
Rural	4	3	1
Urban	2	1	1
68. Sulung			
Total	1,443	745	698
Rural	1,442	744	698
Urban	1	1	0
69. Sulung Bangni			
Total	4	4	0
Rural	4	4	0
70. Tagin			
Total	423	231	192
Rural	118	64	54
Urban	305	167	138
71. Tagin Bangni			
Total	6	2	4
Rural	6	2	4
72. Tanggam			
Total	2	2	0
Rural	2	2	0
73. Tangsa			
Total	100	57	43
Rural	28	22	6
Urban	72	35	37
74. Taram			
Total	2	1	1
Rural	2	1	1
75. Unclassified			
Total	236	120	116
Rural	156	78	78
Urban	80	42	38

Source: Census 1991.

Note: 1. All Scheduled Tribes includes figures for 'unclassified'.

2. Tribes having nil return are not shown.

Table 4
Main Tribes of Upper Subansiri District[9] (1991)

Name of Tribes	Population		
	Total	Male	Female
(1)	(2)	(3)	(4)
All Scheduled Tribes			
Total	43,034	21,642	21,392
Rural	43,034	21,642	21,392
1. Abor			
Total	5	2	3
Rural	5	2	3
2. Adi			
Total	252	140	112
Rural	252	140	112
3. Adi Gallong			
Total	3,224	1,625	1,599
Rural	3,224	1,625	1,599
4. Adi Minyong			
Total	22	12	10
Rural	22	12	10
5. Adi Padam			
Total	3	2	1
Rural	3	2	1
6. Adi Pasi			
Total	2	2	0
Rural	2	2	0
7. Aka			
Total	4	1	3
Rural	4	1	3
8. Apatani			
Total	379	213	166
Rural	379	213	166
9. Ashing			
Total	4	0	4
Rural	4	0	4
10. Bangni			
Total	20	14	6
Rural	20	14	6
11. Bangro			
Total	5	4	1
Rural	5	4	1
12. Bogum			
Total	3	3	0
Rural	3	3	0
13. Bori			
Total	1	1	0
Rural	1	1	0
14. Dafla			
Total	1	1	0
Rural	1	1	0
15. Darok Tangsa			
Total	2	0	2
Rural	2	0	2
16. Deori			
Total	6	4	2
Rural	6	4	2
17. Degaru/Taraon Mishmi			
Total	3	1	2
Rural	3	1	2
18. Dirang Monpa			
Total	6	2	4
Rural	6	2	4
19. Gallong			
Total	1,853	933	920
Rural	1,853	933	920
20. Hill Miri			
Total	4,542	2,206	2,336
Rural	4,542	2,206	2,336
21. Hotang Tangsa			
Total	7	4	3
Rural	7	4	3
22. Idu/Chulikata Mishmi			
Total	16	8	8
Rural	16	8	8
23. Janbo			
Total	4	2	2
Rural	4	2	2
24. Karka			
Total	3	1	2
Rural	3	1	2
25. Katin Tangsa			
Total	1	0	1
Rural	1	0	1
26. Khamiyang			
Total	3	2	1
Rural	3	2	1
27. Khampti			
Total	6	3	3
Rural	6	3	3
28. Komkar			
Total	2	2	0
Rural	2	2	0
29. Kongbo			
Total	32	11	21
Rural	32	11	21
30. Langkai Tangsa			
Total	5	2	3
Rural	5	2	3
31. Lichi Tangsa			
Total	3	0	3
Rural	3	0	3

(Contd.)

(1)	(2)	(3)	(4)
32. Longchang Tangsa			
Total	7	3	4
Rural	7	3	4
33. Longin Tangsa			
Total	1	1	0
Rural	1	1	0
34. Longri Tangsa			
Total	1	1	0
Rural	1	1	0
35. Longsang Tangsa			
Total	1	1	0
Rural	1	1	0
36. Lowang Tangsa			
Total	2	1	1
Rural	2	1	1
37. Mikir			
Total	1	0	1
Rural	1	0	1
38. Millang			
Total	9	3	6
Rural	9	3	6
39. Millang Abor			
Total	7	4	3
Rural	7	4	3
40. Miniyong			
Total	30	15	15
Rural	30	15	15
41. Mishing/Miri			
Total	306	146	160
Rural	306	146	160
42. Mishmi			
Total	2	1	1
Rural	2	1	1
43. Moglum Tangsa			
Total	1	1	0
Rural	1	1	0
44. Momba			
Total	20	9	11
Rural	20	9	11
45. Monpa			
Total	2	1	1
Rural	2	1	1
46. Mossang Tangsa			
Total	2	2	0
Rural	2	2	0
47. Namsang Tangsa			
Total	3	1	2
Rural	3	1	2
48. Nishang			
Total	125	76	49
Rural	125	76	49
49. Nissi			
Total	135	87	48
Rural	135	87	48
50. Nocte			
Total	14	8	6
Rural	14	8	6
51. Nonong			
Total	10	6	4
Rural	10	6	4
52. Padam			
Total	7	6	1
Rural	7	6	1
53. Pongkong			
Total	1	0	1
Rural	1	0	1
54. Rangai Tangsa			
Total	3	2	1
Rural	3	2	1
55. Simsa Tangsa			
Total	12	7	5
Rural	12	7	5
56. Singpho			
Total	2	1	1
Rural	2	1	1
57. Siram			
Total	90	46	44
Rural	90	46	44
58. Sulung			
Total	26	13	13
Rural	26	13	13
59. Sulung Bangni			
Total	3	2	1
Rural	3	2	1
60. Tagin			
Total	31,499	15,845	15,654
Rural	31,499	15,845	15,654
61. Tagin Bangni			
Total	15	7	8
Rural	15	7	8
62. Taisen Tangsa			
Total	5	2	3
Rural	5	2	3
63. Tanggam			
Total	70	28	42
Rural	70	28	42
64. Tangsa			
Total	17	9	8
Rural	17	9	8
65. Taram			
Total	6	3	3
Rural	6	3	3
66. Unclassified			
Total	180	103	77
Rural	180	103	77

Source: Census 1991.

Note: 1. All Scheduled Tribes includes figures for 'unclassified'.

2. Tribes having nil return are not shown.

(a) The Nissi Tribe. Nissi tribe resembles very much Bangni in Kameng. They occupy a vast stretch of hills and forests about half of the western part of the district. They live scattered and attend to shifting cultivation without much liking. They are as such not self-sufficient in foodgrains. When their foodgrains run short, they procure the same either on barter against animals, stone-beads and other valuable things or on loan. Despite the market at Hapoli, they at times purchase cloth from the Apatanis.

This indicates that the Nissis like traditional cloth. The Nissis who also possess a part of the adjoining East Kamang district go on migrating from one area to another and frequently come into clash with their neighbours. In the very nature of things, the economy of the Nissis tribe in Subansiri is therefore, based on cattle rather more than on land. The breeding of livestock is important occupation for these groups of the people. It is unique characteristic of this tribe.

(b) The Tagin[10] Tribe. These people are the inhabitants of the northern and eastern parts of the district of Subansiri, now upper Subansiri district, and are more or less still in the hunting stage undernourished and unhygienic in their look and habits. Their territory extends along the bank of Sipi river on the north of the united Subansiri. They always prefer shady mountain side for the village site. Weaving is known to them. They follow shifting cultivation. They are worse off than other tribes in other parts of the region. But now the things have started moving to brighter side.

(c) The Apatani Tribe. Forefathers of the Apatanis came from a country, situated in north or north-east near Supupad and Pudpumi rivers, according to their current legends. However, their cultural affinities with such people as the Abors and even higher with the Nagas of the hills in the south of Brahmaputra Valley are well recorded.[11] The whole plateau is spread over about 52 square kilometres[12] in the centre of Subansiri district (now Lower Subansiri) where its headquarters is also located is occupied by them. The density of population in this plateau comes to about 247 persons per square kilometre area as against 6 for the entire Arunachal Pradesh in 1971.

Being industrious, compact and highly organised tribesmen, they are mostly cultivators and have always surplus foodgrains. The good and fertile land available to them has intensified their interest in cultivation. They plough their land with instead of bullocks. They have developed extensive indigenous method of irrigation to water their fields from the natural sources. Due to their continuous feuds with the neighbouring tribe, i.e., Nissis and their counter resistance, the Apatanis could not carry out trade till recently. Women folk has been interest in weaving. The Apatanis are almost self-sufficient in cloth. The Apatani coat has achieved reputation amongst the plains people. Their religious belief is confined to traditional tribal forms Dnoyi and Polo. A peculiar practice is prevalent among the Apatani women. The Apatani women put on cane nods on both the sides of the fore front of nose. The fore front of the nose is made of cartilage which expands in conformity with the duration of age. To tighten the nods so that it does not fall down, a round of either cane or straw or something like that is accommodated. This new round tightens their nods and it does not fall. We see it is so regularly done that even age of a can be guessed only by looking at this nod.[13] Now it has stopped.

(d) The Hill Miri People. These people are very much akin to the Bangnis or Daflas or Nissis or Kameng and Subansiri. But what distinguishes them from the latter is their mild temperament. The Hill Miris inhabit parallel to the Tagins in Subansiri and are quite co-operative by their temperament. The singularity of this tribe is that both male and female decorate their bodies with as many as 100 cane-woven bends. They generally practise shifting cultivation and are backward economically.

(e) The Sulung Community. Among them, the Sulungs of Lower Subansiri also live in the high hills but are no more slaves to their masters, Nissis. Now, they have started cultivation. Weaving is their main hereditary occupation but it is restricted to meet their own requirements. They are very much laborious. The Mikirs and Bangros who came to a little more than 2 per cent of the total tribals in the District are similar to other tribes. While sex-ratio of the former is less than the overall one, the counterpart of the latter is the largest one in Subansiri.

III. District of Siang

District Siang, the most populous district full of unusually picturesque scenery, has got the least number of tribes, as tabulated below:

Table 5
Main Tribes of East Siang District[15]

Name of Tribes	*Population*		
	Total	*Male*	*Female*
(1)	*(2)*	*(3)*	*(4)*
All Scheduled Tribes			
Total	68,330	34,116	34,214
Rural	64,525	32,129	32,396
Urban	3,805	1,987	1,818
1. Abor			
Total	939	490	449
Rural	928	484	444
Urban	11	6	5
2. Adi			
Total	15,849	7,919	7,930
Rural	15,259	7,642	7,617
Urban	590	277	313
3. Adi Gallong			
Total	4,561	2,279	2,282
Rural	4,224	2,077	2,147
Urban	337	202	135
4. Adi Minyong			
Total	18,863	9,428	9,435
Rural	18,325	9,156	9,169
Urban	538	272	266
5. Adi Padam			
Total	4,005	1,984	2,021
Rural	3,388	1,701	1,687
Urban	617	283	334
6. Adi Pasi			
Total	2,130	1,047	1,083
Rural	2,024	998	1,026
Urban	106	49	57
7. Aka			
Total	12	4	8
Rural	9	3	6
Urban	3	1	2

(Contd.)

(1)	(2)	(3)	(4)
8. Apatani			
Total	258	144	114
Rural	127	63	64
Urban	131	81	50
9. Ashing			
Total	43	15	28
Rural	39	15	24
Urban	4	0	4
10. Bagi			
Total	3	2	1
Rural	3	2	1
11. Bangni			
Total	10	4	6
Rural	7	4	3
Urban	3	0	3
12. Bangro			
Total	4	1	3
Rural	2	1	1
Urban	2	0	2
13. Bogum			
Total	198	92	106
Rural	198	92	106
14. Bokar			
Total	44	34	10
Rural	29	23	6
Urban	15	11	4
15. Bolok Tangsa			
Total	1	0	1
Urban	1	0	1
16. Bomdo			
Total	3	1	2
Rural	2	0	2
Urban	1	1	0
17. Bori			
Total	101	61	40
Rural	87	53	34
Urban	14	8	6
18. But Monpa			
Total	2	2	0
Rural	1	1	0
Urban	1	1	0
19. Dafla			
Total	10	4	6
Rural	5	2	3
Urban	5	2	3
20. Darok Tangsa			
Total	13	3	10
Rural	13	3	10
21. Deori			
Total	83	54	29
Rural	55	39	16
Urban	28	15	13
22. Degaru/Taraon Mishmi			
Total	18	8	10
Rural	15	6	9
Urban	3	2	1
23. Dirang Monpa			
Total	2	1	1
Rural	1	1	0
Urban	1	0	1
24. Gallong			
Total	1,339	699	640
Rural	1,090	560	530
Urban	249	139	110
25. Haisa Tangsa			
Total	4	1	3
Rural	4	1	3
26. Havi Tangsa			
Total	3	2	1
Rural	3	2	1
27. Hill Miri			
Total	19	12	7
Rural	7	5	2
Urban	12	7	5
28. Hotang Tangsa			
Total	4	4	0
Rural	2	2	0
Urban	2	2	0
29. Idu/Chulikata Mishmi			
Total	283	137	146
Rural	283	137	146
30. Janbo			
Total	1	0	1
Rural	1	0	1
31. Kaman/Miju Mishmi			
Total	4	4	0
Rural	3	3	0
Urban	1	1	0
32. Karka			
Total	451	214	237
Rural	449	212	237
Urban	2	2	0
33. Katin Tangsa			
Total	6	3	3
Rural	6	3	3

(Contd.)

(1)	(2)	(3)	(4)
34. Kemsing Tangsa			
Total	4	0	4
Rural	4	0	4
35. Khamba			
Total	483	234	249
Rural	483	234	249
36. Khamiyang			
Total	6	2	4
Urban	6	2	4
37. Khampti			
Total	11	9	2
Rural	6	5	1
Urban	5	4	1
38. Khrodeng Bangni			
Total	1	1	0
Rural	1	1	0
39. Komkar			
Total	604	306	298
Rural	600	306	294
Urban	4	0	4
40. Langkai Tangsa			
Total	2	0	2
Rural	2	0	2
41. Libo			
Total	1	0	1
Rural	1	0	1
42. Lichi Tangsa			
Total	3	2	1
Rural	3	2	1
43. Lish Monpa			
Total	1	0	1
Rural	1	0	1
44. Longin Tangsa			
Total	1	0	1
Rural	1	0	1
45. Longri Tangsa			
Total	4	1	3
Rural	2	1	1
Urban	2	0	2
46. Longsang Tangsa			
Total	1	0	1
Urban	1	0	1
47. Meyor			
Total	3	2	1
Urban	3	2	1
48. Miji			
Total	26	15	11
Rural	5	3	2
Urban	21	12	9
49. Mikir			
Total	1	1	0
Rural	1	1	0
50. Millang			
Total	1,533	786	747
Rural	1,522	783	739
Urban	11	3	8
51. Millang Abor			
Total	1	0	1
Rural	1	0	1
52. Miniyong			
Total	5,448	2,679	2,769
Rural	5,013	2,441	2,572
Urban	435	238	197
53. Mishing/Miri			
Total	2,274	1,156	1,118
Rural	2,162	1,085	1,077
Urban	112	71	41
54. Mishmi			
Total	46	27	19
Rural	40	23	17
Urban	6	4	2
55. Moglum Tangsa			
Total	9	4	5
Rural	9	4	5
56. Momba			
Total	1,795	842	953
Rural	1,793	840	953
Urban	2	2	0
57. Monpa			
Total	48	30	18
Rural	17	10	7
Urban	31	20	11
58. Morang Tangsa			
Total	44	26	18
Rural	38	24	14
Urban	6	2	4
59. Mossang Tangsa			
Total	1	1	0
Urban	1	1	0
60. Muktum			
Total	4	4	0
Rural	4	4	0
61. Namsang Tangsa			
Total	3	1	2
Rural	3	1	2

(Contd.)

(1)	(2)	(3)	(4)
62. Ngimong Tangsa			
Total	1	1	0
Rural	1	1	0
63. Nishang			
Total	72	54	18
Rural	41	30	11
Urban	31	24	7
64. Nissi			
Total	136	80	56
Rural	80	46	34
Urban	56	34	22
65. Nocte			
Total	36	26	10
Rural	14	12	2
Urban	22	14	8
66. Nonong			
Total	10	6	4
Rural	7	3	4
Urban	3	3	0
67. Padam			
Total	3,381	1,665	1,716
Rural	3,160	1,552	1,608
Urban	221	113	108
68. Panchen Monpa			
Total	2	1	1
Rural	2	1	1
69. Pangi			
Total	1,634	791	843
Rural	1,594	775	819
Urban	40	16	24
70. Pasi			
Total	278	130	148
Rural	242	113	129
Urban	36	17	19
71. Phongle Tangsa			
Total	6	4	2
Rural	6	4	2
72. Pongkong			
Total	1	0	1
Rural	1	0	1
73. Ponthai Nocte			
Total	1	1	0
Rural	1	1	0
74. Ramo			
Total	5	3	2
Rural	4	2	2
Urban	1	1	0
75. Rongrang Tangsa			
Total	3	1	2
Rural	3	1	2
76. Sanke Tangsa			
Total	1	0	1
Rural	1	0	1
77. Sherdukpen			
Total	2	0	2
Rural	1	0	1
Urban	1	0	1
78. Simong			
Total	688	326	362
Rural	686	324	362
Urban	2	2	0
79. Singpho			
Total	1	0	1
Urban	1	0	1
80. Siram			
Total	6	3	3
Rural	1	1	0
Urban	5	2	3
81. Tagin			
Total	42	24	18
Rural	33	18	15
Urban	9	6	3
82. Tagin Bangni			
Total	2	1	1
Rural	2	1	1
83. Taisen Tangsa			
Total	1	0	1
Rural	1	0	1
84. Tanggam			
Total	142	73	69
Rural	141	73	68
Urban	1	0	1
85. Tangsa			
Total	28	18	10
Rural	2	1	1
Urban	26	17	9
86. Unclassified			
Total	227	126	101
Rural	200	111	89
Urban	27	15	12

Source : Census 1991.

Note: 1. All Scheduled Tribes includes figures for 'unclassified'.

2. Tribes having nil return are not shown.

Table 6
Main Tribes of West Siang District

Name of Tribes	*Population*		
	Total	*Male*	*Female*
(1)	(2)	(3)	(4)
All Scheduled Tribes			
Total	70,571	35,160	35,411
Rural	65,039	32,209	32,830
Urban	5,532	2,951	2,581
1. Abor			
Total	15	9	6
Rural	10	5	5
Urban	5	4	1
2. Adi			
Total	935	466	469
Rural	674	324	350
Urban	261	142	119
3. Adi Gallong			
Total	46,062	22,995	23,067
Rural	42,472	21,115	21,357
Urban	3,590	1,880	1,710
4. Adi Minyong			
Total	7,340	3,595	3,745
Rural	6,659	3,257	3,402
Urban	681	338	343
5. Adi Padam			
Total	37	22	15
Rural	27	16	11
Urban	10	6	4
6. Adi Pasi			
Total	14	9	5
Rural	11	6	5
Urban	3	3	0
7. Aka			
Total	5	3	2
Rural	4	2	2
Urban	1	1	0
8. Apatani			
Total	240	154	86
Rural	117	79	38
Urban	123	75	48
9. Ashing			
Total	28	12	16
Rural	26	11	15
Urban	2	1	1
10. Bagi			
Total	1	1	0
Rural	1	1	0
11. Bangni			
Total	1	0	1
Rural	1	0	1
12. Bangro			
Total	5	1	4
Rural	3	0	3
Urban	2	1	1
13. Bogum			
Total	5	5	0
Rural	2	2	0
Urban	3	3	0
14. Bokar			
Total	3,832	1,827	2,005
Rural	3,686	1,746	1,940
Urban	146	81	65
15. Bolok Tangsa			
Total	1	1	0
Rural	1	1	0
16. Bomdo			
Total	21	10	11
Rural	21	10	11
17. Bori			
Total	1,967	922	1,045
Rural	1,822	857	965
Urban	145	65	80
18. But Monpa			
Total	2	1	1
Rural	2	1	1

(Contd.)

(1)	(2)	(3)	(4)
19. Dafla			
Total	14	13	1
Rural	2	1	1
Urban	12	12	0
20. Darok Tangsa			
Total	3	1	2
Rural	3	1	2
21. Deori			
Total	28	19	9
Rural	19	14	5
Urban	9	5	4
22. Dirang Monpa			
Total	15	6	9
Rural	15	6	9
23. Gallong			
Total	3,478	1,751	1,727
Rural	3,433	1,726	1,707
Urban	45	25	20
24. Haisa Tangsa			
Total	3	2	1
Rural	3	2	1
25. Havi Tangsa			
Total	1	0	1
Rural	1	0	1
26. Hill Miri			
Total	98	52	46
Rural	64	37	27
Urban	34	15	19
27. Idu/Chulikata Mishmi			
Total	3	2	1
Rural	2	1	1
Urban	1	1	0
28. Janbo			
Total	2	0	2
Rural	2	0	2
29. Karka			
Total	1	0	1
Rural	1	0	1
30. Khamba			
Total	6	4	2
Urban	6	4	2
31. Khampti			
Total	4	3	1
Rural	2	1	1
Urban	2	2	0
32. Komkar			
Total	2	1	1
Rural	2	1	1
33. Libo			
Total	210	112	98
Rural	187	99	88
Urban	23	13	10
34. Lichi Tangsa			
Total	4	0	4
Rural	2	0	2
Urban	2	0	2
35. Longchang Tangsa			
Total	5	4	1
Urban	5	4	
36. Longin Tangsa			
Total	1	0	1
Rural	1	0	1
37. Meyor			
Total	2	2	0
Urban	2	2	0
38. Miji			
Total	1	1	0
Urban	1	1	0
39. Millang			
Total	1	1	0
Rural	1	1	0
40. Miniyong			
Total	1,341	672	669
Rural	1,274	616	658
Urban	67	56	11
41. Mishing/Miri			
Total	223	120	103
Rural	187	101	86
Urban	36	19	17
42. Mishmi			
Total	18	12	6
Rural	12	9	3
Urban	6	3	3
43. Moglum Tangsa			
Total	1	1	0

(1)	(2)	(3)	(4)
Rural	1	1	0
44. Momba			
Total	1,953	986	967
Rural	1,854	930	924
Urban	99	56	43
45. Monpa			
Total	46	36	10
Rural	18	14	4
Urban	28	22	6
46. Morang Tangsa			
Total	3	0	3
Rural	3	0	3
47. Mossang Tangsa			
Total	2	1	1
Rural	2	1	1
48. Muktum			
Total	2	1	1
Rural	2	1	1
49. Ngimong Tangsa			
Total	2	0	2
Rural	2	0	2
50. Nishang			
Total	40	23	17
Rural	31	18	13
Urban	9	5	4
51. Nissi			
Total	138	85	53
Rural	102	64	38
Urban	36	21	15
52. Nocte			
Total	24	17	7
Rural	20	14	6
Urban	4	3	1
53. Nonong			
Total	7	3	4
Rural	7	3	4
54. Padam			
Total	12	7	5
Rural	4	2	2
Urban	8	5	3
55. Pailibo			
Total	974	475	499
Rural	967	470	497
Urban	7	5	2
56. Panchen Monpa			
Total	1	1	0
Rural	1	1	0
57. Pangi			
Total	7	4	3
Rural	7	4	3
58. Pasi			
Total	4	3	1
Rural	2	1	1
Urban	2	2	0
59. Ramo			
Total	833	399	434
Rural	810	387	423
Urban	23	12	11
60. Sherdukpen			
Total	4	4	0
Urban	4	4	0
61. Simong			
Total	1	1	0
Rural	1	1	0
62. Siram			
Total	5	4	1
Rural	5	4	1
63. Sulung			
Total	15	8	7
Urban	15	8	7
64. Tagin			
Total	447	244	203
Rural	385	207	178
Urban	62	37	25
65. Tanggam			
Total	1	1	0
Rural	1	1	0
66. Tangsa			
Total	14	12	2
Rural	11	9	2
Urban	3	3	0
67. Unclassified			
Total	60	33	27
Rural	51	27	24
Urban	9	6	3

Source: Census 1991.

Note: 1. All Scheduled Tribes includes figures for 'unclassified'.

2. Tribes having nil return are not shown.

(a) The Adi Tribe. The inhabitants of Siang district who once known as the Abor, are now called the Adi which means friendly and progressive, in outlook as they have undergone such favourable transformation over the years. This common title '*Adi*' comprises many groups, namely, Padam, Minyong, Pangi, Shimong, Ashing, Pasi, Karko, Bokar, Bori, Ramo, Pailibo, Milang, Tangam and Tagin.[16] Among them, Padam, Minyong, Gallong, Khamba, Momba and Tagin are major ones according to their different and independent entities. The land of the Adis is of songs and dances.

The Adis community as a whole are less conservative than other tribes. They have, for instance, now started milking the cow to consume milk which was till recently not regarded as edible. In the villages of foot-hills, mithun is almost non-existent. They rear cows and bulls. For milking cows, they construct separate cow-sheds. They plough their fields with bullocks. They know boating and their fishing art is a little better advanced than that of the Adis inhabiting the hills. Now-a-days, average Adis are aware of the happenings of the outside world.

Among the Adis, Mopin, Sulung and Attar celebrations are popular. The Padam and Minyong live in the east and eastern-south of the district which is now East Siang district. These are essentially, cultivators and have adopted recently new methods in agriculture. Their fine weaving and carpet-making are well known and decorate the museum of Arunachal Pradesh. They grew cotton on their fields and weave clothes. But now-a-days, they have almost stopped growing cotton. They are very much rely on the market of Pasighat and Along.

Next the Gallongs being 38,259 in number that is 36 per cent of the total tribals in the united district, it is another interesting group of the Adis. The area inhabited by them is spread from the Subansiri river in the west to the Sindo river in the southern east of the district. The northern and southern boundaries of the Gallongs are confined by the Brahmaputra and the Siyom rivers.[17] In the west of their habitation, the Hill Miris live and in the east, Minyong, Bori, Ramo and Pailibo. As having less sloping land, the Gallongs are luckier than the Boris and the Minyong who are having rocky and steep sloping lands. They follow method of shifting cultivation and are self-sufficient in their food needs. The interesting system of polyandry[18] exists among them. Though polygamy has been common among all the tribes of Arunachal Pradesh for quite some time, the monogymy has been thriving specially among the Padam and Minyong. For the marriage purposes, there are two rigid divisions among the Gallongs such as Niji and Nira. The marriages within these two clans are strictly forbidden. Like the Bangnis, the brideprice among them is very high. But now the practice of polyandry is on the decay among the educated people.

(b) The Tagin Tribe. These people live in the western part of Siang and follow method of shifting cultivation. They have faith in traditional religion, and regard animal sacrifice as being equivalent to offering of flowers to their God. They are not progressive in viewpoint unlike other groups of the Adis.

(c) The Momba Tribe. This particular tribe is very much akin to the Khambas in almost all respects. Inhabiting the northern border of the district, they profess Buddhism and attend to shifting cultivation. Weaving is known to them but in a very odd form. They rear mithun, cow, goat and chicken. They failed to utilise their animals economically unlike other Buddhist tribes.

(d) The Miri Tribals. This is also a tribe having independent entity, though constitutes 1.3 per cent of total tribal population in the District of united Siang. Amongst Miris just the males exceeded females, that is to say, the sex-ratio is less than unity.

(e) The Khamba Community. Khambas resemble the Monpas of Kameng and live along the international frontier in the Tuting area. The prevalent pattern of their cultivation is shifting. Foodgrain production along-with food gathering from the jungles fulfil their purpose. They have got faith in Buddhism.

IV. District of Lohit

Lohit District is the abode of Mishmis, Khamptis and Singphos, each comprising a number of sub-tribes; Mishmi, for instance, comprises Digaru, Miju

Table 7

Total Population, Males and Females[19] of Main Tribes in the District of Lohit

Name of Tribes	Population		
	Total	Male	Female
(1)	(2)	(3)	(4)
All Scheduled Tribes			
Total	40,933	20,660	20,273
Rural	38,065	19,147	18,918
Urban	2,868	1,513	1,355
1. Abor			
Total	5	1	4
Rural	5	1	4
2. Adi			
Total	1,422	723	699
Rural	1,154	572	582
Urban	268	151	117
3. Adi Gallong			
Total	316	164	152
Rural	169	89	80
Urban	147	75	72
4. Adi Minyong			
Total	66	35	31
Rural	34	16	18
Urban	32	19	13
5. Adi Padam			
Total	745	399	346
Rural	624	339	285
Urban	121	60	61
6. Adi Pasi			
Total	28	16	12
Rural	27	15	12
Urban	1	1	0
7. Aka			
Total	2	2	0
Rural	1	1	0
Urban	1	1	0
8. Apatani			
Total	253	128	125
Rural	72	42	30
Urban	181	86	95

(Contd.)

(1)	(2)	(3)	(4)
9. Ashing			
Total	1	1	0
Urban	1	1	0
10. Bangni			
Total	2	1	1
Rural	1	1	0
Urban	1	0	1
11. Bangro			
Total	5	2	3
Rural	2	1	1
Urban	3	1	2
12. Bogum			
Total	7	4	3
Rural	7	4	3
13. Bomdo			
Total	2	0	2
Rural	2	0	2
14. Bori			
Total	2	1	1
Rural	2	1	1
15. But Monpa			
Total	1	1	0
Rural	1	1	0
16. Dafla			
Total	1	1	0
Rural	1	1	0
17. Darok Tangsa			
Total	4	3	1
Rural	4	3	1
18. Deori			
Total	3,378	1,648	1,730
Rural	3,196	1,553	1,643
Urban	182	95	87
19. Degaru/Taraon Mishmi			
Total	6,049	3,030	3,019
Rural	5,940	2,982	2,958
Urban	109	48	61
20. Dirang Monpa			
Total	3	3	0
Rural	2	2	0
Urban	1	1	0
21. Gallong			
Total	160	81	79
Rural	138	71	67
Urban	22	10	12
22. Haisa Tangsa			
Total	5	0	5
Rural	4	0	4
Urban	1	0	1
23. Havi Tangsa			
Total	9	7	2
Rural	9	7	2
24. Hill Miri			
Total	27	13	14
Rural	9	4	5
Urban	18	9	9
25. Hotang Tangsa			
Total	12	7	5
Rural	10	6	4
Urban	2	1	1
26. Idu/Chulikata Mishmi			
Total	287	134	153
Rural	119	54	65
Urban	168	80	88
27. Janbo			
Total	2	1	1
Rural	2	1	1
28. Kaman/Miju Mishmi			
Total	9,814	4,857	4,957
Rural	9,634	4,755	4,879
Urban	180	102	78
29. Karka			
Total	19	14	5
Rural	18	13	5
Urban	1	1	0
30. Katin Tangsa			
Total	5	1	4
Rural	1	0	1
Urban	4	1	3
31. Kemsing Tangsa			
Total	1	0	1
Rural	1	0	1
32. Khalim Tangsa			
Total	1	1	0
Rural	1	1	0
33. Khamba			
Total	9	4	5
Rural	5	3	2
Urban	4	1	3
34. Khamiyang			
Total	830	430	400
Rural	804	418	386
Urban	26	12	14
35. Khampti			
Total	7,490	3,744	3,746

(Contd.)

(1)	(2)	(3)	(4)
Rural	7,029	3,531	3,498
Urban	461	213	248
36. Khowa			
Total	5	4	1
Rural	5	4	1
37. Kongbo			
Total	2	0	2
Rural	2	0	2
38. Lichi Tangsa			
Total	2	2	0
Urban	2	2	0
39. Liju Nocte			
Total	1	1	0
Urban	1	1	0
40. Longphi Tangsa			
Total	2	2	0
Rural	1	1	0
Urban	1	1	0
41. Longri Tangsa			
Total	9	4	5
Rural	9	4	5
42. Longsang Tangsa			
Total	1	0	1
Rural	1	0	1
43. Meyor			
Total	326	163	163
Rural	324	163	161
Urban	2	0	2
44. Miji			
Total	33	16	17
Rural	7	3	4
Urban	26	13	13
45. Mikir			
Total	13	8	5
Rural	7	4	3
Urban	6	4	2
46. Miniyong			
Total	37	20	17
Rural	23	13	10
Urban	14	7	7
47. Mishing/Miri			
Total	4,140	2,090	2,050
Rural	4,070	2,052	2,018
Urban	70	38	32
48. Mishmi			
Total	2,560	1,353	1,207
Rural	2,218	1,163	1,055
Urban	342	190	152
49. Moglum Tangsa			
Total	8	6	2
Rural	8	6	2
50. Momba			
Total	4	4	0
Rural	4	4	0
51. Monpa			
Total	63	35	28
Rural	20	10	10
Urban	43	25	18
52. Morang Tangsa			
Total	3	2	1
Rural	1	0	1
Urban	2	2	0
53. Mossang Tangsa			
Total	4	3	1
Rural	3	2	1
Urban	1	1	0
54. Namsang Tangsa			
Total	6	3	3
Rural	6	3	3
55. Nishang			
Total	8	6	2
Rural	6	4	2
Urban	2	2	0
56. Nissi			
Total	195	99	96
Rural	87	45	42
Urban	108	54	54
57. Nocte			
Total	143	104	39
Rural	73	55	18
Urban	70	49	21
58. Padam			
Total	55	33	22
Rural	39	25	14
Urban	16	8	8
59. Pailibo			
Total	1	1	0
Urban	1	1	0
60. Panchen Monpa			
Total	1	1	0
Rural	1	1	0
61. Pangi			
Total	5	2	3
Rural	5	2	3

(Contd.)

(1)	(2)	(3)	(4)
62. Ponthai Nocte			
Total	5	3	2
Urban	5	3	2
63. Ramo			
Total	2	1	1
Rural	2	1	1
64. Sanke Tangsa			
Total	1	1	0
Rural	1	1	0
65. Sherdukpen			
Total	5	3	2
Rural	1	0	1
Urban	4	3	1
66. Singpho			
Total	891	458	433
Rural	851	436	415
Urban	40	22	18
67. Siram			
Total	22	8	14
Rural	22	8	14
68. Sulung			
Total	5	1	4
Rural	4	1	3
Urban	1	0	1
69. Tagin			
Total	40	23	17
Rural	21	10	11
Urban	19	13	6
70. Taisen Tangsa			
Total	4	1	3
Rural	4	1	3
71. Tangsa			
Total	69	40	29
Rural	52	31	21
Urban	17	9	8
72. Taram			
Total	4	3	1
Rural	3	2	1
Urban	1	1	0
73. Unclassified			
Total	1,295	699	596
Rural	1,156	604	552
Urban	139	95	44

Source: Census 1991.

Note: 1. All Scheduled Tribes includes figures for 'unclassified'.

2. Tribes having nil return are not shown.

(A) Groups Among the Mishmis

This tribe is close to the Bangnis of Kameng and Nissis of Subansiri. The Mishmis are very much individualistic. The village community has got no much meaning[20] to them and their houses are scattered and the social unit is almost their family itself. They cultivate paddy in winter as well as summer, both on shifting fields. Tobacco is also grown by them as they are very much accustomed to smoking. Their women are also very skilled weavers. The Idu group of the Mishmis is keenly interested traders.

This Idu, also known as Chulikata Mishmis, visits the markets of Assam to dispose musk, ivory, skins and Mishmi Teeta (a medicinal root) and purchase salt, cloth and other articles of daily use. They produce also rubber, though in small quantity, specifically for the purpose of sale. The dress of the Mijus and the Digarus comprises a strip of cloth bound in the waist. A coat, without sleeves, reaching down from the neck to the knee, is their common garment made of two pieces of hand-loom cloth woven by the Mishmi women in a harmonious colour combination of red, black, brown and blue colours. The Idus, one of the groups of the Mishmis, call the soul *"megra"* or *"arra"*. According to them, the soul is the vital principle which sustains life in their body. When a woman is carrying, it is the soul which enters the womb kindles the foetus into life. The soul is invincible and not perceived or felt. When the soul withdraws, the body falls dead. This is their traditional belief so strong.

(B) The Khampti People

The Khamptis and the Singphos are the Buddhist tribes, having much affinity with the Burmese culture and traditions. The Khamptis are inhabiting the southern part and are skilled people. Due to constant contacts with outsiders, they are very much progressive in their outlook. They use buffalo-plough and skilfully utilise the flow of streams and rivers to turn their rice-husking machines. Khampti is the sole tribe in Arunachal Pradesh having its own script.

No doubt other tribes, namely, Monpas, Sherdukpens and Tangsas are also having their script, but not absolutely of their own. The Monpas own the script but Tibetan one. The Khamptis also apply manure in their cultivation as the Monpas of Kameng. The Khamptis domesticate animals from commercial angle also. They are good cultivators and keen traders. They also milk the buffalo and cow and consume the milk products. The Khamptis are known to migrate from Shan States of Burma and speak a language of the Tai group.

V. District of Tirap

Leading tribes in this district are Wanchos, Noctes and Tangsas, as borne out from the table given below:

Table 8
Numerical Strength of Tribes[21] in Tirap

Name of Tribes	*Population*		
	Total	*Male*	*Female*
(1)	(2)	(3)	(4)
All Scheduled Tribes			
Total	68,770	34,734	34,036
Rural	66,661	33,675	32,986
Urban	2,109	1,059	1,050
1. Abor			
Total	3	3	0
Rural	3	3	0
2. Adi			
Total	332	194	138
Rural	115	91	24
Urban	217	103	114
3. Adi Gallong			
Total	139	80	59
Rural	128	71	57
Urban	11	9	2
4. Adi Minyong			
Total	52	30	22
Rural	43	24	19
Urban	9	6	3
5. Adi Padam			
Total	28	17	11
Rural	17	11	6
Urban	11	6	5
6. Adi Pasi			
Total	1	1	0
Rural	1	1	0
7. Aka			
Total	2	1	1
Rural	1	1	0
Urban	1	0	1
8. Apatani			
Total	137	81	56
Rural	99	65	34
Urban	38	16	22
9. Ashing			
Total	1	1	0
Urban	1	1	0
10. Bangni			
Total	9	6	3
Rural	5	5	0
Urban	4	1	3
11. Bangro			
Total	1	1	0
Urban	1	1	0

(Contd.)

(1)	(2)	(3)	(4)
12. Bogum			
Total	10	6	4
Rural	8	6	2
Urban	2	0	2
13. Bori			
Total	1	0	1
Rural	1	0	1
14. Dafla			
Total	1	1	0
Rural	1	1	0
15. Deori			
Total	65	31	34
Rural	51	22	29
Urban	14	9	5
16. Degaru/Taraon Mishmi			
Total	2	0	2
Rural	2	0	2
17. Dirang Monpa			
Total	2	2	0
Rural	1	1	0
Urban	1	1	0
18. Gallong			
Total	32	13	19
Rural	7	3	4
Urban	25	10	15
19. Haisa Tangsa			
Total	1	1	0
Rural	1	1	0
20. Hill Miri			
Total	18	12	6
Rural	16	12	4
Urban	2	0	2
21. Idu/Chulikata Mishmi			
Total	10	7	3
Rural	3	2	1
Urban	7	5	2
22. Kaman/Miju Mishmi			
Total	2	2	0
Rural	1	1	0
Urban	1	1	0
23. Khalim Tangsa			
Total	1	1	0
Rural	1	1	0
24. Khamba			
Total	6	1	5
Rural	1	0	1
Urban	5	1	4
25. Khamiyang			
Total	8	5	3
Rural	5	3	2
Urban	3	2	1
26. Khampti			
Total	79	56	23
Rural	55	44	11
Urban	24	12	12
27. Khrodeng Bangni			
Total	2	2	0
Rural	2	2	0
28. Kongbo			
Total	1	1	0
Rural	1	1	0
29. Korang Tangsa			
Total	1	0	1
Rural	1	0	1
30. Liju Nocte			
Total	7	5	2
Rural	6	4	2
Urban	1	1	0
31. Longchang Tangsa			
Total	5	3	2
Rural	4	3	1
Urban	1	0	1
32. Longphi Tangsa			
Total	1	1	0
Rural	1	1	0
33. Longsang Tangsa			
Total	5	1	4
Rural	3	1	2
Urban	2	0	2
34. Miji			
Total	12	5	7
Urban	12	5	7
35. Miniyong			
Total	3	1	2
Urban	3	1	2
36. Mishing/Miri			
Total	34	27	7
Rural	26	21	5
Urban	8	6	2
37. Mishmi			
Total	20	15	5
Rural	14	13	1
Urban	6	2	4
38. Moglum Tangsa			
Total	23	13	10
Rural	15	8	7
Urban	8	5	3
39. Momba			
Total	4	3	1
Rural	3	3	0
Urban	1	0	1

(Contd.)

(1)	*(2)*	*(3)*	*(4)*
40. Monpa			
Total	36	20	16
Rural	13	11	2
Urban	23	9	14
41. Morang Tangsa			
Total	2	1	1
Rural	2	1	1
42. Mossang Tangsa			
Total	2	2	0
Rural	2	2	0
43. Muktum			
Total	4	3	1
Rural	3	2	1
Urban	1	1	0
44. Namsang Tangsa			
Total	1	0	1
Urban	1	0	1
45. Ngimong Tangsa			
Total	1	1	0
Rural	1	1	0
46. Nishang			
Total	4	1	3
Rural	3	1	2
Urban	1	0	1
47. Nissi			
Total	89	43	46
Rural	62	33	29
Urban	27	10	17
48. Nocte			
Total	22,062	11,200	10,862
Rural	20,997	10,631	10,366
Urban	1,065	569	496
49. Nonong			
Total	4	3	1
Rural	4	3	1
50. Padam			
Total	20	11	9
Rural	7	5	2
Urban	13	6	7
51. Pailibo			
Total	16	10	6
Rural	9	6	3
Urban	7	4	3
52. Panchen Monpa			
Total	1	1	0
Rural	1	1	0
53. Pangi			
Total	3	3	0
Rural	3	3	0
54. Pasi			
Total	4	4	0
Urban	4	4	0
55. Phongle Tangsa			
Total	3	3	0
Rural	3	3	0
56. Rongrang Tangsa			
Total	4	2	2
Rural	4	2	2
57. Sherdukpen			
Total	30	21	9
Rural	19	16	3
Urban	11	5	6
58. Simong			
Total	1	1	0
Urban	1	1	0
59. Singpho			
Total	24	12	12
Rural	17	10	7
Urban	7	2	5
60. Siram			
Total	1	0	1
Urban	1	0	1
61. Sulung			
Total	1	1	0
Rural	1	1	0
62. Sulung Bangni			
Total	1	0	1
Rural	1	0	1
63. Tagin			
Total	50	31	19
Rural	31	22	9
Urban	19	9	10
64. Tagin Bangni			
Total	1	1	0
Rural	1	1	0
65. Tanggam			
Total	3	0	3
Rural	1	0	1
Urban	2	0	2
66. Tangsa			
Total	157	86	71
Rural	83	61	22
Urban	74	25	49
67. Taram			
Total	2	0	2
Rural	2	0	2
68. Wancho			
Total	45,182	22,643	22,539
Rural	44,749	22,433	22,316
Urban	433	210	223

Source : Census 1991.

Note: 1. All Scheduled Tribes includes figures for 'unclassified'.

2. Tribes having nil return are not shown.

(A) The Wancho Tribe. The people of the tribe live in the southern-west part of the district, bordering Nagaland and resemble the Konyak Nagas who live in the Tuengang area. The Wanchos practise shifting cultivation and observe principle of polygamy. Though weaving is known to their women folk, the Wanchos are not traditionally fond of clothes. But they make for this by the use of plenty of ornaments of ivory, bones, horns, shells and beads, while the more *ephemeral* grace of feathers and flowers distinguish their ears and hair. They are very fond of wearing decorated head gears, heavy strings of beads on neck, arms, legs and ears. Though Tatooing is prevalent among many tribes, it is found in special fashion among the Wanchos. The males do tatooing heavy over their face, around eyes, elaborate designs on neck, throat, chest, arms, back and on the stomach. Their women make across tatooing over the naval, necklace designs between breasts and draw elaborate designs on the shoulders and dots on both thighs.

One more oddity of this tribe is that the village chief is paid tributes by the villagers for controlling them. Among the Wanchos, in case of unnatural death, disposal of the body is not done in the usual customary method. In such cases, the body is wrapped with mats and fastened to a tree in the jungle. The personal belongings of the deceased are thrown close to that tree.

(b) The Nocte Tribe. They live in the central part of the district of Tirap, nearing the plains of Assam. Their malefolk put on cane belt and bamboo slips around legs and arms as part of their dress. Their hair-style is also separate from that of other tribes. They shave hair on front head and wear the hair at the crown tied in a bun over the nape of the neck. Tatooing and dreadful wardances are highly popular amongst the Noctes as well as the Wanchos. Like the Wancho-village chief, the Nocte village chief is also paid tributes by the villagers, for the same ground. The Noctes profess Vaishnavism.

Their main source of earning is by selling 'pan' *(Betal leaf)* to the plains of Assam and working in the tea-gardens of Assam during winter. They practise shifting cultivation also. Because of being close to the plains, they show keen interest in trade and commerce. It is the only tribe in Arunachal Pradesh, having brinewells for the manufacture of salt.

(c) Community of the Tangsas. People of this tribe lives in the east, bordering Burma as such the Tangsas have similar links with the Burmese, who have influenced even their way of life including style of dresses. The impact of ordinary living of the Burmese on their life is very much borne out of the fact that males put on lungis, shirts and turbans and the females wrap a piece of cloth around the body from the breasts to the ankles and wear blouse. In some cases women put on turbans also.

The 'Tangsas' are another promising tribe of Tirap district and agriculture is their chief occupation. They practise wet rice cultivation and also grow edible fruits. They have started general merchandise shops.

They are industrious and their women are good weavers. Their artistic talents find place in the expression of their textile designs. They also prepare hand bags with diamond design woven thereon and invariably carry them with great feeling of accomplishment. They are sensitive to scarlet red, black and dark green colours particularly. The Tangsas are more elaborately dressed than the Noctes and the Wancho people.

(d) The Singpho Community. They live in the north-east corner of the Tirap District and are Buddhists by religion. This tribe is polygamous, having interesting laws of inheritance under which only the eldest and the youngest sons inherit, while the middle ones are often left out.[22] The eldest inherits the estate and the family title, while the youngest receives the movable property and makes his own setup.

Thus, the middle sons fall under the proletariat class. The Singphos are good cultivators and their women are expert in weaving. They are said to belong to the 'Kachin Clan' of upper Burma.[23] The Singphos who were considered identical with Karus or Kachayens of Burma, had initially their abode in the great eastern branch of Irrawady. Later, they extended as far south as N. Lat 25°—while close to north and eastern border of China in Lat 27.30° with the break-up of the Northern Shankingdom. The Kakhayens entered as aggressor and conquest which practically placed in their hands the past of nation between upper Assam and Burma.[24] However, their language is akin to Manipuri Kuki, Abor and Karen but the script is that of the Shan.

I. Socio-Economic Belt Grouping

We shall now divide the whole habitation of the people in Arunachal Pradesh into three belts, namely, (a) the northern belt, (b) the middle belt and (c) the southern belt.

(a) These living in the northern belt are very much influenced by the Tibetans look in the religion as well as other spheres of life. The people, living in this belt along the Chinese border, were in close touch with the Tibetans and because of that trade could be possible in the past. They used to visit Tibet with skin, Tobacco and other jungle herbs to barter them for salt, utensils and cloth in particular. This connection helped them to broaden their outlook too.

It also helped them to learn knitting of sweater, carpet weaving and ploughing of land etc. The people living in the middle belt remained highly cut off from the outside world. This is the reason that apart from shifting cultivation, no other worthwhile economic activities they could resort to.

In this region, self-weaving has been in vogue. In fact, it continues to be there even now. The people in the soutern belt are traders because of their suitable geographical location. As the inhabitants of extreme northern belt and commercial contacts with the Tibetans, the people of this belt also had the same economic relation with the Assamese people.

Unlike the people in the middle belt region, who are still in primitive stage because of unfavourable geographical location, the people of northern and southern belts are advanced both economically as well as culturally. Despite existence of large number of tribes and sub-tribes in the different parts, there are certain common features relating to all of them in the whole of Arunachal Pradesh. These common features relate to ownership of land, site of villages, village chief system, construction works, shifting cultivation, weaving, food habits, democratic and co-operative social life style, domestic life, domestic animals, religious and cultural affinities, marriage practices, and the absence of money economy. All these may be taken into account to have an appraisal of their financial problems.

1. Formation of a village. In general, Arunachal village is a group of single pattern long thatched huts, either on the top of the hills or in the smaller narrow valleys. While selecting the site for village construction, water source for drinking, security[29] and availability of suitable land for cultivation are significant factors borne in mind.

It is the high hills and rivers that act as boundary lines between the two villages. Now one more aspect is that every Buddhist tribe village must have a monastry which is the heart of their village life and culture. Similarly, an Adi village must have a 'Namghar' or *'Mosup'* which also helps as village male-shed during the day.

2. Setup of houses. The tribesmen generally live in cosy houses, either stone built or thatched. Being the terrain cold, these cosy houses provide them considerable comforts. The houses of the Monpas and Sherdukpens of Kameng are two storyed and constructed of stone or wood with plank floors often with carved wooden doors and window-frames. The other tribesmen usually live in thatched big and long halls erected on poles. These long or small halls are built of bamboo, wood, cane, thatch, banana leaves, cane leaves, straw, millet or jungle grass with either flattened bamboo or wooden planks which lies on poles from two feet to twelve feet above the around. Due to the land being uneven and undulating, the poles are to be used to get a level floor. Doors are few and quite far between the windows are completely absent, barring those of Buddhist tribes.

Their roof is thatched with plantain leaves, cane leaves, other tree-leaves, paddy straw, millet or flattened bamboo. The wall of thatched houses is built of twilled bamboo mats or wooden planks and floor of wooden planks or plain flattened bamboo ceiling of flattened bamboo is also very commonly given where millet for the preparation of Apong (local beer), other household articles such as baskets, dao, ropes and other agricultural appliances are kept. In the rear front of the house, a small verandah is provided to accommodate one or two sets of mortars and pestles for husking and pounding the grown grains.

In the front of the same residential house, big verandahs are left and the half of the same is covered beneath the roof and the remaining half remains open where family members often indulge in gossipping and attend to cane and wood carving, bamboo carving, basketry, weaving, and so on and do take sun-bath during the winter. The front verandah serves a number of other purposes also, namely, for drying grains, entertaining strangers and tourists. To reach the verandah and enter the house, a notched ladder of thick wood is placed at each of the verandahs, joining the ground below.

Thus, there are two doors in each and every residential house for the entrance and exit. The width of this house is from 18 to 20 feet generally, while the length depends upon the number of the living hearths. The front of the residential house is decorated generally.[26] With the skulls of hunted animals and their horns, symbolising economic as well as social status of the family apart from personal achievements of the head of the households. A hut, for storing foodgrain, is constructed quite apart the residential cluster where valuable household articles such as Tibetan bells and Dunki[27] are also kept, only with a view to check fire risk.

In the olden days, the separate construction of cowshed, goatshed and poultry was foreign to them excepting the Buddhist tribes like Monpas. But, now-a-days it is a personal phenomenon and quite common in the foothills. So far the hygiene and sanitation is concerned, the surrounding of each and every house is dirty because of their domesticated pigs and total absence of proper maintenance. Even the interior of their houses is dirty which, in turn, may be attributed to their habit of frequent spitting. But the interior of the houses of the Monpas, Adis and some other tribes are relatively more clean.

The rainy season adds fuel to the fire and, consequently, the interior of the house as well as the surroundings get more dirty. Having returned from the fields and anywhere else outside house, they enter their houses straight way without washing or cleaning their feet. The extent of congestion in rural parti is well borne out from the following data:

Articles inside a house. Their social as well as economic life of the tribesmen is by and large influenced by their habits developed from time immemorial. Their household articles as such include cooking utensils[28] like bamboo jars and pots, brass, aluminium, dishes, wooden pots, earthen pots, weapons of fighting like bow and arrow, spear, guns and big daos, agricultural appliances like baskets.small daos, spade, hatchet, mortars and pestles, their dresses (endi-cloth) and ornaments like stone-beads and silver rings. The other common household articles are Deokahin, Deo-ghanti, Tibetan bells,[29] bamboo woven pots for winnowing grains, lion looms and smoking pipes traditionally possessed. Now-a-days modern amenities like car, T.V. etc. are also possessed proudly.

II. The Social Set-up, Social Hierarchy and Social Organisation

Although a village comprises preferably on tribe and its sub-tribes, other tribes are, however, allowed to live alongwith them. The village chief or headmanship[31] is regarded as an essential element of village administration, designed to make solidarity of the tribes concerned through imposition of certain customs and conventions like marrying within the given tribal groups. Any matter, concerning community as a whole, like organising social functions, is decided at the village level. The individual functions like marriage, religious rites, house-building,[32] selection of land for the purpose of shifting cultivation and individual disputes also involve the entire village in the process of decision making. Even assumption of crimes like taking revenge and murder call for co-operation at village level. Thus, the village, being a unit of social life, is the most integrating force.

(a) Crimes within Society. To err is human as universally accepted. But to restrict the cases of crimes, the society has got certain specific provisions which are based on the principles of compensation. In cases where there is no scope for imposing the fines, the guilty is punished generally. Compensation as well as fine is paid in kind such as animals of their livestock, poultry birds like, mithun, cow, yak, sheep, pig, goat and chicken. The same is also discharged through surrender of stonebeads, valuable metal pots and religious pots. The daos, iron ring stove, hatchet and grain are also acceptable in return of these penalties.

Amongst the fine and the compensation, the latter is of more significance from economic stand point. In case of murder, for instance, the aggrieved party resents to take revenge by killing either the culprit or any other important member of the same family

In case of such development, the offender surrenders himself by compensating the aggrieved party. The amount of such compensation is fixed mutually in accordance with conventions in vogue. The convention[33] is that for each of the limbs, the amount of compensation is determined differently. The traditional village panchayat body, locally known as Kebang, is the judicio-administrative body of an Adi village. This Kebang consists of sensible, mature and influential elders of the Adi village as its usual members and looks after the administration of justice in the society.

The situation of a murder is committed, it is informed to the Kebang. However, the complainant insists on demanding a man for a man. In the past either the offender or any member of family had to turn life-long slave of the complainant. But now-a-days, the Adis are also not allowed by the Administration to demand a man for a man, ultimately the complainant has to remain contented with compensation which can be at exhorbitant rate. Like the Bangnis, the convention amongst the Adis is to seek compensation from the offender at different rate[34] on various grounds.

(b) The family life and formation. Like any other society, family is the primary unit of individuals, in Arunachal Pradesh. Mostly families[35] comprise husband, wife and unmarried children. But married children, mother, father and mother-in-laws, other relatives, servants and slaves[36] are also found as members of a family, but such cases are not many. Male children live with the parents till they attain age of maturity and are ultimately married. The sons so separated are allotted lands by the father for their subsistence. The men stay with the eldest wife.[37] He visits all the wives in rotation, and in return, the husband is fed by all the wives. The husband functions as guardian of all.

Moreover, aforesaid persons, married daughters alongwith their husbands[38] and children are also found in the families. It is at times said that old parents, physically disabled to attend to work, are included within their son's families.

(c) Social Pattern of Tribals. The tribal society in this state is essentially a patriarchal one. The sons are entitled to inherit paternal property. The paternal kins are considered to be nearer and their relationship is considered more important than that of maternal kins. There is a practice in vogue that the daughters who want to settle down in the parent's village alongwith their husband, are allotted a few plots of land by their fathers for providing them some source of subsistence but such daughters do not enjoy, however, legally any claim, thereon. It cannot be taken to mean that women have no position in tribal society.

Apart from polygymy[39] prevalent amongst some tribes, women enjoy a good position. Before a man goes for second wife, he has to consult his present wife whose opinion is ultimately honoured. Women are not just a household wife for bearing children and attending to domestic works, right from cooking to food gathering rather they participate actively with their husbands in different social-religious functions. Due to their vital role in various activities, women are regarded as asset to the family.

Barring administrative affairs as well as war and chasing of animals, they enjoy respectable position in all walks of life. Now, a word about idealism of individuals as a social institution may be mentioned. A person who shows his readiness to extend co-operation in all social matters makes best use of his wealth and other means in helping the destitute and yet does not think much of himself and too has the spirit of service and endurance[40] is considered noble by the villagers.

In spite of aforesaid idealism and individuals' ideology, slavery[41] has been in vogue amongst the Nissis, Akas, Mijis and Bangnis (Daflas) of Kameng district. The slave tribe is of the Sulungs who are known to be outside the master-class social structure.[42] Other than slaves, those who are caught while stealing are subjected to a heavy fine.

In case such guilty persons express their inability to pay fines, they are compelled to serve as slaves to the persons whose things were being stolen. Although the slaves are at times allowed to live in the village and alongwith their masters, they are not accorded the position of family members. The slaves were purchased and sold also by their masters till recently, at the price of 2 mithuns and a piece of cloth.[43] The Akas, generally used to purchase them from the neighbouring Bangnis.[44] We also came to know of a provision that a slave could be set free after their devoted services for a considerable period. The slaves so freed were also allowed to acquire, wealth and settle anywhere they wished. They were, however, to attend to periodic roll-calls made by their masters to testify their loyalty to the latter. In case failed to present themselves before the masters just on their calls, they were searched and reconverted into slaves.

Here, it is a notable fact that despite social stratification like chief, middle, slave or servant class, as well as tribe distinction, as observed for social purposes, we do not see problem of the touchability in the region under study.

(d) Rules Regarding Marriage. As per custom, a tribeman must marry within the tribe but[45] essentially outside the clan. This marriage in their society is a matter to pay the bride heavy price and as such its settlement has at times involved excessive bargaining. It is the bridegroom's party that has to take initiative for the marriage and acceptance is sought in the early phase of negotiation and bride's price is, thus, determined. As soon as an agreement is arrived at, marriage-date is fixed through mutual consultation and thereafter the groom's father sends either Apong, (pig meat), or at least roasted meat of any animal; though the former is mostly preferred roasted rats, dry fish and roasted squirrel[46] to the house of his would-be daughter-in-law.

Rate[47] of bride is paid in kind such as 'mithun, cow, yak, stone-beads, brass bowls, metal pots, big iron ring stove, deokathin, and Tibetan bell etc.

Simultaneously, bride-price is paid in instalments. In certain cases, settlement of such price is done after birth of two to three issues. On the date of the commencement of marriage, many rituals are performed where parents do perform an important role. A feast is offered to the villagers at groom's house sacrificing mithun or cow or any animal, according to their means. On bride's side, a mithun is necessarily sacrificed and rituals are performed. When the girl comes, another ceremony is performed and a feast[48] is thrown to the people concerned. In case a girl gets paralysed or gets, disabled physically after her marriage, the pride-price[49] is either to be returned or another girl is to be offered to the groom.

Thus, physical disability of a bride, after the marriage, causes a peculiar situation for her parents. The idea underlying such compensation arrangement is to meet permanent shortage of labour through refund of bride's price. In case, the girl becomes disabled after giving birth to any child, the girl's father is exempted from the charge.

There is also a custom that in some tribes the marriage of a girl is settled while she is in the lap of mother and the question of settlement of bride-price begins from that time itself followed by the payment of the settled amount in a number of instalments. Having reached the full womanhood, at times she refuses, to agree with such arrangements. Her refusal as such invites trouble for her father as the latter has to return all what he had got as price. In such a circumstance, girls are instead forced to yield to their parents' wishes.

Such enforced marriages lead to elopements which, in turn, involves prosecution of legal proceedings; the eloper is usually made to pay compensation similar to bride-price paid to the girl's father[50] by the first husband. The number of such refusals these days have gone high and this, in turn, has discouraged settlement of marriage during the childhood. Thus, women even a barren one, occupy important position in the society. Once she joins the husband's family, she is taken for granted as its asset. It is, thus, very natural not to part with one's own asset. And this is the mystery behind the fact that son inherits his step mother[51] excepting own mother who begot him, after the expiry of his father. If she does not want to live in the family, another man who marries her pays half price.[52] If she is very old, no-body would marry her as such she remains there as widow. A Census data about age, sex and marital status for scheduled tribes is given on next page.

Though practice of polygymy is prevalent prominently among the Bangnis, Akas, Majis, Wanchos, Tangsas, Apatanis, Tagins and Hill Miri etc. the monogymy

Table 9
Age, Sex and Marital Status for Scheduled Tribes

Age group	*Total*	*Never Married*	*Married*	*Widowed*	*Divor-ced*	*Unsp-ecified*
1	2	3	4	5	6	7
ALL SCHEDULED TRIBES						
Rural						
All Ages	**5,18,222**	**2,85,995**	**2,12,462**	**18,378**	**1,351**	**36**
0 - 9	1,54,877	1,54,877	0	0	0	0
10-14	59,840	58,729	1,065	23	20	3
15-19	46,142	39,251	6,785	45	55	6
20-24	37,126	15,888	20,880	192	164	2
25-29	40,131	7,248	32,267	391	223	2
30-34	31,099	2,686	27,690	540	182	1
35-39	29,186	1,447	26,753	842	143	1
40-44	26,963	1,003	24,379	1,457	122	2
15-44	2,10,647	67,523	1,38,754	3,467	889	14
45-49	24,338	633	21,796	1,803	105	1
50-54	21,770	619	18,361	2,683	107	0
55-59	13,061	339	10,849	1,811	59	3
60-64	13,502	348	10,016	3,069	69	0
65-69	6,468	136	4,673	1,637	22	0
70-74	5,117	134	3,246	1,698	39	0
75-79	2,093	43	1,292	747	11	0
80+	3,259	258	1,687	1,287	23	4
Age not stated	3,250	2,356	723	153	7	11
Rural						
All ages	**32,129**	**20,059**	**11,644**	**338**	**82**	**6**
0 - 9	9,727	9,727	0	0	0	0
10-14	4,171	4,114	53	1	3	0
15-19	4,263	3,778	479	1	2	3
20-24	3,665	1,551	2,099	6	9	0
25-29	3,397	427	2,932	19	18	1
30-34	2,134	112	1,987	18	17	0
35-39	1,647	34	1,559	38	16	0
40-44	1,031	26	954	47	4	0
15-44	16,137	5,928	10,010	129	66	4
45-49	794	14	725	50	5	0
50-54	471	12	409	48	2	0
55-59	211	4	172	34	1	0
60-64	183	6	138	35	4	0
65-69	58	1	42	15	0	0
70-74	51	8	29	14	0	0
75-79	16	2	13	1	0	0
80+	44	10	23	10	1	0
Age not stated	266	233	30	1	0	2

Source : *Census 1991.*

is, on the other hand, followed among the Padam, Minyong, Monpa, Khamptis and Sherdukpens. The polyandry[53] is followed by the Gallongs of the district of Siang due to bride-price being considerable one which cannot be afforded to by those poor people particularly who have got a number of sons. But now-a-days this practice of polyandry is reducing every day.

(e) The birth of a child. As soon as the bride conceives, the task of the husband is taken to be over. In some tribes, like Adis, Sherdukpens, Khamptis, Monpas, husband is, however, supposed to take her special care and pregnant women is not allowed to attend to any heavy work. In some tribes like Bengnis, Sulungs, Tagins, Apatanis, Akas, Mijis and Wanchos, no work is forbidden. But, they are not allowed to go to funeral grounds. Nextly, the pregnant ladies cannot stretch their legs crossed while sleeping towards the sun. The meat of hunted animals is forbidden to be eaten by them. In some tribes, the mithun-meat is also not consumed during the period. A census data of ever married, current married women belonging to scheduled tribes by age, number of their surviving children by sex is given on next two pages.

In almost all the tribes, the lady attends to cultivation even during the advanced stage of pregnancy. In case women feel abnormal labour pain and delivery is delayed, the priest is called to observe some religious rites, sacrificing a chicken. The priest is mostly presents in kind, namely, cloth, dao, pig, chicken or stone-beads in case delivery takes place safely. In the normal delivery priest is not called. Among the Buddhist tribes, the priest is urged to sing certain 'mantras' from religious books for the desired result. Oil massage of the baby is not common. The post-natal precaution is also not undertaken. It is only upto six to seven months that mother takes care of the baby and mother does not care too much thereafter. She goes to the field and the baby is left at home with elder brothers or sisters who are even below 8 to 9 years of age. Though male child as the first issue in the family is preferred in almost in 99 per cent[54] cases children of both the sexes in equal number[55] are welcomed throughout. So far the number of children is concerned, most of the tribals are not at all concerned with their number in the family as they hold the view that both hands and mouth come together.

(f) The Health Issues. Man falls prey to the disease now and then. The region under study is infested with various kinds of communicable diseases like Malaria which alone had been a serious menace to public health. This truth, however, may be illustrated that in 1955 out of nearly two lakhs of patients examined throughout the area, as many as 61,000[56] were found to be infected by Malaria. Further, Tuberculosis has also been affecting health of the general people in a wide area of Arunachal Pradesh. Leprosy also is another infectious disease prevalent in many parts of Arunachal Pradesh.

Before 1951, the services of medical personnel were availed of by the Assam Rifles personnel on duty in the region and very nominal medical services were available to the local residents. But, with the commencement of the First Five

Table 10

Ever Married and Currently Married Women Belonging to Scheduled Tribes by Present Age, Number of Surviving Children and Total Number of Surviving Children by Sex

Present Age	Total ever/ currently married women	Ever/currently married women with number of surviving children						Total surviving children		
		0	1	2	3	4	5+	Total	Males	Females
1	2	3	4	5	6	7	8	9	10	11
ALL SCHEDULED TRIBES										
RURAL										
Ever Married										
All ages	**1,27,127**	**39,382**	**18,580**	**18,577**	**16,514**	**13,148**	**20,912**	**2,84,781**	**1,48,212**	**1,36,569**
Less than 15	706	639	28	37	0	0	0	102	58	44
15-19	5,413	3,683	1,326	289	71	42	0	2,285	1,185	1,100
20-24	14,967	6,049	4,254	2,869	1,241	406	147	16,141	8,242	7,899
25-29	19,601	5,915	3,324	3,956	3,201	1,973	1,232	35,697	18,181	17,516
30-34	15,690	4,252	1,822	2,431	2,505	2,164	2,515	37,299	18,853	18,446
35-39	14,947	3,872	1,318	1,904	2,170	2,060	3,623	41,663	21,197	20,466
40-44	13,851	3,698	1,249	1,580	1,801	1,763	3,759	40,076	20,646	19,430
45-49	11,848	3,036	1,113	1,373	1,563	1,380	3,382	35,142	18,286	16,856
50-54	9,820	2,774	1,044	1,303	1,263	1,106	2,329	26,337	14,077	12,260
55-59	5,847	1,562	657	795	813	700	1,320	15,742	8,515	7,227
60-64	6,068	1,639	912	852	792	677	1,196	15,041	8,231	6,810
65-69	2,983	753	494	422	398	326	589	7,486	4,181	3,305
70-74	2,402	638	467	326	289	282	400	5,494	3,054	2,440
75-79	1,001	221	194	163	152	107	162	2,353	1,343	1,010
80 +	1,468	384	310	217	206	129	220	3,228	1,780	1,448

(Contd.)

(Contd.)

1	2	3	4	5	6	7	8	9	10	11
Currently Married										
All ages	**1,11,951**	**35,310**	**15,890**	**16,174**	**14,405**	**11,518**	**18,644**	**2,50,972**	**1,29,941**	**1,21,031**
Less than 15	682	622	25	33	0	0	0	91	53	38
15-19	5,335	3,638	1,300	286	68	41	0	2,240	1,161	1,079
20-24	14,672	5,925	4,142	2,827	1,228	404	145	15,887	8,111	7,776
25-29	19,142	5,741	3,202	3,867	3,158	1,955	1,219	35,126	17,895	17,231
30-34	15,149	4,079	1,707	2,333	2,443	2,110	2,476	36,373	18,398	17,975
35-39	14,200	3,645	1,210	1,754	2,074	1,981	3,536	40,163	20,437	19,726
40-44	12,612	3,332	1,066	1,409	1,638	1,616	3,551	37,247	19,199	18,048
45-49	10,361	2,697	906	1,160	1,309	1,185	3,103	31,289	16,253	15,036
50-54	7,607	2,167	727	948	948	868	1,948	21,120	11,249	9,871
55-59	4,437	1,215	465	550	601	523	1,083	12,287	6,609	5,678
60-64	3,645	1,014	484	480	453	417	797	9,440	5,145	4,295
65-69	1,696	442	264	220	206	181	382	4,460	2,486	1,974
70-74	1,067	316	187	124	115	121	204	2,496	1,391	1,105
75-79	440	107	74	66	67	45	81	1,061	622	439
80 +	527	166	90	71	63	45	91	1,184	654	530

Source : Census 1991.

Notes

1. All ages includes 'age not stated'.
2. Number of ever/currently married women in column 4 includes women not reporting number of surviving children.
3. The age groups having nil return are not shown.

Year Plan serious efforts were made by the national Government for extending medical benefit to the local inhabitants living in the interior areas of the Union Territory.

Till the end of March 1973, 6 District Hospitals, 39 Dispensary Health Units, 1 T.B. Hospital, and Ayurvedic Dispensaries[57] were functional in the region. Thus, to make available the most modern medical assistance to the tribesmen, the services of specialists in various branches have been provided alongwith the facilities of ambulances and X-rays. Despite these provisions of facilities, it is interesting to note that the local people have failed to utilise them just because of their outlook and superstitious beliefs. The people of Arunachal Pradesh by and large, prefer to go first to the village priest who either reads cutting a boiled egg or looks into the heart of a chicken to find out the cause of his/her disease and thereafter suggests the person concerned to arrange for given sacrifice of animal to suppress the evil spirit. It is learnt in course of personal investigation that very few people who live very close to hospitals used to go to a physician and in case the latter fails to cure patient, their genuine faith in the priest was reinforced. But now the favourable trend is also noticed to have started. Increasingly larger number of tribal people has started visiting doctors.

(g) Faith in Religion. Barring the Buddhist followers, the image worship is not in vogue amongst the tribesmen in Arunachal Pradesh. Although a bamboo image of the spirit to be prayed in traditional style is installed, it cannot be concluded they worship image. It is held that there are separate gods to be prayed for on different occasions like physical disability, rain, hunting and so on. Their religious rites are performed through sacrificing animals.

(h) Disposal of Dead Bodies. The sense of brotherhood is very much evident amongst the tribals in this Union Territory as evident from the fact that when in a given household death takes place, the whole village feels very much aggrieved. The people belonging to a number of tribes like Padam, Minyong and Millang share sorrows by offering even meal to the bereaved members of the village. They even sleep with them to show their heartiest sympathy. The dead humans are, generally, burried. In Sherdukpen tribe only, the dead body of the rich person is cremated.[58] In a few tribes, the dead body is neither buried nor cremated but kept in a thatched hut, built for the same purpose.[59] Amongst some tribes, the dead-body is disposed of on the same day, in some cases on the following day.

Amongst almost all the tribes and sub-tribe like Daflas,[60] the dead body is given a bath like Aryan Hindus before final disposal. They believe that while good deeds take one to the heaven after death, one is supposed to go to hell because of poor act like the stealing, cheating, oppressing others. They have belief that those who die prematurely, or are involved in accident of any type do not go to any of these worlds. Their souls wander aimlessly hither and thither along the painful tracks.

III. Cultural Belt Region

As we know all tribesmen in Arunachal Pradesh have a rich cultural heritage which they can be proud of, the Monpas, the Sherdukpens, the Khamptis and the Adis may be mentioned specifically. In general, all the tribals are devotees of *'Donyi Polo'* (the sun and the moon), the supreme spiritual force in the universe other than the Buddhists tribes. The philosophy of the non-Buddhist tribes is based on the different manifestation of nature and on universalism. This has naturally endowed them with the strength to preserve their own time-old tradition and culture today. As noted by Dr. Verrier Elwin, (erstwhile NEFA) Arunachal Pradesh may conveniently be divided into three artistic and cultural provinces.

The people of the first one are Buddhists by religion. The religion commands the faith of the Monpas, the Sherdukpens, the Singphos, the Khamptis, the Mombas and the Khambas significantly throughout the area, though they could have influenced many other neighbouring tribes such as the Khowas, the Hrusso and Dhammai groups and a few Idu-Mishmis etc. It is important to classify Tibetan-speaking Mombas and Khambas living along the frontier from Mechuke through Tuting Mankhota and Gelling to Wallong in Lohit District. While the artistic tradition of the Khamptis and Singphos has taken a different course and they are geographically isolated from the frontier groups, it would be convenient to include them, here, since they are Buddhists and also have certain points in common, such as the making of masks, which are foreign elsewhere in the region under study.

Next cultural province stretches from west to east that is from Seppa in Kameng and through the greater part of Subansiri, Siang and Lohit districts. This cultural area is populated by tribes of different traditions, yet united from the standpoint of culture in their attachment to weaving, the absence of wood carving and a stress of fine work in cane and bamboo.

After this, third cultural belt is Tirap being populated by the Noctes, who are Vaishnavite by religion, the Wanchos, a brave independent people, and the gentle, opium loving Tangsas, all of whom have come under some what influence of Burma. The Tangsa groups, in fact, still have many contacts across the border, inter-marry, with the Burmese tribes, do their hair and dress in a Burmese style.

In case, a fourth cultural belt, in regard to the region, is talked about, it is a truth to be accepted. Because, in the present years, the religions from outside Arunachal have begun casting their influences on the local population residing in the foothills, except Buddhists. During the field investigation conducted by the present author, the issue of adoption and persuasion was inquired as inspired by the situation present.

In majority of cases, they were found indecisive. In few cases, the advocacy of both the Christianity and Hinduism was heard. Somewhere it was also heard saying that they should limit to their own time-old religion which is gold. This above narrated situation may lead them to either of the three which will be finalised in course of time.

It is also said that those non-Buddhist tribals who have not permitted their faith to shake are modifying their traditional style of worshipping which is vividly visible when the Adis, around Pasighat, observed the 'Mopin' or 'Atar' or 'Solung' festivals, specifically.

About the ceremonies of the local people in the region under study, the same may be divided into three main groups such as the ceremonies connected with the cure of sickness, the ceremonies connected about agriculture and the ceremonies connected with death, including the Buddhist tribes. In addition to the above categories of ceremonies, there are spring festivals, seasonal festivals, harvesting festivals and yearly festivals. These festivals are, generally observed in the mist of much fan-fair and festivity alongwith dances and songs.

For an example, the Monpas perform many pantomime dances. Such dances are displayed during the annual festivals. But their *"Ajilamu"* dance is very popular. Similarly, the war dance by the Wanchos and the Noctes is exhibited which is also attractive. In a nutshell, these dances and songs are socio-religious in nature. Besides, the ceremonies and festivals are too costly affairs due to the sacrifices of expensive animals like Mithun, Cow etc. The important ceremonies and festivals observed by the different tribes may be viewed as below: The Monpas observe Losar, Losar-Khachot, Ngah, Sakadawa, Guru-Rinpoche, Drukpa-Tsejee, Ganden-Nyamchot, Nyanpa-Gozum, Torgya, Ghoikar, Dungyur, Nyungye, Sang-dui, Tsokar and lastly Guthok; Sherdukpens perform Chhekar, Losar, Wang (these three are Buddhist ceremonies) and Khiksaba; the Khowas perform Kshyat-Sowai; the Nishangs Nissis follow Mlokon-yulo; the Apatanis perform Morong, Dree and Yapung; and "Fung-glin" or Chidang and Nechido are respectively observed by the Mijis and the Akas. Similarly "Sangken" is the most significant festival of the Khamptis and "Rren" of the Idu-Mishmis. Most of these festivals are performed on community basis. Nextly, there is no fixed date for celebrating the festivals in any of the tribes; the same is fixed at the village level in accordance with their convenience.

(a) Faith in Religion. As far their religious belief is concerned, it is very much similar to that of the Hindus. They believe in gods and goddesses and worship them on various occasions. They have impeached faith in the concept of rebirth. Their religious restrictions are also similar like their sky-world where the sun lives, there is "SURYAPURAN" in the Hindu religion. But their way of worship is very much costly even beyond ordinary imagination. For instance, one mithun costs average Rs. 1500 which is usually sacrificed without any consideration. This, of course, affects economy. The disposal of dead body is also much expensive because of cow's and mithun's sacrifice.

(b) Gender Based Distribution of Activities. Since, females do not confine themselves to domestic affairs alone like cooking, preparation of Apong, carrying of drinking water, they do take up the work of clearing the burnt-jungle on the current jhum field, dibbling, weeding, act of harvesting fields, winnowing fire-wood collection, weaving, pottery, husking and pounding of grains, and spinning

On the other, matters relating to the household administration as well as that of village, the house-building and repair, tracks and bridges construction and repair, selection of site for the shifting cultivation, felling the jungles on the field, setting them into fire, protecting crops while on the field, settlement of marriage of both the sexes, purchase and sale, war and chase, sacrificing of animals, setting of disputes are the tasks, performed by the male folk.

This division of work between male and female is economic by nature rather than religious. Early to bed and early to rise has been their habit. They generally get up from beds before the sun-rise. While women go to fetch drinking water and start husking, pounding and cooking, the male folk entertain the babies and at the sametime, start drinking home brewed beer. By 7 A.M. or even earlier, specially during cultivation season, they are accustomed to take their meals.

During winter or off-seasons, they have meal a little latter but in no case beyond 8 A.M. After meals, women first go out, taking Apong and rice for the mid-day meal to fields and the men follow them quite later and remain there for sometime. The women work there till 15.00 hours or so. While coming back to their homes the women start collecting fire-wood and vegetables. Further, at the evening, the females fetch water, husk, pound and cook.

Before cooking, Apong is prepared for evening drink. During evening, persons go out on social visits for gossiping and offered Apong through the hosts. They take their dinner[61] also and go their beds early. So far their seasonal engagement is concerned, during cultivation times, usually from the second half of February to the first half of October, cultivation keeps them busy. During slack period of the year they have light work-load. After cooking and taking meal, women attend to weaving for most of the time, the males attend to cane, wood and bamboo carving. They attend to basketry and rope-making. Besides, they go for hunting,[62] fishing, touring and repairing houses and also bridges over the rivers and streams and tracts.

In some area, fire-wood is collected by both the sexes to meet the requirements of rainy season. They maintain well their individual bamboo groves, settle marriages,[63] purchase and sell animals locally; conduct trade and go out to purchase essential commodities, select sites for next jhuming. But those who are in foothills and practice permanent cultivation throughout the year absorb themselves in cultivation.

(c) Diet. Their food consists of cereal, millet, vegetables and meat. Among the grains, paddy, maize and millet are their traditional items. Among the vegetables, chilly, pumpkins, melons, ginger, sweet potato, brinjals, plantain flower, mushroom and also roots are common. Cotton,[64] Pan[65] and Poppy[66] plants are also traditional items grown simultaneously on the same jhum field. Now-a-days barley, wheat, potato, mustard and sugarcane too are grown in same lands.

These tribals have a very little taste for sweets. Except Buddhist tribes, none other tribes like milk.[67] In common, their diet must consist of grain, simply boiled ones with little salt but with heavy dose of chilly, Apong and meat.

They eat meat of any animal including dead, sacrificed and even killed ones. Often they take fried and roasted fish and meat. The reason is that the supply of fish and meat is an occasional one, a matter of chance at all. Again, there was no local market where the surplus quantity might be taken for sale. Due to absence of market and scope for trading, they are either bound to consume whole quantity or to surrender surplus to others or to even store the same for future consumption. The situation is, of course, changing now. The households consuming meat and fish regularly are very few in number. This way, by preserving the surplus quantity of meat and fish drying, they used to derive maximum utility, though at the cost of vitamins. Habit of drinking 'Apong' needs a special mention here from economic standpoint. While, on the other hand, the Apong, being compulsory item in food, enriches the diet of the tribals, it leads on the other hand, the cascity of foodgrains as such they take drink recklessly. When they are at the harvest, the consumption of foodgrains is not given any thought. After the stock of food-grains is finished, they collect whatever they could from the jungles and at times approach their better off neighbours for loan or exchange of goods to bridge over the gap between times of shortage and that of subsequent harvest.

(d) Animals and Poultry. Their animals and poultry, generally, comprise mithun,[68] cow,[69] yak, horse, sheep, goat, elephant[70] and chicken and at times ducks also. These animals are well reared by the Monpas and some other Buddhist tribes, whereas others allow them to roam in the jungles and when required they are caught hold of by them. The state level census data for religion belonging to Scheduled Tribes are as follows :

Table 11
Religion for Scheduled Tribes

Scheduled Tribe	*Rural*			*Urban*		
	Total	*Males*	*Females*	*Total*	*Males*	*Females*
1	2	3	4	5	6	7
ALL SCHEDULED TRIBES						
All Religions	**5,18,222**	**2,58,595**	**2,59,627**	**32,129**	**16,802**	**15,327**
1. Buddhists	62,650	31,365	31,285	2,871	1,513	1,358
2. Christians	72,487	35,748	36,739	2,407	1,263	1,144
3. Hindus	75,544	37,903	37,641	3,759	2,099	1,660
4. Jains 6	3	3	0	0	0	
5. Muslims	134	56	78	20	9	11
6. Sikhs2	2	0	0	0	0	
7.Other Religions & Persuations	2,91,344	1,45,545	1,45,799	22,823	11,802	11,021
8. Religion not stated	16,055	7,973	8,082	249	116	133

Source: Census 1991.

In every week, each mithun must come once to lick salt. If a mithun does not come back, it is supposed missing and search is made for the same. Chicken and Goats are generally provided with necessary shelter. Pigs rest under the floor of the residential house. The same is the fate of cows too. But mithuns do not come to take shelter at night time.

Thus, concludingly the change for the better in the lives of the villagers and the cultural and spiritual renaissance of people that has been brought about in recent times, in Arunachal Pradesh is something to be valued. However, in the light of the needs of the tribal people there is no room for any complacency. The attempt is being made to bring them into main stream of the country's development. As aptly remarked by Dr. Elwin, hunger, disease, ignorance and isolation are evils whose cure cannot be delayed anymore; they must be treated fast and efficiently.[71]

Language (Mother Tongue)

In Mizoram different languages and dialects are spoken by the people representing various tribes. These tribes may be mentioned as follows: The scheduled tribes, chakmas, dimasa, Garo, Hajong, Hmar, Khasi and Jaintia (including synteng or Pnar, War and any Kuki Tribes including Biate. All these have been systematically and comprehensively listed in the Chart entitled 'Mother Tongue for Scheduled Tribes'. These clearly depict almost details including rural and urban, and male and females. For further details, numerical strength about the languages spoken by scheduled tribes in Arunachal Pradesh is given below :

Table 12

Mother Tongue for Scheduled T.ibes

Scheduled Tribe	*Mother Tongue*	*Number of Speakers*					
		Rural			*Urban*		
		Total	*Males*	*Females*	*Total*	*Males*	*Females*
1	2	3	4	5	6	7	8
All Scheduled Tribes							
	Adi	1,41,170	70,338	70,832	12,253	6,397	5,856
	Anal	5	5	0	1	0	1
	Angami	3	0	3	0	0	0
	Ao	8	5	3	0	0	0
	Arabic/Arbi	17	10	7	0	0	0
	Assamese	4,606	2,343	2,263	171	94	77
	Bengali	247	139	108	25	14	11
	Bhili/Bhilodi	4	0	4	0	0	0
	Bhotia	12	8	4	2	2	0
	Bhumij	3	1	2	2	2	0

(Contd.)

(Contd.)

1	2	3	4	5	6	7	8
	Bodo/Boro	76	42	34	24	9	15
	Coorgi/Kodagu	2	1	1	0	0	0
	Deori	1,571	810	761	300	168	132
	Dogri	11	3	8	0	0	0
	English	55	33	22	2	2	0
	Gangte	2	2	0	0	0	0
	Garo	51	21	30	6	4	2
	Gondi	3	1	2	0	0	0
	Gujarati	3	1	2	0	0	0
	Halam	1	0	1	0	0	0
	Hindi	2,098	1,224	874	271	152	119
	Hmar	1	0	1	0	0	0
	Ho	1	0	1	0	0	0
	Jatapu	1	1	0	0	0	0
	Kabui	1	1	0	0	0	0
	Karbi/Mikir	769	428	341	11	3	8
	Kashmire	4	1	3	0	0	0
	Khandeshi	4	2	2	1	1	0
	Kharia	8	3	5	0	0	0
	Khasi	1	1	0	1	0	1
	Kisan	1	1	0	0	0	0
	Korwa	2	0	2	0	0	0
	Kui	2	1	1	0	0	0
	Kuki	2	1	1	0	0	0
	Kurukh/Oraon	4	1	3	0	0	0
	Lahnda	2	1	1	0	0	0
	Lepcha	1	1	0	0	0	0
	Limbu	2	1	1	0	0	0
	Lushai/Mizo	50	26	24	0	0	0
	Malayalam	12	10	2	9	5	4
	Malto	12	7	5	0	0	0
	Manipuri	1	1	0	0	0	0
	Mao	3	1	2	0	0	0
	Marathi	1	0	1	0	0	0
	Miri/Mishing	8,301	4,227	4,074	389	216	173
	Mishmi	26,226	12,985	13,241	1,295	726	569
	Monpa	40,732	20,201	20,531	1,637	840	797
	Munda	16	7	9	2	1	1
	Mundari	14	14	0	2	1	1
	Nepali	202	105	97	23	12	11
	Nicobarese	2	2	0	0	0	0
	Nissi/Dafla	1,58,669	78,554	80,115	12,049	6,207	5,842
	Nocte	26,676	13,389	13,287	1,251	700	551
	Oriya	32	22	10	1	1	0
	Pabha	1	0	1	0	0	0

(Contd.)

(Contd.)

1	2	3	4	5	6	7	8
	Paite	1	0	1	0	0	0
	Parji	4	1	3	0	0	0
	Pawi	1	1	0	0	0	0
	Phom	14	8	6	0	0	0
	Pochury	1	0	1	0	0	0
	Punjabi	4	2	2	3	1	2
	Sangtam	6	4	2	0	0	0
	Santali	75	38	37	1	1	0
	Savara	2	1	1	1	0	1
	Sema	2	2	0	0	0	0
	Sherpa	2	0	2	0	0	0
	Sindhi	1	1	0	0	0	0
	Tamil	2	0	2	2	1	1
	Tangkhul	1	1	0	0	0	0
	Tangsa	18,073	9,037	9,036	245	116	129
	Telugu	8	5	3	0	0	0
	Tibetan	3,402	1,698	1,704	190	93	97
	Tripuri	10	6	4	1	1	0
	Urdu	45	30	15	6	3	3
	Vaiphei	6	3	3	0	0	0
	Wancho	38,473	19,528	18,945	515	281	234
	Yimchungre	1	1	0	0	0	0
	Zemi	1	1	0	0	0	0
	Others	46,383	23,245	23,138	1,437	748	689

Source : Census 1991.

References

1. Census, Arunachal Pradesh: Series-24, Part II-A, General Population Tables, 1972, p. IX.
2. Census Department of Arunachal Pradesh; District Census Hand Book of Kameng District, (unpublished), Monpa is a common name for a group of tribes of same ethnological identity, namely, Monpa, Tawang Monpa, Dirang Monpa, But Monpa and Kalaktang Monpa, etc. Since the data has been collected from Gazetteer also, so the figures here are not the latest.
3. B.K. Roy Burman, (Dr.): Census of India, 1961, Office of the Registrar General, India, Government of India, New Delhi—Demographic and Socio-Economic Profiles of the Hill Areas of North-East India, 1970, p. 90.
4. Raghuvir Sinha: The Akas, 1962, p. 59.
5. Later, in 1848 the British agreed to pay the 'Kapaschor Akas' an annual 'Posa' of Rs. 520.
6. The Bazarikhowas had a right to *'Posa'* originally conceded by the Assamese, while the Kapaschors did not enjoy the privilege. Later the then Assam Government also granted the right of Posa to the Hazarikhowas, at the time of the annexation of Assam (Sinha Raghuvir: *op. cit.*, pp. 4-6).
7. B.K. Roy Burman (Dr.): *op. cit.*, p. 88.
8. R.R.P. Sharma: The Sherdpens, (1961), p. 1.

9. Directorate of Census Operations, Arunachal Pradesh: District Census Hand Book of Subansiri (unpublished) (1971) Census.
10. They inhabit the above portion of Subansiri and Sub-division of Siang. The Tagins at times affiliate themselves with the Daflas and the Adis. The Tagins to Tadadege re ion. (Burman, B.K. Roy Dr. op. cit. pp. 93-94).
11. B.K. Roy Burman (Dr.): *op. cit.* p. 92.
12. N.C.A.E.R.: *op. cit.* p. 12.
13. As legend goes that Apatani women were being kidnapped by Nissi people in the past. For this, many times there had been many fights. But Apatani people being lesser in number comparatively proved weaker. Thus fight also could not solve the problem. Thus, fight also could not solve the problem. Then the Apatani people evolved a formula to make their women distinctive and they brought this into practice their women would wear cane nods on the both sides of the nose. But on account of the practice of nod-wearing the personality of the Apatani women disfigures. In view of this, the young generation took notice and the practice has been stopped now.
14. Hill Miris are considered to be the members of Tibet Burman family and also akin to Bodo or Kachari, Garo, Rabha and Meches. They are sub-divided into endogamous spets, the Barogams and the Dohgams which are again sub-divided into many minor groups [Burman B.K. Roy (Dr.) *op. cit.* 0.94].
15. 1971 Census: District Census Hand Book of Siang (unpublished).
16. Sachin Roy: Aspects of Padam Minyong Culture, (1966) pp. 11-12.
17. L.R.N. Shrivastava: The Gallongs, 1962, p. 1.
18. Verrier, Elwin: A Philosophy of NEFA, (1964), p. 9.
19. Census of India, Arunachal Pradesh: District Census Hand Book (unpublished).
20. N.C.A.E.R, : Techno-Economic Survey of NEFA, 1967, p. 13.
21. Arunachal Pradesh Census Department, District Census Hand Book, Tirap District, 1991 Census. (unpublished).
22. The Director, Publication Division, Ministry of Information and Board-Casting; Government of India, NEFA, (1965), p. 24.
23. A Pamphlet produced by the Director of Information and Public Relations, NEFA, Shillong, (1970), p. 10.
24. B.K. Roy Burman: *op. cit.* p. 97.
25. Census of India, 1991 Establishment Report Part III B. Establishments Tables p. X.
26. Excepting a few Buddhist tribes of Arunachal Pradesh.
27. Tibetan bells and 'Dunki' are religious articles. 'Dunki' is a big pan on which the pictures of lotus, wheels, the sun and their other gods are inscribed. The value of this religious pot depends upon inscription rather than quality of the metal. Due to its religious significance its importance is beyond expectation. Some times one Dunki is equal to more than one mithun, a domestic animal which on average costs Rs. 700 to 800.
28. Among Akas, Mijis, Khowas, Sulungs, Wanchos and Tagins, bamboo jars and vessels and now-a-days aluminium utensils are found. Among the Monpas, Sherdukpens, Noctes, Adis and few other tribes also, brass utensils including aluminium, glass and now-a-days, dish, plates and cups are found.
29. Today also all these are almost non-existent among the Daflas, Sulungs and a few other tribes.
30. Census of India, Arunachal Pradesh. Series 24, Arunachal Pradesh Part III-A Establishments Report Part III-B Establishments Tables, p. xi—
    Number of households : 94, 646.
    Number of residential households : 92, 898.

Number of houseless households : 439.
Number of Institutional households : 1,309.

Number of rooms —	Total	:	136,544
	Rural	:	130,146
	Urban	:	6,398

31. In general, the village chief enjoys high degree of honour and other facilities. But the same of Wanchos and Noctes, is paid tribute by the villagers for controlling them. (NCAER) Techno-Economic Survey of NEFA, 1967 p. 13). The village chief is not hereditary. He is selected by the villagers and later recognised by the administration, providing a distinctive red coat now-a-days. But now the authority of village chief is eroded on account of increasing grip of administration and panchayat urban.

32. In the construction of anyone's house, each and every household in the village sends a representative to help. The representatives are fed and served Apong. No payment is made. Therefore, the construction of even long house also does not take more than a week.

33.

For Head	—	10 mithuns and 1 deokahin.
For Chest	—	1 mithun and 2 cows.
For Heart	—	2 mithuns or 1 deoghanti, i.e., Tibetan bell.
For Lever	—	1 deokahin, i.e., brass plate.
For Stomach	—	2 deo-mani, i.e., valuable beads.
For Skin	—	2 endicloths, i.e., Assam Silk.
For Rib	—	1 deo.
For Ear	—	1 deo-mani (for each).
For Nose	—	1 Zukli (a type of ornament made of alloy of silver).
For Eye	—	1 eling-mani (for each).
For Hand	—	1 Kharu or bangle (for each).
For Leg	—	1 deo-ghanti or 1 cow.

Census of India, New Delhi, Jara, a Dafia village, November, 10, 1966, p. 48—This table gives the account of Daflas in relation to other tribes the rate of compensation differs from the foregoing one.

34.

Taleng Dumbling (Symbolic honour to the deceased)	—	Valuable beads costing about Rs. 500 app.
Taleng Dumten (external pillow for the deceased)	—	Valuable plates costing Rs. 1,000 approx.
Taleng Maapu (eternal bed)	—	Valuable plate costing Rs. 1,000 approx.
Taleng Mangan (symbolises chain of life)	—	A chain of valuable beads costing of Rs. 1000 approx.
Taleng Dodgong (sacrifice for the honour of deceased)	—	An Eso (mithun) costing Rs. 1,000 approx.
Asi Among Todey-Dodney Nape (for purification of environment)	—	An Eso (mithun) costing Rs. 1,000 approx.

AKI AJENG (Payment An Eso (mithun) costing Rs. 1,000 to maternal uncles approximately of deceased).

Directorate of Information and Public Relations, NEFA:

NEFA Information, October, 1971, pp. 15-16. In addition, the aggrieved party demands for expenditure incurred in holding the Kebang and feeding the participants in Kebang from distant villages.

35. According to personal enquiry made by the present author, ninety per cent of families are comprising husband, wife and unmarried children.

36. Were found among the Bangnis of Kameng and among the Akas and Mijis in the past.

37. Brahma Kumar Shukla, The Daflas of Subansiri Region 1965, p. 50.

38. The present author has learnt that the Padam of Siang district has custom according to which the bridegroom is to stay in his 'would be' wife's house, just after the settlement of the marriage through negotiation. In the first visit, the bridegroom is not allowed to meet his wife. In second visit which materialises after a short interval, he is allowed to meet his wife. During this stay he is to attend the cultivation of land belonging to his father-in-law. During this stay, atleast one child is expected. If the couple proves unfertile, after the completion of three years, the bride is allowed to go to her husband's house, specially at the time of new harvest. The idea behind this custom is to compensate the loss of permanent labour in case of girls' father. In other few tribes, bride price is all and everything as such the groom is not supposed to serve in the field of the father-in-law.

39. As per pesonal enquiry, the monogamy is in practice mostly among the Padam and Minyong these days. Still to tame more than one wife at a time is not a bar. The monogamy is thriving among other tribes also. Polygamy is, on the other hand, common among Daflas, Wanchos and many other tribes.

40. Raghuvir Sinha: op. cit., p. 63.

41. *Ibid.,* p. 59.

42. *Ibid.,* p. 63.

43. (a) Mithun is their domesticated animal which average indigeous price is Rs. 700.
(b) The piece of cloth is Assamese Endicloth which in their society costs Rs. 80 to Rs. 150.

44. Raghuvir Sinha: op. cit., p. 59.

45. It is gathered in course of personal visits, the inter-tribe marriage has been thriving these days. The youths of today have encouraged love-marriage too.

46. Sending of roasted squirrel, one pair, is an unavoidable custom among the Padams. If it is accepted, the marriage is taken to be fixed.

47. Among the Padam and Minyong, such practice of payment is almost not in the existence. But one who elopes or kidnapes has to pay heavy price as demanded by the bride's side, as learnt in course of personal talks.

48. Apong, meat and rice constitute the most essential item for above feast.

49. In one way or another the practice of refund of such prices exists among almost all the tribes and sub-tribes, specially, where bride price is high. However, Bangni, Aka and Mijis strict to the return of another girl, if the girl gets disabled physically. The other tribes are not so much adament on this score. But as the tide is taking turn on account of mass awakening this practice shall die out fast.

50. It is the moral duty of every daughter not to refuse and therefore, those who do not refuse, suffer the whole life. Every girl does not refuse is a fact.

51. Brahma Kumar Shukla: The Daflas of Subansiri Region, (1965) p. 67.

52. *Ibid.,* p. 67.

53. The eldest son pays the price collectively and others are allowed to have physically contacts with the lady periodically on mutually agreed basis.

54. As per personal contacts and visits.

55. As per personal enquiry made. They prefer to have equal number of children, male/female, just to equalise gain and loss of the bride-price.

56. Directorate of Information and Public Relations, Arunachal Pradesh on the March, (1972) p. 17.
57. Statistics Department, Arunachal Pradesh, Shillong, Quick Issue of Statistical Hand Book of Arunachal Pradesh, (1972-73) (Provisional) p. 22.
58. R.R.P. Sharma : The Sherdukpens. (1961), p. 88.
59. The answer was given to understand in course of personal investigation that the corpse remains intact.
60. As per personal schedule.
61. Usually, husband and wife take together.
62. In October, individual hunting is more prevalent.
63. There is, however, no particular marriage season.
64. Some Adi group of Siang.
65. Noctes of Tirap.
66. Mismis of Lohit and Noctes of Tirap—Poppy is an opium plant.
67. Now, the Adis have started milking for their personal consumption.
68. The cow and buffalos, semi-domesticated traditional animals, possess considerable social and exchange value. It serves as medium of exchange amongst local people.
69. Yak is Monpas' domesticated animal which carries loads. Now the Monpas keep cow mithun crossed which gives maximum quantity of milk.
70. Elephant is found in foothills, specially in Tirap district of the Pradesh.
71. Verrier, Elwin: The Tribal World, pp. 245-46.

2

Farming and Other Related Functions

After knowing about the social set-up and geographical arrangements, next important aspect is economic one, i.e., livelihood. In Arunachal Pradesh, agriculture is the main source of livelihood and profession of tribal society.

In the state of Arunachal Pradesh where more than 80 per cent of working force (that is 2.16 lakhs, forming 46 per cent of total population) is dependent directly on agriculture and allied activities, about 78 per cent of workers are said to be cultivators. These cultivators, by and large, practise 'Jhum' (shifting) cultivation on 1,66,838 hectares (about 58 per cent) as against 2,84,577 hectares of gross cultivable land between 1973-74. Jhum cultivation is regulated by the Balipara Frontier Tract, Jhum Land Regulation of 111 of 1947[1] which has been akin to the Chin Hills Regulation of 1896.

However, we find a significant distinction between the two and that is that customary right to Jhum land is recognised in case of a village or community or people where the right to cultivate the jhum land has been enjoyed for not loss than five years prior to the adoption of the former Regulation as against thirty years in latter case.

Jhum Cultivation

The strange topographical conditions and unsuitable land available to them have left with no alternative except practising Jhum, i.e., shifting cultivation. Besides, conspicuous absence of technical knowhow on the part of the tribals who remained completely isolated for considerable duration of time is also responsible for considerable dependence on jhuming which is a method of cultivation on a plot of land covered with shrubs and bushes and trees for production of a crop for one or two years merely instead of settled cultivation where the same plot is cultivated year after year. Shifting cultivation is as such not just an occupation providing for subsistence but more notably as a main stay of the tribal life, since all the processes[3] right from site selection to harvesting, are followed a number of religious rites and ceremonies which, involving same basic norm, differ from tribe to tribe in respect of their observance in practice.

When a site, for instance, is chosen, the village priests *chant hymns* in the midst of ceremonial performances like animal sacrifice, with a view to invoke divine blessing for the protection of crops against natural disasters like attack of pests, insects and wild animals and, finally, to ensure good harvest. Shifting cultivation is not peculiar to Arunachal Pradesh alone as it is a largely accepted basic method of cultivation in many of the undeveloped parts of the world.

It is, for instance, practised in the mountainous regions of heavy rain-fall belts of South-East-Asia and the Himalayan parts. This method of cultivation has got its own significance. It quickly renders a dense vegetal cover suitable for growing crops after felling and burning of the forest. The ashes out of burning add fertility to the soil. It is now well established by the scientific knowledge that highly acidic soil of the heavy rain-fall belt is neutralised to some extent by the alike contents of the ashes.

Again, burning also destroys insects, pests and fungii; proved to be a menace to many for settled cultivation. It also means burning of the weeds and rendering the crop to be leading for one season. Now it is clear enough that agriculture, though being technical in character, is moulded by social and cultural aspects as well as by the way of living in the region under study.

Ownership of Lands

The concept of land ownership in the region under study may, broadly, be considered under three heads, namely the individual, the clan and the village common land. As ownership of land differs from tribe to tribe, the same system varies between the tribes practising shifting cultivation only and the other tribes having continuous and permanent cultivation.[2] The land under individual ownership comprises cultivated land such as irrigated rice fields, fields for dry crops, kitchen gardens, plots for crops like maize, vegetables, fruit trees, bamboo groves, pine, other useful trees and homestead site. The land such as meadows close to village, commonly used as pasture as well as burial ground and the tracts of forests come under clan ownership.

According to normal practice existing amongst many tribes of Arunachal Pradesh, a continuous stretch of available land is generally cleared by a single clan who, in turn, is said to be the owners. The members of inhabiting the village are as such treated like tenants. No doubt, the latter are allowed to make the use of land so long they reside in the village without having any right over the transfer of cultivated land even to their descendants.

Notwithstanding they can also transfer provided it is permitted by the village council.[3] Under, the last category of ownership falls the common village land which comprises one or two, generally not extensive stretches of pasture and the forest tracts, for instance, on the periphery of the Apatani villages. In the region, some villages consist of sub-villages inhabited by certain communities other than the dominant community.

In such cases, the sub-villagers are required to pay to the dominating community as mark of political as well as financial relationship of the tribal communities with their territories.[4] It is here worthwhile to mention that strong sense of individual ownership is kept in mind particularly by the Apatanis, the Monpas, the Padams, the Minyongs of foothills and the Khamptis. This sense of individual ownership of land has gained ground these days amongst the other tribes of the downhills as well. It has got momentum in recent days due to introduction of Wet Rice Cultivation (WRC) and Terrace Rice Cultivation (TRC) and horticulture development in various parts of Arunachal Pradesh.

Pattern of Planting Crops

As a matter of fact, their method of crops is very much influenced by three types of climatic conditions prevailing in all the three topographical belts of the region. It is because of this that in the upper belt, particularly in the northern and southern Kameng, (Tawang and Bomdila sub-divisions) barley, wheat, maize, millets and soyabean are grown while the lower belt (now East Kameng) in eastern Kameng is fit for rice cultivation. However, maize and millets are grown in both the reaches of the district. The cereals like paddy, maize and finger millets are the crops regions of Subansiri district.

In Siang, the dominating crops are the same as in Subansiri. Besides, chillies, mustard, kochu, potatoes and sugarcane are also grown in the foothills. It should be mentioned here that crops like mustard, potatoes and sugarcane have, of late, been introduced by the Agriculture Department, in the regions of all the five districts, according to suitability. In Lohit, the people plant wheat, barley and buck-wheat in the upper reaches and rice, millets, *'matikalai,'* sugarcane, potatoes and oilseeds, in the lower one.

So far Tirap is concerned, paddy, millets and maize are the leading crops, while *'Kochu'* (traditional root vegetables) and topioca are the supplementary ones. Besides, cotton and ginger are also grown throughout Arunachal Pradesh as is evinced from the below crop calendar[5] of Arunachal Pradesh. While maize and millet are grown throughout Arunachal Pradesh, paddy, being the staple food, is cultivated on about 60 per cent[6] of land under cultivation.

Table 1
Crop Calendar of Arunachal Pradesh, District-wise

Name of Crops	*Local Name of Crop*	*Sowing Season*	*Harvesting Season*
1	2	3	4
1. Kameng			
Maize	(Pinthang) (Ashum)	March/April	August/September
Paddy	(Bara)	March	November/ December
Wheat			
(a) Wheat	(Shopa) (Strait)	August/September	March/April

(b) Wheat	Bong (curline)	February/March	July/August
Millet	Kongpu	June	December/ January
Konidan	Chhera	March	July
Chillies	Solu	April/May	October/November
Radish	Muli	July	September
Mustard Seed	Memba	April	January
Garlic	Lam	March/April	December/January
Onion	Chong	March/April	August
Potato (Big)	Chong	March/April	
Sweet Potato	Yingong	January	September
Pumpkin	Brumga	March	September/October
Cucumber	Mamphung	March	August
(a) Bean	Orsha	April	July
(b) Bean	Patengursha	April	December
Soyabean	Ligi	July	January
(a) Pepper (Bitter) one)	Khala	October	January (For bread)
(b) Papor (Sweet one)	Gungchung	October	December

2. Subansiri (Apatani Valley)

Paddy	Emo, Pyati, Pyare	April	October/September and Last part of August
Maize	Tanyi	February	July
Chillies	Tero	February/March	May/June
Ginger	Taki	April/May	November/December
Tobacco	Muku	March/April	June/July
Millet	Sarse	April/May	September/October
Bean	Perung	April/May	October/November
Gourd	Tape	April/May	October/November
	(Other Areas)		
Paddy	Timin Amt	March/May/June	August/November/ December
Kachu	Inse	March	December/November
Maize	Top	April	July/August
Sweet Potato	Guria (Ingir)	April	December/January
Chillies	Yamdick	April	May/June

	(Other Areas)		
Millet	Tami Tami	March/April June/July	August/September December/January
Ginger	Taki	March/April	November/ December
3. Siang			
Paddy	Am, Amna	May/June/July	December/January
Foxtail Millet	Mirung	May	December
Finger Millet	Ayak	May	October/November
Maize	Sapa	January/February	May (Last part)
Cotton	Sipayak	April	October/November
Sweet Potato	Hugin-tare	–	October onward
Mustard Seed	Tulang	September/October	March
Country Bean	Peron	April/May	November/ December
Pumpkin	Tapa	April/May	October/November
White-gourd	Pao, par	April/May	October/November
Small Onion	Talap	April/May	October/November
Brinjal	Bayom	April/May	October/November
Bittergourd	Kerala	April/May	September/October
Tomato	Tumpuluk	January/February	August/September
Chillies	Mirsui	April/May	August/September
Tobacco	Kuser, Dumak	January/February	August/September
Arum (Kochu)	Enge	April/May	December/January
Sesamum	Totok	March	October/November
A kind of crop	Angyat	April	January/February
4. Lohit			
Paddy	Keh	March/April	September
Foxtail Millet	Dhu	May	October/November
Wheat	(Not available)	May	September/October
Maize	Nambu	March	September/October
Sweet Potato	Ghihuhla	April/May	November/ December
Mustard Seed	Turi	November/ December	March/April
Country Bean	Ghuleso	March/April	October/November
Pumpkin	Kopra	March/April	September/October
Whitegourd	Thaam	March/April	September/October
Small Onion	Allo	March/April	September/October
Brinjal	Phungcho	March/April	October/November

French Bean	Dhebeh	March/April	November/ December
Potato	Alu	October/ November	January/February
Tomato	Thanahii	March/April	September/October
Chillies	Pachak	March/April	September/October
Tobacco	Dhungwa	March/April	August/September
Ginger	Hodzing	March/April	November/ December
5. Tirap			
Paddy	(Not Available)	May	September/October
Millet (Foxtail variety)	N.A.	February/March	June/July
Finger Millet	N.A.	May	November/ December
Maize	N.A.	February/March	June/July
Arum	N.A.	February/March	October/December

(I) Paddy Crop

We find different indigenous types of paddy suited to slope as well as flat land. While *Amka, Amkel, Amtebara, Kalamdani, Khasia* and *Neoli* are the most important indigenous varieties grown largely around Pasighat, (East Siang) with the average yield of about 2275 kg. per hectare,[6] the traditional varieties of paddy like *Khaomakhy, Khao-yekun, Khao-pakhi, Khao-nu, Khao-ji, and Khao-malin,* grown in Lohit district are also important ones. The rice tract can broadly be divided into two main zones, namely, the rainfed zone and the irrigated zone.

However, according to the capacity to retain moisture, land under paddy cultivation may be grouped under three heads, namely, medium high land (where there autumn paddy is grown; the medium land), medium low land (suitable for growing medium duration of winter varieties) and low land (suitable for growing certain medium and late duration winter types where rain water accumulates in pockets).

Although this account is particularly in regard to Lohit, it is, in fact applicable practically throughout the region. Here it may also be noticed that due to topographical difficulty, provision for irrigation cannot be availed of by most of the fields and as such a large portion of the rainfed rice tract is under shifting function. In case of tracts where irrigational facilities cannot be availed of, it is done so through gravitational flow brought from the streams and rivers in the vicinity through improvised diversification structures, while in case of shifting cultivation depending mainly on monsoons, there are two paddy seasons, from May-June to November-December and between March-April to September. The average yield of paddy on jhum land is estimated to be about 1,100 kg. per hectare

(4.44 quintals per acre) as compared to about 2,285 Kg. per hectare (9.25 quintals per acre) in case of irrigated land which[7] form about 17 per cent of the total cultivated region.

(II) Traditional Crop—Maize

It is the second traditional major crop in the region under study, grown prominently in Kameng, Subansiri, Tirap and Siang. Maize is very favourite crop of the Akas and the Mijis of Kameng. This crop is usually grown in the upper belt. It may be mentioned here that maize is consumed especially in Monpa areas by the people as well as their domesticated pigs. Local bear is also brewed from it in the same manner as done from rice. Like wheat and millets, the yield of maize per hectare is estimated to vary between 700 kg. and 1,000 kg. Maize of orange yellow, roundish and dirty white colours are found in the region. However, the administration has recently introduced cultivation of Shillong variety of maize in some part of Arunachal Pradesh.

(III) Millet Crop

Because of having no substitutes for the preparation of local bear, millet is widely cultivated for its two-fold consumption purposes namely, bear consumption by people and as concentrate food for pigs and chickens. Still, it lags much behind paddy in respect of its out-turns.

(IV) Crops of Barley and Wheat

Both these crops are grown in the western Kameng and Lohit only. However, the administration has been putting efforts recently to popularise the practice of wheat and barley cultivation in other parts of the region too.

(V) Growing of Mustard Seed

This crop is cultivated in Siang and Lohit on forest land after a rough felling of trees followed by burning. Its two varieties are generally met and both are brown in these parts of Arunachal. In Siang its output was guessed around 360 tonnes during 1970-1971, giving average yield of 437[8] kg. per hectare.

(VI) Crop of Sugarcane

Just like mustard seeds sugarcane is also cultivated in Lohit and Siang district at the instance of administration which came forward with various measures of inducement like liberal supplies of sugarcane crushers and those of juice boiling pans. But even then its output has been poor.

(VII) Plantation of Potato and Kochu

The latter one is traditional one and widely practised. It is only the root vegetable which the tribals used to cultivate in all districts. Besides *'Kochu,'* arum and tapioca are also grown in Tirap. In some areas of the region sweet potato is also grown, though not at all proved to be commercial one. Although introduced by the administration, its (potato) production has recently gained ground in Kameng that has got output of 100 tonnes a year.[15]

(VIII) Chilly Crop

Since it forms an important part of the taste of the local people who prefer chilly to sweet, it is cultivated widely in the region. More than 60 hectares of land were for chilly and vegetable in Kameng alone as early as in mid-sixties. Although it is a commercial crop by nature, it is mainly restricted to self-consumption. In recent past, the villagers near the administrative centres have started selling it to the staff.

(IX) Ginger Crop

Ginger, being a traditional crop, is grown largely in some parts of the region prominently and in others less significantly. It is mixed with salt while taking beer and roasted fish or meat. It is also consumed as vegetable suiting their taste. Just like chilli, it is grown for own consumption and taken to the nearby administrative places infrequently from door to door by their women. But now, the attempts are afoot to commercialise its production.

(X) Cotton Crop

The tradition of cotton cultivation is traced in the district of Siang only and in some other parts negligibly. They used to grow on their jhum field simultaneously. But now-a-days, cotton growing is almost abandoned due to availability of readymade threads in the local market. The cotton blankets of Padam and Minyong are commonly available.

Improvement in Agriculture

A quick appraisal of agricultural development programmes like land reclamation, distribution of manures, fertilizers, high yielding seeds and seedlings, improved tools and implements. and adoption of plant protection instruments and maintenance of agricultural farms, as reflected by the tabulated data, may now be made here. Although financial allocation for agricultural development programmes cost around Rs. 32 and Rs. 50.21 lakhs for First and Second Plans respectively, actual expenditure amounted to Rs. 32.77 lakhs and Rs. 24.63 lakhs.

As against allotment of Rs. 63.48 lakhs, real expenditure stood at Rs. 64.90 lakhs during 1961-1966. While Rs. 59.05 lakhs for three Annual Plans (1966-67 to 1968-69) and Rs. 188.32 lakhs for Fourth Plan (1969-74) were earmarked, expenditure came to Rs. 33.83 lakhs and 92.78 lakhs[9] respectively. As borne out from the Table that the acreage of land developed has gone on rising steadily and at declining rate over the period of two decades of planning. Similar has been the case of the acreage of land brought under little irrigation. The use of manures does not show any increase during post-Third Plan period. However, consumption of fertilizer that was initiated after Third Plan is said to have gone on rising markedly in recent years.

A continuous increase in the distribution of tools and implements is also recorded but the same of animals power[17] has been at a speedy rate till the end of Third Plan period and at a lower pace thereafter. The distribution of seeds/seedlings and the amount spent on the scheme of plant protection has also kept the pace of some like. The number of agricultural farms managed by the department rose notably during the Second Plan period. But during the post-Third Plan duration, there was almost no change in their numerical strength. The practical difficulties that have stood in the way of agricultural development programmes are absence of soil survey, experiment and research to discover agronomic practices suited to terrains as well as regional climatic conditions.

Above all, the practice of shifting cultivation, being deep rooted because of social customs and religious rites, has hampered progress. But in recent years, people have preferred scientific cultivation to it in those cases where necessary facilities have been provided for the purpose. It may be advised that increasing provision be made and ensure regular supply of high yielding varieties of seeds and seedlings, improved tools and implements, larger consumption of manures including fertilizers. Certain irrigational potentialities as existed should be well exploited. It is, on the whole, necessary to ensure that agricultural practices are increasingly remodelled to make better the availability of foodgrains. Besides, it may be noted that the increasing provision of these facilities alongwith necessary encouragement to the cultivators through financial subsidies and betterment of marketing would improve image of agriculture as a means of livelihood.

We do not endorse the view, as held by the NCAER, that establishment of agricultural colonies (p. 22) would eradicate shifting cultivation. We contend rather commercialising agriculture as primary means of livelihood by adopting all means to improve upon its contributions.

Owing to above efforts taken by the Administration, it is contended officially that per-capita availability of foodgrain production has risen from 175 kilograms in 1966 to 180 kilograms in 1969.[10] Still, such claim may very well be contested and said to be ill-founded as rate of increase in population has very much outstripped that of foodgrain production. Foodgrain production went up by 32 per cent during 1960-61 to 1971-72, that is, by 2.9 per cent as against annual population increase of 3.9 per cent. It is also well borne out from the foregoing table that sixties witnessed quicker rate of increase in foodgrain production in the region. However, despite it, the unabated population explosion in the region has, in fact, led to decline in per capita availability of foodgrains, from 178 Kg. to below 170 Kg. during the sixties.[11]

With the foregoing table we note the highest percentage of self-sufficient villages in Kameng followed by Siang. The district of Lohit is followed by Tirap. At the same time Subansiri shares the minimum. The percentage of surplus villages in the districts is very much uneven. As such the highest percentage of surplus villages is noticed in Siang and the lowest in Tirap.

Other three districts, called Lohit, Subansiri and Kameng share 32 per cent, 19 per cent and 9 per cent, respectively. As regards the deficit villages, Subansiri tops the list followed by Tirap and Lohit in order with a very few margin. If the percentage of self-sufficient persons is compared to that of self-sufficient villages, the former does not deviate from the above order of the districts except between districts of Tirap and Lohit. But when a comparison is made between the surplus villages and the surplus persons, Lohit surpasses Siang irrespective of its smaller share in surplus villages. Still, the percentage of deficit villages coincides with the deficit population.

This may, it is clear enough that self-sufficiency in foodgrain is far from the reach in the region. As such, the Arunachal Pradesh administration will face a food shortage of 37,000 tonnes at the end of 1974. It has also been found that the total requirement of foodgrain will go to 1,14,000 tonnes[14] by the end of Fifth Five Year Plan (1978-79) assuming about six lakhs of population.

1. Horticulture Development. While the varied topography is ideally suited to fruit growing such as apple, orange, pineapple, banana and pears etc., even the progressive tribes like the Monpas, the Khamptis and the Adis did not know the pursuits till the sixties. It was the administration that took initiative towards the horticultural development during Third Plan period which, in turn, led to the following results in the areas.

Now-a-days these horticultural nurseries are helping the gardens in fruit growing and as such apple-growing in Kameng (specially Bomdila and Dirang areas) and pineapple in the foothills of the eastern districts of the state has made much headway in recent years. For instance, apple production came up from scratch till 1963 to about 10 tonnes[16] during 1971-72. Likewise, vegetables growing improved over the period and output of potato has come to more than 100 tonnes[17] in Kameng alone at present. It is proposed to ensure development of horticulture in as many as around 1,000 villages, that is, more than one-third of the total, during Fifth Plan period. Rightly the programme of horticultural development has assumed priority by virtue of its own financial units in recent years.

2. Livestock. Livestock that used to play an indispensible role in past as the medium of exchange in the local economy due to absence of money do play an important role even today in different parts of the area. Thus, animals serve as the conveyance of their economy. Despite this, no livestock census had been taken till 1978-79. Nevertheless, it is found that every family maintains pigs and chicken, regardless of its tribal distinction, religion and climatic conditions prevailing in various parts of the region. Their livestock comprises mithun, cow, yak, sheep, horse, buffalo (Khamptis) and elephants, especially in the foothills and Tirap and goat. As regards their poultry, it consists of chickens and at times ducks too. A brief account of some of the main constituents of the livestock of the region is given here.

3. Mithun for Beef. This particular animal which is semi-domesticated throughout the region is an excellent source of beef. It is allowed to roam wild and except for periodical provision of artificial salt-licks on palm, the owners do not bother and is brought home only on the day of slaughter, that is, on ceremonial occasions as well as to serve the purpose of using it as medium of exchange for commodities even now. The present practice of leaving mithuns in a semi-wild state in forests full of predatory wild animals is not at all conducive to increase of the stock and as such need to be rejected. Further, necessary measures should be taken to protect them against dangerous epidemics.

4. Yak for Various Purposes. This animals, being a beast of burden, is found in the upper reaches and tamed by the Buddhist tribes residing along the Tibetan frontier. It is the most useful animal, well suited to travel over rough terrain as well as fast adapted to grazing even at steep slopes and high elevation. Besides, yak is used as pack animal. It produces milk and meat. Its skin is used for leather and hair for making ropes and also weaving tents.

5. Cow for Various Purposes. This is an imported animal from the neighbouring state of Assam and used to be found in the foothills only till recently. Now, it has reached even the higher altitudes. Among the Bangnis of Kameng and Nissis of Subansiri and also a few other tribes, it is meant for sacrifice and meat only. But the Monpas and the Adis of the foothills, in particular, plough and milk. The areas where wet rice cultivation has been introduced, the Bangnis also plough but such cases are very few.

6. Domesticated Buffalo. This is domesticated only in Lohit by the Khamptis. They plough their land through buffaloes. They milk them as well. Now-a-days, buffalo-keeping and sale of milk have developed in the region like an industrial one.

7. Horse for Loads. Same are kept by the Monpas of Kameng for taking their loads. Here it should be mentioned that the administration also employ horse and mules as one of the means of transport with a desire to encouraging this procedure on the part of the locals. But the humid climate does not suit the horse so well.

8. Elephant for Firewood. Elephant keeping is popular in the foothills, especially in Tirap and Siang for carrying log from the forests. But such practice is very much restricted one. This animal is useful to the saw mills and also for the forest-timber extractors.

9. Pig for Twin-use. Pig keeping is practised by each and every tribal family in the region. Like mithun, it serves two-fold purposes, namely, slaughtering on religious occasions and medium of exchange. As noted earlier, in settlement, roasted pig meat is a first and due priority, on the occasion of marriages. To improve the local breed, administration distributed fed pigs to many tribes, but this has met with no success as the fed pigs did not to search food from the jungle.

10. Goat for Consumption and Exchange. This may be said that the climate of Arunachal Pradesh is exceptionally suitable for goat-keeping and as such it has very much flourished over the period. But goat does not have sacrifice value. It is kept for exchange and also for consumption. However, goat meat is forbidden amongst few tribes like the Mijis of East Kameng district—they consider the consumption of goat meat as a social stigma.

11. Sheep for Commercial Purpose. This animal has won commercial value in the sense that wool is produced. However, sheep-keeping tradition is prevalent in the upper reaches but significantly amongst the Monpas of Tawang.

12. Chicken. Chicken is their poultry bird, being indispensable in various religious and social rites. However, it is sold too, now-a-days in the nearby markets.

The development that has taken place in regard to animal husbandry in Arunachal Pradesh may be noted from the table given that follows:

As found from the table, the number of cattle farms swelled to six times at the end of Third Plan, but some of them were not in operation in recent years. However, the goat farm remained quite static throughout the plan duration. At the same time we notice that an addition to existing during Third Plan sheep farm proved to be temporary phenomenon. The pig farms have shown definite trend of decline. The background of poultry farms were still worse as all came to closure in recent past. It is notable that irrespective of the wide rearing of pig and chicken these farms have met such infant mortality.

It may here be attributed partly to ignorance of the people and their disinclination to improve the situation and partly to absence of initiative and imagination on the part of administrative staff concerned. However, the veterinary dispensaries as well as the veterinary aid centres have expressed trend of unabated growth throughout the period. It is gratifying to point out here that the Fifth Five Year Plan of Arunachal Pradesh (p. 17) aims to start dairy, poultry, piggery, sheep and goat-keeping in their full multifarious aspects. Besides, a Regional Hill Livestock Breeding-cum-Research Station has been approved of recently for the state by the North Eastern Council. The headquarters of the Station is proposed to be set up at Itanagar, capital of the Territory, alongwith its branches in each of the district. A Regional Fodder-cum-Demonstration Farm too has to be set up at Itanagar, with its sub-branches in all the districts.

The North-Eastern Council has also approved of the expansion of Biological production station at Guwahati, with three useful storage centres in Upper Assam and at Charduar which is at the gate of Arunachal Pradesh. It would undoubtedly provide necessary infrastructure for the growth of animal husbandry in the region. The Arunachal Pradesh Administration has also itself decided to set up one Hill Area Cattle Research Unit on the line of the state of Himachal Pradesh.

13. Fishery for Pond Purposes. We have seen elsewhere that the tribesmen in Arunachal Pradesh follow the pursuits of fishery, through very occasionally rather than often, the administration initiated measures in this context during the Second Plan period only, as transpired from the table given after next paragraph.

Various schemes like setting up of seed multiplication centre, introducing pond culture and providing necessary equipments, have been taken into hand by the administration to cater to yearly demand for fish to the order of 7,000 tonnes. The scheme of pond culture has, however, been given the top priority and a few major schemes like creation of nursery space, starting of demonstration fish farms, village domestic fish pond, people's fish farms, school fish pond, fish ponds in Government institution, expansion of existing fish farms, initiation of intensive fish farming and paddy-cum-fish culture, have been implemented in recent years.

Table 2
Fishery Development, Category-wise[19]

Name of Items⇒ *Agencies ⇓*	*Unit*	*At the end of First Plan 1955-56*	*At the end of Second Plan 1960-61*	*At the end of Third Plan 1965-66*	*As on 31.3. 67*	*As on 31.3. 68*	*As on 31.3. 69*	*As on 31.3. 72*
(1) Government Fish Farms	No.	–	1	2	3	4	5	7
(2) People's Fish Farms	No.	–	1	2	4	6	6	12
(3) Village Fish Farms	No.	–	25	479	524	665	759	1,084
(4) Fingerlings Distributed (in lakhs)	No.	–	–	2.41	2.80	3.31	4.04	5.00

Despite these steps, Arunachal Pradesh, as assumed, possesses the potentiality for fish production to the tune of 2,200 tonnes only, which is far behind the local requirements. This poor potentiality of the region may be ascribed to absence of constant and permanent accumulation of water because of its mountainous terrain. However, the programme of riverine fishery has also been included for execution during the Fifth Plan period which may increase the potentiality for fish production.

14. Hunting and other Related Pursuits. Factually speaking, the system of shifting cultivation in Arunachal Pradesh is a compromise between pure hunting and food-gathering on the part of the men and the quite limited kitchen garden cultivation has been practical for the women folk. It is seen that while working on the jhum fields, trapping of wild animals, even of smaller ones like squirrels and birds, is practiced. All these provide more varied diet as well as a diversification of activity which, of course, contribute to their mental happiness. Moreover, they go on hunting expedition in groups on the eve of socio-religious festivals. The Adis, for instance, go on collective hunting while they celebrate festivals like Atar, and Solung. The time when the people are free from reasonal works of agriculture, all the able-bodied male go for collective hunting. The Adis hunt tigers also, whereas the Nissi-group members avoid tiger hunting.

Thus, Agriculture has been the main source of food and livelihood of tribals. With the passage of time, through governmental efforts, things have improving to a great extent especially regarding allied activities agriculture. But, there is always scope for improvement. The Census data about the cultivators and agricultural labourers is given on next page.

Table 3
Agricultural and Farming Functions including Labourers and Other Workers (Districtwise) : Census 2001

District	Cultivators			Agricultural labourers			Household industries			Other workers		
	P	M	F	P	M	F	P	M	F	P	M	F
Tawang	9,503	4,040	5,463	465	216	249	99	64	35	12,032	9,934	2,098
West Kameng	12,169	6,235	5,934	1,370	722	648	355	147	208	20,459	17,766	2,693
East Kameng	18,389	8,159	10,230	711	376	335	85	42	43	6,732	5,399	1,333
Papum Pare	10,772	5,127	5,645	1,483	744	739	621	301	320	31,338	23,737	7,601
Lower Subansiri	32,533	14,103	18,430	1,511	647	864	279	156	123	10,709	8,561	2,148
Upper Subansiri	15,290	6,888	8,402	457	230	227	112	67	45	6,404	5,259	1,145
West Siang	27,103	13,170	13,933	862	539	323	586	337	249	14,309	11,541	2,768
East Siang	17,537	8,962	8,575	1,940	1,123	817	646	273	373	13,455	10,136	3,319
Upper Siang	11,135	5,325	5,810	409	280	129	29	19	10	5,537	4,722	815
Dibang Valley	13,764	7,219	6,545	1,833	1,043	790	154	124	30	9,745	8,047	1,698
Lohit	34,772	19,444	15,328	3,938	2,229	1,709	416	260	156	21,197	17,756	3,441
Changlang	41,970	21,472	20,498	3,238	1,740	1,498	591	285	306	14,210	11,236	2,974
Tirap	36,885	17,148	19,737	352	208	144	157	71	86	11,558	9,920	1,638

Table 4
Agricultural and Farming Functions including Labourers and Other Workers (Statewise) : Census 2001

Total/ Rural/ Urban	*Persons/ Males/ Females*	*Cultivators Labourers*	*Agricultural Industry Workers*	*Household Workers*	*Other*
Total	Persons	281,822	18,569	4,130	177,685
	Males	137,292	10,097	2,146	144,014
	Females	144,530	8,472	1,984	33,671
Rural	Persons	277,148	17,334	2,922	108,594
	Males	135,257	9,362	1,325	88,489
	Females	141,891	7,972	1,597	20,105
Urban	Persons	4,674	1,235	1,208	69,091
	Males	2,035	735	821	55,525
	Females	2,639	500	387	13,566

References

1. B.K. Roy Burman: Census of India, 1961, Demographic and Socio-Economic Profiles of the Hill Areas of North East India, 1970, p. 178.
2. Planning and Development Department, Arunachal Pradesh Administration, Approach to Fifth Five Year Plan (1974-79) p. 32.
3. B.K. Roy Burman (Dr.): *op. cit.* p. 182.
4. (Directorate of Census Operations, Arunachal Pradesh): Crop Calendar with respect to all tne five districts.
5. Planning and Development, Arunachal Pradesh Administration, Approach to Fifth Year Plan 1974-79, p. 5.
6. Directorate of Information and Public Relations, NEFA, Shillong, NEFA Information, September, 1971, p. 14.
7. NEFA Information, September 1991, pp. 22-23.
8. NEFA Information, September, 1971, p. 14—As the tribals do not take mustard oil, it is precisely produced for cash.
9. Statistics Department, Arunachal Pradesh, Quick Issue of Statistical Hand Book of Arunachal Pradesh, 1971-72 (Provisional) p. 73.
10. Director of Information and Public Relations, NEFA, NEFA Information, August, 1971, p. 4.
11. Worked out by dividing foodgrain production of 60,000 tonnes in 1960-61 and 79,000 tonnes in 1971-72 by total population of 3,36,558 4,67,511 in 1961 and 1971 respectively.
12. Census of India, 1991, Arunachal Pradesh, Village Directory.
13. Assam Tribune, Gauhati, June 22, 1973.
14. Planning and Development Department, Arunachal Pradesh Administration Shillong, Approach to Fifth Five Year Plan, 1974-79, p. 6.
15. Adopted from the data included in Approach to Fifth Five Year Plan, 1974-79, p. 32.
16. Approach to Fifth Five Year Plan, 1974-79, p. 6.
17. The Assam Tribune, Gauhati, the 10th of July, 1973.
18. Approach to Fifth Five Year Plan, pp. 32-33.
19. Planning and Development Department, Arunachal Pradesh Administration, Approach to Fifth Five Year Plan, 1974-79, p. 33.

3

Resources Under Forestry

Natural resources of a state are indicators of prosperity and growth. And, we can say that Arunachal Pradesh is a rich and prosperous state.

Total Area Covered under Forest

We all know that the monsoon discriminates Arunachal Pradesh with heavy rainfall almost throughout the year and this, in turn, creates element weather for the growth of multiple vegetation. Around 60,747 square kilometre (72.70 per cent) of the territory is covered under forests. The district-wise concentration of forest may be seen. It appears that Tirap has recorded relatively good progress in bringing majority of its forest area under reserve. Next comes forest in Kameng District, with almost 42 per cent of area under reserve. While Lohit has got reserved very inconsiderable area of its forest, Siang, with about 90 per cent of its geographical part under forest, have nominal proportion of its forest under the reserved category.

Subansiri with the heaviest concentration of forest has still to open its account for the reserved area. On the whole, Arunachal Pradesh has got a little more than one-ninth of its area under reserve so far. The probe into this achievement shows that first two plan periods did not record any progress whatsoever and reserved forest area remained steady at 527 square kilometres. During Third Plan duration, addition to the order of 1,132 square kilometres could be recorded for the first time. During the first Annual Plan of 1966-67 measures were very much speeded up and also the record addition of 2,954 square kilometres could be effected to. During the subsequent three years, however, no progress was recorded in this direction.

The second year of the Fourth Plan got succeeded in breaking up the steadiness in this regard by addition of 2,173 square kilometres under the reserved category of forests. Very nominal addition could be recorded during 1971-72 and 1972-73 as compared to gone years.

It is sure that the forests in Arunachal Pradesh play their primary role by providing house-building materials, firewood and other forest products. Along with performing usual protective functions like preventing land erosion, controlling and maintaining water supply, civilisation, culture and religion of the natives in Arunachal Pradesh are highly influenced by the forests. They decorate their figures with forests; they delight in forests; they worship in forests; they get land for shifting cultivation in forests; they receive crafts' materials from forests; they get food and vegetables from forests; they get medicinal herbs from forests; they hunt in forests and fish in forest. In view of their dependence on forest, it can be said undoubtedly that their economy is agro-forest based one. The forests, in general, include Hollock, Hallong, Makai, Mekahi, Bola, Bongum, Cham, Amari-Jutuli, bamboo, reeds, Simul, grasses of industrial importances, plantain and veneer. In the higher areas, Blue pine, Psuga, Chir pine and Rir are notably available.

According to their use, we get (1) constructional timber (2) veneer timber (3) furniture timber (4) match-wood and pulp-wood in the forests of the state. Besides, medicinal plants like Mishmi-teeta occur, plants of industrial value are also available and are being utilised by the indigenous paper manufacturers of the Monpa tribe in Kameng District.

Products from Forests

The total outturn of timber from the reserved forests has reached, according to available data, the level of about 1.78 lakh cubic metre in 1970-71, while of fuel to about 0.49 lakh cubic metre in 1969-70. Amongst the list to minor products, mention may be made of agar (802 quintals), boulders (86000 cum), black pepper (1.50 quintals), charcoal (965 million tonnes), dalchini (15 quintals), dunna (12 quintals), stones (229 thousand cum), and lastly of thatches (109 thousand bundles. As a matter of fact, no census of wild-life has been conducted in the region. However, elephants, bisons, barking deer, sambars, scally, monetary lizards, wild buffaloes, and animals like monkeys and 'longoars' are found in these forests. In the higher region, wild life is poor in comparison to that of foot-hills, but black bears and other cold climate animals are seen. In this connection, it should be mentioned here that Tirap is richer than those of the remaining four districts, namely, Kameng, Subansiri, Siang and Lohit Districts.

Forest Administration

At the outset when forest administration stated, the forest was being managed under the forest policy of Assam.[3] In later years, parallel to Nagaland Chin Hills Regulation of 1896, the Balipara Frontier Tract, Jhum Land Regulation, 1947 was made operative in the state which stipulated that no formal acquisition proceedings would be necessary for taking over the forest lands, though reasonable compensation would be payable for this:

All required initiative for the management of forest was taken as early as 1946 through the appointment of Forest Adviser to the Governor of Assam "to aid and advise him on the matters relating to the forest". While in 1947, a Divisional Forest Officer was appointed with his headquarters in Tirap, the Forest Department, in fact, came into being in 1948 with the appointment of Chief Forest Officer in place of Forest Adviser, in order to head the Department of Forest in Tirap. During the same year, three Forest Divisions (Tirap, Sadiya and Balipara Forest Divisions) were created.

Now, under the Northern and Southern circles at Terajuli and deomali, there are as many as 10 territorial forest divisions, from two divisions (functional forest division and utilisation with forest division) at Shillong with the direct control of the Chief Conservator of Forest who happens to be the administrative head of the Forest Department of the Arunachal Pradesh Administration.

Because the system of the Panchayat Raj has been brought into existence, forest policy has undergone drastic change. A draft on the 'constitution of village Forest Reserves' and the views of the Deputy Commissioners were as such investigated by the Administration appreciating the apparent desire of the people to have sizeable areas of forest alloted to the Panchayat.

Contemplating over the 'pros and cons' of the advice that 'Forest Department should look after and maintain these forests; 80 per cent of the revenue may be given to the Panchayats and 20 per cent to the Forest Department, while in the original proposal, it was for the village Panchayats to look after and maintain their own forests; the Forest Department was to give them only technical guidance'. In fact, practically, any Government agency such as Forest Department cannot manage private estate without having any control over it to spend such a large sum of money and vice versa.

This is why, it was suggested finally that forest land in blocks of 500 acres or above may be declared as regular reserves to be known after the particular Panchayats or Anchals, in the wake of the enunciation of the National Forest Policy of India alongwith the observance and enforcement of normal provision for Forest Reserves by the Forest Department. The provision was also kept for the traditional rights of the tribesmen for their bonafide needs. Out of the net revenue from reserves, the Panchayats and the Forest Department would be given 50 per cent each. However, still, the above proposal has already been approved by the Pradesh Council.[4] It is worthwhile to mention here that the Forest Department is the sole Governmental agency earning revenue in Arunachal Pradesh. Its total revenue rose from Rs. 11.54 lakhs in 1955-56 to Rs. 147.80 lakhs in 1971-72. Its source of earning has been the major and minor products from the reserved forests, referred to earlier.

Apart from selling timber and other products, it has been earning through supply of sleeper logs and other conversion products. Railways have been the largest customers in this regard and available statistics reveals that about 122.66 thousand pieces of sleepers were supplied to them in 1970-71 as compared to about 127 thousand pieces of sleepers in the preceding year. Next to railways, saw mills constitute another important group of customers for the Forest Department.

Thus, to sum up, we may say that the vast forest coverage places Arunachal Pradesh on a level with many of the larger units in India and provides good potentiality to meet forest requirements of the nation. Nevertheless, forest resources of the region are not so varied as those of Assam. The forests of the former lack hard woods like sal, while commercial trees like khair are absent. Its timbers may be regarded as medium hard-wood (hollock, for instance), and soft-wood as Simul, with durability life of 15 years and 3 years respectively. The availability of hard-wood such as Nahar (iron wood of the State of Assam) has not been formally traced so far as no relevant survey for the purpose could be conducted.

References

1. Statistics Department, Arunachal Pradesh: Quick Issue of Statistical Hand Book of Arunachal Pradesh, 1972-73 (Provisional) p. 47.
2. Statistics Department, NEFA, Statistical Hand Book of North-East Frontier Agency, 1970-71, p. 63.
3. Registrar General, India, Census of India, 1961: Demographic and Socio-Economic Profiles of the Hill Areas of North-East India, 1970, p. 178.
4. The Director of Information and Public Relations, Arunachal Pradesh, Arunachal News, October, 1972, p. 5.

4

Mineral Resources and Their Use

We have read in the previous chapters that Arunachal Pradesh has rich natural resources[1] more particularly the forests. Here, the tribesmen in the state have an age-old tradition of artistic craftsmanship. Each and every household weaves its own cloth, prepares baskets, makes wooden utensils and bamboo pots, bow and arrows, traps, sleeping benches, wooden mortars and pestles for grinding grains and dehusking paddy. They use what they produce, although tools and techniques are old. Beside cotton carpet and rug-making of Padam in Siang, popular wood-carving of Monpa in Kameng and Nocte and Wancho in Tirap, lion-loom textile goods of the Adis, preparation of Lord Buddha's idol out of clay, manufacturing of paper, traditional carpet-making and woollen garments woven with Rajasthani wool of Monpa, are very famous even outside Arunachal.

As pottery is rarely found these days, they carve wood, bamboo and cane vessels to use as utensils. Rudimentary black smithy and silver smithy are also seen in practice. 'Daos', fire-stand (like ring used as stove), pot-stands are manufactured from iron, while smoking pipes of intricate design are made of silver by the Daflas (now called the Nishang group), Gallongs and Sherdukpens distinctively. Strictly speaking, except a few almost all the activities cannot be called the household industries but they are rather their home-crafts which keep them engaged as well as happy during leisure period. They are taken to be source of entertainment, although, being necessary according to economic needs.

It may be ascribed to, firstly, the practice of their adoption at family level and secondly, non-availability of markets for their production and sale on under scale. It may be noted here that weaving is an occupation confined to females only. But those tribes who are having trade connections with outside do not insist too much on weaving, due to the fact that they purchase clothes from markets. But to those who are not more than 'jhum' (shifting) cultivators, out of weaving has become an imperative aspect of life. The people residing in the middle belt of the terrain belong to this category.

However, it is an important vocation among the Sulungs in the lack of any other alternative to it. The present author has been informed that a Sulung girl cannot be married unless she knows weaving. The basketry, wood and bamboo-carving, while on the other hand, are the crafts generally meant for the male folk. Bamboo baskets, cane, bamboo and wooden jars and vessels are their significant instruments to carry on domestic life, including agricultural pursuits. Another reason for carrying on these crafts is the ample availability of raw materials around them. The skills involved in these crafts are learnt by the persons themselves spontaneously because of their keen interest in them as an important profitable means absorbing them. Certain other crafts like blacksmithy, silver smithy and pottery are not practised by all. For instance, the Yano Bangni residing in the east-southern (Pakke-Kessang circle of Seppa Sub-division now East Kameng) know blacksmithy quite well and the rest of the Bangnis purchase iron made articles from them.

In addition, the Sulungs also know the blacksmithy; their winder made with banana leaves is an attractive one. Despite these wide prevalent practices and non-availability of widespread markets, quite a few crafts are carried out on commercial lines also and good so created are brought to the markets within and outside the region for sale. Some of the crafts practising establishments have as such been categorised as cottage industries. Of the establishments engaged in household industries, the districts of Subansiri and Lohit contribute almost equal being the least number.

Tirap and Kameng came to almost equal and the highest number of such units. Kameng also accounts for about a two and a half times as many manufacturing, processing or servicing establishments that have been called workshops than any other district. The incidence of Government or quasi-Government establishments is also higher in Kameng as compared to other parts of the area, as is evident from the following table. The industrial policy in Arunachal Pradesh as administered by the Cottage Industries Development, established 1953-54, has been to revitalise traditional handicraft, handlooms and sericulture industries through craft and production centres and also to intiate modern tools and techniques of production as well as certain other crafts which were hitherto not known to the tribesmen.

The policy was as such designed to organise widescale production alongwith the opening of new craft centres by the Department. During past two decades, the number of craft centres as set up by the Cottage Industries Department of the State Administration rose to twentyone; six in Kameng, five in Subansiri, four in Siang and Tirap each and two in Lohit.[2] Besides, marketing facilities too have been extended to the village artisans by organising Sales Emporiums at district and also at sub-divisional headquarters. Apart from general administration of funds allotted under Plans to the Department of Cottage Industries, for imparting training in various crafts, running of craft and production centres, as well as payment of subsidies under prescribed conditions could partly be utilised, establishing the fact that achievements behind the fixed targets.

Rs. 6.19 lakhs, Rs. 15.24 lakhs, Rs. 10.62 lakhs, Rs. 24.50 lakhs and Rs. 49.43 lakhs were allotted for First, Second and Third Five Year Plans, Three Annual Plans (1966-69) and then the Fourth Five Year Plan respectively. The actual expenditure, however, amounted to Rs. 4.02 lakhs during Second Plan period, that is, little more than one-fourth of allotment, while it stood at Rs. 14.64 lakhs during 1966-69 and Rs. 30.40 lakhs during 1969-72.

1. Sector of Sericulture. Humid and moist climate because of heavy rainfall during summer has made Arunachal Pradesh a natural home for certain types of indigenous insects and their corresponding food plants. Such helping condition might be the reason that some of the tribesmen, specially of foot-hills, were found to be indigenous silk rearers. However, they used to face difficulties in respect of production and also supply of seeds. Moreover, the silk worms are easily disease susceptive and the ordinary villagers cannot produce their required disease free silk worm seeds to ensure fruitful harvest.

Talking in the context of above situation, the Administration started seed production farms and centres of supply disease-free seeds to the rearers and also extend technical guidance to them through demonstration centres. One centre like this was there in Kameng, two in each of Subansiri and Lohit Districts, three in Siang and four in Tirap.

2. Culture Based Industries. In fact, Arunachal Pradesh's cropping pattern represents as monoculture, with paddy, maize and millet being the principal crops. Commercial crops like jute, sugarcane oilseeds, cotton and then tea plantation on which agro-industries could base themselves are almost non-existent in the region. Of late, some commercial crops like sugarcane and mustard oil seeds have been started by the Administration, but these efforts have not met with much success. Some native individuals have taken initiatives for tea-plantation, but this too is confined to kitchen garden largely for show purpose. Such being the situation, we find only twelve rice mills and oil mills,[3] operating within the region at present. A few flour mills were also started alongwith rice mills some years back which in course of short time itself proved prohibitive for want of raw materials.

3. Industries Based on Forestry. For all these industries, the Pradesh provides ample scope. But the progress made in this direction is poor one. However, the first plywood mill and large industrial plant unit, Assam Saw Mill and Timber Co. was established at Namsai, in Lohit district, during the year 1950. The idea behind it was to supply tea Chests to the tea industry located in Assam.

Kebang Koret Saw Mill, established in 1956, has considerably contributed in building the Pasighat Township in the district of East Siang now. An Adi Kebang Saw Mill, as a co-operative venture of the local people, is located at Likhabali in Siang. NEFA Udyog, a private saw mill, was started at Banderdewa in Subansiri during 1962-63. In Tirap, M/S Nocte Timber Company began installation of Saw-cum-Veneer Mill at Deomali during 1963-64. Another veneer industrial unit, under the name of Narotham Co-operative, has been established at Deomali in December, 1972. Industries and a few other Saw Mills are also in existence. However, the total score of the industries based on forest materials may be put as six saw mills and two plants of each plywood and Veneer Mills. In view of the abundant forest resources in the region, progress made so far is not very much encouraging which may be attributed local situation.

4. More Small Scale Units. Apart from above units, four tailoring shops, two leather factories, one mechanical workshop, one knitting wool factory, one soap-making unit, one carpet making unit, seven candle factories and then two steel trunk and bucket factories[4] could have been set up throughout the region under study till 1971-72. The extent of economic contribution of the various industrial units, located in Arunachal Pradesh, may be well assessed in respect of persons employed as well as type of fuel/power used, from the table that comes next. It is seen that about three-fourths of factories/workshops were run without any sort of power, with average strength of 9.4 persons. Out of these units, nearly four-fifths with personnel strength of 5 were located in rural areas. About 22 per cent of such units, located in urban areas, provided employment, on average, to as many as 24 persons. Amongst the units run with power, four-fifths were located in rural areas and their average employment stood at little more than 24 persons, whereas four of such units in urban parts provided average employment to less than 7 persons.

Only one of the factories run with electric power in rural area provided employment to more than half of the total labour force employed in rural units in the region. In regard to household industries, we note that 85 per cent of them were run by manual power. Their rural focus was also equally large, while such units in rural areas on average, employed as 3 persons, their counterpart in urban areas could have 5 persons on average. Out of 15 per cent of such units run with some power, more than four-fifths were situated in rural areas, employing 3 persons on average.

Their counterpart in urban parts registered average employment of 7 personnel during the period under census report.

5. Different Mineral Resources and Industries Running With Them. While geologically the region is least known in the country, a systematic programme has, of late, been launched in 1970-71 by the Geological Survey of India to explore the feasibility of occurrence of various minerals like lime stone, soap stone, marble, graphite, coal, asbestos, berye, iron ore, copper clay, oil and salt in the region.[6] However, the terrain is divided into two regions mainly; the Himalayan, comprising Kameng, Subansiri, Siang and Lohit districts, and the next Patkoi consisting the district of Tirap only.

While the former (Arunachal Himalaya) is made up of a narrow belt of Tertiary sediments in the outer hills with Gondwana and Archean Metamorphic rocks in the internal and higher ranges, the latter, Patkoi, is constituted of Tertiary sediments, belonging to Disang, Barail, Tipam and Dihing series.

Natural Mineral Resources

1. Coal. Its occurrences are seen in all the five districts of Arunachal Pradesh. However, Kameng and Tirap share significantly. In Himalayan sector, that is, Kameng, Subansiri, Siang and Lohit, the coal occurs in Gondwana rocks, though it is reported to have occurred in Tertiary rocks of Patkoi in Tirap. In Kameng, the occurrences of the above mineral are reported chiefly from two stratigraphic horizons, i.e. Gondwanas and Tertiaries.

The latter coal occurrences are, generally, in the form of lenticular to irregular streakes or pockets of shining black coal material and carbonised to half-carbonised woody, lignitic to peaty material. A belt of the former, that is Gondwana rocks, stretches from east to west, just north of foothills (Siwalik) Zone. In this belt, the coal seams are usually intercalated, associated with sand-stones and slaty shales. Due to tectonic movements, the Gondwana coals are conspicuously crushed and are usually powdery in nature. There are a number of coaly horizons, occurring as intercalatory bonds near Amatulla (26°55': 92°06') near Bhairavkund river part and north of Doimara (27°00': 92°25') in Belsiri river area.

Over and above, the lenses of coal in these areas are reported to be varying from a few centimeters to even 1 to 5 meters. More thin of quite crushed coal within the Gondwana rocks are also observed near 15 kilometre post on Kamengbari, Bomdila road section. The prominent coal deposits too have been brought to notice in Tirap. They seem to occur in Tertiary rocks in continuity with the same of upper Assam coal fields.

In this district two coaly fields have been reported, being, (1) Namchik-Namphuk, and (2) Mia-Bum. The former is located about 10 kilometre north-east of the Makuk coal field of Assam between two tributaries of Buridihing river, i.e. Namphu, Kharsang river in the north and the north-east and Namchik river in the west. The major coal seams occur in Supra thrust block in Tikak Patbat stage (Barail series) as is separated by Bara-golies by the Basal coal horizons.

The Geographical survey has explored eight coal seams (seam I to VIII) in the area of which seam III has a maximum thickness differing from 4.55 to 19.00 meters. The total seam-wise reserves of coal proved in this field amounting to 14.28 million tonnes, through the overall potentiality of the region may be about six times more. The coal reserves of this area contain high potentiality and high sulphur contents similar to those of upper part of Assam. The Mia-Bum coal horizon in Tirap is located in the eastward extension of the Namchik-Namphuk coal field. The two main seams with an average thickness of about 10 metres have been correlated in the area. Its probable deposits may be in the order of about six million tonnes upto 200 metre depth.

Unlike the suitability of Makum coal area as coking blend with Jharia, Raniganj coal, the adjacent Namchick-Namphuk coal fields may be suitable for the manufacture of synthetic petroleum, low-temperature carbonisation plants and power creation as those of Assam. Although Tertiary Coal occurs in Subansiri, it is of limited significance for academic interest only and thought not feasible from economic stand point. Because the occurrence is woody, lignitic to peaty materials in different forms and discernible, according to the different tertiary rocks along various sections.

However, and Ozm thick peaty out-crop within 100 metre-length has been noted through the right bank of the Kale river close to Saro village in Ziro valley. The emergence of Gondwana coal is nil. The district of Siang also shares the occurrence of Tertiary coal, but of low grade in the form of non-frequent streakes, lenses and carbonised to semi-carbonised wood lignitic to peaty materials.

These occurrences are not economically important. Many but small lenticular bodies of coal emerge in Gondwana horizons which are crushed and usually associated with the sandy or shaly partings.

2. Occurrence of Iron Ore. These occurrences have been reported from the opposite to Bana village (27°16': 92°52) about 35 kilometres southward extension of Seppa (Kameng District), comprising ground, short ridge on the right flank of Bichom river Reserve of this area contains boulders of micaceous hematite, some times with magnetic as bloat also being associated with Quartzitic material.

The in-situ reserve has, not been observed. In Subansiri, iron ore reserves have been noticed in many small patches being placed between Landak (27°51': 94°15') and Godak villages (27°49: 94°11) on the western bank of Simi river. Small rolled boulders of iron ore have also been reported from Alluvial terrace in Tertiary belt, close to Kimin 27°19': 93°58') and Jahing (27°18': 94°03'), across Ranga valley. In the district of Siang, the iron ore veins of hematite-magnetite in schists and phyllite boulders emerge within a distance of 5 kilometres from east of Tribin (28°01': 94°35') to near Lete (27°59': 94°35') village. A few minor occurrences are also found close Yomcha village (28°0': 94°34') three kilometres east of it.

3. Dolomite Occurrence. Its prominent occurrence is heard from Dedza (27°12': 92°35') areas/section. In this area it is exposed on the left flank of Tenga river as a highly disturbed zone. The massive and cherty dolomite band constitutes the apex unit of succession of thin blank phyllites and bedded dense dark grey carbonate rocks. The exposed thickness of dolomite is likely to be more than 100 metres with a strike spread of 500 metres or more. The same dolomite has been noticed in Rupa area, about 3 kilometres upstream of Rupa on the right flank of Tenga river close to Gocham bridge. The white-massive crystalline dolomite here contains minor bands of grey variety physically over lies a sequence of highly sheared quartzites and quartz schists etc., although its thickness differs, on average, more than 10 metres.

In Siang, a few bands/specks of dolomite have been observed between Takar (28°13′: 94°55′) and Pangin (28°12′: 94°55′) on Along Pangin route.

Also, a number of out crops of fine grained grey dolomitic lime-stones have been found along Siang river between Pasighat (28°05': 95°20') and Pugging (28°45': 94°57').

4. Availability of Glass Sand. It occurs in Tenga valley of Rupa area associated with a hard and compact quartzite band, probably of the significant importance of glass industry.

5. Limestone Carbonate. A few limestone carbonate specks are reported in Kameng, majority of which are inconsistent and of without any economic significance. The reserves being located on the right bank of Bichom river for almost 20 kilometres are variegated slates, massive and compact limestone, carbonates and sandstones. This calcarious zone is well exposed in the road cutting near 53 kilometres stone on Seppa road. Complete thickness of the zone is reported to be about 30 metres of which limestone is nearly 50 per cent.

The presence of slaty rocks has also been seen in the calcarious bands of Bichom river section/specks down stream of Bana Basti (village). Calcarious dolomitic limestones have been found in Khetabari-yazali area of Ranga valley in Kamla river bed and also between Lamdak and Godak villages. In Siang, the above deposits are seen near Dali (27°54': 94°47') and Kabu (28°12': 94°45').

In Lohit District a reserve of cement grade good quality limestone has been reported at Tadding, near the confluence of Tadding and Tellu rivers. Internally, folded band of nicely bedded, crystilline, some times, massive limestone has been observed to continue for more than 20 kilometres strikewise. The estimated deposits for a spread of 1.70 kilometres with an average thickness of 240 metres of the order of 25 million tonnes down to a vertical depth of 50 metres occur.

6. Crystals and Marbles. In the district of Kameng, roughly white crystalline has been noted, across Bomdila-Tawang road in Dirang area. The presence of crystalline limestone marble has been said to be seen Siang near Dapu (28°33' : 94°36') and Lipushi (28°40': 94°15') villages. The above deposits have also been discovered further upstream close to Mechuke (28°48' : 94°59') from upper reaches of Siyom valley. It occurs within crystalline seduce. The two deposits of marble within metamorphites have been found in Tezu area (27°54': 96°09') occurring from the Tezu plain. The marble in above reserves is, in general, white, medium grained and jointed. Besides the above areas' having numerous reserves, some valleys and river reserves deserve a special mention.

7. Tezu River Deposits. A lenticular reserve of crystlline limestone marble, being located amongst schists, grounlites etc., is situated about 13 kilometres north of Tezu-Dihing road. The road speck has a surface expansion of about 1230 metres with average thickness of 92 metres. About 30.3 million tonnes of marble have been estimated to be the total deposits in this area till a depth of 50 metres.

8. Dara River Reserves. It occurs about 10 kilometres from Tezu towards east through Dara river belt. Two main lenses of this calcareous rocks within Quartz-felsparsericite schist. These lenses vary from 45 metres to 186 metres in thickness and from 160 metres in thickness to in length. Still, the above reserves of carbonate rock are estimated to be 43.3 million tonnes down to a depth of 50 million tonnes. By dint of their physical and chemical properties, the stones of the above reserves seem to be suitable for lime burning and in somewhat selective manner the material can be found suitable as building stone and as marble flats for mosaic flooring.

9. Tellu Valley Deposits. One more marble deposit of 200 metres thickness with an intercalating band of hotublende schist (4 m) is located in the West of

Bambi village (27°58': 96°58') in the valley. Same way, a number of marble specks have been noticed on Tezu-Hayuliang road falling between 40 kilometres and 70 kilometre stones. These are coarse grained and siliceous in nature. Their such character may make them useful for lime processing and building purposes.

10. Dibang valley deposits. The occurrence of twin bands of impure marble of about 40 to 150 metres width is observed along Tangan river in the valley. Another band of about 200 metres thick has been seen at about 3 kilometre north of Gruli (28°40': 95°56') village. The chemical test concludes the reserves to be high and calcic bands with the marble. One thin impure marble has been reported in Inchi Nala.

11. Arse Nopyrite Deposits. Its deposit of one metre thick which is shared with Quartzite and in association with Quartz veins has been reported about 100 metres up stream from the confluence of Kale and Ranga rivers. The reserves are said to be containing some amount of arsenic within the above mentioned zone. The occurrence has not been found anywhere other than Subansiri.

12. Berye Crystals. In Subansiri, the crystals of white berye are seen from small pegmatite veins in the gneisses near Yachali (27°29': 93°46') about 69 kilometre on Kimin-Ziro road. However, it does not take place in other districts.

13. Clay Zones. In Subansiri thin clayed zones in terrace materials have been observed upstream of pit a pol (27°20': 93°48') through Ranga valley. Due to its impurity, it looks grey. Again, clay deposit has been discovered along the Mishmi Thrust in the foot-hills from Chidu (28°12': 95°47') to Koronu (23°3': 95°57') in the Digbang Valley of Lohit. These deposits, being pockety in character, may hardly be called economic exploitation.

14. Cobalty Nickel Reserves. Its deposit of sulphide materialisation has been noted in Ranga Vall near Potin (27°19': 93°48') containing cobalt and nickel. The above speck has been stated to be within a strike length of around 3 kilometres and within a width of 300 to 800 metres.

15. Graphite Deposits. Deposits, Pockety, flaky and amorphous graphite schist objects bodies, in high grade have been discovered in morphic rocks located near La village. It is estimated to be in a depth of 30 metres; and of the order of 21,886 tonnes, with its small deposit also seen near Yachali. It occurs in Siang near Tai (29°59': 94°31') village. It is about 2 kilometres with a width of about 11 metres. Its depth is reported to be 150 metres of the order of 10.35 million tonnes. The district of Lohit also shares the above reserves but of low grade graphic schist near Lalpani (27°56': 96°22').

The major graphic schist body extends for about 1.10 kilometre on surface with an average width of about 300 metres. However, the total deposits are guessed to be depth of 100 metres, being in order of 71 million tonnes.

16. Mica Reserves. Subansiri appears to be a monopolist with regard to the mica's reserves, containing small, highly crushed and fracture and trained biolite and muscovite books, the pegmatites in granite near Ziro, Pitapol and Potin and also close to Maghu on Diro-Daporijo road route. Irrespective of the reserves being small, are exploitable, economically.

17. Deposits of Phosphorite. In Subansiri, dark shales and also carous to cherty bands within Gondwanas, have been traced along Kimin-Ziro road between 25 and 35 kilometres stones. It occurs also in Siang region between Basar and Daporijo.

18. Occurrences of Pyrite and Pyrrhotite. These occurrence containing chiefly pyrite with rare chaleopyrite and specks of malachite and a Zurite has been noted near 20/3 culvert within 20th kilometre and 31/3 culvert within area 32 kilometre from Ziro to Tamen following Ziro-Daporijo metalled road. In Tirap it is found in Disang shales between Bhoga and Pani and Khonsa (27°01': 95°24') and (27°06': 95°32') respectively.

19. Ochre. Most of its deposits are exposed between Bame (28°03': 94°11') and Along (28°11': 94°48') following the road section. Some promising pockets of yellow ochres on initial testing offered Fe 202 ranging from 19.82 to 30.39 per cent. In general, these pockets are low to medium grade as regards the quality.

20. Gold Mines. No authentic information is available in this context. However, the gold occurrences may be related to the historical records of gold panning in the sands of Buridihing river significantly. The tributaries derive rock materials from the area comprising igneous and metamorphic confusions. It is tribal residents of Vijoynagar area, who were, in the past, linked with traditional export gold panners in the adjoining region of Burma.

21. Oil and Gas Deposits. In Tirap District, the Tertiary succession is in continuity with the Assam Tertiary belt which is well known for its oil and gas resources. Many oil and gas seepages ("Pungs") have been reported in Namdeik area. Oil deposits have been observed near Tissa stream south of Kanubari area. But economic finds of oil and gas in the areas (Tirap district) has been established recently.

The map of minerals in doubt of Arunachal Pradesh is in hand by the Geological Survey of India. Tirap is also well known for brine wells and saline springs, locally called 'sum'. The wells/springs are placed chiefly around Borduria (27°02': 95°29'), Khonsa (27°00': 95°30') and Namsang (27°02': 95°28'). Generally, these wells occur along joint planes shear joints, fauls or faulted anticlines and also are placed in the stream valley.

The oozing is mostly in Disang beds but a few in Barail rocks also. Although we have noted the occurrences of a number of minerals in the State study, they are reported occurrences so far.

Here, it would be of much worth to have a glance over the programmes laid down for the industrial development in Arunachal Pradesh during the Fifth Five Year Plan period. The Plan targets at setting up small, medium and large scale industries based on agriculture and forest resources. Further, it provides for the setting up of industrial estate in various trades, and organising marketing through sales emporium alongwith making available finance and raw materials for necessary industries. Several schemes under small and medium scale sectors have also been proposed to bring about solid improvement in the existing pattern of industrial development without sacrificing the traditional values of artistic craftsmanship.

The setting up of a paper and news print unit, one Central Raw-material Depot, a Research and Design Centre as well as some more craft centres is also included under the Plan.

Records show that it has also been proposed to set-up mineral based industries like cement and coal etc. Besides, there is a proposal to drill four exploratary wells, one in each year. The objective depth of each of these wells is about to range from 4,570 to 6,100 metres. Oil India Limited has also taken up a scheme to expand the capacity of its crude oil pipelines by installing additional pumps to transport crude oil to the said refinery at Bongaigaon (in Assam). The crude oil conditioning facilities to Moran are also being expanded to keep the crude oil pumpable during the cold weather. All these jobs are in press.

Thus, to sum up, Arunachal Pradesh is still practically limited to handicrafts and, of course, some agro and forest based medium size industrial units, apart from a few other small scale units in some other fields, have appeared in the region, still leaving much scope to develop them alongwith addition of new units. The geological survey has revealed good potentiality of mineral exploration in the region. In fact, some proposals for development of mineral based industries like cement and coal have, of late, been well contemplated by the authorities concerned, yet it is still true to ensure the observation of Techno-Economic Survey Team, of the National Council of Applied Economic Research, which is that 'mineral development in NEFA (now Arunachal Pradesh) would have to be oriented towards the large needs of India as a whole,' keeping in view of the fact that it would take sometime before local demand for minerals develops. It goes without saying, that the mineral based industries may generate tremendous economy to the state if matching infrastructure also emerges.

References

1. Series—24—Arunachal Pradesh Part III-A Establishments Report & Part III-B Establishments Tables, p. 24.
2. Statistics Department, Arunachal Pradesh: Quick Issue of Statistical Hand Book of Arunachal Pradesh, 1972-73, (Provisional), p. 56.
3. Planning and Development Department, Arunachal Pradesh Administration, Approach to Fifth Five Year Plan (1974-79), p. 21.
4. Arunachal Pradesh Administration, Implementation of the Recommendations of Senior Officers Conference, 1971, p. 90.
5. Census of India, 1971, Series—24—Arunachal Pradesh Part III-A—Establishments Report, Part III-B—Establishments Tables p. XVI.
6. Director of Information and Public Relations, NEFA: NEFA Information p. 13.

5

Economy and Trade

Availability of natural resources and geographical placing of a state guides its finances, trade and commerce. So is true of Arunachal Pradesh too.

A. Brackground

1. Pre-Independence Period. Before the advent of the Britishers to Assam in 1838, trade relation existed amongst the traders in Leh, Sadiya, Lahul, Spiti, Garhwal, Kumaon, Nepal, Assam and the North East Frontier Region who generally used to barter their indigenous surplus products against their requirements. Having taken note of such trade, the East India Company thought of settling themselves in the Asiatic continental markets. The obligation to settle trade deficit in terms of gold and silver facilitated entry of the East India Company to Tibet and as such construction of the roadways from the plains of Simla region to the Sutlej, the Tibetan border, was contemplated around 1850. However, this idea was subsequently abandoned in 1858 in view of the suggested alternative to construct a route to Tibet along Darjeeling or the northern hills of Assam as it was to shorten the route by connecting India with the eastern Tibet in place of the western Tibet[1] region.

While response from the side of the Governor General to the proposal of the Commissioner of Assam and his Agent for the North East Frontier to open the trade route through Tawang Tract in 1840 was highly encouraging, nothing was done in this respect. The importance of Assam route through the erstwhile North-East Frontier Tract was, however, well realised and the issue cropped up time and again. Mr. Cooper who unsuccessfully tried to undertake the journey to Tibet and then Assam or Burma through Western China in 1868 and again in 1869 from Sadiya (Assam) to Tibet via the valley of Lohit, was prompted ultimately to advocate for the route through the Lohit Valley and the Assam Hills between Assam and Central and Eastern Tibet[2] region. The attention of the Britishers engaged in commerce was as such drawn to the Indo-Tibetan trade across the eastern Himalayas and, consequently, it added to the stress on the then British Government in India to open the aforesaid route. Due to rich prospects of trade in the Tibetan markets, the Chambers of Commerce in areas like Manchester, Hudders field, Leeds, Halifax, Brandford, Liverpool, Bristol, Gaoncester, Glasgow and others appealed to the British India office to arrange for the starting of the western China to the English merchants. And, therefore, projects concerning Assam-Tibet route through the region of present Arunachal Pradesh was well thought of. But the British India Office never supported the route through Burma to western China and the Inner Line Regulation of 1873 in Assam proved to be a great deterrent in the way of formation of trade route through the Lohit Valley to Eastern Tibet.

The Inner Line restrictions kept the plains trader at arm's length. Despite certain hurdles to develop trade routes, trade and commerce remained an imperative and pressing necessity for the North-Eastern Frontier like any other region in any part of the world due to their ever increasing economic inter-dependence. Barring a few tribes who carried on their high enterprising ability, lack of mutual trust amongst various tribal groups in the region under present study stood as a huge stumbling block in the way of development of trade and commerce in general. The Apatanis, one among the most prosperous tribal group, could not carry on trade either inside or outside due to the resistance by the neighbouring Nissi in the early time. However, during the middle forties they could continue trade, though accidental, rare and irregular. An Apatani, named 'NIME' used to go to Tibet generally as an interpreter with the British official tourists and take in rubber as much as he could and used to resell it among his own men at a greater margin of profit who, in turn, made water-proof baskets.[3]

In another visit, he used to bring valuable white beads as large as hen's eggs. Such trip trade by Apatani was, however, very occasional, though it reflected their natural and curious interest in trade.

As we shall see, the Akas are famous for their enterprising acts in trade and commerce, as they have been carrying on inter-village trade amongst the tribal mens within Arunachal Pradesh and with the plains of Assam outside for several years. Their inter-village-trade has mainly been in foodgrains[4] being carried on in this way that the surplus villages in foodgrains used to tell their desire to the neighbouring villages that they were prepared to barter.

Having come to know about it, the deficit villages used to respond and fix up time, date and place. As per their mutual convenience on which and where the scheduled barter had to take place. This inter-village trade as such facilitated close more association amongst the Bangnis, the Mijis and the Akas. Another notable feature of such barter trade has been that even stone-beads and slaves[5] were bartered away. The Akas who did not have slaves bought their goods from the neighbouring Bangnis.[6] So far as trade and commerce with the plains was concerned, money transaction used to be continued and the Akas used to sell their indigenous goods like fowls[7] against receipts of cash. With this amount, they used to purchase mill cloth, silver ornaments and utensils. It was on account of this trade with the plains that the currency could reach the Akas earlier as compared to other nearby tribes, like the Bangnis, and the Mijis. Their trade-route to the plains market is traced to Jamiri via Bhalukpong to Charduar (Assam). During the post-independence era, a road has been made following this route connecting Charduar and Tawang via Bhalukpong, Rupa, Bomdila and Dirang Valley. The Sherdukpens, one more tribal group, used to carry on trade among themselves as well as with the people in the plains of Assam. Their annual winter migration to Doimara (in Assam) has also been affected, specially by the trade interest. Even today, they go to Doimara with their cattle, poultry, birds (chicken), chillies, dried radishes, jabrang (local pepper) spice, daos and woven bags[8] for sale through markets of plains and purchase Assamese endi-silk, mill made cloth, salt, rice, beads, bangles and metallic utensils.[9]

So far their internal trade is concerned, they used to exchange their cows for mithuns with the Akas, horses, cows, Assamese endi-cloth, mithuns, and animal skins with the Monpas for butter, coats, shoes, carpets, saddle bags, blanket, face masks and yak-cap and with the Khowas cloth, salt, betalnut and pinerasin[10] for other indigenous goods. The Monpas, a Buddhist tribe, also used to visit Tibet and exchange their musks, rice, chillies and dead animal skins for salt, wool, woollen cloth and Tibetan swords.[11] Such trade enabled them to recognise value of money as exchange. But the Lopas, a sub-tribe, were firm in this regard as they decided to stick to barter exchange,[12] prevailing from time immemorial. Thus, the articles, namely, madder,[13] red dye, skin, tobacco, hurbs and madder dye were taken to Tibet and, in exchange, they used to get salt, wool, woollen cloth, cymbols, bell (a Tibetan religious bell) and white shell beads. These articles were transported by ponies.[15] Various seasons were prescribed to conduct these trades. There were, for example, summer markets during the fifth month, autumn markets during the seventh month and winter markets during the tenth month[16] of the year.

According to suitability of various seasons, the articles for bartering were taken. Salt, for instance, used to be prominent article for winter markets. There were also trade in plank.[17] In the earlier period, the traders were subjected to many hardships as they had to cover long snow clad routes. Again, although the Adis (known as Abor earlier), to note an instance, used to visit Tibet four times during a year in a party of 80 to 100 persons,[18] they were yet not allowed to enter and sleep in any of the Tibetan villages at night and, ultimately, they were to camp on the hillsides.[19]

These Adis people exchanged rice for salt. Again, there was no definite rate for bartering commodities. However, there was a prevalent high rate for exchange of salt; so high as mere one packet of madder dye for one 'tre' (a pot as unit).[20] This trade-relation with Tibet came to an end just after India's attainment of independence. The relation of trade and commerce among the tribesmen in the region under study and the plains of Assam deserves a special mention as even during early period there was an economic intercourse between them. During the days of Ahoms, the tribesmen used to visit the markets and fairs held in the plains of Assam. The Mishmis, for instance, used to come down with their teeta (a root of specific plant valuable as a febrifuge), musk, aconite, bee wax, ginger and chillies to Sadiya and Dibrugarh[21] (both in Assam) for bartering against salt, mill-made cloth utensils, irons and yarn etc.

In the latter half of the 19th century, these border plain markets were regularised with a view to promote trade and, thereafter, fairs were organised at

Sadiya every year. The fair, conducted at Sadiya on the 18th and 19th of the February, 1866, was attended by the Mishmis in a good number. A similar fair was held in 1874 and the same was attended by considerable number of people.

Again, during the year 1876, a fair was held at Udalguri[22] in Assam and was attended by as many as 3,000 tribesmen, belonging to different tribes, namely, Miris, Mishmis, Khamptis and Singphos and many others. It would be of much worth to mention the different places in the plains of Assam which were visited frequently by the different tribesmen, as per their conveniences. The Sherdukpens used to camp at Doimara and visit Mishamari and Rangapara markets. In the same way, the Dirang Monpas and south Monpas used to camp at Amaratola, specially during the winter and visit Darrang, Udalguri and other adjacent places.

The Akas visited Charduar and Balipara. The Daflas were touring through Charduar, Balipara and Itakhola Hat. Dulungmukh, Pathalipam and North Lakhimpur were visited by the Nissis of Subansiri also used to visit Itakhola, Nahalbari. The Gallongs went to Majorbari, Sibsagar, Dibrugarh and North Lakhimpur too. But the rest of the Adis group used to visit Dibrugarh very frequently. The Mishmis and the Khamptis toured to Sadiya, Doomdooma, Tinsukia and Dibrugarh. While the Singphos used to go to Pengri and Margherita, the Tangsas Ledo, Lekhapani and Margherita. Joypur, Naharkatia, Namrup and Margherita were visited by the Noctes, whereas Jorhat, Namrup and Sonari by the Wanchos of Tirap. It is an interesting reality to note here that all the tribesmen other than the Noctes were to depend on outside markets for salt. At the same time, the Noctes used to produce the salt from their wells[23] and supply it to the markets of Assam. They used to pay tributes to the Ahom Kings in salt.

(2) Post-Independence Period. Except their indigenous goods like forest products, animal skins, Mishmiteeta, galle of Adi, carpet, shoes, butter, woollen cloth, for caps of Monpas, Wooden and cane material, chillies, ginger, jabran (local species similar to black pepper) opium, bags, small daggers, tusks, and salt of Noctes, the rest of the commercial articles like torch, battery, shoes, radio, designed mill cloth sweets and numerous other groceries including threads[25] though new to them, are available in today's markets held over they are imported by the small, middle and big traders, shifted to the region by the local tribesmen as well as consumers' co-operatives. All the District Headquarters and Sub-divisional Headquarters have been flourishing as the trade and commercial centres for sometime past. It may be attributed to gradual replacement of barter economy by the money economy and creation of new demand for various goods. It is, thus, very natural to see that demand so created is met through supplies[26] from within.

The district-wise division of trade or business establishments is very much uneven. While Siang district accounting for a little more than 38 per cent of such establishments is about four times more than Lohit District, Tirap and Kameng Districts share almost equally to total business establishments. With a little more than 10 per cent of business establishments in the region Subansiri has relatively the highest concentration of establishments owned and controlled by the Government agencies. Next comes Lohit district, accounting for 20 per cent of such Government establishments.

While share of such establishments in Siang stands unfavourably low, when considered in relation to total number of business establishments in the district, it comes to total as high as 27 per cent of the total number, of Government establishments in Arunachal Pradesh. Subansiri and Lohit districts have got lower shares of their private establishments as against their overall share in the territory. Consumers' Co-operatives, on the whole, have got very weak base in the region, as evident from their low share. Their highest percentage that comes to less than 9 per cent of these establishments in regard to Lohit district. More than three-fourths of the establishments carry on retail trade. There is a sole whole-sale establishment in Siang. Amongst the other category of establishments, educational institutions and public health institutions account for one-fourth of such establishments. The rural urban division of establishments under 'other' category, works out to more than 91 per cent[29] in the rural areas alone. However, the educational and public health institutions form about 8 per cent[30] of the all urban establishments under the category. The census data, having latest figures, relating to workers are given on next two pages.

Thus, to conclude, it may be said that despite various impediments and uncongenial environment like mutual suspicion and feuds, complete absence of transport and communication as well as lack of common medium of exchange, trade relations between the people in this region and outside were there also in the early days. Trade and Commerce has assumed greater significance in the recent past due to money economy and emergence of transport and communication facilities and the changing pattern of socio-economic life of the people in the region. Self-sufficiency is no longer the commodity of the day even in the region not very easily accessible due to topography and difficult terrain. Now, economy is no more isolated and stagnant and economic inter-course has rather become quite common. In Siang, now, 'mithun' is purchased for money and marriage price is paid in cash partially. Although, barter system in its antiquated form has almost disappeared, every money-earner needs indigenous goods such as beads, mithuns etc., to meet the barter requirements for social purposes on the occasions of wedding and money income for outside transaction, on the other hand. Thus, barter system is still not ruled out completely and in the villages barter is still in vogue for purchasing vegetables and grocery objects. The growing tendency amongst the local people to purchase the threads from the markets to weave on lion-loom has resulted in the growth of weaving art in the area. Same is the case of basketry, wood and cane carving, as borne out by the decline of trade of earthen pot-making as a result of availability of metallic utensils through barter-exchange. The above changing socio-economic condition in the region provides ample justification for the decision of the Administration to solve the difficulty in two ways: by encouraging local enterprising people to set-up their own shops and by setting up

Table 1

The Survey of Main Workers, Marginal Workers and Non-Workers (Districtwise) : Census 2001

District	*Total workers*			*Main workers*			*Marginal workers*			*Non workers*		
	P	*M*	*F*	*P*	*M*	*F*	*P*	*M*	*F*	*P*	*M*	*F*
Tawang	22,099	14,254	7,845	18,377	12,506	5,871	3,722	1,748	1,974	17,143	7,827	9,316
West Kameng	34,353	24,870	9,483	28,868	22,464	6,404	5,485	2,406	3,079	40,174	17,715	22,459
East Kameng	25,917	13,976	11,941	23,483	13,227	10,256	2,434	749	1,685	31,148	14,767	16,381
Papum Pare	44,214	29,909	14,305	38,408	27,289	11,119	5,806	2,620	3,186	77,518	34,119	43,399
Lower Subansiri	45,032	23,467	21,565	36,872	20,225	16,647	8,160	3,242	4,918	52,696	25,799	26,897
Upper Subansiri	22,263	12,444	9,819	20,900	11,944	8,956	1,363	500	863	33,093	15,726	17,367
West Siang	42,860	25,587	17,273	36,600	23,035	13,565	6,260	2,552	3,708	60,923	28,769	32,154
East Siang	33,578	20,494	13,084	29,094	18,832	10,262	4,484	1,662	2,822	53,753	24,639	29,114
Upper Siang	17,110	10,346	6,764	15,400	9,501	5,899	1,710	845	865	16,246	7,698	8,548
Dibang Valley	25,496	16,433	9,063	21,840	14,949	6,891	3,656	1,484	2,172	32,047	14,847	17,200
Lohit	60,323	39,689	20,634	50,945	36,771	14,174	9,378	2,918	6,460	83,155	37,563	45,592
Changlang	60,009	34,733	25,276	49,071	31,097	17,974	10,938	3,636	7,302	65,325	31,026	34,299
Tirap	48,952	27,347	21,605	43,663	25,082	18,581	5,289	2,265	3,024	51,275	25,114	26,161

consumer cooperative stores to establish their trading activities. It is well proved that certain tribesmen in Arunachal Pradesh have turned out to be very good businessmen. At district headquarters and a few sub-divisional headquarters, the Administration has set up market places and rent the blocks to local traders which has paid good dividends. Latest census data showing total, main, marginal workers and non-workers is given below :

Table 2
The Survey of Main Workers, Marginal Workers and Non-Workers (Statewise) : Census 2001

Total Rural Urban	*Persons Males Females*	*Total workers*	*Main workers*	*Marginal workers*	*Non-workers*	*Total Workers (main + marginal)*
Total	Persons	482,206	413,521	68,685	614,496	482,206
	Males	293,549	266,922	26,627	285,609	293,549
	Females	188,657	146,599	42,058	328,887	188,657
Rural	Persons	405,998	343,181	62,817	467,635	405,998
	Males	234,433	210,871	23,562	224,049	234,433
	Females	171,565	132,310	39,255	243,586	171,565
Urban	Persons	76,208	70,340	5,868	146,861	76,208
	Males	59,116	56,051	3,065	61,560	59,116
	Females	17,092	14,289	2,803	85,301	17,092

References

1. Major Mountgomery of the Survey of India; India and Bengal Despatches, Vol. 81 to 169: India Foreign Letters No. 74 of Dec. 1852. Accounts and Papers 1857 Session 1. XI: Minutes and correspondance concerning Hindustan-Tibet Road, p. 275.
2. Lamb, Alastair, Britain and Chinese Asia (London) 1960 pp. 125-126—Mr. Cooper also provided a detailed report about the feasibility of trans-Himalayan trade through the North-Eastern Hills, that is, Assam Hills.
3. C.F. Haimendarf; Himalayan Barbary (1955), p. 85.
4. Raghuvir Sinha: *op. cit.*, p. 48.
5. Raghuvir Sinha, *op. cit.* p. 59.
6. *Ibid.*, p. 50.
7. *Ibid.*, p. 59.
8. R.R.P. Sharma,: *op. cit.* p. 9.
9. *Ibid.*
10. *Ibid.*, pp. 9-10.
11. F.M. Bailey,: No Passport to Tibet (1957), p. 162.
12. F.M. Bailey,: No Passport to Tibet (1957), p. 162.
13. *Ibid.*, p. 232.

14. *Ibid.*, p. 214.
15. *Ibid.*, p. 232.
16. *Ibid.*, p. 246.
17. *Ibid.*
18. F.M. Bailey,: *op. cit.* p. 158.
19. *Ibid.*, p. 158.
20. *Ibid.*, p. 214.
21. Government of India, Publication Division, Ministry of Information and Broadcasting: NEFA, 1965, p. 20.
22. Verrier Elwin: "A philosophy For NEFA, (Second Reprint 1964), p. 3.
23. C.F. Haimendorf,: *op. cit.*, p. 90.
24. Census of India, 1971, Arunachal Pradesh, Series 24 Arunachal Pradesh Part III-A—Establishments Report Part III-B—Establishments Tables, p. 26.
25. Series 24—Arunachal Pradesh, Part III-A—Establishments Report Part III B—Establishments Tables, p. 26.
26. Series 24—Arunachal Pradesh, Part III-A—Establishments Report Part III B—Establishments Tables, p. 26.

6

Education, Crafts and Skill-Upgradation

After these basic necessities are fulfilled, the most important requirement of a human being is education. The development of education which, as rightly noted by Plato, is "to give to the body and to the soul all the beauty and all the perfection of which they are capable" is as old in the state as the political independence of India, since two junior basic schools were started only in 1947.

(a) Evaluation of Education Institutional

During the first decade of national independence, that is till 1957-58, the number of educational institutions rose to 105 (that is 93 junior basic schools, 10 middle and 2 high schools) with the total enrolment of 4,443 students in the area. Over the next fifteen years, their number (567) rose to more than five times.

It may be found that the number of junior basic schools which constitute 88 per cent of educational institutions in Arunachal Pradesh has risen more than five times as compared to 1957-58, whereas number of middle schools, forming 8 per cent of the institutions, rose to four and a half times over the corresponding period.

The sole Degree college (Jawaharlal Nehru College) at Pasighat in Siang District, the oldest seat of administrative headquarters (East Siang) and the only solitary town in the region in the strictest sense, provides for education in disciplines Arts and Science courses till the Degree stage to both boys and girls, numbering about a hundred. The break-up of the numerical strength shows that Siang, accounting for more than 31 per cent of them, claims the credit for establishing its superiority over the rest of the region in respect of more than one reasons.

Firstly, the part of the District in regard to middle schools is as high as more than 42 per cent as against 20 per cent of Subansiri, 16 per cent of Kameng, 13 per cent of Lohit and 9 per cent of Tirap. Next, the District enjoys the singular character, imparting collegiate education and lastly, as revealed from Table 2, given below, the District also tops from the standpoint of number of educational establishments in relation to its population. The account of educational establishments in the state would remain incomplete unless reference is not made to other institutions engaged in various forms of educational pursuits for various groups of local population. While a *Buniyadi Siksha Bhavan* at Changlang in Tirap with enrolment in the neighbourhood of eighty is concerned with imparting training to teachers, adult education centres totalling 88 with enrolment of about a thousand are in operation to cope with the growing needs of adult education in the region. There are as may as about 60 centres in different educational institutions with enrolment of 1,400 concerned with promotion of scout and guide movement amongst youths of different age-groups. As many as thirty N.C.C. Units (29 Army Wing and 1 Air Wing) have been performing their jobs in Arunachal Pradesh.

(b) Increase in Enrolment of Students

The percentage of students in the junior basic schools stood at 78.8 as against 15.8 and 4.9 in the middle and high schools respectively. Less than one-half of one per cent constitutes the proportion of boys/girls going for Pre-University and Three-Year Degree Course in Arts and Science. It may be mentioned here that some handful youths (181 during 1972-73) of the region were said to have been studying at different missionary institutes and Sainik Colleges and Universities outside Arunachal Pradesh.

Other thirty one pupils were reported to pursue various technical courses at the Institute of Technology, Engineering Colleges, Forest Research Institutes and Medical Colleges outside the state till the end of financial year of 1973.

(c) State's Full View of Literacy Levels

Inequality in the growth of educational institutions in the region, as revealed from the table, may now be taken into account.

Kameng and Subansiri are the two districts having less than one educational institutions for the population of one thousand. Their average is equivalent to three-fourth of the incredible low figure of the state which is well demonstrated by the lowest percentage of literacy in the region.

It seems from the table that Arunachal Pradesh stands at the lowest ladder in the country as a whole, with percentage of literacy equivalent to less than two-fifths of the country's figure. Notably, the percentage of literacy in the state is one-fourth of that of even Andaman and Nicobar Island and L.M. and A. Islands. It works out to less than one-fifth of the highest percentage of more than 61 per cent in U.T., i.e., Chandigarh, the other union territory.

Considering the neighbouring states in North East India itself, we notc that Arunachal Pradesh's average rate of literacy stands to one-third of states of Manipur and Tripura, and two-fifths that of Meghalaya, Assam and Nagaland.

It is necessary, however, to be pointed out that percentage of literacy related to total populations does not give clear account because of the fact that it includes the literates other than the tribals. This being the situation, unless the same is examined in regard to the base tribal population, the physical achievement of education cannot be assessed correctly.

(d) Number of Drop-Outs

Excessive wastage of human resources involved in the progress of education is, however, well evident from the sharp decline in number of pupils throughout various stages, right from Primary Class II onwards. This may be credited to a number of factors like proverty, apathy of parents, physical and mental handicaps, social norms, early marriage, insufficient number of schools and its dull functioning, uneven age of children in single class, constraints of teachers to hold the students and the absence of ancillary services.

(e) Training for Crafts

The industrial training is an important means for the development of effective work habits and method of work, we propose now to assess provision of such facilities in the region. Regardings the context of the Administration's industrial policy to preserve and revitalise the traditional indigenous handicrafts, handlooms and sericultural products through the functioning of different craft and production units, 21 craft centres and 24 production centres are reported to have been functioning in the Pradesh for imparting training to the tribals in various crafts. The following detail information may enable to have an idea of nature of diversification of training programme in the state. Beside the above craft centres and production centres, one Industrial Training Institute was established during 1971 where motor mechanic, carpentry, plumbing and electrician courses are taught.

The Ministry of Central Govternments Agriculture Department allotted a Farmers Training Centre against Arunachal Pradesh to provide agricultural training to the farmers to facilitate the widespread application of science and technology in the field of agriculture. This centre was located at Pasighat within the campus of Gram Sevak (Village Level Worker) Training Centre.

The centre consists of two wing, called, 'Institutional Training Wing' and the other 'Peripatetic Wing'. The former wing organises institutional training to the farmers in modern agro-practices by way of short duration courses of one week or so while the latter wing imparts training to the farmers on their fields. Besides, the G.T.C. provides institutional training to Village Level Workers. In addition to all this, a centrally-sponsored pilot project on multiple cropping was also allotted to the Union Territory by the aforesaid Ministry of the Union Government, and headquarters of the project started operating from February 1972.

The demonstrating function of the project comprises at present different crops like paddy, wheat, potato and 'moong' with high-yielding varieties, possible within the duration of one year. Although the demonstrations are restricted to three-crop-sequences, another function is also to be carried out like adaptive, research trial on types and new crops. In the absence of any Forest Training Institute within the region under study, the Forest Department sends its staff for training of different forest specialised courses, for example, wild life.

Training, Accounts Training, Refresher Courses and soil and water Management Project Courses, to different Forest Institutes within the country as well as outside India. There is a Health Training and Research Centre at Pasighat set-up in 1956 where local boys and girls are imparted training for skill upgradation of Health Assistants, Anxiliary Nurse-cum-Midwives and Pharmacists. Besides, a training college has been set-up in the territory to train the Police personnel.

(F) Sactioning of Money and Actual Expenditure

Thorough analysis of physical achievements with regard to education and training made may also be supplemented by reforming to financial allocation and actual expenditure on this account.

It may, here, be pointed out that expenditure for various training courses is incurred by the departments concerned which provide for payment of various stipends and other contingent expenditure regarding training in different handicrafts. The plan allocation was to the order of Rs. 41.81 lakhs Rs. 50.00 lakhs, Rs. 82.37 lakhs for the First, Second and Third Five Year Plans respectively, while Rs. 107.33 lakhs were earmarked for three annual plans of 1966-69 and Rs. 205.18 lakhs for Fourth Plan period of 1969-74. The actual expenditure has by and large lagged much behind the abovesaid allotments as is evident from the total expenditure of Rs. 19.07 lakhs, Rs. 43.32 lakhs, and Rs. 84.97 lakhs, for the respective three Five Year Plans. Rs. 131.41 lakhs were incurred during 1969-72 as against Rs. 74.41 lakh during 1966-69. We, however, note some upward trend in expenditure over the period of more than two decades. At present, the plan allocation of fund under education and training sector has increased many fold which may keep on increasing in proportion to growth in population and the development needs emerging from preceding economic growth. Thus, there is a need for serious estimation of requirements, quick funding and committed execution to bring out desired state in the field of crafts.

Table 1

Literates and Literacy Rates by Sex—Arunachal Pradesh: Census 2001

Union Territory/ Districts	*Persons*	*Literates Males*	*Females*	*Literacy Rate of 2001 Persons*	*Males*	*Females*
Arunachal Pradesh	**487,796**	**302,371**	**185,425**	**54.74**	**64.07**	**44.24**
Tawang	11,589	7,318	4,271	41.14	51.05	30.87
West Kameng	38,488	25,864	12,624	61.67	71.02	48.56
East Kameng	18,548	12,072	6,476	40.89	52.66	28.86
Papum Pare	72,021	42,602	29,419	70.89	79.00	61.72
Lower Subansiri	36,025	21,673	14,352	45.01	53.68	36.19
Upper Subansiri	22,623	13,270	9,353	50.89	58.81	42.74
West Siang	52,015	30,176	21,839	60.31	66.72	53.24
East Siang	44,196	25,779	18,417	61.22	69.02	52.87
Upper Siang	13,409	8,655	4,754	49.80	58.64	39.09
Dibang Valley	28,131	17,706	10,425	59.45	68.02	48.96
Lohit	64,899	41,323	23,576	56.05	65.68	44.59
Changlang	52,116	33,248	18,868	51.98	62.83	39.85
Tirap	33,736	22,685	11,051	42.01	53.76	29.00

References

Directorate of Information and Public Relations, Arunachal Pradesh, Arunachal News, October 1972, pp. 3-5.

Statistics Department, Arunachal Pradesh: Quick Issue of Statistical Hand Book of Arunachal Pradesh (1971-72) (Provisional) p. 27.

Quick Issue of Statistical Hand Book of Arunachal Pradesh (Provisional) p. 28—Prior to 1972-73, there were also three nursery schools, putting the number of educational institutions at 570 till then.

Statistics Department, Arunachal Pradesh: Quick Issue of Statistical Hand Book of Arunachal Pradesh (Provisional), p. 30.

Census of India, Arunachal Pradesh, Series-24—Part IIIA—Establishments Report, Part IIIB-Establishments Tables, p. 27.

Registrar General and Census Commissioner, India New Delhi, Census Centenary, (1972) Pocket Book of Population Statistics.

Census of India, Series-24—Arunachal Pradesh Part II-A—General Population Tables, p. XIV.

Quick Issue of Statistical Hand Book of Arunachal Pradesh (Provisional) p. 32: Excludes 22 teaching staff of J.N. College, Pasighat.

Ministry of Information and Broadcasting, Government of India: 1973, p. 63.

The Assam Tribune, Gauhati, July 26, 1973.

Directorate of Information and Public Relations, Arunachal Pradesh, Arunachal News, Twenty fifth Independence Jayanti, August 1972, p. 19.

Section-II
Manipur

7

The Land and the People

Like other states of India and of North-East specifically, Manipur too has a background, a history, a story to tell about its land and the people residing on that land. The sources of the background of Manipur are as rich as those of any part of the country. There are evidences to show that a glorious civilisation took its shape in the valley of Manipur several thousands of years back and there were continuous events enacted by the coming generations for the sustenance and dynamic promotion of this ancient civilisation.

Small Autonomous Kingdoms

The evolution of Manipur as a political entity from the ancient days was identical to our great country, India, which developed into a strong national awakening through the ages. Just as we see that Indian culture and nationhood were not the product of a single administrative power, the growth of Manipur, her culture and political entity were never under one supreme political power. But it is very remarkable that the cultural individuality and the feeling of one nationhood were constructed through a number of small but almost independent kingdoms which grew and functioned in the same manner as the City States of Greece did. During the old days the means of communication were quite poor and the contacts between village and village and kingdom and kingdom were few and far between in this area. Naturally, therefore, even a small village developed during the course of its emergence, its own genius and individuality which almost amounted to a basic civilisation. Orthodoxy and conservatism were at the root of the growth of these variegated cultural as well as political units. These closely guarded individual entities were, somehow, trimmed into harmony to fit into the colourful Manipuri culture, customs and traditions, and will be futile to make an attempt at discovering a supreme political power which might have been instrumental in the promotion and maintenance of Manipuri language and dialects, culture and traditions.

Prior to the advent of a powerful ruler in the person of Rajarshi Bhagya Chandra in the Eighteenth Century, the political history of Manipur was a history of small kingdoms which were in regular competition with one another. These kingdoms must have been small in population and area. Only the histories of those which happened to be strong and made good contributions to the evolution of the regional culture, find place in the chronicles which form the main sources of the history of Manipur.

Special mention may be made of seven clans which more or less could set up stable kingdoms in different areas of the State. These are Khuman, Moirang, Ningthouja, Khaba, Nganba, Luwang, and Angom. The most outstanding contribution seems to have been made by Moirang, and Ningthouja. The contribution of Moirang to the development of Manipur culture and the State craft is outstanding and worth mentioning.

Perpetual Conflict among Kingdoms

During the times of these small kingdoms, the predominant character of the history of Manipur is the perpetual conflict among these kingdoms which not only comprised of accession of territory by means of warfare, but also of inter-kingdom competitions in sports and various kinds of athletic feats. These small kingdoms invariably had fairly strong set-ups for effective administration. The king being the head of the state and the Government, drew his power partly from the consent of the people and partly from his own intellect. The history of many of the kingdoms indicate beyond doubt that law of hereditary rights for kingship prevailed subject to ability of the kings.

The battle for the power was endless and formed the very basis of the right and justification of a person sitting on the throne. It is, therefore, to be observed that both might and right went hand in hand for the maintenance of the throne. A king had to prove his qualification to be on the throne over and above his hereditary right, through his ability. Proper laws and conventions for diplomatic relations prevailed among the small kingdoms which had tremendous mutual respect among themselves, inspite of endless rivalries. After the amalgamation of small kingdoms through one supreme leadership during the time of Rajarshi Bhagya Chandra, who had a wonderful superhuman genius to please and control his people, he maintained memorial chairs for all the lost kings in his big court and these memorial chairs were given limited powers to look after and supervise the affairs of the administration of the zones carrying the erstwhile small kingdoms. With minor modifications from time to time this tradition continued till the British conquest of Manipur.

Unity Against Foreign Invasions

One important question to be raised about the small kingdoms is whether they had a sense of unity and common purpose in the event of having an external enemy? It has been observed earlier that the small kingdoms were perpetually in conflict and competition with one another. This was only one aspect of the political life of this region. The more important and significant aspect of the political life of the people of Manipur since ancient days upto the British conquest of Manipur in the year 1891 was the perpetual situation of war with Burma. Excepting rare cases of betrayal and fifth columnism by some small kingdoms in the whole history of Manipur, the kingdoms were united in the event of wars with the then Myanmar or with any neighbouring country. It is very remarkable that Manipur was held as a powerful sovereign power in the Far-East till very recently.

From this sprang up full her martial tradition and economic life which appear to be different from other States in the country. One can easily imagine the state of ceaseless tension in the minds of the general people for a possible aggression by the neighbours resulting in the development in every individual of a second nature, the instinct of self-defence and the desire for more and more conquest. The value of the individual was tremendous and beyond description. The small country with a small population and practically no ways of communication from the outside world, had to produce all its food stuff. In such a State, it was only natural and constraining that rich culture should have sprung up and a sense of orthodoxy and also conservatism should have reached the highest degree and the value of the individual must have been wonderfully high. It is in this context that we have to understand the life of the masses of Manipur today.

Kings without Palaces

It will not be out of context to make further analysis of the political and economic life of the people in relation to their king. In a place where the form of Government was once monarchy, one can expect, as basis of historical relics, remnants of palaces and rich treasures laid by succeeding kings in this area. Yet no palaces can be seen anywhere nor royal treasures, which could deserve the name of historical relics, are to be found anywhere, Why? The answer is very simple. There have been powerful kings, but no monarch was so rich to leave behind him material palaces and treasures through which he could be remembered. In short, there was no rich king in Manipur. This narrates the socio-economic structure of Manipuri society through the ages.

Justification for Monarchy or Kingship

Monarchy in a region like Manipur during the early days was the natural outcome of the existing social and economic conditions of the region. The absence of proper means of communication inside the state and for outside contacts was to a great extent responsible for the growth of an isolated culture made deep and profound by constant nourishment by the masses who devoted major portions of their time to this aspect. Development of industries and the scientific approach to life were not given due stress. Education, in so far as it meant the modern emphasis on reading, writing and arithmetic, was confined to very few individuals sponsored mostly by the kings. The kings used to be virtual leaders in all aspects of social and political life. They had to lead in culture, wars and religious institutions. They were regarded as visible Gods by the people.

As has been said earlier the kings, however, had to prove their worth and right to hold their offices by their actual performance in every field. In other words the kings were all-rounders and even the persons of the royal family were expected to educate themselves in such a way as to make themselves superior to the common man in every respect. Those who failed to win recognition of superiority in the actual fields did not get a place in the king's court as well as in history. The system had its merits and the present generation has to make laborious analysis about them. What we have and are today are mostly the gifts of the past and it will be futile to attempt at projecting our own superiority to the generations of our ancestors. If we claim any superiority it will be self-styled and shall have no relevance to facts. Opportunities for wider contacts and coming closer to one another have, however, grew all over the world.

Each part of the globe thus gets more or less the benefit of these ever increasing opportunities promoted by scientific developments. We thus observe a speedy revolution all over the world in the mind of man to adjust itself to this new current. But why should we judge the past with our own yardsticks alone? In fact there is much to be appreciated about the glorious past of Manipur even including the type of monarchy that prevailed. The social customs and practices that have come down to this generation from early days amply show that they were introduced with much foresight and due understanding of the social and economic need of the people inhabiting the state.

To what extent the king exercised his powers upon the subjects in other matters is a question which is deeply engaging the time and labour of many scholars in the field. The kings, so long as they were the occupants of the thrones, were regarded almost as super-human powers. The extent of the power they exercised upon the society could be regarded as very large and covered numerous aspects of human life. They had however, to act cautiously. The fear of revolt from some unexpected quarter to challenge them for the throne was always there. The wise kings had to utilise their powers in more in proportion of development of culture and in acts of benevolence than in acts of suppression and exploitation. The social and collective will for equalisation in privileges and avenues played tremendous role in constraining the rulers to use their powers sparingly and towards the promotion of culture and other virtues for the whole society and also for the individuals.

Rulers and Ruled Partners in Social Set Up

The king, as per Manipuri traditions, was never allowed to hoard treasures for himself at the cost of the people. The relation between the king and his ruled was one of partnership in a social set up based on equality and justice. To elaborate this point, it will be worthwhile to make a reference to the system of defence manage in the old days. The king did not provide facilities from his stores to his fighting forces according to modern concept of defence organisation. Members of his fighting forces would come with their own provision of food and weapons at the back and call of the king which was signalled through so many accepted mediums. This set up of running a defence force could easily be criticised as maximum exploitation of the people, if one used the normal standard to judge such systems, but this could as well be seen from other angle and praised as a very good system based on democracy and extreme respect for individuals.

The system of concentration of wealth and power was not to be seen in this case. What was largely predominating was a partnership between the king and his subjects for the common purpose of the defence of the country. In such a system, the degree of determination and sense of commitment with which an individual soldier faced his enemy was very high. This must have been one of the reasons how the small State of Manipur faced its giant neighbours in the state of wars.

Chaos and its Reasons

In the history of Manipur, there have, however, periods of chaos and defeats at the hands of enemies from Burma. Such periods are very few and far between, but the effect of this type of chaos and defeat did stay with tremendous impact on the socio-economic structure of the people of Manipur. To take an instance, there was the period of chaos for seven years, which is currently known as, "Chahi Taret Khuntakpa". During this chaos the entire population of Manipur were utterly confused. Some fled towards Assam, some were caught and transferred to Burma as war prisoners.

The occupation forces from Burma were not able to establish a Government, the king of the land having fled away to an unknown corner of the State or taking political shelter in the court of a friendly king of Assam. This period was the worst point in the history of Manipur. The pertinent question now is why this chaos took place, how the king and the people in Manipur could regain normalcy after such a chaos and also how such chaos explains the basic strength of Manipur in comparison with that of its close by states? The reason was that Burma and Manipur did not stand comparison in respect of population, resources and area. A writer on the background of the Far Eastern Zone had very rightly observed that Burma sometimes woke up like a lion getting up in usual slumber and insolence, to teach Manipur a lesson. When Burma woke up and came all prepared for a revenge against Manipur, a tiny State, the result is obvious. Such awakenings were accidental and casual but instinct of self-defence was in the blood of every Manipuri.

Thus, it was a matter of time when the powerful sleeping lion could be beaten back to its den by the few but determined Manipuri soldiers under an able leadership. In such a social organisation what was significant and essential for a king was not collection of wealth, but the true quality of leadership and ability to lead his country to prosperity and safety against the enemy. So it will be a blunder to hasten to the conclusion that Manipur was a monarchy in the usual sense of the term. This peculiar socio-economic system which prevailed during the time of the kings in Manipur deserve special and deep studies by able scholars. The system as explained above could be called the basic approach to an egalitarian society. The popular belief among the people about any one, not excluding the king, rising too high in anything, was that there was an ancient power in Manipur which equates all facilities and any individual wishing too high and boasting too much about his or her attainment, some day or the other will meet that spiritual force, which is called "Lai Chakhetpa". So, in building up the fabric of the present Manipuri socio-economic structure, this common belief has made its own contribution. Even at present, it is hard to find a very rich man as also a very poor man in Manipur. Socio-economic structure and other traditions and common beliefs are against widening of the gap between the rich as well as the poor.

Rajarshi the Great Integrator

The name of famous Rajarshi Bhagya Chandra deserves special mention and our generation ought to be grateful to this genius of a great unifier of the land of Manipur. He has been a versatile genius and we see his contribution in every aspect of Manipuri life. He was driven out of his kingdom in his early days, by his maternal uncle ruling in Moirang with the support of the Burmese, and took political asylum in Assam for some years. The episode of his stay in Assam in political asylum under the king of Ahom was a very remarkable point in the history of the state and also in the life of this great ruler. His uncle not satisfied with the driving away of his nephew from Manipur, went even to the extent of instigating the monarch of Assam and the people that the person taking asylum in the kingdom was not the real Bhagya Chandra and must be put to a test. The outstanding valour and other qualities of Rajarshi Bhagya Chandra had been known to all the neighbouring kingdoms.

On receipt of the letter of instigation from the king of Moirang. The Ahom king conducted a test prior to the public to verify the extraordinary qualities of Rajarshi Bhagya Chandra. The Rajarshi was put unarmed in the den of a wild elephant just to test, on the one hand, whether he had any divine power, saving him and, on the other, to see that the life of the suspected friend could be put to an end in this cruel way. The night prior to the appointed day of the public ordeal, the Rajarshi had a vision. In this vision he saw Sri Govindji in his full Ras dress. Sri Govindji assured him that he would take special care of the wild elephant and Bhagya Chandra was not to bother about it. Sri Govindji, however, put a condition that immediately on return to his kingdom and recovery of his throne, he should adapt the image of Govindji as presented in vision and Ras Leela as described in the Tenth Chapter of Srimad Bhagvat Mahapurana must be organised.

The vision was said to be very very clear and prolonged. Hints even as to the type of dress and contents of the music in such a Ras performance were given in that vision. The tree from which the image was to be carved out, where it was growing and the manner and time of its cutting down were also indicated. On the fixed day the Rajarshi had only a Tulsimala in his hand when he entered the den of the wild elephant. The entire people and the King of Assam were astonished beyond words and they were compelled to recognise Bhagya Chandra, not only as a king but as a great devotee of God, who was protected by some unseen power under all circumstances.

As an outcome of the triumph of the Rajarshi in this ordeal, the Ahom king offered to help him in raising an army for the liberation of Manipur from the hands of the Burmese. In his attempt to liberate Manipur the king had to move to all the nook and corner of the State in disguise to mobilise the people and also to ascertain his own popularity among his people. It was perhaps for the first time that a king of the valley travelled the entire hill region of Manipur making deep studies of the problems prevailing in different parts and befriending the entire population consisting of several tribes and groups, thereby paving the way for the much needed consolidation of Manipur as one administrative unit. In due course of time he pushed out the Burmese invaders from the soil of Manipur, nay, to several miles beyond the border of Manipur—deep into the territory of Burma. After his success over the Burmese forces, Bhagya Chandra emerged not only as the king of small clan of Manipur, but as the supreme ruler of the entire State. From this rule sprang up the strong current of mainstream of Manipuri culture, glorified by its colourful sub-branches. It is also likely that since then Manipur became more or less the accepted name for the entire area.

Emergence of Ras Leela

The episode of the vision was completely forgotten according to royal chronicles, by the Rajarshi when he regained his throne. It appeared that he was slumbering in total forgetfulness about this highly valuable vision for several years of his reign as a supreme ruler of the entire Manipur. Some incidents led to the recovery of his memory concerning his vision and right steps were taken to fulfil his promise to his God. The result is, we see the image of Sri Govindji today in the royal temple and the glorious classical style of Ras Dance which passes the test of sophistication and other material and wordly illusions. The genius of Bhagya Chandra as a ruler may be seen in many things he did during his period. The principle of exchanging population between two hostile kingdoms was conceived and executed in each purification during his time. The result was that the long drawn hostilities between small kingdoms ceased. The feeling of partial prestige was subdued to the minimum. He could plan a stable and strong Government with full cooperation of the entire population. In these efforts he very successfully blended State craft with religious traditions and cultural sentiments of the masses. To this day the entire people of Manipur remember the Rajarshi with a sense of gratitude and thankfulness. His name will shine as the maker of the modern history of this highly sensitive and complicated area.

Second Chaos in Manipur

From the time of his coming to power, onwards Manipur continued to be ruled under the system of monarchy more or less effectively till immediately before the British conquest of Manipur. Wars went on to be fought more or less in quick succession. The period which deserves special mention is a period of the second chaos which took place during the time of his grandson who had to run like him into Assam and come back again after organising an army there with the help of the British East India Company. It was in the early half of the Nineteenth Century when Maharaja Gambhir Singh, in co-operation with his cousin brother Nar Singh, who also became a king after the death of Maharaj Gambhir Singh, defeated the Burmese and threw them backfar into their own land, and thereby capturing a vast stretch of Burmese area as a conquered land. The success of the Manipuri forces against the Burmese was now decisive. Since this episode there was no further mention of any war between Manipur and Burma in light of the fact that India including Burma became part of the British Empire.

Although Manipur entered the empire only in the year 1891, the extension of the British rule upto Manipur was consequent upon domestic strifes in the royal family in Manipur, on one hand, and the success of British diplomacy, on the other. But the manner in which Manipur lost her freedom in the hands of British forces deserve special mention in this context.

Connections with British Empire

The rulers of Manipur began their contact with the British empire through its agency, the East India Company operating in the Eastern Zone of India in the early half of the Nineteenth Century. Before that there is no indication of any relation between Manipur and the East India Company worth mentioning. Following the retirement of Rajarshi Bhagya Chandra, his successors could not give a stable Government to Manipur and thus the Burmese invaders became more powerful and took full advantage of the chaotic state in Manipur.

A few years after Rajarshi Bhagya Chandra abdicated his throne, his successor had to flee to Cachar and run his Government from a distance. It was during this time that the Manipur princes established their contact with the British East India Company. They entered into an agreement of mutual aid at the time of crisis and external attack. During the early Twenties of the Nineteenth Century the Manipuri forces under the leadership of Maharaj Gambhir Singh came back with full support in new arms and ammunitions from the East India Company to drive away the enemies. The struggle did not last long and the result came in favour of the Manipuri forces. Normal Government was re-established and the masses had a fresh lease of life under the able leadership of Maharaj Gambhir Singh and his cousin brother, Maharaj Nar Singh. Unfortunately Maharaj Gambhir Singh expired young leaving behind his seven year old son, Chandrakirti Singh to the care of his cousin brother, Nar Singh, who ascended the throne to succeed outgoing Maharaj Gambhir Singh.

Succession of Chandrakirti

The case of Maharaj Nar Singh's succession to the throne following the death of Gambhir Singh is a controversial chapter in the history of Manipur. It is said that Maharaj Nar Singh refused to become a king and that he offered to rule the kingdom as an officer of the infant king, Chandrakiriti, but Maharani Kumudini, widow mother of Chandrakirti did not believe in the sincerity and honesty of Maharaj Nar Singh. She, therefore, stealthily fled away with her son to Cachar thereby compelling Nar Singh to take over the throne till the return of Chandrakirti, which, however, did not take place during lifetime of Nar Singh. After the death of Nar Singh his younger brother succeeded him to the throne.

As early as the news of the death of Nar Singh reached the ears of young Chandrakirti and his mother, Kumudini, they decided to go back to Manipur to claim their legitimate control to the throne. Chandrakirti was then sufficiently grown up to be able to take affairs of the State into his hands. The people of Manipur welcomed the return of the young prince who had immediately been put to the throne. Chandrakirti gave to the people a strong and stable Government for more than 40 years.

Spread of British Empire

The contacts between the East India Company and the Government of Manipur became closer and closer although Manipur continued to be a sovereign State. To what extent Chandrakirti Maharaj committed towards the formation of Manipur as a part of the British empire will remain an important aspect of the political history of Manipur. Scholars will no doubt be able to throw light on the subject, but one fact was too glaring to be subdued. The British Government conferred the title of KCSI on Maharaj Chandrakirti who accepted it even during his time. Whatever might have been the material changes in the actual relation between the Government of Manipur and the British Government, the importance of the acceptance of the British title by Chandrakirti must be regarded as a definite step towards acceptance of extension of the British empire upto Manipur. Whether Chandrakirti accepted the title without thinking of its real implications, is a matter of opinion. But a king of his wisdom and ability must have realised what he was doing and there must have been compelling circumstances towards the acceptance of that reality.

System of Posting of Resident

The system of keeping a British Resident Officer in Imphal started during the time of Chandrakirti. The Resident Officer, it appears, never acted in hurry so as not to cause the impression in the minds of the people of Manipur that the British Government were interfering in their internal administration. In fact he was a slow time bomb. The significance of his existence grew day by day during the old age of Chandrakiriti, and especially after his expiry.

Fight between Brothers

Chandrakirti left behind two warring camps of his sons born to different Ranis. One of the camps was led by Maharaj Surchandra who succeeded Chandrakirti and the other camp was led by his step-brother Kulachandra ably assisted by Tikendrajit. In fact there was no real rivalry between Maharaj Surchandra and his step brother Kulachandra. Both virtually happened to be the eldest sons of their mothers. As history has it, at the root of the conflict and serious rivalry there was the bitterness between the younger brothers of both camps. On this the British Government took full advantage of the situation and they lost no time in bringing the conflict into its climax. As a result of an armed fight between the two camps, Maharaj Surchandra and his brothers fled to Calcutta and made an appeal to the Governor-General of India for intervention. The Governmnt-general of India acting through the then Chief Commissioner of Assam tried to intervene in the matter. The British Government supported the cause of Maharaj Surchandra and saw fault with Maharaj Kulachandra and his brothers. It was now known to the British Government that Maharaj Kulachandra's camp will be totally anti-British and that at the basis of anti-British campaign was Yuvraj Tikendrajit and Thangal General. The British Government tried to capture Yuvraj Tikendrajit and General Thangal through many treacherous plots. Tikendrajit was, however, clever enough to detect the inner motive of the British Government. Every attempt was thus foiled through his superior manoeuvres.

Massacre of Innocents

In the early years of the year 1891 the Chief Commissioner of Assam, Mr. Quinton accompanied by a large number of British Officers visited Manipur to see things and evaluate the merits and demerits of events for himself and to advise the British Government about the step to be taken. As history has it, the forces accompanying the Chief Commissioner of Assam enacted the episode more or less equal to the 'Jallianwala Bagh Massacre' at the visit of the Chief Commissioner. One night the British army opened fire on an innocent crowd witnessing the traditional Ras Leela performance in the palace which was organised in respect of the visiting VIPs from Assam. In consequence a large number of innocent people were murdered and the whole population got panicky.

The Manipur Government had to act fast in order to satisfy the demand and pressure of the panic striken population. The Chief Commissioner and his officers were tried on accustion of waging war against the kingdom of Manipur without any provocation according to the law of the kingdom. All the British Officers were condemned to death. The execution of the death sentence took place the following day, thereby putting an end to the long established relation of friendship and mutual understanding between the Government of Manipur and the British Government in India. The news of the death of the Chief Commissioner of Assam and other British Officers accompanying him must have naturally shocked the British Government. The results were, therefore, obvious. The British Government in a few days time made a three pronged invasion on Manipur in the month of August 1891. The British forces outnumbered the Manipuris and it did not take time for them to reach the capital after annihilating the whole Manipuri forces on all fronts.

Battle of Khongjom by Brajabasi

The battle of Khongjom needs special mention in this connection. This was led by Paona Brajabasi, who was a genius in sword fighting. His name and the battle of Khongjm has become a legend today because of the heroism and high sense of devotion that he and his soldiers displayed in the said battle which was destined to be lost. This could be compared against episode sung by Tenyson in his famous poem "Charge of the Light Brigade". Even today Ballad singers of Manipur earn their living by singing the glory of Paona Brajabasi and his heroic feats during the said battle. This has led to the invention of completely new style of singing, known as "Khongjom Parva".

Khongjom Parva implies the Khongjom episode. In this an artist sits, in the middle of a big group, with Dholak in hand and sings the glory of the hero of Khongjom. These days, they also sing the history of Manipur through this style of singing. It will not be, therefore, out of place to make a little mention of Paona Brajabasi and his heroism. As history has it he was persuaded by the king to lead the most dangerous front of Khongjom. Most of the Generals were aware that it was already a lost battle so far as physical prowess was concerned. But they could never concede that it could ever be lost morally. It was, therefore, decided that the best feasible forces should be sent in all directions to defend the freedom of the motherland. As the story has it, Paona was then in his retirement but at the call of the Nation he happily consented to lead the Khongjom front. He took the choicest of his disciples in sword fighting and in the use of fire arms who accompanied him to the battle to die with him.

It is said that the way in which they fought with their meagre supply of arms against the steam roller attack of the British forces earned admiration and respect of the enemy. Almost every one of the whole force sacrificed his life. Only those few who returned alive not for fear, but by the nature of their duties such as washermen or cooks, remembered the events of the battle too clearly to be forgotten. One of them called as Dhobi Madhu was a gifted singer. He was inspired by his memory of the battle to introduce a new style of singing as mentioned before in which the singer sings the glory of the Khongjom war to the beat of a Dholak. The tradition is ever growing today in Manipuri society. A large number of Khongjom Parva singers entertain the Manipuri population with their mellodious performances. These singers enjoy high respect in society and are given high remuneration for their performance. Even during the British days this singing of the glory of our heroes went on to a great extent and to the annoyance of the Britishers. Coming to the political aspect of our history after the Manipuri forces were over-powered, the British Government frantically searched for another line of royal blood to succeed to the throne as more or less a puppet king. This they had to do in order to adjust themselves with a long followed tradition of the region and also show that they have not come to exactly replace the old tradition of monarchy in that region. Following their victory in the war front and before the establishment of a civilian Government, they put all the war heroes of Manipur before a Military Tribunal which in haste, tried and condemned them. As a result, Maharaj Kulachandra and many of his relatives were exiled. Yuvraj Tikendrajit and Thangal General were hanged in an open place before the general public of Manipur. This took place on the 13th August, 1891. With the execution of the two heroes on the gallows on this day an important chapter in the history of Manipur almost came to a close.

British Domination

The next phase that followed was one of slavery and domination under the British empire. The British Government selected an infant grandson of Maharaj Nar Singh to ascend Maharaj Kulchandra who was the grandson of Maharaj Gambhir Singh. Thus, Maharaj Churachand who was hardly five years old was put to the throne of Manipur. Churachand was the youngest of many brothers, thus the wisdom of the British to select the youngest brother in supercession of the elder ones for the throne was worthy of admiration; if could we see it from their angle. But to the people of Manipur and also to any future historian the policy was negative and a complete departure from their general traditions.

It was the British intention of turning the future king more or less a puppet show. The transition from independence to serfdom was the beginning of a complete chapter in the socio-economic and cultural past of Manipur. For many years it looked as if the people were put under the effect of some powerful chloroform. The British Government took full advantage of the geographical condition state of Manipur and were able to maintain Manipuri as a completely isolated individual from the rest of the world. Modern education was not encouraged in the same speed as was done in the remaining India. No measure that could lead to popular consciousness about modern development was adopted. Their policy of divide and rule was implemented in all feasible ways so that the history of Manipur during the British regime is a history of strifes between tribe and tribe in the hill areas, between section and section among the Manipuri Hindus within the valley.

In gone days imagination of the British Government, the king was used as their unfailing instrument. Many outsiders including learned section feel that there is a basic difference between the valley people of Manipur and those who are in hill areas. In fact it is not so. The entire people of Manipur belong to the same ethnic group and find out their origin more or less to the Sino-Tibetan group of human species.

Gap Created between Valley and Hills

Currently, however, the gap between the valley people and hill people appear to be considerably wide. There are two factors which contribute to the widening and also to the practice of this gap. Before the conversion of the major population of the valley into Hinduism about 400 years back the only difference between the valley people and the hill people was that of language and convenience of communication and agriculture.

But the emergence of Hindu religion as a principal faith of the Meiteis who are in the valley, a new dawn of orthodoxy and conservatism arose in the valley—even so the relation between the hill and the valley kept on to be very cordial and cooperative. The virtue of the tolerance and understanding bound the two major sections of the population in spite of their numerous differences. But with the coming of the British rule the difference was given a prominent stamp through their famous divide and rule policy. It is needless to point out how much the British Government through their policies as well as through the conduct of individual officers encouraged sectarianism along with orthodoxy in the state of Manipur. The Hindu orthodoxy became a powerful instrument for keeping the population divided at the roots.

Here in this context it will be interesting to recall the incident of a British officer touching the wall of a newly-constructed Brahmin temple belonging to a high-ranking official of the Government of Manipur. Some section of the orthodox population expressed discontentment at the episode. The British Government, rather than defending their action, encouraged this kind of orthodoxy and consented to pay full compensation with which another new building could be constructed. The result was that a new story glorifying British sense of respect for Hindu orthodoxy was circulated within the Hindu population without realising the full significance of such a gesture. During their long stay in Manipur no British officer went into a Hindu house even through mistake. They took meticulous care to avoid doing so. The Hindus in their turn, most of them new converts, felt flattered and this encouraged more and more orthodoxy. Taking advantage of the situation the British opened Christian Missionaries in the hill areas with their full patronage and increased the apparent gap between the valley and the hills.

Gap between Tribes and Valley People—a Passing Phase

The fact is that the people of Manipur cannot be divided inspite of the existence of several tribes with their own dialects and customs and traditions. Each one among them has contributed more or less to the building up of the great Manipuri tradition. The apparent gap which also exists today must be shortlived and should be regarded as only a temporary passing phase. It will be futile to attempt at further magnification of the difference that exists between the different tribes and also between the plains people and the hill people. The need for joint endeavour for a common purpose and common welfare is being realised more and more, specially among the educated and aware young generation.

Was Manipur Part of India?

Coming back to the issue of Manipur's political history and its relevance to the wider Indian context we are reminded of a question, namely, whether Manipur was at any time a part of Indian subcontinent. This question is valid not only in the case of Manipur, but also in the case of other parts of the great country. In this context one might ask, was India in its present form, ever a nation or a nation in academic concept of the terms. The author is of the strong view that India was a solid entity from the very ancient Vedic times, although its boundaries were not defended with force of arms as it is done in the present day. There should not be any doubt about the continued growth of the cultural and emotional integration inside this sub-continent since times immemorial.

Manipur despite its geographical isolation and development in the light of separate cultural entity drew its inspiration from the common Indian source and civilisation and any gain for the matter of that is rooted in the common soil from which the Vedas sprang up and flourished.

Common Beliefs and Culture

Common culture may be further divided and protected by different administrative units only to intensify the glory that comes out of variegation. If we make efforts at finding administrative boundaries of the ancient India in the light of the modern definition of a State and make our conclusions on the basis of our findings from this angle, probably we are making futile attempts. Cultural and spiritual boundaries can never be protected by force of arms perpetually. People belonging to common cultures and beliefs may have some ad-hoc differences and quarrels resulting in the establishment of small States and Governments from time to time. Our great country amply proves in its chequered long history the validity of this issue. Any way, therefore, it appears that Manipur was never a part of India till its integration with the Indian Union in the year 1949 alongwith other native states. But in case, this formula is pursued further, we might come to the conclusion that there was no place like Manipur as we have it today. What is upper most for our consideration is presently whether the people of Manipur in their past have shared the common beliefs and accepted the principles of truth as explained in the ocean of Vedic literature.

Manipuri Culture Derived from Vedic Civilisation

For the present, however, we might state that Manipur by virtue of its geographical position was in between the two called the Aryan culture and Mongolian. Although in physical features and certain traditional practices people appear to be more akin to the Mongolian camp, the basic principles mentioned in the old scriptures of the Manipuris are much nearer to the Vedic religion than to the Mongolian currents of thought and religion. That is to say Manipuri culture forms part and parcel of the wide Vedic civilisation.

Scholars who have made laborious studies in the field are of the opinion that because of this basis affinity between two cultures, the Vaishnavic movement started in Bengal by Lord Cheitanya Mahaprabhu could be so easily spread to the Manipuri population which absorbed it with willingness and contentment as the fulfilment of a long cherished spiritual aspiration. The Mahabharata also mentions the name of Manipur as a battle ground between Arjuna and his own son Babhrubahana.

Connected with Mainstream of Indian Thought and History

The degree of reality as a historical event has yet to be established but it can be seen that the Rishis of ancient India with their deep and thorough knowledge of the people and regions of the great sub-continent made relevant and meaningful references to different places and people of the country. This is a thread by which we can link up Manipur with the mainstream of Indian thought and history. So far as we judge national boundaries by normal yardstick, Manipur had never been part of any political unit of India. Through ages she has retained her individuality politically and also culturally. The link between the people of Manipur with the rest of India became closer and more frequent after British conquest of her than in the earlier days. The contacts were largely promoted by religious factors. Since the time of Rajarshi Bhagya Chandra the Manipuri kings used to establish their Bhavans at famous pilgrimage places for example, Radha Kund, Brindaban, Nabadwip and Jagannathpuri. It is very remarkable that most of the major temples surrounding Radha Kund in Mathura were set-up and run by the Manipuri kings and their relatives. Even today the Manipuri population in Radha Kund and Brindaban is substantial in view of the smallness of these places.

In Nabadwip also the Manipuri population keeps on to play an important role in furtherance of the Vaishnav cult of Lord Cheitanya Mahaprabhu. Before the emergence of British rule in Manipur, pilgrims would come out in their hundreds towards the same places of India mostly on foot. The pilgrims considered fortunate if they could die on way to Brindaban. Following the opening of vehicular traffic and the railways the flow of pilgrims increased by leaps and bounds so much so that the famous temples in leading places of pilgrimage all over India recognise the features of the Manipuri pilgrims and in certain seasons the sacred places are crowded with Manipuri pilgrims alone. This leads sometimes to exploitation of the simple Manipuri pilgrims by their guides or their Pandas. Manipuri Hindus today form an inseparable part of the great Hindu family. Whatever might have been the factors in the past these are no longer sufficient to divert the Manipuri mind from the mainstream of India's spiritual and literary current.

Merger in India-Popular Movement

When India got independence after her prolonged struggle, Manipur was left to the discretion of the ruling prince who did not earn his right to be a ruler except for being the eldest son of a king nominated by the British to hold the throne during their pleasure. The people did not like the idea of continuing under the dictatorial regime of the king. A number of popular demonstrations in favour of Manipur's merger with Indian Union helped the Government of India, specially the then Deputy Prime Minister of India, Sri Vallavbhai Patel to hurry up with the decision to integrate Manipur with the Indian Union. The integration took place on the 15th October, 1949. The Maharaja was said to have refused to sign Instrument of Accession inspite of repeated persuasion by the Government of India and the popular demands in this behalf. Finally, there was no way out and the Instrument of Accession was signed in Shillong on the said day, thereby putting an end to the long history of monarchy in Manipur and initiating the first step towards democracy and egalitarian society.

Expectations

But the events that followed the integration was not up to the expectations of the people. The people of Manipur naturally expected that after the merger, Manipur would be offered the status of a State inspite of her other limitations. But in view of overruling considerations of her historical background, distinct cultural and ethnic individuality, and absence of affinity with the immediate neighbours in respect of culture and language, Manipur, however, did not give up hope to continue fight for the legitimate right of attaining complete statehood. During the year 1961 the erstwhile Naga Hill district of Assam became a fulfledged State. Nagaland is the immediate neighbour of Manipur and is not superior to Manipur in any case. The few years, preceding to conferment of Statehood to Nagaland, were full of bloodshed and other forms of violence in the Nagaland area.

Fuel Put to Fire

The people of Manipur felt that the Government of India were paying the premium to violence when the new State came into existence. This added fuel to the fire and the dissatisfaction of the masses, of Manipur increased by leaps and bounds, while Manipur had her best wishes for Nagaland. She found difficult to adjust while the national leadership prepared a preferential treatment in respect of an area with the same type of people living under very similar and compelling situations.

As a result the struggle for Statehood was carried on with vigour and renewed determination by all sections of the people. The struggle surpassed party considerations and suppressed sectional interests. The sense of unity and integrity among the people was once again renewed under the common banner of the fighting for Statehood. The pressure from Manipur and also the adjoining like Mizoram, for recognition of their political individuality led the Government of India to see the whole region of North Eastern areas consisting of Assam, Manipur, Nagaland, Tripura and NEFA comprehensively and for the first time during the leadership of the Prime Minister, Srimati Indira Gandhi. The need for a complete reorganisation of the North Eastern areas was realised and adequate steps were taken in this behalf. The completion of measures of reorganisation was very slow and the situation reach nearly its explosive point. Yet it is now seen that reorganisation delayed was not necessarily denial of the same. The genius of Pandit Jawaharlal Nehru had foreseen the compelling situation several years back. He rightly observed that the individuality of Manipur and Tripura should be safeguarded by enabling them to carry on as separate States. He was also of the opinion that these units should not be merged with any bigger province only for administrative convenience. Panditji could praise the depth attained by social and cultural institutions in these small units especially those in Manipur.

Criteria for Formation of New States

The principal criteria for the formation of new States in India was and should normally continue to be economic viability, geographical compactness and stabilised tradition of emotional integration within the people in the said zone. But India, as a vast country comprising different people and places differing from one another, stood in need of protection in the interest of national solidarity. Some small units like Manipur, Tripura, Nagaland, Meghalaya, Goa, Himachal, Andaman and Nicobar Islands, Mizoram kept on to be specially organised where the Government of India had to exercise their discretion to depart from the normal yardstick of measurement. The question is what constitutes these special factors.

It was quite understandable why the Government of India even after their realisation of special factors in the case of Nagaland had to delay further their decision in respect of this small unit. There might be other such units in the remaining country awaiting special attention and indulgence of the nation in the matter of safeguarding their precious individuality. The Government of India had to visualise all these possibilities and take adequate precautionary measures to guard themselves against future risks.

Gratitude to Indira Gandhi's Leadership

The ultimate reorganisation is a bold step in this direction. The people of the units will be benefitted by the measures just introduced, and they must be thankful to a mature and timely leadership provided to them by the Prime Minister, Srimati Indira Gandhi. A new era has dawned not only upon the North Eastern region, but also upon the whole country, with the introduction of new legislative measures raising the political status and facilities of these small units. The state of Manipur in the North Eastern areas is unique. She has common border with Burma in three directions and thus constitutes quite sensitive and strategic international area. The security of the country is closely connected with the prosperity and security of this area. The conferment of the Statehood to her promoted satisfaction and enthusiasm among the people who must now contribute, with added vigour, to the security and prosperity of the country as a devoted sentry on the Eastern gate of the country.

People's Attitude Towards Main Current of Indian Politics

We shall now make an analysis of the development and people's attitude towards the maincurrent of Indian politics in so far as it relates to Manipur. There is a peculiar division among the people in this respect. The people in the valley who form a little more than two-thirds of full population of the State have developed their political thought and action more or less in the same degree and fashion as we see in any part of the country. The population in the hill regions which mainly consists of more than twenty-nine Scheduled Tribes and few non-tribal pockets forming a little less than one-third of the total population have yet to catch up with the leading political currents of the country. The thinking is mostly on tribal lines and is thus confined to narrow communal attitude which decides the direction at the time of fighting and selection of candidates during most of the general elections. It is, however, encouraging to see that during the last few years the response from the enlightened section among the hill inhabitants to the call of All India Political Parties have shown a basic departure from the long drawn practice of tribal or communal thinking in political times.

Plain Vs. Hills

Certain reference has already been made to the changing pattern of relationship between the hill people and the valley people of Manipur. As our chronicles say it, the division between hill and the valley was not so sharp as we see it today. We may divide the whole history of Manipur into three phases while discussing this subject. The introductory phase will consist of the period when the entire population was living in the hill areas. During this time there could be no question of any difference between the hill and the plains. The second phase could cover the period when the population from the hill areas started moving down to the valley and settling there for good. The third phase will cover the period when the difference became noticeably wide and allowed political roles to be played through the instrument of the difference between the hill and the valley. The Manipuri legends record it that in the ancient days the valley of Manipur which today stands at an altitude of 2,600 feet above the sea-level was totally under water for several thousands of years and unfit for human habitation. During that period the seed of civilisation in Manipur was sown in the Koubru Hills in the north-western corner of Manipur region. Upto this day the Koubru Peak continues to be a place of pilgrimage to the Manipuris.

It was here on this peak, according to the common belief of the Manipuris, that whole drama of creation of human-beings was enacted by the Creator several thousand years back. Many stories are told about the episode of creation, about the heroism of the first incarnation of God who guided the human population in this area. Pilgrims who have frequently been to this Koubru Peak testify that there is abundant evidence of this peak having been used in place of the palace of the Divine King who ruled the land from this peak.

Origin and Background of Manipuris in Hills

If this is taken for granted that we have an element of truth in our legends and historical records, one thing is established that the ancient forefathers of the Manipuris had their origin in the hill parts of Manipur. This period of forefathers reigning in hill-tops is too remote from our memory and understanding to grasp it in its fullest details. As time went off, a super-human king performed almost a miraculous feat to drain the water collected in the valley by boring a hole through a hillock with a spear like-weapon. Even now the outlet, called "Chingnunghut" which means hole through the interior of a solid hillock, on the border between Manipur and Burma testifies this legend. This acts as a perpetual outlet of the water of Manipur flowing out of the Manipur valley through the Manipur river. In the absence of this outlet the condition of Manipur valley would have been just a vast lake. As the legend says, after a large part of the valley got dried up after getting the outlet, the people from the hill areas especially from the Koubru peak began to move down towards the valley for permanent settlement.

Certain historians ascribe this complete change in the geographical condition of the area to the benevolent powers of Lord Shiva who manifested himself in the guise of the Divine King to make the big hole for the said outlet on the Indo-Burma border. Whether such a contention will stand the test of scientific scrutiny and systematic historical research is more or less a pure matter of opinion, but something very significant appears to have taken place to bring about a total change in the living pattern of the population.

As a result of the drainage made for the water of Manipur, the population of Manipur moved down to the valley. For a long time they concentrated on certain belts which were fertile for agriculture and offered more facilities for communication and fishing. During this period of early settlement in the valley, the pattern of civilisation and way of living was very much akin to those prevailing in the hill areas. In the famous legend of Khamba and Thoibi the relation with the hill and the valley was one of extreme cordiality and affinity. As the story has it, legendary hero Khamba and his elder sister Khamnu turned orphans during their infancy. Their father was the Prime Minister of the King of Moirang, a small kingdom which flourished on the banks of the famous Loktak lake.

Owing to extreme negligence and also possible fear from the rest of society Khammu fled away with her infant brother to the house of a Kabui Naga Chief.

They returned home after they attained maturity. At their stay in the house of the Naga Chief they were treated with affection and extreme care and learnt all the necessities of State craft and feats of heroism of which Khamba turned the unrivalled champion afterwards. This in a way indicates that the tribal people were not as backward as they appear to be now. They enjoyed due respect from the kings in the valley and had many things that the people of the valley had to learn. Every valley king used to establish fast friendship with his counterparts in the hill areas for mutual benefits. Throughout the history of Manipur state, the element of rivalry and bitterness inside the royal family was more or less prominent at any given time. Suspicious mothers of the heir apparent used to send their sons in concealment to be reared as tribal boys in some distant tribal area under the affectionate care of a hill chief so that he might come back after attaining maturity to succeed his father.

There are many examples of famous kings who had taken shelter in distant hill areas under the disguise of hill boys in the said fashion. In many of the cases when the heir apparents returned to succeed their fathers, they brought alongwith them boys and girls from the hill areas to get settled in the valley and also to get benefit of special honour and distinction in the king's court out of gratitude for the affectionate care the hill communities had shown to the future kings. It is, therefore, very hard to believe that the valley population is unmixed and maintains its crystal purity of generation in light of the close tie of friendship and social contacts between the hill and the valley during the said period. One glaring example of the great respect for their origin and close affinity with the hill people is that kings invariably are dressed in the tribal fashion on the occasion of their coronation, and also on a number of festive occasions associated with the traditional culture of the people. In the local concept of God and his incarnation also, God came down to the plains of Manipur in the disguise of a tribal youth. This is amply demonstrated by the prevailing convention of "Lai Haraoba" in which the God, the Creator, appeared in the guise of a Tankhul Naga to court a divine lady in the valley. The whole story of "Lai Haraoba" is woven round the meeting between God-king in the disguise of a tribal boy and his love with his consort incarnated as a girl in the valley. From this meeting between the two incarnations of God, the story of creation began and such a story is depicted in all its aspects in the form of a dance drama highlighted by sweet music and difficult customs conducted by experts in the line in a traditional "Lai Haraoba" festival. The whole fabric of Manipuri culture is woven round the entire population and it is unthinkable that at any moment of our history the different sections of the people will justify complete isolation and segregation from one another merely on footing of political considerations.

In the course of the tours conducted by the kings in the hill areas, they used to pick up talented young people from among the tribes and bring them up for appointments in deserving posts. This kind of talents received tremendous respect from the king as well as from the general population that even now there are some clans whose origins are traced to such talents from the hill areas. It is thought to be a privilege and a matter of good fortune to enter into matrimonial alliance with such clans. Such events indicated that the hill and the valley were not like water-tight compartments in the body politic and also socio-economic structure of Manipur for several thousands of years. Prior to the conversion of the major portion of the valley population to Vaishnavism it is not known with authenticity whether there was any difference in respect of food habits and manner of dress between the valley and the hills. We hear of many phrases and idioms in the Manipuri language to indicate that they were meat eaters and used wine as one of their essential food habits. Now that the Manipuri Vaishnavs are total strangers to meat eating and the drinking habit, it might be considered an insult to their sense of self-respect if they were told that their forefathers, about a few hundred years back, were meat eaters and had drinking habits.

We have observed that interested parties are trying to widen the gap between the hill and the valley for their political ends. It is unfortunate. It is also seen at the same time that sections of the people in the valley prefer to oversee this problem and contend themselves while sleeping over the problem in profound optimism that there is no danger ahead even if things carry on as they do. Right approach to this problem must be an earnest attempt at understanding and appreciation of the real root of the problem and readiness to make amendments in the proper direction. We may now come to the third and most controversial chapter of the history of Manipuri society covering the period of large scale scale conversion to Hinduism under the patronage of the king and its far reaching consequences in the socio-economic life of the people. Although Hindu saints and scholars came to preach Hinduism from time to time, the impact was not so tremendous as it was during the reign of Garibniwaz, the saint who came as a missionary during his time was clever enough to begin his mission with the monarch himself.

After conversion of the king to his faith, it was easy for him to extend his mission to the general population. The respect and fear with which the king was treated by his people during those days was unique. The conversion of the people to a cult with the patronage of a powerful king was naturally one of advantage for the missionary and at the same time, of compulsion to some extent for the common people. The merits and demerits of this episode will be left for future historians to judge. The author is interested in making an analysis of the incidents that took place during the peak days of the conversion. The people of Manipur with their deep sentimental life and respect for their ancestors and the cult handed down to them through the generation by their forefathers must have raised deep opposition. The manner in which the great cult of Vaishnavism was spread with the support of the royal power and influence; rich treasures of books containing valuable legends and profound knowledge recorded after laborious research by the ancient ancestors were collected with the order of the king and made them into a huge pile in a public place. The pile of books was burnt, as the story has it, in the same ceremony and solemn style in which Hindu dead-body is cremated. This episode dug deep into the sentiments of the scholars and enlightened section of the population although they could not openly revolt against the monarch.

Even after acceptance of great cult of Vaishnavism, the sentiment of bitterness between the preachers and the general population could not subside, after the lapse of hundreds of years. The hollowners and short-sightedness of the preachers leading the campaign of conversion led to a good deal of confusion and misunderstanding between themselves and the latest converts. These missionaries did not realise that with the burning of books a culture cannot be destroyed. What followed the mass burning of the literary treasures of the people was the feeling of the richness of the local culture and traditions which even the preachers themselves were compelled to recognise. The funny part of the situation was that the preachers themselves turned Meiteis and took Manipuri surnames and identified themselves with most of the local customs and traditions while being good Hindus. They failed to admire the depth of the local culture which in fact was not basically hostile to Vedic approach and practice. In order to satisfy the sentiments of the people the ruler had to order re-writing of the burnt books quoting from the memory of the experts, thereby strengthening the basic foundation of the local beliefs and usages. Consequent upon the transition to the common Hindu faith and also consequent upon the introduction of orthodox formalities by the heads of missionaries for the division of the population into watertight clans and tribes, which began as a vigorous process, was taken full advantage of by the British when they ruled Manipur through the puppet king.

The Social Setup, Social Hierarchy and Social Organisation

In the pre-independence period, scant attention was paid to the socio-economic development of the people of Manipur on account being situated in the far-flung difficult terrain. The resources with the government were not upto the mark. But with the dawn of independence, a new developmental schemes were envisaged. The main plank was the all-round development of the residents, including women and children. In fact the creation of a new state has given deep involvements of developments, socio-economic in temperament, to the newly formed government. Whereas the Panchayati Raj was given priority in this regard, the development of education with regard to women and children are considered quite significant. At the younger age, they have been given basic facilities. Primary schools have been opened where the students are given education free of charge along with other basic facilities. It has been felt that they should be provided with trained teachers. Similarly women have been given basic social facilities in their domestic environments. They of course work in fields and industrial establishments in order to solve their economic problems. Any social dispute in domestic environments is resolved by the Panchayat of the village. Thus the social setup and the sense of social organisation are being strengthened in quite a systematic way. People have begun to realise. Their social functions and instead of going to the court of law, they resolve their socio-economic differences in a mutual way. The census data relating to ever married and currently married women belonging to Scheduled Tribes according to their age and number of their surviving childrens is given on next pages.

Table 1

Ever Married and Currently Married Women Belonging to Scheduled Tribes by Present Age, Number of Surviving Children and Total Number of Surviving Children by Sex

Present Age	Total ever/currently married women	Ever/currently married women with number of serviving children						Total surviving children		
		0	1	2	3	4	5+	Total	Males	Females
1	2	3	4	5	6	7	8	9	10	11
ALL SCHEDULED TRIBES										
RURAL										
Ever Married										
All ages	**1,13,450**	**27,149**	**11,033**	**12,244**	**12,850**	**12,510**	**34,730**	**3,51,165**	**1,84,178**	**1,66,987**
Less than 15	450	420	11	11	0	0	0	33	22	11
15-19	2,083	1,312	499	97	27	23	0	866	470	396
20-24	8,884	3,415	2,516	1,577	681	215	122	9,270	4,739	4,531
25-29	17,158	4,561	2,831	3,481	2,973	1,748	1,088	31,893	16,528	15,365
30-34	14,986	3,128	1,287	2,066	2,444	2,451	3,251	41,141	21,199	19,942
35-39	15,378	2,884	721	1,350	1,876	2,287	5,962	54,608	28,456	26,152
40-44	12,408	2,339	531	767	1,165	1,527	5,829	49,882	25,842	24,040
45-49	11,938	2,286	464	634	1,010	1,306	6,024	51,044	26,750	24,294
50-54	9,238	1,785	493	613	800	965	4,369	38,146	20,246	17,900
55-59	6,688	1,254	363	473	608	710	3,131	27,679	14,917	12,762
60-64	5,810	1,346	432	507	560	562	2,223	20,894	11,079	9,815
65-69	3,365	739	296	254	312	300	1,347	12,149	6,610	5,539
70-74	2,286	666	289	178	164	238	677	6,706	3,595	3,111
75-79	1,128	373	114	91	99	77	327	3,062	1,642	1,420
80 +	1,477	536	175	133	121	94	352	3,509	1,935	1,574

(Contd.)

1	2	3	4	5	6	7	8	9	10	11
Currently Married										
All ages	**1,03,291**	**24,479**	**9,448**	**11,098**	**11,808**	**11,563**	**32,480**	**3,25,850**	**1,70,716**	**1,55,134**
Less than 15	408	383	9	8	0	0	0	25	18	7
15-19	2,028	1,277	486	96	27	23	0	851	459	392
20-24	8,608	3,298	2,418	1,543	675	213	118	9,056	4,624	4,432
25-29	16,615	4,377	2,639	3,412	2,938	1,733	1,077	31,330	16,236	15,094
30-34	14,406	2,944	1,149	1,971	2,382	2,416	3,229	40,353	20,781	19,572
35-39	14,690	2,722	609	1,228	1,787	2,214	5,873	53,145	27,687	25,458
40-44	11,555	2,152	397	647	1,063	1,437	5,649	47,714	24,724	22,990
45-49	11,081	2,119	345	536	907	1,181	5,803	48,559	25,420	23,139
50-54	8,057	1,545	349	483	637	833	4,048	34,638	18,395	16,243
55-59	5,805	1,076	263	372	509	612	2,859	24,909	13,422	11,487
60-64	4,483	1,013	270	366	448	428	1,841	17,057	9,068	7,989
65-69	2,594	560	193	188	224	231	1,132	9,968	5,445	4,523
70-74	1,427	415	168	109	99	148	456	4,430	2,358	2,072
75-79	700	248	62	58	56	42	213	1,946	1,059	887
80 +	705	276	82	71	49	47	158	1,632	894	738
URBAN										
Ever Married										
All ages	**10,776**	**2,511**	**1,031**	**1,209**	**1,455**	**1,340**	**2,871**	**31,467**	**16,008**	**15,459**
Less than 15	36	35	1	0	0	0	0	1	1	0
15-19	258	153	66	14	6	2	0	120	63	57
20-24	1,032	379	256	211	88	31	15	1,149	566	583
25-29	1,737	462	214	331	359	208	105	3,382	1,694	1,688
30-34	1,698	370	113	190	351	320	312	4,583	2,303	2,280
35-39	1,545	270	64	146	213	308	498	5,170	2,627	2,543
40-44	1,150	153	65	89	123	176	515	4,593	2,288	2,305
45-49	939	141	52	60	101	99	461	3,837	2,013	1,824
50-54	745	130	54	49	86	68	340	2,966	1,473	1,493
55-59	457	110	31	36	25	39	198	1,662	903	759
60-64	416	96	34	30	35	33	168	1,522	809	713

(Contd.)

1	2	3	4	5	6	7	8	9	10	11
65-69	256	60	27	8	30	21	102	962	472	490
70-74	225	66	19	19	18	20	72	690	373	317
75-79	108	31	16	7	9	9	27	300	163	137
80 +	163	45	19	19	11	6	57	524	256	268
Currently Married										
All ages	**9,685**	**2,274**	**871**	**1,091**	**1,321**	**1,226**	**2,597**	**28,370**	**14,375**	**13,995**
Less than 15	31	30	1	0	0	0	0	1	1	0
15-19	249	145	65	14	6	2	0	119	63	56
20-24	1,002	372	243	210	87	29	14	1,115	541	574
25-29	1,700	450	203	323	355	207	105	3,339	1,672	1,667
30-34	1,635	359	100	179	337	311	308	4,447	2,238	2,209
35-39	1,464	259	57	133	200	292	483	4,950	2,517	2,433
40-44	1,047	139	44	79	99	168	492	4,301	2,127	2,174
45-49	858	128	44	39	95	88	444	3,627	1,896	1,731
50-54	614	114	29	39	69	47	301	2,533	1,266	1,267
55-59	378	90	27	24	21	31	170	1,414	779	635
60-64	275	60	22	22	20	21	120	1,072	567	505
65-69	181	41	18	3	16	19	78	712	337	375
70-74	127	43	7	12	9	6	44	371	186	185
75-79	65	24	7	4	7	3	18	188	102	86
80 +	53	15	4	10	0	2	19	175	79	96

Source: Census 1991.

Notes: 1. 'All ages includes 'age not stated'.

2. Number of ever/currently married women in col.4 includes women not reporting number of surviving children.

3. The age groups having nil return are not shown.

7

The Land and the People

Let's start geographical introduction of the state, i.e., Meghalaya with these words of Prof. G.G. Swell:

> The people who constitute the population of Meghalaya are mainly the Garos and the Khasis. Considering their historical and political background, their progress from isolation has been astounding. There is no written record about their remote past but it is universally accepted that at one time the Garos migrated from Tibet and are classified as a Tibeto-Burman people. Compared to the Khasis, who are confined more or less to their home district, the Garos are more widespread. They are to be found today not only in various parts of Assam but also in considerable areas in East Pakistan.
>
> The Khasis have been inhabiting the Khasi and Jaintia Hills from times immemorial. They are an ancient people and no one is able as yet to say from where they came. Anthropologists and linguists, who have studied their physical features, language and customs and traditions, consider them to be the kin of the Khmer people of Cambodia who, between the 8th and 12th centuries, ruled over the greatest empire in South-East Asia and built the enormous and breath-taking stone structures of Angkor Vat before which, it is said, the splendours of Greece and Rome pale into insignificance.

When we talk of geography of any particular area, the most important aspect to be kept in mind is its surroundings. The same principle applies here in the case of Meghalaya which shares its border with the East Pakistan (non-Bangaldesh). For that, it is obviously subject to the tension between Indian sub-continent and Pakistan. This chapter taken up some of border tension between Meghalaya and the neighbouring country.

"Pakistani leaders", Mr. V.K. Krishna Menon said to Michael Brecher, "looked upon Pakistan as a first instalment, thinking in terms of the English doctrine 'take what you can and fight for more.' They never seem to have accepted the partition as final, as we did. Their main approach to the problem was that India was theirs; India was a Muslim country historically; the British had taken it away from them; now the British had gone away and it should be handed over to them."

Further developing his thesis he said:

> Pakistan will do anything and everything against us. The original Pakistani doctrine of Rehmet Ali, a Cambridge student, was that Bengal was Pakistan,

> Hyderabad was Pakistan, Kashmir was Pakistan, Punjab was Pakistan, and so on. Now, according to these ideas, what haven't they got? They do not have even half of the Punjab, they have not got Kashmir, they have not got even half of Bengal, and they have not got Hyderabad. So when we talk about Kashmir this is only part that Rehmet Ali map—and there is of course the larger map—which could place almost all of India in Pakistan . . .
>
> Pakistan's aggression is not for a place, not for Kashmir alone; the aggression is against India, against secularism. What has Pakistan claimed since we partitioned? They claimed various parts of what was then India. On account of the partition arrangements, we agreed to plebiscites in the North-West Frontier Province, Sylhet, certain villages and so on. We lost them . . .

Facts behind this analysis is becoming clearer day by day. Nehru offered a no-war pact to Pakistan's leaders time and again. Lal Bahadur Shastri concluded his life with a declaration of India's peaceful policy for Pakistan at Tashkent. Mrs. Indira Gandhi has reiterated the desire of India for peaceful co-existence on each day of significance to India and Pakistan and on every occasion for eliminating possible tensions—be it with regard to the river water dispute or diplomatic discussions on political irritants.

What results has our profession of trust in peace yielded? It has caused no change in the basic policy of hatred of Pakistan towards India. But it has confirmed our will to wander for peace until conflicts become necessary. This is in fitness of the things that make us a secular, tolerant republic despite the communal aberrations we encounter every now and then. But to say that professions of peace will obviate the need of keeping the nation guarded and strong is a child like illusion. With the collusion between Pakistan and China, the long border between East Pakistan, and Assam and Meghalaya remains perpetually live. There are frequent intrusions. Meghalaya possesses a longer border stretch than Assam has and, therefore, it it only prudent to take stock of the situation in this area of international tension. Let us look at the geographical placement of East Pakistan.

Geographical Position of East Pakistan

It comprises the eastern territories of the partitioned province of Bengal and the former Assam district of Sylhet, with the exception of certain thanas of the Karimganj sub-division. It is administratively grouped into three divisions and 17 districts: (a) Dacca Division—the districts of Dacca, Mymensing, Faridpur and Bakarganj; (b) the Chittagong Region Division—The districts of Chittagong, Tipperah, Noakhali, Chittagong Hill Tracts and Sylhet; (c) Rajshahi Division—the districts like Rajshahi Dinajpur, Rangpur, Bogra, Pabna, Kushtia, Jessore and Khulna.

After this, let us see the situation of Assam:

Assam first became a British protectorate at the close of the first Burmese war in 1826. In 1832, Cachar was annexed; in 1835 the Jaintia Hills had been included in the East Indian Company's dominion, and in 1839 Upper Assam was annexed to Bengal. In 1874 Assam was detached from Bengal and evolved a separate Chief Commissionership. On the partition of Bengal in 1905, it was united with the eastern districts of Bengal under a Lieutenant-Governor.

Since 1912, the Chief Commissionership of Assam was revived, and in 1921 a Governorship was created. After the partition of India almost the whole of the predominantly Muslim district of Sylhet was merged with East Bengal (Pakistan). Dewangiri in North Kamrup was ceded to Bhutan in the year 1951. The States Reorganisation Act, 1956, effected no territorial changes in the case of Assam.

(a) Nagaland (the Naga Hills-Tuensang region). The Naga Hills-Tuensang region was constituted as a centrally administered area under the Ministry of External Affairs on December 1, 1957. It included the Naga Hills district of Assam and Tuensang Frontier Division earlier under the North-East Frontier Agency.

Nagaland has an area of 6,236 sq. miles.

(b) The North-East Frontier Agency. This agency includes Kemang, Tirap, Subansiri, Siang and Lohit Frontier Divisions, and has an area of 31,438 sq. miles. Our north-eastern borders, we therefore see, is perpetually threatened by expansionists having political ideologies different from ours. Chinese arms poured into Pakistan pass, due to the difficulties of terrain and the nature of forests which provide cover to smugglers and saboteurs and hide-outs to misguided hostile factions of the Nagas and the Mizos, into unreliable hands in West Bengal and Assam. No security can be fool-proof in these regions. Infiltration by East Pakistani miscreants is an often feature and in any long-drawn war between Pakistan and India or China and India the people of Meghalaya will have to shoulder heavy responsibilities.

This was one of the points which the hill leaders stressed while demanding an autonomous state. When the Chinese invaded India in 1962, they suspended their agitation and revealed their power to strengthen the defence system of the country. The Pakistani thrusts in 1965 were confined to the Punjab and Jammu areas. Defence attempts on our Assam front were an obvious deterrent to Ayub Khan's miscalculated plan to walk over the Indian territory. This way, taking into consideration the Chinese game of shifting boundaries on the map and the hate-India bogey launched in Pakistan on every occasion of external pressure or internal problems, the powder will have to be kept dry and the morale of the people kept high in Meghalaya. The borders of the hill states, specifically, that of Assam and Meghalaya with Pakistan should be sealed.

The Burma frontier is particularly troublesome due to the difficult terrain escaping into which Nagas and Mizos step into Chinese territory and get money and weapon for involving in sabotage. But this precaution is not a wholly workable proposition. A sensitive border area cannot be fenced off by barbed wire—the way we fence off a garden against the intrusion of stray cattle. Even expert military vigilance of the highest order has human limitations and logistic handicaps. It is necessary but it is not fool-proof.

Thus, it has to be supplemented by a well-trained force of violent citizens living in peace but ready to meet other eventualities too. For this the entire border region of the North-East India requires a broad economic base for its people. A clear understanding of the political and social problems of some parts of the region, which have not yet been solved, is a basic necessity. If the battle of wits among the leaders of Assam and the hill people would not have been concluded with wisdom by creating the fresh state of Meghalaya, North-East India would have been the poorer for it. There are more or less identical problems in Nagaland and the Mizo Hills, although there is not even a fraction of the consent that was available in the Garo Hills and the United Khasi and Jaintia Hills to take the irritants away from the political situation.

Eco-political Troubles

But with a measure of persistence, intelligence and negotiation for peace with the right kind of local leaders at the right point of time, a sensible solution can be developed and even the dark conceited world of the misguided tribals can be illumined by an era of cooperation between them and the remaining India. Border defence is a politico-military problem and there is no better source of military strength than settling enlightened and financially self-sufficient communities in politically stable conditions in the sensitive areas. Observers often stress two key goals for the under-developed parts—economic development and modernisation on the one hand, and political stability on the other.

The compatibility of these goals, however, is quite limited. Without a constitutional tradition of peaceful change some kind of violence is virtually inevitable. In the underdeveloped areas, the alternatives, broadly speaking, are not constitutional change or violent change, but gradual change through revolutionary style or revolutionary coups d'etat. The enforced absence of change, political "stability" without coups d'etat, is often only the breeding ground for even worse forms of violence. In the border areas we need democratisation of government to which the only alternative seems to be an ostentatious democratisation of violence—if we emphasise on our being called a democracy. And the former order is honourable and not alien to our tradition or national genius, i.e., purely Indian.

The Contributors

(a) Capt Williamson A. Sangma. Whole life of Capt. Sangma is an ingratiating social vignette. Its curvilinear patterns resemble a slender vine twisting round a sturdy oak. He has grown from strength to strength and people and agencies have clung to him for direction and support. One cannot reduce such a meaningful life to a formulated description. His roots are in the soil.

Even prior to he accepted military commission he was a man of the masses. He was helpful to the less privileged people of the community and conscious of their difficulties. He entered active political life in 1952 as a man committed not to politics but to social welfare. He knew the people who practiced a garnished and cumbered existence, harassed by poverty and eking out a miserable living from an unprofitable soil, yet looking at the world from hill-tops, responding to the miracles of nature and taking pride in their tradition and faith. The army had taught him discipline and training in conquering inertia. It was a rigorous spell of education. He learnt the advice of Rousseau to all administrators and his commanders:

> If it is good to know how to deal with men as they are, it is much better to make them what they should be. The most absolute authority is that which penetrates a man's inner being, and concerns itself no less with his will than with his action. Make men, therefore, if you would command men; if you would have them obedient to the laws, make them love the laws, and then they will need to know only what is their duty to do it.

They say that the people responded to his sincerity with abundant affection and his friends gave him their absolute trust. He was elected to be the chief executive member of the Garo Hills District Council. Later came a more intense association with political life when he became the chairman of the Eastern India Tribal Union. In the year 1957, he was elected as a member of the Assam Legislative Assembly. The following year, he joined the cabinet of Assam to look after the departments of the tribal regions, information, publicity and transport.

When the Assamese language bill was passed in spite of opposition from the tribal people, he resigned from the cabinet impressing that it is better to fight for a cause without the trapings of power and be nearer to history than to office. When the A.P. H.L.C. was born, he was elected to become its first chairman. Throughout the peaceful struggle for a separate hill state, Capt Sangma underlined the importance of fairplay, integrity and peaceful, political give and take. He elevated politics from the morass of mean manoeuvres and mischief to the level of faith, efficiency, honesty and ethics. He was convinced with this that the hill people constituted a community which looked ahead of time. For them he conceived a system capable of renewing itself to meet the changing conditions. He evolved in the political temper of the hillman a desire to shun violence and negotiate for peace. This quality has raised the people he leads well above the Nagas and the Mizos who have almost failed to achieve social stability and political strength despite years of existence as groups-in-arms. Meghalaya joined the Indian federation under his imaginative captaincy. Those who are aware of his success as a leader know that his achievements have come from the fountainspring of the belief that leaders must be simple at heart. Their love for the people must be reflected not in rhetoric but in acts and that all their actions, motivated by the necessity of bringing a better life to the people, must come like Eve from somewhere near the third rib and there must be the leader's own heart beating in them.

(b) Prof. G.G. Swell. A great academician, Prof. G.G. Swell, is a world of thought in himself. He has come to politics after a long and distinguished career as a teacher. His beginnings are humble and submissive. He was born in a village called Laityusew, forty miles to the west of Shillong. The family was small and its income was modest. His father ran a small scale business. His education began in the village. From there he went to Ramakrishna Mission School, Cherapunji, where he received sound, liberal education and developed love for art. The Scottish Church College, his alma mater at Calcutta, opened before him the treasure of world literature. Having specialised in the English language, he took many teaching assignments in colleges and brought greater respect to his profession. In Addis Ababa, where he taught English for few days, his erudition and imaginative original methods of teaching are still remembered by his old boys and the teaching community. Politics is a means to the end that is public service to him. Life, thought, social conditions and hopes of the times through which one lives presents the raw material from which can be fashioned the means of helpful change. The invisible and intangible archetypes and prototypes of things, activities and virtues, often expressed by politicians in terms of cliches and conceits, and are mere practices in adolescent mental ability. A politician needs an overall view of the situation he is dealing with and his ability to look into the heart of the matter is the most significant aspect in the struggle for achieving any goal for his people.

Prof. Swell has never got involved in epic celebrations of the lost paradise of the tribal people's culture. He loved the simple folk because he felt about their problems as they have realised. He spoke to them in simple, de-academicised language. He spoke to them the mutations of their failure and extravagance of their conduct. Between him and his people, as he joined the A.P.H.L.C. movement, the great conversation has continued. His main source of inspiration was the affection of the people. His political affiliations are subservient to his high sense of patriotism. Few people know that he was a Congressman at the initial stage of his political career.

Representing the tribal people of Assam in the Lok Sabha with dignity and contagious effability for about eight years, he rose to the office of the Deputy Speaker on December 9, 1969. His belief in the infinitude of the private man and the integrity of the individual mind has endeared him to the members of representatives in Parliament and thinking men and women in the capital. In him the tribal people had, perhaps, the finest interpreter of their culture. He sees the problems of the hill people in the context of the problems of South-East Asia. He says: Of all regions of our country, North-East India lies the closest to the South-East Asian theatre to which the world centre of gravity is gradually shifting, and while we may be disinterested to what may go on, other countries are not.

(c) Mr. Stanley Nichols Roy. They say that personal legacies are always difficult to preserve. In the wider context of the inheritance of nations or communities a sense of lyrical vagueness and impersonalisation acts as a protective membrane. An ideal kept dormant beneath the surface of hallowed time does not claim immediate emulation or action. But a person born to a rich family heritage has to accept many challenges. If he proves equal to them, succeeds in measuring upto the standards set before him or, by personal effort and enterprise, helps enrich it, he adds to the then present glory bequeathed to him. Otherwise, his fall from the sublime to the ridiculous writes him off and corrodes his heritage. Mr. Roy, with his academics, service to the people and high standards in public life, has not only proved himself worthy of the values of his esteemed father, the Rev J.J.M. Nichols Roy, but has also carried forward his mission of service to the tribal people. His country home is in the hills in a village of which he is proud. His work is among the villagers who are proud of him. Educated at Presidency College, Calcutta and at California, U.S.A., Mr. Nichols Roy has praised the beauty and serenity of tribal life against the background of urban civilisation with its traps, tricks and temptations. He witnessed his father's heart and mind crying out for the cherished values of political and social life.

He saw him fighting out with brilliant wit and limitless sympathy the forces of disintegration in the hilly regions and the plains of Assam. He saw him working ceaselessly for ensuring to the tribal people their rightful place in the multi-racial country and, above all, he found him throwing himself, in all humility, on the breast of revealed religion in moments of trial for succour and solace. Mr. Nichols Roy combines in his personal self the discernment of a mature politician and the self-effacing spirit of service of a clergyman. He has held executive positions in business, done pioneering job in providing educational facilities to the tribal people and actively campaigned for the political rights of the hill people. The Union Christian College at Barapani is a great monument to his tireless social work. In recognition of his work for their political awakening, the people elected him as general secretary of the APHLC in 1960—the office which he has held ever since. He has always pleaded for non-violence and practised Gandhi's teachings in his daily life. Scrupulously avoiding moments for upleasantness in personal and political life, he has developed such a persuasive plausibility of speech and manners that he has come to be known as a symbol of friendship between the people of the hills and the plains. He is married to a former American citizen, Miss Helen Randolph. They have four children. But is his family just so small? Mr. Nichols Roy feels that a man who believes in the ministry of Christ and the message of his crucifixion to human kind has the whole world as his family.

Language, Religious Beliefs and Practices

We will endeavour to highlight the social and ethnic characteristics mainly. This is because Meghalaya survives uniformly as the island of matrilineal societies distinct from the patriarchal societies which surround it. Yet Meghalaya with its distinct matrilineal family and social organisation has found enough room to adjust itself to all the situations which have affected the State. Most of the Bodic or Sino-Tibetan speaking people at one time exhibited strongly the matrilineal traits, who at the laps of the long ages, switched over to a patrilineal society. This is proved by the Garo Society which still retains its matrilineal customs of succession and inhertiance.

Mother kinship among the Khasi groups is dominant. The tribe is a conglomerate of clans. The mother is the custodian of family rites and property always to be succeeded by her youngest sister who attains the position of the next custodian entrusted with the post of trust and responsibility. Being instrumental to perform the host of family rites and celebrations and affecting the family gatherings and assemblies, and being care-taker of her parents and other unprotected members of the family. She secures the lion's share of the family including the ancestral residence which she cannot part off, her elder sister (s) also getting the share of property in the shape of lands, jewelleries, ornaments, vessels and articles of household furniture and goods. The elder sisters generaly move with their respective husbands, but the youngest stays in her residence, the custom being matrilocal. The census data regarding language spoken by various Tribes is given below :

Table 1
Mother Tongue for Scheduled Tribes

Scheduled Tribe	*Mother Tongue*	*Number of Speakers*					
			Rural			*Urban*	
		Total	*Males*	*Females*	*Total*	*Males*	*Females*
1	2	3	4	5	6	7	8
All Scheduled Tribes							
	Adi	80	43	37	4	2	2
	Anal	1	1	0	61	39	22
	Angami	3	1	2	7	5	2
	Ao	0	0	0	72	34	38
	Assamese	8,637	4,457	4,180	596	363	233
	Bengali	25,454	12,998	12,456	2,305	1,190	1,115
	Bhili/Bhilodi	8	6	2	4	1	3
	Bhotia	1	0	1	0	0	0
	Bishnupuriya	0	0	0	1	1	0
	Bodo/Boro	2,042	1,108	934	764	441	323
	Chakhesang	0	0	0	2	0	2
	Chakru/Chokri	0	0	0	3	3	0
	Deori	0	0	0	3	2	1
	Dimasa	116	58	58	2	2	0
	Dogri	0	0	0	3	3	0
	English	102	57	45	150	66	84
	Gangte	8	4	4	1	1	0
	Garo	4,97,654	2,51,372	2,46,282	48,025	24,808	23,217
	Gondi	31	12	19	10	2	8
	Gujarati	1	0	1	5	3	2
	Halam	131	65	66	14	7	7
	Hindi	2,778	1,526	1,252	664	388	276
	Hmar	246	134	112	188	116	72

(Contd.)

(Contd.)

1	2	3	4	5	6	7	8
	Ho	26	15	11	5	3	2
	Kabui	668	364	304	67	33	34
	Kannada	19	11	8	0	0	0
	Karbi/Mikir	8,428	4,323	4,105	99	60	39
	Kashmire	4	2	2	0	0	0
	Khandeshi	16	5	11	5	4	1
	Kharia	37	22	15	10	6	4
	Khasi	7,14,409	3,57,376	3,57,033	1,47,161	69,640	77,521
	Khezha	38	19	19	9	4	5
	Khond/Kondh	26	17	9	1	1	0
	Kinnauri	20	9	11	0	0	0
	Koch	17,068	8,484	8,584	560	285	275
	Koda/Kora	2	0	2	1	1	0
	Kom	0	0	0	5	2	3
	Konda	1	1	0	1	1	0
	Konkani	1	0	1	3	2	1
	Konyak	0	0	0	6	4	2
	Kuki	1,021	500	521	339	236	103
	Kurukh/Oraon	4	3	1	2	1	1
	Lahnda	3	2	1	0	0	0
	Lakher	0	0	0	3	3	0
	Lalung	955	483	472	1	1	0
	Liangmei	28	13	15	4	4	0
	Lotha	0	0	0	38	26	12
	Lushai/Mizo	380	205	175	2,352	1,245	1,107
	Malayalam	48	32	16	71	51	20
	Manipuri	17	12	5	22	13	9
	Mao	15	7	8	297	154	143
	Maram	174	87	87	2	0	2
	Marathi	3,117	1,550	1,567	16	11	5
	Maring	7	4	3	0	0	0
	Miri/Mishing	0	0	0	2	1	1
	Mishmi	0	0	0	2	2	0
	Munda	76	41	35	25	17	8
	Mundari	1	1	0	2	2	0
	Nepali	702	539	163	230	138	92
	Nissi/Dafla	27	15	12	6	2	4
	Nocte	4	3	1	7	7	0
	Oriya	6	4	2	9	8	1
	Pabha	19,774	9,878	9,896	216	134	82
	Paite	2	1	1	98	50	48
	Parji	3	1	2	1	0	1
	Pawi	0	0	0	1	1	0
	Punjabi	12	7	5	34	11	23
	Sangtam	2	1	1	1	1	0
	Santali	48	22	26	6	3	3
	Savara	4	3	1	0	0	0
	Sema	11	9	2	27	19	8
	Sindhi	1	1	0	1	1	0

(Contd.)

(Contd.)

1	2	3	4	5	6	7	8
	Tamil	16	12	4	21	17	4
	Tangkhul	1	1	0	57	40	17
	Tangsa	52	24	28	4	3	1
	Telugu	5	5	0	2	1	1
	Thado	1,461	762	699	32	23	9
	Tibetan	13	5	8	9	4	5
	Tripuri	4	2	2	28	22	6
	Tulu	2	0	2	0	0	0
	Urdu	13	11	2	21	16	5
	Vaiphei	383	198	185	41	22	19
	Wancho	0	0	0	3	3	0
	Yimchungre	14	5	9	2	1	1
	Zeliang	2	2	0	3	1	2
	Zemi	0	0	0	5	5	0
	Zou	0	0	0	26	11	15
	Others	5,629	2,918	2,711	948	541	407

Source: Census 1991.

The system in keeping with its original pattern and moral effiacy has been now-a-days largely distorted especially when the female custodian is habituated to neglecting her duty and even disposes of the ancestral property and fails to deliver the goods she ought to do so. The avancular power of the meals has been adversely affected leading sometimes to the deprivation of the youngest daughter by the avaricious manipulation or hatching a plan by her uncles with her to dispose of the ancestral property. The couple on the other hand by virtue of Meghalaya succession Bill 1984 enacted as an Act are eligible to dispose of their self acquired property to sons or daughters and provide education or in the event, the wife is poor, this is usually the husband's entire responsibility. There are exceptions. The sons may have secured other kinds of relief or investment from their mothers to establish themselves in which case, the earnings increased out of it is to be bequeathed to their wives' children although normally sons otherwise get only small gifts with personal belongings when they are married. Now-a-days, if a man shares with his mother any business, he gets a dividend. The father has the right to transmit hsi self-acquired property to his children. He, has the right to conduct his children's affairs; if he earns jointly with his wife, both will manage the house. If through his self-acquired property (*Kamai Khun)* he has made provisions for his children by constructing houses or purchasing plots of lands or groves or fields, they remain until he has made a formal division unto them. But if he has started business with capital supplied by his wife, they latter apparently has a greater voice, if she possesses ancestral or self acquired property in greater proportion, he becomes the adviser or assistant in the management.

A great portion of the bachelors' earing *(Kamai Khynraw)* goes to his mother before marriage but he is not prevented from transferring it on marriage to his wife nor his wife after marriage, can prevent him from transferring a portion of his earning *(Kamai iing khun)* to his mother if she deserves assistance. A man exercises a dual function as *U Knii,* i.e., maternal uncle (councellor) for his mother's *kin and U Kpa* (the father) at his wife's home. In the war (southern) areas, the father has got more authority at his home since his children are eligible to obtain shares of property from him, it might be the one that has been inherited from his mother.

The youngest daughter, in Christian families still exercises her moral duties and obtains the biggest portion of ancentral property today. She is bound to take care of her unmaried brothers and sisters. She is the guardian of the parentless and homeless members; the mother acts are a moral force to unite the family as the spiritual head.

In the Jaintia Hills, the form obtained is not conjugal originally like Garo and Khasi, but the Pnar or Jaintia form is more dualocal as the father is titular, leaving total family responsibilities to his wife, all his earning being integrated with that of his mother's and to his wife he renders a normal provision (*bai kait*) only. Daughters do not inherit to their father's property but get it from their maternal uncle and brothers. But today, the growth of conjugal system as of Khasi pattern and the development of nuclear families is a social trend of noticeable growth among Christians leading to the corporate living and supervisory care of both husband and wife over their children. The census data for various religions adopted by Scheduled Tribes is as follows :

Table 2
Religion for Scheduled Tribes

Scheduled Tribe	*Rural*			*Urban*		
	Total	*Males*	*Females*	*Total*	*Males*	*Females*
1	2	3	4	5	6	7
ALL SCHEDULED TRIBES						
All Religions	**13,12,093**	**6,59,859**	**6,52,234**	**2,05,834**	**1,00,375**	**1,05,459**
1. Buddhists	783	389	394	85	55	30
2. Christians	9,65,680	4,85,920	4,79,760	1,77,606	86,599	91,007
3. Hindus	82,129	41,651	40,478	6,184	3,214	2,970
4. Jains	3	2	1	0	0	0
5. Muslims	874	438	436	753	364	389
6. Sikhs	33	15	18	11	3	8
7. Other Religions & Persuations	2,62,081	1,31,164	1,30,917	20,973	10,028	10,945
8. Religion not stated	510	280	230	222	112	110

Source: Census 1991

The characteristic features which dominate the religious belief and ritual can now be deduced. The theistic elements as such are admixed evidently with the monotheistic principles but to many, the former are subsidiary to the latter. For instance thanks giving to the spirits known as *Phan longkur* (who gives increase to the clan). *Phan longrngiew* (who enhances the concept of the manly dignity or who adds strength to the human nerves), *Phan Longbriew* (identified with a sound moral) are believed to represent to goddess as her agents. These and other spirits are propitiated only when through divination, her permission is obtained. Thanks giving to the Supreme Being or the Goddess representing Him is signalised by casting 9 or 7 or 5 pieces of the entrails of the animals slain at the altar, a small lump or red earth where the leaves of an oak are planted. Therefore, the concept of *blie iing* or deities of the house who guard and defend them is followed. For instance at Shangpung, *Blei Sngi,* the sun goddess, *Blei synshar, Tholang* (a male progenitor), *Thaw Niawbi* (ancestress), *Lukhimi* (spirit of the fire place) are all embodied to be the manifestations of the power of the supreme god. The cult of the dead represented by lawbei (the ancestress), u *Thawlang* (the paternal patriarch), U *Suitnia* (the uncle, brother of the mother) which means the intercessor or advocate are held in reverance. Megalithic culture is intimately connected with the cult of the dead for preserving their reverent memory but this culture not funerary entirely, has created also the other manifestations in architecture. The three persons symbolising the intrinsic household are glorified. The cremation of the dead is a series of the observancy of prayer, intercession, sacrifices and purgatory rite. The post-cremation on a grand scale becomes extended to a festival full of colours, symbolic exchanges and demonstrations. Similarly, agricultural fertility is sustained by the performances of sacrificial rites, dances action songs and feasts.

Agriculture and Irrigation

The people are acquainted to practising both the permanent and shifting cultivation. However, the methods of cultivation are varied and differ according to climatic conditions. The climate itself ranges from sub-tropical to semi-temperate and thence to temperate. 'The soil is lateritic in the foothills and, above 500 meters it is mainly podzolic; while the areas in the southern slopes are in the layer of limestone belts, the northern slopes are mostly podzolic and have red loamy soil"[1]. The Khasi value the settled agriculture more than the shifting. They, therefore, cultivate cereals, vegetables and fruits of a variegated nature. The State is divided into three physical divisions which are the northern valleys and hills (sub-mountain) known as *Bhoi,* the central highlands located amid 900 and 2,000 metres altitude called *Ri Lum* and the southern precipitous mountain tract bordering Bangladesh, named *Ri War.* Garo Hills follow the same pattern of this physical division but a distinct temperate climate occurs only at some selected places.

In the rugged terrain we find that the slash and burn system exists. Under slash and burn system exists. Under slash and burn system, a mixed cropping pattern obtains, the contrast of mono-crop farming. The cultivators have been used to practising a modified system of *Jhumming* since the centuries past. The well known methods of farming are:

(1) *Rep sung:* rice irrigated farming in the extensive valley tracts.

(2) *Rep hali:* rice farming in irrigated valleys.

Table 3
Agricultural and Farming Functions including Labourers and Other Workers

District	*Cultivators*			*Agricultural labourers*			*Household industries*			*Other workers*		
	P	M	F	P	M	F	P	M	F	P	M	F
West Garo Hills	116,213	65,295	50,918	36,295	20,170	16,125	4,706	1,737	2,969	53,499	41,101	12,398
East Garo Hills	74,055	39,599	34,456	15,464	7,829	7,635	2,183	472	1,711	16,032	10,650	5,382
South Garo Hills	28,125	14,251	13,874	6,912	3,486	3,426	837	465	372	11,260	8,151	3,109
West Khasi Hills	81,358	40,570	40,788	30,381	15,235	15,146	691	448	243	18,708	12,373	6,335
Ri Bhoi	51,562	28,670	22,892	16,655	8,802	7,853	1,282	615	667	21,835	15,639	6,196
East Khasi Hills	45,517	25,461	20,056	31,231	18,148	13,083	6,874	3,553	3,321	158,119	103,387	54,732
Jaintia Hills	60,365	36,530	23,835	36,037	16,954	19,083	1,383	695	688	28,846	17,521	11,325

(3) *Rep pynthor:* a terraced cultivation applied in the lower hills and the adjoining valleys.
(4) *Thang ram:* or *rep shyrti* a heavy shift and burn system.
(5) *Thang bun:* a turfing system of cultivation.
(6) *Thang syllai:* which consists of the extraction of light herbage and utilising it for cultivation.
(7) *Rep bri:* which occurs in the south for the cultivation of fruits, banana, tez pat, pepper, betelvines, arcanuts and others.
(8) *Rep lyngkha:* a plot under cultivation, regular, semi-permanent or otherwise.
(9) *Rep kper:* a home-stead or kitchen gardening.
(10) *Rep rnem:* a system of cultivation by hoeing, applying manuring and putting seeds used for various crops.

Table 4
Agricultural and Farming Function including Labourers and Other Workers (Statewise): Census 1991

Total/ Rural/ Urban	*Persons/ Males/ Females*	*Cultivators Labourers*	*Agricultural Industry Workers*	*Household Workers*	*Other*
Total	Persons	457,195	172,975	17,956	308,299
	Males	250,376	90,624	7,985	208,822
	Females	206,819	82,351	9,971	99,477
Rural	Persons	450,097	166,572	16,129	193,536
	Males	246,680	87,530	6,884	129,618
	Females	203,417	79,042	9,245	63,918
Urban	Persons	7,098	6,403	1,827	114,763
	Males	3,696	3,094	1,101	79,204
	Females	3,402	3,309	726	35,559

Education

In Meghalaya, the development of education had been a slow process. The most difficult terain in the Himalayas which badly lacked the means of communication as well, any kind of problem like this remained in the same shape for decades together. The British Raj, in fact, did not feel the necessity of educational development in this region. The significant step in this direction was, however, taken by the Welsh Presbyterian Mission who realised the problem with all seriousness and undertook some useful measures in this direction. The year of commencement of such a social activity was 1841 when the government of the East India Company was in its hay days. In fact the first Welsh missionary entered the district and established his residence at Sohra. The work was started in a moderate way.

The indefagitable labour of that missionary (Thomas Jones I) and his successors paid its dividend. The first missionaries stood alone with hardy any official patronage extended to them. And it was after long decades of their continuity in the field that Government came forward and assisted them. However, the beginning of education is traced to the days of William Carey. A tradition recounts that a few students went to several places in the near and far of plains to prosecute school and college studies. It is not known if any Fort William College in the Bengal Presidency. The historical antecedents to the growth of Education are important for our review.

Although the initiative was underken in a sincere way, the literate community found it difficult to continue such a process in an easy way. In fact they had no script of their own and used Assamese and Bengali and even Persian and Arabic in order to straighten their State records and relevent documents.

The role of Serampore in this direction is conspicuous. Even prior to the arrival of the Welsh Mission, a few students (Khasi and Garo) had read in the colleges of Bengal including the Serampore college. This is referred to by William Carey who said that among the students belonging to different communities, Muslim; Bengalee and others there were two Khasis, three Garos (the latter sent by Scott then Commissioner of Coach Behar); that was in 1819; the Serampore College then being started in which William Carey was its founder. Evidently Scott had not contacted the Khasis yet. The first Khasi Students known were Ram Ringh and B Tham, sons of rich persons.

After Shillong became the provincial capital, there was no headway in the field of education. However, a local educationist, U. Jeelion Roy strove hard to explore the possibilities of starting a High School in 1876-77. He met the finances and expenditure from his own pocket. The hostel accommodation was provided after a few years. In fact the entry of the Roman Catholic and Ram Krishna Mission gave considerable boost to the increase of schools.

The significant steps in this direction were taken by two more prominent educationists, viz., U. Joel and Gatphoh and Oliver Thomas who introduced the famous Dalton method in the Shillong training school.

By the year 1931-32, the government funds were Rs. 1,07,882, Municipal Funds Rs. 5,445.

Fees	Rs. 27,648
Other sources	Rs. 1,57,555
Total	Rs. 2,98,530

The decision mas arrived at to withdraw education from the control of the Church. The new policy was accepted by the Local Assembly held at Wahjajer. In 1947-48, there were altogether 428 schools, 14777 pupils and 557 teachers belonging to the Presbyterian Church.

Inflationary increases against the statistical enumeration can now be reviewed as briefly as possible. A provisional estimate in 1977 shows the overlapping increase of institutions as follows :

(a) Pre-Primary and Basic - 379: (b) Primary and Basic-3,445 : (c) Middle and Sr. Basic-387 : (d) High and Higher Secondary - 155 : (e) Teachers Training : (f) Basic, Non-Basic including U.G. standard - 110 : (g) Schools for vocational, professional, special and other education - 125 : (h) Colleges - 12.

Number of instutions estimated in 1980 - 81 High Schools - 150, Middle or Sr. Basic - 400, Primary - 3,500, High Schools distributed District wise were-East Khasi - 97, Jaintia 19, West Khasi-25, West Garo-80, East Garo-33. In fact the State Council of Educational Research and Training is showing a significant result in the development of education. The Council is conducting multifarious programmes and very often seeks to identify the area of educational wastages and weaknesses and offer remedies to remove these problems.

Shillong Polytechnics caters to Technical Education. There is no College of Engineering of Technology yet established. The Polytechnics offers a three year course which extends mainly to workshop, laboratorical and theoretical management. The elementary course is concerned with workshop management in various trades. Workshop Management at infrastructural level is connected with welding, carpentry, smithery, fitting, mansonary, machinery, furniture, painting, etc. Laboratorical management extends to preliminary components in physical, chemical, mechanical, engineering science, etc. Theory classes mainly relate to management, economics and English. The course is conducted in four terms in which the combination of subjects pertaining to each term is aptly followed. Some departments offer scholarships or stipends to students in which these recipients are bound to execute the Bond of Agreement. It is a diploma course and passed out students can prepare and sit at exams conducted by the All India Council of Technical Education which can offer them certificates equivalent of Bachelor (Engineering), Master (Technical) and Doctorate Degrees. Admission is opened to HSLC passed. A hostel, school and workshop are attached. The Polytechnics was started in 1965. It accommodates a good number of students.

The Industrial Training Institute also caters at infastructural level to Industrial Training. It started initially in 1965 housed at Gauhati then shifted to Shillong housed in a temporary building. The Institute moved to its permanent premises in the city till 1985. It offers course of training to Electricians, Mechanic (Radio and Television), Civil Droughtsmen, Wiremen, Mechanic (MV), Fitters, Carpenters and even Stenographers. It functions under the Directorate of Craftsmen's Training and Employment. The entry qualification is Class VIII or HSLC passed (the latter confined apparently to Electrician, Radio and Television Mechanic, Civil Draughtsmen and Stenographers). The ITI women's branch started only two years ago, caters training in dress making. Subjects offered for Engineering towards trade include Theory, Engineering Drawing, Workshop, Laboratory, Practical and Social study. Simple subjects are not loaded with laboratory and Engineering in their distinct patterns ITI Tura offers courses for Electrician, Mechanic, Plumber, Carpenter, Welder and Stenographer. Most of the trainees are stipendiaries. They enjoy the benefit of free tutions and using the libraries. Hostel facilities exist only in Tura. The annual outturn of trainees is on mild scale. ITI is understood to have qualified trainees for using their experiences consistently. Literates and literacy rates by sex is given below for Meghalaya.

Table 5
Literates and Literacy Rates by Sex—Meghalaya: Census 2001

Union Territory/ Districts		*Literates*			*Literacy Rate of 2001*	
	Persons	*Males*	*Females*	*Persons*	*Males*	*Females*
Meghalaya	**1,789,717**	**1,170,443**	**44.85**	**63.31**	**66.14**	**60.41**
West Garo Hills	213,970	120,871	30.81	51.03	57.51	44.51
East Garo Hills	122,350	68,278	41.70	61.70	67.39	55.74
South Garo Hills	43,659	25,241	34.02	55.82	62.60	48.61
West Khasi Hills	148,868	77,179	47.94	65.64	67.02	64.21
Ri Bhoi	97,473	52,989	35.73	66.07	69.22	62.67
East Khasi Hills	422,329	215,937	61.86	76.98	78.12	75.82
Jaintia Hills	121,794	58,779	36.31	53.00	50.52	55.54

8

Constitution, the Law and the Local Administration

I

Since our Constitution makes special provision for those backward and downtrodden sections, provision of management of tribal areas is one under the Sixth Schedule of the Constitution, which provides certain guidelines for administration of tribal areas all over the country.

The administration of the Tribal Areas of North-Eastern region which were previously known as "Backward Tracts" has a history of its own. The Grant of the Diwany of Bengal to the East India Company in 1765 by Shah Alam II, secured for the British East India Company "superintendence of all revenues" in the Presidency of Bengal. Even prior to the taking over of the territories formerly administered under the East India Company by the British sovereign in 1858, after the Sepoy Mutiny of 1857, the making of laws was entrusted to the Governor General-in-Council by the Government of India Acts of 1833 and 1853.

These statutes allowed laws to be enacted directly for the areas which were earlier under the authority of the East India Company. In the following years, many Acts and Regulations were passed which affected the North Eastern region in diverse ways—like the Inner Line Regulation of 1873, the Scheduled Districts Act 1874, the Government of India Acts 1919 and 1935. As per the scheme of Provincial Autonomy, the hill areas of the then province of Assam fell into two categories, viz., the Excluded and Partially Excluded Areas, as scheduled through the Order-in-Council under the Government of India Act 1935. The main concern of the administration at that period of time was more static than dynamic.

This way, the administrative insulation contributed to the prolongation of backwardness of the North-Eastern region especially the areas predominantly inhabited by the tribal people. The English rulers did everything possible to check the emotional integration between the tribals and non-tribals for the evolution of a spirit of common identity superseding ethnic diversities. There were even abortive trials at keeping the North-Eastern tribal areas outside the Indian Dominion when the Indian Independence Act of 1947 was being passed by the British Parliament. But in independent India, under the inspiring leadership of Jawaharlal Nehru, the policy of winning the confidence of the tribal people and promoting closer contacts and intercourses between the tribals and non-tribals, ensuring the safety of interests of the tribals in their lands and autonomy to shape their lives as they desire, was followed.

In the Constituent Assembly, Jawaharlal Nehru presented the historic objectives Resolution which was adopted on 22 January 1947. These objectives have actually shaped the making of the Constitution. This Resolution proclaimed that India would become an Independent Sovereign Democratic Republic wherein, *inter-alia,* "adequate safeguards shall be depressed and other backward classes." When the Constitution of free India was adopted, it envisaged strong democratic institutions at the grass-root level as well as concerning the affairs of the tribal communities.

Consequently, democratic decentralisation and setting up of Panchayati Raj became one of the Directive Principles of State Policy. However, in the case of the Tribal Areas in the country, especially those in the North-East, there are some specific provisions provided in the Constitution. The Constitution makers also recognised the necessity of a separate political and administrative structure for the hill Tribal Areas of the erstwhile province of State of Assam by enacting the Sixth Schedule to the Constitution of India. In doing so, they were guided broadly speaking by three main considerations:

(a) need to maintain the distinct customs, socio-economic and political culture of the tribal people of the region and to ensure autonomy of the tribal people and to protect their identities;
(b) the necessity to check their economic and social exploitation by the more advanced neighbouring people of the plains;
(c) to allow the people to develop and administer themselves as per their own genius.

Keeping the above in mind, in pursuance of paragraph 20 of the Cabinet Mission Statement of May 16, 1946, an Advisory Committee on Fundamental Rights of Minorities in Tribal Areas, was formed by the Constituent Assembly in India. One of the sub-committees constituted by the Advisory Committee was the North-East Frontier (Assam) Tribal and Excluded Areas Sub-Committee with the chairmanship of Gopinath Bordoloi (popularly known as Bordoloi Sub-Committee). The Sub-Committee visited the tribal areas in the then composite State of Assam and talked with the representatives of the hill people in order to formulate a model administrative set up for these within the State of Assam. When the Sub-Committee studies the difficulties of the tribal people of the region, it realised that these areas needed protection and safeguard so that they might be able to preserve their way of life and at the same time take part in political life of the country alongwith others.

It also noted the existence of the traditional self-governing institutions which functioned democratically and resolved their disputes in accordance with their own customs and traditions. The Sub-Committee sought to evolve a system by which it could be possible to remove the apprehensions of the tribal people, innocent and backward as they were, so that they might not be exploited, subjugated and oppressed by the more advanced people. The suggestions of the Sub-Committee were incorporated in the Sixth Schedule to the Constitution. The idea behind the Sixth Schedule was to provide the tribal people with a simple and chief administration of their own, so that they could safeguard their own customs, traditions, culture, etc., and to provide them maximum autonomy in the management of their tribal affairs.

The Bordoloi Sub-Committee specifically appreciated that the tribal people were particularly sensitive about their lands, traditional system of justice and social rituals. In acceptance of the recommendations of this Sub-Committee, the Sixth Schedule to the Constitution of India was adopted. This provided for the formation of the Autonomous District Councils (ADCs) in certain hills districts of the then composite State of Assam. The Autonomous District Councils (ADCs) in certain hill district (except Naga Hills) of the then composite State of Assam were first introduced in 1952, and in 1955 Regional Councils (now District Councils) were introduced in the then Lushai Hills District (now Mizoram), according to the provisions of the Sixth Schedule. For the last more than forty years, these ADCs have functioned in their respective autonomous districts. Many of these ADCs have enacted from time to time a number of laws, rules, regulations, acts, etc., dealing with and affecting the people of their respective areas in diverse ways—relating to such pertinent issues like land, forest, literacy and primary school education, planning processes, markets, trade, developmental activities, etc., to mention a few of them. Some such Acts have direct effects on the traditional institutions like the chiefs, tribal councils and others. Many changes have taken place since 1952. The role, functions and workings of these constitutional institutions have been studied from time to time by many scholars of the area itself. A number of criticisms have also been levelled against the working and effective functioning of these Councils. The relevance of the ADCs today has been questioned from time to time particularly after the creation of full-fledged States where District Councils are in existence. On the part of the District Councils, they have been asking for more autonomy and direct funding from the Central government itself to strengthen their power and functions. Examining the role of the ADCs from a different angle, it should be noted that it was an institutional innovation of effecting decentralisation of power at the district level covering under its general framework, the troubles and issues down to the village level as devolved under the Constitution of India.

However, soon after the creation and the setting up of the ADCs in the Sixth Schedule regions of North-East India, they have been persistently voicing their grievances against the treatments meted out to them by the different State Governments in the matters of provision of grants, according to approval of the legislative proposals of the ADCs, super session of the ADCs, etc. Before the reorganisation of the then composite State of Assam (pre-1972), those grievances were directed against that State. The situation is not so different today even after the re-organisation of Assam which gave way to the formation/establishment of complete States like Meghalaya, Mizoram, Manipur, Tripura, etc. For instance, in Meghalaya today, a tug-of-war is still continuing between the State Government and the three ADCs over a specific paragraph (paragraph 12A) of the Sixth Schedule.

The ADCs in Meghalaya, Mizoram, Tripura, the hill districts of Assam (Karbi Anglong and North Cachar) are unhappy and not happy with the decisions of their respective State Governments. The ADCs were created in the hill areas of North-East India in reply to the demands of the tribal people for autonomy out of their apprehensions about the preservation of their ethnic identity and their rights over the lands, natural resources, customary laws, traditions, etc. They were conceived to make certain the right of self-rule of the tribal people, to manage their affairs according to their own genius, to enable them to preserve their ethnic recognition, and to face the forces of assimilation squarely from their more advanced neighbours in the plains. The underlying factor contributing to whatever achievements of the ADCs is that of the tribal people's emotional and active involvement in asserting their rights of self-rule and to run the administration by their own elected tribal representatives for promoting, preserving and safeguarding their rights on their lands and natural resources which are so dear to their own hearts and the over-all economic interests in general.

No wonder, the concept of the ADC has served as the root model for meeting the demands for autonomy. The autonomy of the ADCs has been affected in the area of financial independence. They have to rely on their respective State governments in matters of financial allotments. This in turn has reduced and restricted their autonomy and performances. One of the means of finance of the ADCs is the share of royalty accruing each year from licenses and leases for the purpose of prospecting for or extraction of minerals granted by the State Government in respect of any part within an autonomous district. Many ADCs have conplained that they are not given their due share from the collection of royalties and taxes. Secondly, the ADCs alleged that due to the obstructive attitude of the respective State Governments in the matter of the release of fund, they had been forced to adopt undesirable practices so as to raise fund in order to perform their constitutional duties like running of primary schools, dispensaries and even to meet the salaries of the employees. The Sixth Schedule confers fresh developmental functions on the ADCs, though there is an enabling clause whereby the State Governments can entrust such functions with them.

On the occasion of the re-organisation of States in North-East India in 1971, there was some sort of understanding at the political level as a result of which a number of new developmental functions were conferred on the ADCs. In this aspect, certain ADCs in North-East India expertenced subsequently that this arrangement was a fragile one lacking in statutory backing, the ADCs had to depend on the changing political relations with the State leadership. The developmental activities of the ADCs therefore depend very much on the political party or parties that manage the State administration. If the same political party is in power both at the State and District Council levels, the latter may have a smooth sailing in its schedule of developmental activities.

If it is otherwise, a number of obstacles and hurdles may be created by the party in power at the State level to jeopardise the plan of action that might be framed by the District Council for the development of the autonomous districts. The 73rd Amendment of the Constitution relating to Panchayat institutions which was passed by the Parliament in December 1992 and brought into effect on April 24, 1993, will have an effect on the ADCs in the States like Assam and Tripura. The Panchayat Raj institutions would cover as many as 29 subjects within their jurisdiction. When all important provisions of the 73rd Amendment about the power, scope of function and financial support for the existence of power and discharge the responsibilities by the Panchayati bodies are compared against those attached to the ADCs under the Sixth Schedule, it is found that while the ADCs have several regulatory powers subject to State control, the Panchayati Raj bodies are in a more advantageous position in respect of developmental functions.

In fact, in the matter of exercise of developmental function, the ADCs are at the pity of the State governments. However, a large number of developmental functions come within the operational jurisdiction of the Panchayati bodies. In some cases, even the level of function is higher for the Panchayati bodies. A careful comparison of the provisions of the Sixth Schedule as amended from time to time and of the 73rd Amendment of the Constitution, makes it visibly clear that while the Demacles's sword of the State power is moving closer and closer to the ADCs, a liberalisation process has been set in motion in respect of the Panchayati Raj Institutions (PRIs). A comparative study of the Sixth Schedule and the 73rd Amendment of the Constitution has become necessary for certain reasons. Compared to the PRIs, the Autonomous District Councils have few development and welfare functions and those are of lower order. If the PRIs under the Amendment Act are not introduced in the Sixth Schedule areas, these areas will enjoy less power of self-government (in development aspect) than the rest of the country.

On the other side, Panchayati bodies with powers exerciseable on matters listed in the eleventh Schedule as ancillary to the 73rd Amendment Act are introduced in Sixth Schedule areas, these may create political foul whether by arrangement with the respective State Governments. If these powers are also taken away from them, they are left with regulatory functions only. They will have no way out to recoursing to inflammatory politics with narrow focus so as to be able to maintain their influence. Again, when all the provisions of the 73rd Amendment about the powers, scope of function and financial support for the exercise of the powers and discharge of the responsibilities by the PRIs are compared with those attached to the Autonomous District Councils under the Sixth Schedule, it is found that while the ADCs have several regulatory powers subject to State Government control, the PRIs are in a more advantageous position in respect of developmental functions. In fact, in the matter of exercise of developmental functions, the ADCs are at the pity of the State Governments. For example, in the recent meeting of the team from Meghalaya, which consisted of the CEMs, EMs, and other members of the ADCs alongwith the Union Minister and Deputy Chairman, Planning Commission, they appraised him of the need of ADCs of the state for direct funding from the Centre and enhancement of funds.

The result of this meeting was the sanction of Rs. 3 crore for the three ADCs in Meghalaya (one crore each). What is interesting to note is that this amount would be channelised through the State Government, which implies that the latter has an overall financial control over the former. The Eleventh Schedule of the Constitution on the other hand, ensures that a large number of development functions come within the functional jurisdiction of the Panchayati bodies. For instance, whereas the ADC may establish conduct of manage primary schools, the functional jurisdiction of PRIs cover even secondary schools, (incidentally, the management of all the primary schools in Meghalaya has been taken over now by the State Government on the failure of the ADCs to handle the same).

Similarly, whereas the ADCs may have dispensaries established by them, hospitals and primary health centres come within the purview of the PRIs. In the tribal predominant States, the ADCs are facing problems of a different order. In Meghalaya, there are three Autonomous District Councils, called the Khasi Autonomous District Council, the Jaintia Hills Autonomous District Council and the Garo Hills Autonomous District Council. These ADCs cover all the districts of the State. When Meghalaya was created as a separate State, over-riding power was given to legislation enacted by the State over the issues included in the jurisdiction of the ADCs by an amendment of the Sixth Schedule and an insertion of paragraph 12 A in the Sixth Schedule. This paragraph states very clearly that if the State Government and the District Councils enact laws on the same subject, the legislation or laws of the State Government shall prevail over those of the District Councils.

This paragraph lays down the over-riding autohority of a law made by the State Legislature over a similar law made by the District Councils in Meghalaya in case of the question of repugnancy arises. The paragraph writes that in case any provision of a law made by the District Council "is repugnant to any provision of a law made by the Legislature of the State of Meghalaya with respect to that matter, then, the law or regulation made by the District Council . . . shall to the extent of the repugnancy, be void and law made by the Legislature of the State of Meghalaya shall prevail." This paragraph has also agitated the minds and thoughts of the leaders of the Regional Political Parties in Meghalaya. It has found its place in the manifestoes of these political parties from time to time, where they have reiterated all along the immediate need to delete what they call the "discriminatory" Paragraph 12 A of the Sixth Schedule. The main complain is that this paragraph authorises the laws of the State Government to over-ride the laws passed by the ADCs even in matters allotted to the District Councils by the Constitution.' Mr. S.K. Dutta the former Chief Justice of the Gauhati State Court and the Chairman of the Commission of Inquiry on Autonomous Districts Administration in the State of Meghalaya, in his report on this vexed issue said, " . . . the status of the District Councils in Meghalaya has been reduced more or less to that of a Municipal Board by the insertion of Paragraph 12A in the Sixth Schedule . . . The District Council, therefore, can function only if it maintains harmonious relationship with the State Government."

Alongwith having a close comparative analysis of the role, powers and functions between the ADCs under the Sixth Schedule and the Panchayati Raj institutions as envisaged by the 73rd Amendment, we in Meghalaya have possibly to discover suitable adjustment which would fit the traditional socio-political institutions like the Syiemships, Doloiships, Nokmaships and the *Durbars* (Councils) in the whole scheme. As per the Sixth Schedule, the offices of *Syiem, Doloi,* and *Nokma,* in Khasi, Jaintia and Garo Hills respectively are treated as subordinate officials of the ADCs. Most of their old power and functions have either been curtailed or taken away by the ADCs. Under the provisions of Paragraph 3(i)(g) of the Sixth Schedule, the District Council can regulate the appointment and succession of PRIs chiefs and headmen. The United Khasi-Jaintia Hills Autonomous District (Appointment and Succession of Chiefs and Headmen) Act 1959, and its later amendments made provisions for removal and suspension and even debarring the Chiefs, deputy chiefs and acting chiefs from participating in politics and elections either to the Parliament, State Legislature and District Council by the Executive Committee of the District Council if in its opinion these incumbents over-rule the terms and conditions of their appointment. Armed with such constitutional powers, the District Council has, therefore, put under it a complete control over the traditional institutions. Therefore, under the new constitutional set up the traditional chiefs are pushed behind the line of leadership.

New 73rd Constitution Amendment Act has brought out more than anything else the extremely limited power of self-government conferred on the Sixth Schedule. The Sixth Schedule is a long history of tribal struggle for identity efforts. It cannot be easily dispensed with, without causing serious doubt about the intention of Indian State. The whole issue of inter-articulation of the institutional arrangements and functional range under the Sixth Schedule and the 73rd Amendment Act will have to be carefully examined and a substantially altered Sixth Schedule by synthesising the positive thrust of both will have to be included.

The Seventy Third Amendment of 1992 and the State of Meghalaya

New Panchayati Raj Act, legally called the Constitution (Seventy-third Amendment) Act, 1992 was passed with near unanimity by Parliament in December 1992. After its ratification by 17 State Assemblies, it has emerged as the Constitution (Seventy-third Amendment) Act 1992 and came into force from April 1993.

Special features of the Panchayati Raj Act are:

(a) The Gram Sabha will be a body comprising of all the adult members registered as voters in the Panchayat area. There shall be a three-tier system of Panchayat at the village, intermediate and district level. Smaller States with populations below 20 lakh will have the option not to have the intermediate level Panchayat.

(b) Seats in Panchayats at all three levels shall be filled by direct election. In addition, Chairpersons of village Panchayats can be made members of the Panchayats at intermediate level and Chairpersons of Panchayats at the intermediate level can be members of the Panchayat at the district level. MPs, MLAs and MLCs could also be members of Panchayats at the intermediate or the district level.

(c) In all the Panchayats, seats would be reserved for Scheduled Castes and Scheduled Tribes in proportion to their population. One-third of the total number of seats will be reserved for women. One-third of the seats reserved for Scheduled Castes and Scheduled Tribes will also be reserved for women.

(d) Posts of the Chairpersons of the Panchayat at all levels, shall be reserved for Scheduled Tribes in proportion to their population in the State. One-third of the posts of Chairpersons of Panchayats at all levels shall also be reserved for women. It shall be open to the Legislature of the State to provide reservation of seats and posts of Chairpersons in Panchayats for backward class of citizens.

It has also been said that every Panchayat shall have a uniform five years term and elections to constitute new bodies shall be completed before the expiry of the term. In the event of dissolution, elections will be compulsorily held within six months. The reconstituted, i.e., new Panchayat will serve for the remaining period the five year term. It will not be possible to dissolve the existing Panchayats by amendment of any Act, before the expiry of its period. The Panchayats existing on 24th April 1993 will be allowed to complete their full term, except when they are dissolved by the House with a resolution.

It also states that a person who is disqualified under any law for elections to the Legislature of the State or under any law of the State, will not be entitled to become a member of the Panchayat.

It is included that an independent Election Commission will be established in the State for superintendence, direction and control of the electoral process and preparation of electoral rolls.

This Act also indicate a set of items in the Eleventh Schedule of the Constitution which may be entrusted to the Panchayats. This is in addition to any schemes for economic development and social justice that may also be entrusted to these by the State Governments. For the implementation of development schemes, the main responsibility will be entrusted to the Panchayat.

The Act says that the Panchayat will receive adequate funds for carrying out their functions. Grants from the State Government will constitute an important source of funding but State Governments are also expected to saction the revenue of certain taxes to the Panchayat. In some cases, the Panchayat will also be permitted to collect and retain the revenue it raises.

"In each State, a Finance Commission will be established within one year, and then after every five years, to review the financial position of the Panchayats; to make suitable recommendations to the State on the distribution of funds between the State and the Panchayats at every level."

For the purpose of social justice, the 73rd Constitutional Amendment Act, 1992, provides for reservation for women, Scheduled Castes and Scheduled Tribes. In the 500,000 Panchayats with three million members about a million women will get elected to these Panchayats and about half a million representatives will be from socially handicapped and disadvantaged people. Even if they commit mistakes in initial years, they would learn a good deal and would be careful in future. Once they are elected to the decision-making centres they will demand a particular type of development which will be beneficial to the disadvantaged people.

At least 5,000 good grass-root level leaders in the countryside were expected to emerge, knowing local problems of poverty, social exploitation and will function with thc control and supervision of the local people who elected them for a term.

The PRIs at different layers after initial years of mistakes and blunders were expected to revolutionise the rural sectors of our society particularly in the field of education, literacy, agriculture, forestry, horticulture, health and family welfare, housing and co-operative farming and marketing.

It was said that "There will be quiet development of what is known as peoples' power which can bring about changes in institutions and social situation in which a wrong is resisted and existing state of things is changed.

The Law is a charter for empowerment of women. The Constitutional (73rd Amendment) Act provides that not less than one-third of the total number of seats for the offices of the chairpersons at each level, would be reserved for women. This was an effective method to ensure women's position as the head of the institution at every level. This may not immediately any social change in the face of attitudinal, social and structural limits. But at least it will certainly ensure the women of the villages with the release of their potentialities and political contributions in a massive way to the total development of the community. The National Perspective Plan for Women (NPPW 1988) i.e., promised that 30 per cent of executive head positions from the village to district level in all statutory institutions should be reserved for women. The Constitution (73rd Amendment) Act for PRIs under its Article 243M states that the Act in its present form will not apply to (a), (b) the States of Nagaland, Meghalaya and Mizoram, (c) the hills areas in the State of Manipur for which District Councils are there.

However, the Act provides that the Amendment may apply to Nagaland, Meghalaya and Mizoram provided that the State Legislative Assembly of the State concerned appears a resolution to the effect by a majority of total membership of that house and by a majority of not less than two-thirds of the members of that house present and voting. We find similar provisions for urban areas under the 74th Amendment of the Constitution. The Article also may by law extend the provisions of the Amendment to the Scheduled Areas and Tribal Areas subject to certain such modifications and exception as may be specified in such law.

The Sixth Schedule of the Indian Constitution

After independence, the Constitution of India provided for protection of the interests of the tribal peoples of the hills of north-eastern India, including their interest in land and forest resources and granted them autonomy in social and political development. The Sixth Schedule of the Constitution provided the legal framework for this protection. In pursuance of this objective, autonomous district councils were established in the North Cachar and Mikir Hills (now known as Karbi Anglong), Lushai Hills (present-day Mizoram) and in the United Khasi and Jaintia Hills districts and in the Garo Hills. Then the Jaintia Hills District Autonomous Council was set up. All the tribal chiefs and headmen were placed under the jurisdiction of this autonomous district council. The appointment and succession of the chairs, chiefs and headmen was wholly regulated by the district council. On 1 October 1964, this council was bifurcated into two autonomous district councils called, the Khasi Hills Autonomous District Council and the Jaintia Hills Autonomous District Council. All the seven districts of Meghalaya were covered by three autonomous district councils. With the setting up of district council, the traditional arrangement of local self-government became complex, with overlapping jurisdiction. There were in every district councils twenty-nine members elected on the basis of universal adult suffrage and one member nominated by the Governor of Meghalaya. There was a chairperson and a Deputy Chairperson in every district council, who held a position similar to Speaker and Deputy Speaker of the Legislative Assembly.

The District Council was administered by an Executive Council led by the Chief Executive Member and two Executive Members. The tenure of the district council was normally five years but elections were not regularly held. This had eroded its authority. While the society was matrilineal and despite the existence of adult franchise, female representation in local self-government institutions was dismal. In the early 1950s there was just one nominated woman member in the Shillong municipality, which was outside the jurisdiction of the district council.

The Shillong Municipality had its first elected woman member only in the year 1966, while in 1971 the first elected lady Chairperson was appointed. There was the solitary instance of a female Executive Member, Estrice Syiem, in the Khasi Hills Autonomous District Council during 1977-78 but her term lasted only for five months. The Sixth Schedule empowered the autonomous district councils of Meghalaya to make laws and regulations on all subjects relating to the customs, traditions and practices of the tribal people, land tenure systems, water courses, forest and forest management except reserved forests, marriage, divorce, inheritance, appointments and succession of the chiefs and headmen. It also provided a mechanism for prevention of economic exploitation by non-tribals.

The District Councils enjoyed the power to regulate money-lending and trading by the non-tribals. The councils were also empowered to make laws relating to the setting up of town committees and village committee for local administration including the village or town police. All such laws were, however, subject to the consent of the Governor of the State. The autonomous district councils had the powers to assess and collect land revenue, impose taxes on certain professions, trades and employment, animals, vehicles, boats, ferries, entry of goods into a market for sale, and so on, and fees for the purpose of prospecting or extraction of minerals under leases sanctioned by the State Government. They could establish primary schools, dispensaries, markets, cattle pounds, ferries, fisheries, roads, provide road transportation and, subject to the jurisdiction of the Gauhati High Court, exercise certain judicial powers both civil and criminal.

Over and above the aforementioned sources of money, the autonomous district councils received financial help from the Union Government through the State Government besides grants-in-aid from the latter, part of the state taxes and grants for hill development schemes and forest protection schemes.

In this way, the Sixth Schedule provided a compact mechanism for self-government in the tribal state of Meghalaya, safeguarding the traditional customs, rights and practices of the tribal people and preserving their own unique and distinct culture and identity. It gave them an instrument to bring a limited change within a static framework.

This mechanism underwent many changes after 1952 through constitutional amendments, Presidential ordinances and isolations. In 1969, the Sixth Schedule was amended in order to empower the State Government to entrust the autonomous district council with functions relating to subjects like agriculture, animal husbandry, community development projects, cooperative societies, social welfare, village planning, or any matter within the executive power of the State Government.

While the District Councils had powers to make laws for land reforms and land development, they had not taken any steps in these areas. They failed to inject dynamism for social change. The State legislature was empowered to make laws even on those subjects relating to land which had been allotted to the District Councils and the State laws prevailed over the laws of the said District Councils.

The District Council could thus not be said to have been conceived as an organisation for promoting participatory process for formation and execution of socio-economic development plans. It was meant only to provide autonomy to the districts, which were inhabited by fairly homogeneous tribal groups, in social and cultural spheres and matters about tribals' everyday life. In course of time it lost its earlier administrative initiative in matters of social transformation. The State Government had in reality taken over from the District Councils the responsibility for primary education.

Over the last four decades, there was a constant friction between them and the Government of Meghalaya in various spheres. For instance, although the District Councils controlled 95 per cent of the forest area of the State, the central fund for afforestation and forest management was routed via State Government. Inadequacy of financial resources and administrative expertise were other major constraints in the proper functioning of the District Councils. The revenue gathered by them and the grants-in-aid from the State Government were too meagre even to cover their administrative costs. It was also necessary for them to evolve an infrastructure for bringing about social and economic changes in their areas. The traditional tribal land relations were giving way to emerging private property and the peasant economy was getting importance in place of a vanishing *jhum* or shifting cultivation. The local self-government structure in Meghalaya, of which the District Council is the key constituent, needed to be adjusted accordingly in order to maintain the new social balance. An interesting aspect of the working of the District Councils was the effect inter-party rivalries made on their relationship with the State Government, on the one hand, and the traditional tribal chiefs, on the other. In the event of there being separate political parties at the helm at the State and District Council level, the two were often engaged in a tug-of-war and would use the tribal chiefs like their pawns.

The undesirable consequences of this antagonistic bilateral relationship between the two top tiers for the functioning of the institutional mechanism as whole should have been taken care of for a smooth functioning of the entire set up.

Again, the provisions of Sixth Schedule to the Constitution have evolved a separate scheme for the administration of the tribal areas of the composite State of Assam which included the present-day Meghalaya and Mizoram and to which regions were added. Nagaland rejected the scheme from the very beginning and it evolved its own system of functional village councils for local development works. About the composite State of Assam, the scheme provided for institutions of Autonomous District Councils and Regional Councils. Assam has two autonomous district councils at present. There is a qualitative difference among the tribal situation in Autonomous District Council areas in the North-East India and the Panchayati Raj Institutions in the rest of the country. The Autonomous District Council areas are almost located on international borders or nearby like North Cachar Hills of Assam. The socio-political milieu in the Sixth Schedule regions particularly of

Meghalaya in North-East India is entirely different from the rest of the country.

The historical background of the district council areas of Meghalaya, the physical arrangements, functioning and operations have very little semblance with those of Panchayati Raj institutional areas as envisaged under 73rd and 74th Constitutional Amendment areas. The provisions of the 73rd Amendment Act 1993 are wholesome and should be extended to Meghalaya under the enabling provisions of Article 243 M [4(a) & (b)]. A number of tribal societies under Autonomous District Council Areas have their own customary laws, traditional practices, community ethos, political and administrative systems which may go against the provisions under 73rd Constitutional Amendment Act 1992. Their present day predicament of exploitation, deprivation and marginalisation have to be kept in mind and the task of blending on traditional and the Panchayati Raj superstructure is indeed challenging one.

To conclude, the provisions of the 73rd Amendment Act 1992 should be considered as a broad and powerful over-arching frame serving as the fountain head and an essential vehicle for democratisation of tribal society with a tradition of quasi-feudal social set up in rural economy of Meghalaya. The design and content of the Sixth Schedule have failed to inspire the progress of democratisation of society. The near 57 years of operations of Sixth Schedule, although in its initial years promised much to bringing about social changes in Meghalaya, failed miserably in later years. This is primarily because of feebleness of emerging middle class in the tribal social set up. The middle class and the tribal semi-feudal social and economic milieu are antithesis to each other. The clan and tribal chiefs proved to be still quite strong and have asserted themselves in the Autonomous District Council arena during the last two decades. The field operation of the provisions of the Sixth Schedule resulted in evolving an identity syndrome which decelerated the process in social and economic activities in bringing significant changes at the grass root levels. The rural economy is still as backward with declining agricultural productivity as before. This is due to lack of equal access to the basic resources—those of land and forest, the prime assets of the society.

The Sixth Schedule has completely failed as an instrument of self-management and social and economic changes in the rural sectors in Meghalaya. The Eleventh Schedule (under Article 243 G) under the 73rd Amendment of the Constitution promises more democratic way of land and community asset management for a better rural society of economic viability. It provides for empowerment of the socially vulnerable groups and more particularly women. The eighties India has witnessed the process of a significant action in women's development strategy. The National Perspective Plan for Women (1988) is a living testimony of such shift in strategy for women's empowerment and their development. The 73rd Constitutional Amendment Act is an enabling mechanism for bringing women in the national development process in democratising rural set up by raising women's status on an equal footing with that of men. The matriliny in Khasi-Pnar-Garo set up could not protect women's equal right in the polity. Panchayati Raj Institution promises equal status to women in Meghalaya like other states where the laws are applicable and also functional.

References

1. Health for the Millions, *Panchayati Raj*, Vol. I, No. 4, August 1993, Health for the Millions Trust, New Delhi.
2. Datta Ray, B., *Status of Panchayati Raj in the States of India*, 1994, Concept, New Delhi, 1994, Chapter on Meghalaya.

10

Principal Deities of the State

People of Manipur wherever they are have been and are God-fearing people. The form of worship and the concept of God, however, differ from tribe to tribe and clan to clan. In the early days the Manipuris worshipped their forefathers who were considered as Gods, or incarnations of Gods. That old tradition of ancestor-worship continues even upto this day. Each of the clans mentioned earlier had their own special place of worship where the image of their deities were installed. The Manipuri civilisation could not be thought of without its inseparable relation to the form of worship which prevailed from ancient days.

Main Goddesses

Mention may be made of the leading deities who are considered to be living in all their spiritual glory upto this day. They have, on the one hand, helped and guided the masses of Manipur in their struggle to survive the onslaughts from external sources, and on the other, to develop a distinct and glorious branch of human civilisation over the years. The principal goddesses are Koubru, reigning in the North-West, Loiyarakpa, reigning in the West, Thangjing in the south-west Wangbren in the South, Marjing in the East and Chinkheiningthou in the North-East region.

These deities are considered to be the defenders of the principal outskirts of Manipur. Whenever people offer any worship, these deities are remembered and proper homage paid. The king used to offer regular worship to these principal deities ruling his country. The impact of the efficacy of their worship is such, even now, that after every Manipuri wedding, as a consumation of the marriage ceremony, sweetmeats and varieties of seasonal fruits are invariably offered towards the direction of these deities, in order to invoke their blessings for the just married couple. Over and above these deities, there are several other local deities. worshipped by several group of families, big and small. These deities are called Umang Lais, which literally mean Jungle Gods. Umang means Jungle, Lai means God.

This does not, however, indicate that the Gods belong to the jungles. What correctly this title implies is that the place of worship of these Gods are in reserved areas, near or inside the localities. The temples are surrounded usually by a rich growth of trees those look like a miniature forest. The areas reserved for the temple and its surroundings are usually spacious. The reason is that people of the locality, in their large numbers, used to gather close to the deity during the annual festivities, known as "Lai Haraoba". The subject of the festivities is being discussed elsewhere in broad details thus need not be mentioned in this chapter. Special mention may be made of the following important deities over and above those previously mentioned.

(i) Lainingthou Khoriphaba
(ii) Konthoujam Lairembi
(iii) Khamlangba
(iv) Ibudhou Panganba
(v) Heisnam Panthoibi
(vi) Lai Ishing Chaiba
(vii) Thongak Lairembi
(viii) Lai Khurembi.

Old Manipuri Religion

Also important are the local deities that are considered to be ruling over the families of Huidrom Oinam, Mayengbam, Wahengbam, Kangabam, Leishangthem, Yumnam and others. The biggest purpose of our reference to these deities and to the form of their worship is to find their agreement or disagreement with the Vedic concept of God. As has been said earlier, upto the entry of the Hindu cult into the Manipuri valley, the entire population was absorbed in their traditional form of worship and faith of God. They owe so much to their deities and their religious disciplines, for what they have been also are upto this day.

It will not, therefore, be out of place to go a little deeper into the philosophic and theological contents of the traditional Manipuri religion while comparing it with the principles of Hindu Philosophy and Theology, as expressed in the various sects of Hinduism. The Manipuris believe in the theory of incarnation. They also think that the highest God is eternal and also powerful. Whenever they sing the glory of their deities, the main contents are that God is immortal, omnipresent, all powerful and omniscient. The history of certain local deities are that they were men with divine attainments and therefore, the men of God. By worshipping their spirit after their death, the people get the satisfaction of worshipping God, through his human representative, thus the belief in the principle of incarnation of God as man finds expression in the worship of the local deities.

Each deity has his, or her background. At the time of the annual festivities which are performed with due dignity and solemnity and with great pomp and grandeur, the priests sing the deities, legendary glories of the past. The people, by listening to the glories of the deities and their divine exploits, derive tremendous spiritual satisfaction and imbibe the greatness of their famous gods.

Pakhangba and Sanamahi

Besides the deities mentioned earlier, there are two deities who receive special place in the heart of the entire population, in all the clans and localities. They are

Pakhangba, the governing deity of the king, and Sanamahi, the ruling deity in every household. The philosophy pertaining to the concept of these two deities, and the legends attached to them, describes the basic religious attitude of the Manipuris and the basic concept of God in the Manipuri traditional system of faith. The story runs as follows:

"Sanamahi and Pakhangba are the sons of Guru Sidaba and Laimaren Sidabi. Guru Sidaba and Laimaren Sidabi stand for the eternal Godhead and his divine consort respectively. The two brothers possessed divine attainments. When both of them were grown up, Guru Sidaba expressed his desire to retire from his throne. As it was difficult to make a choice between the two equally grown up and qualified sons, Guru Sidaba prescribed the condition that the one who will be able to return earlier after making a round of the whole universe, will succeed his throne. Sanamahi, the elder of the two brothers, was of superior will and better qualified for the feat prescribed by his father. Without the least hesitation he started the pilgrimage, as directed by his father, in full confidence and hope that he will be able to complete the round earlier than his younger brother, who was physically weaker than he. After he had set out on the journey, the younger brother, Pakhangba wept before his mother, in frustration and despair, for his physical weakness and inability to compete with his elder brother. Laimaren Sidabi, his divine mother had compassion with him and told him that there was still time for him to get the prize before the arrival of his elder brother. Pakhangba was considerably consoled and pleaded with his mother for the much needed secret of achieving the feat ahead of his brother. Laimaren Sidabi disclosed the secret to Pakhangba by telling that making a round of the throne seven times would amount to making a round of the whole universe. Pakhangba realised the implication of his mother's advice and made seven rounds of the throne and claimed it from his father, Guru Sidaba. Guru Sidaba knew that the secret must have been told by his divine consort to her younger son and that trouble was in the offing. He, therefore, gave up the throne in favour of his younger son. When Sanamahi returned after completing his round of the universe with all enthusiasm and pride for his feat, he saw, to his utter surprise and dismay, that his younger brother was sitting on the throne of his father with pride and confidence. He found out, after an altercation with his mother, that the secret was revealed by her to his younger brother who now holds the throne in his full right and according to the accepted tradition. The wrath of Sanamahi ran high and he was seen in his most destructive disposition. Guru Sidaba, the divine father, who had just retired from his throne, had to come down to console and soften his enraged son, Sanamahi. Guru Sidaba praised the matchless strength and virtues of his eldest son pursuaded him to reign in every household as the ruling deity, while his brother might be allowed to reign as the ruling deity of every king that might come afterwards."

Custom in Manipur so far is that every ruling dynasty worships Pakhangba as their family deity while every household in Manipur among the Meiteis worships

Sanamahi as its family deity by keeping the South-Western corner of the house for the place of worship of Sanamahi and the Northern portion for Laimaren Sidabi, the mother of Sanamahi.

Conformity with Bhagavat Gita Epic

From these facts, we can draw the conclusion that even before they embraced Hinduism, the Manipuris profoundly believed in the Supreme being who eternally rules in heaven and comes down on earth, at intervals, in human form, to lead and help mankind to attain the highest virtues and glories mundane as well as extra-mundane. Wherever these deities are worshipped and whatever are their names, they uniformly conform to the basic fact and the differences in the way of their exploits and their names and places of birth only confirm the theory of incarnation accepted by the people exactly in the spirit carried in the message of Srimad Bhagvat Gita.

No Difference between Traditional and Hindu Religion

The author is very much constrained to call these ruling deities of the Manipuris as eternally living and also afficacious. We have made reference to the period of transition from the traditional religion to Hindu Vaishnavism during the reign of King Maharaja Garibniwaz. The priest, who came down to the valley of Manipur from remote corners of Bengal, with the message of Lord Cheitanya Mahaprabhu, founder of the Vaishnavic movement within Bengal, had to encounter Himalayan obstacles in driving home the message to the minds of the Manipuris. It was only the natural that they decided to begin with the ruler so that they might preach the cult with the royal power as their sword and shield. The episode has been described and discussed in broad detail elsewhere in this book.

The deities in all their glories continued to reign in the hearts of Manipuris. Now the question is whether the Manipuri Hindus are putting forth double standards in their spiritual life or not? The issue is both pertinent and valid. To be able to make a correct reply to this question we have to understand the basic agreements and disagreements between the two faiths. Besides the difference in language and in the places of occurrance one may fail to trace any basic difference between the Hindu faith and the Manipuri traditional faith. This must be the leading reason why a Manipuri has become a Hindu, and a devout one at that, while he continues to be his own-self with all his reverence for and faith in his great spiritual traditions and form of worship.

In a way the situation could be characterised as a meeting of two apparently different personalities to establish a harmonious and complete individuality for the feeling and fulfilment of the high spiritual principle. The Manipuri tradition found its chance to set itself against a bigger canvass to evaluate itself in the community of religions in the world when it came across the Hindu current of thought. While the Hindu current of thought had its own opportunity to prove its commodiousness and catholicity when it encountered at the soil of Manipur with a deep and determined resistance from the local tradition.

The Manipuri Hindu society is a clear manifestation of Hinduism at the social level in its glorious trust and realisation of the old Manipuri traditions, its rightful place in the broad canvass of universal faith. Coming again to the local deities, it will be educative and interesting to narrate here a few external incidents of the history of Manipur which may be ascribed to the powerful influence of the presence of the said deities. The main deity of the Moirang dynasty is Lord Thangjing. The whole region and history of Moirang is woven round the divine power of this diety. To a citizen of Moirang, even presently, Lord Thangjing is a reality and a living God in the true sense of the term. The story of Khamba and Thoibi, the divine lovers of Moirang is today more than a legend. The whole story looks like a garland made on the thread of unshakable beliefs, deep faith and loyalty to their deity, Lord Thangjing.

This story is full of mysterious and miraculous events, the reality of which could only be explained in relation to the divine power of the ruling deity staging and directing the whole drama for the utility of the future generations. It cannot be wholly untrue. This has been handed down from generation to generation, as a source of inspiration to the downtrodden and for those who are made to suffer and sacrifice for the achievement of the highest ideal life. The temple of Lord Thangjing stands on the bank of the famous Loktak lake near the newly constructed town of Moirang. Over and above its being a place of regular pilgrimage for every Manipuri, it is also a tourist attraction. Any tourist who goes to enjoy the good looking scenery of Loktak must also visit the temple either for historical information, or for spiritual blessings, or for both.

Mention has been made elsewhere that the contribution of Moirang to the folk culture and society of Manipur has no parallel. Although there is difference of opinion among scholars, here and there, about the degree of contribution made to the composite culture of Manipur from the different small kingdoms, there can be no two opinons about the supremacy of Moirang in the field of development of folk art and the indigenous games like Mukna, Khongkangjei and Kang. Great nature and importance of these games have been discussed elsewhere in this book.

Koubru the First Settler

Famous deity of Koubru, who is worshipped mostly by the group of villagers on the northern side of the Manipur valley, is considered to be the founder of the Manipuri civilisation. While his glory is sung, prominent mention is made of his contribution as the first settler, and the literal translation of the prayer to him runs as below:

"O Supreme Lord of the Northern World, Lord Koubru, thou are the first settler as a servant of God. Give us thy blessings."

Again in the southern part of the Manipur valley, Wangbren is the supreme deity. There are many interesting stories about his living impact and effect on the population of the southern part.

There is a story about a British Engineer, who held the position of a

State Engineer during the early British days in Manipur. He took a number of Gurkha Jawans belonging to the 4th Assam Rifles to cut down pine trees from the compounds reserved for Lord Wangbren. It is said that the local population dissuaded the Saheb not to cut down the trees in the said compound without first offering due homage to the deity and also without getting the communication regarding his sanction. Not heeding to the warning given by the local population the Gurkha Jawans started cutting down a few trees. The result was that many of them expired due to some unknown causes. Whether it was a matter of accidental coincidence or not, will be a matter of further research from all angles, scientific as well as spiritual. But the said incident did take place and the State Engineer had to reconsider his step. From his point of view it was essential that the trees must be cut down at any cost and the jungle cleared for a varieties of causes.

However, before he ordered further felling of the trees in the compound, he stood before the deity with folded hands and prayed as below:

"Lord Wangbren, I know the jungle and all trees are your property, but I need them for the welfare of the State and your people. Allow me to cut them down. Stop punishing my men and I promise you that for every tree cut down, I will plant two seedlings so that you will get back your family of trees in due course of time."

Following this prayer, he ordered the Gurkha Jawans to start felling the trees again. As the story has it, the jungle was cleared quickly without any more deaths of the Jawans. For fulfilment of his promise, the State Engineer planted two seedlings in place of each of the trees felled down. Today we see there trees in their full growth and the jungle has again its density and dignity. We hear of other similar stories about the unfailing effect of the power of this deity not only in the southern part of the valley, but through out its length and breadth. The deity is thought to be ruling over the entire rivers and water portions of the lake.

Whenever, cases of drowning take place in the valley of Manipur in large numbers, the people worship Wangbren as per the traditional rites in the belief that there may be no further death in water. Whenever, abnormal signs are seen in the currents of the rivers, particularly, during the flood season, the people proficiate Wangbren and seek his blessings to save them from drowning and other accidents that may happen in water. Many present scholars compare him against the Hindu God, Varuna, who rules over water according to the Hindu traditions.

Cremation of Dead Body was Prevalent

In similar amount of respect and faith Manipuris hold other deities also. We need not mention here in detail these numberless stories, but an episode pertaining to the life of one of the deities called Konthoujam Lairembi deserves special reference here because it gives a clue to a very controversial issue, namely, whether the Manipuris burnt their dead-bodies before they embraced Hinduism or not. The story has it that a beautiful damsel of the Konthoujam family was married to Lord Soraren, the Manipuri counterpart of Indra in the ancient days.

After many years of happy conjugal life in the divine kingdom, one day Konthoujam Lairembi saw the likeness of a cremation, from which smoke came up in visible quantity, thereby causing an apprehension in her mind that somebody related to her must have died. She complained to her Lord that he had betrayed her by not stopping human mortality in her land, while he had promised her that there would be no further deaths in her family. The Lord consoled her that actually nobody had died in her family and what she had seen was not of course, the cremation of a dead man, but something else, adding that it was not becoming of her to entertain such an apprehension. Lairembi, however, refused to be consoled and insisted on her going home to find out the truth. The Lord had to be given in before the persuasion of his consort who enjoyed his unreserved affection and indulgence. On reaching home, however, the Lairembi found out that it was only a plot enacted by her relatives and friends only to attract her attention and thereby to call her down in their midst for a happy reunion. She repented for her failure to rely on the wisdom of her Lord and asked her parents as well as relatives for their permission for her return to her Lord. They insisted that she should return after partaking their usual food and drink which she had forgotten owing to her long absence from her paternal home. She pleaded that she was prohibited by her Lord to take any food or drink in her paternal home and he might not allow her to return to his residence if he came to know of the fact. But inspite of her resistance, the affection and persuasion of her people prevailed upon her. Under cover of a cloth spread over her head, she took away the drink and the items of food offered to her, in the belief that her Lord would not see. But the Lord saw everything from above and sent his message immediately that she was banned from coming back to his abode again. She spent the rest of her life in the midst of her relatives in repentence and ceaseless worship of her Lord.

Nevertheless during her lifetime she kept on to be a representative of the Lord in heaven among her people and after her death she was the sole object of worship by her people who did not repent having cheated her in the said manner, as they thought that it was the will of God that was behind the very plot and by virtue of such a plot God sent his beloved consort to bring solace to the people and offer the much needed spiritual umbrella. Now, there is a spacious jungle standing in the middle of the Kinothujam village with all its dignity signalling the immortal presence of the spirit of the Lairembi as a ruling deity of the whole area. The census data with latest figures about the religions of the scheduled tribes is given on next page.

Table 1
Religion for Scheduled Tribes

Scheduled Tribe	*Rural*			*Urban*		
	Total	*Males*	*Females*	*Total*	*Males*	*Females*
1	*2*	*3*	*4*	*5*	*6*	*7*
ALL SCHEDULED TRIBES						
All Religions	**5,78,930**	**2,95,691**	**2,83,239**	**53,243**	**27,029**	**26,214**
1. Buddhists	54	32	22	0	0	0
2. Christians	5,70,901	2,91,489	2,79,412	46,936	23,802	23,134
3. Hindus	1,085	677	408	1,574	821	753
4. Jains	11	7	4	0	0	0
5. Muslims	323	149	174	47	32	15
6. Sikhs	41	27	14	20	6	14
7. Other Religions and Persuations	6,514	3,310	3,204	4,666	2,368	2,298
8. Religion not stated	1	0	1	0	0	0

Source: Census 1991.

11

Popular Manipuri Dances

Each person or a place has something special which makes it different from others. Therefore, whenever we introduce a person or a place or even an article to a stranger, we mention the most outstanding quality of the place or the most popular aspect of the place or person or article to be introduced. Manipur today can be best introduced through her Dances. Her handloom and other aspects follow afterwards. The dances of Manipur are part and parcel of Manipuri culture, possessing a distinct individuality which was built up during the course of several centuries and carries the stamps of contribution from small kingdoms, which formed the basis of the present Manipur, prior to its consolidation under a powerful supreme ruler and benevolent patron in the person of Rajarshi Bhagya Chandra, in the beginning of the 18th Century.

History and Evolution of Manipuri Dances

The background of the development of Manipuri dances and music may be divided into two parts. The first part will cover the period preceding the entry of Hindu cult inside Manipur while the second will cover the Hindu period. Each of the two aspects has its own importance and glory. Before we start to discuss their details it has to be observed that the first part being the formative period should be considered the more important of the two. The whole foundation of the classical Manipuri dance was laid and thus accomplished in the formative period while the developments in the second period were just like footnotes to the basic concepts formed and practised in the earlier period.

From the very beginning of the history of Manipur, dance, music and religion were inseparably interlinked. This is true of the hills people as much as of the plain people. Dance and music formed inevitable parts of religious festivals and the development of all dances and their musical aspect was thus through the religious festivals. Dancing for the sake of dancing was almost unknown to people. Dance performances were done before the deities of the people with great humility and submission for the pleasure of the deities. From this tradition arose same basic characters of all forms of dancing. They includes

(a) maintenance of the sanctity of the dancing arenas;

(b) avoidance of communication between the dancers and the audience by words or through gestures of the eyes or any part of the body;

(c) observance of strict submission and humility in front of the deities during the presentation of the dance;

(d) The dances are more of ritualistic character than for the pleasure and entertainment of the human eyes;

(e) Dancing as a profession for selected few did never got materialised;

(f) In the early days and even today some items of dance, inspite of their sophisticated developments in choreography and intricate talas, remain folk in character, in view of the truth that any body born a Manipuri is expected to be able to participate in its presentation with or without rehearsals.

Lai Haraoba Festival

The occasion of dances is the changing of seasons. The well known festival of "Lai Haraoba mostly performed between the spring and the rainy seasons is the most comprehensive feast for dancers. The term Lai Haraoba, literally as well as actually, means the festivity of Gods. The festival is performed with great pomp and grandeur in various localities during the said season, before the temples of deities, which have been in existence since ancient days carrying Manipuri names and worshipped in accordance with the old Manipuri traditions that existed before the entry of Hindu cult into Manipur. The tradition continues upto this day with more popular enthusiasm and inspite of the fact that they have came into the Hindu fold, with equal degree of orthodoxy and faith as any other sect of the Hindu community. It is for the philosophers and teachers of religion to ascertain if the Manipuri Hindus are practising double loyality to two different religions or not.

The fact, however, is that the continuance of his traditional worship of the early deities in the Lai Haraoba festivals in their daily life does not prick the conscience of an ordinary Manipuri. He finds a very profound harmony between the two cults and a fulfilment of his spiritual urge by discharging his duties towards his traditional deities and the supreme reality taught by Hinduism. There must be salient points of agreement between the two traditions.

Abovesaid "Lai Haraoba" formed important annual religious festivals of the small kingdoms. The kings and members of the royal family, the main members of the kings' court and the regional chiefs took active part in these festivals, alongwith the common people, not only as spectators and remote promoters but as true participants in the dance and other ritual performances.

One can realise the importance of these festivals as the breeding ground for the Manipuri dances. The story has it that kings danced alongwith their queens, unmarried princes with choicest of girls and princesses with youths of outstanding attainments as their partners. Similarly husbands and wives partnered, suitable matches of boys and girls made for duet presentations. There was the unfailing atmosphere of undeclared competition and rivalry for the best presentation, in respect of not only the dances but also of the dance custumes, which had to be donned strictly in accordance with existing traditions. Thus the society acted as one man in the promotion of a culture which was bound to be recognised as an asset for the entire human race. There are various kinds of dances presented in the course of a "Lai Haraoba". Presentation of solo or duet or even group dances, as separate items of the festival, covers the appearance of kings and queens, husbands and wives, boys and girls in an undeclared competition, as mentioned before. But the more essential part of Lai Haraoba is the enactment of the drama of the entire creation, in the open arena by the vast congeregation, through the medium of dances and singing. The part, full of dignity and solemnity, is a long process which covers almost the entire afternoon. Experts in the subject lead the procession to the arena and participants as well as the audience bother that their attention is not diverted from the rituals. There are many do's and don'ts to be observed strictly by all during this performance. Even a stranger cannot but admire the depth of the feeling of every body present during this episode. The meeting between God and Goddess, sowing of the human seed in the womb, birth of the child, entry of the child into manhood, struggle for the fulfilment of the material needs of mankind, the process of cultivation, weaving, house making and the various arts of discharging human obligations towards God and to his fellowmen are enacted, one by one, with meticulous care lest any mistake occurs.

The popular belief is that in case any mistake occurs, that will have far reaching results in the life of the society, the king and also the individual making such mistake. The prayers sung in the Lai Haraoba festivals are mostly for the welfare and prosperity of the ruler and the people of the land.

Cult of Maibis, i.e., Priests

The role of priests during this ritual is played by a team of Maibis. The Maibis are either men or women living a life dedicated to the practice of some extraordinary spiritual discipline as per the old tradition. They belong to a special cult, entry into which is decided by certain uncommon developments in the individual's mode of thinking and action. We hear of a local convention which guides whether a person has attained the requisite mental aptitude for entry into the cult of Maibis. Members of this cult, in their appearance in front of the deities or for any religious ritual, are to dress themselves like women and they are known only as Maibis whether they are men or women. The term, Maibi, is the female gender of the masculine term Maiba although in meaning they are not necessarily similar. The Maibis require intensive training under able Gurus. They are thought to have vision of the gods and goddesses whom they serve and are able to communicate their messages, during their trances, to the people.

The manner and occasion of these communications are of two kinds. One is the communication before a mass gathering like the Lai Haraoba and predicting the future of the society in general and of the individuals in particular. Sometimes the predictions come out quite true even to the last details of events like death, illness, accident, promotion etc., concerning individuals. If a Maibi suddenly goes into a trance in the process of a dance ritual, the process is stopped for the time being to listen to the utterances of the Maibi. The whole crowd observes pindrop silence and believe themselves as having established contact with the living deity through the medium of the Maibi. The rituals will be resumed after the trance will be over. Even upto this day such functions are not uncommon. Anybody who will have the patience to see the daily routine of a Lai Haraoba from morning till night will not miss such an occurrance.

Promotion of Sports and Atheletics

The Lai Haraoba festivals also have been instrumental for the promotion of sports and several athletic events. The ritual dances are invariably followed by sports and athletic activities in which most of the able bodied young men and women participate. The Manipuris loved games and sports during the old days. The old days' chronicles contain valuable accounts of the attainments of the early generations in this field. Some of the old games and sports continue to be exercised by the present sophisticated generation as important indigenous games. They are Polo, Khong Kangjei (Manipuri style of Hockey) Mukna (a kind of wrestling) and Kang (a game played over the mud floor of big outhouses), which consists of hitting targets fixed on the floor with *hard smooth oblong* shaped flat instruments, known as "kang". The tradition of this game is quite old and there is mention of it in the famous story of Khamba and Thoibi. This particular game is played strictly during the period between the Manipuri New Year's Day and the Rath Jatra Festival.

The popular belief is that the game has other effects on the minds of the people and if played beyond the said period evil consequences may follow. The dominant deity of the game is said to be "Panthoibi', the Manipuri counterpart of the Goddess Durga who rules over wars as destroyer of enemies.

Expansion of Vaisnavic Cult

Coming back to the main subject of this chapter, namely, the dances of Manipur, attention of the reader is drawn to an earlier reference to the contribution made through the generations who lived in the small kingdoms before the advent of the Hindu cult in Manipur. The character of the cultural *revolution* remains more or less the same even despite the transition to Hindu faith. It may, however, be observed that, during the few years of transition, the conditions must have been more or less full of confusion and chaos. Vaisnavic cult starting from Bengal was spread into Manipur through the hard work and sense of dedication as missionaries of a handful of religious teachers who hailed from Bengal.

The name of Santidas Goswami needs special mention. They had to encounter innumerable obstacles in spreading the Gospel of Lord Cheitanya to the people of Manipur, who were deeply plunged into their ancient traditions. The first and foremost difficulty was that of language. The Manipuri language has no affinity with Sanskrit or any Aryan group of languages. Communication of views/concepts between the teachers from Bengal and the disciples in Manipur would have been easier and more natural if either side was conversant with the other's language and social background. In such a case neither side could understand the other and there being no way out, the Goswami and his team began with the king in the hope that through the means of the power and influence of the king the gospel could reach the people. They succeeded in winning over Garibniwaz, the grand father of Rajarshi Bhagya Chandra as their highly effective and valuable convert.

We wish reader could believe that a cult like Lord Cheitanya's Vaisnavism was spread with an element of compulsion and that conversions took place almost at the point of a sharp sword? Many of the new converts accepted the new religion more for the fear of the king than for the love of its profound reality which could not be communicated to the people with success. The Goswamis who led the mission could not come upto the expectations of their office, on the one hand and the local population while on the other, could not feel that there was any spiritual vaccum which needed filling. The new teachers had to encourage the king to take measures which almost appeared like religious persecutions. As they could not teach things by their examples, they took shelter under the royal umbrella and made the succeeding kings their unfailing mouthpieces.

What followed then was a series of formalities and strict rules of orthodoxy. They did not encourage singing of religious songs and prayers in the local language. They brought with them the whole 'Vaisnab Padabali' of Bengal and taught the local singers to sing exactly in the Bengali fashion. The local writers and singers were almost prohibited by the supreme authority of the ruler to contribute to the new current. The result is that even upto this day in the royal temple of Sri Govindji, the use of Manipuri as a medium of religious songs and prayers remain strictly prohibited with the only exception that can be seen is that during the Doljatra festival, unofficial *holi* parties may sing in Manipuri language the holi music. This departure from the strict rules in this behalf was given effect to in the late twenties of this century when the then students of the Johnstone High School staged a protest against the language restrictions in the religious arena and sought the Maharajah's permission, to allow a students' Holi Party to sing the holi theme in their mother tongue. The king was said to have been happily surprised to know that the holi theme could be sung in Manipuri so naturally and effectively as in any other language. He thus kept this exception which further led to other exceptions, in the course of time, in respect of many unofficial holi-parties. There are two categories of holi parties which present themselves for singing in front of Sri Govindji. The one consists of those declared royal parties, during the performance of which the king might participate. There are quite a few such parties. The other category is of those coming voluntarily from all parts of the valley for such presentation. They are comparatively large in number.

Manipuri Language Ignored

The official or royal parties carry to abhor the mother tongue as a medium of religious songs and prayers. In fact the present generation is not to blame for this. This basic cause of the whole mistaken approach was the failure of the pioneers to realise that the new converts could be totally absorbed in the new faith only through the strong medium of the local language which was already sufficiently rich for the purpose. They also failed to realise that there was a basic difference between spreading of a cult and expanding a cultural empire. The Goswamis confused the two issues and persuaded their royal converts with their full spiritual authority that the development of the Manipuri language particularly in the Vaisnavic religious sphere should be totally banned. The story has it that they even spread a curse as follows:

"Whosoever sings the glory of Hindu Gods in Manipuri during day time will reborn as a crow and those who sing at night as owls in their next births."

To what extent this story is true will remain a matter of opinion. But it is difficult to underrate such stories in view of the fact that even today, a large section of the elders in Manipuri society stick to the ancient tradition and justify their stand that they cannot incur the curse of the Guru. The Goswamis themselves settled in Manipur married Manipuri females and ultimately became Manipuris in their food, dress and language. But the wrong advice they had given to their powerful royal disciples kept on to have its stream-roller sway on the cultural life of the Manipuri people. The originality and genius of Manipur found its way only in the evolution of dances and their colourful costumes during the new religious movement. Those who have realised this in the present context of an all-round reawakening, explode obviously with extraordinary vigour and plead with their elders to rise to the situation and bless the younger generation in their urgent endeavour to bring their mother-tongue to her rightful place more especially in the sphere of religious prayers and songs.

Lord Chaitanya Never Envisaged Cultural Empire

There should be no misunderstanding or confusion about this issue. The suggestion is not that those who became Hindus a few centuries back should revert to their ancient faith. It will be highly improper and uncalled for to make any suggestion like this. Manipuri Hindus are now seettled in the faith and they even can stand on their legs. They have in fact derived tremendous benefit from the lead given to them by the said Goswamis in several aspects. But the only point which needs clarification and reclarification is that Lord Cheitanya and his enlightened disciples in Bengal never envisaged the extension of a cultural and literary empire.

They were far from fulfilling any such dream. If some mistake was committed by those who came to Manipur with the profound gospel of love and tolerance, the mistake was totally individual. The present generation of Manipuri Hindus can correct that since the movement has already gathered momentum. Writers and singers have shown good progress in the correct direction. A word of explanation may be necessary why such an extensive digression has been made on this issue in a chapter about Manipuri Dances. In fact dance and music go hand in hand in any dance presentation in Manipuri. The musical aspect has to be studied and grasped in order to judge the merit and demerit of a particular dance item. Since a dance is the enactment of some thought content of a piece of story, the relevance and accuracy of dance is adjudged with careful reference to its musical content. In the case of dances confined to Ras and Hindu themes performed in the traditional fashion in Govindji Temple, on specific days, the music is invariably in some language (mostly Bengali sometimes Sanskrit and even Brajabali) other than Manipuri.

Any inquisitive stranger and even members of the present generation in Manipur are naturally templed to ask, "Why this total lack of Manipuri in the music? Could you not provide suitable composition in Manipuri? Is it not strange?" The foregoing discussion is in reply to such valid issues. The objection to the constant and compulsory use of languages completely ignoring and ignoring the rich Manipuri is not on the basis of any parochial or narrow consideration. The fact of the situation is that these languages are unknown to the population. An artist who learnt the Bengali songs like a parrot, without any academic background, from his Guru, who is also equally ignorant of the language, sings for hours before an audience made of those who are complete strangers to the language of the music, the result must automatically be a complete defeat of the sole purpose of such singing.

Rightly one may question how such a fantastic tradition could survive so long. The reply is that people are used to it and they get the same benefit as one gets from observing a regular japa of a mantra. But the trouble is that in the case of a public singing in Manipur the artists are not doing the normal japa of a mantra. They are singing interesting stories of the divine love of Radha and Krishna and reciting beautiful poetic pieces on important episodes of the immortal story of Krishna and His Divine consort, Radha, in the hope that the audience will admire them. The sweetness of their music and the accepted divinity of the theme captivates the hearts of the audience while the real literary contents of the music is completely missed.

Different Categories of Manipuri Dance

In the foregoing pages, we have discussed at length the nature of the development of the Manipuri dances during the pre-Hindu period. During the said times, the dances developed were more or less within the folk category at best, this period provided only the starting period of a much deeper and far-reaching revolution in the growth of classical Manipuri dance. What categories of dances belong to the classical group remains a subject matter of heated controversy among the Gurus today. The author does not suggest to take the risk of joining issues with any of the warring camps of the authorities on the subject. Separate treatises on the subject by competent authorities may put sufficient light.

We will confine to only broad divisions where the controversies have no access. There are three categories of dance which are more or less of tremendous value and relevance. These being:

(i) Lai Haraoba category of dance;
(ii) The Ras Dance; and
(iii) The Cholom aspect of the Manipuri Nat Sankritan.

Whether the Lai Haraoba group of dances are classical or not remains unsettled. There are strong opinion on both sides. The Ras category is the only undisputed one belonging to classical old form. It is one of the four leading classical dances of India that include, Bharat Natyam, Kathakali, Kathak, over and above Manipuri. During the last few years Kuchipudi and Orissi are also coming up to claim the position of classical dances of our country. Now the question is whether the Cholom aspect of the Manipuri Nat Sankirtan should also be treated at par with the Ras dances. It may be recalled in this regard that the dance authorities in Manipur have moved the Sangeet Natak Academy to recognise the Cholom, Pung, as well as Pala as classical dances of Manipur.

The last Academy award for Manipuri dance went in favour of a Guru in Pala Cholom. We may, therefore, take it that the Choloms have also been treated by the Sangeet Natak Academy equal to the Ras Dances thereby widening the field of Manipuri classical dances. The recognition is very timely and in the right direction. Indeed, the Ras Dances and the Cholom aspects of Manipuri Nat Sankirtan are inseparably linked up as distinguishable aspects of the same whole. The observation in this chapter will be limited to certain aspects of this classical category of Manipuri dance.

Some Aspects of Cholom

When the Manipuris in the valley adopted Hinduism on a mass scale they were taught that, in the Kaliyuga, Hari Nam Sankirtan was the best of yagyas. They had not been taught the Vedic rites of Yagyas and Homas. As a result, the new converts observed the rite of singing Gods' name of any important religious occasion which would have been fit for the performance of Homas and Yagyas. For instance Shradahas performed with simple rites, consisting mainly of the singing of Harinam by a party of singers trained for this purpose. Marriages are also performed in similar atmosphere. The underlying idea was that when Harinam was sung no other Yagya or Homa would be essential in the Kaliyuga. This is the principal message of Lórd Cheitanya. From this a new and rich tradition of Nat Sankirtan and Ras Dances started up in Manipur. The love for dancing already formed the second nature of Manipuris. When the theme of the immortal Ras Leela of Sri Krishna and the pious Gopis was introduced in Manipur, the Manipuri Genius rose to the occasion and produced almogst over night the beautiful Manipuri Ras tradition as we see it now.

Tradition of Rasleela

This Rasleela had its origin in the vision of Rajarshi Bhagya Chandra. After installation of the image of Sri Govindji, in fulfilment of his earlier promise to Govindji, the Rajarshi hurried up with his plan to perform a Rasleela. As the image of Srimati Radha had yet to be installed the role of Radha had to be played by a young girl, while the image of Govindji was kept in the middle of the Rasmandal during the performance. The young daughter of the Rajarshi played the role of Radha. The real name of the princes is not known but popularly she was famous as Sija Laioibi which means a princess, who became goddess or a princess who looked after God. She refused to marry and spent her whole life as a devotee of Krishna.

She passed away in Nabadwip, the birthplace of Lord Cheitanya. Like Bhakta Mira, Sija Laioibi worshipped Govindji as her divine lover and many poignant stories are spoken of the extraordinary devotion of this princess. The first Rasleela was performed at a specially constructed Rasmandal near Rajarṣhi's palace at Langthaban, now called Kanchipur. The sacred spot, as the result of the shifting of the palace site, is totally neglected at present. The government of the new State ought to take initial steps to develop the spot and surrounding areas which were occupied by the palace buildings of the Rajarshi and his successors as a befitting memorial to the historic development.

The very first Ras performance must have created lasting enthusiasm for the king and his team of dance teachers. The Ras tradition grew from strength to strength in the hands of succeeding rulers. It is not known how far the present trend has deviated from the earliest concepts of mudras, talas, music and costumes. No photographs or paintings of that period are traceable.

It is, however, accepted on all platforms that the basic concepts of the Rajarshi remained unchanged in most of the aspects. But it will be unreasonable to believe that no improvements or changes have been made on the root foundation. The present Rasleela dances are the sum total of the contributions made by several generations of master-minds in the line. They carry the unfailing stamps of genius composers in dance and music, master craftsmen who designed and made the immortal costumes and galaxies of artists who enriched the tradition by their masterly performance. But the only credit goes to the Rajarshi who was the master brain of the glorious tradition. Our hats off to him again and again.

The famous Rasleela depicts the story of Sri Krishna's divine love sports with the Gopis of Brindaban, as explained in the 10th chapter of Srimad Bhagabat.

This carries the highest of divine Rosos. Seeing, hearing, performing and even a remote attention to Rasleela are considered by the followers of the Bhagabat cult as tasks of supreme virtue. Manipuri Hindus are worshippers of Radha-Krishna, the divine communion. From the introduction of the tradition of Rasleela performances according to the strict tenets contained in the Srimad Bhagabat the dance talent of the Manipuris found fresh avenue for wider and deeper exercise. The developments of this tradition was on the following foundations:

1. In the matter of dance techniques, the Lai Haraoba and the resources like techniques of spear and sword fightings provided ready materials for the master composers.
2. The basic concept of Manipuri folk dances was immaculately preserved to such extent that in none of the Ras dances even the most critical observer can trace any mixture of the local tradition with outside influence, however strong it might be.
3. The aspect of costumes is a total departure either from life or from existing Indian tradition.

Explanation has already been given, about the unique costumes and the atmosphere which goes with the classical category of Manipuri dances yet some amount of repetition here may not be useless. Reference has again to be made to the miraculous vision which the Rajarshi had during his political asylum in Assam, in which he was given clear instructions about the style in which the Rasleela was to be presented, after his recovery of the throne from the hands of the Burmese invaders.

It is said that he saw the types of costumes to be worn by each of the characters in a Rasleela. The impact of this vision was mixed up with the orthodox outlook of the king himself. He wished to make the presentation to confine itself within the bounds of a strict religious ritual which would have to do nothing with human entertainment. As a consequence the female participants cover all their indentities under very colourful yet stiff and extensive layers of decorative costumes. Màny inquisitive observers often ask—why the costumes of a Manipuri Rasleela are so far away from life and why such an abundance of heavy decorations should render the artist almost circumscribed within a limited sphere for movements and expression of the supreme sentiments associated with the divine play. These are valid questions and the crux of the whole problem is in the replies to these questions. As has been said earlier Manipuri dances have been developed invariably in most of the cases as religious rituals.

4. "Although the bodily movements and the customary aspect remain deep-rooted in Manipuri tradition the theme is total adoptation of the Ras episode, described in the Srimad-Bhagabat Mahapurana. In the process of this adoption, the scientific sources of Indian dances were thoroughly mastered by the composers of the Manipuri Ras dances. It is amazing to see the rich varieties of mudras, intricate talas, subtle movements of the limbs to suit the requirements of the expressions made by the different characters. These Talas and Mudras are known by either Manipuri names or accepted classical definitions of the Indian science of dances. The classical character is, therefore, too prominent to be disputed. The tradition of teaching the Ras techniques has been handed down to the present generation through a line of gifted masters of the subject who dedicated their lives to the promotion of this dance form."

The method of promotion of this dance form consisted of the following factors:

(a) The succeeding generation of rulers patronised the development.
(b) The general population also made their share of contribution in the development.
(c) The secret of the fast and fastidious development of this dance-form in Manipur is that it is an essential ingredient of the socio-religious life of the people whose zeal for beating one another as promoters of the Ras is in their sub-conscious self. This constructive trend is ever on the increase even during these days of extreme sophistication and inspite of the tremendous onslaught got from other trends.

Getting back to the main issue of the chapter *viz.*, the Rasleela, we may now divide this style into two broad categories, *viz.*, Gopa-Ras and Srikrishna's Rasleela alongwith the Gopis. The Gopa-Ras form depicts the story of Shrikrishna with his Gopa friends manifesting himself as a lover of cows and proving his worth as the highly accomplished incarnation of the God-head—during the period of his boyhood. Every year on the day of the Gostastami, Gopa-Ras, with all its captivating details, is presented at the temples kept well with royal patronage. These temples include those of Sri Govindji, Sri-Bijoy-Govindji and the royal temples at Ningthoukhong. These performances at the selected temples on the said day are followed by several similar performances all over the valley. The tradition has it that no performance of Gopa-Ras should be organised in ordinary temples on and prior to the Gostastami, a day specifically reserved only for the performance in the temples mentioned earlier.

Different Categories of Ras

The highly important Rasleela of Srikrishna with his Divine lovers of Brindaban may be divided according to the Manipuri traditions into four categories being Maharas, Kunjaras, Basanta-ras and Nitiras. The first three categories are traditionally presented on specific days in selected temples with meticulous care in the same way as the first Gopa-rasas are presented. Maharas is presented on the full moon of day of Hiyangei (Kartika)—Kunjaras on the full moon day of Mera (Aswin)—Basantaras on the full moon day, i.e., Poornima of Sajibu (Baishakh) and Nitiras, on any day. Nitiras can be sub-divided into Dibaras and Nishiras. The names naturally indicate that the first is presented in the day time, while the next is the usual Rasleela presented at night.

Further, tradition of Sri Govindji's temple which confines to the first three categories is quite unique. The performances are done strictly in accordance with the requirements of the tradition which is thought to have been handed down more or less from the time of Rajarshi Bhagyachandra through his successors. One can see a sharp contrast between these performances and other performances made with some departures from the traditional framework. The traditional framework consists of the aspect of time, music, choreography etc. The differences between these ancient presentations and modified ones is not in the basic concept of the style and theme. It is only in the editorial aspects of the performance and the degree of attachment to the value of the gone days, i.e., orthodoxy. It will, therefore, be wrong to understand that the divisions of the categories are based on root differences.

The departure permitted in Nitiras and other performance done on ordinary days outside the selected temples are,

(a) elaboration of certain episodes, may be with fresh compositions within the framework of classical tradition,

(b) option for alteration and changes in the hands of the directors. These departures do not imply absolute freedom for the organisers and the teachers.

They adjust themselves within the framework of another accepted tradition of these permissible departures. The two currents have worked during the last several generations as mutual compliments and supplements in the constructions of the tradition and its dynamic maintenance. While the initial three categories form a powerful fact for check and balance upon the quick speed of sophistication, the fourth category is the breeding ground for creative tendencies of the mode.

While both aspects are equally exposed to dangers, there is greater and greater realisation in both avenues for the proper sustenance of this classical dance form. While the first category has been exposed to the danger of dead stagnation in the name of tradition and orthodoxy, the second is exposed to the danger of speedy annihilation of the true spirit of the form in the name of creativity and sophistication. The future of the Manipuri classical dance form entirely depends upon the actual co-operation and co-ordination of the two powerful forces, represented by quite well-organised groups in the society.

Ancient Traditional Rasleela

The occasion for staging a Rasleela has been explained in the foregoing paragraphs. Just as there are different categories of Rasleela there are various methods for organisation of these different categories. The categories for which fixed days of the calender year are reserved stand on a special footing in this regard. Interested parties apply to the agencies, incharge of such performances, for permission to enable their children to play the main roles in the said Ras. In the case of Sri Govindji, members of the king's family or children of the top-ranking officials of the State get the preference if there are many such applications. Usually there is heavy rush for this privilege.

The same process of registration in advance, is adopted in the case of Sri-Bijoy Govindji temple and other similar temples, managed with royal patronage, but not with strict adherence to the principle of preference, as found in the case of Sri Govindji temple. Children mostly young girls selected for participation in the traditional performance receive their training from a Guru or a group of Gurus appointed for the purpose. The training and usual preparations are completed within a period of two months at the maximum. In some cases the time spent in the training of the children is hardly one month.

This is a unique characteristic of the Manipuri children. Anybody who does not belong to the social fold of Manipuri Hindus could not take part in these traditional presentations even after prolonged training and repeated rehearsals. It looks as if the whole thing is in the blood of the children taking part in the performances. The process of training may be characterised as the awakening of some dormant talent inherited by the children from their forefathers. It should not, however, be interpreted as starting that every Manipuri child is as good as a professional dancer. Professional dancers have their own footing which ordinary people cannot achieve. The point at issue, however, is the platform of common attainment by the members of the society in this respect. Usually a team of expert artists assist the performance by their participation and contribution for which they are properly remunerated. In a way these artists may be called professionals or full-timers in this field. Their rates of remuneration, in such performances, differ from individual to individual and from class to class. There is no denying the fact that succeeding generations of such artists have created their own tradition.

They enjoy great respect from the society and the best of them in any generation get enviable position in society including from economic angle. The success of these artists depends mostly on their showmanship both being dancers and as musicians. They have to undergo prolonged and intensive training and research under very competent Gurus. Theirs is a life of complete commitment to their trade. In a way they have been the brick and mortar with which the strong and glorious tradition has been built up over the centuries. Upto this day the tradition is in the process of regular building and rebuilding, in which the role of the dedicated artists occupies an important place. The Gurus are also substantial limbs of the tradition. They have succeeded the skill and experience of the earlier Gurus by their devotion, and dedication to the tradition. On the day of performance; the Mandap, which may be either a permanent structure or ad-hoc improvisation for the purpose of the performance, is so decorated as to look aesthetic and solemn. The members of the audience come like pilgrims to the spot.

The atmosphere is these charged with religious feeling of reverence and deep humility. The actual Rasleela is preceded by the performance of a Nat-Sankirtan which confines itself to the singing of the praise of the incarnation of Sri Cheitanya Mahaprabhu and the episode of his life in which he enacted in his divine mood Sri Krishna's Rasleela with the Gopis in Brindaban. This process is invariable and we cannot conceive of a traditional Rasleela unrpreceded by a Nat-Sankirtan as explained. In the performance of the different categories of Rasleela one can see the stress on the aspects connected with the season in question. On the basis of the particular emphasis given to each category, the different names are given. For example, in the Basanta Ras the emphasis is on 'Abir-khel' and sprinkling of coloured water as prevalent during the spring season throughout the length and breadth of the country. Some episodes seen in the Maharas are not to be seen in other categories. The traditional Ras performances begin from early hours of night and invariably carries go upto the time of Mangalarati (twilight before sunrise). The period covering a whole night is considered too short for a complete Ras of the Manipuri tradition, which consists of numerous episodes, marked by variations in the music and dance sequences. The main scenes of Ras include among others the solo dances of Krishna, Radha, Brinda, Chandrabali, group dances and sometimes duet presentations of Radha and Krishna. Rasleelas done in Sri Govindji's temple consist of only the gopis, as the roles of Radha and Krishna are played by the images of Radha and Sri Govindji respectively.

During the performance the pious images are taken out into the Ras arena. The above generalisation of the solo dances does not apply to Govindji's temple.

In some other dances all the characters need not be there uniformly. For instance, the role of Chandrabali is not to be found in Niti-ras. The stock compositions, presentable subject to availability of time, in Rasleela are many and also varied. Like, Bhangi-pareng, Bridaban pareng, Khurumba pareng are beautiful classical compositions which are regarded as the very foundation of Manipuri Rasleela. These parengs (series) are presented in various groups. Once the presentation of Bhangi starts the members of the audience cannot leave the Mandap till the presentation is over. These parengs, specially the Bhangi parengs, are many in number so that it is almost impossible to present all of them in a single night. The Gurus make suitable selection and exercise their talent in editing these to suit particular performances.

Music for Rasleela

The music aspect has an important place in the total structure of a Ras. A team of sutradharis led by the Guru of the performance includes at least two female singers, a flute player, conch blower and other instrumental musicians whose strength and variety may differ from performance to performance according to the taste and capacity of the organisers, sit generally in the north-western corner of the Ras-Mandal to provide musical commentary and background to the performance. The sewers of the costumes also play an important part in the development and maintenance of the Ras tradition. There are many professional costume stitchers in Manipur. Many of them have usually good earning out of this trade. The participants are extremely careful to use the newest costume so that there is an atmosphere of unsaid competition in this respect among them. The costume makers are also in competition with one another in the production of the most attractive designs within the sanctioned tradition. The cases of the professional artists are different. They are not fastidious about the qualities of their costumes. It is so because they come on contract basis against some certain fixed rate of remuneration, part of which has to be spent for their costumes. They usually, select costumes with minimum charges and sometimes there is an unhappy contrast between the skilled artist and the other participants who are sharing the expenses of the presentation or at least have to bear the expenses of their costumes. In the life time of a Manipuri girl it is quite desirable that at least once she must participate in such traditional Rasleela. The mode of sharing expenditures is also interesting. The parents of the children playing main roles must bear the lion's share of the expenses.

Fashion of Collective Patronage of Rasleela

Today, there is an increasing trend of collective patronage of Ras performances. The friends and the relatives of the parents whose children play the main roles come and offer the tokens of their support to the tradition either in cash or in kind, presented during the solo performances of the leading roles, in the Ras-Mandal. Such presents are collected and taken by the parents of the children concerned. It will not be surprising, therefore, in the changing circumstances, a parent with considerable influence in society may get presents in cash and kind, value of which sometimes may exceed his expenditure, but commercial consideration is out of question. There are many critics of his trend. The new fashion of collective patronage, in so far as it adjusts to the sanctity of the tradition, may be regarded as a very encouraging and healthy sign which will go a long way in keeping the tradition not only alive, but correctly remunerative. The very development of the Manipuri Nat Kirtan rests on similar foundation of collective social patronage. It will be unwise to disappoint this trend in the Manipuri society whose economic standard will continue to be low for several years to come. They days of royal patronage to Manipuri or any kind of art are gone for good. The Government, however, will have to discharge its share of responsibility in keeping the flame of Manipuri Ras-tradition burning.

Tribal Dances of Manipur

Before we end the discussion on the subject of Manipuri dances reference ought to be made to the tribal dances of Manipur. There are more than twenty-nine Scheduled tribes in Manipur. All of these tribes are proud of their special cloth-designs and folk dances. The folk dances are extremely colourful. Most of them are simple in respect of stepping, choreography and talas. It is not, thus, difficult to learn them but each form is held in extreme regard and affection by the tribe concerned. The reason is that they are closely associated with the very evalution of the tribes over the ages. Special mention may be made of the Kabui-dance which is definitely the most developed and sophisticated of the tribal group.

During the last some years this particular tribal dance has been enriched with tremendous speed in respect of choreography, intricate movements of hands and feet and colourful costumes. The Kabuis live the North-Western hill ranges of Manipur, but this particular tribal dance has developed and popularised through the labour and dedication of the Kabui-pockets in the valley. One peculiar characteristic of this tribe is its settlement all over the valley in more or less small pockets. Through these pockets the relation between the Kabuis and the valley people has been deep as well as close for the last many centuries. The possibility of mutual influence between the valley people and the Kabuis in respect of language, custom and culture cannot be denied.

Famous Tankhul-dances are also colourful and charming. The steppings are simple but unique. In respect of dances and other social customs one can see many similarities between the Thankuls and the people of the valley. Their unstopped proficiency in the Manipuri language can only be compared with those of the Koms and the Marings. Such affinities must form the subject-matter of further research by committed scholars so that the different peoples of Manipur could be fixed to their proper origins.

It has been found that the Mao-Nagas also have their own distinct folk dances which indicate their talent not only in dancing but also in the art of colour combination. The dances are heroic while the costumes represent rich handicraft and understanding of colour. The Kukis who form the non-Naga group of Manipuri tribals are subdivided into several sub-tribes each of which has its unique design of cloth and unique composition of folk dance. These folk dances have their own individualities. The accompanying music is usually sweet and smacks of the trend of thought of every tribe.

Further Anals, Moyons, and Marings also have their folk dances. The Anals mostly inhibit the Tengoupal areas. This area has its individuality in many respects. The National Highway—Indo-Burma Road, passes through it, and fulfils the purpose of a useful link between the valley and the tribal people in this area. In the early days, when there were frequent contacts between Manipur and Burma the sole road to and from Burma was through foot-paths, running through the Tengnoupal subdivision and the eastern portion of the hill areas of Ukhrul. The contacts between the people of these parts and the people of Manipur valley must have been frequent and of far-reaching consequences in mutual developments. One should not, therefore, be surprised to see the results of such contacts in the Manipuri tradition.

The Manipuri Nat-Sankirtan Dance

It is true that the Manipuri Rasleela cannot be studied in isolation from the Nat-Sankirtan which provides the musical and several other fundamental aspect of the dances. A Sankirtan can be divided into two aspects, *viz.,* the musical aspect and the 'cholom' aspect. Both aspect have their own respective importance. One is complementary to the other. The cholom aspect may again be subdivided into two, viz. pala-cholom and pung-cholom. Pala-cho-lom is a form of dance done by participants in a Nat-Sankirtan. It is a harmonious mix of vigour and softness. Pung-choom is performed by mridanga-artists.

This also is a unique and harmonious combination of masculine vigour and Vaishnavic humility. In light of the Shastric character of the cholom aspects of Sankirtan, the Sangeet-Natak Academy has very rightly recognised them as classical. The music aspect covers all the sixty-four Rosos associated with immortal love of Radha and Krishna and also the singing of glory of Cheitanya Mahaprabhu from whom the Manipuri tradition of Sankirtan originated, if not in its totality at least in its spiritual base, and basic tenets that rules most of the formalities of a Manipuri Sankirtan. As has been explained earlier, the place of Nat-Sankirtan in Manipuri ethical life is of indescribable importance. The story and thought contents of the music explains the basic spiritual outlook of the Manipuris. The language aspect of Sankirtan has been discussed at sufficient length in the start of this chapter. So far as the story and thought contents are concerned a thorough discussion on them, for that purpose of this book, is not called for.

It may, however, be said that the tradition has fixed as to which theme ought to be sung on what occasion. For instance, 'Niti-pareng' which is a composition on the motto of Srikrishna's meeting with Radha during the daytime, is the usual theme for Shraddha ceremony. The choloms which have special relevance to this chapter are the expression of various moods of Radha and Krishna through the medium of dances which form essential parts of a Sankirtan. The Sankirtan artists are very well-versed in both aspects. Thus most of the Rasgurus are well grounded in the Sankirtan tradition. They have been at one time or other Sankirtan-artists with sufficient amount of success. The choloms are performed in extremely intricate 'talas' and movements are confined to the Manipuri tradition of dances.

The renowned artists in this field are full-timers or professionals. They are amply remunerated for their ability and devotion to this profession. But tradition forbids them to enter into any contract for any form of performance. The simple reason is that Sankirtans are sung only on religious occasions. The artists are not supposed to behave like businessmen, calculating in every step about their losses and gains. Still, a system of informal contracts rules their relation with their patrons who never hesitate to give more than what the artist normally deserves. This is a secret behind the dynamic development of Manipuri Sankirtan. The other cholom is mridanga-cholom which also forms another integral part of Nat-Sankirtan. This is masculine in character like the other cholom. This performance is done by two mridanga players taking part in the Sankirtan. The feat of the mridanga players is extraordinary. The profession is confined only to a small number of highly gifted artists of every generation.

In this case also the artist to succeed must devote his entire life to this art. The training is extremely rigorous. The masters in the line are definitely caught young. The stories of the famous gurus in this line are those of complete devotion and lifelong dedication to the culture of this art under the able guidance of intelligent gurus. There is a saying among them that there is no holiday from the routine of rigorous practice of this art form so long as the artist is in the active side of the trade. They are tested everyday and in every public performance. There is nothing like reigning on false prestige of the past. The artist has to defend his title in his every bouts. The depth of the classical character of Manipuri dance can be assessed with special reference to this art form which specialises in the field of the intricate 'talas'.

Numerous Dance Institutions

Where these dances form people's breath of life it is natural that there should be a large number of institutions imparting systematic training in the various dances. The concept of established institutions in the modern sense is only a recent trend in Manipur so far as the dances are concerned. The tradition has been maintained and handed down through the old Indian tradition of Guru and disciple relationship. Traditionally speaking the same old practice is continuing. The emergence of dance training institutions was sole a response to the need of the sophisticated society to adapt some of the Manipuri dances for stage presentation and to train promising dance talents of Manipur as well as from outside to describe and demonstrate the Manipuri art form to the sophisticated public in Manipur and outside. There is tremendous risk involved in the establishment and running a dance institution in a state like Manipur where dance is more of a religious ritual than an entertainment for the audience and where a society is extremely against fast trends in cultural revolution. Presently the only institution which combines in itself the element of creation and the orthodox trend appears to be the Jawaharlal Nehru Manipur Dance

Academy, which was sponsored by the Sangeet Natak Academy. The other institutions are either too weak to be effective or have tried to introduce too much of their own in the name of creative art.

Some of such institutions which hurt in the name of creation are extremely unpopular and dying out. While the institutions which would have been otherwise effective are short of resources and absenting in seriousness. There is, however, no denying of the fact that some good institutions are actually needed. The State Government has a special responsibility for the promotion of such institutions. The gurus who were considered usually outmoded and held rigid views against the modern trends have now shown tremendous understanding and admiration of the need of the hour. They have now realised that by neglecting the modern emphasis on stage adaptation and the element of creation, they have only to encourage self-styled gurus and artists who have no right schooling and footing in the basic traditions to go out performing in all towns and cities, exploiting the name of Manipuris and making all types of misrepresentations. Positive action is necessary to check this destructive trend. It is encouraging that the old gurus have now realised the seriousness of the problem.

There are just two alternatives left for the promoters of the Manipuri dance form, either they totally discourage half-hearted institutions or they go in seriously for setting up and running of really competent institutions. There can be no compromise in the matter.

Reference has been made to the word Meitei. The people of Manipur in the valley, speaking as their mother tongue the Manipuri language, is known in the local language as the "Meiteis." Whenever mention have been made of them the word Manipuri has been used. Scholars have many things to say on the origin and significance of the term "Meites". The Manipuri language is also known as the "Meitei Lol", which means the language of the "Meiteis". In the present context, therefore, the term "Meitei" is synonymous to the Manipuri. The Meiteis are largely divided into Hindus, Muslims, and Scheduled Castes or those of the Meiteis who still continue to follow the old traditions. The Meitei Muslims or Manipuri Muslims have several things in common with their Hindu counterparts, in respect of language, women's dress, house-keeping. These common features are strong bonds for their unity where they are. This ensures for the harmonious coexistence between the Manipuri Hindus and Manipuri Muslims in Assam, Tripura and Bangladesh. Ultimately, whatever are the terms, references or understandings, these dances are expressions of their sense of devotion towards god/goddesses.

12

Economic Development of Manipur

They say that the study of any state or region is incomplete unless we study the economy of that particular political unit. From the previous pages, we have got to know that as far as economic matters are concerned, small States of Indian Union like Manipur, Nagaland, Meghalaya and Tripura stand on a footing altogether different from the rest of the bigger States especially in respect of economic development and viability. The economic factor has been one of the serious obstacles towards ultimate conferment of the new status in the case of every State. Of these small States, Nagaland has the benefit of having gone ahead of the others by almost ten years. During the precious period of ten years she has been able to probe her own strength and weakness in every respect. The Government of India have been giving considerable attention to her problems. Vigorous measures for economic development have so far been taken in that State. Nevertheless it has to be done even in respect of Nagaland.

The fresh States of Manipur, Meghalaya and Tripura, judged by their present positions, are far from being economically viable. The reasons are obvious. So far, proper attention has not been given to the important aspect of economic follow up to the political necessity of confering the status of States to these units. The problems of Tripura and Meghalaya vary from those of Manipur. In fact, each of the three States has its own unique problems. The solution of the problems in the different units will have, therefore, to be achieved through its own ways and genus. The only common resource of finance as well as expertise will be the Government of India for all these non-viable States until they stand on their own legs.

Given below is a study of the current economic situation and the future prospects of economic development of the new State of Manipur. The assessment is an extract of a research conducted by a student in Manipur.

Agriculture Main Profession

The main profession of the population is agriculture. Weaving, fishing and other cottage industries are the main supplements. Employment in the Government and semi-Government establishments and institutions forms hardly 5 per cent of the employment statistics. The main profession of a substantial section of the population in and around Imphal is weaving. The main profession of the entire population of Thanga, covering several islands in the Loktak lake is fishing and collection of Shinghara ('Heikak'). The villages on the bank of Loktak have the mixed profession of agriculture and fishing. The resources of human labour for road constructions, hill cuttings, and similar other unskilled labour, are confined to certain groups of villages along the Indo-Burma Road. More than one thousand families depend for their livelihood on the profession of Nat-music, which confines to the Hindu population to the valley. Costume-making for the different dances give employment in considerably large number of families which also confine in the valley. The cottage industries, viz., carpentry, blacksmithy, goldsmithy, tailoring, embroidery, bamboo and cane works also support a small section of the population. The transport industries for which the Manipuris have a special fascination give a considerable employment to a large number of drivers, fitters and the managerial staff. The services in most of the State Highways are in the hands of the transport co-operatives, so much so that this industry has embraced considerably large number of people in different capacities. Thousands of women both in the urban and rural areas supplement the income of their families by active participation, may, by playing leading role in the small business sectors of the main markets. Reference has already been made in a preceding chapter to this tradition of women's active participation in the socio-economic life of the Manipuri society. The latest census data showing total agricultural workers and their categories is given as follows :

Table 1
Agricultural and Farming Functions including Labourers and Other Workers (Statewise) : Census 2001

Total/ Rural/ Urban	Persons/ Males/ Females	Cultivators Labourers	Agricultural Industry Workers	Household Workers	Other
Total	Persons	492,696	120,991	97,955	357,936
	Males	277,583	53,227	19,603	244,229
	Females	215,113	67,764	78,352	113,707
Rural	Persons	452,841	99,550	69,187	225,017
	Males	250,413	43,655	13,308	157,417
	Females	202,428	55,895	55,879	67,600
Urban	Persons	39,855	21,441	28,768	132,919
	Males	27,170	9,572	6,295	86,812
	Females	12,685	11,869	22,473	46,107

Some of the above mentioned professions deserve elaborate discussion in this chapter. The profession of weaving, its present position, past history and the future possibilities have been discussed at length in this chapter. The agricultural industry in Manipur has tremendous possibilities for future development. While the nature of cultivation in the hill areas differs from that in the plain areas, the future prospects are equally bright in both areas. The system of Jhooming or shifting cultivation is too extravagant and has far reaching after effects in forestry and other development aspects of the hill areas. This method has, therefore, to be replaced by a more stable and settled type of cultivation. The dexterity of the

Table 2

Agricultural and Farming Functions including Labourers and Other Workers (Districtwise) : Census 2001

District	*Cultivators*			*Agricultural labourers*			*Household industries*			*Other workers*		
	P	M	F	P	M	F	P	M	F	P	M	F
Senapati	144,192	75,093	69,099	13,857	6,558	7,299	5,343	1,671	3,672	25,871	17,812	8,059
Tamenglong	40,556	19,349	21,207	881	388	493	756	252	504	9,840	7,491	2,349
Churachandpur	55,408	31,317	24,091	10,101	4,785	5,316	7,109	1,585	5,524	26,644	19,095	7,549
Bishnupur	28,998	20,684	8,314	14,155	5,870	8,285	11,709	2,007	9,702	36,436	23,303	13,133
Thoubal	74,445	45,770	28,675	37,151	15,611	21,540	19,859	3,628	16,231	50,063	32,375	17,688
Imphal West	37,438	23,985	13,453	16,148	6,959	9,189	23,853	5,224	18,629	99,638	65,618	34,020
Imphal East	31,855	22,123	9,732	22,719	10,226	12,493	24,057	3,608	20,449	80,044	57,537	22,507
Ukhrul	46,822	22,059	24,763	1,966	958	1,008	2,180	818	1,362	15,628	12,106	3,522
Chandel	32,982	17,203	15,779	4,013	1,872	2,141	3,089	810	2,279	13,772	8,892	4,880

people of Mao and adjoining areas in rice cultivation on the hill slopes is considered highest among the hill people of Manipur. The State Agriculture Department will do well to introduce a system by which there can be a profitable exchange of skill and experience among the hill tribes in the field of cultivation. The vast areas in the hills can be used at present only for two purposes, namely, forestry and agriculture.

Need for Vigorous Programme of Afforestation

One can imagine the loss from the vast expanse of waste land covered neither by forests nor used for agriculture in the hill areas covering more than eight thousand square miles inhabited by less than one-third of the population. The Government shall have to apply its mind to the maximum use of these areas for either of the two purposes. What one sees today is the horrible picture of indiscriminate burning and cutting of forests without any programme of afforestation and adequate use of deforested areas for other purposes. Nothing can be more painful than this state of affairs. The newly introduced autonomous district councils in the hill areas of Manipur will have to pay their utmost attention to this, because the future development programmes in the hill areas will automatically centre round these aspects in the beginning. We usually forget that the forests are not over-night growths. The massive destruction of forests during the Second World War and after, has to be compensated for, by a vigorous programme for afforestation. The forest-wealth of Manipur was considered to be very rich. Its teak-wood, agar trees, orchids, spices, different species of wild-life, varieties of timbers, canes, bamboos and several other mineral products like lime-stone, stone-quarries, almost inexhaustible sources for road-making and house-construction, deserve special mention. The future programme of economic development for the new State shall have to emphasise the aspect of exploring and exploiting the forest resources including its cultivable areas. The teak industry in Manipur has yet to take its shape. The forest policy adopted in respect of teak-wood remains unproductive and discouraging so far. Possibility of exploring more items of mineral resources in the hill areas has been indicated by competent people from different platforms.

High Time for Geological Survey

The adequate reply to this suggestion should be a thorough geological survey in the hill areas without further delay. The scientific findings of such a survey should form the basis for all future industrial and development plannings. It may be mentioned here that the law and order situation in the hill areas will become more and more favourable to such a survey. It is understandable that there were genuine obstacles in the way of a comprehensive geological survey in Manipur during the last few years. The government and also the people shall have to take full advantage of the changing political climate.

Urgency for Constructive Activities

It is time for the people, who have more or less been misled by undue ambitions in the past, to realise that the attainment of Statehood is in fulfilment of the best possible political aspirations of the people of Manipur. After such attainment it is only logical that they address themselves to constructive activities. If they have had grievances against the National leadership for not conceding to their political aspirations for some time, the grievances are now over. They should not create an occasion in which the National leadership will find the fault, of failure to appreciate the implications of the reorganisation of the North Eastern Areas, with them. The author is very confident that with the willing co-operation of the people a galaxy of development measures could be taken up in the hill areas as well as the plains, to boost up the economy of the region. Coming to the sphere of agriculture in the valley of Manipur the following factors may be attended to:

Need for Full Available Cultivable Land

The pressure on land in the valley includes agriculture, fishing, settlements for homesteads, industrial and business centres, facilities for sports and recreations. All these demands have to be made from the limited space of hardly seven hundred square miles. The concentration of population here is maximum—more than two-thirds of the total population are confined to the valley. Fisheries occupy at least one-seventh of the total valley area. The remaining area is divided between homestead lands, agricultural lands and the reserves for the purposes mentioned above. In spite of this heavy pressure, the situation is not so frightening and gloomy as it appears superficially. The available lands for agriculture can be put to more intensive use by introducing additional facilities for irrigation. The natural fertility of the land is an accepted fact. The agriculture so far has depended on the monsoon and the natural fertility of the land. It is a common feature everywhere that the fields remain dry for six months, thereby throwing the cultivators out of employment during the dry season as well as allowing the lands to remain waste for such length of time in a year. The unique topography of the Manipur valley is solely responsible for this wastage. The sources of the rivers serving the valley are very near their course in the flat areas. The result is that the rivers are invariably in high flood during the six wet months of the year. Floods are always sudden because of the nearness of the sources, thus, damaging enough in every case. When the monsoon is over the valley is completely dry, the rivers thin away in no time so that the annual floods are followed quick on their heels by semi-drought conditions. This perpetual succession of floods by droughts in the valley has been one of the principal causes of agricultural unproductiveness of the area. The principal crop favourable to the valley is rice while vegetables, sugar-cane, pulses, wheat, jute and maize are supplementary crops. Maize cultivation specially suits the hill areas. Manipur produces several varieties of paddy. Some varieties suit the normal areas while some varieties can be grown only in wet areas. Manipuri rice as a whole, has a special quality of its own. It is in demand everywhere because of its special flavour and food content.

Some Suggestions

The suggestions that can be made for development of agriculture in the state are as follows:

(a) Increasing facilities for irrigation:
(b) Providing adequate fertilizers to the agriculturalists;
(c) To enable the agriculturalists to receive the benefit of the improved varieties of seeds and of the latest information on the technique of scientific cultivation, suitable to the region;
(d) Vigorous implementation of the land reform measures to remove obstacles arising out of uneconomic holdings of land and also undue concentration of land in the hands of a few individuals;
(e) Liberal assistance to agriculturalists in cash or in kind or in both according to need and practicability;
(f) Arrangement of sufficient marketing facilities so that the agriculturalists will get entire profit on their products from the middlemen;

Irrigation Deserves Priority

Of the above mentioned measures the first and foremost is the irrigation facilities. Much hope has been given by the authors of the Loktak Hydro-Electric Project about increasing irrigation facilities after its completion. The emphasis is on lift irrigation system. The success of the lift irrigation system will solely depend on the availability of abundant power supply at cheap cost. If the Loktak Project would come up more or less according to the present plan there is no doubt that some power may be available for this purpose. But it will be unrealistic to say that this should be the only solution to the vast problem.

To Check Floods Rivers Need be Controlled

The problems of floods and remedy for droughts can be taken up as a composite programme. Experts in these fields must have seen a number of unique features of the frequent floods followed by droughts in the valley. The remedy appears to lie in damming the turbulent rivers at their sources. Such dammings will, while enable to control the floods, also regulate regular flow of water in the main rivers. Over and above these the serious problem of shortage of drinking water in Manipur may be solved by this scheme. The possibility of utilising these dams for generation of hydro-electric power will also be high. It appears that this aspect has not received due attention of the experts so far. By virtue of such schemes if the rivers in the Manipur valley could be kept navigable throughout the year, thereby making the cost of internal transport cheaper, the entire economy of the valley will be changed. If these measures are taken up the Manipur valley will undoubtedly become a granary of the north-eastern areas in spite of its smallness.

Fishery Deserves Special Attention

Another means of livelihood for a considerable section of the population is fishing. There are two categories of fisheries in the State, viz. (1) free fishing areas which cover the Loktak and several river courses, and (2) Government fisheries sold by annual auction. These include natural water lakes like Pumlen, Kharung-pat. Waithou, Phumnom, Ningthikhong, Ngangou, Yangoi etc. At present Manipur is not self-sufficient in fish in spite of these fishing areas. A total re-thinking on the subject is the need of the hour. In spite of the trend of modernisation in several fields fishing, as a trade, remains totally unchanged in its methods of breeding as well as of catching. The damming of the rivers at their sources and subsequent regulation of the flow of water in the rivers throughout the year, as suggested above, may perhaps improve the fishing trade to a considerable extent. This will also have tremendous impact on the future tourist trade in Manipur.

Industrial Developments

The absence of industry even in the small scale sector in Manipur, is the eloquent commentary on the past attitude taken by the Centre towards Manipur, in the sphere of economic developments. The financial assistance extended to Manipur so far may be characterised as confining to the sphere of routine expenditures like pays and allowances and similar expenditures which cannot be considered long term investment for future economic developments. There is no doubt that many new roads have been constructed and some investments have been made for education which may be regarded as human reconstruction. The only major project taken up after independence is the Loktak Hydro-Electric Project, which is now under construction. Considering the vast forest resources of Manipur priority has to be given to the establishment of some forest industries in order to boost up the economy of the region. The nearest possibilities are paper, pulp, cement and turpentile industries. The bamboo resources of the region are vast. So also limestone reserves are rich enough to feed a considerable size of cement industry. Necessary surveys and deeper investigations are reported to have been completed in respect of a paper pulp factory and a cement factory.

Intentions not Matched with Programmes

While the broad intentions of the Government of India, to remove all disparities in industrial development of the country, are quite clear and do not leave any room for the least doubt about their sincerity in this respect, the programme for immediate future does not indicate that the development of these extremely backward units in the North Eastern region has received the attention due to them. These units in spite of their present economic backwardness have been given special political status. There can be no going back upon this historic step taken by the present leadership after prolonged and mature consideration. It will not be much to say that the National Government has to follow up this historic political measure with prompt and suitable programme of economic development.

Case for Special Central Assistance

The emergence of the North-Eastern Council, which will look after major projects, involving inter-State adjustments and other interests, is looked at with pessimism and suspicion by critical elements in each of the new States. How far the starting of the proposed paper and cement factories in Manipur will have its relevance to the Council and its manifold jurisdictions remains to be seen. The small units in the North Eastern Council cannot forget their experience and bitter lessons learnt from the erstwhile Eastern Zonal Council. The component units, big and small, used to sit across the table during the life-time of the Zonal Council. It is painful to remember that matters involving inter-State adjustments could seldom be decided on merit. The decisions were made on the basis of the strength of political pull of the component units. Naturally, therefore, the fate of the small units was miserable. They were thrown to compete in the tug of war against stronger brothers. The small units have best of intentions for the prospering and development of the bigger states, because the very welfare and prosperity of the smaller units depend on the patronage and liberal assistance of the bigger States. Such assistance will be possible only when the bigger States can command enough surplus and resources. But the point at issue here is—whether the Nation has an obligation to the economic development of the smaller units, which have justified certain departure from the normal yardsticks in fixing their political future. The emphasis is, therefore, on the need for special Central assistance towards the implementation of special economic programmes for the smaller units. The case of Manipur in this context is strong enough and does not stand in need of further amplification.

Early Development of Roads for Economic Growth

The comprehensive programme of economic development referred to above will have to be supplemented by the following items of communications:

(a) Extension of railway facilities to Manipur.
(b) To increase the mileage of roads in the hill areas.
(c) The widening and strengthening of the existing roadways.
(d) Regulation of the flow of the principal rivers so that navigation will be possible more or less throughout the year.

Extension of Railways Upto Manipur

The issue relating to the opening of a railhead in the Jiribam Sub-division of Manipur has been hanging fire for many years. The urgency and justification of the demand have been enhanced to a great extent by the opening of new Cachar Road. The Jiribam Sub-division is situated near Silchar. The proposed extension could be either from Silchar or from any other station which may be linked with Jiribam, at the least cost and within the shortest possible time.

Areas like Manipur, where not an inch of rail line has been introduced, ought to receive priority treatment at the hands of the Central Government. Because all future economic developments and industrial programmes shall have to depend on this aspect of communication. We can visualise the prospects for the development of industries and the tourist trade in the case of lining up Jiribam with other parts of the country through railways. Manipur occupies a strategic position. The extension of railways to this strategic area has, therefore, ample justification from the security angle too.

Cycle Industry

Manipur valley is considered one of the places, in the whole of India, which uses cycles on a mass scale. The manufacture of cycle parts should be one of the items which could be immediately taken up without fear for future market. The Small Scale Sector Unit of the Government of India is understood to have taken up this item in Manipur. It is, however, yet to be seen whether the patronage and guidance of the said unit means serious business or not.

Watch Factory

The suitability of light and precision tools manufacturing in Manipur has been discussed at length. Of all such industries the relevance of a watch factory in Manipur cannot be over emphasised. While considering the opening of an additional unit of the Hindustan Machine Tools, the subject matter of a watch factory should be treated on priority basis.

Other Industries

The peculiar geographical situation and the climatic condition of Manipur have to be taken into consideration in the matter of future industrial developments. Opening of heavy industries, which will require major transport facilities and whose products will be bulky and involve heavy transport expenses, will not be economic now and in near future. The emphasis has, therefore, to be given on the manufacture of light and precision tools. The Manipuris are noted for their inborn dexterity in the mechanical and precision industries. The climate is suitable for such industries. There is a strong case for opening a branch of the Hindustan Machine Tools in this region, as early as possible.

Vast Possibilities for Tea Plantation

The Manipuri variety of tea-seed is famous throughout the world and is used for multiplication. But the tragedy of the situation is that there is no tea-plantation in Manipur. Tea grows wild in many areas of the State so that sections of the local population depend on the wild growths for their domestic consumption. The Manipuri variety of seed was discovered long ago by British tea-planters. Now a pertinent question should be raised why the possibility of tea plantation should not be explored by the Government at the Centre as well as in the State. The need for such an exploration is urgent in view of the following factors:

(a) The production of Indian tea has to be raised in order to meet the internal as well as external demands.
(b) Manipur has vast areas which can be put under tea plantation with profit and considerable ease.

Why the princely regime did not take up this industry, in spite of its close relationships with the British Government, is a matter which requires considerable probe and research. Now that the political climate in the whole State has undergone a thorough change, the issue may be taken up with full vigour, without further loss of time. The experts, guiding the Government in this important trade, have a special responsibility in putting Manipur on the tea-map of India. How much they have to depend upon the sense of initiative of the State Government or the local people has to be decided by reference to the fact that Manipur and her people are total strangers to this trade. They will require a comprehensive education and information on the subject. Mention may be made of the suitability conducting the first trials in the Jiribam Sub-division of Manipur which is in the close neighbourhood of the Cachar Tea Gardens.

Spinning Mills

The Government of India have agreed, according to the latest report to the setting up of spinning mills in Manipur by exempting the general ban on further licensing of similar mills in the rest of India. There has been emphatic demand for such a mill from the people of Manipur for several years. The hill areas can be extensively used for plantation of cotton in case the proposed mills come into existence. The importance of weaving, as one of the leading professions of the population, has been discussed in this chapter in detail. The emergence of the spinning mills will lead to vast employment in cotton growing areas on the one hand, and as factory hands to many people, on the other. Now the anxiety of the people of Manipur is how quickly the matter will be processed at the relevant levels. The Government of India's decision in this behalf, although belated, is welcome. A good well-implemented decision in this case will lead to the fulfilment of a mandate received from the people, viz., the mandate of removing regional disparity in industrial development. The opening of the spinning mills will also be an unfailing booster to the weaving trade of Manipur, on the one hand and the total economy of the State on the other.

Importance of Weaving

Weaving is as essential as breathing for every woman of Manipur, irrespective of the status of her family. The dexterity of the legendary Heroine Thoibi princess of Moirang in the art of weaving and embroidery was considered one of her best qualifications. The tradition continues till today. An outsider should not be surprised to see any Manipuri woman, however well placed she may be, according to social warrant of predence or by virtue of her achievements in the present context, weaving on a traditional loom, as a hobby or for actual business. One rarely comes across a Manipuri house without a loom or some weaving materials.

In the hill areas the weaving pattern is different. While the cloth designs differ from tribe to tribe or even from village to village the weaving pattern is invariably confined to loin-looms. Loin-looms are also used in the valley more or less as essential equipments for weaving certain items of clothes. A bar is put through the holes. The bar forms one end of the loom while the weaver's loin forms the other end. The equipments are few and simple. The quality of the products depend more on the dexterity of the weaver than the equipments. Loin-loom products are lasting, strong and can be extremely uniform and fine. Certain items of Manipuri clothes have to be woven only on the loin-loom. Manipuri women's traditional dress (Phanek) and other varieties of thick chaddars and bed clothes like Ngabong, Leisum, Lashingphi and any cloth belonging to tribal origin are best produced on the loin-loom. Young girls of the present generation in Manipur continue to be familiar with traditional handlooms inspite of their sophisticated outlook. But the use of loin-looms is now confined to certain areas of the Manipur Valley, the women folk of which have specialised in the trade of weaving Phaneks, the traditional woman's dress.

Will the arts of weaving and embroidery die out of Manipur soon, due to the great impact of mill clothes and the fast change in taste for clothing pattern? This question is often asked in many quarters. It is true that weaving has ceased being a paying proposition to many women in Manipur. The price of yarns is rising, higher and higher, day by day. The Manipuri handloom weaver today weaves more out of her zeal to exercise her taunt and dexterity than for profit in a large number of cases. Serious steps have to be taken to keep this profession alive and remunerative. There is vast internal as well as international demand for Manipuri handloom products which have a distinctive character of their own in respect of texture, design and colour. The following measures will enable the trade to sustain itself.

(a) To enable the weavers to purchase yarn at cheaper rates, necessarily the State Government has to make special arrangements.
(b) The margin of profit, on the finished products, must be raised. For this the Government has to provide marketing facilities so that the middle man cannot exploit the poor weavers.
(c) Adequate machinery to control design and quality should be provided to put a stop to cheap imitations and use of non-fast colours which otherwise will have a harmful effect on the trade itself. It has been observed that a lot of goodwill and temptation for Manipur handlooms among outsiders including foreign tourists is diminishing on account of the inability to control and standardise quality and designs and to check cheap imitations by agencies outside the State.
(d) Propaganda and advertisement must be done adequately both for internal and outside markets.

Coming to the main question whether the handloom trade will die out soon, it can be said without hesitation, that it will not. The following are the main among other reasons:

(a) The womenfolk of Manipur will continue to adhere to their own handloom products in the matter of their best and ceremonial dress. No mill cloth has been able to replace the Manipuri hand-woven cloth in respect of texture, strength and design. The tradition remains so far unshaken and has shown signs of revitalisation of wake of modernisation. Nothing can be more encouraging.
(b) The profession of weaving continues to be as respectable as it was in the old days. This is the secret of the sustenance of the trade inspite of the great impact of mill cloths. The life and death of a profession or a trade cannot be

ruled by economic factors alone. At least in the case of Manipuri handloom the social and sentimental value, attached to this trade, has enabled it to sustain itself inspite of several hostile currents including economic. While travelling in the hill areas one is struck by the deep sentiments of respect and care with which each tribal group treats its specific design of cloth. In many cases the type of cloth will indicate the tribe or community of the person in Manipur. This conservative trend has been a blessing in disguise and is likely to grow into its productive height in the region.

In a way the Manipuri handloom tradition is inimmitable. It has been observed that attempts are being made to immitate the Manipuri handloom products by varieties of agencies in many places. They have invariably failed to achieve their end for obvious reasons. The Manipuri weavers are not jealous of those trying to immitate them. But the only fear is that due to misrepresentation by incompetent sources the popularity of Manipuri handloom might be affected thereby giving a death blow to the basic economy of the state of Manipur.

Just as the skill and mastery of the making of Banarasi Sarees and Chaddars are confined to a section of the Banarasi population, who have inherited that from their forefathers, through the ages, the weaving tradition in Manipur is handed down to the succeeding generations from ancient days. The tradition, therefore, carries with it tremendous sentimental value for things inherited. It is also difficult to learn this art for an outsider unless he or she devotes adequate time and labour and works with a sense of complete dedication. The census data about the total workers, main workers, marginal workers and non-workers is as follows :

Table 3

The Survey of Main Workers, Marginal Workers and Non-Workers (Statewise) : Census 2001

Total Rural Urban	*Persons Males Females*	*Total workers*	*Main workers*	*Marginal workers*	*Non-workers*	*Total Workers (main + marginal)*
Total	Persons	1,069,578	756,520	313,058	1,318,490	1,069,578
	Males	594,642	484,240	110,402	621,022	594,642
	Females	474,936	272,280	202,656	697,468	474,936
Rural	Persons	846,595	592,379	254,216	965,509	846,595
	Males	464,793	373,702	91,091	463,418	464,793
	Females	381,802	218,677	163,125	502,091	381,802
Urban	Persons	222,983	164,141	58,842	352,981	222,983
	Males	129,849	110,538	19,311	157,604	129,849
	Females	93,134	53,603	39,531	195,377	93,134

While building up the economy of the new State of Manipur the handloom industry should get top priority. It is agreed on all hands that a State and its population can be developed mainly and quickly on the existing tradition of the

Table 4

The Survey of Main Workers, Marginal Workers and Non-Workers (Districtwise) : Census 2001

District	*Total workers*			*Main workers*			*Marginal workers*			*Non workers*		
	P	M	F	P	M	F	P	M	F	P	M	F
Senapati	189,263	101,134	88,129	144,653	81,885	62,768	44,610	19,249	25,361	189,320	96,298	93,022
Tamenglong	52,033	27,480	24,553	44,672	24,322	20,350	7,361	3,158	4,203	59,826	30,562	29,264
Churachandpur	99,262	56,782	42,480	71,466	46,448	25,018	27,796	10,334	17,462	126,347	59,327	67,020
Bishnupur	91,298	51,864	39,434	56,302	40,682	15,620	34,996	11,182	23,814	116,516	53,502	63,014
Thoubal	181,518	97,384	84,134	114,826	76,902	37,924	66,692	20,482	46,210	185,416	88,428	96,988
Imphal West	177,077	101,786	75,291	126,593	84,948	41,645	50,484	16,838	33,646	267,374	119,722	147,652
Imphal East	158,675	93,494	65,181	107,372	76,305	31,067	51,303	17,189	34,114	237,185	105,744	131,441
Ukhrul	66,596	35,941	30,655	51,569	29,261	22,308	15,027	6,680	8,347	74,024	37,389	36,635
Chandel	53,856	28,777	25,079	39,067	23,487	15,580	14,789	5,290	9,499	62,482	30,050	32,432

people. The question is whether there is enough scope for it or not. As has been maintained earlier the scope and justification for encouraging the handloom industry are ample. A bold approach has to be made and a realistic plan has to be drawn up in order to rush to the rescue of the weakening industry, on one hand, and to strengthen the economy of the state, on the other, through this industry.

Sugar and Cornflake

The other industries which may be taken up in the small scale sector are sugar, cornflake, fruit carning etc. The suitability of Manipur to the production of sugarcanes need not be exaggerated. So also the possibilities of maize production is an approved fact. Opening of sugar and cornflake industries in the small scale sector has adequate justification and will contribute to the development of the economy of the region. The availability of some varieties of fruits in abundance in Manipur is known to the Department of Industries and also to any layman. Pineapples, oranges, guava, heikha, malhei, heitup, chumbrei are found during their seasons, in abundance. Fruit canning industries in the small sector will have tremendous relevance and justification.

The aspect of horticulture remains miserably neglected in Manipur. The lesson of Himachal in production of apples must be an eye-opener to Manipur also. Plenty of fertile soil and human labour is already assured in Manipur. Research and experimentation have to be taken up to utilise the available land and human labour. A few varieties of fruits could be experimented in right earnest in the same manner as the State of Himachal did in the case of apple. There is nothing like something falling down from heaven. Heaven itself is to be created with the sweat of our labour and with the materials available at hand.

Thus, the economy of Manipur has improved with establishment of peace to some extent after conferring of statehood to Manipur but still, there is a long way to go and that is possible not only either by governmental or people's efforts but a balanced combination of both.

Section-III
Mizoram

13

The Land and the People

North East in India is said to have its distinct identity, culture and culture which are quite different from other parts of the country. But within north-eastern states also, this distinction prevails. Each state has identity of its own and certain features which differentiate it from other states of the region and the country. This, then becomes true in case of Mizoram also. Mizo regionalism also is preserved by a number of factors each contributing to its growth in its own way. Such factors which have most evidently contributed to the growth of Mizo regionalism are certain cultural and traditional peculiarities, ethnicity, communalisation of religion, psycho-social factors, language, economic factors, geographical conditions and elite conflict. This chapter is an effort to analyse how these factors together foster and sustain Mizo regionalism.

(a) Culture and Tradition of Mizos

E.B. Taylor defines 'culture' as 'that complex which includes knowledge, belief, art, morals, law, custom and any other capabilities and habits acquired by man as a member of society." Others too have said that "the essential core of culture consists of traditional (i.e. historically derived and selected) ideas, and especially their attached values."[2]

In the light of above definitions of culture we may attempt to identify and analyse the main tenets of Mizo culture and traditions. Mohan Lal Sharma holds the view that the differences of the North East India should be traced to the norms governing the politico-institutional behaviour, which norms are being guided by the concept of 'retaliation' which results in acceptance of violence as a common pattern of behaviour. He would see, among the people of the region, common traits such as love for independent living, undifferentiated structures at local level and local autonomy. He believes that the tribes of Northeast India have those values and norms like liberal universal outlook, plain heartedness, simplicity and high aesthetic tastes.[3]

Mr. Mukherjee, an M.P. once said about the Mizos thus, "These are simple-hearted and genuine people, not the like of you and me who do not always say what we mean."[4] These 'traits', 'norms' and 'values' are strongly evident in Mizo culture and traditions. Typical peculiarities are also realisable in the physical aspects of their culture such as music, dance, literature, habits and artefacts. It is clearly seen that in music, dance, habits, costumes and lifestyle, they are in confirmity to the cultures of the people of East and South-East Asia. Besides these the Mizos have a strong socio-cultural norm of 'tlawmngaihna' which is said to have no equivalent term in English. It is the governing principle of Mizo culture through which every Mizo is expected to be industrious, brave, long-suffering, helpful and to be more concerned about the comfort of others than personal gain.

Their traditional customs are so different from those of the people living in plains that the latter always find it difficult to understand the Mizo sense of justice, fairness and judgement. All these go to differentiate the Mizo outlook on life from those of others that mutual accommodation within the 'out group' and the 'in group' is always characterised with certain amount of frictions.

It is accepted that Mizos are open to the process of modernisation, yet they are also apprehensive of the possible obliteration of their cherished cultural traits, norms and values, in the process if modernisation goes without proper protection to their culture and tradition. When Christianity was introduced, the early Mizo converts thought that many of their cultural and traditional practices were incompatible with Christianity. But, as time passed and when all the Mizos had turned Christians, they gradually adjusted these practices with the new found religion by bringing them into its fold. This process of christianisation of culture and traditions is an ongoing process and effective factor of Mizo regionalism, especially with its religious overtones, by which it is pitched against the ever-shadowing dominant Hindu culture.

The force of tradition and custom is considered by Mathur as "an adhesive force to the tribal identity which no other social identity can match" and this, taken together with certain other factors have "given rise to an isolationist complex . . . and to the feeling that the interests of the tribals can be preserved only if they are political masters of the region in which they live.[5]

Thus, we contend that the peculiar cultural traits and traditional customs contribute in great measure to the reinforcement of regional sentiments among the Mizo people. The acculturation process which have been occurring in Mizoram is more of western than Indian because westernisation came alongwith the spread of Christianity.

Mizos find it difficult to adopt any of the dominant Indian cultures because of their strange culture and traditions as well as their receptivity to western culture. They can conceive of India as a federated union of varieties of people and cultures than being a country where the minority cultures are absorbed by the dominant culture. Had the Hindu saints gone into the hills before the Christian missionaries, the Mizos may have been highly Hinduised. But, once they have adopted Christianity, it does not look feasible or desirable to impose the Hindu culture or for that matter any other strong culture on the Mizos, for this will only result in friction which may escalate into socio-political consciousness of the extreme form.

(b) Ethnic Footings

The Mizo people are an ethnic group formed as a result of the assimilation of many tribes, sub-tribes and clans.[6] The transformation of these tribes and clans into a common ethnic identity is said to be facilitated by the deliberate move for broad-basing of the ethnic identity so as to involve all the tribes living in an area in the struggle for certain basic interests rather than rely on a few hundred or a few thousand people belonging to a single tribe" and this move is ensured by "the adoption of common symbols like Christianity, roman script and western education."[7] According to Nirmal Nibedon, the various uprisings in the North-East India constitute an "Ethnic Explosion". He observes the ethnic base of the tribal movements in the North-East India thus,

> " . . . the feeling of being ethnically and racially different from the rest of the subcontinent was the decisive factor for one major group to launch a defensive guerilla war. Of course the strong feelings of being 'different' would be further galvanised on the mountains by westernised Christianity . . . But, strangely, it was ethnicity that was the prime mover, the fundamental cause for the battles of the future. At best religion played a secondary role. It was not the other way round as claimed later by the plainsmen when the tribal tornado struck."[8]

We find it to be a strong observation of the ethnic ground of tribal movements, yet, it is very true especially in the Mizo case. The transformation of Mizos into a common ethnico-cultural identity, though an established fact, is still an on-going process as a deeper search about identity. The Mizos learn their ethnic lessons from the experiences of Manipuris (Meiteis), the Tripuris and the Cacharis. There is a strong evidence that the Meiteis and the Mizos are similar ethnically, yet, the Hinduisation of the Meiteis has done them to the extent of losing their original ethnic identity. They are now trying to revive their ethnico-cultural identity. The case of the natives of Tripura state is quite sad one in the context of ethnic identity. How they have been rendered strangers in their homeland by the assimilation of their ethnico-cultural identity by a stronger culture is a lesson for the Mizos and they have got it. The Cacharis, the natives of the once flourishing Cachar Kingdom (now a District in the State of Assam bordering Mizoram) are not only minorities in their own land but the least assertive and most centered group in the District because they were not adequately protected from the demographic invasion from other quarters, possibly from across the international boundary with the erstwhile East Pakistan. Surrounded by these developments, the fear of losing ethnico-cultural identity cannot but be very real in Mizo politics.

This is especially so because they are bounded by Bengali parts on the north and west. They are constantly apprehensive of the possible wave of infiltration engulfing them from across the international and state borders. The issue of Chakma Buddhist infiltration from Bangladesh has ever been one of the most burning issues in Mizoram politics. This fear of assimilation by other groups is so real that they even think if the process of economic development is fatal to their ethnic culture and identity, because they are aware that the native ethnic components are often disturbed and dislocated by the massive economic measures, as occurred in cases elsewhere. This is not to say that Mizos do not want modernisation and economic development, but to contend that even material advancement can be detrimental to the ethnic group unless it is well-planned and handled according to the local genius and suitability. We cannot impose our plans just on the ground that they will uplift the people economically if we do not also look into the sensitive ethnic awareness of the people. In deeper analysis, it is found that the 'feeling' of being different is based on the 'reality' of being different. The simple fact that Mizos are often taken to be non-Indians by the general masses in India and people of other countries just by seeing their feature and lifestyle and habits bears out the reality of the difference. This may be due to lack of communication, interaction and understanding among the different various groups in such a vast country like India, yet, it has a repulsive effect on the Mizo psyche. At many places in India, Mizos have to convince their fellow Indians that they are Indians, not to talk about people in other countries.

Another simple fact to affirm the difference is that their names and the names of their capital Aizawl are always written incorrectly in national papers, highly standardised research works and books and government owned mass media and documents. Not only the names of ordinary people but also the names of Chief Ministers, Ministers and other State dignitaries are usually wrongly written in important and well-known papers and documents. If this is not a callousness on the part of the writers, it can at least be their lack of understanding and unfamiliarity with the Mizos.[9] This type of unfamiliarity and lack of knowledge about one part of the country only reflects the indifferent and unconcerned attitudes toward minorities and it is fatal to emotional integration. It is recorded that Prime Minister Desai once asked the Naga elders if they are Indians.[10] One may well ask other Indians if they regard the Nagas (and Mizos) as Indians.

Strong ethnic difference of Mizos from the rest of Indians constitute a base for regional assertiveness and ethnic segregationism. Our respondents give this factor a second place among the bases of Mizo regionalism.[11] About the Mizo attitude towards the plains people, whom they commonly call 'VAI'[12] the responses reveal the fact that Mizos are highly apprehensive of the possible loss of their ethnic identity if the number of 'Vais' settling in Mizoram is not strictly banned. 67.62 per cent our respondents hold the view that the number of plainsmen in Mizoram is too large, and 73.37 per cent want to keep the number always below even 5 per cent of the total population of Mizos. To some, even this percentage is too high. 68.25 per cent do not allow the plains people to hold lands in Mizoram and 65.37 per cent have strong objection to Mizo girls marrying from plains. The plains people residing in Mizoram are mostly Government servants, teachers, traders and labourers. The distinctive feature of Mizoram from the rest of the hill areas in North-East India is that most of the shops and business establishments in Mizoram are owned by the Mizo themselves, but only time can tell whether it will continue to be like this. It is in the context of this that trading non-tribals is restricted in Mizoram.

However, we find a number of cases of non-tribals carrying on trades in Mizoram in the name of Mizos. This is an eyesore to the more conscious and sensitive Mizos, because they think that this backdoor way of economic infiltration can ultimately lead to economic infiltration can ultimately lead to economic subservience of Mizos and through it to the loss of Mizo ethnico-cultural identity.

(c) Religion

Religion can be a very strong base for regionalism as seen in the creation of a Muslim majority District of Maloppuram in Kerala which leads Mathur to say that "a case of regionalism generated and sustained by a religious identity and such demands for political regionalism are likely to go up (and not down) as a result of this success."[14] He further observes that "religious identity has proved to be a potent bulwark of regionalism in North-East India where the spread of Hinduism . . . would almost certainly take much fire out of the militant regionalist activist.

The Mizo people had their own religion which was a mixture of animistic beliefs and a consciousness of a Supreme God whom they called *"PATHIAN"*. Protestant Christianity was introduced into the Lushai Hills by the Welsh Presbyterian and also English London Baptist missionaries since 1894.[14] *The Mizos were so receptive to the Gospel message of Christ that within a period of five decades, the whole tribe was converted into Christianity,*[15] and now Christians in the state of Mizoram are 83.81 per cent of the total population of Mizoram, Buddhists (mainly Chakmas) are 8.19 per cent Hindus 7.14 per cent, Muslims 0.45 per cent and Sikhs 0.09 per cent. People who follow religions other than christianity are those coming into Mizoram from outside, except a few cases of indigenous Buddhist Chakmas and animistic tribes. The Mizos consider themselves to be cent-per-cent Christians. Large scale conversion of the whole tribes to a new religion is a peculiar phenomenon and the conversion of the whole of Mizo tribes into Christianity is regarded by many as God's miracle.[16] *The story of this phenomenal conversion to Christianity is taken as very significant "because it is also in a way story of the political and administrative development of the people of the region.*[17]

Having become the sole religion of the Mizos, Christianity acted as a strong agent of modernisation and N.E. Parry, the Superintendent of the Lushai Hills during 1924-28 could observe that "A more active instrument of change than the government is the Christian mission."[18] The impact of the Christian teaching on Mizo society is much greater than in any other Christian areas in India. This has led Ray to state that "Nowhere-else in India religion has so much influence on social, political and other temporal aspects of life."[19] It brought changes to their primitive customs, gave them formal western education and thus indirectly made them socio-politically conscious. How Christianity has brought about far-reaching changes in the Mizo society cannot be expressed in statistical form. Suffice it to say that it is Christianity and its fellow agent of education that have made the Mizo people what they now are socially, economically and politically. How, then, Christianity, being a modernising aspect, can also be one of the causes of the growth of regional sentiment, is a question we have to examine in the context of this book. Christianity, as a universal religion of "peace" and "goodwill towards humanity" is not directly contributive to and responsible for the narrow domestic regional feeling. But, it is some sort of 'territorialisation' or 'communalisation' of it that becomes a mobilising factor for Mizo identity.

Such instances of territorialisation of religion fomenting regional feeling are often seen in other state and national political system, be it the case of Hinduism or Islamism, or Buddhism. This is true about the Mizos. The concept of Mizoram being a 'Christian Land' (which virtually it is) and the politicisation of Mizos with religious overtones result in 'communalisation' of Christianity, and it is in this manner that religion becomes a base for Mizo regionalism. The Church never advocates officially the secession of Mizoram from the Indian Union on the basis of Christianity. It rather encourages its adherents to live as responsible citizens and to contribute to the happiness and prosperity of India. It is also true that Mizo people, especially the educated group are aware that Christianity is not a religion exclusively of the people and that there are many other Christians in different parts of India. But, the knowledge of this simple fact does not effectively govern their political orientation. It is the capitalisation of the sensitive religious fervour propping up Christianity as the Mizo symbol that reinforces their regional sentiments. This form of capitalisation of religious zeal is more evident in the movements of regional political parties in general and in that of the Mizo National Front (MNF) in particular which popularised the slogan "For God and for our land."

Why the Indian National Congress and the Leftist Parties cannot strike deep bases in Mizoram is due to the people's consideration of them as Hinduised party and Atheistic parties respectively. Christianity taken in this way, therefore, becomes a base for Mizo regionalism and a factor for the strength of regional level parties. In this way, Christianity fosters regionalism in Mizoram. It is a time, therefore, that some thinkers revise their opinion that christianity *per se* is responsible for the regional/secessionist movements in those parts where Christians are dominant. It may be beneficial to realise the possibility and necessity that Christianity can be an agent of integration of Mizos if it can be taken out of its communal frame. A close insight into the MNF secessionist movement reveals that it was for the sake of Christianity that the MNF underground army could not enter into a close collaboration with the Communist China. Christianity acts as a border sentinel of an Indian national territory of Mizoram against the possible attempts of territorial aggrandizement on religious ground by the neighbouring Buddhist Burma (Myanmar) and Muslim Bangladesh. Thus, we can rather be thankful that Mizos are Christians. The census data about the religions of the Scheduled Tribes of Mizoram is as follows :

Table 1
Religion for Scheduled Tribes

Scheduled Tribes	*Rural*			*Urban*		
	Total	*Males*	*Females*	*Total*	*Males*	*Females*
1	2	3	4	5	6	7
ALL SCHEDULED TRIBES						
All Religions	**3,58,113**	**1,82,212**	**1,75,901**	**2,95,452**	**1,47,607**	**1,47,845**
1. Buddhists	51,831	26,908	24,923	412	230	182
2. Christians	2,97,026	1,50,413	1,46,613	2,92,615	1,46,063	1,46,552
3. Hindus	7,836	4,090	3,746	773	450	323
4. Jains	3	3	0	3	3	0
5. Muslims	200	128	72	136	85	51
6. Sikhs	14	7	7	10	5	5
7. Other Religions and Persuations	987	503	484	816	442	374
8. Religion not stated	216	160	56	687	329	358

Source : Census 1991.

(d) Psycho-Social Responsible Factors

The Mizos are very close-knit society and a minority group in all respects in the national context, yet having great pride in their culture and traditions. They remember their heroes who have become legendary figures for their deeds of valour. The hills have shaped their mental frame and social behaviour in such a way that they are so different from the plains people in psycho-social system and pattern. They are also so conscious about their being not to match for the plains people in an open socio-economic competition not necessarily because they lack in capabilities but because of their environmental constraints. These conditions have moulded the Mizo psyche in such manner that they are sharply prejudiced against the people in the plain areas.

It is observed by Mathur that

> "The Shiv Sena certainly drew upon the historical pride and prejudices of the Marathas and turned the 'Shivaji Cult' into a powerful political weapon against the South Indian residents of Bombay who were successfully stereotyped as economic usurpers. . . the very success of the Shiv Sena strategy . . . shows that it drew strength from psychological prejudices rather than territorial regionalism."[20]

The Mizos, though even without a written record of their distant history also remember the deeds of their legendary heroes through the oral traditions passed on from one generation to another drawing inspirations from the remembrances of their fruitful campaigns against their enemies. Nibedon comments on this legacy thus,

> "A few in whom the patriotic spart smouldered, finding themselves isolated and temporarily helpless, bided their time, clinging all the while to the ancient legends of their heroes. A new generation was coming up in the Mizo Hills. Would legend survive history?
>
> In general, the hillmen were perplexed, full of scepticism and suspense. Only one thing remained clear to them in the changing course of history—they had these heroes whom the whitemen never knew, nor would the 'vais' when they came later."[21]

Even if not as well-known as Shivaji, the legendary heroes of Mizos were the source of inspiration to the young generation towards courageous deeds. One Mizo poet composed a song which used to be sung widely thus,[22]

> "Kan pi kan pu mihuaite dan tha kha kan ti,
> Thian chhan thih an ngam fo thin
> An hming a thang bawk si;
> Keinin chu dan chu zawmin huai taka din kan tum,
> Mizo kan ni kan hmel a tha kan tum a sang bawk si.
>
> which in its English rendering may mean somewhat like this,
>
> We admire the beauty of the good rule
> That our forefather heroes followed,
> Always daring to die to rescue friends,
> Spreading their fame far and wide;
> True to this rule of valour, we still stand up courageously
> We are Mizos we look so good,
> And our aspirations are high"

Moved as they are by the examples of their heroes, the new generations of Mizos take it upon themselves as their right obligation to fight the 'enemies' with the same spirit of their forefathers. Their inter-village and inter-tribal feuds being the issue of the past, their "enemies" happened to be the British intruders and later the Indian plains people. Their tribal spirit of valour combined with a sense of tactfulness in war caused them to be proud and prejudiced against the plains people. Their spirit is such that they would rather die fighting than give themselves over to the enemies in defeat. How this sense of valour, activated in their various movements, have aided in preserving their identity is undeterminable.

Observation on this aspect of Mizo politics may be possible only after some time when we can look at the course of future developments in the lack of this deterrent force. It will be nationally productive if the Mizos are not provoked to activate again this sense of valour and pride in their heroic past. The Mizos are always suspicious of outsiders. They regard their Mizoness as based on their strong principle of life known as *'tlawmngaihna'* which is explained elsewhere.

They take Indianness as something tricky, crafty, fraudulent and foul. This impression of India prejudiced them against all Indians though they know well that the plains are much better-off economically. The remarks that Mizos are "simple hearted and genuine people, not the like of you and me who do not always say what we mean"[23] is too true in their social grouping of people. They, therefore, find it difficult to have full confidence in the genuineness of plains people and cannot repose full trust on them when the latter, especially those among them who show some form of concern for their welfare, try to win their confidence in various ways.

Due to a close-knit, egalitarian and free society, they are apprehensive about the possible inroads of undesirable elements into their society. Their social freedom is so high that they are often taken to be a society where sexual freedom exists in the loose sense of the term. But, a close look at their social norms and practices would prove otherwise. Men and women mix freely but they do not necessarily misbehave, whereas in the plains, women are limited at home and are allowed to enjoy limited freedom, though whether this practice is a better means of ensuring the chastity, fidelity, dignity and honour of women is difficult to say. Mizo society is very egalitarian, on account of the high level of socialisation. There is no social barrier between high and low. There is neither caste nor dowry system. Very frequently, the peon will be seen in the chair at Church services and other social gatherings while his 'boss' in the office where he works will be sitting as an ordinary member of the audience. Quite often, the drivers, officers and government ministers will eat together at the same table. These are rare sights among the caste-ridden societies of India. Census data is given on next pages showing marital status and no. of children.

Mizos are happy to have this type of society and they are sensitively on guard from any possible inroads of unwanted socio-cultural behaviour into their egalitarian society. It is no exaggeration to say that the original Mizo society was very close to the attainment of the utopian society of idealists' dream. Much of the degradations which have set into the Mizo society can be generally considered as the consequence of the infiltration of outside-value and norm systems, which in turn result in the heightening of the regionalist sentiments. Hmartawnphunga, father of the Chief Minister Lalthanhawla wrote a pamphlet in 1947, wherein he disclosed his opinion as to how he thought the Mizos would not be able to live with *'vais'*. According to him, the danger of joining India lies in the fact that the *'vais'* cannot be made true friends of the Mizos and they are much more selfish than the British.[24]

It is also known to the Mizos that the plains people are too conscious of economic gains and they are afraid that, provided equal opportunity, they would not be able to compete with them. This fear gives rise to a "defensive nationalism" and "it was the same defensive posture and a bit of scepticism which seem to characterise the budding political attitudes" of the Mizo people.[25] Thus, the psycho-social milieu of Mizos not only differentiate them from the plains people but also alienates them from the rest of the country.

Table 2

Ever Married and Currently Married Women Belonging to Scheduled Tribes by Present Age, Number of Surviving Children and Total Number of Surviving Children by Sex

Present Age	*Total ever/ currently married women*	*Ever/currently married women with number of serviving children*						*Total surviving children*		
		0	*1*	*2*	*3*	*4*	*5+*	*Total*	*Males*	*Females*
1	2	3	4	5	6	7	8	9	10	11
ALL SCHEDULED TRIBES										
RURAL										
Ever Married										
All ages	**75,374**	**18,733**	**7,807**	**8,810**	**8,658**	**9,468**	**21,117**	**2,25,102**	**1,15,162**	**1,09,940**
Less than 15	184	169	4	9	0	0	0	22	10	12
15-19	1,996	1,255	527	92	7	9	0	768	414	354
20-24	8,799	3,083	2,661	1,984	677	189	40	9,633	4,876	4,757
25-29	12,946	3,064	1,821	2,757	2,522	1,838	821	26,854	13,580	13,274
30-34	10,822	2,262	757	1,260	1,898	2,239	2,340	30,979	15,591	15,388
35-39	9,085	1,815	466	663	1,047	1,724	3,322	31,424	16,071	15,353
40-44	7,164	1,459	314	451	599	985	3,297	28,138	14,444	13,694
45-49	6,048	1,159	252	403	527	682	2,979	25,460	13,046	12,414
50-54	5,183	1,084	258	397	435	509	2,459	21,401	11,211	10,190
55-59	3,805	823	157	227	334	415	1,829	15,863	8,221	7,642
60-64	3,317	793	201	232	264	297	1,509	13,017	6,677	6,340
65-69	2,088	506	141	121	120	207	966	8,219	4,298	3,921
70-74	1,494	370	102	84	80	155	682	5,766	2,939	2,827
75-79	884	274	48	33	41	69	398	3,240	1,679	1,561
80 +	1,111	355	73	68	72	123	406	3,594	1,779	1,815

(Contd.)

(Contd.)

1	2	3	4	5	6	7	8	9	10	11
Currently Married										
All ages	**65,814**	**16,024**	**6,525**	**7,683**	**7,769**	**8,570**	**18,645**	**1,99,107**	**1,01,888**	**97,219**
Less than 15	177	164	3	9	0	0	0	21	10	11
15-19	1,839	1,171	460	91	6	9	0	696	371	325
20-24	8,183	2,866	2,399	1,883	662	186	38	9,100	4,627	4,473
25-29	12,228	2,837	1,637	2,576	2,454	1,807	811	25,917	13,099	12,818
30-34	10,172	2,068	636	1,131	1,808	2,179	2,298	29,851	15,031	14,820
35-39	8,569	1,677	377	564	983	1,660	3,262	30,357	15,534	14,823
40-44	6,584	1,326	258	372	523	890	3,172	26,509	13,600	12,909
45-49	5,393	1,000	178	321	433	610	2,822	23,642	12,045	11,597
50-54	4,343	883	184	293	346	413	2,198	18,706	9,847	8,859
55-59	2,965	612	93	155	220	335	1,541	13,109	6,780	6,329
60-64	2,252	485	121	126	173	198	1,136	9,608	4,940	4,668
65-69	1,355	321	83	80	62	123	676	5,652	2,948	2,704
70-74	718	166	43	31	35	62	376	3,044	1,551	1,493
75-79	358	121	21	12	18	30	154	1,325	702	623
80 +	294	101	11	14	16	43	105	967	526	441
URBAN										
Ever Married										
All ages	**62,669**	**12,158**	**7,700**	**8,344**	**9,838**	**9,408**	**14,901**	**1,85,157**	**93,060**	**92,097**
Less than 15	141	132	1	6	0	0	0	13	6	7
15-19	1,706	1,103	478	75	5	8	0	675	362	313
20-24	7,986	2,361	2,709	1,885	749	155	37	9,556	4,773	4,783
25-29	11,704	2,201	1,889	2,852	2,840	1,436	436	24,348	12,264	12,084
30-34	9,532	1,518	843	1,228	2,364	2,195	1,346	26,437	13,547	12,890
35-39	7,495	1,095	436	654	1,429	1,920	1,932	24,695	12,608	12,087
40-44	5,761	804	330	442	758	1,256	2,154	21,296	10,576	10,720
45-49	4,501	598	211	320	479	837	2,044	18,575	9,128	9,447
50-54	4,124	585	232	234	420	570	2,073	17,586	8,731	8,855

(Contd.)

(Contd.)

1	2	3	4	5	6	7	8	9	10	11
55-59	2,816	460	129	197	239	306	1,477	12,356	6,212	6,144
60-64	2,762	492	180	147	204	303	1,431	12,119	6,017	6,102
65-69	1,548	279	97	85	122	126	830	7,090	3,612	3,478
70-74	967	175	60	69	84	125	451	4,126	2,092	2,034
75-79	584	118	37	36	47	57	282	2,500	1,272	1,228
80 +	857	173	53	76	83	99	370	3,341	1,638	1,703
Currently Married										
All ages	**53,015**	**10,150**	**6,069**	**7,047**	**8,689**	**8,356**	**12,428**	**1,57,086**	**78,893**	**78,193**
Less than 15	124	116	1	5	0	0	0	11	5	6
15-19	1,554	1,026	407	74	5	8	0	602	321	281
20-24	7,348	2,151	2,423	1,794	711	147	36	8,935	4,458	4,477
25-29	10,716	1,956	1,599	2,565	2,731	1,396	422	22,913	11,533	11,380
30-34	8,641	1,311	607	1,047	2,232	2,102	1,308	24,869	12,767	12,102
35-39	6,723	950	293	530	1,282	1,790	1,850	22,894	11,683	11,211
40-44	5,044	698	229	319	646	1,128	2,012	19,253	9,553	9,700
45-49	3,846	476	152	229	377	713	1,889	16,566	8,079	8,487
50-54	3,254	437	138	161	308	450	1,752	14,544	7,247	7,297
55-59	2,058	321	58	111	167	233	1,162	9,561	4,816	4,745
60-64	1,787	328	69	65	101	175	1,045	8,495	4,214	4,281
65-69	868	177	36	41	56	86	469	3,951	2,022	1,929
70-74	451	66	28	37	24	72	224	2,076	1,034	1,042
75-79	233	40	10	16	11	21	133	1,152	568	584
80 +	237	47	7	35	28	22	98	955	456	499

Source: Census 1991.

Notes: 1. 'All ages includes 'age not stated'.

2. Number of ever/currently married women in col.4 includes women not reporting number of surviving children.

3. The age groups having nil return are not shown.

Table 3
Age, Sex and Marital Status for Scheduled Tribes (Manipur)

Age group	Total	Never Married	Married	Widowed	Divorced	Unspecified
1	2	3	4	5	6	7
ALL SCHEDULED TRIBES						
RURAL						
All ages	**3,58,113**	**2,15,788**	**1,28,237**	**9,021**	**5,020**	**47**
0 - 9	99,235	99,235	0	0	0	0
10-14	48,381	48,059	306	4	9	3
15-19	37,045	34,738	2,121	20	158	8
20-24	27,944	15,946	11,180	108	710	0
25-29	28,663	6,896	20,737	195	833	2
30-34	23,809	2,806	19,989	237	777	0
35-39	20,720	1,440	18,426	358	483	13
40-44	15,648	774	13,984	425	465	0
15-44	1,53,829	62,600	86,437	1,343	3,426	23
45-49	13,277	543	11,809	547	376	2
50-54	11,142	428	9,434	927	350	3
55-59	8,359	263	6,879	958	259	0
60-64	7,440	228	5,646	1,372	194	0
65-69	4,474	142	3,207	997	128	0
70-74	3,159	65	1,968	1,017	107	2
75-79	1,746	22	928	745	51	0
80+	2,095	67	886	1,044	98	0
Age not stated	4,976	4,136	737	67	22	14
URBAN						
All ages	**2,95,452**	**1,79,672**	**1,02,345**	**7,413**	**5,998**	**24**
0 - 9	73,694	73,694	0	0	0	0
10-14	38,086	37,816	208	5	57	0
15-19	34,253	32,249	1,836	16	152	0
20-24	29,327	17,903	10,641	131	649	3
25-29	28,223	8,544	18,306	238	1,131	4
30-34	20,884	3,101	16,436	346	1,001	0
35-39	16,642	1,447	14,095	388	712	0
40-44	12,661	719	10,959	425	558	0
15-44	1,41,990	63,963	72,273	1,544	4,203	7
45-49	9,822	415	8,516	480	410	1
50-54	8,712	336	7,202	789	384	1
55-59	6,268	209	5,041	700	317	1
60-64	5,697	212	4,142	1,081	262	0
65-69	3,321	103	2,260	811	147	0
70-74	2,114	97	1,242	676	99	0
75-79	1,147	30	594	485	38	0
80+	1,571	84	617	816	54	0
Age not stated	3,030	2,713	250	26	27	14

Source : Census 1991.

(e) Linguistic Aspects

In India, language is not just a factor but also a politically recognised base for States Reorganisation since 1917. The Indian National Congress accepted the principle of linguistic provinces in its annual session at Nagpur in 1920.[26] This was since the Congress party took the non-linguistic administrative areas as the arbitrary arrangement of the British as a part of their 'divide and rule' policy.[27] Language was then considered standing for and representing culture, race, history, individually and finally a sub-nation. After independence, there was a controversy over the question of the criterion to be followed for states reorganisation. The Dar Commission of the Constituent Assembly (1948) favoured 'administrative convenience' than 'language' to be determining factor in states reorganisation. The J.V.P. Committee of the Congress party also led down the demand of linguistic provinces but allowed its experimentation with the creation of Andhra Pradesh on linguistic basis, which took place in 1953.

The States Reorganisation Commission set up four main factors including "linguistic and cultural homogeneity" as one of them for the reorganisation of States. It followed two major principles of: (a) language as the broad factors of reorganisation, and (b) administrative undesirability of too many states. It is this Commission's "pre-occupation with linguistic issue . . . which later on released forces powerful enough to challenge the validity and viability of the map of India drawn in 1956." From then, "The SRC was literally inundated with pleas and petitions for carrying states on the basis of one-language-one-state principles but it did not concede the demand that language must be treated as the sole criterion for demarcation of state boundaries."[28]

Still, the linguistic pressures and demands were so strong that Bombay was split in 1960, Punjab in 1966 and Assam since the mid-sixties, all on linguistic basis. Such splittings of states "gave further impetus to linguistic regionalism in national politics.[29]

The past seven decades in India have been characterised by the preponderance of language-related or language-based regionalism.[30] In Mizo state politics, language, even if not a prominent factor of regionalism, has its role in fostering it as a negative consequence of the Assamese linguistic chauvinism, this also in relation to all hill areas in the then Assam and not in relation to Mizoram only. On November 9, 1947, Nichols-Roy, the initiator of the hills-plains unity week at Shillong urged, in front of 450 delegates of hill leaders from all the hill parts of Assam, that the hill people would better learn the Assamese language. A negative reaction came from Williamson A. Sangma who desired Assam to be a composite state and opposed the imposition of the Assamese language on the hill people. Bawihchhuaka, a popular Mizo Union Party delegate also opposed to the imposition of Assamese on the hill people.[31] In a meeting of all the Chief Executive Members of all the District Councils of Assam convened by himself, Williamson Sangma cited a resolution of the Asom Jatiya Mahasobha taken shortly before, to the effect that the areas opposed to Assamese as State Language should be severed from

Assam. He cited this in order to justify a demand for Hill State. A deputation of hill leaders gave their opinion to Prime Minister Nehru when he visited Shillong on August 28, 1955, to the effect that imposition of Assamese was undesirable for the hill people.

Despite all these oppositions, the Assam Pradesh Congress Committee passed a resolution on April 22, 1960, demanding immediate introduction of Assamese State Language Bill which was complied with by the Assam Government. The Eastern India Tribals Union (EITU) which was also joined by the Union Mizo Freedom Organisation (UMFO) vehemently opposed the move. The All Party Hill Leaders Conference (APHLC) taking place in July 1960 demanded the dropping of the language Bill. The third meeting of the APHLC in November, 1960 at Haflong viewed the passage of the Assamese Official Language Bill being "a clear proof of unfair attitude and firm determinaton of the Assamese community to avail themselves of undue advantages and thereby enhance their domination over the hills people . . . ."

During all these developments, the Mizo leaders actively participated in the hill leaders' opposition to the Assamese Official Language move. This move, thus, indirectly reinforced the regional sentiment of the Mizos, for they soon realised that so long as they continued to remain under a linguistically dominant group, their linguistic identity and all other identity were at risk. During the Janata rule at the Centre, in 1979, the proposal to have a compulsory paper of any Indian major language found in the Eighth Schedule in the competitive tests conducted by the UPSC agitated by Mizos. When President Sajeeva Reddy visited Aizawl, the Mizo Zirlai Pawl (MZP), Mizo Students' Association, demonstrated their opposition for the proposal by wearing black clothes, standing in lines all along the road from the 'gateway' to Aizawl town and turning their backs to the President as soon as the motorcade passed by them. T.C. Kapmawia, the then President of the MZP said to the President of India in a short interview that if the proposal was not dropped it would have serious consequences in Mizoram.

The President of India showed an appearance of being annoyed by such threatening statements. But, it appeared that being a shrewd politician, he could see the harm that could be done to the Union by such imposition of language on the weaker sections. It was learnt that he later expressed sympathy to the non-Hindi speaking people and he demonstrated this on certain occasion. The Mizoram (UT) Assembly enacted the Mizoram Official Language Act, 1974, which received the President's assent on 17.2.1975. By this Act, Mizo Language was made the Official Language of Mizoram with scope for the use of English in official purposes where required.[32] Regional sentiment with linguistic overtones was seen in the Mizo Union Party's "Aims and Objectives."[33] *In 1947, D. Ronghaka issued a pamphlet "Zoram Independent" in which he spelt out the reasons why Mizoram should become independent from India, wherein he gave the following argument: "The fact that we speak one language is itself a good reason why we should strive for independence."*[34]

Attempts are being put in to popularise Hindi in Mizoram through formal and non-formal methods of education. Besides providing regular simple courses at the elementary level of formal education, propagation of Hindi is formed a Wing in the Education Department of Mizoram and there is post-graduate level Hindi Training Institute at Aizawl. There is also a special Hindi Lesson Programme through the All India Radio, Aizawl Station for 30 minutes time in a week and much more. The census data for the languages spoken by various Scheduled Tribes for Mizoram state is as follows :

Table 4
Mother Tongue for Scheduled Tribes

Scheduled Tribe	*Mother Tongue*	*Number of Speakers*					
		Rural			*Urban*		
		Total	*Males*	*Females*	*Total*	*Males*	*Females*
1	2	3	4	5	6	7	8
ALL SCHEDULED TRIBES							
	Adi	4	2	2	2	2	0
	Angami	0	0	0	1	1	0
	Ao	3	1	2	132	82	50
	Arabic/Arbi	2	2	0	2	0	2
	Assamese	7	7	0	78	52	26
	Bengali	51,084	26,566	24,518	695	433	262
	Bhotia	1	0	1	1	0	1
	Bodo/Boro	8	4	4	11	9	2
	Coorgi/Kodagu	116	69	47	4	4	0
	Dimasa	0	0	0	2	2	0
	Dogri	51	24	27	28	21	7
	English	253	123	130	106	48	58
	Gangte	0	0	0	3	3	0
	Garo	4	3	1	12	8	4
	Gondi	3	1	2	0	0	0
	Gujarati	1	1	0	0	0	0
	Halam	226	115	111	2	2	0
	Hindi	446	298	148	578	334	244
	Hmar	7,289	3,704	3,585	328	197	131
	Juang	5	1	4	0	0	0
	Kabui	0	0	0	1	1	0
	Karbi/Mikir	3	0	3	9	5	4
	Khasi	31	21	10	428	222	206
	Khiemnungan	1	0	1	3	2	1
	Kisan	0	0	0	2	2	0
	Koch	1	1	0	0	0	0
	Koda/Kora	12	2	10	2	0	2
	Kom	0	0	0	1	1	0
	Konyak	79	34	45	1	1	0
	Koya	2	2	0	1	0	1

Kuki	10	10	0	34	17	17
Lahauli	1	1	0	2	0	2
Lahnda	20	12	8	11	4	7
Lakher	18,002	9,052	8,950	6,258	3,177	3,081
Lalung	2	2	0	0	0	0
Liangmei	2	2	0	2	0	2
Limbu	1	1	0	0	0	0
Lotha	197	103	94	0	0	0
Lushai/Mizo	2,30,638	1,16,433	1,14,205	2,80,227	1,39,555	1,40,672
Malayalam	7	7	0	51	36	15
Manipuri	29	27	2	14	12	2
Mao	21	13	8	787	422	365
Marathi	0	0	0	2	1	1
Mishmi	4	0	4	4	2	2
Mogh	29	25	4	0	0	0
Munda	38	23	15	11	10	1
Mundari	46	46	0	0	0	0
Nepali	250	201	49	283	178	105
Nicobarese	1	1	0	0	0	0
Oriya	1	1	0	8	8	0
Paite	5,305	2,739	2,566	1,186	602	584
Parji	1	1	0	4	3	1
Pawi	13,135	6,581	6,554	2,433	1,217	1,216
Pochury	13	6	7	7	3	4
Punjabi	9	7	2	3	3	0
Santali	257	255	2	109	92	17
Sema	63	28	35	2	0	2
Tamil	3	3	0	9	8	1
Tangkhul	1	0	1	0	0	0
Tangsa	1	1	0	2	1	1
Telugu	3	2	1	4	2	2
Thado	2	1	1	3	1	2
Tibetan	90	42	48	0	0	0
Tripuri	25,864	13,306	12,558	427	222	205
Tulu	40	16	24	2	1	1
Urdu	45	45	0	15	13	2
Vaiphei	0	0	0	1	0	1
Zou	1	1	0	0	0	0
Others	4,349	2,237	2,112	1,118	585	533

Source: Census 1991.

(f) Monetary Factors

Mathur has suggested a theory that regionalism based on the economic factor alone is less potent if it fails to evoke primordial loyalties, as seen in experience of Telenganna regionalism.[35] This may lead one to think economic factor is lacking or less strong in Mizo regionalism for it is a case of regionalism of great potence. On the other hand, there is an opinion held by some scholars that economic factor is mainly responsible for Mizo regionalism that the best way of tackling with it is economic measures.[36] It is, therefore, imperative on our part to examine the question how far economic factor has been contributive to Mizo cultural confinements?

One fact that cannot escape from the eye of any scholar on Mizos is that the British administration of the Hills had done a little to the economic uplift of the people. It is correct that McCall, one British Superintendent of the Lushai Hills entertained certain ideas of improving the economic conditions of the Mizo people. But, his progressive ideas were fruitless mainly due to lack of financial support in the absence of political commitment. Ray has aptly commented that "Policy formulation towards development administration remained pious wish during the British rule."

Thus, when the British left Lushai Hills their economy remained primitive and static. The precarious conditions of the economy acted as a constraint on Mizo political aspirations and it was mostly because of this constraint that they dared not opt for independent existence. The Mizos were aware that their primitive and village based economy of subsistence would be inappropriate and too fragile for the changed situation. The British administration had not prepared them for independent economy.

We, therefore, contend in light of these facts that it was economic constraint which stopped the Mizos from opting for independent polity and it was the same economic consideration that induced them to prefer joining India through the province of Assam.

This is clear from the memorandum submitted by the Mizo Union Party on April 22, 1947, to His Majesty's Government and the Government of India and the Constituent Assembly through the Bordoloi Sub-Advisory Committee when they demanded, *inter-alia,* that "special financial provision" be kept "by the Centre from year to year until such time as the Mizos shall assert that they are able to maintain their territorial integrity and self-determination without this financial provision."[37]

This would go to recommend that while being compelled to join India, they had strong reservations about their regional sentiments. It further suggests that the Mizos had high hopes of economic progress by joining Indian national Union. But, before economic measures could gain momentum, the Mizo economy deteriorated further.

The Assam Government appointed a Committee to enquire into the consequences of partition on the border districts and to suggest remedies. The Committee submitted its recommendations in January, 1951. However, the well-intended comprehensive development programme proposed by the Committee for the Mizo District could not materialise. Ray gives 'financial difficulties', 'organisational problems' and 'lack of trained personnel who would like to go into the interior', like reasons for the non-implementation of the Committee's recommendations. This appears to be genuine but in view of the provisions of Article 275(1) of the Indian Constitution with the special financial assistance to the Government of Assam for expenditure in the hill districts, the claim that it was due to 'lack of funds' appears to be weak.

Whatever be the purpose causes for its non-implementation, this was taken by the Mizos as an instance of lack of interest on the part of the Government of

Assam in launching massive drive for the economic betterment of the deprived Mizo people. The financial assistance in the form of grants-in-aid for Mizo Hills and the expenditure of the same for the years 1947-48 and 1948-49 showed an average excess of expenses over receipts to be Rs. 10,43,231/-. The gulf between the receipts and expenditures kept on widening as the years went by. Therefore, right from the initial stage, Mizo Hills economy was a dependent one. We found no provision for direct financial assistance from the Central Government to the District Councils. This provincial dependency in economy partly belied the Mizo hopes for economic upgradation by joining Indian Union and it provided a lever for the provincial government to manipulate economic power so as to reduce the dependent districts to the status of mere beggars. The Assam Government was, therefore, directly responsible for the economic development or otherwise of Mizo Hills District. In October, 1952, when Prime Minister Nehru went to north-eastern region, the District Councils of the hill areas requested him to make additional funds available to them so that they could take up the functions of the District Councils envisaged in the Constitution. Mr. Nehru immediately made an ad-hoc grant of Rs. 10 lakhs for all the District Councils out of which Rs. 2.25 lakhs (22.5 per cent) was given to Lushai Hills.

The subsequent history of the financial relations between the Government of Assam and Mizo District Council and the development process in the District, however, brought about a feeling of dissatisfaction on the part of both. The ordinary features of the District Council period under Assam in the context of developmental progress may be summed up thus :

1. The resources of the District Council did not match its heavy responsibilities, and, whatever resources the District had, were not adequately exploited, as confirmed by the finding of the Vaghaiwalla Committee in 1959.
2. The taxation system was not effective.
3. There was an administrative gap between the State Government and the District Council leaving ample scope for disharmony and misunderstanding. The appointment of a Commissioner for Hill Areas did not help much because his headquarters was at Shillong and the District Leaders could not maintain close contact with him.
4. The District Council general staff was too big and uneconomical. The revenue staff was too small to be effective. This necessitated spending of development grant on general administration. It was found that the local revenue had to be spent on establishment and general administration, leaving nothing for the development works.
5. The grants-in-aid received by the District Council was more than double the revenue receipts from local sources.
6. It was a dependent economy lacking in development drives.

Owing to these reasons, the development schemes in Mizo District could not yield tangible and far-reaching results. The District Council Leaders blamed the Assam Government for the failure of the programmes. The Assam Government charged the District Council for poor implementation of the programmes and for low exploitation of local resources. Apart from this disharmony and absence of co-operation between the Government of Assam and the Mizo District Council, the real cause of the economic lag in Mizo Hills after Independence was the inherent constraints on both the Assam Government as well as the District Council. On the part of the Assam Government, it was constraints on geography, remoteness and lack of manpower which acted as a handicap for accelerating the development process.

It was a mental handicap on the part of the Mizo District Council. The District Council leaders who were now sitting on the seats of power had been the ones who had taught the people not to pay taxes or tributes to the chiefs/heads. It was by capitalising on the "unbearable taxes" paid on the chiefs that they could replace the traditional elites. Thus, they were politically forced to start the drive for exploitation of local resources, because the people considered any such move as a revival of the unwanted system of chief's rule, which very mentality was the by-product of the politics of their leaders who were now in the District Council. Moreover, the economy of Mizo Hills having been so dependent, the local leaders were not thinking in terms of self-sufficiency in various resources. This mentality has not been erased even till today. This psycho-social handicap of Mizos in relation to economic self-sufficiency has always been the factor for their inability to assert themselves politically. To make the matter worse, a large-scale famine occurred in Mizo District following a *"MAUTAM"* (death of bamboos) in 1959. Before they die to produce fresh generation of their species the *"mau tak"* a species of bamboo which grow in plenty in Mizo Hills bear flowers and then seeds. The scientific name of this species of bamboo is known to be *"melocanna rambueoides"*.

The theory is like this, that when rats eat the seeds of the bamboo, their fertility increases with a result that their number increases suddenly. After eating up the bamboo seeds, they turn to the paddy fields which have been sufficiently for harvest. "The bamboo fruit is much relished by the rats. The fruit acts as a fertility pill to the female rats. The rats thus eat away all the crops. The rats menace increases to such an extent that it requires an army to destroy them."[38]

Anticipating the famine generated by such rat havoc, the Mizo District Council issued passes for the cultivation of flat lands of the 'phaisen area' bordering Cachar District to encourage Mizo cultivation of paddy there as a preventive step, for it was known that rat menace used to be less serious on paddy of flat land cultivation. But, the Forest Department of Assam in Cachar objected to the cultivation of paddy in the area. Eleven Mizo farmers were arrested with an order of the Hailakandi court. Ch. Chhunga and Lalsawia, then Presidents of the Mizo Union and Eastern India Tribals Union, respectively issued a joint pamphlet condemning the order of the Hailakandi court. Despite subsequent attempts, the cultivation on that area could not be continued because the Deputy Commissioner of the Mizo District himself was in the way of the move, perhaps since he wanted to avert law and order problem.

It was said that the Assam Government shifted on its own the boundary between the Cachar and Mizo District far into the Mizo territory. The repeated warnings and requests made by the District Council for the taking of precautionary measures were not properly heeded to by the Assam Government who were reluctant to accept the theory that such a large-scale famine would take place, based on the simple belief that the population of rats increases when the bamboo bears flowers. It was only after the famine did break out and Williamson Sangma visited Mizo Hills being Tribal Areas Minister that the Assam Government was convinced that there was a large-scale famine in the hills and relief measures were taken.

Despite relief measures were taken, the attitude of the Assam authorities was that they would not like to channel the measures through the District Council alone. Part of them were channelled through the Deputy Commissioner. Chaliha also, keen to bypass and humiliate the Mizo Union leaders, who were running the District Council, patronised the Mizo National Famine Front and "relief turned out to be a salient form of patronage in the famine-affected hills. Nag comments thus,

> "Cases of starvation deaths officially reported by the District Council were denied by the Assam Government. Discontentment grew bigger and bigger in the minds of the people . . . they felt that the Government did not pay much attention nor did they attach so much importance to the District Council as expected . . . Against this background . . . the Mizo National Famine Front transformed itself into the Mizo National Front and raised the demand for sovereign Independence of Greater Mizoram."[39]

Nibedon writes about the situation in the following words,

> The Mizo Union sent an SOS and then a delegation to the plains for expert advise (sic). The Assam Government sent an entemologist who camped for a couple of nights at Aizawl finding no evidence whatsoever to connect the increase in the rat-population to that of the flowering of the bamboo groves . . . What the Assam Government could have done and never did was to take some kind of normal precautionary measures. The Chief Executive Member and his colleagues wanted an immediate supply of rice to be stocked in the interiors knowing full well that at the height of the crisis they would not be able to move the foodgrains to the interiors for lack of proper roads. The Assam administration, in its typically slow and indifferent manner, had not grasped the situation."[40]

On this, the Mizo people felt humiliated when the Assam Government showed them a very indifferent attitude in their times of greatest need. They felt hurt by the fact that they were treated thus in spite of their earlier support to the Greater Assam Movement in the light of the Greater Bengal Movement. Capitalising on this general discontent, the MNF which was originally patronised by Chaliha Government of

Assam to minimize the popular Mizo Union or probably to apply the 'divide and rule' policy among Mizos, grew to size and ultimately launched the Mizo Independence Movement. Chaliha's attempt to minimize the Mizo Union and to bypass the Mizo District Council therefore boomeranged on him and he had to lament later that Laldenga had betrayed him. However, the deeper fact was that Mizos had not at all shed off their regional feelings and the administration of the District by the District Council and the Assam Government made the soil too fertile for the culmination of their regional sentiment into an independence movement through the leadership of the MNF party.

All these developments in Mizoram over a period of two decades would compel us to contend that the economic factor, which induced the Mizos to join India turned out to be the reason for their dislike for Assam and also whole nation. Such estrangement on economic ground reinforced Mizo regionalism in great measure.

(g) Geographical Situations of Mizoram

One may not have to give quite many arguments to support the fact that geography is a strong factor in moulding the habits and political orientation of the people. Mathur considers the sharp difference in life-style between the hills people and the people from plains and the occurrences of tensions between them as a 'general tendency' all over the world and that the hill tribes of North East India are no exception to this. The impact or influence of geography and topography over culture and civilisation can take shape in different ways.[41] The physical barriers in the hill areas are so great that small areas witness the flourishing of autonomous regions. As a chain of secluded living and social heterogeneity, the people, especially of the hills, could maintain a spirit of independence. The bounty of fauna and flora helps the people develop straight-forwardness bereft of quite a lot of artfulness which goes with developed civilisations. Topography, the hill terrains and deep river basins prove to be constraints on means of transport and communication rendering it difficult for a regional economy to grow. Inter-elite and inter-mass co-operations were impossible in the independent village system. The above factors are too immensely present in Mizoram. The perpetuation of the British administrative boundaries left Mizoram in such a location where approximately 70 per cent of its boundaries are international, yet, with many of the Mizo kinsmen just immediately across such boundary lines. This has made Mizoram geo-politically, strategical and internationally susceptible and sensitive. The meeting of the Myanmar-Mizoram and the Bangladesh-Mizoram border limits at the south-end of Mizoram has made it possible for rebel groups in the region to meet with ease.

In this way, Mizoram is too favourable for the growth of regionalism and secesionist movement. Had it not been so, the MNF movement may have been an impossibility. When viewed in the context of geography and demographic regionalisation, it appears more logical to relimit the international and state boundaries around the present Mizoram so as to put all Mizo ethnic groups under one administration within the Indian Union because the ethnic affinity of Mizos with those groups immediately across the borders may even render the border areas vulnerable possibly having adverse effects on the Mizoram economy and politics directly and on the Indian politics as a whole indirectly. The Mizo people on all sides around Mizoram borders are now looking toward Mizoram for leadership and with certain amount of envy, as they have so many socio-economic problems under the administration of their respective regions.

(h) Conflicts between Regional Elites

Sense of Regionalism, studied as an expression of competitions and struggle for power among the elites of the region will be a novel approach to the problem, especially in relation to the North Eastern Region. Such approach is, however, essential not only as an academic exercise but also because it is likely to be rewarding "particularly in the context of the North Eastern region where history has been a witness to the continued hold of a distinct elite strata over isolated and small territories."[42] Sharma writes thus,

> " . . . irrespective of the perspective on or dimensionalities of regionalism, it may commonly be understood as a form of elite conflict at certain levels. In that sense regionalism is not something which is irrational and impulsive, but it is a cover or a plank through which the elites compete and fight for power . . . It is noted that mass of the people may be hypnotized by talk of emotive issues; but this is cunningly raised as an ideological plank by a group of elite to generate mass pressures and control levers of power."[43]

Here it is claimed that the Committee on National Integration constituted by the Government of India offers a similar acknowledgement like this, "what often appears as a conflict between different castes is at bottom only a struggle among the educated people for obtaining jobs and political power.[44]

Our evaluation of Mizo regionalism will not be complete unless some attempt is made to examine its base from this speech. It is pointed out earlier that in the Mizo traditional system, the independent chiefs, the elders, the *'zalen'* and *'ramhual'* and the village level blacksmith constituted the elite class, the bulk of the villagers constituting the traditional masses. In that system, co-operation among the inter-village elites were constrained by the socio-geographical handicap, but, inside the village system, there was a very limited circulation of elites and the elite composition remained static.

In extreme case, there used to be a possibility of a villager deserting his chief and migrating to an acceptable/accepting chief of another village. Otherwise, inter-village mobility in the form of migration was limited. When some chief's family expanded, some form of inter-village chiefs' co-operation developed. The chief of Village 'A' may instruct the chief of Village 'B' not to accept any of his villagers willing to migrate to his village and the latter will oblige because such act will deter his own villagers from attempting to migrate. This form of elite cooperation existed only among few friendly chiefs and had no importance on the whole situation of Lushai Hills. When the British came, the traditional privileges and power of the chiefs were considerably reduced and the traditional elite co-operation which had existed in its rudimentary form suffered a setback.

Impact of British administration, the spread of Christianity and education set the process of modernisation and as a result a new educated Mizo elites began to emerge. The emergent elites soon became a potent force. They enjoyed more advantage in terms of cooperation and interaction than the traditional elites because they were more educated. They soon formed a political party (Mizo Union) by which they started a political movement which at last brought about the end of chiefship, the traditional elitism. The emergent elites adopted pro-Indian stance and could impress upon the people that the traditional elites were pro-British and thus reactionary to any move for modernisation.

Taking highly of the autonomous status under the province of Assam, they exploited chiefs—commoners antagonism and soon occupied seats of political power. But, when they felt that the Assam Government, whom they had been looking to for their own sustenance, became unappreciative of the workings of the Mizo District Council which they were running, the emergent elites then came up and joined the 'Hill State' movement in the early fifties. Again, the hill state movement also did not very well suit their attempt to hold power because such movement was highly broadbased and their power equation with the other hills leaders was poor. They then switched over to the policy of Mizoram state. During this, the traditional elites became resilient and found a new forum in the Mizo National Council and then in United Mizo Freedom Organisation (UMFO) and then again in Eastern India Tribals Union (EITU) to reassert themselves in the fresh situation. They propounded 'Crown Colony' and then 'Join Burma' and then again 'Hill State' movements. The struggle for power between the old and the new elites was so sharp in the beginning of the latter half of the fifties, the Mizo politics was divided into two main streams. The emergent elites' hold on the masses, however, was so strong, being cemented by the active support of the Assam Pradesh Congress Committee, that the resilient traditional elites and their supporters could not make any tangible achievement in their interest.

Those who did not remain in politics soon found well-well placed government vacancies remained in active politics were artful enough to take advantage of the new situations that even when they left politics, they found themselves in economically sound positions. But, the old elites soon receded into the background. A fresh elite class again emerged, whose members were taken from all sides. It is this new elite class which spearheaded the independence movement through the MNF party. It is in this situation that "hypnotization of the masses by the talk of emotive issues . . . to generate pressures and control levers of power" is too evident. Those who led the rebel movement in the beginning appealing to the emotion of the people were later comfortably holding power under the Constitution of India which they had once sought to boycott. This is a case of tactful adjustment of one's policy and programme in order to capture power by any means than being a case of *volte face* on the part of the third group of Mizo elites.

Of course, the regionalist elites, having come to power just by exploiting the regional sentiment of the people, often take the side of the Central Powers when their regionalist stance is going to estrange them from their central masters, thus betraying their regional support structure. This would, however, create a fresh opportunity for the emergence of a new elite group or for the revival of the old one by appealing to the same regional sentiment of people.

Thus, to conclude, Mizo statehood has drawn sustenance from different sources and not from only one or two factors. Whatever be the measure of contribution of each of these factors, Mizo regionalism remains a strong force. History is a witness also to the truth that whatever regional party that comes up in Mizoram, it cannot take a strong stand in opposition to the Central Power. It is also seen that while they want to maintain regional autonomy in terms of political power and also socio-cultural factors, the Mizos always try to draw as much economic advantage of being in Indian Union as possible, because of their inherent economic backwardness. In order to deal with this type of situation, therefore, it is necessary we have a comprehensive policy handled with patience and due recognition of factors that involve, as a result of which we may expect Mizoram State to become a model state for others to emulate.

References

1. E.B. Taylor, as quoted in G. Duncan Mitchell (ed.): *A new Dictionary of Sociology,* London & henley, Routledge & Kegan Paul, 1979, p. 45.
2. A.K. Kroeber & Clyde Kluckhohn, quoted in Mitchell, *Idem.*
3. M.L. Sharma. *"The Troubled North East"* in Iqbal Narain (ed) *State Politics in India,* Meerut and New Delhi, Menakshi Prakashan, 1976, pp. 451-2.
4. Parliamentary Debates, Lok Sabha, 3rd Series, Vol. 51, March 1-51/66.
5. P.C. Mathur, *"Regionalism in India, An Essay in Dimensionalisation of State politics in India",* in Ramakant (ed). *op. cit.* p. 16.
6. The leading sub-tribes and clans under the generic term 'Mizo' are Lusei, Rálte, Pawi Hmar, Paite, Chawngthu, Khiangte, etc.
7. M.L. Sharma. *"Ethnicity and Regionalism in North-East India-Problems of Multiple identities and Inter-Elite Conflicts,"* in Pant (A.D.) & Gupta (S.K.) (ed.) *Multi Ethnicity and National Integration.* Allahabad, Vohra, 1985, pp. 163-64.
8. N. Nibedon, *North-East India-The Ethnic Explosion,* New Delhi, Lancers Publishers, 1981, p. 16.
9. In 1980 a group of college lecturers wanted to send telegraphic message from Calcutta to Aizawl and entered AIZAWL in the form, which was the correct spelling. But, the booking clerk asked them to write it AIZWAL because that was how it had been written in the Directory.
10. Nibedon. *op. cit.,* p. 80.
11. See Table IV in Appendix A.
12. Many plains people tend to regard the term 'VAI' as derogatory because of its common use with prejudicial tone. But, informed sources say that it originated from the Hindi term 'bhai'

(brother) which term was picked by early Mizos to identify the plainsmen apart from Mizos because they often heard them call themselves 'bhai'.

13. Idem
14. P.K. Bandhyopadhyay, *Leadership Among the Mizos*, Delhi, B.R. Publishing Corporation, 1985, p. 260.
15. *Ibid.*, pp. 60, 61.
16. Rev. Zairema. *God's Miracle in Mizoram,* Aizawl, Synod Press, 1978.
17. A. Ray. *op. cit.* p. 70.
18. N.E. Parry. The Lakhers, *London Macmillan & Co. 1932,* p. 19.
19. A. Ray, *op. cit.* p. 62.
20. P.C. Mathur, *"Regionalism in India . . ."* Ramakant (ed) *op. cit.* pp. 41-42.
21. N. Nibedon. Mizoram-The Dagger Brigade, New Delhi, Lancers Publishers, 1980, pp. 20-21.
22. Rokunga. *Thalai Hlabu* (Songs of Youth) No. 13.
23. Mukherjee, Member of Parliament, quoted earlier.
24. Hmartawnphunga's *Pamphlet* dated 5.5.47 (*Vaihozawn nge i duh mahnia din).*
25. M.L. Sharma. *"Elite Conflicts, Regionalism and the Compatibility Crisis: A Study of the Autonomy Movements in North-East India"* in Ramakant (ed) *op. cit.* p. 70.
26. R.N. Mishra. *Regionalism and State Politics in India,* New Delhi, Ashish Publishing House, 1984, p. 14.
27. *Idem.*
28. P.C. Mathur. "Regionalism in India . . ." In Ramakant (ed.) *op. cit.*, p. 8.
29. *Idem.*
30. Mathur. *Ibid.*, p. 9.
31. S. Chaube *Hill Politics in North East India,* Calcutta, Orient Longman, 1973, p. 73.
32. *Government of Mizoram,* Law and Judicial Department's Complication of Acts passed by the Mizoram Legislative Assembly, Vol. I, p. 84.
33. *Mizo Union Party Constitution* (original) 1946, p. 1. (We are indebted to Mr. R. Vanlawama for making the copy available to us).
34. R. Samuelson. Love Mizoram, Imphal, Goodwill Press, 1985, p. 44.
35. P.C. Mathur. "Regionalism in India . . ." in Ramakant (ed), *op. cit.* pp. 19-20.
36. B.B. Goswami & Mukherjee. "The Mizo Political Movement in *Tribal Movemens in India,* K.S. Singh (ed), New Delhi, Manohar Publications, 1982, p. 148.
37. A.K. Nag. *The Mizo Dilemma,* Calcutta, Tribal Mirror Publications, 1984, p. 24.
38. J.D. Baveja. *The Land Where the bamboo Flowers,* Gauhati, Assam Publication Board, 1970, p. 63.
39. A.K. Nag. "The Ups and Downs of Mizo Politics", in North Eastern Affairs, Shillong, October-December Issue, 1972.
40. N. Nibedon. *Mizoram—The Dagger Brigade,* New Delhi, Lancers Publishers, 1980, pp. 34-35.
41. M.L. Sharma, "Elite Conflicts, Regionalism and the Compatibility Crisis: A Study of the autonomy movements in North East India", in Ramakant (ed). *Ibid.*, pp. 56-58.
42. *Ibid.*, p. 51.
43. *Ibid.*, p. 50.
44. N.S. Gupta. *"Unity in Diversity: A Clue to National Integration"* in M.R. Sinha (ed.), Integration in India, Bombay.

14

Political Parties in the State

In a modern democratic set-up, it is even far from imagination of a political order without the existence of political parties. Thus, study of political parties also became an indispensable part of the study of any particular state or government. Approaches to the study, and idea of political parties, have been undergoing gradual change from the 'traditional method' of their study before the Second World War. The traditional approach was guided by questions relating to the life histories of the parties, members who matter in the party's movement, basic views about political society, programmes and interaction of parties in a country and electoral battles fought' Ostrogorski and Robert Michels are the more popular among writers applied this method. With the publication Maurice Duverger's *Les parties politiques* in 1951, Neumann's article "Toward Comparative Study of Political Parties" in 1956, and many of works on political parties after the Second World War, there has been a breakthrough in the approach to the study and in the understanding about political parties.

The current approaches to the study of political parties are concerned more with the process of public policy-making through the parties. One important characteristic of the new trend in the approach to the study of political parties is such that there is no more a dichotomy between party and government in the twentieth century parliamentary party system. Cabinet, parliamentary party, electoral organisation, make up the certain political party. With the change in approach came the change in the meaning and functions of political parties as well as in the nature and determinants of party systems. Party is no more conceived of merely as a body of men united for promoting national interest on some agreed principles, as Burke would like us to understand it. Recent writers like Dean, Schumann, Neumann, La Palombara, Myron Weiner and Jean Blondel etc. emphasise such aspects which concern with specialisation, partnership, durability, power-orientation and public policy-making process, while defining the nature of political party. About their functions, parties are more and more conceived of as uniting, simplifying and stabilising political process, always struggling for power, providing a link between the government and the people, ever growing the scope of political activity and widening popular participation, presenting issues and setting value goals for the society, serving as broker of ideas, always leading in the task of political modernisation and performing different social welfare functions. Likewise, the determinants of party-system and party-structure also increase with the growing importance of parties. These determinants differ in category from being historical to socio-economical and ideological. Such factors as religion, race, sub-nationalism, linguistic chauvinism, caste, attractive leader, dissidence, confederation of like minded organisations, etc. have become quite relevant in the determination of the structure of parties and the development of party-systems. Parties and party system are now studied not only from Michels' "iron law of oligarchy" or Duverger's "natural dualism" at the same also as "Clientele-oriented stratarchies."[2]

Inside this broad framework of the conceptualisation of political parties, an attempt is made in this chapter to analyse the bases, natures, programmes, functions and movements of Mizo political parties with an idea to identify where and how Mizo regionalism has governed their orientation and how the parties have been trying to strike a compromise between the constant factor of Mizo regionalism and the demands for the task of building an integrated Indian Nation. This chapter, therefore, may throw some light as to which type of parties are likely to hold the mass-support in Mizoram, and which will be the best link between the regionalist Mizo masses and the nationalist Indians.

There have been identified as many as 24 political parties (including factions) and 5 party alliances having been in existence in Mizoram. However, out of this great number of parties, just a few have been able to emerge and remain for some time as major parties in terms of following and electoral achievements. Others have come but gone out of existence or mingled with bigger parties. Among the major ones, only the Indian National Congress is popular in Mizoram as an all-India level party; Mizo Union (MU), United Mizo Freedom Organisation (UMFO), Mizo National Front (MNF) and People's Conference (PC) etc. popular in their respective periods as Regional parties. The PC party converted itself into a national party viz. Janata Dal but could not make much headway as such.

(a) The Mizo Union, the pro-Congress Regional Party

The Mizo Union (MU) was the first Mizo political party set-up on April 9, 1946. The principal objectives of the party were to achieve a rightful status for the Mizos; to develop better understanding between chiefs and commoners; to unify the common masses; general uplift of the Mizo people; to become the democratic representative and spokesman for the whole of Mizo people; and to popularise Mizo language.[3] These objectives well assess the socio-political conditions that brought the party into existence. Though open to all Mizo-chiefs and commoners, it became popular only among the commoners, because of its basic but unofficial anti-chiefs orientation.[4] The strong hold of the party on Mizo people was so strong that it could capture and maintain power throughout the District Council period except for a short interregnum during 1970-71, when the Congress party could formulate a shaky 'government' of the District Council by a small margin of seats, the MU being the opposition party.

When Mizoram was made a Union Territory, the first Assembly Elections were conducted in April 1972 in which the Mizo Union again came to power capturing 21 seats in the 30 elective seats of the Mizoram (UT) legislative Assembly. The party initially had all the hues of the political figures among the commoners Mizo within its fold. The chiefs were having their own forums in the Chiefs' Council and the District Conference, through which they tried to impose their rule by advocating a 'Crown Colony' for the Mizos after the British had left. In the Mizo Union party also, the original leadership was more inclined to this aspiration. But, they were soon replaced with the pro-Indian leadership who capitalised on the commoners' anti-chiefs fervour.

The Mizo Union Movement since then became an anti-chiefs-pro-Indian-regionalist movement. Those who advocated 'Crown Colony' or 'Mizo Independence' did not have any place in the party, thus paving a way for the formation of a second party to pursue the anti-India inclination. The future of the Mizos, as per the leadership of the Mizo Union, lies with the Indian Union. They held a strong opinion that the welfare and modernisation of Mizos would be achieved best within Indian Union. At its first general Assembly on September 24, 1946 at Kulikawn, Aizawl, the party resolved that in the event of India attaining independence, the Lushai Hills must be included within the province of Assam. The Assembly was against the idea of the Lushai Hills being treated as an Excluded area. It wished to be represented in the Assam Assembly adequately. "At the same time . . . no legislation of the provincial legislative Assembly should apply to the Lushai Hills automatically. The internal affairs of Lushai Hills should be managed by its own legislature."

This Assembly also resolved that all the contiguous areas occupied by the Mizos should be united under one administration. These demands were confirmed by the next conference of the MU at Lakhipur, Cachar District on November 21, 1946. This conference was attended by representatives of Mizos in Cachar, Manipur and Lushai Hills, some Congressmen from Cachar also came to attend. While confirming the previous resolutions, the conference demanded the widest possible autonomy for Mizoram and that the Mizos should be represented in the Constituent Assembly. Their demand of representation was communicated to the President of the Constituent Assembly on January 3, 1947, with a warning that if Mizos were not included in the Constituent Assembly, the Mizo Union would formulate a separate constitution for the Mizos. "They also said that they would decide whether they should be under the British protection for the time being, or form an independent state or join the Chin Hills in Burma and form a separate province within Burma."

In line with these resolutions, the party submitted a lengthy memorandum to His majesty's government, the Government of India, and the Constituent Assembly through the Bordoloi Committee in which two main MU leaders were co-opted members. They made the following points in the memorandum.

(a) Mizos are a family of numerous tribes spreading over Lushai Hills, Manipur, Cachar, Tripura, Chittagong Hill Tracts and Burma.

(b) The creation of Lushai Hills comprising only Luseis, a Mizo tribe, was effected for the British administrative convenience, leaving other Mizo tribes outside it. Quoting various authorities like Shakespeare, Stevenson, Liangkhaia, Shaw, Kingdanward and Kim of the Statesman, they maintained that the Mizos within Lushai Hills and without it had strong solidarity.

(c) The Mizos were distinct from the plains people as well as from the Nagas and Manipuris.

(d) Migrating to their present habitats from the east, the Mizo villages lay within the areas covered by the border of the present Falam Sub-Division in Burma in the east.

(e) The area occupied by Mizo tribes was as big as 15,993 square miles and the population was about 328,400.[5]

(f) It is, therefore, imperative that His majesty's Government, the Government of India and the Constituent Assembly do the "just and proper thing" and grant the Mizos their "just demand" for Territorial Unity and Solidarity.

(g) The Mizos were never subjugated by the Maharajas of Manipur, Tripura, Chittagong and Cachar. When the British annexed their land, they became loyal to the British, as proved by their willing participation on their side during the Two World Wars, Abhor Expedition and Haukip rebellion.

(h) The Mizos had efficient system of administration and discipline as a distinct group governed by their traditional laws, customs and organisations.

(i) Mizos had never been under the Indian Government and never had any connection with the politics of the various groups of Indian Dominion. So, they could not be thrown on a common platform with the rest of India, because their ways were too different from those of others.

(j) It is, therefore, important to the highest degree that the Mizos be given self-determination in its fullest form.

(k) On account of all the problems and its strategic location, lack of developmental facilities, it is all the more imperative that Mizoram be given special financial provision by the Centre while allowing them their territorial integrity "as anything short of this will be detrimental to their upbringing."

(l) The District shall join Assam through legislature with adequate representation and be also eligible to the provincial services with due reservations of posts at the same time retaining her territorial integrity and self-determination; as otherwise, thrown among forty crores of Indian, the 3,28,400 Mizos with their unique system of life will be wiped out of existence.

Alongwith these points, the MU demanded for (i) Territorial Unity and Solidarity of the whole Mizo population to be known henceforth as *MIZO* and *MIZORAM* for *Lushai* and *Lushai Hills District* retaining the sole proprietory rights for the land. (ii) Full self-determination within the province of Assam with a National Council having the supreme legislative authority and an Executive Body and a Judiciary inside the District, the composition and functions of which will be prescribed by rules. Any concurrent subjects in which the district may be connected with the Autonomous province of Assam or country as a whole shall be by negotiations with the National Council which will be set up according to the wishes of the general public, any legislation may be applied to the District only with the approval of the National Council with any modification. (iii) Special Financial provision by the Centre from year to year until such time as the Mizos shall assert that they are able to maintain their old integrity and self-determination without this financial provision. The memorandum was concluded with the following words: "All the above items shall be subject to revision according to the future trends of events even to the extent of seceding after ten years. For this end, it is to be understood that the democratic system of government in its purest form shall at the very outset be introduced."

A 'Draft Constitution of Mizoram' was also submitted alongwith the memorandum in line with the demands expressed in the memorandum. It will be seen from these that the Mizo Union Party, based on the primordial loyalties minus chiefship, laid the foundation for moderate regionalism or an integrationist form of regional politics in Mizoram. Such considerations as economic limits, regional autonomy in legislation and administration, preservation of distinct ethnico-cultural identity, historical independence, geographical isolation, linguistic distinctness are present in numerous measures in the sentiment of the Mizo Union Party.

It is also evident that the Mizo Union's option to join India through Assam was not without conditions. They reserved the possibility of opting out again after the passage of ten years, if the future trends did not seem to favour the fulfilment of their aspirations. The party took the reins of power in the autonomous District Council of the Lushai Hills, that was changed to Mizo Hills in 1954. While they could foster some sort of Mizo Unification within the Mizo Hills, the Mizo Union leaders soon forgot about some of their demands, Unification of complete Mizo groups within and without the then Lushai Hills, for instance.

The party was gradually more occupied with internal administration and struggle for power, and it suffered major split in 1956. It did not perform so well on the developmental front. It put an end to traditional chiefship and introduced an elective system of Village Council in 1954. When the "ten year period" elapsed, it did not care to renew the issue of determining the political future of the Mizos. Instead, true to its original pro-India stand, it became highly instrumental in the hands of the Assam Government and the Government of India in their efforts to check the secessionist movement of the Mizo National Front (MNF). Though it was a regional party, it soon joined the Assam Congress Legislature party at the state level in 1952.[6] It broke company with the Congress party following sharp differences on the famine (1959-60) relief and Assamese official language issues since 1960.[7] It then joined the Hill State Movement with other hill district parties for some duration. The leadership, however, soon became disinterested in the movement and at the party's general Assembly held during March 8-10, 1963 it was resolved to fight for Mizoram state.[8]

The party's committed pursuit of this objective made it a counter-force against the MNF's secessionist movement resulting in serious antagonism between them. That the Mizo Union Party, at least its leadership, was though regional in form but pro-India and pro-Congress in practice was evident on many occasions.[9] It appears to us that the Indian National Congress also did not bother to form its unit in Mizoram for a long duration because the integrationist pro-Congress Mizo Union party was there. Mr. A. Thanglura, the first Mizo Cabinet Minister in the Government of Assam and the founder of Congress party in Mizoram, could observe that Mr. Ch. Saprawnga, the most tenacious and prominent leader of the party "appeared to be ready to follow the Congress party" from the very beginning.[10]

On one occasion, in 1964 at Vaphai village, while on their campaign tours for the Assam MLA by-election, it is reported by A. Thanglura that Ch. Saprawnga was saying then in public to the effect that:

> "It is not proper for us to scorn the Congress party. It is not only the oldest party but the one which successfully fought for Indian Independence. Our only contention is whether it is time to form its unit here in Mizoram. If you do not want to cast your votes for our MU candidate, you better vote for the Congress candidate than for MNF candidate."

This statement ascribed to Ch. Saprawnga, show the pro-Congress stance, at least of the leadership, of the Mizo Union. The Congress Party was formed in Mizoram on August 10, 1961, under the leadership of A. Thanglura. But, the Government of state Assam and Government of India put more trust on the Mizo Union than on the Mizoram Congress because the latter was considered to be pro-MNF. After a loss of power at the last District Council election in 1970 with a small margin, the party assumed power for the fast time in the first Mizoram (UT) Assembly Elections in 1972. It completely merged itself with the Congress on January 12, 1974.[11]

At first, the merger did not become very popular especially in the villages, and the leaders had to take lot of painsd to convince the villagers about the "advantage" of the merger. Some leaders of the erstwhile Mizo Union attempted to revive the party. But, their attempts yielded no practical result and the party went out of existence after a 27 year period of popularity. The merger of such a popular and significant regional party with the Indian National Congress is explained by the leaders of the erstwhile Mizo Union as a move to obliterate the feeling of antagonism between the chiefs and their descendants and many ex-MNF men on the one hand and the Mizo Unionists on the other. It is too said that it was time for the Mizos to broaden their political vision to the extent of aspiring for Ministership at the Centre through the national party. Another argument is that as the Central Government could not restore full confidence in any regional party, it was thought better to merge the Mizo Union in the Congress party in order to win the confidence of the Central Government and thereby to quicken the process of negotiation for peaceful settlement of the MNF's secessionist problem. These arguments appear to be reasonable on certain grounds.

But, one may observe that had the Mizo Union waited till the another Assembly Elections which were due in 1978, they were likely to concede power to the pro-MNF Congress party which was the gaining popularity day by day. So, the merger was of same advantage to the party for it could continue to be in power for some years more, by retaining its hold of the rein of power and sharing some with the 'original' Congressmen. But, the later course of events showed a way for the rise of another regional party in the People's Conference, perhaps much contrary to the expectation of the Merger Congress leaders.

(b) The United Mizo Freedom Organisation (UMFO)

It has been said that at the beginning, all the shades of public opinion were within the Mizo Union, but, those who had the idea of having Mizo political future away from the Indian Union soon became unacceptable to the Mizo Union Party. Meanwhile the commoners-chiefs antagonism developed into an extreme form of enmity. The factional group of the Mizo Union adopted the name of the Mizo Union Council and talked of Mizo Independence, from April 1947. The Mizo Union was practically a commoners' party and the chiefs generally did not join it. Some leading citizens then felt that a new party was necessary in order to forge a forum wherein all commoners and chiefs could be united. The result was the United Mizo Freedom Organisation (UMFO). It came into existence under the leadership of Lalbiakthanga and Rev. Zairema on July 5, 1947. It attached everyone, the chiefs, the dissatisfied Mizo Unionists and those who disliked the pro-India anti-chief anti-British stance of the Mizo Union. So, the party was essentially in opposition to the Mizo Union and it was made with a view to provide an alternative to the first Mizo political party.

The main objectives of the UMFO were:[12]

1. In looking for a country with which to identify ourselves we should seek one we admire and which can give us some benefits.
2. We must promote a true democracy where the people can choose their own leaders; we must try hard to avoid any taint of fascism.
3. We must make our country as strong as possible so that we need not be dependent on other countries.
4. We must seek to improve, in creative ways, our present culture.
5. We must seek for better communication and understanding between the people who rule and those who are ruled.
6. We must develop the best and most efficient ways of administering ourselves.
7. We insist on freedom of speech and of the press.
8. We insist on freedom of religion.

Like this, the party was at first open to joining any country. But, it bided time to observe as to the desirability of joining any country or to remain independent or a British colony. When its President Lalbiakthanga went to Government service, Lalmawia, an ex-Burmese Army Officer became its president. Under Lalmawia's leadership, the party resolved that it would be to the greatest advantage of Mizos to join Burma. The reasons given for this opinion were that (a) Burma being smaller than India, the Mizos might have a larger voice in affairs generally; (b) Mizo participation in public affairs may have greater scope in Burma; (c) Mizos are highly close to the Burmese ethnically; (d) Mizos would have greater autonomy in Burma; (e) It was said that the Draft Constitution of Burma had a provision for the possibility of opting out of Burma by any of the hills-people after the passage of ten years.[13]

Also, 'join Burma' policy could not gain popularity on account of the fact that Mizoram had legally become part of India. The party then dropped the policy and functioned within the Indian Constitution. It captured only the joint constituency of Lunglei and capital Aizawl townships out of 18 constituencies in the 1952 District Council Elections and failed to return any candidate in the Assembly Elections of the same year. It polled 18 per cent and 31 per cent of votes at the District Council and Assembly Elections respectively, the rest being bagged by the Mizo Union.

The UMFO party almost captured power by winning in 8 constituencies in the 1957 District Council Elections and also two members from Pawi-Lakher Region giving their support to it. It also bagged two of the three MLA seats of Mizo District. In terms of votes polled by the parties, it became almost equal to the Mizo Union's 50 per cent in the District Council Elections; 46 per cent against the MU's 46 per cent in the Assembly Elections, the remaining percentages going to the MU factional group. The possible causes for the UMFO's ascendency in 1957 were:

(a) It had left its 'join Burma' policy and adopted 'Hill State' policy since 1954.
(b) The split of the Mizo Union Party in 1956 on the question of leadership turned in the UMFO's favour.
(c) The MU leaders who were handling the District Council had displeased many people.
(d) The MU had lost its true fervour which was inspired by anti-chiefs feeling.

After having lost by a small margin in the 1957 District Council Elections, the UMFO and the Mizo Union (Right Wing), as the Mizo Union faction was then known, merged into Eastern India Tribals Union (EITU) on October 2, 1957,[14] to advocate the 'Hill State' policy of the Mizo Union and with the formation of the MNF and the growing popularity of the Mizo Independence movement, the Hill State movement became quite unpopular and the EITU also receded into the background. The UMFO has been a regional party representing largely the resilient traditional elites and the anti-Mizo Union leaders which even attempted to let Mizos join Burma instead of India but failed to do so due to unfavourable circumstances. In terms of its regionalistic ground, it was no much different from the Mizo Union. But, in terms of orientation and direction of movement, it was just the opposite of the Mizo Union. In a way, it was the second version of the Mizo feelings. The factors of regional autonomy and self-assertion were highly present in its formation and movement.

(c) The Secessionist Mizo National Front

The "ten-year" duration of the "experimentation" of association with the Indian Union through the state of Assam was well over and the conditions brought about by the "future trends of events" were too fertile for the rise and growth of secessionist sense among the Mizos. The Mizo Union's expectation that the lot of the Mizos would be best when Lushai Hills was made an autonomous district under state of Assam had been belied by the Assam government's general attitude and particularly during the famine of 1959-60. The general feeling of the people was against the District Council for its incapability of facing real situations, and against the Government of Assam for its "step-motherly treatment" and against the whole of India because they held a general opinion that India could not be much different from Assam, though the Mizos had not had any direct relations with the Central Government. Vanlawma says that many Mizos had been nurturing a separatist feeling since very long time but kept it undercurrent.

Some politically conscious Mizos had formed social organisations on an implicit separatist sentiment—the Mizo Cultural Society (1959) and also the Mizo National Famine Front (1960) were such organisations. The MNF was the manifestation of the sentiment in an organised form with political overtones. The Mizo National Famine Front was very converted into a political party as Mizo National Front on October 22, 1961. Thus one may observe that while being a product of the regionalist sentiment reinforced by many societal factors, the secessionist movement in the form of MNF was immediately caused by the 'Mautam' famine in Mizoram. It will be a far-fetched argument, however, if one thinks that the famine was the 'sole' cause of the Mizo Independence movement, for such a serious development cannot be caused just by a passing event like the *'Mautam'* famine. The discontentment of a big section of the Mizo population had roots deeper than in the famine conditions. "Fear of losing ethnico-cultural identity", and "lack of civilisational pull and poor interaction of the plains men with the hill people",[16] and also feeling of frustration among certain sections of the Mizo people, were significant factors for the rise of the MNF. When the MNF emerged, it drew following from among the members (or ex-chambers) of the erstwhile UMFO/ EITU and Mizoram Congress parties. In other words, it attracted all those who had strong hatred for the Mizo Union. The Mizo Union was not much affected. In fact, the Mizo Union stood alone as a party in opposition to the MNF movement. This may compel one to observe that the Mizo Union was higher pro-India and more Congress than the Mizoram Congress party itself. One may also find here that there can be different forms of regionalism—a moderate form as the Mizo Union and an extreme one like the MNF. The MNF movement was joined, besides those mentioned, by 'neutral' in regards to party affiliation but who by nature regionalist. Many ex-servicemen, educated people, students and even professionals joined the movement with some peculiar enthusiasm. The party, in other words, just appeal to the emotion of the large part of the Mizo people. Those who actively participated in its armed movement wore from the age group of 20-35 years.

In the words of Dr. V.V. Rao,[17] the MNF was able to enlist the tacit sympathy and open support from all types of persons." and the factors for this "large scale rebellion", the disbandment of the Mizo dominated Second Battalion of the Assam Regiment in 1964, the presence of a large number of discontented ex-chiefs and unemployed youth, the readiness of the Pakistan Government to help the MNF, Chaliha's patronage of the MNF in order to weaken the Mizo Union, the growing number of juvenile delinquents, and the Assamese language issue." He understands the MNF movement like a popular movement rather than being a stray incident of lawlessness perpetrated by a few sections of Mizo people. He writes, "the number of persons that participated in the revolt was some thousands, and not a few as was stated in the press."

Though the reasons for the rise of the MNF given by Dr. V.V. Rao are generally true, one should not have the impression that the MNF was a mere collection of unwanted and jobless people and delinquent youths. Various successful Government servants and promising youths and students left their careers and joined the movement. It is also a fact that the "spirit of Mizo Independence" haunted the minds of many Mizos, and the MNF party clearly enjoyed the admiration of different sections of the Mizo people. For youngmen, it was shameful not to be an MNF volunteer. The old people, whose memories of the tales about their forefathers' lives in Burma were ever fresh, and whose minds had always been longing for reunification with their brethren across the borders, gave approving support to the movement. Such was the wave of the MNF when it emerged in the Mizo political front.

The disbandment of the Mizo-dominated Second Battalion of the Assam Regiment in 1964 was also originally caused by the mishandling of the situation arising out of the Mizo discontent on the issue of the type of items served to them as army ration supply. The Mizos were forced to change their food habits overnight, instead of patiently waiting for them to adjust themselves. It was a simple question of rice or wheat. The Mizo people, who had been rice eaters since time immemorial were given *'chappati'* for a number of days at a stretch, giving them no option to eat rice or *'chappati'*. One can observe, thus, that the Mizos felt humiliated and unaccepted on all aspects of life—political, socio-cultural and government services. The original aims and objectives of MNF, as per a booklet published by the party were:[18]

1. Integration of all the Mizo ethnic groups under one government possessing the highest degree of freedom.
2. Upgradation of the status, and the development of the economic conditions, of the Mizo people.
3. Safeguard of the Christian Religion.

Sense of regionalism of the MNF, thus, was fundamentally based on ethnic, political, socio-economic and religious factors. In regard to the first objective, the party understood the past life of the Mizos as politically independent. The Mizo freedom was somewhere lost when "foreign rule" was imposed by the British. Mizo Independence was the only way to do away with the foreign domination. Re-unification of all Mizos in different parts of India, Burma and the Bangladesh, i.e., then East Pakistan would be a step towards the attainment of Mizo Independence. The socio-economic problems of the Mizos were, according to the MNF, due to the "foreign infiltration" as long as the "foreign yoke" was on their shoulders, there would be no socio-economic liberation for the Mizos. The party considered the Mizos fortunate for having found the "only true God" through Christianity spread by the British missionaries, in the midst of the "idol worship".

It considered the Buddhism of Burma and the Islamism of Pakistan as unsuitable and undesirable for the Mizo people. It took Indian Secularism as a "tricky way of Hinduisation." By spreading such propaganda effectively, the MNF could win the support of the Mizos. The MNF contested the Assembly by-elections in two of the three Mizo District Constituencies in 1963 and won in both by a comfortable majority of votes. During the same year, it captured 145 village councils out of 411 in the elections in Aizawl subdivision.[19] The party at first professed non-violence, Laldenga wrote like this,

> "The Mizo people are religious-minded and peace-loving. They love peace in as much as they need it . . . Though known as martial race, Mizo nation commits itself to a policy of non-violence, not to resort to violence for their liberation . . . They have witnessed and clearly seen the result of violence and its futility in Kashmir and in Nagaland. They do not want such things to happen in Mizoram: Mizoram being landlocked and taking into consideration its supply routes and economic conditions, the leaders know that military victory over India is not possible and they hope that the problem would well be solved through negotiations."[20]

This being the position of the MNF, one can question why they took up arms and rebelled? The MNF's taking to arms has at least three versions. One is that the common membership forced for it and the leadership had to yield. The second version is that the extremist group in the leadership wanted to start armed-insurrection and Laldenga could not resist the pressure. Thirdly, it is also said that the MNF went on and on for violence but was only buying time to collect more weapons and to find more excuses for the strike. Even before they attacked various security posts and government installations, it was an open secret that the MNF was collecting arms and training its volunteers in their use. The MNF declared Mizoram a Sovereign and Independent State with effect from the midnight of February 28-March 1, 1966 and started to attack important government installations and security camps at various places. They could capture important places except Aizawl. When the Security Forces were almost forced to surrender, the IAF came to their rescue.

The main market area of Aizawl was in flame after heavy strafing from the IAF Hunter jet fighters. The MNF and all its subsidiary organisations were said unlawful under Rule 32 of Defence of India Rules, 1962, and the MNF and its shadow "Government of Mizoram" and the "Mizo National Army" which were organised on the American model had to go underground and start operating its guerilla warfare from across the international borders. The MNF justified their armed movement by saying that all their formal pleadings for the solution of Mizo issue with the Assam and Indian leaders and commissions had not only been unheeded but also reciprocated with callous and indifferent attitudes in most cases: One of their pamphlets contained these words:

"All the attempts to effect peaceful negotiation and settlement on the principle of fairness have become futile. The fate of the Mizo people has now been clear. The intention of India is to apprehend all the leaders who work for freedom, and to suppress the people in order to discourage them so that they dare not speak about freedom. Therefore, the only way that remains for national liberation is to declare independence and form Mizoram Government on our own."[21]

Laldenga said thus,

> "Blind with insatiable thirst of territorial ambition and maddened by the feeling of big power chauvinism, the Indian leaders in colossal disregard of human rights and dignity sent their troops into Mizoram to suppress the political rights of the people in the month of February 1966.

The party was not, therefore, wanting in finding grounds for their armed insurrection. The events that followed the MNF's declaration of Mizoram Independence cannot be dealth with in this book.[22] The 'counterstrikes' and some measures were so severe that it would take a long time for the Mizos to forget their sufferings and loss during the 20 year period of their history wherein they had to live between the symbols those are 'Hammer' (the Indian Security Forces) and the 'anvil' (the MNF). One thing that one can observe, however, is that Mizo problem, being a political problem, could not be solved militarily. It had been through a prolonged and chequered process of political negotiations that a Peace Accord could be signed between the Government of India and the MNF in a form of Memorandum of Settlement dated June 30, 1986. Mizo regionalism developed into an extreme form with the MNF movement. Their demands were not simply autonomy or financial provisions, but complete separation from the Indian Union. To the MNF Mizoram was not just a regional entity but a 'national' polity. They conceived of Mizo as a "nation" and attempted to vindicate "Mizo nationalism" through appealing to the ethnic, socio-cultural, historical, political and religious sentiments of the people. The movement suffered a [set back] on the fall of East Pakistan, their main foreign base.

Then, the party, having signed the Memorandum of Settlement, have dropped its original aims and objectives so as to make itself acceptable to the Government of India. The 'new' MNF was installed and afterwards elected to the seats of power in the new State of Mizoram. Time will tell how meaningful is the role of the MNF in the process of the socio-economic development of Mizoram and in serving the interests of the Mizos while including them with the 'mainstream' of the national life. The present leadership appears to be serious in working for the socio-economic uplift of the people, so as to catch up with other hill states thus making up the loss suffered during the 20 years of its underground movement.

The greatest challenge for the MNF party now could be how to fulfil the Mizo people's expectations of it and wishes for socio-economic reconstruction.

The liberal financial support from the Central Government may be utilised for the acceleration of the speed of socio-economic advancement. But, what Mizos have to learn is how to become more and more self-sufficient. It is everybody's question whether the MNF, which has even attempted to form an independent Mizoram, will be sufficiently effective enough in bringing about the real healing of the wounds suffered by the Mizos. The aspirations of the Mizos are still high. 53.87 per cent of our respondents still wish to have an Independent Greater Mizoram, while 29.50 per cent are satisfied with a state in Indian Union with special provisions. The moral support given to the party even when it went underground was so apparent as borne out by the success of any overground party blessed by the MNF. It will be counter-productive for the party if it fails the Mizo people who have all along been entertaining hope in it.[23]

(d) The People's Conference of Mizoram

The Mizo Union, the dominant regional party at over-ground politics merged itself into the Congress Party in January 1974 and the Merger Congress had been running the Mizoram U.T. Ministry for one year and two months. But, it made hopeless performance, and the expectation that the socio-political conditions would improve if the Mizoram Government was run by the same party as that possess power at the Centre, was belied. The Mizo people had the impression that the Merger Congress minister was no better than the Mizo Union Ministry.

The formal merger of the two parties was not followed by an emotional union. The Mizo Union group and the 'original' Congressmen continued to have different mentalities. There were also an internal power-struggle between the two groups. People in the rural parts who had completely identified themselves with the Mizo Union for years did not find it easy to become Congressmen overnight. The pro-MNF people who had rallied round the Congress party had neither very enthusiastic about having the anti-MNF Mizo Unionists in their midst. So the merger was practically useful, whatever be the intentions of the leaders of the two parties in having them merged. In the midst of these conditions, the MNF underground movement still went on and the sufferings of innocent people at the hands of the atrocious military being beyond description, the people were yearning for effective leadership in order to ameliorate their untold sufferings. After the dominant regional party (MU) had become a national party and the MNF was still underground, there was a vacuum in the regionalist politics of Mizoram.

There were talks of setting up a new regional party everywhere. Meanwhile, Brig. Thenphunga Sailo had retired from the Indian Army and formed a Human

Rights Committee, and as the president of the committee, gave a strong memorandum to Prime Minister Indira Gandhi in the following terms,

> "It must be accepted that the present trouble in Mizoram is not a military problem. It is a political problem and consequently a human problem—a battle of the hearts. The most ruthless measures were . . . the so-called grouping centres, reminiscent of a concentration camp. The Security Forces have tried to intimidate the public with all manners of atrocities and ill-treatment. However, this strong arm method has not brought about any solution. On the contrary, it has driven solution even farther away. It has only engendered bitterness and hatred against the Security Forces and consequently, India."[24]

Due to being a retired Brigadier of the Indian Army with good service record, the Mizo people looked up to T. Sailo to deliver them from their sufferings under the strong-arm policy. With the co-operation from a new educated elite group, a joint invitation was largely circulated on March 18, 1975 for holding a conference on the general people to discuss the prevalent political conditions of Mizoram. The conference was took place at Aizawl on April 16-17, 1975, in which 882 representatives of 192 villages and towns participated.[25] Most of the speeches were from the representatives of villages. On the second day, April 17, 1975, a unanimous resolution was made to form a new regional party. It was given a tentative name of "People's Conference", which was later approved by the first General Conference of the party. Brig. T. Sailo was unanimously chases president of the ponty. The people wanted to form a 'regional' party particularly for the following perceived reasons of the undesirability of either the Congress Party or Mizo Union.

1. There was no special advantage as people had generally believed in having a Congress Government in Mizoram as was evident from the performance of the Merger Congress Ministry in the spheres of law and order, economic development and political solution to Mizo problem.
2. The membership and organisational set up of the Congress were not in tune with Mizo mentality and practices. They were undemocratic.
3. In the Congress party, the Mizoram Pradesh Committee did not have full authority in party affairs e.g., in making party candidates for elections, and there is greater scope for infighting within the party. Even the Chief Minister and other Ministers had to be the choice of the party High Command at New Delhi, so it was alleged.
4. The Mizo Union had outlived its utility. Mizos were economically at a much lower level than their fellow hill-people in the North-East India because of the poor performance of the Mizo Union on the economic front.
5. The moral degeneration of Mizos was thought to have come about due to politicising within the dominance of the Mizo Union.

6. Inter-party antagonism was too much because of the Mizo Union's long-standing handling of politics.[26]

There were many others who would not join Mizo Union at any cost. The inevitable outcome of all these developments was a new regional party formed by the people themselves and led by effective leaders. The People's Conference under the leadership of Brig. T. Sailo was just the type of the regional party the people were looking for. Another plus point was that people had the impression that it was having a friendly relationship with the Underground MNF. Brig. T. Sailo's son was still in 'Mizo National Army'. A leadership that could assert itself and boldly speak against the army atrocities and maintain good relations with the underground MNF enjoyed all the uses to come up during those days. The party put down its aims and and objectives like this :[27]

1. The party will endeavour to prepare grounds for the peaceful solution to the Mizo political problem.
2. The party aims at the unification of all Mizo inhabited contiguous areas now forming parts of India under a single administrative unit.
3. The party stands for the wishes of the people to preserve their distinct identity ethnically, culturally and socially.
4. The interests of the people and Mizoram shall be the guiding principles with over-riding priority and precedence over those of the party.
5. The party will work for speedy economic advancement with special emphasis on rural development.
6. The party will uphold the aims and objects of the Human Rights Committee.

Above said aims and objects depict the nature and orientation of the PC as a strictly regional party, founded on the ethnico-cultural base. Two points of its difference from other regional parties were that it put down in black and white its interest in the peaceful way of Mizo problem, and that it respected human rights. It began to popularise itself and soon drew following in all parts of Mizoram excepting the Chakma areas. Its fast rise caused for them a problem with the Merger Congress and seven PC leaders including Brig. T. Sailo were soon arrested under the Maintenance of Internal Security Act (MISA) during the Emergency dated June 3, 1976 and were released in May 1977.[28] While the seven leaders were still in jail the party contested the Lok Sabha Elections in March 1977 and its candidate defeated his Congress rival by polling 52.93 per cent of votes. The Congress voted 37.70 per cent, the Mizo Union (who did not accept the 1974 merger) polled 8.47 per cent and Independents 1.48 per cent. It won the 1978 (May) Assembly Elections with an overwhelming majority of 23 seats out of 30. The party suffered a major split in October 1978 when 8 PC MLAs withdrew their support from the Chief Minister Brig. T. Sailo. They contended that he had gone far from the party policy No. 1, that is, "to prepare grounds for peaceful settlement of Mizo political problems."

The Speaker of the Assembly himself was trying to form an alternative government of the PC. When the situation was very uncertain, Prime Minister Morarji Desai visited Aizawl and Mizoram was soon kept under President's rule. The rebel MLAs claimed they were still People's Conference party. Others called them as PC(B). According to Sailo loyalists, the split was only due to the personal ambitions of the rebel MLAs. They were dissatisfied since they were not included in the ministry. Sailo's group were called by others as PC(A). A fresh Assembly election was held in April, 1979 in which Brig. T. Sailo's group PC(A) came up with lesser majority, bagging 18 out of 30 constituencies. In 1982, by-elections were held in four constituencies on account of the resignation of PC(B) MLAs. According to them, the resignation had been to strengthen the hands of Laldenga in his bargain with the Government of India. Mr. Lalsawia (then Rajya Sabha member) told the author at New Delhi that the resignation would make it feasible for the PC(B) to test the strength of PC(A). Sailo loyalists PC(A) took three and the fourth went to a 'Mizo Union' candidate with the support of the PC(A). The Sailo group then became free of the faction issue. Losing hope, the PC(B) converted itself into Mizo Convention in the same year. Sailo's People's Conference Government became stable once more.

But, with the increasing popularity of the party, the rift between T. Sailo and Laldenga which began sometime after the PC won the 1978 Assembly Elections by an overwhelming majority became wider. It is known that Brig. Sailo himself used to be invited to participate in certain talks between the Government of India and the MNF at the beginning. It could well be that Laldenga and T. Sailo had differences in regards to the modalities of settlement of peace in the state of Mizoram. Anti-Sailo groups charged that Sailo made a *Volte face* and turned against the MNF all on a sudden. Pro-Sailo groups said that Laldenga was by nature intolerant of any rival and he was making efforts to dislocate Sailo by any means. One point that the PC always made clear in public was that it could not understand why the MNF continued killings after having undertaken that it would look settlement within the framework of Indian Constitution. The rift between Sailo and Laldenga became so wide and deep that in 1978 a huge chunk of the MNF came over-ground and joined Sailo's PC party. It remains everybody's guess whether all these developments, between the PC and the MNF in general and between Sailo and Laldenga in particular, were because of Sailo's plan to finish Laldenga so that he could not hold any power after the settlement of peace, or were all these the consequences of Ladenga's clever tactics to dislocate Sailo before he could turn overground, in order to make his way to power safe and easy.

One thing that remains very clear in Mizo politics, however, is that any leader or party which has opposed the underground MNF stands a poor chance of winning elections. In the 1984 Assembly Elections, the Congress party won 19 out of 30 elective seats polling 40 per cent of votes, the PC could win only in 8 constituencies. The victory of the Congress was not necessarily due to people's deliberate support to it as a national party but because the leaders promised that they would step down from power when peace had been concluded between the Government of India and the MNF. The Congress candidate for the Lower house at Centre Election was elected unopposed. In the first Election to the full-fledged Mizoram State Legislative Assembly of 40 members, held in February 1987, the PC got only 3 candidates returned, one of them immediately defected to MNF and became a Minister of State in Laldenga's ministry. One may, therefore, suggest that a substantial number of the regionalist Mizos always give support to the MNF and the further division of the regionalist camp into two big groups would always result in the ascendency of the Congress party. If the regionalist camp can be solidly brought within the fold of a big regional party, the Congress has no possibility in Mizoram. The stand of the People's Conference on the question of regionalism is explained by Brig. Sailo himself thus,

> ". . . the Mizo people are deeply wedded to the concept of regional party as opposed to all-India party. I want to take this opportunity of once again clarifying our party stand vis-a-vis all-India party. For some valid and special reason we want to retain regional party. Though regional in character the People's Conference party has a positive national outlook and stands fully committed to the integrity and solidarity of the Indian Union and will work towards strengthening the fibre of national unity and territorial integrity. Further, we have a working understanding with the ruling party at the Centre . . . we have pledged full cooperation with the ruling party both inside and outside Parliament in their pursuit of the principle of secular democracy based on respect for human rights and the protection of the interests of the tribal groups and other backward classes and religious minority. This last election (1979) is a victory of regional party over all-India party."[29]

He explained the "regional in character but national in outlook" concept at another place like this,

"I wish to point out two possible extremes. Firstly, some of our people may tend to look at things too much in compartmental fashion and overlook matter of national importance. This will not be the right attitude because main events at national level also concern us intimately because we are a part of the same country. Secondly, and vice-versa, national leaders in Delhi, looking at things from an overall picture may tend to submerge our identities in the swirling current of national activities and altogether obliterate our regional character. Apart from that, it is the wish of our people to maintain our respective identity-ethnically, socially and culturally.[30]

This party took up many issues during its hold of power. On the economic front, it started the process of meeting what it called Six Basic Needs such as food, drinking water, road, transportation, power and issue of rural development.[31] It took the question of "Assimilation" very seriously. Drawing examples from the experience of Tripuris and Cacharis, the party tried hard to educate the public about the risk of being assimilated by larger groups. It spoke of assimilation as having physical (demographic), economic, cultural and social dimensions. It took a lot of pain to make the Mizos more aware of this problem and urges them to be watchful about it. The party took the infiltration of Bangladeshi Chakmas into Mizoram seriously. Brig. Sailo sent a memorandum on this to the Prime Minister of India on June 14, 1982, wherein he pointed out that "the Mizo people" can perhaps reconcile themselves to the idea of accepting those Chakmas who came into Mizoram in the 40s and 50s but are largely exercised about those who came into Mizoram in the 60s and 70s. The party took some measures in pushing back illegal infiltrators and in preventing further infiltration of foreigners into the state. It even talked of issuing identity cards to Mizoram Chakmas.[32] The party also took up the questions of Mizoram-Cachar boundary and Inner Line reserves and then a study group for these.[33] While settlement of peace between the Government of India and the MNF was still pending, the PC demanded special status for Mizoram with constitutional safeguards to Mizos and Mizoram regarding ownership and transfer of land, socio-cultural protection and economic provisions. Now, the PC party had conceded power to the Congress and become a minority party in terms of seats in the State Legislative Assembly. It had only two sitting members in a house of 40 and is busy 'reviewing' its poor performance in the Assembly Elections 1987. It had therefore, been submerged by the 'MNF wave', if this will be just for a while or for good is everybody's question. This development may give us an opinion that no two strong regional leaderships can co-exist in the state politics, and if they are divided equally, the national party will come up.

(e) The Indian National Congress (Mizoram)

Within the All India Parties, only the Congress has been able to establish some hold in Mizoram. This is mainly because of its secularistic liberalims which permits adjustment of various forces within its fold. Admitting that "regional ideology is highly appealing to the people", the party thinks that "regionalism is a passport to secessionism."[34] Regionalism gives birth to communalism and communalism in its extreme form breeds separatism", so says the party and warns that if the forces of regionalism which "erode the national unity" are not destroyed, "a time may come when the total North Eastern Region may plunge into a predicament where the centre and state leaders would become helpless."

It holds regional parties responsible for fanning up communal tensions in the region. The concept of "regional in character but national in outlook" is dismissed as one "that does not stand scrutiny", for "no one can have an outlook bigger than his character". A possible compromise of "regional in character" and "national in outlook" has been, the party states, attempted, but without success, from the platform of the Mizo Union which, as the Congress leaders would say, was a "well-disciplined regional party". Its merger with the Congress party in 1974 is therefore justified. The leaders of the Congress party hope to fulfil their commitment to bring the Mizo people into the 'mainstream' of national life through the party. Still, the party does not favour assimilation of Mizos and total obliteration of regional identity. It would even speak of "safeguarding the special and distinctive interests and aspirations" of the Mizo people. The Mizoram Congress is known to have a constitution of its own by which it has a "functional autonomy".[35] It has even been in alliance with third (regional) parties on some occasions. But, it would not support regional parties beyond a point where it would stand to lose its all-India character. The Mizoram Congress was formed, as already said, on August 10, 1961.

According to A. Thanglura, its founder in Mizoram, the attempt to popularise the Congress party among Mizos in those days was something like "trying to sell human excreta" and also like "trying to get a bird-lime stick on the trunk of a plantain",[36] because it was by nature opposed to Mizo Union and MNF movements. But, after sometime, the ex-MNF (or MNF returnees) and pro-MNF people started to join the Congress. Though Congress in form, the party was looked upon as 'overground MNF' because of its policy of peaceful settlement of Mizo problem and its effort to act as a mediator between the Government of India and the underground MNF. It captured majority of seats in the District Council Election of 1970 by a small margin of one over the Mizo Union and formed a highly shaky 'Government' in the last Mizo District Council. It swallowed the Mizo Union in a merger in 1974 and was in the opposition to Sailo's PC Government during 1978-83. During the 1984 Assembly Elections, it bagged 19 out of 30 elective seats, thus, turning the table on the PC. The Congress victory in the 1984 Elections was nothing but a result of its pledge to the people that it would finalise the talks for peace between the Government of India and the MNF and with the finalization, would step down from power in favour of the MNF.

This pledge was so appealing to the Mizos since they remembered Mrs. Indira Gandhi's remark earlier that if Mizoram Government was of the Congress, she could have directed it to step-down any moment the MNF would come to front. The people wanted to try them on this promise. When the Government of India and MNF came to the conclusion of the negotiation, the Congress Ministry could share power with the MNF, the Chief Minister coming down to Deputy Chief Ministership and three other ministers being replaced by MNF-men. The Congress captured 13 constituencies in the 1987 State Assembly Elections, polling 33 per cent of votes against the 24 seats and 37 per cent of votes taken by the MNF. It is interesting to note that all the Congress ministers who had vacated their positions in favour of the MNF got re-elected and all those who remained in the coalition Government (except Mr. Lalthanhawla who remained as Dy. Chief Minister in Laldenga Ministry) got defeat in the 1987 Elections.

We should observe from this fate of the Mizoram Congress that Mizos have been all along regionalist-minded. They put the Congress party up simply because they wanted to try their genuineness in their promise to step down in favour of the MNF. The said promise was productive in the politics of the day because Brig T. Sailo's ministry was, as it appeared to the general public, unlikely to hand over power to Laldenga's MNF. Even the Congress Ministry's yielding to the MNF was not a smooth process. It took place after the party's Lok Sabha M.P. Mr.

Lalduhawma pressed for the finalisation of peace talks even to the extent of leaving power-seats for Laldenga and as a result, he had to leave the party with one MLA and some followers. The various attempts of the Congress to penetrate the regionalistic politics of Mizoram have so far yielded no permanent results. It is also true that the members of the Congress party cannot go beyond a certain point where they would lose their Mizoness. When the then ruling MNF party had lost its solidarity as an organisation, largely over the question of liberalised issue of liquor permits, the Congress party was elected to power in 1989 followed by allegations of corruption in politics, which was difficult to establish. The party had promised the people a Christian society in Mizoram.

To sum up, the factors in order of importance as considered by people are as follows:

1. Mizo Union	Situation, policy, members, leadership, church support, Central Support, (No respondent gives 'money power' as a factor).
2. People's Conference	Leadership, policy, church, circumstances, members, money power, central help.
3. MNF	Policy, leadership, members, circumstances and church (No respondent gives 'Central Support' and 'money power' as important factors).
4. Congress	Central Support, money power, policy members, leadership and circumstances, church.

The factor of 'policy', holds the first place only in the case of the MNF, second place in MU and PC, third place in the Congress. 'Leadership' occupies first place in PC, second place in MNF, fourth place in MU and fifth place with Congress. 'Central Support' and 'money power' take particularly high places in the case of the Congress. 'Church Support' is at the lower side except in the case of PC, and it has just the last place in the cases of Congress and the MNF. These would suggest that in Mizoram politics, a party that is most likely to enjoy mass support is such which has a policy acceptable to the regionalist Mizos, possessing effective leadership and conscious members, enjoying some church support and also favourable socio-political circumstances. It may also be seen that 'central support' and 'money power' do not matter much in winning the support of the general masses as somewhere else.

Now that after the last assembly election, the scenario has changed at platform of State politics in this new 21st century, it is yet to be concluded what shape the whole state political set-up will take.

References

1. Frederick C. Engelmann. "A Critique of Recent Writings on Political parties, in Eckstein and Apter (ed.) *Comparative Politics. A Reader,* New York, Free Press, 1963, p. 379.
2. Samuel J. *Eldersveld's Political Parties: A Behavioral Analysis*, Chicago, Rand McNally, 1964 and
   Nageshwar Prasad's *Ideology and Organisation in Indian Politics—A study of Political Parties at the Grass-Roots,* New Delhi, Allied Publishers, 1980, where the new approaches are applied.
3. The original *Constitution of the Mizo Union* 1946, p. 1.
4. V.V. Rao. *A Century of Tribal Politics,* New Delhi, S. Chand and Co., 1976 (First Ed.) p. 495.
5. The total population of Lushai Hills alone according to 1941 Census was 1,52,786.
6. R. Vanlawama. *Ka Ram leh kei (My Country and I)* Aizawl, Zalen Printing House, 1972 (Second Impression), p. 177.
7. Amit Kumar Nag. *The Mizo dilemma,* Silchar, Tribal Mirror Publications, 1984, p. 27.
8. R. Vanlawama, *op. cit.,* p. 205.
9. The independence of India was enthusiastically welcomed by the Mizo Unionists. In December 1948, January 1949, the Mizo Union lauched a mess demonstration against the fast British Superintendent L.L. Peters.
10. A. Thanglura, *Zoram Politic Lumlet Dan,* Aizawl, Thankthing Bazar Press, 1983, p. 151.
11. Chaltuahkhuma, *Political History of Mizoram,* Aizawl, 1981, p. 120.
12. Ramchuani Sena Samuelson (Mrs.) *Love Mizoram,* Imphal, Goodwill Press, 1985 (First Impression), p. 54.
13. Lalchungnunga, *Parties and Politics in Mizoram: A Study of the Development of a Regional Party System* (unpublished M.Phil. Dissertation) JNU, 1982, p. 80.
14. R. Vanlawma, *op. cit.* p. 188.
15. Nirmal Nibedon, *North-East India-The Ethnic Explosion,* New Delhi, Lancers Publishers, 1981, p. 38.
16. B.B. Goswami, *Mizo Unrest: A Study in Politicization of Culture,* Aalekh, 1979, p. 84.
17. Dr. Animesh Ray, *Mizoram, Dynamics of Change,* Calcutta, Pearl Publishers, 1982, pp. 156 ff.
18. *MNF Pawl Thiltumte Hrilhfiahna,* (An Explanation of the MNF's Aims and Objectives) November 16, 1972, p. 1.
19. C. Nunthara, *The Politics of the Mizo Hills,* (Unpublished Dectoral Thesis) Delhi University, 1980, p. 138.
20. Laldenga, *Mizoram Marches Towards Freedom,* published by the "Government of Mizoram" (MNF), recent cyclostyled copy, p. 25.
21. *Mizoram Politics Chanchin,* a pamphlet published by the MNF, December 29, 1973, p. 52.
22. Nirmal Nibedon, *Mizoram, the Dagger Brigade,* contains some of the main events.
23. Biswanath Ghosh, *"Laldenga taking an uphill task" Amrita Bazar Patrika,* Thursday, May 7, 1987, p. 8.
24. *Memorandum* submitted to the Prime Minister of India by the Human Rights Committee, Mizoram, Aizawl, 1974, p. 2.
25. *Message No. 2* of People's Conference, dt. 22.4.1975.
26. *People's Conference's Message No. 3,* dated 21.5.1975.
27. *People's Conference Party Constitution,* Aizawl, Lianchhungi Book Stores, October 22, 1976, p. 3. These aims and objectives were retained when the Constitution was amended in 1981.

28. P.C. Ghos. Letter No. PC 25/75/3656-3660 dated Aizawl 20th July, 1976, and Order No. III-14025/4/76-NE, Govt. of India, Ministry of Home Affairs, North Eastern Division, New Delhi, 5th March, 1977.
29. *Public Speech* delivered by Brig. T. Sailo at Assam Rifles Parade Ground, Aizawl, on May 5, 1979, published by PC General Headquarters.
30. Brig. T. Sailo, in his *opening address* to the convention of North Eastern Hill Areas Regional Parties (NEHARP) at Shillong on May 19, 1977.
31. Brig. T. Sailo, *Speeches and Writings,* Aizawl Mizoram Government Press, 1981, p. 50.
32. PC Office Bearer's Meeting on 9-12-75. *Resolution No. 4.*
33. PC *Central Working Committee Meetings* of March 26, 1976, (Res. No. 1) February 7, 1979 (Res. No. 3) and February 9, 1979-Res. No. 1 (ii).
34. *Write-up* issued by Mr. Lalsangzuala, General Secretary, Mizoram Pradesh Committee (I), dated July 19, 1980. Congress Committee (I), dated July 19, 1980. Congress.
35. A leaflet issued by the Mizoram Congress (I) under Memo No. MCC. 6/83/pt. dated Aizawl, December 5, 1983.
36. A. Thanglura, *op. cit.* p. 172. "Ek zawrh ang chauh a ni", p. 178, *"Changela sawi bel ang chauh a ni"*. These are Mizo phrases to say that the act does not look hopeful of success.

15

Impact of Terrorism on Politics and Administration

After independence, resettling of the country had to undergo numerous problems in states. The most important factor which has determined the course of political development in the Mizo Hills area is undoubtedly the occurrence of insurgency. Insurgency has disrupted the normal administrative system and the counter-insurgency steps have again affected the system in the feed back process. Many incidents have taken place in this area during the last decade and inspite of the counter-insurgency measures followed by the government sporadic incidents are taking place even now.

(a) Leading Incidents

One of the main incidents is as below:

"Between 10-30 a.m. of February 28 and 3 a.m. of March 1, 1966, large scale disturbances broke out in different places in the Mizo Hills. In reply to a calling attention motion in the Lok Sabha on March 2, 1966, Gulzarilal Nanda, Home Minister made a statement in the House giving the details of the incidents[1]: A number of armed Mizos led by the Mizo National Front (MNF) resorted to lawlessness and violence at Aizawl, Lunglei, Vairengte, Chawngte, Chhimluang and other places to disrupt communications and overawe public servants. He stated that the first attack was on the Sub-Treasury at Lunglei. A gang of about 1000 armed Mizos attacked the Assam Rifles post at Lunglei. Some attackers and two Assam Rifles men were killed and three Assam Rifles men were wounded. The whereabouts of the Subdivisional Officer were not known. At 2 a.m. on March 1 a gang attacked the Telephone Exchange at Aijawl. About 100 to 150 people attacked the Aizawl Treasury and took away cash from the cash boxes under single lock, and ten rifles and ammunition from the guard room.

At Vairengte, the first Mizo village on Silchar-Aizawl road, at 1-30 a.m. on the March 1 about 150 armed Mizos went to the houses where the non-Mizos were residing and asked them to leave Mizo district immediately. They took away the jeep of the Subdivisional Officer, Public Works Department and took over the PWD stores which had explosives, petrol and other stores useful to the rebels. Two culverts between Vairengte and Lailapur, the first village on the Cachar side in the plains, on the Aizawl-Silchar road were blown up and huge trees were cut down and placed on the road which completely disrupted road communication between Sichar and Aizawl which was the only road communication Mizo district had with the rest of India.

Disturbances continued in all important centres of the district on March 1. At Lunglei heavy firing from both the sides continued. The post of the Border Security Forces was captured by the rebels. R.V. Pillai, SDO, Lunglei, and many other officers were kidnapped by the rebels. Far in the interiors in the south, firing between posts of the Border Security Forces and the rebels continued throughout the day. At Champhai on the Burma border, the Wing Headquarters of the Assam Rifles with two platoons of forces fell to the rebels and the post was destroyed."

(b) Declaration of Freedom

It came to be heard on March 1 that the MNF had declared independence. Declaring the district as 'independent Mizoram', they had put armed volunteers of the so-called Mizo National Army (MNA) to set free Mizoram from the Indian Government. Cyclostyled copies of the 'Declaration of Independence' signed by Laldenga and sixty others were circulated[2]. The news of the Mizo rebellion reported shortly on the March 2 issue of some of the newspapers, were flashed in headlines all over the country on March 3. *The Assam Tribune* of March 3 also reported in banner headline—'Administration in Mizo paralysed following widespread subversion by the armed volunteers of the MNF.'

Just after receipt of the information of the trouble the government sent a team of high officers to Aizawl. On March 1 the commissioner of the Division, the Inspector General of the Assam Rifles and a senior Army officer went to Aizawl for an on-the-spot assessment of the situation.

On March 2 the Government of Assam declared the district as a "disturbed area" with immediate effect as per the Assam Disturbed Areas Act, 1955. It was also declared as a "disturbed area" under the Armed Forces (Assam and Manipur) Special Powers Act, 1958. On March 3 of same year, J.L. Hathi, Minister of State for Home Affairs, told the Lok Sabha that as a result of the on-the-spot assessment the Army had been asked to deal with the situation in the Mizo Hills. Transport of troops to Aizawl by helicopters were going on since the morning of March 3 and troops left Silchar for Aizawl also by road.

The armed police forces were placed under the operational control of the Army for handling the disturbances. The Army was to remain in charge of operation as long as necessary in support of the civil administration.[3] By the evening of March 6 troops reached Aizawl by clearing obstacles on the way. The Silchar-Aizawl road was opened to traffic. On the same day the MNF was declared an unlawful organisation as per rule 32 of the Defence of India Rules, 1962, on the ground that the MNF was an organisation indulging in activities prejudicial to the security of Mizo district and the adjoining areas. Any person, who managed, promoted or attended meetings of the organisation, published any notice regarding such meetings and invited persons to support such organisation was liable to seven years' imprisonment and also to certain fine.

The State Government dropped one lakh leaflets to apprise the people of the situation.[4] However, the rebels' pressure upon the Assam Rifles Post at Lunglei mounted. They disrupted communication to all the interior centres, damaged government property and set fire to the Aizawl market. Presenting all these details of the atrocities in the Lok Sabha the Minister for Home Affairs told the House on March 8, 1966:[5]

> "Although the Prime Minister had kept herself in constant touch with the developments from Delhi, she decided to pay a flying visit to Gauhati yesterday (March 7) to get a first-hand report on the happenings and the latest detailed information on the situation in Mizo Hills."

Then, on March 7 Lalnunmawia, Vice-President of the MNF, sent a letter to the DC offering peace talks with the government. The DC rejected the offer and demanded unconditional surrender of the rebels within 24 hours. The rebels were in control of Lunglei, Champhai and a number of other interior centres. The troops entered Lunglei on April 13 and relieved the town without any opposition from the hostiles. Champhai had been freed from the rebels on April 14 and Demagiri on April 17. The Minister of Home Affairs told the Lok Sabha on March 25.[6]

> "All the important posts and towns have been rid of the influences of the armed Mizo gangs and the Mizo National Front volunteers have either gone into hiding in jungles or are trying to escape into Pakistan or Burma. Mopping up operation are now continuing."

Complete figures of casulties of the troops till March 25, 1966, showed one Commissioned Officer, five Junior Commissioned Officers and 192 persons of other ranks missing or kidnapped. Besides, the headquarters of the 1st Assam Rifles at Aijawl all other areas of Mizo district fell in the hands of the MNF. It took more than a month for the troops to gain control over the major centres of administration.

On April 6, 1966 the Chief Minister of Assam told the State Legislature:[7]

> "Apart from capturing officers, large quantities of arms and ammunition, it is feared, cash from Lunglei has fallen into the hands of the members of this banned MNF organisation. The pressure against a number of posts continued, both on the Burma border as well as on the Pakistan border. Columns of the Defence Forces have gradually been going over to the areas under pressure. The Government has rushed in supplies of essential food stuffs and are in the process of restoring and strengthening the Administration. While determined organised attacks on any significant scale have not been reported, yet intimidation, threats, sniping, ambushes and other activities indicate that the lawless elements are still active in many parts of the Mizo District."

(c) Sporadic Cases

The atrocities of the Mizo rebels went on sporadically in the interiors of the district and in the border areas. On September 26, 1966, about 100 armed Mizos attacked the police outpost at Jairampunji in Cachar District bordering the Mizo Hills, with the help of rifles, grenades and automatic weapons. Three constables died in the encounter[8]. On November 9, 1966, in the morning a batch of Mizos armed with rifles and LMG looted valuables, properties and committed arson at the bus stand of the Gharmura village in Cachar District. Simultaneously, another batch looted properties on the eastern bank of the river Dhaleswari[9]. Due to the strong military action in the Mizo Hills the MNF activists took shelter in the neighbouring Chittagong Hill Tracts in the then East Pakistan.

Then, on November 9, 1966 the Deputy Minister for Home Affairs stated in the Lok Sabha: "A provisional Government by the Mizo National Front is operating from East Pakistan and directing subversive activities in Mizo and Cachar Districts[10]. State government had information that the Mizo rebels set up camps in East Pakistan for organisation and training. The Government of India protested Pakistan about this matter; no reply was received, but Pakistan publicly declines giving arms or training to the Mizos.[11]

(d) Factors Behind the Insurgency

On the reasons of these disturbances there had been so many theories and opinions that it is difficult to give a comprehensive picture. Some criticisms were regarding the policy of the government and some were against persons in the government. A persistent one against Bimala Prasad Chaliha, Chief Minister of Assam, was that he was too soft to the MNF even when he knew that they planned to stick down to subversive activities. He was accused of too lenient a treatment when in 1964 he ordered the release of Laldenga and Lalnunmawia, President and Vice-President respectively of MNF, only after they had been arrested by the district administration while returning from East Pakistan.[12]

The Chief Minister clarified his stand in the Assembly on March 5, 1966, while replying to a discussion on the state in the Mizo Hills. He said that the President and the Vice-President of MNF gave him an assurance on February 19, 1964, in writing that they would not get into any anti-social activities and that they regretted very much their visit to Pakistan without any valid document. They said that they wanted to visit their brethren in Pakistan where they were facing troubles and not for any political purpose.[13] The Chief Minister said that there were three ways of dealing with the MNF—politically, administratively and by police action. Owing to the troubles in the border, the government decided to deal with it politically. Accordingly, discussions with the MNF were held. It was the consensus that most of the problems were economic and thus, development projects should be taken up. The MNF leaders promised to co-operate with the government in the economic development programmes. On this assurance of cooperation the MNF leaders released from Jail.

The Chief Minister took the entire responsibility of what happened in the Mizo Hills and stated that the government was not in any way influenced by any evaluation of the situation by the local officials. Thus the Chief Minister absolved the DC, Mizo district, of the accusation, commonly being levelled, that he did not assess the situation rightly. It was also being talked that the DC did not advise the government correctly and failed to take adequate precautionary measures. It was generally stated that although a Superintendent of Police was posted in the district in 1963, he was transferred in 1964 and on the advice of the DC no other SP was posted in the district. Clarifying the position in this context, Fakhruddin Ali Ahmed, Minister for Irrigation and Power, told the Lok Sabha on March 3, 1966 that from the beginning the DC in the Mizo Hills also discharged the duty of the SP. He was assisted by the Commandant of the 1st Assam Rifles, posted at Aizawl, in maintenance of land and order in the district. As the DC became increasingly busy with same other work, in 1963 he enlisted the help of an SP. But the new system was not found practicable and hence the SP was reverted to the State Government.

On the Chief Minister's attitude, Ahmed said that Chaliha, because of being a kind man, did not like to use force. But, because of deteriorating law and order situation, a second battalion of the Assam Rifles was posted in the district dated September 1965[14]. P.C. Barroah, MP, traced the root of the trouble to the British. He said that Coupland gave a proposal before the independence of India that the hill regions of Assam should be separated from India and converted into a British colony. The communists had access to these areas, being friendly to the British and they sowed the seed of self-determination. The Sixth Schedule of the Constitution was accepted by the five hill districts of Assam but the Nagas did not accept it. Some sections of the Nagas wanted a different State, some others demanded independence.

Concessions given to the Nagas in the form of Statehood encouraged the other tribals to demand more. Mizos wanted a different Mizoram which would also comprise the adjoining areas of Burma and Pakistan. When the second Assam Rifles battalion was to be sent to Mizo district, they started a movement against the induction of the said additional force.[15] The view of G.G. Swell, MP, was that Laldenga was not an extremist to start with; he was with the All Party Hill Leaders' Conference (APHLC) when it was emerged in 1960 with the demand of a Hill State. He attributed the Mizo trouble to the wrong policy of introducing Assamese language by the Assam Government. Hem Barua, MP, varied from him saying that even in 1954, before the policy regarding the Assamese language was announced, some Mizo youngmen gave a booklet to Nehru, in which a separate independent land for the Mizos was asked for. Hence, he said, the demand made by the insurgents was neither sudden nor abrupt. Jyotsna Chanda, MP, held that the rivalry between the MNF and the Mizo Union was the beginning point of the movement by the MNF in 1962 for separation from Assam and in 1964 led to violence in which a Border Roads Officer was murdered in the Border Roads headquarters at Zemabak near Aijawl. Replying to the debate, Gulzarilal Nanda,

Home Minister, traced the development of the political activity by the MNF. The MNF, he said, had enunciated some political line which was wholly unacceptable, but "at the same time they were following a Constitutional course. They have been able to win election in 143 out of 420 villages as against 277 by the Union. Also they have got a majority of seats in the Assembly".

The issue was when to apply force. It was thought that the moderates would be able to guide the Mizos, but contrary to the expectation, the situation got worsened.[16]

After this, the second batallion of Assam Rifles moved into the district. The extremists thought that the government was about to take action against them and hence they struck. Nanda observed that fast economic development which had just started in the Mizo Hills was another reason why the extremists had taken up arms. There was an impressive increase in the Plan expenditure in the Mizo Hills. The Plan-wise figures were as below: First Plan—Rs. 63 lakhs, Second Plan—Rs. 211 lakhs and Third Plan—Rs. 562 lakhs. Big stepping up of the plan expenditure enhanced also the administrative facilities. The *per capita* expenditure in Mizo district at the end of the Third Plan was Rs. 314/- against the Rs. 166/- for the whole state.

During 1963-64 the Adviser to the Planning Commission toured the area and formulated comprehensive development programmes. The extremists were afraid, Nanda said, that by the newly started schemes of development the Mizo people would become accustomed to normal peaceful way and hence, if delayed, the contemplated revolt would not materialise at any cost. On the MNF's attempts to justify their stand by claiming that the Mizos had all along been independent, Ram Monohar Lohia, MP, read out in the lower house[17] from an alleged letter from Laldenga to President Sukarno of Indonesia:

> "Historians claim that we, the Mizo people are the Mongoloids originated from time immemorial from the southern part of China and migrated towards the present habitat between India and Burma through the Shan State of Burma in about (*sic.*) fifteenth century.
>
> Our Chiefs ruled over separate hills and valleys with supreme authority and their administration was very much like that of the Greek City-States of the past. India's top leader and spokesman late Pandit Jawaharlal Nehru released a press statement on the 9th August 1946 and stated: 'The tribal areas are defined as being those along the frontiers of India, which one neither part of India, nor of Burma, nor of an India State, nor of any foreign power."

On this, Lohia commented that he did not know whether Nehru made such comments and even it he did, he must have said something else which was not in this quotation. He went on with the letter and said that it appeared that there was a proclamation by the British to the Mizos.[18] He quoted further from Laldenga's letter as said below:

> "Consequent upon the proclamation the Lushai Brigade and the Lushai Scouts actually fought in the Burma Front against the Japanese aggression. In fact, we were in semi-independent State during the British period."

Nanda said that this letter was seized at the time of a search.[19] The trouble in the Mizo Hills followed the course of events as occurred in the Naga Hills. The genesis of trouble in these border parts—Nagaland and Mizoram—may be traced to the deliberate and successful attempt on the part of the British to keep these separate from the rest of India.[20] The pattern of development within these hills also contributed to these developments. The essence of the tribal society was undergoing a drastic transformation because of very quick conversion of the Mizos to Christianity. The extinction of same Mizo way of life symbolised by *zawlbuk* (bachelors' dormitory), *tlawnmaihna* (a spirit of selfless cooperation and help to the fellow beings), etc., introduced individualistic life instead of the collective tribal life. The spread of primary education was extremely rapid. But the scope for higher or professional education was confined. The educated youngmen aspired for the government jobs which were not enough in number. All these led to the coming up of a generation of youngmen whose roots were loose and the future not sure. These frustrated youngmen spearheaded the uprising. A majority of them were in their teens, and although politically conscious, they did not have the voting rights. So the MNF, which largely comprised of young people, could not come to the District Council. This also resulted in the adoption of a destructive attitude by these yougmen.

(e) Role of Ex-servicemen in this Act

There was a huge number of ex-servicemen in the district. During the second world war about 5,000 Mizos were enrolled in the army and the allied services. Most of them went to serve in other places in the country and some also served outside India. Back home after the war they were unhappy to get back to the arduous but uneconomic *jhums* and the feudal system of the village life. There was not much scope of suitable employment of all these people in the stagnant economic life of the district. There were again a few hundred Mizo soldiers of the Assam Regiment who were sent back after their regiment had been disbanded following an incidence of insubordination. They had a grudge against the government and this ill-feeling prompted them to join their hands with the MNF.

The MNF utilised the service of all these trained ex-servicemen in organising the youngmen in the villages and giving them military training. The atmosphere of guerilla training provided to the villagers during the second world war also helped the MNF. There was a source of huge quantities of arms and ammunition as the villagers were permitted, from Shakespeare's days, one gun for every fifteen households in a village. There were also many guns, left-overs from the war, and many were clandestinely made locally. It was assumed that at the time uprising occurred there were about 7,000 guns in the district. The MNF hoped to capture all these weapons, once the uprising started.

The MNF counted much on the assistance from the foreign countries, particularly Pakistan. It appears that they had an assurance of military, political and moral support, once they start the rebellion. Indeed, following the security operations in the district after the initial disturbances, the hard core of the MNF left the district and took shelter in East Pakistan. Their subsequent operations inside the Mizo Hills and the close by areas in Cachar and Tripura were conducted by infiltration of trained batches from these bases.

Regarding the development of events, Roy Burman says:[21]

> "The uprising in Mizo Hills was patering out and the rebels were trying hard to regroup their forces with foreign assistance. Their contacts with Pakistan were of long standing but a new development was an effort to seek China's help.
>
> The Mizo rebels have been to touch with Peking through the Chinese Consulate in Dacca, which has been taking an interest in them right from the beginning of the uprising in February 1966. Laldenga, President of the Mizo National Front, is known to have been in communication with the Consulate during the period he and his family were staying in Dacca. It is known that Peking had extended invitations to the rebel leaders to visit China for direct discussions with the Chinese leaders.
>
> The Mizos may also be seeking the help of the Naga underground to get to China overland via Nagaland and Burma. This collusion gains added significance from the fact that traffic between Nagaland and China has already been established by the extremist section of the underground.
>
> In the meanwhile, Mizos continued to receive help from Pakistan by way of arms as well as training facilities. Instructions in guerilla warfare techniques is being given at camps functioning in the areas adjoining Mizo Hills lying within the districts of Sylhet and Chittagong Hills tracts. Apart from these Pakistan-run camps, the Mizos have been allowed to locate their operation bases inside Pakistan territory outside the reach of Indian force."

(f) New Outbreak

There occurred temporary lull in 1968 and the major part of 1969. But towards the end of 1969 about 150 to 200 armed Mizo rebels entered Mizo district from the Chittagong Hills Tracts. These armed people in groups of three to five men infiltrated deep into the interiors with light arms and sleeping bags. Their presence increased the anxiety of the administration which was facing the problem of acute food shortage in the district.[22] There were incidents of clashes between them and the security forces. One Major of the Indian Army and six other armymen were killed in Marpara region in the border of the Mizo Hills with East Pakistan, on the night of February 16, 1970, in an ambush by the armed gangs.

It was reported that the Mizo, the Naga and the Kuki insurgents camping in East Pakistan (Bangladesh) were being reared up by China as a joint military command to aid extremist movement in north-eastern India. Their number was estimated at 1,500.[23] The insurgents started a programme of intensified guerilla activities. On July 2, 1970, a large number of armed Mizos crossed from East Pakistan into three border villages of Tripura and started heavy mortar and machinegun fire as a result of which three persons died, seven were injured and the Central Reserve Police camp was damaged. They were believed to have went across from the Sajik range where Pakistan was maintaining a large number of training for them.[24] There were reports of hostile activities by small batches of rebels who infiltrated into Mizo District.

During a mopping operation by the security forces in August 1970 six rebels were killed and 31 others were captured. "The documents seized from the captured hostiles revealed that they had returned with specific instructions from the Pakistan authorities to sabotage road communications, blow up bridges, ambush army convoys and stimulate the moribund secessionist movement with the help of the leaders of the outlawed Mizo National Front. Two explosives were recovered from the premises of the Deputy Commissioner's bungalow at Aizawl. Timely detection prevented a serious explosion. As a large number of people turned up to celebrate the Independence Day at Aizawl an explosion took place in a *nullah* (drain). Another explosion took place near the bungalow of the Assistant Deputy Commissioner at Saiha".[25]

All above incidents revived the hostile atmosphere throughout the whole district. During the Christmas of 1970 Mahendra Mohan Choudhury, Chief Minister of Assam, went to Aizawl and expressed the State Government's keen desire to accelerate economic development of the district.

(g) Counter-Insurgency Arrangements

The extraordinary situation of immediate rebellion throughout the whole district required immediate action under the different special provisions of law which were designed to meet such situations. The whole district was said disturbed area under the Assam Disturbed Areas Act, 1955, to enable the government to make adequate provision for the suppression of the disturbances, maintenance of the public order and communication system and for the protection of life and property of the loyal citizens in the area. This Act empowered magistrates, officers of the Assam Rifles of the rank of Havilder and upwards and also police officers of the rank of Sub-Inspectors and above to fire upon or otherwise use force even to the causing of death, against any person who is acting in contravention of any law or order side the disturbed area prohibiting the assembly of five or more persons or carrying of weapons.[26] Under this Act magistrates and officers of same rank of the armed forces have powers to destroy arms dumps, fortified positions or shelters, training camps for armed volunteers, hideouts or shelters of armed gangs. The armed forces could exercise these powers under the Armed Forces (Assam and Manipur) Special Powers Act, 1958, if an area is declared a disturbed area under the Act.

State Government of Assam declared the whole of Mizo district a disturbed area under this Act, as the government was of the opinion that Mizo district was in such disturbed and risky condition that the use of armed forces in aid of civil power was necessary. This enabled the officers of the armed forces to use force for the enforcement of prohibitory orders and to harm arms dumps, hideouts, etc.[27]

This Act also empowered the officers of the armed forces to arrest without warrant any person who has committed a cognizable offence or against whom a reasonable suspicion is there that he has committed or is about to commit a cognizable offence.[28]

> "This is a very wide power and so that it may not lead to unreasonable restrictions to the liberty of citizens, it has been laid down under the Act that the arrested person shall be handed over to the officer in charge of the nearest police station with the least possible delay, together with a report of the circumstances occasioning the arrest. In case of delay in release of the arrested persons, their relations and the friends would move the DC for their release. Writ petitions for *habeas corpus* were also often submitted to the High Court of Assam and the Supreme Court. Although the number of such arrests and detention by the armed forces was quite large during the early stages of the counter-insurgency opeations, it gradually decreased as the conditions settled down."

Compliance with the legal provisions became easier when Administrative Officers (AOs) with magisterial powers were posted in the villages. They enjoyed the powers to order detention in custody beyond twenty four hours. The armed forces had also the power to enter and search, without warrant, any premises, to make an arrest or even to recover any person wrongfully restrained or confined or any stolen property or any arms, ammunition or explosive substances unlawfully kept in such premises.

A special protection to officers acting under these Acts was given by the provision that no suit, prosecution or other legal proceedings could be instituted except with the previous sanction of the State Government of Mizoram against any person in respect of anything done under the Assam Disturbed Areas Act, 1955,[29] and without the previous sanction of the Central Government for anything done as per the Armed Forces (Assam and Manipur) Special Powers Act, 1958.[30] The powers of the armed forces have been elaborated above, as under the ordinary Indian law, the armed forces do not have any power over the civilian population. But in the case of emergency, special statutes and provisions of law may be invoked to put the military forces operation in a disturbed situation occurring within the country. The army called in aid of civil power has to act within the strict confines of the law. The people jealously guard their civil rights even in absolutely abnormal condition of rebellion or insurgency. A democratic government based on the principles of equality and liberty can hardly militate against the accepted code of conduct setup by law.

The Government of India and the Government of Assam were evidently keen to see that however great might be the provocation and the necessity of restoring normalcy in the largely disturbed areas, the democratic processes of law were strictly adhered to. All the executive actions taken by the district administration in the perspective of the disturbances too had to conform to the standards of the established legal norms. As a matter of fact, to meet the insurgency the entire administrative pattern of the district went through a quick change, both in structure as well as function.

(h) Movement Restrictions, Curfew and Other Orders in State

Among the security measures taken by the government was the restrictions of movement from one place to another. The Government of Assam declared the area within ten miles of both sides of Silchar—Aizawl—Lunglei road as protected area as per Sub-Rule (1) of Rule 80 of the Defence of India Rules, 1962.[31] By these orders persons entering the protected area would require permits from the authorised government functionaries. This was a measure to prevent infiltration of hostiles into the most vital area of the district, i.e., the road connecting Silchar, Aizawl and Lunglei by which all the supplies into the district shifted from the plains of Assam. The most pervasive order in the counter-insurgency operation in the district since March 1966 was the enforcement of curfew all over the district directing that no person should remain or be out of doors during the period between 6 p.m. and 4 a.m. in any part of the district. At the initial stages, these curfew orders were passed under the Defence of India Rules, 1962 but later on these orders were regularly passed under the Code of Criminal Procedure i.e., Cr.P.C. in Mizo district the gun register in March 1966 indicated that there were about 5,000 licensed guns in the district. But estimates would put the correct number at about 7,000.

The Mizos had been making guns indigenously for more than a century. They were also clandestinely importing guns from the neighbouring foreign nations, i.e., Burma and East Pakistan. A gun was a prized possession and a status symbol among the hill people. Prior to the British rule guns were freely used by the Mizos while in warpaths and also head-hunting expeditions. Later the primary use of guns became protection of crops from the depredations of wild animals.

Although the trigger-happy Mizos practically left no fauna in the area, the number of guns went on to increase in the district. In the state of rebellion, this big number of guns provided a nice opportunity to the insurgents to arm themselves and they took as many guns as possible from the villagers for use against the government. As per a very moderate estimate, not less than 6,000 guns passed on to the hands of the rebels for such use. Hence it was necessary to pass restrictive orders regarding possessions of guns. According to Rule 81 of the Defence of the India Rules, 1962, the DC prohibited the possession, carrying, use and sale of arms and ammunition in the district and directed the gun licence-holders of the district to submit their guns and licences with the government authorities.

Contravention of the order was made rigorously punishable.[32] The MNF volunteers were organised well like regular armed forces. They wore military uniforms, had camp offices in which they used typewriters and duplicating machines not only for internal communication amongst themselves but also to create propaganda literature. For communication between distant places they adopted a very old and traditional method of transmission of messages from hill top to hill top with signals of torch lights. Orders were passed prohibiting production, import, storage, sale and purchase of torch lights, torch cells, jungle boots/shoes, jungle hats, olive green or khaki fabric wool, typewriters and duplicators, excepting under a permit from an authorised officer.[33]

(i) Forming of Villages Clusters

The villages in the Mizo hills areas were reorganised after the insurrection. The twin objectives of the reorganisation were to contain the rebel activities of the MNF and also to accelerate economic growth of the district. After the rebellion was crushed in the main centres and the big villages the hostiles fled to jungles where they had an ideal hiding place. To meet their necessary requirements of goods, clothes, medicine and other consumer articles they would swoop on the interior villages and extort from the people the articles and cash they would need. The rebels would threaten the people by show of force and also by committing heinous crimes like murder, kidnapping and dacoity. They would leave the village when a column of security force was expected to arrive at the village and would reappear when the security patrol had moved out of the village. The villagers would virtually be at the pity of the rebels and even while the security column might be passing through the villages, the people would really be at ransom of the rebels who could demand anything including joining of volunteers, supply of free labour and accommodation under pain of cruel reprisals.

These rebels would also collect information regarding movement of the security force and the government's counter-insurgency measures and would lay ambushes to break security covers, countermand the government's orders to the people and would virtually run a parallel government in the interiors. To stop all these harassments to the people and to bring in lasting peace, it was essential to post pickets of armed forces in all the interior villages. But these would have required deployment of disproportionately large number of armed forces as the villages numbered around 1,000, most of which had population of only about a 100 or so each.

It was, therefore, considered reasonable to shift the people from the small interior villages to some vantage points specifically by the side of the main roads. Small villages which were already by the main roads could also be grouped together to form big units. These big villages could be conveniently saved from the ravages of the hostiles by posting of static armed guards in each of these villages. Shifting of the villages from the interiors would give wider scope of operation to the security forces as they could focus on combats without being saddled with the duty of protecting innumerable places of habitation. It would also deny the hostiles easy havens as they would no longer be able to generate food and other essential articles in the deep interiors devoid of any human habitation.

As they would not be in touch with the masses, the propaganda value of their existence in defiance of the lawful government would also be lost. In the Mizo hills, the villages are situated on hill tops and as such they are highly distant from one another. Alongwith the difficulty of the terrain, the distances of the villages from the centres of development make the development projects non-viable. Then, most of the small hamlets were yet untouched by development processes. In this context Tarlok Singh, a Member of the Planning Commission, who led a study team to the Mizo Hills in January 1966, just prior to the outbreak of the disturbances, observed that the economic benefits could not reach the innumerable interior villages having small populations, situated as they were over distant and scattered hills and he suggested that these small villages should be reconstituted into large units with road communication which would bring the people within easy reach of technical know-how of development and monetary and other assistance from the government.

Thus grouping of villages was considered necessary for fast economic development, that alone could defeat the main plank of the rebels who had gained implied popular support to insurgency on ground of economic backwardness due to alleged negligence of their area by the Government of Assam and also by the Central Government. These circumstances led to the decision of the government to shift the population of the interior villages to some selected places on the road side and also to reorganise the small road side villages into compact and big units.

A regrouped village was called "Protected and Progressive Village" or in short, PPV. At the first step, PPVs were organised on the main road of Silchar-Aizawl-Lunglei, starting from Vairengte, the first village in Mizoram from the Silchar side, and stretching over a length of some 400 kilometers.[34] Actual shifting of the population and rehabilitation in the PPVs were done under the supervision of the security forces. With meticulous care, a well-laid-down plan of the changing and rehabilitation was carried out very quickly. With the help of the security forces the people carried their personal effects to the new sites where they were given free construction material including galvanised corrugated iron sheets, free medical aid and free ration till they could gather harvest in the new cultivations.

After about a month from the beginning of the shifting operation, the security forces handed over the villages to the civil administration. The organisation of the PPVs brought a new chapter in the administrative pattern of the district. Whereas in the earlier days, the villages were more or less left undisturbed in their routine life and administration touched only the fringe of the village life, the new set-up brought the villages in the closest feasible touch with the main function of the government, viz., security, welfare and development.

(j) Administrative Machinery

Every PPV was put under the charge of an Administrative Officer who soon came to be known all over, by the abbreviation of AO. Officers of the Junior Assam Civil Service (ACS), i.e., Sub-Deputy Collectors and Block Development Officers (BDOs) were appointed as AOs. A small administrative office was set up in each PPV with the AO in charge and under him were given an extension officer and a *gram sevak* (village level worker of the community development block) for agricultural development and other extension service, a medical unit under a pharmacist, a midwife and a health assistant, office staff of two clerks, and five porters for transport. The staff of the other government department, like, forest rangers, soil conservation officials and school teachers were also placed at the disposal of the AO. The AO also had under him the civil supplies officials which included a supply sub-inspector, a storekeeper, a watchman and also a few porters.

In order to give stature to this new set-up and in view of the urgent necessity of inculcating the national spirit and emotional integration, the administrative offices were allowed, as a very special case, to hoist the national flag which was normally allowed only at the level of the court and office of the Subdivisional Officer and above. The singing of the national anthem, *Jana Gana Mana,* by the public in general and the students in particular, was also made a very popular ceremony by the AOs. The Mizos, a people having a natural gift for music, would lustily sing the national anthem on any eve of importance like visit of a high official, village meetings, sports gathering, etc. In the administrative hierarchy, just above the Administrative Officer, had been kept the Area Administrative Officer (AAO). The AAOs were drawn from among the junior IAS officers who were cender district training or the ACS officers who were of the rank of Extra Assistant Commissioners or even Deputy Magistrates.

The AAO functioned as the AO of the headquarters village and also supervised the work of the AOs and the other officers under the PPVs within his jurisdiction. The main function of the AO was to represent the DC to the people of the PPV. He was accountable for the proper functioning of the units of the various government departments located at the PPV. He was constantly in touch with the security forces and saw to it that no unnecessary harassment was caused to the people in course of security operations. One of the very important functions of the AO was to ensure employment of the villagers under the growing activities of the government. The security force required a number of daily labours to work as porters to carry ration, ammunition and other equipment. Although, there was an innate antipathy of the Mizos to be employed as porters, here was an opportunity to get large-scale employment and because the people were in economic distress, the AOs were fruitfully able to utilise this opening for ad hoc employment.

(k) Relief Measures by the Government

The disturbances in the district badly affected agriculture to a great extent as the people could not go to the jungle for *jhum* cultivation because of uncertain security conditions and also due to the restrictions on movement necessitated by the inevitable security operations. The government, therefore, had to come forward in a big way to feed the people by providing them rice, wheat, and also other essential commodities e.g. salt and kerosene. These supplies were arranged on the scale of two kilograms of cereals per adult per week, given on cash payment if the recipient had the purchasing power, otherwise in the form of gratuitous relief. All these commodities had to come from the plains of Assam.

It was the duty of the AOs to receive the commodities at their centres, store and distribute them according to the government order from time to time. An AO was expected to take all the measures necessary to prevent starvation in his village. He had to report the food situation of the village on weekly basis to the Aizawl headquarters which coordinated the supply and distribution arrangements. The relief operation could only be a temporary measure and permanent solutions had to be searched for the food problem by developing agriculture on the proper lines. This could be done by making extensive *jhums* possible and also by permanent cultivation. The AO was needed to facilitate *jhumming* in consultation with the security forces, guide and assist the people to have permanent terrace cultivation and encourage undertaking of piggery, poultry and cottage industries in the form of subsidiary occupations.

(l) Public Participation in Administrative

In every PPV an administrative advisory committee was set up to associate the people in the village administration and to involve them in implementation of the development and the welfare schemes. These committees comprised of the village council president (VCP), local leaders of the two most prominent political parties of the district—the Mizo Union and the Congress, and the local church leaders. The committee met once a week under the chairmanship of the AO and discussed all matters regarding development and village administration, excepting matters concerning security.

The Committee operated in an advisory capacity and it acted informally. It was, however, a very useful link between the administration and the people as it acted as a channel of communication between the two. People's participation in village administration through this committee was a morale booster for the people during these years stress and tensions. The village councils were recognised were reorganised through the District Council to suit the changed situation. Bigger village councils were formed in the PPVs amalgamating the village councils of the shifted villages. Villages communities were also remodelled to take in the new arrivals within their folds. The Young Mizo Association (YMA), having branches in almost all the villages, immediately reorganised their branches in the PPVs, joining the separate units of erstwhile separate villages.

The gestures of the village councils, the YMA and other voluntary social and cultural organisations brought in a quite healthy atmosphere of inducing community life, cohesion and integration of people belonging to different subtribes, clans and groups.

(m) Security Post in PPVs

In all PPVs a security post each of the armed forces was set up. The post was under the command of an officer, designated as Post Commander. It was the duty of the Post Commander to safeguard the loyal villagers from the vengeance of the hostiles, to prevent infiltration of the hostiles into the villages and to stop all rebellious activities within the jurisdiction of operation of the post. Besides, the strict armed operations, the post also had to function as the police agency for maintenance of law and order, in places where was no regular police force.

(n) Grouping into Further Interiors

After the PPVs had been consolidated on the main road between Vairengte and Lunglei, steps were taken to group villages in the further interiors of the district. In 1969 the DC passed an order for grouping of 182 villages into same 40 group centres.[35] These group centres were organised on the three borders of the district—two of which were international borders, one in the west with East Pakistan where several hostiles had taken shelter in camps provided by the Pakistan Government and the other in the east, with Burma where in the Chin hills the hostiles were finding an easy way for journey to China. The border in the north-west was an internal one with Tripura which had ranges of low hills and deep jungles continuous with the terrain in the Mizo Hills region. This regrouping was necessary to prevent hostile activities of the MNF volunteers who took temporary shelters in these areas away from Mizo district where army operation was concentrated. Thus, although the villages in the borders could not be immediately connected by roads with the other administrative centres in the districts, it was considered expedient to have complete grouping of these villages to give protection to the people and deny the hostiles the opportunity of growing roots in these far-flung areas. There was still one more set of grouping of villages in the interiors where villages were shifted to the secondary roads. These roads were Lunglei—Lawngtlai road, Selling—Champhai road and Darngawn i.e., Khawzawl—Bungzung—Khawbung—North Vanlaiphai—Serchip road. In fact, shifting of the population in these areas started immediately after the PPVs were organised and were completed by October 15, 1969.

Around 50,000 people were shifted to forty grouped villages organised in the two sectors. The shifting of the population was conducted by the security officials in association with the civil liaison officers who explained the objectives of shifting and cushioned the rigidity of the army orders to prevent hardship to the people. The army authorities also appointed some commissioned officers as army administrative officers for these grouped villages. During the process of grouping and rehabilitation the villagers were given free food, medical arrangements and other amenities as were given to the villagers while PPVs were formed.

After the initial work of organisations of these grouped villages was over the centres were handed over to civil administration in month of December 1969. These forty grouped villages came to be known as new group centres (NGCs). At about the same time, a general movement ranging from small villages to bigger ones and from the interior villages to the road-side villages was taking place all over the district. One such movement occurred in the villages in between the PPV along the main road between Variengte and Lunglei and the new group centres established on the borders. In these areas 110 villages were groups into 26 villages.

As the grouping of the villages according to this category was not organised strictly on the lines of the PPVs and the NGCs and the movement to one or the other of the centres was left to the desire of the villagers, these centres were called Voluntary Group centres (VGCs). The process of grouping in the VGCs started in 1968 and continued till the end of 1969. Like the PPVs and the NGCs, the VGCs too were organised under the supervision of the security forces and at the initial stage of settlement the security forces provided all the necessary support to the people. The army authorities handed over the administration of these centres to the civil administration of these to the civil administration in the middle of the year 1970. Another area of the district where grouping was going on was the area bordering Manipur in the north and Burma in the east. There were same 63 villages in the area and a population of 40,000. The grouping was done in 17 centres organised in the area which came to be known in the official parlance as the extended loop area (ELA). The act of grouping was completed by the end of 1969 and the group centres were handed over by the army authorities to the DC in the middle of 1970. This grouping in the extended loop area facilitated operation both in the Mizo Hills and in Manipur, where in the Churachandpur subdivision bordering the Mizo Hills concentrated army operation against hostile Nagas and Kukis continuing.

A large portion of the district was reorganised by the grouping of the villages. There were, however, certain areas where grouping was not done. The urban areas of Aizawl and Lunglei having population of 40,000 and 10,000 respectively had not been grouped as there were adequate security arrangements in the towns. A stretch of 40 miles from Aizawl to Thenzawl also escaped grouping as the villages in these parts, twenty in all, could be adequately covered by security columns patrolling from the Aizawl town. There was a third area where grouping was not done—the central and the south-eastern region of the Pawi-Lakher region, the reason being the absence of hostile activities in these areas.

This grouping affected about 80 per cent of the rural population and about 65 per cent of the total population of the district. It was, therefore, a major event in the history of the district. Most of the people bemoaned their luck in leaving the ancestral hearth and home and the village the singers would sing pathetic songs of their loss of habitat where they were born and brought up. Although the Mizos were migratory in their habits till the initial years of this century and the British got them settled in permanent villages with difficulty, they took their fixed habitations with a lot of attachment and the current shifting hurt their feelings. Still, this antipathy continued irrespective of the facilities available in the group centres vis-a-vis the ungrouped villages. Each of the interior group centres had one air dropping zone; food and other civil supplies were carried and dropped by the Indian Air Force at the centres at government cost and most of the time distributed free of cost to the people. The villagers of the ungrouped villages had to trek a long distance to draw their rations from the group centres. Indeed, most of the people of the ungrouped villages were not being given ration by the government, as they were presumed to be continuing with their *jhums* undisturbed. Being the central points in the development efforts, the group centres also provided more scope for employment. Medical, educational and other welfare measures were focussed in the group centres.

The State expenditure on grouping came to about two crores of rupees. Only on free ration in the 19 PPVs from January 1967 to June 1968 an amount of Rs. 71 lakhs was spent. Also, the government gave one bundle of galvanised corrugated iron sheets to each family. Agricultural implements and seeds were liberally distributed. All these were given free of cost. In the other group centres rehabilitation amount of Rs. 400/- and above per family was given by the government. The government spent Rs. 64 lakhs on the rehabilitation grant. As the group centres had a sufficient government staff the development work could be initiated in these centres in spite of the general disturbed condition in the district.

The people in the ungrouped villages found the contrast in government's attention to them and to the grouped people which led them to demand the same facilities, although they at the same time wanted to continue in their small villages, without adopting the process of grouping. In view of the administrative convenience and widening scope of development activities, and of course, keeping the paramount need of security in view, it was then decided by the government in the later part of 1970 to group the villages in the remaining areas in the district.

By that time, some people led by the political parties had constantly been agitatating against grouping of villages. They took this opportunity of catching popular support by opposing the move for grouping and at the same time assuring the masses of the facilities which were available only to the grouped villages. When the Chief Minister of Assam, Mahendra Mohan Choudhury, visited Aizawl during the Christmas of 1970, the event was made use of by the people opposing grouping.

In December 1970 the government of Assam kept the order of grouping for the remaining area in abeyance. This may, the processes of grouping in Mizo district came to a halt leaving a small part of the district uncovered. Although popular opinion in general was against grouping and all the political parties wanted that the villages should be reestablished in the old sites, the grouped villages continue as such even after a popular government came in power following the election in Mizoram in 1972.

There are obvious advantages of populous villages situated on the lines of communication. Administration has therefore, preferred the people to keep on in the group centres, rather than moving back to scattered hamlets away from the main currents of developmental and administrative activities.

Thus, we can say that, in one way or the other, insurgency is almost a continuous phenomenon now in many of the developing countries. In the process of nation-building the developing countries are facing not only the gigantic task of accelerating the economic development but also the responsibility of closing in all the groups and sub-groups inside the nation. The internal wars have caused a serious threat to the integrity and hampered the growth of unified country in many developing countries. In all these countries internal warfare could not be brought under control by the usual show of force or even by the rude actions by the superior armed forces. The military might was not the decisive force in such struggles. In India also the insurgency in the north-east frontier of the country created a serious problem to the nation-building process and economic development in this section. As yet no study has been made to find out the deep roots and measure the reasons of insurgency in the Naga Hills and the Mizo Hills. Political aspirations or economic ambitions only highlighted the problems which rose probably from social and institutional controversies, and emotional imbalance between the different segments of the population. Deployment of the army in a condition of insurgency, sometimes acentuates the problem. The army functions not only against the rebels, but it also has to take many restrictive actions against the civilian population which generate resentment in the ordinary masses against the government and its forces. It is difficult for the army to act efficiently, respecting, at the same time, the civil and the political norms of the people. Thus, operation by the army may make the otherwise neutral civilian population an ally of the rebels. The counter-insurgency measures have, therefore, to be specifically oriented from the standpoint of civil administration. It is the indigenous civilian population of the area which has to meet the challenge, and hence they have to be prepared for the target—economically, socially and politically. Economic ways and means are provided by the development plans. Social development takes place by educational and contain welfare projects. The most effective tool is, however, the political settlement. In the Mizo Hills all these measures have been put into action. Reorganisation of the villages, launching of widespread economic development plans and social welfare projects, and introduction of a new political unit in the shape of the Union territory of Mizoram are all geared to meet the problems thrown up by the terrorism. The process at work in the mizo Hills is essentially a process towards nation-building. Hence, it requires the closest attention and the highest consideration at all levels of decision-making process and implementation.

References

1. *Lok Sabha Debates,* Vol. 1, 1966, Columns 3426-27.
2. The 'Declaration' was exhibited in the courts during trial of the arrested hostiles.
3. Statement by the Minister, *Lok Sabha Debates,* March 3, 1966, Columns 3685-86.
4. Calling Attention Motion on the Situation in the Mizo Hills, Statement of Minister of Home Affairs, March 25, 1966, *Lok Sabha Debates,* Vol. L II, Column 7894.
5. Calling Attention Motion on the Situation in the Mizo Hills, March 8, 1966, *Lok Sabha Debates,* Vol. L II, Columns 4256-57.
6. Statement of the Minister of Home Affairs on Calling Attention Motion on the situation in the Mizo Hills, *Lok Sabha Debates,* March 25, 1966, Vol. L II, Columns 7893-94.
7. The Chief Minister's statement on the concluding day of the Budget Session, *Proceedings of the Assam Legislative Assembly,* April 6, 1966, Secretariat of the Assam Legislative Assembly, Shillong.
8. Written Reply to an Unstarred Question given in the Lok Sabha on November 6, 1966, *Lok Sabha Debates,* Vol. LX.

9. Statement of Minister for Home Affairs on the situation in the Mizo Hills given in the Lok Sabha on November 8, 1966, *Lok Sabha Debates,* Vol. LX.
10. Written Answer to an unstarred question given in the Lok Sabha on November 9, 1966, *Lok Sabha Debates,* Vol. LX.
11. Reply to an Unstarred Question, April 18, 1966, *Lok Sabha Debates,* Vol. LIV.
12. B.K. Roy Burman, *Demographic and Socio-Economic Profiles of the Hill Areas of North East India,* Department of Publication, Delhi, 1970, p. 134.
13. *Proceedings of the Assam Legislative Assembly,* Shillong, March 5, 1966.
14. Debate on the Adjournment Motion on the situation in Mizo district March 3, 1966, *Lok Sabha Debates,* Vol. LI, Column 3728.
15. *Lok Sabha Debates,* March 3, 1966. Vol. LI, Column 3706.
16. Minister's reply to the Adjournment Motion, *Lok Sabha Debates,* March 3, 1966, Vol. LI.
17. *Lok Sabha Debates,* April 20, 1966, Vol. LIV, Columns 11834-35.
18. It is probably a reference to the alleged assurance given to the Mizos by A.G. McCall Superintendent, Lushai Hills district, in 1943 that if the Mizos actively supported for the British war effort against the Japanese who were close to the Lushai Hills, they would be given independence after the war.
19. *Lok Sabha Debates,* April 20, 1965, Vol. LIV.
20. "Mizo Uprising Follows Years of Naga Unrest", *The Assam Tribune,* Gauhati, March 21, 1966.
21. B.K. Roy Burman, *op. cit.* p. 134.
22. *The Assam Tribune,* Gauhati, January 14, 1970.
23. *The Hindustan Standard,* Calcutta, May 19, 1970.
24. *Amrita Bazar Patrika,* Calcutta, July 4, 1970.
25. *The Statesman,* Calcutta, August 17, 1970.
26. *The Assam Disturbed Areas, Act 1955,* Section 4.
27. Assam Government Notification No. PLB 69/66 dated 2nd March 1966.
28. *The Armed Forces (Assam and Manipur) Special Powers Act, 1958,* Section 4, Sub-Section (c).
29. *The Assam Disturbed Areas Act, 1955,* Section 6.
30. *The Armed Forces (Assam and Manipur) Special Powers Act, 1958,* Sec. 6.
31. Government of Assam Notification No. PLB 70/67/5 dated 3rd May 1967.
32. Deputy Commissioner's Order No. GCD 6/66/4-5, dated Aizawl, the 26th May 1966.
33. Deputy Commissioner's Order No. ASLO/1/67/1 dated Aizawl, the 19th June 1967.
34. Orders No. CLD 1/1-67/1, dated Silchar, the 2nd January 1967, and No. CLD 1/1-67/1-80 dated Silchar, the 27th February 1967, passed by the Central Government Liaison Officer for Mizo district, under Rule 57 of the Defence of India Rules, 1962.
35. Order No. APGC/28/69/196, dated the 22nd September 1969, passed by the Deputy Commissioner under Section 13D of the Assam Maintenance of Public Order Act, 1953.

16

Administrative Set-up

Indian republic has a written constitution and a political system that has a written Constitution some of the norms of the system are set down in the document itself and the political structures are, to a large extent, shaped by the Constitution. Likewise, the Constitution of India has helped to the genesis and growth of many political structures. The District Councils in Mizoram may be cited as instances of such structures. Prior to the commencement of the Constitution, the Lushai Hills district was administered as an Excluded Area. As in the other Excluded Areas in the Lushai Hills also the administration was patriarchal and powers vested in the Deputy Commissioner. In all the hill districts of Assam, there were certain indigenous institutions on which the district administration was based. They were the chiefs and the headmen known as *syiems, lyngdohs* and *sardars* in the Khasi and Jaintia Hills, *nokmas* and *laskars* in the Garo Hills, and *lals* in the Lushai Hills.

There was no political organisation at the district level through which people's will could be expressed. After 1935 the Partially Excluded Areas of Jowai, the Garo Hills and a portion of the Mikir Hills were allowed to send elected members to the provincial legislature. The Lushai Hills, the Naga Hills and the North Carchar Hills continued as Excluded Areas without any representation in the provincial legislative body.

(A) Bordoloi Sub-committee of the Constituent Assembly

One Sub-committee of the Constituent Assembly, the Bordoloi Sub-Committee,[1] carefully studied the administrative set up in these areas, particularly in the perspective of conservation of the tribal way of life and at the same time making it feasible for the tribal people to participate fully in the political life and the administration of the Stat, alongwith the rest of the people of the State. The Sub-Committee felt that due to the strategic position of the tribal areas, the people living there should be free from any fear of exploitation or domination by the advanced sections of people from the plains and that they should have complete freedom in repsect of their own manners, customs, inheritances, social organisations, village administration, etc., and unless they could be guaranteed proper safeguard in maintaining their characteristic way of life their bonds of unity with the rest of the country would not be consolidated and strengthened.

It was appreciated that the tribal people were specifically sensitive about their land, forests, systems of justice, etc., and it would be necessary to help them preserve their way of life in those matters. It was accordingly recommended that their legitimate desires regarding the management of their own affairs in these and allied matters should be fulfilled to the extent it was necessary without affecting the unity of the State and uniformity in broad policy making. The Sub-Committee recommended a set-up for the administration of the hill areas, based on the concept of regional autonomy in all matters influencing their customs, laws of inheritance, administration of justice, land, forest, etc.[2] This pattern of administration took shape in the outline of the Sixth Schedule of the Constitution.

The view behind the Sixth Schedule was to provide the tribal people with a simple and inexpensive administrative set-up of their own which would safeguard their tribal customs and ways of life and get them management of characteristically tribal affairs. These areas were to continue as parts of Assam and the Sixth Schedule was not to affect the unity and integrity of the State. The proposed autonomy was merely in respect of the peculiar tribal customs and it was not to disturb the unity of administration. The State and the Union Government would continue to have the responsibility to obtain to them the benefits of progressive and liberal administration by promoting with special care their educational and economic interest and protecting them from social injustice and all kinds of exploitation as envisaged in the Directive Principles of State Policy.

(b) Sixth Schedule of the Constitution

As per the Sixth Schedule of the Constitution, the following six autonomous districts were created in Assam: United Khasi and Jaintia Hills, Garo Hills, Lushai Hills, Naga Hills, North Cachar and Mikir Hills. There was planned to be a District Council for each autonomous district consisting of not more than twenty four members, of whom not less than three-fourths should be elected on the basis of adult suffrage. Had there been different scheduled tribes in an autonomous district, the Governor could divide the areas inhabited by them into autonomous regions. Only one autonomous region, *viz.,* Pawi-Lakher Region, was generated. The administration of an autonomous district/region vested in the District/Regional Council.

According to the Constitution the Council has law-making powers with respect to :

(a) the allotment, occupation or use, or setting apart, of land other than any land which is a reserved forest, for the purpose of agriculture or grazing or for residential or other non-agricultural purpose or for any other purposes likely to promote the interests of the inhabitants of any village or town, subject to the power of compulsory acquisition of any land for public purposes by the Government of Assam;

(b) the management of any forest not being reserved forest;

(c) the use for any canal or water-course for the purpose of agriculture;

(d) the regulation of the practice of *jhum* or other forms of shifting cultivation;
(e) the establishment of village or town committees or councils and their powers;
(f) any other matter relating to village or town administration, including village or town police and public health and sanitation;
(g) the appointment or succession of chiefs or headmen;
(h) the inheritance of property;
(i) marriage; and
(j) social customs.

The District/Regional Council enjoys the power of constitution of village councils or courts, appointment of members and presiding officers of village councils and courts and appointment of officers essential for administration of laws made under Paragraph 3 of the Sixth Schedule. The District/Regional Council or courts constituted by it exercise power of court of appeal. The Council may make rules regulating procedure to be observed by different courts and enforcement of the decisions of such courts. The District/Regional Council has been given the power to (a) assess and collect land revenue, (b) levy and collect taxes on lands and buildings, and toll on persons resident in the district, and (c) levy and collect these taxes: (1) taxes on profession, trades, callings, and employments, (2) taxes on animals, vehicles and boats, (3) taxes on the entry of goods into a market for sale therein, and tolls on passengers and things carried in ferries, and (4) taxes for the maintenance of schools, dispensaries or roads. The District/Regional Council may also make rules regulating (a) the formation of subordinate local Councils or Boards and their procedure and the conduct of their business, and (b) generally all matters concerning to the administration of the district or region.

These general provisions should however, be taken to mean the rule making powers of the Council with regard to the functions assigned to the Council through the Sixth Schedule. Hence these powers cannot be invoked for making rules with regard to functions not falling within the jurisdiction of the said Council. The jurisdiction and the functions mentioned above are those of the Regional Council over the areas in the Region and of the District Council over the area in the whole district even excluding the Region. There are certain other functions which have been given only to the District Council and hence the District Council's jurisdiction concerning these functions is the whole district.

Within this exclusive jurisdiction the District Council has the authority of establishment, construction and management of (a) primary schools, (b) dispensaries, (c) markets, (d) cattle pounds, (e) ferries, (f) fisheries, (g) roads, and (h) waterways and the like in the district. The District has also been given the powers to prescribe the language and the manner in which primary education was to be imparted in the primary schools in the district. The District Council enjoys authority to regulate and control money lending and trading within the district by persons other than those belonging to the scheduled tribes resident in the district. It has the power to prescribe for licence, maximum rate of interest and books of accounts for the business of money lending. It can also prescribe that no person who is not a member of a scheduled tribe member in the district shall carry on wholesale or retail business in any commodity excepting under a licence released by the District Council. After the commencement of the Constitution the first general election in the country was conducted in February 1952. In the Lushai Hills this was the first ever election on the basis of adult franchise.

Alongwith the election to the House of the People and the Legislative Assembly of Assam, election took place to the autonomous District Council of the Lushai Hills. The District Council was inaugurated on April 25, 1952. The Pawi-Lakher Regional Council was set-up on April 23, 1953. Jawaharlal Nehru, Prime Minister of India, visited the north-eastern frontier areas in October 1952. During his visit representations were made for special financial sanctions to the District Councils. The District Councils requested the Prime Minister for additional funds which would enable them to take up all the functions as envisaged through the Constitution. In response to this request, immediately an ad-hoc grant of Rs. 10 lakhs was given from the Central Government. This amount was equally distributed among the four District Councils and also the Lushai Hills got Rs. 2.25 lakhs.

(c) Barve Report on District Councils

In accordance of the Prime Minister's visit it was decided that an official study of the financial and administrative requirements of the District Councils should be made. Accordingly, S.C. Barve, Joint Secretary in the Finance Ministry, went to the autonomous districts in May 1953. In his report Barve brought out the characteristic features of the District Councils as compared to local bodies like the District Boards at the level of the local self-government. The District Councils were much more widely conceived than District Boards and they were endowed with legislative powers, had allotted sources of taxation, were conferred powers to set up and administer a system of justice and establish and maintain beneficient as well as general administrative services in education, public health, medical relief and administrative of land as much as forests, etc. These are powers and functions not of local authorities, but something approaching the jurisdictional principalities. Thus, there was possibility of conflict of functions between the District Councils and the State Government. In his report, Barve observes:[3]

> "It is difficult to foresee at present exactly what kind of administrative set-up by the State Government would remain in the Autonomous Districts when the District Councils have fledged out their organisation fully to the limit of their powers and duties. Thus, if the Deputy Commissioner has no responsibility for administration of land and forests or the raising of land revenue and other taxes and if he has also no duties relating to the administration of criminal and civil justice and is not to function as a court of appeal over subordinate courts of justice as at present, it is difficult to visualise how he would have enough to do and whether District Officers of the usual seniority of a Deputy Commissioner would be justified in these districts."

During the initial period the Government of Assam continued to run such administration and was also engaged in expanding the administrative services. This had to go on as the District Councils were not able to take up their functions completely because of financial and administrative constraints. Thus the State Government took up plans for the expansion of primary as well as secondary education, for the setting up of dispensaries, and for the development of communication, etc., in these districts. It maintained an establishment for administration of forests and a skeleton staff for engineering and also for agricultural development. All these activities fall in the sphere of competence of the District Council, but the District Councils were not in a position to take over these responsibilities rightaway.

It was, however, necessary to prepare the Councils to take over "all these administrative duties and the related machinery". In course of time most of these responsibilities were taken over by the District Councils but they always continued to suffer from the handicap of inadequacy of funds. Lack of trained personnel and technical people also stood in the way of adequate functioning of technical services for forest development, road building, municipal services and the like. Commenting on the their existing set up of administration in the autonomous districts, Barve observed that there was a need for contact between the State Government and the District Councils at a level higher than the Deputy Commissioner of the District.

The District Councils were vested with considerable powers and duties which had so far been the domain of the Deputy Commissioner. Obviously, the "District Council quarters viewed the Deputy Commissioner's Office and particularly its subordinate functionaries" with "jealousy and suspicion". The Tribal Areas Department in the Secretariat was far quite distant and impersonal and its relations could only be formal. It could not be in touch with the day to day problems, movements of thought and opinion in the various District Councils. Thus, there was "scope for generation of avoidable disharmony and misunderstanding".

The District Councils required formal approval of the State Government on many subjects. It was better to avoid confrontation over these matters and guide and counsel the District Councils on such matters which could be done if there was a Divisional Commissioner to keep intact liaisoning between the State Government and the District Council.

About the basic issue of subventions, Barve recognised the need for financial assistance to the District Councils and he recommended that the Government of Assam itself should make such a grant for administrative costs if there was justification for it and for the performance of the District Council was "otherwise satisfactory".

In the year 1955, in a letter to the Home Minister of India, Dr. Rosiama, Chairman, Mizo District Council, pointed out the urgent need for financial assistance from the government. He said that the economic state of the district, perhaps the worst in the whole of India, stood in the way of increasing the rate of any taxes.

The Government of Assam had also been compelled by this economic situation to exempt the district from Sales Tax Act. The District Council could not afford to impose any additional taxes over and above the taxes already introduced. If the District Council was to carry on to function in a proper shape and manner required under the Sixth Schedule adequate grant-in-aid must be given. Dr. Rosiama pointed out that because of financial difficulties the District Council could not obtain charge of forests, primary schools, dispensaries, roads and waterways as prescribed by the Sixth Schedule. As a result of the partition of the nation, the Lushai Hills lost markets of Rangamati and Chittagong to which their forest produce could be taken easily by riverine routes. This resulted in a fall in the revenue. The average annual revenue collection by the Deputy Commissioner in 1947-48 and 1948-49, the pre-Council years, was Rs. 2,65,473/- whereas the total revenue collected by the District Council in 1954-55 was exactly Rs. 2,41,753.

(d) States Reorganisation Commission of 1995

During this time there was a demand among some sections of the tribal people for creation of a Hill State comprising the autonomous districts of Assam. In 1955 the States Reorganisation Commission examined this demand. It did not get any justification for the demand and recommended maintenance of the *status quo,* with closer liaison between the Assam Government and the District Councils.[4] The Commission also realised the necessity of economic development of the hill districts and suggested the appointment of a Commissioner for better liaison and also for overseeing economic development. In this connection, the Commission observed:

> "It is clear to us that a great deal of misunderstanding, is now due to lack of adequate contact between the Assam Government and the District Councils as regards both ordinary administration and development work. We are surprised to note that no use was being made at present of the district officers by the District Councils and that no provision had been made in the Sixth Schedule for the maintenance of any contact between them. An important step in the direction of providing better liaison, in our opinion, will be the appointment of a Commissioner to be in charge of the administration and development of all Hill Districts. We envisage that the Commissioner would act as the Governor's agent for the various purpose laid down in the Sixth Schedule and that he, with the assistance of the district officers, would help the District Councils in their various day-to-day problem so as to remove difficulties speedily. He may be assisted by a development board consisting among others of representatives of the different District Councils. This should help to focus attention on the economic need of this area and promote rapid development."

Based on this recommendation, the State Government appointed a Commissioner for Hill Areas who was also made ex-officio Secretary of the Tribal Areas Department. The headquarters of the Commissioner being situated at

Shillong, the problem of communication, however, continued for the councils in Mizo District. Shillong was two days' journey from Aizawal and four days' away from Saiha, the headquarters of the Mizo District Council and the Pawi-Lakher Regional Council respectively. Hence the Deputy Commissioner continued to be the principal figure of the Assam Government regarding its contact with the councils.

(e) Vaghaiwalla Committee for District Councils

At the State level there used to be an Advisory Council for Autonomous Districts consisting of the representatives of the District Councils and the local MLAs and MPs. The Minister for Tribal Areas Department was the Chairman of this Council. On the suggestion of this Council the Government of Assam appointed a Committee on June 11, 1959, under the chairmanship of R.B. Vaghaiwalla, Commissioner of the Hills Division. Main objective of the Committee was to examine the financial condition and the administrative machinery of the District Councils and also of the Pawi-Lakher Regional Council. The Committee prepared an exhaustive list of the sources of revenue of a District Council as provided under the Sixth Schedule of the Constitution. The direct means of revenue of District Councils are:[5]

Land revenue, taxes on land and buildings, and employment, taxes on sale and purchase of animals, taxes on vehicles, taxes on the entry of goods into a market for sale therein, tolls on passengers and goods carried on ferries, taxes for the maintenance of schools, taxes for the running of dispensaries, taxes for the maintenance of roads, and royalties on timber. Indirectly the Council can augment the resource position by levying the following fees: fees for giving of permission for transfer, lease, etc., of land, fees for distribution of *jhum* lands, fees or rents for the use of any canal or water course for the purpose of agriculture, fees for administration of the laws related to inheritance of property, fees for administration of the marriage laws, fees in lieu of voluntary labour in connection with the administration of certain social customs, fees or fines in relation with the administration of justice, and fees in connection with administration of the regulations for the control of money lending and trading by non-tribals in the region. This Committee particularly studied as to what extent the different District Councils exploited these various sources.

In case of the Mizo District Council it was observed that although it had jurisdiction over an area of around 6,919 square miles, only about 70 square miles had been brought under assessment of land revenue. Of the sources of revenue mentioned earlier, the Council had tapped these ones: 'land revenue, house tax, taxes on profession, trades and calling, taxes on animals, taxes on vehicles and boats, tolls on ferries, fees on land transfer, royalties on unclassed State forests, fees on establishment of markets, and rent on fisheries.'

Between 1953-54 to 1958-59 the Council's estimates of revenue and demand were about Rs. 16 lakhs and the collection was about Rs. 11.50 lakhs. On the other hand, the total expenditure of the Council during this time, was Rs. 22.72 lakhs of which on establishment alone the expenditure came to Rs. 16.22 lakhs.

The deficit in the administrative expenditure was usually met by diverting funds got as grants for development from the State Government. On the administrative side the Council was elaborately organised with three regular departments—being executive, legislative and judicial. The Council had three Executive Members and a Chief Executive Member. It also had a Chairman and a Deputy Chairman who conducted the meetings of the Council. The general establishment of the Council consisted of a secretary to the executive committee, five officers and 87 other members of the staff in the revenue department, some 89 lower primary school teachers in the education department, 23 members of the subordinate staff in the public health department and 10 persons for the civil works.

The legislative wing also had a secretary and 11 other employees. Administration of justice engaged 7 judicial officers and 22 subordinate staff. The forest department had a staff of 33 in total. The Committee felt that the administrative machinery could be streamlined to effect economy. The Council could easily do away with the present strength of its happens by about one third. It observed:

> "The Council should immediately do away with the bench system of its judiciary which has little work to day. The present system of complete separation of the judiciary from the executive is rather too expensive for the Council when judicial officers have not a day's work to occupy their time. The District Council should, therefore, reduce its bench system to a one man Court, and the judicial officers may be made to do executive work as well."

The district did not possess known mineral resources. One viable source was revenue on wet cultivations which was not tapped. The Committee felt that the old system of collection of six tins of paddy from each household by chiefs for *jhumming* could be conveniently restored. The new system introduced by the Councils of collection of only three tins and allowing the village councils to appropriate the whole collection was not satisfactory. The Council's income from tax on professions, trades and callings was only Rs. 4,188/- in 1956-59. With increase in employment, trade and contracts, this collection should have been much more. Market should also be a good source. Apart from Aizawl and Lunglei no other place in the district had markets. The Council should establish markets at a distance of 10/15 miles. Royalty on timber and taxes on vehicles should yield substantial revenue. The Committee also studied the financial status of the Pawi-Lakher Regional Council.

Whereas the Regional Council covered an area of 1,230 square miles, the area under assessment was even below two square miles. The Council too had utilised only five sources of revenue, viz., land revenue, house tax, shop tax, grazing tax and royalty on timber. In 1958-59 total revenue collected was Rs. 23,761/- and the complete expenditure was Rs. 48,181/- of which establishment alone accounted for Rs. 44,703/-. The Council consisted of a Chairman, a Chief Executive Member and an Executive Member. In the Secretariat of the Council there were three departments, *viz.,* executive, judicial and legislative. The staff in the executive department comprised of a secretary, two other officers and 76 other members.

The judicial department had a judicial officer and a staff of 7. The legislative department had a separate secretary who had a pair of assistants to help him. The Council received Rs. 1.06 lakhs from the State Government as grants-in-aid for administrative reasons, from 1953-54 to 1959-60. For improvement of markets, water supply, local development works, rural communication, social welfare works, primary schools, housing etc., during six years time from 1954 to 1960 the Government of Assam gave loans and grants to the Council amounting to Rs. 3,86,018/-. But the amount was not properly spent.

The grants-in-aid for development activities had not been always fully utilised for the purpose for which they had been given. The Council had to meet the pay and allowances of the staff out of these development grants that the Council tried to reimburse later whenever specific grants-in-aid or loans were received from the State Government towards the expense of the administrative staff. The committee acknowledged the special difficulties faced by the Council when it observed:

> "The Committee is painfully aware that the resources of this Council are extremely slender with no prospects of improvement in the near future. There are very few educated people also to man the Council or the office. The Secretary who appears to be trying his best was an Assistant from the SDO's office. The Secretary seems to be quite alive to his duty, but the Committee feels that this post should be filled by an experienced and qualified officer who can reasonably be expected to be in a position to help and guide it. But it is doubtful if such a person will have the missionary spirit to serve in this remote region like the Lorrains of Serkwar who have served for three generations in this outlying region where people are friendly but the most rudimentary facilities and amenities for educated persons are non-existent."

This Committee was contented that the Council, in spite of so many handicaps, tried to implement the provisions of the Sixth Schedule and hence it recommended that all possible help should be given to this Council for many years. The study of the Committee revealed that in general the District Councils had been spending almost their entire revenue receipts for general administration. In certain cases even the grants received from the State government for development purposes had been spent on general administration.

Hence, the Committee proposed that the State Government should give adequate financial assistance to the District Councils to meet their administrative costs, till they were able to augment their own resources specially in light of the fact that in most of these districts the District Council staff was of immense help to the general administration. On the imbalance between the general administration and the revenue administration, this Committee noted that the defects of the administrative machinery were seen in the "hypertrophy of the office clerical staff and the atrophy of the revenue staff."

This was borne out with the fact of the extent of the arrears in revenue which had been allowed to remain unrealised over a number of years. On the general working of the democratic institutions established for the first time in the erstwhile Excluded and Partially Excluded Areas of Assam, the Committee said: "Though the tribal people are endowed with democratic traditions most of the elected representatives who man the Councils are, however, not experienced in the art of public administration through democratic machinery. It is not, therefore, surprising that Councils should meet, in the course of their work, with many difficulties, some of which might have arisen because of the inexperience of the members and the dearth of experienced officers, to run their administration."

The committee recommended that the government should lend to the Councils the services of qualified and experienced officers. The Committee was convinced with the special nature of the difficulties in the Mizo Hills and recommended that the State Government should give annually Rs. 2.50 lakhs to the Mizo District Council and Rs. 0.50 lakh for the Pawi-Lakher Regional Council as grants-in-aid for normal administration and Rs. 1 lakh to the District Council and Rs. 0.25 lakh to the Regional Council towards the construction of inter-village paths for the purpose of maintenance of rural communication. The Government of Assam accepted the recommendations of the Committee and advised the Councils to take right action as suggested by the Committee.

This was the first comprehensive study of the administrative set-up and the financial position of the Councils. The Committee rightly stressed on the fact that the Councils did not have enough financial resources to sustain the full-fledged administrative structure they erected. This imbalance hampered the realisation of the major purpose of these autonomous bodies, i.e., the fulfilment of the hillmen's aspiration of self-administration and at the same time bringing them within the fold of the national life.

All the these District Councils, soon after they were set up, built up a large administrative machinery to giver these concrete shape. But their financial resources did not match the spreading machinery. It was also extremely difficult to tap effectively fully the different sources of revenue set apart for them by the Constitution. New taxation is a difficult and unpopular step and it is specifically so in the economically backward tribal areas. On the other hand the awareness of development in the hill people a new hope and expectation and they expected the District Councils to deliver to them the benefits of economic development.

(f) Monetary Aid to District Councils

Members of the Constitution could envisage the special financial requirements of the hill districts of Assam and hence provided for financial assistance to the Government of Assam for expenditure in the hill districts. As per Article 275 (1) of the Constitution the State Government of Assam received grants-in-aid from the Central Government equivalent to (a) the average excess of expenditure over the revenue during the two years immediately preceding the commencement of the Constitution in respect of the autonomous district of Assam;

and (b) the costs of development scheme taken up by the State Government with the approval of the Centre, for the purpose of raising the level of administration of these areas to that of the administration of the rest of the areas of the State.'

Alongwith these funds, the Government of Assam would also get shares of funds available under the same same Article to all the States for development schemes for promotion of welfare of the Scheduled Tribes i.e., S.Ts., For the Mizo Hills the grant-in-aid was based on the following figures:

	1947-48	*1948-49*
(1) Total receipts	Rs. 2,67,621	Rs. 2,63,326
(2) Total expenditures	Rs. 10,20,679	Rs. 15,96,730

Thus, during the two years immediately preceding the commencement of the Constitution, the excess of the expenditure over revenue of the district in respect of administration were Rs. 7,53,058/- and Rs. 13,33,404/- respectively, reaching the average of Rs. 10,43,231/-. The Government of Assam was entitled to receive this amount annually from the Centre for meeting the administrative expenditure incurred in Mizo District. The State Government was also receiving grants-in-aid expansion and development of administration as envisaged in Article 275 (1) (b). But there was an ever-growing gulf between the revenue collection and the administrative costs in the hill districts. In the Mizo Hills in 1952-53 and 1953-54 the per year normal revenue was Rs. 1.11 lakh and the expense amount was Rs. 28.37 lakhs. There was no provision for direct financial assistance by the Centre to the District Councils. The Councils were to approach the State Government for financial assistance to meet their budget deficits. Particularly the Mizo District Council was in a bad financial shape and had to approach the State Government frequently for financial aid.

The State Government, on the other hand, had to look after four other Councils and also they had to guard against competition for grant and subsequent dependence mentality. For functioning of the normal administration in the hill districts, the State Government itself was short of funds. As pointed out by the State Government to Barve, for the years 1952-53 and 1953-54 the total annual normal revenue for the five autonomous districts was Rs. 11.58 lakhs whereas the total normal expenditure annually was 127.02 lakhs making an annual deficit of Rs. 115.44 lakhs for functioning of the administration of the five hill districts.

About the raising of resources, all the commissions and committees which enquired into the administration of these areas were of the same opinion that they must raise more funds from the sources at their disposal than what they were doing in the past. The latest comment was by the Commission on the Hill Areas of Assam (1965-66) headed by H. V. Pataskar. It said: "The district councils' own efforts to raise funds from the resources available to them have been on the whole unimpressive."[6] It is accepted, for example, that because of the peculiar physical features of these districts, not much part could be brought under direct assessment of land revenue, but the District Councils had not done all that was possible in this regard. In the Mizo Hills only 0.19 per cent of the full areas were brought under assessment; the respective figures for the other hill districts were the North Cachar Hills 0.44, the United Khasi and Jaintia Hills 0.76, the Garo Hills 4.85 and lastly the Mikir Hills 4.86.

Similarly, there could be greater income from the markets. The Mizo District Council could have derived substantial income from Aizawl and Lunglei markets. Mere 0.63 per cent of the total revenue of the Mizo Hills was from markets, as against 25.94 per cent in the North Cachar Hills and 12.34 per cent in the Garo Hills. The resultant dearth of finances badly affected the development works. One of the major contributing factors towards the stagnation in the economy of the Mizo Hills was the lack of any main development activity by the Mizo District Council. The District Council wanted that the State Government should provide sufficient fund to enable it to take up suitable development schemes. The state Government of Assam, on the other hand, expected the District Council to meet the finances for development, at least, partly from their own resources.

Almost the entire resources of the Mizo District Council were spent on establishment and administration. In this regard, compared to the other District Councils in Assam, the position of the Mizo District Council was not at all satisfactory. The grants-in-aid were more than double the revenue receipts of the District Council.

(g) Laws

The District Councils had sufficient law making powers under the Constitution. In the matter of legislation the Mizo District Council went far ahead of the other District Councils. It passed a number of laws on different subjects. It was the first Council to pass laws on management forests. Only the Mizo and the Garo Hills District Councils passed laws on social customs. The Mizo District Council, for that matter also the Pawi-Lakher Regional Council, made enactments on land and revenue administration, forests, social customs, house sites, inheritance of property and establishment of village councils.

Different amenities to these Acts and Regulations were made by the Councils. For example, six amendments were made to the Mizo District Forest Act which was passed in 1955. The number of amendments was rather large. But, probably, this was necessary in the fast changing tribal society. The Councils wanted to codify the changes necessitated by the quickly changing circumstances. Old customs and rituals were losing the sanctity. With the abolition of chieftainship, it was necessary to set up a new system of authority.

Hence it appears that the Councils did well in bringing forth laws covering the major social, economic and political issues. It was, of course, inescapable that there would be some defects in drafting the legislations, as the Councils did not have any skilled draftsman for this purpose. However, the fact that the legislations of the Councils did not evoke any serious controversy or caused any major conflicts establishes that the District and the Regional Councils in Mizo District performed their legislative functions satisfactorily. In administration, the Councils have jurisdiction over all the matters in which they have the law enacting powers as provided in Paragraph 3 of the Sixth Schedule of the Constitution. In addition, paragraph 6 of the Sixth Schedule authorises the District Council to administer primary education and maintain dispensaries, markets, etc.

In Paragraph 4 of the Sixth Schedule administration of justice in respect of suits and cases between the parties all of whom belong to the scheduled tribes vest in the District/Regional Council.[8]

(h) Overall Performance of District Councils

About the overall performance of the District Councils, the State Reorganisation Commission discussed the general opinion that the scheme of the Sixth Schedule was not working satisfactorily. The Commission faced two diametrically opposite views on rectification. One section of opinion representing the tribal interests desired greater measure of autonomy. This section complains of absence of sympathy from the administration, inadequacy of financial resources, interference from above, neglect of tribal areas by the Government, imposition of the Assamese language and culture and the starting of tribal lands to the settlers from the plains."[8]

The contrary view was that the administration of these Councils had tended to be bureaucratic, that the powers delegated to the said bodies regarding primary education had been used only to benefit certain classes and that the Councils had adopted an unnecessary expensive judicial system which was not also suited to the special necessities of the tribal people. The Commission did not examine the merits of the opposite views. But it observed that no proposal for the amendment of the Sixth Schedule that would have the effect of encouraging disruptive tendencies should be entertained. It recommended that the question of the working of the Sixth Schedule should be examined widely by a body specially constituted for this purpose as envisaged under Paragraph 14 of the Sixth Schedule which empowered the Governor to appoint such a body.

The Commission realised that this body should consist of persons of adequate standing from outside the State and these people should be chosen from among those who had sympathy with the tribal people and understood their difficulties. The commission felt that the question should be examined with regard to the promotion of the best interests of these people and the need for checking disruptive tendencies and ensuring good administration.

This position did not change in the next ten years. In their report the Pataskar Commission observed in 1966 that "the evidence placed" before them "was severely critical of the performance of the District and Regional Councils."[9] The major points of criticism were as follows:

(i) The Councils failed to accomplish any substantial welfare and development work for the tribal people.

Again two contrary explanations were given to the Pataskar Commission which were substantially the same as were given to the States Reorganisation Commission ten years back. One was that the Councils did not have sufficient power and authority to take an effective part in the development programme and the other was that the Councils did not make proper use of their powers of legislation and taxation, and their administration tended to be top heavy.

(ii) The Councils suffered from inadequacy of financial resources and lack of sympathy from the State Government and administration.

(iii) The majority tribes controlling the Councils did not pay due regard to the needs and requirements of the other smaller tribes.

(iv) Non-tribals in the hill district complained of discrimination against them in matters of land, taxation, franchise, etc.

The Commission recognised the power of this criticism and observed:

"The performance of these Councils had generally not been satisfactory. We consider it particularly unfortunate that no enquiry into the administration of these bodies, for which a provision exists in the Sixth Schedule, was undertaken although complants about their unsatisfactory working have been there for a number of years. Had such an enquiry been undertaken and suitable steps taken to improve the administration, the Councils might have become more useful to the tribal people".

The Commission suggested the continuance of the District Councils with wider powers, to satisfy the demand of the hill people for a full measure of autonomy. They did not suggest any great change in the legislative sphere of the Councils in view of their suggestion to bring about a Hill Areas Committee of the Assam State Legislature which should look after the legislative needs of the hill areas. Certain minor changes were suggested, like the inclusion of 'fixation of ceilings on agricultural lands' within the legislative jurisdiction of the Councils.

It, however, recommended a wide expansion of the administrative and executive functions of a District Council by inclusion of the following: land and revenue administration, education upto higher secondary stage, roads and waterways, community development projects and development blocks, agriculture and minor irrigation, animal husbandry and veterinary, co-operatives, fisheries, small scale and rural industries, sericulture and weaving, water supply in villages, public health, rural manpower, and commercial business or other enterprises, including means of transport and industries authorised by the Governor of the State.

(i) Reorganisation of Hill Areas

The Central Government accepted the main recommendations of the Pataskar Commission and widened the jurisdiction of the District Council. For this purpose in 1969 a new provision was made in the Sixth Schedule stating that "The Governor may, with the consent of any District Council, entrust either conditionally or unconditionally to that Council or to its officers functions in relation to agriculture, animal husbandry, community projects, co-operative societies, social welfare, village planning or any other matter to which the executive power of the State extends."[10]

The matter of 'road transport' was also brought within the purview of the District Council. Under the plan of reorganisation of the hill areas, states of Meghalaya was formed with the three autonomous districts of Garo, Khasi and Jowai. The District Councils of two other districts, viz., Mikir Hills and North Cachar Hills were given the option to join Meghalaya or to remain with Assam. These two districts preferred to remain in Assam and the Government of Assam transferred to them the development functions alongwith essential budgetary provisions.

The State Government also lent them the services of two senior IAS officers for appointment as Chief Executive Officers and some Assam Civil Serivce Officers to be appointed as Executive Officers for adequate implementation of the development programme. In the scheme of reorganisation the Mizo Hills did not figure so far as joining Meghalaya was concerned. No even single provision was made for the Mizo District Council to decide whether they would join Meghalaya or not. It meant that the Mizo district was to continue in Assam, at least for the time being. This particular decision was partly due to the fact that the public opinion in the district was rather in favour of the creation of a separate Mizo State and mainly due to the faith that no political settlement was possible in the prevailing distressed condition in the district. The Mizo District Council, however, could have been given additional functions concerning development and deed, the District Council moved the Government of Assam for these additional powers. But as the future set-up of the district was under consideration of the Government of India, no change was made in the activities of the Mizo District Council.

(j) Dissolution of the Mizo District Council

Under the scheme of reorganisation of the north-eastern region prepared in 1971, in which Mizo district was to become the Union territory of Mizoram, it was envisaged that the Mizo District Council would stand dissolved and stop to exist from the date on which the Legislative Assembly of the Union territory of Mizoram would be continued. After an election in the territory, the Mizoram Legislative Assembly was formed on April 29, 1972 and on this date the Mizo District Council stood dissolved. The Administrator of the Union territory, Chief Commissioner of Mizoram, passed several orders transferring the assets and liabilities of the Council to the Government of Mizoram. The staff of the Council was taken over by the Government of Mizoram. Provisions were also kept for the continuance of the laws made by the District Council and in force imemdiately before the dissolution.

(k) Three Fresh District Councils

The position was quite different in the Pawi-lakher Region. The Central Government was sympathetic to the demands of the three tribes in the Region—

the Pawis, the Lakhers and the Chakmas—for protection of their own distinct tradition customs and culture. The Mizos could protect their own way of life by suitable legislations passed by the Mizoram Assembly and hence there was no necessity of carrying with the duplicate machinery of the District Council for the Mizos, but it was felt that the Pawis, the Lakhers and the Chakmas should have District Councils of their own for the distinctive functions mentioned in the Sixth Schedule of the Constitution.[11] After the Union territory of Mizoram was set up, the Administrator passed an order creating three autonomous regions, one each for the Pawis, the Lakhers and finally for the Chakmas, in place of the Pawi-Lakher region.

As it has been provided under Paragraph 205[12] of the Sixth Schedule that every autonomous region existing immediately before the date on which the Mizoram Assembly was constituted would become an autonomous district on the same date and the Regional Council would become the District Council of the corresponding new district, on April 29, 1972 the District Councils for the said three autonomous districts of Pawi, Lakher and Chakmas came into existence with headquarters at Lawngtlai, Saiha and Vaseitlang respectively.

The Acts, Regulations and Rules made by the Pawi-Lakher Region Council are to remain in force under all these new District Councils till amended or even replaced by the corresponding District Council. Regarding regular constitution of these three District Councils the Lieutenant Governor of Mizoram, passed orders specifying the numbers of members in each of these Councils.

The Pawi District Council is to have 14 members, of whom 12 are to be elected on basis of adult suffrage and 2 are to be nominated by the Administrator, the Lakher District Council is supposed to have a total of 10 members—9 elected and 1 nominated and the Chakma District Council, 9 members—8 elected and 1 nominated. Under the dual administrative set-up written in the Sixth Schedule on one side, the Deputy, Commissioner representing the State Government and on the other, the District Council elected by the people of the district, it was necessary factor that the applicability of laws made by the different legislative bodies should also be clearly defined.

It was laid down in the Sixth Schedule that no Act of the State Legislative assembly on any subject within the purview of the District Council would apply to the autonomous district. The District Council, could, however, direct its application, if necessary, with certain modifications. The other Acts of the State Legislature and all Acts of Parliament would apply to the autonomous district, unless the Governor issued a notification barring the application of this type of laws in the area.[13] These provisions continue to remain in force so far as the autonomous districts under Assam are concerned. But a change has been introduced in case of Meghalaya and Mizoram by giving an overriding character to the Acts passed by the State/Union territory Legislature. Thus, in Mizoram, if any provision of law made by a District Council for subject assigned to it under Paragraph 3, 8 or 10 of the Schedule is repugnant to any provision of law made by the Mizoram Assembly, the former will be void to the extent of the repugnancy.

This shift in the position was necessary because of the change in the legislative organisation in the territory. The Mizoram Assembly itself is an Assembly mainly of the tribal people, and it is the best judge of the necessity of the people resident in the territory. The District Councils of the minority tribes—the Pawis, the Lakhers and the Chakmas are to act more as local councils and administer the local matters as per their own customs so long as these do not clash with the laws made by the Mizoram Legislature. With respect to the Acts of Parliament the position continues to be same that all Acts of Parliament apply to the autonomous districts unless specifically banned; the only difference is that earlier the Governor had the power to debar and now only the President can pass this kind of an order. The evolution of the District Council has shown that it was well conceived and hence in spite of large scale reorganisation in the area, the basic structure of the autonomy generated by the Sixth Schedule of the Constitution continues as the administrative framework in the area.

Mainly two planks, first, the efficacy of the traditional customs in administration of a tribal society and secondly, the reliability of democratic institutions to streamline the currents of change in the tribal socities in transition, made the District Councils beneficial institutions both to the government and to the people. In spite of constant financial hardship from which the Mizo District Council suffered, it worked well in codifying the customary law and legislating on most of the 'subjects' within their authority. The District Council also did well in organising village councils all over the districts. The truth that one political party—the Mizo Union, remained in power in the District Council contributed to a great extent to the consistency and balance in the functioning of local administration. The Mizo District Council and Pawi-Lakher Regional Council both had to suspend their activities when the insurgency started in 1966. For the next two to three years their functions were confined largely to the big administrative centres. The District Council leaders were always under constant threat from the rebels for their co-operation with the government. Whatever might have been the losses or failures of the District Councils, these failures could not be called considerable in view of the limited scope and responses of the Councils. The Mizo District Council, it should be said, was loyal to the objectives set out in the Sixth Schedule for the national unity amidst the mainfold diversity of the people and now after the commencement of new Panchayati Raj system in persuance with the 73rd Amendment to the Constitution, there is hope for improvement in both administration as well as governance at local and grassroot level.

References

1. This Sub-Committee was set up under the Chairmanship of Gopinath Bordoloi, Premier of Assam. The members of the Sub-Committee were: Rup Nath Brahma, A.V. Thakkar and Aliba Imti. Khawtinkhuma and Saprawnga were co-opted as members for the Lushai Hills area. R.K.

Ramdhiyani was the secretary of the Sub-Committee.

2. *Report of the North-East Frontiers (Assam) Tribal and Excluded Areas Sub-Committee* (Bordoloi Sub-Committee), 1947, Manager of Publications, Delhi, 1950.
3. S.C. Barve, *Report on the Autonomous District Councils of Assam,* Government of Assam, Shillong, 1957, pp. 14-15.
4. *Report of the States Reorganisation Commission,* 1955, Ministry of Home Affairs, New Delhi, 1936, p. 184.
5. *Report of the Committee to Examine Financial Conditions of each District/Regional Council* (Vaghaiwalla Committee), Government of Assam, Shillong, 1960, pp. 2-3.
6. *Report of the Commission on the Hill Areas of Assam* (Pataskar Commission), Ministry of Home Affairs, New Delhi, 1966, p. 62.
7. *Supra,* Chapter 4, Administration of Justice.
8. *Report of the States Reorganisation Commission,* p. 188.
9. *Report of the Commission on the Hill Areas of Assam, op. cit.* p. 66.
10. *The Constitution of India,* Sixth Schedule, Paragraph 6, Sub-Paragraph (2). This is a new provision made by the Assam Reorganisation (Meghalaya) Act, 1969. It came into effect on April 2, 1970.
11. The demands of separate District Councils for these three tribes were placed by them in several memoranda submitted to the Government of India at the time of the formation of the Union territory of Mizoram.
12. *The Constitution of India,* Paragraph 20B. This provision, like that under Paragraph 20A, is a transitional provision for Mizoram inserted in the Sixth Schedule by the Government of Union Territories (Amendment) Act, 1971.
13. *The Constitution of India,* Paragraph 12.

17

New Plannings

Basic difference between a state and a society is that rules and regulations in a state are clear, well designed and more strictly implemented so that order can be maintained. For that matter, law and order have always been the main concern of a government. Any government worth the name would try its best to put down an insurgency. As we have noted in the earlier chapter it would also have to provide against a new outbreak in the future. That would mean an attempt to analyse the root causes of these disturbances. A proper understanding of the evolution and the troubles of the administration of Mizoram, therefore, necessitates a look at the condition—economic and otherwise prevalent in the state. The economic activities of the Mizos are mostly confined to *jhum* or shifting cultivation. Their wants were few till new demands came up by introduction of western style of living by the missionaries.

At the time of British occupation Shakespear found the Mizos self-sufficient in meeting whatever they considered essential for life. There were no shop-keepers, and, except the blacksmith, no craftsmen either. Each household was capable of subsisting on its own. The men built their houses themselves, had rice and vegetables grown in their own *jhums* and procured fresh meat by their skill in setting snares and hunting. Periodically they visited the *bazars* (markets), sometimes after a walk for several days to purchase some necessities like salt, brass cooking pots and iron to make *daos* and weapons.

It was through these *bazars* that the British frontier officers kept contact with the Lushais before their territory was annexed. The *bazars* provided good means of communication with the hill people, helped to maintain friendly relations with them and were very remunerative to the traders bartering salt, cloth and iron for rubber and other forest products. There was, however, no certainty about these *bazars* which would dwindle or flourish depending on the availability of indigenous forest produce and also on the relationship between the chiefs and the British and between the chiefs themselves. The Lushais leaned heavily on economic help from outside when there was a widespread famine in 1881. Many people migrated to Cachar during the famine, most of them returned to the hills by the commencement of the rainy season of 1882 and resumed their cultivation. This economic calamity brought the hill people in close contact with the British

Government and the plains people but it was only for a very temporary period. The isolation was resumed after the economy of the hills revived.

Even after a few years of British occupation, trade with the Lushais continued to be in the rudimentary stage. Their wants of the outside goods did not go beyond salt, coloured yarns, brass vessels and small quantities of iron. In 1895 the amount of trade done was however, sufficient to support nine shops in the Sairang *bazar*. There were three shops in Aizawl, but the Lushais were yet to start dealing with them.

The economic position of the Lushais started improving with the government expenditure in the hills. The government paid in cash for the *coolie* (porter) which had to be liberally employed for carriage of government stores and also for road and building constructions. The Administrative Report of 1902-03 says: "The people are contented and happy having more than enough for their wants, which are few. Fines when imposed are paid up readily and the people must be accumulating a certain amount of cash, for their cash expenses once they have paid their house-tax are almost nil". In 1904 the SDO, Lunglei, reported that the people in his subdivision were having a surplus of money, which they did not know how to spend and, therefore, their natural dislike to work was increasing. The Lushais being nomads did not accumulate goods as they moved from one place to another every four to five years.

Hence they really did not have much use for cash. Throughout the district, the state condition of the people was improving but in those parts which were far removed from any of the government posts, there was not much accumulation of surplus capital, the means being the government expenditure. Slowly, the demands of the people started increasing with the adoption of a new life style with premium on comfort and luxury. More and more items were added to the list of imports which in 1915 were: cotton and woolen yarn, salt, metals like brass utensils, chewing tobacco, *daos,* umbrellas, enamelled ware, plates, glass, cigarettes, condensed milk, iron pans, soap and beads. There was, however, no appreciable growth in the list of items for export. Exports mostly consisted of bee wax, cotton, chillies, and forest produce. By and large, the Lushais continued to have a very simple economic life without much dependence on outside support. The first world war had little effect on the economic life of the Lushais—their only dependence on the outside world had been for salt. Thus the major changes in the economic life in the country left the Lushai Hills unaffected.

(a) Static Economy

Financial condition in the Lushai Hills did not change much during the British rule. It was a static economy without much demand or supply. The people were placid and complacent in their limited means alongwith low level of consumption. The policy of the British administration towards the economic betterment of the people was negative in the sense that apart from keeping the Lushais protected from the feasible economic and cultural exploitation by their powerful neigbours, it did not give much positive lead. This gap was keenly felt by McCall,

Superintendent, who in the 1940s introduced some economic and welfare measures.

By this time the Lushais were sufficiently educated and adjusted to the life under one settled administration which provided enough leisure but not much scope to involve in activities which would come into conflict with law. On the other hand, the social and customary bonds were weakening. The old ethics had lost sanction but there was no fresh code of conduct accepted by all. Hence there was a vacuum in the life of a Lushai and he did not know how to fill it up.

The economic position of the people had never been satisfactory, but the masses had hardly been conscious of it earlier. Now they were gradually becoming frustrated comparing their own conditions with those existing in the rest of the country where at least the ground of economic development had been laid. Considering all these aspects McCall drew up a plan of allround economic development in which the lead was to be given by the administration. To raise the economic status McCall suggested the adoption of cottage industries and he took steps to start the first cottage industries in the region. For the welfare and economic well-being of the villages he organised in each village a village welfare committee. These committees functioned under the guidance of the District Red Cross Committee at Aizawl.

The objective was to improve public health and living conditions in the villages, with the technical guidance of the Civil Surgeon. To give moral and social base to the welfare attempts, McCall suggested adoption by everyone of a code of conduct, which included love for indigenous culture, keeping the demands reasonable in relation to own natural sources and industry, strengthening health, home, crops, industry and possession by modern scientific technique as would suit well with the traditional life and fruitful use of leisure time. McCall felt that there should be a well defined government policy towards the Lushais which had been absent so far. There should be a policy statement which, *inter alia,* should lay down the following principles and objectives.

(i) Medical, industrial, educational, agricultural and all development measures should be specifically designed and directed to ensure that the people would be able to absorb them as part and parcel of their own cultural system.

(ii) All departmental budgets should be submitted through the District Officer as coordinating centre of all efforts.

(iii) Educational curriculum should be so designed as to ensure that education reached the masses and would suit the genius of the people.

(iv) Adequate public health measure should be taken.

McCall's ideas, however, were not very useful. The village welfare committees could not do much mainly because of the lack of financial support. Policy formulation towards development administration remained holy wish during the British rule.

(b) Consequences of Partition

When the British left, the economy of the Lushai Hills was obviously no better than what they found when they had annexed the territory. In fact, in many aspects it was worse. The population had grown a rapid pace. Due to the spread of general education there were many educated youngmen who were not ready to follow agricultural pursuits.

By gradual denudation of the hills, the *jhums* were yielding less and less. Further, the partition of the country hit hard the economy of the Lushai Hills, when the Chittagong Hill Tracts and Chittagong district went to Pakistan, disrupting a quite vital link of the Lushai Hills with the outside markets. The Government of Assam appointed a Committee to enquire into the impact of partition on the border districts and to suggest remedies. In its report on the Mizo Hills submitted to the government in January 1951, the Committee gave the following picture of financial life in the South Mizo Hills, before and after the partition. Before partition the Lushais produced rice, cotton, *til,* oranges and chillies in large quantities in their *jhums* for the purpose of trade in the Chittagong Hills Tracts.

Forest produces like bamboo, timber and cane were also exported. The Lushais would get in exchange consumption articles like food items except rice and vegetables, clothing, kerosene, betel nut and also agricultural implements, utensils, medicines, and stationery articles.

Because of partition this inter-dependent economic set-up was artificially separated in the Mizo Hills area it adversely affected the whole of the southern hills. The entire economy of the south and west side of the district was shaken. The prices of the commodities which the Lushais obtained from the Chittagong side, like mustard oil, sugar, *gur* (molasses), salt, dry fish, coconut oil and kerosene, went up six to ten times whereas the prices of the commodities which they had for export—cotton, oil seeds and oranges fell appreciably. The deteriorated economic situation was also reflected in the family budget which in the border areas near Demagiri, showed, on the average, a deficit of Rs. 159.05 per year, the yearly consumption expenditure being Rs. 696.07 and the income Rs. 537.02.

The random sample survey conducted by the Directorate of Statistics revealed that 57.5 per cent of the families were indebted, the means of credit being the traders who charged exhorbitant rates of interest. The government took a number of steps to give relief to the affected people. A fleet of jeeps was run by the DC in order to transport sugar, mustard oil and kerosene from the neighbouring plains district of Cachar to Lunglei. The Government met the transport cost as a subsidy and the commodities were given through fair price shops. This was the beginning of economic relief measures undertaken by the government in the Mizo Hills which, in some shape or other, have been going on over since. The Committee suggested an intensive development programme for the district which included the following steps:

(i) intensive cultivation of non-perishable crops like clove, castor, black pepper, ground nut, seasum and mustard; (ii) cultivation of onion, chilly and cashew nuts at places below 1,000 feet; (iii) cultivation of oranges; (iv) cultivation of vanilla, walnut, pineapple, resin, figs of good quality and medicinal plants such as those grown in Kulu Valley; (v) terracing and contour bunding of the cultivable areas; (vi) intensification of cultivation. Other suggestions of the committee were—(a) settlement of the Chakmas in permanent villages; (b) subsidy for improving cultivation; (c) organisation of cooperative societies with provision for subsidy for making warehouses for the seasonal excess paddy; (d) setting up blacksmithy centres for supply of agricultural implements; (e) starting of paper pulp and juice extracting industries; and (f) organisation of subsidiary occupation in poultry and animal husbandry.

Suggestions of the Committee offered a comprehensive development programme for the district. The measures suggested were all feasible and attuned to the resources and the needs of the district. There were, however, problems with regard to finances and organisation at the ground level. The programme envisaged a huge outlay and a complete change in the economic behaviour. Organisation of a fresh pattern of agriculture and the setting up of industrial units, although of a small scale or cottage type, required a good number of trained personnel who would be prepared to serve in the malaria affected remote locality like Demagiri. These constraints stood in the way of immediate all round development but this nevertheless was the starting point of development administration through the Mizo Hills.

(c) Agriculture

As we have already said that the Mizos practise *jhum* or shifting cultivation. Each year they clear a patch of jungle and cultivate the land, moving on in the next year to another area in the jungle. Prior to the British occupation the Lushais in general were migratory with their habits, leaving one village site for another after a few years. This was a convenient habit as they moved on when all the areas near the village has been *jhummed.* At the initial stage of British occupation it was felt by the administrators that until the Lushais abandon their migratory habits little improvement could be hoped for.

It was, however in the interest of the heads to perpetuate the migratory habits as with permanent cultivation the tendency would have been for the existing large communities to split up, which would have diminished the authority of the heads over their people. The migratory habit had an adverse effect on the economic stability of the people. One of the early reports states:

> "Owing to the improvidence of the Lushai as a result of their migratory habits, and the impossibility of carrying about with them large stocks of grain there is never a surplus share of rice in any village, and the failure of a single harvest breaks it up, the inhabitants dispersing to the villages of chiefs more fortunately situated."

The state government was keen to introduce permanent cultivation primarily to facilitate law and order enforcement because it was difficult to contain migratory tribes to peaceful behaviour. Due to the terrain, it was, however, difficult to introduce permanent cultivation everywhere.

But some suitable areas were found where long stretches of flat lands were available. A lot of interest was created in agricultural experiments. Reclamation of valley lands was taken up. Experimental cultivation of many new crops was being undertaken. Potatoes were doing well. Little quantities of wheat were also successfully raised. Experiment in rubber cultivation was started. Terraced cultivation was introduced as this was the only scientific way of agriculture in the steep hills. The census data about the male and female agricultural labourersand household workers is given as follows:

Table 1
Agricultural and Farming Functions including Labourers and Other Workers (Statewise) : Census 2001

Total/ Rural/ Urban	*Persons/ Males/ Females*	*Cultivators Labourers*	*Agricultural Industry Workers*	*Household Workers*	*Other*
Total	Persons	253,167	27,494	6,572	182,364
	Males	128,836	13,010	3,164	119,152
	Females	124,331	14,484	3,408	63,212
Rural	Persons	200,316	10,086	2,166	44,920
	Males	101,594	4,793	1,093	31,631
	Females	98,722	5,293	1,073	13,289
Urban	Persons	52,851	17,408	4,406	137,444
	Males	27,242	8,217	2,071	87,521
	Females	25,609	9,191	2,335	49,923

As terracing was an excellent success in the Naga Hills, a party of Lushai chiefs was taken by the Superintendent to the Naga Hills to show them the benefits of terracing method. Most of these programmes were, however, only amateurish and were taken up in a half-hearted way. There was neither any financial support nor any technical support. In 1933-34 the agriculture staff in the district consisted of only a demonstrator who was in charge of the Dhobinala vegetable farm and an inspector for the entire district. The progress in modernisation of agriculture was far from satisfactory. An another census data relating to agricultural and farming functions including labourers and other workers is given on next page.

After experiments on a wide scale over a decade it was observed in the Administrative Report of 1933-34 that the progress of agricultural activities in the district was very slow mainly because of scarcity of water in the district and also due to the fact that with the exception of a few places there were no arable lands, no available parts for making water canal irrigation, nor were there suitable places for cattle grazing. The administration realised that as the people migrated in search of *jhum* lands, new crops which would serve as staple crops of permanent nature suitable in the locality and could be carried out without *jhumming,* should be tested.

Table 2
Agricutural and Farming Functions including Labourers and Other Workers (Districtwise) : Census 2001

District	*Cultivators*			*Agricultural labourers*			*Household industries*			*Other workers*		
	Persons	Males	Females	Persons	Males	Females	Persons	Males	Females	Persons	Males	Females
Mamit	19,663	10,365	9,298	1,816	875	941	287	181	106	13,603	8,226	5,377
Kolasib	18,921	10,248	8,673	3,029	1,261	1,768	367	247	120	10,071	6,821	3,250
Aizawl	56,845	28,747	28,098	7,805	3,697	4,108	3,125	1,580	1,545	104,336	65,341	38,995
Cham-phai	43,932	22,003	21,929	6,839	3,299	3,540	591	344	247	11,640	7,445	4,195
Serchhip	25,574	12,652	12,922	1,458	736	722	757	218	539	6,562	4,710	1,852
Lunglei	46,203	23,451	22,752	2,780	1,289	1,491	557	306	251	22,230	15,853	6,377
Lawn-gtlai	23,838	12,656	11,182	2,370	1,259	1,111	640	145	495	6,837	5,335	1,502
Saiha	18,185	8,707	9,478	1,397	594	803	248	143	105	7,091	5,428	1,663

It was hoped that fruit cultivation will not only encourage the people to be permanent, to dig and plough, to sow and plant and harvest, to feed and milk the cows and to rear all kinds of domestic storage, but it will also open the way for various related industries that are dependent on agriculture. The administration was thus alive to the problems in agriculture and general economic conditions in particular, in the Lushai Hills; it also had the likely solutions, but there was no concerted and wide-based move from the government to tackle the difficulties.

(d) Post-Independence Time and Developments

Following independence, agriculture was given the prime place of attention in all the development plans in the Mizo Hills. A glance at the staffing and the programmes of agriculture in 1957-58 will reveal the extent of the importance given to agriculture. At the district level there was a District Agriculture Officer at Aizawl. A post of Subdivisional Agricultural Officer at Lunglei was also created. There were three kinds of agricultural schemes in the district—normal schemes, development schemes under Article 275 of the Constitution and Grow More Food schemes. Under the normal schemes there kept one agricultural inspector and two demonstrators.

For the schemes under Article 275 there were four inspectors, two assistant inspectors and 17 demonstrators mostly posted in the deep interior villages. Tools and implements for agriculture were issued to primary schools on loans; demonstration-cum-experimental farms were started and subsidies were given to the cultivators for the purpose of growing cash crops like black pepper, cardamom, coffee and cotton, for extension of wet paddy cultivation and for starting model farms. For the Grow More Food programme some employees of the irrigation staff were posted in the district. Steps were taken to start minor irrigation projects and soil conservation measures. But the programmes suffered from many handicaps.

Owing to transport difficulties and exhorbitant freight charges many things had to remain in Aizawl godowns. Again many schemes were not suited to the special terrain of the Mizo Hills. Loan scheme could not be initiated as people did not have ownership right over land. In the development programme for the then Union territory of Mizoram the foremost priority has been given to agriculture.

Certain crops have done well in some areas and not in others, although the physical conditions including quality of soil are more or less the same all over. It is expected that with improvement of transport and input arrangements there will be balanced development all throughout the territory.

There has, however, been considerable progress including new areas in cultivation. The following figures will show that the acreage under different crops has almost doubled in the couple of decades.

During 1969 a team of agricultural experts of the Government of India visited the Mizo Hills and prepared a comprehensive programme of intensive agricultural development of the entire district. It was planned that throughout whole the district, terrace cultivation would be introduced, and modern farms started. The present agricultural programmes are based on the lines of development indicated by this team. The Union Government has also started State farms at two places, *viz.*, Lakichherra, and Hortoki. There is a good prospect if such farms are started at Palak lake area in the south and Demagiri in the west region.

Till then, it had proved difficult to introduce permanent and settled cultivation in Mizoram. As has been pointed out earlier, the British had tried to introduce terrace cultivation in the Mizo Hills from the very initial days of the administration. The attempt did not bring in any significant result. The present thinking is that because of difficult terrain *jhumming* cannot be given up in Mizoram. The research team on Tribal Development Programme for the Fourth Plan said:

> "The only way of improving agriculture in the area is to induce the villagers, by the offer of financial assistance and technical guidance, to take up the cultivation of lower slopes which may, if necessary, be allowed to be jhummed initially and later terraced. To enable them to assess the relative merits of terrace and jhum cultivation, a part of the area may be thrown open for their traditional jhum cultivation and the rest terraced. When they see for themselves that terrace cultivation gives better results, they will voluntarily give up jhum cultivation in favour of cultivation on terraced land."

Further, in the agricultural sector animal husbandry and poultry-keeping engaged the attention of the government from the very early period. In 1906 Cole, Superintendent, introduced poultry farming in the district. Besides, starting government poultry farms the Lushais were encouraged to start individual farms. In fact, the poultry which is abundant in the territory now is primarily the outcome of all these experiments, particularly, of cross-breeding. Pig-rearing wars also started quiet early and it has proved a great success in the territory.

(e) Industrial Development

Development of industry is a difficult act in Mizoram mainly because of the lack of transport facilities and the scarcity of raw materials. It was, however, felt that cottage and small industries could be developed to some extent. The thoughts of administration in this regard were expressed in the Annual Administrative Report of 1935-36 in the following manner:

> "As the villagers are familiar with the art of spinning and weaving their clothes, attention towards better development of this art is also being paid by encouragement of sheep breeding that will produce good wool and sericulture that will produce good silk for their clothes. Industries and economy are virtues of a civilised life. As the district, which is still raw and penniless, is awakening and feeling the need for money, it is hoped that these new indutries will become village industries suitable for local conditions."

The very first organised attempt to develop cottage industries in the Lushai Hills was made by McCall, Superintendent, in 1940s with very active and encouraging help from his wife. They started a unit in Aizawl. Villagers were inspired to take up making of rugs, money bags, cane work, luncheon mats, ladies hand bags, aprons and many other articles of same type. But there was virtually no development in this regard. On analysing the position shown by the 1961 census, Roy Burman states,

> "Mizo district is one of the most industrially backward districts of Assam. The few industries found in the district are the traditional cottage and village industries like weaving (loin loom), carpentry, etc. In 1961, 0.28 per cent of the industrial establishments in the district were run on electricity but there was no registered factory."

During the year 1971 the Lal Khama Committee said that there was no industrial unit worth the name in the Mizo Hills. According to the report submitted by the Rural Industries Project Office, Aizawl, there were 119 units under the RIP Aizawl.

These units, besides a handful of them, could not be said to be industries in the real sense of the term. The development of industries started under the Community Development Projects suffered a set-back because of the disturbances of 1966. The Lal Khama Committee listed a number of industries which could be easily developed in the Mizo Hills. The census data about total , main, marginal and non-workers is given below. Some data is given on next page.

Table 3
The Survey of Main Workers, Marginal Workers and Non-Workers (Statewise) : Census 2001

Total Rural Urban	*Persons Males Females*	*Total workers*	*Main workers*	*Marginal workers*	*Non-workers*	*Total Workers (main + marginal)*
Total	Persons	469,597	363,858	105,739	421,461	469,597
	Males	264,162	226,637	37,525	195,621	264,162
	Females	205,435	137,221	68,214	225,840	205,435
Rural	Persons	257,488	202,257	55,231	192,530	257,488
	Males	139,111	120,915	18,196	94,607	139,111
	Females	118,377	81,342	37,035	97,923	118,377
Urban	Persons	212,109	161,601	50,508	228,931	212,109
	Males	125,051	105,722	19,329	101,014	125,051
	Females	87,058	55,879	31,179	127,917	87,058

Some of these were: manufacture of sugar, fruit preservation, tapioca starch-making, oil-expelling, bamboo pulp and bamboo board, saw mill, and processing of maize, banana, chilli and ginger. Apart from these agro-based industries, there are possibilities according to the Committee, of many other small industries like

Table 4

The Survey of Main Workers, Marginal Workers and Non-Workers (Districtwise) : Census 2001

District	*Total workers*			*Main workers*			*Marginal workers*			*Non workers*		
	Persons	Males	Females	Persons	Males	Females	Persons	Males	Females	Persons	Males	Females
Mamit	35,369	19,647	15,722	27,515	17,649	9,866	7,854	1,998	5,856	26,944	13,119	13,825
Aizawl	32,388	18,577	13,811	24,958	16,580	8,378	7,430	1,997	5,433	28,589	13,297	15,292
Cham-phai	172,111	99,365	72,746	131,835	83,604	48,231	40,276	15,761	24,515	167,701	74,565	93,136
Serchhip	63,002	33,091	29,911	45,830	26,567	19,263	17,172	6,524	10,648	38,387	18,778	19,609
Lunglei	34,351	18,316	16,035	26,150	15,024	11,126	8,201	3,292	4,909	21,188	10,129	11,059
Lawn-gtlai	71,770	40,899	30,871	60,930	37,201	23,729	10,840	3,698	7,142	65,385	30,454	34,931
Saiha	33,685	19,395	14,290	25,986	17,139	8,847	7,699	2,256	5,443	39,365	19,030	20,335

type-retreading, radio assembling and repairing, and manufacture of plastic articles, footwear, hosiery goods, readymade garments, aluminium utensils and the like. After the Union territory has come into existence, high priority has been given to industrial development.

The stress is also evident from the fact that on January 21, 1972 when the Union territory of Mizoram was set up the Industries establishment in the territory did not have any class one post among total six class two posts five were vacant. Two class one and one additional class two posts have since been created. Most of these posts, including that of the Director of Industries, have been fulfilled.

(f) Transport and Other Facilities of Infrastructure

Whole system of transport in Mizoram includes roads, waterways and airways. Road development got the attention of the British since the starting of the military expeditions inside the Lushai Hills. The difficult terrain came in the way of making wide and permanent roads. Hence mostly paths were made. The following table shows the roads and the paths in the district in 1936.

Table 5
Length of Roads in the Year 1936

Unmetalled roads (fit for animal-drawn carts) (in miles)	
Aizawl – Sairang road	13.50
Aizawl station road	6.75
Sairang station road	2.00
Lunglei station road	2.38
Demagiri station road	1.00
Total	25.63

Bridle paths (fit for loaded ponies) (in miles)	
Sairang – Changail	6.25
Aizawl – North Vanlaiphai	80.25
Aizawl – Falam (Burma)	102.50
Aizawl – Dwarband (Cachar)	78.50
Aizawl – Lunglei	102.50
Aizawl – Tipaimukh	71.87
Lock's trace road	51.75
Lunglei – Demagiri	42.14
Lunglei – Haka (Burma)	58.00

(Contd.)

(Contd.)

Lenglei – Sherkawr	67.14
Dokhma – Kolodyne	31.25
Zongling – Tongkolong	42.00
Tuipang – Chakhang	45.00
Total	779.15

Source: Report on Administrative of the Lushai Hills for the year 1935-36, Government of Assam, Shillong, 1936, p. 17.

All these paths had been constructed mainly for maintenance of supply lines in the interior posts of Assam Rifles which maintained law and order in the district. Communication with Burma was maintained through some among these paths which reached to the administrative headquarters in Chin Hills district. Hence the Lushais could maintain a close contact with the Chins, which was subsequently obstructed after India and Burma became independent States.

Very first jeepable road was made during the second world war, connecting Silchar with Aizawl, a distance of 120 miles. Some jeep tracks were also made between Demagiri and the neighbouring areas. In the year 1950 S. Barkataki, DC, got a 128-mile-long jeep road between Aizawl and Lunglei constructed by the villagers on self-support basis. The Border Roads Task Force (BRTF) was inducted in the district in 1963. The regular PWD also started functioning in the district; earlier there was only a small PWD set-ups under the DC. There has been tremendous development in this regard since then. The progress in road-building is shown in the table given below.

Modern transport is an indication of economic development. The rapidly increasing number of motor vehicles in Mizoram is an index of the economic growth in the territory. In 1970 the DC introduced a scheme called the Employment Generation Scheme for constructing jeepable roads connecting all the villages of the district with one another and with the main roads.

Within just two years about 400 miles of jeepable roads were constructed under the scheme with an expenditure of Rs. 90 lakhs spent in terms of food ration to the villagers who were suffering from food shortage. This scheme was greatly appreciated not only as a relief measure, but also as a big and successful venture in road making. Recently the scheme has been expanded to cover construction of further 525 miles to make a total of 925 miles of jeep road. This scheme is particularly significant because of popular participation involved in the programme. It mobilised the huge idle human power and organised them for a massive road-building programme throughout the district.

(g) Waterways Development

Besides, the communication by roads there is a good scope for development of waterways in the territory. Before independence the south Lushai Hills had an excellent waterways connection by the Karnafuli river starting from Demagiri to Rangamati and Chittagong. When Pakistan built the Kaptai dam near Rangamati huge areas on the Indian side near Demagiri were submerged in water. But this catchment of water and resultant rising of water level has made it possible to develop riverine transport in the Demagiri area. The Koladyne river which passes through the southern part of the land can also be made nevigable with some planning and improvement. In the north, the Dhaleswari, the Sonai and quite a few other rivers are navigable. All these water courses were made use of with the DC in 1970 and 1971 when large scale relief operations were organised and a few thousand tonnes of rice and other commodities were moved by river from Silchar to the deep interior centres of the Mizo Hills. The total waterways in the territory have, however, remained more or less static, increasing by only 30 Kilometres within three years from 170 Kilometres in 1969 to 200 Kilometres in 1972.

(h) Air Service for Mizos

The Mizo Hills had the first air service when in 1966 helicopters hopped from village to village mainly as a part of the anti-insurrection measure, transporting personnel of the security forces, and also moving civil officials, doctors, medicine, food, etc. and evacuating civilian patients from the interiors to the town hospitals. Helipads were constructed in each group centre and essential communications were maintained with the helicopter services. The Mizo Hills got an air-strip in 1967 built by the army engineers near Aizawl and there was a passenger air service between Aizawl and Calcutta *via* Silchar functioned by a private airliner.

(i) Postal Service Communications

The Mizo Hills got an excellent postal service before the disturbances. Each of the big villages had a branch post office. There were telegraphic lines connecting Aizawl, Demagiri, Lunglei and Champhai. The disturbances gave a great jolt to the postal network and it took a few years to restore the services. At present there are two post offices with telegraphic facilities and 128 post offices without this kind of facilities. During the disturbances, the administration started their own courier services and communication by wireless. The wireless system covered the entire district and it largely facilitated restoration of administration in the interior villages.

(j) Medical Provisions

The time when the British administration was setup in the Lushai Hills the post of Civil Surgeon was created alongwith the post of Superintendent. In 1898 the district had four civil dispensaries, one station hospital and also four military police outpost hospitals. Although these medical facilities were primarily for the government employees, the Lushais also were encouraged to use the services.

Indeed, the number of Lushais coming to the dispensaries was regarded as an index of pacification and normalisation. The total number of Lushais cured in all the hospitals and dispensaries in 1900 was 11,528 against 5,497 in the previous year. This steady increase in the number of Lushai patients was indicative of the growing confidence of the Lushais in the government.

Within the next two years the attendance doubled, 22,941 being the number of Lushais treated in 1902-03. Vaccination against disease of small pox was also taken up extensively. In 1935-36 there were nine civil hospitals and two travelling dispensaries in the district. The most common diseases treated were malaria, round worms, respiratory and digestive troubles.

Alongwith education in the Christian missionaries provided medical facilities to the Lushais. In fact most of the missionaries had some knowledge of medicine and would give relief to the sick villagers.

The missionaries were running some very good hospitals in the district. At Serkawn near Lunglei and at Durtlang, five miles away from Aizawl, the missionaries had two excellent hospitals and both ran training centres for nurses. In spite of efforts both by the government and the Christian missions the medical facilities existing in Lushai district was not adequate as there was dearth of medical personnel. The location of the villages on hill tops, one far away from the other, also contributed towards the problems in providing adequate medical coverage to the people. Medical facilities had been increased considerably after independence.

Complete the medical and public health services came to a halt during the disturbances. The dispensaries and the staff had to be withdrawn from the interior villages and only the medical centres in the towns went on to function. With the grouping of villages, a pharmacy was set up in each group centre and a doctor was placed in charge of three to four villages. But it was difficult to get the necessary number of medical staff, which in the minimum was 150 pharmacists and 70 doctors. The position has not improved much even now. This definitely, is a common feature all over the country. Even in the developed plains areas it is difficult to get adequate number of doctors prepared to serve in the rural areas. In Mizoram, apart from the general backwardness, the disturbed condition acts as a deterrent to the doctors to serve in the deep interiors.

(k) Water Supply for Drinking Purpose

Availability of supply of drinking water in the villages is a common problem in Mizoram. All the villages are situated on hill tops. The courses of rivers running through the valleys, the village women have the arduous job of drawing water from the valley to the hill top, collecting water in bamboo pipes and walking up a thousand feet or so every day. In Aizawl township area, the people have to depend mostly on their own water reservoirs. Each family has the arrangement to collect rain water from roof of the house and store it for the entire year. Special arrangements are made for the government employees at Aizawl. During the monsoon a part of the requirements is met from an old reservoir which was made for the handful of government functionaries during the British administration. Apart from this, water is fetched by tank trucks from the Dhaleswari river, 15 kilometres from Aizawl. During the winter 60 to 70 trucks have to be busy daily for this purpose.

These arrangements are obviously inadequate. Water supply, therefore, got a high priority in the development programmes of the district. A public Health

Engineering Division with an Executive Engineer and a couple of Assistant Engineers was set up in the district. The Aizawl Water Supply Scheme was introduced for drawing water by pipes from the Dhaleswari river and arranging supply to all the inhabitants of the town. In 13 villages schemes were taken up for impounding water of the streams and thus supply throughout the year. Schemes were prepared for 65 other villages. But all these works had to be halted in 1966 when the insurgency started. While reforming the villages after the disturbances, water supply was given the highest consideration. But often it was found that the water points available near the villages were not adequate for the huge number of people brought together in a group centre. Hence in 1971 the DC took special steps in implementing an emergency water supply scheme in all the villages. These schemes are now under implementation and some have been executed.

(l) Educational Achievements

The Christian missionaries began their work in the Lushai Hills by setting up primary schools. In fact primary education was the base created by the missionaries for the spread of Christianity. The administrative reports reveal the tremendous progress made by the missionaries. The Administration Report of 1896-97 says:

"Messers Savidge and Lorrain, the pioneer missionaries, have been in these hills since the Spring of 1893 and have been wonderfully successful in introducing education. These two missionaries have done most valuable work. They are about to produce a Hand Book and Dictionary of the Lushai language which is badly needed."

During 1897 a school was opened for the first time in Aizawl in which 68 boys were enrolled. Next year three government primary schools were started. During the year 27 young chiefs and chosen men from villages were put through a course of instruction in the government school in Aizawl. They were given free ration during their stay in Aizawl. The government expenses for administration of the Lushai Hills was expected to be substantially reduced by the expansion of education. The administration felt: "Education is another of government's good investments, one of the many aids to pacification which bring nearer the date when the garrisin can be safely reduced".

The cost on education was, however, fantastically low compared to the expenditure on police. In 1898-99 the expenditure on education was Rs. 888-12-9 as compared to Rs. 4,93,357-0-8 spent on police. In 1890-1900 the figures of expenditure under these heads were Rs. 1,793-9-11 and Rs. 5,00,330-8-1 respectively. In 1903 the Chief Commissioner of Assam, during his trip to Aizawl, decided that the government schools for the Lushais should be handed over to the missions.

This was a momentous decision. From that year onwards till the taking responsibility of the schools by the Government of Assam and subsequently by the District Council, missions were the official agencies of education among the

Lushais for some 50 years. The missionaries were working as the honorary Inspectors of Schools in the district. In 1906 Rowlands, honorary Inspector of Schools, Aizawl, complained that education was obstructed because of migratory character of the people and suggested that when a village migrated, the village school should be erected first.

The Superintendent consented that the school should be erected as soon as the villagers had housed themselves. Six scholarships of Rs. 10/- per month for 10 years were introduced by the government in 1907 and provided in Shillong to provide higher education to promising Lushais until there was a high school in the Lushai Hills. The objective was to make trained Lushai youngmen available for joining as clerks, sub-overseas, hospital assistants, etc. With the spread of primary and middle education it was realised that practical education in agriculture and also vocation would be more befitting the requirements of the Lushais. Savidge, honorary Inspector of Schools, Lunglei, stated in 1916:

> "The Lushais are keen on education and the progress made during the year has been satisfactory. It is important, however, to remember that when we have educated sufficient boys to fill the Government posts available, there will be little for educated youths to do unless their education has been such as to enable them to develop agriculture and other resources of the district. I think the educational authorities of the district realise this."

Reality is that not much of importance was ever given to vocational education. The widespread primary and middle level education ultimately brought a big chunk of the young people away from agricultural pursuits. They, however, left without any employment as there was practically no other economic activity in the area. These frustrated young people were the main catalytic agents for causing the disturbances in 1966. The rate of growth in education after independence is higher than that under the missionaries. During the British regime the stress was only on primary education and no encouragement was given for further education. After 1947 positive steps were taken to correct the imbalance created by this neglect.

Many primary schools have been enhanced to middle and and high school levels. With the grouping of villages, the number of primary schools has decreased but the enrolment per school has increased. Grouping has made it feasible to restructure the educational institutions from the point of view of viability and effectiveness. Next table shows the progress in education in the post-independence period—the years for which the figures are given being chosen at random.

For the last few decades the Mizos maintained this status of being most educationally advanced people in Assam. The high rate of literacy among women was also a significant feature. Since the beginning of the British administration and the missionary developments in the district, the Mizos have been taking keen interest in education. Every village has a primary school and all school-going children attend the school.

Each village takes pride in the maintenance of its school. Education is regarded by the Mizos as one of the essential services in a village. The number of educational staff has considerably rose after the coming up of the Union territory. This is shown in the table given below.

Figures of census has brought out the fact of regional disparity in the development of education. The following table shows the literates and literacy rate in the State districtwise.

Table 6
Literates and Literacy Rates by Sex : Census 2001

Union Territory/ Districts	*Literates*			*Literacy Rate of 2001*		
	Persons	*Males*	*Females*	*Persons*	*Males*	*Females*
Mizoram	**663,262**	**351,851**	**311,411**	**88.49**	**90.69**	**86.13**
Mamit	41,161	22,837	18,324	80.09	84.04	75.66
Kolasib	46,346	24,623	21,723	90.49	91.50	89.37
Aizawl	282,523	145,727	136,796	96.64	97.20	96.06
Champhai	77,466	40,621	36,845	91.88	94.00	89.64
Serchhip	44,642	23,210	21,432	96.16	97.24	95.02
Lunglei	96,513	52,314	44,199	84.20	87.36	80.74
Lawngtlai	33,478	20,463	13,015	56.45	65.13	46.68
Saiha	41,133	22,056	19,077	82.43	86.28	78.39

Pawi-Lakher Region, presently the Chimtuipui district, is educationally far backward compared to the other areas in the territory. It is, therefore, necessary to give special attention to this area for balanced advancement in education. The fast development in school and college education has created the problem of unemployment of the educated youngmen. It is realised that the bulk of these people will have to be employed in agriculture which should be organised on a scientific basis to attract the educated people. On social education also there has been sufficient progress. Under the village development scheme initiated by the DC in 1971, as a part of the relief measures, every village was encouraged to build a community centre and a library. The All India Radio Station at Aizawl, started in 1968, has been a great help in adult and social education.

(m) Newspapers in the State

The Mizo people are avid newspaper readers. The following table shows the number of newspapers, district-wise in Mizoram.

Table 7
Number of Newspapers in Mizoram

Newspaper	*Aizawl*	*Lunglei*	*Chimtuipui*	*Total for Mizoram*
Daily	8	2	1	11
Weekly	3	1	1	5
Fortnightly	1	–	–	1
Monthly	6	1	–	7
Total	18	4	2	24

Source: Mizoram – Some Facts, Directorate of Information and Public Relations, Aizawl, 1973.

Great number of newspapers in the territory as shown in the table indicates the great interest a Mizo has in current affairs.

(n) Voluntary Organisations for Education

Various social welfare organisations are also excellent agencies for social education. With the gradual extinction of *zawbulk,* the tribal institutions of bachelors' dormitory, an association called the Young Lushai Association (YLA) was set-up in 1935 under the sponsorship of the missionaries for inculcating the spirit of social service among youngmen. This association, now called the Young Mizo Association (YMA), is highly popular and the biggest social organisation in the territory.

In the development of the state the role of these organisations in very important. The people in general and the youngmen in particular can be properly oriented through these organisations for fast social and economic development. It may be observed that the high degree of political and social consciousness among the Mizos generated by the extensively circulated newspapers representing different shades of political opinion and the widely spread-out welfare organisations provide a suitable infrastructure for mobilising public opinion in favour of development and progress of the Mizos as an indispensable part of the Indian nation.

(o) Community Development Programmes

Alongwith the other areas in the country Mizoram also had community development blocks organised on the all-India pattern. There were six CD blocks in the Aizawl subdivision, viz., Aizawl, Kolosib, Mamit, Serchip, Saitual and Champhai and also three in Lunglei subdivision, viz., Lunglei, Lawngtlai and Hnathial. The CD blocks in the tribal areas were gradually converted into tribal blocks organised under a special scheme introduced by the Ministry of Home Affairs in 1956.

The purpose of this scheme was to utilise the blocks for determining the development progress suitable for tribal life. The tribal blocks had been made intensive development blocks. The State governments were authorised to transfer amounts from one head to another. One of the objectives of the special scheme was to deviate away the tribal people from the practice of shifting cultivation and to induce them to take settled agriculture. Special attention was given towards terracing, irrigation, agriculture, horiculture, drinking water facilities, public health, medical facilities, communications, education, and arts and crafts.

During the year 1958 the Ministry of Home Affairs appointed a Committee with Dr. Verrier Elwin as the chairman to study the working of the tribal development blocks. The study revealed that, by and large, the programme of special multipurpose tribal betterment blocks had developed, contrary to the requirement, on the same lines as in the normal CD blocks. The Committee reported:

(i) The programme introduced in most of these blocks did not reflect the specific needs of the tribals.
(ii) The surveys conducted in some of these blocks for the purpose of introduction of programmes did not seek any data on the specific cultural pattern of the tribals residing in these blocks, their social and economic practices and their specific needs.
(iii) Generally, the staff did not have adequate background knowledge and understanding of the tribal problems.
(iv) By and large, the programmes had been developed on the same general pattern as in other areas. In other words, little "tribal touch" had been given to the community development programme in the special multipurpose tribal blocks.

Based on the grounds of these findings of the Elwin Committee, the Ministry of Community Development and Co-operation revised the approach to community development in the tribal areas. The new approach stressed the growth of the tribals by their own efforts and by the efforts of the extension workers. This approach sought to recognise the totality of the community life of the tribals, the integrated life of the person with the community, and the culture and tradition of the tribals.

The approach avoided a stereotyped outlook and included identification with the tribal life, understanding their institutions and agencies, the motivating factors for development activities and suggesting changes acceptable to them in terms of their value system. In his report for the period 1960-61, L.M. Shrikant, Commissioner for Scheduled Castes and Scheduled Tribes, observed that the very sound line of approach indicated by the Elwin Committee had not yet been shifted into action everywhere. The Commissioner fully endorsed the view expressed in the Epilogue of the Elwin Report.

> "We agree that we should 'hasten slowly', advance with caution, give the tribes a breathing space to adapt themselves to the new world . . . . Hunger, disease, exploitation, ignorance, isolation are evils whose cure cannot be delayed, they must be treated rapidly and efficiently.
>
> We believe that in the programme of the special tribal blocks, if it is planned wisely and implemented sincerely, India has an effective instrument

to save her tribal people from poverty and fear, and develop them along the lines of their own genius."

To begin with, Lunglei in the Mizo Hills was converted into a Tribal Development Block during the Second Plan period. During the third Plan period the other blocks were made Tribal Development Blocks. Detail about the Blocks and the stages of conversion are given in Appendix 7(i). The Blocks started functioning well, but before the full benefits of the new approach and the additional funds could mature, disturbances took place in the district and all the good works done so far was almost completely lost. During the period 1966 to 1972 all the headquarters of the Blocks had been transferred either to Aizawl or to Lunglei as it was not possible to undertake effectively the development functions in the interiors. There was also the shortage of staff who had, in the meantime, been engaged by the DC for running administration of the group centres. In 1973 the entire structure of the Blocks was reorganised. In the year 1976 there were 20 Blocks functioning all over the territory.

(p) Plan Expenditure for Mizoram

The Plan expenditure for Mizo Hills against the total expenditure for the State of Assam and for the hill areas are shown below:

Table 8
Details of Plan Expenditure in the First Three Five Year Plans in the Hills Parts of Assam

Five Year Plan	*General Plan*	*Welfare of Backward Class (Hills)*	*Total (Rupees in lakhs)*	*Expenditure in the Mizo Hills*
First	111.79	313.02	424.81	63
Second	395.63	537.73	933.36	211
Third	929.69	668.45	1,598.14	423

Additional grants were sanctioned in the hill districts for implementation of centrally sponsored schemes. This additional expenditure amounted to Rs. 2.23 crores in the Second Plan and Rs. 6.02 crores during the Third Plan. During this time, out of the total population of 13.15 lakhs in the four autonomous districts of Assam, the Mizo population was 2.15 lakhs. The figures in Table 16 will show that the expenditure in Mizo Hills during this time was more than the pro rata entitlement based on population. In the First Plan expenditure in the Mizo Hills was 15 per cent in the Second Plan 22.60 per cent and in the Third Plan 26.40 per cent of the complete expenditure in the hill areas.

(q) Finding of Krishnaswamy and Tarlok Singh

About study of the problems of development in the Mizo Hills by R.S. Krishnaswamy, Adviser to the Planning Commission, in March 1963, a Three-

Year Integrated Plan for the development of the district was started in 1963-64 providing for a total outlay of Rs. 150 lakhs with an emphasis on road development (Rs. 64.10 lakhs), education (Rs. 20.74 lakhs) and health (Rs. 12 lakhs). Intensive development was also started in respect of rural water supply, soil conservation, agriculture, inland water transport and electricity.

To implement the Integrated Plan a Special Board was established with the Deputy Commissioner as Chairman and a senior IAS Officer as the Secretary of the Board. The Board had the local MP, MLAs and other local leaders as members and started from headquarters in Aizawl. It was expected that this accelerated development programme would be able to bring up the Mizo Hills economically at par with other areas in the nation. But, unfortunately, by the time there could be a well-concerted move for development, rebellion broke out in the district. In February 1966 some days before the disturbances started, Tarlok Singh, Member of the Planning Commission, visited the Mizo Hills alongwith a team of experts in different streams of development.

Although schemes had been formulated on the basis of his study for the intensive development of the district, nothing could be done for the next few years because of the disturbed conditions and thus there was not much development in the district during the Fourth Plan period. The planned development again started effectively in recent years. The outlay has considerably grown after the Union territory came into existence. The plan outlays for the years 1973-74, 1974-75 and the Fifth Plan are shown in the next table.

Table 9
Outlay for 1973-74 and 1974-75 Annual Plans and Fifth Five-Year Plan

Head of Expenditure	*1973-74*	*Fifth Plan (74-79)* (*Rupees in lakhs*)	*1974-75*
1. Agriculture	129.00	1,567.00	209.10
2. Irrigation and Power	60.00	390.00	60.00
3. Industry and Mining	17.00	312.00	25.00
4. Transport and Communications	202.00	1,163.00	214.00
5. Social Service	185.00	1,043.00	167.00
6. Miscellaneous	6.50	84.00	14.90
Total	599.50	4,559.00	690.00

Presently, the annual Plan expenditure in Mizoram is more than the total annual expenditure in any of the earlier Five-Year Plans. Alongwith the increase in expenditures, staff in all the development departments has been strengthened. Compared to the total 21 Class I posts and 144 Class II posts existing on January 21, 1972 when the Union territory came into existence, there were 87 Class I posts and 239 Class II offices on November 1, 1973. This shows that in less than two years, the number of Class I posts had trebled while that of the Class II posts has almost doubled.

While there continues to be a large number of vacancies in these posts, mainly because it is difficult to get technical people to serve in these remote areas, attempts to fill up the newly-generated posts have succeeded to a great extent. The constraints in these regard were noted by R.S. Krishnaswamy, when he wrote: "As a general rule (there are some commendable exceptions) officers are averse to posting in the district and when posted, are impatient to get away. The difficulties of development in the area seem to consist of what may be called external factors such as non-availability of technical officers in adequate numbers, lack of implements, etc."

Undoubtedly, this is a vicious circle. Unless an area is developed personnel and equipment are not adequately available for the technical agencies and on the other hand without these factors development is not feasible. It is possible to break the vicious circle by organising task of development personnel and the implementation of the development plans on a war-footing.

To sums up, development administration as a strategy of process modernising the society in an underdeveloped economy is of recent origin. The colonial powers left the countries under their control in a disarray of political, social and economic values. It was left up to the new powers to bring in all the forces together in a newly organised system with a fresh orientation towards the means and the end. This process involved close understanding of the interacting forces and proper strategy had to be worked out by trial and error. This is a continuing process and it is under evolution in all the developing nations in Asia and Africa, particularly those which were under colonial rule. This fascinating phenomenon is at work on a miniature scale in Mizoram.

References

J. Shakespear, *The Lushai-Kuki Clans,* Macmillan & Co. Ltd., London, 1912, p. 17.

E.R. Elles, *Military Report on the Chin-Lushai Country,* Government Central Printing Press, Simla, 1893, pp. 33-34.

Annual Report on the Native States and Frontier Tribes of Assam, 1895-96, Government of Assam, Shillong, 1896, p. 25.

Administration Report of the Lushai Hills for the year 1902-03, Government of Assam, Shillong, 1903, p. 2.

Administration Report of the Lushai Hills for the Year 1903-04, Government of Assam, Shillong, 1904, p. 2.

Administrative Report of the Lushai Hills for the year 1915-16, Government of Assam, Shillong, 1916.

A.G. McCall, *Lushai Chrysolis,* Luzac & Co., London, 1949, pp. 260-269.

Report of the Committee appointed to examine the measures required to be undertaken for the rehabilitation of the economy of the people living in the borders of Mizo district adjoining East Pakistan, Government of Assam, Shillong, 1959, p. 6.

The author always found it difficult to get suitable personnel who were ready to be posted in the interior areas in the district. Demagiri and areas in the west side of the district, the Chakma areas, were particularly unpopular.

Administration Report of the North Lushai Hills for the year 1895-96, Government of Assam, Shillong, 1896, p. 1.

Administrative Report of the Lushai Hills for the year 1907-08, Government of Assam, Shillong, 1908, pp. 18-19.

Administration Report of the Lushai Hills for the year 1933-34, Government of Assam, Shillong, 1934, pp. 26-32.

Report on the Administration of the Lushai Hills for the year 1935-36, Government of Assam, Shillong, 1936, p. 34.

Report on the Administration of the Mizo Hills for the year 1957-58, Government of Assam, Shillong, 1958, pp. 3-14.

Source: Development Commissioner, Government of Mizoram, Aizawl.

Source: Development Commissioner, Government of Mizoram, Aizawl.

Source: Development Commissioner, Government of Mizoram, Aizawl.

Figures are for the year 1972-73. *Source:* Director of Agriculture, Government of Mizoram, Aizawl.

Report of the Study Team on Tribal Development Programmes, Committee on Plan Project, Planning Committee, New Delhi, 1969, p. 142.

Administration Report of the Lushai Hills for the year 1916-17, Government of Assam, Shillong, 1917, pp. 32-33.

Annual Report on the Administration of the Lushai Hills for the year 1935-36, Shillong, 1936, pp. 34-35.

A.G. McCall, *op. cit.,* p. 278.

B.K. Roy Burman, *Demographic and Socio-Economic Profiles of the Hill Areas of North-East India,* Department of Publications, Delhi, 1970, p. 279.

Report on Development Industries in Mizo Hills, Small Scale Industries Development and Internal Trade, New Delhi, 1971, p. 23.

The author as Deputy Commissioner, also functioned as Executive Engineer, PWD.

Information collected from the Development Commissioner, Government of Mizoram, Aizawl.

It is the author's personal experience that fast communication through wireless telegraph (WT) and radio telephone (RT) is of immense help to administration in the hill areas, particularly in the frontier.

Administration Report of the Lushai Hills for the year 1900-01, Government of Assam, Shillong, 1901, p. 5.

Administration Report of the Lushai Hills for the year 1902-03, Government of Assam, Shillong, 1903, p. 2.

Report on Administration of the Lushai Hills for the year 1935-36, Government of Assam, Shillong, 1936, p. 32.

Compiled from *Statistical Abstract, Mizo District, 1961,* District Statistical Officer, Aizawl, Department of Economics and Statistics, Government of Assam.

Information collected from the Director of Health Services, Government of Mizoram, Aizawl.

Annual Report on the Native States and Frontier Tribes of Assam, 1896-97, Government of Assam, 1898, p. 21.

Administration Report of the Lushai Hills for the year 1898-99, Government of Assam, 1899, p. 14.

Letter No. 355 For/2419/P dated Shillong, the 27th June 1900, from Secretary to Chief Commissioner of Assam to Secretary to Government of India, Foreign Department, appended to *Administration Report of the Lushai Hills for the year 1899-1900,* Government of Assam, Shillong 1900.

Administration Report of the Lushai Hills for the year 1906-07, Government of Assam, Shillong, 1907, p. 11.

Administration Report of the Lushai Hills for the year 1915-16, Government of Assam, Shillong, 1916, p. 16.

Source: India, A Reference Manual, 1975, Publication Division Ministry of Information and Broadcasting, 1975, p. 53.

The acting figures are difficult to get at any particular time as there are many ventures and experiments.

Report of the Committee on Special Multipurpose Tribal Blocks, Manager of Publications, Delhi, 1960.

Index

ENCYCLOPAEDIA
OF
NORTH-EAST INDIA

(In 3 Volumes)

(Assam, Meghalaya)

(Vol. 1)

T. RAATAN

KALPAZ PUBLICATIONS

DELHI-110 052

Encyclopaedia of North-East India

Rs. 2200 (In 3 Volumes Set)

ISBN: 81-8205-051-0 (Set)
ISBN: 81-8205-052-9 (Vol. 1)

Published in 2008 in India by
Isha Books, D-43, Prithviraj Road
Adarsh Nagar, Delhi-110 033

Lasertypesetting by: Varsha Graphics, Delhi
Printed at: Vishal Kaushik Printers Delhi

Contents

Section–II
MEGHALYA

Preface

The series *Encyclopaedia of North-East India* seeks to bring together in one place all information on North-Eastern States in India and particularly included in the Indian Union with great trouble and then finally conferred the status of statehood one by one.

Having always suffered with one lacunae or the other may it be terrorism or below average economic development, these states of store house of rich natural resources and moreover very distinct tribal culture. Despite all this, not much documentation has been done on presenting all the information about North-East in one volume or one series.

Present volume, Vol. I, of the series which is about Assam and Meghalaya is as said, a collection of significant information about the States. Both the States have contributed immensely not only to distinct culture and economy of the North-East region but of India as a whole.

Assam is said to be sentinel of North-Eastern part of India and also a gateway to North-Eastern States. Another significance of the State is that it is very close to India's international borders touching Bangladesh and Bhutan. Assam is surrounded by Bhutan and Arunachal Pradesh in the north, Manipur, Nagaland and Arunachal Pradesh the East and Meghalaya, Tripura and Mizoram in the South.

Now coming to Meghalaya, the other State of the present volume, it came into existence as full fledged State on 2nd January, 1972. Meghalaya is surrounded in north and east by Assam and on the south and west by Bangladesh. It is predominantly a hill state and inhabited by Garo, Khasi and Jayantia tribal communities and thus contains important elements of distinct tribal culture.

Having such significant character and so strategic location with international boundaries it becomes highly important to document important information about these states and present them in front of those to whom this is of any use.

Divided in two sections on Assam and Meghalaya each, Chapter 1 of both the sections, i.e., Land and the People—is about basics about the state and people living in Assam and Meghalaya respectively. All other chapters give description of specific of each state.

Chapter 2 of Section I is about problems that Assam had to face in post-1947 period and Chapter 3 about Identity Crisis, crisis of dominant community with inflow of refugees. Chapter 4 and 5 respectively present dialectics of the Assam movement and chronology of sequential development between 1978 to 1981. Last, i.e., 6th chapter is about culture and linguistic set up of Assam.

About Section II, i.e., Meghalaya, Chapter 8 and 9 are on constitutional provisions about local self governance in tribal areas and efficacy of autonomous district councils respectively. Chapter 10 and 11 are regarding traditional tribal political system and a comparison between marking of old and new self-governing institutions. Chapter 12 is about role of women in newly revived system of local self-governance. Lastly, Chapters 13 and 14 are about emergence of bureaucratic class facing political pressures and; deficiencies with their own functioning styles.

We are sure that the Volume will be of great use to researchers, academicians and to libraries especially in providing all basic important information together at one place.

T. Raatan

Introduction

Assam and Meghalaya are among most significant and naturally affluent States of North-East in India. They are both not only geographically close to each other but they have a lot in common. They share similar culture and tradition, Assam even has strong economy and both the States are very important to India from the international security point of view. We have already given geographical location of each State in the Preface. Here, we shall discuss some important points of each State of the volume that find detailed description in the various chapters of the book.

We shall start with the origin of **Assam**. Term 'Assam' as interpreted by some scholars have been extracted from the Sanskrit word *Asom* that means peerless and unparalleled. Some academicians also claim that the term has come from the original name of Ahomas who ruled over the land for some six hundred years before the entry of the Britishers. Races like Austric, Mongolian, Dravidian and also Aryans who came on the land centuries ago have made great contribution to the composite culture of Assam.

It is said that Assam was also known as *Pragjyotisha* or the place of eastern astronomy in epic period and later came to be known as *Kampura*. The advent of Ahom across the eastern hills in 1228 A.D. became a turning point in the history of the State. They ruled over Assam for almost six centuries. Assam became a British Protectorate in 1826 under the provisions of Treaty of Yandabo.

Assam is basically an agricultural society and its economy is more or less based on agriculture only. Principal food crop has been rice. Besides many cash crops are also grown. According to 2001 statistics, the State has an estimated 39.44 Lakh hectares gross cropped area and new area sown is around 27.10 lakh hectares.

Assam is famous for its rich forest resources also and of total forest area. 21.2 per cent is the reserved forest area. There are also five national parks and eleven wildlife sanctuaries in the State. Kaziranga and Manas National Parks enjoy popularity even at international level.

Despite the fact that Assam has undergone numerous political troubles both in the pre- and post-independence era and the continuous movement for long time shattered its economy and trade to a large extent, there are numerous tea-based industries in the State. Exploitation of mineral resources in the State comprise largely petroleum, natural gas, limestone and coal. There are six industrial growth centres in the State and two such centres are going to be established in near future at Balipara and Natia each. A Central Institute for Plastic Engineering Technology has been established at Amingaon near Guwahati.

Table 1
Population, Decadal Growth Rate, Sex Ratio and Density : 2001

District	*Population*			*Decadal growth rate*		*Sex Ratio*		*Density*	
	Person	*Male*	*Female*	*1981-91*	*1991-01*	*1991*	*2001*	*1991*	*2001*
	(1)	(2)	(3)	(4)	(5)	(6)	(7)	(8)	(9)
Assam	**26,638,407**	**13,787,799**	**12,850,608**	**NA**	**18.85**	**923**	**932**	**286**	**340**
Kokrajhar	930,404	478,242	452,162	NA	15.05	940	945	255	294
Dhubri	1,634,589	840,673	793,916	NA	23.42	950	944	473	584
Goalpara	822,306	420,707	401,599	NA	23.07	947	955	366	451
Bongaigaon	906,315	465,970	440,345	NA	12.23	940	945	322	361
Barpeta	1,642,420	846,106	796,314	NA	18.53	939	941	427	506
Kamrup	2,515,030	1,327,717	1,187,313	NA	25.75	879	894	460	579
Nalbari	1,138,184	587,668	550,516	NA	11.98	936	937	450	504
Darrang	1,503,943	773,982	729,961	NA	15.79	938	943	373	432
Marigaon	775,874	398,930	376,944	NA	21.29	941	945	375	455
Nagaon	2,315,387	1,194,327	1,121,060	NA	22.30	929	939	494	604
Sonitpur	1,677,874	864,125	813,749	NA	17.80	912	942	268	315
Lakhimpur	889,325	455,689	433,636	NA	18.34	931	952	330	391
Dhemaji	569,468	294,105	275,363	NA	18.93	927	936	148	176
Tinsukia	1,150,146	602,515	547,631	NA	19.52	891	909	254	303
Dibrugarh	1,172,056	609,470	562,586	NA	12.43	905	923	308	347
Sibsagar	1,052,802	546,565	506,237	NA	15.95	907	926	340	395
Jorhat	1,009,197	530,240	478,957	NA	15.84	913	903	306	354
Golaghat	945,781	490,370	455,411	NA	14.21	920	929	236	270
Karbi Anglong	812,320	422,599	389,721	NA	22.57	907	922	64	78
N. Cachar Hills	186,189	98,899	87,290	NA	23.47	857	883	31	38
Cachar	1,442,141	741,580	700,561	NA	18.66	932	945	321	381
Karimganj	1,003,678	516,408	487,270	NA	21.35	946	944	457	555
Hailakandi	542,978	280,912	262,066	NA	20.92	929	933	338	409

Assam has always enjoyed highest admiration for her arts and crafts associated with the cottage industries of the State. These industries like handloom, sericulture, cane and bamboo articles, carpentry, brass and bell-metal crafts. Assam is also famous for production of varieties of silk, Endi, Muga, Tassar, etc. For Muga silk, Assam is the only centre in the whole world.

Assam celebrates an exclusive range of colourful festivals. *Bihu* is the chief festival celebrated on three different occasions. Rangoli Bihu/Bohag Bihu indicates the beginning of cropping period and it also ushers in the Assamese new year.

Bhogali Bihu/Magh Bihu is the festival of harvest season. Further, religion accounts for a large variety of festivals. Vaishnavites observe birth and death anniversaries of leading Vaishnav saints with a whole day long singing of hymns and staging theatrical performances in their traditional way.

Table 2
Population, population in the Age Group 0-6 of Assam : 2001

District	*Total Rural Urban*	*Population*			*0-6 Population*		
		Person	*Male*	*Female*	*Person*	*Male*	*Female*
1	*2*	*3*	*4*	*5*	*6*	*7*	*8*
Assam	**Total**	**26,638,407**	**13,787,799**	**12,850,608**	**4,350,248**	**2,215,104**	**2,135,144**
	Rural	**23,248,994**	**11,983,157**	**11,265,837**	**3,981,910**	**2,024,362**	**1,957,548**
	Urban	**3,389,413**	**1,804,642**	**1,584,771**	**368,338**	**190,742**	**177,596**
Kokrajhar	Total	930,404	478,242	452,162	169,032	86,482	82,550
	Rural	866,772	444,800	421,972	162,090	82,905	79,185
	Urban	63,632	33,442	30,190	6,942	3,577	3,365
Dhubri	Total	1,634,589	840,673	793,916	331,164	166,907	164,257
	Rural	1,444,043	742,566	701,477	306,551	154,323	152,228
	Urban	190,546	98,107	92,439	24,613	12,584	12,029
Goalpara	Total	822,306	420,707	401,599	155,804	78,883	76,921
	Rural	755,017	385,769	369,248	147,031	74,505	72,526
	Urban	67,289	34,938	32,351	8,773	4,378	4,395
Bongaigaon	Total	906,315	465,970	440,345	160,072	80,933	79,139
	Rural	796,028	408,175	387,853	148,156	74,805	73,351
	Urban	110,287	57,795	52,492	11,916	6,128	5,788
Barpeta	Total	1,642,420	846,106	796,314	301,095	153,339	147,756
	Rural	1,517,280	781,559	735,721	287,526	146,378	141,148
	Urban	125,140	64,547	60,593	13,569	6,961	6,608
Kamrup	Total	2,515,030	1,327,717	1,187,313	335,231	172,922	162,309
	Rural	1,614,512	836,945	777,567	242,107	123,609	118,498
	Urban	900,518	490,772	409,746	93,124	49,313	43,811
Nalbari	Total	1,138,184	587,668	550,516	161,616	82,372	79,244
	Rural	1,110,706	573,269	537,437	158,689	80,845	77,844
	Urban	27,478	14,399	13,079	2,927	1,527	1,400
Darrang	Total	1,503,943	773,982	729,961	261,802	132,598	129,204
	Rural	1,430,099	734,788	695,311	253,439	128,318	125,121
	Urban	73,844	39,194	34,650	8,363	4,280	4,083
Marigaon	Total	775,874	398,930	376,944	144,388	73,472	70,916
	Rural	737,813	378,674	359,139	139,923	71,163	68,760
	Urban	38,061	20,256	17,805	4,465	2,309	2,156
Nagaon	Total	2,315,387	1,194,327	1,121,060	414,086	209,071	205,015
	Rural	2,037,466	1,048,764	988,702	383,266	193,406	189,860
	Urban	277,921	145,563	132,358	30,820	15,665	15,155
Sonitpur	Total	1,677,874	864,125	813,749	264,449	133,365	131,084
	Rural	1,530,043	786,356	743,687	250,404	126,189	124,215
	Urban	147,831	77,769	70,062	14,045	7,176	6,869
Lakhimpur	Total	889,325	455,689	433,636	145,572	74,196	71,376

(Contd.)

(Contd.)

1	2	3	4	5	6	7	8
	Rural	824,196	421,028	403,168	137,235	69,855	67,380
	Urban	65,129	34,661	30,468	8,337	4,341	3,996
Dhemaji	Total	569,468	294,105	275,363	94,166	48,108	46,058
	Rural	530,138	273,148	256,990	88,628	45,274	43,354
	Urban	39,330	20,957	18,373	5,538	2,834	2,704
Tinsukia	Total	1,150,146	602,515	547,631	179,111	91,208	87,903
	Rural	925,972	481,255	444,717	154,890	78,603	76,287
	Urban	224,174	121,260	102,914	24,221	12,605	11,616
Dibrugarh	Total	1,172,056	609,470	562,586	164,384	84,139	80,245
	Rural	952,080	491,339	460,741	143,428	73,200	70,228
	Urban	219,976	118,131	101,845	20,956	10,939	10,017
Sibsagar	Total	1,052,802	546,565	506,237	142,253	72,363	69,890
	Rural	955,701	493,116	462,585	132,124	67,072	65,052
	Urban	97,101	53,449	43,652	10,129	5,291	4,838
Jorhat	Total	1,009,197	530,240	478,957	124,293	65,395	58,898
	Rural	838,549	439,282	399,267	106,179	56,018	50,161
	Urban	170,648	90,958	79,690	18,114	9,377	8,737
Golaghat	Total	945,781	490,370	455,411	138,178	70,324	67,854
	Rural	866,625	447,942	418,683	129,320	65,789	63,531
	Urban	79,156	42,428	36,728	8,858	4,535	4,323
Karbi Anglong	Total	812,320	422,599	389,721	145,000	73,504	71,496
	Rural	719,569	372,586	346,983	132,420	67,062	65,358
	Urban	92,751	50,013	42,738	12,580	6,442	6,138
North Cachar Hills	Total	186,189	98,899	87,290	29,944	15,349	14,595
	Rural	128,110	67,052	61,058	22,823	11,754	11,069
	Urban	58,079	31,847	26,232	7,121	3,595	3,526
Cachar	Total	1,442,141	741,580	700,561	220,497	112,727	107,770
	Rural	1,240,723	638,561	602,162	199,344	101,885	97,459
	Urban	201,418	103,019	98,399	21,153	10,842	10,311
Karimganj	Total	1,003,678	516,408	487,270	171,185	86,509	84,676
	Rural	930,131	478,582	451,549	164,607	83,118	81,489
	Urban	73,547	37,826	35,721	6,578	3,391	3,187
Hailakandi	Total	542,978	280,912	262,066	96,926	50,938	45,988
	Rural	497,421	257,601	239,820	91,730	48,286	43,444
	Urban	45,557	23,311	22,246	5,196	2,652	2,544

Among worthseeing places of tourism are *Kamakhya temple, Umanand, Navrag, Basishta Ashram, Dolgobinda, Gandhi Mandap,* state zoo, state museum, *Sukheshwar* temple, Gita Mandir and many more. Other important tourist places in Assam are; Kaziranga National Park and Manas Tiger projects (already mentioned), wildlife sanctuaries like *Pobi-tor* and *Orag* Sibsagar and Tezpur temples, Hajo—meeting point of Buddhism, a picnic spot, i.e., Chandubi lake, etc., also appear very attractive to the tourists. In short, the State has all that lures a person to visit the State.

Meghalaya, having its capital in hill town Shillong literally means 'residence of clouds'. This name was given by the great Indian geographer, Sh. S.P. Chatterjee. Meghalaya became a State in the year 1972. One of world's wettest region is found in Meghalaya, i.e., Cherrapunji which has the maximum rainfall recorded in Asia and second highest in the whole world. The climate of the State generally remains mild.

Besides accounts of more important Khasi Kingdom in the Chronicles of neighbouring Ahom and Kachari, not much is known about Meghalaya prior to the advent of British in the region. It has been recorded that in the early 19th century, the Britishers' desire to construct a road through the State in order to link Bengal and Assam facilitated a treaty in 1827 with the ruler. Opponents of this treaty persuaded the ruler to abandon it in 1829 and following this, an attack on the British led to British military operations against the Khasi. For following one century, the English exercised complete political control over the area called them the Garo and Khasi states, but the tribal clans left to themselves, were able to preserve their traditional style of living in seclusion.

After 1947, struggle for autonomy and self-rule led to agitation and finally Meghalaya was created as full State within Assam which attained full statehood in 1972.

This area is very rich in tribal culture and folklores. Both drinking and dancing are indispensable parts of religious celebrations and social gatherings. Marriages are exogamous. Penetration of Christianity in the mid-nineteenth century accompanied with strict morals has affected many of the tribal and communal institutions. According to a custom among Gaoras, by used to live in father-in-law's house as clan representative after marriage and at the death of father-in-law, he would marry his mother-in-law also, thus husband of both mother and daughter. This custom is now almost dead. Human sacrifice was also initially practised by them. Total population, decadal growth rate, sex ratio, density and population between 0-6 years of age are given as follows :

Table 3

Population, Decadal Growth Rate, Sex Ratio and Density : 2001

District	*Population*			*Decadal growth rate*		*Sex Ratio*		*Density*	
	Person	*Male*	*Female*	*1981-91*	*1991-01*	*1991*	*2001*	*1991*	*2001*
	(1)	(2)	(3)	(4)	(5)	(6)	(7)	(8)	(9)
Meghalaya	**2,306,069**	**1,167,840**	**1,138,229**	**32.86**	**29.94**	**955**	**975**	**79**	**103**
West Garo Hills	515,813	259,440	256,373	31.06	27.98	959	988	108	139
East Garo Hills	247,555	126,312	121,243	38.29	31.10	958	960	73	95
South Garo Hills	99,105	51,051	48,054	23.61	28.59	963	941	42	54
West Khasi Hills	294,115	149,159	144,956	36.26	33.59	951	972	42	56
Ri Bhoi	192,795	99,315	93,480	27.40	51.44	941	941	54	81
East Khasi Hills	660,994	333,187	327,807	30.72	22.88	948	984	191	234
Jaintia Hills	295,692	149,376	146,316	40.97	34.12	973	980	58	77

The population of the State is predominantly rural, with a few towns existing in Meghalaya. Shillong, the capital city, also happens to be the largest town. Plateau region being the hilly with rugged topography, physical and location factors are such that it has resulted in isolation of tribal communities. Almost 80 per cent of the population is of Scheduled Tribes. Khasi and Garo are the main languages and Jaintia and English are the official languages.

Table 4
Population, Population in the Age Group 0-6 of Assam : 2001

District	*Total Rural Urban*	*Population* *Person*	*Male*	*Female*	*0-6 Population* *Person*	*Male*	*Female*
1	2	3	4	5	6	7	8
Meghalaya	**Total**	**2,306,069**	**1,167,840**	**1,138,229**	**457,442**	**231,571**	**225,871**
	Rural	**1,853,457**	**939,803**	**913,654**	**392,305**	**198,408**	**193,897**
	Urban	**452,612**	**228,037**	**224,575**	**65,137**	**33,163**	**31,974**
West Garo Hills	Total	515,813	259,440	256,373	96,482	49,276	47,206
	Rural	457,422	229,592	227,830	88,425	45,100	43,325
	Urban	58,391	29,848	28,543	8,057	4,176	3,881
East Garo Hills	Total	247,555	126,312	121,243	49,242	25,000	24,242
	Rural	211,652	107,935	103,717	42,892	21,735	21,157
	Urban	35,903	18,377	17,526	6,350	3,265	3,085
South Garo Hills	Total	99,105	51,051	48,054	20,892	10,730	10,162
	Rural	90,462	46,449	44,013	19,480	10,005	9,475
	Urban	8,643	4,602	4,041	1,412	725	687
West Khasi Hills	Total	294,115	149,159	144,956	67,321	34,005	33,316
	Rural	260,595	132,293	128,302	59,792	30,130	29,662
	Urban	33,520	16,866	16,654	7,529	3,875	3,654
Rai Bhoi	Total	192,795	99,315	93,480	45,257	22,760	22,497
	Rural	179,630	92,573	87,057	42,449	21,309	21,140
	Urban	13,165	6,742	6,423	2,808	1,451	1,357
East Khasi Hills	Total	660,994	333,187	327,807	112,374	56,775	55,599
	Rural	383,027	193,854	189,173	77,592	39,249	38,343
	Urban	277,967	139,333	138,634	34,782	17,526	17,256
Jaintia Hills	Total	295,692	149,376	146,316	65,874	33,025	32,849
	Rural	270,669	137,107	133,562	61,675	30,880	30,795
	Urban	25,023	12,269	12,754	4,199	2,145	2,054

Like other north-eastern States, in Meghalaya also, religion and festivals are integral part of their life. A five day religious festival of Khasis the Pamblang Nongkrem popular with short name Nongkrem dance is performed every year at village Smil 11 km. away from Shillong. Shord Sukmyniesm is another important festival of Khasis that celebrated at Shillong during the second weak of April. Behdiengkhalm is the most colourful festival of Jaintias. But later, with the spread of Christianity, changes in religious community of the region have been brought with the immigration of Hindus and Muslims to the State. Christianity, Hinduism and the aministic Hinduism are the leading religions in the State. In very small number, Muslims, Buddhists and even Sikhs are found.

Agriculture is the dominant economic activity of the State upon which 80 per cent of the population depends for livelihood though the net area grown is less than 9 per cent. Land is owned in common but Jhum cultivation has left people poor and also caused soil erosion. The main crops are rice, millet, maize, potatoes, pepper, chillies, cotton, ginger, betal nuts, fruits and vegetables, etc.

The transition in the state from a nomadic to settled life have been due to abundance of labour. The State has unlimited natural resources that have not been tapped well. Its sillimanite deposits are especially the best in the world. Meghalaya has no heavy industries. Small-scale industries include the manufacture of cement, plywood and beverage factories, etc., along with a newly set up electronics plant.

As it is evident that the State is one of the most underdeveloped in India. Only about half, i.e., 49.1 per cent people are even literate. Literacy in urban areas is much higher as compared to the rural ones. There are at present 5,517 institutions in the State for education: North-East Hill University at Shillong is the State's sole university.

In short, though the State is underdeveloped, there is a great scope for development and betterment with awareness generation among the people and development plans and programmes.

Section-I
Assam

1

Land and the People: A Background

Whenever, there is an attempt to study North-East in India, one cannot help starting with Assam because it is not only one of the biggest States of the region but also among the richest and well-developed ones. Assam has contributed a lot to the economy of the region as well as of the country.

Brief History

Assam was famous as Kamrupa and its capital was Pragjyotishpura. King Narakasura and his son Bhagadatta were famous rulers in the 1000 B.C. The Varman Dynasty was established by Pusyavarman in 355 A.D. The Chinese traveller Hiuen Tsang visited the country in 640 A.D., Bhaskaravarman invited this Chinese traveller. He left a clear account of the Kingdom and its people. Then it is known as Kamrupa, was about 1,700 miles in circuit and included the Brahmaputra Valley, Bhutan, Rangpur district (now in Bangladesh), and Cooch Bihar (now in West Bengal) and extending western part of the river Koshi in Bihar. After at Assam was ruled by various dynasties: Plas, Koches Kacharis, and the Chutiyas, etc. There was no stable Government during this period. In 1236 A.D., a Mongolian tribe Ahoms from Thailand came through Burma and conquered upper Assam. Sukapha was the Ahoms leader who entered Assam with some nobles and about 800 men, women and children. After the Ahom defeated the Koches, the Kacharis and other local rulers of lower Assam including Goalpara. So the whole country was named "Assam" after the Ahoms. The Ahoms had a very good administrative system and Cabinet Ministers under Bargohain and Buragohain. Ahoms reached its top rank during the reign of King Rudra Singha (1696-1715).[1]

The Mughals invaded Assam for seventeen times. In the 13th and 17th centuries, the Assamese people are successfully resisted the incorporation of Assam into the Mughal Empire. Lachit Barphukan defended Assam from the Mughals. For tardiness in building a rampart for defense against a Mughal attack, Barphukan who was himself slayed his own maternal uncle, the reason being: "My maternal uncle is not greater than my country." In the seventeenth and last battle, he went to the battlefield of Saraighat riding in his sick bed to fight the Mughals. In the Assamese history his name sparks even today.

Hindu Vaishnavaism was known throughout Brahmaputra Valley in the sixteenth century during the time of sage Sankardeva (died 1568). That time Muslim influence was growing all over in India. The Maharaja of Cooch Bihar was a promoter of Sankardeva's Vaishnavaism. That's why Sankardeva spent later part of his life in the court of Maharaja and he wrote most of his valuable works. He was also a social reformer.

The Ahoms were originally Buddhists, but married local girls and tried to take up local language and religion. The Brahmins and Kalitas moved to Assam after the invasion of Ahoms from the area around Kanauj in Uttar Pradesh. Thirty years before the Ahoms came to Assam the Muslims came to Kamrup with the invading Army of Mohammad Ibn Bakhtiar in 1206. The historian Dr. H.K. Barpujari said that Muslim settlements might have originated in western Assam before the 16th century. Their movement into upper Assam cannot be discovered the marks of the invasion of Nawab Mirjumla, in 1662. They were employed to make out what obscure and interpreting Persian documents as craftsmen and artisans.

The vocabulary of the Assamese language was enriched by Persian and Arabic words. The 'Zikir' and 'Zari' songs which are known as 'Azan Fakirar Geet'. These songs occupy an eminent place in Assamese literature. Shihabuddin Talish had accompanied Nawab Mirjumla, found nothing similar among the Assamese Muslims of Islam except the name; their hearts were inclined far more towards mixing with the Assamese than towards association with the Muslims, he claimed[2]. Some Sikhs, who came with the Mughal invaders settled themselves in Nowgong District. They observe their religion, but culture is quite similar to communicate. During that time Burmese soldiers also settled at Singimari in the Goalpara District. These different ethnic groups mixed up with Assamese society and became one nationality during the 600 years of Ahom rule.

British Period

The Ahom princes were very weakened to rule the Ahom administration. So, Prince Gaurinath Singha welcomed the British in 1786. The British tried to bring peace and returned to Calcutta. The rival Governor, Barphukan Badan Chandra, called the Burmese to fight against the king in 1817. The Burmese invaded Assam three times and brought destruction and misery all over the country. At the request of king Purander Singha the British drove out the Burmese invaders. As a result treaty of Yandabo with Burma, settled down on the 24th of February, 1826. So Assam became a part of British India. The Burmese did not have the right to give up Assam to the British since their sovereignty was not established. Assam was free of the Burmese rule when the treaty was being signed. Any agreement on Assam, should, therefore, have been on tri-lateral basis. Thus the British possessed Assam through evil spirit.

British Agent was administered in 1839 in Assam. The devastated area of Assam was incorporated into the Bengal Presidency. The entire Assam Valley has come under British rule in 1842. The Sylhet district (now in Bangladesh) and the Cachar district were created in Assam and administered by a Chief Commissioner with its capital at Shillong in 1874. The people of Sylhet protested the merger with Assam. The cultural identity and historic association with Bengal, and Sylhet, i.e., the golden calf. The calf was being sacrificed for a new idol called the province of Assam. The Viceroy did not give up to the protestors. Lord Curzon declared a new province called 'Eastern Bengal and Assam' in 1905. The partition of Bengal was in 1912. This arrangement was turned back to the old province of Assam until 1947.

During the British rule several things were marked revolt against British. Gomdhar Konwar, Roopchand Konwar and Peoli Barphukan in 1828-29. Peoli Barphukan was hanged in 1828. India, revolted against the British in 1857. The Assamese leader, Maniram Dewan was also hanged by British in 1859.

The Bengali language was very popular in Assam from 1831 to 1872. Dr. Miles Brown prepared the first Assamese-English dictionary for Assamese community and published the first Assamese monthly *Orunudoi*. Sir Henry Cotton, Chief Commissioner, who established Cotton College in Gauhati in 1901. The Assamese language was recognised by the Calcutta University in 1903 by Chief Commissioner Fuller.

In 1839, the tea cultivation started by the British. The establishment of saw mills, coal mining and explored oil at Digboi in 1890. The construction of railroads began in 1881. There were 715 miles of railroads. Between 1874 and 1905, the development of tea, coal, oil, saw mills and railways Rs. 315 million were invested.[3] Bengalees were to engage for wages as administrators and also operators of railways and other industries started to Assam during British rule.

Bengalee immigration started the Assam Legislative Council was comprising the British, Bengalees, and Assamese. On January 2, 1913, first sitting. It served only in an advisory capacity encountered by were divided by the council. Many problems were political parties. Along the lines of Hindu-Muslim and Assamese Bengalee. The Assamese and the Bengalees wanted linguistic provinces and transferring Sylhet and Cachar to Bengal during 1917-1926. Planned to Saiyid Muhammad Saadulla who was a prominent Muslim leader of Sibasagar district. January 6, 1926, he said that as Sylhet remained in Assam, Muslims who constituted one-third of the provincial population, would remain a minority and hold of Assam's electoral politics in January. If Muslim majority district of Sylhet goes to Bengal, Sylhet would lose that position in Assam forever. The proportion of Muslims in Bengal's population would not have increased. Do not even by one per cent. Sylhet remained in Assam serving the interest of the Muslims.[4]

Self-governing power in 1937 got the Assam. The first Chief Minister was Saadulla. Saadulla had five terms in the next ten years. Gopinath Bardoloi served as Chief Minister for two terms. The National Congress high-command decided not to participate in self-government by Bardoloi to resign. In the absence of prominent Assamese leaders in the Council and Saadulla was a Muslim League leader and for that he took advantage of grafting thousands of Muslims in Assam.

Assam Under Independent India

It was also decided to give independence to India and partition India. The founder of Pakistan was M.A. Jinnah. He demanded that Assam be included in Pakistan. Assam was almost handed over to Pakistan at the time of partition. The Cabinet Mission included Assam and Bengal were to decide by a simple majority vote and for which one of the two domains they would like to join. Assam would have been outvoted and included in Pakistan. Gopinath Bardoloi, who became Chief Minister of Assam during that year and decided not to sit in the section with Bengal. Backed by Gandhi, this decision also defended Assam's right to provincial autonomy and fought for maintaining its political and cultural identity. He wrote in *Harijan* on December 29, 1946:

> No one can force Assam to do what it does not want to do. Not only a Province but even a single individual can rebel against Congress and by doing so, serve it, assuming that the Province or the individual is in the right. I have done so myself. That would be a kind of *Satyagraha* against the Congress for the good of the Congress . . . for the independence of India it is the only condition. Each unit must be able to decide and act for itself.

The Muslim League declared direct action against the Assam Government for its aforesaid decision. Khiliji Dastas of the Muslim League was sent from East Bengal to occur raids on Assam lands. Gandhi by stood Assam at this critical moment and saved her from inclusion in Pakistan.

Assam and the North-East region remained isolated from India for Last two and one-half years. All communications were linked to India, through the Rangpur district. This district had situated Pakistan. Assam was connected to the rest of India by railways and roads through Siliguri.

About 273,000 Hindu refugees, from East Pakistan moved to Assam during the partition of India. The Assamese people were unhappy. But Government of Assam settled them against their wishes. According to M.V. Kamath:

> There are other events that the Assamese have not forgotten such as a demand to incorporate the district of Goalpara in West Bengal and to carve out a new State from Assam by the name of the Purbachal, made before the States Reorganisation Commission (1953-55) or efforts to convert Assam into a bilingual State in 1960, at the time of adopting Assamese as the State language of Assam. The Assamese people believe these demands would not have become possible if they were politically strong and economically viable.[5]

The new oil fields were discovered in Assam in the year 1950. The Government of India decided build a refinery at Barauni, Bihar against export-opinion and unemployment and industrial backwardness of Assam. After protests and demonstrations a small refinery was built by the Government of India in Gauwhati, Assam.

In 1962, China invaded Assam. The Chinese Army crossed the Himalayas only 49 miles from Tezpur. Rana K.D.N. Singh, Deputy Commissioner of Darrang district started the evacuation of Assam by destroying currency notes, coins and records in the State Bank on November 10, 1962. Telephone installations were to be destroyed before his departure. Many of the families who had homes outside Assam evacuated. But the permanent inhabitants of Assam preferred to stay home and face the enemy than die of possible fatigue, starvation and disease on their way to or in refugee camps outside the State.

The Muslim immigrants who came from the East Pakistan by raising the flag of Pakistan to welcome the Chinese. Prime Minister Jawaharlal Nehru virtually abandoned Assam. He made a grief of sorrow and speech farewell address over the radio. On November 12, 1962. "My heart cries for the people of Assam," he said. Due to unknown causes the Chinese restrained back. Assam remained with India. The invasion by the civilians of Bangladesh and Nepal began after that. Assam has been splited into five States in 1963.

In the liberation movement, East Pakistan as Bangladesh was born during 1971. Assam gave refuge to millions who left to save their lives from Pakistani soldiers. Some of them returned to Bangladesh, few of them came back. Since, Bangladeshis can easily move into Assam. The thousands of people are trying to come in the North-eastern Region. In spite of repeated requests by the Assamese people since independence, the Government of India has not decided to take prevention of infiltration and deport illegal immigrants. Since middle part of 1979 popular upsurge against foreign domination was take place in Nepal and Bangladesh.

Consequences of English Rule

In this first half of the chapter, we have seen in brief, how British interference torn of economy and policy of the State. This particular part concentrate on the positive as well as negative consequences of control of Britishers over Assam which last from 1826 to 1947.

English rule in Assam during the 18th century brought tremendous changes in social and political life. The rigidity of the closed society during Ahom period became open to outside influx, destroying the traditional system of aristocracy and the new pattern of social system had come into existence. The British rule had done both destructive and constructive roles during a period of almost more than a century.

System of Education. The indigenous system of education or centre of Sanskrit education under the Brahmin teachers of the Ahom period was discontinued. The main objective of introducing the western education was to make the young people fit for junior posts in administration. The British Government gave little patronage toward the persisting system which did not contribute anything for mass educational movement. The British thought that the western educational system alone could alter or remove the orthodoxy and superstitions from the society.

However, the Brahmin section was not happy at all and they had been disappointed. When people showed their eagerness to learn, the Government had to start village schools in different parts of the province. The census data relating to literates and literacy rates by sex district wise is as follows :

Table 1
Literates and Literacy Rates by Sex—Assam Census 2001

Union Territory/ Districts	*Literates*			*Literacy Rate of 2001*		
	Persons	*Males*	*Females*	*Persons*	*Males*	*Females*
Assam	**14,327,540**	**8,324,077**	**6,003,463**	**64.28**	**71.93**	**56.03**
Kokrajhar	400,123	242,482	157,641	52.55	61.90	42.65
Dhubri	649,944	381,442	268,502	49.86	56.61	42.64
Goalpara	390,278	223,407	166,871	58.56	65.36	51.40
Bongaigaon	449,754	264,957	184,797	60.27	68.81	51.16
Barpeta	769,225	456,870	312,355	57.35	65.95	48.16
Kamrup	1,628,088	938,144	689,944	74.69	81.24	67.31
Nalbari	664,886	389,686	275,200	68.08	77.12	58.40
Darrang	694,570	412,510	282,060	55.92	64.32	46.95
Marigaon	375,465	215,215	160,250	59.46	66.13	52.36
Nagaon	1,184,140	675,105	[illegible]9,035	62.28	68.52	55.57
Sonitpur	852,201	494,298	357,903	60.29	67.64	52.43
Lakhimpur	517,607	298,539	219,068	69.59	78.26	60.47
Dhemaji	313,511	184,856	128,655	65.96	75.15	56.11
Tinsukia	614,461	368,978	245,483	63.28	72.16	53.40
Dibrugarh	717,603	418,053	299,550	71.21	79.58	62.10
Sibsagar	685,949	389,242	296,707	75.33	82.08	68.00
Jorhat	689,414	384,685	304,729	77.91	82.76	72.54
Golaghat	568,250	327,692	240,558	70.36	73.01	62.07
Karbi Anglong	392,589	237,761	154,828	58.83	68.11	48.65
N. Cachar Hills	107,173	63,991	43,182	68.59	76.59	59.40
Cachar	835,888	481,106	354,782	68.42	76.51	59.85
Karimganj	559,512	317,584	241,928	67.21	73.87	60.09
Hailakandi	266,909	157,474	109,435	59.84	68.47	50.65

In this durations, the American Baptist Missionaries pioneered to open hospitals, orphanages and schools for boys and girls. Rev. Nathan Brown and Oliver Cutter started a school at Sadiya in 1837. Various schools had been established in many parts of the province. The people, particularly in Assam, were initially apathetic towards the medium of instruction both in schools as well as courts. On the other hand, the Christian Missionaries, while they tried to bring the gospel closer to the people, they disregarded the Government's language policy and pushed the people to educate themselves through their own mother-tongues. At the same time, there had also been a persistent demand for English education among the middle class motivating for government jobs. After restoring the position of Assamese language in 1873, the percentage of successful candidates had remarkably increased. Also, the Christian Missionaries like Mrs. Brown, Cutter, Robinson and Barker had initiated for setting up schools for girls. The first girls school was started at Sibsagar in 1840 and then at Nowgong and Gauhati consequently. However, many young girls of orthodox background had lost their privilege of attending schools and their social block had stood as obstacles to their freedom and progress.

The missionaries had tried their best efforts to face the prevailing situation and to encourage female education. They "went out into the highways and byways and sought the orphane and homeless". Even then, the response of the people was very poor. The importance of the western education included scientific knowledge which enabled the people to shed superstitions, magic power and sorcery for healing of sickness. The medical education had become popular among growing generation in spite of contempt for the caste-Hindus. The impact of the western education touched the grass-root of Caste-Hindu society and their way of life. The orthodox Brahmins began to send their sons and daughters to schools "having their half-cut in the English fashion and giving up the time-honoured custom of keeping a pig-tail."

(ii) Education of Girl Child. The female education brought forward new awareness of women status in society which had assumed great importance. Because of this awareness women could participate in the national struggle for freedom, shed the rigid forms of *sati* system and the prohibition of widow re-marriage. The liberal ideas received through the western education made women folk, particularly the upper class, to invite an open challenge to the societal attitude of men towards women. Some of them had realised that liberation of women from social prejudice was inseparable from the struggle for national liberty of India.

(iii) Financial Transformation in Assam. After establishing a stable Government the British turned their interest to economic policy in Assam. The British had taken over the trade and industries and the sources of communication system in the province. But due to prolonged uprising, internal dissensions and Burmese invasions Assam was impoverished.

When the British came to administer, they did not immediately start the land revenue measure but maintained the traditional system of 'paik' which was rendering of personal service to the state at the rate of Rs. 3 per head per annum. When this traditional system was not successful, the Government implemented the Revenue Regulation of 1880 and the revenue paying lands were settled with rayats' yearly till 1883. A thorough land survey was made and classified it for revenue assessment. Land was divided into basti, rupit and faringati and in 1838 the Mouzdari system was accepted for collection of revenue.

The lands were again divided into Devottar-lands (revenue-free known as Lakhiraj), Brahmottar-lands and Dharmottar-lands (half revenue paying popularly known as Nisfkhiraj), and other lands of full revenue paying (khiraj or Rayatwari). This new arrangement of land revenue system had affected the interest of the Ahom nobility and aristocracy. At the same time, the prestige and status of Ahoms were lowered down to the level of ordinary land owners.

The old rigid form of social distinction of the feudal sections and the ordinary people was removed. Meanwhile, the increase of land tax, the ban on poppy cultivation, and a permit for sale of opium from Government treasury on high prices were some of the issues of distress among the people. The cottage industries like textile, smiths and artisans were ruined and the country was flooded with the machinery textile products from Lancashire and England on lower rates. The indigenous industries were not encouraged and the prosperity of the country was greatly affected resulting in outbreaks of peasant's problems in various places in the province.

(iv) Internal Regulation. During the Ahom administration there was free intercourse between the people of the plains and the hill tribes in trades and commutation. But in 1873 the Inner Line Regulation Act was introduced to check the free accessibility of the British subjects to the hilly countries. Because of the unrestricted Ahom rule, there had been quarrels which sometimes caused serious disturbances. This was specially mentioned with the traffic in rubber brought down from the hills. In order to stop the recurrence of troublesome disputes with the frontier tribes in their vicinity a Regulation in 1873 had been adopted by the Government to prohibit British subjects generally from going ahead of a certain line, known as "Inner Line" which was not necessarily territorial line but "only the limits of the administered area".

For the first time the internal carved Inner Line Regulation was promulgated in Assam under the Statute 33 Vict. to empower the Executive government to deal with the backward areas. Regulation is distinguished from the Acts or laws enacted in the legislature. Under this Regulation the tea planters were not allowed to acquire land beyond the Inner line. Indirectly therefore this policy also influenced the national unity and integrity.

(v) Means of Communication and Transporation. The British felt the necessity of road-transport in the province from both commercial and defence points of consideration. The unchecked exploitation of industries, the exploration of coal mines and petroleum, the large scale of the plantation were prominant factors which were responsible for network growth of transport and communication lines. In 1842 the Assam Tea Company opened a steamboat service between Gauhati to Calcutta. After 1884 a direct service of steamers was made between Dibrugarh and Calcutta. From 1880 onward railways began to serve the Company's works. The Public Works Department started operating in 1868 for road construction and maintenance following which post and telegraph offices were established in different parts of the province.

Impact of Gandhi and his Movements in Assam

No state was left unaffected with movements of Gandhi, so was Assam. Here are some Gandhian efforts and ideas which made impact.

(i) Faith in Non-violence. Mahatma Gandhi had voiced for spontaneous upsurge of the people throughout the country into a single anti-British mass movement. He decided that the movement should be based on the principle of non-violence and he persuaded the Indian National Congress session held in Calcutta in September 1920 to adopt a resolution on Non-Cooperation with the alien Government. The object of the INC resolution was to attain Swarajya (self-rule) as interpreted by Gandhi as "self-government within the Empire if possible outside, if necessary." Initially, movement in Assam was commenced from the middle class, but quickly touched the entire peasantry and the working masses.

(ii) Communal Unity. The leaders of Assam started to organise a Hindu-Muslim unity movement. On March 19, 1920 a Khilafat meeting was convened at Gauhati to observe strike under the chairmanship of T.R. Phukan, but an unanimous decision could not be made. Later, on October 11 in the same year, members of the Assam Association had made unanimous decision to support Gandhiji's draft resolution on Non-cooperation.

The Assam Valley Muslim Association also supported the resolution. The Khilafatists were oathed to Swadeshi and worked for the unity of the Hindu-Muslim in the country against the British rule. Within a short time Non-cooperation became the leading theme of the movement in every household. To spread the idea of Non-Cooperation, leaders like N.C. Bardoloi, T.R. Phukan and Chandranath Sarma escorted by volunteers held meetings in several places in Assam Valley.

(iii) Famous Montague-Chelmsford Reforms 1918. The well-known reforms proposed by Montague and Chelmsford were published in July 1918. It was also popularly known as Montford Reforms. Mr. Edwin Montague was the Secretary of State of India and Lord Chelmsford was the Viceroy. In order to ascertain the public opinion of Indian masses, they visited different parts of the country meeting different political parties and delegations. In the proposed Montford Reforms certain political concessions had been made, but put down the popular demand for self-government.

The Montford Reforms created a mixed feeling among the Indian Nationals. In a special Congress session conducted at Bombay in August 1918 the Montague scheme was termed as "disappointing and unsatisfactory." Further the Congress demanded for self-government within the Empire or Swaraj like that of the U.K. In spite of different opinions between the moderate and the radical groups, the Reforms had been accepted for implementation. However, Annie Besant declared the reforms as "unworthy of England to offer and unworthy of India to accept." In November 1918, the Assam Association sent delegations led by N.C. Bardoloi to

Calcutta to put forth Assam's case before Montague for awarding the major provincial status.

In fact, Assam tacitly supported the Montford Reforms without reservation. On the other hand, due to other communal forces being played up against each other the question of inclusion of Assam in the scheme had become a mess. Meanwhile, the national patriotic feelings among the people of Assam was more vigorously pushed forward and plunged themselves wholeheartedly in the national struggle for freedom. They had joined the Non-Cooperation Movement started by the Congress under the leadership of Mahatma Gandhi.

(iv) Holding of Assam Chatra Sanmilan. The first session of the new Assam Chatra Sanmilan was held at Gauhati in 1916 under the presidentship of Lakshminath Bezbarua. The objective of the organisation was to announce their demands of measure for social development and reforms. Later many members of the Sanmilan became prominent during struggle for India's Independence. They were quite active in the Non-Cooperation Movement and identified themselves with the greater interest of the country. Their organisational activity had been expanded to the whole Assam forming the Surma Valley Students' Federation in 1926.

Since students had put their great assertion in favour of the movement they had to leave their studies for propagating the message of Non-cooperation to all sections of the people. During one of their meetings, shopkeepers were forced to make a bonfire of cigarettes to mark protest against the use of forced foreign goods.

(v) Civil Disobedience Satyagraha of 1929. In December 1929 in the Lahore session, the INC had launched a programme of Civil Disobedience declaring complete independence as its goal. The Congress had made decision to boycott the Simon Commission to be held in London in a Round Table Conference and demanded that India should be given a full Dominion Status. Consequently, the whole nation observed the Independence Day (now Republic Day) on January 26, 1930 till the independence was finally achieved. In Assam there was a mixed reaction about the outcome of the Lahore Congress. As expressed by veteran Congress leaders like T.R. Phukan, Bardoloi and B.K. Choudhury, Assam was not agreed to join the Civil Disobedience Movement. In the crisis of the Provincial Congress Office, Bishnu Ram Medhi came forward to accept the responsibility of the President of the APCC.

Certain enthusiasts like Md. Tayebulla, the General Secretary, Sidhinath Sarma, Ambikagiri, Hem Chandra Barua and Omeo Kumar Das conducted a fresh movement. Thus Assam was prepared to have mass Civil Disobedience Movement in the province. When the news of the arrest of Mahatma Gandhi and Jawaharlal Nehru reached Assam an intensified programming had been taken up both by school children and villagers by observing hartal and cease-work. In Surma valley a response came to the appeal for Civil Disobedience forming independent organisations like Sylhet District Congress Committee led by Brajendranarayan as the president and the Socialist Youth Conference led by Darikanath Goswami, a pupil of Murari Chand College. For the cause of the national freedom even women were not spared, they were dragged into imprisonment. The movement was liquefied on 4 March 1931, for some time.

(vi) The Latter Phase of Movement. In the absence of Gandhiji, the Government let loose its repressive measure on the movement. On the arrest of Jawaharlal Nehru and Khan Bahadur Khan the Working Committee of Indian National Congress had to resume the Civil Disobedience Movement on January 1, 1932. In response to the call of the movement, Assam Congressmen defied the repressive steps of the Government and thousands of people were arrested including 80 women. Subsequently, the Congressmen in Assam suffered due to oppressive and repressive measures taken by the English Government, even Congress offices were burned down. On hearing the news, the AICC led by Pandit Motilal Nehru, Pandit Madan Mohan Malviya and Dr. Rajendra Prasad came to Gauhati for spot investigation.

(vii) Impact in the Hills. In fact, Nagas as a whole were not very much affected by the Indian National Congress and the Muslim League movement because of the strained relations between the Assamese and the Nagas in spite of having been immediate neighbours. In between, the Zeliangrong Nagas living in Manipur, Cachar, North Cachar Hills and the Naga Hills got political inspirations from the plain people, who were fighting for their freedom guided by the Indian National Congress. The name of Mahatma Gandhi was spread out as a great freedom fighter. The visit of Mahatma Gandhi and the Congress session which took place at Pandu in December 1926 left a significant impact in many respects. It inspired the hill peoples to follow the movement for national independence.

(viii) Jadonnang and Freedom Struggle. The news of Indian freedom movement was spread rampant in the Surma and the Brahmaputra valleys, when the presence and integrity of the Zeliangrong Nagas were threatened by the invasion of British as well as the infiltration of Kukis from outside into the hills. Jadonnang emerged as a committed 'Messiah' for the Nagas. He organised some trusted followers including Gaidinliu to establish Naga Raj and to spread the ideology of his movement for independence. Jadonnang did not have a direct link with the INC, but its activities inspired by him to launch a political movement independently.

The first contact he made with the plain people, e.g., Manipuris and Bengalis was very disgusting because they called the Nagas uncivilised and untouchable, and did not allow them to mix with the Hindus. Jadonnang also felt that the spread of Christianity was the policy of the British raj to denounce the tribal religion. He was arrested on February 19, 1931 at Jirighat in Cachar on false allegations of assassination of two Manipuri travellers. Jadonnang was tied and taken to villages and towns to demonstrate to the people that their leader was captured. He was kept in the Imphal jail for more than two months and hanged publicly on Saturday, 29 August 1931 at 6 a.m. on the bank of Nambul river. The last words before he stopped were, "I have done nothing wrong to anybody, whatever I had thought and done was for the cause of my people."

(ix) The Movement of Rani Gaidinliu. The expiry of Jadonnang was not the end of the movement. The leadership of freedom movement had passed to Rani Gaidinliu, who became the spiritual and political heir of Jadonnang. Like Jadonnang her cousine, Rani Gaidinliu also urged the people to stop payment of house-tax to the British Government. At this moment, Non-Cooperation and Civil Disobedience Movement was launched in full swing throughout the country. She knew well that violence would not respond against the mighty forces of the British. By any means, she had to adopt a method of propaganda saying, "Nagas are free people, the alien pale-race (the British) had no right to rule over us".

She told the people that this pale-race would leave the Naga country sooner or later. She appealed to all the Zeliangrong people not to bow before the British rule. When the British saw the gaining momentum under the leadership of Gaidinliu, she was declared as a "wanted woman" by the Deputy Commissioner of the Naga Hills of Assam State on a deliberate charge of murder, and a warrant was served for her arrest. The Assam Government ordered for the military punitive operation against Gaidinliu.

For three consecutive months desperately, the detachments of Assam Rifles were pursuing her and her party. Finally, an encounter occurred at Hangrum village in North Cachar Hills on February 16, 1932 between the sepoys and Gaidinliu's followers.

In that encounter some persons were killed and entire village was burnt down including paddy granaries so that the people might not get shelter any more. She had escaped and could not be traced out. On March 2, 1932 the Government of Assam gave another report to the Government of India that the escape of Gaidinliu had signalled a grave danger of mass outbreak in Naga Hills, Manipur and North Cachar Hills. As an outcome of the report, the Government was determined to take every possible step for capturing her alive or dead and nib the movement in the bud. To take hold of Gaidinliu was now not as easy as that of Jadonnang. The hunt was very expensive, to quote Ursula Graham Bower, it was "something almost comparable to the hunt for Prince Charlie".

The state Governor-in-Council had sanctioned a large scale operations for the capture of Gaidinliu and her followers. J.P. Mills, ICS the Deputy Commissioner of the Naga Hills District was entrusted to conduct the operation with the 3rd and 4th Assam Rifles. Captain Macdonald, the Commandant of the 3rd Assam Rifles had worked out an elaborate plan to meet the objective. He arranged a column of one hundred Rifles and one hundred Naga, Kuki and Napalese porters from Kohima to proceed to Pulomei village as per the secret report.

On October 18, 1932 she was arrested after frantic search and dismantling houses. Then she was sent for life imprisonment at Nowgong jail and some other places. The arrest and life imprisonment could not bring the movement to an end. The movement was again revived by her followers like Dikeo, Masang, and Haidua of Jengpa village in Tamenglong area of Manipur. Haidua claimed to be the priest who succeeded Gaidinliu. He also preached not to pay house-tax to the British

Government, and not to serve as officials' coolies. It was a kind of Non-Cooperation Movement.

For this cause, he was arrested in May 1932 by the Assam Rifles. After long imprisonment and torture Haidua was released, but shortly after his release he took his last breath. The Assam government put its oppressive and violent hands on the Zeliangrong people, yet the movement had died hard to keep alive the ideals of Jadonnang and Gaidinliu. A number of follow up leaders were either arrested or shot dead. As a precautionary measure to keep under control any uprising or revivals of the movement a bold outpost was maintained at Henima in the Zeliangrong area.

(x) 1942 Movement. The advancement of Japanese forces toward the frontiers of India through Burma caused a mixed feeling among the National leaders of Congress. At this time, the British Government sent Sir Stafford Cripps to India on a conciliatory gesture. He repeatedly offered the proposal in August 1940 for main changes in the constitution. The mission failed because the Congress as well as the Muslim League had refused to accept the offer, resulted in intensified hostility for the British.

At the same time, confusion held sway among leaders like Subhas Chandra Bose, Jawaharlal Nehru and Abul Kalam Azad because of the rapid advancement of the Japanese forces. Abul Kalam Azad recommended that India should resist the Japanese movement and that a non-violent movement was impracticable at that situation. When INC looked to Gandhiji for his opinion, he concluded that so long as the British domination persisted, the internal problem of India would not be solved. The British must quit India.

On August 8, 1942, the Congress accepted resolution on 'Quit India' which led to the mass civil disobedience throughout the country. In Assam, within a week of announcement of the 'Quit India' Resolution, many important leaders like Md. Tayebullah, G.N. Bardoloi and others who took part in the movement were arrested. The people of Assam had to defy the creed of non-violence and many lost their lives before armed atrocities. In many places like Dhekiajuli, Gahpur and Chaiduar thousands of people marched to the Police stations to hoist the Congress flag and the demonstrators were shot down. In the Surma valley people had responded to the INC's appeal and the Congress workers formed a war-council. The arrest of the top Congress leaders and assassination of the demonstrators could not change the course of the movement. There were leaders among the youths and students who played active role both in open and as underground. They carried on the struggle for independence unabated. About this time, Assam witnessed a new era of pressure when the *Azad Hind Fauj* or Indian National Army (INA) led by Subhas Chandra Bose appeared on the eastern region into Manipur and Naga Hills in March 1944.

Heavy fighting occurred at Imphal, Kohima and elsewhere. However, the British Government suppressed both the 'Quit India' and 'Azad Hind Fauj'. But at the end of the Second World War, one more revolution spread in the navy and the armed forces.

(xi) Attainment of India Freedom and Partitions. At last, the British had to recognise the right of India to freedom. The British had agreed to transfer power to the Indians. A British Cabinet Mission was sent to India in 1946 for a dialogue with the Indian leaders. At last, in the midnight of the 14th August 1947, Mountbatten, the Viceroy, on behalf of the British Government, declared India's freedom. Jawaharlal Nehru expressed precisely, "At the stroke of midnight hour, when the world sleeps, India will awake to life and freedom . . ."

Still, the declaration of Indian Independence was followed by the division of the country. The Muslim League had carved out their separate independent country forming West Pakistan and East Pakistan from India. State of Assam had to receive fresh immigration or refugees due to partition of the country. Just after Independence, Lokapriya Gopinath Bardoloi took over as the first Chief Minister, when Sir Akbar Hydari took over as the first Governor of Assam in 1947. Thus the long cherished hope of the Assamese people had been fulfilled. But the unexpected death of Mahatma Gandhi on 30 January 1948 was not only a great shock to the nation but also an irreparable loss to Assam as the Mahatma had a soft corner for Assam and was a means of inspiration to the people in particular.

References

1. *Encyclopaedia Britannica,* 15th edition, Knowledge in Depth, Volume 2, p. 307.
2. Dr. H.K. Barpujari, *Assam: In the Days of Company,* Gauhati, Lawyer's Book Stall, 1963, pp. 264-265.
3. Amalendu Guha, *Planter-Raj to Swaraj: Freedom Struggle and Electoral Politics in Assam 1826-1947,* Indian Council of Historical Research, 35 Ferozeshah Road, New Delhi—110 001, 1977, p. 35.
4. *Ibid.,* p. 167.
5. M.V. Kamath, "Neglected Assam", *The Illustrated Weekly of India,* Bombay, January 20, 1980.

2

Assam in Post-1947 Period

We have already seen that pre-independence development made great impact upon Assam also but post-independence period is even more important since it shaped statehood of Assam.

Problems after Partition: Inflow of Refugees

India was declared Independent on 15 August, 1947. With the declaration of independence, the immediate problem was the carving out of Sylhet district from Assam, which opted for East Pakistan. Following the partition of the country, thousands of refugees had flown into Assam from East Pakistan (now Bangladesh). To deal with this heavy pouring of refugees, the National Government passed the Immigration Act on 13 February 1950 and authorised the Assam Government to expel all non-bonafide immigrants from Assam. Moreover, the Indo-Pak Agreement of 8 May 1950 for rehabilitation of the refugees even more than two lakhs compelled Assam Government to allot about one and a half lakh *bighas* of land.

(a) Difficulties of Immigrants. The large number of immigrants became a serious threat to Assamese people culturally, politically and economically. Over and above, a communal tension started to hatch resulting in about a lakh of Muslim refugees quitting Assam to East Pakistan in 1950. Very soon a large number of educated immigrants managed to get jobs in Government offices, and a number of them were also settling in both rural and urban areas. As a result, more than ten thousand indigenous inhabitants became landless.

With the dawn of independence, Assam has been passing through severe economic crises due to the industrial strikes, peasants struggle like that of the pre-independence, natural calamities like the great earthquake of 1950 and natural disaster like floods that have been more frequent and devastating.

(b) Fresh Planning for National Development. In 1950 the Planning Commission was formed to plan out for utilisation of resources to raise the standard of living and national income. Various improvement measures and schemes have been launched such as Panchayat and Cooperative Societies, industries, and trade and commerce have been established. A new Opium Prohibition Act for solution of illicit trade in opium, and the Assam Adhiar Protection and Regulation Act for recognising the rights of tenants to land were passed in 1948. The road-transport was nationalised.

The state level court at Guwahati, technical colleges like Medical College at

Dibrugarh, Veterinary College at Gauhati, Agriculture College at Jorhat and the Gauhati University were established. The Plantation Labour Act was also enacted in 1951 for certain welfare measures in favour of the tea garden labourers.

Disintegration of States. After the reorganisation of the states, the Union Government declared that there would be no further disintegration of states. But under special circumstances Assam was to be conferred a special consideration for the general aspirations of the hill people. A Hill Sub-Committee was formed led by G.N. Bardoloi as Chairman in 1948. This Committee paved the way for the hill people to perform their own affairs according to their social customs and life. Accordingly, a large amount of autonomy was granted to the hill people according to the Sixth Sçhedule of the Indian Constitution in the form of the District Councils. But the Nagas were isolated from this scope because of their ambitious movement for full independence of Nagaland.

(d) Emergence of Nagaland. The Nagas asked for an independent Nagaland both outside Assam and the Indian Union. The Naga National Council would not agree to anything less than total independence. The NNC declared the independence of Nagaland on 14 August 1947. They had brought out a journal *The Naga Nation* as an official part to draw the attention of the general public. They also boycotted the first general election of India. While Jawaharlal Nehru had himself supported the cause of Nagaland for self-determination in 1944 he oft-quoted to the NNC, "It is obvious that Naga territory in eastern Assam is too small to stand by itself politically and economically".

In 1953, when the Nagas rose in arms and set a parallel government underground, the Central Government let loose armed forces to crush the movement immediately with a strong hand. In fact, in the month of June 1947, the British India Government represented by Sir Akbar Hydari, the Governor of Assam, entered into an agreement with the NNC to take a special job for a period of ten years interim and at the end of this period the Nagas would be free to decide for their future. Unfortunately the Indian Government had bypassed various provisions of agreement. However, a section of Nagas formed the All Tribes Naga Peoples' Convention and demanded for an Administrative Unit consisting of the three districts of Kohima, Tuensang, and Mokokchung. In 1960, the Naga Peoples' Convention (NPC) led by Dr. Imkongliba Ao, the President of the Convention and the Central Government, after the sequence of talks, reached an agreement for granting the state of Nagaland and to place it under the Ministry of External Affairs. Thus, the Naga Hills District was separated from State of Assam and became a full-fledged state in 1963. However, the NNC, who formed the Federal Government of Nagaland (underground) continued to fight for their full independence.

(e) Re-organisation of the State of Assam. On 13 January 1967, the Union Government had decided to recognise the state of Assam. On this decision Assam leaders felt that it was not mere reorganisation of Assam nor division but destruction of Assam. The proposal of the Central Government was to break up Assam into various units and unite them into a federation. However, there were widespread protests against such decision on Assam as undemocratic and unconstitutional. The All Party Hill Leaders Conference (APHLC), however has been demanding a separate State within the Indian Union so that they can enjoy full scope of developing their language and culture.

In this context, the Prime Minister Indira Gandhi explained to some delegations that there would be more than one unit in the Hills as well as more than one unit in the Plains. Consequential demand for independent units of Cachar, Tai Ahom and the Kamatapur Plain Tribal lands came into picture. In 1970, the Khasi-Jaintia and the Garo Hills were separated from Assam and formed into single State called *Meghalaya,* (the abode of clouds) and Shillong became its capital. In 1972, the North East Frontier Agency (NEFA) now known as *Arunachal Pradesh* (Land of Sunrise) earned the status of a Union Territory. In March 1966, the Mizo National Front led by Laldenga demanded an independent Mizoram or 'Chinland' consisting Mizo-Chin areas of India, Pakistan and Burma. However, the armed revolt was suppressed by the Indian army. Then Mizoram became union territory along with the organisation of Tripura and Manipur as states.

Thus, the North Cachar Hills and Karbi Anglong (Mikir Hills) remained within the State of Assam. For the factors of constituting federation and the departure of various Hill districts to form separate States, there was widespread agitation in Assam against the declaration of 13 January 1967 and the Home Minister, Sri Chavan was about to come to Gauhati for meeting with the representatives as well as political leaders.

In this meeting APHLC did not participate as mark of protest. All the nascent States and Union Territories namely Assam, Manipur, Nagaland, Meghalaya, Mizoram, Tripura, and Arunachal Pradesh were placed under the North Eastern Council in August 1972 for common uniform development plans and the Council was inaugurated by the Prime Minister, Mrs. Indira Gandhi on 8 November in the same year.

Targets under the Five Year Plans

(i) Introducing Five Year Plan. For this, the Planning Commission was asked to draw up the Colombo Plan for India. The Commission was also asked to formulate integrated Five Year Plans termed as quinquennial plans. In the year 1951, the First Five Year Plan was launched in Assam along with the rest of India. It envisaged for developing the economic condition of the country such as increased food productions and evolution in agriculture, to control inflation, to build up an economic infrastructure, and to build up administrative and other organisations for carrying out plans for future development. A sum of Rs. 420 crore had been spent during the plan period. Many new roads and bridges were constructed and improved in the state. The plan started from the first April 1950 and ended on the 31st March 1956.

(ii) Five Year Plan from 1956-61. The next Five Year Plan came into effect on first April 1956, which emphasised on the industrialisation of Assam. The most important achievement during this plan was the bridge above the Brahmaputra near Pandu which opened in 1960 and the establishment of an Oil Refinery at Noonmati near Gauhati. The census data of various types of working industries (statewise and districtwise) are as follows :

Table 1
The Survey of Main Workers, Marginal Workers and Non-Workers (Statewise): Census 2001

Total Rural Urban	*Persons Males Females*	*Total Workers*	*Main Workers*	*Marginal Workers*	*Non-Workers*	*Total Workers (main + marginal)*
Total	Persons	9,557,064	7,083,046	2,474,018	17,081,343	9,557,064
	Males	6,884,451	5,839,050	1,045,401	6,903,348	6,884,451
	Females	2,672,613	1,243,996	1,428,617	10,177,995	2,672,613
Rural	Persons	8,473,127	6,078,938	2,394,189	14,775,867	8,473,127
	Males	5,963,601	4,968,101	995,500	6,019,556	5,963,601
	Females	2,509,526	1,110,837	1,398,689	8,756,311	2,509,526
Urban	Persons	1,083,937	1,004,108	79,829	2,305,476	1,083,937
	Males	920,850	870,949	49,901	883,792	920,850
	Females	163,087	133,159	29,928	1,421,684	163,087

Since the basic principle of the plan was to enter the 'take-off' stage setting up a socialistic pattern of society, there had been tremendous effort for pushing ahead to its goal. In Assam all the defunct cooperative societies were once revived in 1958 and during the plan period more than two thousand Co-operative Societies and thirty one Co-operative Credit Societies were set up. One of the leading achievements was the Umium-Umtru Hydro-Electric project which was opened in 1960 under the auspices of the Assam Electricity Board. A jute mill, a cement factory, a paper pulp mill and a sugar mill were set-up. Many technical schools and colleges like Engineering College at Gauhati, Medical Colleges at Gauhati and Silchar were opened in 1960-61. Besides, several bills concerning to occupancy of land were passed and enforced land ceiling act to meet the need of the general people. Many other developmental works had been implemented successfully during the Second Five Year Plan.

(iii) Five Year Plan of April 1961 to 31 March 1966. Underlying principle of Third Five Year Plan was to take up an intensive development programme leading to self-reliance and self-sufficiency in economy. Despite envisaged plan there had been no corresponding growth in trade/industries in the State, and on the other hand a problem of unemployed youth rose suddenly. Only very few polytechnics training centres and a regional Engineering College and also an institute at Silchar and Gauhati were set up. The development programme in Assam was not satisfactory. After completion of the three quinquennial plans, there were

Table 2

The Survey of Main Workers, Marginal Workers and Non-Workers (Districtwise) : Census 2001 (Districtwise) : Census 2001

District	Total Workers			Main Workers			Marginal Workers			Non Workers		
	P	M	F	P	M	F	P	M	F	P	M	F
Kokrajhar	345,586	231,316	114,270	242,062	190,258	51,804	103,524	41,058	62,466	584,818	246,926	337,892
Dhubri	471,941	408,148	63,793	400,030	367,124	32,906	71,911	41,024	30,887	1,162,648	432,525	730,123
Goalpara	274,150	203,679	70,471	208,844	178,564	30,280	65,306	25,115	40,191	548,156	217,028	331,128
Bongaigaon	294,184	227,125	67,059	233,168	202,008	31,160	61,016	25,117	35,899	612,131	238,845	373,286
Barpeta	516,108	404,536	111,572	408,464	363,083	45,381	107,644	41,453	66,191	1,126,312	441,570	684,742
Kamrup	821,144	645,695	175,449	672,549	576,785	95,764	148,595	68,910	79,685	1,693,886	682,022	1,011,864
Nalbari	383,594	284,102	99,492	287,618	243,554	44,064	95,976	40,548	55,428	754,590	303,566	451,024
Darrang	541,543	390,003	151,540	405,878	346,462	59,416	135,665	43,541	92,124	962,400	383,979	578,421
Marigaon	263,238	201,696	61,542	199,703	177,798	21,905	63,535	23,898	39,637	512,636	197,234	315,402
Nagaon	726,952	589,715	137,237	562,947	503,386	59,561	164,005	86,329	77,676	1,588,435	604,612	983,823
Sonitpur	631,663	433,570	198,093	462,880	367,187	95,693	168,783	66,383	102,400	1,046,211	430,555	615,656
Lakhimpur	499,245	282,888	216,357	287,817	205,537	82,280	211,428	77,351	134,077	390,080	172,801	217,279
Dhemaji	252,507	147,316	105,191	156,255	112,562	43,693	96,252	34,754	61,498	316,961	146,789	170,172
Tinsukia	468,952	305,182	163,770	351,131	253,396	97,735	117,821	51,786	66,035	681,194	297,333	383,861
Dibrugarh	473,233	307,795	165,438	339,419	251,365	88,054	133,814	56,430	77,384	698,823	301,675	397,148
Sibsagar	430,277	280,348	149,929	287,162	218,736	68,426	143,115	61,612	81,503	622,525	266,217	356,308
Jorhat	419,816	279,040	140,776	287,509	223,375	64,134	132,307	55,665	76,642	589,381	251,200	338,181
Golaghat	393,215	252,502	140,713	270,279	206,423	63,856	122,936	46,079	76,857	552,566	237,868	314,698
Karbi Anglong	329,595	207,149	122,446	229,390	172,764	56,626	100,205	34,385	65,820	482,725	215,450	267,275
North Cachar Hills	69,892	48,582	21,310	54,546	43,021	11,525	15,346	5,561	9,785	116,297	50,317	65,980
Cachar	464,022	368,990	95,032	363,006	310,323	52,683	101,016	58,667	42,349	978,119	372,590	605,529
Karimganj	305,224	247,461	57,763	234,427	208,609	25,818	70,797	38,852	31,945	698,454	268,947	429,507
Hailakandi	180,983	137,613	43,370	137,962	116,730	21,232	43,021	20,883	22,138	361,995	143,299	218,696

then three One-year plans (April 1966 to March 1969). This period was known as 'a Plan Holiday' which had separate annual plans having no continuation of any fresh objectives and special strategies. Agricultural and farming functions and including labourers and other workers (statewise) are given below :

Table 3
Agricultural and Farming Functions and Including Labourers and Other Workers (Statewise) : Census 2001

Total/ Rural/ Urban	Persons/ Males/ Females	Cultivators Labourers	Agricultural Industry Workers	Household Workers	Other
Total	Persons	3,741,912	1,289,902	328,541	4,196,709
	Males	2,661,619	849,434	117,647	3,255,751
	Females	1,080,293	440,468	210,894	940,958
Rural	Persons	3,722,180	1,280,776	300,014	3,170,157
	Males	2,645,554	843,146	100,794	2,374,107
	Females	1,076,626	437,630	199,220	796,050
Urban	Persons	19,732	9,126	28,527	1,026,552
	Males	16,065	6,288	16,853	881,644
	Females	3,667	2,838	11,674	144,908

A plan-gap was felt necessary to regenerate the confidence of the people because during the Third Five Year Plans the curses of the Indo-Chinese War of 1962 and the Indo-Pak War of 1965-66 had done huge damage. One of the notable programmes was the introduction of the Green Revolution, the new agricultural strategy. For the development of the hill districts a separate Committee was formulated. In Assam, 1823 miles of roads connecting the hills with the plains were nationalised and air-fields were also constructed at NEFA, Manipur and Nagaland. In the year 1968, the Agricultural University was set up at Jorhat.

This particular plan was followed by more five-year plans: the Fifth and the Sixth (The Janata Government's Sixth) Plan operated for two years only from April 1979 to March 1981. The next Sixth Five Year Plan was carried on in the hand of the Cong-I Government from April 1981 to March 1985. Thus the planning era has completed by March 31, 1985.

(iv) War for Formation of Bangladesh. The Independence War of Bangladesh of 1971-72 from Pak had been a great setback to the economy of Assam. After signing of the 'Treaty of Friendship, Co-operation and Peace' at Dacca between the Indian Prime Minister, Mrs. Indira Gandhi and Prime Minister of Bangladesh Sheikh Mujibur Rahman, several lakhs of Bengali immigrants poured into Assam. In fact, Assam hailed with joy on the victory of Bangladesh independence but in the aftermoath of the war a few Bangladesh nationals returned home.

As a result Assam had to raise the issue of foreigners, and it was first raised by the All Assam Students Union in 1974 against deporting all the foreign nationals.

Table 4
Agricultural and Farming Functions and Including Labourers and Other Workers

District	Cultivators			Agricultural Labourers			Household Industries			Other Workers		
	P	M	F	P	M	F	P	M	F	P	M	F
Senapati	144,192	75,093	69,099	13,857	6,558	7,299	5,343	1,671	3,672	25,871	17,812	8,059
Kokrajhar	146,992	99,340	47,652	79,866	48,838	31,028	11,316	4,746	6,570	107,412	78,392	29,020
Dhubri	175,104	158,269	16,835	112,356	94,347	18,009	16,879	10,202	6,677	167,602	145,330	22,272
Goalpara	100,492	78,532	21,960	50,370	32,708	17,662	12,536	3,871	8,665	110,752	88,568	22,184
Bongaigaon	113,558	87,815	25,743	52,794	34,597	18,197	8,312	3,630	4,682	119,520	101,083	18,437
Barpeta	209,863	177,196	32,667	83,668	61,149	22,519	27,229	9,690	17,539	195,348	156,501	38,847
Kamrup	205,324	168,918	36,406	77,400	50,107	27,293	44,610	14,972	29,638	493,810	411,698	82,112
Nalbari	141,586	109,101	32,485	56,154	35,164	20,990	21,142	5,581	15,561	164,712	134,256	30,456
Darrang	246,522	186,639	59,883	85,936	54,679	31,257	15,956	5,125	10,831	193,129	143,560	49,569
Marigaon	138,368	109,945	28,423	53,391	36,295	17,096	7,781	1,982	5,799	63,698	53,474	10,224
Nagaon	278,086	233,697	44,389	146,763	116,687	30,076	23,513	9,550	13,963	278,590	229,781	48,809
Sonitpur	211,927	151,926	60,001	84,466	46,317	38,149	17,110	6,665	10,445	318,160	228,662	89,498
Lakhimpur	339,236	175,763	163,473	35,715	16,938	18,777	11,290	3,108	8,182	113,004	87,079	25,925
Dhemaji	184,276	102,669	81,607	20,100	8,666	11,434	5,598	1,319	4,279	42,533	34,662	7,871
Tinsukia	146,339	84,147	62,192	29,066	15,226	13,840	7,264	3,565	3,699	286,283	202,244	84,039
Dibrugarh	137,486	80,668	56,818	37,419	18,986	18,433	11,490	3,789	7,701	286,838	204,352	82,486
Sibsagar	155,222	90,618	64,604	30,918	15,817	15,101	11,910	4,413	7,497	232,227	169,500	62,727
Jorhat	157,426	93,379	64,047	33,794	16,973	16,821	16,969	5,752	11,217	211,627	162,936	48,691
Golaghat	183,873	115,100	68,773	42,135	20,457	21,678	10,366	3,353	7,013	156,841	113,592	43,249
Karbi Anglong	195,323	124,805	70,518	45,970	20,549	25,421	10,931	2,404	8,527	77,371	59,391	17,980
North Cachar Hills	34,509	21,077	13,432	3,600	1,980	1,620	1,480	387	1,093	30,303	25,138	5,165
Cachar	103,985	91,295	12,690	55,769	46,179	9,590	15,565	7,141	8,424	288,703	224,375	64,328
Karimganj	73,598	67,822	5,776	46,267	37,450	8,817	14,013	4,728	9,285	171,346	137,461	33,885
Hailakandi	62,817	52,898	9,919	25,985	19,325	6,660	5,281	1,674	3,607	86,900	63,716	23,184

Many problems such as socio-economy, slow progress of industries, scarcity of land in the State and serious threat of unemployment and alarming level of corruption in all social strata had been cropping up unabated. There was a sharp decline of the agricultural products. The condition of the tenants was pitiable, and the Land Ceiling Act failed to solve the problem of illegal possession of surplus lands over eighty thousands hectares. The State could see a large number of farmers become wage-earners or even beggars. Thus, to conclude, if on one side, war brought freedom to Bangladeshis, on the other hand, it also brought lot of destruction for them as well as remaining Pakistan and ultimately it affected the economy of the State of Assam also.

ASU Movement from 1979-85

(i) Subject of Foreign Nationals. Assam has been passing through the difficult years of political turmoil and instability for the last two decades. It was not a fresh thing that the student community directly participated in the mass movement since Independence. They intermittently played a leading role in several movements whenever situation asked for. From the 19th century onwards, there has been a clear trace of steady influx of immigrants from Bengal into Assam, and because of heavy influx of foreign nationals there have been numerous occasions of trouble and clashes between Bengalis and Assamese. The issue of expulsion of the foreign nationals has become a heating point of struggle of the Assamese people for their own survival.

On the other hand, the struggle for power among the political parties like Cong-I, Janata, CPI-M, etc., had also encouraged the unchecked flow of the foreigners into the State. Seeing the helpless situation in Assam that has turned from bad to worse, the All Assam Students Union (AASU) spear-headed to raise their sixteen point charter of demands in July 1978. Among the major points of their demands was for expulsion of all foreign nationals. The students Union put forward a formula so called 'three Ds' . . . which are detection, deletion and deportation with immediate effect; other points of their demands were checking of price-rise, better employment opportunities to local citizens, release of illegal confinement of political prisoners also. They resorted to non-violent methods like picketing, satyagraha, hunger-strike and bandhs throughout the State. There was tremendous response from all walks of life to the appeal of the AASU right from the beginning of the movement.

(ii) Success and the Downfall. From Independence the Congress had been in power in Assam till 1978 without any interruption. But the Congress lost in the Assembly Election of 1978. Janata Party came to power in the Assembly under Golap Borbora, and the short-survived Assam Janata Dal (AJD) with J.N. Hazarika as a leader. But the Ministry collapsed soon and Assam was put under the President's rule for a quite long period, then a short-lived of Congress Ministry too headed by Mrs. S.A. Taimur and another period of the President's rule before a second short-lived of Congress Ministry headed by K.C. Gogoi.

Very fast, another President's rule came to hold the fort. The total period of the President's rule in Assam was 26 months all together during agitation. The mini-general elections for the Assam Assembly took place in February 1978. In the polling to the 126 Assam assembly seats, the Janata won by 53 and compelled the Congress-U Ministry led by S.C. Sinha to resign and leave the chair. Then a Janata Ministry headed by Golap Borbora came to power on the 12th March 1978. The Ministry was supported by the Plains Tribal Council of Assam (PTCA), the CPI-M, and also the Independent group so-called Popular Democratic Front (PDF). Unfortunately the days of the Janata Government in the Centre as well as in the states were numbered.

The split, of course, came again. An uncertainty came to Janata Ministry in Assam. On the 22 June, the Janata Parliamentary Board directed the Chief Minister to reorganise of the Ministry for reconstitution in the Assembly. In fact, Mr. Golap Borbora was not willing to drop any member of the ministry, rather he would prefer to expand it. But he had to abide as per the instruction of the High Command of the party.

Perhaps, the question of the foreigners issue was one of the causes of the reshuffling and that eventually led to the failure of the Janata Government in the State. In July 1979, some Cabinet Ministers had resigned and a group of Janata MLAs too had withdrew support to the Borbora Ministry. On the 11th August four members of the PTCA including the PDF withdrew support from the Ministry. When the Janata Party in Assam was supporting the Charan Singh faction, the dissidents charged that Mr. Borbora was too secular. The whole mess in the Janata Party in Assam was at best mere prelude to the anti-foreign movement.

(iii) Updating of Rolls for Mangaldai. The real agitation started in the first half of 1979 when the Election Commission began to update the Mangaldai parliamentary constituency electoral rolls. While following the process of checking, deleting and adding the names of new arrival, complaints came to the electoral officers alleging that a number of aliens had been included on the voters' lists illegally. Within a short duration as many as 70,000 complaints were registered. The tricky question which disturbed the minds of responsible Assamese was that, if the Election Commission, after a sincere scrutiny of the objections, upheld 64.28 per ccnt of the charges, and if this was the case in a single constituency, was about the rest of the 13 constituencies? The first organisation to take lead in that situation was the All Assam Students Union (AASU) supported by a number of regional parties like Jatiyatabadi Dal, the Purbanchalya Lok Parishad, and the Asom Shitya Sabha.

In the year 1979, the All Assam Gana Sangram Parishad was formed better known as AAGSP consisting of AASU, ASS, PLP, and later the Jatyabadi Dal known as JD, the Asom Jatiyabadi Yuba Chatra Parishad (AJYCP), the Asom Yuva Samaj (AYS), and the Young Lawyers' Forum (YLF) also joined the composite new organisation AAGSP. The student leaders then took up the foreigners issue as a nationalist and patriotic duty with sincerity and dedication in the interest of national unity and integrity. They studied the problems in depth before they set the matter in challenge.

They made sure that they were on solid ground, legal and constitutional. Meanwhile, there were many objections from the various political parties about the style of revision of the electoral rolls being done, and the final Electoral Rolls for the bye-election were never published because of the arrangements for all bye-elections to the Central Lok Sabha being cancelled on the 22nd August. The AASU leaders namely Prafulla Mahanta (24), the President, Brigu Phukan (22), the General Secretary, and also Bharat Norah (20), the Assistant Secretary called a meeting of all the organisations which supported their demands for removing the aliens and revision of the electoral rolls with a view to make the agitation broader-based.

When Phukan was arrested, both Mahanta and Norah, the Acting General Secretary, went "underground" to evade detention. They continued to release joint statements urging the people to put greater efforts and condemn the government's attitude towards the movement or the people would assert a fresh plan of mass agitation. Committed efforts and the patriotic movement of the young people have touched the depth of feelings and stirred the hearts of Assamese women.

Another Mr. Lalit Rajkhowa and K.N. Sharma were chief advisers to AASU. The student leaders' general conducts were praiseworthy. When they went to New Delhi for talks with Mrs. Gandhi and her colleagues, the Government offered them to live in a five-star hotel to stay on free. But they turned down the offer, instead they would stay together at Assam House. Again the Government wished to put cars at their (leaders) disposal for pleasure trips to different places, but they rejected saying that they had come "for business, not for pleasure." These are good examples for all political leaders also.

(iv) Severe Step of Agitation. The State Government met all the representatives of the movement leaders and urged them to give time to the Government to settle the issue and requested not to resort to fresh agitation so that the foreigners issue could be solved through constitutional and judicial procedure. But the efforts of the political leaders were unsuccessful. The AASU-AGSP had prepared a full programme of mass-picketing in front of all Central and the State Government establishments in Assam for a four-day agitation with effect from the 19th November 1979.

They put forth their demands for immediate deportation of foreign nationals and deletion of their names from the electoral rolls. This phase of satyagraha had kept whole people in enigma. The Central Government offices, banks and many other establishments throughout Assam remained closed and deserted; life of cities and towns got paralysed. The Government banned processions and alerted army in many parts of the Brahmaputra valley. The picketing was so exciting and enthusiastic that the bulk of officers and staff abstained from duties. Government employees defied threats of suspension and transfers, coming out to join hands with the mass movement in their hundreds.

The agitation was initially peaceful but on the 20th November, there were clashes between a large number of Bengalis some of whom supported and other did not favour the movement. There were also cases of stabbing and stray incidents of assault and intimidation in several parts of the State. The election was drawing closer and time was running short because the last date for filing nominations was scheduled on the 10th December. On the other hand, there were instructions of the Government that the machinery should accept passports even without individual's photographs.

As a result, there were plenty of such forged passports detected. The Assamese people felt that they might be cut down to minority by Bengali immigrants like in Tripura where the local tribal inhabitants have been reduced to that state. The fact was that Marxist Government of West Bengal and Tripura had granted citizenship certificates to the recent influx of Bangladesh nationals into Assam. To this mounting problem, the AASU-AGSP made a fateful decision to step up a further agitational programme to give a new thrust and meaning to the movement. They called on responsible citizens to boycott the elections and not to participate because there would be no free and fair elections since the voter lists were fraudulent and needed revision.

According to the Newspaper the number of foreigners on the electoral rolls varied from 5,00,000 to 25,00,000. There was also an indication that if the agitation failed to achieve its ends, there might be a possibility of setting up a parallel Government in the State of Assam by referring back to 1826 and form an independence Sovereign Republic of Assam by reunification of all the frontier States of North-eastern India.

(v) Arrangements for Mid-term Polls. Inspite of representations and memorandum submitted to the President of India, the Central Government and the Election Commission had gone ahead with the preparation for conducting mid-term polls for Lok Sabha in Assam. The students organisations had to oppose it in every possible manner to stop the election. But Dev Kanta Barooah, the ex-Congress President, Begum Abida Ahmed, widow of the late President F.A. Ahmed, and Nihar Laskar were adamant.

The worst things came up when these personalities refused to concede to the protest and they were ready to file their nomination papers. On December 10, thousands defied the curfew orders and marched to the Circuit House at Nowgong at which the Congress leader was staying and he was unable to file his papers. In the case of Begum Abida, things turned a different shape. A strong police contingent and also the paramilitary Central Reserve Police Force escorted her to Barpeta for filing her nomination papers. But it was hurriedly done, her papers were found not in order. Thus, the returning officers rejected her nomination. On the way to Barpeta, CRP clashed with demonstrators and as an outcome, in Bhabanipur, a 20-year-old leader Khargeswar Talukdar was beaten to death by the CRP. In Cachar, Laskar and S.M. Deb, Congress I-contestents won handsome victories and were elected without getting any trouble because Cachar went on at the normal life when the rest of Assam witnessed thousands of Satyagrahis giving arrest. This students agitation could be regarded as one of the greatest moments and political developments in the modern history of the north-east since Independence.

It is important landmark in the history of Assam which achieved victory through the non-violent method.

(vi) The Second Phase of the Protest. On 27 December, the AASU and the AGSP launched a non-cooperation movement for three days. As a consequence refineries at Digboi, Gauhati and Bangaigoan shut down for want of crude oil. The student organisations announced that picketing of oil installations would continue and no oil would be given to outside Assam through pumps. At the same time, the Janata Legislative Party also went on a hunger strike in Dispur protesting against the decision of CEC. At the same time, Assam Sahitya Sabha announced that it would file a case against the CEC in the Gauhati High Court for violating the Constitution. The student agitators knew very well that picketing of oil installations would affect the country. But they told, "But without it, you in Delhi or Bombay would never have realised the magnitude of the problem here."

On January 1980, when thousands were picketing the oil installations at Narengi, the CRP opened fire and four youths were killed and several were injured. It was condemned as a barbaric behaviour of the guardians of law. Immediately, Robi Mitra, a top executive of Oil India Ltd. who was masterminding the firing at Duliajan, was sent to the hospital by an anonymous phone call. He came straight to the hospital for looking at those injured people. Mitra was dragged out of his car by a mob and was beaten black and blue to death.

3

Identity Crisis

As we have seen in the last chapters, the partition of India and then of Pakistan in Bangladesh led to a inflow of a number of foreign nationals in Assam. This badly shattered the economy of the State and affected their social and political interests, what else, even their identity came into crisis. Asamiya identity is the crux of this chapter. In the present chapter, we propose to comprehend the question of the Asamiya identity vis-a-vis the Bengalis, the Nepalis and the *Bohiragatos,* the Indian "outsiders" in Assam. In contrast to the initial internal groups, these three groups are external to the Asamiya-nationality. They are not members of the Asamiya nationality, but, they live side by side with the Asamiyas in the same economically backward regional society. In the course of process, they came into conflict with the Asamiya ruling class and the Asamiya middle class. We will be discussing these points in detail when we talk of each group in terms of their relations with the Asamiya nationality. It is hoped that our group-wise discussion would enable us to understand the issues involved in the controversy and competition and the Asamiya identity crisis. In addition to these groups, we are also attempting to analyse the status of Asamiya language, the most sensitive symbol of the rising Asamiya nationality.

Bengalis in Assam

The issue of the Asamiya nationality vis-a-vis the Bengalis in Assam has remained controversial, ever since the arrival of the Bengali *baboos* in the wake of the annexation and consolidation of the British control in Assam in 1826. However, this does not mean that Assam had no connection at all with Bengal. Geographically, Assam's connection with the rest of the Indian sub-continent has ever been through Bengal. Being a neighbour, Assam and Bengal have had social, cultural, economic, diplomatic and political connections since the beginning of human civilisation in that region of the sub-continent. Many of the present day Asamiya caste-Hindu families came originally from Bengal during the later Ahom days.

While Asamiya was the dominant language in pre-British Assam. Bengali was also widely used for diplomatic relations with neighbouring kingdoms of Cachar, Darrang, and Tripura (Bhuyan 1949: XXII, Barpujari, 1987: 14, Hamilton 1807-14: 7). It has been noted that Ahom rulers preferred to maintain Assam's isolation and distance from mainland India. However, at times, they allowed a selected few from outside Assam to enter the state after a very alert scrutiny (Bhuyan 1949: 57). However, king Rudra Simha (1696-1740) gradually deviated from the traditional Ahom policy of maintaining isolation as he was planning to form an united Hindu force in the east to fight the powerful Mughals—the Indian rulers (Barpujari 1987: 34). He patronised immigration of artisans, scholars, musicians and religious priests, etc., from Bengal. During the rule of Siva Simha (1741-44), the successor of Rudra Simha, the influence of Bengali culture became very remarkable in the State of Assam. He brought Krishnaram Bhattacharyya, a Sivaite priest from Bengal and later became his disciple. The neo-Hindu king Siva Simha appointed this Bengali Brahmin as the chief priest of the popular Kamakhya temple of Guwahati. A large amount of land was presented to this priest which is still being occupied by his present successors in Guwahati (*Ibid*: 35).

These Bengali priests who migrated to Assam under the aristocratic patronage, significantly contributed in sanskritizing/brahminising the non-caste Asamiyas like the Ahoms. This also helped to improve the connections between Assam and India/Bengal. Therefore, we can see from the historical evidence that Assam had a small number of Bengalis, particularly the Brahmin priests who were highly influential in the medieval Asamiya society and polity. Those who migrated during the pre-British period assimilated and integrated with the medieval Asamiya society, and in the progress they left their Bengali identity—the way the Muslims and the Ahoms became Asamiya earlier, after settling-down permanently in Assam.

And, therefore, obviously, there was no such difficulty like Asamiya-Bengali conflict in pre-British Assam. However, Assam's incorporation into the British Indian colony, radically improved the Asamiya-Bengali relations in Assam. The conditions under which the British colonialism incorporated Assam through a treaty with the Burmese invaders at Yandaboo in 1826. Prior to the British colonisation, Assam witnessed internal disturbances of severe intensity in the 18th century against the Ahom rulers (for details see Neog 1982 and Bora 1983). Perpetual feuds among the Ahom rulers made them incapable of countering the mass rebellion which transformed into a long-drawn civil war. This precarious situation led to the military intervention of the neighbouring Burmese rulers. The intervention was highly brutal and barbarous. These events perniciously frustrated the entire Asamiya society. It was surrounded by uncertainties, pathos and gloom. At this point, the British rulers who were looking for colonising Assam from Bengal where they consolidated their rule long back, got a real opportunity to grab. In order to save Assam, they accepted the responsibility of driving out the Burmese invaders from Assam. The British colonization of Assam under the mask of the saviour was so tacid that many Asamiyas could not even notice that they were being made dependent subjects of the British colonialism after they forced the Burmese invaders out.

The realisation of being subjugated by colonialists came late to the Asamiyas. By the moment they realised their subjugated position, the Asamiyas were in no position to offer any significant resistance to the British colonialism. The situation under which the English rulers colonized Assam, saved the Asamiyas from the brutalities of the invading Burmese soldiers; the Asamiyas as a highly disorganised and disappointed community at that time, felt relieved and rescued from a long-drawn turmoil. Anandaram Dhekiyal Phukan (1829-59), the second Asamiya to receive western education in Calcutta and to take over an important office in the colonial administration, who contributed a note on the administration of Assam as an appendix to a report prepared by a colonial administrator in 1853, stated:

> Our countrymen hailed the day on which British supremacy was proclaimed in the province of Assam, and entertained sanguine expectations of peace and happiness from the rule of Britain. For several years antecedent to the annexation, the province groaned under the oppression and lawless tyranny of the Burmese, whose barbarous and inhuman policy depopulated the country and destroyed more than one half of the population which had already been thinned by intestine commotions and repeated civil wars. (Mills 1854: 92, Appendix J).

Apart from this, the apparent loyalist tone, Phukan's observation expressed that at the early stage of colonisation, the British emerged as the saviour of the Asamiyas. The colonisation gradually ended the isolation of Assam by making it a part of British India, and thereby, linking it with the colonial/capitalist world economy. This break with the traditional isolation is, historically a very important event for Assam and the Asamiyas. The penetration of colonialism added new complexities with serious socio-political and economic ramifications into the semi-feudal and semi-tribal Asamiya community. Assam's incorporation into the colonial system led to the abandonment of the Ahom way of administration which was replaced by a new British-Mughal set up of administration. Initially, the colonisers in the interest of their colony, patronised the pre-British Asamiya aristocracy in their administration. Though Assam possessed the rich tradition of writing *buranjis* (chronicles) since the arrival of the Ahoms in 1228, the pre-British aristocracy had neither knowledge nor experience of keeping written and formal records of administrative functioning revenue of land, hence, this aristocracy did not fit into the new system based on modern bureaucratic principles like maintaining formal and written records. Moderate English education became a pre-condition for entry into jobs in the new colonial administration. The British colonisers had no intention to educate or train the Asamiyas immediately with a purpose to ensure their continuity in the new colonial set up. This led to the decline of the pre-British Asamiya aristocracy immediately and more significantly, it delayed the process of the evolution of the middle class among the Asamiyas. This also pertinently explains the reason behind the import of the *baboos* from neighbouring Bengal to hold the junior level positions of the colonial administration in Assam.

Without any investment in western education in Assam, the colonisers profitably availed the services of the already surplus educated unemployed individuals from the Bengal Presidency. It would be worthwhile to recollect that the British colonised Bengal much earlier and a new middle class emerged with the spread of western education in Bengal Presidency from the Bengali Hindus mainly drawn from the high castes like Brahmins, Kayasthas, Vaidyas etc. (see Misra 1961, Seal 1971, Broomfield 1968, etc.).

The Muslim answer to the middle class formation was feeble and very slow in Bengal Presidency. Therefore, those who came to Assam to work in the colonial administration were more or less Bengali Hindus. In the absence of an Asamiya middle class in the early colonial Assam, the Bengalis virtually monopolised nearly all the jobs meant for the Indians in the colonial administration. Moreover, many more Bengalis came to Assam as lawyers, private doctors, small traders and shopkeepers, jewellers and tailors. They became quite conspicuous in the colonial administration and emerging urban centres in Assam. Gunaviram Barua, a highly distinguished Asamiya literacy figure of the late 19th century Assam, wrote: "The social status of the Bengalis stood next to the British in Assam" (Barua 1985: 95, translation ours). He observed similarities between the Asamiyas and the Bengalis (*Ibid:* 96).

Sociologically speaking, the Bengalis became a reference group of the Asamiyas who were looking for upward social mobility within the emerging social hierarchy in British Assam. Many of the Bengali sweetmeats, eating habits, dress pattern, manners, rituals and behaviour found acceptance among them. They used to talk proudly in Bengali, read Bengali papers and literature. Some of them even wrote in Bengali even prior to the consolidation of modern Asamiya literature in the late 19th century. Apparently, they developed love and respect for Bengali language and culture. And due to this factor, Choudhary observes "the British got the courage, rationale and opportunity to introduce Bengali language in Assam" (Barman and Choudhary 1986: 9).

One more prominent Asamiya scholar of literature and language observed similarly (Neog 1967: 233). Many of the Asamiya writers of the early and mid-19th century Assam wrote and published their works in Bengali. For instance, Maniram Dewan, an Asamiya aristocrat who later tried to link Assam with the first Indian War of Independence in 1857 and sacrificed his life at the colonial gallows, used to write in Bengali newspapers. Yogyaram Kharghoria Phukan, the first western educated Asamiya wrote in *Samachar Darpan,* a Bengali paper in 1831. Holiram Phukan also wrote a book on Assam's history in Bengali language in 1829. Jaduram Deka Barua also frequently wrote in Bengali magazines like *Samachar Darpan* and *Samachar Chandrika.* Even the doyen of the modern Asamiya literature stock. Lakhminath Bezbarua, attempted his first writings in the Bengali language. Even in his autobiography, he had admitted that his family used Bengali for communication within its members (Bezbarua 1965). The Asamiya-Bengali relations have been irreductably involved with the question of Asamiya language and nationality. It would be pertinent to point out here that, just after colonisation, the colonisers made Assam a part of the Bengal Presidency. In 1831, Bengali replaced Persian as the medium of instruction at the school level and the language of the judicial court in Bengal. Similarly, Bengali was also given the same status in Assam in 1837 by suppressing the Asamiya language in Assam itself.

This event is of great importance and should be comprehended seriously and objectively without any prejudice to the Asamiyas and the Bengalis. Bengali replaced Persian, simply since Bengali was the most popular and dominant language of Bengal. If the same rationale was applied, Asamiya should have been the official language of the court and also the medium of instruction at the school level in, at least, Assam proper, that is, the Brahmaputra Valley. However, the colonisers acted otherwise because of the colonial constraints.

This matter has been utilized raucously by a very large number of the Asamiya scholars, journalists, literary figures, politicians and even social scientists, of both the 19th and 20th century. Even at present, the blame continues to be on the Bengalis/Bengali *baboos* for decisively misguiding the British colonial rulers against the legitimate right of the Asamiya language in the State of Assam (Gohain Barooah 1917, Goswami and Gohain Barooah 1907, Bezbarua 1965, 1924, Neog 1962, Sarma 1965, Sarma 1972, Talukdar 1975, etc.). They believe that a handful of the Bengali *baboos* were a success in persuading the British rulers to accept Bengali as the official language of Assam. And, their conspiracy led to the suppression of the Asamiya language during 1867-1873, Myron Weiner too observed similarly, "Since Bengali and Assamese language and the scripts are similar, the *Bengalis were able to persuade the British government* that Assamese was only a corrupt and vulgar dialect of Bengali" (Weiner 1978:93, emphasis ours).

Apart from this, these conservative scholars, surprisingly, an Asamiya Marxist (CPML) scholar wrote in *Economic and Political Weekly* quite similarly. . . "British policy makers with the support of Bengali chauvinists in the administration made Bengali the official language of Assam in 1830s" (Sharma 1980: 1392). This conspiracy theory is still being sincerely followed by a larger number of Asamiyas cutting across the class and political barriers. Even the Asam Sahitya Sabha, the most respectable among the different components of the All Assam Gana Sangram Parishad which led the Assam movement, together with the All Assam Students Union, in a memorandum submitted to the Union Home Minister on 23rd February 1980, which was highly circulated inside and outside Assam, alleged that it was not the *baboos* but the entire Hindu Bengalis of Assam who were responsible for this: "there were Bengali-speaking people and on their advice Bengali was introduced in the courts of justice and other government offices and schools in Assam" (Asam Sahitya Sabha, 1980).

This particular theory became all pervasive, and has been used in the socialisation process, even through the university level text-books. This theory has contributed very solidly in forming and continuing the hate/anti-Bengali tendency among a large section of the Asamiyas. The propagators and the supporters of the conspiracy theory grossly under-estimated the colonial context, and could not situate the all powerful role of the colonial rulers as the real decision makers in their colony. Consciously or unconsciously, they regarded the British rulers as 'native', 'innocent', and manipulable by a group of their subordinated subjects—the Bengali *baboos.* There is no tangible historicity about the successful Bengali conspiracy in opposition the Asamiya language. The colonial rulers made several surveys prior to and after colonising Assam in 1826. Therefore, it would be very highly simplistic to guess that the British had no knowledge about the existence and popularity of the Asamiya language. Even then the colonial rulers had gone in non-indigenous Bengali language in Assam. Gohain has described the reason behind such exercise:

> . . . the colonial rulers had introduced Bengali in 1837 not out of their interest in any language dispute but for administrative convenience only. Assam was being ruled as part of Bengal administration and the British were introducing new land laws, law-courts and official procedures in Assam. Bengali had already been in use in Bengal for these purposes and it was more economical to use that ready made instrument and pupils trained in its use than flounder about with Assamese which lacked such terminology" (Gohain 1980: 14).

Apart from this, at that particular stage, the Asamiyas lacked a western educated middle class, conscious of their identity and capable of resisting the oppression of their mother tongue. Till the beginning of a national movement for freedom from the colonial rule, the Asamiya middle class was largely a class of loyalist collaborators of colonialism. Because of their class position in a specific colonial situation and their loyalist nature, they failed to comprehend adequately the language policy of the colonial rulers and found the scapegoat in Bengali *baboos.* Sarma states that unfortunately the Asamiya intellectuals and a large number of the Asamiya literary figures still do not blame for British rulers for the suppression of the Asamiya language (Sarma 1980: 9-10).

The colonial rulers were capable of playing their game well, to antagonise one subject nationality against another in order to ensure and prolong their own rule. The Bengali conspiracy theory has remained quite dominant among the Asamiyas, particularly among the middle class. They have very successfully articulated this theory to the cultural, political and national identity of the Asamiya people. This theory even contributed very significantly in backing and solidifying the ideology and praxis of the Assam movement, the movement for formal recognition of Asamiya language in 1960 and the 1972 movement for making Asamiya the sole medium of instruction upto the graduate level with English as sole alternative medium of instruction for a limited period.

The leadership of the Assam movement, too, has exploited this theory in a similar way. They repeatedly reminded their observers about the successful conspiracy against the Asamiyas in the early colonial Assam. This helped in politically socialising a large section of the Asamiyas to brand the Bengalis as inimical to the interests of the Asamiya culture, language and nationality. All historically dominant ideology of a particular period ultimately come across a counter ideology as part of ideological struggle of various classes and forces. Recently, quite a few Asamiya scholars have taken up the Bengali conspiracy theory for serious scrutiny from historical angles (Choudhury 1973; Gohain 1977, 1980; Neog 1967; Guha 1977, 1979, 1980; Barman 1980; Barman and Choudhury 1986). All of them have taken into consideration the colonial connection and the class factors involved in the language question in Assam. We would like to add and emphasise that even in the wake of colonial excesses Asamiya, like any other live language, did not lose its base and popularity in the Brahmaputra Valley. The most significant event after the suppression of language was the entry of the American Baptist Mission in the Assam in 1838. In most colonial situations, the missionary activity can be observed which is paralleled to colonisation or complementary to it (Rocher 1972: 509). We all know that the Baptist Missionary did not succeed in converting the Asamiyas from their earlier faiths to Christianity. However, they played a very positive role in evolving Asamiya language and literature which virtually did not grow during the post-*Vaisnava* movement. The missionaries published the first ever Asamiya magazine *Aroonoday,* from Sibsagar in 1846. The magazine was highly secular and modern in its approach and content. As they had the policy to use native language to preach Christianity, they had to go in for Asamiya in Assam. They also released an Asamiya grammar in 1846, and an English-Asamiya dictionary in 1867 authored by Miles Bronson. These activities helped to establish the distinct and independent identity of the Asamiya language.

The second western educated and first Asamiya officer of significant rank in the colonial administration, Anandaram Dhekiyal Phukan also quite sincerely tried to establish the status of Asamiya language as the language of schools and courts in British Assam. He very assiduously researched and demonstrated the distinctive and independent identity of the Asamiya language through a book published by the American Baptist Mission (A Native 1856: Neog 1977). He was the first Asamiya to ask for replacing Bengali with Asamiya in British Assam. However, very significantly unlike many of his successors who later took up the cause of Asamiya language, literature, culture and nationality, famous Anandaram Dhekiyal Phukan did neither preach Asamiya exclusiveness nor involved himself in inciting national hostility, contempt and hatred against the non-Asamiyas; though he was very strongly demanding replacement of the Bengali language with the Asamiya language in British Assam. He wrote:

> . . . by the substitution of Assamese, we do not mean to suggest that Bengalee should be altogether abolished from the schools. On the contrary, we are of

> opinion that it should be cultivated as a language indispensable to complete the course of vernacular education and the standard Bangalle works should likewise be introduced in the higher classes. We are only opposed to its exclusive adoption as the medium of instructing the people in literature, science and other useful branches of knowledge (Phukan in Mills 1854: 106).

Attempts of the Baptist Missionary and Anandaram Dhekiyal Phukan proved beyond doubt the autonomy and distinctiveness of Asamiya from Bengali language though both had a common parentage—Sanskrit. Due to the strong support rendered by the Baptist Missionary, their most trusted ally in the colonial Assam, the British rulers gradually changed their position and policy on language. A renowned scholar of Asamiya language and literature observed that the British rulers . . .

> . . . were not moved till there was agitation of the people and that this agitation took shape much after Phukan's efforts and publication of Mill's report. The Baptists held the line of this agitation as evident from such fact that of the continuation of their Assamese medium schools and that of Bronson's leading a representation of 216 educated Assamese on 9 March 1872 (Neog 1977:21-22).

At last, the British rulers replaced Bengali with Asamiya in 1873 as the language of schools and courts in all the districts of the Brahmaputra Valley excluding Goalpara district. Historically this was a very significant achievement for the Asamiya language alone but also for the emergence of the modern Asamiya nationality. Though the colonial suppression of language was over, Asamiya was re-established and the path was paved for its growth, yet the injury inflicted by the colonial suppression continued in a distorted form among the nascent Asamiya middle class. This pulls us to the point of the middle class dimension, in addition to language, in determining the Asamiya-Bengali relations in Assam.

Though the Bengalis had become a reference group for the rising Asamiya middle class, paradoxically, the Asamiya fear of the Bengalis continued. A leading Asamiya intellectual of the late 19th century wrote, "though the Asamiyas accepted many aspects from the Bengalis, they still continued to hate the Bengalis" (Barua 1885:100). What was the factor behind such hatred against the Bengalis at that time, that is in 1885? Meanwhile, a western educated Asamiya middle class was gradually emerging and they faced stiff competition for limited jobs reserved for the Indian subjects from the non-native Bengalis. The colonial system envenomed the relationship between the Bengali and the Asamiya middle class in Assam. What was necessarily a competition for jobs and patronage from the colonial system transformed itself into an ugly fight between two oppressed nationalitie, of course standing at unequal levels within the same colony. Though the colonial rulers declared the reintroduction of the Asamiya language in 1873, it took almost two decades to fully implement the new language policy in Assam. It ended the long-standing uncertainties of the Asamiya language in its homeland.

From then, there is no looking back. Both the Asamiya language and literature developed substantially by the end of the 19th century. This, in turn, contributed significantly to the growth of a small but very distinct modern Asamiya nationality. The number of Asamiya speakers rose from the estimated 7 lakhs in 1826 to 15 in 1901. In the present century, not only has the population of Assam grown fast but the Asamiya population, too, has been growing at a very fast rate. Asamiya has been the official language of the state since 1961. Asamiya also very significantly gained the status of the medium of instruction upto the graduate level together with English in 1972. Many scholars are aware of the abnormally high growth rate of population in Assam, but surprisingly number of them are ignorant of the very high growth rate of the Asamiyas and other autochthon tribals in Assam. Alongwith the development of the Asamiya nationality, the Asamiya middle class has consolidated its position very strongly. After Independence and the separation of Sylhet, the Asamiya middle class had won a position whereby they could exert their hegemony over the entire society in Assam. Needless to say, many a times, their imposition of hegemony over the whole state acted against the Asamiya nationality itself, besides antagonizing and violating the democratic rights of demographically and the socio-economically weaker groups in Assam.

Here, we are mainly concerned with the problem of identity crisis faced by the Asamiya nationality vis-a-vis the Bengalis of Assam. Directly or indirectly, consciously or unconsciously, the threat of Bengali dominance over the Asamiyas dominated the psychology of masses who supported the Assam movement. Besides, the foreign national issue largely overlapped with the Bengalis since most of them came from East Bengal/East Pakistan or Bangladesh. This added a new dimension to the existing relationship between the Asamiyas and the Bengalis in state of Assam. The leadership of the movement, directly or indirectly, patronised the colonial legacy, the Asamiya fear against the Bengali dominance. This obviously sharpened the antagonism between these two groups within the State. This found manifestation in onesided killings of civilians by civilians.

The census data show that the Asamiya speaking population is three times larger than Bengali speaking people in Assam. The Bengalis constitute about 20 per cent of the total population of the state. Anyway, if we exclude, the predominantly Bengali speaking Cachar district/Barak valley, the Asamiya constitute an overwhelming 72 per cent of the total population of the Brahmaputra Valley, the old homeland of the Asamiyas which they have been sharing with the autochthon tribal population. If we include the autochthon tribals living in the Brahmaputra Valley in the category of the Asamiyas, their strength becomes as high as 80 per cent of the total population of the Brahmaputra Valley. The Bengalis in Assam are definitely not threatening the linguistic identity of the Asamiyas in Assam. The Asamiyas are the largest linguistic group in Assam. Their position in their historical homeland is quite higher, that is, 72 per cent compared to 61 per cent of the State. The Bengalis are the second single largest group, and they constitute only 11.5 per cent of total population of this Valley. The Bengalis are neither threatening the linguistic balance of the state nor the identity of the Asamiya language. The demography of Assam has shown a very progressive growth of the Asamiyas, both in terms of absolute number and percentage over the years till 1951. This indicates the absorption of various migrant communities into the rising Asamiya nationality during the colonial period. The Na-Asamiya Muslims and the black-tribals of Assam's plantations together gave the Asamiyas a dominant single majority status in a highly multilingual State.

The large scale identification of the Bengali Muslim peasants from East Bengal with the Asamiyas which very significantly increased the Asamiya population in their state. During this period, the black-tribals of Assam's tea plantations started identifying with the Asamiyas. Besides, the people of Goalpara too joined in. Being the western most district of Assam neighbouring Bangladesh and West Bengal, which had all the sociological features of a frontier region having no single well defined culture to identify with the people of Goalpara after freedom have begun increasingly identifying themselves with the Asamiyas.

Needless to say that after Independence and the separation of Sylhet, there were some socio-political compulsions on them to identify themselves with the largest group—the Asamiyas. The Bengalis were 13 per cent in 1951, and reduced to 9.8 per cent in 1961 and grew marginally to 11.48 per cent in 1971 of the total population of the Brahmaputra Valley. It is very clear that the Bengali population did not increase at any alarming rate to cause language or cultural identity crisis of the Asamiya nationality. By and large, the demographic structure of 1951 has been maintained unaltered.

After 1947, consequently, refugees from East Pakistan started moving to the eastern Indians states, West Bengal, Tripura and Assam. The large scale acceptance and entry of the Hindu Bengali refugees dramatically transformed the demographic equation of Tripura within a short period of time wherein the autochthon tribals became a minority and the refugees a majority. We shall talk about this issue later in more details.

Like other States, Assam also accepted the refugees as a part of the national commitment to the Hindu minorities in Pakistan. The Assam government under the leadership of Gopinath Bordoloi took very active role in settling the displaced refugees in Assam. The successive high caste dominated Congress government at the state level continued to offer very active help in settling down the East Pakistani refugees in Assam. Already, Assam had a good number of Hindu Bengalis, therefore, the refugees did not find Assam an alien land. Even with the refugees, the Bengali population did not go up to the extent to warrant identity crisis among the Asamiyas. The percentage of the Bengalis remained 13 to

11.5 per cent between 1951-71 in the Brahmaputra Valley. The major amount of the refugee burden fell mainly on the Barak Valley/Cachar district which, both geographically and historically, has never been a part of Assam or Asamiya culture. Some of the Bengali Hindu farmers and non-middle class segment of refugees who settled down in the Brahmaputra Valley tried and gradually assimilated with the Asamiyas.

This phenomena also explain to some extent the stability and continuous balance of Assam's demographic structure between 1951-71 in spite of large refugee influx to Assam. Regarding the percentage of people who were migrants from outside India, according to their last place of residence, the percentage is not as alarming as the leadership of the Assam movement would wish us to believe. Such people constitute only 5.6 per cent of the total population of the State. This also includes those who were born in the Sylhet district which was a part of colonial Assam till Independence of India; but the partition made it a part of a foreign country, that is, East Pakistan. This too failed to change the demographic structure of Assam and cause an identity problem of the Asamiya nationality in Assam.

The Asamiyas as a nationality has been growing very fast, assimilating and integrating many migrant groups and autochthon tribals together. Though the census data has been compartmentalising the linguistic groups, it would be improper on our part to measure the Asamiya-Bengali equations in terms of dead statistics alone: it goes far beyond that. The Bengalis residing in Assam, particularly in the Brahmaputra Valley, besides their mother tongue, can express/communicate well in the Asamiya language (Hussain 1988 B: 283).

The prevailing social and economic scenario constantly forced not only the Bengalis but also the other non-Asamiyas to learn the Asamiya language in their own interest, the way many non-Hindi speaking people are learning Hindi language. The tribals of Assam are already bilingual. In addition to their language/dialect, they know Asamiya, though some of them are struggling hard to set up their distinct tribal identity vis-a-vis the Asamiyas. The Asamiyas together with non-Asamiyas including the Bengalis of the Brahmaputra Valley and the autochthon plains' tribals are extending the Asamiya language its due popularity and wider acceptance in Assam.

Besides Assam, the Asamiya language is reasonably popular in other north-eastern states. It is very highly used in Meghalaya, Nagaland and Arunachal Pradesh. The present Chief Ministers of Arunachal Pradesh, Nagaland and Meghalaya can speak Asamiya as fluently as the then Chief Minister of Assam. 'Nagamese', a pidgin of the Asamiya language has been in use as the lingua-franca among the various tribes, speaking different dialects/languages in the tribal Nagaland. Acharya states that the Nagas have accepted Asamiya as their second native language (Acharya 1988: 1073). Similarly, Asamiya based pidgin, earlier called *Nefamese*, now renamed as *Arunachali* is extensively used in Arunachal Pradesh (*Ibid.* 1023 also see Sreedhar 1974). In these two predominantly tribal States also with a multiplicity of tribal dialects/languages and their mutual unintelligibility, the Asamiya based pidgin language has solved the problem of inter-tribal and tribal and non-tribal interactions and communications at the well-known level. So, in spite of the perpetual enforcement of the inner line system, both in Arunachal Pradesh and Nagaland, in order to separate the people of the hill from the people of plain areas, both in colonial and post-colonial India, and the existence of not so cordial relations between Assam and Nagaland on one hand, and again, between Arunachal Pradesh and Assam on the other hand, at the government level, the Asamiya based pidgin language has remained popular among all the tribals of Arunachal Pradesh and Nagaland. Besides, most of the Garos of Meghalaya can communicate very well in the Asamiya language. For us, it would be sociologically important to note that Asamiya language is not just the official language of the State of Assam and of Asamiyas but its fame today is much wider than it looks. All autochthon tribals of the Brahmaputra Valley and most of the non-Asamiyas, including the Bengalis in the Brahmaputra Valley, use Asamiya language as their second language. Besides, the Asamiya based pidgins *Arunachali* and *Nagamese* are extensively used at the popular level in Arunachal Pradesh and Nagaland respectively.

The significance of the Asamiya language has not decreased with the gradual decrease of Assam's territorial size, rather it has increased its popularity both in terms of numbers of speakers and also its use inside and outside Assam. Besides, we should not overlook the irreductable historical status of Asamiya as a language of the market and exchange in Assam and the north-east. None among the leaders of the Assam movement tried to comprehend and explain these positive developments and inculcate confidence among the Asamiyas, on the strength and some of the Asamiya language. They acted in the opposite direction which only served to increase the historical weakness of the Asamiya nationality—threat against the Bengalis.

In the wake of the Assam movement, the Bengali conspiracy theory gained more popularity and currency. Along with this, the leadership of the movement, in connection with the Asamiya bourgeois press, took up another issue which also propelled the Asamiya fear.

The matter was the transformation of Tripura to a Bengali majority State where the autochthon tribals lost their identity to the Bengali refugees. They argued that the state of the Asamiyas was quite similar to the Tripura tribals who lost their identity and majority status in their traditional homeland, and that the same fate was awaiting the Asamiyas in the wake of regular immigration from Bangladesh. A large number of Asamiyas seriously believed that the Bengali influx would destroy Asamiya's cultural, linguistic and political identity and that their status would become the same as that of the Tripura tribals. Therefore, they participated in various protest actions en masse and supported the movement on the honest idea of defending their national identity in their traditional homeland. A superficial look at the Tripura case would present an ostensibly similar case as that of Assam. Still, an objective look makes the scene qualitatively different and noncomparable. The argument that the Bengalis can destroy the Asamiya identity is not grounded on history or sound demographical understanding. The case of Tripura shows that the Tripura tribals had no developed language. They neither had a script nor written literature. The Asamiyas kept the tradition of writing since the 6th century. Asamiya literature developed very significantly during the medieval period and was at its peak during the great *Vaisnava/Bhakti* movement in the past 15th and 16th century. In spite of colonial suppression of the Asamiya language between 1838-73, it continued to develop defying the artificial suppression, due to its historically well-entrenched position and popularity in the Brahmaputra Valley. Since 1972, the Asamiya language has also attained the status of medium of instruction upto the graduate level in educational agencies.

The Asamiya language and literature continued to develop during the post-independence period. The contemporary Asamiya literature is as rich as any other rich leading Indian language. At the time when the Asamiyas were fearful of their linguistic identity, surprisingly, an Asamiya writer, B.K. Bhattacharya was awarded the honoured 'Jnanpith' award for his novel *Mrittunjoy*. Besides, in contrast to the Tripura tribals, the Asamiya nationality has its very strong middle class, conscious and capable of defending its any linguistic identity. The comparison between the Asamiya and the Tripura tribals vis-a-vis the Bengali is highly simplistic and erroneous. An Asamiya scholar has disclosed very pertinently that the case of the Bengalis versus the Tripura tribals is not at all comparable to the existing relationship between the Bengalis and the Asamiyas; instead, the case is very much comparable to the existing relationship between the Asamiyas and the autochthon tribals, like Bodos, Mishings, etc. (Barman 1980: 42). From the above discussion, we have found that the Bengalis as a community, is in no way threatening the Asamiya nationality. The data that we have presented unmistakably suggests that the Bengali population in Assam is not growing alarmingly so as to cause a numerical crisis of identity of the Asamiyas in Assam. Though, the growth of population is very high in Assam, we must also notice, at the same time, that the Asamiyas are also growing at a higher rate demonstrating the historical capacity of the Asamiya nationality to absorb and assimilate various permanent migrants to its fold. Then why is there this slogan and utterance that the Asamiyas are losing their identity? We have noted earlier that there was no Asamiya-Bengali conflict in pre-British Assam. It came to existence only under the transformative processes Assam experienced under peculiar colonial conditions. The colonial system envenomed the relationship between two suppressed nationalities, standing at uneven levels wherein the middle class dimension sharpened the antagonism deeply. The nascent Asamiya middle class directed their fear and disappointment, paradoxically, against their own reference group—the Bengali middle class in colonial Assam.

In the post-colonial period, though the colonial hangover perpetuated, the political map of Assam changed very drastically. The separation of Sylhet from Assam in the wake of Independence and partition, substantially decreased the number of Bengalis, both Hindus and Muslims. After Independence, the Asamiya middle class consolidated their position from where they could exert their own hegemony over other classes in Assam. This has obviously led to a further reduction of Assam's size from 2,23,590 sq. kms. to 78,523 sq. kms. by 1972. However, the reduction of its size has caused more homogenisation of its population and the increase of the Asamiya speaking population and their demographic dominance in Assam. The division of Cachar, North Cachar Hills district and Karbi Anglong Hills district would further help to strengthen the demographic authority of the Asamiya nationality in Assam (Hussain : 1972). Barua, too, pleaded for a separation of the predominantly Bengali speaking Cachar district/Barak Valley from Assam in order to ensure better demographic status for the Asamiyas in Assam (Barua 1984: 303). We, too, feel that the separation of Cachar would particularly help to reduce the Asamiya-Bengali conflict in Assam to a great extent. Besides, the separation of North Cachar and Karbi Anglong, the remaining two hill districts with a predominantly tribal population and historically non-Asamiya region, would fulfil the interests of the hills tribals and the Asamiyas better.

Now, in order to understand the Asamiya insecurities against the Bengalis, we must go back to history. Since its birth, the Asamiya middle class has been competing for jobs with the Bengalis. Relatively speaking, the giant-like size of the neighbouring Bengalis, as a nation with a very strong middle class backing and their conspicuous presence in Assam was itself a cause for fear among the educated categories of the smaller nationality like the Asamiyas. The colonial society, because of its inherent limitations and the post-colonial society, because of its capitalist path of development, have obviously got defeated to meet the aspirations of the emerging Asamiya middle class. The Asamiyas lack a class of strong bourgeoisie. The Asamiya bourgeoisie is weak and nagging. Therefore, of course, it is incapable of offering job opportunities to its own middle class. The Asamiya bourgeoisie lacks a strong capitalist class of its own, with a little exceptions of about 10 families owning tea plantations in Upper Assam. There are a few small capitalists, owning Assam's powerful regional press, with English and Asamiya publication works, and a few rich transport operators.

Therefore, the Asamiya bourgeoisie is composed mainly of the Asamiya middle class, which is fundamentally dependent on government vacancies and patronage in various forms. The inherent limitation in the absence of industrialisation has forced them to desperately try to dominate the state government. Needless to state that they have been largely successful in doing so. The Asamiya middle class is, by and large, composed of the Asamiya high caste Hindus who would not like to give share of this small cake to the autochthon tribals, black-tribals Asamiya Muslims, Na-Asamiya Muslims, non-caste Ahoms,

Koch-Rajbanshis and other backward classes (OBCs) of the same nationality, not to speak of the Hindu Bengalis. The Hindu Bengalis in Assam, being largely educated and largely middle class in its composition, obviously becomes competitors with the Asamiya middle class. Any way, compared to the Muslims, black-tribals, non-caste Hindus and autochthon tribals, the position of the Bengalis are relatively better because of their pre-partitioned foothold in some types of employment controlled by the agencies outside the State but in the post-partitioned era, they too have fallen progressively behind the Assamese in all spheres of fresh employment. In fact, urban unemployment among them is now highest.

Because of being largely middle class in composition, the concentration of Bengalis in urban Assam is very conspicuously significant. There are quite few small towns in the Brahmaputra Valley where the Bengalis were more than the Asamiyas. There are a few observable Bengali pockets in Guwahati city too. The Asamiya-Bengali conflict and its periodic violent manifestations have increased the importance of such 'safe' and segregated pockets for Bengalis in Assam. This has significantly decreased the scope of interaction and integration process. Though the Bengalis feel 'safe' in such pockets, it generated apprehensions among the Asamiyas about their intention. Many Asamiyas feel that such segregation is aimed to create a mini-Bengal/Bengali island in Assam. A large part of the Asamiyas refuse to accept the Bengali 'safety' rationale, and similarly, their Bengali counterparts do not share the Asamiya apprehensions about them. And, hence there is a continuity of doubt, hostility and conflict in urban Assam. In this connection, it would be important to note that Assam is one of the highly under-urbanised States in India. The percentage of urban population in Assam is just 8.82 per cent (Census of India, 1971) and the percentage of Bengalis living in urban Assam noticeably goes the percentage of the Asamiyas. Their respective percentage is 18 and 6 per cent. It is an undeniable fact that the emerging Asamiya nationality is the cumulative outcome of a long ongoing process of assimilation and integration of innumerable migrant groups, belonging to various racial, linguistic and religious affinities. The Asamia language has been the most significant symbol of the Asamiya nationality. Besides, the nationality formation process is still incomplete and going on gradually.

Therefore, we see that there are old Asamiyas and Asamiyas and neo-Asamiyas, together making the contemporary Asamia nationality. The history of Assam demonstrated that the immunerable permanent migrant groups have inter-mingled, integrated and identified with the Asamiya nationality. Therefore, we can observe that in spite of massive growth of population in Assam since the beginning of the 20th century, the Asamiya nationality goes on to grow surprisingly at a higher rate, ensuring its distinct and dominant identity in Assam. This has been a very positive trend in the Asamiya nationality formation and its development. However, the Bengali Hindus, particularly a large section of the middle class have been maintaining their distinct Bengali identity without identifying with the

Asamiyas. This carries on to disturb a large section of the Asamiyas psychologically. We have noted that the Bengali Muslims and even Hindu Bengali peasants in the Brahmaputra Valley have mingled and identified themselves with the Asamiya nationality.

Being largely middle class, the Bengali Hindus are obviously very conscious about their cultural heritage and linguistic identity, just like the Asamiya middle class.

It has been noted that secular and democratic sections of the Asamiya nationality have been assiduously struggling to bridge the gap between the Asamiyas and the Bengalis in Assam. Many persons feel that there are still numerous rabidly ethnocentric Bengalis in Assam who look at the Asamiyas as inferior to them, and, therefore, refuse to mix or assimilate with them. Many of the Bengalis, with the support of the bourgeois press in Calcutta tried to characterise/demand Assam as a bilingual state. Even during the hey days of the Assam movement in 1980 when all kinds of restraints were required very seriously, an Assam based Bengali scholar very surprisingly in a 'Governor financed' colloquim organised by the North East India Council for Social Science Research, pleaded for the formation of a Union Territory for the Bengalis in the Brahmaputra Valley in addition to another in the Barak Valley, as a solution to overcome the impasse created by the Assam movement (Bhattacharjee 1982: 133).

We come across many such utterances from the Bengali chauvinists. It would be highly improper to undermine the role of the Bengali chauvinism in understanding the Asamiya-Bengali connections in Assam. Both the Asamiyas and the Bengali chauvinists have been helping each other in raucously envenoming the Asamiya-Bengali relationship, both in the pre-colonial and the post-colonial Assam. Needless to say, chauvinism inherently represents the interests of the recreationary classes or class at a particular stage and not of the whole nationality or nation. But chauvinism, depending on its strength is capable of inflicting injuries to the entire nation deeply. Though not an oppressor community in relation to the Asamiya nationality, the Bengalis form a large population of the Indian sub-continent and have a rich culture, language and literature. The Bengali chauvinism, even on a small scale, is quite capable of energising chauvinism of a bigger intensity among the Asamiyas. The irrational demand to change the present linguistic status of Assam or their demand for the formation of an union territory for the Bengalis in the Brahmaputra Valley would hurt the Asamiya nationality very deeply, and increase its fear and suspicion against the Bengalis in Assam. Such threats and suspicion would provide solid base for continuity and consolidation of the Asamiya chauvinism. Such chauvinism will definitely go against the interest of the ordinary masses of both the Asamiyas and the Bengalis in Assam.

After a long-drawn struggle, the Asamiyas established their language and literature in colonial Assam. Psychologically speaking, the Asamiya language has remained the most important symbol of the Asamiya nationality. Many demanded/

characterised Assam as a multi-lingual, twin-lingual or an Asamiya-Bengali state but not as an unilingual state. If one applies the same yardstick then all other Indian states should be characterized as multi-lingual or bi-lingual States in that sense. Apart from this, the principle of the linguistic States in India has to be abandoned immediately. But in reality, no one is prepared, as yet, for that. And no one should try to do that in Assam; that is what the Asamiyas as a nationality feels very strongly. However, as the Asamiyas share their traditional homeland, the Brahmaputra Valley, with numerous distinct autochthon tribals like the Bodos, Mishings, Tiwas, and the Rabhas, their underdeveloped languages/dialects also deserve a legitimately justful status in Assam. As the autochthon tribals are bilingual, they can speak Asamiya, besides their own tribal language/dialect. The Asamiya language is already well-entrenched with the support of a rich literary tradition, its status as the official language of the State and medium of instruction upto the graduate level; more significantly Asamiya as the language of market and exchange has already gained a permanent popular status. This status is historical, and is unlikely to affect/reverse, even if the Asamiyas confer special status to the indigenous tribal languages, and initiate honest and sincere steps to protect and develop their languages.

Conclusion

Thus, in order to understand the Bengali question vis-a-vis the Asamiya nationality, language and identity, it is imperative to comprehend objectively the peculiar colonial situation under which a half-tribal and a semi-feudal Asamiya society experienced a highly distorted and uneven social transformation. We have also tried to link the middle class dimension, both in colonial as well as post-colonial developments, besides exploring the roots of the Asamiya fear against the Bengalis. One of the recent expressions of this unending fear against the Bengalis was the beginning of the Assam movement which ostensibly aimed at deporting foreign nationals. The Assam movement's ideological indoctrination is that the Asamiyas are facing a severe crisis to their identity due to the large influx of Bengalis/Bangladeshis to Assam which justified the movement and its resultant huge cost and human sacrifices. Our analysis of history and society on the ground of available data, has led us to think otherwise. The Bengalis are not threatening the identity of the Asamiyas. We have noted that in spite of the massive growth of population in Assam throughout the past century, the number of the Asamiya population is also increasing very significantly at a higher rate than that of the others, ensuring a dominant demographic status for the Asamiya people in Assam. Historically, a ruling class led-movement, is inherently incapable of safeguarding the interest of the masses. Though it pleads a national cause, it represents only its own limited class interests. It articulates its own class interests as the interest of the whole nation/nationality. In order to protect and enhance its class interest and hegemony over the society in Assam, and wrest more concessions from their big brother—the big Indian dominant class, the Asamiya ruling class led the Assam movement very tacitly. The big Indian bourgeoisie and the little Asamiya bourgeoisie, together, had given birth to psycho and structural conditions in the State of Assam for the emergence of such a massive movement like the Assam movement. Both of them have immensely benefited from the movement and its ideology. Their class interest is also obvious to be spelt out in details here.

The Nepalis as Foreigner/Indian

Movement in Assam brought into sharp focus the question of the Nepalis as foreigner/Indian together with the 'question of East Pakistanis and Bangladeshis in Assam. Once the movement switched over from the question of the *bohiragatas*—the outsiders—to the issue of the *'videshis*—the foreigners,—the question about the status of the Nepalis was raised, as the country of their origin happens to be a foreign country called Nepal. The leadership of the Assam movement demanded the deportation of all the Nepali foreigners together with the East Pakistani/Bangladeshi foreigners residing in Assam illegally. Here in this part, we propose to comprehend the Nepali question in Assam vis-a-vis the Assam movement and the question of the Asamiya national level identity in Assam.

(a) Socio-Legal Status of Nepalis in India. Their status in India has been overlapping both legally and sociologically. We must take a distinction between (a) the Nepalis of Nepal; and (b) the Indian Nepalis, that is, the people of Nepali origin residing in India for a reasonably long period of time and participating in the socio-economic and political processes in India. The second group of Nepalis has been experiencing the process of assimilation, certainly, in uneven degrees, depending on the situation of demography, place and areas of their residence in India. While technically Nepal is a foreign country, the Nepalis were never treated as foreign nationals in India. So was the status of the Indians in Nepal. This was obviously a mutually accepted understanding between two neighbouring nations with a history of cordial, social, political and economic relations and without a natural physical boundary to demarcate them distinctly. The ongoing trends saw manifestation formally in the Indo-Nepal Friendship Treaty of 1950, the Tripartite Delhi Agreement of 1951, and the revised Indo-Nepal Agreement of 1956. All these ensured the state of equal rights for the Indians with the Nepalis in Nepal and the Nepalis with the Indians in India. Accordingly, both the Indians and the Nepalis can seek employment, engage in agricultural or business sector besides their right to movement, settlement and acquisition of property without hindrance.

Therefore, a Nepali can come to India without a passport and visa, and an Indian can in the same way go to Nepal without a passport and a visa. Though at the technical level, Nepal and India are two separate countries, they have preferred to overlap the vital questions like citizenship/nationality. This overlapping has given the right to immigrate without any restrictions for the citizens of both the countries. Historically significant migrations with following serious socio-political ramifications in Assam are the migrations of (a) the Bengali *baboos* to run the subordinate levels of the colonial administration in the State of Assam, (b) the black-tribals from the Jharkhand-Chotanagpur region to Assam's tea-plantations, (c) the migration of the East Bengal peasants to Assam's vast wasteland, (d) the migration of the Nepalis nationals to Assam had a common link, that is, the colonial context under which Assam experienced social transformation. However, it should be noted that Assam's connection with Nepal is historically quite old. There were matrimonial connections between the medieval ruling families of Assam and Nepal. Historical evidences suggest that some limited migration of the Nepalis occurred before the British colonisation of Assam.

According to a scholar, one group of *Pandas* (priests) of Assam's famous *Kamakhya* temple owe their origins to Nepal (Chetri 1983: 13). Those who migrated from Nepal in confined number gradually assimilated with the emerging Asamiya society, abandoned their past Nepali identity and connections like other migrants in pre-British Assam.

Apart from these historical linkages, Assam had ethnic/racial connections with the Nepalis. There are large number of the sub-ethnic groups what Prof. Suniti Kumar Chatterji (1951) refers to *Kiratas,* to whom, the Limbu, the Tamong, the Lepcha, the Mogor, the Gurung and the Sherpa belong. Traditionally, they live in the eastern region of Nepal which is geographically not very far from the western border of Assam. Similarly, Assam too, has a larger number of the *Kirata* people like the Bodos, the Kacharis, the Rabhas and the Mishings, who are known as the Scheduled Tribes of the Assam plains. They are all very similar in their physical appearance. A few scholars have found that the Morans of Upper Assam originally hailed from Nepal in the seventh century AD (Benudhar Sarma, Kedernath Brahmachari, etc., quoted in Chetri 1983:5). From this brief historical account, it would not be very difficult to guess that the historical and ethnic/racial relationship between Assam and Nepal is much deeper than what is really visible at the popular level.

(b) Heterogeneous Nature of Community of Bengalis. Like the Muslims of Assam, contrary to popular assumption, the Nepalis of Assam, empirically speaking, do not belong to a single monolithic homogeneous community; instead, they are divided and sub-divided among themselves on the basis of caste, sub-caste, ethnicity, regional identity, language and dialects. 'Gorkhali' is not only the main language of Nepal but also the lingua-franca of many other Nepalis who have their own dialects. The linguistic composition of the Nepalis in Assam reflects the original linguistic conditions of Nepal. The Nepalis in Assam besides their Gorkhali dialects, use Hindi and Asamiya as their second and third languages respectively. Despite these historical and ethnic connections, as the Asamiya society during the pre-British period was semi-tribal and semi-feudal in nature, there was obviously neither substantial migration nor emigration. All the main migrations to Assam with serious political ramifications took place, we must note, under the colonial context. After colonising India, the British rulers realised the suitability of the Nepalis as very honest soldiers of the colonial army. The colonial historian Gait

(1905: 292) recorded that in 1817, nine years prior to the formal annexation of Assam, the colonial army which entered Assam, ostensibly to form the marauding Burmese army, had many Hindustani and Gorkha soldiers. The British found the Nepali most suitable for their colonial army, and exploited them accordingly in their colonial spread, and consolidation in north-eastern India. Gradually, the Nepali soldiers became the most loyal servants of the British colonial army. In many civilian jobs also, the Nepalis proved their loyalty very strongly. This was obviously a part of their manifested social behaviour. What made the entire community dependable and faithful to their masters? A scholar wrote very pertinently: "The only political systems they are acquainted with are that of paternalistic feudal and theocratic rulers. As a result, obedience, loyalty, conformity and subordination are inseparable of the Nepali personality and character".

Being an integral part of the British expansion and consolidation, many Nepalis migrated to Assam. The colonial rulers naturally encouraged the Nepali soldiers to settle down in Assam, after their discharge or retirement from the services in army. This led to the Nepali settlement on the foothills between Arunachal Pradesh and Assam, the Naga hills and or Assam's forest fringes and river banks. Besides, a significant number of them settled down in Meghalaya and Manipur. Such ex-armymen later became agriculturists, and some of them engaged in small dairy business. Apart from finding the suitability of the Nepalis for the colonial army, the British rulers also found them to be very hardly hill cultivators. They encouraged the Nepali settlement in tribal hills to generate a buffer against the unadministered and rebellious tribals of the Assam hills. The British policy of encouraging the Nepali migration to the hills, Dutt observed, ensure their majority status in Sikkim and they composed about 40 per cent of the total population of Bhutan (Dutt 1981: 1054).

(c) Factors behind Migration from Nepal. Needless to say, there were some strong push factors in Nepal which constantly pressurised a large number of the Nepalis to seek livelihood outside Nepal. The economic forces behind their migration were: (1) growing fragmentation of landholding, (2) indebtedness, (3) ecological crisis through deforestation, (4) rising population without further land to cultivate; and finally (5) chronic deficiency of food production in the hill areas of Nepal (*Ibid:* 1981: 1053). These push factors together with certain pull factors in Assam propelled the Nepali migration to Assam and the north-east. Leading pull factors were: (1) the colonial patronage, (2) abundance of land both in plains and hills of Assam, (3) thinness of the local population and their refusal to work in some hard fields opened up after colonisation, (4) similarity of natural environment and (5) scope for employment in the colonial army and police, in the offices, as *chaukidars, darwans, chaprasis* and peons. Apart from these, there were avenues in agricultural sector, dairy, transport and construction of roads and buildings. The negative push factors in Nepal and the positive pull factors in India/ Assam caused conditions for their emigration from Nepal.

By the end of 1950, one in every 10 Nepalis had immigrated (*Ibid:* 1053). In India only, by 1970, there were 1.5 million Nepalis out of a total population of 11.55 million in Nepal (*Ibid:* 1053). The annual rate of migration of 1961 was 82,000 a year and 20,000 of them remained in India every year.

These facts demonstrate the very strong tendency among the Nepalis for migration, both temporary and permanent. Naturally, this is not a brain drain to worry the Government of Nepal. This is a migration of various oppressed people struggling for a dignified survival. The very problem of survival forced them to move out of Nepal. The existing laws in India and Nepal have helped them to look for alternatives outside their motherland. They can very easily venture, even as an experimental migration. This is definitely highly impossible for a Bangladesh national. Dutt (1981: 1053) has observed that the Nepali migration has taken place throughout South Asia, not merely in north-eastern India alone, and as such must be viewed on an international basis. With the above background in mind, we can now move to explain the magnitude of the Nepali migration to Assam. The data of nineteenth century Assam on the Nepalis is extremely scanty, and sometimes not very reliable too. However, to have an idea, we can use the figures provided by Hunter (1879) who based his account on the basis of first Census Report of India, 1872.

Needless to say, the massive migration of various groups to Assam served the colonial interests very well. The colonial rulers encouraged the great migration of several groups of oppressed people to Assam. We must note here that the British did not encourage such migration out of their desire to liberate them from oppression but to transfer them to another kind of exploitation—colonial exploitation. The exploitation of the black-tribals in tea-plantations benefitted the British investors. The migration of East Bengal peasants contributed to the growth of colonial land revenue in which the colonial rulers were fundamentally interested.

The influx of the Nepalis also helped to increase the colonial revenue in Assam. One economic historian elaborated this aspect in his study (Guha 1977: 91-94). He pointed out:

> In land abundant Assam, peasants enjoyed from time immemorial the traditional right to graze their cattle freely on the village commons and neighbouring forests. Hence never before were there any habit of growing fodder crops on their private lands. Under the British regime, the right was gradually encroached upon to bring forth additional revenue to the exchequer (*Ibid:* 91).

During the initial stage, the revenue collected from grazing fees was not very significant. However, with the gradual influx of the Nepalis and other graziers alongwith their cattle to Assam the revenue went up substantially, from a meagre Rs. 15,640 in 1895 to Rs. 86,325 by 1920 (*Ibid:* 92). This also explains one of the reasons behind the colonial encouragement to the Nepali migration to Assam.

From the massive migration of different oppressed groups, the British rulers succeeded in their main colonial interest, that is, to raise the quantum of revenue without any investment in Assam. Even the Nepali population continued to grow during the post-colonial period too. The growth rate of the Nepali population in Assam was quite high during 1951-71. Numerically they rose from 1,01,338 in 1951 to 3,49,116 in 1971, indicating a nearly 3.5 times growth within a span of 20 years only. Their percentage in the total population of Assam also almost doubled during the same period. During 1951-71, the Nepalis became a demographically significant group in Assam. They started sending their own elected leaders to the Assam Legislative Assembly, and played an important role in ensuring the electoral success of the Congress Party in Assam to some extent. This was possible because of their numerical strength in some constituencies. How do we explain the very significant migration of the Nepalis to Assam? As stated before, the push factors in Nepal remained very strong and forced a very significant number of the Nepalis to migrate. Second, the Indo-Nepal Friendship Treaty 1950 and two similar more treaties of 1951 and 1956, conferred upon the Nepalis equal rights with the Indian citizens in India, free movement, permission to seek employment, engage in business, possess property and settlement. Third, in the wake of the Chinese aggression of 1962, the government had to build-up a new communication network, besides improving the then existing ones in Assam and NEFA (now Arunachal Pradesh). A sizeable number of the Nepalis were already in the Indian army and Assam Rifles posted in Assam and the NEFA, besides the Nepali civilians.

The construction of more roads, particularly the strategically important border roads and link roads and the construction of 350 km long new Ranagapara-North Lakhimpur-Jonai-Murkoke-Selek railway line generated tremendous scope for the employment of the Nepalis, both in Assam and NEFA. It must be accepted that the border road construction inside NEFA was an extremely arduous task and that the Nepali labourers were regarded as the best for such a gigantic task. As a result, many Nepalis migrated to Assam and NEFA. Number of them later settled down in Assam. The NEFA did not share the burden of the migrants because of the operation of inner-line system which did not permit non-indigenous people to settle down permanently there. Therefore, Assam had to accommodate a large number of the Nepali labourers. In Assam, they turned into marginal farmers-cum-small dairymen. Certain among them continued to engage in road and building construction, as labourers and woodcutters. Still, some of them were absorbed as securitymen, *darwans, chowkidars,* peons, drivers and in skilled jobs like carpenters, both in the government and non-government sectors. A Nepali used to get the benefit over others including the indigenous population for some jobs. The protest against the Nepali migration to Assam has never been strong. In the wake of the Chinese aggression of 1962, many Nepali soldiers sacrificed their lives to safeguard the north-east frontier of India. This generated tremendous sympathy for the Nepalis in Assam. They were largely well-accepted and well-treated in the larger Assamese social order. However, the emergence of the Assam movement, which raised the foreigners issue, radically transformed the existing relationship of the Nepalis with the Asamiyas in Assam. The Nepalis, irrespective of their length of stay in Assam virtually became dangerous, unwanted foreigners in Assam who had been "threatening the socio-cultural and political identity of the Asamiyas" in their traditional homeland. The powerful Asamiya bourgeois press successfully labelled all the Nepalis in Assam as outsiders.

Needless to say, the Assam movement had a very wide mass base, both in urban and rural Assam. The demand for removing the names of the Nepalis for voting rights expelling them from India/Assam, and labelling them indiscriminately as foreigners very deeply affected the Nepalis of Assam.

It obviously propelled the sharpening of the old Nepali identity consciousness. The Indian Nepali leaders from Sikkim and Darjeeling, added fuel to the anger of the Nepalis living in Assam. The Nepalis in Assam began to mobilise themselves under separate organisations, and distinctly aligned with the right-wing political forces opposed to the ideology and praxis of the Assam movement. Along with some other aggravated groups, the Nepalis were forced to assert their distinct identity in Assam as Indian citizens. It is worthwhile to note here that till the enforcement of the 'Restricted Area Permit' in 1976 for entry into Assam and other north-eastern States, they had the right to enter Assam. Therefore, those who entered Assam prior to the imposition of permit system in 1976, realised themselves as Indian citizens. In spite of abrasions between the Nepalis and the Asamiyas in the wake of Assam movement, we would like to stress that though the Assam movement demanded deportation/expulsion of the Nepalis from Assam, together with the East-Pakistanis/Bangladeshis, the depth of demand and also of feeling against the Nepalis were definitely not as vociferous as against the East Pakistanis/ Bangladeshis. The last two categories obviously overlapped with the Na-Asamiya Muslims and also the Hindu Bengalis in Assam. This brings us to the middle class dimension of the problem.

The Asamiya middle class is mainly composed of caste Hindus and they highly monopolised the middle class jobs and opportunities in Assam. Therefore, the dominant section of the Asamiyas does not consider the Nepalis as a growing threat to their middle class monopoly, very unlike the Hindu Bengalis in Assam. The Nepalis of Assam are at present in no position to threaten the Asamiya middle class. Besides this, Barman (1980:12) has said that numerically the Nepalis are insignificant as compared to the Bengalis in Assam, hence, there is less vociferosity against the Nepalis. On the other hand, the Nepalis play a secondary role in Assam, and most of them are toiling masses; therefore, they are unlikely to create an identity crisis among the Asamiyas (*Ibid:* 12). All these accounts for lesser scare against the Nepalis in Assam.

(d) Less Backlash from Bourgeoisie

This also brings to focus one more aspect of the Nepalis living in Assam, that due to their weaker position in the class structure of Assam, and their near-total failure in responding to the middle class formation in Assam, the Nepalese have, very paradoxically, helped themselves to draw lesser backlash from the Asamiya bourgeoisie. It seems clear that if they continue to play the same subordinate role, and fail to enhance their class position significantly, they are unlikely to face severe backlash in the near future. The data also do not show any kind of threat by the Nepalis to the Asamiya nationality. However, their migration pattern hás shown unmistakably that their growth rate has been very fast during the post-independence period. This makes a section of the Asamiyas apprehensive. Like the Bengali Hindus, the Nepalis are also very sensitive about their language, customs and culture. The Nepalis of Assam, alongwith other Indian Nepalis, have been demanding the inclusion of Gorkhali/Nepali language in the Eighth Schedule. In recent times, the Nepalis have been quite very conscious of their identity, whether in Sikkim or in West Bengal or in Assam. That has to some extent affected their relationship with other groups in the states concerned.

In the wake of the Assam movement just like the Bengali Hindus and the Na-Asamiya Muslims, they too were opposed to certain demands and actions of the movement. Though, there were conflicts, none of these groups opposed to the deportation of foreigners from Assam through due legal process. Of course, the Nepalis as a community did not suffer the way the Bengali Hindus and then the Na-Asamiya Muslims suffered civil violence and the Asamiyas suffered state violence. The earlier generation of the Nepalis in Assam have deeply assimilated and integrated with the Asamiya set up and nationality. They prefer to identify themselves as the Nepali Asamiya. The Nepalis of the earlier generation had significant records of fighting for India's Independence in Assam. Together with the Asamiyas, they fought against the notorious grouping scheme. They also fought for the official recognition of Asamiya language as the medium of instruction upto the graduate level at par with English and "therefore for all practical purposes, the Nepalis are Asamiyas" (Neog: 1974).

However, their concentration in some pockets, and continuous migration have affected their assimilation process deeply. Unlike the earlier Nepali migrants, the new migrants prefer to keep their social and economic relations with the place of their origin in Nepal. The duality of their social roots hinders their assimilation with the larger Asamiya society and they suffer a kind of alienation both ways.

It has been seen that the migration of the Nepalis to Assam, like the migration of the Bengali *baboos* to man the subordinate status meant for the Indians in the colonial administrative structure, black-tribals to Assam's tea-plantations and the oppressed East Bengal peasants to Assam's wasteland had a common connection—the colonial context under which Assam experienced social transformation.

The growth of the Nepali population has been very remarkable, both numerically and percentage-wise in the post-independence period. Obviously, this was a part of the entire development process itself. The strong push factors in

Nepal have been compelling a large number of the Nepalis to move out of Nepal every year. Several treaties between the government of India and Nepal, the massive construction of road and rail track in Assam and NEFA in the wake of the Chinese aggression of 1962, have propelled the migration of the Nepalis to Assam and the north-east. The Nepalis are not threatening the geographic, social, economic, cultural and political identity of the Asamiya nationality.

The earlier generation of the Nepalis has already identified with the Asamiyas and have maintained their relationship with Nepal. The later migrants perhaps would take a little more time to assimilate. If the social compulsions are removed, the Asamiya nationality is likely to achieve more from the assimilative process.

However, this is not our intention to say that as the Nepalis are not threatening the Asamiya national identity, the Nepali immigration should be permitted to continue. The present Assam is neither land-abundant nor is thinly populated. Over the years, Assam has transformed radically. Therefore, we would prefer to say that by both energising the assimilative and the integrative processes in a democratic manner and calling a halt to the immigration from both Nepal and Bangladesh, one would hope to heal the genuine or imaginary injury to the Asamiya nationality caused by their fear of losing their identity in their old home—Assam.

Bohiragatos—The Indian Foreigners in Assam

Apart from the question of foreign nationals in India, the Assam movement also sharply raised the question of "outsiders" in Assam. At the initial stage, as we have noted earlier, the movement was targetted at building up opinion for expulsion and restricted entry of *bohiragatos*—the outsiders in Assam. As the concept *bohiragotes* includes all outsiders including the Indian citizens residing in Assam, it was realised that sending back or restricting the entry of outsiders Indians would not be possible within the present political constitutional framework. Thus, the leadership gave up the *bohiragato* issue, and took up *videshi*—the foreigners issue, to launch a movement. This gave a better rationale and respectability to the movement. Along with this, the issue did not look like a chauvinist one. The change of issue, focus and target gave the remaining non-Asamiya, non-Bengali, non-Muslim Indians living in Assam, a sense of relief. Some of them even pushed the movement by providing necessary financial and material backing, besides participating in various protest actions, giving the movement an apparently wider support base. That's why, we can see the Marwaris as an important sector who patronised and participated in the movement. In this section, we propose to talk about the non-Asamiya Indian outsiders like the economically dominant Marwaris and other groups of Hindi-speaking origins in Assam. Besides the Marwaris, this category too includes the migrants from Uttar Pradesh, Haryana, Delhi and particularly from Bihar. Obviously, the outsiders as a category is not homogenous—they are multi-caste, multi-state/region and also of a multi-class background. The data on them are overlapping which makes it difficult to specify each of their exact or near demographic status, due to categorisation of all of them together, as Hindi-speakers in Assam.

The Marwaris in Assam

If we see among the outsiders, the Marwaris are the most conspicuous and economically dominant community in Assam. It is difficult to assess the number of Marwari population in Assam since they are clubbed together with the remaining Hindi-speakers. The Marwari traders were among the very early group of migrants to colonial Assam. Captain Jenkins said that he saw Marwari traders even at Sadiya—the eastern-most town of Assam as early as in 1831 (Barpujari 1987: 29). It would not be wrong to think that the Marwari traders arrived in Assam immediately after the colonisation of Assam in 1826. In 1841, a British officer wrote in his work on Assam—"at present whole of commerce of Assam is engrossed by *Kaiah,* a very enterprising class of men, resident in the principal towns. They are emigrant from Marwar and seem to have been induced to settle in Assam for the sake of trading merely" (Robinson 1841: 245).

It is not very difficult to assume that within a very short span of colonial period, the Marwaris emerged very strong in the trade and commerce in Assam. So phenomenal was the success of the Marwaris, that it did not fail to draw the attention of the British administrators.

(a) Factors Behind their Success

There were some historical and sociological reasons behind the phenomenal success of Marwaris in Assam. The pre-British Asamiya society as noted earlier, was a semi-tribal and semi-feudal in nature wherein trade and commerce naturally did not grow much. This was further handicapped by the continuous policy of successive Ahom rulers to maintain Assam's isolation from the rest of India. This ensured the persistent of Assam's semi-tribal and semi-feudal society without much surplus and trade. Besides, the caste Hindu/Aryan population in the State of Assam had never been very strong demographically. Still, the caste Hindu/Aryan population in Assam would not exceed 35 per cent of the total population of the State. And, also there has been a conspicuous absence of a real trading caste in Assam. Pre-colonial Assam did neither produce significant surplus to develop a market nor developed a trading caste or class among the Asamiyas able to take-up trade and commerce in the early colonial period. It would also be worthwhile to recollect that the British colonised Assam at a time when it was a demoralised, disorganised and a depopulated State. Naturally, in such a situation, historically the Asamiyas were in no position to take up trade and commerce. As a result of colonisation, Assam's isolation was broken, and it was slowly made a part of the world capitalist system. The British colonilism led to the monetisation of Assam's economy. As we have noted, the conditions created by the inherent rules of colonialism, paved the way for growth of an organic market. And, in such situation, the Asamiyas were in no position to take up trade, and obviously, there was a vacuum.

The neighbouring Bengalis also, were in no position to fill up this vacuum in Assam. Such a vacuum gave the enterprising Marwaris a chance to grab the opportunity offered by the early colonial Assam, which was till then not open to them. The Marwaris already expanded their business significantly in the major parts of British India—their penetration to Assam was obvious and inevitable. Within a small duration, from the westernmost Goalpara district to the easternmost small town Sadiya, the Marwaris established their supremacy in trade and business activities.

Betterment of road communication, massive plantations and its resultant massive migration to Assam, the exploitation of Assam's petroleum, coal and forests, under the colonial aegis, offered great scope for the Marwaris in the growing market. The Marwaris stood next to the British in the emerging colonial market in Assam. The Marwaris were engaged as bankers and agents to the increasing European tea-estates in Upper Assam. In selling hardware and equipment for building construction, dealing in clothes and rice and grains in colonial Assam. Many scholars have missed the role performed by the Marwaris as moneylenders to the rural peasantry. Guha has made observations in their role in the colonial economy:

> The fact that the market sector of the peasant economy was completely in the grip of well-entranched Marwari trading capital ever since the advent of British rule is beyond dispute. Peasants used to receive cash advances from the Marwari traders against pledged crops, to a considerable extent. These traders and their agents were mostly put in census under the category of petty shopkeepers rather than moneylenders. The numerous shops provided for a network for the filtration of credit into the rural areas (Guha 1977: 49).

(b) Moneylenders' Role of Marwaris

Being moneylenders, the Marwari also helped the East Bengal peasants to settle down in certain places in Assam, together with the Asamiya *mahajans* and the landed aristocracy. Alongwith this, their grip over trade and commerce in Assam, a few *Marwaris* were also successful in getting appointment from the British rulers as *Mauzadars*—the land revenue collection members for a cluster of villages known as *mauza,* on a commission basis. The *mauzadars* were normally appointed from the influential Asamiya landed aristocracy. The appointment of Marwaris for *Mauzadars* led to a conflicting situation in the mid-19th century. In a petition to the Judge Member of Saddar, Moniram Dewan, an Asamiya aristocrat who afterwards had to sacrifice his life at the colonial gallows for his alleged attempt to link Assam with the first Indian War of Independence 1857, alleged in a very clear language:

> . . . while a number of respectable Assamese are out of employ, the inhabitants of Marwar and Bengalees of Sylhet have been appointed to *Mauzadarship*, and for us respectable Assamese to become a ryot of such foreigners is a source of deep mortification" (Mills 1853 Appendix: KB 607).

Through our discussion, it is not very difficult to realise that it was the consolidation that the Marwaris had made over trade, and even on certain influential jobs like the *mauzadar,* that led to the disappointment from the Asamiya aristocracy, whose powers declined severely after the colonisation of Assam. The number of Marwaris in Assam is difficult to ascertain, because of their overlapping with Hindi language speakers from North India and other trading castes. In Assam, most of the Hindu trading castes from northern India, and particularly from Rajasthan, are called *Kainah* or Marwari. It is non-controversial that they penetrated into Assam immediately after the British annexation of Assam. The Marwaris consolidated their position in the absence of a competing local trading group, i.e., caste or class without a very short period of time. For the first time, the Census was conducted in Assam in 1872. W.W. Hunter, then Director General of Statistics of the Government of India, assumed the number of the Marwaris in the Brahmaputra Valley at 5,234 including other north Indian trading castes.

Now it is evident from Table 3.10 that the Marwaris were present at that time throughout the Brahmaputra Valley. In 1872, Brahmaputra Valley's population was only 18,79,650 (Census 1872). Again in 1881, the urban population of Assam was merely 62,212 (Census of India 1931, Vol. 3, Assam Part II, p. 8). From this we can infer that the Marwaris were a significant component of the urban population. While the number of Marwaris was higher in lower Assam in 1872, than in Upper Assam, this demographic position was reversed later with the large scale tea-plantations, exploitation of petroleum, coal and forests and the expansion of road and rail communication network. As these provided scope for the Marwaris as a comprador partner of the British colonialism in Assam to victimise the trading opportunities in Upper Assam. Upper Assam gradually drew more Marwaris compared to Lower Assam. However, the Census of later stage overlapped the Marwaris with other Hindi-speaking migrants to Assam. Both Barman (1980:8) and Weiner (1978: 103) found that the number of Marwaris in Assam has been underestimated. Barman estimated their number at 70,000 and 0.05 per cent of total population of the State (Barman 1980: 8). Despite their smallness in number and in percentage of Assam's total population, one can very easily feel the presence of Marwaris in Assam—particularly in urban parts. Even if we examine the number of the entire Hindi-speaking population in Assam get to see that they were in no way threatening the demographic status of the Asamiyas in Assam. But, still, the relationship between the Marwaris and the Asamiyas is very far from cordial.

The Assam movement though does not explicitly demonstrate any apparent manifestation of competition and conflict between these two communities that does not also reflect the latent competition and conflict with its full explosive potential. We have already noted the economic status of the Marwaris in colonial Assam. What was their status in the post-colonial Assam? The class structure and composition has changed significantly in the post-colonial Assam. In the absence of the British, the Marwaris improved and even further consolidated their economic position in Assam radically. During the colonial period, they played a comprador role in tea-plantations. Today, they play a leading role in the tea-industry, together with the Indian big bourgeoisie. Most of the Marwaris in Assam are the agents of the Indian bourgeoisie.

This status has made them economically very dominant in an otherwise industrially backward state, and blocked the process of growth of an economically powerful Asamiya capitalist class. From the angle of trade, some of the Marwaris have also become industrialists of whatever visible industries that have come up in the private sector in Assam. They also own a large number of petrol pumps and cinema halls. As an outcome of the present development process, and Guwahati being the gateway to the north-east, it has emerged as the largest business centre of the entire north-east.

The Marwari dominated Fancy Bazar (See Weiner 1978:102-3 for a vivid note) which is the largest wholesale and retail market of various essential commodities and hardware. The Marwaris, being the dominant one in trade in Assam, have been able to economically exploit the entire north-eastern region. The network of the Marwari business, trade and industry has further developed radically during the post-colonial era.

(c) Relations with Local Asamiyas

Have the Marwari assimilated with the Asamiyas like other migrants to Assam? Like the Bengali Hindus, they have not been able to assimilate with the Asamiyas. It would be very important to recollect that only the oppressed migrants groups like the black-tribals from the Jharkhand region and the oppressed farmers from East Bengal, and other autochthon tribals, mainly because of their class position have assimilated deeply with the emerging Asamiya nationality. This also explains the counter assimilative tendencies among the huge section of the Hindu Bengalis and the Marwaris, because of their priviledged class position—the former being mainly of culture conscious middle class, and the latter, the economically affluent class.

The development of Asamiya nationality confirms that the oppressed groups take less time to assimilate and integrate as a part of their survival strategy—to live with dignity. They are interested in survival, not on identity. The Marwaris in Assam have built up their own Hindi schools, hospitals, temples, *vivah-bhavans,* community halls, and what else even newspapers—wherever their number is large. Besides, some of them have donated liberally to build schools and colleges at various places. They have also been very liberally donating for the Asamiyas national festival like *Bihu.* In every locality/town, the top Marwari businessman normally becomes the chief patron of the *Bihu* celebration committees. But does that make them well-wishers of the entire Asamiya nationality? An analysis from the class point of view, would situate the bigger section of the Marwari community as the exploiter class and/or the collaborator class in Assam.

Now the question is, if they fall into the category of exploiter class, why is the Asamiya influence weak against the Marwaris? Why is it not as vociferous as against the Bengalis? This simply exposes the limitations of the Asamiya middle class leadership. Since till they attain more strength, they would hesitate to fight against the Marwaris. This was also the lesson they have learnt from their violent outburst against the Marwaris in Guwahati on 26th January of the year. The Asamiya middle class does not find any significant competition from the Marwaris for jobs in the government sectors. An average Marwari educated boy would always prefer to go in for business rather than go in for jobs. The Marwari boys who now go in for medical education would prefer to start a profitable nursing home/private hospital instead of joining or waiting for jobs in the government sector. The proliferation of nursing homes/private hospital business in Assam would confirm this tendency. Apart from this, an average Marwari youth gets married much earlier, and earns illegally from dowry which is widely practised within the community. This amount is enough to initiate a modest business. By the time, his Asamiya friend/counterpart manages a job, the Marwari youth becomes well-established in his business, and financially far ahead of them.

Along with Assam's economy, the Marwaris also indirectly play a decisive role in the state politics too. Besides financing all right wing political parties, inclusive of the Congress and the R.S.S., the Marwaris contributed economically and materially to the Assam movement significantly. Their interest was obvious, because, the movement was started by the socially, politically and demographically strong sections of the State, the Marwaris did not want to antagonise them when they were desperately looking for any non-Asamiya supporters. Secondly, the Marwaris felt relieved when the movement was shifted from the *bohiragata* to the *videshi,* which categorically kept the Marwaris out from the target group. Thirdly, they were intelligent enough to know that this issue like "foreigners" and identity crisis among the Asamiyas would lead to conflicts between the Bengalis and Asamiyas, the Hindus and the Muslims, the Nepalis and the Asamiyas.

The beginning and continuity of such conflict, entirely on non-class issue, would present the Marwaris, a fertile time and opportunity to exploit Assam economically to the maximum feasible extent. The help extended by the Marwaris enabled them to hide their class position and patronised the blurring of class consciousness among the Asamiyas. All these shows the reasons behind the Marwari's support to the Assam movement.

Though they supported the Assam movement, it would be important to state that in the elections to the State legislature in 1985, the Marwaris did not support the pro-movement Asom Gana Parishad (AGP) candidates. This was evident from the voting pattern of the Marwari dominated parts like Fancy Bazar in Guwahati. This has shown that they would support the Asamiya bourgeoisie led movement to a certain point only, after which they would not support them. They would not let the Asamiya bourgeoisie to grow stronger or emerge as a threat to their total dominance over the economy. The leadership of the Assam movement did not wish to antagonise all the non-Asamiyas, together with a section of the Na-Asamiyas and the Bengalis at the same time. They were well aware of the Marwari's economic power in Assam. Therefore, instead of making them a target, they were made an allied force. The politically powerful Asamiyas had also tacit links with the Marwaris, particularly in getting jobs in the Marwari dominated business, industry or tea-gardens. That was an additional business, industry or tea-gardens. That was an additional insurance/second line of defence against unemployment of their children. Moreover, pertinently, the Asamiyas seriously lacked a class of businessmen capable of competing with the Marwaris.

Therefore, they had to accept the support of the Marwaris which mutually supported each other's class interest in Assam. This also explains as to why initial zeal for *bohiragata* transformed into *videshi* only. But, only the emergence of a Asamiya bourgeoisie stronger than what it is at present would be able to challenge the Marwari dominance in certain sectors of trade and business. However, the Marwaris are likely to remain where they are today economically, unless and until there is a radical shift in the class dominance of Assam's politics and economy. In spite of a not so cordial relationship between the Marwaris and the Asamiya at present, it must be admitted that some of the earlier generations of the Marwari assimilated and integrated with the Asamiya nationality fully. They played very important role in the formation and progress of modern Asamiya nationality. The famous "Agarwalla" family of Tezpur contributed significantly to the enrichment of modern Asamiya literature and culture.

Haribilas Agarwalla (1842-1916), just like the American Baptist Missionary, took up the responsibility of publishing books in Asamiya. He brought for the first time into the print the masterpieces of spiritual and literary writings of the Vaisnavite movement. His son Chandra Kumar Agarwalla became a very prominent literary figure of the late 19th century and early 20th century. Besides, he himself published and also edited an Asamiya magazine *Jonaki* (The Moonlight) which played a renascent role in the modern Asamiya literary movement. 'Jonaki' also helped in raising the national awakening among the Asamiyas. The influence of *Jonaki* was so high, that even the periodization of history of modern Asamiya literature starts with the "Jonaki Yug" the Jonaki decade. From the same family came another gigant Asamiya of modern Assam—Jyoti Prasad Agarwalla (1903-51).

He was famous as a great artist, a freedom fighter, a prolific writer who turned to radicalism at the later stage of his life. He fought for Independence, as dedicated by Congressmen, questioned the significance of Gandhian philosophy of non-violence, and was prepared to take revolutionary methods for attaining Independence. He was a revolutionary poet, lyricist and a music composer of quite high calibre who radically transformed the modern Asamiya music. He wrote several dramas which are still very famous. He produced and directed the first ever Asamiya cinema with sound at a time when Hindi/Hindustani Cinema with sound was hardly three years old. He appealed for breaking the isolation of the

Asamiyas, and to assimilate the migrants like the Nepalis, Bengalis, black-tribals, autochthon tribals, East Bengal peasants, etc., to the fold of Asamiyas (Sarma ed. 1986: 739-741).

He too was highly disillusioned with the post-independence development, which made him radical in his ideas and approach. He led the Indian Peoples' Theatre Association (I.P.T.A.) in Assam to prepare a mass oriented progressive cultural movement in Assam. But he died prematurely in 1951. His monumental contribution to the Asamiya culture, literature, and performing arts crowns him one of the greatest men that the Asamiyas have ever produced. Even today a few Marwaris are giving writing in Asamiya language. Quite a few of them have married Asamiyas, but, the assimilative progress has remained weak. The new generation of the Marwaris in Assam then preferred to remain as Marwaris. Wherever the Marwaris are relatively large in number, they have built-up Hindi medium schools at Guwahati, Dibrugarh, Tinsukia and Jorhat, which differentiates a Marwari from an Asamiya boy, hampering the process of assimilation and integration. Today, famousmost of the Marwaris neither know the contribution of nor the name of Jyoti Prasad Agarwalla.

However, wherever, the number of Marwari is few, they send their children to Asamiya medium school, together with Asamiya boys. A large number of the Marwaris are, anyhow, apprehensive about the Asamiyas. The 1968 experience is too bitter for them to forget. Many of them are still sceptical of investing more capital in Assam. They are diverting their capital to outside Assam. Besides, a large number of them are living in Assam in a semi-permanent manner. Dass (1981: 854) has rightly observed that the Marwaris are responsible for the drainage of the big savings and, also, for the poor accumulation of capital in Assam. It is needless to specify the importance of saving/capital for an industrially less-developed State like Assam. The Marwaris, as agents of the Indian big bourgeoisie, are an inseparable part of their operational network of the exploitative set up in which the Asamiya nationality, alongwith others in Assam are lugubriously rotating. For our requirement, it would be worthwhile to point out that, very paradoxically, though the Marwaris are dominating the economy of Assam very visibly and state politics very indirectly, they are not threatening the Asamiyas numerically, and culturally. The Marwaris, though very conspicuous in urban Assam, are quite small numerically, like any other exploiter class or community.

The Biharis as Hindi Speakers in Assam

The Biharis are the largest group among Hindi speakers in Assam. They are mainly engaged in laborious and toilsome jobs like-rickshaw pulling, *thela*-pushing, portering, brick-making, earth-filling, constructing roads and embankments, and as construction labours. Now, some of them are engaged in petty business like vegetable-selling, fruit-selling, hawking and running small hotels and pan-shops. The Biharis are quite a lot in number and a significant component of Assam's unorganised labour force. Their migration to Assam is temporary and they are not interested in

Assam's politics. They simply toil to feed themselves and save money to support/ supplement the income of their families in Bihar. They belong mostly to the abjectly poverty ridden low castes of rural Bihar. The Biharis are an oppressed section of migrants struggling very hard to earn a livelihood in Assam. So the economic position of most of the Biharis in Assam is pathetic, they cannot even think of sending their children to school, and cannot bring their families with them to live together. Obviously, they suffer from a high degree of alienation. Similar is the state of the poverty ridden migrants from eastern Uttar Pradesh.

Along with the Marwaris and the Biharis, there are a numerically insignificant number of migrants from Haryana, Rajasthan, Punjab and Uttar Pradesh. Most of them are engaged in business and commerce. All the above communities are migratory in nature. Together with the Marwaris, they too are responsible for draining out the savings from Assam which results in poor accumulation of capital, and therefore low investment which is again the cause of the perpetual backwardness of Assam. Now, it would be important to see the growth of the Hindi speaking population in Assam.

Numerically speaking, the Hindi speakers are in no way threatening the Asamiya nationality. The Asamiya nationality has shown a phenomenal growth rate as compared to others in Assam. This shows the capacity of the Asamiya nationality and its culture to successfully absorb certain migrant groups into its fold. However, Hindi speakers have a problem in Assam, as noted earlier, they just want to earn their *roti* in Assam, their nature of living remains by and large, migratory and quasi-permanent. That makes them inherently less responsive to the assimilative process. Those who are doing business in Assam for a longer period, have learnt the Asamiya language in the well-being of their business. Those who send their children to schools, normally send them to Hindi medium schools.

As the economically powerful Marwaris came under the category of Hindi speakers, under their patronage a large number of Hindi schools have come up in Assam. Besides, the establishment of several central schools in Assam, also partially fulfilled the demand of Hindi schools. The Hindi movies, Doordarshan programmes, radio programmes, besides Hindi as a compulsory subject in all secondary schools, has contributed largely towards the growing popularity of Hindi in Assam. The imposition/popularisation of Hindi in Assam has been very tacit indeed. The Asamiya middle class does not dislike Hindi, not because it is the official national language of India, but because the Hindi speakers are not their rivals for middle class jobs and avenues unlike the Bengali speakers in Assam. Simply put, the cultural issue like language does not come into the scene, while determining the relationship between the Hindi speakers in Assam and among the Asamiyas. The successive Assam governments have patronised the ongoing process of popularisation of Hindi in Assam. An average Asamiya may not be able to speak Hindi accurately, but he understands the language, even if he refuses to learn, because of common parentage of both the languages.

At the popular level, there appears to be antagonism between the Hindi and Asamiya speakers as the Hindi speakers do not threaten the identity of Asamiyas, both numerically and culturally. However, the question of economic identity of the Asamiyas is yet to be handled, and yet to be raised more objectively by the political leadership. We must note that the relationship between the big Indian bourgeoise and the emerging angry and nagging Asamiya bourgeoisie is quite far from cordial at the present stage. The sharpening of their conflict in the coming days may lead to anti-Marwari manifestations in Assam. As we have noted, the Assam movement has made the economically weak Asamiya bourgeoisie politically more powerful. The Marwaris, as agents of the Indian big bourgeoisie, are standing at an economically dominant status in Assam. The sharpening of conflict and competition for dominance in the regional market between these two classes is likely to make their competition and conflict more visible and naked. Lastly, though economic conflicts of an intra-class nature exists between the Indian big bourgeoisie and their agents—the Marwaris in Assam on one hand and the Asamiya bourgeoisie on the other. It seems there exists no cultural conflict between the Hindi speakers and the Asamiyas in Assam itself.

Non-Hindi Speaking Indians

This specific category of outsiders in Assam are non-Asamiyas, non-Nepalis, non-indigenous tribals, non-Bengali and non-Hindi speaking Indians living in Assam. They represent almost all the languages included in the eighth Schedule of the Constitution. The total number of population of this category was 1,88,456 persons according to the 1971 census. Their percentage in the total population of Assam was at 1.3 per cent (computed from Census 1971 Assam). A large majority of them are Oriya speakers, working in tea-plantations. Their position is similar to that of the black-tribal labours of Assam's plantations. They migrated to the state of Assam long back. Some of Oriya speakers are also engaged as labourers in construction, mainly earth filling and also as cooks and priests. The non-plantation category of Oriya labourers are ad-hoc migrants to Assam. The remaining 38,760 Indians are mostly employed in various central government, quasi-government, defence and missionary establishments. Some of them are engaged in small trade. Needless to say, their stay in Assam is largely temporary in nature. Even the smallness of their number would speak for itself. These outsiders are not threatening the socio-cultural or political identity of the Asamiya nationality.

To conclude, from our analysis in this chapter, we have found that the Bengalis, the Nepalis and the *bohiragatos* are not threatening the distinct identity of Asamiya nationality. Their time to time migration to Assam was linked with the colonial expansion and consolidation. Asamiya language, the most sensitive symbol of the Asamiya nationality is also facing no problems. Rather, it has shown the sign of rapid growth in Assam. These points demonstrate the existence of serious gap between the ideology of Assam movement and the empirical fact. It seems, it is not essential to have an ideology which corresponds to the empirical reality for building up a famous social movement. The ideologues of the movement, have distorted the reality to suit their class interest. They very successfully mixed their class interests with the interest of the Asamiya nationality. From our analysis, it is not at all difficult to say that the nationality question in Assam is a very complex one, perhaps most complex in India today. The Indian State has failed to solve the nationality question because of the class limitations of its operators. They have always attempted at only adhoc or ephimeral solutions to the unresolved problem like the nationality issue. Any long-term solution to the nationality question is inseparably related to the question of radical transformation of Indian society and polity. Unless such transformation occurs in India, the nationality question is likely to remain lugubriously unresolved, and a grim reality.

4

Positive Side of Assam Movement

The Description

We have already gone through various developments that took place in the context of Assam Movement but, it is also said that any significant social movement is always closely embedded in history and society from where it emerges. In our study of Assam movement, we have tried to situate its roots in Assam's specific society and history. We have tried to go beyond the title of this study in order to comprehend the nature of social transformation that Assam has been experiencing since the beginning of colonial era so as to understand the Assam movement from a larger perspective.

(a) Historical Transformation

The annexation of semi-tribal and semi-feudal society in Assam by the colonial rulers into British dominated India in 1826 paved the way for a different historical transformation which had broken Assam's long isolation of the pre-colonial period. The traditional social structure changed a lot. The aristocracy, particularly the ruling clan, the non-caste Ahoms weakened. However, a small fraction of upper caste groups managed to escape the onslaught on the surviving pre-colonial aristocracy propelled by the mechanisms of colonial system. They produced the first group of the western educated Asamiya middle class, by the end of the 19th century. The success of upper castes/classes and the failure of non-caste groups, like the Ahoms, rested on the question of acquisition of land. The priestly class had acquired large tracts of land by the expiry of the Ahom period, which the colonial rulers allowed them to retain. However, unlike the upper castes, the pre-colonial Ahom aristocracy could not retain their ownership of large tracts of land. Thus, those who could produce some surplus from their land could afford liberal western education by sending their children away from home to Calcutta and Dhaka. The Asamiya middle class section which was numerically very small had to face stiff competition from the Bengali class in colonial Assam. In Assam's colonial administration, the Bengalis had almost monopolised all the jobs meant for the Indians. It had two pertinent reasons; first, by the time Assam was incorporated into British India, its neighbour Bengal, already had a huge western educated middle class. When Assam was annexed, relatively advanced Bengalis came in together with the British rulers. Secondly, a thickly populated area of Bengal, that is, Sylhet was amalgamated with the province of Assam.

Therefore, being the subject of the same province, many educated Hindu Bengalis shifted to Assam proper. The British-owned sector of Assam's economy, particularly the tea-plantations had grown remarkably; but, it failed, even in accommodating the growing Asamiya middle class which had been facing competition from the Bengalis. It had obviously led to an anti-Bengali feeling among the nascent Asamiya middle class which failed to realise the colonial limitations. The British rulers succeeded in envenoming the Asamiya-Bengali relations in colonial Assam.

(b) Enhancing Land Revenue

We have seen that pre-colonial, and even colonial Assam, of course excluding Sylhet, was a land-abundant and thinly populated province.

Thus, its contribution to the colonial coffers was far below the expectations of its rulers. In order to augment the contribution to the colonial coffers, the rulers encouraged migration of different groups, so as to bring more and more land under habitation and cultivation, to enhance the land revenue. Many people, in order to avoid dual oppression of colonialism and feudalism, shifted to Assam where feudal oppression was far below the level of East Bengal, because of abundance of land and thin population. On the other hand, in the lack of local labour, the colonial rulers patronised the massive migration of black tribals from the Jharkhand region, in order to meet the growing need of cheap labour for the British dominated tea-estates. The poverty-ridden and oppressed black-tribals migrated to Assam in search of better living. The colonial situation in Assam opened the floodgates of migration, and in the same process, it transformed the social composition of Assam's population. As a part of its "divide and rule" policy, the colonial state provoked and patronised the Asamiya and non-Asamiya issue in colonial Assam, though paradoxically, colonialism created the conditions of massive migration to Assam. Besides, it did not allow the Asamiya nationality to grow, and obstructed the process of assimilation in Assam. Similar to its middle class, the Asamiya nationality, too, had to experience distorted growth under the colonial limits.

After independence and partition of the country, the Bengali inhabited Sylhet region became a part of East Pakistan. With Sylhet's incorporation into Pakistan, the Asamiyas became the biggest group in the post-independent Assam. This also strengthened the Asamiya ruling class, and it started exerting its hegemony over all other ethnic groups and minorities. In the process, it underwent severe backlash, and Assam became smaller in size by 1972, compared to 1947. However, we must note that the Brahmaputra Valley is the old homeland of the Asamiyas which they have been sharing with the autochthon tribals of the plains.

What we have emphasised in the encyclopaedia is that the Asamiya ruling class have been decisively shaping the politics of post-colonial Assam. It has been perpetuating its dominance in an economically backward, territorial reduction and poiitically disturbed State. Though India has developed a large public sector it is persuing basically a capitalist track of development to overcome its socio-economic backwardness. As an inevitable result of this path of development, strong economic disparities have emerged among various parts in India. Assam has remained largely backward. However, Assam has gradually transformed over the years, from a land abundant and thinly populated State to virtually a land-scarce and a densely populated State. The high rate of population growth without significant corresponding economic development has compounded further the burden of backwardness.

As a consequence, popular discontent was building up, and reached its peak around the time of the beginning of the Assam movement. It seems that the Assam movement quite successfully tapped the popular discontent to the advantage of the class of the people who led the movement.

(c) Dominance of Dominant Class

We think that behind the edifice of the movement stood the dominant class of Assam. Analysis of class dimension is very important to understand the nature of social movement. The masses participated in the movement out of their resentment, therefore, the leadership had to highlight some of the problems of Assam's economic backwardness, and negligence of the centre. However, we must note that the movement did not target at addressing itself seriously to the legitimate aspirations of the people for overcoming Assam's economic backwardness. The massive blockade of oil for almost one year was effected to pressurise the government to send back the "foreigners" who had come to Assam after 1951. The blockade was neither related with the abysmally low royalty paid to Assam by the central government, nor with better utilisation of this precious resource for Assam's industrialisation and economic development.

The leadership of this movement indoctrinated the Asamiya masses by emphasizing that the root of Assam's all problems lies in the continuous immigration from across the border. We do not refuse the existence of such a problem, but that problem alone was not fundamental to Assam's backwardness. Since 1971, the upper caste groups of the Asamiya ruling class declined in Assam's politics as they were marginalised with the emergence of non-caste leadership in the Congress Party. Since then, the upper caste leaders were waiting to an alternative organisation with a new ideology to recapture their lost status in the power structure of the State. The emergence of the Left political force as a potential way out to the Congress Janata formations in Assam alarmed them terribly. And, the decline of the Congress at the grass-root level helped them to join the leadership. Their road to political power has not been straight, they had to come through a zig-zag way, with ups and downs. In the process, they created a new ideology, and tailored it to fit their class interests in Assam. Not only had their ideology to undergo transformation but they also had to significantly transform their organisational establishment before embarking upon a massive social movement.

(d) Use of Persuasive Methods

Like many other social movements, the Assam movement, too, used its own methods to push the government to fulfil the demands. It used persuasive methods backed by massive protest actions, like strike, bandh, boycott, procession, rallies, *satyagraha,* blackouts, squatting and the like. The movement very successfully resisted the government's plan to hold Lok Sabha elections in the Brahmaputra Valley in 1980, hindered the flow of crude oil and made mockery of 1983 elections to the State legislature. Though apparently, the movement was led by a political student leaders, the Asamiya bourgeoisie stood firmly behind the movement. For instance, the Asamiya bourgeois press played a very decisive role in massive indoctrination, creating restlessness and fear among the Asamiya locals. The press which did not support the AASU movement of 1974, virtually became the mouthpiece of the AASU led Assam movement.

The leadership of the Assam movement was largely confined to the Asamiya middle class. The AASU, the Assam Sahitya Sabha and two regional political parties together provided the organisational ground for the movement. Geographically, the support-base of the movement was confined to the Asamiya homeland, that is, the Brahmaputra Valley. Socially, most of Asamiya upper-caste people were the maximum vocal supporters of the movement. The response of other social groups ranged from opposition to lukewarm support. However, it must be admitted that at the starting, the movement had a wider support base. Behind the apparent leadership stood solidly, the weak and nagging Asamiya bourgeoisie, composed of a few tea-planters, holders of Asamiya bourgeois press, Asamiya professionals, bureaucrats, middle class, contractors, owners of influential mobile theatres, transport operators and rural gentry. The rural gentry was successful in bringing a section of Asamiya peasantry to the fold of the movement. Additionally, the movement received support from the educated, semi-educated and unemployed youths from rural parts. They provided aggressiveness to the movement in rural areas.

The Assam movement reached its peak in November 1979, and continued till the mid-1980. This was the time when the Asamiya masses had shown the power of the people; lakhs of people offered *satyagraha,* resisted the elections to the Lok Sabha in 1980, hindered the flow of crude oil outside Assam and came out in large numbers on the streets to make curfew inoperative which was imposed to curb their participation in oil-blockade. It was the great participation of the people that made the Assam movement a very remarkable social movement that post-Independent India ever witnessed.

Assam witnessed the unprecedented violence. Both the leadership and the government failed to contain violence. Like many powerful social movements, the Assam movement also encountered a counter-movement. Apart from this, it had a very strong anti-Left tendency, both in ideology and in practice. It also destabilised the parliamentary politics in Assam; leading to collapse of four state governments within a duration of four years. Ultimately, the Assam movement gave birth to a Right Wing regional political party 'Asam Gana Parishad (AGP)' which captured political power in Assam, disproving one of its main ideological assumptions that the Asamiyas are facing a crisis of political identity in the wake of immigration of foreigners and inclusion of their names in the voters' list.

The career of the movement was also affected by a gradual transformation in goals. The leadership initially demanded 1951 as the cut-off, and later on they accepted 1971 as the cut-off year, for all practical purposes. The change in the target year was the result of gradual erosion of its support base. However, the leadership of the movement maintained an unstinting support base among the dominant groups of the Asamiyas and therefore, it could bargain for certain concessions. Ultimately, an accord was signed between the central government and the leadership of the movement. The accord recorded the official understanding between two contending parties. However, under the surface, the Asamiya ruling class came into a fresh working agreement with the Indian ruling class redefining their relations at the State level.

The emergence of the AGP as a ruling party in Assam with main leaders of the movement leading the State Government, led to the institutionalisation of the Assam movement. The Assam movement became a part of the establishment. Though the party got to taste power soon after its birth, and the leaders who operated the government machinery were young, they had to, however, accept the hard fact of operating within the same old institutions. Because of their severe class limitations, they failed to create new institutions, or change tangibly the nature of the old institutions. The new party and its young workers proved too weak before the old institutions. They lugubriously relied on the old institutions to accommodate them solidly. And, the goals of the Assam movement remained as away as they were before the beginning of the movement.

Here, we have tried to comprehend the question of Asamiya identity crisis vis-a-vis the Muslims, the Bengalis and the Nepalis, besides the autochthon tribals, the black-tribals and other Indians residing in Assam.

(e) Neglible Identity Crisis

The local Asamiyas in Assam, particularly in their traditional homeland Brahmaputra Valley, are facing no threat to their socio-cultural, linguistic, demographic and political identity. In spite of large-scale migration during the colonial and post-colonial period, the Asamiyas are not losing their identity, rather, such migration has propelled economic growth and better utilisation of land and other natural resources. Significantly most of the oppressed groups have identified themselves with the Asamiya nationality. This shows the capability of the Asamiya nationality to absorb and accept migrant groups into its fold. It should be observed that the demographic structure of 1951 census has been largely maintained in the census of 1971. Over the years, the Asamiyas have been growing faster than any other group or section in Assam, maintaining their numerical dominance. Thus, we find the existence of a serious gap between the ideology of the Assam movement and the empirical reality. We have noted that the Asamiya nationality is growing strength over the years, and even massive migration during the colonial and post-colonial period has virtually failed to check the growth of the Asamiya nationality. However, it is not our intention to say that as the Asamiyas are not facing a crisis situation, migration/immigration to Assam should be permitted to continue; the present Assam, as we have observed already, is neither land-abundant, nor thinly populated—over the years, it has changed radically. And, its regular economic backwardness has compounded the problem further. Therefore, we would prefer to say that by energising the ongoing assimilative and integrative processes in quite democratic manner and halting further immigration, together, would heal the real or imaginary injury of the Asamiya nationality, caused by the fear of loosing their distinct identity in their old homeland. In its long career of six years whenever the Assam movement generated certain bellicosous tendencies, numerous politicians characterised the Assam movement as a secessionist one. However, from our understanding, we do not feel so. As noted earlier, behind the Assam movement, the local Asamiya ruling class stood solidly, which is a partner of the Indian ruling class. They would not like to sever their coalition with the Indian ruling class, though at times, they wished for a re-definition and a re-arrangement of their relationship. In order to wrest certain concessions from the Indian ruling class, this class might have used its secessionist card at times. Assam's integration with rest of India was complete long back, unlike Nagaland or Mizoram. An indigenous capitalist class, capable of challenging the Indian big-bourgeoisie on equal terms is also not present. The Asamiya ruling class is neither capable of leading a secessionist movement, nor would they like to become nihilistically ambitious. The Assam movement was, of course, not a secessionist movement.

Thus, needless to say, the Assam movement has become a reference movement for tribal movements that have emerged in the hills and plains of Assam. It seems the issue of group identity at different levels has become very important since the beginning of the Assam movement. In the process, some fundamental issues related to Assam's economic growth has been relegated to the background as non-issues or issues of no fundamental importance. It seems, the Assam movement has affected the growth and beginning of a broad based democratic mass movement capable of uniting the people of Assam, irrespective of nationality, religion, caste, language or ethnicity, on certain legitimate economic issues and demands, to overcome Assam's severe economic backwardness and popular discontent.

The Text of the Memorandum Submitted to the Chief Election Commissioner by Certain Distinguished Members of Parliament, 1979

We the following members of Parliament take this opportunity of inviting your attention to various illegalities and irregularities in preparation of voters' list of Mangaldai Parliamentary Constituency of Assam. These illegalities and irregularities have caused serious tension and panic in the area and the situation demands immediate remedial measures.

"The Mangaldoi constituency is composed of a large population coming from the minority communities. The Government of Assam, as it appears from the recent developments decided to use their police machinery of deprive large section of these populations of their democratic rights. So far as information goes the police officials on instruction from the Government procured objection forms in large numbers. From the Election Office at Dispur they could collect about 10,000 forms, and as these were not sufficient in their view another 40,000 forms were printed. The police officials took these forms to the rural areas and got the blank objection forms signed by village headmen and secretaries of village defence parties in some cases under intimidation and threat also. The blank spaces were then filled up by police officials themselves.

On personal enquiry made by some of us a number of objectors categorically stated that they did not know the purpose for which their signatures were obtained and they had no reason to object. The inclusion of names in the voters list of persons whose names appear in the objection forms, we want to draw your attention to statutory provision that to make a statement in an objection from knowing or believing it to be false or knowing to be not true is liable to penal action under the provisions of the Representation of the Peoples Act of 1951.

"The police authorities by their action have made the innocent people subject to penal consequences. Panic and uncertainty have gripped the area. Mostly the poor persons without any resources have become the victim of this operation. They apprehended that the deletion of their names will be followed up by deportation notices. Most of these people have no resources to fight for their rights in courts of law. However, some persons have already approached courts of law, including the High Court at Gauhati, and obtained stay order against the operation of these notices. Citizens of our country are being deprived of their valuable democratic rights by this dubious method by the Government of Assam. We urge upon you to make an immediate enquiry and set things right at the earliest."

The same memorandum was signed by Y.B. Chavan, C. Subramaniam, D.K. Borooah, Ahmad Hussain, Hitendra Desai, K. Gopal, V.B. Raju, K.P. Unnikrishnan, Bedobrata Barua, Dinesh Goswami, Saugata Roy, B.P. Das, H. Bhumij, Jaharlal Banerjee and Dr. Rafiq Zakaria.

This Extract is about Violence Occurred during the Assam Movement

They are Burning the Bridges

The novel which won the Nobel Prize for lvo Andric, the Yugoslav writer, was called, "The Bridge over the Drinar." Bridges, in fact, appear over and over again in all of Andric's writings, because to him, the bridge was the symbol of unification and merger; and unity between man and man, culture and culture, the past and the present. If there are no bridges or if they break down, then the unifying threads between men snap and, as a result, even those who are close, slowly drift apart. That is why the history of civilisation is, from a certain point of view, the history of building bridges. The animal forces within man try continuously to create huge distances of hate and hostility between men; the great men always try with immense patience to build bridges of unity between men. Building of bridges

Table 1
Social Groups of Assam
(Ground: Religion and Language)

Religion	*Language*	*Assamese*	*Bengali*	*Tibeto-Burman*	*Hindustani*	*Others*
HINDU	Upper Caste	1. Brahmin including Gosain	31. Brahmin	48. Meitei of all castes	64. Rajasthanis of	75. Bishnupriya
		2. Suryyavipra Ganak	32. Suryyavipra		65. North Indians,	
		3. Kayastha	33. Kayastha		66. Nepalis of all castes	
		4. Kalita (Bar and Saru)	34. Vaidya			
		5. Keot (Halwa)	35. Sonari			
		6. Mali (Malakar)	36. Guwala			
		7. Saloi	37. Kumar			
		8. Suri	38. Saha (Vaisya)			
			39. Teli			
	Backward Caste	9. Koch (Bar and Saru)	40. Nath			
		10. Ahom	41. Napit			
		11. Nath	42. Dhobi (Suklavaidya)			
		12. Koch-Rajbanshi				
		13. Patia				
		14. Teli				
		15. Chutiya				
		16. Kumar				
		17. Mukhi				
		18. Napit				

Religion	Language	Assamese	Bengali	Tibeto-Burman	Hindustani	Others
		19. Matak				
		20. Sut				
	Scheduled Caste	21. Brittial and Bania	43. Namasudra		67. Dhobi	
		22. Hira	44. Bhuimali		68. Dungia and Dholi	
		23. Jalkeot	45. Patni		69. Muchi/Rishi	
		24. Kaivartta	46. Jhalo Malo		70. Mahara	
		25. Sutradhar			71. Basphor	
		26. Namasudra			73. Mehtar/Bhangi	
Muslim		27. Indigenous	47. Indigenous		74. North Indian Urdu speaking	
		28. Peasant Immigrant	47a. Immigrant			
Christian		29. Indigenous				76. Austro-Asiatic Monkhmer speaking Khasi & Pnar
Buddhist						77. Siamese

(contd.)

(contd.)

Religion	*Language*	*Assamese*	*Bengali*	*Tibeto-Burman*	*Hindustani*	*Others*
						Chinese; Aiton, Doania, Khamti, Khamyang, Phake, Turung
SIKH		30. Indigenous			Sujourners from Punjab	
TRIBAL	Plains		49. Barman 50. Boro-Kachari			78. Austro-Asiatic; (Mundari- Speaking)
			51. Deori 52. Hojal 53. Kachari 54. Tiwa 55. Mech 56. Mishing 57. Rabha			Munda, Santal, Ho, Savara, Oraon, Bhuyan, etc.
			58. Dimasa 59. Karbi			

Religion	*Language*	*Assamese*	*Bengali*	*Tibeto-Burman*	*Hindustani*	*Others*
	Hills		60. Chakma 61. Garo 62. Kuki/Hmar/ Mizo 63. Nath			

N.B. 1. Only major castes have been shown, without old social precedence.
2. Hinduised and christianised tribals and those following tribal religions are not differentiated.

Source: Taher 1988: 17.

is the work of those who love man and create his cultures: destroying bridges is the work those who hate man and lead the Vandals.

As part of the recent agitation against elections in Assam, many bridges have been burnt. This bridge-burning has so matched the overall character of the anti-foreigner agitation that it would have been quite discordant if such burnings had not taken place. Perhaps the agitationists did not burn the bridges with any deep meditation or planning, wooden bridges are easy to burn, so they burnt them. But unbeknownst to them, this orgy of violence has revealed the real aims deeply buried in their subconcious minds. By burning the bridges which appeared in Ivo Andric's imagination as the symbol of unity between human communities and cultures the agitations have proved that they do not want the great unity and merger between different societies and cultures, that they want alienation, hatred and hostility. These merchants of hatred and violent may want to display themselves as the keepers and guardians of a particular culture, but in fact they :

RCPI

1. Baneswar Saikia
2. Budha Baruah
3. Khagen Barbarua
4. Md. Shamsul Huda

PTCA

1. Binoy Kumar Basumatari
2. Kamal Ch. Basumatari
3. Panchanan Brahma
4. Samar B. Choundary

JANATA-S

1. Ramesh Mohan Kouli
2. Anil Das

INDEPENDENTS

1. Atul Chandra Goswami
2. Dewan Jainul Abedin
3. Nazim-ul-Haque
4. Phani Medhi
5. Premadhar Bora
6. Siraj-ul Haq
7. Sheikh Chand Mohammad

Assam Accord 1985
(Memorandum of Settlement)

1. The government have all along been most anxious to find a satisfactory solution to the problem of foreigners in Assam. The All Assam Student Union (AASU) and the AAGSP have also expressed their keenness to find such a solution.
2. The AASU through their memorandum dated 2nd February, 1980 presented to the late Prime Minister, Mrs. Indira Gandhi, conveyed their profound sense of apprehension regarding the influx of foreign nationals into Assam and fear about adverse effects on the political social, economic and the cultural life of the state.
3. Being full alive to the genuine apprehensions of the people of Assam, the then Prime Minister initiated the dialogue with the AASU and the AAGSP. Subsequently, the talks were held at the Prime Minister's and home minister's levels during the period 1980 to 1983. Several rounds of informal talks were held during 1984, Formal discussions were resumed in March 1985.
4. Keeping all aspects of the problem including constitutional and legal provisions, international agreements and national commitments and humanitarian consideration it has been decided to proceed as follows:

Foreigners Issue

5. (i) For purposes of detection and deletion of foreigners 1.1.1966 shall be the base date and year.
   (ii) All persons who came to Assam prior to 1.1.1966 including those amongst them whose names appeared on the electoral rolls used in 1967 elections, shall be regularised.
   (iii) Foreigners who came to Assam after 1.1.1966 (inclusive) upto 24.3.1971 shall be detected in accordance with the provisions of foreigners Act 1946 and the foreigners (tribunal) order 1964.
   (iv) Names of foreigners so detected will be deleted from the electoral rolls in force. Such persons will be required to register themselves before the registration officer in respective districts in accordance with registration of foreigners Act 1939 and registration of foreigners rules 1939.
   (v) For this purpose Government of India will undertake suitable strengthening of the government machinery.
   (vi) On the expiry of a period of 10 years following the date of detection, the names of all such persons which have been deleted from the electoral rolls shall be restored.
   (vii) All persons who were expelled earlier but have since re-entered illegally into Assam shall be expelled.

* Later, he became leader of the AGP group in Lok Sabha, and a Cabinet Minister during the V.P. Singh Government.

(viii) Foreigners who came to Assam on or after March 25, 1971, shall be detected, deleted and expelled in accordance with law. Immediate and practical steps shall be taken to expel such foreigners.

(ix) Government of India will give due consideration to certain difficulties expressed by the AASU and AAGSP regarding implementation of illegal migrants (determination by tribunals) Act, 1983.

Safeguards and Economic Development

6. Constitutional, legislative and administrative safeguards as may be appropriate will be provided to protect the cultural, social and linguistic identity and heritage of the Assamese people.
7. Government takes this opportunity to renew the commitment for the speedy, all-round economic development of Assam, so as to improve the standard of living of the people. Special emphasis will be placed on education, science and technology and establishment of national institutions in Assam.
8. (i) Citizenship certificates in future will be issued only by the authorities of the Central Government.

   (ii) Specific complaints made by AASU and AAGSP about irregular issuance of citizenship certificates will be looked into.

   (iii) International border will be made secure against future infiltration by erection of physical barriers such as walls, barbed fence and other obstacles at appropriate places. Patrolling of security forces on land and river along the international border will be adequately intensified.

   In order to further strengthen the security arrangements and prevent future infiltration, adequate number of check posts will be set up. Besides, a road all along the international border will be constructed so as to facilitate patrolling by security forces.
9. The land between border and the wall will be kept free of human habitation wherever possible, patrolling along the international border will be intensified and all effective measures will be adopted to prevent infiltrators from crossing/ attempting to cross international border.
10. It will be ensured that relevant laws for prevention of encroachment on government land and lands in tribal belts and blocks are strictly enforced. Unauthorised encroachers will be evicted under such laws. It will be ensured that relevant laws restricting acquisition of immovable properties by foreigners in Assam will be strictly enforced.

    It will be ensured that birth and death registers are duly maintained.

Restoration of Normalcy

AASU and AAGSP will call off the agitation and take up themselves towards the development of the country.

Centre and state governments have agreed to:

(a) view with sympathy and withdraw cases of disciplinary action taken against its employees in the context of the agitation to ensure that there is no victimisation.
(b) frame a scheme for ex-gratia payment to the next of kin of those killed in the course of the agitation.
(c) give sympathetic consideration to the proposals for extension of age limit for purposes of employment in public services, having regard to exceptional situation prevailed in holding of academic and competitive examinations, etc., in the context of the agitation.
(d) undertake review of detention cases, if any, as well as cases against persons charged with criminal offences in connection with the agitation except those charges of commission of heinous offences.
(e) consider withdrawal of prohibitory orders/notification in force, if any.
(f) the Union Home Ministry will be the nodal ministry for the implementation of the accord.

Government has agreed to the following:

(a) Election Commission will be requested to ensure preparation of fair electoral rolls;
(b) Time for settlement of claims and objections to be extended by 30 days, subject to this being consistent with the election rules; and
(c) Election Commission will be requested to send Central Observers.

In order to accelerate the industrial and educational development, the Government of India has agreed:

(a) to establish an oil refinery in Assam. Government will render all possible assistance in terms of institutional and Bank finance to facilitate the establishment of a refinery in the Private Sector.
(b) Central Government will render full assistance to the State Government in their efforts to reopen:

    (i) Ashok Paper Mill
    (ii) Jute Mills

(c) An IIT will be set up in Assam.

The Aims and Objectives of the AGP

1. Establishment of a progressive society free from exploitation and based on a political equality, economic development and social justice
2. To work for the achievement of secularism, democracy and socialism, to strive for peace, progress and social harmony and integration and to promote these causes among the people.
3. To secure more rights for the State in a real Federal Union.

4. Full utilisation of Assam's natural resources in the interest of all round benefit for the people and on that basis to strive for strengthening the state's economic foundations.
5. Protection of forests and reserved area and adoption of measures for cultivation of fallow lands and increase productivity.
7. To provide for full protection of the interests of local candidates in all matters of employment.
8. Restructuring of State's Plan so that the benefits of a planned economy serve the interests of the poorest sections of the society and thus ensure maximum welfare for the people of Assam.
9. Protection of the interests of local peasantry and workers by revising land laws and policy relating to industries.
10. Equal opportunities for all in the field of education, introduction of employment-oriented educational courses, and ensuring autonomy in the field of higher education.
11. Strengthening understanding and goodwill among different ethnic groups and sections of people, and adoption of all measures for the development of all indigenous languages, art and culture.
12. Extension of health care facilities to the poorest sections also through decentralisation of public health service measures.
13. To accelerate the pace of rural development by making improvement in the field of transport and communication.
14. Promotion of the scientific temper in the society in order to keep pace with future industrial development and for all this, to lay emphasis on science and technology.
15. In order that national and international problems could be faced appropriately, to seek to extend cooperation with all democratic secular and such other political parties and are opposed to regional imbalance and respect the legitimate rights of small nationalities: such cooperation would depend on the merits of the issues.
16. To seek to build up unity in action with all like minded parties of the north-eastern states for facing problems of common concern.
17. To adopt all measures to realise in practice the constitutional safeguards provided for in the Constitution for all comparatively backward people including SC/ST categories irrespective of their habitation, in hills or plain areas.

5

Dawn of Consciousness 1978 to 1981

This chapter presents sequential development of the movement focussing on the period between July 1978 to 1981. Total number of voters in Assam increased by 744,933 or 10.3 per cent in 8 months from March 1977 to November 1977. This phenomenal growth in the number of voters was due to the infiltration of about 1.7 million illegitimate immigrants from across the border and their inclusion in the voters' list by unscrupulous politicians. In the February 1978 election, the 'Janata Party' came up as the ruling party and Golap Borbora became the Chief Minister of Assam. In the 126-member Legislative Assembly, for the first time, the Muslims captured 28 seats. In this process, the Communist Party of India—Marxist (CPI-M) also captured 11 seats for the first time with the help of the foreigners' votes.

It was a clear indication, and as will be described later, that the newly-arrived 'foreigners' had gathered considerable political strength. The election results also were eye openers for politically sensitive Assamese people, especially the students of educational institutions. The representatives of the All Assam Students' Union (AASU) held a conference in July 1978 at Jorhat.[1] They made a 16-points list of demands, including the identification and deportation of illegal foreign nationals from Assam. These demands were submitted to the Government of Assam and the Government of India. To stress their demands, they started picketing on August 8, 1978, in front of the Deputy Commissioners' offices throughout Assam. There were *Satyagraha* (a grasping for truth; the political principle of Mahandas K. Gandhi, which favoured passive resistance and non-cooperation) from 12th to 14th August, a hunger strike on 21st August, Assam Bandh on September 22nd, *Satyagraha* on 8th, 9th and 10th October, and a 13-hour Assam Bandh (closure) on 11th December, 1978. On 21st December, the Executive Committee of the AASU began a 'fast unto death'. On 23rd December, the Government of Assam had a discussion with them and sought some time to consider the demands to which the AASU consented. The Government of Assam could do nothing in the next few months. Up to this point the movement was confined mostly to student community. As a consequence of these events, Atal Behari Vajpayee, then Minister of External Affairs and Shyamlal Shakdher, the Chief Election Commissioner (CEC) of India made some very significant statements which are now widely quoted. Shakdher in the conference of the Chief Electoral Officers of the States held at Ootacamund from October 24 to 26, 1978, declared as follows:

> I would like to refer to the alarming situation in some States specially in North-Eastern Region wherefrom disturbing reports are coming regarding large scale inclusion of foreign nationals in the Electoral Rolls. In one case (Assam) the population in 1971 recorded an increase as high as 34.98 per cent over the 1961 figures and this increase was attributed to the influx of a very large number of persons from the neighbouring countries. The influx has become a regular feature. I think it may not be a wrong assessment to make, on the basis of the increase of 34.98 per cent between the two census, the increase that is likely to be recorded in the 1991 census would be more than 100 per cent over the 1961 census. In other words, a stage would be reached when the State may have to reckon with the foreign nationals who may probably constitute a sizeable percentage, if not the majority of the population of the State.
>
> Another disturbing factor in this regard is the demand made by the political parties for the inclusion in the electoral rolls the names of such migrants who are not Indian citizens without even questioning and properly determining their citizenship status. This is a serious state of affairs.

With this, he proposed to the Home Ministry to initiate identification cards to the Indian citizens in the North-East Region. The entire population of the region welcomed the proposal, but it was not executed. The foreigners' lobby argued that it would create unnecessary harassment to the genuine Indian citizens.

Atal Behari Vajpayee on August 21, 1978, while responding to a call attention motion on the floor of the Upper House on the issue of the influx of foreigners, said as follows:

> If infiltration took place in any part of the country, whether it was Kashmir or Assam the security of the whole nation was jeopardised and Government would not allow monetary considerations to stand in the way of safeguarding the security of the country . . . this problem of infiltration is a recurring phenomenon and we must sit together and devise ways and means so that the North-Eastern Region could be made secure and the people there should feel that their sorrows and worries are shared by the rest of the country.[2]

Once again on November 27, 1979, Mr. Vajpayee made the following written reply to a question on the floor of the Parliament:

(i) It has come to the notice of the Election Commission from time to time that large-scale inclusion of foreign nationals in the Electoral Rolls, specially in the North-Eastern Region has been taking place.

(ii) In August 1975, the Ministry of Home Affairs instructed all the State Governments and the Administrations of all the Union Territories that the

> State Criminal Investigation Departments might be instructed to take immediate steps to check the electoral rolls and if they discover the names of foreigners in the rolls, that fact might be brought to the notice of the concerned Electoral Registration Officers for getting such names deleted from the electoral rolls. The Election Commission have also issued instructions to the Chief Electoral Officers of the State/Union Territories concerned that if it is found that a large number of foreigners have managed to get their names registered in the electoral rolls, recourse should be had to the provisions of Section 22 of the Representation of the Peoples' Act 1950, for getting the names of such persons deleted from the electoral rolls on the ground that they are not Indian citizens.[3]

Then Prime Minister Morarji Desai and Vajpayee made reassuring statements to the Borbora that the issue of foreign nationals would be settled but nothing was really done. They themselves had the problem of staying in power. The *Statesman,* a major newspaper in India, had thrown sufficient light on the potential threat to sovereignty by reporting on January 16, 1979:

> An offshoot of this population explosion has been a sudden change in the composition of the district's (Goalpara) electorate. The immigrants are in an absolute majority in seven of the nineteen Assembly constituencies in the district. In five more constituencies they are numerous enough to be crucial for an electorate victory. There is almost a similar transformation in the small border district of Cachar, which returned 15 legislators to the 126-member State Assembly.

By elections of 1979

During March 1979, a by-election was to be held following the death of Hiralal Patowary, the Janata Party's Member of Parliament (MP), in the Mangaldoi constituency of Darrang district. The voter's list was then updated for this constituency. Out of 600,000 names on the voters' list, objections were raised against 70,000 names as foreigners. The CEC directed the Government of Assam to take the required steps to correct the voters' list. Chief Minister Golap Borbora set up a tribunal which declared 45,000 as foreigners. This news transmitted a shock wave among the masses of Assam. If there could be that many foreigners in one constituency, how about the other 13 parliamentary constituencies, specially in the Goalpara district, the Nowgong district, and the Barpeta subdivision the place where infiltration is at an extremely high level.

To make matters worse, two Muslim Ministers, Zahirul Islam, A.F. Golam Osmani and some other political leaders who would have benefited from the "foreign" vote objected to the deletion of the names. The AASU discussed this serious situation in its annual conference conducted from 7th to 10th March, 1979. The AASU called for a 12-hour Assam Bandh on June 8, 1979, demanding deportation of foreign nationals. This Bandh was extremely successful and the people of Assam advocated the movement. On June 21, 1979, an AASU delegate handed a memorandum to the CEC at Dispur, a suburb of Gauhati and capital of Assam, demanding the removal of foreigners' names from the voters' list and their deportation. The people of Assam believed that in thirty-two years of independence, progress and prosperity had not come to Assam since millions of foreigners had come to settle on their land. The people of Assam boycotted the celebration of August 15, the Independence Day of India. The by-election at Mangaldoi was delayed for the forthcoming mid-term election.

Various Organisations/Agencies and Leaders Behind the Movement

The All Assam Students' Union made what came to be seen as an extremely intelligent decision by calling a meeting of all organisations who were actively supporting "detection and deletion" (of names from the voters' list), and deportation of foreigners. The AASU wanted to create a broader base to the movement. The three-day meeting was held at Kanoi College, Dibrugarh from 25th to 27th August, 1979. The same was attended by the AASU, the Assam Sahitya Sabha (ASS), Assam Yuvak Samaj and the Purbanchaliya Loka Parishad (PLP). On 27th, the All Assam Gana Sangram Parishad, i.e., AAGSP was formed. Three convenors were chosen: Bhrigu Kumar Phukan (AASU), Jatin Goswami (ASS) and Atul Bora (PLP) to lead the AAGSP for coordination. Soon the Assam Jatiyatabadi Dal, the Assam Jatiyatabadi Yuva Chhatra Parishad and the Assam Yuvak Samaj joined the AAGSP. By the expiry of December 1979, the Plains Tribal Council (Progressive), the All Assam Tribal Sangha, and the Young Lawyers' Forum joined the AAGSP. Ironically, the AAGSP is a forum which has been struggling on behalf of the Government of India for a national cause of security and integrity. Organisations mentioned below did not formally join the AAGSP but have given their whole hearted support: The Tea Garden Workers, the Banga-Bhasiya Asamiya *Samaj,* the teaching community like Assam College Teachers' Association, Local Teachers' Associations, the All Assam Employees' Parishad, (which is the top body of the All Assam State Employees' Parishad, the State Electricity Board Employees' Parishad, the famous All Assam Public Undertakings Employees' Federation, the All Assam Bank Employees' Parishad, and the All Assam Non-Government Employees' Parishad), Women's organisations and institutions, Sreeguru Singh Sabha of Gauhati, and the Assam unit of the All-India Sikh Students Federation. The AASU has a long track record of putting demonstrations, struggles, and *Satyagrahas* for various genuine causes such as: establishment of Gauhati University in 1948, the refinery in Gauhati, the sole bridge across the Brahmaputra, promotion of Assamese as the State language, Assamese as a regional language of education and deportation of illegal foreigners.

In fact, the AASU has been asking for deportation of illegal foreigners since 1974, when it submitted a 21-point list of demands to the Government. Some pro-foreigners try to discredit the then movement, calling it only a student-led movement. But there is relevance and justification to the students' involvement.

The national political parties did not protect the interests of Assam. The students thus lost faith in the political leaders and the Governments they form. Even many Assamese politicians betrayed the people of Assam. The AASU has organised a local level movement in towns and villages. Every college and high school has its own Students' Union. The 35-member AASU executive body has among its representatives from seven districts, Gauhati University and Dibrugarh University and includes Hindus, Muslims, Tribals and other minorities. They have an absolutely interesting and effective method of decision-making and implementation of decisions. The executive body discusses the strategy, coordinates with AAGSP and passes the decisions on to grassroot leaders for implementation the members were sincere and dedicated. President Prafulla Mahanta is a post-graduate student of economics, soft spoken and moderate. He is also a visionary thinker and a very effective communicator in precise words. Vice-President Atul Koch is an efficient organiser. General Secretary Bhrigu Kumar Phukan, 23, is quite shrewd and a very good orator. He is careful in his choice of words and how much he says, Assistant General Secretary Bharat Noroh, 21, is a Miri-Tribal. He is an eloquent speaker who can bind audience spell-bound for hours. Phukan and Noroh made several joint statements urging people to greater efforts, announcing new plans or criticising the Government. There are Muslim student leaders such as Gulam Murtazo Ahmed, Abu Nasser Iftekhar Hussain Bora, Nekibur Rahman, Altafur Latif, Abdul Jabbar, and others who have committed themselves for the just cause of Assam without bringing religion into the picture. The AASU also have able advisers such as Lalit Rajkhowa, K.N. Sharma and also Brindaban Goswami. The Purbanchaliya Lok Parishad (PLP) was founded in 1977, because some people felt that the national political parties did not protect the interests of the North-Eastern Region and they felt the need for a political party. This party has regional appeal and has thrown itself fully into the movement. President Nibaran Bora, 60, previously a socialist. He has also been called a 'human computer' because of his mastery over intricate facts and figures and ability to reel them off without referring to notes. The Assam Sahitya Sabha (ASS) has been very active in presenting and promoting Assamese language, literature, culture and identity over three quarters of a century.

It has given complete support to the present movement and is an active and committed partner in the present movement headed by its president Jatin Goswami. The Assam Jatiyatabadi Dal is a regional party. President Girin Barua is an old Ranji Trophy cricketer, present Deputy Mayor of Gauhati and an out-spoken person. He has been quoted as saying: "Whenever they (Bengalees) get a chance they try to suppress us. This is why we have clashes with the Bengalees since 1837. Whenever there is a movement or demand they always say the movement is against Bengalees. Almost all the foreigners speak Bengali and that is why the Bengalees are supporting them."[4]

Some critics accuse him of being parochial. The Assam Yuvak Samaj founded by Ambikagiri Raichowdhury, has been in life since 1965 and has been raising its voice for various causes of Assam. Khanindra Chandra Barua, who is in his seventies now, has been the president of this "youth" organisation for more than twelve years. He is a retired Commissioner of Assam"—a book containing various articles by the author on critical difficulties of Assam during 1960-72. The AYS is an active partner in the movement. The Assam College Teachers' Association has not formally joined the AAGSP, but at the same time, supports the movement wholeheartedly. It has submitted memorandums to the President of India and the Home Minister and prepared some literature on the movement. Satish Bhattacharya has remained the general secretary of ACTA. The All Assam Employees' Parishad's President is Debeswar Bhattacharya and the convenors of the same were: Dinbandhu Choudhury, Khanindra Chandra Das and Atul Chandra Sharma. There were also hundreds of local organisations and units of the above mentioned parties and organisations which are actively involved in the present movement throughout the State.

Collapse of the Borbora Ministry

We have mentioned earlier, Chief Minister Golap Borbora had set up tribunals to delete the names of foreigners from the voters' list. Under public pressure, he was also considering a deportation plan. For criticising his plan he dropped his Muslim Ministers: Zahirul Islam and A.F. Osmani from his cabinet. But the members of Legislative Assembly (MLA) from the Muslim block, Communist (CPM), Congress (Indira), and Congress (Urs), and also some others pulled the rug from underneath Borbora's feet. His ministry resigned on September 4, 1979. Jogendra Nath Hazarika became the next Chief Minister of Assam and after three months he also met the same fate. The fall of the Borbora ministry is a significant turning point in the history of Assam.

It explains the treacherous way most of the politicians work. The Muslim MLAs acted communally and opposed Borbora for his plan, which would have affected the Muslim foreigners most. The Communists, most of whom were Hindus, criticised him because the landless foreigners provide a fertile ground for the growth of communism. And the rest who "pulled the rug" were simply concerned about their own power. All of them wanted the foreigners for their own selfish reasons and do not care for the citizens in Assam and their votes. If we divide the total house of 126 MLAs along linguistic and religious lines, Assamese (Hindus and Muslims) are in a majority, and Hindus are in majority. Neither the language future nor the communal future of the State is of any concern to a collective group of MLAs. But that is what some groups of MLAs are fighting for. The result is that foreigners are going to stay and some more will too come. One characteristic common to most of the MLAs is disregard for the Constitution, laws, security and welfare of the State and the country. Had there been unity among the State MLAs and if the Borbora Ministry had been allowed to go ahead with the plan, the history of Assam would have been different, at least in the short duration.

The Movement Gains Strength

The making of the AAGSP boosted the morale of the students and the Assamese public. Regional and local AAGSP unit offices were formed all over the Brahmaputra Valley. The people got organised for a popular movement. The main demands were: (a) deletion of foreign nationals on the basis of the 1951 National Register of Citizens, (b) striking their names off the electoral rolls, (c) their deportation, (d) subject of identity cards to citizens, and (e) no election without striking out the names of foreigners from the voters' list. The AAGSP called for a Statewide protest and sit-ins in front of Government offices such as the offices of the Deputy Commissioners and Sub-Divisional Officers on September 6th and 7th, 1979.

The reply was overwhelming. People turned out in different towns by the thousands. The demonstration was peaceful, but some people were arrested. Mass *Satyagraha* began on September 10, and there was mass picketing of offices from 12th to 14th September, 1979, all over the Brahmaputra Valley. At the appeal of the Assam Jatiyatabadi Yuva-Chhatra Parishad, there was a convention of All Assam Employees' Parishad at Namrup on 14th and 15th September, 1979. The convention ended in an emotional outburst of complete support for the movement.

Mid-Term Election Issue

The Janata Governments of Morarji Desai and Charan Singh failed one after another in New Delhi. The President of India called for a mid-term election to be conducted at the end of December 1979, to elect Members of Parliament in all States of India. For this election, preparation of voters' list began over the country including Assam.

As mentioned earlier, the people of Assam had demanded that foreign nationals must be dropped from the electoral rolls and until that took place the election should be postponed in Assam. Following an appeal by the Congress (I), the Congress (U), and the CPM, the CEC took a 180° turn from his previous instruction of deleting the names of the foreigners. He directed the Electoral Registration Officer of Assam to stop the deletion of foreigners' names and stated, "A person whose name has been included . . . shall be presumed to be a citizen of India." The instruction said that objections could continue to be made but Section 22 of the "Representation of Peoples Act" (1950) might be inoperative until the balloting was completed.

Section 22 of the Act empowers Electoral Registration Officers to delete names of foreigners at their own discretion. On September 18, 1979, a Press Note (No. 88) released by the Government of Assam read:

> The Commission has instructed that no person whose name was included in the electoral rolls shall be eliminated on the grounds of citizenship as the process of establishing citizenship is time consuming. The Commission further advised scrutiny of electoral rolls after the election is over.

In thousands, Assamese perceived the administrative decisions as an insult to the Constitution of India and felt it was an absurd proposition to include foreigners in the voters' list and then assume them to be citizens. It is of benefit to remove the names once representatives are put in power to protect them.

Soon after this unconstitutional verdict, a full scale movement started. Students left schools and colleges, women left homes and employees left offices to take part in mass rallies in the District and Sub-divisional headquarters on September 25, 1979. There was spontaneous response from all sections of the masses. From 26th September to 9th October, there was a mass signature collective drive in support of the demands. In a meeting at M.C. College, Barpeta, on 2nd October, the election enumerators decided not to submit the electoral rolls until the CEC reversed his decision. The Master Printers' Association also refused to make publish the electoral rolls if the foreigners' names were not deleted.

The AASU, AAGSP, AAS, AJD, PLP, ACTA and other organisations called for an all Assam people's rally on 6th October, 1979 at Judges' Field in Gauhati. This mammoth rally was attended by people coming from all over Assam.

A torch of flame and a big silhouette portraint of Lachit Barphukan, the symbol of bravery and patriotism, were relayed by runners from Shadiya to Gauhati, a distance of over 300 miles. This novel idea was highly successful in inspiring the people all the way. Thousands of people waited at Judges' Field until midnight when the torch arrived. The runners were garlanded. In the middle of seriousness the masses still enjoyed themselves. They garlanded the dog which accompanied the relay for a very long distance.

The overall message of the meeting was that if the Assamese people want to live with respect, they must win this battle. Otherwise the Assamese as a sub-nationality might be dead forever. From 11th October to 18th October, there were acts like picketing and strikes. From 20th October to 3rd November, complaints were registered about illegal voters. A total of 320,000 complaints had been filed. This is trusted to be a fraction of total illegal voters in the State. A week-long All Assam *Gana-Satyagraha* started on November 12, and ended on November 27, 1979. The AASU and the AAGSP pledged to hold this movement on peaceful, non-violent, secular, democratic and Gandhian principles. The natives of Assam, the assimilated section of the Assamese society such as the tea plantation workers and others, Biharis, Rajasthanis, U.P. men, Sikhs, Tamilians, Malayalees, some Bengalees, and other Indians joined the *Satyagraha*. It is worth mentioning that old Bengalee settlers in Assam took part in the present movement under the banner "Banga-bhashi Asamiya Samaj".

Bengalee intellectuals such as Dr. Biman Kar and Professor Suhag Chattopadhyay supported this righteous and constitutional movement. A Bengalee young man, Ashutosh Dev Nath, also gave his life for the cause. Manipuri girl-students in Gauhati came out in procession and also joined the *Satyagraha*. The Khasi students also came from Shillong to join the *Satyagraha*. The response was massive. During the seven days of opposition over 700,000 persons courted arrest in Gauhati alone. Police authorities had a problem: where to keep the thousands of *Satyagrahis* who courted arrest daily? The then jail accommodation were inadequate. The Police converted all the open spaces in the city into temporary jails. Even those became inadequate. The authorities began to release *Satyagrahis* after a few hours of jail to make room for new arrivals. Mass picketing of offices continued from the 17th to the 19th and again from the 22nd to 28th of November, 1979, through the volunteers. Arrests and imprisonment also continued as before. Memorandums were submitted by Assam Sahitya Sabha (ASS) and Assam College Teachers' Association (ACTA) and other organisations to Sanjiva Reddy, President of India. The ACTA memorandum contained eleven points which included itself: "identification of foreigners on the basis of National Register of Citizens of 1951 and voter's list of 1952, postponement of mid-term election in Assam until the electoral rolls were corrected to become constitutionally valid, refusal to allow foreign nationals into Assam to whom West Bengal and Tripura issued citizenship certificates, protection of the North-East Region for the next 15-20 years from the influx of migrants and necessary constitutional amendments and some permanent measures to protect the border."[5]

On his, the President took no action. J.N. Hazarika, then Chief Minister of Assam, and other leaders met the President and the CEC in October. A group of student representatives hailing from the five States and two Union Territories of the North-East Region also went to New Delhi in November and submitted a joint memorandum to the Prime Minister of India Ch. Charan Singh. They also met the CEC, but the President did not grant them an interview. Y.B. Chavan, the then Deputy Prime Minister during the caretaker Union Government, visited Assam on November 1, and talked to the leaders of the AASU, AAGSP and other parties.

He informed them that the number of checkposts on the Bangladesh border was being increased to over 300 and the number of patrols was also increased. But he did not go to the heart of the problem. On his return to New Delhi he conducted a round table conference on Assam on November 28, 1979. The Conference concluded that the Lok Sabha (Parliament) election should be conducted in Assam as planned. The Government of India thus did not accede to popular demands in Assam and turned a blind eye to the illegal practice of using fraudulent electoral rolls. The only alternative left was to boycott the mid-term election. In protest against the Government's decision, a 34-hour Assam Bandh was observed on December 3 and 4, 1979, which paralysed the whole State. December 3 to 10 were the dates for filing nomination papers. The AASU and the AAGSP requested to the political parties not to file nominations. The volunteers started mass picketing in front of the offices accepting nomination papers. The candidates of all the political parties had been also kept under *gherao* (house arrest) by the volunteers of AASU and AAGSP and no one could file nomination papers.

The boycott was successful at a loss of one life, injuries to many and public arrests. No nomination paper was filed except in the Bengalee speaking district of Cachar. The Khasis in Shillong, Meghalaya also boycotted the election. The Government neglected the voice of the people by holding elections in two constituencies of the Cachar district. The Bengalee dominated Cachar district did not accept the movement against the non-Indians because almost all foreigners are Bengalees. Nihar Laskar and S.M. Deb. both of Congress-I (I stands for Indira), easily won the elections. The indigenous citizens of Cachar district: Dimacha Kacharis, Manipuris and Muslims did not participate in the election.[6]

Uncompromising Twin Leadership

Begum Abida Ahmed, the wife of late President of India F.A. Ahmed was the stubborn nominee of Congress-I. Another stubborn candidate was the Congress-U. nominee Deva Kanta Borooah, former Congress President. They led down the appeal of the public to boycott the election and not to submit nomination papers. December 10, 1979, was the cut off day for the submission of nomination papers. Begum Abida Ahmed, who is a non-Assamese and never cared to learn Assamese even though her husband was an Assamese reached in Gauhati on December 6, from Delhi to file nomination papers.

She rejected the appeals of the round-the-clock picketers outside her Gauhati residence not to file her nomination papers. She had no sympathy or concern for the movement and decided to go to Barpeta, her husband's constituency and a migrant Muslim majority area, to file her nomination papers. A curfew was enforced around her house on December 9. Anwara Taimur, who became the Chief Minister of Assam a year later, also tried to accompany Mrs. Ahmed. K.P.S. Gill, DIG of Police, ordered a Lathi-charge on the picketers and many men and women were seriously injured. At one point he ordered firing without the grant of permission of the Deputy Commissioner Jyoti Rajkhowa. Timely intervention by Rajkhowa saved people from being fired upon but the next day he was transferred to another job. Without the knowledge and order of higher officials who were Assamese like, Home Secretary, Deputy Commissioner and Inspector General of Police, their non-Assamese subordinates Narasimhan (Commissioner of Lower Assam), Malik, then ADM and Gill (DIGP) went ahead to help Mrs. Ahmed. At the order of Narasimhan, Gill and Malik took Mrs. Ahmed in a convoy of Central Reserve Police (CRP). About their 80-mile journey to Barpeta on December 9, picketers resisted their movement and many of them injured including two Cotton College ex-principals.

In the small duration of December 10, picketers stopped the Police convoy at Bhabanipur. Mrs. Ahmed disguised herself in a Police uniform but Khargeswar Talukdar, a pupil of B.H.B. College, Sorupeta, identified her. The Police immediately resorted to Lathi-charge. They brutally killed Talukdar and seriously injured several others. They threw Talukdar's body in the roadside ditch and went off. To cover up the Police brutality, the Government tried to prove that Talukdar's death was by drowning. The Government has not bothered to investigate the expiry of Talukdar on the attacks on the protesters. Assam Bandh on December 10, and a week long mourning followed.

Thousands turned out in silent processions in Gauhati and other towns in Assam. Public sentiments grew deeper. A curfew was imposed at Barpeta on December 10, and Indian Army troops patrolled the streets with automatic weapons with orders to shoot demonstrators at a particular sight. Mrs. Ahmed submitted her nomination papers on December 10, 1979, at Barpeta. The Returning Officer, after close scrutiny, declared that the papers had not been entered properly and the nomination was cancelled.

Deva Kanta Borooah is an Assamese and he was the President of the Congress Party at the moment of the controversial emergency rule by Mrs. Indira Gandhi. He was also the author of the "Indira is India" campaign during that time. The call of the public to boycott the election did not affect Mr. Borooah's political ambition. He was at the Nowgong Circuit House (Government Guest House) for filing his nomination papers. On December 10, curfew was enforced in Nowgong such that Borooah could file nomination papers without hindrance. But thousands defied the curfew order and surrounded the circuit house. Borooah was not in a position to file his papers. He called the incident "sheer intimidation" and accused the Police of collaborating with the students to prevent him contest the election.

Emergency in Assam and Presidential Rule

Chief Minister Jogendra Nath Hazarika included the two dismissed Muslim Ministers of the Borbora ministry in his cabinet. But he got opposition from them again when Hazarika reactivated tribunals for detection and deportation of foreign nationals under public agitation and pressure. His ministry did not run when the Congress-I, the Congress-U, and the CPI-M, who competed for the foreigner's vote, joined the block of Muslim legislators. None of the contending factions commanded a majority to form a fresh ministry. President's rule was imposed in Assam on 12th December, 1979, and the legislature and the ministry were suspended but not dissolved.

Agents of Movement; Victims of Atrocities

Renowned Khargeswar Talukdar was the first martyr at the hands of the Central Reserve Police (CRP). But others such as Purna Nirmalia, Kameswar Bora, Promod Kalita and Mukunda Boro lost their lives at the hands of immigrants from Bengal in 1979. Purna Nirmalia, teen-aged school boy was mercilessly beaten to death by a Bengalee restaurant owner for the pitiful sum of one rupee but twenty paise. At Lumding, a Bengalee stronghold, Police constable Kameswar Bora was killed by an armed gang. There was no retaliation.

Anti-social Elements

In the isolated case, some immigrants also lost their lives. On December 12, Dr. Anjan Chakravarti, a Bengalee doctor, was killed by some radical and impulsive anti-social elements in the Gauhati Medical College. The details and the depressed are not known. Timir Majumdar also lost his life in Dibrugarh.

The AASU and AAGSP have been condemning such violence and said that such violence would affect the image of the non-violent movement. They have been demanding an enquiry into the violent acts but the Government has not responded. The tea garden workers in the Doomdooma region who migrated generations ago and have been assimilated into the Assamese society were misinformed by some left-political workers that the movement was designed to throw them out. It was then explained that they had nothing to worry about since they are part of the Assamese society. The disturbances then reduced.

Open Pledge in Public Meetings

On 18 December, 1979, the people of Assam took the following pledge in public meetings:

> We pledge today to sacrifice our lives for the national cause of Assam and promise that we will remain active participants of the national movement launched by the All Assam Students' Union and we will save our motherland from the clutches of the foreigners and from any danger that may come.

And then, on December 19 and 20, there was a non-cooperation demonstration. On December 21, *adya shradha* (death ceremony) of Khargeswar Talukdar was observed all over the Brahmaputra Valley region.

Oil as an Effective Measure

Then the leaders of the movement realised that oil is a powerful weapon which could be used to put effective pressure on the Government to draw attention of the press and the people of India to their deplorable plight. On December 27, 1979, thousands of men, women and children squatted, stood and shouted slogans outside the gates of various oil installations throughout the State. The volunteers successfully hindered the functioning of the refinery in Bihar.

Later on the decision was revised to allow the Digboi and the Gauhati refinery to function. The flow of crude oil to Bongaigaon and Barauni areas remained closed. Assam produced 5.25 million metric tons of crude oil per year, which is over 50 per cent of India's oil production and over 15 per cent India's requirement. This oil is worth 70 trillion a year. Assamese people are also very unhappy that Assam receives only Rs. 54 per tonne (metric ton) as royalty and tax whereas the Government of India receives 991.03 per tonne. Seventy per cent of the oil is refined outside Assam and as a result Assam has been losing sales tax and employment opportunities. There was not even single petro-chemical industry in Assam. The oil blockade, however, got the attention of the Indian press. Previously the press, the leaders and the people of India did not extend any attention to the movement in Assam. The oil blockade got front page coverage in newspapers. Oil is as important to the AAGSP as salt was important to Mahatma Gandhi at the time of the 'Quit India' Movement.

Violence and Victimisation in North Kamrup

Violence broke out at Barikadanga village (about 10 miles from Nalbari) on January 3, 1980. A small group of students of Baganpara High School went to Barikadanga the same day. According to one version, they had been there to supervise a three-day strike in response to a call given by the AASU. According to another version, the students went there to gather money for the movement. The village of Barikadanga has a mixed Hindu and Muslim Bangalee population, most of whom are non-Indians. They attacked the students. A student named Dilip Huzuri, who was a member of the executive body of the Dhamdhama regional students' union, was speared to death and some of his friends received injuries. Dilip was a brilliant student who contributed articles to his school magazine regularly and wrote an inspiring poem called "Bhabanipur" on Khargeswar Talukdar's untimely death. The situation was thought to be an excellent opportunity by some of the infiltrators to start an Assamese-Bengalee riot. The Bangladeshi Muslims began fires in villages of Assamese and Bengalee Hindus on January 5. (It should be remembered that in 1960, at the time of language riot Bangladeshi Muslims put to fire the houses of Bengalee Hindus in Assam). An Assamese village called 'Arrah' was completely gutted. There were attacks and counter-attacks. About 12 Jawans of the Central Reserve Police were present there on the site. The Hindus returned to their houses but the Bangladeshi Muslims, whose number swelled to about ten thousand, refused to return and attacked the Jawans. One police Jawan was killed and others took shelter in Assamese villages.

In Barama Thana, 15 villages were burned. There were repercussions at 'Chawlkhowa' and violence spread into North Kamrup in the next two days. On the 7th, the CRP and BSF opened fire and people were gunned down. About four to five thousand Assamese then became refugees in their homeland. They took shelter in High School buildings at Barsimla, Helona, and Nalbari. There were also around six to seven thousand Bengalee Hindus and six to seven thousand Bengalee Muslims who became refugees. According to Calcutta news media 12,000 refugees went to West Bengal, around 30 Bengalees were killed and 3,200 houses were burned. These acts of violence are certainly condemnable whoever might be responsible. Perhaps only a judicial enquiry can bring out the truth. The incidents were the result of a colossal amount of group prejudice which has built up during the past 30 years. Mob psychology appeared to justify anti-social activities such as arson, mass killing and destruction even in a civilised society.

This happened not only in North Kamrup but in Moradabad and many places in India and the whole world. The root cause is the rivalry in a heterogenous society.

In certain areas of North Kamrup, most of the people affected by the violence were immgrants, both legal and illegal, as well as Hindus and Muslims from East Bengal (Bangladesh). The legal immigrants gave shelter to illegitimate immigrants. Therefore, without investigation it is impossible to identify how many legal immigrants who had been settling there for over thirty years were affected.

As far as mob-psychology matters, it did not make any difference to either of the parties whether the immigrants were legal or illegal. For this reason it is unfair that West Bengal should have mounted a full propaganda campaign that the movement in Assam was anti-Bengalee. All the blame was put on the Assamese villagers by the national press, particularly by the Calcutta newspapers and some politicians. The Government took severe action against the Assamese villagers.

The Government enforced a curfew on North Kamrup and called the military to aid the civil administration. But the military did not consult with the civil administration, entered into the interior villages, and committed unbelievable atrocities on January 10 and 11, 1980. The military and the CRP raped, beat and tortured over 200 women and men in 29 villages. The press gave very little coverage and termed them 'so-called atrocities'. The details of the atrocities are discussed later. Upto January 15, 1980, about 44 persons were reported killed, maximum of them were infiltrators but a few Indian Bengalees, six Assamese and one CRP constable were also the victims. Neither the AASU nor any other organisation or agency of AAGSP was responsible for this violence. It is unjustified to call the movement violent. Similar "incidents" happened during the freedom movement in India for which the Congress Party could not be blamed.

Incidents of Duliajan

On January 18, 1980, 12,000 picketers gathered in front of an oil installation at Duliajan. Picketing had been going on since December 27, 1979. It was not an unusual day. But in absence of the chief officer in the duty of the installation, who was an Assamese, an extra CRP force was brought and they fired at the picketers. Only four persons: Nagen Deka, Kumud Gogoi, Ajit Neog, and Nripen Bora were reported killed. Many of the injured became crippled for life and some are missing. Dr. Rabi Mitra, who was in-charge of the oil installation that day, was killed one hour after the firing.

26th January Tragedy

January 26, 1980, the Republic Day of the country, was observed all over Assam with the programmes laid down by the AASU. The Government programme was boycotted.

Letter of the P.M. and the First Round of Talks

Mrs. Indira Gandhi took office as Prime Minister of India on January 14, 1980, after a big success by her Party in the mid-term election. Yashpal Kapoor and S.D. Sharma, emissaries of Mrs. Gandhi, met the AASU leaders on January 17, and persuaded them to go to New Delhi for meeting with Mrs. Gandhi.

On January 22, Mrs. Gandhi's letter of invitation was given to the AASU and a meeting was called for February 2, 1980, in the capital. Eight student leaders including Prafulla Mahanta, Bhrigu Kumar Phukan and Bharat Noroh came to New Delhi. They also took for the meeting Lalit Rajkhowa and K.N. Sharma, advisers to the AASU, as interpreters. At the request of the student leaders, the meeting started with a minute's silent prayer remembering those who lost their lives during the movement. Indira Gandhi, then Indian Home Minister Zail Singh and top officials of the Home Ministry attended the meeting. The students handed over a memorandum consisting of papers, clippings and photographs which mere covered in 119 pages.

This carefully prepared memorandum contained eight familiar demands: (a) detection and deportation of foreigners, (b) deletion of names of foreigners from the voters lists before holding any election in Assam, (c) security of the border, (d) issuance of identity cards to citizens, (e) constitutional protection to Assam, (f) rejection of citizenship certificates issued by West Bengal and Tripura, (g) transfer of authority in granting citizenship from States to the Central Government, and (h) new nominations in the districts of Karbi Anglong and North Cachar when an election would be announced after detection and deportation of foreigners. They also made proposals like use of the National Register of Citizens of 1951 and electoral rolls of 1952 for the purpose of establishing citizenship, and a free zone devoid of trees and houses on the border. The Prime Minister was pressurised but agreed only on five demands (the first four and the eighth) in principle and offered 1971 as the cutoff date for identification and deportation of foreigners and denied the use of NRC-51. The meeting ended after 80 minutes. There are some interesting points which need to be mentioned about the meeting. After initial discussions, Mrs. Gandhi left the room and Zail Singh joined the discussion. The students were taken off guard when Singh had shown extra enthusiasm in deportation of foreigners. In Prafulla Mahanta's words: "He told us, 'Why should only those who came after 1951 be expelled? I think we should throw out all those that came illegally immediately after independence."[7]

Some time after that, Singh conversed with Mrs. Gandhi and said, according to Mahanta: "within half an hour he was back and said in a rather embarassed manner that 1951 was not acceptable to the Government and why could not we settle for 1971 as the base year?"[8] The straight thought "lost its tail" in the political setup. The students thought that their own spoken English was poor and hence they needed interpreters. But it turned out that they could speak much better than some leading persons at the meeting. Mrs. Gandhi claimed that they could speak fluent English. She asked who was their leader. The students pointed at a portrait of father of nation Mahatma Gandhi. The Government arranged for their stay in a five star hotel in New Delhi but the students decided to stay in Assam House, a guest house meant for Assam Government officials in New Delhi. They were also given cars to visit Delhi, Agra and Fatehpur Sikri but they declined the offer and a student leader aptly snapped at Yashpal Kapoor and said: "Have we come here on a picnic?"

This gave the impression of trying to bribe the students. Back home morale was boosted because of these declines. The student-delegation requested to Mrs. Gandhi to visit Assam and see the situation for herself. "We all look forward to a speedy and just solution. The loss of so many lives must not be in vain. We hoped you would feel the pangs of our bleeding hearts."

After this, on January 15, 1980, Assam Jagriti, a cultural organisation, also submitted to a memorandum to Indira Gandhi, Zail Singh and the members of Parliament. After the defeat in the talk on February 2, agitation continued in double vigour.

Visit of Giani Zail Singh

The Assam movement was relaxed from February 14, 1980, for a week for the forthcoming visit by Zail Singh, but the oil blockade continued. Singh came to Assam on February 22. The ASS, the ACTA, the AAGSP and certain other organisations submitted memorandums to Singh. After two days of discussion, nothing new emerged. The Government stand was firm on 1971, as the date of identification. Singh also visited Meghalaya in this trip. In a press conference in Shillong he was asked how many foreigners he thought were living in Meghalaya. His reply was: "A hundred and twenty". That was because he saw 120 persons in a refugee camp. In Meghalaya there are about 150,000 foreigners. Singh's remark was based on ignorance and drew that decisions are made the same way.

AIPP Conference and Third Round of Talks

On March 2, 1980, Indira Gandhi held a conference of leaders of All India political parties in New Delhi. This conference appealed to the movement leaders to stop their demonstrations. The appeal was rejected. At the invitation of Mrs. Gandhi, an AASU delegation again travelled to New Delhi on March 6, 1980. Nothing extra happened during two days of talk. The students suggested inclusion of the AAGSP in the discussion. On invitation an AAGSP delegate also went for New Delhi on March 9, 1980. The talks failed. The Government did not give any reason why the demands were unacceptable. The AASU and the AAGSP submitted a draft of an agreement between the two for acceptance and offered to suspend the civil disobedience. But the Government never responded to this draft agreement. Zail Singh said to students: "You can agitate to your hearts content but let the oil flow."[9] This was, of course, turned down by the students.

The movement activities then further intensified. *Satyagraha* continued all over the Brahmaputra Valley. Women of all ages came out and joined in the demonstrations. Thousands courted arrest.

Beginning on 24th March of the Blockade by the Congress—I

After consultation with Mrs. Gandhi, West Bengal Chhatra Parishad (Cong-I) leader Subroto Mukherjee launched a one-week long Assam blockade beginning March 24. Assam bound rail and road traffic was blocked in areas near Siliguri. Mukherjee declared on April 1, in Calcutta, that as far as he was concerned a blockade of Assam would continue in retaliation for the anti-Bengalee agitation there. They gave slogans like: "No oil, no food." West Bengal Chief Minister, Jyoti Basu called it a just cause. He flew to New Delhi and held talks with

Mrs. Gandhi and mentioned the Assam movement "communal and secessionist." He made snide remarks about Assamese women taking jam sandwiches and tea as if they were going on picnics rather than on *Satyagraha.* The Assamese women said: "If Mr. Basu wanted to participate in the picnic, standing for hours at a stretch in the blazing sun, going without food and drinking water in the heat and facing the Lathis of the CRP, he was welcome."[10] Even Mrs. Gandhi justified the blockade.

Formation of All Assam Minorities Students' Union (AAMSU)

On March 29 and 30, 1980, a convention took place at Jaleswar in Goalpara district by some Bengalee-Muslim and Bengalee-Hindu leaders and they formed the All Assam Minorities Students' Union (AAMSU). In April, the union office of the AAMSU was inauguranted at Howli, a Bengalee-Muslim stronghold. Two Assamese leaders of Congress (I), Lolit Doley and Dhrubanarayan Barua, also addressed the said convention. The professed aim was "to protect and strengthen the rights of religious and linguistic minorities by the Constitution of India."

This aim was not in conflict with the movement by AAGSP and AASU since they were not fighting against minority Indian citizens, but the actual aim of AAMSU is different. It was to assert that constitutional rights must be given to foreigners. The AAMSU opposed the detection and deportation of foreigners. They also opposed eviction of foreigners from illegally encroached Government land, forest land, railway land, etc. They also formed a sister organisation called All Assam Minority Yuva Parishad known as AAMYP.

State Government's Stand Against the Movement

On April 1, 1980, Governor L.P. Singh called a meeting with four AASU leaders. He offered 1967 as the date of identification of foreigners subject to the approval of the Central Government. He felt this would include the refugees who came to Assam during Indo-Pak war of 1967. According to Mahanta and Phukan, Singh's proposal was to identify foreigners from 1967, but the actual deportation was to start from 1971. This was not any different than Government proposals made earlier. Thus, this was not acceptable to the AASU. On April 3, Chief Secretary R.S. Paramasivam, who was sympathetic to the movement declared that the agitators will "face stern measures" if the oil blockade was not suspended. At a press conference he accused the leaders of the movement of cowardice and taking shelter behind women and children. He also stated: "This is a typically cowardly manner in which senseless leaders try to avoid consequences of their own mischief."

This was considered an underhand attack because when he had been sent on leave during the Hazarika Government in the last part of 1979, the students had agitated for his reinstatement and succeeded.

As a direct challenge to Paramasivam, common mass *satyagraha* was launched and picketing at the oil installations was intensified. The movement leaders asked the women of Assam to join the movement with more determination to give a fitting reply to the Chief Secretary's assessment. The response was overwhelming and thousands of men, women and children were imprisoned. It would be appropriate to mention here that during the Independence movement of India some Congressmen objected to the involvement of women in *Satyagraha.* But Mahatma Gandhi encouraged participation of women, saying that the women who can take the agonies of childbirth are fit for *Satyagraha.* The women of Assam, particularly the elderly women, have been on the front line of the movement. They argue: "Let us go to the front, let the military kill us first, the young generation must live, the young generation would otherwise blame us that we did nothing for them."[11]

Following this, on April 5, 1980, Governor L.P. Singh declared all of Assam except North Cachar district a "disturbed area", effective from April 6. The Assam Disturbed Area Act and the Armed Forces (Special Power) Law were brought into force.

This would have given power to the military to enter any house, shoot, strafe, bomb, and annihilate the Assamese people. Indrajit Baruah, a private citizen, observed the declaration was unconstitutional and submitted a petition in the Assam High Court. After hearing arguments by P.G. Baruah, the petitioner's lawyer, the then Justice B.L. Hansaria issued a stay order on April 7, and gave the government ten days in which to appeal. Soon Singh left for consultation with Mrs. Gandhi. On April 7, 16,000 persons, many among them women and children, were arrested but not charged. George Fernandes of the Lok Dal called the declaration of "disturbed area" just like a "declared war on the people of Assam." Chandra Shekhar, leader of the Janata Party and Atal Behari Vajpayee, leader of the Bharatiya Janata Party, condemned the act. On April 10, Government employees numbering more than 85,000 took leave from their offices and joined *Satyagraha.* They risked dismissal, suspension and even imprisonment in this regard.

Visit of Prime Minister to Assam and Meghalaya

On the occasion of Assamese New Year's day, April 12, 1980, Mrs. Gandhi came to Assam. *The Assam Tribune,* Northeast's main daily welcomed her visit saying ". . . the Prime Minister's present visit is certainly a silver lining in the otherwise cloudy atmosphere." She had a jam-packed schedule to visit places like Gauhati, Shillong and Nowgong in 9 hours only, including helicopter flight time from and to Gauhati airport. In Gauhati, a pile of memorandums were given to her by various organisations. Her meeting with Prafulla Mahanta, Nibaran Bora, Girin Baruah and other leaders lasted only 20 minutes because she stuck to 1971 as the year to begin detection. In a press conference, she claimed that some persons had "very exaggerated figure" on the number of foreigners. She also stated "One need not consider history but take a human approach. We have a certain international obligation." But she did not mention which international obligation.

During the meeting, she delivered a lecture that development programmes in Assam suffered as a result of the agitation. Disappointed Mahanta also declared: "Here we were talking about the deportation of foreigners, and she gave us a lecture on the problem of malaria in Assam." Out of 20 minutes how much time was actually devoted to the main issue is anyone's assumption. In Shillong Mrs. Gandhi had a meeting with B.B. Lyngdoh, Chief Minister of Meghalaya, and other leaders.

The Meghalaya Government presented her a memorandum which urged her to solve the problem of large-scale influx of Bangladeshis and Nepalis. It said some of the foreign nationals might be "agent provocateurs and potential sources of disorder" in the region. In Nowgong, Mrs. Gandhi was greeted with slogans like "Indira Gandhi go back", "We want 1951 as base year." Police dispersed the crowd, she had sufficient time (two hours) to talk to Nurul Hussain and other anti-Assam group of people. Thirty-seven members of the AAMSU and AAMYP had a meeting with her and told that they had been tortured and persecuted. They said: "Save us from the hands of those fanatics."

Bhumi Putra wrote:

> What was the purpose of this visit to Nowgong, of all place? What was the earthly reason for not granting an interview to such groups at Gauhati? Witnesses may lie, but circumstances cannot, so goes the old adage. The very strong suspicion in the public mind is that she blessed the catastrophe to befall Assam in the last week of May 1980, particularly in the areas predominantly inhabited by the people of the East Bengal origin and their ever-increasing brethren from Bangladesh.[12]

During return to Gauhati, on her way back to New Delhi, the Prime Minister addressed the people of Assam by radio. She said:

> Today your normal tranquility is somewhat ruffled. I have seen your deep feelings and I understand your wish to preserve your local identity. Solutions to the problems that are agitating your minds must be found and will be found. They should be arrived at in goodwill and in a spirit of give and take . . . You have apprehensions and I am anxious that these should be allayed speedily. We are determined to deal with infiltrators. But any action we take must be in accordance with the due process of law, humanitarian considerations, and legal and constitutional obligations.
>
> It is my duty to mention that a large number of people in the State have told me that they feel insecure because some looked upon them as foreigners.
>
> The agitation today is like a quarrel within a family. It has to be composed. You can be sure of my own sympathy. The government which I happen to head will always be responsible to any grievance that is genuine.[13]

During her speech, Mrs. Gandhi mentioned about due process of law, and legal and constitutional obligations. But her actions do not comply with what she preached. It appears that her humanitarian consideration overweighed rest of all considerations which is probably most beneficial for her politically. On one hand, she said the number of foreigners has been exaggerated, on the other hand she said that a huge number of people in the State felt being looked upon as foreigners. Judicial inquiry would be the best way to determine who are and how many are non-Indians.

Suspension of Oil Blockade

The State Governments of India and Assam challenged the Assam High Court's stay order. On April 16, after listening to the counsels for the Governments and the defence, a Division Bench of the Supreme Court refused to intervene in the High Court ruling. The Judges asked the High Court to hear the two parties.

On April 18, Justice K.N. Saikia of Assam High Court ruled that the two acts could become functional but stay would continue with regard to two key provisions which empowered the Army to shoot to kill. Regarding the provisions of search and arrest without any written warrants, Justice Saikia told the authority to take "sufficient precaution" when using these provisions. The Government did not waste time following this verdict. Within hours of the judgement, Governor L.P. Singh promulgated the Assam Preventive Detention Ordinance (APDO) even though there was no violence. The strategy behind this whole was to crack down on oil picketers. During the night of April 19, 1980, armed Police made arrests of Bhrigu Phukan, Nagen Hazarika, Nibaran Bora, Khanindra Chandra Barua, Nekibur Rahman, Rabindra Deka, Pranab Das, Atul Bora and other leaders totaling over 50.

On tip-offs, some leaders like Prafulla Mahanta, Bharat Noroh, Girin Barua and many others went "underground". On April 20, at 5 a.m. the Army and local Police arrested 2,500 picketers in order to tear off the four-month-old oil blockade. Early in the morning Government jeeps went around and declared a curfew through megaphones in Gauhati. The Army also established machine-gun nests around the oil installation of Narengi. The oil workers refused to obey the order to turn the taps on against the will of the people. The news of the crackdown and arrest of leaders spread fast. People left home and went to the street defying the curfew. All the roads leading to Narengi were filled with people. Bus loads of people came from villages. In the morning a tide of around 300,000 demonstrators, including women and children, marched to Narengi chanting slogans and carrying photographs of Mahatma Gandhi. Volleys of objects like teargas shells, baton charges, and barricades could not stop the tide. A total of 63 people were treated or hospitalised at Gauhati Medical College Hospital. Deputy Commissioner Kameswar Bora was forced to withdraw the curfew when a huge crowd surrounded him. Dulal Sarma, a youth, had further stirred the crowd's sentiment by slashing his chest and writing down with his own blood: "We will give blood but not oil." Once this picketing was allowed, life returned to normal. After eight hours of the crackdown, the oilhead was taken over by the demonstrators. Troops were gradually withdrawn. There was no sign of violence on the part of the demonstrators.

April and May Developments

On April 22, the AAGSP and the AASU announced their plan to screen and deport the foreigners if the Government failed to do so before May 10. Picketing of the Government offices also started on April 22 and continued for five days. Simultaneously the demonstrators started a blockade of wagons and trucks exporting things like tea, plywood, jute and bamboo. A student picketer was killed and another injured on April 24, by a speeding truck carrying jute. Thirty persons were injured in a Police baton charge on a crowd trying to look into railway wagons at Kampur to see if they contained tea or jute. About 1,200 wagons loaded with these goods were held at different places. On the last day, April 26, 2000 demonstrators were arrested. April 28 was observed as 'Non-Cooperation Day'. April 29 was observed as 'Martial Sound Day'. Church bells were rung and drums were beaten at 11 a.m. in the whole State. The protest was designed to draw attention to the issue. All air, rail and road transportation was suspended.

All Central and State Government offices like banks, and post offices joined in the non-cooperation. In a major shake-up, the Government sent Chief Secretary R.S. Paramasivam and DIG at the Border Hiranya Bhattacharya on unexpected leave and suspended more than 100 officers for sympathising with the agitation. Mr. H.C. Sarin, who is known for his heavy hand in suppressing the Telengana Movement, was appointed Principal Adviser to the State Governer, in fact, the Chief Adviser to Mrs. Gandhi on the Assam movement. The AAMSU called for observing May 5 as a protest day with rallies and demonstrations against the detection and the deportation plan announced by the AAGSP and the AASU.

On May 2, the deadline of May 10 was extended to May 25 and the AAMSU postponed its 'protest day' programme.

On 5th May 1,700 demonstrators had been arrested in front of the Deputy Commissioner's Court in Gauhati. Only on May 6, did H.C. Sarin, Chief Adviser to the Government of Assam announce that the Government had thought to step up border checks to stop infiltration and six motor boats had been ordered from Calcutta to stop infiltration through the Brahmaputra River. On May 10, the student leaders declared for a demonstration and meetings. Many student leaders were arrested and fifty were taken to Bhagalpur jail in Bihar. The Government employees protested against the Government's 'repressive measures' against their colleagues by abstaining from the offices for one day. The new Chief Secretary, Mr. Ramesh Chandra, suspended 60 high level officials which also included five Deputy Secretaries for abstaining from the office. On May 14, the evening before the deadline expired, the AASU announced that it would not go ahead with its programme to deport foreigners but the AAGSP maintained that the deportation should start.

The same evening, the AAMSU decided to stage a demonstration on May 26. On May 16, there was a communal riot at Tinsukia and five peoples were killed by Police and 14 were injured. Jyoti Basu observed "Bengal Bandh" on

May 17, referring to it a protest against harassment of Bengalees in Assam. The Bengali-speaking Cachar District of Assam and Tripura joined the Bengal Bandh move.

Protest by Foreign Nationals of Bangladesh

On May 26, the AAMSU led processions in certain regions which include Barpeta subdivision, the Goalpara district and the Nowgong district. In the Barpeta subdivision alone there were nine rallies which were reported to have also attracted 300,000 foreigners and their supporters. The Government relaxed curfew for two hours in Barpeta to permit the procession organisers to submit memoranda. Mr. K. Rammurthy, advisor to the Governor, accepted that lethal weapons were found in their possession. The foreign nationals in their rallies shouted "Joy Bangla," unfurled the national flag of Bangladesh, carried the portrait of Sheikh Mujibur Rahman, and inscribed 'Joy Bangla' on running vehicles.

In Nowgong, Kamrup and Goalpara the foreigners attacked the Assamese population. On May 28, some 4,000 foreigners, carrying weapons, made a planned attack on some villages in the Nowgong district. Before the Police could take action, they had set fire to 300 homes, making 1,200 Assamese people homeless. In another violent attack at Athgaon Chapari in the Nowgong district, they killed ten Indian citizens and injured 300 people. When Police gheraoed 250 of the foreign nationals, 68 lathis, 18 daoes, 26 daggers and 87 spears were recovered. The foreign nationals also stopped buses, attacked passengers and kidnapped some passengers, some among whom could not be found later. They were so defiant and violent that the Police had to resort to firing resulting in the death of several persons. In the six days of violence that ended on May 29, 39 persons were heard killed in Nowgong district.

The Defeat of Government in Another Legal Battle

The student leaders who had been still free sought legal remedy in the Assam High Court. On April 29, 1980, J.C. Medhi moved a 'habeas corpus' motion before Justice Ibotombi Singh on behalf of the other detained leaders. Medhi described the ground of conspiracy and instigation of people to paralyse Government functioning, as blamed by the Government, as "totally vague and unrelated to maintenance of public order." He hammered away at the prosecution grounds of detention describing them as violation of the Constitution and a serious attack on personal liberty. He further argued:

> Such meagre safeguards as the Constitution has provided against the improper exercise of power must be jealously watched and enforced by the court . . . Our country is taking singular pride in democratic ideals enshrined in the Constitution and most cherished of these ideals is personal liberty. It would be ironic, if in the name of social security, we would sanction the subversion of this liberty . . . no freedom is higher than personal freedom and duty is higher than to maintain it unimpaired.

Then Justice Ibotombi Singh dismissed the prosecution case and held that the detenus were detained improperly without adequate grounds for their arrest and ordered their release.

Talks between the Government and Students

On May 31, a joint gathering of seven political parties of India appealed to sponsors of the movement to call off their agitation as a first step towards a negotiated settlement. The leaders said there was no reason of either calling off or suspending the agitation until an acceptable solution had been formulated. They called it a deceptive strategy of Mrs. Gandhi. Also they said that unless the repressive measures were taken back, there could be no negotiation. A delegation from Assam met Mrs. Gandhi on July 2, in New Delhi but could resolve nothing. During the second week of July, more than 5,000 persons had been arrested for picketing Government offices. The student leaders asked Mrs. Gandhi on July 12, to withdraw all repressive measures in order to clear the way for negotiations. Mrs. Gandhi did not agree to this proposal until the student leaders would agree to her proposal deciding 1971 as the date of inquiry. At the initiative of Manipur Minister Mr. Dorendra Singh, a congenial atmosphere was created for a meeting on August 11, in Imphal, between the Central Government and the leaders of the All Assam Gana Sangram Parishad and the All Assam Students' Union. The Government of India carried M.L.S. Chhabra, a Joint Secretary of the Home Ministry and Mr. Dorendra Singh. The leaders agreed to lift the embargo on tea, jute, bamboo and timber and to suspend agitation during the talks and demanded that by the 15th, the Government of India should free all detainees, lift the curfew and reinstate State employees suspended for taking part in the agitation.

The representatives of the Central Government agreed and a full-fledged meeting was scheduled on the 18th of August in Shillong. After three hours of discussion the Shillong meeting ended only in a stalemate. After the meeting Bhrigu Kumar Phukan, General Secretary of the AASU, said that the Government did not fulfil its promises. Curfew was not lifted from the Narengi oil installation and other repressive measures were not fully withdrawn. Phukan also said in a public meeting at Sibsagar that the Government had a "half-hearted and insincere attitude". Yogendra Makwana, the then Minister of State for Home Affairs who attended the meeting, said that 179 out of 207 Government employees who were suspended for supporting the agitation had been reinstated in their Government jobs and the process of reinstating the rest was continuing.

The movement leaders were determined that Dorendra Singh attended the meeting. Mr. Makwana said that the demands could not be fulfilled and that the leaders "beat about the bush and never came near the main issue." Mrs. Gandhi informed a general body meeting of the Congress (I) Party in Parliament that vested interests were creating hurdles in the Government's efforts to bring about a peaceful solution of the foreigners' question in Assam. The Government arrested five student leaders on August 20, and two more student leaders including Vice-President Atul

Koch on August 23.

The leaders asked the release of the seven students and said that such 'bureaucratic excesses' might lead to a difficult situation. According to Sitaram Kesari, Minister of State for Parliamentary Affairs, a total of 1,609,157 persons had been arrested for participating in the Assam Movement; 17,612 arrested persons had been put on trial in the law courts; 28 persons were killed in Police firing and one constable of the Central Reserve Police (CRP) was killed in mob violence between January 1 and June 18, 1980. As per news reports based on official figures, a total of 189 persons were killed and 243 were missing. According to Mr. Makwana, as stated earlier, 207 Government officials had been suspended.[15] The total number of detainees under the Prevention Detention Ordinance could be above one hundred, 82 of whom were reported released by August 14, 1980.

In November 1979, 700,000 during a week-long *satyagraha,* persons were arrested. Therefore, a total of 2,309,000 persons had been arrested in this movement, including men, women and children upto June 1980. Around 3,700 houses had been burned, of which about 500 belonged to the Assamese. There have been no incidents of burning or destroying public property.

Development in October and November, 1980

In October of 1980, the Government said it was ready to start work to identify foreigners who entered the State after 1975. There was a talk in New Delhi which failed again. Home Minister Zail Singh consented to use in the NRC alongwith other relevant public documents to detect the foreigners and correct the voters' list. But the talks broke down when he expressed inability to remove any foreigner coming in between 1961-71 even after identification of visa. On this, agitation leaders had taken a rigid and obstinate attitude and let themselves fall prey to "vested interests". The agitation leaders said the Centre was not sincere and the negotiations were an "exercise in futility." There were general strikes and picketing. At least 17 persons were arrested under the controversial National Security Ordinance and over 300 persons had been arrested under other laws. On October 30, ten persons were injured at Barpeta in a clash between the AAMSU demonstrators and local supporters of this movement. There were talks on forming a new Government in Assam to replace the President's rule. The people of Assam objected to this area since many of the representatives were elected with the help of foreigners' votes and they failed to take action on the issue when they were in power.

Volunteers gheraoed the hostel of the legislators at Dispur, Gauhati and kept them under *Gherao* (house arrest). On November 1, the CRP was called to disperse the volunteers. The CRP lathi-charged and many persons were injured. Dilip Chakravarti, a mild-mannered upper division clerk of Assam secretariat while walking through the corridor of his office was fired and shot dead by a CRP without any provocation.

This added to the furore. People took the clerk's body in a procession in

Gauhati. There were protest marches throughout the Brahmaputra Valley. On November 2, the Army was called out to help the Police and protect the legislators. The Government arrested picketers at the oil wells the same day and began to pump oil to the Gauhati refinery. The AASU asked the oil workers to stop working in protest against Dilip's death. On November 3, a 12-hour strike crippled Assam.

In this protest, 1,200 workers of Gauhati refinery stopped working for the next 26 days. Mass picketing of oil installations started again on November 5. The CRP tried to raid the Gauhati Medical College hostels at 11 p.m. on November 27. The campus is on a hilly terrain and there is no other way in except through the main gate which was locked. The watchman refused to open the gate without permission of the college principal. Principal Dr. Jogesh Mahanta refused permission at the hour of the night specially when there were girl students. After two days Mahanta was transferred to Assam Medical College in Dibrugarh.

This unwarranted transfer was protested by the students and the teaching faculty of the medical college. Dr. Mahanta was already in the black list for not performing, as the Government wanted, a post-mortem test on Dilip Chakravarty in the night. He was killed in Police firing on November 1. On November 28, at 4 a.m., the CRP raided 7 boys' hostels of Cotton College, Gauhati without search warrants, even without an accompanying magistrate and without informing the principal of the college. They smashed doors and windows, entered rooms, beat and pulled the students numbering 468, loaded them in six buses and took them to a Police Station. Many students were injured and five of them were hospitalised. They were remained in the buses for ten hours without food, water and sanitary facilities. Some charges were brought against 64 students and others were released at 4 p.m. The CRP took away cooking knives and biology dissection boxes as dangerous weapons. They also took gold rings and watches away from the students and did not give the items back. The same day the CRP totally ransacked the Gauhati AASU office at Sudmerson Hall, Cotton College. For the next few days there were protests against the inhumanly CRP attack on Cotton College students. The CRP also took over Bhagawati Prasad Bhavan Gauhati office of the Assam Sahitya Sabha.

Elections after the Emergency

We have already mentioned that the President's rule was imposed on Assam on December 12, 1979. According to the Constitution of India, the President's rule cannot be extended beyond one year. But it could have been extended in any case, provided two conditions were satisfied: (a) the State Assembly, which was in suspended animation, had to be dissolved, and (b) the Chief Election Commissioner had to certify that fresh elections were not possible. Both of these conditions could have been met. But Mrs. Gandhi tried and succeeded in putting her party in power through elections. In the State Legislature, of 126 members there were only Ex-Census Commissioner C.S. Mullan: "Wheresoever the carcass, the vultures be gathered together. Where there is power thither flock the politicians."

Almost 43 Legislators defected to Mrs. Gandhi's Congress-I Party making it the largest group of 51 Legislators. The following persons were contenders for the office of Chief Minister: Anwara Taimur, Lolit Doley (who took initiative in forming the AAMSU and led a delegation to New Delhi to demand a tribal State), Bipin Pal Das (a member of upper home), Hiteswar Saikia (Former Home Minister in Janata Government) and Keshav Gogoi. A group from Cachar headed by Altaf Hussain Mazumdar, a former Minister, boldly opposed the choice of Mrs. Taimur on the plea that this would "greatly complicate" matters in the State in regard to the position of Muslims at a time of agitation against the foreigners. Still, some other Congress-I leaders from Cachar, namely S.M. Dev, M.P. and A.F. Golam Osmani and several others supported Mrs. Taimur. Mrs. Gandhi picked Mrs. Taimur, with masters in economics from Aligarh Muslim University, as Chief Minister of Assam. People reacted sharply to the announcement. The strike called by the AASU and the AAGSP was so huge and successful that two new Ministers-designate were unable to reach the Janata House in the capital to take the oath of office on December 6, 1980.

Assam was almost paralysed including blackout on December 7 by a 24-hour total non-cooperative movement. The movement leaders said the new Government was created with the help of "defectors elected on the votes of foreign nationals". Prafulla Mahanta said that by deciding to install a new administration Gandhi's Government had treated the Assamese people with "utter contempt" and disregard. Mrs. Taimur's legitimacy as an elected legislator has also been questioned. She won the 1978 election from Dalgaon in Darrang district, by mere 9,206 votes.

In 1979, the Election Commission deleted 14,406 names of foreigners from the same voters' list. It is also known that the foreigner nationals voted for Mrs. Taimur. It was claimed that there were 51 MLA of Congress-I Party and the CPI-M supported the Taimur Government. It is customary that a Governor asks a new ministry to call Assembly in a short duration to test the strength of support. But in this case it was not done until the end of March 1981.

Since the ministry of Hazarika was in suspended animation and was not dissolved, therefore, the formation of the Taimur Government was improper. Mrs. Taimur included A.F. Golam Osmani, who strongly opposed the detection and deportation attempts of Assam Janata Government of Borbora and Hazarika, in her ministry as the Minister of Public Works Department and as righthand person in the administrative setup.

The Atmosphere of Terror

Then the AASU and the AAGSP started a 13-day *Satyagraha* on December 18, 1980, demanding an early solution to the problem of foreign nationals. On the very first day, the CRP resorted to firing and lathi-charges at Barpeta, Patacharkuchi, Nalbari, Rangia, Tamulpur, Gauhati, Nowgong, Tezpur, Jorhat, Dibrugarh and various parts of Assam. At Barpeta, the CRP turned fire engine hoses on girl *Satyagrahis*, who peacefully squatted on roads. When the girls were unable to run with their long wet dresses the police lathi-charged and gunned fire. Thakur Ojah at Barpeta and Akhendra Talukdar at Patacharkuchi were killed in Police fire. Critically wounded were eleven persons including girls who had been brought to Gauhati Medical College and Hospital. In Gauhati, Kalpanath Bhattacharya, head assistant of the Handique Girls College, died following Police brutality. In Gauhati, 515 persons including 110 members from the Gauhati Lawyer's Association were arrested with intention to prosecute.

For the first time some Assam Janata Party members joined the *Satyagraha* and courted arrest. At Dibrugarh region Atul Chandra Koch, Vice President of the AASU, Biman Bijoy Gogoi and 18 other leaders were arrested. Temporary jails were constructed in Judge's field and various other parts in Assam. In North Lakhimpur 185 persons were arrested. On December 19, an 11-hour Gauhati Bandh was observed in protest against Police firing and inhuman attack on unarmed *Satyagrahis.* L. Ganesan, a DMK member of the Rajya Sabha, visited Assam and witnessed atrocities by the CRP. A group of movement leaders also went to the capital and briefed some opposition leaders such as Atal Behari Vajpayee, Y.B. Chavan, and Bhupesh Gupta.

On December 18 leaders of the movement Borbora, Deva Bora and Arun Sarma said:

> Assam has not seen such repression till today after the launching of the movement 18 months ago . . . The repression can be no solution to the foreign nationals problem nor could it stop the people from continuing their movement.[16]

Again on December 21, Ramesh Chandra Saharia, Assam's Home Minister, appealed to the people to support and cooperate with the Government to ensure peace and law and order in the State. He said:

> The issue of foreign nationals had already received serious attention of the Union Government and particularly of the Prime Minister . . . The renewal of the agitation will thus only raise doubts about the sincerity of the agitating organisations to see the problem resolved . . . It is the Government's sacred duty to match up to such threats to law and order and the steps taken by the Government and those that may be taken in future have to be viewed only in this light.[17]

Following this, December 22, the fifth day of the 13-day mass *Satyagraha,* six Satyagrahis were killed in Police firing at Rangiya and Mirza including Chandra Dhar Kalita, Rajen Kumar, Sunanda Haloi and Jogen Kalita. Hundreds of persons were injured. At Tezpur, 76 persons were reported injured. In Gauhati, 14 Assam Janata Party MLAs including Golap Borbora, Shanker Bhattacharjya and also Renuka Devi Borkotoki were arrested for joining the *Satyagraha.* Avtar Singh, the President of Sreeguru Singh Sabha of Gauhati and Gurdip Singh, the convener of Assam unit of AISSF, i.e., All-India Sikh Students Federation, led a procession of Sikhs at Panbazar, Gauhati and joined the *Satyagraha.* Earlier Santa Singh Legh, Supreme Commander of the All India Akal Sena, visited Assam and expressed support in different public meetings. The killings and CRP brutality were protested all over Assam. In the capital, Indira Gandhi told a meeting of the North Eastern Council that preaching of narrow loyalties was against the interest of the people. The agitators had unfortunately not understood the great ingredient of India's national genius, and that any violence has to be strongly dealt with.

Ban on Press

The Government felt uncomfortable when newspapers on December 23, reported the killing of six Satyagrahis by the CRP. On the same day the Governor of Assam invoked Assam's Special Powers (Press) Act of 1960. The Government order said that "the maintenance of communal harmony is threatened by publication of the matters in the printing presses."

On December 24, two main newspapers of Assam. *The Assam Tribune* and *The Dainik Assam,* were not published. *The Dainik Assam* of December 25 was almost one-fourth blank (See Appendix B). After both these papers were seen with blank columns. Authorities also expelled foreign and national news reporters from Assam except reporters of the Calcutta newspapers. Here are some instances of censorship. On December 26, 1980, a PTI news item saying that "The All-Assam Students Union today appealed to the people to observe the 34-hour bandh beginning on December 29", was also censored in Assam but most national newspapers carried the news. Another PTI news item saying that the Bharatiya Janata Party had decided to observe "Assam Day" was cut down. Birendra Bhattacharya's statement criticizing the use of "State violence" in Assam was censored in Assam newspapers but printed in many major newspapers in India. An *Assam Tribune* correspondent's report of a meeting of Assam Lawyer's Association, which consisted of four paragraphs found this paragraph censored: "The meeting also condemned unprovoked firing on peaceful Satyagrahis at Rangia, Mirza and other places of Assam and further condemned the brutal attack of CRP on peaceful people throughout Assam.

In the first week of January, the Government asked newspapers not to print blank space. The All India Newspaper Editors Conference (AINEC) condemned the assumption of special powers by the Assam Government under which reports "affecting or likely to affect public can be censored. It said in a statement that the powers "cut at the roots of the freedom of the press." On this, AINEC said that imposition of press censorship was not the way to deal with the agitation in Assam and with this added: "Press censorship generally recoils on those who impose it."

Restoration of Oil Flow

In the month of November, 1980, under heavy guard, military engineers began to flush out about 80,000 tonnes of crude oil in the 465-mile pipeline which had been in the pipe since December 1979. Officials said the operation was required because the pipeline might be damaged when the stagnating oil solidifies in the cold winter weather. The military engineers also learned the operation of the pipelines such that the Government did not have to rely upon oil workers, who continued on strike. Finance Minister Ramaswamy Venkataraman said in January 1980, that the country suffered a loss of $1.25 billion due to Assam oil embargo. During the embargo only two refineries, Gauhati and Digboi, were allowed to operate intermittently. In the last week of February, the Government got success in pumping oil to Barauni refinery in Bihar. There was bomb blast damage to the oil pipeline near Gauhati on February 13, 1981. All India Radio transmitters close to Gauhati and near Dibrugarh were also blown up on February 12, 1981. In February, the railway track at Bamunimaidan, near Gauhati was hurt by a bomb.

On March 18, 1981, two powerful bomb explosions rocked the Assembly Members' housing complex at Dispur, Gauhati. But there were found no casualties. On April 4, an oil pipeline exploded near Nowgong. In the first week of April, E.S. Parthasarthi, Upper Assam Division's Commissioner, was killed at Jorhat when a bomb exploded in his office. Then Governor Lallan Prasad Singh told reporters that by mid-April there were 42 blasts in the past three months. Nobody claimed responsibility for the series of bombings.

Appeal of the Taimur Government

Mrs. Taimur first requested to the people of Assam to cooperate with her Government. She said on December 8, 1981, that she would give top priority to finding a solution to the foreigner's issue and her Government would make that no foreigner stayed in Assam illegally. It was not explained, however, whether the foreigners would be deported or their stay would be legalised. She also stated that she would try to resolve the problem through negotiations within the Constitution of the country. But her Government did nothing to resolve the issue. Instead, the Government was assumed to terrorising people, trying to create a 'fear psychosis', resuming the flow of oil to Barauni and strengthening the Government against the movement.

By the end of December 1980, a large inscription on the wall of the Judges' Court House in Gauhati said "Save Assam from the AASU". Atrocities under Taimur had definitely increased. People standing on the roadside for city buses had been beaten by the CRP as a violation of Section 144, which makes assembly of more than four persons illegal. People could not go shopping either. They could not get out on the street. In the Gauhati Veterinary College hostel selectively Assamese Hindu students were beaten by the CRP.

There were charges that many key officers, specially in the Police Department, had been replaced by Muslims. The movement leaders observed a general strike on January 26, 1981, and asked people to boycott the Republic Day celebration. The State Government warned it would punish public employees boycotting the

26th January celebration. But the boycott was successful. Chief Minister Anwara Taimur performed the ceremony under heavy military guard which was attended by certain officers of her administration and inmates from Gauhati jail. There was practically no public participation. On the other hand, Mrs. Taimur said in the first week of February 1981, that the movement no more had the mass support it once enjoyed and the situation was under control.

Therefore, it appeared that the Government saw no reason to deport any foreigner and the foreigner's question was shelved. The Taimur Government for the first time called the Assembly in March 1981. On March 24, the Government survived a no-confidence motion by 53 to 43 votes. After having claimed a strength of 66 in the Assembly, her Government could master only 53 votes following intense lobbying. In June 1981, several leftist groups decided to withdraw their support from the Minority Government of Mrs. Taimur. She resigned on June 18. She said during a speech at Dispur: "The horse-trading will begin once again." This way, Taimur's Government succeeded neither in establishing a rapport with the movement leaders nor in destroying that leadership by weaning the masses away from the movement.

On the other side, the 205-day Anwara Taimur ministry has left a deep scar in the communal harmony. It lowered party politics to the level of haggling in the fish market and thus shaken the people's faith in their elected representatives. The Centre imposed Presidential rule again on the State.

Duration of Low Profile

During the first half of 1981, the movement kept a low profile in the sense that there were no demonstrations or picketing. After a loss of one academic year, the students started going to schools and colleges in October 1980. Examinations were conducted in April-May 1981. This was part of the reasons for the calm. The people also appeared to be tired of the long drawn out movement. However, attempts for a solution continued in political circles and there were several rounds of talks between the Government of India and the leaders of the movement but without any result. Thus, the fall of the Taimur Government was the only victory for the movement. The students demanded that the Government provide full written clarification of its offer to resettle outside Assam all illegal immigrants. But the Government refused, saying this was not normal procedure. The Government stressed that Assam accept all authorised refugees and those settled under administrative instructions (who do not have any legal or constitutional right) who entered the State between 1961 and 1971. In the month of May, the student leaders rejected the proposal, saying it would legalise the entry of about 1.2 million people into Assam. They wanted all of them shifted out of the State. The movement leaders also threatened to revive the movement and mobilise farmers and tea plantation workers if the rounds of talks failed. The movement leaders were called for five rounds of discussions/but there was no agreement. On September 23, 1981, in response to a suggestion made by the Government of India, the movement leaders submitted present counter proposals containing 17 points.

Five points were accepted by the Government but when the basic point of foreigners (point no. 8) who entered Assam during 1961-71, came for discussions, there was no agreement and the talks did not go beyond. Suspension of the movement and the peaceful situation prevailing in the State led the Government to believe that the movement was petering.

References

1. The All Assam Gana Sangram Parishad, *The Foreigners' Problem, An Analysis,* Gauhati, 1980, pp. 17-18.
2. *Ibid.,* p. 18.
3. *Ibid.,* p. 18-19.
4. Sanjayya, *Assam: A Crisis of Identity,* Gauhati, United Publishers, July, 1980, p. 20.
5. Hitesh Deka, *Asamiya Jati Tikibane,* Gauhati Deka Prakashan, 1980, p. 27.
6. *Sanjayya, Assam: A Crisis of Indentity,* Gautami, Spectrum Publication, July 1980, p. 27.
7. See full text in Chapter 9.
8. Sanjayya, p. 35.
9. *Ibid.,* p. 36.
10. *Ibid.,* p. 38.
11. *Ibid.,* p. 39.
12. *Ibid.,* p. 44.
13. *Ibid.,* p. 53.
14. *India Tribune,* Chicago, September 1, 1980. In answer to a question raised by K.C. Sebastian in Rajya Sabha.
15. *India Abroad,* New York, August 15 and 22, 1980.
16. *The Assam Tribune,* Gauhati, December 29, 1980.
17. *Ibid.,* December 22, 1980.

[illegible]

[illegible] 10 points.

[illegible] was accepted [illegible] during 1905-11 [illegible]

[illegible]

References

[illegible]

[illegible]

[illegible]

6

Socio-cultural and Linguistic Set-up of Assam

Any act of a community or society is affected by the culture, customs and tradition of that societal group. The Assamese language, literature, and culture are almost similar to those of the Bengalees. For that matter all Indian languages, literatures, and cultures have some similarities: yet they are different. Until the British control, Assam was always independent and isolated from the rest of India. The Assamese language, literature, and culture have influences of Indo-Aryans as well as Tibeto-Burmese. The Assamese group stands out as a distinct ethnic group as do Bengalees, Oriyas, Biharis, Gujaratis, Maharastrians, Malayalees, and other sub-nationalities in India. In many respects Assamese language, literature and culture had been more progressive than those of other sub-nationalities as will be revealed in this chapter.

Linguistic Position of Assamese

The Assamese language is derived from mother of all languages, sanskrit, a deviation from "Udra Magadhi" was its source. In the course of time there took place in this language the healthiest assimilation of Tibeto-Burmese, Austric and other factors. In 1848, Reverend Brown wrote that the Assamese language was derived from Sanskrit and not from Bengali. In 1891, Bains wrote in the census report that Assamese and Oriyas successfully struggled against the claims of Bengalees that these two languages are dialects of Bengali. In the 1901 census report, Sir Edward Gait wrote that like Oriya, the Assamese language is a co-language of Bengali and not a daughter. Dr. Grierson wrote in "Linguistic Survey of India" that if grammar is the basis of determining language, then the Assamese language has no connection to the Bengali language, Nicholas, professor of ancient language in Oxford University, wrote that the Assamese language is an independent language and derived from the joint origin as Bengali.[1]

Script of the Language of Assam

It is also wrong to say that the Assamese borrowed the Bengali script. The Assamese have been using these scripts for centuries as well as the Bengalees have. K.C. Barua outlines the development of the Assamese script in this manner:

> The alphabets used in the languages of Northern India with Sanskrit, Pali and Prakrit as their origin are practically the same. But in the absence of

standard printing types, the scripts are used to be varied. The script originally used is known as Brahmi script. In the course of time, this script converted itself first into Kushan script and then into Gupta script. That is to say, with the progress of the art to writing, the letters changed their shapes gradually in order to effect speed, legibility and beauty. Later Gupta script gave birth to Kashmiri and Gurmukhi, Devanagri, Gujrati and Kutila. From Kutila the present Assamese script evolved. Devanagri is in the fourth state of evolution from Brahmi; whereas Assamese is the fifth stage.[2] The census data for various types of languages spoken by Scheduled Tribes is given below :

Table 1

Mother Tongue for Scheduled Tribes

Scheduled Tribe	Mother Tongue	Number of Speakers Rural			Urban		
		Total	Males	Females	Total	Males	Females
1	2	3	4	5	6	7	8
All Scheduled Tribes							
	Adi	233	115	118	8	3	5
	Anal	2	1	1	0	0	0
	Angami	32	17	15	20	7	13
	Ao	661	338	323	15	7	8
	Arabic/Arbi	1	1	0	0	0	0
	Assamese	6,12,930	3,10,145	3,02,785	39,567	21,345	18,222
	Bengali	7,958	4,134	3,824	667	360	307
	Bhili/Bhilodi	63	32	31	10	6	4
	Bhotia	25	14	11	1	0	1
	Bhumij	6	3	3	0	0	0
	Bishnupuriya	7	5	2	13	10	3
	Bodo/Boro	11,80,767	5,97,429	5,83,338	19,447	10,371	9,076
	Chakhesang	7	3	4	2	1	1
	Coorgi/Kodagu	5	3	2	0	0	0
	Deori	20,258	10,333	9,925	269	139	130
	Dimasa	71,426	36,126	35,300	3,955	2,170	1,785
	Dogri	784	376	408	3	1	2
	English	609	325	284	208	117	91
	Gadaba	8	6	2	1	0	1
	Gangte	14	11	3	36	21	15
	Garo	18,178	9,425	8,753	485	259	226

(Contd.)

1	2	3	4	5	6	7	8
	Gondi	8	6	2	4	2	2
	Gujarati	79	38	41	9	6	3
	Halabi	1	0	1	0	0	0
	Halam	561	282	279	11	5	6
	Hindi	3,350	1,794	1,556	488	289	199
	Hmar	8,631	4,518	4,113	2,888	1,539	1,349
	Ho	160	92	68	0	0	0
	Jatapu	931	464	467	1	0	1
	Juang	1	1	0	3	2	1
	Kabui	78	32	46	117	61	56
	Kannada	1	1	0	4	2	2
	Karbi/Mikir	2,65,351	1,35,553	1,29,798	19,926	10,564	9,362
	Kashmire	13	6	7	0	0	0
	Khandeshi	5	1	4	0	0	0
	Kharia	111	70	41	4	2	2
	Khasi	11,818	5,991	5,827	362	179	183
	Khezha	3	1	2	0	0	0
	Kinnauri	2	2	0	0	0	0
	Koch	38	19	19	3	1	2
	Koda/Kora	2	0	2	0	0	0
	Konda	2	1	1	8	3	5
	Konkani	5	2	3	3	1	2
	Korku	16	7	9	0	0	0
	Koya	1	0	1	0	0	0
	Kui	3	3	0	3	3	0
	Kuki	13,817	7,236	6,581	2,338	1,206	1,132
	Kurukh/Oraon	139	78	61	3	1	2
	Lahnda	15	8	7	3	1	2
	Lalung	14,459	7,371	7,088	370	194	176
	Lepcha	6	3	3	1	1	0
	Liangmei	1	0	1	0	0	0
	Limbu	2	0	2	0	0	0
	Lotha	33	19	14	5	5	0
	Lushai/Mizo	182	96	86	688	341	347
	Malayalam	2,127	923	1,204	314	179	135
	Malto	1	0	1	0	0	0
	Manipuri	114	31	83	0	0	0
	Mao	17	13	4	19	10	9

(Contd.)

1	2	3	4	5	6	7	8
	Marathi	107	58	49	5	2	3
	Miri/Mishing	3,93,737	2,01,213	1,92,524	1,901	1,106	795
	Mishmi	5	3	2	1	1	0
	Monpa	2	1	1	3	2	1
	Munda	152	73	79	9	6	3
	Mundari	106	58	48	4	2	2
	Nepali	641	342	299	68	39	29
	Nissi/Dafla	3	2	1	1	1	0
	Nocte	1	0	1	0	0	0
	Oriya	88	43	45	4	1	3
	Pabha	1,13,584	57,472	56,112	743	420	323
	Paite	514	263	251	26	14	12
	Parji	118	64	54	1	1	0
	Pochury	1	1	0	0	0	0
	Punjabi	12	6	6	9	7	2
	Rengma	1,787	970	817	98	56	42
	Sangtam	6	5	1	0	0	0
	Sanskrit	1	1	0	0	0	0
	Santali	622	363	259	8	4	4
	Savara	9	6	3	0	0	0
	Sema	219	122	97	3	3	0
	Tamil	75	46	29	2	2	0
	Tangkhul	3	2	1	12	4	8
	Tangsa	16	10	6	4	3	1
	Telugu	19	13	6	41	22	19
	Thado	1,425	724	701	28	17	11
	Tibetan	48	25	23	3	2	1
	Tripuri	1,254	666	588	9	6	3
	Tulu	21	8	13	2	2	0
	Urdu	171	100	71	2	2	0
	Vaiphei	117	60	57	124	62	62
	Yimchungre	2,217	1,122	1,095	0	0	0
	Zeliang	63	30	33	8	5	3
	Zemi	5,546	2,791	2,755	173	93	80
	Others	18,560	9,197	9,363	1,559	897	662

Source : Census 1991

Literature of Assam

Assamese literature dates back to as old as 600 A.D. Pandit Hemchandra Goswami divided the Assamese literature into six different periods on historic and philologic considerations. The first period begins about 600 A.D. when the famous Chinese traveller Hiuen Tsang visited the country and extended upto 800 A.D.

when the aphorisms of Dak were first reduced to writing. During this time, the literature remained in an unwritten state and it was entirely lyrical in its nature. The cradle songs, the pastoral songs, the Bihu songs and the ballads of Assam belonged to this era.[3] The second period (800 A.D.—1200 A.D.) is called "Period of Mantras and Aphorisms", when the writing of Mantras started and later when written literature evolved. The third period (1200 A.D.—1450 A.D.) is known as "Pre-Vaisnava Period", in which Hem Saraswati, Madhab Kandali, Pitambar Dwija and others translated Ramayana and Purana from Sanskrit to Assamese and paved the way for Vaisnavaism in Assam. The initial text in a language that is uncontestably Assamese is the Prahlad—Charitra of Hem Saraswati in the 13th century. Poet Madhab Kandali (14th century) translated the Sanskrit Ramayana and produced Devajit. The fourth period (1450 A.D.—1600 A.D.) is called "Vaisnavite Period", in which the great sage Sankardev's 27 creations of poetry and devotion and "Bhaona' (Folk Operas) transformed the Assamese culture, literature, and Vaisnavaism into a golden era. He and Madhabdev wrote *Namghosha* (A Book of Hymns) and *Bargeets* (Devotional Songs). Bhattadev wrote *'Katha Gita',* the first prose book in India in 1593-97 at Barnagar and Patbaushi Shatra close to Barpeta.

The Buranjis (chronicles) were written since the 13th century in Tai language (language of the Ahoms) and in Assamese from the 19th century. Assamese people are proud of this Buranji literature which is not found anywhere else in India. Pandit Goswami called the fifth period (1600 A.D.—1800 A.D.) known as the "Period of extension" and he wrote, "This period was marked by great literary activity and numerous books were written on a variety of subjects by writers of all levels and grades; but on the whole it was a period of deterioration owing to the depredation caused by the Burmese and the Moamarias.

As the literature of this period lost in depth, it gained in surface and so we call this "the period of extension."[4] The sixth period (1800 A.D.—1900 A.D.) is called the 'modern period' in which influences of English literature can be found. Because of the imposition of the Bengali language, the Assamese literature did not develop to a great extent. Outstanding Bengalee literary men like Sir Prafulla Chandra Roy, Sir Asutosh Mookerjee, and Kabiguru Rabindra Nath Tagore praised the Assamese literature. After reading *Katha Gita* (Gita in Prose) of Bhattadev, which was edited and compiled by Pandit Hemchandra Goswami in 1918, they wrote the following in 1919, to Pandit Goswami.[5] Sir Prafulla Chandra Roy wrote:

> Indeed the prose Gita of Bhattadev composed in the sixteenth century is unique of its kind. I had an opportunity of coming across an excellent edition of this book, which we owe to the patriotism and scholarship of Pandit Hemchandra Goswami. It is a priceless treasure. Assamese prose literature developed to a stage in the far distant sixteenth century, which no other literature of the world reached except the writings of Hooker and Latimer in England. There has been a controversy for long about the independence and identity of the Assamese language. This is extremely foolish. This is due, I

hold, to the provincial patriotism and the national conceit of the Bengalees living in Assam. The Katha Gita shows clearly that the Assamese literature developed to a standard in the sixteenth century which the Bengali literature had reached only in the time of Iswar Chandra and Bankim Chandra. In fact, if some Assamese scholars now get up and say that it is the Bengalee who had borrowed his prose from Assamese literature and enriched his own, it will be very difficult to dislodge him. I think the question may now be considered as solved and settled for good. I say this not as a representative Bengalee but as the Ex-President of the Bengal Literary Conference."

Also, Sir Asutosh Mookerjee wrote: "The people who could write Gita in such prose in the sixteenth century was not a small people." As per Kabiguru Rabindra Nath Tagore, "... You may very well be proud of the author of this book who could handle prose in such a remarkably lucid style more than a century before we had any prose book in Bengal. The Census data for various religions adopted by Scheduled Tribes is given below:

Table 2
Religion for Scheduled Tribes

Scheduled Tribe	Rural			Urban		
	Total	Males	Females	Total	Males	Females
1	2	3	4	5	6	7
ALL SCHEDULED TRIBES						
All Religions	**27,77,308**	**14,09,364**	**13,67,944**	**97,133**	**52,196**	**44,937**
1. Buddhists	5,597	2,927	2,670	71	42	29
2. Christians	2,06,642	1,06,076	1,00,566	12,781	6,709	6,072
3. Hindus	25,58,031	12,96,939	12,61,092	84,117	45,343	38,774
4. Jains	186	93	93	13	7	6
5. Muslims	851	434	417	69	39	30
6. Sikhs	114	60	54	11	7	4
7. Other Religions and Persuations	5,885	2,834	3,051	71	49	22
8. Religion not stated	2	1	1	0	0	0

Source: Census 1991

The very first Bengali prose book "Pratapaditya" was written by Ram Ram Basu in 1801, two hundred and four years after *Katha Gita.* Sir Asutosh Mookerjee, while he was Vice Chancellor of Calcutta University, prepared a scheme for the 'Advanced Study of the Indian Vernaculars." The objectives were: to study the origin and growth of both the language and the literature, to collect and compile the literature, and to make materials available to teachers and students for M.A. degrees. On this mission he went to Assam is 1918, and met Pandit Hemchandra

Goswami and other Assamese scholars. He also introduced Assamese language in M.A. degree in Calcutta University in spite of strong criticism from other Bengalees.[6]

The Assamese people are grateful to this magnanimous, unselfish and great scholar for his remarkable contribution in conserving both Assamese language and literature. The Assamese people wish that other Bengalees would follow the great ideas of Sir Asutosh Mookerjee and learn to respect the language, literature, culture, and identity of certain other ethnic groups in India.

Special Features of Assamese Society

The Assamese people are famous for being traditionally gentle and hospitable. There have been no social evils like Dowry, *Sati,* communal riot, and caste conflicts.

Virtually there is no evil of dowry in the Assamese society. Thousands of families are affected by this evil system in the rest of India. Dowry for a medical doctor has gone up to Rs. 425,000. A college graduate asks Rs. 50,000 as dowry. Thousands of poor and middle class families sell property for dowry, and thousands cannot get married for lack of dowry money. Even after marriage, wives are battered for insufficient dowry.

There are suicide and murder cases. The victims are newly wed-wives. In marriages in Assam it is still the custom that the groom's side send ornaments, bridal dress and cosmetics according to their capability, which would come back with the bride anyway. It is up to the bride's parents to offer what they want to their daughter. Both sides arrange their own wedding reception separately at their own expense.

There are instances where one side helps the other financially with the marriage expenses. Giving a dowry is considered a bribe to get a good son-in-law when the girl is inferior, and therefore, it is considered an insult to the parents who are, in reality, conceding that their daughter is inferior. Throughout history there has been no instance of *Sati* (custom of widow burning herself on the funeral pyre of her dead husband) in the Assamese set up. The *Sati* custom was prevalent throughout India, especially among the Rajputs and Bengalee Brahmins. In 1829, the British abolished this custom by law, but the custom continued for almost more than 30 years. It is shocking that in October 1980, a 16-year-old widow committed *Sati* at a Jhadi village in Rajasthan. It is also amazing that in contrast to the rest of the country, there is no serious caste conflict in Assam. Hindu saye Sankardev preached in the 16th century not only Vaishnavism but against untouchability and for respect for religion of Islam. Caste has hardly been a factor in politics in Assam. The census data relating to women (married, unmarried, divorced, ever married, currently married) belonging to Scheduled Tribes is given on next few pages.

There is no instance of communal riots among the Assamese Hindus and the Assamese Muslims. They lived peacefully throughout history enjoying each others' festivities. The Hindu-Muslim riot in Assam just after the partition of India was between Bengalee-Hindu refugees hailing from East Pakistan and the Bengalee-Muslims, who migrated to Assam in the pre-partition period. Every Assamese

Table 3
Age, Sex and Marital Status for Scheduled Tribes

Age group	*Total*	*Never Married*	*Married*	*Widowed*	*Divorced*	*Unspecified*
1	*2*	*3*	*4*	*5*	*6*	*7*
ALL SCHEDULED TRIBES						
Rural						
All ages	**27,77,308**	**17,34,317**	**9,64,432**	**75,256**	**3,217**	**86**
0 - 9	8,00,932	8,00,932	0	0	0	0
10-14	3,68,201	3,64,542	3,481	111	63	4
15-19	3,12,692	2,85,447	26,893	221	125	6
20-24	2,46,661	1,51,366	94,114	817	364	0
25-29	2,33,890	69,901	1,61,575	1,894	516	4
30-34	1,71,473	22,287	1,45,833	2,878	473	2
35-39	1,56,638	8,156	1,43,881	4,201	398	2
40-44	1,10,954	3,882	1,01,106	5,672	294	0
15-44	12,32,308	5,41,039	6,73,402	15,683	2,170	14
45-49	95,273	1,911	86,021	7,071	268	2
50-54	76,331	1,554	64,899	9,667	209	2
55-59	50,272	648	42,143	7,371	110	0
60-64	53,549	997	40,011	12,395	146	0
65-69	26,365	256	19,614	6,429	66	0
70-74	23,554	593	15,859	7,029	73	0
75-79	10,608	162	7,126	3,291	29	0
80+	17,837	2,219	9,579	5,978	58	3
Age not stated	22,078	19,464	2,297	231	25	61
URBAN						
All ages	**97,133**	**60,394**	**34,731**	**1,883**	**118**	**7**
0 - 9	23,123	23,123	0	0	0	0
10-14	12,126	11,967	153	4	1	1
15-19	12,243	11,244	975	8	15	1
20-24	10,907	7,328	3,542	21	16	0
25-29	10,234	3,588	6,555	71	20	0
30-34	7,132	1,121	5,903	89	19	0
35-39	6,181	338	5,712	118	12	1
40-44	4,099	191	3,732	164	12	0
15-44	50,796	23,810	26,419	471	94	2
45-49	3,278	111	2,974	187	6	0
50-54	2,099	84	1,778	236	1	0
55-59	1,279	33	1,083	163	0	0
60-64	1,165	45	850	264	6	0
65-69	599	8	438	151	2	0
70-74	542	14	368	156	4	0
75-79	211	8	146	56	1	0
80+	720	168	368	182	2	0
Age not stated	1,195	1,023	154	13	1	4

Source: Census 1991

Table 4

Ever Married and Currently Married Women Belonging to Scheduled Tribes by Present Age, Number of Surviving Children and Total Number of Surviving Children by Sex

Present Age	*Total ever/ currently married women*	*Ever/currently married women with number of serviving children*						*Total surviving children*		
		0	*1*	*2*	*3*	*4*	*5+*	*Total*	*Males*	*Females*
1	*2*	*3*	*4*	*5*	*6*	*7*	*8*	*9*	*10*	*11*
ALL SCHEDULED TRIBES										
RURAL										
Ever Married										
All ages	**5,50,646**	**69,992**	**66,615**	**81,468**	**85,903**	**77,223**	**1,67,523**	**18,67,248**	**9,78,850**	**8,88,398**
Less than 15	2,411	1,927	185	265	0	0	0	715	380	335
15-19	23,418	12,423	7,691	2,246	504	306	0	14,919	7,646	7,273
20-24	72,037	16,477	22,542	18,684	9,350	3,230	1,472	1,09,085	56,086	52,999
25-29	1,00,725	11,445	15,070	23,980	24,471	15,302	10,106	2,54,935	1,30,365	1,24,570
30-34	78,241	6,221	5,610	11,592	16,594	16,280	21,766	2,69,897	1,37,928	1,31,969
35-39	68,433	4,507	3,152	6,879	11,068	13,167	29,534	2,84,660	1,45,971	1,38,689
40-44	49,803	3,297	2,134	4,182	6,474	8,064	25,538	2,27,630	1,18,868	1,08,762
45-49	42,229	2,677	1,699	3,283	4,759	6,275	23,439	2,03,514	1,07,770	95,744
50-54	34,585	2,621	1,854	2,876	3,867	4,623	18,646	1,62,736	87,550	75,186
55-59	22,522	1,747	1,367	1,805	2,435	2,999	12,105	1,06,819	58,226	48,593
60-64	22,995	2,275	1,870	2,214	2,562	2,996	10,962	1,00,498	55,034	45,464
65-69	11,564	1,204	968	1,101	1,277	1,394	5,555	50,270	27,729	22,541
70-74	9,580	1,241	1,049	1,014	1,076	1,153	3,990	37,920	21,152	16,768
75-79	4,285	595	468	457	495	510	1,736	16,618	9,218	7,400
80 +	6,490	1,008	816	722	777	769	2,330	23,132	12,872	10,260

(Contd.)

1	2	3	4	5	6	7	8	9	10	11
Currently Married										
All ages	**4,93,760**	**62,565**	**60,008**	**74,497**	**78,233**	**69,541**	**1,47,297**	**16,61,933**	**8,67,955**	**7,93,978**
Less than 15	2,309	1,867	167	241	0	0	0	649	344	305
15-19	23,153	12,299	7,590	2,236	495	287	0	14,695	7,539	7,156
20-24	71,172	16,218	22,174	18,552	9,293	3,211	1,451	1,08,082	55,583	52,499
25-29	99,033	11,071	14,586	23,607	24,205	15,193	10,028	2,52,033	1,28,839	1,23,194
30-34	75,862	5,789	5,160	11,105	16,184	15,990	21,464	2,64,329	1,35,058	1,29,271
35-39	65,186	4,137	2,748	6,333	10,479	12,634	28,735	2,74,580	1,40,763	1,33,817
40-44	45,436	2,813	1,721	3,598	5,724	7,358	24,123	2,12,165	1,10,863	1,01,302
45-49	36,673	2,157	1,261	2,652	3,906	5,369	21,245	1,81,717	96,096	85,621
50-54	27,071	1,890	1,223	2,007	2,867	3,539	15,486	1,32,700	71,386	61,314
55-59	17,004	1,157	888	1,256	1,796	2,194	9,668	84,084	45,894	38,190
60-64	13,621	1,164	938	1,189	1,414	1,745	7,117	63,545	34,811	28,734
65-69	6,849	580	476	615	712	786	3,643	32,111	17,776	14,335
70-74	4,606	517	439	476	464	532	2,157	19,809	11,082	8,727
75-79	2,104	262	225	205	222	253	926	8,676	4,876	3,800
80 +	2,565	387	292	279	297	322	964	9,437	5,297	4,140
URBAN										
Ever Married										
All ages	**18,455**	**3,035**	**2,727**	**3,443**	**3,430**	**2,438**	**3,371**	**50,738**	**26,405**	**24,333**
Less than 15	96	73	11	11·	0	0	0	33	16	17
15-19	853	478	279	71	14	10	0	503	267	236
20-24	2,767	760	906	670	324	62	45	3,718	1,916	1,802
25-29	4,251	649	792	1,158	942	475	235	9,219	4,729	4,490
30-34	2,903	303	307	621	768	490	409	8,203	4,178	4,025
35-39	2,442	215	121	370	563	540	630	8,484	4,382	4,102
40-44	1,519	143	70	188	297	303	517	5,728	2,969	2,759
45-49	1,105	80	59	108	198	216	444	4,547	2,444	2,103
50-54	731	75	55	67	91	105	338	3,088	1,664	1,424
55-59	454	50	20	35	57	77	215	1,988	1,072	916
60-64	479	59	27	37	68	68	220	2,043	1,060	983

(Contd.)

1	2	3	4	5	6	7	8	9	10	11
65-69	259	40	23	36	37	31	92	964	502	462
70-74	233	27	24	24	28	29	101	984	509	475
75-79	87	16	5	6	11	8	41	366	208	158
80 +	195	31	22	23	25	18	76	736	405	331
Currently Married										
All ages	**16,913**	**2,813**	**2,552**	**3,249**	**3,192**	**2,230**	**2,867**	**45,369**	**23,567**	**21,802**
Less than 15	93	71	11	10	0	0	0	31	14	17
15-19	836	469	272	71	14	9	0	492	261	231
20-24	2,738	750	896	665	322	61	44	3,682	1,898	1,784
25-29	4,189	631	777	1,141	936	470	234	9,125	4,675	4,450
30-34	2,813	287	287	602	746	481	405	8,017	4,083	3,934
35-39	2,339	203	114	349	540	521	609	8,160	4,225	3,935
40-44	1,371	120	52	168	272	273	486	5,285	2,724	2,561
45-49	944	69	42	90	171	180	392	3,944	2,103	1,841
50-54	539	51	38	43	63	80	264	2,376	1,288	1,088
55-59	334	37	11	24	43	61	158	1,490	791	699
60-64	272	33	15	26	33	41	124	1,186	623	563
65-69	142	25	7	19	17	22	52	533	301	232
70-74	110	13	14	11	12	12	48	463	241	222
75-79	40	6	2	3	8	3	18	182	102	80
80 +	82	18	9	10	9	10	26	282	163	119

Source: Census 1991.

Notes: 1. 'All ages includes 'age not stated'.

2. Number of ever/currently married women in column 4 includes women not reporting number of surviving children.

3. The age groups having nil return are not shown.

woman, irrespective of caste or religion, is supposed to know weaving. Not knowing how to weave used to be a disqualification for a woman in getting married. Traditionally every woman gives at least a hand woven *gamosa* towel to her husband and children on the New Year's day.

They also spin cotton and silks on their own. Many widows took weaving as a profession to support their children. Mahatma Gandhi was amazed to find skillful and artistic weaving talents among the Assamese women when he went to Assam in 1921, especially when he was putting embargos on the use of foreign clothes and was asking everyone to spin and weave their own clothes. This tradition is not seen in any part of India. There is a little story about an Assamese student in Calcutta, somewhere at the turn of the 20th Century. The student lived with some other Bengalee students. For New Year's Day he received a parcel from his mother. Proudly he showed the New Year's Day present to his roommates, a beautiful cloth woven by his mother. The roommates immediately said that he belonged to a low caste, *Tati* (weaver) family and asked him to move out. He had to comply. The Assamese people have been called lazy from the beginning of British rule, because they did not take labour jobs in tea plantations and railroad construction. Labour had to be imported to Assam. Some academicians have also accused the so-called laziness on the humid weather in Assam. However, even though humidity limits hard labour to some degree, this does not seem to be the main cause for not taking labour jobs. The main reason for the apparent "laziness" was that Assam was a land of plenty and the people had an easy going life.

Traditionally, the Assamese economy was self-sufficient. The food was home grown; fish and game was plentiful; cloth was woven from muga, paat, and eri worms had been reared at home; every family had its own loom; and they built their own homes with wood, bamboo and thatch, all of which were plentiful. Beggars were almost non-existant. Only some widows who had minor children used to beg while continuing to live in their own huts on their own land. Assamese society has been truly Gandhian in household labour, village self-sufficiency and social harmony. Therefore, it is wrong to assert that the Assamese people are lazy and deserve some of the misfortune that has befallen them. Even assuming that the Assamese people are lazy, there is no justification that more hardworking foreigners should be allowed to settle in their land to share resources and face constant confrontation and controversy.

References

1. Benudhar Sharma, *Asamiya Sahityar Paramacharjya Pandit Hemchandra Goswami,* Jorhat, Assam Sahitya Sabha, 1972, pp. 70-71.
2. Khanindra Chandra Barua, *Critical Days of Assam,* Maligaon, Gauhati, Sreeguru Press, 1972, pp. 144-145.
3. Hem Bora, *Pandit Hemchandra Goswamir Sahitya Pratibha,* Goladghat, Navajoti Prakash, 1972, p. 45.
4. *Ibid.,* p. 46.
5. Hemchandra Goswami (ed.), *Katha Gita,* 3rd Edition, Gauhati, Assam Book Depot, 1961, p. 7-8.

Part–II
Meghalaya

Table 2
Age, Sex and Marital Status for Scheduled Tribes

Age group	Total	Never Married	Married	Widowed	Divor-ced	Unsp-ecified
1	2	3	4	5	6	7
ALL SCHEDULED TRIBES						
RURAL						
All ages	**17,705**	**10,260**	**6,628**	**717**	**98**	**2**
0 - 9	4,597	4,597	0	0	0	0
10-14	2,179	2,153	24	1	1	0
15-19	1,661	1,534	123	0	2	2
20-24	1,497	953	529	1	14	0
25-29	1,482	500	952	17	13	0
30-34	1,338	171	1,128	18	21	0
35-39	1,126	56	1,015	41	14	0
40-44	864	22	775	55	12	0
15-44	7,968	3,236	4,522	132	76	2
45-49	726	15	639	64	8	0
50-54	471	10	389	68	4	0
55-59	479	4	412	61	2	0
60-64	426	15	273	133	5	0
65-69	239	2	161	75	1	0
70-74	189	7	109	73	0	0
75-79	101	2	52	47	0	0
80+	111	3	45	63	0	0
Age not stated	219	216	2	0	1	0
URBAN						
All ages	**19,400**	**11,367**	**7,182**	**765**	**83**	**3**
0 - 9	4,584	4,584	0	0	0	0
10-14	2,478	2,469	9	0	0	0
15-19	2,095	1,924	168	0	0	3
20-24	1,780	1,272	504	2	2	0
25-29	1,688	580	1,059	15	34	0
30-34	1,420	227	1,163	24	6	0
35-39	1,330	77	1,194	46	13	0
40-44	862	20	755	77	10	0
15-44	9,175	4,100	4,843	164	65	3
45-49	695	4	641	41	9	0
50-54	535	12	433	87	3	0
55-59	582	2	511	69	0	0
60-64	524	3	399	119	3	0
65-69	181	1	114	63	3	0
70-74	219	2	105	112	0	0
75-79	155	0	103	52	0	0
80 +	84	8	18	58	0	0
Age not stated	188	182	6	0	0	0

Source : Census 1991.

8

Education, Literature and Linguistic

Education

The literacy drive in Manipur has been a remarkable feature since the creation of this new State. Proper care has been taken, under the developmental scheme, to promote education and culturein this far-flung hill region. In fact the government showed the sense of keenness to promote literacy in the age group ranging from six onward.

If we browse through the details of Tables, appended here, we find the child population in the age group of 0-6, literates and literacy. All the districts have been covered upto 2001 detail of different headings like literates, persons, males, and females, literacy rate of 2001, persons, males and females. For example, the literacy rate of 2001 among males and females in the district of Senapati is 77.87 for the former and 59.70 for the latter. This indeed gives the reader the impression about the significant changes for the better standard.

Manipur has been styled as a kingdom without much of historical relics and monuments. As per the belief of the people, there cannot be secular buildings as the publicis not allowed to have brick buildings. Obsessed by the action that private and secular residences must not be compared in grandeur or excellence with the temples of god, the kings used to destroy the buildings by letting the elephants destroy them. Added to this was the attitude of the ancient monarchs who did not care to leave behind them material palaces and rich treasures through which they could be remembered by the posterity. There have been powerful monarchs but they were not rich enough to build monuments on account of other worldly attitude and socio-economic structure of Manipuri society. Most of the buildings made of bamboo and straw, were of combustible materials. But they had their style of house building and skilful craftmenship in the sacred palatial building locally known as *Yamjao*.

There were ten temples before the war of 1891. The Buddhists, Burmese motifs are discernible in the ornamentation of the *Kyangs* or early temples. In the later period, the Hindu style and decorative style have been introduced by the architects and artists from British India. The ruins of the ancient capital of Kangla and temple of General Thangal are the instances in point in showing the combination of Hindu and Chinese styles. The Maharaja's palace on the eastern bank of Imphal river and Sri Govindaji's Golden Temple (1894) are noteworthy.

Building activity has been remarkable in and around the city since 1960. The notable ones include Gandhi Memorial Hall, Imphal Tourist Lodge, R. Medical College, Lamphelpat, New Secretariat Building and a series of Government Quarters, PWD Office, Dance College and Cinema Halls in Khwairamband Bazar and Lamphelpat, Shaheed Minar in Sir Tikendrajit Park, Gurudwara, Jain-temple, INA Memorial Hall in Moirang etc. Gandhi Memorial Hall shows an attempt at evolving an organised relation between the *rath* shape of the old and the modern design of architecture. It is a case of combination of contacts. Tourist lodge is built on modern Indian style. The series of government quarters and churches at Amphelpat and Imphal show a trend towards the western style of architecture. One sees the Muslim, Sikh and Jaina architectural styles in the concerned buildings in the main bazar. The INA Memorial Hall has the statue of Netaji Subhas Chandra Bose, a replica of the monolith erected by Netaji at Singapore in 1945. The groves or mounds which were supposed to be the abode of Lai (deity) remained as isolated patches of wooded land in the midst of open area with the passage of time. After the Second World War, black temples of Umanglais were built throughout the valley where the local committees took charge of them from a particular family. Many Hindu temples were also built in plain villages and hills of the valley of which the Siva Temple at the top of Nongmaiching Hill, as we see in connection with Maharaja Bodhachandra's reign is prominent. Cemetaries and tombs raised over the graves of the forefathers are considered to be of great religious merit to the relatives. But they have fallen into neglect and can now be seen in various stages of dilapidation. The Roman Catholics are the first to introduce their architectural style in church buildings at their centres. Other churches in the hill villages are constructed like Hindu temples by the Meitei workers with little knowledge of the church design. Thus one will see in Manipuri buildings of various styles and varieties.

Sculptures

Judged by the examples of structural works such as *Kangla Sa* (animal of the sun, personification of divine power symbolising the luck of the state. It is built of masonry to resemble stone installed in front of the gate of the capital), art objects of handicrafts and handloom products (artistry in house roof, leaf plates and cups, ornamental products and other objects of the hill areas) as well as the traditions that have come down to us. Sculptures must have reached a distinctive place. Drawing, painting and sculpture usually coexist and are inseparable. It is a deep rooted belief that any error in painting/carving will give him a handicapped child. Carving is connected with a deep knowledge of philosophy and psychology. The artists have accepted the current view of the open environment. The images are made after the human forms showing the intimate relation between human being and god. Sex symbol in the deity is the soul in their belief.

Artisery in colour of suitable objects caught the eyes of the great people and they became popular in Congress *Swadeshi Mela* and British exhibitions although the work has declined much since the abolition of the monarchy. The products of today are mainly confined to types of dollmaking of wooden, earthen, paper and cloth products at the time of exhibitions. They depict artists such as drum player, fiddle player, Khamba and Thoibi in dance, Radha-Krishna Jugal Milan, swordman, spearman, etc. The tribal clothes and weapons have a symmetrical and artistic design. Among the Meiteis, the long shield used by as spearman (called *Chung*) is painted in fearful figures. The war sword had floral designs over the handle made of copper and of different colours, and such is the case with *Pena* tiddle and *Pung* (drum). The numerical strength with latest figures of census 2001 is given below which shows the literates and literacy rate of manipur (districtwise).

Table 1
Literates and Literacy Rates by Sex : Census 2001

Union Territory/ Districts	*Literates*			*Literacy Rate of 2001*		
	Persons	*Males*	*Females*	*Persons*	*Males*	*Females*
Manipur	**1,429,656**	**815,944**	**613,712**	**68.87**	**77.87**	**59.70**
Senapati	171,100	99,583	71,517	50.47	56.39	44.04
Tamenglong	56,269	33,640	22,629	58.46	67.04	49.11
Churachandpur	148,829	84,537	64,292	74.67	84.98	64.40
Bishnupur	127,667	72,751	54,916	71.59	82.25	61.09
Thoubal	208,464	123;372	85,092	67.90	80.50	55.34
Imphal West	312,125	171,350	140,775	80.61	89.10	72.24
Imphal East	260,573	147,617	112,956	76.38	86.44	66.30
Ukhrul	83,284	47,625	35,659	68.96	75.40	61.91
Chandel	61,345	35,469	25,876	57.38	66.12	48.57

Language and Literature

Manipuri and English are the langauges of the State. Hindi is spoken and understood by most of the people. Manipuri language has been the court language of Manipur since time immemorial. It has also a separate script of its own which is found in old manuscripts and began to evolve about 17th century. The Meitei language and the script under the able kings brought about a great unification. Under the influence of Bengal Vaishnavism and the British rule, the people accepted the Bengali script for their language though the number of books reached its height in the 19th century. The modern Manipuri literature starts from the beginning of the 19th century after English pattern of administration had found a share among the people. The establishment of a first High School, i.e., Johnstone and its reorganisation in 1891 and affiliation to Calcutta University, are important steps. Important works had been done by English officials and Meitei educationists who started writing about Manipur. The census data about the types of languages spoken by various tribes of Manipur is given as follows:

Table 2
Mother Tongue for Scheduled Tribes

Scheduled Tribe	*Mother Tongue*	*Number of Speakers*					
		Rural			*Urban*		
		Total	*Males*	*Females*	*Total*	*Males*	*Females*
1	2	3	4	5	6	7	8
ALL SCHEDULED TRIBES							
	Adi	1	1	0	2	2	0
	Anal	11,869	5,831	6,038	258	127	131
	Angami	8	2	6	77	77	0
	Ao	7	5	2	137	59	78
	Arabic/Arbi	30	17	13	2	0	2
	Assamese	247	182	65	3	0	3
	Bengali	112	58	54	35	21	14
	Bhili/Bhilodi	8	2	6	2	1	1
	Bhumij	28	11	17	0	0	0
	Bishnupuriya	7	3	4	1	1	0
	Bodo/Boro	2	2	0	1	1	0
	Chakhesang	1,278	654	624	11	6	5
	Chang	2	2	0	0	0	0
	Coorgi/Kodagu	5	2	3	9	2	7
	Deori	9	3	6	9	5	4
	Dimasa	11	4	7	0	0	0
	Dogri	23	17	6	8	5	3
	English	687	374	313	245	134	111
	Gangte	10,150	5,267	4,883	2,503	1,245	1,258
	Garo	4	4	0	0	0	0
	Gondi	4	2	2	1	0	1
	Gujarati	322	169	153	115	53	62
	Halabi	0	0	0	1	1	0
	Halam	6	2	4	1	1	0
	Hindi	2,920	1,640	1,280	744	410	334
	Hmar	30,749	15,732	15,017	5,583	2,687	2,896
	Ho	5	2	3	3	3	0
	Jatapu	3	2	1	0	0	0
	Juang	17	8	9	10	4	6
	Kabui	55,446	27,992	27,454	7,907	4,061	3,846
	Kannada	30	17	13	6	6	0
	Karbi/Mikir	177	91	86	6	5	1
	Khandeshi	3	0	3	16	8	8
	Kharia	4	4	0	7	3	4
	Khasi	53	26	27	40	17	23
	Khezha	676	331	345	7	4	3
	Khiemnungan	16	4	12	0	0	0

(Contd.)

(Contd.)

1	2	3	4	5	6	7	8
	Khond/Kondh	1	0	1	0	0	0
	Kisan	1	1	0	2	1	1
	Kom	12,953	6,683	6,270	290	176	114
	Konda	8	3	5	30	17	13
	Konkani	5	3	2	12	5	7
	Konyak	8	6	2	0	0	0
	Korku	1	0	1	3	0	3
	Korwa	11	5	6	1	0	1
	Koya	1	0	1	1	0	1
	Kuki	26,360	13,597	12,763	3,295	1,674	1,621
	Kurukh/Oraon	23	15	8	5	4	1
	Lahauli	1	0	1	1	0	1
	Lahnda	3	2	1	0	0	0
	Lakher	2	2	0	0	0	0
	Lepcha	0	0	0	2	1	1
	Liangmei	27,084	13,991	13,093	40	19	21
	Lotha	8	5	3	77	38	39
	Lushai/Mizo	4,098	2,102	1,996	3,089	1,540	1,549
	Malayalam	165	127	38	16	8	8
	Malto	2	2	0	0	0	0
	Manipuri	296	189	107	488	220	268
	Mao	73,164	37,500	35,664	986	555	431
	Maram	9,101	4,738	4,363	76	42	34
	Marathi	191	88	103	0	0	0
	Maring	14,674	7,518	7,156	126	72	54
	Miri/Mishing	0	0	0	1	1	0
	Mishmi	3	1	2	0	0	0
	Mogh	0	0	0	4	4	0
	Monpa	5	1	4	0	0	0
	Munda	2	1	1	23	10	13
	Mundari	12	4	8	1	1	0
	Nepali	245	124	121	26	13	13
	Nissi/Dafla	0	0	0	14	14	0
	Oriya	1	0	1	0	0	0
	Pabha	2	2	0	7	4	3
	Paite	28,861	14,784	14,077	11,820	5,994	5,826
	Parji	5	2	3	0	0	0
	Pawi	4	3	1	1	0	1
	Phom	11	4	7	9	4	5
	Pochury	2	2	0	0	0	0
	Punjabi	7	6	1	3	2	1
	Rengma	0	0	0	36	14	22
	Sangtam	9	4	5	2	2	0
	Santali	8	4	4	0	0	0
	Savara	1	1	0	0	0	0

(Contd.)

(Contd.)

1	2	3	4	5	6	7	8
	Sema	5	2	3	14	7	7
	Sindhi	9	4	5	0	0	0
	Tamil	2	2	0	27	14	13
	Tangkhul	1,01,464	51,818	49,646	2,682	1,399	1,283
	Tangsa	69	43	26	6	4	2
	Telugu	33	19	14	19	12	7
	Thado	91,407	46,226	45,181	4,095	2,056	2,039
	Tibetan	6	4	2	6	5	1
	Tripuri	0	0	0	9	9	0
	Tulu	2	0	2	4	3	1
	Urdu	788	414	374	9	6	3
	Vaiphei	21,774	11,196	10,578	2,556	1,295	1,261
	Wancho	8	6	2	3	1	2
	Yimchungre	22	15	7	28	17	11
	Zeliang	1,247	641	606	7	5	2
	Zemi	5,536	2,811	2,725	14	4	10
	Zou	12,973	6,457	6,516	2,362	1,158	1,204
	Others	31,327	16,050	15,277	3,165	1,650	1,515

Source : Census 1991.

In the beginning of the 20th century men like Rev. W. Pettigrew, Mr. Wince, Bengali teachers like Babu Ramsundar Roy and the educated Manipuris like H. Maker Singh, Munal Singh, Jatiswar Singh and Haodijam Chaitanya began to print Manipuri books is Bengali. Maharaja Sir Churachand Singh was a great pattron of Manipuri literature and culture. At first the Manipuri literature was confined to writing text books for the beginners. New books were later written and published on a variety of subjects. A steady output of books on Bengali model also appeared.

Manipuri Sahitya Parishad was established in 1935 with Ibungohal Singh as its President and H. Irabot Singh as Secretary, with the purpose of promoting Manipuri language on the lines of Bangiya. Sanskrit Prisad. It helped the coming of some talent in creative writing. Says poet Kh. Chaoba Singh, "Our vernacular is a humble tongue to an unknown head, Manipuri poet is yet to come out." In his estimate the nucleous of the future of Manipuri which if nurtured properly will make a great leap. By 1947-48, Meitei writers such as Atom-bapu Sarma, L. Ibungohal Singh, H. Irabot Singh, O. Gokulchandra Singh, Ch. Mayurdhwaja, M. Jhulon Singh, etc., who for many years until their death built up their literature, were prolific. Their writings cover all aspects of creative literature. Poetry has ever been the favourite form of literary expression in Manipur and seems to be so now-a-days too, though it has changed very much. Poets of the old generation like Dr. Kamal, H. Anganghal, Kh. Chaoba Singh, A. Dorendra, A. Minaketan wrote lyrics and poems by drawing inspiration from folk songs, tradition and glory of Manipur. Dr. L. Kamal's *Leipareng,* Kh. Chaoba's *Thainagi Leirang,* Minaketan's

Vasant Sheireng, Ch. Mayurdhwaja's *Sheireng Anouba,* H. Irabot's Sheidam Sheireng contain collection of poems. They have gained tremendous popularity. H. Anganghal Singh has written an epic poem containing 38 thousand lines on the legend of *Khamba* and *Thoibi* which was published in eight volumes under the title *"Khamba Thoibigi Sheireng."* His "Singhel Indu" is another long narrative poem. A. Dorendro Singh produced his "Kamsa Bodha" on the model of Michael Modhusudan Datta's "Meghanad Bodha Kavya."

Post independent Manipuri poetry is negligible. The poets and writers have no *Sadhna.* There have been Manipuri translations of *Meghanad Bodh Kavya, Gitanjali, Meghaduta, Raghuvamsa, Rape of Lucreces, Kumar Sambhava,* etc. Daily papers with their supplements, magazines of different types in Manipur encourage new creative writers and accelerate the new course of literature.

Jahera by H. Anganghal is on the theme of the love between a Manipuri Hindu youngman called Kunjo and a Muslim girl called Jahera. Short story as a distinct literary form is hardly fifty years old in Manipur. Rajkumar Shitaljit Singh is regarded as the pioneer of short-story writer in Manipuri literature. In the Forties of this century two volumes, namely *Leikonungda* and *Leinun gshi* were published by him. He has also to his credit a number of novels like *Thadokpa,* and *Ima Rohini.* Now we have the numerous important novelists and short-story writers but they have not achieved a degree of success. Attempts are being made to introduce English, Bengali, Hindi and Russian works to Manipuri readers of the present generation.

Dictionary

Manipuri dictionary is well developed. N. Dinachandra's *Khunung Longi Artha* (Meaning of Archaic Manipuri), N. Khelchandra Singh's Manipuri to Manipuri and English Dictionary. *Ariba Manipuri Longei* (Dictionary *Ariba Manipuri Longei* (Dictionary of old Manipuri), H. Dijwamani Sharma's Anglo-Manipuri Dictionary, Hindi-Manipuri Dictionary, L. Ibungahol's Beginners' Anglo-Manipuri Dictionary, R.K. Shitaljit's Pocket Manipuri-English Dictionary, Friends's English to Manipuri, are worth-mentioning.

L. Radhamohan' Hindi-Manipuri Dictionary, L. Narayan Sharma's Manipuri to Hindi Shabdakosa, Dr. M. Kirti Singh's *Darsangi Longei* (Dictionary of Philosophy of Manipuri) etc. have enriched this branch of literature. The terminology committee set up the Government of Manipuri in 1975 has coined suitable Manipuri words in different subjects upto the Pre-University Standard.

Historical and Cultural Works

Scholars of Manipuri have written different types of histories: (1) General History of Manipur, (2) Cultural and Literary History, (3) Dynastic Histories, (4) Critical edition of texts written in Meitei script of the Purana's. Manipur has produced a number of historians/research scholars who have concentrated their critical faculties exclusively on Manipuris political history, developments in literature and culture, histories of several dynastic clans-such as Khumals, etc.,

Scores of traditional historians can also be mentioned who have enriched historical research by their addition of ancient Meitei text with transliteration, modern Manipuri translation and explanations of the texts. Late M. Chandra Singh, Kh. Yaima Singh Pandit, R.K. Sanahal Singh, N. Khelchandra Singh, Pandit Ng. Kulachandra Singh, etc. are well-known in this field.

The musicians and dancers have worked diligently over the last 20 years to provide the important works on the systems of *Tals* dance forms. The more important names are Guru Maisnam Amubi Singh, I. Gulamjat Singh, R.K. Iboton Singh, Pandit Pariskhit Sharma etc.

The institution which sought to promote ideological studies were Vivodha-Janani Sabha of Maharaja Sir Churachand Singh, *Manipur Itihas Goveshna Samiti* (Historical Research Society of Manipur), etc. which had been active in collecting manuscripts on medicine, astrology, clan traditions and rites until the Second World War when they had to close doors. The period from 1948 up to the present has been the period of founding many voluntary institutions with grants from the Government of Manipur. The editions and publications of the manuscripts (originally in Meitei script) now in Bengali script have started to be produced very swiftly. The number of such treatises is over six thousand.

Essay and Translation Works

The essay and translation forms of literary works in Manipuri developed mainly after 1947. Editions of daily papers and columnists of several news papers and journal have successfully handled essay writing. A foretaste of the conditions before and after the Second World War, Indian Independence and Manipur's integration with India has been given in them. This aspect has some high literary works of great values.

Atombapu Sarma made translations into Manipuri of the entire Shakti and religious texts of the Hindus viz. *Candi, Gita, Govinda, Sarasvata-Vay-akarna,* etc. Kalachand Sastri had published his 30 volumes translation of the entire Sanskrit *Mahabharata.* The translation of literacy, poetical, religious and philosophical books into Manipuri from English, Hindi, Sanskrit, and Bengali have penetrated Manipur. The translation of the works of Michael, Bankumchandra, Rabindranath, Krishnadas Kaviraj etc., from Bengali into Manipuri was completed and sold in Manipuri. Some people have published the editions of the works of Shakespeare, Ibsen, Tolstoy, G.B. Shaw, copies of which can still be seen in some college libraries. Persons having education in Hindi got as far as the works of Tulsidas, Premchand, etc. There have been attempts by them to do the job on the translations of Khamba and Thoibi (epic story of hero Khamba and heroine Thoibi) into Bengali. W. Yumjao Singh devoted years to the English translation of the royal chronicle 'Cheitharol Kumbaba.' Unfortunately, he died before its publication. The translocation of the old Testament, with the help of a local Pandit, was done as early as 1810 by Srirampur Christian Mission. The Light of Life, Baskandi, Cachar, published the entire New Testament in Manipuri in 1930 for the students of the Bible correspondence course. The English version of some gospols has been brought out by S. Don Bosco, Imphal. They have studied Manipuri language to do their work. Coming to the philosophical translations the author under took faithful and paraphrase translations of philoslophical treatise such as *Sankhya Karika, Republic* and *Tractatus Logico-Philosophicus* which are suited to the needs of students of philosophy.

The various religious groups and communities like the Muslims, the Sikhs, the Jaina brought parts of their scriptures (the Holy Quran, Guru Granth, Mahavira's Teaching) through their private finance and printings. They have stressed the Manipuri lawyers and Brahmin Pandits go the credit of getting legal texts such as the India Penal Code (IPC), and the Criminal Procedure Code (CrPC), Indian Constitution, Police Act, Panchayat Act and *Manu Samhita* translated to Manipuri. They are rather difficult for the common people to understand. They have retained a high percentage of English terms and phrases.

Philosophical Thought and Literature. The peculiarity of Manipur belief and religious concepts, however, is its great influence on almost all fields of cultural life, literature, art, pedagogies and even political life. The *Maibis* (traditional priests and priestesses) and an intoxicated Vaishnavas who represented the living tradition of prewar days came to dominate and seemed to have dominated the field ever since. They were too old to change their views; they continued the teaching of Hindu philosophy in the form of Gaudiya-Vaishnavism as found in Manipur. Atombapur Sarma had published his volumes of the *Rig Veda,* the *Gita,* the *Bhagavata, Chaitanya Charitamitra* etc. Teaching of Gandhi, Aurobindo, Vinoba, Gaudiya Vaishnava, Missionaries were available in Manipuri with texts, notes and commentaries.

The development of philosophical literature is linked with the Sanskrit scholars and Manipuri philosophy professors who not only taught them in schools and colleges but wrote versions of works nearest to the originals than those already current and translation work of Rabindranath, Gandhi, Aurobindo, Vivekanand, and Rama Krishna etc. They promoted the centenary celebrations and jublees of these contemporary thinkers. This glance on philosophical thought cannot be complete without mentioning polished books and journals of Vivekanand Kendra, Aurobindo Society, Imphal branches, Gita Mandal, Sarbodaya Mandal, Imphal, Divine Life Society of Swami Sivananda, Imphal branch of ISCON and anti-Hindu organisations such as Apokpa Marup, Meitei National Front.

Prose and Criticism

The post-Independence era has given a brilliant batch of young essayist and critics. Most of them are college and University lecturers, who are in touch with Manipuri modern literature. But none of them has made a critical and serious study of old manuscripts and texts. They have yet to write books and submit research papers on different aspects of literary progress and essays.

Journalism in Manipuri language is popular. There are thirty daily papers, two English weekly papers, numerous fortnightly and monthly papers/magazines.

Manipuri language, at given at the outset, is the State language. Its script is also recognised by the Government for teaching. The publication of Manipuri magazine has considerably increased. Publication of Manipuri Government's *Angangsingi Numit* (Children day on November 14), Manipur (fortnightly) from the Director of Information and Public Relations, Bulletins of different Government Departments and souvenirs of many literary organisations are not-worthy. The important names in all these magazines include *Matamgi Khongthang* published by the United Literary Association, Lamlong Bazar, *Yeningtha* published by Young Writers' Forum, Imphal. They have been successful in creating taste for Manipuri magazines in the intelligentsia.

As far as the prospect of Manipuri literature is concerned, there are better hopes. With the spread of literacy, production of research degree holders, study of old *Meitei Puranas* through the culture of Meitei Script by different sections, better conditions for writers and scholars through the patronage and cooperation of ministers will put Manipuri literature on the path of progress.

Manipuri Sahitya Parishad which has completed its 49 years of active existence is trying to make Manipuri literature up-to-date through collection of old books, publishing books, organising annual sessions in different places and conferring suitable titles on the artists of traditional Manipuri School. Among other institutions are Naharol Sahitya Sabga, Naharol Sahitya Samiti, Premi Samiti, Cultural Forum, Astrological Society, Universal Literary Association etc., all of them have rendered significant service to the Manipuri language and literature.

The Manipuri Student Union is an association of Manipuri young students who live in the state. The tradition of heroic deeds, chivalry and distinctive culture has developed strong regional consciousness in them. The sacred land and its history remain a source of inspiration to the young Meitei mind. The members have taken up arms against any humiliation, to do within their power by strikes, agitations and propaganda, to restore. Manipur's ancient glory, to include Manipuri language in the 8th Schedule of Indian Constitution, to recognise it as a subject in Manipur Public Service Examination and to continue research work in this language. They impress in the mind of Manipuris an interest in treating Manipur as the land of the ancient people and expelling new comers by an Act of the State.

The resultant effects of their efforts have been the measures adopted by the state in these demands.

Manipuri literature has the credit of receiving recognition of the Sahitya Akademy almost every year. Some of the Manipuri writers have been awarded the Akademy's prizes though the traditions of pre-War output have not been kept in the same spirit in there fields.

9

Administrative and Political Struggle

Like other states of North East, Manipur too has a political background of its full statehood. Departure of Britishers even worsened the problems by giving the option of leaving India Union. Thus, Sardar Patel had to work hard to include Manipur in India by persuading the Monarch. It was only from the year 1945 and afterwards that Manipur began to witness a large number of political movements. The basic objective of the movement was to bring a new political system in the state. Therefore, the period from 1946 to 1949 was a big landmark in the political history of the state. During this short period the people began to witness two unprecedented political movements, the first one was for the setting up of a full responsible government in Manipur and the second one was for the merger of this state into the Dominion of India.

The first one aimed at a drastic change in her political structure and administrative system without disturbing her political identity and the latter was for the end of the era of the autonomous kingdom of Manipur.

(a) Movement for the Setting up of a Responsible Governments

The growth of these progressive political movements was closely associated with the growth of political and national consciousness among the people of Manipur. In this regard, the formation of the 'Nikhil Hindu Manipuri Mahasabha', on the 30th May 1934 may be regarded as a stepping stone for the growth of political consciousness in the country. Basically this organisation was a social and religious organisation and its only objective was for the upliftment and strengthening of the social and religious life of the people. The chief patronage of this organisation was the Maharaja of Manipur. However, if the nature of the organisation and political affiliation of certain leading members of the organisation is to be studied it can be observed that the basic undisclosed motive of the establishment of this organisation was for a social unification among the Meitei ethnic group for the strengthening of a political force. This was quite evident from the welcome address of Hijam Irabot Singh, a prominent leader of the Mahasabha. On the inaugural day of the organisation he particularly mentioned that one of the most important objectives of the organisation was to promote social unity for the strengthening of the Meitei nation.[1]

So, to achieve this goal, he strongly stressed the social unity among the same ethnic group. Therefore, there was no scope for a political action in the policy and programme of the organisation. Finding this lack of chance for political activities, some leading members, mostly educated elite group, who were influenced by the political programme of the Indian National Movement, strongly felt the immediate necessity of a political organisation in Manipur. They were fully convinced that a sweeping political change in the state could be possible only when there was a political organisation. So, in order to continue a mass movement, they wanted to change this social and religious organisation into a political party. Their desire was successfully materialised on the 29th and 30th December 1938 when the 'Fourth Session' of the said organisation was held at Chinga in South Imphal. In this session, this social and religious organisation became a political party and the original name of the organisation was also changed to new era, i.e., 'Nikhil Manipuri Mahasabha'. In the opening session, the party adopted some important political resolutions and among them the most important demand was the issue of the establishment of a responsible government in Manipur.

This new political development was a serious concern to the government of Manipur. As per resolution of the Manipur State Durbar, the government released an order that no employee of the state would be allowed to be a member of this party and it was further stated that no state pensioner was allowed to participate in it, subscribe in aid of it, and assist it in any way.[2] Thus according to the order of the Maharaja, all the government employees, who were the members of the Mahasabha except H. Irabot Singh and E. Tompok Singh, then President and General Secretary, resigned from the party. Thus the emergence of Mahasabha as a political party was a significant development in the history of the political movement in Manipur.

Activities of Mahasabha as a first step of the beginning of the political movement in the Nikhil Manipur Mahasabha made a petition to the authority with 356 signatories, for the setting up of a Legislative Council in the state. Such a political movement, initiated by the new political party was a great challenge to the existing political system in the state. The Maharaja also took it very sincerely. He wrote a letter to MacDonald the President of the Manipur State Darbar and enquired about their opinion in this matter. But surprisingly the Darbar was of the opinion that the setting up of a Legislative Council would not contribute anything to the solution of the existing problems of Manipur.[3] Regarding the establishment of a democratic political institution in the state, C. Gimson, the Political Agent gave a very damaging opinion not in favour of the wishes of the people. In a confidential letter to the Maharaja he stated that "Manipur is yet ripe for a large experiment in democracy. Her people have no experience in democratic institutions which are foreign to them and have no roots in her history and in my opinion it has not yet either the requisite electorate or a sufficient member of qualified legislators to make democratic institution a success."[4]

He again suggested to establish a Municipal Committee in Imphal as an experiment for a democratic political institution. However, in spite of this, all the responsible people of the colonial British government admitted that the mismanagement in the administration was the main reason for the dissatisfaction of the people and so they wanted to bring some positive changes in the administrative set up. A.R.H. MacDonald, President of the Manipur State Darbar, took a keen interest in bringing some positive changes in the administration. He was very much against the trend of Mangba-Sengba (clean and unclean social ostracism) which was exercised by the Maharaja and the Brahma Sabha. He took it as the most important reason for the dissatisfaction of people. So, he expressed his wish to remove all the social evils from the administration of the state. He disclosed that the state made a huge amount of expenditure for no benefit. Under this understanding he suggested the sale of the State's property in British India, the abolition of all grants for 'Puja ceremonies and allowances to temples, reduction in the staff of H.H. the Maharaja's Palace Office and Revisional Court etc.[5]

After this, the Darbar adopted a resolution asking all the members of the Darbar to submit their suggestion for reforms in Manipur before the end of April 1939. Meanwhile, H. Irabot Singh, the President of the Nikhil Manipuri Mahasabha submitted an outline of the Legislature. "There he specifically pointed out the immediate need for the establishment of the legislature as first step to responsible government.[6] Besides this, he also pointed out the possible power and duties of the proposed legislature.

Thus just after the establishment of this political party, the people began to come across a series of political movements for the establishment of a responsible government in Manipur as a state.

(b) Split in the Party

In the year 1939, the Nikhil Manipuri Mahasabha got split into two. The outbreak of Nupi Lan was the immediate cause of this split. The radicalist group in the party led by H. Irabot Singh supported the cause of the movement. But the latter group did not share his view. Due to this difference the party was split into two and Irabot and his group came out and formed a new party. H. Irabot himself took over as the president of the party. The name of the party was the 'Praja Sanmeloni'. The main objective of this party was the abolition of the colonial and feudal administrative system and setting up of a responsible government in Manipur. Under the banner of these two political demands the 'Praja Sanmeloni' started a peaceful and non-violent political movement against the feudalism and colonialism. But between 1941 to 1945 there was no political movement in Manipur, during which the Japanese and INA forces fought several battles in Manipur. The battle of Imphal was among the decisive battles of Second World War in the South East Asian Theatre.

Again in 1945 another party was formed in Manipur at the initiative of H. Irabot Singh. All the left oriented leaders in the state joined as the members of this party. The name of this party was known as the "Praja Sangha". The fundamental aim and objective of the party was to endeavour for the attainment of independence of Manipur from the hands of the colonial Britishers, abolition of the existing feudal system, establishment of responsible government and introduction of adult universal franchise. With these aim and objectives the party started to work on the line of a left oriented party. Besides this, the party also strongly stressed for the establishment of classless society in the state. At that time there was a peasant organisation called 'Krishi Sanmeloni' and its headquarter was at Nambol, a place situated at about nine miles from Imphal. The basic objective of the organisation was to endeavour for the welfare of the Agricultural class in the state. At that time they had no political objective. H. Irabot Singh wanted to strengthen the activities of the organisation and with this understanding he joined as a member of this peasant party. On the 16th May 1946 the second session of the Krishi Sanmeloni was held at Nambol. In this session the original name of the organisation was changed to 'Krishak Sabha' and Irabot was chosen its President and Ibomcha Singh (Ibomcha Kabiraj) became the Secretary.

Thus, after this session, the Krishak Sabha became one of the most significant left oriented political organisations and with the co-operation of other like minded political organisations they began to launch political movement against the colonial and feudal administrative order. Just like other political parties they had also strongly demanded for the establishment of a responsible government in Manipur. Their other demands were the introduction of adult franchise, administrative oneness between hill and plain people, and that land must belong to the tillers. In the meantime the Cabinet Mission Plan came to India with certain new administrative proposal. About the position of the state, the Cabinet Mission Plan categorically mentioned for the establishment of a representative institution in order to have a close and constant touch with the public opinion in the state. This opinion was also endorsed by the standing committee of the Chamber of Princes and expressed their desire to implement the decision within twelve months.

Taking the opportunity of this latest political development of the post-war period in India the Nikhil Manipuri Mahasabha adopted a very strong resolution and urged the Maharaja of Manipur to make an immediate announcement for early establishment of a responsible government in Manipur state.[7] They further asked the authority to take up an immediate step so that the complete implementation of the declaration would be made within a year. They further requested the Maharaja to install an interim government during the formulative period with responsible government.

(c) Birth of Manipuri State Congress Party

Then the political movement for the setting up of the responsible government was further intensified with the birth of the Manipur State Congress Party. On the 18th September 1946, a joint meeting of all the existing political parties in Manipur was held at the Aryan Theatre Hall of Imphal. This move was initiated by some educated youths of Manipur. The main objective of the meeting was to develop a common platform which could represent the general feeling of the masses. All the representatives of the different political parties warmly welcomed this idea and they all agreed to have a joint meeting on 4th October 1946. Regarding this meeting, a 'Conciliatory Committee' was formed and all the representatives of the parties was the member of this committee.

But it is very interesting to reproduce that when the meeting was about to start some participants in the meeting made a strong objection to the presence of H. Irabot Singh, because they charged him that he was a communist. As a consequence of this a very bad scene was created and finally, as a mark of protest against the mismanagement of the organisers all the members of the Krishak Sabha and the Praja Sangha went off the meeting hall and abstained permanently from the meeting. But the remaining members in the meeting hall continued the business and finally they all agreed to form another political party in Manipur. The name kept for this party was the Manipur State Congress Party and one Rajkumar Bhubon Singh became its first President. Later on this party became a unit of the All India Congress Committee.

In its plan the party strongly emphasised for the abolition of social injustice prevailing in the state and establishment of a responsible government in Manipur on the basis of democratic principles. Thus, the effort for the polarisation of all the political parties in Manipur for the establishment of a common political platform in the country was not materialised. However, the commencement of this new party undoubtedly gave a great impetus to the activities of the political movements in Manipur.

Thus, the emergence of left-oriented parties and political activities of the said party produced a positive sweeping change in the political system of the country. Indeed, the birth of these political parties tremendously enhanced the political and national awakening among the people of Manipur and under the banner of the demand for the establishment of a responsible government they began to fight for the attainment of their political right.

Beginning of the Second World war was of a great significance particularly in the history of the liberation movement in India. Now every Indian began to feel that just after the end of this war the British officers would hand over the administrative responsibilities to the Indian leaders. So, they felt that the impending independence of India from the colonial rule was now only a matter of time. This news spread quite soon and sensing the mood of the time every princely state in India also began to prepare for a separate administrative unit of their own. Taking the opportunity of this advantageous latest political development the Maharaja of Manipur took an initiative in urging the colonial authority to allow him to make a royal proclamation about the new administrative report to the people of his State.[8] Another copy of the letter was also sent to the Chancellor, Chamber of Princes in India. C. Gimson, the British political Agent in Manipur, also welcomed this idea and he asked the Maharaja to send a draft copy which he proposed to announce and assured that he would forward it at once for the order of the Governor.

After consultation with his top officers, the Maharaja sent a letter to the British Political Agent on 30th October 1946 and he explicitly expressed his desire to establish a democratic system of administration with an 'Elected Advisory Assembly' consisted of the representative of both 'hills and plains'. He also stated that the proposed constitution should have a comprehensive idea for the establishment of a full understanding between hill and valley people in future. But it seems that Maharaja was not in favour of the demand of the establishment of responsible government in Manipur. So in order to realise his idea, he submitted the 'Draft Manipur Administrative Rule' to the Political Agent on 6th November 1946. This proposed 'Draft Rule' mentioned the rules of the relationship between the State Darbar and the Maharaja and also powers of the individual members of the state council. The Rules also provided for a 'Council' of six members in addition to the President and two members would be chosen from the representatives of the hill people. Another provision given by the said rules was to regulate the operation of the 'State Courts', and for this a separate 'Draft Court Act' was prepared. One more important power of the Maharaja which was mentioned in the proposed draft rule was that the Chief Minister and members of the Council would be appointed by the Maharaja.

However, as per the letter of Pearson, the PMSD, the appointment of the Chief Minister and other members had to be made on the advice of His Excellency, the Agent to the Crown Representative. But nothing was discussed in the whole body of the proposed draft administrative rules about the establishment of a full responsible government in Manipur on the basis of democratic principle. Instead of this, the proposed draft clearly indicated the room of the political right of the British in the future administration of the state. The 'Draft Administrative Rules' proposed by the colonial authorities was not at all acceptable to all the political parties in Manipur because they felt that it did not fulfil the demand of the parties. Their main objective was to establish responsible government under a different constitution of the state. The first reaction came from the Manipur State Congress Party. They urged the Maharaja to kindly make a royal declaration for the establishment of Legislative Assembly based on democratic principle.[10]

The Maharaja also was fully aware of the growing political consciousness among the people of his state. He mentioned that to implement the responsibilities for the governance of the state would not be possible for him without the co-operation of the people. So, he clearly mentioned that "democratic form of government is the order of the day"[11] and with this objective he was preparing to initiate a new system of democratic principle in the light of the existing political circumstances in the state. At the same time he was also of the view that since the constitution was meant for popular and responsible government, the people must also be involved in the framing of the constitution.[12] Therefore he proposed a basis under which the "Constitution Making Committee" had to be constituted.

According to his proposal: "the committee should be constituted of the following members: (1) three members nominated by the President of the Manipur

State Darbar including the President himself as Chairman, (2) one member deputed by the Chairman, Chief Court, (3) one representative deputed by each of the Tahsil Circles from the five Tahsils, (5) one representative deputed by each of the areas viz., Ukhrul, Mao, Tamenlong, Churachandpur and S.E. Areas.

Thus, sensing the flow of the time and without any delay, he began to prepare for the establishment of a new administrative system on the basis of the democratic norm. And on the 12th December 1946 Maharaja released a formal order to constitute a 'Constitution Making Committee'.[13] He mentioned that the new constitution would provide enough room for the amalgamation of the tribal parts with the government of the state. The Election Committee was formed and it constituted of three members: S. Somorendro Singh, Jail member of the Darbar as Chairman, L. Ibungohal Singh and Quazi Walliulla as their members. Then on 24th December 1946 the Chairman of the Election Committee issued a notice to submit the names of the candidates of the respective Tahsil circles on or prior to 5th January 1947. It is mentioned that such an unimaginative order from the authority brought a lot of misunderstanding and confusion among the people, except the leaders of the Manipur State Congress. Still, whatever it may be, the order of the Chairman of the Election Committee was strongly protested by the Krishak Sabha and Praja Sangha. They were of the opinion that the time given for the notification was too short and it would not be possible for the people to decide within such a limited time about the fundamental common issue on which should be based the future constitution of state of Manipur.[14]

Therefore, as a mark of resentment against this hasty and ambiguous terms of the Election Committee, they launched a series of protest meeting from the 1st to 11th January 1947 at various places of Manipur. They adopted a resolution and a copy was sent to the Maharaja for necessary action. But the Maharaja did not respond to their request. So as a mark of revolt to the attitude of the authority they abstained from the preparation of the Constitution Making Committee. Contrary to this and taking the opportunity of this new political development the Congress Party was completely prepared to join the committee. Thus the abstention from the committee of the two parties left the field open for the Manipur State Congress Party.

(d) Party Election and Afterwards

The election was conducted on 21st January 1947 and the following persons were elected to the committee. They were as follows Dr. N. Leirem Singh (Congress), Imphal East, Sinam Krishnamohan Singh (Congress), Imphal West, Laishram Jugeshwar Singh (Congress), Thoubal Tahsil, Dwijamani Dev Sharma from Congress, Bishenpur Tahsil and Irom, Mera Singh (Independent), Mayang Imphal. However, the election of the hill areas was not held because of the confusion in regard to the method of the selection of tribal representatives. In the meantime, some leaders of the hill areas submitted an application to the Maharaja and requested that they should be allowed to elect their representatives clearly as it was done in the valley area. The Maharaja immediately asked the President of the Manipur

State Darbar to look into the matter. But later on the authority invited five educated hill people to join the Constitution Making Committee.[15]

Thus, in the midst of widespread dissatisfaction to the functioning of the authority, particularly in regard to the selection of hill representatives, the Maharaja formed the 'Constitution Making Committee' consisting of fourteen members. They were S. Somorendro Singh, Md. Quazi Walliulla, L.M. Ibungohal Singh, A. Minaketan Singh also known as Ibotombi Singh, Dwijamani Dev Sharma, S. Krishnamohon Singh, Dr. N. Leiren Singh, L. Jugeshwar Singh, Irom Mera Singh, Daiho, Thangkhopao, M.K. Shimray, Teba Kilong, and Tiangkham, F.F. Pearson, the then President of Manipur State Darbar was appointed the Chairman and thus on the 10th March 1947 Maharaja formally inaugurated the Committee.

The preparatory work of the 'Manipur State Constitution' was accomplished in the month of July 1947 and on the 27th of the same month the proposed draft constitution was submitted to the Maharaja. Thus despite, many irregularities in the process of the constitution of the committee and strong objection from the major political parties, the government successfully prepared a separate constitution of the Manipur State. And the enactment of this constitution provided the solid foundation for the establishment of a responsible government in the state. On the day of the inauguration of the 'Constitution Making Committee', the Maharaja disclosed his desire to have 'a prosperous, happy, peaceful and progressive Manipur under the responsible government which was constituted by the representatives of the masses.[16]

(e) Setting up of Manipur State Council

Anyway, the Maharaja was not prepared to fulfil completely the desire and demands of the political parties. Just after the end of the Second World War, the British authorities were fully determined to hand the administrative responsibilities over to the Indian leaders. All the princely states in India also were prepared to take over the responsibilities of administration from the British. Taking this advantage the Maharaja also got ready to form an 'Interim Government' in Manipur. On the 1st July 1947 the Manipur State Darbar which was established in 1907 was abolished and in place of the Darbar the 'Manipur State Council' was established.

On the 15th July 1947 F.F. Pearson, the President, Manipur State Darbar was appointed as the first Chief Minister of Manipur. But surprisingly, within a short span of time of thirty days, i.e., on the 13th August 1947 the Maharaja issued a new order and accordingly Manipur State Council was dissolved and a new 'Interim Council' was set up with Maharajakumar Priyobrata Singh, the younger brother of the Maharaja, as the Chief Minister of Manipur. The other ministers appointed were K. Gouro Singh (Education), Bashiruddin Ahmed (Jail, Medical, P.W.D.), R.K. Bhubon Singh (Revenue), S. Krishnamohan Singh (Commerce and Industry), Major Khathing (for handling Hill Affairs), T.C. Tiangkham (Forest, Veterinary). On the 15th August 1947, with the independence of India Manipur became independent. The policy of constituting of 'Interim Council' was not a desirable decision to other political parties. The basic demand and desire of the people was to establish a responsible government in Manipur on democratic principle. Even a huge section of the Congress Party also severely criticised the policy of the authority in regard to the formation of 'Interim Council' and they also expressed their unhappiness to the method of the appointment of two Congress members in the 'Council'. It is mentioned that some opportunist leaders in the Congress Party met the Chief Minister Pearson and suggested to form a government. In their view, the basis of the constitution of ministry would be two from the official and two from the Congress Party of Manipur because they claimed that the Manipur State Congress party was the largest party in Manipur which could represent the masses. The intrigue of some Congress leaders was highly condemned by the Praja Sangha, another political party in Manipur. They boldly asserted that since there were many political parties in Manipur, the Congress Party could not be treated as the only party which could represent the masses.

And they again claimed that all the members of the 'Interim Government' should be selected by the people through a proper election.[17] On the other side, the sizeable section of the Congress Party also had badly criticised the motive of some leaders of the party. As a result of this the Congress Party was split into two groups. On the 22nd July 1947, Elangbam Tompok Singh and Chandrahas Singh issued a hand-bill in which they declared about the removal of the President and General Secretary and some leaders of the Congress Working Committee. They further emphasised that the new Working Committee was formed under the Presidentship of E. Tompok Singh, But their claim was not recognised by Pearson. In a letter to Chandrahas Singh, he categorically stressed that if Tompok Singh carried on to call himself the 'Manipur State Congress' then he would be liable to get punishment liable to a criminal charge of mispresentation and cheating.[18] The action of Pearson was largely condemned by "Tompok Congress". In the Working Committee meeting held on 31st July 1947 they condemned the Chief Minister as a man who ignored the wishes and demand of the people.[19] They strongly urged that a 'Popular Interim Government' should be established without any further delay otherwise the progress towards the formation of a responsible government would be obstructed and delayed. Finally they mentioned that if the state authority failed to do so, the State Congress would take up proper steps to achieve the goal.

(f) Interim Council

But without giving any answer and response to the demand of "Tompok Congress", the Maharaja inaugurated the 'Interim Council'. Seeing the negative attitude of the Maharaja, the Congress Party led by Tompok Singh, immediately thought to take up political movement against the Government. On the 4th October 1947 the meeting of the Working Committee was held and they adopted a resolution to urge the government to make an urgent declaration of granting a 'Responsible Government' before the 1st April 1948.[20] The resolution further stressed that if the government did not respond to their demand till 31st October 1947, they would immediately take up political agitation from the 1st November 1947. On the other side they also demanded to establish an 'Interim Council' immediately and further said that the steps should be taken up for framing a 'State Constitution' so that a full responsible government could be established under the constitution. On the 12th October 1947 a meeting was conducted with the representatives of the State Council, Legal Remeberancer to His Highness the Maharaja of Manipur and some members of the Manipur State Congress Party led by Tomal Singh.

On part of His Highness the Maharaja of Manipur, K.C. Chakravarty, the Legal Remebrancer, assured that the demand of the Congress Party (Tompok Congress), i.e., the provision of voting, elected members of the legislature and ministers elected by the legislatures would be included in the constitution.[21] But the meeting was not able to meet the basic demand of the Tompok Congress about the setting up of responsible government of the state. In the meantime, the Manipur State Congress (Tomal Congress), also strongly asserted that the alternative of this draft constitution must be to pave way for the establishment of a full responsible government to the people. Therefore, they requested the Maharaja to make an announcement for the establishment of a responsible government, grounded on adult franchise and all the executive responsibilities should be in the hands of the legislatures.[22]

They further demanded that the responsible government should be set up not later than the 26th May 1948. However, they were not prepared for a political movement. Thus, since no positive reply was received from the government, the Manipur State Congress (Tompok) began agitation from the 6th November 1947. As a part of their political movement they adopted the method of civil disobedience movement and the volunteers started demonstration band, and picketings in front of the state offices and at the residence of the government officials. As a result of this the normal life of the functioning of the state was completely paralysed. At the moment of the outlook of this agitation, the Dominion Agent Debeswar Sharma was not in Manipur. He was in Shillong. So, the Registrar of Dominion's Office immediately sent a telegraphic message about the whole situation. He said that as the situation getting grave and tense the immediate presence of the Dominion Agent was required.[23] The political movement for the setting up of full responsible government launched by the Tompok Congress was supported by the Praja Sangha, the Krishak Sabha, the Mahila Sanmeloni and the Student Federation etc.

At this point the Congress Party (Tomal) adopted a resolution in which they urged the government to make a declaration within 48 hours that the full responsible government would be established within May 1948. They were of opinion that if the government made such an announcement immediately the trouble created by the Tompok Congress would die down.[24] At the same time, they also demanded to give the responsibilities of the whole interim administration of the state to their party. On the other hand, the intensity of the movement became very serious. Therefore, the government used police forces to control the movement. As a result of this three people were injured by shooting incident. However, according to an unofficial report the number of casualties was 25 persons and all of them were moved by the other volunteers. Chief Minister Maharajkumar Priyobrata Singh then wrote a letter to the Dominion Agent for requisition of the Assam Rifles to guard the council office, Revenue Office and also the Secretariat[25]. The police firing upon the demonstrators was highly condemned by E. Tompok Singh, Director, Satyagraha Council of Action Manipur State Congress. He stated that during the course of the movement his volunteers were strictly observing the principle of non-violence.[26] Seeing this situation Debeshwar Sharma, the Dominion Agent in Manipur made a request to the people to suspend the agitation and on behalf of the Governor of Assam he assured the people that full responsible government would be set up in Manipur' not later than 1st June next[27] i.e., the year 1948. Then he immediately gave a telegraphic information to the Governor of Assam about the political development in Manipur. He said that the people were not interested to suspend satyagraha without an unequivocal declaration from the Maharaja granting full responsible government with elected 'Interim Arrangement'. After this he again sent a letter to the Maharaja and suggested that the proclamation announcing the grant of responsible government should not be delayed any longer.[28] Meanwhile the government released a notice in which it was mentioned that "the distribution of war compensation would be stopped from today, i.e., 10th November, of the Tompok Congress did not call off this agitation.

But this threat did not stop the activities of the movement and it became more serious. Then the Chief Minister of the Interim Council finally made an official announcement on the 23rd November 1947 that a complete responsible government would be established in Manipur by April 1948. The official declaration of establishment of responsible government was warmly welcomed by every political parties in Manipur. They regarded it as a positive gesture on the part of the authority and thought that it was very good for the attainment of their goal. On 25th November 1947 Tompok Singh wrote a letter to the Dominion Agent and showed his appreciation to the decision of the government. But he sought further classification from the authority about the proposed administrative system which was talked by the chief minister of Manipur. The Dominion Agent explained that the election of the state assembly would take place according to the constitution and the proposed assembly would be a sovereign body so that it could have that power to modify and draft the constitution. The leader of the majority party in the 'Assembly' would be the Chief Minister of the State.

Thus, after receiving this clarification from the Dominion Agent the political movement for the establishment of a full responsible government launched by Tompok Congress with the support of other political parties was withdrawn on the 26th November 1947.

(e) Franchise Sub-Committee

The state government had already constituted a 'Franchise Sub-Committee' on the 14th October 1947 and it was constituted of nine members. The duty of this 'Committee' was to enact rules for the election. As per the draft rule the valley areas were divided into twenty five constituencies and out of this the three constituencies in which there are numerous Mohammedan population was given a plural voting method, i.e., one Voter would have the right to cast one Vote for Mohammedans and other for non-Mohammedans[3] and the hill reserve areas also divided into eighteen constituencies. About the qualification of voters and candidates, the draft rules mentioned that any bonafide Manipuri who attained an age of twenty five could contest the election and a person who reached an age of twenty one was eligible to cast their vote. However, a person who was alleged as guilty of corruption, an offence relating to election, criminal offence etc. was not qualified to contest election. Then to resolve the election dispute or case the committee formed an 'Election Tribunal' consisting of three members. Thus after having a full preparation, the date of election was fixed on the 11th June 1948 and P.C. Deb had been appointed as the Returning Officer on the 3rd April 1948. In the meantime the two groups of the Manipur State Congress Party were again reunited and with a resolution of the Working Committee the four Congress members in the Interim Government were withdrawn with effect from the 1st April 1948.[31]

Election was held according to the scheduled time but in the election no party was able to win an absolute majority in the 'Assembly'. However, the Congress party was lucky to secure the position of a single largest majority party in the 'House'. But although the Congress Party was single biggest party in the election, they were not able to form the government and a coalition ministry was formed with Maharajkumar Priyobrata Singh as the first Chief Minister of "Independent" Manipur. Some other Ministers were Major Khathin, Arambam Ibotomcha Singh, Ningthoujam Leiren Singh, Ayekpam Gourabidhu Singh, T-eba Kilong, Md. Alimuddin, T.C. Tiangkham and T. Bokul Singh got elected the Speaker and Deputy Speaker of the House. The maiden session of the Manipur Legislative Assembly was held on the 18th October 1948. In his inaugural address before the Assembly, the Maharaja sincerely expressed his happiness to the establishment of a Legislative Assembly in Manipur which according to him was a long cherished desire of the public of Manipur. The establishment of this Legislative Assembly which was constituted by the elected representatives of the people on the basis of democratic line, was a great landmark in the political history of Manipur. It fulfilled a long standing desire and demand of the people for a full responsible government in the state.

However, if we make a closer observation about the character of the leadership of the movement, it can be said that the political movement for a responsible government was mainly carried by the same elitist group of the society. Their only desire was to get a political right from the hands of the colonial and feudal authority in Manipur. But they were not very much clear regarding the existing economic problem in the state. This was clearly evident by the course of their movement. Their only demand was to establish a full responsible government so that they would enjoy certain political right in the administration of the state. But they never asked for any change in the economic policy in the state in order to remove the economic hardship borne mainly by the peasant section of the society. Therefore, it can be said that the establishment of full responsible government does not serve completely the aspiration of the people. Just to the opposite, it served only the interest of the elitist section, a new emergent class in the society.

Merger of Manipur in Indian Union

The most significant epoch epoch development in the political history of Manipur was the movement for the merger of Manipur into the Indian Union. This historic event marked the end of an era of 'Independent Kingdom of Manipur and start of a new one that of a Constitutional state' of the Indian Union. Two important factors were responsible for this compelling phenomenon. One inportantance was the rule of the leaders of the Manipur State Congress Party and other one was the pressure of the psychological invasion of the ruling party of the government of India. Just after the announcement of independence in the year 1947 the Government of India adopted a policy to bring all the princely states, either protectorate or colonial state during the British regime into the boundary of the Indian Union.

At a session conducted on the 15th June 1947, the Indian National Congress declared that no princely state in India should be allowed to keep aloof as a sovereign independent state.[32] From this fact it can be said that the only objective of the leaders of the Congress Party of India was to amalgamate all the native and princely states into the Indian Union as early as possible.

This above said merger movement in Manipur was directly related to the political development that emerged in the state from the year 1947. A few days before the transfer of power took place, the British authorities called a meeting of all the princes and suggested them to establish close relationship with Indian Government in future. Maharaja Bodhchandra Singh also desired to establish a relationship with the Indian Government and with this view he signed the 'Stand Still Agreement' with the Indian Government on the 11th August 1947. According to the agreement the Maharaja of Manipur consented to hand over all the responsibilities of defence, communication and external affairs into the care of the Indian Government and the responsibilities of the democratic administration was fully in the hands of Maharaja. The communication between the government of Manipur and India was made through an agent which was known as 'Dominion Agent'. The power and the function of the Dominion Agent was almost the similar with the position of the political Agent but only difference was that the British Political Agent acted as an administrative agent of the British Government to handle Manipur whereas the Dominion Agent has got the power to act all the relevant matters related between the Government of India and Manipur. So, it is mentioned that owing to this advantageous position he was able to play a game in the domestic politics of the state. The first Dominion Agent in Manipur was Deveshwar Sharma who was the Chief whip of the Assam Congress Legislative party.

His appointment for the Dominion Agent may be said to be a deliberate calculative move of the Congress leaders of India because through this political position of the leaders of the India and Manipur State Congress had able to play a big role in the state. It is alleged that sometimes the Dominion Agent misused his power and so Sir Akbar Hydari, the Governor of Assam had very poor impression about him. He even decided to abolish this post. In this regard he made a discussion with Sardar Patel, the Home Minister of India. He submitted three basic charges against the conduct of the Dominion Agent. He said that the Dominion Agent had given encouragement (1) to the leaders of the movement among the tribals (2) he was trying to disturb the arrangement under which the Tulihal Airfield and suitable area surrounding it would be handed over to in return for the old British reserve area, and (3) he was taking an active part in return for the manoever of the different portions in Manipur adding to the confused politics which are a constant affiction to the state government.[33]

Thus, after the approval of the Home Minister, Governor Sir Akbar Hydari abolished the post of Dominion Agent on the 22nd August 1948. Then he urgently wrote a letter to the Maharaja and asked him to appoint a 'Dewan'. The duty of this new post was to watch the treaty obligation between the state and Indian Dominion.[34] Therefore, he proposed the name of Maharajkumar Priyobrata Singh, the younger brother of the Maharaja for the post. At this juncture, Sir Akbar Hydari died and he was succeeded by Sri Prakash. Like his predecessor, Sri Prakash also suggested the Maharaja to appoint a 'Dewan'. Then on the 21st March 1949, Governor Sri Prakash arrived in Manipur. He was accompanied by A.B. Chatterjee, the Joint Secretary to the Ministry of states and also Nari Rustamji the Advisor to the Governor of Assam. Nobody know about the purpose of his visit. But his surprise visit created an alarming situation in the political circles of Manipur.

At that point of time, there was a strong apprehension in the minds of the people of the state about the possibility of losing their political identity very soon. Seeing the feeling of the people, Sri Prakash said that his tour was not related at all to the merger issue and he further stated that the Government of India had no intention to destroy the political identity of the Manipur state. However, without disclosing any reason he further pressed the Maharaja of Manipur to appoint a 'Dewan'. Thus he put the Maharaja in a very embarrassing position. The Maharaja wanted to know the administrative condition of the proposed office.[35] He further said that "since there is no provision for the appointment of the Dewan in the state Constitution Act, I could not make any commitment independently of the provisions of the constitution in the absence of any reference to and consent from the state Assembly Council of Minister . . ."[36]

But Sri Prakash simply answered that the appointment of 'Dewan' would strengthen the relationship between Manipur and India. Then he went back very soon and on the 10th April the Maharaja received a telegraphic information from the Governor of the Maharája received a telegraphic information from the Governor of Assam regarding the appointment of Major General Rewal Amar Singh as the Dewan in Manipur.[37] Again on the 14th April Governor Sri Prakash sent another letter in which he talked of the power and position of Dewan. In the first place he mentioned that the administration of Manipur State be carried on under the general superintendence, guidance and control of the Dewan and he would enjoy the power to call paper from any of the ministers in charge of any Department, secondly, the Dewan would have to direct charge of portfolios of law and order administration of hill tracts, state forces and link with the Government of India and thirdly, distribution of portfolios of the ministers was to be done subject to the approval of Dewan.[38] In his letter Sri Prakash further reiterated that the appointment of Dewan would not effect the integrity and unity of Manipur State. But on the other hand, he again pressed the Maharaja to hand over all the administrative works to the Dewan. The appointment of Major General Rewal Amar Singh as the 'Dewan' in Manipur was a great political achievement of the Governor of Assam and Manipur State Congress Party specifically. Indeed, this appointment was a good step for the fulfilment of their Plan. Then on the 14th April, Thakur Nathu Singh, General Officer Commanding of Eastern Command and also Brigadier E. Habibuluah, G.O.C., Shillong Sub-Area and Ridant, I.G.P. of Assam Rifles arrived in Manipur. Earlier a batch of military personnel had already arrived and was put up at 'Kabaw Leikai' near Minuthong in Imphal. This unprecedented military movement created a great alarming situation in Manipur, because, at that time there was a great doubt among the people of the state that the political identity of the Manipur State would be lost very soon. They spread a news that the purpose of their visit was to check the communist insurgency in Burma which caused disturbances to the law and order situation in the border area. Then Governor Sri Prakash, in order to materialise successfully the plan of the Indian Government, began to arrange his political pawns with lot of precaution.

Besides, the activities of the Government of India, the role played by the Manipur State Congress Party, in favour of the merger movement, further strengthened the position of the Indian Government. After getting a deplorable loss in the election of the Manipur Legislative Assembly, the Manipur State Congress Party brought a new political dimension in the State. It is a fact that their only desire was to take over a position in the administration of the State. So, to get this opportunity they began to have a direct relationship with the leaders of the All India Congress Committee. At that time there was a proposal to amalgamate the areas of Manipur, Tripura, Cachar and Lushai Hills and formed a separate province. The Manipur State Congress also was in favour of this proposal. Then in order to provide a proper shape and to get favour from the leaders of the Congress Party of India, they even invited Prafulla Chandra Ghose, an eminent Congress leader of West Bengal to Manipur.

In the public meeting convened on 22nd August, P.C. Ghose, supporting the decision of the Manipur State Congress Party, stressed that "Manipur State in order to make equilibrium according to the motto of Congress Party, required to be amalgamated with the three places, Tripura, Cachar and Lushai Hills."[39] Certain other political parties in the state were against this move. In the meeting held on the 18th September, all the leaders of both plain and hill area strongly opposed the idea of a new province and announced that the people of Manipur would resist and type of imposition of proposed province.[40] The Government of Manipur also was against this move and thus because of the strong opposition from all corners, except for Manipur State Congress Party, the move for the creation of the 'Purbanchal State' was not materialised.

It generated an indirect positive impact in favour of the Manipur State Congress Party. That in the first place the Manipur State Congress Party was able to establish a direct contact with the leaders of the All India Congress Committee and then with the help of the State Congress Party, the leaders of the ruling party of India got a very good advantage to interfere in the domestic affairs of the state. Thus, the role of the State Congress Party gave a successful cause for the merger of Manipur into India. As a move against the political intrigue between the Manipur State Congress Party and leaders of the Government of India, the certain other political parties in the state began to oppose the merger movement. A strong and serious reaction come from the Praja Santi Sabha, an important party in the state. Through a resolution adopted by the party members in the Legislative Assembly, they strongly stressed that if the integration be imposed by taking the advantage of the helpless circumstances of the state and without the desire of the people might lead to the growth of a serious political handicap in the relationship between India and Manipur.[41]

Just to the contrary of the resolution of Praja Santi Sabha, the then Manipur State Congress Party adopted a resolution in favour of the merger. In a meeting held on the 29th April 1949, they pointed out three basic reasons in favour of their resolution, one, the inability of the government of Manipur to maintain law and order situation of the country, and then, the apprehensions from the activities of the communist revolution in Burma and thirdly, the integration of Manipur into India would bring peace and development.[42] They even decided to send a delegation of the party comprising of three members, to meet the leaders of the Congress Party of India and the concerned Ministers to discuss about the possible ways and means of the merger of Manipur. This way, the Manipur State Congress Party gave a very good, encouraging support to the leaders of the Indian Government. When such an unhealthy political state was in Manipur, a serious conflict was developed between the 'Dewan' and 'Maharaja' on the issue of the administrative position and power between the two important offices. It is said that at time the 'Dewan' always interfered in the internal administrative affairs of the state. The Maharaja was very much annoyed at the repeated intervention of the Dewan and he wished to remove this confusion. So, in order to make a permanent solution over this issue, Maharaja left Imphal on 15th September 1949 for Shillong and reached there on the 17th. But the time he reached there he was completely upset to see the unexpected policy adopted by the Government of India. Governor Sri Prakash informed him that he was directed by the Government of India to finish negotiation with Maharaja by 20th September 1949 and the Governor pressed him to accept it. Maharaja Bodhachandra Singh was in a very awkward position. So, on the 18th of September, he wrote a letter to the Governor and pointed out that he was only a constitutional head of the Manipur State. Therefore, he stressed that since the sovereignty of the state had been vested in the general people, it would be in the fitness of things to hear the people's voice and learn their sentiments so that the time of action may not in any case be unconstitutional.[43]

But the Governor instead of giving a response to the Maharaja, took up various methods to implement the instruction of the Indian Government. He put soldiers in the surrounding area of 'Red-lands' where the Maharaja used to inhabit and all the communication between 'Red-land' and other places were totally cut off. As a result of this the Maharaja of Manipur was in helpless position and without having no way out, Maharaja Bodhachandra signed the merger agreement on the 21st September but it was officially announced on the 15th October 1949. Then after this official declaration, the political status of Manipur was changed from a sovereign independent Kingdom to the political unit of the Indian Union.

Thus, from the above facts it can be concluded that the merger of Manipur into the political boundary of the Indian Union was successfully implemented with the help of the Indianised political attitude of the Manipur State Congress Party and also the chauvinist attitude of the leaders of the Government of India. However the role played by the Indian leaders was more dangerous than the internal factors. That if they really wanted democratic process, they would have taken the opinion of the people into consideration. In this respect we find a serious contradiction in the official decision. That when the Constitution of Manipur was prepared, the Indian Government suggested that the Maharaja should follow the path as a constitutional monarch and should not ignore the provision of the constitution[44] while when the question of the appointment of Dewan was there Sri Prakash said that the Government of India did recognise neither the Manipur State Council nor the State Assembly but the king only.[45] Again when there was a discussion about the integration in the constitutional Assembly on 15th March 1948. V. N. Gadgil the then Minister of Works, issued an official statement on behalf of the Home Ministry in which he said that" there is no desire on our part, in any way, to compel or the coerce them into merger or integration. If they wish to remain a separate autonomous unit was could have not objected but if the Ruler and the people of any of these states desire to merge with the neighbouring province or from a Union with the neigbouring states on a voluntary basis obviously the Government of India cannot say 'No'. Jawaharlal Nehru also strongly emphasised the need of integration not at the top level of the people.[46] But when the Maharaja refused to sign the agreement on the ground of his inability to act against the constitution, Sri Prakash categorically stressed that the Government of India would deal with the Maharaja as a ruler of the state and he further mentioned that if here was any objection which might be realised by the people, the Government of India would take a complete responsibilities.[47] So, here we find a serious unconstitutional act on the part of the Government of India and their deliberate insensitive ignorance of the voice of the people was also definitely undemocratic on their part. Then the merger movement led by the Manipur State Congress Party with the help of the leaders of the Indian Government was successfully materialised. Giving the justification from the Government's point of view V.P. Menon wrote, "In view of its position as a border state and its under developed character, it was decided to take over Manipur as a Chief Commissioner's Province.[48]

Therefore, from the above two cases it can be drawn that the outbreak of these political movements was indeed a great significant development in the political history of the state. It gives tremendous help to the growth of political and national awakening among the people of Manipur. The movement for the establishment of a responsible government had undoubtedly made an eye-opener to every citizen of the state for the evolution of a new political idea. With the help of this new political concept the people began to demand their political right and at the same time they also asked to maintain a separate political identity of the state on the ground of the democratic principle. However, the only objective of the people, i.e., the aim of a separate political identity of the state and for this the people were struggling against the colonial and feudal ruler, was completely shattered by the merger movement of Manipur into India. This movement brought a new political status of the state. The outbreak of the merger movement in reality put an end to the history of political movements which was launched by the people from the year 1938. Therefore, the integration of Manipur into the political boundary of the Indian Union ended the chapter of the political movement of sovereign independent state of Manipur and on the other hand it opened new chapter, i.e., Manipur being a constitutional state of the Indian Union.

References

1. Nikhil Hindu Manipuri Mahasabha and Manipur Pradarsini, p. 23.
2. Darbar Resolution No. 78, 16.10.39.
3. Darbar Resolution No. 8 of 22.2.1939.
4. A confidential letter from C. Gimson to the Maharaja in July, 1939 (Reproduced in *Resistance,* August 31, 1976).
5. Letter from MacDonald, PMSD to the members of the Darbar, Memo No. 2913-18G dated 30.3.1939.
6. An outline of the Legislature, submitted by H. Irabot Singh, President of Nikhil Manipur Mahasabha to the Maharaja of Manipur, Memo No. 124 NMM, 2.11.1939.
7. Resolution of the Working Committee of the Nikhil Manipuri Mahasabha, held on 2nd August 1946, (Reproduced in *Resistance,* January 4, 1977).
8. Letter from Maharaja to the Political Agent. Memo No. 456, pp. 11-1 dated 21.9.1946 (*Resistance,* January 11, 1972).
9. Letter from Pearson, P.M.S.D. to the Political Agent in Manipur vide letter No. 4/CONST/46-47 dt. 6.11.1946 (*Ibid*).
10. Letter dated 21.11.1946 from Yumnam Khoimacha Singh, general Secy. Manipur State Congress to Sanasam Gourahari Singh, Secretary to the Maharaja of Manipur.
11. D.O. letter No. 728p.11-1 dated 23.11.1946 from the Maharaja to Gimson, Political Agent in Manipur.
12. Confidential letter No. 803-p.11-1 dated 23.11.1946 from the Maharaja to Pearson PMSD

(Reproduced in *'Resistance,* 15 February 1977).

13. Order No. 30, p. of 1946 dated 12.12.1946 by the Maharaja of Manipur.
14. Proceedings of the meeting of the working Committee, Manipur Praja Sangha, held on 28.12.1946.
15. Confidential Letter No. 8141 from Political Agent Mr. Stewart to the Maharaja of Manipur on 28.2.1947.
16. Excerpts from the announcement made by the Maharaja to the people of Manipur on the day of the inauguration of the 'Constitution Making Committee' on 10.3.1947.
17. Resolution of the emergency meeting of the Working Committee of the Praja Sangha held on 20.7.1947.
18. Letter from Chief Minister Pearson to Chandrahas Singh Memo. No. 720-2 (C), dated 23rd July 1947.
19. Resolution of the Working Committee of the Manipur State Congress, dated 31.7.1947.
20. Resolution of the Working Committee of Manipur State Congress Party (Tompok Congress) held on 18th October 1947.
21. Minutes of the meeting of Representative of the State Council, the Legal Remembrancer to H.H. the Maharaja and the Manipur State Congress held on 12th October 1947 (File No.C/POL/1/47).
22. Resolution No. 7 of the Manipur State Congress Council (Tomal) held on November 2, 1947.
23. Telegram from the Registrar, Dominion Agent's Office to Dominion Agent C/O Government House, Shillong.
24. Resolution No. 1 of the Working Committee of the Manipur State Congress held on 8.11.1947 (Tomal Congress).
25. Letter of M.K. Priyobrata Singh, Chief Minister of Manipur to Dominion Agent on 8.11.1947.
26. Letter Ref. No. 186-L/MSC dated 9.11.1947 from E. Tompok Singh, director Satyagraha Council of Action Manipur State Congress to Dominion Agent in Manipur.
27. An appeal of the Dominion Agent to the people of the Manipur State (File No. C/POL/1/84 Political Movement of Congress in Manipur, Manipur Secretariat Library).
28. Letter from the Dominion Agent to the Maharaja of Manipur, 10.11.1947.
29. Notice issued by the Publicity Officer, Manipur dated 11.10.1997.
30. Resolution No. 2 of the meeting of the Franchise Committee held on the 8th to 9th December 1947.
31. Letter from the General Secretary, Manipur State Congress Party to Private secretary to His Highness the Maharaja on 1.4.48 No. 647-53 L1(C).
32. R.C. Majumdar, H.C. Roychoudhury, K.K. Dutta, *An Advanced History in India,* p. 998.
33. Letter from Sri Akbar Hydari to Sardar Patel on 24th May 1948 (Sardar Patel's Correspondence 1945-50, Vol. 6), p. 126.
34. Letter of Akbar Hydari to the Maharaja of Manipur 2.8.1948.
35. Letter of the Maharaja of Manipur to the Governor of Assam vide D.O. No. 1986 p.11-1 dated 23.3.1949.
36. Secret Memorandum No. 2601 p. 1-1 dated 25.6.1949 from Maharaja to Sri Prakash.
37. Lamyanba' (A monthly journal published PANMYL) No. 48, September 1973.
38. Letter from Sri Prakash to Bodhachandra, Maharaja of Manipur on 14.4.49.
39. Report of the Police retgarding the public meeting held on 22.8.48 at Imphal Polo Ground (*Resistance,* July 11, 1978).
40. Resolution No. 1 of the meeting of both hills and plains leaders under the Chairman of Mr.

Parijat Singh on 18.9.1948 (*Resistance,* July 18, 1978).

41. Resolution of the meeting of the MLAX belonging to the ruling Praja Santi Sabha on 25.8.1949.
42. Ksh. Shyamkanhai, *Manipuri Leingaklon Amasung Leingak Pathapki Itihas, 1762-1949,* p. 105.
43. Letters from Maharaja to Sri Prakash, 18.9.1949.
44. Letter from Sri Prakash to Maharaja, 4.7.1949.
45. Secret Memorandum No, 2601, p. 1-1 dated 25.6.1949. from Maharaja Bodhachandra to Sri Prakash, Governor of Assam.
46. *Jawaharlal Nehru's Speech,* 1946, Vol. I, p. 22.
47. Letter from Sri Prakash to the Maharaja, dt. 19.9.49.
48. V.P. Menon, *The Story of the Integration of the Indian States.*

9

Efficacy of Autonomous District Councils

Efficacy of ADCs in Meghalaya

Present chapter is the edited version of a paper presented in a seminar about the functioning of various administrative agencies of local self governance. Here, in this chapter, we are focussing on the efficacy of Administrative District Councils (ADCs) in the light of 73rd Amendment. Functioning of these ADCs alongwith provisions of Sixth Schedule of the Constitution (which provides for ADCs) is being evaluated in the chapter. Second part of the chapter is about Paragraph 12A of the Sixth Schedule according to which any regulation made by ADC is, if not in line with the law of the State Legislature, it will be considered void and the law of the State of Meghalaya shall prevail arising out of this provision is the focus of the second part.

I

"The Autonomous District Councils were constituted on line with the provisions of the Sixth Schedule of the Constitution of India since 1950s, initially for a period of ten years. Since then there are many changes and amendments in Indian Constitution. It is our opinion that the time has come to go for detail evaluation of the working of the District Councils. A peculiar situation is now reached to the fact that, where there is a Council its existence and continuity is being questioned, on the other hand, demand for implementation of this constitutional scheme arises and the people demand for it where there is no council of this kind. Therefore, this constitutional scheme is debated on many platforms and some of its provisions are discussed on the floor of the high courts in the country and numerous interpretations of the provisions are made accordingly.

Paragraph 2(1) of the Sixth Schedule says that "the council shall consists of not more than 30 members, of whom not more than four persons shall be nominated by the Governor and the rest shall be elected on the basis of Adult Suffrage."

All the political parties, National or Regional can participate in the election. A person not belonging to Scheduled Tribe shall not be entitled to vote unless he is permanent, or resident within the territorial limits of the said Autonomous Council and for the purpose of this rule, a person shall be deemed to be permanently resident within the territorial limits of an Autonomous District if he has taken up his fixed or permanent habitation with his family or made his permanent home in that district and resided continually therein for a period of not less than twelve years on the qualifying date."

Thus, many non-tribals are today listed as voters in the Council elections and they are playing very important roles in the Council Administration.[2] But at the same time, the provision for nomination of a person as a member of the Council has created a controversy between the District Council and the Government on many occasions. [The case of *Daolagupu and 3 others* vs. *Government of Assam* (AIR 1974) Gauhati High Court in Karbi Anglong Council, and Khasi and Garo Hills District Councils]. Abovesaid provisions for nomination of a person as member of the Council is always utilised in favour of the party in power in the State. District Council made rules and passed resolutions for nomination of a member as per the advices of the party in power under the council but such rules and resolutions of the Council are always not accepted by the State Government.

This way, the party in power in the State can effectively interfere in the formation of the Government in the Council. This provision may be examined in depth and some say that this provision should be deleted, so as to have a fair play in the game of politics.

Under para 3, the District Councils are vested with the power to enact laws. The subjects are listed in the Constitution.

"All the District Councils made rules for the administration of the listed subjects. The laws made by the Council for administration of the aforesaid subjects shall have the force of law only when assented by the Governor."

After this, now let us examine the limitations of the Council laws with reference to adaptation of State Laws, e.g., Assam Land and Revenue Manual 1886 and Assam Forest Act 1891. As the allotment, occupation or use, or the setting aside, of land, other than any land is the language of the Constitution for Revenue Administration for the Council as per the provisions of the Assam Land and Revenue Regulation.

Still, many of the provisions of the Assam Land and Revenue Manual cannot apply for Revenue Administration under Council specially for the A'khing Lands in Garo Hills for Village lands situated in hill parts of the North Cachar Hills district of Assam. For this purpose the cases of Plain area or settled area and A'khing lands may be examined separately. Settled areas can be brought within the purview of Assam Land and Revenue Manual but appropriate settlement rules are not yet framed by the Councils till date, so far, information available to me for giving settlement in the village lands.

The extent of the power given to the Council for land administration is limited. As for example, the District Council is not a competent authority to pass Land Transfer Act (*Sawian* vs *Bhandari*). Therefore, the State Government passed Land

Transfer Act to restrict transfer of land from tribal to non-tribal wherein Deputy Commissioners are notified as competent authority to effect transfer of land which shows that the Deputy Commissioners are the heads in revenue administration. The brief note above, clearly indicated the limitation of legislative powers of the Council for revenue administration.

Further, adoption of Assam Forest Act 1991 by the District Councils for administration of unclean. Forest A'khing land as in Garo Hills or in North Cachar Hills is full of limitation as to how the provisions of the Assam Forest Act 1891 can be applied in those areas.

The point I want to bring home is that application of revenue laws including forest laws for Council administration may further be examined and appropriate rules and regulations based on ground reality may be framed.

Para 10 provides power to the District Council to make regulations for the control of the money lending and trading by non-tribals. Therefore, the business activities by the non-tribals are controlled by the District Council within Sixth Schedule areas by issuing license. Penalties for illegal trades are also provided in the Act and also list of commodities as well as name of trades are given in the Act alongwith rate of fees payable by the traders.

(a) Judiciary

Paras 4 and 5 of the Sixth Schedule provides for the Administration of Justice and empowers the District Councils to constitute courts—the Village Court, Sub-ordinate Court and the District Councils Court and appeal from Village Court goes to Sub-ordinate Court whereas appeal from Sub-ordinate Court goes to District Court and appeal from the District Court goes to the High Court. All the Council courts are under the jurisdiction of the High Court.

As you all know the Council courts are instituted for trial of suits and cases between the parties belonging to Scheduled Tribes within the autonomous areas.

As per the provision the Governor may also invest with these courts the power for trial of offences punishable with death, transportation for life or imprisonment for a term not exceeding five years under the Indian Penal Code.

The Governor may also confer such powers to the courts under the provisions of the court of civil procedure or the court of criminal procedure.

It appears from the above provisions the Courts under Council are powerful but in actual practice Council courts suffer from various limitations for trial of cases. The Council courts cannot try any cases connected with security-related matters, even, if the offence committed by the members of the Scheduled Tribe, e.g. cases under Sections 124-A, 197, 153, 193, and Chapter X of IPC, and cases under Sections 107 to 110 and 144-145 of CrPC.

Meghalaya brings 125 CrPC and issue of succession certificate under concurrent power to be tried by the State Court under the Deputy Commissioner and the District Council Court.

The Autonomous District Councils of Karbi Anglong in Assam and Tripura

Hill areas have not yet framed rules for administration of justice.

Further, procedures are very long for the Council courts to utilise the services of the State police and the district jails for court works. To make the procedure simple and easy amendment of Police Manual and Jail Manual may be made, so that Council courts may function smoothly. Involvement of chief executive member in the judicial process in connection with the execution of lower court degree may be reviewed, so that the lower courts are able to function freely without any political influence.

The power for trial of 302 IPC by the Council or any other cases where the State is represented by the police is still debatable in terms of jurisdiction because of the involvement of the State which is non-tribal.

There is general opinion that Council courts are constituted for the purpose of administration of laws made by the District Council but in actual practice the situation is reversed. The Council courts do not have any jurisdiction to try cases where the District Council is a party.

The Council Court cannot sanction anticipatory bail for the offences tried by the court (the *State of Meghalaya* vs *the Judge District Council Court and others,* Gauhati High Court Rules 1993). Therefore, the status of the judge of the Council court cannot be equated with the status of the session judge in terms of power. In Garo Hills A'khing cases are kept outside the judicial power of the Council courts. Such cases are tried by the executive member of revenue and appeal against executive member's order goes to chief-executive member and then order from chief executive member can be appealed in the High Court. But in many cases the High Court transfer such cases to the court of the Deputy Commissioner.

But on the other hand, as per provision of the Assam Land and Revenue Manual, adopted by the District Council in 1954, the chief executive member was made equivalent to the status of the Commissioner. Therefore, there is no clear-cut demarcation of power for revenue administration vis-a-vis Council court. The judicial officer Sub-ordinate District Council court (Mizoram) admitted a case where the complainant was Nepali and the accused was a local tribal and the case was tried by the judicial officer and the accused was convicted and sentenced to pay a fine of Rs. 100 U/S 325 IPC. In this case a non-tribal complainant appears to have accepted the jurisdiction of the Council court.

Further even after dissolution of the Council at Aizawl, the courts under the District Council are still functioning. (Reference LRI).

(b) Administrative Control of the District Council Exercised by the State Government through the Deputy Commissioner

The Autonomous District Council cannot exercise a free hand for day to day administration. The Deputy Commissioner is still playing very important role within the four walls of the Council. The Deputy Commissioner prepares electoral rolls for Council election and conducts election as Returning Officer. He plays a very important role for constitution of the Council and administers the oath of affirmation to the members in the Council Hall. As in the case of Meghalaya, all the funds sanctioned by the Government are issued directly to the Deputy Commissioner who releases such amount to the District Council for implementation of rural development programmes and the Council in turn submits utilisation certificates to all the State Governments through the Deputy Commissioner.

The Deputy Commissioner is entitled under the rule for copy of the Assembly proceedings and also Assembly questions and answers. He can refuse admission of Assembly questions on valid grounds. In case of difference of opinion with the Council, he can refer the same to the State Government for final decision.

The Deputy Commissioner is always notified as administrator when the Council is superseded and in that case he assumes all the powers vested with the executive committee. The Council is to report to the Deputy Commissioner all cases of fund embezzlement.

In case of sanction and release of funds thereof, the position of rules regarding the Deputy Commissioners in Assam is different.

The Council exercise powers to assess and collect land revenues and impose taxes to raise funds for its administration, the revenue sources are as follows:

1. Land revenue.
2. Forest royalty.
3. House tax including local rates.
4. Sale of local markets, fishery ponds, including cattle ponds.
5. Grazing tax including residential toll.
6. Royalty on minerals shared with the State Government 60/40 basis.
7. Motor vehicle tax share with State Government on 60/40 basis.
8. Fees for trading licence (TNT).

The District Council received share of development fund from State Government out of state plan scheme for rural development programmes and also grant-in-aid for land records staff

Professional tax is also collected by the Garo Hills District Council without sharing with the Government but in Hill State Government, the collected professional tax is shared with the District Council.

The District Council pass rules on fund for maintenance of accounts, etc. more or less on uniform system for all the Councils. The accounts for the Councils are subject to audit by the CAG/AG. But the account system appears to be very weak as per my experience gathered during my period of service on deputation. The procedure needs to be examined in greater detail, so as to plug the loop-holes and system to be built up for greater involvement of the Accountant General, so that proper audit can be conducted. As per existing procedure the audit of the Council Account is conducted with the support of the Council documents only.

Operational system with the State Treasury and State Bank of India may be received.

Opening of two heads of accounts:

PL-1 and PL-2 is not sufficient to strengthen the account system.

There should be proper delegation of financial power and orders for executive of business may be introduced for internal administration of the Council.

(c) Provision of 12(a) and 12(b)

The 12 (a) is for Councils in Meghalaya and 12 (b) for Councils in Mizoram, eroded the autonomy of the District Councils in Meghalaya and Mizoram while retaining the original provision for Councils in Assam. The Meghalaya Government invoked this provision in connection with realisation of royalty of coal by Notification No. MG.50/89/192, dt. 20.7.93.

The District Councils in Meghalaya recently demanded more functional powers from the State Government and the power to issue Schedule Tribe certificate and to raise the rank and status of the chief executive member and chairman and also direct funding of the development programme by the Central Government.

The provision for extension of the terms of the Council beyond 5 years term may be reviewed. Right now, the ADC of Kharbi Anglong and North Cachar Hills are on extension.

(d) Relevance of 73rd Amendment

The provisions of the 73rd Constitutional Amendment 1992 excluded the Sixth Schedule areas. In case of Assam also, the Assam Panchayat Act, 1994 covered only plain areas. A brief study on the applicability of the provisions of the 73rd Constitutional Amendment is made in this paper with reference to Garo Hills District.

First, let us examine the existing traditional institutions and also the process of their evolution. It is a fact that liberal democracy has taken its roots in the country and that it is spreading rapidly even in the remote areas under reference but a campaign is not yet started to familiarise the people in rural areas about the aims, objectives and the philosophy of Panchayati Raj. I firmly believe that the clock cannot be put back as far as liberal democrative values are concerned.

In the light of the above observation, let us examine the existing traditional institution at the grass root level in Garo Hills.

(1) The institution of Lasker is a part of history and there are as many as 65 or so within the district under the administrative control of the District Council. The Lasker is having two functions—judiciary and executive for non-judicial works. He is assisted by the Secretary, who is on the pay roll of the District Council. One eleka consists of some members of villages. Besides the institution of Lasker, there are Hill Mouzadars under the Council for revenue works as well as miscellaneous works. Each mouza consists of some number of villages.

Besides the above traditional institution there are Nokmas, A'khing Nokmas are the most powerful Nokmas as they control the village land. The A'khing Nokma is the head of one revenue village. The A'khing Nokmas are under the administrative control of District Council.

The plain areas of Garo Hills are more or less on a different footing as the entire areas are settled areas and at the village level the head of the village is Gaubura who is also under the administrative control of the District Council and there are some members of mouzadars in plain areas who are engaged for revenue works, they are also under the administrative control of the District Council.

Now let us examine the institutions under the direct control of the State Government at the grass root level that there are community development blocks which are the lowest centre of civil administration and they are entrusted with development works and many other miscellaneous works including revenue works but excluding land matters. Each development block consists of 15 Gram Sevak Circles—each Gram Sevak Circle consists of 15-20 villages at the district level. There are district rural development agencies. But the district rural development agencies are implementing many programmes through the development blocks only.

There are a number of development committees at the block level and in the district level there are district planning and development council for each district, chaired by the ministers and all the development programmes are discussed in such meetings. This is briefly the policy of decentralisation of power at the grass root level in Meghalaya.

We have brought out briefly the administrative structure at the grass root level and now let us examine the applicability of the provisions of 73rd Constitutional Amendment as follows:

The first issue for consideration is the size of the village panchayat, whether we will favour three tier system of the panchayat or two tier system. If we will consider to have three tier system such as village level, block level and the district level, then it is necessary to examine the village set up. The present situation as of today is that, village-wise Council cannot be set up because the villages are scattered and they are small in terms of population and poor communication. It is therefore suggested that a group of villages may form one village area panchayat. We may take one Lasker area on Gram Sevak Circle to form village council at the grass root level.

The institution of block administration at the middle level may serve the purpose with a little bit modification, the extent of which may be examined in detail for suitable adjustment.

At the district level or Jilla Parishad, it is my opinion that the provisions of 73rd Amendment can be introduced by making administrative arrangement and detailed examination of the administrative infrastructure at the district level.

But when we examine and study the allotment of subjects for the panchayats as in Assam or elsewhere as well as the allotment of subjects to the District Councils under the Sixth Schedule, there is an area of contrast. Therefore, suitable amendment in respect of allotment of subjects either for the District Council or Panchayati Raj should be made to define clearly their respective areas of operation-line of demarcation.

Unlike the plain areas it is felt necessary to examine in greater detail, the situation of existing administrative institution, traditional or otherwise as obtained in the scheduled areas for introduction of the provision of 73rd Constitutional Amendment.

It is my opinion that the system of dualism in the field of administration should be avoided, as far as practicable and attempts should be made to introduce uniform system of administration throughout the length and breadth of the country.

II

Politics behind Para 12A of the Sixth Schedule

The Autonomous District Councils in Meghalaya were first introduced in 1952 in the then United Khasi-Jaintia Hills District and the Garo Hills District alongwith other Autonomous District Councils in the other hill districts of the then composite State of Assam. A separate District Council for the then Jowai sub-division (now Jaintia Hills District) was created in 1964 (but started actual functioning) in 1967 after its bufercation from the then United Khasi-Jaintia Hills District. At present there are three Autonomous District Councils as per the Sixth Schedule to the Constitution of India for the seven districts in Meghalaya.

When the North-Eastern Reorganisation Act of 1971 came into force in 1972, a full-fledged state of Meghalaya was born. This Act has also its effect on certain paragraphs 12 of the Sixth Schedule, where a new sub-paragraph was added, thus making it paragraph 12A. This paragraph state thus:

> Notwithstanding anything in this Constitution if any provision of a law made by a District or Regional Council in the State of Meghalaya with respect to any matter specified in Sub-paragraph (1) of Paragraph 3 of the Schedule or if any provision of any regulation made by a District Council or a Regional Council in the State under Paragraph 8 or Paragraph 10 of this Schedule, is repugnant to any provision of a law made by the Legislature of the State of Meghalaya with respect to that matter, then, the law or regulation made by the District Council or, as the case may be, the Regional Council whether made or before or after the law made by the Legislature of the State of Meghalaya, shall, to the extent of repugnancy, be void and the law made by the Legislature of the State of Meghalaya shall prevail.

Paragraph 12A of the Sixth Schedule states very clearly that if the State Government and the District Councils make laws on the same subject, the legislation or laws of the State Government shall prevail over those of the District Councils'. This Paragraph therefore lays down the over-riding authority of a law made by the

Legislature of the State of Meghalaya over a similar law made by the District Councils in the State in case of the question of repugnancy arises. The Paragraph spells out that in case any provision of a law made by the District Council "is repugnant to any provision of a law made by the Legislature of the State of Meghalaya shall prevail."

This Paragraph has agitated the minds and thoughts of the leaders of the Regional Political Parties in Meghalaya, especially that of the Hill State People's Democratic Party (HSPDP). This party has for several years been demanding for the deletion of Paragraph 12A from the Sixth Schedule of the Constitution. True to what those leaders spoke in public, this certain Paragraph found its place in the election manifesto of this party in the elections to both the Legislative Assembly and District Councils. The demand for deletion of this Paragraph also appeared almost every year in the Annual General Meeting of the party and in its memoranda and appeals to various bodies, organisations and the public in general. This particular political party has not as yet stopped to make fervent appeal and demand for the deletion of Paragraph 12A. The other major Regional Political Parties in the State like the Hill People Union (HPU) and the Public Demands Implementation Convention (PDIC) have also demanded the same. These three Regional Political Parties have reiterated all along, the urgent need to delete what they call the "discriminatory" Paragraph 12A of the Sixth Schedule. The main complain is that this Paragraph empowers the laws of the State Government to override the laws passed by the Autonomous District Councils 'even in matters allotted to the District Councils by the Constitution.'

The leaders of the Regional Political Parties have been trying for the last many years to do away with Paragraph 12A of the Sixth Schedule by appealing to the Central Government to do something to meet their demand. They feel that the State Government have already had enough powers under the State List as well as in the Concurrent List. They are therefore of the opinion that the State Government should concentrate on those subjects and leave the District Councils alone with whatever powers and functions and subjects as empowered and entrusted by the Sixth Schedule to them. The former Chief Executive Member of the Khasi Hills Autonomous District Council, Mr. G.S. Massar, even went to the extent of suggesting that the District Councils in Meghalaya should be given the same powers enjoyed by the Panchayats in Assam.

The Regional Political Parties in Meghalaya put the blame on the Congress (I) Government both at the Centre and the State for the indifferent attitude shown on this issue. This problem is more acute when different political parties are ruling at the State and District Council level. With two different political parties ruling the respective administration set up, the clash of interests is bound to take place. While the Opposition-ruled District Councils feel that the State Government [under Congress (I) rule] might discriminate against them, the State Government obviously wants that its writ should run large in important matters, including the District

Council affairs.

In 1990, when the Congress (I) was in power in the State of Meghalaya, one of the issues over which a tug-of-war took a serious turn between the two camps, was Paragraph 12A of the Sixth Schedule. The Minister for District Council Affairs at that time when asked of his opinion about the demand of the Opposition to delete Paragraph 12 A said that if their demand is granted, it could create complications as both the State Government and the District Councils would exercise their powers independently of each other. This according to him could happen because of the fact that in Meghalaya both the State Government and the District Councils exercise their powers over the whole State. Under the circumstances, the State Government feels that if the District Councils are entrusted with powers to make their own laws, the authority of the State would be diluted. The Opposition leaders however, would not like to draw such conclusion as to them Paragraph 12A is a threat to the powers of the District Councils in the State. These leaders have since been fighting for the deletion of this particular Paragraph so as, according to them, to gain a truly 'autonomous status' for District Councils.

The question of deleting Paragraph 12 A (or for that matter any paragraph in the Constitution) of the Sixth Schedule does not depend entirely on the State Government. If such a paragraph is to be deleted, it has to be done by the Parliament because of the fact that the Constitution itself has to be amended. The leaders of the Regional Political Parties in the State understood this constitutional requirement very well. They therefore tried to seize the opportunity during the National Front rule hoping that unlike the Congress (I), they would be more sympathetic towards their demand and get things done under the National Front Government at the Centre. They therefore went on delegation to Delhi to meet V.P. Singh, the then Prime Minister of India and other Central Ministers too. They also met V.P. Singh at Guwahati during his visit where they raised the issue and pleaded for the need to delete this Paragraph. However, not much headway came in this respect.

Way back in 1988-89, a Commission of Inquiry on Autonomous Districts Administration in the State of Meghalaya was appointed which was headed by the former Chief Justice of the Gauhati High Court, Mr. S.K. Dutta. One of the interesting recommendations of this Commission was on this vexed issue of Paragraph 12A. The Report of the Commission indicated its recommendation 'for the deletion of Paragraph 12 A of the Sixth Schedule relating to application of the Acts of the Legislature of the State to Autonomous District Councils'. Further, in the same Report which was also placed in the Meghalaya Legislative Assembly in 1989, the Commission pointed out certain difficulties under which the Autonomous District Councils are functioning and recommended that there should be statutory provisions to remove them. "But", the Report stated, "the main reasons for the failure of the administration of the District Councils appear to be their want of realisation about their sphere of duty and responsibility. They seem to devote their time and thought to development works rather than to the enactment of laws for the protection of healthy customs and usages relating to their democratic systems of administration, inheritance of property, marriage and divorce and other social customs . . . Indeed, the District Council members do not appear to have realised that with the formation of Meghalaya, the status of the District Councils in Meghalaya has been reduced more or less to that of a Municipal Board by the insertion of Paragraph 12 A in the Sixth Schedule . . . The District Council, therefore, can function only if it maintains harmonious relationship with the State Government."

Analysis

All these reactions came when 73rd Amendment to the Constitution has just been declared and everybody had some apprehensions about the effectiveness of Panchayat laws made after the said Amendment. Though some doubts, some fears are still existing but new system has started taking its shape and in all respects, it is undoubtedly better than the previous one. The need is overcome the difficulties of implementation and make new arrangement of local self governance a reality.

References

1. *The Assam Panchayati Act,* 1994.
2. Study of the Administration of Justice among the Tribes and Races of the North Eastern Region by LRI Gauwhati.
3. *Assam and Meghalaya Autonomous Districts* (Constitutional District Councils Rules, 1951 including Relevant Rules as required for holding Election to Garo Hills District).
4. The Constitution of India Seventh Edition by D.K. Singh.
5. My Experiences on the working of the Provisions during the Period of My Service under G.D.C.
6. The North Cachar Hills Autonomous District Council CODE, 1977.

10

Old Tribal Set-up

Advent of British rule, in the case of Meghalaya, disturbed the old system of leading tribal communities of the state—mainly Garos, Khasis and Jaintias. Sixth schedule of the Constitution deal with three areas through certain provisions in the post-independence governance. Famous 73rd Amendment to the Constitution further shook the functioning of these scheduled areas. Here, in the present chapter, which is basically a presentation at a seminar conducted in order to examine if the 73rd Amendment has any relevance to the areas covered under the abovesaid schedule.

This chapter intends to deal with "attempts to describe and analyse three related questions: (a) What had been the nature of traditional political systems among the Khasis, Jaintias, and Garos of Meghalaya prior to the advent of the British? (b) What was the impact of British rule on the traditional political institutions of these three tribes? and (c) What happened to these institutions after the commencement of the Sixth Schedule in the post-Independent India?

(a) The Traditional Political Systems: A Generalised Approximation

Long before the advent of the British, the indigenous people in the hills of north-east India had organised themselves under the political systems of their own which had been the natural outcome of their social evolution. Two distinctly different types of system of governance had been evolved in the hills, i.e., democratic system in the clan-based village societies controlled by the village councils and village headmen, and autocratic system of chieftainship controlled by the clan or village chiefs. The extent of power and authority of these traditional political institutions in relation to their people used to vary from tribe to tribe. While in certain communities these traditional institutions were well-organised and well-structured and even, in few cases, they led the formation of miniature states, in some communities these institutions were loosely organised without any central authority.

Unlike other hill tribes, the Khasis evolved a unique three-tier democratic system of governance with villages at the bottom, *Raids* at the middle and *Syiemships* at the top. The Jaintias in the hills, though ruled by the *Dolois,* had a titular king who actively ruled the plains portion from Jaintiapur, the capital of his Kingdom. Unlike the Khasis and Jaintias, the traditional political system of Garos was not institutionalised beyond the village boundaries. However, the Garo system of governance of clan based village community seemed to be much immature compared to that of the Khasis and Jaintias.

It may be noted that no written records pertaining to the functioning of these traditional political institutions were maintained by the indigenous people. And except a few casual reference in the chronicles of neighbouring Kingdoms like Assam and Cachar,[1] no written documents were available on the traditional tribal system of governance prior to the advent of the British in the hills of north-east India. In fact, it was the British who first studied the traditional political institutions of the hills for their administrative interest. Based on the various reports and other writings of the British administrators associated with the task of administering the hill tribes of north-east India, the scholars of social science in post-Independent India have tried to construct the models of age-old traditional political systems that had hitherto been existing among the different tribal communities prior to the colonial intervention.

It may also be noted that neither the Khasis nor the Garos could evolve any uniform pattern of administration under a common supreme authority. In fact, there were twenty-five petty Khasi states before the advent of the British. Fifteen of them were under the *Syiems,* one was a confederacy jointly administered by *Wahadadars,* five were under the *Sirdars* and the rest four under the *Lyngdohs.*[2] The largest states were those of Khyrim, Mylliem, Nongkhlaw and Nongstoin having a population of 31,327, 17,863, 9,715 and 9,606 respectively as per the census of 1901.[3] The smallest state was Nonglewai with a population of only 169 persons in 1901.[4] The Jaintia Hills were administered by twelve *Dolois* almost independently.[5] There was hardly any uniform and well-defined code of conduct between the *Dolois* and the Jaintia king as well as between the *Dolois* and the village headmen. The highest political institution among the Garos was the office of the *Nokma,* i.e., the village headman. In fact, there were as many *Nokmas* as the number of villages in the Garo hills. And again, no uniform pattern of relationship could be found between the *Nokmas* and the people ruled by them. Practically, the relationship varied from village to village depending upon the local customs, clan tradition, and above all the personality and efficiency of the *Nokmas per se.*

In view of the above facts, it may, however, be noted that no uniform system of governance was there in any case of these three tribal communities. However, in spite of the local specificities, broad structural as well as functional similarities between the different units of administration within a particular tribe provide the scope for tribe specific generalisation of the traditional political system. No doubt that such generalisation represents the dominant trend and hence an obvious approximation to the actual situation. We shall now present the outline of the generalised approximation of the traditional political system of the Khasis, Jaintias and Garos.

(i) Traditional Political System of Khasis. The evolution of the traditional political system among the Khasis is interwoven round the process of growth of the Khasi race *per se.* The Khasis belief that the *Hynniew Trep Hynniew Skum* were the progenitors of the Khasi race where *trep* is equivalent to a *Kur* or clan. In fact, the *Kur* had been the nucleus of all traditional socio-cultural and political institutions.[6] Initially, in the villages founded by the different *Kurs,* the village boundary was coterminus with the clan boundary. But as the marriage was strictly exogamous, i.e., marrying within one's own clan was socially prohibited, the coincidence of these two boundaries gradually broke down by way of marriage to accommodate multiple clans within the village boundary. This process had led to the emergence of separate village administration cutting across the clan boundaries.

With the growth of population in the original villages, some people shifted to some other places and thereby established new villages. While the newly established villages used to have village level administration, they remained under the overall control of the parent villages. The office of the *Basan Raid* was evolved to look after inter-village issues.[7] This process had resulted into the emergence of *Raids* as a larger territorial unit comprising of a number of villages and the *Raid* level institutions like *Durbar Raids* and *Basans.* The congregation of such *Raids* finally gave birth to the institution of *Syiemships.*[8] However, the actual process of transition from the *Raids* into *Syiemships* needs further investigation in order to confirm the existing notion that the mutual agreement among the former had given birth the latter.

Thus the traditional political system of the Khasis basically functioned at three levels, *viz.,* (i) village, (ii) *Raid* and (iii) State. Again at the village level clans used to function as sub-system to the overall system of village administration. Each clan had its own *Durbar* or Council known as *Durbar Kur* presided over by the *Rangba Kur,* i.e., clan headman. Male members of each clan used to elect the *Rangbah Kur.* The institutions of *Durbar Kur* and *Rangbah Kur* used to manage all the internal affairs within a clan. In fact both the clan-based institutions basically seemed to be social units under the political jurisdiction of the village level institutions.

Every Khasi village had its own local assembly known as *Durbar Shnong,* i.e., village *Durbar* or Council which was presided by the *Rangbah Shnong,* i.e., village headman who had been elected to his office by the adult male inhabitants of the village irrespective of their clan affiliation. The *Rangbah Shnong* used to run the village administration following the local customs and traditions as well as rules and regulations as legislated by the *Durbar Shnong.* Both the village Durbar and the village headman played the role of development agency as all the items of collective interest, e.g., village sanitation, water-supply, health, roads, education, etc., were under the jurisdiction of the Durbar. Both the institutions played pivotal role in conflict management at the village level as the Durbar enjoyed legislative power and the village headman used to discharge the dual functions of magistrate and police officer.[9] Apart from these, the village headman also performed religious and ceremonial functions in absence of the village priest. He also acted as a subordinate executive to the higher political authority as it was his duty to see to the payment of tributes to the *Syiem* by the village community. His loyalty to the concerned *Syiem* lay in the fact that his election to the office had to be confirmed by the latter. As a subordinate executive he transmitted the messages and orders of his political superiors to his village people and referred the unsettled cases to the higher political authorities.

However, the issues relating to the inter-village interests were beyond the jurisdiction of the village administration. These were dealt at the *Raid* level. *Raid* was a political unit comprising a number of adjacent Khasi villages organised into a political system for the purpose of social control and harmonious civil and judicial administration. In fact, this was the largest political unit under the *Syiemship.*[10] There was *Durbar Raid* at the *Raid* level which had been presided over by an elected headman variously known as either *Basan* or *Lyngdoh* or *Sirdar* at various *Raids.* The institutions of *Durbar Raid,* its headman and other elected officials used to settle the inter-village disputes and look after the interests of the *Raid.* However, the disputes which could not be settled at the *Raid* level and cases involving sentences of life imprisonment and death for commission of serious crimes were referred to supreme political authority, i.e., *Syiem*. In fact, all the *Raid* officials were subordinate to the office of the *Syiem* as the election to their respective offices needed to be confirmed by the *Syiem.*

The *Syiemship* with an elected chief known as *Syiem* was the supreme political institution among the Khasis which had been the result of the congregation of several *Raids.* The *Syiem* with the assistance of other elected officials ruled the Khasi state under the overall supervision of *Durbar Hima,* i.e., the state assembly, the supreme authority in the Khasi political system. The *Syiem,* presided over the *Durbar Hima* and also over his own Durbar, i.e., *Syiem's Durbar* or *Durbar Myntri* or council of ministers. All the officials like *Myntries, Lyngskors, Basans* and *Lyngdohs* elected from different clans under the *Syiemships* were the members of the *Durbar Myntri.*[11] They were collectively known as *Bakhraws,* i.e., noblemen. However, besides the *Bakhraws,* representatives and elders of the villages used to be present in the *Durbar Hima.*[12]

In spite of much similarity in succession to *Syiemship* in most of the *Himas,* i.e., Khasi states, the method of election of *Syiems* differed from State to State. Generally, the *Syiem* was elected from the *Syiem's* family or its legitimate branch. The electoral council besides *Myntri's* also comprised of other heads of clans. This electoral council used to elect and appoint the *Syiem.* In some cases, the *Bakhraws* only proposed the name of the candidate whereas the people themselves choose the *Syiem.*[13]

The *Syiem* as the head of the state or *Syiemship* performed administrative, military, religious, ceremonial and judicial functions in consultation with the members of the *Durbar Myntri* along the desired line of the *Durbar Hima.* His was the highest court in the State. All unsettled disputes either at the village level or at the *Raid* level and all serious cases involving severe punishment like life imprisonment and death were referred to his court where the *Syiem* acted as a judge and the whole body of the durbar as the jury.[14] There was no land revenue and the *Syiem* had no power to confiscate public and clan property as it was not he who owned the land but the clans, villages and individuals. The main sources of income of the state were the crown or *raj* lands, *pynsuk* or state subscription, market toll or *Khrong,* judicial fines, registration fees, etc.[15]

The three-tier hierarchy of the traditional Khasi political system was, thus, interdependent and interlinked with each other in such a way that the relative autonomy was guaranteed at every sphere. As a result, the legitimacy of the system was not questioned. Since at every sphere the *Durbar* was much powerful than the institutional head, the will of the people was always upheld than the individual interest.

(ii) Traditional Political System of Jaintias. Similar to the Khasis, the Jaintias also evolved a three-tier system of administration with the King (*Syiem*) at the top as the supreme political authority of the Jaintia Kingdom, the *Dolois* at the middle as the head of the *Raids* or *Elakas* and the *Wahehchnong,* i.e., village headmen at the bottom. Like the Khasi political system, administrative heads at different spheres also had their own *durbars* or councils. The King was assisted by the highest *durbar* known as *Durbar Hima* or Raj Durbar, i.e., National Assembly and a council of ministers headed by a *Laskor.* The Dolois at the Raid level had their own councils known as *Durbar Raid* or *Durbar Elaka.* And the *Wahehchnong* was assisted by the village Durbar or *Durbar Chnong.*[16]

The village, usually organised along the clan lines, was the basic unit of administration where the village headman looked after the administrative and judicial matters and the *Lyngdoh,* i.e., the priest performed the religious and ceremonial functions. The *Wahehchnong* was elected by the *Durbar Chnong* where all the adult male members of the village used to have active participation. Unlike the *Dolois* there was no such custom that the *Wahehchnong* need to belong to the original or founding clan of the village.[17]

Raid or *Elaka,* consisted of a number of villages, was the immediate higher administrative unit next to village. Every *Elaka* had a *Doloi* as its head. A *Doloi* was usually elected from among the adult male members of the original clan(s) of the Elaka. Moreover, even among these clans, the candidate for the post of *Doloi* was chosen mostly on ascriptive criteria rather than on grounds of achievements.[18] Generally, the term of office for a *Doloi* was continued for life. He was assisted by a council of officials *viz., Pator, Sangot, Bot Sangot, Chutia, Dan,* etc. These officials were generally elected by the *Durbar Elaka* which was presided over by the *Doloi* and in some cases they were appointed by the *Doloi* himself. The *Dolois* used to perform the executive, political, magisterial, religious and ceremonial functions.[19] In fact, the office of the *Doloi* wielded much power over their respective Elakas as the administration of the hill areas of the Jaintia Kingdom was left entirely to it.[20] The only symbol of their allegiance to the King was an annual tribute of one he-goat from each and every village under their administration.[21] Thus, in all practical purposes, the *Doloi's* were the *de facto* heads of the hill section of the Jaintia Kingdom.

The confederation of all the *Raids* or *Elakas* ruled by the *Dolois* had ultimately gave birth to the institution of *Syiemship* or kingship among the Jaintias in the historical past. The Sutnga dynasty, the first dynasty of Jaintia Kingdom, had brought all the *Elakas* under one central authority with wide autonomy to the units. With the conquest of the Jaintia plains in the thirteenth century and subsequent shifting of the headquarters from Sutnga to Jaintiapur, all the affairs in the hills were completely left to the *Dolois,* while the plains section of the kingdom was under the direct control and supervision of the King. In fact, the Jaintia Kingdom was a sort of loose federation where the doloiships were completely independent in internal matters and only the areas of common interest like foreign affairs, defence, communications and currency were looked after by the King.[22]

It may be noted that while the Jaintia King was an absolute monarch in the plains section of his Kingdom, he was merely a titular head for the hill areas. Though the Khasis and Jaintias have the same origin[23] and have evolved the similar three-tier political structure, the status and position of the *Raid* level institutions in relation to people as well as to the supreme authority, i.e., the *Syiem* or King, were significantly different in them. In fact, it appears that the office of the *Dolois* among the Jaintias was more powerful than the office of the *Basan* or *Lyngdoh* or *Sirdar* among the Khasis. Moreover, though the political system of the Jaintias seems to be more advanced than the Khasis in view of the state formation, the internal cohesion of the Khasi system of administration appeared to be much stronger than that of the Jaintias. However, the Garos, being a branch of the Tibeto-Burman Bodos,[24] lagged far behind the Khasis and Jaintias in terms of polity formation to which we shall now concentrate.

(iii) The Traditional Political System of the Garos. Unlike the Khasis and Jaintias, no well-organised political system evolved among the Garos. Indeed the traditional political system of the Garos were embedded in the process of social evolution and hardly any clear cut distinction is possible between the social and political institutions in the Garo traditional society.

The Garo society has divided into a number of exogamous sects known as *Chatchi.*[25] Every *Chatchi* was again divided into a number of strictly exogamous sub-groups or clans known as *Machong.* Within *Machong* there were a number of *Maharis,* i.e., smaller homogenous groups consisting of brothers and sisters, mother, maternal uncles, aunts, grandmother and her brothers and sisters, etc. i.e., all the members who could trace their blood relationship from a common brother. Every *Machong* had a well-defined area under its ownership called *Akhing.*[26]

This *Akhing* might be an equivalent to a village or a group of villages. The villages of the *Akhing* were loosely bounded by common interest of using land for shifting cultivation within the *Akhing.* Each village had a definite area within the *Akhing* to which it had to confine its operations. The area earmarked for a particular village within the *Akhing* was known as *Adok.* It was possible to adjust areas between the *Adoks* but no such adjustment was possible outside the *Akhing* without involving in a feud.[27]

All the land within the *Akhing* belonged to a particular lineage. Inheritance passed through the mother to the chosen daughter. The husband of the inheritress daughter (nokna) of the oldest family of the *Machong* i.e., the *Akhing* owning family, used to be the custodian of the *Akhing* land.[28] He is called *Nokma,* i.e., headman or chief. Though the ownership of *Akhing* land was held by the oldest/ founding family on behalf of the *Machong* members, the uses of the land had been socialised as every households had use-rights over *Akhing* resources.[29]

The entire Garo Hills was divided into a number of *Akhings* under the supervision of the *Nokmas.* In fact, office of the *Nokma* was the only political and administrative authority. The *Nokma* administered the political, social and economic life of the people as a custodian, religious head and the highest executive of the *Akhing.*[30] He had to lead his people in case of inter-*Akhing* feud.

It appears that there were no legislative and judicial organs among the Garos in their *Akhings.* Functions of both the organs used to be discharged by the *Nokma* with the common consent of the *Akhing* elders as his council of advisers. The composition of the council varied with the nature of disputes and the parties involved therein. If any member of wife's *Mahari* involved in the dispute, the council would be predominated by her *Chra* consisted of all brothers, their maternal uncles and great uncles. If several *Maharis* within the *Akhing* were involved, all the important members of the concerned *Maharis* would participate in the council proceedings. In case of inter-Akhing disputes, these were settled by the representatives of the concerned *Akhings* led by the respective *Nokmas.*[31]

Unlike the Khasis and Jaintias, there was no well-organised village council among the Garos. However, in matters of common interest the *Nokma* was assisted by two councils *viz, Mela-Solbonga* and *Jigma-Changga.* The former consisted of the adults from all the *Maharis* within the *Akhing* and was convened for disposing of inter-*Mahari* disputes, initiating legislation, executing administration, distributing lands and deciding other issues of common interest. The latter was the war council which decided all questions of war and peace and included the active male inmates of the *Akhing.*[32]

However, there was no political unit beyond the *Akhing* and no higher administrative authority above the *Nokma.* Thus compared to the traditional political system of Khasis and Jaintias, the evolution of the same was too immature to make any sorts of distinction between the social and political systems of the Garos.

(b) Incorporation, Colonial Intervention and Consequent Distortion of the Traditional Political Systems

After the assumption of Dewani of Bengali in 1765, the British came in contact with the Khasis, Jaintias and Garos living in the north-eastern border hills of Bengal. Until the Burmese occupation of Assam and Manipur in 1824, the British followed the Mughal policy of non-intervention towards these bordering hill tribes. Following the British annexation of Assam in 1826, its policy underwent a drastic change from one of non-interference to intervention. The plains section of the Jaintia Kingdom was annexed in 1835 and the institution of Kingship was abolished leaving the hills section in the hands of the *Dolois*. All the Khasi states were brought under subjugation by 1839. And finally, the entire Garo Hills was annexed in 1873.

Incorporation of the Khasi, Jaintia and Garo Hills into British Indian Empire led to the colonial intervention into the traditional political systems of the respective communities. Of course, the nature of intervention and subsequent distortion of the traditional system were not uniform in all cases. While the Jaintia and Garo hills were annexed and brought under the direct control, no Khasi State was annexed into British India except the three smaller tracts *viz.,* Mawsmai, Mawmluh and Sohbar where a new office of *Sirdar* had been created to administer the villages on behalf of the British administration.[33]

However, the British had reduced the office of the *Syiem* to a subordinate to the paramount power by treaties and agreements and granting sannads to the *Syiem*. British intervention into the succession to *Syiemship* necessitated formal recognition of the office of the *Syiem* by the paramount power which ultimately legitimised the indirect colonial rule. Though the hereditary and elective succession, as was in vogue, was recognised, for the formal recognition of their office by the paramount power made the *Syiems* largely dependent on the colonial power. The British took away from the *Syiems* the right to wage war or enter into any independent treaties, and the right to try cases involving murder and homicide. Appeals against the judgement of the *Syiem* were allowed in the court of the Deputy Commissioner. The *Syiems* were also made to submit implicity to all orders promulgated by the Deputy Commissioner. With the growth of British backed Christian missionary activities and growing number of new generation of Christian *Syiems* who were more loyal to British than to Khasi tradition, traditional power structure became subservient to the British administration.[34]

Thus, the British rule, although, did not distort the overall functioning of the traditional Khasi political system in relation to internal administration where the village and *Raid* level institutions were left undisturbed, the status and authority of the office of the *Syiem* was significantly reduced to make it loyal and to act according to British interest. The office of the Deputy Commissioner was superimposed upon the Khasi States to act as guardian power and to administer the indirect British rule.

Unlike the Khasi states, soon after the annexation of the plains section of the Jaintia Kingdom in 1835, the British abolished the office of the Jaintia King and brought the plains under direct administration leaving the hills section to continue under the *Dolois*. Subsequently a number of changes had been made in relation to the administration of Jaintia hills in order to control the power and authority of the *Dolois* that had ultimately led them to be mere agents of British authority.

Following the reorganisation of the *Elakas,* their number had gone up from twelve (before the British annexation) to nineteen in 1858 as recorded by Allen. Of these, fifteen were *Doloiships* and the remaining four *Elakas* were under the charge of thirteen headmen called Sirdars. It appears that throughout the British rule these *Elakas* were frequently adjusted within themselves for the convenience of administration as the number of *Dolois* was differently mentioned in different administrative reports published during the British rule.[35]

The judicial power of the *Dolois* was reduced as the British authority prohibited them from trying all criminal cases involving any sorts of personal interests of their own. The power of the *Dolois* to adjudicate cases of serious and henious nature were taken away and the same were vested in the hands of the Deputy Commissioner.

The tenure of office of the *Doloi* was reduced from lifetime to three years only. Of course, the same *Doloi* might seek re-election at the end of his tenure. Moreover, besides the election to the office by the people, the assumption of the office of the *Doloi* needed to be approved and confirmed by the British authority.[36]

A house-tax of one rupee per house was introduced in the Jaintia hills in 1860 and the *Dolois* were entrusted the duty to collect it who, as remuneration for their efforts, were to receive a percentage of the amount collected.[37] The *Dolois* were required to submit a list of the number of houses annually to local British authority.[38] In fact, following the curtailment of their judicial and administrative powers to a large extent, the *Dolois* were essentially reduced to that of "Commission agents" of the British Government.[39]

Thus, unlike the Khasis, the Jaintia hills were brought under the direct colonial supervision. Though the *Dolois* were allowed to continue to administer the *Elakas* and to perform certain judicial functions in relation to their own people, their allegiance towards their king had made to shift the British authority. In spite of curtailment of some of their traditional powers and privileges, the *Dolois* appear to have gained much power and authority as the agent of the British government in their new role as collector of house-tax.

In Garo hills, the British not only recognised the office of the *Nokmas,* they were also granted the documents of possession.[40] As a result, the status of the *Nokmas* was raised from a mere custodian under the traditional system to that of a legal authority under the British rule. However, as there was no superior political authority above the office of the *Nokma* in the traditional Garo society, the British created the institution of *Laskarship* and *Sarbarakar* to deal with the inter-village issues.

Laskars were appointed to exercise police and revenue duties over a group of clans or villages. They were to report to the British authority about all sorts of heinous offences, inter clan feuds, and the overall situation in their respective jurisdiction. In return of their services, the *Laskars* were entitled to commission not exceeding twenty per cent of the gross collection.[41] They were also empowered to try civil and criminal offences not of a heinous nature. A *Panchayat* was constituted in every village with the leading persons headed by the Laskars to assist the latter in the trial of cases. The criminal offences of heinous nature and the civil cases involving persons belonging to different villages or clans were referred to the local British authority.[42] Generally, the influential *Nokmas* were selected for the office of *Laskar*. The office of the *Sarbarakar* was created to supervise the activities of the *Laskars*.

Thus, although the British allowed the traditional institution of *Nokmanship* to continue and strengthened it further by issuing legal documents of possession, the introduction of the office of *Laskar* and *Sarbarakar* without any linkage to the Garo kinship system and the superimposition of these institutions upon the office of the *Nokma* had changed the whole fabric of the traditional Garo political system.

While the traditional political institutions of the Khasis, Jaintias and Garos, completely lost their external sovereignty as well as certain internal administrative and judicial powers to the colonial state, with the growth of Christian missionary activities and large scale conversion, the religious and ceremonial functions of the traditional chiefs were taken up by the Church.

As a result, these were left with limited administrative and judicial powers in relation to internal administration to play the comprador role under the colonial power. It may, however, be noted that though the power of the traditional authority under British rule declined much in relation to colonial authority, the power of the former was largely enhanced in relation to the people they ruled over as it was backed by the latter.[43]

(c) Independence and Integration: Sixth Schedule and the Traditional Political Institutions

Unlike the Jaintia and Garo hills, Khasi States were not annexed to British India and hence these were not made a part of His Majesty's Dominion, but for general administrative purposes these were brought under the Khasi and Jaintia Hills district. Following the Standstill Agreement signed by the Federation of Khasi States on August 8, 1947, and the Instrument of Accession signed in December 1947, the Khasi states joined in Indian Union. The Agreement gave the Federation of Khasi States judicial, administrative and legislative powers for the period until new or modified arrangements would be arrived at.[44] Prior to the commencement of the Constitution of India in 1950, the administration in Khasi, Jaintia and Garo Hills remained as before under the charge of Deputy Commissioners as Political Officers under the Governor of Assam.

Following the recommendations of the Bordoloi Sub-Committee, both the United Khasi and Jaintia Hills district and Garo Hills district were brought under the Sixth Schedule which resulted into the formation of the Autonomous District

Council in both the districts in 1952.

Later on with the bifurcation of the United Khasi and Jaintia Hills district, a separate District Council was set up for the Jaintia Hills known as the Jaintia Hills Autonomous District Council in 1967.

Under the Sixth Schedule, the District Councils are provided considerable executive, legislative, financial and judicial powers in relation to internal administration of the concerned areas within the jurisdiction of the respective councils. Following the provision of Paragraph 3(1)(9) of the Sixth Schedule where District Councils have been empowered to make laws on the appointment or succession of chiefs or headmen, the District Councils passed laws resulting into subordination of the traditional institutions under these constitutional bodies. As a result, the office of the *Syiem, Doloi* and *Nokma* in Khasi, Jaintia and Garo hills respectively turned into subordinate officials of the respective district council.

In exercise of the powers conferred under Paragraph 4 of the Sixth Schedule, the District Councils passed laws in order to set up (i) Village Courts, (ii) Subordinate and Additional Subordinate District Council Courts, and (iii) District Council Court. At the village level, the *Doloi, Sirdar, Basan, Lyngdoh, Lyngskor, Laskar,* or village headman as the case may be acts as the Chairman of the Village Courts. In Khasi Hills District, the Additional Subordinate District Council Courts are composed of the *Syiems, Lyngdohs, Wahdadars* or *Sirdars* Courts as their territorial jurisdiction being co-extensive with *Syiemship, Lyngdohship, Wahdadarship* or *Sirdarship* as the case may be.[45] In Garo hills, the Subordinate District Council Court is presided over by a judicial officer appointed by the District Council. The District Council Courts are presided over by a first class Magistrate appointed by the District Council. Thus, the offices in the traditional political systems are also integrated with the new judicial arrangements under District Councils.

Thus, the District Councils having wide ranging legislative powers covering almost every aspect of the material and cultural life of the people have created a socio-political field where the role and function of the traditional political institutions are well-defined by making them accountable to the constitutional bodies.

(d) Concluding Remarks

With the formation of the State of Meghalaya in 1972 comprising of the Khasi, Jaintia and Garo Hills, the district councils have not only lost much of their relevance but have also stood on the way of vertical administrative integration. In fact, the power and function of the district councils have been designed in such a way so that they can enjoy wide ranging autonomy in relation to land and people of the concerned areas under the jurisdiction of the respective councils. As the state has no constitutional power to control and supervise the functioning of the District Councils, both the institutions exist parallely with overlapping legislative powers within a single socio-political field. As the Sixth Schedule has empowered the District Councils to regulate and supervise the traditional political institutions at the grass root level, the State exercises its powers without having any direct linkage with the local bodies at the village level.

Moreover, the multiplicity of legislative authority has made the legal system too complex, particularly in relation to resource management, to undertake development activities. In fact, the hills which were hitherto under administered during the British rule are now over administered. This calls for urgent administrative rearrangements to make the administrative structure conducive to economic development for which establishment of the vertical administrative linkage and elimination of the multiple authority structure may prove to be useful. It is in this context that the Seventy-third Amendment Act 1992, on the Panchayati Raj that has proposed to provide wide ranging roles to the village level institutions may prove to be beneficial, if adopted, in Meghalaya as well. Although the Act directly encroaches into the constitutional jurisdiction of the district councils it no way affects the tribal political ethos. As the basic unit of traditional political system, the village level institutions used to exercise wide ranging powers which had gradually been reduced in the process of their integration with the Constitutional bodies. The Act envisages not only political empowerment of the village level institutions but also wants to empower them financially without which the former hardly bears any importance.

References

1. L.M. Simon, (ed.), *Meghalaya District Gazetteers: Khasi Hills District,* 1991, Government of Meghalaya, Shillong, p. 208.
2. *Ibid.*
3. B.C. Allen, *Gazetteer of the Khasi and Jaintia Hills District,* 1905, (1980, reprint), Gian Publications, Delhi, pp. 44-49.
4. *Ibid.*
5. H.L. Deb Roy, *A Tribe in Transition: The Jaintias of Meghalaya,* 1981, Cosmo Publications, New Delhi, p. 56.
6. Helen Giri, *The Khasi Under British Rule (1824-1947),* 1990, Akashi Book Depot, Shillong, pp. 10–14.
7. H.O. Mawrie, *The Khasi Milieu,* 1981, Concept Publishing Company, New Delhi, p. 18.
8. *Ibid.*
9. P.R.G. Mathur, *The Khasi of Meghalaya,* 1979, Cosmo Publications, New Delhi, p. 66.
10. *Ibid.,* p. 67.
11. H.O. Mawrie, *op. cit.* p. 93.
12. *Ibid.*

13. Hamlet Bareh, "Ancient Khasi Polity", in Jayanta Sarkar and B. Datta Ray, (ed.), *Social and Political Institutions of the Hill People of North-East India,* 1990, Anthropological Survey of India, Calcutta, p. 70.
14. P.R. Gurdon, *The Khasis,* 1990 (Reprint), Low Price Publications, Delhi, p. 69.
15. *Ibid.,* p. 67.
16. B. Pakem, "Social and Political Institutions of the Jaintias of Meghalaya," in Jayanta Sarkar and B. Datta Ray, (ed.), *op. cit.,* pp. 81-82.
17. L.S. Gassah, "The Emerging Political System and Its Effects on Traditional Leadership in Jaintia Hills of Meghalaya," in the *Proceedings of the North-East India Political Science Association (NEIPSA)*, Second Annual Conference, 1992, Guwahati, p. 221.
18. *Ibid.,* p. 232.
19. S.K. Chattopadhyay, *the Jaintias,* 1988, Cosmo Publications, New Delhi, p. 100.
20. L.S. Gassah, "The Emerging Political Elites in Jaintia Hills," in the *Proceedings of North-East India History Association* (NEIHA), Fifth Session, 1984, NEIHA, Shillong, p. 198.
21. L.S. Gassah, "The Emerging Political System . . .," *op. cit.,* p. 223.
22. B. Pakem, *op. cit.* p. 81.
23. S.K. Chatterjee, *Kirata-Jana-Krti,* 1957, (1974, reprint), Calcutta, p. 166.
24. *Ibid.,* pp. 45-46.
25. Earlier there were three septs, *viz.,* Sangma, Marak and Momin. Following the process of fission two more new *Chatchis* viz., Shira and Areng came later. This process is still continuing in the Garo society.
26. Jayanta Bhusan Bhattacharjee, *The Garos and the English (1765–1874),* 1978, Radiant Publishers, New Delhi, p. 10.
27. D.N. Majumdar, "The Changing Role of the Nokma in Garo Hills," in Jayanta Sarkar and B. Datta Ray, (ed.), *op. cit.,* p. 43.
28. Parimal Chandra Kar, *British Annexation of Garo Hills,* 1970, Naba Bharat Publishers, Calcutta, p. XVI.
29. Parimal Chandra Kar, *Glimpse of the Garos,* 1982, Garo Hills Book Emporium, Tura, p. 21.
30. *Ibid.,* p. 13.
31. Parimal Chandra Kar, *"Outlines of Akhing Polity among the Garo of Meghalaya,"* in Jayanta Sarkar and B. Datta Ray, (eds.), *op. cit.,* p. 52.
32. Jayanta Bhusan Bhattacharjee, *op. cit.,* p. 17.
33. David R. Syiemlieh, *British Administration in Meghalaya* 1989, Heritage Publishers, New Delhi, p. 66.
34. P.R.G. Mathur, *op. cit.* pp. 72-73.
35. For details, see L.S. Gassah, "The Concept of Ka Ri Khadar Doloi: A Critical Assessment," in *Proceedings of NEIHA,* Seventh Session, 1986, NEIHA, Shillong.
36. L.S. Gassah, "The Emerging Political System . . .," *op. cit.,* p. 224.
37. David R. Syiemlieh, *op. cit.,* pp. 88-96.

38. H.L. Deb Roy, *op. cit.*, p. 57.
39. L.S. Gassah, "The Emerging Political System . . .," *op. cit.* p. 225.
40. D.N. Majumdar, *op. cit.*, p. 46.
41. Jayanta Bhusan Bhattacharjee, *op. cit.*, p. 190.
42. *Ibid.*
43. Gurudas Das, *Tribes of Arunachal Pradesh in Transition,* 1995, Vikas Publishing House, New Delhi, p. 186.
44. D.R. Syiemleih, "Integration of the Khasi States into the Indian Union," in *Proceedings of the NEIHA,* First Session, 1980, NEIHA, Shillong, pp. 58–68.
45. L.S. Gassah, *"Self-Management of Structures of Tribals in the Urban Context of Meghalaya,"* 1991, (mimeo).

11

Comparison of Functioning of Old and New Self-Governing Bodies

In the previous chapter, we have focussed at the famous three tribes and their difficulties due to British and post-independence interventions. This chapter is specifically focussed on comparison between old Khasi and new Panchayati Raj Institutions. Idea of self-government right upto the grassroot level is present in most tribal societies of the past. In the Khasi polity too the practice of self-government was well-defined and universal in all the Khasi-Jaintia Hills regions. Bareh (1985) distinguishes between the earlier state systems such as Basanship, Doloiship and Lyngdohship, and the later ones such as Syiemship, Wahdadarship and Sirdarship. In the past, the evolution of Syiemship came about when Basans, Lyngdohs and the petty rulers combine to form a confederation of States, i.e., a Syiemship, the Syiemship was used to be nominated and elected by an electoral council comprising the State Officials—Basans, Lyngdohs, Sirdars, Lyngskors, Metabors, etc., as well as elected representatives. Such senior members of ruling clans are jointly known as *Ki Bakhraw* (the great ones).

Below are given the four-tier structures of Khasi Institutions:

1. ***Full State Darbar i.e., Ka Darbar ka Hima Pyllum.*** It was the supreme authority of the state, and the highest legislative, judicial and executive body. It was convened when the State faces natural calamities, epidemics or to discuss issues like extra-territorial rights, defence and foreign policies. A Cabinet or Executive Council handled other State subjects like trade, communications, trading markets, rivers, forests and day-to-day administration. The Dorbar Hima acted as a supreme court and had judicial functions such as disposal of cases of petitioners and also land disputes. Ki Myntri, Basan, Lyngdoh, Lyngskor, Metabar, were attached to the Syiem to carry out their various duties and submit judicial reports to the Syiem. *U Syiem Khynnah* (Deputy Syiem) also helped the Syiem in administration, while *Ka Syiem-Sad* helped in the preparation and organisation of State rituals. In addition to the Chief and *Ki Bakhraw* Ka *Dorbar Hima* it included representatives of the *Dorbar Raid, Dorbar Shnong* and *Dorbar Kur*.

2. Dorbar of Thirty Villages i.e. Ka Dorbar Raid **or** ***Ka Dorbar Laiphew Shnong.*** It coordinated the affairs of constituent villages, (not necessarily 30 in numbers, but it included the whole commune or circle). All in the village were members of *a Dorbar*

Raid, with additional representatives whenever necessary. The Dorbar elected the *Rangbah Raid* (Head of the Raid) as Chairman and also the executive head, while members acted as advisors. The Dorbar supervised administration, improvement of markets, roads, collection of common market levies, maintenance of Raid lands and sanction of the same to landless people. It also arranged rituals and ceremonies, and sent offerings (such as a goat for sacrifice) at festivals. Village representatives from various localities were at times summoned to the Syiem's headquarters to resolve common issues. Once a verdict is given, it cannot be resolved through any other authority.

3. Council called Ka Darbar ki Kyntoit* or *Ka Darbar Pyllun is a small council of a group of villages or localities, with more or less the same functions as the above, with lesser jurisdiction within *ki Kyntoit* (literally, 'units').

4. Village Level Darbar, i.e., Ka Darbar Shnong (Village or Local Darbar). Because of being smallest council of people at the village level, it met more frequently than the above Darbar. As the *Hima, Raid* and *Kyntoit darbars,* it had administrative, financial and adjudicatory functions. In Baren's words, it gave "directives for day-to-day administration" and functioned as a "court to dispose of cases and inflict penalties upon all wrongdoers". These *Dorbar Shnong* meet at any time of the day, morning (Ka Dorbar Step), day (Ka Dorbar Sngi) or night (Ka Dorbar miet). The *Dorbar Shnong* were formed and set up by all resident villagers. It had the highest authority in all matters related to the village. The power and authority of the *Dorbar Shnong* was derived from the traditions of autonomy and traditional practice, which had the force of law. As self-governing bodies, the *Dorbar Shnong* can be compared to old Greek city-republics "(P.R. Mawthoh, personal communication).

5. Clan Council, i.e., Dorbar Kur. At the lowest end, the *Kur* (clan) council nonetheless functioned as an organised political unit. Male members of each *Kur* (clan), *jait* (sub-clan) and sometimes every *kpoh* (lineage) were sent as representatives. The *Rangbah Kur* (clan headman) was also the *Kni Rangbah* (head uncle) as he was the eldest member of the clan. He used to the president, executive and judicial head, as well as the clan priest. The council looked after the clan lands (*Ri Kur*) and the welfare of all clan members, especially those who had been destitute or unfortunate. It also settled disputes between clan members, disciplined the wayward ones, and generally exercised control over all the members of the clan.

Then, the hierarchy of five different councils at different levels of jurisdiction and operation, points to the fact of grass-root democracy practised by the Khasis from ancient times. All democratic norms like election, majority, consensus, accountability, representation and so on, operated at all levels. The five councils were also connected to each other by representations and common agenda, as well as religious observances. The *Kur* (clan) as the nucleus of Khasi society was also the crieteria for some elected representatives. It might be fruitful to study and research ancient democratic institutions like those of the Khasis, to put some light on administration and social cohesion among the 'primitive' indigenous peoples of the world. This chapter is an attempt, at a very small level, to do this by comparing the *Dorbar Shnong* with Panchayati Raj Institutions. The *Dorbar Shnong* is taken since very little has been said about it.

As the chapter concerned mainly with the *Dorbar Shnong* vis-a-vis the PRIs, the details of this "resourful Dorbar" will be discussed in subsequent pages.

A Brief Description of the Dorbar Shnong and PRIs and Comparison between them

Set up

Khasi Context		*Indian Union Context*
Past (5 tier)	Present (Multi Tier)	(3-Tier) or (6-Tier)
Traditional Institutions	*(i) Constitutional Institutions*	
(a) Dorbar ka Hima Pyllum	(a) Houses of Parliament	(a) Houses of Parliament
(b) Dorbar Raid or Dorbar ki Laiphew Syiem	(b) Legislative Assemblies	(b) Legislative Assemblies
(c) Dorbar ki Kyntoit or (Dorbar Pyllun)	(c) District Councils	(c) PRIs
	(ii) Traditional Institutions	
(d) Dorbar Shnong	(d) Dorbar Hima Pyllun	(i) District
(e) Dorbar Kur	(e) Dorbar Raid or Dorbar Ki Laiphew Syiem	(ii) Intermediate (Block)
		(iii) Village
	(f) Dorbar Ki Kyntoit or Dorbar Pyllun	(iv) Gram Sabha
	(g) Dorbar Shnong	
	(h) Dorbar Kur	

In above all the three structures, the different tiers show an acknowledgement of decentralisation as political principle. Secondly, it acknowledges the principle of local self-government.

1. Origin and the Background

The institution may have originated and been necessitated by the geo-political contexts in the past. Generally, isolated by lack of proper communications, the governance of the villages was in the hands of the village people themselves.

Villages under the Syiemship/Doloiship/Wahdadarship were more or less autonomous, the relationship with the Syiem and his representatives being rather loose and irregular. The *Dorbar Shnong* coming out of needs at the grassroot level had from times immemorial placed power with the people.

This may also be true of the indigenous Panchayats of the past. However, the origin of present-day PRIs lies in the enactments of the Highest Council (Parliament) by the Constitution (Seventy-third Amendment) Act, 1993, and the Seventy-fourth Amendment. The existence of PRIs by this type of "Legislative and administrative actions" of the Parliament and State Legislatures indicate a 'Top-Down' approach.

However, PRIs enjoy constitutional status and are also at par with Central and State governments. The motivations for the third tier in the Indian political structure include "the democratisation of our pluralistic society . . ." (p. 29, *Issues for Discussion*), shifting of "Power to the people" (p. 29) i.e., peoples' empowerment, devolution of power and decentralisation by establishing grassroot political institutions in every nook and corner of this vast country. Being a "Top-Down" approach, constitutional and legislative acts also require mobilisation of support and awareness. The Task Force on PRIs suggests "NGOs, academic and professional bodies, trade unions, political parties and other groups and individuals should involve themselves in exerting pressure 'to restore power where it belongs."

2. Locality

Though PRIs are instituted for rural areas, the *Dorbar Shnong* which originated in rural villages have also been made applicable to some localities in urban areas like Shillong and Jowai in the present time.

3. Criteria for Membership

The old institution practises male suffrage since all males who have reached around eighteen years of age, are admitted to the *Dorbar Shnong* as voting members. Young males function as "Ki Nongpyrta Shrong" to announce meetings of the *Dorbar* and other community matters. They are also sanctioned light duties and responsibilities. Howerver, there was no representation of women in the past. Women would come to the *Dorbar* only when cases or matters relating to them were discussed. In many *Dorbar Shnong* in the present times, women also take part (one village in West Khasi Hills, elected a women as *Rangbah Shnong* and a number of *Dorbar Shnong* in urban Shillong areas include women in the Executive Committees or elect them as office bearers. Representatives in PRIs are elected from within the geographical constituencies, in the Panchayat area [Article 243-C (2)]. There is also a mandatory one-third representation by women, and reservations also for SCs and STs [Article 243-D (1)] of Constitution. By such provisions the Act ensures "universal" representation by all sections of a community.

4. Institutional Leaders

The *Dorbar Shnong* follows the democratic process of election for the office

U Rangbah Shnong (Headman). If there are more than one *Rangbah Shnong,* one is then elected as Chairman. In many cases, especially when the village or locality is large in area, some *Rangbah Dong* (Area Elders/Leaders) help the *Rangbah Shnong* in administration. Article 243-C (5) states that the Legislature of a State shall pass a law for the election of a Chairperson at the village level, while at the intermediate and district levels the Chairperson should be "elected by, and from amongst the elected members thereof".

5. Written/Unwritten Laws and Practices

We knows that the institutions of PRIs are encoded in Parliamentary and Legislative Acts, along with detailed provisions in well-discussed Constitutions. PRIs therefore enjoy constitutional status. On the other hand, the *Dorbar Shnong* in the past days, functioned purely on uncodified customary laws and practices, which were more or less binding on all citizens of the village. Nowadays the trends have changed, and many *Dorbar Shnong* too have their own written constitutions, rules and regulations.

6. Area of Functioning

Dorbar Shnong in the past had jurisdictions only within the villages. In the present time there are agreed areas within the jurisdiction of each local *Dorbar Shnong*. For example, Nongthymmai being a fairly large area, has eleven *Dorbar Shnong* each every one operating within well-demarcated boundaries. However, in some matters of common concerns the different localities come together as *Ka Dorbar Pyllun Nongthymmai*. On these occasions. Nongthymmai is taken as a single constituency. Similarly, *Ka Sanda Tynger* is the Council comprising of various neighbouring villages in the War area.

7. The Staff

Except from the *Rangbah Shnong* (Headman), *Rangbah Dong* (Area Elders), and Committee members, other responsible people including women, can be given duties and responsibilities. In some cases, e.g., funerals, cleaning up the areas etc., the whole community takes part. Though the ideal is for PRIs to "have personnel of their own", in fact, the key functionaries such as Secretaries and Executives officers at all levels are government appointees who are liable to transfers and deputations, thus affecting the functioning of the PRIs. Moreover, absolute autonomy cannot be maintained.

8. Party Politics

During the traditional *Dorbar Shnong* days, there is no question of party politics in the case of elections, etc. This is still true in present day practices by and large. However, in urban localities a particular party has been setting up its candidate for the office of *Rangbah Shnong*. This may not be a healthy trend since party politics encourages power play, corruption, nepotism, and the unsavoury nexus among the politicians, functionaries and unwanted elements in the locality. Since parties are generally connected to the highest echelons of power, the "top-down" control will defeat the very purpose of grass-root level. In the case of PRIs, elections are contested on party lines. There are also provisions for interlocking membership among the different tiers of the Panchayat bodies, e.g., the Heads of intermediate Panchayats represent at the intermediate level, the Heads of intermediate Panchayats in the district level bodies while M.Ps and M.L.As (party leaders) are voting members in the intermediate and district bodies. Such being the case, there is scope for party-politics.

9. Power, Autonomy and Control

Here, traditional *Dorbar Shnong* was entirely autonomous, since there was no funding nor personnel assistance from other sources. By and large, present day *Dorbar Shrong* are still autonomous bodies, with unchecked decision-making processes and implementations. In very recent times, some control (through persuasions and incentives) may have been attempted by the State Government which met the famous *Synjuk Ki Rangbah Shnong* (Council of Headmen) at different times. The *Synjuk* itself is a newly constituted body in Shillong.

Secondly, if a *Rangbah Shnong* or significant functionaries in the *Dorbar Shnong* are party men or actively affiliated to the ruling party, control is possible. The spirit behind Panchayats as instilled by Gandhiji, Rajiv Gandhi, etc., is for autonomy and self-government, with minimum control and interference from State Governments. However, the Task Force on PR has given that the four parameters of PRIs for local self-government have been tampared with by State Acts, thus undermining the autonomy of Panchayats and making them "a pawn in chess of power-politics." The Task Force says that any enquiry should be made by "an independent body." The fact that a sizeable amount is allocated by the State Government from its consolidated funds and through taxes, etc. (Article 243-H), it's quite possible for a loophole to occur in the question of autonomy or control in PRIs.

10. Monetary Aspects

In the old set up, *Dorbar Shnong* can levy contributions, duties (e.g., from markets) etc., from householders within its jurisdiction, to meet expenses such as, construction of roads, bridges, defence purposes, parties and cultural festivals, etc. The *Dorbar Shnong* can also impose fines on defaulters. Nowadays, some villages/localities levy a mandatory "*bairung shnong*" (duty paid on buying land, building a house to help a family with funeral expenses, or if a family or families meet with misfortunes (failure of crop, houses destroyed by calamities like fire and wind, etc.).

PRIs according to Article 243-H are authorised by State Legislatures to "levy, collect and appropriate" taxes, duties, tolls and fees. State Legislatures also assign taxes, etc., to Panchayats and make grants-in-aid from the Consolidated Fund of Meghalaya Since State funding is provided for, the financial matters of a Panchayat are to be reviewed by a Finance Commission as per the Provision of 243-I of the Constitution.

11. Possessions

Some villages own some community land e.g. *Ki Khlaw Shrong* (village forests), usually those forests having water sources, streams, etc., and *Ki Khyndew Shnong* (viliage land) used for religious purposes, cremation grounds, sports fields and archery-fields, schools, etc.

12. Activities

The Eleventh Schedule of Article 243-G lists some twenty-nine functions and areas to be taken up by PRIs. However, it is left to State Government acts to allocate the various functions to the various tiers of PRIs. Police and adjudicatory functions have also been recommended by the Task Force.

In the old set-up, functions of the *Dorbar Shnong* necessarily arise out of the socio-cultural, politico-economic milieu of rural villages. In the past village defence was an important agenda in the *Dorbar Shnong.* Other functions also include the establishment of markets (Hat), usually organised by several neighbouring *Dorbar Shnong* (e.g., *Hat Shella; Iew-Dor,* a recently established market place near Mawrong), which then receive the approval signal from the *Syiem/Wahdadar.* In the past such *Hat* or market function one day in a week, care being taken that different *Hat,* in the area do not fall on the same day. The villages used to be responsible for collecting duties from the market, its maintenance, and settling disputes. Developmental works such as the construction and maintenance of roads, bridges, water sources, acts of sanitation, etc., were taken up by the *Dorbar Shnong.* For example, poisoning of river fish was strictly prohibited. If fish was required, some fishing and netting was permitted (which was shared by the community). To keep the village clean, stone-walls were usually erected to keep the pigs confined to a particular corner.

The practice of timely *Pynkhuid Shnong* (cleaning the village) is still continued, even in urban localities (usually accompanied by a community feast). Welfare works, such as help rendered to the distressed or unfortunate and community work in construction of roads houses, Dorbar Hall, schools, etc., are still an important part of village life. The *Dorbar Shnong* also functions as village/local courts to try small cases such as land squabbles, fights, divorces, ex-communications of incestuous couples (*Shong sang*), boundary disputes, petty thefts, etc. In the days of *U Thlen,* a man/woman suspected of being a *Nonghohnoh* (ritual murderer) can be beaten to death by the village, with the tacit consent of *Ka Dorbar Shnong.* At the religio-cultural level, the *Dorbar Shnong* may introduce and organise functions such as dances, festivals, hunts, archery etc. Rules and regulations, *'Ki Adong Shnong'* passed by the *Dorbar Shnong* were strictly followed. For example, in times of plagues or infectious diseases, no one was allowed to enter the village.

Similarly, to stop the spread of diseases among animals, villages were not allowed to sell or buy pigs/cows/chicken, whatever the case may be. In cases of death having occured in the village, it was (as is still in most villages) mandatory for each house to send its adult representatives, and some young men are given the duty of digging the grave, etc., a member of *Shnong* as a community could not deny such obligations. To cut wood, even to take a fallen branch and to disturb the flora, fauna and all living things within *Ki Law Kyntang* (sacred groves) was strictly banned. Christians as well as non-Christians alike consider such acts as sacrilege. Such practices clearly show the innate capability of tribals to manage natural resources from where they get their sustenance.

Same way, rules that forbade drinking or drunks, as well as disorderly conduct in the *Ing Dorbar* (Dorbar House) indicate a sense of propriety and seriousness of old institutions. It may be well to restore such practices again in this more 'advanced' age! Bareh observes that "because of the total village participation it became itself a training ground in citizenship, welfare, oratory and in the resumption of economic activities. It channelised different means of village education acquainting young men in welfare, dance, music, social service and specialisation in their subjects including the use and veterance in martial arts."

Today, especially in the urban setting some of the functions of the *Dorbar Shnong* have been modified to suit the needs and context. In several areas the *Dorbar Shnong* work together with the Government agencies/functionaries and NGOs like for obtaining and maintaining drinking water supply, electricity, roads, schools, etc., to deal with anti-social elements such as bootleggers and drug peddlars, maintenance of law and order in the area, etc. *Dorbar Shnnong* also collaborate with Church organisations to construct Lower Primary and Primary Schools (which usually serve as the *Ing Dorbar* when needed), shrines like Churches, cremation grounds, etc. Recently, the KJP Synod sponsored by the NEC was instrumental in bringing non-conventional solar energy to a few villages in the West Khasi Hills. The *Dorbar Shnong* is generally approached to implement other government programmes like Adult Literacy and non-formal education, IRDP, Public Distribution System, Nova Vidyalayas (schools), etc.

13. Issue of Accountability

The said *Rangbah Shnong/Dong* and executive members of the *Dorbar Shnong* are accountable to the villagers/householders. *Dorbar Shnong* is held whenever the need arises, which may be two-three times a year, or more. At such ordinary meetings, questions or clarifications may be put forward by any member relating to any matter-financial, administrative or executive. Collective decisions are given after long and detailed pondering.

Even PRIs are accountable to the people, and to Vigilance Agencies if such exist. In financial matters a Finance Commission also acts as a review committee. However, since PRIs are politically connected, the wishes of political masters may over ride the voice of the people and "accountability to the people" may be perfunctory.

The Recommendations

Here, it has been suggested by the Workshop on Traditional self-governing Institutions among the Hill Tribal Population Groups of NE India, that "the 73rd Amendment could be adopted by the exempted areas in order to *reinforce their existing system of autonomous self-governance* in its scope, functions, resources as well as democratic context."

To put it the other way, since the Khasis and other tribal groups in North-East India already have the age-old grass root democracy and traditional institutions of self-government with which they are conversant, certain provisions of PRIs can be adopted or modified to strengthen the existing institutions to suit the regional or local contexts. This will truly hand over power into the hands of the people :

(a) This way, with regard to functions of the *Dorbar Shnong,* a few functions listed in Schedule II (Article 243-G), e.g., rural housing, adult, non-formal and vocational education, libraries, PHC and government dispensaries, family and social welfare, public distribution system, women and child welfare and development, can be introduced and experimented as new programmes for the *Dorbar Shnong.*

(b) In certain *Dorbar Shnong* which still debar women from participation, there should be reservation for women.

(c) Since *Dorbar Shnongs* are based on customary laws and practices, they are usually unstructured. Some DS nowadays have written constitutions. There is a need for more well-defined and well-demarcated specifications on the various aspects of these local self-governing institutions. This will ensure non-overlapping of jurisdiction, functions, powers, etc.

(d) Various resources and finances of *Dorbar Shnongs'* can be enhanced by district and state funding, along the lines suggested for PRIs, alongwith a Finance Commission. However, accountability will have to be towards the people.

(e) All schemes, programmes and plans should be people or village-centred and sponsored. Such schemes should be sent to the next level, i.e., District Council or to the State Government, for ratification, deliberation and funding of these.

(f) Committed efforts should be made to educate the people and re-establish the rules of conduct and orderliness in *Dorbar Shnongs.* This will enhance the prestige of *Dorbar Shnong,* and also link the present with the old rich tradition of the Khasis in matters of conduct and social behaviour.

(g) The relationship and co-operation of the *Dorbar Shnong* with the State and District bodies, as well as their customary traditional links with the *higher Dorbars,* e.g., *Dorbar Hima,* can be studied and recommendations made.

To conclude, a Study Group from the Political Science, Sociology, and History Departments as well as those involved in administration can be constituted to thoroughly research all aspects of the *Dorbar Shnong* and give their findings towards public awareness and implementation. The above views and suggestions are those of a layman, with a view to start the ball rolling, for better and more just administration at all levels.

12

Women and the System of Local Self-Governance

Self Rule and then total independence have been the dreams of our freedom fighters. Even more than this, it was the dream of Mahatma Gandhi, to have a fully decentralised form of Government in Independent India. He lamented at the non inclusion of the Panchayati Raj set up in the Constitution, as to him independence must begin at the bottom and every village will be a republic or Panchayat. Gandhi wrote in India of my dreams that, "true democracy cannot be worked by twenty men sitting at the Centre. It has to work from below by the people of every village".

Rajiv Gandhi, in the course of his short span of political life, took the major step in achieving the objective of decentralisation of power, when he introduced the Constitution 64th Amendment Bill in the lower house in May 1989. The Lok Sabha supported and passed it, but the Rajya Sabha could not enact it. Again, it was in 1991, under the government led by Prime Minister P.V. Narasimha Rao, that the Constitution 72nd Amendment Bill was brought in the Lok Sabha, which passed it on December 22, 1992, and the Rajya Sabha approved it, the following day.

After the ratification of more than fifty per cent the states the President gave his assent to the Bill on April 20, 1993, and it became an Act with effect from April 24, 1993. The 73rd Amendment Act targets the decentralisation of political administration, as well as decentralisation of institutions for development. It also aims at achieving grassroot democratic polity, by making the Panchayati Raj *Vyavastha* an instrument of local self-government and community development. The Act provides for a constitutional status to the Panchayats and gives reservation to women and other weaker sections, to establish their active participation at all levels of the Panchayati Raj system. This decentralisation is of great significance as people have been given so much of responsibility in undertaking the development programmes which will bring about a quick rural development.

(a) The State of Meghalaya and The Constitution 73rd Amendment Act

The makers of the Constitution of India realised the necessity of a separate political and administrative structure for the hill areas of the erstwhile Province of Assam. Therefore, certain provisions were made in the Sixth Schedule to the Constitution, to maintain the distinct culture of the hill people, to prevent them from socio-economic and political exploitation, and to permit them to administer according to their own genius. In the states of North-East India like Nagaland, Mizoram and Meghalaya, the people have their own traditional system of self-government since time immemorial.

Within the areas covered by the Sixth Schedule, where the Autonomous District Councils have been established, the traditional system remains undisturbed. The 73rd Amendment Act contains Article 243 M[1], which states that the Act is not applicable to the states of Nagaland, Meghalaya and Mizoram.

The Act does not also extend to the District Council areas of Manipur and the areas that come under the Gorkha Hill Council in the Darjeeling District of West Bengal. It is not applicable to the Fifth Schedule areas in the country, and the Sixth Schedule district and regions. The national Parliament has been authorised by law to extend it to these two categories of areas, subject to such exceptions and modifications as may be specified. It has also been clarified that such enactment is not to be deemed as Amendment of the Constitution. While enacting the Constitution 73rd Amendment Act, it appears that the Parliament decided consciously that the provisions of the Act should not be imposed to the Fifth Schedule areas and the Sixth Schedule districts and regions. The reason is that they have their traditional system, almost to the Panchayati Raj, that must be disturbed but require a carefully considered treatment.

Now let's talk of Meghalaya. In Meghalaya, the people have their own traditional socio-political system since the earliest time. They have their self-governing institutions beginning from the grassroot at the village level, which function in a very democratic manner. In the Khasi and Jaintia Hills, the traditional Chiefs are the Syiem, Lyngdoh, Sirdar, Wahadadar, Doloi, Pator and the Rangbah Shnong or even Village Headmen. They look after the administration of the Syiemship, elaka and villages according to customs and traditions.

The will of the people and the *Dorbar* or old councils are supreme and they play a very important role in the administration and decision making. In Garo Hills, the famous institution of Nokmanship and the Village Council are the two traditional institutions. However, the Nokma does not enjoy autocratic powers as all the decisions are taken at a joint group of the village elders. These traditional institutions play a very important role in the socio-economic and political life of the people of Meghalaya.

Through the Sixth Schedule of the Constitution, the Autonomous District Councils have been established in the United Khasi and Jaintia Hills in 1952. Later, the people of Jaintia Hills felt that a separate District Council was required for the Jowai Sub-division. In 1963, the Jarman Commission was appointed in connection with the bifurcation. The history of the United Khasi and Jaintia Hills Autonomous District Council made a new turn when in 1966, the Commission recommended a separate Autonomous District Council for Jowai Sub-division, for administrative convenience and the first election was conducted in 1967. Thus Meghalaya has three Autonomous Districts Councils, one each in Khasi Hills,

Jaintia Hills and Garo Hills. The District Councils play a supervisory role and function as guardians of the customs and traditions of the people.

However, since independence, under the new administrative set up, the powers of the traditional heads have been reduced. The different acts enforced from time to time by the District Councils effect the appointment and succession of Chiefs and headmen in the Khasi and Jaintia Hills. As a consequence, there are misunderstandings between the Districts and the traditional heads. There is no smooth sailing between the State Government and the District Councils, the latter are asking for direct funding, removing of Para 12A and other demands, so as to improve the functioning of the District Councils and to make them more effective to carry on their responsibilities and liabilities.

Reservation for Women and the 73rd Amendment Act

Women's participation in the Panchayati Raj institutions is considered essential, for their political participation in the democratic process and to ensure their overall development. The 73rd Amendment Act provides 33 per cent, i.e., 1/3rd of total seats for women in the Panchayati Raj institutions. This constitutional innovation is a significant step towards empowerment of women by giving them a say in the decision making process.

The Constitution 73rd Amendment Act[2] contains Article 243 D (1) "seats shall be reserved for (a) the Scheduled Castes and (b) the Scheduled Tribes."

(2) Not less than one-third of the total number of seats reserved under Clause (I) shall be reserved for women belonging to the Scheduled Castes or as the case may be the Scheduled Tribes.

(3) Not less than one-third (including the number of seats reserved for women belonging to the Schedurled Castes and the Scheduled Tribes) of the total number of seats to be filled by direct election in every Panchayat shall be reserved for women and such seats may be allotted by rotation to different constituencies in a Panchayat.

(4) The Offices of the Chairpersons in the Panchayats at the village or any other level shall be reserved for the Scheduled Caste and Scheduled Tribes and women in such manner as the Legislature of a State may by law, provide.

Provided further, that not less than one-third of the total number of offices of Chairpersons in the Panchayats at each level shall be reserved for women.

This 33 per cent reservation for women is based on social justice and thus guaranteed the Constitutional rights for women.

Organisations Working for Women in Meghalaya

Special feature of Meghalaya is the matrilineal system where descent is traced from women and they also inherit property. The society is free from many of social restraints of the larger Indian society. There is no caste system and also the evil of untouchability or social inequality. They do not have problems like dowry, bride burning, female foeticide and others. However, there are other social stigmas like illiteracy, dropouts, unemployment, broken marriages and divorce, lack of family welfare programmes for women and children, particularly in the rural areas and other kinds of deficiencies. Women in Meghalaya enjoy social and economic freedom but politics and administration are considered man's domain.

Traditionally, women are not permitted to attend Dorbar and the Village administration is headed by men. But women can act as moral force behind men and can give views and suggestions to menfolk on different issues. Presently, women also attend Dorbar in some localities, for instance the Laitumkhrah, Nongrim Hills and Lachumiere *Dorbar* do include women in the executive commitees. Some women organisations, e.g., Ka Seng Longkmie Laitumkhrah and Seng Kynthei Nongrim Hills send two representatives to the Executive Committee of their local Dorbars. Recently, in Lachumiere locality of Shillong, a woman was elected as a treasurer of the Executive Committee of the Dorbar. A number of women organisations were formed prior to the creation of Meghalaya. One of the oldest women organisations is the Mother's Union, founded in 1941, at Tura in Garo Hills.

This organisation has performed an important role bringing about radical changes in the socio-economic life of the Garos. Ka Synjuk Kynthei, an association of women is the oldest voluntary welfare organisation in the areas like Khasi and Jaintia Hills formed in 1947. This organisation is still continuing to work effectively for the upliftment of the society in general and the females in particular.

One most premier women organisation is Ka Synjuk Ki Kynthei Riewlum or the Tribal Women Welfare and Development Association of Meghalaya, popularly known as TWWADAM which was formed in 1979. The leading concerns of the organisation are the protection of the tribal lands, and trade, foreigners issues, unemployment, social evils and other problems. The TWWADAM has taken up many issues, and even now is continuing to work for the social and cultural upliftment. Ka Lympung Ki Seng Kynthei is a Central Branch or apex body and functions as a coordination body of 22 (Twenty-two) women organisations of the various localities of Shillong and its suburbs. Since it is the Central co-ordination issues and problems of the various women organisations. Besides the above organisations, women organisations exist in different areas, like the Seng Kynthei or Seng Longkmie of Mawlai, Jaiaw, Riatsamthiah, Laban, Laitumkhrah, etc. Their nature and activities are very much localised in their areas. There are more women organisations like the Meghalaya Women Forum, Meghalaya Women Alliance, Talents Club, Eastern India Women Association, Mizo Women Organisation and some others. Women organisations also exist in the various Churches, like Ka Synjuk Ki Seng Kynthei Katholik, Seng Kynthei Synod, Young Women Christian Association, etc. These various women organisations either religious or secular contribute in their different ways to the social upliftment and general welfare of the society as a whole.

1. Political Parties and Women in Meghalaya. Along with the social and voluntary organisations, the political parties whether national or regional have their affiliated Women's Wing like the Mahila Congress Committee I and the Women's Wing of the Hill Peoples' Union. Their leading objectives are to strengthen their political parties through their social and political activities. It is the women's wing of the political parties that are raising certain issues on the significance of giving political and administrative representations to women. As early as 1987, the Congress I Women Front in Garo Hills in a resolution accepted at the first conference in Mendipathar, presided over by M.D. Shira, demanded that at least five seats should be reserved for women in the ensuing Meghalaya Assembly election. Again, they demanded that five seats to be kept for fair sex in the District Council.[4] The Tura City Congress I Women Committee even took up steps to eradicate corrupt practices in some departments of the Garo Hills Autonomous District Council and to reform its administrative system.

They met the Executive Committee of the GHADC to discuss with them on certain burning issues. They were more sore with the Forest Department for issuing free permit to cut a number of Teak Trees from the Eden Bari Plantation area. This action was very much praised by the general public and to the great embarrassment of the Council. In 1994, the North-East Mahila Congress Coordination Committee I, demanded the government for establishing a State Women Commission which will function as a watchdog for Women's rights and to formulate appropriate policies for the socio-economic growth of women.[6] When Mrs. J. Patnaik, Chairperson of the National Commission for Women and Mrs. Padma Seth, a member NCW, visited Meghalaya in 1994, they expressed astonishment that there was not a single women representative in the District Council and only one women in the Legislative Assembly. Besides discussing other problems, they said that trials should be made to include women in the important decision making forum of the State as well as in the region.[7] Further it was at the first North East Mahila Congress Convention held at Shillong in September 14, 1994, that a resolution was adopted calling for 30 per cent reservation for women as public representatives in almost all spheres including the Council of Ministers and assignment in public undertakings to encourage women to come forward and participate in the political process right from the village level, up to the National Union Level.

Mrs. Margaret Alva said that more than 7,50,000 women would soon be participating all over the country as public representatives once they are elected to the Panchayats as per 30 per cent reservation. It is a social revolution and women must take full part in the socio-economic development process of the country. She urged upon the women of the region to struggle for reservation in the Autonomous District Councils. The women of other States have already got representation in the Panchayats and so should the tribal women get the similar in the Councils.

In this manner, the various women organisations, both social and political have been voicing their opinions on the various issues and act as pressure groups on various public matters.

(b) Women in District, State and Central Level Politics

Since politics is considered as a male prerogative, very few women came forward to contest in the election, as a result of which the decision-making and administration is concentrated in the hands of men. During the British rule, the Government of India Act 1935, women were given the right to vote, but very much restricted or limited. The Act provided for the representation of women through the reservation of a seat from the Shillong Constituency in the Assam Legislative Assembly. The Act also permitted women to contest not only from the reserved seats but also from the general seats. In the year 1937, two women contested the reserved seat, Mrs. Berlina Diengdoh and Miss Mavis Dunn Lyngdoh. The latter was elected and it was for the first time that a woman became a member of the state Legislative Assembly. Miss Mavis Dunn Lyngdoh was included in the Muhammad Saadulla's Ministry in 1939 till 1941 and again from 1942 till 1945. Mavis Dunn Lyngdoh was the first lady to become a cabinet minister in the North-East. In 1946, five women stood in the elections, they were Mrs. Bonniely Khongmen, T.W. Shadap, Berlina Diengdoh, Padma Kumari Gohain and Miss Mavis Dunn Lyngdoh. Except Mrs. B. Khongmen who was a Congress nominee, all four female contested as independents. Padma K. Gohain contested the general seat, the others, the Shillong women seat, Mrs. B. Khongmen got elected.

Further, the first general election of free India was held in 1952. There were six women who filed their nominations. Of these, four were from the plain districts of Assam and two from the Khasi and Jaintia Hills. In 1952, there was no reservation of seats for women, they could contest any seat. Miss Mavis Dunn Lyngdoh and Manorama Mehta contested the Shillong seat against J.J.M. Nichols Roy, both got defeated.[9] In the Lok Sabha election, Mrs. Bonniely Khongmen was nominated by the Congress for the seat reserved for the hill tribals. She had to contest against two male contestants, Donaldson Basan and Wilson Reade.

Mrs. B. Khongmen was elected and became the first and only women from Assam in the Lok Sabha. Mrs. B. Khongmen was a member of the Assam State Legislative Assembly from 1946-1952, and was elected Deputy Speaker in 1952. In 1957, she returned to State politics but was defeated. In 1962 and 1967, no women fought the election to the Assam Legislative Assembly. After the creation of Meghalaya in 1972, a number of women came forward to contest in the first general election to the Meghalaya Legislative Assembly. Of these, Miss Silverene Swer, Mrs. Muriel S. Dunn, Mrs. P.S. Marbaniang, Maysalin War, Louisiana Brosila Lamin who contested from the constituency Khasi Hills. In Garo Hills a number of women contested the election, these were Miriam D. Shira, Percylina Marak and H.B. Sangma.

Only Percylina Marak was elected from the Garo Hills and none from the Khasi Hills constituency.

In 1978, Mrs. Neena Rynjah, Maysalin War, Drosila Mukhim and Usha Bhattacharjee contested the election from the Khasi Hills and Miriam D. Shira,

Percylina Marak and finally Friedna Marak from Garo Hills. Only Miriam D. Shira from Garo Hills came out successfully. In 1983, there were eight women contestants. These were Mrs. Ivoryna Shylla, Nongbri, Naramai Langstieh, Evandalyne Massar, Maya R. Kyndiah, Louisiana Brosila Lamin and Maysalin War from Khasi Hills and Miriam D. Shira from Garo Hills.

During this election no lady was elected and the Meghalaya Legislative Assembly is a hundred per cent male-dominated. In 1988 elections, a number of ladies contested, some of them were Maya R. Kyndiah, Maysalin War and Ivoryna Shylla. Only Maysalin War was elected from Mawthengkut constituency and she was appointed in the ministry.

Again, in 1993, Mrs. Roshan Warjri was elected from the prestigious Mawkhar Constituency and she is the only woman legislator in the present Meghalaya Legislative Assembly. Being the only woman, she accepts the challenge to give her best, and she is performing very well. She contested the election in 1993 due to public demand and of too much public pressure, earlier she had refused to contest. In the Autonomous District Councils, there were a number of women representatives who were either elected or nominated. Mrs. Lariam Shullai's name was nominated to the first Khasi and Jaintia Hills Autonomous District Council in 1952-57. Dr. (Mrs.) K. Rymbai was nominated to the Jaintia Hills Autonomous District Council. Mrs. Louisiana Brosila Lamin and also Mrs. Etris Syiem contested and won the election in 1972. In 1984, Mrs. Maysalin War contested and won the election to the Khasi Hills Autonomous District Council with the Congress I ticket.

In 1972, Mr. L.G. Shullai was elected as the Chief Executive Member of the KHADC. He selected Mrs. L. Brosila Lamin as one of the executive members. The involvement of a woman as an executive member is very significant as the KHADC was the first of all the District Councils in the North-East to have a lady as the executive member. Mrs. E. Syiem too was also an executive member for a brief period in 1977.[10] In the first election to the Garo Hills Autonomous District Council in 1952, there were two women members in the district house of twenty four, Mrs. Sujomoti W. Momin who was elected as an independent candidate and Mrs. Roneswari Marak who was nominated by the Governor. During 1957, Mrs. Sujomati W. Momin contested against two male candidates and polled an absolute majority. In 1962, the election was not held due to the Chinese aggression, it was held in 1964. The census data for age, Sex, Marital status, Ever and Curreh married women with their no. of surviving children is given on next page.

Sole female member Mrs. Ewinel Marak contested against three male rivals and was defeated. As there was no woman member, a lady Bisadini Sangma was nominated by the Governor to represent females. in 1972, only one woman candidate Evangeline Shira contested as an independent, but was defeated. However, two lady members Alleswary Momin and Janje Marak had been nominated. There was no female member in 1978–1983. In 1983 two women were elected, Enilla D. Shira and Reboti Barman. In 1989 election, there was sole female member Mrs. Reboti Burman who was elected. In 1994, there was no female

Table 1
Age, Sex and Marital Status for Scheduled Tribes

Age Group	*Total*	*Never Married*	*Married*	*Widowed*	*Divor-ced*	*Unsp-ecified*
1	2	3	4	5	6	7
ALL SCHEDULED TRIBES						
RURAL						
All ages	**13,12,093**	**7,85,888**	**4,74,604**	**35,061**	**16,437**	**103**
0 - 9	4,13,790	4,13,790	0	0	0	0
10-14	1,63,610	1,61,457	1,737	344	64	8
15-19	1,24,213	1,10,785	12,354	251	808	15
20-24	1,02,960	50,396	49,164	930	2,465	5
25-29	1,08,401	21,146	83,433	1,146	2,663	13
30-34	80,298	7,119	69,530	1,666	1,982	1
35-39	77,303	3,406	70,285	1,968	1,641	3
40-44	56,141	2,020	49,940	2,650	1,529	2
15-44	5,49,316	1,94,872	3,34,706	8,611	11,088	39
45-49	50,120	1,307	44,090	3,351	1,368	4
50-54	38,097	976	31,443	4,454	1,221	3
55-59	23,860	491	19,560	3,085	722	2
60-64	25,214	614	18,616	5,116	867	1
65-69	13,595	248	9,865	3,046	436	0
70-74	10,430	243	6,720	3,143	324	0
75-79	4,950	90	3,197	1,513	150	0
80+	6,014	341	3,242	2,271	157	3
Age not stated	13,097	11,459	1,428	127	40	43
URBAN						
All ages	**2,05,834**	**1,31,954**	**67,210**	**4,212**	**2,429**	**29**
0 - 9	55,796	55,796	0	0	0	0
10-14	26,965	26,721	183	51	9	1
15-19	25,496	23,801	1,587	20	81	7
20-24	21,423	13,227	7,784	91	320	1
25-29	18,264	5,476	12,285	112	390	1
30-34	13,010	1,742	10,743	193	332	0
35-39	11,602	885	10,164	244	308	1
40-44	8,203	496	7,118	322	267	0
15-44	97,998	45,627	49,681	982	1,698	10
45-49	6,604	294	5,680	398	230	2
50-54	4,988	259	3,998	557	174	0
55-59	3,041	151	2,399	403	88	0
60-64	2,935	151	2,146	541	97	0
65-69	1,681	68	1,185	377	51	0
70-74	1,284	76	815	363	30	0
75-79	683	28	421	218	16	0
80+	903	101	465	308	26	3
Age not stated	2,956	2,682	237	14	10	13

Source: Census 1991

Table 2

Ever Married and Currently Married Women Belonging to Scheduled Tribes by Present Age, Number of Surviving Children and Total Number of Surviving Children by Sex

Present Age	*Total ever/ currently married women*	*Ever/currently married women with number of serviving children*						*Total surviving children*		
		0	*1*	*2*	*3*	*4*	*5+*	*Total*	*Males*	*Females*
1	2	3	4	5	6	7	8	9	10	11
ALL SCHEDULED TRIBES										
RURAL										
Ever Married										
All ages	**2,82,569**	**48,808**	**38,191**	**40,416**	**37,980**	**32,940**	**72,555**	**8,30,321**	**4,20,168**	**4,10,153**
Less than 15	1,326	1,106	70	72	0	0	0	214	96	118
15-19	11,246	4,787	3,406	878	190	122	0	6,220	3,197	3,023
20-24	38,427	9,069	11,714	8,508	4,015	1,364	730	50,345	25,480	24,865
25-29	53,810	8,670	8,514	11,784	10,552	7,007	5,370	1,21,910	61,848	60,062
30-34	37,846	5,221	3,370	5,245	6,457	6,385	10,165	1,18,584	59,800	58,784
35-39	35,506	4,323	2,336	3,681	4,744	5,387	14,245	1,35,593	69,026	66,567
40-44	25,968	3,340	1,687	2,422	2,943	3,406	11,589	1,06,475	54,052	52,423
45-49	23,027	3,024	1,632	2,013	2,641	2,828	10,380	95,379	48,471	46,908
50-54	17,542	2,461	1,511	1,855	2,096	2,141	6,983	67,015	33,862	33,153
55-59	10,861	1,528	937	1,113	1,301	1,304	4,326	41,350	20,829	20,521
60-64	10,869	1,794	1,216	1,171	1,246	1,229	3,842	37,634	18,758	18,876
65-69	5,929	1,066	597	682	648	674	2,031	19,948	10,019	9,929
70-74	4,582	917	551	426	552	523	1,413	14,365	7,198	7,167
75-79	2,178	447	250	225	240	246	659	6,629	3,295	3,334
80 +	2,603	598	348	278	290	267	683	7,175	3,494	3,681

(Contd.)

1	2	3	4	5	6	7	8	9	10	11
Currently Married										
All ages	**2,45,203**	**42,315**	**31,685**	**35,166**	**33,355**	**28,845**	**63,902**	**7,28,341**	**3,69,311**	**3,59,030**
Less than 15	1,108	924	57	57	0	0	0	171	76	95
15-19	10,382	4,442	3,055	847	178	109	0	5,719	2,939	2,780
20-24	35,845	8,450	10,625	8,067	3,882	1,328	705	47,689	24,133	23,556
25-29	51,055	8,190	7,630	11,177	10,211	6,813	5,273	1,17,453	59,582	57,871
30-34	35,415	4,820	2,890	4,762	6,084	6,089	9,873	1,13,158	57,118	56,040
35-39	33,006	3,989	1,966	3,258	4,380	5,033	13,669	1,28,391	65,388	63,003
40-44	23,064	2,956	1,320	1,983	2,547	3,015	10,757	97,256	49,393	47,863
45-49	19,482	2,577	1,200	1,554	2,123	2,359	9,259	83,469	42,533	40,936
50-54	13,302	1,872	1,002	1,260	1,535	1,593	5,688	53,147	27,025	26,122
55-59	7,979	1,128	565	797	912	949	3,400	31,788	16,084	15,704
60-64	6,448	1,094	611	641	679	710	2,538	23,868	11,935	11,933
65-69	3,375	606	317	354	337	361	1,277	11,947	6,018	5,929
70-74	2,067	427	213	174	220	234	713	6,915	3,458	3,457
75-79	1,003	215	92	94	103	106	351	3,298	1,628	1,670
80 +	936	231	98	91	107	98	268	2,732	1,334	1,398
URBAN										
Ever Married										
All ages	**40,996**	**4,755**	**5,746**	**6,138**	**6,082**	**5,372**	**10,755**	**1,27,013**	**63,637**	**63,376**
Less than 15	148	114	9	17	0	0	0	43	16	27
15-19	1,435	477	512	115	23	18	0	883	446	437
20-24	5,838	911	1,810	1,486	719	245	120	8,619	4,345	4,274
25-29	7,526	833	1,213	1,606	1,495	1,121	843	18,271	9,345	8,926
30-34	5,950	558	563	823	1,118	1,088	1,602	19,401	9,888	9,513
35-39	5,344	426	408	603	845	814	2,097	20,803	10,521	10,282
40-44	3,754	310	271	368	539	577	1,573	15,432	7,658	7,774
45-49	3,091	276	201	297	361	449	1,417	13,326	6,680	6,646
50-54	2,392	205	196	239	282	346	1,047	9,914	4,931	4,983

(Contd.)

1	2	3	4	5	6	7	8	9	10	11
55-59	1,524	144	127	142	190	238	620	6,148	3,008	3,140
60-64	1,433	136	152	150	196	174	560	5,471	2,650	2,821
65-69	882	84	88	103	114	106	352	3,354	1,573	1,781
70-74	667	94	70	63	90	80	229	2,266	1,118	1,148
75-79	382	51	53	39	42	52	126	1,276	586	690
80 +	486	76	56	67	55	58	145	1,544	739	805
Currently Married										
All ages	**35,554**	**4,143**	**4,815**	**5,387**	**5,379**	**4,727**	**9,216**	**1,09,948**	**55,306**	**54,642**
Less than 15	120	89	8	16	0	0	0	40	15	25
15-19	1,345	445	471	109	20	16	0	813	411	402
20-24	5,499	856	1,652	1,422	692	240	117	8,214	4,160	4,054
25-29	7,130	794	1,078	1,519	1,445	1,084	816	17,497	8,954	8,543
30-34	5,534	513	474	744	1,064	1,029	1,538	18,380	9,392	8,988
35-39	4,892	388	333	535	761	755	1,978	19,370	9,796	9,574
40-44	3,276	276	210	303	467	510	1,410	13,726	6,816	6,910
45-49	2,569	231	137	226	311	385	1,209	11,333	5,688	5,645
50-54	1,792	154	124	179	195	267	820	7,643	3,808	3,835
55-59	1,102	105	76	100	139	172	472	4,624	2,273	2,351
60-64	893	96	87	92	110	110	358	3,445	1,663	1,782
65-69	518	47	53	49	67	60	224	2,057	963	1,094
70-74	347	42	34	31	48	44	129	1,273	649	624
75-79	191	25	32	14	21	19	70	643	285	358
80 +	220	37	29	29	26	31	52	639	305	334

Source: Census 1991.

Notes: 1. 'All ages includes 'age not stated'.

2. Number of ever/currently married women in col.4 includes women not reporting number of surviving children.

3. The age groups having nil return are not shown.

member in the Garo Hills Autonomous District Council.[11]

After examining the statistics given of the women representation in the Parliament, State Legislature and district Councils, their participation is negligible. It is surprising that women who play an active role in the social and economic spheres, yet very few come forward to contest in the election. Women do participate actively in political parties both National and Regional. During election, they take part in political campaigns, like processions, public meetings, giving public speeches and other works. Women turn out in large numbers to exercise their franchise and in some polling booths women voters exceed those of men.

Some women political workers hold important and big posts in the political parties. The question is, if women can take part in all political activities, why not fighting for the election? If women do not contest and get elected in the State Legislature and District Councils, that would deprive them of being involved in the policy and decision making level.

(c) Summing Up

Above said 33 per cent reservation for women in the Panchayati Raj institutions in the country, is a significant step, as it provides opportunities and empower them. In the system, women can raise their voice at the decision making level. The constitutional innovation is necessary as women constitute half of the country's population, and are involved in the economic life of both the rural and urban India. Even the solid financial management of the family is the responsibility of women, as they know better how to be economising and thrifty, as that quality is inherent in women.

The presence of females in large numbers in the Panchayats will make the self-governing institutions more representative, more efficient, disciplined and responsible. In their significant role as mothers and educators, the women of India, have throughout the ages been the custodians of Indian culture and traditions, and of transmitting the same to the coming generation. There is an effort in most States of India, to make the Panchayat more effective and to ensure the participation of women for the democratic process, but there are states where women participation is negligible or does not exist at all. In Meghalaya, in spite of the matrilineal system, and the social and economic freedom, yet when it comes to politics ever long held traditions still prevail. Traditionally, women both in the Khasi and Jaintia Hills do not have a role to play in political matters, they are not permitted to attend a Dorbar. There is a common saying in Khasi, *"haba la k̄ynih ka 'iar kynthei la wai ka pyrthei"*, meaning, when the hen crows, it will be the end of the world or the world will be in trouble. In Garo Hills, women have no part at all in the administration, the Nokma, Laskar and Sardar who administer justice like magistrates in rural areas and all men and women can never be chosen as village headmen. In early days, traditions tell us that there were female rulers which show that initially women were not debarred from taking part in political matters. In the *hima* or state of Nobosohphoh, there was a female named Ka Lar, who became the ruler as there was total absence of male heirs.[12] In the writing in the Calcutta Review, regarding ancient Assam, the author said that after the visit of Hieun Tsang to Assam, Lalitaditya, a King of Kashmir invaded the Jaintia kingdom, which they called "Stri Rajya", a woman's kingdom in which Lalitaditya had been repulsed.[13]

There was also a female ruler named Ka law Saring in the Raid lapngar in the Bhoi Area. The story of Ka Latympang is well-known, she was a wise and strong ruler of a small state of Manar in Jaintia Hills, she settled at a place called Barato. The existence of these female rulers suggest that women were accepted as rulers and that they definitely participate in political affairs. Now, women in Meghalaya have come up in every field, in professional studies, in business and trade, in civil services and other spheres. Besides the women in politics, that we have referred earlier, there are other prominent women like Mrs. Rose Millian Bathew Kharbuli, Chairman of the UPSC, Mrs. Alvareen Dkhar, Chairman MPSC, Mrs. M.R. Mawlong, first woman Deputy Commissioner, Miss Silverine Swer and Mrs. E.N. Shullai, Padmashree awardees, Mrs. Queenie Rynjah, Mrs. Verna Ingty and other noted social workers. This establishes that there is no dearth of women in the various fields in Meghalaya.

In the State of Meghalaya, the representation of women in the Legislative Assembly and District Councils is dismal. It appears that women themselves are not very keen or interested in contesting the election, may be the traditional feeling, is still bold. In spite of the rapid changes that are going on in the society, yet politics is still considered as a male prerogative. Women feel that their first priority is towards the family and again they feel overburdened with family works, and they cannot undergo the stress and strain of political life. The women organisations do not enlighten the people on the significance of their representation in the decision and policy making level. Most of the women organisations begin their constitution by mentioning that their organisation is purely social and does not involve in politics, their struggle is mainly social and economic, little do they realise that their isolation and exclusion from this important area affects them.

Thus, reservation of seats will be meaningless, if the women donot assert themselves. Women of Meghalaya are competitive, intelligent, practical, hardworking and very creative, and these values and qualities will be appropriately used in the decision-making level, if they are represented in the local, State and National politics. Women activists should come forward and enlighten the women folk on the significance of women participation in public life. If there are wider entry of women into the Legislature and Councils, that would be of immense contribution to the State and the nation as a whole.

The system of Panchayati Raj envisaging power to the people has come into force throughout the country. An amendment to the Constitution was effected to enable the State Governments to pass legislations giving one-third representation to women at all levels of local self-government. In Meghalaya, neither the State

Government nor the District Councils are initiating the process of discussing the Constitutional 73rd Amendment Act for giving reservation to women and empowering them, or how the spirit of the Act will be enforced in Meghalaya. In the District Council election of 1994, there are no women members in the three District Councils. There is a provision for nomination. It is expected that prominent women in any field would be nominated, but it was not done. Although no one is very much in favour of reservation, because women should get anything through competition and merit, yet for the general interest of the fairer sex, women should come forward to fight for their share of 33 per cent reservation not only in the District Councils but also in the State Assembly. That would provide a balanced and speedy development in all fields.

An appropriate step would be 33 per cent reservation of seats through direct election. In case women do not come out through election, they must be accommodated through nomination. Another way out and effective step to encourage women initially would be to declare a certain percentage of constituencies as exclusive women constituencies. Women need support and encouragement, we cannot deny the truth that without the 33 per cent reservation as provided under the 73rd Amendment Act, we would not have women representatives at all levels of the Panchayati Raj Institutions.

Thus, in a nutshell, for an all round development of women, in Meghalaya a strong women movement is needed for asserting their rights and to impress upon the political authority the necessity for a 30 per cent reservation for women. This will enable them to work and share side by side with men and women who constitute nearly half the State's population can also participate actively in the policy and decision making process at all levels and thus double the performance alongwith men.

References

1. *The Constitution Seventy Third Amendment Act, 1992 on the Panchayats,* Reprinted for circulation by Rajiv Gandhi Foundation New Delhi, n.d., pp. 9–10.
2. *Ibid.*, p. 4.
3. Lyngdoh, M.P.R., "Women Movements in Meghalaya with reference to some selected women organisations" *Seminar on Social Movements in North East India",* 26th to 27th August, 1994 organised by the NEICSSR, Shillong.
4. *Shillong Times,* April 28, 1987.
5. *Shillong Times,* May 26, 1994.
6. *Meghalaya Guardian,* May 2, 1994.
7. *Shillong Times,* May 6, 1994.
8. *Shillong Times,* May, 26, 1994.
9. Rao, V.V. and Hazarika, N., *A Century of Government and Politics in North East India, Vol. I (Assam),* New Delhi, 1993, pp. 171-178.

10. Information provided by Mr. W. Kharkrang, Secretary, Khasi Hills Autonomous District Council.
11. Information provided by the Secretary, Garo Hills Autonomous District Council, Tura.
12. Lyngdoh, H., *Ki Syiem Khasi bad Synteng,* p. IV, Introduction, Shillong, 1938.
13. Lyngdoh, H., *Ka Niam Khasi, Introduction,* pp. X-XI, Shillong, 1970.

13

Concept of New Class

Bureaucracy is considered fourth and inevitable organ of government after legislature, administrative and judiciary. All work (good or bad) which Government gets the credit, it is actually done by bureaucracy. As Prof. Ramashray Roy aptly says:

> . . . the factors relating to the administrators as individuals and those relating to the functioning of the administrative system alone will not give us a complete understanding of the role of bureacucracy in . . . development. We need to know the nature of interaction between the administration and the environment it operates in. In this process of interaction the organisation has to contend with the operational limitations the environment imposes on the desirability as well as on the feasibility of certain actions proposed or undertaken by the organisation.[1]

Therefore, the study of bureaucracy is not complete without a study of the environment in which the bureaucracy functions. And also, the goal realisation of the system is dependent upon the proper relationship between the political leaders and the bureaucrats, and the exploration of certain critical dimensions of their relationship is central to any investigation about bureaucratic performance.[2]

In this chapter, we are going to study the various kinds of pressures exerted upon the bureaucrats by the politicians and political leaders and the way the bureaucrats deal with these pressures. We shall also study the consequences of these pressures on the bureaucrats as individual and bureaucracy as an institution designed to serve the goals of nation-building and socio-economic change.

In order to gain a clear understanding of the problem posed above, it is necessary to start with the politico-bureaucratic relationship in India in its historical context. The bureaucracy in its modern form was set up in India by the Britishers and it was with the help of bureaucracy that the Britishers maintained their hold in India. During the British period, the bureaucracy was not subject to political control and therefore, a bureaucrat was accorded full protection to sustain his authority as the pivot of colonial administration. Although the Governor-General was at the helm of affairs and was conferred with the power of supervision and control, he was not given the authority to initiate disciplinary action against a delinquent bureaucrat.

That power was reserved with the Crown exercisable via the Secretary of State for India. Secure within this framework, a bureaucrat had little or no problem in assisting the government with diligence, probity and to the best of his self. But such a role of the bureaucrats was resented by the political leaders in India. To the political leaders, the bureaucrats were the agents of alien imperialist rulers, working in the interest of foreign power at the cost of national interest. They were critical of the bureaucratic machinery and had a feeling of suspicion, distrust, and hostility towards the same.

But after the achievement of independence in 1947, there took place a radical change in the situation. With independence, we adopted the parliamentary process of government where the bureaucracy had to function under the direction and control of the political leaders. The politicians, after independence, found the bureaucracy as the sole instrument available to them in their programmes of development and the bureaucrats, on the other hand, had no other alternative but to accept their new role of operating under political direction. Moreover, the achievement of independence and the adoption of democratic and parliamentary system of government have changed the role of both the politicians and the bureaucrats. The role of the politicians has been changed from organising agitation to managing the matters of the State, and operating government and fulfiling peoples social and economic aspirations and demands. The bureaucrats, on the other hand, are to come down to the level of people, not with the idea to rule, but with the idea to serve, and in this task of service they are to be guided and directed by the political leaders. Herein lies the significance of the relationship of mutual trust, understanding and co-operation between the political leaders and the bureaucrats. But how far such relationship of mutual trust and understanding has developed our country is a matter of anybody's guess. If the accounts given by the national dailies and the public discussions are of any indication, then it can be said that such relationship of mutual trust and of understanding has not only developed in India but also worsened.[3]

Frequently, it is found that ministers and political leaders, when faced with the criticism of below level performance, generally blame the administrative machinery and civil servants who cannot defend themselves in the legislature.[4] The bureaucrats are often made a scapegoat by the politicians, press and the society in general. As Prof. Subramaniam writes:

> Too often, there is a tendency on the part of the political leaders to be contemptuous about the role of the Civil Servants. Too often also, there is a tendency on the part of the interested sections in the press to paint the image of the Civil Service and the political system in lurid colours. Sensationalism and scandalising are the order of the day. Good, honest work, amelioration of distress, and positive achievement in welfare administration do not get any recognition in the press whereas minor deviations from established procedures are magnified beyond all proportion. Official arrangement for

> propaganda are treated with scorn and the press. . . plays to the gallery to get cheap popularity by contemptuous comments on administration and securrilous attacks against the political and administrative executives. The same is true in the references made to the services in Parliament and in the State Legislatures. The Civil Service ought to be nameless and faceless so far as legislature is concerned, but it is a matter of disappointment that in this country, ill-informed and irresponsible criticism of the Civil Service, which is not in a position to answer back, is indulged in the legislatures. Parliamentary and Legislative immunity are excellent principles but our democracy must also learn that irresponsibility and impunity in criticism of administration is likely not only to lead to a weakening of initiative and to develop frustration among the administration but also to ineffectiveness in the political system to translate the ideas of democracy into practice.[5]

In the same manner, G.D. Khosla, a reputed ex-civil servant, presents an alarming and distressing picture of the state of affairs regarding the relation between political leaders and civil servants in the words given below:

> I have spent no less than fifty years in various departments of the Establishment, and I have been associated with hundreds of civil servants. I have a deep and enduring feeling for them, and I am grievously pained to see them collapsing and disintegrating under the incessant buldgeoning [sic.] of self-seeking politicians. They are corrupt. They are arrogant. They are hungry. 'They are unpatriotic, reactionary, obstructionist, and they are (the Devil take them) disloyal'.
>
> When I survey the administrative scene I find it barren of ideas (where is the time to sit down and think when you have to dance attendance on these morons?); the old dedication and efficiency vanishing (chaltahai); a total lack of initiative (why should I stick my neck out?); integrity and probity mere shadows of their past reality (what is there in it for me?); and a general overall flabbiness (I am trying to be loyal).[6]

While the above mentioned quotations from V. Subramaniam and G.D. Khosla indicate the nature and extent of political pressures upon the bureaucrats, they are not something unique to India or the State of Meghalaya. They are an inherent feature of the democratic system and are all-pervasive in administration in all developing countries.[7] In a democracy, two sets of functionaries with separate training and attitudes need to function in close cooperation with one another. One set of functionaries is that of the politicians and political leaders, the other set being that for the bureaucrats. The bureaucrats are the permanent executives who, by habit and training, are required to judge the merit of particular cases in the light of impersonal and universal standards which are already laid down for their guidance. The politicians, on the other hand, are not the permanent executives. They are not selected but elected and for getting elected, they rely upon the verdict of the people. Since their future depends upon the people, they spend a substantial amount of money, time and also of energy in nurturing their respective constituencies and the people whose verdict they seek from time to time in order to continue in power. For nurturing the constituency or keeping the people contented, the politicians must bestow some favours (may be legal or extra-legal) on the people or at least on their supporters in the constituency. But the politicians by themselves cannot bestow any support directly.

In doing this they depend upon the bureaucrats and consequently, they put pressure upon him. This poses a dilemma for the bureaucrats since if they stick to rules and regulations, they are bound to create dissatisfaction in the minds clientele and invite displeasure of the politicians who are in a position to take revenge on them. And the other hand, if they depart too much from the bureaucratic rules and regulations and succumb to such pressure, legal rational criteria of bureaucracy will have to be sacrificed, resulting in "... highly personalised administration creating in its wake a situation where favouritism, power considerations and extra-organisational criteria are likely to influence the decision-making process."[8]

This will also endanger the organisational viability of the administration as well as its goal achievement.[9] After a discussion of the nature and mechanics of political pressures and influence on the administration in general, now an attempt is made in the remainder of the chapter to study the political pressures which operate on the higher bureaucracy in Meghalaya. In studying these political pressures, a number of questions need to be answered: How frequently do the politicians exert pressures upon the bureaucrats? What are the various types of pressures? What are the assumed consequences a bureaucrat has to face if he does not submit to pressures? How does a bureaucrat deal with political pressures?

For the purpose of a study of the frequency of political pressures, a question regarding the operation and frequency of political pressure[10] was asked to the bureaucrats and it was found that none of the bureaucrats refused the operation of political pressures, although they differed in identifying the degree of frequency. While 34.55 per cent of the bureaucrats consider political pressures to be quite frequent and frequent, 19.09 per cent of the bureaucrats consider them to be less frequent and 11.82 per cent consider them to be least frequent.[11] As a whole, in this study, 69.10 per cent of the bureaucrats find high frequency of political pressures.

Another thing to be noted here is that bureaucrats working in the field consider political pressures to be more frequent rather than the bureaucrats working in the Secretariat or headquarters. The bureaucrats working in the headquarters are engaged in policy formulation and not policy implementation, and as a result, they are relatively free from political pressures. The task of policy implementation is vested in field units and, hence, they are more pressurised by the politicians. Also, no marked difference is found between the responses of technical and non-technical bureaucrats about the frequency of political pressures.

Still, a question that arises here is: for whom do the politicians exert pressures upon the bureaucrats? Do they seek their own interest or the interest of their supporters or of the members of the constituency in general or of all the three? In a democratic set-up, politicians being the representatives of the people, are expected to look after the interests of the people whom they represent. This is the universalistic principle followed in a democratic set-up.

But politicians, being human, may deviate from this universalistic norm and may follow the particularistic norm, i.e., they may think of only their own interests or the interests of their supporters, friends and relatives. But how frequently do the politicians deviate from this universalistic norm?

In order to examine this aspect of political pressures, we asked a question to the bureaucrats about the nature and frequency of demands the politicians made upon the bureaucrats.

An analysis of the answers to this question shows that politicians most frequently approach the bureaucrats with the demands of their supporters. This is not surprising as in a democratic set-up politicians must keep their supporters satisfied in order to be in power or to come to power. It is with the help of the supporters only that the politicians can make headway in politics of elections. However, in the frequency distribution next to the demand of the supporters, we find the demand of the relatives and friends, the demands of the people of the constituency and finally, the demands concerning the politicians' interests and the interests of the members of their family are pointed out by the bureaucrats. Though the demands regarding politicians' personal interests and the interests of the members of their family stand last in the frequency distribution, it is widely considered that politicians in the State of Meghalaya do follow particularistic norms and pursue parochial interests. It can safely be asserted that the politicians in the State tend to pursue narrow parochial interests both for themselves and others, and accordingly, frequently pressurise the bureaucrats in either furthering or protecting such interests.

Different Kinds of Political Pressures

After going through the nature of demands the politicians make upon the bureaucrats, the next question is: how do the politicians pressurise the bureaucrats? Do they themselves contact the bureaucrats to get done what they want or do they approach them through some other functionaries? It would be of considerable significance to study the ways and means adopted in exerting political pressures upon the bureaucrats, and for studying this aspect, we asked the bureaucrats to identify the important ways through which politicians exerted pressures upon them. This particular question elicited a wide variety of responses which we classified into six categories:

(a) Ensuring approach through the political leaders at the higher level (M.L.A., M.D.C., Minister, etc.).
(b) Ensuring approach through administrative officers at the higher level.
(c) Persuasion with the help of administrators' friends or relatives.
(d) Threat of consequences for non-obeyance.
(e) Promise of better career avenues to bureaucrats.
(f) Pressure through demonstrations like gheraos, dharnas, and the like.

It is evident from the aforesaid categories of responses that in the case of first three categories, pressure is brought upon the bureaucrats not directly but indirectly; whereas, in the case of last three categories, pressure is exerted upon the bureaucrats directly by the politicians themselves. An analysis[14] of the responses we received reveals that indirect political pressures account for 84.73 per cent of the answers while direct type of pressures account for 15.27 per cent of the total responses. Among the indirect kinds, 'making approach through political leaders at the higher level' accounts for the highest percentage of responses (38.17 per cent) followed by 'approach through administrative officers at the higher position' (30.53 per cent) and 'persuasion through administrators' 'friends and relatives' (16.03 per cent).

Within the direct types of pressures, 'threat of consequences accounts for 6.87 per cent of the responses followed by promise of better career opportunities' and 'pressure through demonstrations like gheraos, dharnas, etc.' which come to 6.11 and 2.29 per cent of the responses, respectively.

This way, we find that making approach through political leaders at the higher level is the most commonly used type of political pressure upon the bureaucrats. This is obvious as politicians are closer to the political leaders who are more easily accessible to them. The political leaders are dependent upon the local politicians for their political strength. Consequently, the political leaders, for keeping their political support base properly, try to fulfil the demands of the politicians. This finding corroborates our earlier finding in this chapter that politicians generally approach the bureaucrats with the demands of their supporters (according to 61.82 per cent of the bureaucrats). Pressure through political intervention may follow different forms of approach. As one bureaucrat commented:

> For getting something done from the administration, the politicians contact the political leaders at the higher level who bring pressures in many ways. Starting from telephone call or recommendation on an application, there may be personal visits and pressure may be in the form of request or order depending upon the rank in the hierarchy wherefrom the order comes.

In this regard, we may refer to an instance cited by A.D. Gorwala in his *Report on Public Administration in India.* In his *Report,* Gorwala pointed out that an "M.L.A. made a request to the Division Collector. The M.L.A., on enquiry, was informed by the Collector that his request could not be entertained because it would detrimentally affect other people. The M.L.A. telephoned the Minister from the Collector's chamber and informed the Minister that his request was not accepted. The Minister phoned back the Collector and told him that what the M.L.A. had asked for should be done. The Collector wanted to argue but the Minister ended by saying "well you know my views. You can do what I want or . . ."[13]

Handling of these Pressures by Bureaucracy

Through the above discussion, it is clear that political pressures and influences operate extensively in the administration, making the position of the bureaucrats delicate and difficult. If the pressure is exerted for right demands, the bureaucrats do not find much difficulty. What they need to do is only to speed up the matter. But if the pressure is for some illegitimate demands or irregular reason, the bureaucrats find themselves on the horns of a dilemma and it would be interesting to study how do the bureaucrats deal with such dilemma.

Here, in this study, the bureaucrats had been asked to identify the important courses they generally adopt when political pressures exerted upon them.[14] The responses we received can be divided into seven categories:

(a) Express inability due to rules and regulations.
(b) Try to handle the situation themselves but by seeking support from the higher level bureaucrats so as to avoid risk.
(c) Refer the case to the higher-ups.
(d) Try to handle the situation themselves but by seeking support from the higher level political leaders.
(e) Deal with the situation themselves.
(f) Seek transfer to another place.
(g) Appeal to the good sense of the politicians.

Analysis of the responses reveals that the bureaucrats follow two courses of action when subjected to political pressures.

Firstly, they try to express their inability due to existing rules and regulations and thus appeal to the good sense of the politicians.

Secondly, the bureaucrats either push up the matter or deal with it by seeking support either from higher level bureaucrats or political leaders, so as to avoid any kind of risk. There may be two reasons behind the seeking of support from the higher authority. One, if anything goes wrong with a bureaucrat's decision, then he alone cannot be held responsible for that; and two, the dissatisfied politician cannot take retaliatory measures against him without the support of higher level authority who has already been consulted by the bureaucrat in making his decision.

Study[15] of the responses shows that 27.98 per cent and 2.98 per cent of the responses account for the first (express inability) and seventh (appeal to the good sense of the politicians) courses of action respectively as given above. The course of dealing with the situation themselves but by seeking support from the higher level administrators accounts for 23.83 per cent of the responses, during the period of dealing with the situation themselves but by seeking support from the higher level political leaders accounts for only 14.93 per cent of the responses.

Thus, we see that bureaucrats, confronted with political pressures, prefer to apprise more the administrative superiors than the political superiors. This is because a bureaucrat is closer to his bureaucratic seniors than to political leaders. Besides, a bureaucrat can understand the difficulties of another bureaucrat better than what a political leader can in such situation.

Further, the percentage of responses (22.39 per cent) for the course of 'referring the case to the higher-ups' shows that there is a process of what is called 'upward deference'. This upward deference takes place because of tension which is one of the most compelling human drives. Anxiety appears when something threatens the individuals' relations with persons important to him.[16] Political pressures generate anxiety in the minds of the bureaucrats as it threatens their relationship with the political leaders and the politicians. "The mechanism used to reduce anxiety" as per Robert Presthus "includes avoiding responsibility by dependency upon one's superiors".

This is done generally by forcing the task upward in the hierarchy, so that all account for their performance may be disclaimed. But this is often dysfunctional to the organisation because it reduces the ability to handle anxiety realistically.[17] Again, the process of upward deference also results in the congestion of work at higher level of the hierarchy causing inefficiency and delay.

Results of Unfavourable Reaction to Political Pressures

What can be the consequences if bureaucrats fail to meet the demands of politicians and to respond favourably to political pressures and influences? For studying this aspect, we asked the bureaucrats to specify leading consequences that follow their failure to meet the demands of the politicians.[18] The answers received were divided into four categories:

(a) Their job will be adversely affected by transfer, complaint to higher authorities, etc.
(b) Co-operation from the politicians will be withdrawn.
(c) Their service records will be spoiled.
(d) They will be made subject to public denigration, or criticism.

As we shall see, an analysis[19] of the different categories of responses reveals that the consequence of 'adversely affecting their service by transfer and complaint to higher authorities' is the most frequently-named outcome which alone accounts for 37.45 per cent of the total responses. Transfer is one of the most important means available to the political leaders for punishing a bureaucrat.[20]

In a democratic set up, transfers and postings of higher bureaucrats are mostly determined by the political executive, but this is not always done on the basis of merit. In certain cases, purely political criteria determine the posting of higher bureaucrats. While answering an Assembly question the Chief Minister of Meghalaya himself admitted a case of transfer under political pressure.[21] However, transfer under political pressure is not something unique in Meghalaya. It is the usual practice followed by the politicians in different States and different political set-ups to pressurise the upper echelon of political hierarchy to get an officer transferred if they do not get alongwith him. Thus, a writer mentioned a minister named Kroma as saying to a young I.A.S. officer about one of his colleagues named Avasthi: "People of your service are good; but very difficult to get alongwith. Look at Avasthi. He is so honest and competent upright, but he is no use to us—whenever I ask for something, he opens the book. I shall have to get him transferred, if we have to win the election."[22] Like this only, about the Civil Service of Pakistan Goodnow wrote:

> If the officer went alongwith the request, the favour-seeker would see that the officer was praised at the right time and in front of the right people. If the officer stuck to his principles and refused the request, pressures were applied at the political level to have him transferred to another—perhaps much undesirable post.[23]

Such transfers under political pressure are a common feature of personnel administration in every State in India, adversely affecting the morale of the administrators and the efficiency of the administrative set-ups. Transfers, especially forced transfers, cause a lot of personal inconvenience and difficulties to a public servant and, consequently, they undermine the honesty and integrity of these public servants. This point was well brought in the comment of an administrator in our sample who said:

> Officers are not solely responsible for the lack of honesty and integrity in the public service. It is the system which sometimes makes an officer dishonest. If an officer is honest and follows the ethics of Civil Service and does not cow down to the political demands he will have to suffer a lot. Instead of being rewarded, he will be subjected to harassment. One of the methods to harass an officer is to transfer him to the interior, so that he gets a lesson. The education of his children will suffer, financial burdens will go up. All these are the rewards for his honesty and integrity . . . and make the officer feel that honesty and integrity are hollow words.

Apart from leading to frustration, frequent transfer of an officer under political pressures prevent him from gaining mastery over his job and do not permit him to execute his tasks completely. The other consequences which result from the non-fulfilment of political demands, 'lack of cooperation' accounts for 29.96 per cent of the answers, 'spoiling service records' accounts for 20.60 per cent of the responses, and 'public denigration and criticism' accounts for 11.99 per cent of the responses. The lack of cooperation from the politicians badly hampers the goal achievement of the organisation. The desired national goals in a democratic system cannot be achieved by the bureaucratic structure unless and until it is supported by the political structure.

The implementation of the goals of nation-building and development depends upon the cooperation between the politicians and the bureaucrats. On one hand, the bureaucrats implement the authoritatively-determined development programmes, the politicians on the other articulate and aggregate public demands and mobilise public support for the programmes. So long as this cooperative relationship does not exist, the development programmes are sure to suffer.

More other consequences of 'spoiling the service records' and 'public denigration' also affect the functioning of bureaucracy. While spoiling service records makes the bureaucrats hostile towards the politicians and also governmental programmes, public denigration undermines self-confidence, and the spirit of enterprise-qualities which are essential for development administration. While analysing the administrative weaknesses in India, H.V.R. Iyengar, an eminent ex-Civil Servant, said:

> As a result of certain recent events, the impression has been created that the structure which we adopted from the British, namely, a Civil Service which is non-political and which can serve a government of any complexion and is able to preserve continuity and tradition, has no longer any validity. Civil Servant no longer feel that they will be protected by their Ministers against attacks in Parliament. The consequence of all this is a slowing down in the whole process of decision-making, a reluctance to take bold decisions and a tendency to "pass the buck" around as far as possible.[24]

Sum Up

Thus, bureaucracy does not operate in a vacuum but in close interaction with society and the political system of which it is a part. In this process of interaction, the bureaucracy has to work within the functional limitations the environment imposes upon the desirability as well as the feasibility of the development programmes. No study of bureaucracy can, therefore, neglect the bureaucratic interactions with its environment. In a society's environment, the political environment is important because it is the political leaders who determine the systemic targets in a democracy. And since the goal realisation of the system is dependent upon a proper relationship between the political leaders and the bureaucrats, the exploitation of certain critical dimensions of their relationship is focal to any enquiry about bureaucratic performance. One of these dimensions is the nature and extent of political pressures on the bureaucracy and their consequences for the operating of bureaucracy as an instrument of development programmes.

Certain important questions related to the study of political pressure are:

(a) How frequently do the politicians exert pressures upon the bureaucrats?
(b) For what purposes do the politicians exert pressures?
(c) What are the different sources through which the politicians bring pressures?

(d) What consequences do follow for the bureaucrats for not submitting to political pressures?

Of course, interestingly enough, no bureaucrat in the sample denies the exertion of political pressures, although they differ among themselves in identifying the frequency of political pressures. It is surprising that around 70 per cent of the bureaucrats consider political pressures either to be frequent or very frequent. This study also reveals that pressures are brought frequently upon the bureaucrats by politicians for furthering the interests of their friends and relatives. Further, the politicians also pursue the interests of the people of their respective constituency or locality besides their own interests and those of their family members.

By pursuing their own interests and the interests of their family members, politicians in Meghalaya mostly deviate from the universalistic norms. In bringing pressures upon the bureaucrats, politicians prefer indirect sources to direct sources. As indirect source of pressures through higher level political leaders, higher level administrators and the administrators' friends and relatives come to 84.73 per cent of the responses, the direct sources of pressures like threat consequences, promising better career opportunities and organising demonstrations like gheraos, and dharnas are almost 15.27 per cent of the responses. Irrespective of the sources or sources used, the exertion of political pressure put the bureaucrats on the horns of a dilemma. If the bureaucrats bow before political pressure, the legal-rational criteria of bureaucracy are sacrificed and, if they do not, the politicians, who are in a position to take revenge, will be dissatisfied. In such a dilemma, the common courses usually reported to by the bureaucrats are: 'expressing inability due to rules and regulations' dealing with the situation themselves but by seeking support either from higher positioned administrator or higher level political leaders', and 'pushing the matters upwards in the hierarchy'.

The other courses of action observed by the bureaucrats are: 'dealing with the situation themselves', and 'seeking transfer to some other place'. Among the courses, 'pushing up the matter' and 'seeking transfer to some other place' are fatal to the efficient functioning of bureaucracy. While the former results in the congestion of work at the higher level, causing organisational delay and inefficiency, the latter then develops as escapist tendency not conducive to healthy bureaucratic functioning.

To conclude, the consequences which follow for not submitting to political pressures such as transfers, spoiling of service records, and non-co-operation and public harassment by political leaders dampen the confidence, initiative and enterprising spirit of the bureaucrats and are detrimental to the development of sound morale and a sence of commitment among them. All these outcomes weaken the bureaucracy and do not permit it to act as a vital instrument of socio-economic change. Therefore, our politicians too should understand the bureaucrats in the interest of nation and of people so that functioning of bureaucracy goes unaffected and unhampered.

References

1. Roy, *op. cit.*, p. 20.
2. *Ibid.*, p. 82.
3. On this subject, see the recent letter by Shri A.K. Chatterjee, a senior officer of the Bihar Cadre of the IAS addressed to the Chief Minister of Bihar, reproduced in Appendix D.
4. P.V.R. Rao, *Red Tape and White Cap,* (First ed., New Delhi: Orient Longman Ltd., 1970), p. 8.
5. V. Subramaniam, "Role of Civil Service in Indian Political System," *The Indian Journal of Public Administration,* Vol. XVII, No. 2, (April-June, 1971), p. 262.
6. G.D. Khosla, "Civil Servants Dilemma: Salvaging a Noble Legacy", *Statesman,* (Calcutta), September 3, 1980.
7. For a vivid picture of political pressure upon the bureaucrats in a developing country see Ataur Rahman Khan's *Ozaratir Du Bachar* (Two Years of Ministry), Dacca, Naoroj.
8. Roy, *op. cit.*, p. 80.
9. *Ibid.*, p. 97.
10. For the question, See Appendix C.
11. See Table 5.2.
12. See Table 5.3.
13. A.D. Gorwala, *Report on Public Administration,* (Planning Commission, Government of India, 1951), pp. 23-24.
14. For question, See Appendix C.
15. See Table 5:4.
16. Presthus, *op. cit.*, p. 4.
17. *Ibid.*, p. 106.
18. For question, See Appendix C.
19. See Table 5.5.
20. Ataur Rahman Khan's *Ozaratir Du Bachhar,* (Two Years of Ministry), *op.cit.*
21. *Meghalaya Legislative Assembly Debate,* Vol. III, No. 2 (Winter Session, 1972), p. 34.
22. Quoted by Anon *"Transfer of the Collector of Matsyapura", New Challenges in Administration,* ed., Committee on Case Studies, (New Delhi: Indian Institute of Public Administration, 1972), p. 8.
23. Goodnow, *op. cit.*, p. 236.
24. H.V.R. Iengar, *Administration in India: A Historical Review,* (First ed., Bombay: Bharatiya Vidya Bhavan, 1967), p. 41.

14

Defects with Bureaucratic Functioning

In the previous chapter, we have seen that bureaucrats have to undergo certain political pressures which affect their smooth functioning. But sometimes, it is due to bureaucratic officials itself that the working is affected. Thus, in study of problems of bureaucratic structure with dysfunctioning is an import aspect to be taken up. Although Max Weber considered bureaucracy to be superior to all other forms of organisation because of its precision, impersonality and rationality which are important for efficient administration,[1] his analysis was of the nature of ideal type bureaucratic functions. He was not concerned with the operational aspect of the ideal-typical features of bureaucracy and thus ignored its dysfunctional aspects.

> In his analysis of bureaucratic structure, Weber focused on official regulations and requirements and their significance for administrative efficiency. Of course, he knew that the behaviour of the members of an organisation does not precisely correspond to its blueprint. But he was not concerned with this problem and did not investigate systematically the way in which operations actually are carried out. Consequently, his analysis ignored the fact that in the course of operations, new elements arise in the structure that influence subsequent operations.[2]

And this type of elements might be dysfunctional to the bureaucratic organisation. Although contemporary scholars like Robert Merton have stressed the dysfunctional aspects of bureaucratic organisation,[3] there are very few scientific, sociological studies of bureaucratic dysfunctions in the Indian context. Referring to corruption as a dysfunctional component in the South Asian countries Gunnar Myrdal points out that it is almost a taboo as a research topic.[4] It is rarely mentioned in scholarly discussion of government and planning disclosing a general bias which has been characterised by Prof. Myrdal as "diplomacy in research".[5]

Still, bureaucratic dysfunctions in terms of corruption and inefficiency are on the increase in our country, and have "become so much a part of everyone's life that people have evolved strategies and styles of operating such a system and the insecurity of dealing with an uncorrupt administration is perhaps what makes people loath to tamper with the existing arrangements".[6]

The growing corruption and inefficiency not only cause loss of time and public money but also affect the stability of the government. If not already, in the near future, it can pose a threat to our democratic setup because the post-war history gives ample evidence of the rise of dictators on the pretext of fighting corruption. As Prof. Myrdal observes:

> The problem is . . . of vital concern to the governments in the region (South Asia). Generally speaking, the habitual practice of bribery and dishonesty tends to pave the way for an authoritarian regime, whose disclosures of corrupt practices in the preceding government and whose punitive action against offenders provide a basis for its initial acceptance by the articulate strata of the population . . . The elimination of corrupt practices has also been advanced as the main justification for military take overs. Should the new regime be unsuccessful in its attempts to eradicate corruption, its failure will prepare the ground for a new putsch of some sort. Thus, it is obvious that the extent of corruption has a direct bearing on the stability of South-Asian governments."[7]

We can say that the bureaucratic dysfunctions in terms of corruption and inefficiency are inter-related and affect not only the day to day life of the citizens but also raise vital obstacles and inhibitions to development. It often promotes irrationally in planning and limits the horizons of plan. The usual way to make money by corrupt practices is to scare obstruction and delay in official functions and this causes slowing down the wheels of administration in developing countries.[8] Keeping the above considerations in mind, an attempt is made in the following sections to study the bureaucratic dysfunctions in terms of the corruption and inefficiency.

The study is not be an abstract one. Instead, we shall try to answer the questions: What do the bureaucrats think to be the causes of corruption and inefficiency and what remedies ways out do they suggest for removing them from public bureaucracy.

Corruption in Functioning

This is an oft-discussed subject in Meghalaya. It pervades all spheres of society in some form or other in varying degrees. Both public discussions and newspaper accounts accord considerable significance to the growing phenomena of political and bureaucratic corruption and inefficiency. The debates in the State Legislation Assembly have quite often dealt with corruption in significant places and amongst the bureaucrats and politicians. Stressing the administrative reform as an immediate necessity one Congress M.L.A. Late Shri P.N. Chaudhury thus observed:

> . . . Corruption is very rampant in our state [Meghalaya]; this evil is deep-rooted and unless we can fight against this evil and try to eradicate it from the society we cannot give the real benefits to the people for whom the development programmes are meant to be taken up."[9]

Anyway, corruption in public bureaucracy is not a phenomenon peculiar to

Meghalaya, though its ramifications are pervasive in Meghalaya. Corruption in public bureaucracy is also not something of latest origin, but an age-old phenomenon. Kautilya in his *Arthasastra* prescribed measures to be adopted to check corruption.

The Mughal period was characterised with bribery, corruption and extortion which led Akbar in 1681 to complain that the clerks and officers of the state have taken to the practice of traders and buy posts with gold and then sell them for shameful considerations.[10] During the period of the East India Company, the British Officers and clerks who were virtually the rulers augmented their income through corrupt practices such as gathering of graft on taxes and receipt of gifts.[11]

But, soon the Britishers realised that unless they had an honest administration, they would not be able to continue their political power in India and consequently, they enforced a strict code of integrity. However, the Britishers could not fully eradicate corruption from the public service.

There was corruption but upto the World War II, corruption was mostly prevalent amongst the lower officials. The higher echelons of bureaucracy were mostly free from this evil. But the immense war efforts during the time of 1939-1945 involved an annual expenditure of hundreds of crores of rupees and the war time controls and scarcities provided possibilities for corruption and bribery.[12] This was probably the beginning of mass corruption in India which got its full sway after independence when economic planning and rapid expansion of government actively in fresh fields involved gigantic public expenditure.

There has been a phenomenal increase in corruption in the public service in India since independence. While writing on this subject, G.D. Khosla has pointed out: ". . . with the realisation of our right in the kind of democracy we had chosen, came the freedom to lie, to cheat, to give and take bribes, to circumvent and to defy the law, to buy positions and power and abuse the power so acquired".[13] In our efforts to analyse the forms and causes of bureaucratic corruption as perceived by the bureaucrats in Meghalaya, we asked them to identify the important types of corruption prevalent in public bureaucracy in the State of Meghalaya.[14] The question elicited a wide variety of responses which were classified as follows:[15]

(a) Benefitting from official position for personal purposes.
(b) Using government vehicles for personal purposes.
(c) Bribery.
(d) Extending favours to friends and relatives.
(e) Using official staff, stationery, etc. for personal work.

On this aspect, we further sought to enquire into the causes of corruption, irrespective of the forms of corruption, as perceived by the bureaucrats by asking them to identify the leading causes of corruption.[16] The responses received stand as follows after classification.[17]

(a) Ethical factor.

(b) Monetary factor.
(c) Political factor.
(d) Structural factor.
(e) Socio-cultural factor.

Prior to entering into a discussion of these factors separately, it needs to be said that these factors are inter-related and cannot be studied independently of one another.

(I) Ethical Factor

Answers like 'no morality', 'no religious faith', 'lack of conscience', etc. are included in the category of 'moral factor' and it is found that 34.78 per cent of the responses account for moral weakness and turpitude to be the reason of corruption in public bureaucracy. The factor of moral weakness has been considered from two viewpoints by the respondents: religious belief and social values. Some among the respondents believe that the morality of the people is becoming weak day-by-day with the advance of modern civilisation, and this is because of the fact that people are losing belief in their religions. As one respondent said:

> Lack of religious belief is the main cause of corruption in both our public and private life. Earlier, people had faith in religion and it was the fear of religion which made them abstain from doing immoral things. Today, religious hold is becoming loose day-by-day. No longer people think about the day of judgement and they value the present more than the future.

One more cause of moral weakness is the replacement of social values, like 'service', 'sufferings' and 'sacrifice' by the new acquisitive values. New acquisitive values are in turn the outcome of a complex combination of factors. People's aspirations were raised during the nationalist movement by promising them a high standard of living. After independence, the programme of economic advancement and modernisation promised eradication of poverty and increase of national income.

Though goals were proclaimed, the means to realise the goals were lacking. This imbalance between objectives and means resulted in the adoption of extra-legal means. Besides, the model of modernisation envisaged by planners is based on the affluent and advanced societies of the West. In order to follow this model, the norms and values of traditional society have been undermined, and the society have come to acquire a new set of norms and values. Status in the modern society is judged with economic success rather than traditional indices. People have developed increased desire for consumption of newer articles which not only provide comfort but are also regarded to be a status symbol. And this desire for consumption can be met only through acquiring wealth. "Wealth, however, acquired is an effective passport to honour, power and influence".[18]

It is certain that a oureaucrat being a part of the society cannot be expected to develop values different from those of society. They are in constant interaction with the society, and as a result of this interaction they affect and, in turn, are influenced by the society. "The standards of people influence those of public officials and it is hard to develop honest officials in a corrupt society. But it is equally true that high standard on the part of officials and public leaders raise the level of the whole community."[19]

The bureaucrats, because of being the executors of various development programmes, have more opportunities to misuse their power and indulge in the acts of corruption more than others. In material society, where people are judged by what they have rather than what they are, bureaucrats cannot be expected to develop personal virtues or a sense of morality. This absence of a sense of morality has led to a scramble for the acquisition of material gains and prizes irrespective of the means adopted.

(II) Monetary Factor

After moral factor is the economic factor which accounts for 30.43 per cent of the responses. In this category of economic factor we included responses like 'poor salary', 'family burden', 'greediness', etc. Respondents who had been interviewed were found to be vocal about the gap between the cost of living and the salary they received, although, in the same breath, they pointed out that severe poverty was not always responsible for corruption. According to most of the respondents, poverty, alongwith lack of honesty and integrity, causes corruption. Thus, it is neither the financial factor nor the moral factor alone, but a combination of the two that causes corruption. This aspect is well-reflected in the following comment of one of the respondents:

> Presume for example that I am a corrupt officer. I take bribes. I use my official position for non-official purposes. But why do I do all these things? I am an officer having a family of five members. I have a status not only in my office but also in the society. Corresponding to this status, some social roles are assigned to me. I must have a servant, I must attend parties and other such social get-togethers (both official and non-official). When I go out for marketing or on a social courtesy visit, I should not walk, and even if I do, my wife must not walk because an officer's wife is more or less a 'maharani'. My wife must be well-dressed when she goes out, otherwise, salesmen at the counter will address her 'Didi' instead of 'Madam' and her host will not see off at the road-side. Besides, I have social obligations and the responsibility to educate my children. But wherefrom I will do all these things? From my salary! It is too little an amount. So, I have two alternatives open to me. Either I shall be a role-deviant (but in this case there is every possibility of disturbing family peace) or I must adopt some extra legal means. This is not something unique in my case, but common to most of the officers. In such a dilemma, either of the two alternatives is to be followed, and mostly the second, because it promises a happy life and probably a bright future.

One more aspect of this economic factor as emphasised by some respondents is the greediness for acquiring more and more money and other material benefits. Although this is a common human desire, in some situations, it is insatiable and leads to increasing illegal gratification of the same.

(III) Political Factor

Answers like 'political interference', 'favours shown under political pressure', 'illegal things done under political direction', etc., are grouped under political factor which accounts for 20.87 per cent of the replies. The respondents have not pointed out cases of bribery among the politicians. Cases most frequently mentioned by them relate to illegal greed of the demands of the relatives of politicians. Illegal gratification can be of various types and forms. Ranging from providing numerous fringe benefits, it may include granting of an industrial licence, export-import licence or issuing contracts to the family members, relatives, friends and favourities of the politicians in power.

At one point, the researcher was present when an officer was instructing the son of the ex-Chief Minister how to apply for a contract and what would be the charge to be shown in the tender. Such favours are expressed under unwritten instructions of political bosses which influence the decisions of the bureaucrats while issuing lincences, permits, and contracts. The ruling party have to oblige those who give donations to their election funds which cannot be done without the support of the bureaucrats. The President of a State Chamber of Commerce once said: "Political leaders pressurised the trades and industry to make unlimited donations . . . which resulted in price rise . . . These are realised on the grounds of licencing, quota and permits, not out of affection, but to protect trade and industry".[20]

If any bureaucrat acts at the behest of the politicians, he is rewarded, and if he sticks to principles, rules and procedures and refuses their requests, he is subjected to harassment. The bureaucrats who act with a purpose to please the politicians, thus, violate the bureaucratic norms of impartiality and neutrality.

(IV) Structural Factor

This category of 'structural factor', responses like 'delay', 'redtapism', 'complicated rules and regulations', etc., are included and these account for 12.61 per cent of the responses. The bureaucratic system in India carried on with the complex set of rules established by the colonial rulers as a means of maintaining control over their Indian subordinates with various levels of training, outlook and targets. The diversity and complexity of these rules have led to an 'administrative jungle'. In Meghalaya, separate set of rules for the tribal areas framed by the various District Councils have further added to this complexity. This complexity of rules and regulations, sometimes, becomes a source of corruption. The bureaucrats, sometimes, deliberately make delay in their decisions so as to get bribes and other pecuniary benefits.

The clients, on the other hand, offer bribes to the bureaucrats in order to be free from or circumvent the bureaucratic web of cumbersome and complicated rules and procedures.[21] Besides, most of the people do not know much about the governmental rules and procedures and find it important to take recourse to the unwritten but more effective ways of getting things done by governmental agencies.

(V) Socio-Cultural Factor

In cultural factor we included responses like 'habit' and 'familial tradition' which account for only 1.30 per cent of the responses. Although negligible from the numerical point of view, such responses show that corruption can be habitual and such a habit can be influenced by the familial background of the bureaucrats. As one of the bureaucrat commented:

> There are two types of corrupt persons not only in the bureaucracy but also in society. Some people are corrupt by nature or habit, others are made corrupt by their poor economic conditions or by the environment in which they work. Persons in the first category are not born with corrupt habits but familial traditions make them corrupt. In most of such cases, you will find either the parents or other members of the family earning through dishonest means and this behaviour of the elders influences the young who start considering such a thing as a natural way of living. And, if such a person enters the government service, he cannot give up his habit which is formed during the early years of his life.

Steps that can be Taken for Removal of Corruption

After analysing causes of corruption, we will now discuss the measures for the removal of corruption from the bureaucracy, a problem which is of great concern to both the people and the government. For this purpose, we asked the bureaucrats to suggest some important remedial measures for removing corruption from the public services.[22] In response to this, a wide variety of recommendations were provided which we categorised into four: Social, Economic, Political and Structural.

(I) Societal Structure

Astonishingly, almost half of the responses (48.15 per cent) account for a change in societal value-structure as a remedy of corruption in public bureaucracy. This emphasis upon social values is because of the fact that bureaucracy being a sub-system of social system cannot undergo basic changes without bringing about changes in the value structure of the society.[23] Again, the lack of morality, as highlighted to be a cause of corruption, is relative and depends upon societal values. Not only morality, but also economic, political and cultural factors are affected by the value structure of society. Nearly 50.00 per cent of respondents, therefore, lay emphasis upon a basic change in social values as a remedial measure for eradicating corruption from public bureaucracy. A bureaucrat commented thus:

No such measure like vigilance commission[24] or enactment of stringent laws will be an adequate answer to the menace of corruption. Though law cannot be made foolproof but even if it can be, its implementation depends upon man who is social animal and who, in due course of time, will become corrupt. Income-tax, Sales-tax, Police, Customs and Central Excise—such half-a-dozen examples can be readily given. If the evil is to be eliminated, we must go to the root of it, and that root lies in society. Today, the society has lost its values. Honesty and integrity no longer count much. A man is judged by what he has—rather than by what he is. There was a time when society looked down upon its dishonest and corrupt members. But today it is not the case. When parents arrange the marriage of their daughter, they consider the material possessions of the bride-groom more than his honesty and integrity. So, what can a young man do? Instead of being rewarded, a honest person is punished by the society. Until and unless our social values are changed and society itself wages a war against its corrupt members, we cannot hope to eliminate corruption from the bureaucracy.

In this context, social value system is inevitably an important factor in the establishment of a clean and efficient administrative system. Its importance has also been emphasised by the Chief Minister W.A. Sangma when he stated:

> . . . unless and until there is a change of character in our society is it possible to talk about a clean and efficient administration? I would very much like to have it and I am sure everyone would like to have it, but where lies the responsibility? The responsibility lies with you and me, with the masses of the people in the State . . . it is a fact that if one wants to get more than what is due to him it means corruption and exploitation. Is it possible for the government alone to rectify this? . . . this problem concerns the entire society. Unless the society itself wants to have a clean and efficient administration it will not be possible to bring about the type of administration simply by trying to remove certain officers from government machinery.[25]

(II) Financial Measures

These accounts for 27.28 per cent of the responses. Responses like, 'more salary', 'more monetary benefits', etc., are included in this category. It believed that if bureaucrats are well paid or paid proportionately to the expense of living, the rate of malpractices will diminish. Earlier, while pointing out the economic strain upon the bureaucrats, a reference was made to the gross disparities of salary-scales and other monetary benefits between the State Government employees and the Central Government employees as well as between the higher and lower officials.

In the course of our discussion we raised the questions: Is it justified to pay more to the Central Government employees than their State counterparts when they live in the same town or same regional part and perform the same functions?

Table 1
The Survey of Main Workers, Marginal Workers and Non-Workers

District	Total Workers			Main Workers			Marginal Workers			Non Workers		
	P	M	F	P	M	F	P	M	F	P	M	F
West Garo Hills	210,713	128,303	82,410	166,240	111,204	55,036	44,473	17,099	27,374	305,100	131,137	173,963
East Garo Hills	107,734	58,550	49,184	77,093	48,579	28,514	30,641	9,971	20,670	139,821	67,762	72,059
South Garo Hills	47,134	26,353	20,781	30,167	19,819	10,348	16,967	6,534	10,433	51,971	24,698	27,273
West Khasi Hills	131,138	68,626	62,512	98,180	51,882	46,298	32,958	16,744	16,214	162,977	80,533	82,444
Ri Bhoi	91,334	53,726	37,608	72,608	47,236	25,372	18,726	6,490	12,236	101,461	45,589	55,872
East Khasi Hills	241,741	150,549	91,192	203,451	133,871	69,580	38,290	16,678	21,612	419,253	182,638	236,615
Jaintia Hills	126,631	71,700	54,931	95,023	59,239	35,784	31,608	12,461	19,147	169,061	77,676	91,385

Such disparities cause a feeling of deprivation in the minds of the State Government employees, and consequently, lead to the following unfair means by them to compensate for their inadequate salaries. According to some of our respondents, this malady can be remedied by raising pay scales of the State Government employees at par with the Central Government employees as it has already been done in the case of some States. It is to be noted here that an increase in the salaries of the State Government employees alone will not solve the problem. There are no equal economic opportunities in India. Economic power has been concentrated in the control of a few, and this has led to an alliance among industrialists-capitalists, politicians and bureaucrats. Further, concentration of economic power in the hands of a few provides them control over vantage positions in the government and even on policy making. Unless a reasonable degree of economic equality is established, a more reduction of disparities in pay-scales will not remove corruption from the bureaucracy. The census data for various types of industrial workers is given below:

Table 2
The Survey of Main Workers, Marginal Workers and Non-Workers (Statewise): Census 2001

Total Rural Urban	*Persons Males Females*	*Total Workers*	*Main Workers*	*Marginal Workers*	*Non-Workers*	*Total Workers (main + marginal)*
Total	Persons	956,425	742,762	213,663	1,349,644	956,425
	Males	557,807	471,830	85,977	610,033	557,807
	Females	398,618	270,932	127,686	739,611	398,618
Rural	Persons	826,334	629,401	196,933	1,027,123	826,334
	Males	470,712	392,511	78,201	469,091	470,712
	Females	355,622	236,890	118,732	558,032	355,622
Urban	Persons	130,091	113,361	16,730	322,521	130,091
	Males	87,095	79,319	7,776	140,942	87,095
	Females	42,996	34,042	8,954	181,579	42,996

(III) Political Aspect

This aspect includes responses like stopping 'political interference' and 'political pressure' and accounts for 12.50 per cent of the responses. It is said that if political interference in the day-to-day administration come to standstill, there would be a decrease in corruption and malpractices. Related to this is the wider question of the nature of political leadership and the values and standards followed by ministers and other political leaders. It is of utmost importance that the leaders set an example by refraining from indulging in acts of corruption and favouritism.

The underlying cause of corruption in the bureaucracy lies in the political sphere—corruption at the highest level in government and political parties. This, however, involves problems which are beyond the scope of the present enquiry.

Need for Structural Reforms

This includes responses like 'avoidance of delay',[28] introduction of simple rules and regulations', etc., which account for 11.57 per cent of the responses. It is suggested that instead of lengthy and cumbersome process and procedures, simple procedures should be introduced in order to avoid delay which is one of the basic causes of corruption in public bureaucracy. Complex procedures and detailed and excessively lengthy rules not only cause delay but also result in dampening individual initiative and ability.[27] Time limits should be prescribed for dealing with receipts, files and the performance of certain other duties and these should be strictly enforced. Superior officers should consider it their responsibility to find out whether in any particular matter there has been avoidable delay and call to account the person accountable for delay.

Speaking on the subject of cumbersome, complex and unimaginative procedures in administration, Dr. Paul H. Appleby made the following observation which need special attention:

> The rules of business, Secretariat Instructions and Office Manuals seems to me to be generally too didactic and confusing, too detailed and unimaginative. They might be connected to contribute to the extreme insistence on following formal channels too literally and invariably. They seem to assume and encourage that liberal mindedness which damps the spirit, imagination and judgement which are important to good administration.[28]

Lack of Efficiency

Lack of efficiency is another aspect of bureaucratic dysfunction in India. The study of the perception of inefficiency is important because it affects the goal achievement of the system. It is also responsible for making the administration an unpopular, and in turn, the government, because the people judge the governmental performance through the efficacy of its administrative machinery. The complexities of a modern democratic government demand, more than before, an efficient administrative set up and competent and capable administrators to operate that machinery. However, according to many observers and critics, growing corruption and inefficiency are the most notorious and distinguishing characteristics of Indian administration.

As Prof. Rajni Kothari has observed ". . . if there is any arm of the Indian polity that is ridden with confusion, indeterminacy and inertia, it is the administration. Nothing is more urgent than infusing change and dynamics to this arm of government. But nothing is more neglected and more resistant to change."[29]

Among the important questions relating to inefficiency in Indian administration is: what are the causes of bureaucratic inefficiency and how can it be removed? For studying the reasons of bureaucratic inefficiency, we asked the respondents to specify some important causes of inefficiency.[30] The question elicited different responses which were classified into the following groups:

(a) Administrative
(b) Political
(c) Social
(d) Personal
(e) Economic.

(I) Administrative Reasons

Of total, 24.25 per cent of the respondents were found to consider bureaucratic inefficiency as resulting from administrative causes like 'complicated procedures', 'lack of co-ordination', 'red-tape', etc. Procedures, rather than serving as a means to an end, sometimes become an end in themselves. Robert Merton has drawn attention to this tendency in the words below:

> "Adherence to the rules, originally conceived as a means, become transformed into an end-in-itself; there occurs the familiar process of displacement of goals whereby an instrumental value becomes a terminal value".[31]

Approximately everyday, some or other new rules, regulations and procedures are introduced which result in the creation of a jungle of procedures. These procedures are 'archaic, unimaginative, anachronistic, and cumbersome' and cause red-tapism and delay in making decisions, in the movement of files and accomplishment of other work. A matter of minor importance passes through half-a-dozen hands; making almost everyone busy for nothing. This aspect of cumbersome rules and regulations has been graphically illustrated by L.K. Jha. He writes:

> If someone asks me a question, the first thing I ask myself is whether it is within my competence to give him a reply, this is never easy for everyone to know. So, I start consulting everybody else who might possibly be concerned or interested. Before they give me any answer, they ask me a number of questions. I fling them back at the chap who approached me first. If he still persevers and comes back with answers, I pass them back to my colleagues. If they can find no flaw in the answers, they take a decision. And usually, the decision is to put to the matter up to the officers above them. And so the game goes on. Do you think I like it? When I retire, the very rules and procedures which I apply will result in my pension being held up for months and even years. And when it is sanctioned, I shall have to prove by producing certificates on the prescribed forms that I am alive and also that I was alive in each of the intervening months during which my pension was under consideration; yet what am I to do? People think I exercise authority. They do not know that I have no authority. Where the authority lies, no one knows. All I know is that if I do nothing, no one will blame me, but if I do something, then many people will ask me whether what I did was correct. Correct, mind you, not right. If I help someone, my motives may be questioned. If I say no,

I am safe. So, I take the line of least assistance.[32]

Just not cumbersome procedures, but also the lack of coordination causes inefficiency. Modern welfare administration requires coordination between different departments, and hierarchies and between various units or branches of the same department. But in Meghalaya, there is no rational system followed in co-ordinating the work of different ministries and departments, and as a result, there is delay and inefficiency in the administration.

(II) Political Reasons

Replies like 'political interference', 'political pressures', 'political victimisation', etc., are included in political causes which account for 21.64 per cent of the total responses. Politicians often interfere in administration and exert pressure upon the administrators to get things done according to their whims and interests. Faced with such pressures, the administrators take recourse to the act of 'passing the buck' or take shelter under the sanctuary or rules and regulations. Victimisation of the bureaucrats on political grounds dampens their initiative and morale.

There evolves a tendency towards 'playing safe' and one of the most commonly-adopted ways of 'playing safe' is to follow the precedents. Though the observance of precedents in taking decisions is an element of bureaucratic rationality,[33] sometimes regard for precedents verges on morbidity. Precedents, therefore, are no longer treated as one of the ingredients in a rational decision but degenerate into a means for avoiding new thinking and quick decisions. "Routine, red-tape, and long-noting take the place of initiative, ingenuity and innovation".[34]

(III) Social Reasons

Social reasons like 'groupism', 'communalism', etc., are also considered to be responsible for bureaucratic inefficiency which account for 20.90 per cent of the responses in this study. As we have discussed earlier, the Meghalaya Society as well as the administration is divided into two hostile camps of 'insiders' and 'outsiders' (the 'tribals' and 'non-tribals') on the grounds of region and community. This 'insiders'-'outsiders' relationship sometimes takes to form of cliques leading to mutual hostility and mistrust, thereby, adversely affecting bureaucratic work performance and efficiency.

(IV) Personal Factor

Such factors like 'lack of initiative', 'devotion to one's duties', 'punctuality', etc., are also considered to be a factor responsible for administrative inefficiency and account for 18.66 per cent of the total responses received. Initiative and interest are personal traits and depend upon the complex interaction of different factors like family up-bringing, the influence of social and educational institution and bureaucratic norms and culture. Included in the individual factor are such traits as 'devotion to one's duties', 'ability to perform one's task', 'punctuality' and 'diligence'. These traits are needed to be assessed at the stage of recruitment. With a policy of large-scale reservations in government service (85 per cent), it cannot be said that the best talents available possessing the qualities of devotion, diligence, etc.) are recruited in the public services of Meghalaya.

(V) Financial Factor

Two, i.e., 'Bribery' and 'monetary benefits' are included in the category of economic factor which accounts for 14.55 per cent of the responses. And here we come across the interaction between corruption and inefficiency—another two inter-related aspects of bureaucratic dysfunction. Corrupt practices result in delay, and in turn, it is delay that causes corruption. A corrupt official deliberately makes delay in making decisions or disposing of a matter, so that he can earn something by way of grease money.

Very often, a bribe-giver does not wish to get anything done unlawfully, but only wants to speed up the movement of files and communication from department to department or from branch to branch of the same department. In some offices, especially the executive offices, every movement of files is facilitated by 'speed money'. Unless and until 'speed money' is paid, the official will not be seen in his seat, and even if he is found, he will not give any attention to the client or will be unable to locate the relevant papers. Sometimes, even the needy needs to be paid for locating the file in the chamber of the officer. The amount of speed money varies from case to case and from person to person. This has become such a matter of day-to-day that a complaint becomes totally infructuous, its only effect being that it may invite harassment to the complainant. Besides being one of the most unhealthy corrupt practices, it rests the wheels of bureaucratic machinery and is one of the most important causes of delay and inefficiency.

Remedial Measures against Inefficiency

Having discussed the causes of inefficiency, the corollary question is: what measures are necessary for making bureaucracy efficient? It is not easy to answer this question. However, we asked the respondents to name leading remedial measures to be adopted for removing inefficiency from the public bureaucracy.[36] The responses received were categorised into three:[37]

(a) Administrative.
(b) Political.
(c) Individual.

Above responses show that none of the respondents suggested social and economic measures as a remedy for bureaucratic inefficiency, although some of them considered social and economic factors to be accountable for bureaucratic inefficiency. They did not suggest social measures probably because they considered society an independent variable. The reason for not suggesting economic measures is possible for the close affinity between corruption and inefficiency.

They perhaps thought that if one was eliminated, the other would not exist.

(a) Administrative Steps. Among the administraive measure, we included responses like 'simplification of rules and regulations', 'proper coordination', 'proper personnel planning', etc., which accounts for 36.50 per cent of the responses. This stress upon administrative measures is because of the fact that it is the immediate sphere with which they are concerned and that much can be done in the administrative sphere for betterment of its efficiency. This aspect has been discussed at some length in the preceding pages.

(b) Political Steps. These account for 33.08 per cent of the responses and include responses like 'non-interference by the politicians', 'code of conduct for politicians', 'demarcation of political and administrative functions', and the like. As we have already discussed, it is believed that there would be efficiency in the administration if politicians behave responsibly and do not interfere in the day-to-day functioning of the administration. Further, it has also been pointed out that if bureaucracy is to function efficiently, bureaucrats should not be made scapegoats. As one respondent said:

> Half of the bureaucratic inefficiency would be eliminated our politicians are trained in a training school in the art of behaving with the administrators in a parliamentary democracy.

Steps for Improving Personal Standard and Ability

Steps in this category account for 30.41 per cent of the responses. In this category, respondents emphasised the importance of recruitment of suitable candidates which relies upon the recruitment policy of the Government. It was suggested that Government policy should be made objective and scientific, so that, only the best candidates would be recruited. Apart from the need for training has also been emphasised. Recruitment of the best talents by itself is not an effective guarantee for increasing efficiency in the administration. Talented candidates must have right and thorough training in the art of administration. In this connection, it may be pointed out that, excepting the Police Training School for subordinate police officials, there is no arrangement for training Civil Servants in Meghalaya.

To conclude dysfunction is an important aspect in the study of bureaucracy, which manifests especially in the bureaucracies of developing societies. Corruption and inefficiency have been the two leading manifestations of bureaucratic dysfunction. There is cause and effect relationship between corruption and inefficiency, and hence, neither of these can be studied in complete isolation of the other. The bureaucratic perception of corruption includes bribery, using official position for non-official goals, using official staff, stationery and vehicles for personal use, and showing favours to relations and friends, all of which are opposed to the norms of Weber's ideal logical bureaucracy. The bureaucrats consider moral, economic, political, structural and cultural factors as being responsible for corruption in public bureaucracy. Among the remedial steps to eradicate corruption, they suggest societal, economic, political and structural measures. The absence of any remedial of any measures in the shape of individual morality is probably due to the fact that morality is dependent upon the value structure of society and it is because of this fact that societal measures have been stressed by the bureaucrats. The other aspects of bureaucratic dysfunction, namely, inefficiency, is a major obstacle in implementing various programmes of development. In this study, it is found that the respondents consider administrative, political, social, individual and economic factors responsible for bureaucratic inefficiency; and for eradicating inefficiency, they suggest administrative, political and individual measures. The respondents do not suggest social and economic measures for removing inefficiency, though they hold social and economic factors responsible for inefficiency. The absence of social measures can be attributed to the fact that they regard society as an independent variable, while the absence of economic measure can be accounted for by the close affinity between corruption and inefficiency.

References

1. Blau, *op. cit.*, p. 1.
2. *Ibid.*, p. 27.
3. Robert K. Merton's "Bureaucratic Structure and Personality" in *Social Theory and Social Structure,* (New Delhi: Amerind Publishing Co. Pvt. Ltd., 1975), pp. 249-260.
4. One such study has been made by N.K. Singhi, in his book *Bureaucracy: Positions and Persons, op. cit.*
5. Gunnar Myrdal, *Asian Drama: An Inquiry into the Poverty of Nations,* Vol. II (London: Allan Lane, The Penguine Press, 1968), pp. 938-939.
6. "Corruption: Third Time Lucky" *Economic and Political Weekly,* Vol. XIII, No. 40 (October 7, 1978), p. 1684.
7. Gunnar Myrdal, *op. cit.*, pp. 937-938.
8. *Ibid.*, pp. 951-955.
9. *Meghalaya Legislative Assembly Debates,* Vol. IV, No. 4 (Budget Session, 1973), p. 38.
10. G.D. Khosla, "Corruption Down the Ages", *Corruption in India,* ed. Suresh Kohli (First ed., New Delhi: Chetna Publications, 1975), p. 19.
11. Bansal, *op. cit.*, p. 2.
12. *Report of the Committee on Prevention of Corruption,* (New Delhi: Ministry of Home Affairs, Government of India, 1964), pp. 6-7.
13. G.D. Khosla, "Corruption Down the Ages", *Corruption in India,* ed. Suresh Kohli, *op. cit.*, p. 20.
14. For the question, see Appendix C.
15. For analysis of the responses, see Table 6 : 1.
16. For the question, see Appendix C.
17. For analysis of the responses, see Table 6 : 2
18. John B. Monteiro, *Corruption: Control of Maladministration,* (First ed., Bombay: Manaktalas, 1966), p. 64.

19. *Ibid.*, p. 67.
20. Dev Dutt, "*In Politics,*" *Corruption in India,* ed., Suresh Kohli, *op. cit.*, p. 94.
21. Singh: *op. cit.*, p. 202.
22. For the question, see Appendix C.
23. For analysis of the responses, see Table 6:3.
24. In this connection, it may be pointed out that though there is an anticorruption wing of the CID under the Deputy Inspector General of Police in Meghalaya, its functionings are beset with certain difficulties. In the words of the Chief Minister "... the work of the branch is too difficult because we do not have trained personnel with sufficient experience in this specialised work ... Our difficulty is that specific instances are not coming forward, and we do not get witness to substantiate the allegations". See *Meghalaya Legislative Assembly Debates,* Vol. X, No. 2, (Budget Session, 1975), p. 83.
25. *Meghalaya Legislative Assembly Debates,* Vol. I, No. 1, (April Session, 1970), pp. 58-59.
26. K.N. Butani, "*Leadership in Administration*", *The Indian Journal of Public Administration,* Vol. II, No. 4 (October-December, 1956), pp. 325-326.
27. Appleby, *op. cit.*, p. 14.
28. Rajni Kothari, "Foreword" *Administrative Change in India,* ed. Ramesh K. Aurora, *op. cit.*, p. 111.
29. For the question, see Appendix C.
30. For analysis of the responses, see Table 6 : 4.
31. Merton, *op. cit.*, p. 253.
32. L.K. Jha, "Mr Red Tape", *The Indian Journal of Public Administration,* Vol. XI, No. 4 (October-December 1965), pp. 681-682.
33. R.P. Khosla, "Bureaucrats: The Loss of Vision", *The Indian Journal of Public Administration,* Vol. XI, No. 1, (January-March 1965), pp. 36-39.
34. N.V. Gadgil, "Accountability of Administration", *The Indian Journal of Public Administration,* Vol. 1, No. 3, (July-September, 1955), p. 195.
35. *Meghalaya Legislative Assembly Debates,* Vol. I, No. 1, (March-April Session, 1972), p. 89.
36. For the question, see Appendix C.
37. For challenges of the responses, see Table 6 : 5.

Index

C

D

I

J

K

L

N

O

P